The Interdisciplinary Council on
Developmental and Learning Disorders

Clinical Practice Guidelines

D0874760

The Interdisciplinary Council on Developmental and Learning Disorders gratefully acknowledges the following people who contributed to the production of this book: Charlotte Ball, Scott Baur, Marilyn Fenichel, Marla Fogelman, Sharon Markus, Janet McCaslin, Betty McDonald, Sue Morrison, Penny Ripka, and Jan Tunney. Cover design by Kristen Mosbaek Communications.

The Interdisciplinary Council on Developmental and Learning Disorders (ICDL)

Clinical Practice Guidelines

Redefining the Standards of Care for Infants, Children, and Families with Special Needs

ICDL Clinical Practice Guidelines Workgroup

Stanley Greenspan, M.D., *Chair,* Clinical Professor of Psychiatry, Behavioral Sciences and Pediatrics, George Washington University Medical School

Serena Wieder, Ph.D. *Associate Chair,* Clinical Psychologist

Margaret Bauman, M.D., Associate Professor of Neurology, Harvard University

Nanci Bell, M.S., C.C.C.-S.L.P., Director, Lindamood-Bell Learning Processes

Lois Black, P.d.D., Director, Center for Psychological and Neuropsychological Services

T. Berry Brazelton, M.D., Clinical Professor Emeritus, Pediatrics, Harvard University Medical School

Leon Cytryn, M.D., Clinical Professor of Psychiatry and Pediatrics, George Washington University Medical School

Georgia DeGangi, Ph.D., O.T.R., F.A.O.T.A., Clinical Psychologist, ITS for Children and Families, Inc.

Sima Gerber, Ph.D., C.C.C.-S.L.P., Assistant Professor of Linguistics and Communication, Queens College, CUNY

Barbara Kalmanson, Ph.D., Clinical Psychologist

Harold Koller, M.D., F.A.A.P., F.A.A.O., Clinical Professor of Opthalmology, Thomas Jefferson University Chair, section on Opthalmology, American Academy of Pediatrics

Karen Levine, P.h.D., Instructor, Harvard University Medical Center

Pat Lindamood, M.S., C.C.C.-S.L.P., Director Lindamood-Bell Learning Processes

Toby Long, Ph.D., P.T., Director, Division of Physical Therapy, Georgetown University Child Development Center, Associate Professor of Pediatrics, Georgetown University

Jane Madell, Ph.D., Director, Hearing and Learning Center, Beth Israel Medical Center

Arnold Miller, Ph.D., Executive Director, Language and Cognitive Development Center

Nancy J. Minshew, M.D., Associate Professor of Psychiatry and Neurology, University of Pittsburgh School of Medicine

Barry Prizant, Ph.D., C.C.C.-S.L.P., Director, Childhood Communications Services, Adjunct Professor, Brown University

Ricki Robinson, M.D., M.P.H., Clinical Professor of Pediatrics, University of Southern California

Mark Rosenbloom, M.D., President, The Unicorn Children's Foundation, Assistant Professor, Clinical Medicine, Northwestern University Medical School

Rebecca Shahmoon Shanok, M.S.W., Ph.D., Director, The Early Childhood Group Therapy Service and Training Program & Director, Institute for Clinical Studies of Infants, Toddlers & Parents, Jewish Board of Family and Children's Services, N.Y.

Stuart Shanker, Ph.D., Professor of Psychology and Philosophy, York University

Richard Solomon, M.D., Clinical Associate Professor of Pediatrics, University of Michigan Medical School

Gerry Stefanatos, D. Phil., Associate Professor of Neuroscience, NJ Neuroscience Institute at JFK Medical Center

Liz Tsakiris, Ed.M., Doctoral Candidate in Psychology, University of Maryland

Harry Wachs, O.D., Director, The Vision and Conceptual Development Center

Robert H. Wharton, M.D., Chief, Developmental and Behavioral Pediatrics, Massachusetts General Hospital and Spaulding Rehabilitation Hospital, Harvard University Medical School

G. Gordon Williamson, Ph.D., OTR Project ERA, JFK Medical Center

Parviz Youssefi, Ed.D., Director, G.M.S. Institute

Andrew Zimmerman, M.D., Associate Professor of Neurology and Psychiatry, Kennedy Kreiger Institute, Johns Hopkins University School of Medicine

Contents

Page

Part One: Overview and Recommendations

Chapter 1.   Introduction - *Stanley I. Greenspan, M.D., Chairman,*
Interdisciplinary Council on Developmental and Learning Disorders   3

Chapter 2.   The Need for a Comprehensive, Individualized Approach   7

Chapter 3.   Overview and Recommendations   13

Chapter 4.   Principles of Clinical Practice for Assessment and Intervention –
Stanley I. Greenspan, M.D., and Serena Wieder, Ph.D.   55

Part Two: Language and Communication

Chapter 5.   Speech, Language, and Communication Assessment and Intervention for Children –
Sima Gerber, Ph.D., C.C.C.-S.L.P., and Barry Prizant, Ph.D., C.C.C.-S.L.P.   85

Chapter 6.   Auditory Disorders in Children with Developmental Learning Disorders –
Jane Madell, Ph.D.   123

Chapter 7.   Children with Special Needs in Bilingual Families: A Developmental Approach to
Language Recommendations – *Robert H. Wharton, M.D., Elizabeth Miller, Ph.D., M.D.,*
Joshua Breslau, Ph.D., Karen Levine, Ph.D., and Stanley Greenspan, M.D.   141

Part Three: Motor and Sensory Functioning

Chapter 8.   Assessment of Sensory Processing, Praxis, and Motor Performance –
G. Gordon Williamson, Ph.D.,O.T.R., Marie Anzalone, Sc.D., O.T.R.,
and Barbara Hanft, M.A., O.T.R.   155

Chapter 9.   Screening, Evaluating, and Assessing Children with Sensorimotor Concerns and
Linking Findings to Intervention Planning: Strategies for Pediatric Occupational and
Physical Therapists – *Toby M. Long, Ph.D., P.T., and Kirsten M. Sippel, M.P.P., P.T.*   185

Chapter 10.   An Integrated Intervention Approach to Treating Infants and Young
Children with Regulatory, Sensory Processing, and Interactional Problems –
Georgia A. DeGangi, Ph.D., O.T.R., F.A.O.T.A.   215

Chapter 11.   An Ophthalmologist's Approach to Visual Processing/Learning Differences –
Harold Koller, M.D., F.A.A.P., F.A.A.O.   243

Part Four: Home, School, and Family Approaches

Chapter 12.   Developmentally Appropriate Interactions and Practices –
Stanley I. Greenspan, M.D., and Serena Wieder, Ph.D.   261

Chapter 13.   Educational Guidelines for Preschool Children with Difficulties in Relating and
Communicating – *Serena Wieder, Ph.D., and Barbara Kalmanson, Ph.D.*   283

Chapter 14.   The Action is in the Interaction: Clinical Practice Guidelines for Work
with Parents of Children With Developmental Disorders –
Rebecca Shahmoon-Shanok, M.S.W., Ph.D.   333

Part Five: Clinical Evaluation Process: Classification and Biomedical Evaluation and Intervention

Chapter 15.   Developmentally Based Approach to the Evaluation Process –
Stanley I. Greenspan, M.D., and Serena Wieder, Ph.D.   375

Chapter 16.   Developmentally Based Approach to the Classification of Infant and Early
Childhood Disorders – *Stanley I. Greenspan, M.D., Serena Wieder, Ph.D.,
and Andrew Zimmerman, M.D.*   389

Chapter 17.   Medical Evaluations of the Child with Autistic Spectrum Disorders –
Ricki Robinson, M.D., M.P.H.   411

Chapter 18.   Neurophsychological Assessment of Developmental and Learning Disorders –
Lois Black, Ph.D. and Gerry Stefanatos, D.Phil.   425

Part Six: Innovative Models that Work with Especially Challenging Functional Developmental Capacities

Chapter 19.   The Miller Method®: A Cognitive-Developmental Systems Approach for Children with Body
Organization, Social, and Communication Issues –
Arnold Miller, Ph.D., and Eileen Eller-Miller, M.A., C.C.C.-S.L.P.   489

Chapter 20.   Visual-Spatial Thinking – *Harry Wachs, O.D.*   517

Chapter 21.   Sensory-Motor Integration: A Perceptual-Motor Approach For Enhancing
Motor Planning In Children with Special Needs – *Parviz Youssefi, Ed.D.,
and Arousha Youssefi*   537

Chapter 22.   Mediated Learning Experience, Instrumental Enrichment and the Learning
Propensity Assessment Device – *Reuven Feuerstein, Ph.D.*   557

Chapter 23.   Speech-Language Development: Oral and Written –
Patricia Lindamood, M.S., C.C.C.-S.L.P., and Phyllis Lindamood   579

Chapter 24.   Technologies to Facilitate Language, Sensory Processing, and Motor
Planning Capacities – *Patricia Lindamood, M.S., C.C.C.-S.L.P.*   605

Chapter 25.   Imagery and the Language Processing Spectrum – *Nanci Bell, M.A.*   615

Chapter 26.   Adolescents and Adults with Special Needs: The Developmental,
Individual Differences, Relationship-Based Approach to Intervention –
Stanley I. Greenspan, M.D., and Henry Mann, M.D.   639

Part Seven: Neuroscience and Neuropsychological Foundations for Clinical Practice

Chapter 27.   Neuromechanisms in Autism – *Andrew Zimmerman, M.D.,
and Barry Gordon, M.D., Ph.D.*   659

Chapter 28.   Autism as a Disorder of Complex Information Processing –
Nancy J. Minshew, M.D., and Gerald Goldstein, Ph.D.   671

Chapter 29.   Autism: Clinical Features and Neurobiological Observations –
Margaret L. Bauman, M.D.   689

Chapter 30.   The BOLD Approach: A Multimodal Approach for Understanding Communication
and Learning Disorders – *Mark Rosenbloom, M.D., and Galina D. Kitchens, M.A.*   705

Part Eight: Functional Developmental Approach to Intervention Research

Chapter 31.   Evaluating Effective Interventions for Children With Autism and Related Disorders:
Widening the View and Changing the Perspective – *Elizabeth Tsakiris, Ed.M.*   725

Conclusion   821

Part One:

Overview and Recommendations

◄ 1 ►

Introduction

Stanley I. Greenspan, M.D., Chairman
Interdisciplinary Council on Developmental and Learning Disorders

Increasing numbers of young children are presenting with non-progressive developmental disorders involving compromises in the capacities of relating, communicating, and thinking. These developmental disorders include autistic spectrum disorders, multisystem developmental disorders, cognitive deficits, severe language problems, types of cerebral palsy, and others. They involve many different areas of developmental functioning, ranging from planning motor actions and comprehending sounds to generating ideas and reflecting on feelings. New research and clinical observations are making it possible to more fully identify these different capacities and, thereby, characterize each child and family according to their unique profile of functional developmental capacities. These new observations also make it possible to subdivide complex developmental disorders, such as autism, based on different configurations of functional or dimensional processes (e.g., auditory processing, motor planning, and reciprocal, affective interactions). Most important, they enable clinicians to individualize assessment and intervention approaches in response to the child-and-family-specific question: "What is the best approach for a given child and family?" Answering the child-and-family-specific question makes it possible for clinicians to tailor the approach

to the child, rather than fit the child to the program.

Too often, however, the clinical practice is to fit the child to a standard program. The rationale for fitting the child to the program is, in part, driven by theory and belief (e.g., all children with autism should receive a specific approach, regardless of their individual developmental profiles). It is also driven by the mistaken assumption that children who share a diagnosis because they display some similar symptoms also have a similar central nervous system processing profile and underlying neurobiology.

There are, however, different neurobiological patterns, in addition to different functional developmental or dimensional processes, within each broad diagnostic group, such as autism. These findings make it timely and imperative to formulate clinical practice guidelines that go beyond traditional diagnostic categories and are based on functional developmental or dimensional differences.

Over the years, the disciplines that work with developmental disorders have constructed a large body of research and clinical experience based on these functional developmental or dimensional processes. This knowledge, however, needed to be brought together and organized. In response to this need, the Interdisciplinary Council on Developmental and Learning

Disorders (ICDL) launched an initiative to systematize the current clinical knowledge, including both research and clinical experience, of disciplines such as speech pathology, developmental and behavioral pediatrics, pediatric neurology, occupational and physical therapy, psychology, social work, special education, early childhood education, early intervention, and child psychiatry. The result of this effort is *The ICDL Clinical Practice Guidelines*.

The ICDL Clinical Practice Guidelines is unique in three ways. First, the guidelines go beyond syndrome-based approaches and build on emerging knowledge of different functional developmental patterns within broad syndromes, such as autism. This specificity enables the identification of each child and family's unique developmental profile, including strengths and vulnerabilities, and the development of an individualized intervention plan that works with all the relevant functional developmental and processing capacities.

Second, *The ICDL Clinical Practice Guidelines* addresses a level of clinical complexity, detail, and depth not often attempted with such efforts. The guidelines recognize the need to go further than simply documenting, in broad strokes, the value of interventions such as special education, social skills training, and/or communication and speech and language therapy. The guidelines recognize that there is enormous variation in clinical goals, techniques, and therapist/child interactions within similarly named interventions (e.g., speech and language therapy), based on the individual challenges of a particular child and family and on the practitioner's personality, training, skill level, and interactive patterns with a particular child and family. The guidelines, therefore, attempt to describe specific strategies and interaction patterns for the different functional areas: For

example, how to work with a child who is very overreactive to touch, underreactive to sound, has poor motor-planning skills, is very avoidant, and moves away from adults and other children to help him learn to enjoy caregiver and peer relationships, interact, communicate, and problem solve. This type of child-specific clinical work requires enormous clinical skills. These skills, which will often determine the success of the overall intervention program, can only be captured by in-depth clinical descriptions that go significantly beyond the identification of a generic intervention category.

Elaborating upon and systematizing in-depth clinical strategies to guide intervention efforts require a broad knowledge base supported by both research and clinical experience. The third unique feature of *The ICDL Clinical Practice Guidelines* is that the guidelines are based on both current research and clinical experience (i.e., expert opinion) from all the disciplines that work with developmental problems. A number of organizations have issued, or are issuing, guidelines based predominantly on reviews of current research (or evidence). Although increasing research is an important long-term goal, the current research base is too incomplete to fully guide clinical decisions. It lacks the scope and specificity necessary to guide interventions tailored to the individual child and family's unique developmental profile. (See Tsakiris, Chapter 31, this volume, for a review of current intervention research.) Current research is only able to ascertain, in broad terms, that (1) intervention programs tend to be helpful, (2) intensive and comprehensive programs tend to produce better results, and (3) a few of the related areas of functioning (e.g., language and social skills) have been studied to some degree. There are no comparative clinical trial intervention studies of major intervention models and no definitive clinical trial intervention studies of comprehensive interventions for representative populations of individuals with autistic spectrum disorders or other disorders of relating and communicating that demonstrate clinically meaningful outcomes. Only selected assessment and intervention procedures have been researched, and many important areas of functioning and related interventions that belong in a comprehensive assessment and treatment program have not been sufficiently studied.

At present and for the foreseeable future, clinical experience together with research is necessary to provide the clinical knowledge needed to individualize approaches to the child and family's functional or dimensional profile. Both are also necessary to work with all the areas of developmental functioning that form the critical foundations for intellectual and emotional growth.

The ICDL Clinical Practice Guidelines addresses the identification, assessment, and treatment of all relevant areas of developmental functioning, including child-caregiver relationships and developmentally appropri-ate interaction patterns; speech and language, including auditory processing; motor functioning, including planning and sequencing; visual-spatial processing and thinking; other types of sensory processing; and sensory modulation, including patterns of hypo- and hypersensitivity; the functional-emotional developmental capacities of attention and regulation, engagement, purposeful, two-way communication, complex problem solving, the creative use of ideas, and abstract, logical thinking; areas of cognitive functioning; social skills; family patterns; and peer relationships.

The ICDL Clinical Practice Guidelines further addresses how these functional developmental capacities become incorporated into the process of a comprehensive evaluation, the construction of the developmental profile, and the formulation of a child-and-family-specific comprehensive intervention program. The functional developmental approach serves as the basis for recommendations for changes in screening, assessment, and intervention services and local, state, and federal policies.   ■

— 2 —

The Need for a Comprehensive Individualized Approach

As indicated in Chapter 1 of this volume, infants and children with non-progressive developmental and learning disorders evidence challenges as well as strengths in many different areas of functioning. Each of these areas must be worked with as part of a comprehensive assessment and intervention program. Such a comprehensive program involves a number of disciplines working together, guided by the unique developmental profile of the child and the child's family.

Although seemingly self-evident, these basic tenets have been surprisingly difficult to put into practice. For many developmental and learning disorders, disagreement exists about what areas of functioning should be addressed, the best ways to observe and assess them, and the interventions most likely to be helpful. In addition, each child and family is quite unique, and each clinician, regardless of background and training, has a personal way of practicing his or her craft. These challenges are formidable, but dealing with them is necessary to creating an individualized interdisciplinary approach that tailors the program to the child rather than fits the child to the program.

For discussion purposes, non-progressive developmental and learning disorders can be divided into two groups. One group involves disorders that significantly interfere with a child's basic abilities to communicate (preverbally and verbally), to relate to others in an age-appropriate manner, and to think creatively and logically. A second group involves disorders that are more circumscribed and interfere with different aspects of learning (including regulating activity and attention) but do not significantly interfere with the child's basic ability to communicate, relate, and think. This edition of *The ICDL Clinical Practice Guidelines* will address the first group of disorders, which includes many forms of autistic spectrum disorders (pervasive developmental disorders), multisystem developmental disorders, language disorders, motor disorders, severe cognitive deficits, Down syndrome, fragile X syndrome, fetal alcohol syndrome, severe forms of regulatory disorders and attention deficit disorder, and others. Rather than address each disorder separately, *The ICDL Clinical Practice Guidelines* will focus on the functional developmental deficits, such as speech and language problems, motor-planning dysfunction, affective processing and regulation problems, and sensory processing and modulation difficulties, that are often present in varying degrees across them.

The current state of clinical practice with the non-progressive developmental and learning disorders that interfere with communicating, relating, and thinking is best described by Charles Dickens's often-quoted statement about this being "the best of times, the worst of times." New understandings of central nervous system mechanisms, processing differences, and innovative practices exist alongside clearly inadequate programs for the majority of children with these disorders.

New understanding of how different behaviors and symptoms are dynamically related to functional developmental and processing differences in many of these disorders (such as autistic spectrum disorders) is providing a basis for improved assessment, diagnostic, and intervention practices. At the same time, neuroscience investigations are revealing dynamic interactions between genetic expression, levels of environmental interaction, and the formation of neurostructures. For example, throughout infancy and childhood, the brain can develop new neuropathways to deal with interruptions, such as a hemispherectomy. Furthermore, individually different, dynamic relationships exist between different areas of the brain. Processing capacities, such as auditory or visual-spatial, may compete for cortical access, depending on functional use. Interactive experience or functional use, including strategically tailored family, education, and therapeutic experiences may, therefore, play a significant role in the development of expectable, new, and alternate pathways (Chugani, 1999; Zimmerman & Gordon, Chapter 27, this volume).

Recent clinical observations and research suggest that there are three interrelated processes that are essential for mobilizing a child's development. The first process is working with each child's individually different underlying processing capacities, such as sensory modulation, auditory and visual-spatial processing, and motor planning. The second process is working with a child's most important functional developmental capacities (the building blocks of intelligence and emotional health), such as shared attention; relating with intimacy; engaging in gestural and affective reciprocal and social interactions; and using

ideas meaningfully, creatively, and logically. The third process involves utilizing new insights into the role of relationships and emotional interactions in facilitating a child's intellectual and emotional growth. For example, the earliest cognitive structures and sense of causality do not, as Piaget believed, first arise from early sensorimotor (cognitive) explorations but from even earlier affective interactions between a baby and his or her caregiver (e.g., a smile begetting a smile). At each stage of early cognitive development, emotional interactions lead the way. The meaning of words, early quantity concepts ("a lot" to a $2^1/_2$-year-old is more than he expects; "a little" is less than he wants), logical and abstract thinking, and even important components of grammar depend on specific types of emotional interactions (Greenspan, 1997; Greenspan & Wieder, 1999). These new observations make it possible to construct individualized, affectively based, learning interactions and relationships to promote intellectual and emotional growth. These individualized interventions are based on each child's unique profile of processing differences and functional developmental capacities.

Even though emerging evidence appears to favor this dynamic model, the vast majority of children with major developmental and learning problems have access only to approaches that are based on older, static views. Many of these approaches have not been very helpful and, for the most part, have not changed over many years. These approaches tend to focus on surface behaviors, symptoms, and syndromes and often assume that children having similar symptoms or surface behaviors also have similar underlying processing mechanisms. These approaches do not sufficiently deal with each child's (and family's) unique developmental and processing profile and the child's potential for growth.

Examples of widely used approaches that are not sufficiently based on dynamic developmental concepts and have not been sufficiently helpful to the majority of children with non-progressive developmental disorders include:

- *Limited educational programs that work with isolated educational skills*, such as matching shapes, without sufficient attention to the developmental stages of pre-verbal relating and communicating and the steps involved in building motor sequencing, visual-spatial processing, auditory and language processing capacities, and imaginative and logical thinking.

- *Behavioral approaches that attempt to be a primary, complete intervention* by working predominantly with surface behaviors and without sufficient attention to critical relating, developmental, and processing capacities.

- *Isolated biomedical approaches* involving various diagnostic procedures and medication without sufficient emphasis on constructing a complementary, comprehensive, functional developmental intervention program. An example is when a diagnostician gives parents their child's diagnosis, offers some recommendations for additional tests and/or a particular medication, and simply tells them to contact representatives of their local special education program (which only offers the limited program just described). Approaches that work intensively and comprehensively with each child's and each family's functional developmental profiles have generally been unavailable.

The challenges many families face in dealing with a service system that lacks the capacity to fully individualize a child's assessment and intervention program is illustrated by the following brief clinical vignette about Roger and his dedicated mother.

"Newly diagnosed with an autistic spectrum disorder, 3-year-old Robert was recommended for speech therapy, a special education program, and a social skills and relationship group. Robert's mother was told that these approaches were often helpful for children with autistic spectrum problems.

On the advice of her pediatrician, Robert's mother looked at a number of speech, special education, and social skills programs to see which would be best for Robert. 'But they are all so different, even though they are called the same thing,' she exclaimed. One speech pathologist was very structured, working on repeating sounds and words and labeling pictures. Since Robert was already repeating in a rote manner what he heard on television, his mother worried that this type of therapy might make his speech even more rote. Another speech therapist was very interactive, trying to get Robert to want to communicate with gestures or words, enticing Robert to imitate her when he really wanted something. This type of approach was more appealing to Robert's mother, but she didn't want to be the one who decided. The special education and social skills programs were even more varied in their approaches. Furthermore, none of the programs she observed seemed able to engage children who, like her Robert, always moved away from others. 'Could they work with a child who was so avoidant?' she wondered.

The mother also thought Robert might need additional services. He had slightly low muscle tone and had difficulty holding a pencil and copying shapes. He couldn't find his toys or even search for them. Furthermore, he tended to be underreactive to pain, but was overreactive to sound and held his ears whenever there were loud noises. At home, he always walked away from his parents and siblings and isolated himself with aimless wandering or repetitive activities, such as watching a video over and over. After researching these issues, his mother wondered if Robert also needed occupational therapy and/or work on his visual-spatial processing. What sort of a program should he have for the many hours he spent at home? Without a home program, he would continue to spend most of his time in relative isolation from others. No one had recommended additional approaches or therapies.

Robert's mother recognized that he was unique and not necessarily like other children who shared his diagnosis. She wanted to know what would be best for her son, based on his unique developmental profile. However, she was told that, at present, research could only answer some of her most general questions. It could tell her, for example, that speech therapy, education, and social skills programs were often helpful. It could not tell her what particular principles, or ingredients, or therapists, or educator personality patterns within these approaches would work best for her Robert. Nor could research tell her if he also needed additional programs, or what she and Robert's family should be doing with him at home, to help him learn to engage and become more reciprocal with others and work on motor planning or visual-spatial processing. Seeing how different the similarly named, recommended interventions were and how many unanswered questions she had, Robert's mother, understandably, felt abandoned by the professional community."

To answer this mother's critical questions, it is vital that the service system:
1. Determine the specific clinical principles and ingredients that should guide interventions for complex developmental disorders.
2. Develop methods to determine how to construct an individualized, comprehensive intervention program for a unique child (such as Robert) with his own profile of functional capacities and processing differences.

Meeting these two goals requires an unusually subtle level of clinical detail. It is a level of detail that recognizes:
- *Vital differences in therapies and educational programs that go by the same name*, but which vary widely in practice due to different interpretations of their intervention principles, different practitioner's personal characteristics, and the variety of situations that call for unplanned therapeutic actions that even the most detailed intervention curriculum can't anticipate.
- *Critical differences in the needs and intervention requirements of children* (and families) who may share the same diagnosis, but nonetheless have very different functional developmental capacities (e.g., one child is just learning to engage with others whereas another is working on using words more abstractly) and processing patterns (e.g., one child evidences strong auditory memory and weak visual-spatial processing capacities, whereas another child evidences just the opposite).

The guidelines presented in the chapters that follow systematize clinical knowledge at a level of clinical detail that focuses on individual patterns in an effort to answer the central question about what approach is best for an individual child and family. This is the question posed by Robert's mother and countless other parents as well as by practitioners from all the disciplines that work with non-progressive developmental disorders involving problems in relating, communicating, and thinking. ∎

REFERENCES

Chugani, H.T. (1999). Metabolic imaging: A window on brain development and plasticity. *The Neuroscientist, 5*, 1.

Greenspan, S. I. (1997). *The growth of the mind and the endangered origins of intelligence.* Reading, MA: Addison Wesley Longman.

Greenspan, S. I., & Wieder, S. (1999). A functional developmental approach to autism spectrum disorders. *Journal of the Association for Persons with Severe Handicaps (JASH), 24*(3); 147-161.

◄ 3 ►

Overview and Recommendations

Chapters 1 and 2 of this volume describe the clinical observations that suggest that functional developmental, or dimensional, profiles of the child and the child's family should guide the assessment and intervention process for complex, non-progressive developmental disorders. It is apparent that these disorders, which include autism, multisystem developmental disorders, cognitive deficits, and other disorders, involve limitations in a number of areas of functioning, such as language, motor planning (sequencing actions or behaviors), aspects of cognition, and social interaction. At present, research into the underlying etiology of many of these disorders, including autism, has not revealed a single cause or neurological pathway for the variety of these observed deficits in functioning (Bauman, Chapter 29, this volume; Cohen & Volkmar, 1997). In addition, there are no definitive clinical trial studies on comprehensive interventions for representative populations that show a clinically significant change in the course of these disorders, nor are there much-needed clinical trial studies comparing different intensive interventions. (See Tsakiris, Chapter 31, this volume, for a review of intervention research.)

It is also apparent that different disorders can involve similar deficits, and the same disorder can evidence different deficits. Thus, each child, regardless of the disorder diagnosed by symptoms, often evidences his own unique pattern of functional capacities (Cytryn, 1998; Greenspan & Wieder, 1997, 1998, 1999; Tanguay, Robertson, & Derrick, 1998). Each child, therefore, requires a highly individualized, comprehensive functional developmental approach. (A functional approach is already used in most complex medical disorders, such as heart disease, which also involves multiple causes and physiologic pathways in comparison to the rare complex disorder with a single etiology, such as syphilis.) Growing awareness of these challenges is reflected in a recent study conducted by the National Early Childhood Technical Assistance System (NECTAS), which revealed that a consensus is emerging on the importance of individualizing interventions to each child's developmental patterns and family needs (Hurth, Shaw, Iseman, Whaley, & Rogers, 1999).

RECOMMENDATIONS

Conceptual Framework: A Functional Developmental Approach

The overriding, conceptual framework for all the following recommendations is a comprehensive, developmentally based model for assessment of and intervention with children with special needs, rather than restricted approaches limited to selected surface behaviors and cognitive processes. For complex syndromes, in addition to exploring underlying etiological mechanisms, it is essential to work with the different functional developmental areas, including their deficits and strengths and the relationships among them. Full adoption of this *functional developmental approach* requires changes at a number of levels, including clinical services, special education, prevention and screening, national and community policies, and research. This chapter discusses these recommendations as well as challenges to them.

Components of a Functional Developmental Approach

In using a functional developmental approach, clinicians should include the following areas in an evaluation and intervention program.

- *Functional emotional developmental capacities,* which identify how the child integrates all her separate abilities (e.g., emotional, language, sensory modulation, spatial, and motor skills) to relate to the social and cognitive world in a purposeful and emotionally meaningful manner. They include the capacity to attend and regulate; relate to others; initiate purposeful interactions with gestures and/or emotional cues; engage in long, social, problem-solving sequences; create ideas, words, and imagine; and think, abstract, and learn. Mastering these critical functional developmental capacities depends on the child learning to connect her emotional interests, intent, or goals with her emerging motor-planning, cognitive, language, and sensory skills. These critical connections enable the child to create purpose and meaning in her world.

Children with complex developmental and learning problems, including autistic spectrum disorders, often only learn skills in an isolated, unpurposeful, or nonmeaningful way (e.g., memorizing scripts). They tend to have a harder time integrating these different capacities meaningfully. An appropriate intervention program must, therefore, focus not on isolated skills but on the most essential functional developmental capacities. Specific skills are embedded in these functional developmental foundations. More and more studies are identifying these capacities for shared attention, intimate relating, affective reciprocity, and the emotionally meaningful use of actions and ideas as the building blocks for logical and abstract thinking, including higher levels of empathy and reflection.

- *Individual differences in the functioning of the central nervous system,* with a special focus on how these differences are expressed in the way a child reacts to and processes experiences, as well as how she plans and organizes responses. This area typically includes sensory modulation (e.g., over- or underreactivity in each sensory modality, such as touch, sight, and sound); sensory processing (e.g., auditory [receptive language], visual-spatial, tactile, vestibular, and proprioceptive); motor planning and sequencing (e.g., planning and organizing actions, behaviors, and ideas); and other affective, cognitive, and learning processes (e.g., special talents and executive functions).

- *Child-caregiver interactions and family and service system patterns,* particularly as they mobilize developmental progress by working with the child's individual differences at the child's functional developmental level. In working with developmental, emotional, and behavioral problems, there is a tendency to lose sight of the functioning of the whole child and her family. Instead, the tendency is to work with isolated behaviors or processes (e.g., compliance, aggression, or matching shapes or colors), with insufficient attention paid to the child's emotional relationship to her caregivers, her ability to engage in a continuous chain of back-and-forth affective and gestural interactions, or her capacity to generate creative ideas. For example, teaching a child to carry out a particular task in a rote manner may decrease her capacity for relating with joy and warmth, expressing a range of feelings, and communicating meaningfully.

In general medicine, it is axiomatic that all systems of the body are relevant and interrelated. Therefore, clinicians routinely assess all areas of functioning (e.g., kidney, liver, and other organ systems) when conducting an evaluation or assessing an intervention such as a new antibiotic.

A comprehensive program that deals with the whole child and his family (as well as his community and culture) provides a framework within which specific techniques that work selectively on different behaviors or areas of functioning can be employed. In fact, the same technique may be quite effective as part of a comprehensive approach and ineffective, or even deleterious, as an isolated intervention.

- *A team approach* to an individualized, comprehensive functional program that works with each child's unique pattern of functional deficits and strengths and often includes, as needed, speech therapy, occupational and/or physical therapy, special education, biomedical interventions, and mental health or developmental work with the child, and child-caregiver interactions and/or family patterns—with all team members working together.

A Functional Developmental Approach to New Interventions and Research

A comprehensive, functional developmental approach can guide the development of new interventions. In a functional developmental approach, interventions developed for functional limitations in one syndrome can be applied to similar functional deficits even when they are part of another syndrome. For example, strategies developed by speech pathologists to facilitate expressive language by using oral-motor exercises can be employed with children with autism, fragile X and Down syndromes, and language dysfunctions. The same is true for strategies developed by occupational therapists to foster motor planning and sensory modulation. Such cross-syndrome applications favor innovation.

Research also can be defined by functional developmental areas rather than by only a specific syndrome. Autism research reviews (see Tsakiris, Chapter 31, this volume) can go beyond studies on children with autism and include research on different functional developmental problems across syndromes (e.g., motor planning, visual-spatial processing, sensory modulation, and auditory processing). Etiological factors and pathophysiologic pathways can be explored for each functional deficit (e.g., auditory processing and motor planning) as well as for whole syndromes. In short, given current knowledge, the best practice is for a team of clinicians to work with each child and family using a model that conceptualizes functional developmental deficits and strengths and constructs individually oriented clinical strategies based on all available knowledge from each of the disciplines that work with developmental problems (see Greenspan & Wieder, Chapter 4, this volume, for additional discussion of a comprehensive developmental approach to assessment and intervention).

Research Support for a Comprehensive Developmental Intervention Approach

In addition to clinical observational support, there is considerable research support for an individualized, comprehensive functional developmental intervention approach. This support emerges from an examination of the complex nature of the intervention process and a careful scrutiny of the strengths and limitations of current research.

Nonbiological intervention research on autistic spectrum and other developmental disorders involving problems in relating, thinking, and communicating faces challenges similar to those the psychotherapy field has been struggling with for the past 40 years (Greenspan & Sharfstein, 1981). These include:

- Characterizing the aspects of therapeutic relationships that are efficacious.
- Validating what actually occurs in a complex intervention.
- Determining and measuring a broad range of relevant outcomes that relate to the important domains of human functioning rather than to a particular theoretical orientation.
- Delineating clinically meaningful subgroups to permit appropriate matching or randomization and interpretation of results (i.e., relating outcomes and patterns of progress to different clinical subgroups within a large heterogeneous disorder, such as autism).

There is, however, no comparative clinical trial intervention studies on the major interventions. Due to the lack of comparative intervention studies on different approaches, there is, at present, therefore, no way to tease out the therapeutically and educationally active elements from all the other elements. For example, several factors of an educational/therapeutic approach could be facilitating development, either individually or in combinations. One could hypothesize that it is the general attention, curriculum, support, or intensity (number of hours per week) of treatment that is having an effect. Alternatively, it

could be the therapist's or teacher's characteristics or personality, the amount of empathy and warmth, or the general practice effect (i.e., simply working on an area, such as speech or motor skills, or on a certain set of behaviors). It might also be a particular therapeutic or educational technique.

Furthermore, if the hypothesis is that a particular intervention technique is responsible for developmental progress, it is difficult to document that the technique is actually practiced in a reasonably similar manner by the different therapists and/or educators who are purporting to use the technique. Videotape studies of therapists performing their craft to separate out tactical variables from personality and relationship variables are rarely, if ever, carried out.

In addition, currently used outcomes in most intervention studies rarely cover the full range of important functional developmental capacities relevant to autistic spectrum and other developmental disorders. For example, few intervention studies have systematically intervened with and measured outcomes for joint attention and symbolic play deficits in children with autism (Mundy & Crowson, 1997), despite the fact that progress in these areas predicts positive outcome in longitudinal studies (Mundy, Sigman, & Kasari, 1990; Sigman & Ruskin, 1999) and deficits in these areas are clinical indicators for the disorder. Most intervention studies have not measured subtle aspects of abstract thinking, in-depth emotional and social functioning, and visual-spatial processing. Instead, these studies have focused on limited outcome variables related to IQ and circumscribed cognitive tasks. Reliance on benchmarks such as cognitive and language scores as sole indices of progress in interventions causes the more obscure, but ultimately more significant, constructs that rely on the integration of skills and abilities to be overlooked (Guralnick, 1991).

These constructs include reciprocity, shared pleasure, empathy, and other elements that are necessary for social competence, as well as arousal, emotional regulation, planning, organization, and attention that are involved in the executive processing of information (Casey, Bronson, Tivnan, Riley, & Spenciner, 1991; Guralnick, 1998; Klinger & Dawson, 1992).

The importance of including hard-to-measure outcome variables is supported by research showing that, when matched for IQ scores, individuals with autism compared to individuals without autism tend to show selective difficulties in the mental processes associated with higher-level abstract thinking capacities, such as the ability to make inferences, interpret information, generate new ideas or perspectives, and generalize (Minshew, 1997, 1999, in press), as well as empathize with and understand the perspective of others (Baron-Cohen, Tager-Flusberg, & Cohen, 1993).

Furthermore, most current intervention research does not create clinically meaningful subgroups within the autistic spectrum. These subgroups could be based on functional developmental capacities, such as social and affective reciprocity and level of symbolic functioning, individually different processing capacities (e.g., auditory processing, visual-spatial processing, motor planning), and child-caregiver and family interaction patterns (see Greenspan, Wieder, & Zimmerman, Chapter 16, this volume). Since children within the autistic spectrum differ, meaningful subgroups would permit teasing out an answer to the important clinical question: What approach is likely to be helpful for a given child and family with their own unique profile?

In summary, current research has not teased out the active therapeutic and educational ingredients, validated the techniques being practiced to determine what is actually being evaluated for efficacy, employed the broad range of outcomes necessary to measure developmental capacities most relevant to autistic spectrum and other disorders of relating and communicating, or used clinically meaningful subgroups. In addition, as indicated, there are no comparative clinical trial outcome studies on the major interventions and no clinical trial outcome studies on comprehensive approaches showing clinically meaningful changes in the course of the disorder on a truly representative population of children with autism. At present, therefore, it would go beyond the currently available research to try to recommend interventions solely from research evidence, despite the fact that this is common practice for many educational systems (see Tsakiris, Chapter 31, this volume, for a more detailed discussion of these issues and a review of relevant intervention research.

The issue is, then, how can intervention programs be initiated without overstepping the existing data? Current research can provide important clues. These can be refined by clinical experience provided from the different disciplines working with developmental problems as well as by additional research. Together, research and clinical experience can provide a model to guide clinical practice. Such a model needs to move beyond which approach is best for a heterogeneous disorder and answer the more important question of how to develop interventions for a child who exhibits his own unique pattern of development and symptoms. It also must allow for, and encourage, a wide range of relevant research outcomes.

Creating the Basic Model

It is important to begin with a basic model that derives from both research and clinical experience. To do less runs the risk of providing less thoughtful interventions and of spending valuable research funds on studies of intervention programs that are unlikely to be helpful. For example, one may compare an intervention that has a modest effect on approximately 30% of the children with autistic spectrum disorder s with an intervention that has a modest effect on only 5% of the children. On the surface, it would appear that the intervention that modestly helps a third of the children is quite potent. However, the primary result of many confirmatory studies may be a well-documented intervention that is, nonetheless, unable to significantly help most of the children with the disorder. Alternatively, it is possible to begin with a robust model that builds on promising research and clinical practice observations. Such a model may create an opportunity to begin from a higher baseline and then study and fine tune an intervention model that is more likely to be helpful to more children.

There are a number of research and clinical practice observations that can contribute to conceptualizing a comprehensive developmental approach for autistic spectrum and other disorders of relating and communicating. One of these is the importance of working with the *different processing areas* compromised in these developmental disorders. These processing areas include work with (1) speech and language, which is well-documented in both research studies and clinical practice descriptions (Goldstein & Hockenberger, 1991; Law, 1997; McLean & Cripe, 1998; Wetherby & Prizant, 1993, 1995) and (2) the motor and sensory systems, including visual-spatial processing, which also is supported by research and clinical practice (Blackman & Goldstein, 1982; Case-Smith & Bryan, 1999; Chez, Gordon, Ghilardi, & Sainburg, 1995; Lincoln, Courchesne, Harms, & Allen, 1995; Williamson & Anzalone, 1997; Wachs, Chapter 20, and Feuerstein, Chapter 22, this volume).

There also is considerable research and clinical support for working with important *functional developmental capacities* (Greenspan, 1992; Tanguay, Robertson, & Derrick, 1998),

including attention and preverbal gestural interactive problem solving (e.g., joint attention [Mundy, Sigman, & Kasari, 1990]), reciprocal affective interactions (Dawson & Galpert, 1990; Lewy & Dawson, 1992; Tanguay, 1999), different levels of symbolic functioning in affective, interpersonal, cognitive, and language domains (e.g., theory of mind [Baron-Cohen, 1994] and the pragmatic [i.e., social functional] use of presymbolic and symbolic communication [Wetherby & Prizant, 1993]). These important areas of developmental functioning can be systematized clinically into six basic functional developmental capacities, which also have support from the normative child development literature (Greenspan, 1992; Greenspan & Lourie, 1981). These six functional developmental capacities are:

1. *Shared attention and regulation.*
2. *Engagement.*
3. *Affective reciprocity and gestural communication.*
4. *Complex presymbolic, shared social communication and problem solving,* including imitation, social referencing, and joint attention.
5. *Symbolic and creative use of ideas,* including pretend play and pragmatic language.
6. *Logical and abstract use of ideas and thinking,* including the capacity for expressing and reflecting on feelings and having insights into self and others.

A review of 200 cases of children with autistic spectrum disorder s demonstrated that there were individual differences (i.e., variations) in these functional developmental and processing capacities among the children, further supporting the importance of working with them in the unique configuration that characterizes a given child and family (see Table 1) (Greenspan & Wieder, 1997).

There also is considerable support for focusing on *child-caregiver interactions and working with the family* (McCollum & Hemmeter, 1998; Krauss, 1998; Turnbull & Turnbull, 1982). In addition, two other elements appear to have importance. One is employing *a very intensive approach to working with children and their families.* In an intensive program, the majority of the child's time is involved in various types of pleasurable, soothing, and learning interactions, leaving very little time available for self-absorption or perseverative activities. In most studies, the intensity factor (30 to 40 hours a week) appears to discriminate between greater and lesser outcomes (Lovaas, 1987; McEachin, Smith, & Lovaas, 1993; Scheinkopf & Siegal, 1998) at least in terms of IQ levels. This is the one finding of the Lovaas study that, based on the design,

Table 1. Chart Review of 200 Cases of Children with Autistic Spectrum Disorders		
Functional Developmental and Processing Capacity	**Percent of Patients**	**Description of Functional Developmental and Processing Pattern**
Attention, engagement, purposeful and problem-solving behavior, and use of symbols	24%	Partially engaged, purposeful problem solving, with limited use of symbols (ideas)
	40%	Partially engaged, purposeful, with very limited complex problem solving, and inconsistent or no use of symbols
	31%	Partially engaged with only fleeting purposeful behavior
	5%	No affective engagement and minimal attention
Sensory modulation	19%	Overreactive to sensation
	39%	Underreactive to sensation (with 11% craving sensation)
	36%	Mixed reactivity to sensation
	6%	Not classified
Motor-planning dysfunction	52%	Mild to moderate motor-planning dysfunction
	48%	Severe motor-planning dysfunction
Low muscle tone	17%	Motor-planning dysfunction with significant degree of low muscle tone
Visual-spatial processing dysfunction	22%	Relative strength (e.g., can find toys, good sense of direction)
	36%	Moderate impairment
	42%	Moderate to severe impairment
Auditory processing and language	45%	Mild to moderate impairment with some abilities to imitate sounds and words or use selected words
	55%	Moderate to severe impairment with no ability to imitate or use words

can be supported clearly and unequivocally. The Lovaas study compared a 40-hour per week intervention program with a 10-hour per week intervention program and found the more intensive program was associated with better outcomes in regard to IQ and selective adaptive scores.

However, defining the active ingredients of a more intensive approach and the threshold levels of very intensive programs is not yet clear from available research (Rogers & DiLalla, 1991; Venn, Wolery, & Graco, 1996; Zelazo, 1997). Intensity is not defined just by the number of hours spent in one-on-one instruction, but also by the amount of time spent during a child's day in helping him generalize skills through the more spontaneous experiences and interactions of daily life and the classroom.

It also appears that *one-on-one child-caregiver interactions,* especially for children who are not yet social and interactive, is essential for significant progress (Dawson & Osterling, 1997; Powers, 1992). Additionally, as children become available for social interaction, it appears that balancing adult-child one-on-one work with peer-to-peer and small-group work is also quite helpful (Hoyson, Jamison, & Strain, 1984; Strain & Cordisco, 1994).

The Developmental, Individual Differences, Relationship-Based (DIR) Approach

The promising elements just identified can be conceptualized as part of a comprehensive developmental model (Greenspan, 1992; Greenspan & Wieder, 1998, 1999) by systematizing the elements into the three broad categories described in a previous section. These broad categories are:

1. *D – Developmental capacities* that integrate the most essential cognitive and affective processes. These are the six func-

tional developmental capacities described previously on page 18 of this chapter.
2. *I – Individual differences* in motor, auditory, visual-spatial, and other sensory processing capacities.
3. *R – Relationships* that are part of child-caregiver and family interaction patterns and which provide:
   - ongoing nurturing support;
   - orchestration of the specific educational and therapeutic elements incorporated in 1 and 2 above;
   - provision of ongoing interactive learning opportunities geared to the child's individual differences and current functional developmental capacities throughout most of the child's waking hours (at an appropriate intensity); and
   - a balance between one-on-one caregiver-to-child interactions and peer-to-peer interactions appropriate to the child's individual differences and functional developmental capacities.

In the Developmental, Individual Differences, Relationship-based (DIR) approach, functional developmental capacities, individual differences in processing capacities, and relationships embedded in the child-caregiver and family patterns are utilized together in clinical decision making to create an individualized program for a given child and family.

In conclusion, there is a wide range of research and clinical experience not just from the field of autism but from the field of early intervention and child development at large, which, when taken as a whole, provides considerable empirical support (far more than for more circumscribed approaches) for a comprehensive developmental model.

The Challenge to a Functional Developmental Approach

Restrictive frameworks that ignore a child's relevant processing capacities, critical functional developmental abilities, necessary family support, and involvement of all relevant disciplines present a special challenge. Although there are many types of restrictive approaches, two are especially visible and often are mistakenly presented as comprehensive. One involves using applied behavioral analysis (ABA), or discrete trial behavioral approaches, as a primary approach rather than as one possible part of a comprehensive effort. In this approach, limited areas of behavior are targeted for modification. The full range of functional developmental deficits and strengths is often not assessed or worked with, nor is the expertise of key professionals sought to facilitate development in these critical areas of functioning (i.e., occupational therapists or speech pathologists are not typically involved in a discrete trial behavioral program). In-depth family and child-caregiver dynamics also are often not a part of this framework.

ABA was the first method to advocate hopeful, intensive one-on-one work and, for a long time, was the only approach to work in this way. During the last 15 years, however, as indicated earlier, there is new research and understanding of differences in underlying processing capacities, the functional developmental capacities that lead to intelligence and emotional health, and the importance of emotions, spontaneous child-caregiver interactions, and family patterns for healthy development. These findings have enabled the field to progress beyond a focus on discrete behaviors and construct intensive, one-on-one and small-group approaches that are comprehensive, developmentally based, and tailored to the individual profile of the child and his or her family. Within such a broad developmental framework, behavioral techniques can be used when needed as part of a larger comprehensive program. For example, children with severe motor-planning problems who are having difficulty learning to imitate motor actions, sounds, and/or words may benefit from more structured work. Behavioral analysis of the environmental factors influencing adaptive and problem behaviors and some of the newer behavioral approaches that focus more on spontaneous or incidental learning opportunities can also be helpful for particular children at a specific time in their development as part of a comprehensive program. Behavioral approaches in and of themselves, however, should not be the primary organizing approach for a program. The primary approach should use a broad developmental framework that conceptualizes all of the vital developmental processes.

In many treatment programs and educational settings, however, behavioral approaches are still used as the primary approach. At times, proponents of ABA (discrete trial) approaches go beyond the available data in discussions of their effectiveness. It is, therefore, necessary to briefly examine the limitations of the research on these approaches.

Proponents of discrete trial behavioral approaches cite the longitudinal Lovaas study (Lovaas, 1987; McEachin et al., 1993) and a number of shorter-term studies. Many professionals and organizations, however, point out the limitations of these studies (Bristol et al., 1996; Greenspan, 1998; Gresham & McMillan, 1998; Rogers, 1996; Schopler, 1987). The Lovaas study had many limitations. Most important, it did not include a representative sample of children with autism. The selection criteria eliminated children who presented with the most typical autistic patterns and, instead, only allowed children who evidenced certain cognitive capacities and had better prognoses. Furthermore, the study used limited outcome measures, focusing on the children's performance on selected, structured, cognitive tests. These tests, however, do not distinguish autistic and nonautistic individuals who are matched for IQ. The outcome measures did not sufficiently assess the variables that research has shown to distinguish autistic and nonautistic individuals and that are specific to autistic functioning. When autistic and nonautistic individuals are matched for IQ, the autistic group shows deficits in the capacity for higher-level abstract thinking, such as making inferences and creating new ideas and solutions (Minshew, 1997, 1999, in press), and understanding one's own and others' feelings (Baron-Cohen et al., 1993). The autistic group also shows deficits in emotional reciprocity and shared attention (Baranek, 1994; Dawson, 1992; Dawson & Galpert, 1990; Lewy & Tanguay, 1999; Mundy et al., 1990; Osterling & Dawson, 1994). The outcome measures used in the Lovaas studies, however, did not assess these autistic-specific deficits involving abstract and creative thinking and emotional flexibility, awareness, and relatedness. In addition, the children in the comparison group did not have precisely the same cognitive and social functioning as the intervention group at the start of the study, the study did not involve random assignment, and participants knew the group to which they were assigned. Furthermore, in another study of discrete trial behavioral interventions with children with more typical patterns of autism involving severe cognitive deficits, the results were not encouraging. Although the intervention group did better than a control group, the changes in the children's behavior did not pass clinically mean-

ingful thresholds; that is, the children retained most of their autistic patterns (Smith, Eikeseth, Morton, & Lovaas, 1997). Furthermore, behavioral studies that show short-term, selected behavioral changes do not sufficiently look at long-term, clinically meaningful changes in important areas of functioning such as empathy and creative, logical, and abstract thinking—the areas of functioning that are impaired in autism.

The limitation of the ABA-discrete trial and related behavioral approaches as the primary approach is perhaps best illustrated, however, by contrasting its wide use in various forms in educational and other settings in most communities during the past 25 years with the lack of progress by most children receiving these approaches. The majority of children with typical patterns of autism in behavioral programs generally have been unable to learn to live independently, work, and participate in a range of age-expected social relationships.

The question then becomes: Should many clinicians and educators continue to use a primary approach that is restrictive, that evidence suggests is of limited value, and that excludes emerging, promising knowledge from the different disciplines, such as occupational therapy and speech pathology? Or, is it time for the entire field to progress to a broader-based approach through which all the knowledge available from different disciplines and levels of research can be used and interventions can be tailored to the child's profile of functional developmental deficits and strengths? This dilemma is not just of theoretical interest. The New York State Department of Health, based on what could be a serious misreading of current research on interventions (see Tsakiris, Chapter 31, this volume), has recently issued a report recommending the restrictive behavioral approaches as a primary approach. The recommendations in that report may severely limit the services available to children and families when developmental problems are present.

The second restrictive approach that is widely used and often mistakenly presented as comprehensive is for a therapist to work with only a limited number of a child's cognitive skills, on the assumption that these are the only skills relevant to a community's educational responsibilities. Typically, such a restrictive educational approach focuses on a very limited number of surface behavioral, cognitive, and social goals, such as rote behaviors or phrases, matching exercises, and social compliance. Only a minimal amount of speech or occupational therapy is provided to work on a child's underlying processing problems.

In a field of incomplete knowledge and no definitive comparative intervention studies, a clinician can provide each child and family the best possible approach only when the option is available to orchestrate a broad-based developmental approach tailored to each child's unique profile of functional developmental deficits and strengths.

The next sections present a series of additional recommendations on the implementation of an appropriate assessment and intervention program, including needed changes in current policies. Subsequent chapters will further amplify these and related recommendations. (See Appendix A of this chapter, "Outline of the DIR Model: How to Use *The ICDL Clinical Practice Guidelines*" for a schematic outline to the functional developmental approach to assessment and intervention.)

Assessment Program

Recommendations For Assessment

- *A comprehensive developmental approach.* A comprehensive individual or team-based approach involves all the relevant functional areas, including a child's individual processing differences, functional developmental level, child-caregiver interactions, and family functioning. A clinician must observe these areas of functioning for a reasonable period of time, with special emphasis on the child's interaction with primary caregivers in order to assess the child's capacity to relate to others and to tease out the full degree of the child's strengths and challenges. A recent chart review of 200 cases revealed that more than 90% of evaluations, including evaluations conducted at university medical centers, clinics, educational settings, and individual practitioners' offices, did not include direct observations of child-caregiver interactions for longer than 15 minutes (Greenspan & Wieder, 1997). In these settings, there tends to be an emphasis on administering structured tests with insufficient attention given to child-caregiver interactions and family functioning.

- *A clinical evaluation process.* Assessment should be the initial phase as well as part of an ongoing clinical process of observation and discussion. The evaluation of infants and children with disorders of relating, communicating, and thinking is a complex process involving careful reports of a child's current developmental functioning, a detailed developmental history, and direct observations of the child interacting with parents as well as the clinician, with a focus on the child's six primary functional developmental capacities, individual processing differences (e.g., motor planning, auditory and visual-spatial processing, sensory modulation), and interaction patterns with caregivers and other family members (see Greenspan & Wieder, Chapters 4 and 15, this volume). Additional assessments must build on this clinical core and often may include assessments of language, motor and sensory functioning, visual-spatial capacities, and different cognitive skills, as well as a biomedical evaluation.

The evaluation process must also include a careful review of family functioning, including discussion with the parents about family relationships and the ability of the family to support the child's different functional developmental capacities as well as work with processing vulnerabilities. In addition, for children with significant developmental challenges, the evaluation process must create a working relationship between the family and the clinician(s) conducting the evaluation. If an intervention is recommended, this relationship will facilitate the family's transition into an intervention program. The working relationship emerges from an understanding of family patterns and a consensus between parents and clinician(s) on the child's developmental profile. An extended evaluation may be required to reach consensus and enable a family to support a comprehensive, individually tailored intervention program.

Although observation and discussion are at the core of the evaluation process, structured protocols and developmental tests may play a supplementary role if needed for a particular child and family. There are a number of reasons why structured assessment protocols or developmental tests should not be used as the primary core of the assessment process. At present, there is not sufficient evidence that they can elicit the full cooperation of a child with severe developmental challenges (i.e., bring out the child's highest level of functioning in each capacity). In addition, there is also insufficient evidence that they can address the range of subtle distinctions during all the phases of infancy and early childhood in critical

functional developmental capacities and important processing abilities (e.g., visual-spatial, motor planning, sensory modulation) more effectively than a comprehensive clinical evaluation utilizing observation, discussion, and clinical judgement. At present, therefore, structured tools should be reserved for research (to establish common ground for a diagnosis) and/or to supplement, on an as-needed basis, the core clinical evaluation.

- *Diagnosis should be a dynamic, ongoing process involving a functional developmental profile of the child and the child's family.* Syndrome-based diagnoses, if required, should initially be provisional and play a secondary role unless the syndrome involves a clear etiology, biologic pathway, and highly effective treatment.

- *In addition, diagnoses of syndromes such as autism and mental retardation should be made only after working with a child for a significant time interval in an optimal program and after observing the child's response to intervention.* Children who quickly learn to relate and interact, for example, may not require a diagnosis of autism even if they initially meet the criteria. Similarly, a diagnosis of mental retardation, which suggests chronic, fixed, global deficits, should not be made unless a child's ability to learn has leveled off for 2 to 3 years in spite of an optimal, individually tailored program. During the time a clinician spends on observation of a child, services can be justified either by the degree of the child's functional deficits that can be documented or with a "provisional" diagnosis.

- *Distinguishing specific and nonspecific symptoms in autistic spectrum disorders is essential to making a proper diagnosis.* With an increasing number of children being diagnosed with austistic spectrum disorders, clinicians and parents are understandably attempting to identify this problem as early as possible. Proper early identification, however, requires a clear understanding of the nature of the deficit that is specific to the disorder and the ability to distinguish this deficit from symptoms seen both in autism and other disorders (i.e., nonspecific symptoms). The deficit that is specific to autism involves the inability to relate to caregivers and engage in a continuous flow of back-and-forth (reciprocal) affective gestures in a variety of contexts (e.g., flirting, getting help and collaborating to solve problems, seeking admiration or approval, or pointing out something of interest).

A common mistake, however, is to make the diagnosis of autism based on a symptom or group of symptoms that are not specific to autism; that is, symptoms that are found in many developmental and learning problems. Examples of symptoms or behaviors that are seen in both autism and other disorders—but are often mistakenly thought to be specific to and, therefore, a sign of autism—are hand-flapping, echolalia, perseverative or repetitive behavior, difficulty relating to peers, and problems with understanding one's own and others' feelings (i.e., the capacity for empathy or theory of mind). Hand-flapping and other unusual motor behaviors can be seen as part of a variety of motor-planning and coordination difficulties, particularly during times of excitement. Echolalia is often seen as part of receptive language problems, in response to which the child may repeat what he hears both because he has difficulty processing it and to hold it in mind as a first step in processing it. Repetitive behavior is often seen in children who tend to become overloaded by sensory

input combined with dyspraxia (motor planning problems). Peer problems can be seen in children who lack opportunities to practice relating to peers, are sensory under- or overreactive, are very anxious, have receptive language problems, or who have severe motor-planning difficulties. Problems with empathy and theory of mind can be seen in many children with severe receptive language, cognitive, regulatory, and/or antisocial behavior problems.

Children who are capable of engaging caregivers with deep intimacy and can participate in a continuous flow of affective (gestural) signaling in a variety of problem-solving contexts are, at times, misdiagnosed with an autistic spectrum disorder because of the presence of some of these nonspecific symptoms. Based on a misdiagnosis, they may be placed in an inappropriate treatment program (e.g., a very controlled and repetition-oriented behavioral or educational program that does not sufficiently emphasize affective relationships and dynamic problem solving interactions) that can undermine their very strength, which is the ability to relate to and reciprocate with a range of affective signals and gestures (i.e., communicate purposefully and creatively). Therefore, only the deficits that are specific to autistic spectrum disorders should be used as primary criteria in making a diagnosis. As indicated earlier, however, working with a child over a period of time is the best way to observe the extent and degree to which a child evidences and can change these primary autism-specific deficits.

Challenges to the Recommendations for Assessment

- *Special challenges to the assessment recommendations include approaches that focus on limited areas of functioning and/or isolated surface behaviors* and do not assess and fully incorporate underlying individual processing differences, spontaneous child-caregiver interactions, the intimacy and affective reciprocity involved in the child-caregiver relationship, or in-depth family functioning.

- In addition, *developmental test-oriented evaluations, which do not fully assess child-caregiver interactions or family patterns,* may omit important observations that are essential for planning interventions. While developmental tests may be part of a comprehensive approach, IQ or other structured developmental tests should not be used as a primary way to categorize or label children or organize an intervention program. While such tests have a long tradition behind them, they may only measure selected cognitive capacities at a point in time. Furthermore, they do not measure all the critical processing capacities that relate to intellectual functioning. In addition, performance on them can be undermined by selective processing deficits such as severe motor-planning and sequencing problems. For example, we have clinically observed children with severe motor-planning and sequencing problems improve their performance on IQ tests by 30% to 50% during a 5-year period as their motor planning and sequencing improved (Greenspan, 1992; Greenspan & Wieder, 1998). IQ and other structured developmental tests, therefore, should not take the place of observing a child over time as he learns through interactions tailored to his developmental profile of processing strengths and weaknesses. In fact, labeling a child and treating him as though he is similar to others in his category tends to decrease the likelihood of

individualized learning interactions. In contrast, working with a child and constantly attempting to find better and better ways to understand his differences and create dynamic, individualized learning interactions often creates continuing opportunities for growth.

- Therefore, *time- and context-limited evaluations that do not include or integrate observations of the child's functioning over time in multiple contexts,* including the child's response to a comprehensive intervention program, may unnecessarily limit the scope of needed observations.

Intervention Program

Recommendations for Intervention

- *A Development, Individual Differences, Relationship-based (DIR) approach.* The intervention program must work with all essential functional developmental capacities (regulation and attention, engagement, two-way purposeful interaction, problem-solving interactions, the creative use of ideas, and logical thinking), individual processing differences (auditory, language, visual-spatial, motor planning, and sensory modulation), and child-caregiver interactions and family functioning, as well as additional cognitive and learning skills. The functional developmental intervention model, which is described more fully in Chapter 4 of this volume, is characterized by a number of additional features.

- *Three types of learning involved in a comprehensive functional developmental intervention program.* The first type of learning involves following the child's lead and engaging in child-initiated interactions that are based on the child's natural emotional interests (floor time). The goal of these spontaneous interactions is to mobilize and improve attention, engagement, purposeful and problem-solving interactions, and, if the child is ready, the creative and logical use of ideas and words. The second type is semistructured problem-solving interactions that meet specific language, cognitive, and social goals. An example of this is an adult enticing a child to try to open a door to get a favorite toy, and using the child's motivated state to teach her to say "open." Semistructured learning can also be relatively structured, if needed. A child with severe challenges in motor planning and sequencing that are interfering with his capacity to imitate and use words, for example, will often require, together with dynamic interactions, a very structured program for a period of time to strengthen motor planning and imitative capacities. Techniques worked out by Arnold Miller (see Miller & Eller-Miller, Chapter 19, this volume) and many of the imitative exercises developed through behavioral approaches can be especially useful in this circumstance. For children unable to engage in complex verbal or gestural interchanges, but with relative strengths in visual pattern recognition, elements of the TEACCH program, which emphasizes visual processing, may be especially valuable. Each of these structured elements, however, needs to be embedded in a comprehensive, functional developmental program that works with all the child's important functional capacities and his family relationships. The third type of learning that characterizes a functional developmental intervention program is motor, sensory, and spatial learning activities oriented toward facilitating motor planning and sequencing, sensory modulation, and visual-spatial thinking. (See Greenspan & Wieder,

Chapter 12, this volume, for a more detailed description of the three types of learning interactions.)

- *All-day and evening programs.* Children with severe developmental problems, including autistic spectrum disorders, often cannot, on their own, initiate or carry through developmentally appropriate interactions or learning practices as recommended by the National Association for the Education of Young Children (NAEYC). If left alone, children with developmental challenges may perseverate, become self-absorbed, or self-stimulate. Therefore, they often require one-on-one or small-group interactive and learning opportunities throughout their waking hours, either in school or at home, geared to their unique developmental profiles. These should include relationship-based interactive, relaxing, and soothing times.

- *Individual therapies,* including speech and language and occupational and/or physical therapy at *sufficient intensity (based on the child's developmental profile) to facilitate optimal progress.* Often, three or more individual sessions of 45 minutes each is required for each therapy.

- *Integrated education program and peer interaction and play opportunities.* Once children with special needs can imitate gestures, sounds, and words, and interact with others, they often benefit from an integrated education program. If they are in a home-based educational program, they benefit from daily opportunities for substantial social interaction during which the other children can understand and respond to their communications. They also require four or more one-on-one peer play dates a week. The education program at school or at home should also be based on the three types of learning described earlier in one-on-one and small-group contexts. In this way, the child can learn through ongoing interactions with others rather than in isolation or through watching.

- *An appropriate education program.* The child's Individual Education Plan (IEP) should include the main funtional developmental capacities of attention and regulation, engagement, purposeful two-way circles of communication, problem-solving interactions, the creative use of ideas, and the capacity to build logical bridges between ideas, as well as work on each processing capacity (i.e., audit, visual-spatial, motor planning, and sensory modulation) as the primary goals. Often, a child can master these developmental goals in conjunction with specific academic or pre-academic skills.

- *Biomedical approaches* should be tailored to each child's individual differences and developmental capacities, including consideration of medication and/or nutritional approaches.

- *Technology-based learning opportunities* should be geared to each child's individual profile.

- *Consultations by a developmental and/or mental health specialist to help construct and monitor the overall program* including the three types of learning and child-caregiver and family interactions.

- *A full evaluation and, if required, an intervention program should be initiated immediately if functional developmental capacities, as outlined in the screening approach are not progressing* (see Appendix B, Figure B1, this chapter, for the Functional Developmental Growth Chart). A wait-and-see approach should only be an option for a short period of time and for circumscribed difficulties that do not interfere with relating, functional communication, or thinking.

- *An intervention program should offer the potential of continuity.* The typical change from an infancy to a preschool program at age 3 is often disruptive for children who are working on learning to relate to others and trust relationships.

Challenges to the Recommendations for Intervention

- Special challenges to the preceding recommendations include a*pproaches which purport to be comprehensive but which do not work with the most relevant functional developmental capacities and related family patterns.* Noncomprehensive approaches include *programs that only work on isolated behaviors and/or language and cognitive skills* and do not sufficiently help a child master core functional capacities, such as shared attention, relating, reciprocal affective cueing, self-initiated problem solving, and the creative, logical, and meaningful use of ideas, or strengthen underlying processing difficulties, or work on relevant family patterns. Therefore, noncomprehensive interventions—which include behavioral and limited educational approaches—should not be used as the primary intervention program for children with disorders of relating, thinking, and communicating, including autistic spectrum disorders. As indicated earlier, however, elements of various approaches may be incorporated into a comprehensive developmental approach tailored to a child's unique profile.

- Further challenges to these recommendations include *programs that are not sufficiently intensive, do not create necessary one-on-one and small-group learning opportunities, and do not contain sufficient learning or interactive opportunities for the child's day and evening time.*

Many children require one-on-one and/or small-group interactive learning opportunities throughout the day and evening in their school and home programs. Too much time spent alone or watching television, as well as passive observation of other children, often results in a child's increasing self-absorption, perseveration, and lack of adequate progress. Some states, such as Pennsylvania, provide "wrap-around" services that can be tailored to the child's developmental profile to help parents create an appropriately intensive home or after-school program.

Prevention and Monitoring Development

Recommendations for Prevention and Monitoring Development

- *An early, universal, prevention and developmental monitoring program.* Through routine well-baby and child pediatric care, early education, daycare, public health and education dissemination efforts, and other programs, all families with children should have access to information, advice, support, and back-up clinical services to promote the child's mastery of (and prevent difficulties in) each expected functional developmental capacity. As part of these efforts, every parent should be offered help to identify the child's emerging functional developmental strengths and challenges.
- *There should be three levels to this program.* At the first level, a series of readily observable functional milestones that integrate the different important functional developmental capacities can be used for observing and asking questions about an infant and child's development as part of well-baby and child care, in early educational settings, and by parents. At the

second level, if needed, a more detailed screening questionnaire can be used to further document a potential problem and determine if a full evaluation is needed. At the third level, if needed, a full evaluation should be conducted and an appropriate intervention program should be available. (See Appendix B, this chapter, for the Functional Developmental Growth Chart and Questionnaire.)

The Challenge to Recommendations for Prevention and Monitoring Development

A special challenge to the preceding recommendations is a *wait-and-see approach that does not distinguish serious emerging functional developmental deficits from circumscribed challenges that the child and family may master on their own.* Waiting to see if a child "grows out of it" is not recommended when critical functional areas, such as relating, interacting, or communicating, are involved because these critical capacities build on one another and are much harder to master later in development. When critical capacities are not developing, delay in evaluating or implementing appropriate interventions tends to increase the challenges. In contrast, circumscribed difficulties, such as a mild expressive language articulation problem, may be observed for a short period of time to see if the difficulties diminish on their own or after advice to parents.

Community and National Policies Affecting Children and Families with Special Needs

Policy Recommendations

Full implementation of the comprehensive functional developmental approach recommended here would require changes to several community and national policies.

Appropriate policies would stress the following actions:

- *Early identification and intervention for functional developmental impairments.* Early intervention minimizes a child's ongoing functional developmental impairments and missed opportunities for mastering critical skills.
- *Flexible criteria for early intervention services.* Resources should not be used to "guard the door." Parents, pediatricians, or developmental specialists should determine if interventions are needed based on their potential to help a child, not on the child's degree of impairment. Most parents will not seek unneeded services, and children in the "gray areas" will be less likely to need intensive services later if help is provided early.
- *Parental involvement.* Parents should be leaders or co-leaders at all levels, including planning an intervention program for their individual child.
- *An "optimal," rather than "adequate," standard for education and special education.*
- *Equality of insurance coverage with other medical disorders, including all recommended therapies, for developmental disorders.*
- *Programs that tailor the approach to the unique characteristics of the child and the child's family* rather than having the child and family fit to the program.
- *Special curricula and programs for pre-professional training based on a functional developmental model.*
- *An emphasis within the training programs of various disciplines to include cross-training in the theories and techniques of other professions.*
- *Efforts to help programs with different philosophies embrace a comprehensive developmental framework and work together* so that, when appropriate, ele-

ments of different programs can be harnessed to meet the individual needs of a given child and family.
- *Recognition of the lack of a single etiology for most non-progressive, complex developmental disorders, including autistic spectrum disorders.* Therefore, support is needed for a broad range of program options with efficacy reviews based on functional developmental areas, and on different levels of knowledge. Practitioners and parents should then determine the type of program for a particular child based on that child's unique profile.

Challenges to the Recommendations for Policy Changes

- Challenges to the preceding policy recommendations include *adversarial interactions between educational or service system professionals and parents.* These conflicts often stem from attempts to justify an "adequate" rather than "optimal" program model or to delay the initiation of appropriate intervention services.
- Challenges also include *restrictive policies supporting a particular intervention approach rather than generic support for constructing an individualized approach that will be best for a particular child* (see Tsakiris, Chapter 31, this volume).

Research

Research Recommendations

- *Research into the etiology and biological pathways involved in autism and other disorders of relating, communicating, and thinking should focus on the etiology and biological pathways associated with specific functional developmental deficits, such as in the connection between affect and motor planning and symbol formation, visual-spatial thinking, motor plan-*

ning and sequencing, and auditory processing, as well as entire syndromes.

Because children with autism and other disorders of relating, communicating, and thinking differ a great deal from one another in their functional developmental capacities, it is highly likely that we are dealing with heterogeneous disorders with many subtypes. Therefore, in order to make sense of biological findings, *more research must be conducted on constructing subtypes based on functional developmental patterns* (see Greenspan & Wieder, Chapter 16, this volume).

There are many clinical challenges affecting large numbers of children that are under-researched. These include self-absorbed, aimless, and fragmented patterns of relating and communicating for preverbal children and concrete, rigid, polarized, and constricted ideational patterns for verbal children. They also include problems in motor planning, visual-spatial thinking, auditory processing, and sensory modulation.

- *Exploratory research in the different disciplines to generate improved clinical strategies is needed.* At present, there is support for evaluation and outcome research but not for research to generate clinical intervention strategies worthy of being evaluated.
- In addition to exploratory studies, *there is a need for comparative clinical trial studies of the major intervention models.* Such studies would help the field identify the critical therapeutic variables by controlling for such factors as intensity and positive expectations.
- *A cumulative central nervous system challenge model should guide a significant portion of the research effort* because the causes and pathways involved in autistic spectrum and related

disorders of communicating, relating, and thinking include the interactions among many factors. Among under-researched factors that need to be studied in interaction with each other are genetic susceptibility and prenatal exposure to toxic substances, such as dioxin and PCBs. These toxic substances, which are associated with increased risk of developmental, immunologic, and reproductive dysfunction, are found in soil, air, water, and, surprisingly, at unsafe levels in maternal breast milk in the United States and most industrialized countries. Other factors that need greater study are postnatal precipitants of regressions in developmental functioning, which occur in one-third to two-thirds of children diagnosed with autistic spectrum disorders (e.g., autoimmune phenomena, various types of physiologic and/or psychological stress). It is likely that genetically susceptible children undergo a series of insults, as just described, which present cumulative challenges to the central nervous system, resulting in developmental regressions and various symptoms of sensory, language, cognitive, affective, and motor dysfunctions.

- *The field must refrain from overstepping current research and advocating narrow "evidence-based" guidelines for clinical practice and, instead, advocate broad knowledge-based guidelines that utilize both available research and clinical experience.*

Acknowledging limitations in the evidence, however, far from leaving the field of interventions for developmental problems vulnerable, creates an important foundation for progress. A number of important facts are part of this foundation. One is that over 20 years ago there was already overall support for the value of early intervention for developmental problems (Greenspan & White, 1987; White and Greenspan, 1987). But historically as well as in the last 20 years there is not sufficient data on specific interventions. Nor are there enough comparative studies on different interventions for the same problem. Therefore, the critical question on which approach will work best for an individual child with a unique developmental profile cannot be answered with definitive data. The proper scientific approach in such a circumstance is to develop broad, knowledge-based guidelines rather than narrow, evidence-based ones.

There are four criteria based on clinical experience that can help determine if there is sufficient evidence for truly evidence-based clinical guidelines:

1. There are a sufficient number of outcome studies on representative populations of the disorder. These studies include different clinical subtypes and use a clinical trial methodology to draw definitive conclusions about relative efficacy.

2. Differences between the intervention group and the comparison group meet a clinically meaningful threshold; that is, they constitute significant gains in the core functional developmental areas germane to the disorder.

3. Interventions are clearly definable. Their operative elements can be identified, measured, and verified, and alternative hypotheses about the operative elements can be ruled out.

4. The disorder is sufficiently understood, including the relationship between its components and its causes. If it is a complex disorder, the interventions can be related to the range of underlying processing deficits and individually different patterns and modes of expression, in addition to surface behaviors.

At present, intervention research on disorders of relating and communicating (e.g., autistic spectrum disorders) do not meet these criteria. Therefore, a broad knowledge-based approach is needed to inform current research and guide clinical practice.

Challenges to the Recommendations for Research

• *The clinical practice and research cultures need to work together more effectively.* Building a body of clinical knowledge needs to draw upon both available research and the expert opinion of all the clinical disciplines working with developmental disorders. A working partnership between the cultures of research and clinical practice could clearly move the field forward. There are a number of challenges, however, to the research and clinical practice cultures being able to work together as fully as possible. The culture of clinical practice is guided by day-to-day clinical challenges. It employs clinical reasoning and decision making, based on an understanding of the nature of the disorder, clinical experience with a range of cases, expert opinion, and available research. The culture of research, although guided by clinical challenges, is defined by available methodologies, data sets, and funding. Areas of developmental functioning and intervention techniques that available research methods are unable to quantify or that have not been identified by existing data sets, or simply lie outside current funding priorities, may be left unstudied, even though they have enormous clinical implications. By its nature, therefore, research contributes more fully to some areas of clinical practice than to others. In general medicine, for example, research often provides helpful data on circumscribed potent interventions, such as specific pharmacologic interventions or defined surgical procedures. Interestingly, however, even for well-defined disorders and interventions, there is rarely enough research on clinical subgroups within a broad diagnostic category to guide clinical management decisions for an individual patient. Clinical experience, in the form of expert opinion, is still required.

Expert opinion based on clinical practice and an understanding of the disorder in question, together with available research, is especially important in the clinical management of complex disorders that are only partially understood. These disorders make up the bulk of clinical practice and include the treatment of conditions such as heart disease and diabetes. For example, for more than 20 years, clinicians recommended tight control of blood glucose for diabetes treatment, based on case studies and an understanding of the pathophysiology of diabetes. Only recently was this clinical management decision confirmed by a large, federally funded study.

Most developmental disorders involving problems in relating and communicating, including autistic spectrum disorders, fit into this group of complex, partially understood disorders that require long-term clinical management.

- *To improve knowledge for the treatment of complex developmental disorders, including autistic spectrum disorders, the research and clinical practice communities will need to work together on a number of levels.* The clinical practice community will need to use case studies and collections of cases to systematically describe problem areas, different functional capacities, intervention methods, and relative courses of progress. As indicated, in the history of medical practice, there is a long tradition of employing expert opinion to discuss and systematize clinical principles in the face of incomplete, but developing, knowledge. The research community will need to apply rigorous methods at the current level of limited knowledge and build from there, working closely with the emerging body of clinical descriptions.

Specifically, clinicians and researchers will need to work toward the following goals:

1. Descriptive case studies to identify more fully all the relevant functional areas derailed in developmental disorders.

2. Exploratory clinical case studies to develop improved assessment and intervention methods for the clinically relevant functional areas.

3. Program descriptions to identify potentially helpful therapeutic elements.

4. Descriptive intervention studies (initially without necessarily involving control groups) to identify promising approaches that appear to facilitate a better-than-expected developmental course for a particular disorder.

5. Methods-development studies to improve techniques to measure difficult-to-quantify developmental and intervention variables.

6. Refinement of assessment and intervention practices based on in-depth clinical descriptions of a wide range of clinical cases.

7. Determining when intervention strategies are sufficiently developed and

helpful to warrant large-scale definitive clinical trial outcome studies.

8. Clinical trial intervention outcome studies for those interventions and areas of functioning that preliminary studies have identified as sufficiently promising to warrant this type of study.

SUMMARY OF A FUNCTIONAL DEVELOPMENTAL APPROACH PROGRAM ELEMENTS

Chart 1 is a brief summary form looking at whether or not a program incorporates the preceding recommendations in its capacity to offer assessments and interventions tailored to the unique developmental profile of each child and the child's family. ∎

Chart 1. Report Card on Assessments and Interventions for Complex Developmental Problems, Including Autistic Spectrum Disorders

	YES	NO
Does the assessment program include all the relevant functional areas?	❑	❑
Does the assessment include significant observations of parent-child interactions and family functioning over time and in multiple contexts?	❑	❑
Is there a functional developmental observation and screening program for all infants and children?	❑	❑
Does the intervention program work with all the relevant functional areas, as well as child-caregiver and family interaction patterns?	❑	❑
Does the intervention program provide a home-based, intensive after-school or full-day program of developmentally appropriate interactions?	❑	❑
Are appropriate therapies, such as speech and language and occupational and/or physical therapy, offered at sufficient intensity (e.g., 3 times/week)?	❑	❑
Does the intervention program provide an integrated educational program for children who are interactive and can imitate, as well as daily peer play?	❑	❑
Does the intervention program provide biomedical approaches based on the child's individual differences?	❑	❑
Does the intervention program provide access to appropriate technology-based learning?	❑	❑
Are consultations by a developmental or mental health specialist available to help construct and monitor the program and work on the three types of learning interactions and on family patterns?	❑	❑
Does the intervention program begin immediately after problems are assessed?	❑	❑
Do the same therapist and teacher(s) work with the child and family throughout infancy and early childhood, without a disruptive change when the child reaches age 3?	❑	❑

REFERENCES

Baranek, G. T. (1999). Autism during infancy: A retrospective video analysis of sensory-motor and social behaviors at 9-12 months of age. *Journal of Autism and Developmental Disorders, 29*(3), 213-224.

Baron-Cohen, S. (1994). *Mindblindness: An essay on autism and theories of mind.* Cambridge, MA: MIT Press.

Baron-Cohen, S., Tager-Flusberg, H., & Cohen, D. (1993). *Understanding other minds: Perspectives from autism.* London: Oxford University Press.

Blackman, S., & Goldstein, K. M. (1982). Cognitive styles and learning disabilities. *Journal of Learning Disabilities, 15*, 106-115.

Bristol, M., Cohen, D., Costello, J., Denckla, M., Eckberg, T., Kallen, R., Kraemer, H., Lord, C., Maurer, R., McIllvane, W., Minshew, N., Sigman, M., & Spence, A. (1996). State of the science in autism: Report to the National Institutes of Health. *Journal of Autism and Developmental Disorders, 26*, 121-154.

Case-Smith, J., & Bryan, T. (1999). The effects of occupational therapy with sensory integration emphasis on preschool-age children with autism. *American Journal of Occupational Therapy, 53*, 489-497.

Casey, M. B., Bronson, M. B., Tivnan, T., Riley, E., & Spenciner, L. (1991). Differentiating preschoolers' sequential planning ability from their general intelligence: A study of organization, systematic responding, and efficiency in young children. *Journal of Applied Developmental Psychology, 12*, 19-32.

Chez, C., Gordon, J., Ghilardi, M. F., & Sainburg, R. (1995). Contributions of vision and proprioception to accuracy in limb movements. In M. S. Gazzaniga (Ed.), *The cognitive neurosciences* (pp. 548-564). Cambridge, MA: MIT Press.

Cohen, D. & Volkmar, F. (Eds.). (1997). *Handbook of autism and pervasive developmental disorders.* (2nd ed.). New York: Wiley and Sons.

Cytryn, L. (1998). Classification of childhood disorders: The need for developmental-dimensional approaches-A personal historical perspective. *The Journal of Developmental and Learning Disorders, 2*, 139-153.

Dawson, G., & Galpert, I. (1990). Mother's use of imitative play for facilitating social responsiveness and toy play in young autistic children. *Developmental and Psychopathology, 2*, 151-162.

Dawson, G., & Osterling, J. (1997). The effectiveness of early intervention. In M. Guralnik (Ed.), *Early intervention in autism.* Baltimore: Paul H. Brookes.

Goldstein, H., & Hockenberger, E. H. (1991). Significant progress in child language intervention: An 11-year retrospective. *Research in Developmental Disability, 12*(4), 401-424.

Greenspan, S. I. (1992). *Infancy and early childhood: The practice of clinical assessment and intervention with emotional and developmental challenges.* Madison, CT: International Universities Press.

Greenspan, S. I. (1998). Commentary: Guidance for constructing clinical practice guidelines for developmental and learning disorders: Knowledge vs. evidence-based approaches. *The Journal of Developmental and Learning Disorders, 2*(2), 171-192.

Greenspan, S. I., & Lourie, R. S. (1981). Developmental structuralist approach to the classification of adaptive and pathologic personality organizations: Application to infancy and early childhood. *American Journal of Psychiatry, 138*(6), 725-35.

Greenspan, S. I., & Sharfstein, S. S. (1981). The efficacy of psychotherapy: Asking the right questions. *Archives of General Psychiatry, 38*(11), 1213-1219.

Greenspan, S. I., & White, K. R. (1987). Conducting research with preventive early intervention programs. In J. D. Noshpitz, J. D. Call, R. L. Cohen, S. I. Harrison, I. N. Berlin, & L. A. Stone (Eds.), *Basic handbook of child psychiatry.* New York: Basic Books.

Greenspan, S. I., & Wieder, S. (1997). Developmental patterns and outcomes in infants and children with disorders in relating and communicating: A chart review of 200 cases of children with autistic spectrum diagnoses. *The Journal of Developmental and Learning Disorders, 1,* 87-141.

Greenspan, S. I., & Wieder, S. (1998). *The child with special needs: Intellectual and emotional growth.* Reading, MA: Addison Wesley Longman.

Greenspan, S. I., & Wieder, S. (1999). A functional developmental approach to autistim spectrum disorders. *Journal of the Association for Persons with Severe Handicaps (JASH), 24*(3), 147-161.

Gresham, F. M., & MacMillan, D. L. (1998). Early intervention project: Can its claims be substantiated and its effects replicated? *Journal of Autism and Developmental Disorders, 28*(1), 5-12.

Guralnick, M. J. (1991). The next decade of research on the effectiveness of early intervention. *Exceptional Children, 58*(2), 174-183.

Guralnick, M. J. (Ed.) (1998). *The effectiveness of early intervention.* Baltimore, MD: Paul H. Brookes.

Hoyson, M., Jamieson, B., & Strain, P. S. (1984). Individualized group instruction of normally developing and autistic-like children: The LEAP curriculum model. *Journal of the Division of Early Childhood, 8,* 157-172.

Klinger, L. G., & Dawson, G. (1992). Facilitating early social and communicative development in children with autism. In S. Warren and J. Reichle (Eds.), *Communication and language intervention series, Vol. I: Causes and effects in communicating and language intervention* (pp. 167-186). Baltimore: Paul H. Brookes.

Krauss, M. W. (1998). Two generations of family research in early intervention. In M. Guralnick (Ed.), *The effectiveness of early intervention* (pp. 611-624). Baltimore: Paul H. Brookes.

Law, J. (1997). Evaluating intervention for language impaired children: A review of the literature. *European Journal of Disorders of Communication, 3,* 1-14.

Lewy, A. L., & Dawson, G. (1992). Social stimulation and joint attention in young autistic children. *Journal of Abnormal Child Psychology, 20(6),* 555-566.

Lincoln, A. J., Courchesne, E., Harms, L., & Allen, M. (1995). Sensory modulation of auditory stimuli in children with autism and receptive development language disorder: Event–related brain potential evidence. *Journal of Autism and Developmental Disorders, 25,* 521-539.

Lovaas, O. I. (1987). Behavioral treatment and normal educational and intellectual functioning in young autistic children. *Journal of Consulting and Clinical Psychology, 55,* 3-9.

McCollum, J. A., & Hemmeter, M. L. (1998). Parent child interaction intervention when children have disabilities. In M. Guralnick (Ed.), *The effectiveness of early intervention* (pp. 549-578). Baltimore, MD: Paul H. Brookes.

McEachin, J. J., Smith, T., & Lovaas, O. I. (1993). Long-term outcome for children with autism who received early intensive behavioral treatment. *American Journal on Mental Retardation, 97,* 359-372.

McLean, L. K., & Cripe, J. W. (1998). The effectiveness of early intervention for children with communication disorders . In M. Guralnick (Ed.), *The effectiveness of early intervention* (pp. 349-428). Baltimore: Paul H. Brookes.

Minshew, N. J. (1997). Autism & the pervasive developmental disorders: the clinical syndrome. In B. K. Shapiro, P. J. Accardo, & A. J. Capute (Eds.), *Behavior belongs in the brain: Neurobehavioral syndromes* (pp. 49-68). Baltimore: York Press.

Minshew, N. (1999). *Autism as a disorder of complex information processing and underdevelopment of neocortical systems.* Paper presented at the Interdisciplinary Council on Developmental and Learning Disorders' Third Annual International Conference on Autism and Disorders of Relating and Communicating, November 12-14, McLean, VA.

Minshew, N. J. (in press). The core deficit in autism and autistic spectrum disorders. *Journal for Developmental and Learning Disorders.* Bethesda, MD: Interdisciplinary Council on Developmental and Learning Disorders.

Mundy, P., & Crowson, M. (1997). Joint attention and early social communication: Implications for research on intervention with autism. *Journal of Autism and Developmental Disorders, 27*(6), 653-676.

Mundy, P., Sigman, M., & Kasari, C. (1990). A longitudinal study of joint attention and language development in autistic children. *Journal of Autism and Developmental Disorders, 20*(1), 115-128.

Osterling, J., & Dawson, G. (1994). Early recognition of children with autism: a study of first birthday home videotapes. *Journal of Autism and Developmental Disorders, 24*(3), 247-257.

Powers, M. (1992). Early intervention for children with autism. In D. Berkell-Zager (Ed.), *Autism: Identification, education, and treatment* (pp. 223-251). Hillsdale, NJ: Erlbaum.

Rogers, S. (1996). Brief report: Early intervention in autism. *Journal of Autism and Developmental Disorders, 26,* 243-246.

Rogers, S., & DiLalla, D. (1991). A comparative study of the effects of a developmentally based instructional model on young children with autism and young children with other disorders of behavior and development. *Topics in Early Childhood Special Education, 11*(2), 29-47.

Scheinkopf, S. J., & Siegal, B. (1998). Home-based behavioral treatment of young children with autism. *Journal of Autism and Developmental Disorders, 28*(1), 15-23.

Schopler, E. (1987). Specific and non-specific factors in the effectiveness of a treatment system. *American Psychologist, 42,* 262-267.

Sigman, M., & Ruskin, E. (1999). Continuity and change in the social competence of children with autism, Down's syndrome, and developmental delays. *Monographs of the Society for Research in Child Development, 64.*

Smith, T., Eikeseth, S., Morten, K., & Lovaas, I. (1997). Intensive behavioral treatment for preschoolers with severe mental retardation and pervasive developmental disorders. *American Journal on Mental Retardation, 102,* 238-249.

Strain, P. S., & Cordisco, L. K. (1994). LEAP preschool. In S. Harris & J. Handelman (Eds.), *Pre-school education programs for children with autism* (pp. 225-252). Austin, TX: PRO-ED.

Tanguay, P. E., Robertson, J., & Derrick, A. (1998). A dimensional classification of autistim spectrum disorder by social communication domains. *Journal of the*

American Academy of Child and Adolescent Psychiatry, 37(3), 271-277.

Tanguay, P. E. (1999). *The diagnostic assessment of autism using social communication domains.* Paper presented at the Interdisciplinary Council on Developmental and Learning Disorders' Third Annual International Conference on Autism and Disorders of Relating and Communicating, McLean, VA, November 12-14

Turnbull, A. P., & Turnbull, H.R. (1982). Parent involvement in the education of handicapped children: A critique. *Mental Retardation, 20,* 115-122.

Venn, M. L., Wolery, M., & Graco, M. (1996). Effects of everyday and every-other day instruction. *Focus on Autism and Other Developmental Disabilities, 11*(1), 15-28.

Wetherby, A. M., & Prizant, B. M. (1993). Profiling communication and symbolic abilities in young children. *Journal of Childhood Communication Disorders, 15,* 23-32.

Wetherby, A. M., Prizant, B. M. (1995). Facilitating language and communication in autism: Assessment and intervention guidelines. In D. Berkell (Ed.), *Autism: Identification, education, and treatment* (pp.107-133). Hillsdale, NJ: Erlbaum.

White, K., & Greespan, S. (1987). An overview of the effectiveness of preventive early intervention programs. In J. D. Noshpitz, J. D. Call, R. L. Cohen, S. I. Harrison, I. N. Berlin, & L. A. Stone (Eds.), *Basic handbook of child psychiatry.* New York: Basic Books.

Williamson, G. G., & Anzalone, M. E. (1997). Sensory integration: A key component of the evaluation and treatment of young children with severe difficulties in relating and communicating. *Zero to Three, 17,* 29-36.

Zelazo, P. R. (1997). Infant-toddler information processing treatment of children with pervasive developmental disorder and autism: Part II. *Infants and Young Children, 10*(2), 1-13.

Appendix A

OUTLINE OF THE DIR MODEL
How to Use *The ICDL Clinical Practice Guidelines*

Screening (Functional Developmental Growth Chart)

If at any time during the early years, a child experiences a loss or lack of progress in developing long chains of emotional cueing—regardless of other symptoms—proceed to a **full, functional developmental evaluation.** Most commonly, the loss or lack of progress in developing a continuous flow of reciprocal emotional cueing is seen between 8 and 18 months of age. *(*See the *Functional Developmental Growth Chart* (Chapter 3, Appendix B*).

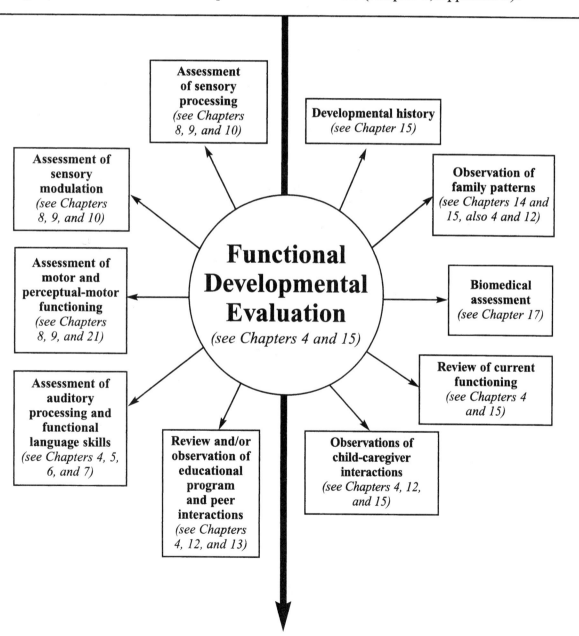

Assessment of sensory processing *(see Chapters 8, 9, and 10)*

Developmental history *(see Chapter 15)*

Assessment of sensory modulation *(see Chapters 8, 9, and 10)*

Observation of family patterns *(see Chapters 14 and 15, also 4 and 12)*

Assessment of motor and perceptual-motor functioning *(see Chapters 8, 9, and 21)*

Functional Developmental Evaluation *(see Chapters 4 and 15)*

Biomedical assessment *(see Chapter 17)*

Review of current functioning *(see Chapters 4 and 15)*

Assessment of auditory processing and functional language skills *(see Chapters 4, 5, 6, and 7)*

Review and/or observation of educational program and peer interactions *(see Chapters 4, 12, and 13)*

Observations of child-caregiver interactions *(see Chapters 4, 12, and 15)*

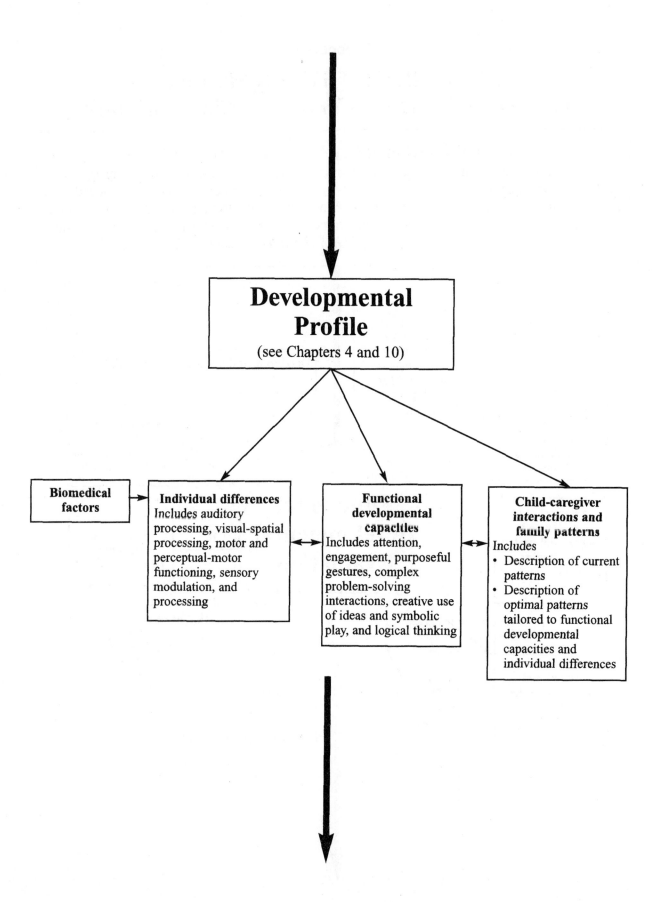

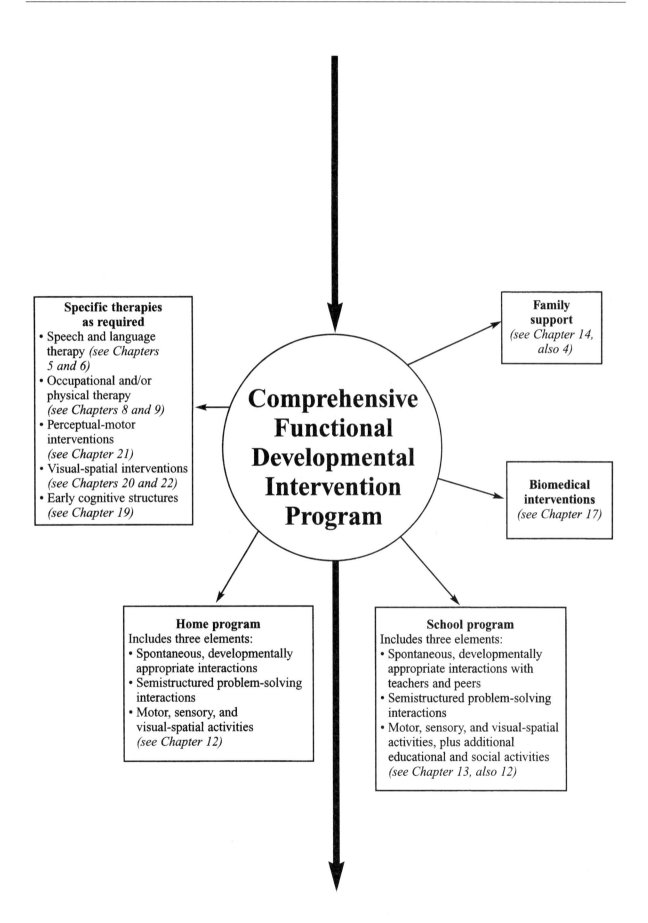

Specific therapies as required
- Speech and language therapy *(see Chapters 5 and 6)*
- Occupational and/or physical therapy *(see Chapters 8 and 9)*
- Perceptual-motor interventions *(see Chapter 21)*
- Visual-spatial interventions *(see Chapters 20 and 22)*
- Early cognitive structures *(see Chapter 19)*

Family support
(see Chapter 14, also 4)

Comprehensive Functional Developmental Intervention Program

Biomedical interventions
(see Chapter 17)

Home program
Includes three elements:
- Spontaneous, developmentally appropriate interactions
- Semistructured problem-solving interactions
- Motor, sensory, and visual-spatial activities *(see Chapter 12)*

School program
Includes three elements:
- Spontaneous, developmentally appropriate interactions with teachers and peers
- Semistructured problem-solving interactions
- Motor, sensory, and visual-spatial activities, plus additional educational and social activities *(see Chapter 13, also 12)*

Home Program
(see Chapter 12)
Includes three elements:
- Spontaneous, developmentally appropriate interactions
- Semistructured problem-solving interactions
- Motor, sensory, and visual-spatial activities

Semistructured problem-solving interactions involving cognitive, language, social, and emotional skills

Often recommended: six or more 20-minute sessions per day *(see Chapter 12)*
- If child is able to imitate readily and use complex problem-solving gestures, then semistructured learning should focus on dynamic problem-solving interactions orchestrated by the caregiver to enable the child to master specific cognitive, social or educational goals *(see Chapters 4 and 12)*
- If a child is not yet able to imitate readily and use complex problem-solving gestures, consider more structured exercises to teach specific cognitive, language, social, and emotional skills. The initial goal of more structured approaches should be mastery of gestural, problem-solving interactions and complex imitation. This often requires work on motor planning and sequencing, visual-spatial processing, as well as on affective gesturing. Use augmentative communication strategies and consider TEACCH, the Miller Method, ABA, and exercises focusing on imitative skills, motor planning and sequencing *(see Chapters 4, 19, and 24)*

Spontaneous, developmentally appropriate interactions mobilizing the six functional developmental capacities (floor time)

Often recommended: eight or more 20-minute sessions per day *(see Chapter 12)*

Motor, sensory, and visual-spatial activities

Often recommended: three or more 20-minute sessions per day. Sessions include the following elements:
- Sensory-integration occupational therapy exercises, such as running, jumping, spinning, firm tactile pressure *(see Chapter 8, 9, and 10)*
- Perceptual-motor exercises (e.g., looking/doing games), such as throwing, catching, kicking, tracking *(see Chapter 21)*
- Visual-spatial problem solving, such as hide-and-seek, treasure hunt, and flashlight games *(see Chapters 20 and 22)*
- Once child can answer "why" questions, consider adding visual-spatial thinking activities *(see Chapters 20 and 22)*
- If the child is verbal and getting ready for school, consider adding preacademic, conceptual reasoning, reading, and math exercises *(see Chapters 22 and 24)*

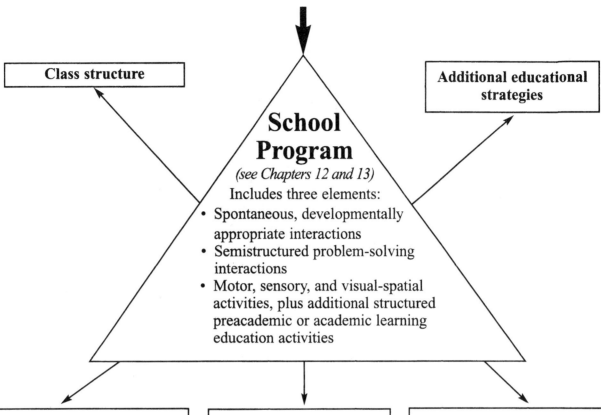

Class structure

School Program
(see Chapters 12 and 13)
Includes three elements:
• Spontaneous, developmentally
  appropriate interactions
• Semistructured problem-solving
  interactions
• Motor, sensory, and visual-spatial
  activities, plus additional structured
  preacademic or academic learning
  education activities

Additional educational strategies

Semistructured problem-solving interactions involving cognitive, language, social, and emotional skills
• If child is able to imitate and use complex problem-solving gestures, then semistructured learning should focus on dynamic problem-solving interactions orchestrated by the educator to enable the child to master specific cognitive, social, or educational goals *(see Chapters 4 and 12)*
• If a child is not yet able to imitate and use complex problem-solving gestures, consider more structured exercises to teach specific cognitive, language, social, and emotional skills. The initial goal should be mastery of gestural, problem-solving interactions and complex imitation
• A cognitive curriculum should involve pragmatic conversation groups, cooperative learning, and social stories

Spontaneous, developmentally appropriate interactions mobilizing the six functional developmental capacities (floor time)
Includes social interactions with teachers and peers, social games, and play dates with "expert peers" *(see Chapters 4 and 12)*

Motor, sensory, and visual-spatial activities
Often recommended: three or more 20-minute sessions per day. Sessions include the following elements:
• Sensory-integration occupational therapy exercises, such as running, jumping, spinning, firm tactile pressure *(see Chapters 8, 9, and 10)*
• Perceptual-motor exercises (e.g., looking/doing games), such as throwing, catching, kicking, tracking *(see Chapter 21)*
• Visual-spatial problem solving, such as hide-and-seek, treasure hunt and flashlight games *(see Chapters 20 and 22)*
• Once child can answer "why" questions, consider adding visual-spatial thinking activities *(see Chapters 20 and 22)*
• Once child is ready for preacademic work, consider adding preacademic conceptual reasoning, reading, and math exercises *(see Chapters 23 and 25)*

Class Structure

Inclusion or regular school program with an aide
If preschool child is able to use complex gestures to problem solve and is beginning to imitate or use words, priority should be given to an inclusive preschool program or a regular preschool with an aide

Inclusion or special-needs class
If the child is not yet using complex gestures to problem solve and is not beginning to imitate or use words, priority should be given to a program where there is a 1:1 ratio of teacher or aide to student in either an inclusive or special-needs class

Additional Educational Strategies

PECS
When language lags behind visual-spatial thinking, consider the PECS to augment communication. Visual communication aids should be used as part of the three elements of a dynamic education

Augmentive communication strategies as needed

ABA
Structured exercises to facilitate imitative skills and basic motor planning and sequencing in children who have difficulty learning imitation skills dynamically *(see Chapter 4)*

TEACCH
Use TEACCH visual communication strategies to establish routines and to reduce frustration. TEACCH educational approaches are especially useful when language is very delayed and motor-planning challenges impede gestural communications *(see Chapter 31)*

Miller Method
Structured and semi-structured exercises to master early, basic cognitive capacities *(see Chapter 19)*

Visual-spatial thinking, perceptual-motor exercises, and visualization-based concept building
For children with challenges in these areas who have progressed to being able to understand and follow directions and answer "why" type questions *(see Chapters 20, 21, 22, 23, and 25)*

Appendix B

MONITORING DEVELOPMENT, PREVENTION, AND EARLY INTERVENTION:

The Functional Developmental
Growth Chart and Questionnaire
Stanley I. Greenspan, M.D.

One of the most important components of a functional approach to intervention is for clinicians to initiate the interventions at the earliest possible time. Early intervention minimizes a child's ongoing functional impairments and missed opportunities for mastering critical functional developmental skills. For example, many children who are diagnosed between ages 2½ and 4 with autistic spectrum disorders began evidencing a subtle deficit in affective reciprocity and complex, preverbal, interactive problem-solving patterns between 12 and 16 months of age (Greenspan & Wieder, 1997) and by 18 months of age often are unable to engage in joint attention tasks, purposeful pointing, and early forms of pretend play (Baron-Cohen, Frith, & Leslie, 1988). The children who are not helped to learn how to engage in complex, social problem-solving interactions at this age (e.g., leading Daddy by the hand to the toy area and pointing to the desired play object) miss an opportunity for mastering critical social, emotional, language, and cognitive milestones that build on these problem-solving interactions during the second year of life.

There is mounting evidence that the absence of critical functional developmental capacities is associated with increased likelihood of severe developmental disorders. For example, in studies of autistic spectrum and related developmental disorders, the following capacities are often not present: joint attention (Mundy, Sigman, & Kasari, 1990),

social reciprocity (Baranek, 1999; Dawson & Galpert, 1990; Lewy & Dawson, 1992; Osterling & Dawson, 1994; Tanguay, 1999; Tanguay, Robertson, & Derrick, 1998;), functional language (Wetherby & Prizant, 1992), selected early motor capacities (Teitelbaum & Teitelbaum, 1999), motor-planning and sequencing capacities (Williamson & Anzalone, 1997), and early indications of symbolic functioning (e.g., pretend play, empathy) (Baron-Cohen, 1999; Baron-Cohen et al., 1988).

There is a confluence of studies showing the presence of certain milestones in healthy development and their absence in children at risk for or evidencing disorders of relating, thinking, and communicating. These studies, together with the growing road map of social, emotional, cognitive, language, and motor milestones, provide the basis for delineating essential functional developmental landmarks (Greenspan, 1992; Greenspan & Lourie, 1981). Therefore, just as a child's physical growth can be charted, the progression of functional developmental capacities should be monitored to help identify difficulties and strengths at the earliest possible age.

There are three levels to monitoring a child's functional developmental capacities. The first level involves broadening and updating the frame of reference pediatricians and other primary health care professionals, educators, and parents use for clinical observations and/or questions about an infant and young child's development. This involves using the functional developmental milestones outlined earlier and in the Functional Developmental Growth Chart and the Questionnaire that follow. These milestones incorporate the well-known motor, language, social, and cognitive landmarks such as crawling, walking, first sounds and words, smiling, and imitating, as well as developmental indicators described by the Child Neurology Society of the American Academy of Neurology as being "nearly universally present by the age indicated" (no babbling by 12 months; no gesturing, pointing, or waving "bye-bye" by 12 months; no single words by 16 months; no two-word spontaneous (e.g., functional) phrases by 24 months; and any loss of language or social skills at any age) (Fillipek et al., 1999). The functional developmental milestones, however, go beyond these well-known indicators and focus on integrated functional developmental capacities identified in more recent studies and clinical observations (Greenspan 1992, 1997; Greenspan & Wieder, 1998, 1999).

Historically, clinicians have approached children's development in terms of isolated areas, such as motor development, the functioning of the senses, aspects of language and cognition, spatial problem solving, and social functioning. When looking at separate areas of development, a child can operate at a relatively advanced level in one area (e.g., motor development), and yet have significant challenges in another area (e.g., language development). Although specific aspects of development are very important to identify and assess, it is more useful for monitoring purposes to look at the full range of a child's functional developmental capacities and the way in which the child uses all her abilities together.

The child's functional, emotional developmental capacities require a coming together of the child's motor skills and her sensory processing, cognitive, and language capacities, under the guidance of her emotional intent and proclivities. These functional emotional developmental capacities include the child's ability to focus and attend, engage with others, initiate reciprocal interactions to intentionally communicate needs (such as reaching to be picked up), and move on to complex problem-solving interactions (such as taking the caregiver by the hand to find the desired toy). They also include the child's ability to use ideas and words to communicate basic needs, as well as to explore imaginative thinking (make-believe) and to use logical bridges to combine ideas as a basis for rational thinking, advanced logical communication, and symbolic problem solving.

Each of these functional developmental capacities has an emotional, language, motor, sensory, and cognitive component. For example, the capacity for back-and-forth interaction (reciprocity) has a social and emotional component (the child's desire or intent to communicate, get a toy, or smile), a motor component (purposeful smiles or hand movements), a language component (using sounds for communicative intent), a sensory component (visual and auditory processing and responding to the gestures of the other person), and a cognitive component (engaging in "means/ends" [i.e., purposeful] interactions). The clinician, however, does not need to consider all the separate components or all possible examples of a particular milestone. He needs only to ascertain through a simple question or observation if the milestone is present or absent; for example, if a 9-month-old infant can initiate and respond to purposeful actions. Each of these readily identifiable milestones (no more difficult to ascertain than a child's ability to walk) can be easily asked about and/or observed. For example, a simple question or observation could elicit the presence or absence of this back-and-forth interaction.

When a child is unable to master these functional developmental milestones, different components of development might be contributing to the child's difficulty. Simply having a mild motor delay, for example, may not derail relating, communicating, or thinking. On the other hand, a mild motor delay coupled with severe family dysfunction or a very severe motor delay might derail one or more functional developmental milestones. The functional developmental milestones are the common pathways or the doors through which the child navigates. The child's ability or inability to walk through these doors provides an important picture of his adaptive and maladaptive development and the need for further evaluation and, possibly, intervention.

If observing and/or asking about a child's functional developmental capacities raises questions about appropriate progress, a second level of monitoring should be considered. This should involve screening questionnaires which have been used with a large number of children and shown to identify different types of developmental problems. Screening questionnaires that cover a broad range of developmental competence include the Communication and Symbolic Behavior Scales Developmental Profile (Wetherby & Prizant, 1998) and the Ages and Stages Questionnaire (ASQ), A Parent-Completed, Child-Monitoring System, Second Edition (Bricker & Squires, 1999).

If a systematic screening questionnaire supports the impression from clinical observations and questions, then a third level should be considered—a comprehensive developmental evaluation to determine the nature and extent of a suspected problem (see Greenspan & Wieder, Chapters 4 and 15, this volume).

In order to broaden the frame of reference and implement the first level of monitoring an infant or child's progress, it may prove

helpful to have a functional developmental growth chart and questionnaire that identifies the milestones to be observed or asked about. The growth chart and screening questionnaire must provide straightforward, clear descriptions that can readily be observed by parents, health care providers, and educators. It must cover all the areas of developmental functioning—emotional, social, cognitive, language, motor, and sensory in an integrated manner—and all the stages of infancy and early childhood.

Figure B1 presents a functional developmental growth chart (followed by a functional developmental screening questionnaire) that is similar to a physical growth chart. The Functional Developmental Growth Chart enables clinicians to look at the pattern of a child's growth rather than simply at a few items at a certain age. Patterns of change over time often provide the most useful information about a child's abilities.

In Figure B1, the functional developmental capacities to be monitored are listed on the horizontal axis. The child's age is on the vertical axis. A 45-degree line shows the expected age range at which a child is expected to master each capacity. As can be observed on the chart, the child's functional developmental accomplishments can be charted in relation to the age at which the accomplishment is expected to emerge and the age at which it does emerge. When a child does not evidence the next milestone during the expected time interval, the last functional capacity mastered is recorded on the chart. The next milestone, if it occurs, is then recorded at whatever later time it is manifested. The 45-degree line indicates a typical developmental curve. A child who is precocious in a predictable manner (e.g., 3 months ahead of expectations) will have a functional developmental curve that parallels the typical one and is a little above it. A child who is a

Figure B1. The Functional Developmental Growth Chart

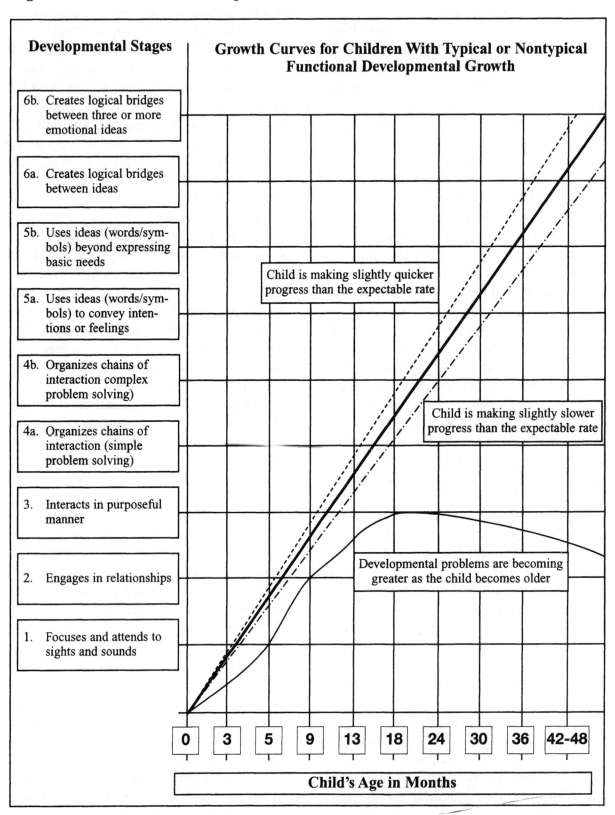

Developmental Stages

6b. Creates logical bridges between three or more emotional ideas

6a. Creates logical bridges between ideas

5b. Uses ideas (words/symbols) beyond expressing basic needs

5a. Uses ideas (words/symbols) to convey intentions or feelings

4b. Organizes chains of interaction complex problem solving)

4a. Organizes chains of interaction (simple problem solving)

3. Interacts in purposeful manner

2. Engages in relationships

1. Focuses and attends to sights and sounds

Growth Curves for Children With Typical or Nontypical Functional Developmental Growth

Child is making slightly quicker progress than the expectable rate

Child is making slightly slower progress than the expectable rate

Developmental problems are becoming greater as the child becomes older

0   3   5   9   13   18   24   30   36   42-48

Child's Age in Months

little behind the expected curve (e.g., 3 months behind on the functional developmental milestones) will have a curve that parallels the typical curve but may fall just below it. When a child's curve is below the norm, the child should be evaluated to identify which factors may be contributing to the developmental lag and what may be helpful in responding to them.

Most worrisome, and a red flag, is a curve that arcs away from the line, that is, the distance from that line keeps growing, indicating a delay that is increasing as the child becomes older (shown as the lowest line on the chart). At the point the curve begins arcing is the point at which immediate assessment and possible intervention is indicated. It is also a red flag if the developmental curve is running parallel to the typical curve but is significantly below it.

Some children master these milestones a little bit later than expected but, as time goes on, they move closer to the expected functional developmental curve. Other children, however, may begin on the expected curve but gradually slip behind. The key is to watch the child's pattern over time and, if for example, the child is slipping further behind, even if it is not dramatic, a full screening and possible evaluation is usually indicated.

The age expectations for each milestone are deliberately set up at the outer boundaries of the expectable range for that capacity to allow for a great deal of individual variation.

This developmental chart can be used by parents, educators (including daycare staff), and other childcare facilitators to monitor a child's functional developmental capacities. In general, a child will have mastered the milestone when she can engage in the behavior associated with the milestone most of the time. Mastery is not indicated in a child who only occasionally is able to mobilize the age-appropriate milestone or requires extraordinary support to perform it. The Functional Developmental Growth Chart Questionnaire follows the chart and provides questions that can be asked to parents or which parents can ask of themselves. These questions can help in determining the child's functional developmental level. ∎

Functional Developmental Growth Chart Questionnaire

The purpose of this questionnaire is to assess whether a child has achieved a new functional developmental milestone. The child has mastered a milestone if the answer is "yes" to all the questions under that milestone. If the answer is "no" to even one question, the child has not yet mastered the milesotne. Remember, the growth chart is simply a visual tool to draw attention to those developmental areas where a child is progressing as expected and those where he or she may be facing some challenges.

By 3 Months (Stage 1- Focusing and Attention)
- Does your infant usually show an interest in things around him/her by looking at sights and turning towards sounds?

By 5 Months (Stage 2 - Engaging in Relationships)
(Ask the question from the prior category plus the new one from this category.)
- Does your baby seem happy or pleased to see you and/or other favorite people: looking and smiling, making sounds or some other gesture, such as moving arms, that indicates pleasure or delight?

By 9 Months (Stage 3 - Interacts in a Purposeful Manner)
(Ask the questions from all prior categories plus the new ones from this category.)
- Is your baby able to show what he/she wants by reaching for or pointing at something, reaching out to be picked up, or making purposeful special noises?
- Does your baby respond to people talking or playing with him/her by, for example, making sounds, faces, or initiating gestures (reaching)?

By 14 to 18 Months (Stage 4 - Organizes Chains of Interaction; Problem Solving)
(Ask the questions from all prior categories plus the new ones for this category.)
- Is your toddler (by 14 months) able to show what he/she wants or needs by using actions, such as leading you by the hand to open a door or pointing to find a toy?
- Is your toddler (by 18 months) able to orchestrate more complex chains of interaction as he/she solves problems and shows you what he/she wants, including such things as getting food. For example, does he/she take your hand, lead you to the refrigerator, tug on the handle, and point to a particular food or bottle of juice or milk?
- Is your toddler (by 18 months) able to use imitation, such as copying your sounds, words, or motor gestures, as part of a playful, ongoing interaction?

By 24 to 30 Months (Stage 5 - Uses Ideas—Words or Symbols— to Convey Intentions or Feelings)

(Ask the questions from all prior categories plus the new ones for this category.)

- Does your toddler (by 24 months) ever respond to people talking with or playing with him/her by using words or sequences of sounds that are clearly an attempt to convey a word?
- Is your toddler (by 24 months) able to imitate familiar pretend-like actions, such as feeding or hugging a doll?
- Is your toddler (by 24 months) able to meet some basic needs with one or a few words, such as "juice," "open," or "kiss"? (A parent may have to say the word first.)
- Is your toddler (by 24 months) able to follow simple one-step directions from a caregiver to meet some basic need, for example, "The toy is there," or "Come give Mommy a kiss."
- Is your toddler (by 30 months) able to engage in interactive pretend play with an adult or another child (feeding dollies, tea parties, etc.)?
- Is your toddler (by 30 months) able to use ideas—words or symbols—to share his/her delight or interest ("See truck!")?
- Is your toddler able to use symbols—words, pictures, organized games—while enjoying and interacting with one or more peers?

By 36 to 48 Months (Stage 6 - Creates Logical Bridges Between Ideas)

(Ask the questions from all prior categories plus the new ones for this category.)
- Is your toddler (by 36 months) able to use words or other symbols (for example, pictures) to convey likes or dislikes, such as "want that" or "no want that"?
- Is your toddler (by 36 months) able to engage in pretend play with another person in which the story or drama makes sense? (e.g., in the story, do the bears go visit grandmother and then have a big lunch)?
- Is your toddler (by 36 months) able to begin to explain wishes or needs. For example, a conversation may contain an exchange such as: "Mommy, go out." "What are you going to do outside?" "Play." The child may need multiple choice help from the parent, such as "What will you do, play or sleep?"
- Can your preschooler (by 48 months) explain reasons for wanting something or wanting to do something (e.g., "Why do you want the juice?"…"Because I'm thirsty")?
- Is your preschooler (by 48 months) occasionally able to use feelings as a reason for a wish or behavior (e.g., "I don't want to do that because it makes me sad")?
- Is your preschooler (by 48 months) able to engage in interactive pretend dramas with both peers as well as adults in which there are a number of elements that logically fit together (e.g., the children go to school, do work, have lunch, and meet an elephant on the way home)?
- Is your preschooler (by 48 months) able to engage in a logical conversation with four or more give-and-take sequences about a variety of topics, ranging from negotiating foods and bedtimes to talking about friends or school?

APPENDIX B REFERENCES

Baranek, G. T. (1999). Autism during infancy: A retrospective video analysis of sensory-motor and social behaviors at 9-12 months of age. *Journal of Autism and Developmental Disorders, 29*(3), 213-224.

Baron-Cohen, S. (1999). *The early detection of autism.* Paper presented at the Interdisciplinary Council on Developmental and Learning Disorders' Third Annual International Conference on Autism and Disorders of Relating and Communicating, McLean, VA, November 12-14.

Baron-Cohen, S., Frith, U., & Leslie, A. M. (1988). Autistic children's understanding of seeing, knowing, and believing. *British Journal of Developmental Psychology, 4,* 315-324.

Bricker, D., & Squires, J. (1999). *Ages & stages questionnaires: A parent-completed, child-monitoring system* (2nd ed.). Baltimore: Paul H. Brookes

Dawson, G., & Galpert, I. (1990). Mother's use of imitative play for facilitating social responsiveness and toy play in young autistic children. Developmental and *Psychopathology, 2,* 151-162.

Dawson, G., Warrenburg, S., & Fuller, P. (1982). Cerebral lateralization in individuals diagnosed as autistic in early childhood. *Brain and Language, 15,* 353-368.

Fillipek, P. Accardo, P., Baranek, G., Cook, E., Dawson, G., Gordon, B., Gravel, J., Johnson, C., Kallen, R., Levy, S., Minshew, N., Prizant, B., Rapin, I., Rogers, S., Stone, W., Teplin, S., Tuchman, R., Volkmar, F. (1999). The screening and diagnosis of autistic spectrum disorders. *Journal of Autism and Developmental Disorders 29(*6), 439-84.

Greenspan, S. I. (1992). *Infancy and early childhood: The practice of clinical assessment and intervention with emotional and developmental challenges.* Madison, CT: International Universities Press.

Greenspan, S. I. (1997). *The growth of the mind and the endangered origins of intelligence.* Reading, MA: Addison Wesley Longman.

Greenspan, S. I., & Lourie, R. S. (1981). Developmental structuralist approach to the classification of adaptive and pathologic personality organizations: Application to infancy and early childhood. *American Journal of Psychiatry, 138(*6), 725-35.

Greenspan, S. I., & Wieder, S. (1997). Developmental patterns and outcomes in infants and children with disorders in relating and communicating: A chart review of 200 cases of children with autistic spectrum diagnoses. *Journal of Developmental and Learning Disorders, 1,* 87-141.

Greenspan, S. I., & Wieder, S. (1999). A functional developmental approach to autistim spectrum disorders. *Journal of the Association for Persons with Severe Handicaps (JASH), 24*(3), 147-161.

Greenspan, S. I., & Wieder, S. (1998). *The child with special needs: Intellectual and emotional growth.* Reading, MA: Addison Wesley Longman.

Lewy, A. L., & Dawson, G. (1992). Social stimulation and joint attention in young autistic children. *Journal of Abnormal Child Psychology, 20*(6), 555-566.

Mundy, P., & Crowson, M. (1997). Joint attention and early social communication: Implications for research on intervention with autism. *Journal of Autism and Developmental Disorders, 27*(6), 653-676.

Mundy, P., Sigman, M., & Kasari, C. (1990). A longitudinal study of joint attention and language development in autistic children. *Journal of Autism and Developmental Disorders, 20*(1), 115-128.

Osterling, J., & Dawson, G. (1994). Early recognition of children with autism: A study of first birthday home videotapes. *Journal of Autism and Developmental Disorders, 24*(3), 247-257.

Tanguay, P. E. (1999). *The diagnostic assessment of autism using social communication domains.* Paper presented at the Interdisciplinary Council on Developmental and Learning Disorders' Third Annual International Conference, Autism and Disorders of Relating and Communicating, McLean, VA, November 12-14.

Tanguay, P. E., Robertson, J., & Derrick, A. (1998). A dimensional classification of autistim spectrum disorder by social communication domains. *Journal of the American Academy of Child and Adolescent Psychiatry, 37*(3), 271-277.

Teitelbaum, P., & Teitelbaum, O. (1999). *Motor indicators of autism in the first year.* Paper presented at the Interdisciplinary Council on Developmental and Learning Disorders' Third Annual International Conference on Autism and Disorders of Relating and Communicating, McLean, VA, November 12-14.

Wetherby, A. M., & Prizant, B. M. (1992). Profiling communication and symbolic abilities in young children. *Journal of Childhood Communication Disorders, 15,* 23-32.

Wetherby, A., & Prizant, B. (1998). *Communication and symbolic behavior scales developmental profile – research edition.* Chicago, IL: Applied Symbolix.

Williamson, G. G., & Anzalone, M. E. (1997). Sensory integration: A key component of the evaluation and treatment of young children with severe difficulties in relating and communicating. *Zero to Three, 17,* 29-36.

—◄ 4 ►—

Principles of Clinical Practice for Assessment and Intervention

Stanley I. Greenspan, M.D., and Serena Wieder, Ph.D.

The discussion in Chapter 2 states that developmental and learning disorders involve varying degrees of impairment in critical central nervous system (CNS) functions, such as motor capacities, language, cognition, sensory, and social and emotional functioning. This chapter continues the discussion by describing the functional developmental approach and its relationship to general principles of clinical practice.

THE FUNCTIONAL DEVELOPMENTAL APPROACH

Most non-progressive developmental and learning disorders, including disorders of relating and communicating (e.g., autistic spectrum or pervasive developmental disorders [PDD], multisystem developmental disorders, severe language and cognitive deficits) are nonspecific with regard to their etiology and pathophysiology. Non-progressive developmental disorders are, therefore, best characterized by types and degrees of functional limitations and processing differences as well as by symptoms that often are only one expression of a functional limitation (e.g., echolalia is a symptom; pragmatic language is the functional limitation).

Yet, as indicated in Chapters 2 and 3, both historically and recently, clinicians have

focused on symptoms and groups of symptoms comprising syndromes, giving only partial attention to a broad range of important functional capacities and their related processing differences. For example, a mother was told by the senior clinician overseeing an evaluation team that because her child was "autistic," he could not interact with purpose and meaning. The clinician concluded that, because an intensive intervention would not be helpful, the therapeutic effort should be modest. Yet, this clinician did not assess the relative strengths and weaknesses of all the child's areas of functioning and underlying processing capacities to see which ones required work and which ones could be harnessed immediately for interacting and learning. For example, was this child's lack of purposeful interaction related to auditory processing and motor problems? Did he have some relative strengths in visual-spatial processing that could be partially harnessed to enable him to interact with others more purposefully? Would working with him on activities that were associated with high motivation (e.g., his eagerness to go outside) help him become more purposeful? Or, was his lack of purposeful interaction part of a biologically based CNS impairment which, by definition, would remain chronic and relatively untreatable?

Cases such as this one suggest the importance of looking at functional capacities. In fact, there is mounting evidence that:

1. Most complex, non-progressive developmental and learning disorders involve processing dysfunctions, each with its own natural history and complex, poorly understood etiology and neurobiology (see Zimmerman & Gordon, Chapter 27, and Minshew & Goldstein, Chapter, 28, this volume).

2. Key functional capacities, as well as related symptoms, learning problems, adaptive capacities, and a variety of surface behaviors, in turn, are often the result of the interaction between early and ongoing interactive experiences and these biologically based processing dysfunctions.

3. The resulting functional capacities, symptoms, or behaviors are not tied to these underlying processes in a rigid, fixed manner. For example, a child who cannot use words to symbolize a wish for juice may be able to learn to use a sign or a picture to symbolize her wish, suggesting many alternatives to symbolization.

Observed behavior, therefore, is often the result of dynamic interactions between the environment and genetic, prenatal, perinatal, and maturational variations. For example, genetic expression is influenced by a number of cellular and extracellular biological processes, including different hormones and toxic substances. Resultant physiologic levels are modified by different levels of interaction with the physical, cognitive, and social environment. Resultant functional capacities and behaviors are further influenced by interactions with different aspects of the environment. (These processes, which can be systematically described in terms of Biomedical traits, Original traits, Learned coping mechanisms, and Derived behaviors [BOLD] are more fully

discussed by Rosenbloom, Chapter 30, this volume).

Many practitioners, especially those in speech and language pathology, occupational therapy, physical therapy, education, and psychology have been expanding a dynamic functional approach that takes into account the dynamic relationship between behavior and the CNS. These practitioners are demonstrating that interactions geared to individual differences can facilitate important functional capacities such as relating, thinking, and communicating.

For example, motor-planning (including oral-motor) exercises can help develop a child's preverbal vocal, motor, and affective gesturing, imitation, and language development. Visual-spatial, problem-solving approaches can aid logical thinking and abstract academic challenges. Sensory modulation work can help a child learn to relate to others and with receptive language, whereas auditory discrimination work can facilitate the child's phonemic awareness as a basis for reading.

In spite of an expanding functional approach, however, many clinicians continue to focus predominantly on symptoms and only a few of the functional areas (e.g., more on verbal development and less on intimacy, relating, and preverbal affective gesturing). Similarly, there is a tendency to focus only on a few of the critical underlying processing differences. For example, some clinicians focus more on auditory processing and less on motor planning and sequencing, which is essential for imitation, social interaction, play, and language. Others may focus more on rote cognitive and social skills and less on spontaneous interaction to promote affective processing.) (See Tsakiris, Chapter 31, this volume).

Consequently, it is important to further systematize and expand a functional approach. In this approach, assessments and interventions must include the contributions of all relevant areas of functioning, processing differences, and interactive relationships (see Chapter 2). Chart 1 summarizes the relevant areas.

THE FUNCTIONAL DEVELOPMENTAL APPROACH TO ASSESSMENT

Implementing an appropriate assessment of all the relevant functional areas requires a number of sessions with the child and family. These sessions must begin with discussions and observations. Structured tests, if indicated, should be administered later to further understand specific functional areas. The sessions should include:

- *Review of current functioning* with parents and other caregivers, looking at both problems and adaptive capacities.

Chart 1. Relevant Areas to Consider in a Functional Developmental Approach

The functional developmental level of the child's communicative, cognitive, and emotional capacities (i.e., how the child integrates all his capacities to meet emotionally meaningful goals, such as using a continuous flow of social problem-solving gestures to get Daddy to reach for and get him a desired toy).

Includes:
1. Shared attention and regulation
2. Engagement
3. Purposeful preverbal/gestural and affective communication
4. Complex social problem-solving interactions
5. The creative and meaningful use of ideas
6. Building logical connections between ideas or symbols (Greenspan, 1992)

Individual differences in the functioning of the child's motor, sensory, and affective patterns

Includes:
1. Sensory modulation (e.g., the degree to which the child is over- or underreactive to sensations in each sensory modality such as touch, movement, sound, sight)
2. Auditory and visual-spatial processing
3. Motor planning and sequencing and affective processing (i.e., the connection between affect, motor planning, other processing capacities, and emerging symbols)

Relationship and affective interaction patterns, including developmentally appropriate interactions (which utilize understanding of the child's functional developmental level and individual differences) or inappropriate interactions

Includes:
1. Existing caregiver, parent, family patterns
2. Educational patterns
3. Peer patterns

- *Review of prenatal, perinatal, and post-natal developmental history,* including development in all the functional areas.
- *Observations of child-caregiver interactions* for 45 or more minutes, including "coaching" or interactions with the clinician to elicit the child's highest adaptive level. There should be at least two observation sessions, with additional sessions scheduled if there is a discrepancy between parental reports and observed functioning. These sessions should serve, together with a history and review of current functioning, as a partial basis for a preliminary impression of the child's functional developmental capacities and individual processing differences, including those that are often underemphasized, such as motor planning, visual-spatial processing and affective processing, and current as well as potentially optimal child-caregiver interaction patterns.
- *Discussion of caregiver personality patterns and child-caregiver interactions,* including identification of strengths and vulnerabilities as well as family and cultural patterns.
- *Review of all current interventions, educational programs, daily activities, behaviors, and interaction patterns.* There should be review and consideration of developmentally appropriate interaction patterns and practices at home, in school, with peers, and in different interventions in regard to their capacity to foster the next level in the child's functional abilities.
- *Review and assessment to rule out (or identify) concurrent and/or contributing medical disorders.* This includes conducting appropriate biomedical assessments to identify biological interventions that may contribute to clinical management (e.g., a 24-hour EEG may reveal the potential usefulness of Depakote or other antiseizure medications). (See Robinson, Chapter 17, this volume).
- *Additional developmental and learning assessments,* such as speech and language functioning, motor and sensory functioning, and specific aspects of cognitive functioning, should be conducted as needed (as opposed to routinely) to answer specific questions. For example, a child with a circumscribed receptive language difficulty may benefit from structured language assessments to tease out more precisely the nature of the deficit. A child with a circumscribed learning problem may benefit from specific structured tasks to tease out areas of strength and weakness, such as visual-spatial processing or motor planning (e.g., a neuropsychological battery). Specific assessments, however, must always build on a basic evaluation because even circumscribed processing difficulties often make it more difficult for a child to process and understand important functions of social relationships. Therefore, the processing difficulties may be associated with emotional, behavioral, and/or family challenges.

In contrast, a child who is only fleetingly engaged or aimless and has receptive as well as expressive language problems may be best understood through ongoing interactive observation and the child's response to a comprehensive intervention program. Such a child may not be able to fully cooperate in a structured developmental assessment and even the best evaluator may only be able to describe the child's behavior in the assessment situation. In such circumstances, clinical observation of caregiver- and clinician-child interactions to observe functional capacities coupled with a review of current and past functioning provide an initial picture of strengths and challenges. Further profiling may then best done as part of the intervention process. (See Gerber & Prizant, Chapter 5; Long & Sippel, Chapter 9; Greenspan & Wieder, Chapter 12, this volume.)

THE FUNCTIONAL PROFILE

The functional assessment leads to an individualized functional profile that captures each child's unique developmental features and serves as a basis for creating individually tailored intervention programs. The profile describes the child's functional developmental capacities, contributing biological processing differences, and environmental interactive patterns, including the different interaction patterns available to the child at home and at school, with peers, and in other settings. The profile should include all areas of functioning, not simply the ones that are more obviously associated with pathologic symptoms. For example, a preschooler's lack of ability to symbolize a broad range of emotional interests and themes in either pretend play or talk is just as important, if not more important, than that same preschooler's tendency to be perseverative or self-stimulatory. In fact, clinicians have often seen that as the child's range of symbolic expression broadens, perseverative and self-stimulatory tendencies decrease. Similarly, a child's areas of special strength may also be critical to the intervention program. For example, visual-spatial thinking capacities may enable a child with severe language problems to interact with others, learn, and reason.

Because the functional profile captures each child's individual variations, children with the same diagnosis (e.g., PDD) may have very different profiles, whereas children with different diagnoses may have similar profiles. The functional profile is updated continually through clinical observations, which serve as a basis for revising the child's intervention program.

The Affect Diathesis Hypothesis

Looking at children with autistic spectrum disorders within the context of their functional profiles highlights a number of important findings. These findings provide clues regarding a core psychological mechanism that may express the neurological differences characterizing autistic spectrum disorders. When children with autism are compared to children without autism, and level of intelligence as measured with IQ tests is controlled for, there are a number of autism-specific functional deficits. These include deficits in the ability for empathy (theory of mind) (Baron-Cohen, 1994); higher-level abstract thinking and skills in making inferences (Minshew & Goldstein, 1998); and shared attention, including social referencing and problem solving (Mundy, Sigman, & Kasari, 1990). In addition, deficits in the capacities for affective reciprocity (Baranek, 1999; Dawson & Galpert, 1990; Lewy & Dawson, 1992; Osterling & Dawson, 1994; Tanguay, 1999; Tanguay, Robertson, & Derrick, 1998), and functional (pragmatic) language (Wetherby & Prizant, 1993) also appear specific to autism.

These functional deficits have a feature in common that may suggest an overriding or core psychological deficit. Clinical work with infants and children without challenges and those with biological challenges and environmental challenges demonstrates that the capacities for empathy, psychological mindedness, abstract thinking, social problem solving, functional language, and reciprocity all stem from the infant's ability to connect affect or intent to motor-planning capacities and emerging symbols (Greenspan, 1979, 1989, 1997). Relative deficits in this core capacity lead to problems in these higher-level emotional and intellectual processes.

A child's capacity to connect affect to motor planning and emerging symbols becomes relatively apparent between 9 and 18 months of age as the infant shifts from simple patterns of engagement and reciprocity to complex chains of affective reciprocity that involve problem-solving interactions. Consider a 14-month-old child who takes his father by the hand and pulls him to the toy area, points to the shelf, and motions for a toy. After Dad picks him up, he nods, smiles, and bubbles with pleasure. For this complex, problem-solving social interaction to occur, the infant needs to have a wish, desire, or intent (i.e., inner affects or emotions) that indicate what he wants. The infant then needs an action plan (i.e., a plan to get his toy) that may involve many steps. However, the direction-giving affects must connect to the action plan in order for the child to create a pattern of meaningful, social problem-solving interactions. Without this connection between affect and action plans (i.e., motor planning), complex interactive problem-solving patterns are not possible. Action plans without affective direction or meaning will tend to become repetitive (perseverative), aimless, or self-stimulatory, which is what is observed when there is a deficit in this core capacity.

As the ability to form symbols emerges, inner affects (intent) need to connect to symbols to create meaningful ideas, such as those involved in functional language, imagination, and creative and logical thought. The meaningful use of symbols usually emerges from meaningful (affect-mediated) problem-solving interactions that enable a toddler to understand the patterns in her world and eventually use symbols to convey these patterns in thought and dialogue. Without affective connections, symbols such as action plans will be used in a repetitive (perseverative) manner (e.g., scripting, echolalia).

Affectively guided problem-solving interactions and symbols are necessary for all the unique capacities that distinguish individuals with autism from individuals without autism, as outlined earlier. For example, long chains of social reciprocity depend on affect guiding interactive social behavior. Shared attention, which includes social referencing and shared problem solving, also depends on affect guiding interactive social behavior. Empathy and theory of mind capacities depend on the ability to understand both one's own affects or feelings and another person's affects or feelings, and to project oneself into the other person's mindset. This complex emotional and cognitive task begins with the ability to exchange affect signals with another person and, through these exchanges, emotionally sense one's own intent and sense of self in interaction with another. Similarly, higher-level abstract thinking skills, such as making inferences, depend on the ability to generate new ideas from one's own affective experiences with the world and then reflect on and categorize them (Greenspan, 1997).

In observations of infants and toddlers heading into autistic patterns and in taking careful histories of older children with autism, we have noted that children with autistic spectrum patterns did not fully make the transition from simple patterns of engagement and interaction into complex affect-mediated, social problem-solving interactions. They, by and large, did not progress to a continuous flow of affective problem-solving interchanges. Even affectionate children who were repeating a few words or memorizing numbers and letters, and who went on to evidence autistic patterns, did not master, for the most part, this early capacity to engage in a continuous flow of affect-mediated, gestural interactions. These children were then unable to develop higher-level capacities for empathy and creative and abstract thinking unless an intervention was initiated that focused on facilitating affect-mediated interactions.

In a review of the functional profiles of 200 cases of children with autistic spectrum disorders, we observed that most of the children shared this unique processing deficit. At the same time, the children differed with regard to other processing deficits involving their auditory, motor-planning, visual-spatial, and sensory modulation abilities. Approximately two-thirds of the children who developed autistic spectrum disorders had this unique type of biologically based processing deficit that involved the connection of affect or intent to motor planning and sequencing capacities as well as to emerging symbolic capacities (Greenspan and Wieder, 1997).

The hypothesis that explores this connection between affect and different processing capacities is called the *affect diathesis hypothesis*. In this hypothesis, as indicated previously, a child uses his affect to provide intent (i.e., direction) for his actions and meaning for his words. Typically, during the second year of life, a child begins to use his affect to guide intentional problem-solving behavior and, later on, meaningful use of language. Through many affective problem-solving interactions, the child develops complex social skills and higher-level emotional and intellectual capacities.

Because this unique processing deficit occurs early in life, it can undermine the toddler's capacity to engage in expectable learning interactions essential for many critical emotional and cognitive skills. For example, she may have more difficulty eliciting ordinary expectable interactions from her parents and the people in her immediate environment. Without appropriate interaction, she may not be able to comprehend the rules of complex social interactions or to develop a sense of self. A child normally develops these skills and capacities at an especially rapid rate between 12 and 24 months of age. By the time a child with processing difficulties receives professional attention, her challenging interaction patterns with her caregivers

may be intensifying her difficulties. She is likely to perplex, confuse, frustrate, and undermine purposeful, interactive communication with even very competent parents. This loss of engagement and intentional, interactive relatedness to key caregivers may cause a child to withdraw more idiosyncratically into her own world and become even more aimless and/or repetitive. What later looks like a primary biological deficit may, therefore, be part of a dynamic process through which the child's lack of interactions has intensified specific, early, biologically based processing problems and derailed critical social skills.

Biologically based processing (regulatory) difficulties, therefore, often contribute to, but are not decisive, in determining relationship and communication difficulties. When problems are perceived early, appropriate professional help can, to varying degrees, teach children and caregivers how to work with the processing (regulatory) dysfunctions, including helping the toddler connect affect to emerging action plans and their associated relationship and communication patterns. Such children can often become capable of forming warm relationships and climb the developmental ladder leading to language and thinking capacities.

There are many children who do not evidence autism but have developmental problems in which intentionality or purposeful action is difficult in its own right and results in less practice or use (e.g., severe motor problems). These children may either have difficulty forming or may secondarily lose their ability to connect intent or affect to motor planning. In these circumstances, creating purposeful interactions around any motor skill (e.g., head or tongue movements) may strengthen the affect-motor connection, reduce aimless, repetitive behavior, and facilitate problem solving and thinking. Recent

MRI studies suggest that practicing and improving motor skills may enhance the developmental plasticity of neuronal connections (Zimmerman & Gordon, Chapter 27, this volume).

In our review of 200 cases, we also found that, although many children with autistic spectrum disorders shared a primary deficit (i.e., connecting affect to processing capacities), they differed in the levels of developmental functioning of their different processing capacities or "component parts." We noted that the relative strength of each component part tended to determine symptoms and splinter skills, such as whether a child lined up toys (which requires some motor planning) or just banged them, or scripted TV shows (which requires some auditory memory) or was silent. It was also found that children with relatively stronger component parts tended to make rapid progress once they were helped to connect affect or intent to their other processing capacities. Children with weaker component parts tended to make more gradual progress and required more intensive, specific therapies, such as speech and occupational therapy, in order to work with the component part directly.

These observations are consistent with recent neuroscience studies suggesting that different processing capacities may compete for cortical access, depending on functional use (Zimmerman & Gordon, Chapter 27, this volume). They are also consistent with neuropsychological studies of individuals with autism but without mental retardation that show that "within affected domains, impairments consistently involved the most complex tasks dependent on higher-order abilities (i.e., concept formation, complex memory, complex language, and complex motor abilities) (Minshew & Goldstein, 1998). Higher-level capacities tend to depend more on "meanings" which, in turn, depend on affective interactions with the world. Furthermore, these observations are also consistent with work on the shifts to a more complex central nervous system organization, including hemispheric connections that occur at the end of the first year of life and early part of the second year, just as the ability to engage in affect-mediated chains of social problem solving are on the ascendancy (Benson & Zaidel, 1985; Courchesne et al., 1994; Dawson, Warrenburg, & Fuller, 1982; Sperry, 1985).

Dynamic Assessments over Time and in the Context of Interventions

The assessment of the functional processing and developmental capacities just described cannot be implemented based only on structured tests or a short observation. A child's "functioning" involves her ability to learn over time and in contexts that provide learning opportunities. For example, observing how a child responds to interventions that foster engagement and interaction reveals more about the child's relationship capacity than a one-time evaluation of how she relates to the clinician in an office. Similarly, the child's ability to learn to gesture, imitate words, and use words purposefully is best assessed by observing her at home, in school, and in the clinician's office when the child is highly motivated and provided with developmentally meaningful, interactive opportunities.

Traditional ways of assessing children with developmental problems, which include time-limited observations and structured tests, may often present a misleading picture because they do not deal with the child's variability and range of functioning by looking at the child's functioning in a dynamic learning situation over time. In fact, the use of structured tests raises an interesting paradox. Because many children with special needs are quite variable in their functioning, fixed (i.e., standard) presentations of stimuli, which may appear attractive from a research point of view, are likely to produce a great deal of variability in functioning or bring out the child's lowest level of possible functioning. In contrast, optimal levels and stability of performance are enhanced by the flexibility of the presentation.

Criteria for Immediate Evaluation vs. "Wait and See"

A child with functional developmental impairments involving foundation-building capacities, such as relating and using gestures to communicate and problem solve, often requires *immediate* attention, not a "wait-and-see" attitude. Because functional capacities build on each other and there is mounting evidence of age and time limits to developmental, neurobiological plasticity in a child's brain, delaying evaluation can increase functional impairments. Delaying intervention until a child is 3 or 4 years old and evidences a clear syndrome tends to increase the therapeutic challenge and may affect the ultimate prognosis. As the child falls further and further behind, there are more missed opportunities. Therefore, a determination of developmentally significant functional impairment in and of itself should serve as a criterion for initiating an appropriate evaluation and intervention. This is especially true for functional impairments that derail the child's ability to attend, relate, communicate, play, or think. Because the functional impairments are the focus of the intervention, it is possible to begin the therapeutic work even while observing the child over time to determine an appropriate diagnosis. As new observations are made, the intervention program can be revised. In assessing functional impairments, distinctions must be made between circumscribed problems that do not derail the basics of relating, communicating, and thinking and more substantial challenges that do derail them. For example, a toddler with a mild articulation problem who relates and communicates with purposeful gestures (e.g., takes Dad to the toy chest) has a circumscribed difficulty. This child is significantly different from a toddler who cannot use social gestures to show what he wants, even if he can repeat words and is being derailed in his fundamental ability to relate and communicate.

RETHINKING AUTISM, MENTAL RETARDATION, AND SEVERE ATTENTIONAL AND LEARNING PROBLEMS

Moving from standardized, one-time assessments to observing functional impairments in the context of truly helpful interventions over time will certainly change how therapists diagnose problems. It may, at times, change the ultimate diagnosis chosen for a child. These ongoing observations are especially relevant for autistic spectrum disorders, mental retardation, and many types of attentional and learning problems.

Autistic Spectrum Disorders

Some children who meet DSM-IV criteria for autistic spectrum disorders have responded very quickly to developmentally based, comprehensive intervention programs and become warmly related, interactive, and verbally communicative (Greenspan, 1992; Greenspan & Wieder, 1997, 1998). Within 1 year, for example, many of these children became engaged and interactive, overcoming their perseverative and self-stimulatory patterns. After 2 years of intervention, many used language flexibly and creatively, though still with delays. If the diagnosis of these children had been delayed for a year while their response to intervention was observed, the diagnosis for this group of rapidly improving children would be language disorders and motor-planning problems, rather than the autistic spectrum disorders with which they initially presented. If diagnosis were delayed for 2 years, the diagnosis would be a less severe language disorder. Many of these children subsequently developed excellent language and learning abilities as well as a solid capacity to relate to others, including peers, with warmth, empathy, creativity, and a sense of humor. They often evidenced in their later school years more circumscribed processing problems involving motor planning and sequencing.

Other children who initially met the criteria for autistic spectrum diagnoses have made much slower progress: 1 and 2 years into the intervention, they continued to meet the criteria for autistic spectrum disorders, although with a greater capacity to relate and communicate. Still others have made extremely slow progress or no progress at all, continuing to meet the criteria for autism after many years.

Although each of these groups had a different presenting profile in terms of developmental capacities (e.g., relatedness, motor planning and sequencing, and visual-spatial processing), the most distinct difference among the groups is the way in which they have responded to an optimal intervention program. The response to intervention can further classify problems in relating and communicating. It raises a question of whether or not children who make extremely rapid progress and no longer meet DSM-IV criteria for PDD should be diagnosed as having an autistic spectrum disorder or a separate type of neurodevelopmental dysfunction. Should these children be diagnosed based on their initial presenting patterns or should therapists take into account their response to an intervention program, thereby leading to alternative diagnostic considerations? Further complicating the

diagnostic challenge is that many symptoms used by clinicians to diagnose autistic spectrum disorders, such as hand-flapping, repetitive behavior, and self-stimulation, are not specific to autism. These behaviors are also seen in children with severe motor-planning problems and sensory-modulation difficulties. Lack of relatedness and affective reciprocity is a more specific symptom, but it is often the first behavior to improve, especially in the children who respond quickly to treatment.

Mental Retardation

Because mental retardation implies relatively permanent cognitive deficits, observing the response to intervention may be even more important then with autistic spectrum disorders. Often, children who have a number of cognitive deficits are assessed as having relatively permanent global deficits and are diagnosed with varying degrees of mental retardation. Historically, intelligence tests (e.g., two standard deviations below the norm constitutes mild retardation) have been used to make this determination. This method, however, tends to look at the child only at one point in time and not take into account her learning curve over a longer period of time, which is essential for observing changes in her many functional capacities. Contrary to traditional expectations, many children who are diagnosed with mental retardation evidence different patterns of growth and, on close scrutiny, evidence relative strengths and weaknesses even if their intelligence subtest scores are all low.

The most accurate method for making a proper diagnosis is, therefore, to observe a child's progress while fostering her growth with a truly optimal program. If the child's learning curve levels off in spite of the best efforts of a comprehensive, intensive, intervention approach, it then might be reasonable to conclude that the child has stopped making progress. Therefore, although cognitive problems should be noted and described, a diagnosis of mental retardation should only be given if the child is in an optimal program with family involvement, and her learning curve has leveled off in all functional areas for 2 to 3 years.

Severe Attentional and Learning Problems

There are two challenges in working with children with severe attentional and learning problems. The first challenge is working with them in relation to their underlying processing patterns rather than working only on their symptoms or behaviors. For example, a motor-planning and sequencing problem will make it difficult for a child to plan and organize actions, such as doing homework or lining up the numbers to do math problems. An auditory processing problem may make learning to read difficult because of poor sound discrimination (i.e., poor phonemic awareness). Underreactivity to sensations such as touch, pain, and sound may lead to sensory craving, increased activity, and poor attention.

The other challenge for clinicians is to look at all areas of functioning. There is a tendency to focus only on the circumscribed learning, attentional, or processing problems and ignore how, for example, they may influence areas of social and emotional functioning. For example, the same visual-spatial and motor-planning problems that may make planning and organizing school work and math difficult may also make it difficult for a child to interpret other people's facial expressions and body posture, which leads to social and emotional misperceptions. This type of emotional problem is not a reaction to frustration or feelings of failure but a direct consequence of the same processing problems that make school-

work difficult. Therefore, circumscribed attentional and learning problems, even if seemingly localized to school, require a comprehensive functional developmental evaluation.

A child's cognitive challenges and changing abilities should be continually assessed. Access to services should not be delayed pending a definitive diagnosis but provided to a child based on the individual profile of functional developmental impairments. If necessary for administrative purposes, a provisional diagnosis can be used.

A COMPREHENSIVE, DEVELOPMENTALLY BASED APPROACH TO INTERVENTION

A functional approach to assessment leads to a comprehensive approach to intervention that deals with all the relevant functional areas in an integrated manner. An essential part of intervention is a review of the child's functional developmental profile based on assessments of the child's functional developmental level and capacities, individual processing differences, and the different interaction patterns available at home and school, with peers, and in other settings. The functional assessment is updated in an ongoing manner with continuing clinical observations as part of the intervention. These ongoing observations are the basis for revising the child's intervention program.

A comprehensive intervention program involves working with the emotional interactions between the child and family to support each of the child's critical developmental capacities and related underlying processing differences. This Developmental, Individual Differences, Relationship-based (DIR) approach can be conceptualized as a pyramid. Each of the components of the pyramid build on each other and are described briefly in the following sections and by Figure 1.

Protective, Stable, Secure Relationships

At the foundation of the intervention pyramid are the protective, stable, developmentally supportive relationships and family patterns that all children require, especially those with developmental challenges. This foundation includes physical protection and safety and an ongoing sense of security. Some families require a great deal of support, therapy, or both in order to stabilize and organize these basic family functions. For example, some families may be dealing with extreme poverty and chronic states of fearfulness, abuse, and neglect. Some families require counseling to explore family patterns and relationships, particularly in connection to the challenges of coping with a child with special needs and the effects on relationships between spouses and siblings.

Intervention programs require staff trained to assess family needs, develop alliances, problem solve, and advocate, including advocating for social and economic support. They also need to provide family counseling and family or personal therapy where indicated (Barber, Turnbull, Behr, & Kerns, 1988; Bronfenbrenner, 1986; Dunst & Trivette, 1988; Powell, Hecimovic, & Christensen, 1992; Robbins, Dunlop, & Plienis, 1991; Turnbull et al., 1986; and Shanok, Chapter 14, this volume).

Ongoing, Nurturing, Trusting Relationships

At the second level of the pyramid are the ongoing and consistent relationships that every child requires. Typically developing children require nurturing relationships to help them achieve emotional and cognitive competency. Children with special needs, who often already have compromises in their capacities to relate, are in even greater need of warm, consistent caregiving. Their caregivers, however, often face challenges in sustaining intimate relationships because it is so easy to misperceive their children's intentions. Understanding their children's behavior as attempts to cope with their difficulties or as being overwhelmed by their difficulties can often help caregivers recognize these misperceptions and develop more creative and empathetic ways of relating to their children. For example, children who are hypersensitive to touch may not be rejecting their parents' comfort and care. For such a child, parents may have to avoid light touch and use deep pressure to help the child feel more comfortable. Or, parents may need to understand that the child who jumps on a toddler who is crying may not be primarily aggressive but is so sensitive to the sounds of the cry that he panics and wants the noise stopped. Similarly, the child who has difficulty comprehending words may become confused and avoid communication. He may benefit from pictures or gestural signs to understand his environment and predict what will happen next in his interactions with caregivers. The child who is generally avoidant or self-absorbed may be underreactive to sensations, have low muscle tone, and need greater "wooing" to get beyond his self-absorption.

The importance of interactive relationships cannot be underestimated. Almost all learning occurs in relationships, whether in the classroom, with the family, or in therapeutic sessions. No one would deny that the ability to enjoy and participate in relationships is pivotal for learning to relate to others, experience intimacy and positive self-esteem, and develop healthy coping strategies. In addition, most cognitive or intellectual capacities learned in the first 4 or 5 years of life are also based on emotions and relationships (Greenspan, 1997a). For example, infants

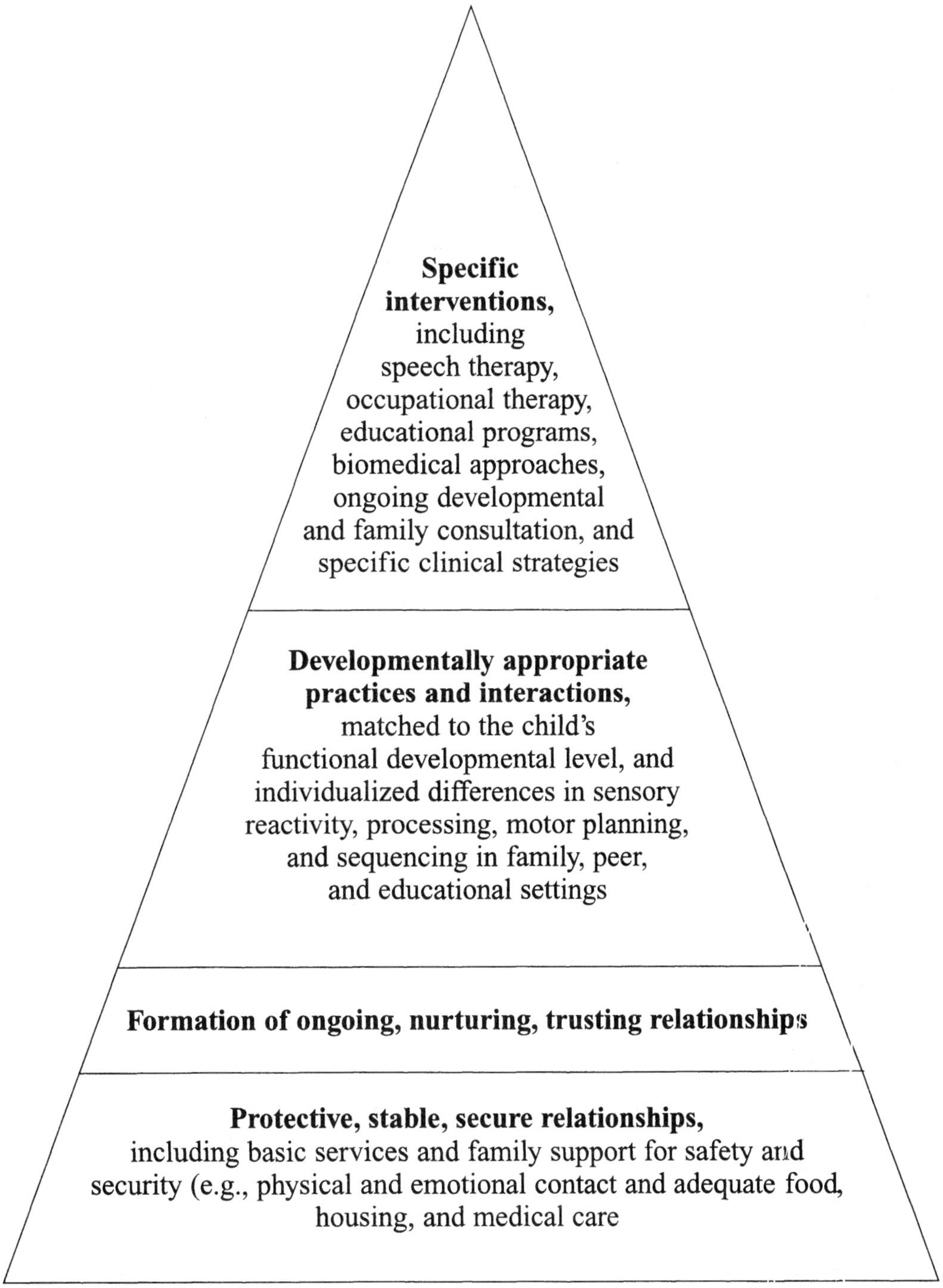

**Specific
interventions,**
including
speech therapy,
occupational therapy,
educational programs,
biomedical approaches,
ongoing developmental
and family consultation, and
specific clinical strategies

**Developmentally appropriate
practices and interactions,**
matched to the child's
functional developmental level, and
individualized differences in sensory
reactivity, processing, motor planning,
and sequencing in family, peer,
and educational settings

Formation of ongoing, nurturing, trusting relationships

Protective, stable, secure relationships,
including basic services and family support for safety and
security (e.g., physical and emotional contact and adequate food,
housing, and medical care

Figure 1. The Intervention Pyramid for Children with Special Needs

first learn initial concepts of causality in early relationships, as a smile lead to a smile back, crying leads to comfort, or reaching out leads to being picked up, rather than in activities such as banging objects on the floor, which leads to learning that this action makes a sound. Similarly, the meaning of words and gestures, the sense of time, and concepts of quantity are also learned as part of interactive, affective relationships early in life (Greenspan, 1997a). For example, for a toddler, "a lot" is more than she expects; "a little" is less than she wants. Words are connected to the emotional experiences that define them, and gestures become organized into patterns associated with emotions and expectation. For example, Dad's smile leads to a hug and tickle.

Relationships serve a number of functions for young children. Most important, they must foster warmth, intimacy, and pleasure. In addition, relationships provide the context in which children experience security, physical safety, protection from illness and injury, and fulfillment of their basic needs. The regulatory aspects of relationships (for example, protection of the child from over- or understimulation) help the child maintain pleasure in intimacy and a secure, alert, attentive state that permits new learning and development to occur.

Relationships provide the basis for communication. Initially, the infant's communication system is nonverbal. It involves affect cueing (smiles, assertive glances, frowns), contingent behavioral interactions (pointing, taking and giving back, negotiating), and the like. From the earliest reciprocal smiles to a child taking her mother's hand, walking to the refrigerator, and pointing to a favorite food, there emerges a complex system of affective, gestural, and behavioral interactions that continues throughout the life of the individual. Even though this nonverbal system eventually works in conjunction with symbolic-verbal

modes of communication, it remains more fundamental: for example, adults tend to trust a person's nonverbal nod or look of approval more than words of praise. The system of reciprocal affective gesturing enables the child to negotiate with his caregivers (environment) in small, graduated increments. Therefore, self-regulation improves and becomes context-dependent, and learning can become subtle and highly differentiated.

Relationships are, therefore, the context for learning which behaviors are appropriate and which are inappropriate (Greenspan, 1974, 1975). As children's behavioral repertoires become more complex in the second year of life, discriminative and reinforcing properties of relationships define which behaviors increase and which behaviors decrease. Repertoires are built up through the give-and-take between children and caregivers (i.e., discriminative learning). In addition to behaviors, relationships help organize a child's wishes, emerging self-perceptions, and a sense of self. The emotional tone and subtle affective interactions of relationships are, therefore, just as important as more easily observable behaviors.

Relationships enable a child to learn to symbolize experience. The first objects with which the child has a highly emotional experience are not playthings, but rather the human "objects" with which he interacts. In his interactions, the child goes from "acting out" his desires or wishes to picturing them in his mind and labeling them with a word. He goes from desiring Mom and grabbing her to saying "Mom" and looking at her lovingly. This transformation heralds symbolic awareness.

The ability to picture an object when it is displaced in both time and space is a much-used marker for the child's achievement of *object permanence* and the emergence of symbolic capacities. Pretend or imaginative play involving emotional human dramas (e.g., the dolls are hugging or fighting) helps the child learn the types of affective-based symbolization that will enable her to connect an image to a wish or intent and then use this image to think, "If I'm nice to Mom, she will let me stay up late." Figuring out the motives of a character in a story as well as the difference between ten cookies and three cookies will depend on the child's capacity for affective symbolization (Greenspan, 1997a).

The child's ability to create mental pictures of relationship and, later, other objects, forms the basis for more advanced symbolic thinking (Greenspan, 1997a & b). For example, a key element essential for future learning and coping is the child's ability for self-observation, problem solving, and creative thought. The ability to self-observe is essential for self-monitoring of activities as simple as coloring inside or outside the lines, or matching pictures with words or numbers. Self-observation also helps a child label rather than act out feelings. It helps her to empathize with others and match behavior to the expectations of the environment.

Self-observation is essential for advanced learning and social negotiation. The ability for self-observation emerges from the ability to observe oneself and another in a relationship and is a product of the same emotional interactive relationships as earlier abilities. Similarly, advanced cognitive skills involving numbers, reading, and analytic thinking build on fundamental, relationship-based capacities. As relationships embrace symbolic capacities, language grows from words to sentences and concepts derived from daily affective experiences. Similarly, cognitive capacities involving time and space emerge out of the day-to-day negotiation of waiting or not waiting, or of having a little more or less of this or that. Even reading comprehension abilities blossom from the natural give-and-take of

dialogue with parents. The child can only understand the meaning of the words or pictures in a book in the context of her daily emotional experiences with others. Without emotional experience to abstract from, there would be no symbolic meaning.

The starting point for mobilizing growth involves meeting a child at his current functional developmental level and forming a relationship and engaging in emotional interactions at that level. Children will vary; some are unrelated and unpurposeful and require work on engaging and intentional communication whereas others are purposeful but require extra help in using symbols. Still others use symbols or ideas in a fragmented way and need to learn how to be logical and more abstract. For each developmental level, special types of interactions can enable a child to master that level and its related capacities.

To support the child's ability to relate requires a significant amount of time, consistency, and understanding. Family difficulties or frequent turnovers among childcare staff or teachers may compromise the requirement for consistency in a child who is beginning to learn how to relate to others.

Developmentally Appropriate Practices and Interactions

At the third level of the pyramid lie consistent relationships and interactions that have been adapted to the individual differences and functional developmental needs of each child, which can be thought of as *developmentally appropriate practices and interactions* for the child with special needs.

Developmentally appropriate practices must characterize family and all other interactions, including home and educational programs. They should also be integrated into the different therapies. Developmentally appropriate interactions and practices, however, are not always easy for caregivers, educators, and therapists to implement. The child's tendency for self-absorption, perseveration, self-stimulation, impulsive actions, or avoidance often elicits counterreactions that attempt to alter the child's immediate behavior rather than to build interactions that will both promote growth and alter the immediate behavior.

Children who do not have special needs often involve themselves in what the National Association for the Education of Young Children (NAEYC) has described as developmentally appropriate practices: that is, they play on their own (part of the time) or with peers, siblings, or parents interactively and using developmentally appropriate toys, games, and puzzles in a constructive, growth-facilitating manner. For children with special needs who, because of their processing difficulties, may find it very hard to interact with people or toys in a way that facilitates their development, the challenge is to help them become involved in their own special types of developmentally appropriate practices and interactions. Doing this involves using the profile of the child's functional developmental level, individual differences in sensory processing, sensory modulation, motor planning and sequencing, and caregiver and family interaction patterns to construct interactions that will be pleasurable as well as developmentally meaningful and facilitating. For example, a 4-year-old may only have the intermittent functional capacities of a 2-year-old, understand visual-spatial experiences better than auditory ones, and be oversensitive to sensations. The focus, therefore, should involve working on engaging, gesturing, and beginning to elaborate symbols by using a lot of visual support and pretend play in a very soothing and regulating context. (See Greenspan & Wieder, Chapter 12, this volume.)

Home-Based Component

Children spend many hours at home. When a child has severe processing difficulties, his choice of activities may *not* be developmentally appropriate or facilitating, such as hours of television-watching, perseverative behavior, or repetitive computer games. Children generally are happier, more productive, less stressed, and make more progress when involved in *developmentally appropriate interactions and practices*. In fact, these types of interactions in the home can become the most important factor for aiding a child's growth.

Developmentally appropriate practices often require one-on-one work with the child. Parents must decide how much they can do on their own and how much help to elicit from volunteers, hired students, or home visitors from community, state, or county-supported intervention programs (e.g., wrap-around services in the state of Pennsylvania provide a very useful model in which bachelor's and master's level professionals often spend more than 20 hours a week supporting the program at home).

The home-based component of developmentally appropriate interactions and practices can be divided into two parts. One involves developmentally appropriate interactions based on following the child's natural interests and emotional inclinations. The other focuses on semistructured problem-solving interactions that also harness the child's "affect" but involve semistructured created situations to facilitate mastery of specific processing capacities, and emotional, cognitive, language, and motor skills. These two components of the home-based program are described in the following sections.

Following The Child's Lead

The caregiver should follow the child's emotional interests to engage him at his functional developmental level and challenge him to move to the next level, thereby gradually moving the child toward negotiating the six levels outlined in Chart 1. These spontaneous interactions in which the caregiver follows the child's lead will often take on two qualities. First, the caregiver helps the child move in the direction that interests him by, for example, putting the ball the child is interested in on her head. The child may then take the ball off the caregiver's head, thus being drawn into focusing on the caregiver and engaging in pleasurable relating and purposeful, two-way communication. Second, the caregiver can become playfully obstructive. For example, if the child perseveratively opens and closes doors, the caregiver could get "stuck" behind the door. This action leads the child to focus on the caregiver as he tries to push her away from the door, giggling as he succeeds—only to have the caregiver run back to the door again to resume the game. In this way, the caregiver facilitates focus and engagement. As the child purposefully tries to engineer moving the caregiver away from the door, intentional, two-way communication is facilitated. Eventually, complex problem-solving behaviors and even the use of words, such as "go" or "away" can be elaborated off of the child's spontaneous, emotional interest in the door. (Strategies for the spontaneous use of developmentally appropriate interactions to help the child master each of the six core functional emotional capacities are described in detail in Greenspan & Wieder, Chapter 12, "Developmentally Appropriate Practices and Interactions.")

Semistructured, Problem-Solving Interactions

The caregiver should create learning challenges for the child to master. These may involve social, motor, sensory, spatial reasoning, language, and other cognitive skills. For example, if the goal is to help a child learn a new word, such as "open," the caregiver might put the child's favorite toy outside the door so that she would want to open it. The caregiver may then help the child imitate the word "open." The child, in this way, is practicing gesturing and using words together. Imitating the sounds "ope" for "open" while opening the door also provides the child with immediate meaning. Tying the word to affect or intent (and meaning) facilitates generalization. This approach is in contrast, for example, to the child saying the word "open" in response to a picture card and only later trying to use the word in real life to solve a problem.

In addition to working on language and cognitive and social capacities, semistructured problem-solving interactions should focus on activities that enable the child to engage in (1) sensory modulation and motor-planning exercises, such as jumping on a trampoline or mattress, running, spinning, appropriate roughhousing with deep tactile pressure, and obstacle courses; (2) perceptual-motor exercises and looking and doing games, such as throwing and catching a big Nerf ball, kicking, and reaching for moving objects; and (3) visual-spatial exercises, such as treasure hunt games, hide-and-seek, and building complex structures from visual cues.

In general, it is most effective for the child's therapeutic team, including parents, educators, speech pathologists, and occupational therapists to meet weekly to design the functional goals for the semistructured aspect of the home-based intervention. At least one-third to one-half of the child's available time at home should be spent on spontaneous interactions (following the child's lead and working off of natural affect and inclination to foster the six functional levels described earlier) and the remaining two-thirds to one-half on developmentally appropriate, semistructured problem-solving activities.

Semistructured, problem-solving activities also need to be geared to each child's unique profile. When put into a problem-solving context with emotional intent, the following types of activities may also be included:

- *Imitating new words and using concepts* that help the child solve a problem he wants to solve, for example, "open," "up there," or "go."
- *Motor-based challenges,* such as gross-motor movement, balance, movement in space, running, jumping, spinning, perceptual-motor activities (involving looking and doing and crossing the midline).
- *Spatial problem solving,* such as treasure hunt games in which the child is given clues about how to find her favorite toy, first in the box in front of her and, eventually, in the box upstairs near another box behind the blue chair.
- *Motor-imitation exercises,* such as copying the caregiver by touching eyes, ears, nose and, eventually, vocal (sound) imitations leading to word development.
- *Spatial and quantity concepts,* such as "here," there," "big," "little," and, eventually, including "more" or "less," and association of numbers, time, or distance (e.g., finding Mommy in different parts of the house, negotiating one versus three cookies, or showing with hands the difference between a little and a lot).
- *Facilitation of conceptual understanding* by using cards where the word is under the picture and is used to help the child get the juice or a favorite toy, or as a cue for pretending what the word or sentence conveys.
- *Visualization exercises,* as the child becomes older, to help the child picture words, sentences, or quantities ($2 + 2 = 4$) to facilitate a deeper understanding of concepts. These concepts may also be acted out.

Specific therapies often work in a semistructured manner on these types of important capacities. (See the Table of Contents for related chapters.) Team meetings should suggest the goals of this part of the home program.

Peer Interaction

Peer play is especially important once the child has mastered preverbal problem-solving skills and is moving into the early stages of using ideas in a functional and spontaneous manner. The now-engaged, intentional, partially verbal, and imaginative child needs to practice his emerging skills not only with adults but also with other children who are at a similar or higher developmental age (i.e., the other children need to be interactive, somewhat verbal, and imaginative). However, the playmates need not be the same age as the child. For example, if the child is 4¹/₂ years old, but has a functional, emotional developmental capacity of 3 years, he might prefer the company (and vice versa) of 3-year-old playmates.

At this point, individual, one-on-one play dates should occur four or more times per week for one hour or more. Initially, an adult may have to facilitate the interactions to help deter the children from drifting into parallel play. The adult may create a game to help the children work jointly, such as having both children hide together while the adult tries to find them. While following the children's lead, the caregiver is also free to create games that facilitate interactions among the children. The goal is to help the children "rub shoulders" with each other and to communicate with gestures and words.

The need for peer play occurs at about the same time that a child needs to be integrated, often with an aide, into a regular preschool program or into an ongoing inclusion or integrated program.

Setting Limits, Facilitating "Compliance"

Developmentally appropriate practices used to foster new functional capacities can help parents, clinicians, and educators with one of their most difficult challenges—how to integrate the process of setting limits and compliance with other clinical and educational goals. Following rules and maintaining safety are understandable goals. Not infrequently, however, the need for compliance and control takes the form of strapping a child into a chair, physically forcing him to walk to the bathroom, or using other types of restraint.

The key to teaching a child to follow rules is to provide developmentally appropriate practices and interactions that meet the child at his functional developmental level in the context of his individual differences. For example, for a child who is impulsive and is not yet capable of logical, verbal thinking and conversation, developmentally appropriate interactions mean a one-on-one aide working with the child on the basics of relating and purposeful interaction. The back-and-forth signaling, which will include limits, however, will be of the type one would implement with a 1- to 2-year-old child. Through this type of one-on-one interaction, the child gradually learns how to be a purposeful, preverbal communicator. Gradually, responding to limits becomes a part of this purposeful communication. Expecting a child who can not yet negotiate basic needs with a series of back-and-forth signals to follow group-oriented rules will often result in frustration, anger, impulsive behavior, and, more importantly, slower progress. Developmentally appropriate practices are more likely to tap into potential plasticity from within the individual child's own brain than will externally-imposed structured techniques (i.e., too complex or restrictive) that bypass neural networks already in place.

As a child makes progress and is purposefully interactive, both encouragement and sensitive limits can help him work with groups of children and follow expectations. Dangerous, as opposed to noncompliant, behavior needs to be dealt with immediately with firm but gentle limits. These limits should be based on the child's functional developmental capacities, not on actual age or expectations for the other children in a group. Just as Congress has appropriately mandated that a child be educated in the least restrictive environment, therapists should teach the child the *least restrictive, developmentally appropriate* tactics to control his behavior and be sensitive to the needs of others.

Specific Therapies and Educational Strategies

At the apex of the pyramid are the specific therapeutic and educational techniques that build on and also facilitate the child's basic capacities for attention, engagement, intentional two-way communication, and the creative use of symbols. In this way, new capacities are tied to the child's sense of purpose and self (i.e., his affects). Integrating therapeutic strategies into the child's naturally occurring interests and activities can be very helpful in simultaneously fostering her capacities to initiate, engage, communicate, problem solve, and think, as well as learn new functional skills. While new skills are on the ascendancy, perhaps in relation to maturational shifts, is an optimal time to intensify a particular therapy that supports that skill, such as physical therapy to facilitate walking.

A variety of strategies have been advocated. Some attempt to offer a comprehensive approach whereas others focus on specific issues. However, an approach cannot be truly comprehensive unless it works with all the levels of the pyramid. Both focused and partially comprehensive approaches must build on the foundation previously described. These include educational approaches (e.g., Bailey & Wolery, 1992), cognitive, language, sensory, and motor processing approaches (e.g., Prizant & Wetherby, 1988; Bricker, 1993), peer models (Odom & Strain, 1986; Strain, Shores, & Timm, 1977), behavioral approaches (Lovaas, 1980, 1987; Durand, Berotti, & Wiener, 1993; Haring & Lovinger, 1989; Odom & Haring, 1993), work with family patterns (e.g., Barber et al., 1988; Bronfenbrenner, 1986; Dunst & Trivette, 1988; Powell et al., 1992; Robbins et al., 1991; Turnbull et al., 1986), interactive "floor time" approaches (Greenspan, 1992; Greenspan & Wieder, 1998), and work with the social milieu (e.g., Ostrosky, Kaiser, & Odom, 1993; Wolfberg & Schuler, 1993).

Speech and Language Therapy

Speech-and-language therapy is especially helpful for preverbal, as well as other types of symbolic communication (e.g., verbal, pictures, signs). It can also be especially valuable for oral-motor work and related expressive language challenges. Three or more individual sessions per week of 30 to 60 minutes each is often required, in addition to consultation to and integration with the home and educational program. (See Gerber & Prizant, Chapter 5, and Madell, Chapter 6, this volume, for further discussion.)

Occupational and Physical Therapy

Occupational and physical therapy are especially helpful for motor problems, motor-planning and sequencing difficulties, and sensory modulation and processing challenges. Two to three individual sessions per week of 30 to 60 minutes each is often required, in addition to consultation to and integration with the home and school programs.

There is often confusion between very helpful clinical strategies that foster sensory modulation, muscle tone, and motor planning and debates about the explanatory value of sensory integration theory. Like all broad theories, time and continuing research will be needed for further refinement of sensory integration theory. In the meantime, clinical techniques that enable children to master functional developmental capacities should be employed based on their clinical usefulness. (For further discussion, see Williamson, Anzalone, & Hanft, Chapter 8; Long & Sippel, Chapter 9; Koller, Chapter 11; Wachs, Chapter 20; Youssefi & Youssefi, Chapter 21; Feuerstein, Chapter 22, this volume.)

Educational Program

An educational program should be geared to a child's functional developmental capacities and processing profile and must involve developmentally appropriate practices for children with special needs. For example, some programs attempt to have a child learn in a group even though the child requires a highly individualized approach. Often, children are able to learn in groups only after they have advanced to the point of mastering individual relationships and preverbal problem-solving interactions and are already beginning to use words. Nonetheless, school settings with other children can be very enriching, even if initially most of the work is conducted on an individual basis. Gradually, learning can move more toward group interactions.

A child who is not yet engaged or purposeful needs to be involved in one-on-one interactions with a teacher, aide, or volunteer throughout most of the school day. The aide's role is not to sit behind the child or help the child conform to noninteractive routines, but rather to "woo" the child into learning interactions (i.e., two-way purposeful interactions and a constant flow of back-and-forth communication). Once a child progresses to purposeful gestural communication, complex imitation and, over time, to using symbols (e.g., words, pictures, and signs) and is able to relate to and communicate logically with peers, two-way symbolic interactions need to be facilitated to promote logical thinking. As a child becomes more logical and abstract, group learning and routine academic activities can provide constructive learning opportunities. This stage, however, is the culmination of a long learning process.

Many programs are not equipped to provide the needed one-on-one interaction for most of the school day, which is required by the child who has not yet fully learned to engage with peers and adults or communicate and problem solve with gestures. In addition, education for children with special needs may take many forms. Often, goals are derived from the academic objectives for older children. When this occurs, there is often little attention given to the sequence by which young children acquire the core functional abilities that will enable them to relate, communicate, think, and learn, including mastering traditional academic tasks. Typically, there is an overemphasis on compliance in a group situation before a child has learned to negotiate one-on-one relationships or even understand simple expectations. For example, a child may be taught in a rote manner to match shapes before she can engage in basic multistep, preverbal, problem-solving interaction sequences, such as getting a toy out of a box, bringing it over, and motioning for an adult to play.

The child who is already attentive, engaged, purposefully interactive, involved in complex, ongoing preverbal problem-solving communication (i.e., gesturing), and is beginning to use words presents special opportunities. She needs to learn to elaborate and build bridges between ideas in a variety of contexts. To meet this goal, the child requires opportunities to interact with peers (one-on-one and in small groups) who are related, interactive, and verbal (often with an adult mediating). She requires an integrated setting or an aide in a mainstream setting.

It is important to emphasize that educational programs for a child with special needs should not comprise a series of disconnected cognitive learning opportunities. The important academic goals just stated do not emerge as isolated cognitive skills by simply practicing them. Having a child sit and look does not mean he understands or that he can learn from listening. Nor does having a child memorize a passage mean he understands it. These skills are part of a progression where each step builds on another. Comprehension, relating, communicating, reading, math, writing, and engaging in higher-level problem solving must build on the six functional capacities described earlier. Education programs should identify where each child is in his unique progression, meet the child at his level, and work on the next steps. *Only this type of logical progression constitutes developmentally appropriate practices for a child in school.*

For example, to read with meaning or to understand math, a child must learn how to:

- *"Want" to attend and engage with others* (first with one person at a time and then a few) in order to be part of experiences that will enable him to discriminate sounds and sights necessary for reading and math, and to eventually give words and quantity concepts meaning.

- *Communicate logically with simple gestures and affect cues,* and then with complex problem-solving behaviors in order to understand patterns of cause-and-effect relationships and different levels of logic. These capacities are essential for any type of academic work.

• *Represent or symbolize emotional experiences and build logical bridges between them.* What a child knows from preverbal experience as well as new verbal experience must be understood, communicated, and thought about logically with words, pictures, or other symbols. This is necessary for creative and logical thought, abstract thinking, and all academic tasks requiring the comprehension of words or the ability to reason with symbols.

In addition to the difficulties in providing one-on-one interaction, most educational programs, due to administrative policies, change intervention teams for a child and family when the child is 3 years old. For a child with autistic patterns who is learning to relate to and trust others, this change can undermine educational progress. Therefore, continuity of staff and program is critical during the infancy and preschool years.

Developing the most appropriate educational program for children with special needs is extremely challenging and often requires one-on-one or very small group learning. To increase one-on-one learning opportunities that enable children to climb the developmental ladder and eventually learn and communicate in groups, school programs should provide more aides and allow parents to volunteer, as they do in cooperative preschools. (See Wieder and Kalmanson, Chapter 13, this volume, for further discussion.)

Children with learning and attention problems who have progressed and mastered their basic challenges in relating and communication, as well as children who have already mastered these skills but have problems with attention, learning, or both, require an educational program that provides opportunities to resolve specific processing challenges and progress to high levels of abstract thinking and academic proficiency. Promising techniques

to strengthen processing capacities such as visual-spatial, auditory, and motor planning are being developed and are available in innovative schools and programs but are not yet sufficiently available in all education and special education programs. (See Miller and Eller-Miller, Chapter 19; Wachs, Chapter 20; Youssefi & Youssefi, Chapter 21; Feuerstein, Chapter 22; and Bell, Chapter 25, this volume.)

In addition, many intelligent children with moderate to severe circumscribed learning and/or attention problems who are fully capable of being mainstreamed often require both participation in regular classes and one-on-one and very small-group (two to four children) learning opportunities to master specific processing challenges. Many require special learning opportunities for as much as half of the day, during which they can work on their processing challenges with the most up-to-date techniques. At present, unfortunately, many children with learning and attention problems do not get the adequate time or techniques they require.

Exploration of Biomedical Interventions

Certain children with special needs will benefit from biomedical assessments and considerations of interventions, including medications. For example, medications in the selective serotonin reuptake inhibitor group may facilitate motor planning, sequencing, and attention and reduce perseverative or repetitive behavior. To determine if a biomedical intervention should be a part of the therapeutic regimen, a basic biomedical assessment needs to be implemented, as described by Robinson, Chapter 17, on biomedical approaches.

In exploring a trial of medication, it is essential to look carefully at the side effects and weigh the benefits and risks. Medications are not designed as precisely as would be optimal and will often affect nontargeted areas. In addition, exceptional caution and close monitoring are required if more than one medication at a time is being considered.

Ongoing Developmental and Family Consultation

In addition to conducting the initial diagnostic evaluation and monitoring progress, developmental specialists (e.g., a psychologist, behavioral or developmental pediatrician, or child psychiatrist) may be helpful in facilitating or coaching the family in constructing developmentally appropriate interactions at home and at school. For some families, this consultation may take the form of regular meetings one or more times per week, during which the therapist works with the parents and other caregivers on their interactions with the child and, if needed, works directly with the child. Consultations may also involve periodic home visits. In addition, intensive family work with supports and coordination from community agencies will be necessary for some families. The form the consultation takes will vary depending on the needs of the child and the family. (For a more detailed discussion, see Greenspan, 1992; Shanok, Chapter 14, this volume)

Family Support and Dynamic Family Processes

Special clinical techniques are often needed to support families. Although there is a long tradition of family-based programs for children with special needs, many of these programs offer only minimal help to the whole family, including siblings. Marital conflicts, misperceptions of the special-needs child or her siblings, and higher levels of stress may characterize the family functioning. It is also difficult for a family to orchestrate an entire

intervention program. Often, various levels of support are needed.

SPECIFIC CLINICAL TECHNIQUES

Specific clinical techniques to deal with difficult symptoms or behaviors are often needed as part of an overall program. There are two primary philosophies that tend to guide parents, educators, and clinicians. The behavioral approach attempts to decrease the target behavior directly by ignoring it, using negative consequences, or both, and attempting to replace it with another behavior supported by positive consequences (e.g., interrupting perseverative behavior and insisting on and reinforcing another activity). Intensive behavioral approaches are often suggested as an overall treatment method. Although they have a circumscribed role for selected children, they do not address many important functional capacities, including the capacity to relate with pleasure and warmth, to connect affect or intent to motor planning and emerging symbolic capacities (for creative and reflective thinking), and to process sensory information and plan actions.

Although behavioral approaches are widely used in most communities, as indicated in Chapter 3, children with typical patterns of autism who are in these programs generally do not make clinically meaningful progress. They are often unable to learn to live independently, work, and participate in a range of age-expected social relationships. (See, Chapter 3; and Tsakiris, Chapter 31, this volume, for a full discussion.) Nonetheless, specific behavioral exercises can be useful for a child who has severe motor-planning problems and, therefore, is having difficulty learning to imitate actions, sounds, and words. When the child can begin using imitative capacities at the moment he is trying to solve a problem, such as copying the act of opening a door to get out, or saying "up" to get his toy from a high shelf, he can move into more dynamic, interactive learning approaches. Therefore, as one part of the semistructured component of a broad comprehensive program, some children may, for a period of time, require behavioral exercises in conjunction with dynamic, interactive work.

Intensive behavioral intervention techniques by themselves tend to be almost antithetical to harnessing the child's natural affect and intent as a basis for internal control and initiation of behavior and language. They have as their strength the external control of behavior through external discriminative and reinforcing stimuli (prompts and reinforcers). External control can help get some behaviors started. While there has been the hope that internal prompts and reinforcers can take over as part of a generalization process, the child does far better if she can learn new behaviors and concepts under the influence of internal affect cues. These give her actions immediate meaning and direction.

Intensive behavioral intervention techniques can be compared to the strategy of a tennis coach using hand-over-hand learning. In this approach, the coach holds the racket with the student and drops the ball in front of the student *only* when teaching a difficult, new handgrip or stroke. Most of the learning occurs either through playing actual games or in dynamic drills where the student is learning to use his forehand or backhand while on the run. The behavioral strategy is similar to the hand-over-hand approach because a therapist uses it temporarily to shore up a skill such as imitative capacities. Once the child reaches a certain level, however, most of the learning needs to occur in the semistructured learning situations (such as the dynamic tennis drilling) and in the spontaneous learning interactions (such as playing games). The more structured approach would remain

available on an as-needed basis. In this way, behavioral strategies are part of the tactics that are available to the clinician.

Interestingly, developmentally appropriate practices can be conceptualized in behavioral terms. In this model, the focus is on developmental processes (i.e., classes of behavior), such as creative, ongoing reciprocal interaction (circles of communication) rather than on specific behaviors, such as "looking." The processes selected for focus are from a hierarchy of developmental capacities that need to be mastered. The cues (discriminative stimuli) and reinforcers are based on internal affect states rather than on external events (i.e., natural social cues and reinforcers). Interactions are continuous rather than stop-start. Some intensive behavioral approaches are moving toward such a developmentally based model (e.g., Pivotal Response Training [(Schreibman, Stahmer, & Pierce, 1996]).

The functional, developmental approach attempts to understand the broad category of functioning that the worrisome behavior is part of, and the broad functional categories that may be missing. In this context, functional means a broad developmental capacity essential for the child's progress, such as purposeful gesturing or using ideas. It does not refer to a narrow functional behavior, such as dressing. Developmentally appropriate interactions and practices are used to help the child master new functional capacities. For example, repetitive opening and closing of a door is part of the larger category of repetitive and rigid ways of dealing with the world. The missing functional category is the developmentally more advanced capacity for flexible, creative interactions in the world. In this model, the worrisome, repetitive behavior serves as an opportunity for progressing to higher functional developmental levels of flexible, creative interactions. Therefore, as described earlier, a perseverative behavior, such as opening and closing a door, is turned into a purposeful interaction. The functional developmental approach keeps the larger therapeutic goal of higher-level functional developmental capacities in the forefront.

Both philosophies can be used in an integrated manner. For example, a caregiver can interrupt a child's self-injurious behavior while simultaneously drawing him into interactions that serve a similar sensory need, such as deep tactile pressure coupled with warm engagement and two-way intentional communication.

SUMMARY

This chapter reviewed the general clinical principles that characterize a functional developmental approach to assessment and intervention. The chapters that follow review intervention research, examine the evaluation and intervention process for each functional area, and explore the evaluation and diagnostic process as well as the intervention process in more detail. Relevant neuroscience research also is considered. ■

REFERENCES

Bailey, D. B., & Wolery, M. (1992). Normalizing early intervention. *Topics in Early Childhood Special Education, 10,* 33-47.

Barber, P. A., Turnbull, A. P., Behr, S. K., & Kerns, G. M. (1988). A family systems perspective on early childhood special education. In S. L. Odom & M. B. Karnes (Eds.), *Early intervention for infants and children with handicaps: An empirical base* (pp. 179-198). Baltimore: Paul H. Brookes.

Baranek, G. T. (1999). Autism during infancy: A retrospective video analysis of sensorimotor and social behaviors at 9-12 months of age. *Journal of Autism and Developmental Disorders, 29*(3), 213-224.

Baron-Cohen, S. (1994). *Mindblindness: An essay on autism and theories of mind.* Cambridge, MA: MIT Press.

Benson, F., & Zaidel, E. (1985). *The dual brain.* New York: Guilford Press.

Bricker, D. (1993). Then, now, and the path between: A brief history of language intervention. In A. P. Kaiser & D. B. Gray (Eds.), *Enhancing children's communication: Research foundations for intervention* (pp. 11-13).

Bristol, M., Cohen, D., Costello, J., Denckla, M., Eckberg, T., Kallen, R., Kraemer, H., Lord, C., Maurer, R., McIllvane, W., Minshew, N., Sigman, M., & Spence, A. (1996). State of the science in autism: *Report to the National Institutes of Health. Journal of Autism and Developmental Disorders, 26,* 121-154.

Bronfenbrenner, U. (1986). Ecology of the family as context for human development research perspectives. *Developmental Psychology, 22,* 723-742.

Courchesne, E., Akshoomoff, N., Egaas, B., Lincoln, A. J., Saitoh, O., Schreibman, L., Townsend, J., & Yeung-Courchesne, R.

(1994). *Role of cerebellar and parietal dysfunction in the social and cognitive deficits in patients with infantile autism.* Paper presented at the Autism Society of America Annual Conference, Las Vegas, NV.

Dawson, G., & Galpert, I. (1990). Mothers' use of imitative play for facilitating social responsiveness and toy play in young autistic children. *Developmental and Psychopathology, 2,* 151-162.

Dawson, G., Warrenburg, S., & Fuller, P. (1982). Cerebral lateralization in individuals diagnosed as autistic in early childhood. *Brain and Language, 15,* 353-368.

Dunst, C. J., & Trivette, C. M. (1988). A family systems model of early intervention with handicapped and developmentally at-risk children. In D. Powell (Ed.), *Parent education as early childhood intervention: Emerging directions in theory, research, and practice* (pp. 131-180). New York: Ablex.

Durand, V. M., Berotti, D., & Weiner, J. S. (1993). Functional communication training: Factors affecting effectiveness, generalization, and maintenance. In J. Reichle & D. P. Wacker (Eds.), *Communicative alternatives to challenging behavior: Integrating functional assessment and intervention strategies* (pp. 317-340).

Greenspan, S. I. (1974). The clinical use of operant learning techniques: Some complex issues. *American Journal of Psychiatry, 131*(8), 852-857.

Greenspan, S. I. (1975). A consideration of some learning variables in the context of psychoanalytic theory: Toward a psychoanalytic learning perspective. *Psychological Issues,* IX(1): Monograph 33. New York: International Universities Press.

Greenspan, S. I. (1979). Intelligence and adaptation: An integration of psychoanalytic and Piagetian developmental psychology.

Psychological Issues (Monograph 47/68). New York: International Universities Press.

Greenspan, S. I. (1989). *The development of the ego: Implications for personality theory, psychopathology, and the psychotherapeutic process.* Madison, CT: International Universities Press.

Greenspan, S. I. (1992). *Infancy and early childhood: The practice of clinical assessment and intervention with emotional and developmental challenges.* Madison, CT: International Universities Press.

Greenspan, S. I. (1997a). *The growth of the mind and the endangered origins of intelligence.* Reading, MA: Addison Wesley Longman.

Greenspan, S. I. (1997b). *Developmentally based psychotherapy.* New York: International Universities Press.

Greenspan, S. I. (1998). Commentary: Guidance for constructing clinical practice guidelines for developmental and learning disorders: Knowledge vs. evidence-based approaches. *Journal of Developmental and Learning Disorders, 2*(2), 171-192.

Greenspan, S. I., & Wieder, S. (1997). Developmental patterns and outcomes in infants and children with disorders in relating and communicating: A chart review of 200 cases of children with autistic spectrum diagnoses. *The Journal of Developmental and Learning Disorders, 1,* 87-141.

Greenspan, S. I., & Wieder, S. (1998). *The child with special needs: Intellectual and emotional growth.* Reading, MA: Addison Wesley Longman.

Gresham, F. M., & MacMillan, D. L. (1998). Early intervention project: Can its claims be substantiated and its effects replicated? *Journal of Autism and Developmental Disorders, 28*(1), 5-12.

Haring, T. G., & Lovinger, L. (1989). Promoting social interaction through teaching generalized play initiation responses to preschool children with autism. *Journal of the Association for Persons with Severe Handicaps, 14,* 255-262.

Lewy, A. L., & Dawson, G. (1992). Social stimulation and joint attention in young autistic children. *Journal of Abnormal Child Psychology, 20*(6), 555-566.

Lovaas, O. I. (1980). Behavioral training with young autistic children. In B. Wilcox & A. Thompson (Eds.), *Critical issues in educating autistic children and youth* (pp. 220-233). U.S. Department of Education, Office of Special Education.

Lovaas, O. I. (1987). Behavioral treatment and normal educational and intellectual functioning in young autistic children. *Journal of Consulting and Clinical Psychology, 55,* 3-9.

McEachin, J. J., Smith, T., & Lovaas, O. I. (1993). Long-term outcome for children with autism who received early intensive behavioral treatment. *American Journal on Mental Retardation, 97,* 359-372.

Minshew N., & Goldstein, G. (1998). Autism as a disorder of complex information processing. *Mental Retardation and Developmental Disabilities, 4,* 129-136.

Mundy, P., Sigman, M., & Kasari, C. (1990). A longitudinal study of joint attention and language development in autistic children. *Journal of Autism and Developmental Disorders, 20*(1), 115-128.

Odom, S. L., & Haring, T. G. (1993). Contextualism and applied behavior analysis: Implications for early childhood education for children with disabilities. In R. Gardner et al. (Eds.). *Behavior analysis in education: Focus on measurably superior instruction.* Pacific Grove, CA: Brookes/Cole.

Odom, S. L., & Strain, P. S. (1986). A comparison of peer-initiation and teacher-antecedent interventions for promoting reciprocal social interaction of autistic preschoolers. *Journal of Applied Behavior Analysis, 19,* 59-71.

Osterling, J., & Dawson, G. (1994). Early recognition of children with autism: A study of first birthday home videotapes. *Journal of Autism and Developmental Disorders, 24*(3), 247-257.

Ostrosky, M. M., Kaiser, A. P., & Odom, S. L. (1993). Facilitating children's social-communicative interactions through the use of peer-mediated interventions. In A. P. Kaiser & D. B. Gray (Eds.), *Enhancing children's communication: Research foundations for intervention: Vol. 2.* (pp.159-185). Baltimore: Paul H. Brookes.

Powell, T. H., Hecimovic, A., & Christensen, L. (1992). Meeting the unique needs of families. In D. E. Berkel (Ed.), *Autism: Identification, education, and treatment* (pp. 187-224). Hillsdale, NJ: Erlbaum.

Prizant, B. M., & Wetherby, A. M. (1988). Providing services to children with autism (ages 0 to 2 years) and their families. *Topics in Language Disorders, 9,* 1-23.

Robbins, F. R., Dunlap, G., & Plienis, A. J. (1991). Family characteristics, family training, and the progress of young children with autism. *Journal of Early Intervention, 15,* 173-184.

Rogers, S. (1996). Brief report: Early intervention in autism. *Journal of Autism and Developmental Disorders, 26,* 243-246.

Schopler, E. (1987). Specific and non-specific factors in the effectiveness of a treatment system. *American Psychologist, 42,* 262-267.

Schreibman, L., Stahmer, A. C., & Pierce, K. L. (1996). Alternative applications of pivotal response training: Teaching symbolic play and social interaction skills. In L. Koegel, R. Koegel, &. G. Dunlap (Eds.), *Positive behavioral change.* Baltimore, MD: Paul H. Brookes.

Smith, T., Eikeseth, S., Morten, K., & Lovaas, I. (1997). Intensive behavioral treatment for preschoolers with severe mental retardation and pervasive developmental disorders. *American Journal on Mental Retardation, 102,* 238-249.

Sperry, R. W. (1985). Consciousness, personal identity, and the divided brain. In F. Benson & E. Zaidel (Eds.), *The dual brain* (pp. 11-27). New York: Guilford Press.

Strain, P. S., Shores, R. E., & Timm, M. (1977). Effects of peer social initiations on the behavior of withdrawn preschool children. *Journal of Applied Behavior Analysis, 10,* 289-298.

Tanguay, P. E. (1999). *The diagnostic assessment of autism using social communication domains.* Paper presented at the Interdisciplinary Council on Developmental and Learning Disorders' Third Annual International Conference, Autism and Disorders of Relating and Communicating, McLean, VA, November 12-14.

Tanguay, P. E., Robertson, J., & Derrick, A. (1998). A dimensional classification of autism spectrum disorder by social communication domains. *Journal of the American Academy of Child and Adolescent Psychiatry, 37*(3), 271.

Turnbull, A. P., & Turnbull, H. R., with Summers, J. A., Brotherson, J. J., & Benson, H. A. (1986). *Families, professionals and exceptionality: A special partnership.* Columbus, OH: Merrill.

Wetherby, A. M., & Prizant, B. M. (1993). Profiling communication and symbolic abilities in young children. *Journal of Childhood Communication Disorders, 15,* 23-32.

Wolfberg, P. J., & Schuler, A. L. (1993). Integrated play groups: A model for promoting the social and cognitive dimensions of play in children with autism. *Journal of Autism and Developmental Disorders, 23,* 467-468.

Part Two:

Language and Communications

◄ 5 ►

Speech, Language, and Communication
Assessment and Intervention for Children

Sima Gerber, Ph.D., C.C.C.–S.L.P.,
and Barry Prizant, Ph.D., C.C.C.–S.L.P.

This chapter outlines guidelines for developmentally based "best practices" in speech-language pathology. As in many other fields, inconsistency exists in the familiarity with and use of a developmental framework for the assessment of and intervention with children who demonstrate speech, language, and communication challenges. These guidelines reassert the principles which guide assessment and intervention for children, particularly those functioning at early stages of language and communication development, regardless of their chronological age.

Although the field of speech-language pathology recognizes that a full understanding of typical development serves as the basis for the assessment and treatment of children with atypical development, the breadth of this perspective is often missed. First, there seems to be some confusion as to the different components of speech, language, and communication and the kind of developmental information that is available in each specific domain. Second, norms and standardized measurements are often used to determine if a child is demonstrating a problem in the development of speech, language, and/or communication.

In this approach, behaviors expected at particular chronological ages and which focus on either receptive or expressive language (e.g., comprehends "in," "on," "under;" produces first words; correctly articulates certain sounds; can retell stories) are tapped through the use of checklists or standardized testing. Information gathered in this way is often seen as the total body of information that a clinician needs in order to embrace a developmental perspective. In fact, the primary use of this kind of information should be to identify those children who are falling behind their chronological peers and therefore are in need of services. The critical next step involves moving from the identification of what the child *is not yet doing* to an understanding of what the child *is doing* to begin to approach the child from his or her current developmental level or stage. Beyond this, for an in-depth developmental assessment of what the child's strengths and challenges are in language, and for an informed understanding of where to begin intervention with a child, clinicians must refer to the rich body of developmental literature, which details the qualitative nature of and processes of language acquisition and communication development. For example, if a child has been identified as being delayed in the development of first words, the clinician will want to understand, on the one hand, the nature of first words in typical development child and, on the other hand, the nature of this particular child's current vocal-verbal repertoire including phonology, semantic categories, and pragmatic functions. This understanding will provide the clinician with the basis for determining which first words to begin working on and in which contexts to begin teaching this child. In fact, by using developmentally based assessment models, a clinician can move seamlessly from assessment to intervention, a step that is not possible following the use of formal testing, which generally yields quantitative information about a child's performance.

Furthermore, the developmental speech-language pathologist broadens the scope of inquiry beyond language for both assessment and intervention. Since the acquisition of language is embedded in, dependent on, and related to other developmental domains, the speech-language pathologist determines where the child is in the process of language acquisition by assessing where the child is in the development of cognitive schemas, affective development, social interaction, prelinguistic communication, and of course, language comprehension, processing, and production. The comprehension and production of language can not be disassociated from other related developments. From the perspective of the developmental speech-language pathologist, an understanding of the course of cognitive development, social-emotional development, and affective development, as well as the developmental relationship between comprehension and production, is crucial to assessment and intervention with the young child.

DETERMINING THE CHILD'S STAGES OF SPEECH, LANGUAGE, AND COMMUNICATION DEVELOPMENT

Similar to determining the stages of emotional development discussed by Greenspan (1992), the developmental speech-language pathologist must determine a child's general stage of language acquisition. In the more developmentally based assessment, the speech-language pathologist begins by observing the child in natural interactions with familiar caregivers and then in the child's interactions with the therapist, with an eye toward determining if the child is at one of the following seven stages of language and communication development.

1. Preintentional Stage
(Intention inferred by the communicative partner)
The child demonstrates a variety of behaviors, including gazing, crying, touching, smiling, laughing, vocalizing, and grasping; the adult responds to these behaviors as if they were intentional.

2. Prelinguistic Intentional Stage
(Emergence of intentional communication)
The child now communicates intentionally using a combination of gestures, vocalizations, and eventually, words.

3. First Words
(Emerging symbolic communication)
The child begins to understand and use language within the contexts of his daily life.

4. Two-Word Stage
(Vocabulary explosion and early multi-word combinations)
The child begins to combine words to form utterances that are governed by semantic-syntactic rules.

5. **Early Syntactic-Semantic Complexity**
*(Later multiword, beginning
multiverb combinations)*

The child develops the basic syntactic structures of the language, talks about many ideas and notions, and uses language for a broad range of communicative functions

6. **Later Syntactic-Semantic Complexity**
*(Multiverb utterances, complex
sentences, and discourse)*

The child uses more complex language to talk about events and engages in various kinds of discourse.

7. **Communicative Competence**

The child's syntactic, semantic, and pragmatic abilities are well developed and sophisticated.

Although each stage is primarily identified by the child's "production"—or, in the case of the preintentional and prelinguistic stages, by "performance"—this approach helps to capture the overall developmental stage which the child has mastered. Within each of these stages, the clinician must further evaluate the child's particular profile of strengths and challenges for both assessment and intervention purposes. For example, within the prelinguistic intentional stage, the clinician is interested in answering the following questions:

- Does the child communicate a range of communicative intentions?
- Does the child use a variety of communicative forms?
- Are the child's interactions specific to particular routines and contexts?
- Is the child's comprehension of language limited to familiar words in familiar contexts or can the child understand the words in different contexts?
- Does the child attempt to vocalize?

- Are these vocalizations best described as babbling, jargon, or phonetically consistent forms, and are they coordinated with the use of gestures?
- Does the child engage in joint reference, turn-taking, interactive play?
- Does the child interact with objects and delight in these interactions?

Each stage of language development brings with it a developmentally appropriate list of behaviors to assess, (see Charts 1 and 2) which will reveal if the child is solidly within a particular stage or more splintered in her skills within that stage. These charts indicate the kinds of information that the speech-language pathologist would be interested in collecting in order to assess the child's current speech, language, and communication abilities. Chart 1 covers the first three stages just listed: *The Preintentional Stage, The Prelinguistic Intentional Stage, and First Words.* Chart 2 covers the *Two-Word Stage, Early Syntactic-Semantic Complexity, Later Syntactic-Semantic Complexity,* and *Communicative Competence.* A chapter appendix specifies the major developments for each of the seven stages.

Basic to the model being presented in this chapter is the notion that developmentally based assessment leads directly to developmentally based intervention. Once the speech-language pathologist has determined the stage of language and communication development that the child is at and the child's strengths and challenges within that stage, starting points for intervention are easily determined. Philosophically, the following guidelines serve as the basis for determining principles of both assessment and intervention from a developmental perspective:

- Information from research on the language acquisition of typically developing children serves as the framework for

Chart 1. Speech, Language, and Communication Assessment for Children at Prelinguistic and Early Language Stages

I. PRELINGUISTIC, LINGUISTIC, AND PRAGMATIC DEVELOPMENT

A. EXPRESSIVE LANGUAGE AND COMMUNICATION

1. *COMMUNICATIVE MEANS*
   a. *Vocalization*
      - syllable structure (CV, VC, CVC)
      - range and complexity
      - frequency and diversity
   b. *Gaze/Facial Expression*
      - use of gaze and gaze shifts for referencing and regulating
      - frequency and diversity
   c. *Gesture/Body Posture*
      - conventional (pointing, showing, giving) or idiosyncratic
      - contact or distal
      - frequency and diversity
   d. *Coordination of Vocalization, Gaze, and/or Gesture*
      - frequency and diversity
   e. *Linguistic Forms*
      - first words - object names, actions, routines; individual styles
      - lexical repertoire
      - word combinations
      - syntax (Subject + Verb; Verb + Object)
      - semantic relations (codes existence, recurrence, location, action, etc)
      - frequency and diversity
   f. *Unconventional Vocal or Verbal Behavior*

2. *COMMUNICATIVE FUNCTIONS AND RELATED SOCIAL-PRAGMATIC DIMENSIONS*
   a. *"Proto-conversations"/"True" Conversations*
      - initiating, responding, turn-taking, adjacency, contingency
      - frequency and diversity
   b. *Communicative Intentions*
      - behavior regulation -requesting, protesting
      - social interaction - showing off, calling, greeting
      - joint attention - commenting, requesting information
      - frequency and diversity
   c. *Speaker-Listener Roles - Awareness of Listener's Needs*
      - persistence and repair strategies
      - frequency and diversity

3. *SPEECH PRODUCTION*
   a. *Syllabic Shape*
      - inventory of consonants and vowels
      - consonant + vowel combinations
      - juxtaposition of syllables (monosyllabic or multisyllabic)
      - frequency and diversity

Continued

Chart 1. *Continued*

      b. *Voice Quality*
      c. *Fluency of Speech*
      d. *Oral Motor Function*

B. *COMPREHENSION/ RECEPTIVE LANGUAGE*

  1. *Nonlinguistic Response Strategies*
     – attends to object mentioned
     – do what is usually done with the object
  2. *Early Comprehension*
     – responds to "no," "bye-bye," "name"
     – responds to single words in context; familiar names; simple actions
     – responds to "Show me _____."
     – understands up to 150 words
    Later Comprehension
     – understands words when the referent is not present
     – understands the language of routines and scripts
     – understands word combinations; simple directions
     – understands simple *Who, What, Where* questions
     – understands up to 500 words

II. LANGUAGE RELATED COGNITIVE, AFFECTIVE, AND SOCIAL-EMOTIONAL DEVELOPMENTS

A. COGNITIVE DEVELOPMENTS

  1. *Conceptual Structures and Schemas*
     – interactions with objects - search, act on, combine
     – exploratory and sensory-motor play
     – relational and functional play
     – frequency and diversity
  2. *Symbolic Play*
     – props, themes, organization, roles
     – frequency and diversity
  3. *Constructive Play*
     – frequency and diversity
  4. *Attention and Focus*
  5. *Spontaneous Imitation*
     – non-verbal behavior
     – vocal and verbal behavior
     – frequency and diversity

B. AFFECTIVE AND SOCIAL-EMOTIONAL DEVELOPMENTS

  1. *Affective Development*
     – expresses positive and negative affect
     – frequency and diversity
  2. *Social-Emotional Development*
     – demonstrates engagement, attachment, intentionality
     – demonstrates interest in peers
     – frequency and diversity

Chart 2. Speech, Language, and Communication Assessment for Children at Early Stages Through Later Stages of Linguistic Complexity**

I. LINGUISTIC AND PRAGMATIC DEVELOPMENT

A. EXPRESSIVE LANGUAGE AND COMMUNICATION/PRODUCTION

1. *LINGUISTIC DEVELOPMENT*
   a. *Lexical Repertoire*
      - develops a diverse vocabulary
      - uses relational (*big/little; tall/short*) and contrastive terms (*more/less; before/after*)
      - uses kinship terms
      - developing pronominal system
      - frequency and diversity
   b. *Semantic-Syntactic Relations*
      Early semantic-syntactic development,
      - MLU (approximately 2.0 at 2 years and 5.5 at 5 years)
      - codes basic semantic relations such as Agent + Action + Object
      - codes a range of meaning relations
      - codes grammatical morphemes (see order of acquisition)
      - codes three constituents Subject + Verb + Complement
      And later syntactic-semantic development,
      - codes basic sentence types- negatives, interrogatives, imperatives
      - further elaboration of sentence types to express meanings
      - coordination and embedding to talk about events and ideas
      - frequency and diversity
   c. *Unconventional Verbal Behavior*

2. *PRAGMATIC DEVELOPMENT*
   a. *Conversational Development*
      - produces spontaneous, responsive, contingent utterances
      - initiates, maintains, terminates topics; adds new information
      - talks about past, future, other people
      - engages in longer conversational exchanges
      - eventually, uses longer and more elaborate discourse turns
      - uses narrative sequences
      - by 7 years, creates narratives with a beginning, end, problem, and resolution
      - frequency and diversity
   b. *Communicative Intentions*
      - expresses a wide range of communicative intentions or functions
      - uses a variety of forms for all functions
      - eventually, uses language to inform, report, plan, and for social functions
      - frequency and diversity
   c. *Speaker-Listener Roles – Awareness of Listener Needs*
      - plays conversational roles of speaker and listener
      - offers conversational repairs, from phonetic revisions to paraphrase
      - determines the information the listener needs

Continued

Chart 2. *Continued*

        – modifies talk to different listeners, e.g., politeness markers to strangers and simplifies language to younger children
        – frequency and diversity

3. *SPEECH PRODUCTION*
   a. *Phonological Processes*
        – many processes used until 4 years of age
        – produces a growing repertoire of consonants; complete repertoire by 7 years
        – by 7 year, produces all consonant clusters
        – uses syllable structure, including two- to three-syllale words
        – frequency and diversity
   b. *Voice Quality*
   c. *Fluency*
   d. *Oral-Motor Function*

4. *METALINGUISTIC ABILITIES*
   Early in this stage,
        – metaphonological skills begin such as rhyming, playing with sounds
   Later in this stage,
        – growing awareness of meaning and structure such as phonological awareness, morphological awareness, multiple meanings in humor, grammatical judgments

B. COMPREHENSION/RECEPTIVE LANGUAGE

1. *Nonlinguistic Response Strategies (early in this stage)*
        – does what is usually done
        – puts things where they usually go (in, on, under, beside)
        – supplies missing information to questions not understood
        – supplies explanation to questions not understood
        – infers most probable speech act

2. *Early in this Stage*
        – understands sentences based on morphological and syntactic rules
        – understands a range of questions - sequence of development:
          Yes/No; What, What doing, Where, Whose, Who, Why, How many
        – understands "he" vs. "she"
   Later in this Stage
        – understands word order cues to Agent + Action + Object relations
        – understands questions such as *How* and *When*
        – responds to multi-step commands
        – understands location and time relationships such as *behind, in front, before,* and *after*
        – understands connected discourse and narratives
        – develops a large receptive lexical repertoire

Continued

Chart 2. *Continued*

II. LANGUAGE RELATED COGNITIVE, AFFECTIVE, AND SOCIAL-EMOTIONAL DEVELOPMENT

A. COGNITIVE DEVELOPMENT

1. *Symbolic Play*
   - props, themes, organization, roles
   - frequency and diversity

2. *Constructive Play*
   - frequency and diversity

3. *Games with Rules*

4. *Attention and Focus*

B. AFFECTIVE AND SOCIAL-EMOTIONAL DEVELOPMENT

1. *Affective Development*
   - expresses a range of affective states (with linguistic and nonlinguistic means)
   - expresses a range of themes (e.g., separation, power, aggression)
   - frequency and diversity

2. *Social-Emotional Development*
   - interacts in a range of social situations beyond home
     enjoys peer relationships
   - engages in parallel, associative, cooperative, and eventually, competitive play
   - assumes a range of social roles
   - frequency and diversity

**At the late stages of childhood, between 7 and 12 years of age, the child's ability to *comprehend* language is characterized by his ability to understand an infinite number of sentences; his *production* of language is characterized by his ability to express an infinite number of sentences. In terms of *Lexical, Syntactic, and Semantic Abilities,* the child demonstrates linguistic complexity relative to word structure, phrase structure, clause structure, complex sentences, and discourse structure. In terms of *Pragmatic Abilities*, the child can use language to accomplish sophisticated functions such as persuading, teasing, and arguing. The child can abide by conversational rules and acquires knowledge of who can say what to whom, when, where, and how. Narratives are elaborated in both content and structure and the child learns different narrative formats, such as plays, jokes, letters, and reports. In terms of *Speech Production,* the child now has a complete phonetic repertoire and can produce all consonant combinations in all positions. Finally, the child's *Metalinguistic Abilities* continue to develop.

determining what to assess and, eventually, what the child needs to learn.

- Parents, caregivers, and teachers' understanding of the child's strengths and challenges, communicative needs, and priorities should be considered integral to the assessment and intervention process.

- The use of language and communication can best be understood and facilitated across contexts of the child's daily life. By embracing the idea of contextual variation (different settings, agendas, participants), the clinician will gain a clearer profile of those factors which support the child's language and communication development and those which may contribute to the difficulties that the child is experiencing.

- A child's conventional and unconventional behaviors are assessed and honored on the way to facilitating the child's development of communication and the acquisition of a language system.

- A child's language and communication development is embedded in and related to other developmental areas, such as cognitive development, social-emotional development, affective development, and motor development. Therefore, all of these areas must be assessed and, ultimately, addressed during intervention.

- The assessment and intervention process, while based on principles that apply to all children and all learning, is seen as an attempt to discover each child's unique profile of strengths and challenges.

- The assessment and intervention strategies best suited to any particular child will be chosen from a range of possibilities and should be based on the child's developmental level; the goals of assessment or intervention; the child's interests, preferences, and response capabilities; and varied assessment and intervention contexts.

- The child should be seen as an active participant and given an active role during both the assessment and the intervention processes.

- Family variables, including but not limited to family structure, resources, informal and formal supports, and critical factors (including language proficiency), must be accounted for in assessment and intervention efforts.

These guidelines, which will now be discussed in more detail as they apply to assessment and intervention, serve as starting points for developmentally based assessment and developmentally based intervention for children who are experiencing challenges in the development of speech, language, and communication.

ASSESSMENT

A comprehensive communication and language assessment is an essential component in planning appropriate educational services for young at-risk children, children with disabilities, and their families. Assessment and intervention of language, communication, and related abilities for young children should be viewed as interdependent processes. Ideally, caregivers should be integrally involved in assessment by participating in activities, sharing their perceptions of their child's abilities, and prioritizing intervention needs.

Purposes and Goals of Assessment

The most obvious goal of a speech, language, and communication assessment of a young child is to determine whether a problem exists. Children who are suspected of having delays in speech, language, and/or communication development should be referred for an initial screening and, if deemed necessary, a comprehensive speech, language, and communication evaluation.

Establishing a child's age equivalent of communicative and language functioning helps to determine whether a problem exists and the child's eligibility for services. However, this type of information in and of itself provides minimal specific direction for intervention planning or for supporting caregivers. The focus of this discussion will be on goals and strategies of assessment that contribute most directly to intervention planning and the intervention process. These goals include determining the child's developmental stage of language and communicative functioning, identifying the child's unique learning and communication style, clarifying his strengths and needs, and identifying functional intervention targets.

In summary, speech, language, and communication assessment of children may be considered at three levels:

1. *Screening* to identify children who have a high probability of developmental delay in speech, language, and communication abilities and need further assessment.
2. *Diagnostic assessment* to determine the existence of a communication delay or disability and identify a child's strengths and needs, usually by using formal and informal assessment instruments.
3. *Assessment for individual program planning* to determine a child's mastery of skills as well as developmental and functional needs.

Principles of Assessment

Communication and language assessment should be based on a number of basic principles, which evolve from the guidelines described earlier. These principles reflect the complexity and multidimensional nature of the process of communication, the fact that communication is first and foremost a social activity, and that language and communication development is closely related to other aspects of development, including cognitive, affective, and social-emotional domains. Thus, assessment should address these relationships. A discussion of each major principle follows.

Developmental research on the sequence and processes of typical language and communication development should provide the framework for assessing a child's speech, language, and communicative abilities.

Familiarity with sequences and processes of communication and language development is essential for a number of reasons. First, although clear individual differences exist in some aspects of language acquisition, nearly 30 years of research has documented relatively invariant sequences and stages of development. This information can provide an organizational framework for documenting a child's abilities and progress in development (see chapter appendix: "Stages of Development of Speech, Language, and Communication"). Second, an intervention plan should be based on a child's current level of ability with developmentally appropriate skills targeted in setting short and long-term goals. Of course, goal setting is greatly influenced by a child's functional needs and caregiver priorities. However, unless these factors are cast within a developmental framework, goals and expectations may be unrealistic and, in the short term, would likely be unattainable.

Parents or primary caregivers should be considered expert informants about a child's communicative competence.

It is not uncommon for caregivers to report that they observe different patterns or levels of communication in their children than may be observed directly by professionals during an assessment. When assessment includes observations of a young child during familiar routines in the home environment, discrepant opinions about the child's abilities may be precluded to a great extent. However, home visitation may not always be possible.

As noted earlier, language development and communicative competence naturally varies across contexts, and caregivers have opportunities to observe and interact with their child far more frequently, and in far more familiar and emotionally secure situations, than do professionals. Thus, a general underlying assumption in language and communication assessment is that caregivers are most knowledgeable about their child's abilities. Professionals must refine their interviewing skills and use appropriate language and communication assessment interview tools and strategies to tap into such knowledge.

Assessment involves gathering information about a child's communicative behavior across situational contexts over time. Assessment is an ongoing process, not a one-time episodic event.

It has been well documented that a child's communicative abilities vary greatly as a function of many factors including, but not limited to, the environment or setting in which a child is observed, the persons interacting with the child, and the familiarity of the situation. Thus, language and communication assessment should account for the normal variability observed in communicative functioning in young children across contexts. Assessment ideally involves gathering and coordinating information from persons who regularly interact with a child in different contexts, whether they are direct care staff at a daycare center, parents, educational staff in preschool and school settings, or speech-language pathologists.

To ascertain a child's communicative strengths and needs, therapists should utilize a variety of strategies, including direct assessment, naturalistic observation, and interviewing significant others.

The use of a variety of strategies reflects currently recognized "best practices" in early childhood assessment for all assessment domains. Direct assessment involves professionals interacting with a child, typically using standardized instruments or checklists, or less structured natural play interactions to collect a language and communication sample for later analysis. Naturalistic observation is characterized by observing or videotaping a child while he or she interacts with familiar persons during relatively familiar life routines and activities. Finally, information may be collected by interviewing significant others who have the opportunity to observe and interact with the child on a regular basis. It is important to recognize that each of these strategies has the potential to provide qualitatively different information about a child's communicative abilities, which can ultimately be integrated to construct a more holistic picture of a child's language and communication system.

Another positive feature of using different assessment strategies is that it allows for cross-validation of findings. That is, a clinician can be more confident in assessment findings if similar language and/or communication patterns are observed across contexts. Information also may be gathered by interviewing caregivers, or by having caregivers present and involved in direct assessment and providing subsequent feedback as to whether a child's communicative behavior as observed is representative of behavior in other contexts.

A variety of instruments or tools may be used in assessment, and should be selected based upon a child's developmental level, the purpose of the assessment, and the assessment strategies used.

A language-communication interview protocol with predetermined questions regarding a child's functional communication abilities (C.S.B.S. Caregiver Questionaire, Wetherby & Prizant, 1993), and/or a developmental checklist focusing on milestones in development (Rossetti, 1990), may be used when interviewing caregivers or other persons familiar with the child. These tools provide information for determining eligibility for services as well as for planning intervention. An observational checklist of communicative behavior may be used during naturalistic observation or during direct assessment, and also can provide information regarding eligibility for services and intervention planning. Checklists of developmental milestones and standardized tests are used primarily for determining eligibility for services and general developmental levels.

Typically, more direct and formal language and communication assessment strategies, such as the use of standardized tests, are most appropriate for developmentally more sophisticated children (e.g., children at conversational language levels or with greater comprehension) and chronologically older preschoolers. They are less appropriate for developmentally and chronologically younger children. Areas assessed in standardized tests include a range of linguistic domains, such as receptive vocabulary (e.g., Peabody Picture Vocabulary Test—Revised, Dunn & Dunn, 1981) and the comprehension of morphological and syntactic structure (e.g., Test for Auditory Comprehension of Language—

Revised, Carrow-Woolfolk, 1998), as well as more general expressive and receptive language abilities (e.g., Clinical Evaluation of Language Functions, Semel, Wiig, & Secord, 1995). Indirect observational approaches are appropriate for both developmentally or chronologically younger children, as well as older children.

Although standardized tests are frequently used, this kind of assessment has a number of limitations. First, there tends to be a focus on communicative milestones and forms (e.g., gestures and words), with limited attention paid to the wide range of preverbal communicative strategies available to young children (e.g., range of conventional gestures) or to the functions or purposes of communication (e.g., is the child using words or gestures to request objects, comment on objects, greet people). Second, when direct formal assessment is used, a child is typically placed in a respondent role (e.g., responding to commands, required to name objects) with little opportunity to be observed in more natural reciprocal interactions. Third, a child's use of social-affective signals (e.g., communicative gaze, expressions of positive and negative affect), which play an important role in regulating communicative interactions, are rarely considered as an aspect of communicative competence. Finally, standardized instruments most typically provide developmental ages or quotients rather than a profile of a child's relative strengths and weaknesses. Thus, a range of assessment strategies that are most appropriate to a child's developmental capacities and provide useful information to families and professionals should be considered.

Language and communication assessment must account for conventional as well as unconventional communicative behavior.

For some children, the acquisition of conventional verbal or nonverbal means of communication is especially difficult or challenging. Due to their disability, some children may develop idiosyncratic and even socially unacceptable means to communicate their intentions. Idiosyncratic means may include subtle or difficult-to-read behaviors that can only be understood by those who know a child well (e.g., the child produces "ay o, ay o" to request singing of "Old MacDonald Had a Farm"). Such behavior has been documented in children with multiple disabilities and in children with social-communicative challenges such as autistic spectrum disorders. Socially unacceptable forms of communication, including aggression and throwing tantrums, have been observed in children and adolescents with developmental disabilities. Frameworks and instruments are available that document intentional but idiosyncratic or socially unacceptable forms of communication (Donnellan, Mirenda, Mesaros, & Fassbender, 1984; Schuler, Prizant & Wetherby, 1997) as well as conventional forms of communication. These tools provide a more complete picture of a child's communication system.

Assessment should always provide direct implications and directions for intervention, and should be viewed as a form of intervention.

Decisions regarding program planning should be made on the basis of an ongoing assessment that documents changes in a child's communication and language behavior. Such documentation serves as the baseline for determining goals and the appropriateness of goals, and for evaluating the effectiveness of approaches to enhance communicative competence. Alternative strategies, if needed, can be developed in collaboration with caregivers to address a child's emerging communicative needs within the context of the child's developmental strengths and weaknesses.

The caregivers' active involvement and participation in assessment activities may contribute significantly to their understanding of their child's communicative strengths and needs, which may ultimately benefit their child. Thus, assessment may serve as one form of intervention. For example, caregivers may become more aware of their child's communicative signals and their level of comprehension. As a result, they may develop interactive strategies that are conducive to sustaining social and communicative exchange.

Assessing and responding to the needs of the family will contribute to the child's ultimate progress.

Working with children with speech, language, and communication challenges necessarily brings with it the understanding that the parents and/or caregivers of these children will be experiencing their own issues and challenges. Although each family and each parent respond in a unique way to the reality of having a child who is delayed, all families will need some kind of support to move through the process and realities of raising their child. In the most comprehensive models of assessment and intervention, therapists recognize that in order to effectively help children with speech, language, and communication problems, they must assess and understand the strengths and challenges of the child's caregivers. From this vantage, the therapist can determine what supports would be most helpful as the family moves through the stages of recognizing, accepting, and living with the "shattered dream" (Moses, 1985) of having a child who is less than perfect.

Whether the speech-language pathologist feels equipped to deal with the needs of the parent or whether the parent is referred for counseling, it should be clear that part of the assessment process involves determining how best to facilitate the caregivers' emotional well-being. From this perspective, helping the parents regain or maintain their equilibrium is critical to the child's well-being and, ultimately, to her development of speech, language, and communication.

Assessing the interactions between the child and the child's communicative partners to determine which behaviors help or hinder the development of language and communication skills.

A child's communicative partners may include parents, other caregivers, educators, therapists, or any other people who interact with the child on a regular basis. Typically, partners demonstrate a wide range of strategies and behaviors that may serve to support and facilitate a child's communicative growth, or in some cases, may hinder communicative exchanges. For young children, the caregiver's style and the degree of match or mismatch with the child's language and communication abilities is of primary interest during the assessment process.

Partners' strengths and weaknesses in supporting communicative interactions may be observed and documented during observations of familiar daily living and play activities. Dimensions of partner style that may be documented include degree of recognition of a child's communicative attempts, use of directive versus facilitative styles of interaction, and use of specific interactive strategies such as responding contingently to child behavior, providing developmentally appropriate communicative models, maintaining the topic of child initiations, and expanding or elaborating on communicative attempts. The primary purpose of assessing partner style is to help

partners develop an awareness of strategies that facilitate successful and positive interactions and to help them recognize and modify interactive styles that may limit productive communicative exchange.

During the process of assessing interactions, the partner's level of comfort using a particular style and the cultural influences on interactions with young children must be considered. Child-rearing practices may vary significantly with families of diverse cultural backgrounds, and such differences must be taken into account in both assessment and intervention efforts. Literature on approaches and strategies for assessing different dimensions of partner-child interaction should be referred to during this part of the assessment process (Duchan, 1989; McCollom & Hemmeter, 1997; Peck, 1989; Van Kleeck, 1994).

Domains of Assessment

A speech, language, and communication assessment framework delineates those specific content areas or domains of communicative behavior to be assessed. When considered in total, the assessment will provide a portrait or profile of a child's linguistic and communicative strengths and needs. Some information may be developmental in nature (e.g., developmental level of a child's linguistic comprehension or understanding), whereas other information may be more qualitative (e.g., use of nonverbal signals such as communicative gaze in interactions). Charts 1 and 2 present two generic frameworks delineating specific content areas for (1) children at prelinguistic and early language levels who are communicating developmentally from birth to the 24-month-old level (Chart 1), and (2) for children beyond emerging language who are communicating developmentally from approximately 2- to 7-year-old levels (Chart 2). The specific type of information provided in each area will vary according to a child's developmental level of linguistic and communicative functioning.

The authors recognize that the framework presented, although comprehensive, is not exhaustive. That is, the framework may not include all specific aspects of communication, language, and related abilities relevant to the assessment of a particular child.

Speech, Language, and Communication Assessment for Children at Prelinguistic and Early Language Stages

I. Prelinguistic, Linguistic, and Pragmatic Development

A. Expressive Language and Communication (Production). The primary focus in this domain is documentation of: (1) communicative means, or the behaviors by which information is communicated; (2) communicative functions, or the purposes for which a child communicates; and (3) speech production, or the quality and variety of a number of parameters of speech, and related oral motor function.

1. Communicative Means. When considering communicative means, the first determination that must be made is whether a child is using signals to influence the behavior of others to accomplish a specific purpose or goal. In other words, is a child communicating with intention? Evidence of intentional communication includes the use of vocal, facial (gaze), or gestural, and/or verbal communicative means directed to other persons with the expectation of a specific response. Further evidence of intentional communication includes a child persisting in

communicative attempts if the intended goal is not initially reached.

For developmentally young, preintentional children, communicative means may include nonverbal and vocal behaviors such as body posture, facial expression, limb extension, hand gestures, directed gaze and gaze aversion, cry and cooing vocalizations, and intonated vowel and/or babbling vocalizations. These signals may function to inform a receiver of the child's physiological and emotional state, level of alertness, focus of attention, interest in interacting or receiving comfort from other persons, interest in obtaining objects, or desire to have events continue or cease. Although a young child may not produce signals with the intention of affecting another person's behavior in specific ways, it has been documented repeatedly that caregivers respond to such signals as if they *were* intentional. The caregivers' assigning or imputing intent to early communicative signals is considered to be an important process in fostering communicative development.

For developmentally more advanced children who communicate intentionally through prelinguistic means, the child's use of vocalizations, gaze and gaze shifting, and intentional use of idiosyncratic (e.g., physically manipulating or leading others) and conventional gestures (e.g., pointing, giving, pushing away, or showing objects, waving, head nods and head shakes) should be documented. Frequency and diversity of vocal, gaze, and gestural means, and coordination of such means should also be noted.

For children using linguistic forms, including speech, sign language, or pictorial or graphic systems (e.g., communication boards), the clinician should document the range of vocabulary (i.e., lexical repertoire), form-content categories, and semantic and syntactic complexity (i.e., word combinations). For range of vocabulary, the number of different words and word classes (e.g., nouns, action words, modifiers or descriptors) used meaningfully also should be documented.

2. Communicative Functions and Related Social-Pragmatic Dimensions. For children at prelinguistic and early language stages, the ability to engage in early aspects of conversational competence, including the ability to initiate communicative interactions, respond to the initiations of others, take turns in interactions, and respond contingently to others should be documented. It also is important to document the relative frequency and diversity of categories of communicative intentions, such as behavioral regulation (e.g., requesting objects or actions, protesting), social interaction (e.g., calling, greeting, requesting comfort, requesting social routines), and joint attention (e.g., commenting, providing information, requesting information). Finally, a child's awareness of the listener and of communicative success can be documented by noting the frequency and diversity of strategies in a child's ability to persist and repair communicative breakdowns.

3. Speech Production. For children using speech as a primary mode of communication, it is essential to document syllabic shape and inventory; that is, different types of consonants and vowels and combinations of consonants and vowels in syllables. Any abnormalities in voice quality such as harshness, or aberrations in quality of vocal resonance such as excessive nasality, should be noted.

Abnormalities in fluency of speech production relative to a child's developmental level should also be noted. For example, it is important to differentiate between the normal dysfluency typical of early stages of language development and problematic disruptions in fluency.

Many young at-risk or developmentally delayed children may not be able to acquire and use speech as a primary mode of communication. This may be due to severity of cognitive impairment or severe to profound hearing loss. It may also be due to specific neuromotor speech disorders, including: (1) dysarthria, a paralysis or paresis (i.e., weakness) in the oral musculature often observed in children with cerebral palsy or other identified neurological disorders; or (2) developmental dyspraxia, a dysfunction in the ability to plan the coordinated movements needed to produce intelligible sequences of speech sounds. Dysarthria and dyspraxia may co-occur in young children, and may range from conditions mildly affecting speech intelligibility to severe conditions rendering speech unintelligible or precluding speech development.

Factors that should be considered when evaluating the potential for speech as a primary mode of communication include
- The child's current level of intelligibility in spontaneous speech
- The child's ability to imitate words with a variety of speech sounds
- The past or recent history of problems in chewing or swallowing,
- The presence of abnormal reflexive patterns (e.g., hyperactive gag reflex), and
- The child's motivation to use speech

A complete oral function assessment should be conducted by a qualified speech-language pathologist and/or occupational therapist; however, informal observations about vocal control for speech, patterns of chewing and swallowing, and other indicators of oral motor function are useful in making decisions about the use of non-speech systems. Assessment should address the status of speech and vocal production to determine whether an augmentative non-speech mode of communication may be beneficial at a particular point in the process of language development.

B. Comprehension of Language/Receptive Language. A child's ability to receive and respond to communicative signals from others is another major domain that should be addressed in assessment. Initially, an audiologist should conduct a full audiological assessment relevant to a child's chronological age and developmental level to assess hearing status. Informal behavioral observation of young children and parental report may also contribute information about a child's functional hearing. For children who are developmentally young, relevant observations would include whether a child shows any startle response to loud environmental sounds, localizes or orients to speech or environmental sounds, or can be soothed or comforted by a caregiver's voice. The ability of preverbal children to approximate sounds or intonation patterns in imitation also provides informal evidence of auditory functioning.

At higher prelinguistic levels of ability, children demonstrating "non-linguistic response strategies" are able to respond to communicative gestures and vocalizations of others and—with the support of situational cues—to demonstrate comprehension of words used in highly routine and familiar activities.

True early linguistic comprehension is evidenced when children can comprehend words without situational or nonverbal cues, especially when words refer to persons, objects, and events not present in the immediate environment. A child's ability to comprehend more complex utterances (e.g., word combinations, "Wh" questions) with a wider range of vocabulary referring to spatially and temporally distant events is assessed for developmentally more advanced children. Miller and Paul (1995) provide a more detailed discussion of informal procedures for assessment of receptive language and communication.

II. Language-Related Cognitive, Affective, and Social-Emotional Development

A. Cognitive Development. Communication and language abilities should always be considered in the context of a child's cognitive and social abilities. Profiling a young child's communicative abilities relative to nonverbal cognitive abilities and capacities provides information about the nature of a communication or language delay. Nonverbal cognitive knowledge is evident by observing how a child interacts with objects, including exploratory, sensory-motor, functional and relational play, as well as imaginative or symbolic play. For example, a child with age-appropriate symbolic play and limited expressive language development may be showing evidence of a more specific expressive language delay not due primarily to a cognitive impairment. Such information would have important implications for education and intervention planning.

Communication and language use is also the means by which children express their knowledge and understanding of other persons and events in their world. Thus, language use is a reflection of as well as dependent upon a child's world knowledge. Finally, the choice of augmentative communication systems, which may be influenced by levels of cognitive/representational ability, requires some estimation of cognitive abilities. Linder (1993), and Patterson & Westby (1994), and Westby (1988) provide guidelines for play-based assessment of language-related cognitive abilities in young children.

Finally, social-cognitive abilities that should be addressed relative to language and communicative abilities include attention and focus, and spontaneous imitation in nonverbal, vocal, and verbal modalities.

B. **Affective and Social-Emotional Development.** Communicative interactions are regulated by social-affective signaling and relationship variables. It is important to document a child's use of facial expression, vocalizations, and other observable behavior reflecting emotional and physiological states, both positive and negative. It is also important to assess children's use of gaze to socially reference or monitor the attention of others and signal attention to others. Furthermore, a child's level of engagement and attachment to others, and level of interest in peers will impact greatly on communicative competence and should be documented relative to both familiar and unfamiliar persons.

Speech, Language, and Communication Assessment for Children at Early Stages Through Later Stages of Linguistic Complexity

Chart 2 outlines the developmental stages of linguistic complexity that children would normally progress through between 2 to 7 years of age (see note relative to children at 7 to 12 years of age). Children with developmental disabilities may be well into adolescence when they reach these stages.

I. Linguistic and Pragmatic Development

A. Expressive Language/Production

1. Linguistic Development. Various aspects of linguistic development are considered in the assessment of expressive language. First, the diversity of the child's vocabulary is important to consider as the increase in lexical development is a hallmark of a developing linguistic system. For children using speech, sign language, or pictorial or graphic systems, the child's lexical repertoire would be documented, including the number of different words and the range of word classes. The child's use of relational (e.g., tall/short), contrastive (e.g., before/after), and kinship (e.g., brother, sister) terms is explored to assess later vocabulary development. The child's use of the pronominal system, such as subjective (he, she, I, you), objective (him, her, me), and— eventually— reflexive pronouns (himself, herself, myself) is analyzed.

The child's semantic-syntactic development can be analyzed in a number of ways. First, the child's mean length of utterance (MLU) is computed as an overall measure of the child's linguistic stage and is compared to chronological age norms. Morphological development is assessed by documenting the child's acquisition of 14 grammatical morphemes (including plural *s*, present progressive *ing*, and past tense *ed*) at increasing MLUs. The child's coding of semantic-syntactic relations, which moves from the basic Agent + Action + Object relations and Subject + Verb + Object structure to a range of meaning relations, sentence types (negatives, interrogatives, imperatives), and complex sentences (coordination and embedding), is analyzed. The child's coding of form-content categories such as state, action, notice, and — eventually—additive, causality, and adversative would also be analyzed. Once again, the frequency and diversity of use of the structures and meanings of the language are addressed as these quantitative and qualitative measures capture the generative aspects of language acquisition.

2. Pragmatic Development. Assessment within the area of pragmatic development includes conversational development, expression of communicative intentions, and the development of speaker-listener roles. The clinician also analyzes the child's ability to engage in conversations with spontaneous, responsive, and topic-related utterances, as well as the child's ability to talk about a range of topics beyond the "here and now" and to expand conversational turns across interactants and within his own turn is also analyzed. Later in this stage, children begin to produce narratives. By 7 years of age, the children's stories have components such as beginnings and ends, a statement of the problem, and resolution.

Children at early through later stages of linguistic complexity express a wide range of communicative intentions, such as requesting, commenting, labeling, greeting, and protesting. Eventually, they express more sophisticated functions of language, such as informing, reporting, planning, and engaging in social functions. The child's ability to use a greater variety of forms to express these functions, which speaks to the interaction of the child's linguistic and pragmatic abilities, is evaluated. In terms of speaker-listener roles and the awareness of the listener's needs, the child's ability to determine the kind of information he must provide his listener, based on an understanding of the information which is shared between the speaker and listener and the information which is not shared, is a developing skill throughout the period being discussed. The child's response to requests for clarification can be assessed by first looking for phonetic revisions, and later for substitutions and paraphrase. The pragmatic ability to adapt to different listeners can also be assessed by noting the child's use of politeness markers to strangers and her simplification of language to younger children. The frequency and diversity of all pragmatic skills will be analyzed in order to develop a rich profile of the child's abilities in this area of language acquisition. In fact, many children with autistic spectrum disorders find these interactive aspects of language use to be most challenging. Even children who develop linguistic systems often struggle with how to appropriately use their lexical, syntactic, and semantic knowledge for communicating in interpersonal interactions.

3. Speech Production. The child's use of phonological processes is assessed relative to the norms available on the typical development of the sound system. The use of a variety of phonological processes as well as the presence of articulation errors is expected at different ages and linguistic levels; however, by 7 years of age the child's phonological repertoire should be complete. Other aspects of speech production, such as voice quality and fluency, would be observed and assessed. (See earlier discussion of the assessment of oral motor function and the consideration of augmentative non-speech modes of communication.)

4. Metalinguistic Abilities. During the preschool years, children begin to develop metalinguistic abilities, or the ability to "play with sounds," and, later, to reflect on language. These skills, particularly metaphonological abilities such as segmenting words into syllables and eventually into phonemes, are evaluated as they are considered important for the development of reading. Eventually, children's abilities to understand humor and to make grammatical judgments reflect their developing ability to think about the language itself and all are important later linguistic developments to explore.

B. Comprehension of Language/Receptive Language. As the child progresses in terms of comprehending language, the child will rely less on nonlinguistic strategies for comprehension and more on her linguistic knowledge. However, it is important to remember that preschool children continue to respond to language with response strategies that are based on their knowledge of the world (e.g., put things where they usually go in response to directions that include "within," "on," or "under") before they respond to these terms on the basis of meaning only. Assessment of a young child's comprehension will acknowledge the use of these strategies in the course of development.

Children at this stage of language also begin to understand sentences based on the morphological and syntactic rules of the language (e.g., word order rules).

Understanding of language is often assessed by exploring the child's response to a range of question types, moving along a developmental continuum from *yes/no* questions, to *what* and *where* questions, and eventually *how* and *when* questions. Children's lexical comprehension is most easily evaluated with standardized tests of receptive vocabulary although, wherever possible, attempts should be made to assess a child's comprehension both in natural contexts as well as decontextualized ones. Later in this stage, the child's ability to understand narratives and connected discourse can be assessed in both semi-structured and more naturalistic interactions.

II. Language-Related Cognitive, Affective, and Social-Emotional Development

A. Cognitive Development. As at earlier stages of development, analysis of the child's symbolic play and constructive play provides the cornerstone of the speech-language pathologist's cognitive assessment of a child. In addition to evaluating the various dimensions of play (props, themes, organization, roles [Patterson & Westby, 1994]) relative to developmental stages, the clinician evaluates the frequency of the child's play interactions with objects and with people as well as the diversity of his play themes. Because many children with developmental difficulties are challenged in the development of play, the careful evaluation of this area is critical to gaining an understanding of the child's knowledge of the world. It is this knowledge which, in turn, serves as the foundation for the development of language.

B. Affective and Social-Emotional Development. As at earlier stages of development, the use of language and communication is significantly affected by and, in turn, significantly impacts on a child's affective and social-emotional development. For example, the child's language and communicative behavior must be understood in the context of his emotional development and his need to express the emotional themes that are typical of all children (e.g., separation, power, control). The child's range of affective states and his ability to communicate these states linguistically and nonlinguistically, conventionally or with idiosyncratic means, will be an important part of the speech-language pathologist's assessment. The child's strategies for regulating emotional arousal, such as using language for negotiating and explaining, should be assessed. In addition, the child's ability to participate in a variety of social situations beyond the home and beyond the caregiver-child relationship will be explored, as will the child's interactions with peers in dyadic and, eventually, small- and large-group contexts. The child's interactions in various types of social play with peers, such as cooperative and competitive play, will be considered. In other words, the frequency and diversity of the child's affective communication, engagement in social interactions, and participation in various social roles will be assessed on the way to developing a profile of language and communication strengths and needs.

INTERVENTION

Basic to the model being presented in this chapter is the notion that developmentally based assessment leads directly to developmentally based intervention. A discussion of each major principle follows.

Principles of Intervention

Intervention goals should be individually determined, based on the assessment of the child's current developmental level in speech, language, and communication and based on what is known about the language acquisition process in typically developing children.

This intervention principle rests on the view that once a clinician has determined the child's developmental level in prelinguistic communication in each component of language (phonology, morphology, syntax, semantics, pragmatics), and/or in each of the developmental domains that are related to language acquisition (cognition, social-emotional development), goals of intervention based on the child's current strengths and challenges can be generated. In other words, intervention goals will be determined relative to the language and language-related behaviors which the child is exhibiting and according to where these behaviors place him on the developmental map of language acquisition (See chapter appendix). This approach can be distinguished from practices where goals are chosen based on the child's current chronological age or on a predetermined program of language and language-related behaviors, or on a more arbitrary determination of what is "missing" from the child's linguistic repertoire. A developmentally based approach focuses on goals that will more easily be accomplished because they are based on what the child is ready to learn next, in conjunction with an understanding of the child's functional communicative needs and the parents' priorities. Again, developmentally based decision-making rests on what is known and well documented about the typical sequence of behaviors in the acquisition of speech, language, and communication. In this way, appropriate expectations are placed on the child, easing his way in the language-learning process.

Beyond this, children with similar behaviors may be at different stages of development. For example, all nonverbal children are not at the same point in communication development. Some nonverbal children are functioning at a preintentional level of communication; other nonverbal children are functioning at an intentional and prelinguistic level; and some nonverbal children are at the symbolic level but are not able to produce speech—a pattern of development which is not easily compared to any stage of typical acquisition. Individually determined goals for nonverbal children can look quite different depending on whether the child is at the preintentional, prelinguistic, or symbolic level.

Use of the developmental approach to intervention can best be illustrated with an example. Imagine that the clinician, having observed the child's play interactions, knows what meanings are available to the child; that is, as a result of her assessment, the clinician can make some assumptions about what the child knows in general (his ideas about the world of objects and events and his ideas about the world of people) and more specifically, what the child knows relative to language. The clinician will then choose goals related to the production of words and structures that fit what the child is bringing to the language-learning task. For example, if the child knows about space and movement (early cognitive notions), as observed by his interest in filling and refilling containers and putting objects in and taking them out of drawers, the clinician can begin to talk about locations with the child (e.g., "in" and "out"). If the child, however, has not demonstrated this conceptual understanding and/or linguistic comprehension (i.e., when asked to take the socks out of the drawer, the child does not respond), then the clinician might:

(a) choose something the child does know about (e.g., the recurrence of objects) to attach language to; and/or

(b) begin to expose the child to experiences that involve putting things in and taking things out in an effort to teach him underlying cognitive notions. If the child is not yet ready to talk about "in" and "out," it will not be in the child's best interest to prematurely begin working on his production of these words. Even if the child begins to imitate these words, little has been taught if the true meaning stages of language-learning have been bypassed.

To summarize, the developmental assessment of the child's language abilities leads to an understanding of where this particular child is on the "map" of language and communication development. From here, knowing what the child has already learned and what is next in the language-learning process, the clinician generates an individualized program for the child, with appropriate developmentally based starting points to ease the child's move into the next language-communication stage.

Intervention strategies should embrace a wide range of possibilities, including those that are more child-directed as well as those that are more clinician-directed. The specific strategies chosen will be individually determined based on the child's developmental level, the goals being addressed, the nature of the child's learning style, the contexts of intervention, and the stage of language intervention that the child is in.

The range of intervention strategies available to the speech-language pathologist includes a continuum of possibilities that are chosen as the clinician comes to know the child and her learning style. As with the goals, these strategies are individually determined based on the clinician's experience with, and sense of, what the child will respond to best. Parent and teacher reports that indicate which strategies have been most successful in other contexts will be adapted for use in individual or small-group sessions with the speech-language pathologist (and vice versa).

The particular strategies being used must be individually determined child by child; this ensures that the child's developmental level, together with her particular profile of strengths and challenges, are the basis of this aspect of therapeutic decision making. For example, for some children, modeling in salient contexts will facilitate the acquisition of new behaviors; for other children, elicited imitation of new behaviors at pragmatically appropriate moments will be more effective. Further, the modalities that are used to enhance language and communication learning must also be determined based on a sense of the child's developmental stage and his individually determined strengths. For example, for some children who are functioning at early prelinguistic stages, the use of picture symbols will be premature; for other children at this same stage, the use of visual materials will be the key to the development of a communication system. Intervention strategies that facilitate language learning at all developmental levels include repetition, timing, simplification, salience, frequent learning opportunities, and positive reinforcement.

Language should be taught in contexts that clarify meaning, in contexts that are natural as well as contrived, in contexts where real messages are being communicated, and in the child's world (Johnston, 1985). The child should be an active participant in the intervention contexts.

In a developmentally based approach to language intervention, the interactive contexts in which typical language acquisition occur are often used as starting points for teaching language to atypically developing children. In other words, the speech-language pathologist begins teaching language in natural, playful interactions; these are the same kinds of spontaneous, child-initiated contexts in which typically developing children begin and continue to learn language. Those approaches that depart from this view emphasize the point that since the child with challenges has not learned language in more typical contexts, alternatives must be sought. In a developmental approach, the clinician rejects this thinking, at least at the initial stages of intervention or, alternatively, provides a combination of natural and more structured learning contexts. When naturalistic contexts are used, they are always altered in some aspects (e.g., frequency of focused input) to provide the language-learning opportunities that define the contexts as "therapeutic." Similarly, when more structured contexts are used, they are altered to provide some aspects of naturalistic contexts (e.g., inherently motivating to the child).

The interest in the use of naturalistic contexts as intervention contexts derives from a number of sources. First, a naturalistic context has the advantage of potentially being most meaningful and functional for the child. Within the context of breakfast or bathtime or play, the child will generally have the most elaborated meanings and understandings, since these activities have been experienced frequently with many nonlinguistic (objects, materials, participants) and linguistic supports. As a result, natural contexts are often the most supportive for and facilitative of language learning. Further, from a pragmatic point of view, when the child learns in natural context, he is learning language in the very situations where he will be using it. The functional advantages of this kind of teaching are apparent. There is no need to add a generalization step to the intervention process if the child has learned language in the contexts of his everyday interactions with people.

It also should be noted that some of the goals considered of the highest priority for children with pervasive challenges can only be taught in the context of natural, spontaneous, and reciprocal relationships and interactions. For example, if the clinician has identified the child to be at the preintentional stage of development, then engagement, attention, intentionality, and use of nonlinguistic communication become the therapeutic goals. Natural contexts where the child's interests lie or where her expectation of particular events is strongest can be used to build intentionality. In fact, it will be easiest for the child if the development of intentionality is embedded in contexts that delight and excite her. Here, the clinician is working from the child's internal life to find the right moment for attaching communication goals, rather than from a more arbitrary moment chosen by the clinician.

Once the child is involved in more formalized instruction (e.g., in a school program), then this too becomes a natural context of the child's life. For those children who attend school, opportunities to guide appropriate language and communication development (given their abilities and the pragmatic expectations of the classroom context) can be incorporated into the children's language intervention program.

Language development is best facilitated by all the significant people in the child's life (i.e., parents, teachers, clinicians) throughout the course of the child's daily activities. A collaborative approach that involves parents, clinicians, and teachers is most effective when working with young children.

For young children, the parents, teachers, and other clinicians must be an integral part of the language therapy team. Clinicians who work in the home have the advantage of seeing the parents on a regular basis. Those clinicians who work in schools can build a team feeling with the parents through frequent

contact and by exchanging ideas and information on a regular basis. Parents should be encouraged to participate in sessions or to observe so they begin to understand the complicated process of language development and the priorities that are being addressed. Differences between the parents' and the clinician's views of what might be best to teach the child need to be monitored constantly. In this way, an integrated approach that reflects the parents' deepest concerns for their child can be provided.

Beyond this, the speech-language pathologist can develop a continuum of priorities, specifically related to language and communication, that is based on the input from the child's parents and teachers. This input can be used as a starting point for understanding where the significant people in the child's life are placing their energies in the development of the child's language and communication. Since the priorities of the teacher, parents, and clinician do not always overlap, the speech-language pathologist can embrace and fine-tune the teacher's priorities to increase the child's opportunities to be a part of the classroom community, and can embrace and fine-tune the parent's priorities to increase the child's opportunities to be a part of the family.

Individually determined intervention plans for supporting the emotional well being of families and caregivers should be developed.

As noted previously in the assessment section, the needs of each family should be evaluated to determine how the therapeutic environment can best be used to support the family as they move through the stages of raising their child. Intervention with these families will be as individual as intervention with the children themselves, and may range from counseling sessions with the speech-language pathologist, to psychotherapy with a social worker, to support groups. Although the speech-language pathologist will be keenly aware of where her training allows her to go in the supportive work with families (and where the families' needs require other kinds of professional intervention), the necessity for a comprehensive intervention plan to address these aspects of the family's needs is undeniable.

Communicative partners such as parents and teachers should be supported in their efforts to facilitate communicative interactions with children with speech, language, and communication challenges.

One of the most positive outgrowths of the extensive research on the social-pragmatic models of language acquisition has been the discussion of those aspects of the parent-child interaction that enhance language and communication development. Based on this information, the modification of parents', caregivers', and teachers' interactive styles as a means of facilitating linguistic and communicative growth has become a primary intervention goal. Several excellent intervention programs have been designed to help parents understand:

- The nature of their child's communicative initiations.
- The importance of increasing their responsiveness to nonlinguistic and linguistic communicative attempts.
- The need for well-matched linguistic and communicative interactions.
- When to prioritize engagement and interaction over linguistic performance.
- The range of strategies that can be used to enhance contingent responding.
- The interactive techniques that underlay the development of linguistic comprehension and production (McDonald, 1989; Manolson, 1992; and Sussman, 1999).

In light of the previous intervention principle, it should be noted that work with many families will begin by focusing on and supporting the parents' own emotional path rather than specifically on improving their communicative interactions with their children. It should be clear that, in either case, the stage is being set for promoting positive social and learning experiences for both parent and child.

Language development is enhanced by providing opportunities for children with challenges in communication to learn from peers who can serve as models of and partners for language and social interactions.

Within the context of speech and language intervention, clinicians can design opportunities for children to interact with peers whose skills in the targeted areas are further developed than their own. Both typically developing and atypically developing children can serve as models and partners in communicative exchanges. Beyond the natural opportunities for these kinds of interactions which may occur in the child's educational program, the need for small-group interactions should be considered a priority in speech-language therapy sessions. With the appropriate pairing and grouping of children, peers can serve as "natural" models and can spontaneously initiate the kinds of communicative interactions that are so important for further progress in social and language development. In this regard, interactions with peers who are not experiencing challenges as well as with peers who are can be facilitating.

The child's preferences, style of learning, and unconventional behaviors are considered the best starting points for understanding and facilitating the language-learning process.

One of the most frequently asked intervention questions is what to do about those behaviors that seem odd or inappropriate. Often, a great deal of energy is spent trying to eliminate or extinguish these behaviors and preferences (e.g., immediate and delayed echolalia, spinning wheels, lining up the seven dwarf dolls). In the approach presented here, these behaviors are looked at as windows into the child's bodily needs, interests, compensations, and joys, rather than as oddities. As a result of this shift in perspective, the clinician can now consider how he might use these windows for the greater good. For example, the child who is self-absorbed and repetitively lines up the seven dwarfs is more likely to become engaged in an activity involving the dwarfs than in an activity with a baby doll or trucks. The child is demonstrating where his interest lies and, in an effort to address one of the first intervention goals— engagement and interaction—the clinician can use those dwarfs as an entree into his world. Even at higher stages of development, these interests can be used to facilitate the comprehension and production of language.

In a somewhat different vein, children with challenges in language and communication often demonstrate obvious strengths in other domains of development. For example, some children are particularly captivated by visual material, showing both focused interest in and unusual skill in dealing with pictures and visually presented information (e.g., books, puzzles, videos, and computers). When individual styles and strengths are identified, they can be transformed into potential teaching-learning strategies. In the example just given, picture symbols and augmentative communication can be used to facilitate participation in and learning of language and communication. Similarly, children who delight in and have a talent for music, numbers, letters, and physical movement can be approached with an eye towards incorporating these skills into the child's educational program.

In summary, the child's preferences, interests, passions, and strengths are starting points for intervention programs, regardless of how unconventional they may seem. From a therapeutic and educational point of view, they serve as windows into children who are sometimes difficult to know and should be thought of as inherent in each child's sense of self. Without a doubt, they serve some human function. At the same time that clinicians work with the child's preferences and unconventional behaviors, they continue to move toward expanding the child's repertoire of interests and strengths to include those that are productive for further learning, conventional, and more socially acceptable. ∎

REFERENCES

Bates, E., Benigni, L., Bretherton, I., Camaioni, L., & Volterra, V. (1979). *The emergence of symbols: Communication and cognition in infancy.* New York: Academic Press.

Bloom, L. (1991). *Language development from two to three.* New York: Cambridge University.

Bloom, L. (1993). *The transition from infancy to language: Acquiring the power of expression.* Cambridge: Cambridge University Press.

Bloom, L. (1997). Language acquisition in its developmental context. In D. Kuhn & R. Siegler (Eds.), *Cognition, perception, and language (Vol. II),* in W. Damon (Series Editor), *Handbook of child psychology.* New York: Wiley & Sons.

Brown, R. (1973). *A first language, the early stages.* Cambridge, MA: Harvard University.

Carrow-Woolfolk, E. (1998). *Test for Auditory Comprehension of Language (3rd ed.).* Circle Pines, MN: American Guidance Service.

Donnellan, A., Mirenda, P., Mesaros, R., & Fassbender, L. (1984). *Analyzing the communicative functions of aberrant behavior. Journal of the Association for Persons with Severe Handicaps, 9,* 201-212.

Dore, J. (1975). Holophrases, speech acts, and language universals. *Journal of Child Language, 2,* 21-40.

Duchan, J. (1989). Evaluating adults' talk to children: Assessing adult attunement. *Seminars in Speech and Language, 10,* 17-27.

Dunn, L., & Dunn, L. (1981). Peabody picture vocabulary test—revised. In D. Bailey & M. Wolery (Eds.), *Teaching infants and preschoolers with disabilities.* Circle Pines, MN: American Guidance Service

Greenspan, S. I. (1992). *Infancy and early childhood: The practice of clinical assessment and intervention with emotional and developmental challenges.* Madison, CT: International Universities Press.

Johnston, J. (1985). Fit, focus, and functionality: An essay on early language intervention. *Child Language Teaching and Therapy, 1,* 125-134.

Lahey, M. (1988). *Language disorders and language development.* New York: Macmillan Press.

Linder, T. (1990). *Transdisciplinary play-based assessment.* Baltimore: Paul H. Brookes.

Linder, T. (1993). *Transdisciplinary play-based assessment–(Rev. ed.)* Baltimore: Paul H. Brookes.

Manolson, A. (1992). *It takes two to talk.* (2nd ed.). Toronto: Hanen Early Language Resource Centre.

McCollum, J., & Hemmeter, M. (1997). Parent-child interaction intervention when children have disabilities In M. Guralnick (Ed.), *The effectiveness of early intervention* (pp. 549-578). Baltimore: Paul H. Brookes.

McDonald, J. (1989). *Becoming partners with children: From play to conversation.* Chicago, IL: Riverside.

Miller, J. & Chapman, R. (1981). The relation between age and mean length of utterance in morphemes. *Journal of Speech and Hearing Research. 24,* 154-161.

Miller, J. & Paul, R. (1995). *The clinical assessment of language comprehension.* Baltimore: Paul H. Brooks.

Moses, K. L. (1985). Dynamic intervention with families. In E. Chenow (Ed.), *Hearing impaired children and youths with disabilities.* Washington, D.C.: Gallaudet College.

Nelson, N. (1993). *Childhood language disorders in context.* New York: Merrill.

Owens, R. (2000). *Language development: An introduction* (5th ed.). Boston: Allyn & Bacon.

Patterson, J., & Westby, C. (1994). The development of play. In W. Haynes & B. Shulman (Eds.), *Communication development.* NJ: Prentice Hall.

Peck, C. (1989). Assessment of social communicative competence: Evaluating environments. *Seminars in Speech and Language, 10,* 1-15.

Prizant, B., & Bailey, D. (1992). Facilitating the acquisition and use of communication skills. In D. Bailey & M. Wolery (Eds.), *Infants and preschoolers with disabilities: Communication development.* Englewood Cliffs, NJ: Prentice Hall.

Prutting, C. (1979). Process: The action of moving forward progressively from one point to another on the way to completion. *Journal of Speech and Hearing Disorders, 44,* 3-30.

Prutting, C., & Kirchner, D. (1987). A clinical appraisal of the pragmatic aspects of language. *Journal of Speech and Hearing Disorders, 52,* 105-119.

Rossetti, L. (1990). *Infant-toddler language scale.* East Moline, IL: LinguiSystems.

Schuler, A. L., Wetherby, A. M., & Prizant, B. M. (1997). Enhancing language and communication: Prelanguage approaches. In D. Cohen & F. Volkmar (Eds.), *Handbook of autism and pervasive developmental disorders* (2nd ed.).

Semel, E., Wiig, E., and Secord, W. (1987). *Clinical evaluation of language fundamentals (CELF-R)* (Rev. ed.). San Antonio, TX: Psychological Corporation.

Sussman, F. (1999). *More than words.* Toronto: Hanen Early Language Resource Centre.

Van Kleeck, A. (1994). Potential cultural bias in training parents as conversational partners with their children who have delays in language development. *American Journal of Speech-Language Pathology, 3,* 67-78.

Velleman, S. (1998). Assessment and treatment of developmental verbal dyspraxia: A phonological perspective. Presented in Long Island, NY.

Westby, C. (1988). Children's play: Reflections of social competence. *Seminars in Speech and Language, 9,* 1-13.

Wetherby, A. (1992). *Communication and language intervention for preschool children.* Chicago: Riverside.

Wetherby, A., & Prizant, B. (1990). *Communication and symbolic behavior scales.* Chicago: Applied Symbolix.

Wetherby, A., & Prizant, B. (1993). Profiling young children's communicative competence. In S. Warren & J. Reichle (Eds.), *Causes and effects in communication and language intervention* (pp. 217-253). Baltimore: Paul H. Brookes.

Wilcox, M. J. (1989). Delivering communication-based services to infants, toddlers, and their families: Approaches and models. *Topics in Language Disorders, 10,* 68-79.

Appendix

STAGES OF DEVELOPMENT IN
SPEECH, LANGUAGE, AND COMMUNICATION

PREINTENTIONAL STAGE

(0-8 months)

INTENTION INFERRED BY THE COMMUNICATIVE PARTNER

The child demonstrates a variety of behaviors including gazing, crying, touching, smiling, laughing, vocalizing, and grasping; the adult responds to these behaviors as if they were intentional.

EARLY

(0-3 months)

Startles to sound	Gazes at caregiver
Reacts to sound	Cries, makes pleasure sounds
Turns head to human voice	Vocalizes -mostly vowel sounds
Responds to tone of voice	Coos single syllable
	Smiles
	Responds vocally to speech of others

MID

(4-6 months)

COMPREHENSION	**PRODUCTION**
Responds to name	Babbles strings of sounds
Smiles at persons speaking to him	Varies pitch
Discriminates angry vs. friendly voices	Imitates tones & sounds
Localizes sounds further away	Experiments with sound
	Smiles & vocalizes to image in mirror
	Vocalizes to toys
	Varies volume, pitch, rate
	Vocalizes pleasure and displeasure
	Pays attention to faces
	Joint attention
	"Proto-conversations"

	COMPREHENSION	**PRODUCTION**

LATER

(7-8 months)

COMPREHENSION	**PRODUCTION**
Listens to vocalizations of others	Begins to fill turn in joint action routines
Listens selectively	Plays vocally
Recognizes some words	Reduplicated babbling
Looks at objects that mother looks at	Imitates gesture and tonal quality of adult speech; echolalia
	Joint reference
	Pointing, showing without reference to adult for confirmation
	Reaching with gaze shift between object and caregiver

PRELINGUISTIC INTENTIONAL STAGE

(8-12 months)

EMERGENCE OF INTENTIONAL COMMUNICATION

The child now communicates intentionally, using a combination of gestures, vocalizations, and eventually words.

RECEPTIVE LANGUAGE/ COMPREHENSION	**EXPRESSIVE LANGUAGE/ PRODUCTION**
Laughs at familiar interaction sequences	Imitates coughs, hisses, clicks, raspberries
Inhibits action in response to "No"	Uses social gestures
Responds to "bye-bye"	Uses jargon
Follows caregiver's gaze to labeled objects	Imitates adult speech if sounds in repertoire
Follows some directions	Imitates inflections, rhythms, facial expressions
Recognizes name	Uses one or more words
Follows simple motor games, especially if accompanied by visual cues ("Peek-a-boo")	Uses conventional gestures-pointing, showing, giving
Understands a few words in context (e.g., "bath")	Mixes words and jargon
Acts on objects at hand; imitates ongoing actions	Expresses communicative intentions (requests, "comments," and protests) with gestures, vocalizations, gesture + vocalizations
	"Practices" words he knows
	Produces distinct sentence-like intonational patterns

FIRST WORDS

(12 - 18 months)

EMERGING SYMBOLIC COMMUNICATION

The child begins to understand and use language within the contexts of his daily life

RECEPTIVE LANGUAGE/COMPREHENSION

– Responds to single words in immediate context
– Understands one word in sentence when referents are present
– Points to objects and body parts in response to "Show me _____"
– Will get an object if told to when object is in view
– Will perform some actions (e.g., kiss, hug) with verbal instruction alone
– Knows names of familiar people
– Strategies used to respond to commands
    – Attends to object mentioned
    – Does what is usually done in a situation (e.g., objects in containers)
    – Gives evidence of notice
    – Takes objects offered
– Comprehension exceeds production
    – child understands 50 words before he produces 10 words
    – the words comprehended are not necessarily the words produced
– Average receptive vocabulary size
    12 months – 3 words
    15 months – 15 words
    18 months – 100-150 words

EXPRESSIVE LANGUAGE/PRODUCTION

- Phonology
    – monosyllabic CV or VC or reduplicated CVCV units
    – labial (*p, b, m*) and alveolar (*t, d*) sounds predominate
    – /a/, /i/, /u/ vowels established
    – phonological preferences influences first words

- Pragmatics
    – primitive speech acts are expressed with words, prosodic patterns, gestures, and vocalizations
        – requesting objects, requesting actions, labeling, repeating, answering, calling, greeting, protesting, practicing
    – verbal turn-taking emerges
    – increased rate of communication and greater persistence

- Lexicon
    - 13 months is the mean for first words
    - first words are often general nominals, specific nominals, action words
    - underextensions and overextensions of meaning occur
    - small core of the child's total vocabulary is used frequently
    - Individual styles and preferences are noted ("noun-lover" vs. "noun-leaver")

- Semantic
    - substantive words, such as *mommy, cookie, hat* and relational words such as *more, up, all gone* are typical
    - talks about *existence, recurrence, nonexistence, rejection, action,* and *locative action* with first words

---

THE TWO-WORD STAGE

(18-24 months)

VOCABULARY EXPLOSION AND EARLY MULTIWORD COMBINATIONS

The child begins to combine words to form utterances that are governed by semantic-syntactic rules

---

RECEPTIVE LANGUAGE/ COMPREHENSION

- understands word combinations before producing them (e.g., Action + Object; Agent + Action; Entity + Location)
- comprehension is based on semantic relations and contextual cues, such as routines and scripts
- understands words when the referent is not present
- understands action words out of the context of routines
- understands and responds to routine forms of *Who, What, Where* questions
- nonlinguistic strategies used to respond to commands
    - locates the objects mentioned
    - gives evidence of notice
    - does what you usually do with objects - (objects in containers)
    - acts on the objects in the way mentioned (Child as agent)
    - receptive vocabulary: 150 - 500 words

EXPRESSIVE LANGUAGE/PRODUCTION

- Phonology
    - phonological processes are employed from 18 months to 4 years. They are simplifying processes and affect classes of sounds, such as final consonant deletion and consonant cluster reduction.
    - the phonetic repertoire of consonants includes *m, b, p, n, w, h*

- Pragmatics
  - expresses a range of communicative intentions
  - talks about the "here and now"
  - aware of his listener – may talk less to strangers
  - begins to repair unintelligible utterances upon request
  - most utterances are adjacent (follow adult's in time); some utterances are contingent (related to the adult's in topic)

- Lexical
  - rapid expansion of vocabulary

- Semantic-Syntactic
  - begins to produce successive single words on the way to word combinations
  - 19 months is the mean for onset of word combinations
  - talks about *existence, nonexistence, recurrence, action, location, possession, state,* and *attribution* with two-word forms
  - codes two constituents of the Subject-Verb-Complement structure
  - individual styles are noted - pronominal vs. nominal

EARLY SYNTACTIC-SEMANTIC COMPLEXITY

(2 years to 3¹/2 years)

LATER MULTIWORD, BEGINNING MULTIVERB COMBINATIONS

The child develops the basic syntactic structures of the language, talks about many ideas and notions, and uses language for a broad range of communicative functions

---

RECEPTIVE LANGUAGE/ COMPREHENSION

- understands sentences based on morphological and syntactic rules (e.g., uses word order strategy for Agent-Action-Object relations)
- responds to Yes/No questions (2 years)
- responds to What, What doing, and Where questions (2¹/2 years)
- responds to Whose, Who, Why, How many questions (3 years)
- follows two-step commands (3 years)
- understands "he" versus "she" (3 years)
- uses a variety of comprehension strategies including:
  - does what is usually done
  - put things where they usually go (in, on, under, beside)
  - probable event strategy for active reversible sentences
  - supplies missing information to questions not understood (2 years)
  - supplies explanation to questions not understood (3years)
  - infers most probable speech act in the situation
- receptive vocabulary: 300-1000 words

EXPRESSIVE LANGUAGE/PRODUCTION

- Phonology
  - phonological processes are employed from 18 months to 4 years. They are simplifying processes and affect classes of sounds. These are syllable structure processes, assimilatory processes, substitution processes, and multiple processes. Processes include Consonant Cluster (CC) reduction and Final Consonant Deletion, and, later, some Stop + Glide Consonant Cluster; medial and final CC reduction; use of final consonants
  - the phonetic repertoire of consonants includes the above + *t, d, k, g, ng* and later, *y, f, v, s, sh, ch, l, r*
  - syllable structure

- Pragmatics
  - uses language for a variety of communicative functions including the above + regulating, planning, reporting, projecting feelings, commenting on imagined context, requesting information, requesting confirmation
  - greater variety of forms for all functions
  - child responds to contingent queries with revisions that reflect level of linguistic development, e.g., phonetic recoding and deletions
  - an increasing number of utterances are about the immediate past and immediate future
  - an increasing number of utterances are about other people
  - increase in the number of non-adjacent utterances
  - adjacent utterances still most frequent
  - more contingent utterances add to the prior utterance of the other speaker
  - by 3 years, child can determine information the listener needs
  - by 3$^1/_2$ years, greater ability to maintain the topic
  - recoding of prior utterances with pronominalization of object and agent
  - by 3 years, children use sequences in their narratives

- Lexical
  - begins to learn relational terms such as *big/little, hard/soft, tall/short*
  - begins to learn kinship terms such as *mother, father, sister, brother*
  - uses pronouns including *I, it, my, me, mine, you, your, she, he, yours, we, they, us, hers, his, them, her*

- Semantic-Syntactic
  - predicted MLU - 2.5 - 3.75
  - begins to develop grammatical morphemes; order of acquisition is *present progressive -ing, on, in, plural s, past irregular, possessive s, copula (to be), articles, past regular, third person singular regular, third person singular irregular, auxiliary*
  - talks about semantic relations such as Agent-Action; Action-Object; Agent-Object
  - talks about form-content relations such as *existence, recurrence, nonexistence, location, possession, rejection, denial, attribution, quantity, state*
  - codes three constituents of the Subject-Verb-Complement structure

- at 2¹/₂ to 3 years, further syntactic development includes producing declarative, negative, imperative, interrogative, and complex sentences
- clausal conjoining with *and* emerges
- talks about immediate future, e.g., "gonna"
- individual styles of pronominal vs. nominal disappear

LATER SYNTACTIC-SEMANTIC COMPLEXITY

(3¹/₂ years - 7 years)

MULTIVERB UTTERANCES, COMPLEX SENTENCES, AND DISCOURSE

The child uses more complex language to talk about events and engages in various kinds of discourse

---

RECEPTIVE LANGUAGE/COMPREHENSION

42-48 MONTHS
- understands word order cues to Agent+Action+Object relations
- word order strategy over-generalized to passive
- receptive vocabulary: 1000 - 3000 words

4 years-7 years
- follows three-step commands
- understands syntactic cues in basic sentence forms
- responds to two-stage action commands
- responds to *how* and *when* questions
- comprehends locational and temporal relationships such as *behind, in back of, in front of, before, after*
- responds to order of mention of clauses
- comprehends connected discourse and narratives
- average receptive vocabulary: 3000-8000 words

EXPRESSIVE LANGUAGE/PRODUCTION

- Phonology
  - some remaining phonological processes used to 4 years. Stop + Glide initial CC used; some medial and final CC used; final consonants produced; by 7 years, all CC except *thr*
  - the phonetic repertoire of consonants includes *j, z, th,*
  - syllable structure includes use of two- to three-syllable words

- Pragmatics
  - uses language to request information, to inform, and to report
  - increase in use of social functions
  - learns the rules that underlie conversational exchanges
  - number of spontaneous utterances is greater than responsive utterances
  - sustains topics across several turns
  - maintains topics and conveys new information
  - more of the child's utterances are related to and add information to his prior utterance, i.e., longer and more elaborate discourse turns
  - adjusts speech and language to different listeners
    - simplifies language to younger children
    - politeness markers to strangers
    - more explicit information
    - get listener's attention prior to making a request
    - repairs communicative breakdowns with above + substitutions
  - uses contingent queries to maintain the conversation
  - recounts stories and recent past; anecdotal narratives most frequent
  - between 3 and 5 years, narrative sequences are time-based with no plot or causality

- by 7 years, narratives have a beginning, end, problem, and resolution

- Lexical
  - contrastive word pairs - *more* and *less*, *before* and *after*
  - use of pronouns such as *its, our, him, myself, yourself, ours, their, theirs, herself, himself, itself, ourselves, yourselves, themselves*

- Semantic-Syntactic
  - predicted MLU – (for $3^1/_2$ - $5^1/_2$-year-olds)
  - further elaboration of the basic sentence forms - declarative, negative, interrogative
  - new syntactic structures at clause and phrase levels such as recursion and embedding
  - clausal conjoining with *because*; past MLU of 5.0, clausal conjoining with *when, but, and so*
  - acquisition of the 14 grammatical morphemes

- Metalinguistic
  - develops metalinguistic awareness of structure and meaning, such as making grammatical judgments, resolving lexical ambiguity, using multiple meanings of words in humor, and segmenting words into phonemes

---

COMMUNICATIVE COMPETENCE

(7 years - 12 years)

The child's syntactic, semantic, and pragmatic abilities are well-developed and sophisticated.

RECEPTIVE LANGUAGE/COMPREHENSION

- understands an infinite number of sentences from a finite set of rules
- understands conditional conjunctions *if* and *when*
- understands causal conjunctions *because* and *so*
- responds to contrastive *but* and *although* as though they mean *and* and later as contrastive terms
- understands idioms and proverbs (late childhood)

EXPRESSIVE LANGUAGE/PRODUCTION

- Phonology
  - all CC including *thr* all positions; CCC in all positions
  - multisyllabic words
  - complete phonetic repertoire
  - morphophonemic development

- Pragmatics
  - learns to abide by conversational rules to be clear, concise, informative, and polite
  - eventually develops adult knowledge of who can say what, in what way, where and when, to whom
  - uses language to converse, explain, imagine, persuade, tease
  - aware of various narrative types - recounts, event casts, accounts, stories
  - narratives develop relative to both the content and structure of stories that are created and retold
  - story length increases across elementary school years - embedding of plots, inclusion of multiple themes, increasing command over cohesive devices
  - by 8 years of age includes character's emotions and thoughts in literary stories
  - increasing knowledge of different narrative "formats" – plays, jokes, poems, letters, reports
  - experience with narrative types affected by cultural and contextual differences
  - use of figurative language such as idioms
  - additional strategies for conversational repair - e.g., provides additional information
  - language use affected by gender differences and individual style

- Semantic-Syntactic
  - generates infinite combinations from finite set of rules
  - spoken sentence length matches chronological age between 7 and 9 years; longer sentences
  - more clauses per sentence
  - sentence complements and infinitival complements
  - areas of syntactic growth for school-age children and adolescents:
    word structure – prefixes, suffixes, nominalization
    phrase structure – complex noun phrases; complex verb phrases
    clause structure – increasing number of adjective and adverbial clauses
    complex sentences – subordination
    discourse structure – adverbial connectives; ellipsis patterns; word order
      variation for theme and focus

- Metalinguistic
  - further development of metalinguistic awareness - humor, idioms, metaphors
  - word definitions shift from functional to categorical; eventually adult-like definitions

— ◄ 6 ► —

Auditory Disorders in Children with Developmental Learning Disorders[1]

Jane R. Madell, Ph.D.

THE IMPORTANCE OF ASSESSING AUDITORY FUNCTIONING

Children learn language through the auditory channel; therefore, it is critical for learning that a child's auditory system functions well. For children who are developing normally, hearing is assumed to be normal. For children who are developing differently, hearing needs to be questioned and fully evaluated. The effect of hearing loss or auditory function disorders should not be underestimated because almost any hearing loss will negatively impact on a child's ability to learn language and on his academic development. Obviously, the more severe the disorder, the more serious the impact. However, children with even mild, conductive, or unilateral hearing losses have demonstrated communicative and academic problems (Bess, Tharp, & Klee, 1986; Fry 1978; Rosenfeld & Madell, 1996; Yoshinaga-Itano, 1987).

Hearing is a complex function. It is not safe to assume that a child's hearing is normal if she occasionally turns to her name, runs into the living room when a favorite video is turned on, or repeats some words. If a child responds to some sound, the child has some hearing. The child may not, however, have sufficient hearing to participate in the variety of different listening situations and social interactions necessary for successful language and academic

learning. Only by assessing all the components of audition is it possible to determine if a child has normal hearing or if an auditory problem is contributing to a learning disorder and remediation is needed.

AUDITORY DISORDERS IN CHILDREN WITH DEVELOPMENTAL LEARNING DISORDERS

Children with developmental learning disorders can demonstrate significant auditory function problems. Although most have hearing within normal limits (meaning that their kind of hearing loss does not make them deaf or even hard of hearing), many have difficulty tolerating loud sounds, are very sensitive to soft sounds, have auditory processing disorders, or disorders of auditory attention (Delcato, 1974; Greenspan, 1992; Powers, 1992; Rapin, 1991).

Hearing Loss

Some children with developmental delays have hearing loss. Hearing loss is identified by assessing pure tone thresholds in both ears separately, at octaves from 250 to 8,000 Hz

---

[1]Some of the material in this chapter has been adapted with permission from Madell, J. R. (1998). *Behavioral evaluation of hearing in infants and young children.* New York: Thieme Medical Publishers.

(i.e., 250, 500, 1,000, 2,000, 4,000, and 8,000 Hz), through air and bone conduction testing. This testing determines the degree and type of hearing loss. Children with normal hearing will have thresholds at each frequency measured between 0 and 15 dB throughout the frequency range for both air and bone conduction. Hearing loss is calculated by averaging the thresholds obtained at 500, 1,000, and 2,000 Hz. Some calculations also include thresholds at 3,000 Hz. Table 1 lists different degrees of hearing loss.

Table 1. Degree of Hearing Loss Thresholds in dB

Hearing Level	Thresholds in dB
Normal hearing	0-15
Borderline hearing	15-25
Mild hearing loss	25-40
Moderate hearing loss	40-55
Moderately severe hearing loss	55-70
Severe hearing loss	70-90
Profound hearing loss ≥	90 dB

Air conduction thresholds (obtained using earphones or through loudspeakers in a soundfield) measure the entire auditory system. Bone conduction testing (obtained using a bone vibrator placed on the mastoid bone behind the outer ear) bypasses the outer and middle ear and tests only the hearing in the inner ear. When a child has normal hearing, air and bone conduction thresholds are 15 at dB or better at all frequencies (see Figure 1). A conductive hearing loss is one caused by damage to the outer or middle ear. In a conductive hearing loss, the bone conduction thresholds are normal but air conduction thresholds are poorer than normal (see Figure 2). Some common causes of conductive hearing loss are ear infections or physical malformations of the outer or middle

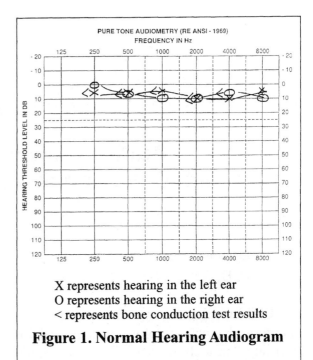

X represents hearing in the left ear
O represents hearing in the right ear
< represents bone conduction test results

Figure 1. Normal Hearing Audiogram

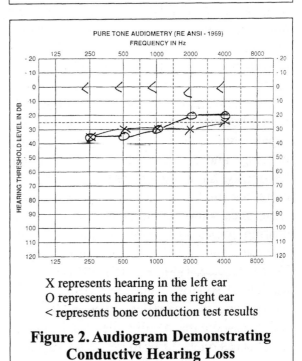

X represents hearing in the left ear
O represents hearing in the right ear
< represents bone conduction test results

Figure 2. Audiogram Demonstrating Conductive Hearing Loss

ear. A sensorineural hearing loss is caused by damage to the inner ear. In a sensorineural hearing loss, both air and bone conduction thresholds are measured at poorer than normal levels (see Figure 3). Common

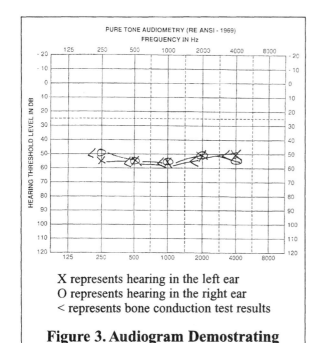

X represents hearing in the left ear
O represents hearing in the right ear
< represents bone conduction test results

**Figure 3. Audiogram Demostrating
Sensorineural Hearing Loss**

causes of sensorineural hearing loss are viral or bacterial infections, high fever, medication reactions, or heredity. (Hayes & Northern, 1996; Silman & Silverman, 1991).

Auditory Processing Disorder

A child with an auditory processing disorder usually has normal peripheral hearing but has difficulty processing auditory information when the signal is in any way degraded. This may occur when there is competing noise, the speaker is speaking from a distance of several feet or has an unusual accent, or when speech is muffled. Children with auditory processing disorders frequently function very well when it is quiet but have reduced functioning in complex listening situations. Children with auditory processing disorders may have difficulty functioning in any situation in which the auditory message is not clear. This can include all classroom situations, dinner table conversations, or whenever there is background noises, such as when the dishwasher is running, dishes are being washed in the sink, or when the

TV or radio is on. The negative effect that unclear auditory messages will have on a child's ability to learn is evident.

Auditory Attention Disorder

Some children with developmental learning disorders have difficulty attending to auditory information, which is sometimes referred to as hyposensitivity to sound. Some attend easily to visual stimuli but cannot consistently attend to auditory stimuli. Others have difficulty attending to any stimuli consistently. In an extreme case, the child appears to be deaf. The inability to attend to auditory stimuli will make language and academic learning very difficult because the child will not be able to learn by listening to conversation.

Sound Sensitivities

Some children with developmental learning disorders have sound sensitivities, which they demonstrate through unusual responses to either very soft sounds or to loud sounds. These children may be uncomfortable hearing sounds that are not uncomfortable to others (such as the noises from a vacuum, blender, dishwasher, or hair dryer). This reaction is sometimes referred to as hypersensitivity. Sounds that are annoying to others (such as fire engines or firecrackers) may be so uncomfortable that these children express pain or fear. Some children will be distracted or even distressed by very soft or distant sounds, such as the phone in the next house, a car down the street, the hum of neon lights, or talking in another room. As a result, these children will be unable to attend appropriately to the auditory stimuli in their immediate environment. Some children will be so distracted that they will be unable to attend to any stimuli consistently (Madell, 1998; Powers, 1992; Rapin, 1991).

ASSESSING AUDITORY FUNCTIONING

A complete diagnostic work-up is essential for fully understanding a child's auditory functioning and developing a treatment plan. Every child must have a complete audiologic evaluation. All components of auditory function should evaluated, including:

- Threshold for sound
- Auditory processing
- Auditory attention
- Sound sensitivities

Measuring Hearing Thresholds

Hearing thresholds need to be measured throughout the frequency range to be certain that hearing is normal across frequencies. A child may have normal hearing at certain frequencies and appear to hear because she will turn to some sounds, but may not have normal hearing at other frequencies. Speech perception requires hearing across the frequency range because different phonemes have energy at different frequencies. If a child does not hear at all frequencies, she will have difficulty perceiving speech clearly.

Hearing testing may be performed behaviorally, which requires a behavioral response from the child (such as dropping a toy into a bucket), or electrophysiologically, which requires no cooperation from the child. Although both procedures are useful, they do not provide the same information. Both procedures may indicate how well the auditory system is working, but only behavioral testing can provide information about how the child is able to use auditory information for attending, processing, and listening.

Behavioral Testing

Audiologists basically use three behavioral techniques to assess pure tone thresholds.

Observation audiometry is used to assess hearing in children with a cognitive age of birth to 6 months. Testing consists of the observation of changes in a child's sucking or respiration after presentation of a sound stimulus. It is the most difficult of the behavioral techniques to perform reliably and should be used only when it is not possible to use other techniques.

Visual reinforcement audiometry is used to assess children with a cognitive age between 6 and 36 months. Testing consists of pairing an auditory stimulus with a visual reinforcer, such as a toy bear playing the drums or a short video segment. As the child associates the sound with the visual reinforcer, she will turn towards the reinforcer when she hears the sound. The test response measure is a consistent head turn. This is an extremely reliable test protocol. Some children with developmental learning disorders will reliably perform visual reinforcement audiometry tasks significantly beyond the 36-month cognitive age.

Play audiometry is used when assessing children with a cognitive age between 30 months and 5 or 6 years, although the protocol will frequently be used for children with developmental disabilities who are more than 6 years old. Play audiometry consists of teaching the child to perform a motor task when he hears a sound. The child begins by holding a toy to his ear to indicate that he is ready to listen. Then, when a sound is presented, the child puts a toy in a bucket or a ring on a ring stand, indicating he has heard the sound.

Electrophysiologic Testing

Electrophysiologic testing (auditory brainstem response [ABR] testing or brainstem evoked response [BEAR] testing) measures electrical responses from electrodes placed on the child's scalp. The child must remain still during testing, so the test is frequently performed with the child under sedation. Testing may utilize click or tonal stimuli. Click stimuli are broad frequency stimuli, which usually have the majority of the energy in the high frequencies but have some energy covering a large portion of the frequency range. When a child responds to click stimuli, the child has some hearing, but this does mean that the child hears well throughout the frequency range. Figure 4 is the audiogram of a child with a significant hearing loss who passed an ABR test using click stimuli.

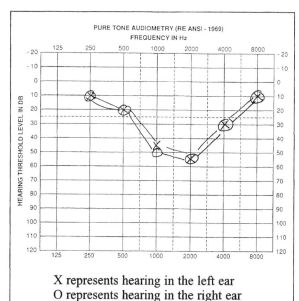

X represents hearing in the left ear
O represents hearing in the right ear
< represents bone conduction test results

Figure 4. Audiogram of a Child with a Hearing Loss Who Passed an ABR Test

Tonal bursts, or filtered tone pip stimuli, are more frequency specific and provide important information about how a child hears at different frequencies across the frequency range. Earphones are used for testing to obtain information about hearing in each ear separately. If earphone testing indicates that the child has a hearing loss, bone conduction testing may be attempted to provide information about whether the hearing loss is conductive (caused by problems in the outer or middle ear) or sensorineural (caused by problems in the inner ear).

Otoacoustic emissions testing measures functioning of the outer hair cells in the cochlea (inner ear). A probe, placed in the child's ear canal, emits a sound. When the hair cells in the cochlea receive this sound, they respond by making an echo. A receiver in the probe measures the echo. The information provided by otoacoustic emissions provides some frequency-specific information.

The advantages of electrophysiologic testing are that it can be easily administered within a few minutes and, because it does not require a response, it can be performed on patients who are not cooperative. A disadvantage is that it does not provide information about function; that is, about how a child uses auditory information. In addition, electrophysiologic testing requires that the child be quiet during testing, which requires that some children be sedated.

Immittance Testing

Immittance testing assesses functioning of the middle ear. A tympanogram is conducted by placing a probe in the child's ear, varying the air pressure in the ear, and measuring the movement of the eardrum. A tympanogram will provide information about the functioning of the middle ear: it *does not* provide information about hearing. Immittance testing also measures movement of the middle ear muscles in response to loud sounds; that is, the ear's acoustic reflexes. Although this information provides some clues about hearing, it is not a measure of hearing and cannot be used to determine how well a child hears.

SELECTING THE APPROPRIATE TEST PROTOCOL

A critical factor in obtaining reliable test results is the selection of an appropriate test protocol. The two essential components guiding selection are (1) the child's cognitive level and (2) the child's physical abilities.

Cognitive Age

The three behavioral techniques described previously are each appropriate for children at different cognitive levels. Observation audiometry is the appropriate behavioral technique for infants from birth to 6 months cognitive age. Visual reinforcement audiometry is the appropriate technique for infants ranging between 5 and 6 months to 30 to 36 months cognitive age. Play audiometry is the appropriate technique for children 36 months and older. Knowing the child's cognitive age allows the tester to select the appropriate test method, but a tester can not always rely solely on chronological age to determine cognitive level. Although many children function at the same levels cognitively and chronologically, not all do. Information about cognitive age can be determined from a thorough case history, an assessment of speech and language and motor development, and psychological evaluations.

If a child's cognitive and chronological levels are too far apart and an inappropriate test is selected, the child cannot respond appropriately to the test protocol. Consequently, the test results may indicate a hearing loss or auditory function problem when none exists. For example, some children with developmental disorders have difficulty cooperating for play audiometry. It may be tempting to use visual reinforcement audiometry, which appears easier to administer to a difficult child. However, this test does not hold the attention of an older child. When the older child does not respond, it may erroneously appear that the child has a hearing loss.

Physical Status

Once a child's cognitive level is established, the child's physical condition must be evaluated to determine if the child is capable of performing the test task. Observation audiometry primarily utilizes changes in sucking. Visual reinforcement audiometry utilizes a conditioned head turn in response to presentation of a sound stimulus. This response measure requires that the child have sufficient neck control to turn and look for the reinforcing toy. This test is most often performed with the child sitting either in a highchair or on a parent's lap. If the child cannot sit, the child is placed in a supported position, such as an infant seat, in which he can still make a conditioned head turn. Visual reinforcement audiometry also requires that the child be able to see the reinforcement toy. If the child has a visual impairment, the test situation is adapted. Play audiometry requires that the child perform a motor task in response to the presentation of a sound. The ability to do this task is limited only by the creativity of the tester. If the child cannot hold a toy and drop it in a bucket, she may, for example, be able to blink her eyes, move a finger, or push a button. Some children who are uncomfortable using toys may be willing to do a task such as jumping when a sound is presented (Madell, 1998).

INFANTS AND CHILDREN WITH DEVELOPMENTAL DELAY

Many children with developmental disabilities also have auditory problems. Some of the syndromes and disorders associated with developmental disabilities (e.g., Down syndrome, cytomegalovirus, and premature birth) are also associated with impaired hearing. As a result, every child identified with any developmental disability or developmental delay should be followed audiologically until ear and frequency-specific information is obtained. If no hearing loss is identified, and if the disorder is not a progressive one, the infant can be discharged from follow-up. However, if the disorder has the potential for being progressive (e.g., cytomegalovirus or central nervous system dysfunction) or fluctuating (e.g., conductive hearing loss commonly associated with Down syndrome), the child's hearing should be monitored on a regular basis.

It is very helpful for the clinician to learn as much as possible about the specific disorder that the child has. This information indicates what may be expected from the child, what types of auditory disorders are expected, and the prognosis for the child's development of speech and language. However, every disorder presents in variable ways. The developmental delay may be mild or severe, and the auditory disorder may be mild or severe. Information about the developmental disorder is a starting place, but only a start.

As with all children, the cognitive age of an infant or young child determines the appropriate test protocol. Flexor and Gans (1985) demonstrated that by carefully assessing the developmental age of profoundly multi-handicapped children, they could obtain thresholds at the same levels obtained with normally developing children of the same developmental age. This finding confirms that the hearing of developmentally delayed children can be accurately assessed if their developmental age is accurately assessed. Thus, assumptions made when evaluating the developmental age of normally developing children cannot be made when evaluating children with developmental disabilities. If the child is in an educational program, the staff should be able to provide information about the child's developmental age. The pediatrician may also be able to provide this information. A number of developmental scales are available to assist in making this determination. (Katoff, Reuter, & Dunn, 1978) Once the child's cognitive age is known, the audiologist can select the appropriate test protocol: observation, visual reinforcement, or play audiometry.

Positioning

Positioning a child for hearing testing is critical for obtaining accurate results. The infant needs to be positioned so that he is comfortable and not straining, and can attend to auditory stimuli. If the child does not have good trunk control, he needs to be seated in a chair that will provide trunk stabilization. Infants can be placed in standard infant seats or leaned against a parent. Older children will need adaptive chairs or strollers, which can provide the necessary support to facilitate head and neck control. Many children will be able to turn toward a reinforcement toy if seated in a chair that provides stabilization.

The audiologist needs to exercise a great deal of care when testing a child with any neurological disorder to keep the child centered. Normally developing children who have good control of their trunk, neck, and head will have no difficulty turning more than 90 degrees to look for a reinforcing toy. However, children who have a neurological disorder and for whom motor activity is difficult will have trouble making a significant head turn. These children must be focused straightforward with the visual reinforcer presented in a way that requires no more than a 90-degree head turn.

For children who are tested through play audiometry, positioning needs to permit an optimum range of arm and hand motions. Some children may need to be held upright to provide enough upper body support to allow them to use their arms and hands for the play activity. Play tasks should be carefully selected to ensure that they are within the child's skill range. Putting pegs into a pegboard may be too difficult, whereas throwing pegs into a basket may be fine.

Timing of Test Presentation

Delivery of the test signal may require a little more consideration with special populations. Because motor control is an issue with many of these children, the audiologist needs to carefully observe each infant to be certain that the infant is stabilized and comfortable prior to presenting a stimulus. If the child is squirming and trying to obtain a stabilized position she may not be able to respond to a stimulus. In that case, absence of response does not mean that the child is unable to hear the stimulus. Stimuli presented too close together may result in the child "tuning out" to the stimuli. Stimuli presented too far apart may also cause the child to "tune out."

Difficulties in Obtaining Responses

There are several problems with obtaining reliable responses from children with developmental disabilities. The responses the children make may be qualitatively different than those obtained from normally developing children. For example, children with developmental disabilities may take longer to focus on a reinforcer and longer to re-focus on the distraction toy. There may be a longer latency between presentation of the test stimulus and the child's response. The audiologist will need to be sensitive to such delays and change the timing of stimulus presentation accordingly. In some cases, the children may demonstrate a very short latency, turning almost as soon as the stimulus is presented. This quick response may indicate sound sensitivities. Motor responses may be slower than with normally developing children. Children with developmental delays may fatigue more quickly, or

they may habituate more quickly to test stimuli and to visual reinforcers. They may fixate on the visual stimulus, thereby making it difficult for the test assistant to center the child's attention after each stimulus presentation. To maximize test results, the test assistant needs to be very alert to the child's mood and change distracters, reinforcers, and play toys quickly to keep the child interested and alert. Social reinforcers, such as saying "Good listening!" or hand-clapping after a response, can be very helpful in sustaining the interest of some children. In addition, the audiologist or test assistant working with the child will need to be certain that the child remains seated upright. Using toys to entertain the child will help keep the child's attention focused straight ahead.

Some children with neurologic disorders react negatively to visual reinforcers. When this happens, the audiologist needs to react quickly. Most visual reinforcers allow the audiologist to set the reinforcement toy so that it can be presented with a light only, with light and motion, or with light, motion, and sound. Obviously, if the sound is frightening for the child, the audiologist needs to turn off the sound and use only the light or light and motion.

INFANTS AND CHILDREN WITH PERVASIVE DEVELOPMENTAL DISORDERS

Children with auditory attention disorders, such as those associated with autism, pervasive developmental disorders, multisystem developmental disorders, or regulatory disorders, usually have normal hearing but may be unable to attend consistently to auditory stimuli. This inconsistency is frequently part of their typical difficulties in responding to a variety of sensory stimuli. With a little extra effort, these children can be tested reliably. For this population, the test set-up needs to be very well controlled. The child needs to be seated so that he will not be able to walk away easily. The highchair is ideal. A strong wooden highchair will hold children as old as 7 or 8 years. Although audiologists normally use visual reinforcement audiometry with children between 5 and 36 months old, this population of children will frequently continue to respond to this test for several more years.

Since these children may "tune out" to voices, it is frequently best to avoid using speech stimuli during hearing tests, at least initially, and to have the test room as quiet as possible. Music, such as the Sesame Street theme or other familiar children's songs, played through the loud speaker will frequently gain the child's attention. Once the child seeks out the stimulus, the reinforcer is activated. Timing of test stimuli is very important with this population because these children frequently habituate quickly. Stimuli should not be presented too closely together because they frequently tune out auditory stimuli. When a child seems to have tuned out, it is often useful to try different stimuli (noise bands or warble tones), change the reinforcer toy, or present a few very loud stimuli to reorient the child. These techniques may reclaim the child's attention, enabling the audiologist to obtain more threshold responses.

Distraction toys can be a problem with this population. It is important to have the child focused forward and interested but not too involved with the toys. This group of children can be difficult to entertain. If they are more visually than auditorially attentive (which is frequently the case) an interesting toy may absorb all their attention, causing them to tune out the auditory stimuli. Finding the right type of distraction for the individual child will require some effort.

Many of these children are sensitive to loud sound. Their parents will report that they have difficulty tolerating sound and will cry when there are loud sounds, party conversations or singing, or noises from some household appliances. Other children will "shut down" if there is too much auditory stimulation. Therefore, it is important that loud stimuli be carefully controlled during testing to keep the child tuned in, but not frightened. The audiologist should present stimuli at soft levels, and then gradually increase intensity. Some children with these disorders tune out sound and almost appear "deaf." For these children, the use of a loud stimulus sometimes helps them tune in again, become alert, and continue responding to soft stimuli.

The speech pathologist, occupational therapist, educator, and parent can provide very useful information to the audiologist by describing how the child uses audition outside of the test situation. This will assist the audiologist in obtaining accurate test results.

PURPOSE OF SPEECH AUDIOMETRY

Speech audiometry, appropriately used, can be an extremely valuable part of the clinical audiologic test battery, particularly for evaluating and monitoring auditory function in children. Pure tone testing provides information about degree and type of hearing loss. It does not, however, provide information about function, which is the ability of a person to use hearing for speech perception. Perception is essential for the development of language and for accurate speech production. Speech perception testing is the only method available for assessing how a child hears speech. Unfortunately, it is frequently overlooked or only used in a limited fashion, thereby failing to maximize its potential usefulness.

Assessing speech perception can be very helpful in determining what kind of difficulties a child may be having and in planning remediation. Word recognition scores that are poorer than expected when compared with pure tone thresholds can be strong indicators that aggressive medical or audiologic treatment is needed. Testing at soft conversational levels and in the presence of competing noise can effectively demonstrate if a person has an auditory processing disorder and/or the need for hearing aids, an FM system in the classroom, or auditory training. Information available from evaluating large numbers of adults indicates that word recognition ability decreases as the degree of hearing loss increases. This pattern is also true for children (Boothroyd, 1984).

Evaluating Auditory Speech Perception

The child's speech-language pathologist will have a great deal of information about the child's speech perception, but he or she works from a different perspective. The speech pathologist will understand the child's language skills working with auditory, visual, and situational prompts combined. The audiologist is not assessing language, but rather the perception of speech, using only audition and language that the child understands.

The goal of speech audiometry is to obtain as much information as possible about a child's speech perception abilities. There are several ways to evaluate speech perception and each procedure provides different information. Erber (1979) describes an auditory skills matrix that is useful when thinking about the different components of speech perception testing and auditory listening tasks.

There are four different response tasks that can be used to assess perception. *Detection* is the ability to tell when a stimulus is present. *Discrimination* is the ability to determine if two stimuli are the same or different. *Identification* is the ability to recognize the stimulus being presented and to identify it by repeating, pointing, or writing. *Comprehension* is the ability to understand

what the stimulus means. (This last task is frequently the speech pathologist's, rather than the audiologist's, responsibility).

Each response task can be assessed using a number of different stimuli, from phonemes, syllables, words, phrases, and sentences to connected discourse. Phoneme testing is the most difficult task in the stimulus hierarchy because it is less redundant and provides the fewest cues. However, it can be presented in either a closed- or open-set format, provides specific information about which sounds are not correctly perceived, and tests many stimuli within a short period of time. Connected discourse, on the other hand, is easier to understand but provides very little information about which specific phonemes are causing perception difficulties because the listener may use contextual clues to correctly extrapolate words she does not correctly perceive. When making a determination about what a child hears, the clinician must be very aware of what kinds of stimuli are being used. If sentences are the stimuli, the tester must be conservative when concluding that speech perception is not a problem because context or situational cues will be contributing to the child's response.

THRESHOLD SPEECH TESTS

There are two types of tests that assess speech thresholds. A *speech awareness threshold* (SAT) assesses a person's ability to detect that a sound is present, similar to testing thresholds for tones. By using different low (baba), mid-high (sh), and high (s) frequency speech stimuli, it is possible for an audiologist to get some information about how a child is able to hear speech at different frequencies. A *speech reception threshold (SRT)* measures the softest level at which the listener is able to recognize different words 50% of the time. There are standardized lists of words designed for this test, but testers can substitute familiar pictures, words, or body parts when the standardized lists are too difficult for children.

WORD RECOGNITION TESTING

Word recognition tests are designed to evaluate a child's ability to understand speech under different listening conditions. Unlike threshold testing, word recognition testing is performed at supra-threshold levels. Testing may be conducted at different intensities and under varying conditions of competing noise. The selection of test materials and test conditions will depend on the child's vocabulary level and the child's ability to cooperate. To score a correct response, the child must accurately perceive all the phonemes in any word. Audiologists can learn a great deal about a child's speech perception skills by modifying the response task and types of reinforcement. No audiological evaluation is complete without obtaining some speech perception information.

Testing may be performed in an open- or closed-set format. Closed-set testing uses a small set of materials from which the listener may select the correct response. The tester's option to limit the number of selections makes the task easier. In open-set testing, the number of possible answers is limited only by the child's vocabulary. Any word, or even a nonsense syllable, is a possible response, as long as the vocabulary is appropriate for the child. Selecting a test that has a vocabulary that is too difficult for the child may produce invalid test results because response errors will be viewed as perception errors when they are really related to the child's lower vocabulary level. Children who are echolalic may be able to repeat words they do not know. Although they may have very limited vocabulary, the ability to "echo," or repeat words, can provide extensive information about auditory perception by simply evaluating the child's errors.

Closed-Set Tests

There are several closed-set tests for measuring word recognition, each involving words familiar to most young children. *Number identification* may be the easiest word recognition task because the vocabulary is familiar to most children and only requires vowel recognition. *Pointing to body parts or other familiar objects* also is an easy task, even for very young children, and can usually be made into an interesting game. The child can point to his, a doll's, or a parent's body. This same task can also be accomplished using pictures or objects with which the child is familiar. Because only a limited number of stimuli are being used, the results must be interpreted with care. The *Alphabet Test (APAL)* was developed to overcome the difficulties caused by a reduced vocabulary in many children with impaired hearing, as well as to evaluate the type of errors the child is making (Ross & Randolph, 1990). The APAL requires that the child be able to identify spoken letters of the alphabet. Responses may be made orally, using finger spelling, or by pointing to a response board.

The *Northwestern University Children's Hearing in Pictures (NU-CHIPS),* developed by Elliot and Katz (1980), is a four-item, forced-choice picture identification test. This test has the vocabulary appropriate for a normally developing 3-year-old. The *Word Intelligibility by Picture Identification (WIPI),* developed by Ross and Lerman (1970), is a 6-item, forced-choice picture identification test with 25 items and 4 test forms. This test requires the vocabulary level of a $3^1/_2$-year-old. It is slightly more difficult than NU-CHIPS because it is a six-item test and the vocabulary is more difficult. It is a good alternative for slightly older children.

Table 2. Conditions for Testing Auditory Function	
Test Condition	**Stimulus Level**
Normal conversation in quiet	50 dB HL
Soft conversation in quiet	35 dB HL
Normal conversation at +5 S/N*	Speech at 50 dB HL/noise at 45 dB HL
Normal conversation at 0 S/N	Speech and noise at 50 dB HL
Soft conversation at 0 S/N	Speech and noise at 35 dB HL

* S/N is signal to noise level, and refers to the relationship between the primary signal (speech) and the competing noise. +5 S/N means that speech is 5 dB louder than the noise; 0 S/N means that speech and noise are at the same level.

Open-Set Tests

There are three basic open-set tests for evaluating word recognition. The vocabularies used in the *NU-CHIPS* (3-year-old level) and in the *WIPI* (3½-year-old level) are excellent for testing young children who can perform using an open-set format.

The *Phonetically Balanced Kindergarten List (PBK)* (Haskins, 1949) consists of 50-item, phonemically balanced, monosyllabic word lists selected from the spoken vocabulary of kindergarten children with normal hearing. The test should not be used with children younger than kindergarten age because the vocabulary will be too difficult, resulting in depressed scores (Sanderson-Leepa & Rintelman, 1976).

Soundfield Evaluation

Every child should have auditory functioning evaluated in soundfield, regardless of the basic reason for the evaluation. Testing should be conducted routinely at normal (50 dB HL) and soft (35 dB HL) conversational levels (Madell, 1990, 1996, 1998). If a child's test results are extremely poor at normal levels, testing need not be conducted at soft levels. After testing is conducted under quiet conditions, it should be repeated at normal and soft conversational levels in the presence of competing noise. (See Table 2 for test conditions.) The most useful competing message is recorded speech babble. Because the stimulus is speech, it will be more distracting than speech noise or white noise, and more like the message competition that the child faces every day. Babble containing only one or two voices will be the most distracting because it is easy to understand some of the words spoken. Twelve-talker babble will be easier to ignore than one-, two- or four-talker babble because it is harder to recognize any individual voices. Four- or 12-talker babble is most commonly used. A child whose word recognition drops significantly in the presence of competing noise may be demonstrating auditory processing difficulties. Even a child with a mild conductive hearing loss who performs well under earphones at 40 dB SL may have difficulty with word recognition at soft conversational levels or in the presence of competing noise. Figure 5 demonstrates test results for such a child. The information obtained by testing at soft conversational levels and with competing noise will be valuable in helping physicians, parents, speech pathologists, classroom teachers, and the children themselves recognize the effect of a mild hearing loss on classroom functioning and in determining when medical or other treatment is indicated.

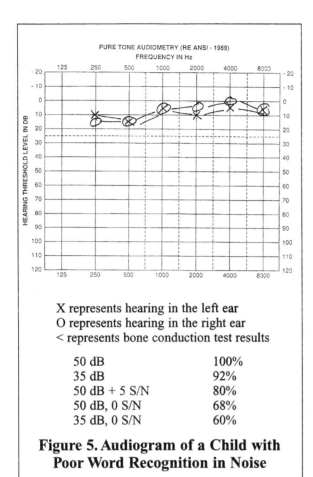

X represents hearing in the left ear
O represents hearing in the right ear
< represents bone conduction test results

50 dB	100%
35 dB	92%
50 dB + 5 S/N	80%
50 dB, 0 S/N	68%
35 dB, 0 S/N	60%

Figure 5. Audiogram of a Child with Poor Word Recognition in Noise

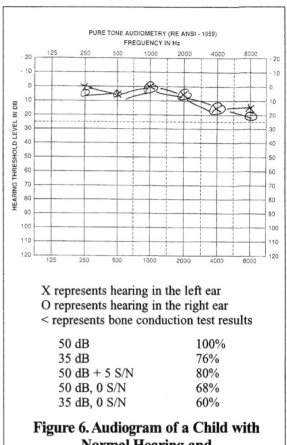

X represents hearing in the left ear
O represents hearing in the right ear
< represents bone conduction test results

50 dB	100%
35 dB	76%
50 dB + 5 S/N	80%
50 dB, 0 S/N	68%
35 dB, 0 S/N	60%

Figure 6. Audiogram of a Child with Normal Hearing and Speech Functioning Test

Figure 6 demonstrates test results of a child with normal hearing, good word recognition at normal conversational levels, but poor word recognition at soft levels and in the presence of competing noise. Identification of this problem helps the parent, teacher, therapists, and child understand that some aberrant academic and behavior patterns do not stem from attention or behavior problems but rather from a very real perception problem.

ASSESSING AUDITORY PROCESSING

An auditory processing disorder is the inability or reduced ability to discriminate, identify, or comprehend auditory stimuli when the auditory signal is in any way degraded. Degradation can occur when speech is muffled; the speaker is at a distance from the listener, is facing away, or has an unfamiliar accent; there is more than one speech signal being presented concurrently; or when there is competing noise. Auditory processing needs to be specifically evaluated. The initial auditory function test is the assessment of speech at normal and soft conversational levels in quiet and in competing noise. After selecting a word recognition test that is appropriate for the child's vocabulary level, the child is tested under all five test conditions (see Table 2). If a child can perform the task at a normal conversational level in quiet, the task and vocabulary level are appropriate. If the child demonstrates reduced scores at soft conversational levels or with competing noise, the child has demonstrated an auditory processing disorder. (Madell, Bodkin, & Rosenfeld [1999] have demonstrated that normally developing children as young as 3 years old are capable of performing this task successfully, with scores of 86% or better in all conditions.) Other auditory processing tests include tests of dichotic listening, filtered speech, competing words, competing sentences, pitch-pattern sequence testing, and various electrophysiologic tests.

DESCRIBING AUDITORY FUNCTIONING

A part of each audiologic report should be a description of the child's auditory functioning. This description will assist the reader in understanding what to expect from the child in a variety of different situations and will assist the teacher and therapist in planning remediation, if needed. Both the audiologist and speech pathologist can provide the information needed to answer the following questions.

- What can you expect from the child when speech is presented at normal and soft conversational levels?
- What happens in the presence of noise?
- Can the child perform in an unclued (open-set) situation or is it necessary for the child to be clued (using a closed-set or topic information) in order to understand?
- Does the child require paragraph or sentence material to follow conversation or can she follow single words?
- Can the child understand the message on first presentation or does he require repetition to understand?

ASSESSING AUDITORY ATTENTION

Auditory attention is the ability to focus on and attend to an auditory message. Normally developing children will occasionally "tune

out" and attend only to the TV but, for the most part, they respond when called and attend to sounds in their environment. Children with auditory attention problems do not attend consistently to auditory information. They may appear not to hear and may almost appear deaf. They may respond inconsistently to stimuli and fail to attend if there are visual or tactile stimuli to distract them. They may be able to "tune in" again after being presented with a loud stimulus. They may respond to sound for a short period of time and then stop responding.

During hearing testing of a child with a possible auditory attention disorder, it is important that the audiologist control the test stimuli carefully and keep all distractions (auditory, visual, and tactile) to a minimum. There should be very little talking. The audiologist should keep the child focused and centered, using toys that will keep her attention but not be too interesting. Stimuli should be presented with sufficient time between each stimulus so that the child is not over-stimulated. If the child stops responding, the audiologist should alter the stimulus (change from tones to noise bands), and use an occasional loud stimulus. For a child with a significant auditory attention disorder, it may not be possible to complete testing in one visit because the child cannot attend for a long time period and may need a significant number of breaks during the test session.

ASSESSING SOUND SENSITIVITIES

Testing for sound sensitivities should include testing of both soft and loud sounds. Some children hear very soft sounds that most listeners do not hear. It is important to identify this because it may explain why some children are so distracted by auditory stimuli. If a child is very sensitive to sound, he may be distracted by sounds that are relatively soft to most people. Sound sensitivity is tested during the measurement of auditory thresholds by continuing to make sound softer than normal and determining the level at which the child responds. Children who hear at several thresholds less than 0 dB may be considered hypersensitive to sound.

Sensitivity to loud sounds is determined by observing a child's response to sound as the volume is increased. Testing can be accomplished in a soundfield. The audiologist presents noise band stimuli, one frequency band at a time, beginning at a soft level and gradually increasing the sound to a loud level (not to exceed 90 dB HL). If the child is verbal, he should be instructed as follows: "I am going to be making some sounds now. They will get very loud. If it gets too loud, you should tell me to stop and I will stop right away. Do not tell me to stop if you don't like it. Tell me to stop if it is uncomfortable." When the child says "stop," the audiologist stops the sound, and then asks the child if the sound level is really uncomfortable or if he just doesn't like it. After several practice attempts, many children can learn to respond correctly. If a child cannot respond in this way, the audiologist, parent, or therapist can observe the child as the sound becomes louder and determine at which level the child seems uncomfortable. She may cry, cover her ears, or try to leave the room. Parents, because they know the child well, will be able to recognize what seems like discomfort. The test should be repeated several times at each level to determine the discomfort level. Before beginning loudness discomfort testing, the tester should ask parents how the child responds to pain or discomfort. This will make observations of the child's responses more accurate.

CONCLUSION

Audition is critical for both language and academic development for all children.

Although everyone who works with a child will have some information about how a child hears and uses hearing for communication, a complete audiologic evaluation is essential to fully understanding a child's auditory functioning. A complete evaluation should begin by obtaining information about auditory and language functioning from parents, teachers, and others who work with the child. It should include an assessment of thresholds for different frequencies, speech perception, auditory processing, auditory attention, and sound sensitivities. Test protocols selected to obtain all the necessary test information will depend on the child's cognitive age, physical status, and interactional skills.

Information obtained from the audiological evaluation will be helpful in selecting an appropriate educational program. For example, a child who has clearly identified auditory processing problems would benefit from being placed in a small, acoustically treated classroom and from using a listening system (e.g., hearing aid) in the classroom and in other situations where listening is difficult. The child also should receive additional therapies (e.g., speech and occupation) through a pull-out program, so that the distractions of a regular classroom will not interfere with the child's ability to hear and benefit from the therapies. Children with sound sensitivities, especially when these interfere with attention, may benefit from a small class with good acoustic treatment and from earplugs or other sound protectors when noise cannot be controlled. Children with auditory attention disorders may need specific training in using audition without visual or situational prompts.

Hearing is only one factor in auditory functioning, but it is a critical one. By fully evaluating auditory functioning and treating it appropriately, it is frequently possible to significantly reduce the negative effects of many auditory disorders. Evaluation and treatment require the cooperation of all clinicians working with the child, the parents, and frequently, the child. ■

REFERENCES

Bess, F. M., Tharp, A. M., & Klee, T. M. (1986). Unilateral sensorineural hearing loss in children. *Ear and Hearing 7*(3), 3-54.

Boothroyd, A. (1984). Auditory perception of speech contrasts by subjects with sensorineural hearing loss. *Journal of Speech and Hearing Research, 27,* 134-144.

Delcato, C. H. (1974). *The ultimate stranger: The autistic child.* Novato, CA: Arena Press.

Elliot, L., & Katz, D. (1980). *Development of a new children's test of speech discrimination.* St. Louis: Auditec.

Erber, N. P. (1979). An approach to evaluating auditory speech perception ability. *The Volta Review, 81,* 16-24.

Flexor, C., & Gans, D. P. (1985). Comparative evaluation of the auditory responsiveness of normal infants and profoundly multihandicapped children. *Journal of Speech and Hearing Research, 28,* 163-168.

Fry, D. (1978). The role and primacy of the auditory channel in speech and language development. In M. Ross & T. Giolas (Eds.), *Auditory management of hearing impaired children.* Baltimore, MD: University Park Press.

Greenspan, S. I. (1992). *Infancy and early childhood: The practice of clinical assessment and intervention with emotional and developmental changes.* Madison, CT: International Universities Press.

Haskins, J. (1949). *Kindergarten phonetically balanced word lists (PBK).* St. Louis: Auditec.

Hayes, D., & Northern, J. L. (1996). *Infants and hearing.* San Diego: Singular Publishing Group.

Katoff, L., Reuter, J., & Dunn, V. (1978). *The Kent infant developmental scale manual.* Kent, OH: Kent State University.

Madell, J. R. (1990). Audiological evaluation. In M. Ross (Ed.), *Hearing-impaired children in the mainstream* (pp. 95-118). Parkton, MD: York Press.

Madell, J. R. (1996). Speech audiometry for children. In S. E. Gerber (Ed.), *The handbook of pediatric audiology* (pp. 84-103). Washington, D.C.: Gallaudet University Press.

Madell, J. R. (1998); *Behavioral evaluation of hearing in infants and young children.* New York: Thieme Medical Publishers.

Madell, J. R., Bodkin, K., & Rosenfeld, R. (1999). *Word recognition testing of children at normal and soft conversational levels in quiet and with competing noise.* Unpublished paper presented at the American Academy of Audiology Annual Conference, Miami, April 27 to May 2.

Powers, M. D. (1992). Early intervention for children with autism. In D. E. Berkell (Ed.), *Autism: Identification, education, and treatment* (pp. 225-252). Hillsdale, NJ: Erlbaum.

Rapin, I. (1991). Autistic children: Diagnostic and clinical features. *Pediatrics, 85,* (Suppl. 5), 751-760.

Rosenfeld, R. M., & Madell, J. R. (1996). Auditory function in normal hearing children with middle ear effusion. In *Recent advances in otitis media.* Hamilton, Ontario, Canada: Decker.

Ross, M., & Lerman, J. (1971). *Word identification by picture identification.* Pittsburgh: Stanwick House.

Ross, M., & Randolph, K. (1990). A test of the auditory perception of alphabet letters for hearing impaired children: The APAL test. *The Volta Review, 92,* 237-244.

Sanderson-Leepa, M. E., & Rintelmann, W. F. (1976). Articulation function and test-retest performance of normal-learning children on three speech discrimination tests: WIPI, PBK 50, and NU auditory test No. 6.

Journal of Speech and Hearing Disorders, 41, 503-519.

Silman, S., & Silverman, C. (1991). *Auditory diagnosis: Principles and applications.* New York: Academic Press.

Verpoorten, R. A., & Emmen, J. G. (1995). A tactile-auditory conditioning procedure for the hearing assessment of persons with autism and mental retardation. *Scandanavian Audiology, 24,* (Suppl. 41), 49-50.

Yoshinaga-Itano, C. (1987). Aural habilitation: A key to acquisition of knowledge, language, and speech. *Seminars in Hearing, 8*(2), 169-174.

—◄ 7 ►—

Children with Special Needs in Bilingual Families: A Developmental Approach to Language Recommendations

Robert H. Wharton, M.D., Karen Levine, Ph.D.,
Elizabeth Miller, M.D., Ph.D.,
Joshua Breslau, Ph.D., and Stanley Greenspan, M.D.

In the United States, bilingual parents of children with special needs are widely counseled by physicians, speech and language pathologists, teachers, and often even by members of their own family to speak to their children in English rather in their native language. This advice appears to be almost universally offered to parents of children with disorders of language and communication, such as pervasive developmental disorder (PDD)/autism, as well as to children with cognition limitations. Since no studies in the literature seems to analyze either the rationale behind or the effect of these recommendations, these directives apparently must stem from a theory that parents speaking in their native language to children who have difficulty learning even one language will interfere with the child's ability to learn the language of common usage. Further, it is relatively certain that what appears to providers to be a benign and narrow linguistic recommendation actually initiates a ripple effect that alters the environment of children in ways that may have more significant negative

consequences for the development of linguistic, cultural, and social competence.

There can be distinct language and social disadvantages to this population of children with special needs when parents are constrained from communicating with them using their native language. Specifically, regarding language, this restrictive recommendation may limit a child's ability to access and master initial gestural preverbal communication as well as the early verbal abilities that serve as the foundation of communication. This recommendation may also restrict the child's expansion of language and appropriate use in social encounters. In addition, the recommendation to use English only may limit affective interchanges between parents and children, which then inhibits a child's opportunities for maximum social and emotional growth.

This chapter presents three case studies exploring language development and social connection in children with PDD/autism. These cases will illustrate the difficulties encountered by children at three levels of development: a child with severely limited social interaction and language, a child with emerging social interaction and language abilities, and a child with limited competence in social interaction and language. Each case analysis also discusses the relationship between language and social development and child development theories. Finally, each case study concludes with recommendations for bilingual, bicultural families related to their use of a native language when communicating with their children with special needs.

Based on the evidence of families studied by the authors, facilitating a family's use of their native language can have positive effects on the child's growth in the domains of communication, social interaction, and competence. Further, a parent's or relative's use of a native language can enhance that person's emotional involvement with the child and so better achieve one of the most crucial developmental missions of parents and children.

BACKGROUND INFORMATION

Evidence exists that neonates have a preference for their parents' native language (Bahrick & Pickens, 1988; Best, 1994; Mehler, Jusczyk, Lambertz, Bertoncini & Amiel-Tison, 1988). Moreover, infants appear to recognize a phonetic distinction in their parents' native language even within their first several months of life (Miller & Eimas, 1995; Werker, 1993). An infant's sensitivity to a specific native language is present not only to the distinct vowels and consonants, but also to the prosodic or rhythmic quality of the language (Jurszyk, 1997). Therefore, the infant's language processing system is highly developed, showing an early sensitivity to the specific sound patterns of the parents' native language (Best, 1994). Moreover, although the infant's abilities initially seem highly instinctual in nature, his or her experience

over time with a native language modifies phonetic perceptual abilities during the first year of life (Kuhl, Williams, Lacerda, Stevens, & Lindblum, 1992; Polka & Werker, 1994).

On a broader level, infants and young children are not only acutely sensitive and responsive to specific sound patterns found in their native language, but research on language acquisition and socialization demonstrates that the social organization of language also plays an important role in language development. Ochs and Schiefflen (1984) argue that "the processes of language acquisition and the process of socialization are integrated." Individual languages have specific grammatical constructions that convey information concerning how the listeners see their own social positions and roles. As children acquire language, therefore, they are also learning the social meaning of the linguistic structures. Patterns of language use, according to Ochs and Schieffelin (1984; Schieffelin & Ochs, 1986), become important resources for children in the process of becoming competent members of their communities.

Although the highly sophisticated abilities of infants to perceive speech are innate, the ability of children to actually acquire and use language appears to be within some time constraint (Chugani, 1998). Children who have not been exposed to language from birth, such as feral children, can best acquire language skills if intense speech and language therapy is introduced before the age of 10 (Curtiss, 1981). Similarly, children who receive an injury to the language-dominant hemisphere have better recovery if the injury occurs before they are 8 to 10 years of age.

Several issues emerge from these studies. First, it is clear that infants and young children have an innate propensity to preferentially learn not only specifics of the language spoken by their parents, but the prosody and intonation as well. Second, the process of language acquisition and socialization are integrated. And, third, there is a critical period for language acquisition after which the potential to acquire language skills is considerably reduced (Lenneberg, 1967). Therefore, for all children—both typical as well as those with developmental disabilities—the development and growth of the their language and social abilities will be intertwined. However, first the children's innate capacity must be targeted by providing access to the language of their biological preference—namely, the language they have been hearing *in utero*, and second, by stimulating the expansion of the children's social attachments. Enhancing exposure and facilitating attachment will enable a child to develop the desire to begin to use communication strategies that will support ongoing social interactions.

CASE STUDIES OF CHILDREN WITH PDD AT THREE LEVELS: PREVERBAL, MINIMAL VERBAL, AND ADVANCED VERBAL

Case Study #1: Initiating the Ability to Connect

Maria is the Cuban-born mother of Eduardo, a 3-year-old child with autism. When Eduardo was an infant, Maria spoke to him only in Spanish, as she had done with her older son, Joseph, who is now 5 years old. Maria emigrated from Cuba with her family when she was 10 years old. Feeling the pressures to learn English, she rapidly became fluent in both Spanish and English. Having personally experienced the joys and advantages of bilingualism, she made a conscious effort to raise her first son bilingually, speaking to him only in Spanish, whereas her husband (also a bilingual Cuban-American) spoke to him only in English. Joseph now

moves smoothly between both languages, equally comfortable in either tongue. When Eduardo was born, Maria and her husband took the same approach to bilingual language instruction with him.

When Eduardo reached the age of 2 and was not using any words, he was referred to early intervention. Shortly thereafter, he was diagnosed with PDD. From the beginning of the early intervention evaluation and throughout the entire process of developing recommendations for treatment, Maria was told to stop speaking to Eduardo in Spanish and to start speaking only in English. She was given this virtually identical advice by his speech pathologists, occupational and physical therapists, physicians, and teachers. Each stressed that she needed to "stop Spanish completely;" that she would "confuse him." "It was really hammered into me that I should speak only in English, no Spanish," Maria recalled. "I wanted what was best for him. What mother wouldn't? If they had told me to learn Chinese, I would have, if they told me that that would help him. I would have stood on my head. Anything!"

At home, Maria reported, she speaks only in Spanish to Eduardo's older brother Joseph, and she lets Joseph watch Spanish programs and videos on television. Her concern for Joseph's language development remains strong and she consistently reminds him to speak Spanish, rather than English, to her. "I want him to be proud of being bilingual," Maria states. Dinner conversations tend to be primarily in Spanish, or a fluid mix of the two languages. When any member of the family addresses Eduardo, however, they must only use English.

At first Maria found it difficult to force herself to speak English at home, but now this situation has reversed itself and she has to make a conscious effort if she wants to use Spanish with Eduardo. "I would love to speak

Spanish to him," says Maria, "but it has been hammered into me. ... I am afraid of what it might do to him [to speak in Spanish]. ... He already has such a confusing world, ... I'm afraid to add to the confusion."

Eduardo rarely makes eye contact, gestures, or uses words. Recently, Maria has been encouraged to begin speaking with him in Spanish, and she has begun to introduce a few relatively simple phrases. "I'm introducing just a taste," she exclaimed. Sometimes she will sing to him in Spanish: "He really smiles and sings along ... with a very dramatic 'ma ma!' " On walks along the beach, Eduardo and his mother will stop to feed the seagulls. After the bread is all gone, his mother will wave dramatically to the birds, "Bye bye birds," then will follow with "Adios parahitos!" Maria then helps Eduardo to wave, too. Now, when she says "water," Eduardo will respond by saying "agua" and laugh, seemingly sharing a joke with her, as if acknowledging their game. Yet even with these moments of connection with her son in her native language, Eduardo's mother still feels great unease. "I want some proof that this is the right thing to do."

Preverbal Gestural Abilities

Children begin to communicate using gestures, facial expressions, and variation in vocal intonation. The affective or emotional component of this preverbal communication will convey a large degree of the intent and meaning of their efforts at communication. Greenspan (1996) has postulated that this affective gestural system best conveys a child's communication goals. The solid development of this system will enhance the child's ability to use language as a major carrier of social and emotional content as well as cognitive information. Parents and other caretakers need to help a child to progress from the gestural stage of communication

into verbal language by first entering into the child's world through highly interactive gestures. This interactional character of language is critical to the psychosocial development of children (Wetsch, 1985).

For children who are not able to use ideas and words meaningfully, such as Eduardo, the parents' first task is to help them master preverbal gestural abilities. George Herbert Mead, a scientist writing in the early part of this century, attached central importance to the vocal gesture, using the metaphor "the conversation of gestures" to describe this critical interaction. Since Eduardo's gestures and vocalizations currently lack social content, however, his parents must first capture his attention and then facilitate his attachment to them. They can assist this process by creating an interactive sequence significant for both its gestural qualities as well as rhythmical motor patterns. However, the key to capturing his attention and, therefore, facilitating engagement will be the development of emotional interplay between him and his parents. Without layering of affect between children like Eduardo and their parents, the development of the children's supportive affective and emotional abilities might remain unavailable.

Eduardo's mother comments that, although he rarely makes eye contact or uses words, "he smiles and sings along" when she sings in Spanish. It is likely that when she sings, her voice carries a sense of her own emotionally enriched experiences that are connected with her traditional lullabies and other emotionally engaging themes. Therefore, she is likely to be communicating at these times with bright facial expressions, supportive gestures, and other forms of enhanced emotional expression. By communicating, more out of habit and experience than design, in this emotionally engaging fashion, she is better able to stimulate a response from Eduardo. She then will have a template upon which to work to capture and expand on his attentional and interactional abilities.

In addition to her efforts to capture Eduardo's attention through vocalizations, his mother has been using the feeding and watching of birds to engage him. While they share the task of feeding the birds, which sets up an interactive, rhythmical pattern during this pleasurable game, the mother adds a vocal component. With much affect, she first waves dramatically to the birds and says, "Bye-bye birds." She then takes his hand and helps Eduardo wave, too. She further expands on her own affect and works to continue the interaction by adding "Adios parahitos!" Eduardo's participation in this emotionally compelling back-and-forth rhythmical interaction—enhanced by his mother's strong affective energy—helps his imitative, and then independent, use of language in all forms. It is likely that this progress will be pushed along by his mother's affect, which is more available to her both consciously and subliminally when she uses her native language.

Affective Memory

Motor movements, once learned and made familiar, can subsequently be performed automatically, without conscious or volitional efforts at motor planning. For example, motor activities such as reaching out a hand to shake with others, giving a "high five," or even walking or running are generally produced without conscious thought. These automatic movements have been referred to by Oliver Sachs as "kinetic memories;" that is, movement memories.

The hypothesis here is that interactions that are performed with high affect have the potential to create specific memories in children with autistic spectrum disorders. However, similar to the development of a "kinetic memory" that can enable someone to reproduce a complex motor movement in response to something so simple as a gesture, a memory of a feeling can produce an emotion in response to a communicated intent. These reactive memories, these memories of affect or emotion, are "affective memories." Raising someone's affect provides a person with a heightened opportunity to establish interpersonal connections or attachments. These affective memories can be used in a way similar to the way in which rhythmical interactive motor sequences can pull children into patterns of engagement and purposeful interaction, expanding their imitation and verbal potential.

When Eduardo's mother tries to engage him, drawing from the well of her own strong cultural feelings and memories will heighten her potential to connect to her socially disconnected son. Using her own emotionally strong memories will increase her affect, thereby expanding her potential to engage Eduardo. When Eduardo responds to her, when he is able to match her affect, he is likely to create an affective memory which the mother can then often rely on to engage him in future play sessions. It is likely that as he smiles and sings along to her songs, he is feeling connected to her, recognizing the feeling of a strong and good emotion, while not yet at the developmental stage where he could generate the same feeling spontaneously. Similarly, whereas a person with a brain injury that has resulted in a disorder of motor planning can automatically shake an outstretched hand, yet not make the same movement if thought is required, a child with autism can demonstrate attachment to an emotion and affective interaction, without the ability to initiate the emotion. A repertoire of affective memories can, therefore, serve as a springboard to facilitate the preverbal interactions that will then support the child's ability to achieve successful verbal interactions.

When Eduardo's parents and other bilingual families with children with special needs share their own emotionally enriched experiences, they are likely to be communicating in an emotionally engaging fashion that will stimulate the children's emotional learning. Therefore, by using their native language at these times of more intense social interaction, they are intuitively enhancing their children's ability to respond to, learn, and remember the particular information, thoughts, and feelings being shared. In this way, their children will have access to the social and emotional competence that forms the structure for shared language.

Case Report #2:
Expanding the Connections

Vladimir, a 4-year-old boy with autism whose parents emigrated from Russia only 5 years previously, had been making consistent progress following his diagnosis and was starting to use language. When his mother played with him, however, she felt her play was too formal and lacked the warmth she felt was necessary to fully engage her somewhat-aloof preschooler. In addition, when speaking to him using her newly learned English, her speech as well as her gestures were somewhat intermittent and constricted, rather than spontaneous, continuous, and rhythmical. She would try to engage her son in English, then fall silent, and then try to re-engage him with more vocalizations and facial expressions. This "in-and-out" staccato pattern paralleled the child's in-and-out disconnected pattern, which was one feature of his autistic behavior.

Vladimir's mother said that when she played with her child she occasionally engaged him using her Russian language, although she had been told by the child's

speech therapist and educators to use English only. When playing with him while using her native language, however, she believed her affect and her entire communication style underwent a dramatic transformation. She felt she displayed an enhanced rhythm in her vocalizations, fuller gestures, and more intimate and inviting facial expressions. Within minutes of starting to interact, she believed her partially aloof, formal, "in-and-out" play pattern gave way to an increasingly warm, nourishing, rhythmical, and rich interaction. When she engaged her child in this manner, she noted he would stay more focused on her face and words and would become more purposeful in his interactions. He also would vocalize and imitate her sounds and words to a greater degree than when she used English.

When commenting on how she felt about speaking Russian in addition to English, Vladimir's mother said that although she loved him the same whether she was talking to him in Russian or in English, she felt warmer and closer to him, and more relaxed, when using her Russian. She commented that when she used English, she needed to stop and think about what she was going to say and that this searching for the right words made her tense and anxious. In comparison, when using Russian with her son, she believed her words had a more natural "flow." She became elated that she could make her child smile and laugh when she used the affectionate and playful "silly talk" she had learned as a youngster, and for which she had no English words.

Verbal Abilities
Once a child such as Vladimir begins imitating sounds and words, the parent or other provider will want to continue to maintain an interactive sequence of sounds and words as part of a purposeful back-and-forth dialogue. Even as the child becomes able to use words

regularly, as well as to use short phrases and sentences, it is essential for others to use these words or phrases to help achieve long sequences of back-and forth-communication with the child.

Vladimir's mother noted two significant changes when using her native language with her son. First, she observed that when she was feeling more natural, relaxed, and spontaneous, she was able to help him become more engaged with her. She observed this through his smile, laughter, and increased imitation. In particular, Vladimir seemed to respond when she engaged in her native "silly talk." This more affectively laden interchange with her child, whereby her affect becomes the vehicle through which language is delivered, is the key to her child's ability to achieve an interactional interchange. In contrast, when she tries to speak with him using only her English, her difficulty feeling comfortable with the language forces her to focus more on finding the right words with which to speak to him, rather than on trying to help expand his attention and affect. The consequence is that even when she and other parents in similar situations are able to find the "correct words" to use, the words themselves—without the necessary heightened affect—lack the ability to stimulate an effective response.

Second, Vladimir's mother noted that using her native language enabled her to sustain interactions and, therefore, have more frequent back-and-forth interchanges with her son. She found that her play initiatives as well as her responses were more available to her when she was not required to first think and translate her planned interactions from Russian into English. As she was able to be continuously spontaneous, she was able to provide Vladimir with the ability to stay connected to her for a sustained period. This expanded opportunity for serial interchange seems critical for normal language development.

Affective Memory

Vladimir's mother stated that using "silly talk" from her own youth helped her make Vladimir smile and laugh during their play. At these times, she felt more emotionally connected to Vladimir and believed that her enthusiasm helped his attachment to her as well. The mother can, therefore, take advantage of this silly talk and use it as an "emotional or affective high five" at the start of their play, or when she feels that Vladimir is having a more difficult time engaging with her during play.

The use of silly talk can be used in specific ways to maximize the advantages for Vladimir and his mother when his mother is attempting to engage him in play. First, the silly talk itself should have the same words, prosody, and affect each time. In this way, its use will form not only a greeting but a verbal marker that will help Vladimir achieve a comfortable transition into play. Second, his mother can silly talk during the course of play should Vladimir start to lose the thread of their interactive give-and-take communication. In this way, she can gently but effectively reconnect to him on an emotional level while helping to regain his attention and his attachment to the interactive episode. Third, Vladimir's mother can also help teach others her specific affective strategies to help them initiate and sustain social engagement with Vladimir during his therapy and play sessions.

Case #3: Refining the Connections

Freddy, a 4-year-old boy with quite mild PDD, lives in a more complex language environment than either Eduardo or Vladimir. In terms of his diagnosis, Freddy had difficulties in the areas of his communication, social interaction, and behavioral style that supported a diagnosis of PDD. Nevertheless, Freddy did have some relevant strengths regarding his social abilities and attachment, but lacked an adequate ability to either comfortably initiate social encounters with other children or family nor, once engaged, to easily or successfully sustain social interactions.

Freddy's parents are from different countries outside the United States and, although they can converse together in both English and French (the father's native language), the mother is more comfortable speaking in her native Danish. Because the family has been told to speak to Freddy in English only, this means that the parents and extended family members who speak English will likely reduce their verbal interactions with the child. Family members who cannot speak English or are not comfortable speaking English may even lose their ability to converse with the child with PDD.

Freddy had made excellent progress in his development in the 2 years since his diagnosis. However, although his PDD was considered relatively mild, he was not making advances in responding consistently or staying engaged for the multiple consecutive verbal interchanges that could result in sustained social interactions. Although his mother enjoyed his enthusiastic initial response to her efforts to connect with him in play, she would become frustrated when his eagerness faded after one exchange. She and Freddy's father had similar difficulties expanding his play when joined together to engage him. She and his father both felt uncomfortable using English. They had expressed a desire to each use their own language in their play with him, but they were worried about confusing him if they used their own or too many different languages.

Nevertheless, with much encouragement, his parents had the following play session with him.

> *Freddy to mother: (in Danish)*
>   *I want to draw an elephant.*
> *Mother to Freddy: (in Danish)*
>   *Yes, lets draw a big, big elephant!*
> *Father to Freddy: (in French)*
>   *Lets take your chalk outside to draw.*
> *Freddy to father: (in French)*
>   *Yes, like yesterday.*
> *Freddy to mother (in Danish)*
>   *You jump on the big elephant*
>   *yesterday.*
> *Father to mother (in French)*
>   *Yesterday we drew on the sidewalk.*
> *Mother to Freddy: (in Danish)*
>   *You jumped on the big elephant*
>   *yesterday? Like this?*
> *Freddy to mother: (in Danish)*
>   *I jumped on it like this.*
> *Freddy to father: (in French)*
>   *Papa, I jumped like this!!*
> *Freddy to mother: (in Danish)*
>   *We take my chalk and make a big*
>   *elephant and we jump! Like this!!!*

Drawing from his parents' enthusiasm, Freddy had no difficulty responding to each parent in turn and maintaining a seamless conversation. He readily switched between French and Danish, unencumbered by concerns about grammar or vocabulary. His parents, in turn, acting from their own comfort with their own languages, relayed their affect to Freddy, becoming increasingly comfortable with the success of this strategy the longer the interchanges lasted. As they ended this play interlude with Freddy, he looked at each of them in turn and, as he went running off with his chalk, said *"au revoir, papa; tak, mama!"*

Verbal and Affective Linkages

Following the reported success of Applied Behavior Analysis (ABA), Greenspan introduced a new behavioral intervention (Lovaas, 1987; Greenspan & Wieder, 1998). "Floor Time," described elsewhere in this book (see Greenspan & Wilder Chapter 12, this volume), uses animated play to intrude into a child's solitary activity and engage the child socially. This strategy makes use of the fact that raising a child's level of emotion helps enhance the child's attention and social attachment.

In general, an effective treatment of children with autism uses adult emotions as a tool to stimulate a child's emotions. Eduardo's mother was encouraged by the successful, enhanced interaction between her and her son as he began to smile and join in her song when she sang to him in her native Spanish. Valdimir's mother expressed equal elation at sharing a smile and a laugh with her child. Both parents recognized that in using their native language they quite naturally used extensive nonverbal communication, including more facial animation and other interactive gestures, and incorporated more emotion into their words. While one might have expected Freddy to become confused by his parent's free-wheeling play session during which they used their own languages, this did not occur. Instead, the parents' linguistic comfort enabled them to maintain the level of heightened affect necessary to keep him engaged.

Freddy's alternating use of languages—a process known as "code switching"—was defined by Gumperz (1982) as "the juxtaposition within the same communication exchange of passages of speech belonging to two different grammatical systems or subsystems." As Freddy had already mastered the

ability to use words to label, his parents' challenge to help him extend the length and complexity of verbal and, therefore, social interchanges did not involve teaching him to develop words into sentences. Rather, their goal was to help him find and then maintain the affect, not the words, for extended communication. As the strength of his attachment grew in direct proportion to the length of the verbal interchange, a focus on the specific language used was less important than the child's and family's emotional contact when using their own languages. A parent's natural and affectively rich communication is vital to orient children with autism to the use of language and to attract their attention in order to stimulate a response that facilitates learning and attachment.

SUMMARY

This chapter explored how bilingual parents can effectively use their native language to help their children expand not only the length and complexity of their linguistic interchanges but also their social and emotional attachment. Eduardo, Vladimir, and Freddy—children with varying levels of disability due to their PDD—all benefited significantly when their parents used their native languages in play situations.

The focus of this chapter has been on what parents can do in the home setting to facilitate improvement in language and social interactions for their children with PDD/autism. The discussion intentionally avoided the subject of using the parents' native language when the children are in the classroom, or on the playground, or in other settings. Instead, this discussion stressed throughout that the major principles of communicating with a child should be adhered to independent of the setting. The key is to use a person's heightened affect and emotion to first capture a child's attention and then support his or her attachment. When providing recommendations to families, the important concept is to reassure them that "it is what you say, and *how* you say it!"

RECOMMENDATIONS

Although this discussion has focused on parent interactions with children with PDD/autism, the following recommendations are suitable for parents of children with other developmental disabilities, including mental retardation.

1. As no known information suggests that use of a parent's native language conveys any risks to that child, and as there may be clear and significant benefits to the child and family from its use, therapists and other health care personnel should refrain from recommendations that restrict the parents' use of their native language with their child. Instead, parents can be cautiously encouraged to try using their native language in specific situations, such as nighttime rituals, certain play situations, and other interactions of high emotional content.

2. Family members, such as grandparents, who do not speak the language of common usage, should be encouraged to interact with the child with PDD/autism or other developmental disabilities using their native language so they will not be cut off from the child.

3. Clinical personnel working with children with developmental disabilities in bilingual settings should explore the development of specific strategies that promote ways to increase opportunities for parents to use their native language in their interactions with their child.

4. Early intervention programs, school programs, and other service providers should undertake efforts to recruit multilingual and multicultural staff. ∎

Acknowledgments

The authors would like to express their sincere gratitude to the many bilingual/bicultural families whom they have had the good fortune to serve over the years. These families have taught them much. To these families, the authors would say, *"merci," "gracie," "tak," …*

REFERENCES

Bahrick, L. E., & Pickens, J. N. (1988). Classification of bimodal English and Spanish language passages by infants. *Infant Behavior and Development, 11,* 277-296.

Best, C. T. (1994). The emergence of native language phonological influences in infants: a perceptual assimilation model. In J. C. Goodman & H. C. Nusbaum (Eds.), *The development of speech perception: The Transition from speech sounds to spoken works.* Cambridge: MIT Press.

Chugani, H. T. (1998). Biological basis of emotions: Brain systems and brain development. *Pediatrics, 102,* 1225-1229.

Curtiss, S. (1981). Feral children. In J. Wotis (Ed.), *Mental retardation and developmental disabilities, XII,* (pp. 129-161). New York: Brunner/Mazel.

Greenspan, S. I. (1996). *The growth of the mind.* Reading, MA: Addison Wesley Longman.

Greenspan S. I., & Weider, S. (1998*). The child with special needs.* Reading, MA: Addison Wesley Longman.

Gumperz, J. J. (1982) *Discourse strategies.* Cambridge: Cambridge University Press.

Jurszyk, P. W. (1997). *The discovery of spoken language.* Cambridge, MA: MIT Press.

Kuhl, P. K., Williams, K. A., Lacerda, F., Stevens, K. N., & Lindblum, B. (1992). Linguistic experience alters phonetic perception in infants by 6 months of age. *Science, 255,* 606-608.

Lenneberg E. (1967). *Biological foundations of language.* New York: Wiley.

Lovaas, O. I. (1987). Behavioral treatment and normal educational and intellectual functioning in young autistic children. *Journal of Consulting and Clinical Psychiatry, 55,* 329-341.

Mehler, J., Jusczyk, P., Lambertz, G., Halstead, N., Bertoncini, J., & Amiel-Tison, C. (1988). A precursor of language acquisition in young infants. *Cognition, 29,* 143-178.

Miller, J. L., & Eimas, P. D. (1995). Speech perception: From signal to word. *Annual Review of Psychology, 46,* 467-492.

Ochs, E., & Schieffelin, B. (1984). Language acquisition and socialization: Three developmental stories and their implications. In R. A. Shweder and R. A. Levine (Eds.), *Culture theory: Essays on mind, self, and emotion, 20,* 276-320.

Polka, L., & Werker, J. F. (1994). Developmental changes in perceptual nonnative vowel contrasts. *Journal of Experimental Psychology: Human Perceptual Performance, 20,* 421-435.

Schieffelin, B., & Ochs, E. (1986). Language socialization. *Annual Review of Anthropology, 15,* 163-191.

Werker, J. F. (1993). Developmental changes in cross-language speech perception: Implications for cognitive models of speech processing. In G. T. M. Altmann and R. Shillcock (Eds.), *Cognitive models of speech processing* (pp. 411-418). East Sussex, U.K.: Erlbaum.

Wertsch, J. V. (Ed.) (1985) *Culture, communication and cognition: Vygotskian perspectives.* Cambridge: Cambridge University Press.

Part Three:

Motor and Sensory Functioning

◄ 8 ►

Assessment of Sensory Processing, Praxis, and Motor Performance

G. Gordon Williamson, Ph.D., O.T.R., Marie E. Anzalone, Sc.D., O.T.R., and Barbara E. Hanft, M.A., O.T.R.

This chapter discusses the domains of sensory processing, praxis, and motor performance. Sensory processing is the organization of sensory input from the body and the environment for use. Praxis is the ability to plan and sequence unfamiliar actions. Motor performance is the actual execution of the gross and fine motor coordination. This chapter provides general assessment guidelines that serve as the foundation for observing individual differences in sensory and motor functioning. It then presents qualitative and standardized evaluations for each of the three domains. The assessment process begins with an initial screening of the child. If findings are significant, qualified specialists need to conduct a more in-depth assessment. Extensive tables provide descriptions of available instruments and their sources. This discussion assumes that the child's vision and hearing have been previously evaluated for a primary sensory deficit.

GENERAL SCREENING AND ASSESSMENT GUIDELINES

This section provides general considerations for the screening and assessment of sensory processing, praxis, and motor performance. A screening provides an overall measure of the child's functioning in a particular domain and identifies whether there is a need for further assessment. A professional knowledgeable about child development from a variety of disciplinary perspectives is capable of conducting a screening. In contrast, when an assessment is necessary, a professional with specialized training in the area of concern is necessary. For example, a teacher could screen whether a child is having problems in fine motor control and sensory modulation, but an occupational therapist would be the most appropriate professional to complete the comprehensive assessment. The following guidelines, summarized in Box 1, establish important parameters for performing quality screening and assessment.

The key to assessment is to focus on *how* the child processes sensory information and manages environmental challenges and not to focus solely on the specific skills or milestones the child displays. This approach entails a dynamic *process* orientation to assessment in addition to a *product* focus typical of most developmental evaluations (Coster, 1998; Greenspan & Meisels, 1996). For instance, the milestone of building a block tower (product) may be analyzed in terms of the child's attention, task persistence, grasp patterns, problem solving, and other qualitative aspects

---

Box 1. General Screening and Assessment Guidelines

1. Focus on how the child processes sensory information using a dynamic *process* orientation.
2. Use parent interview and natural observation to gather information regarding sensory processing.
3. Do not look at the child in isolation, but observe the relationship between the child and the environment.
4. Remember that the influence of sensory input is not always immediately observable; there is cumulative effect and a latency of response.
5. Observe for autonomic signs of distress during or after sensory experiences.
6. Expect variability of responses to sensory input and behavior.
7. Keep in mind that sensory-based stereotypic behaviors serve different functions depending on the child's current sensory threshold.
8. Design the assessment process to provide the child with opportunities for choice, self-initiation, creativity, and flexible problem solving.

---

of performance (process). Likewise, assessment of repetitive rocking would include an analysis of what environmental conditions precede or follow this behavior. Such qualitative information enables the practitioner to understand the child and design meaningful intervention.

There are many ways to gather information regarding a child's capacity to process sensory information. The most effective methods are parental interview and natural observation of the child within the context of relationships, play, and functional activities. These primary approaches are supplemented by the administration of standardized tests. Observation of the following situations is particularly informative in understanding the child's sensory and motor processing: independent and social free play, mealtimes, bathing and other functional activities, structured and unstructured peer interaction, parent-child interaction, and transitions between activities.

An examiner does not look at the child in isolation during the assessment process, but at the relationship between the child and

environmental challenges (Hanft & Place, 1996). The practitioner should avoid focussing on pathology and recognize that functional difficulties can arise from a poor fit between the child's needs and available resources. The fit may be complex, subtle, and dynamic. For example, a child who is distractible during play may be responding to glaring lights or a chaotic playroom instead of to internally driven impulsivity.

The influence of sensory input is not always immediately observed. There is both a cumulative effect and a latency of response. The response to sensation builds up over time and is cumulative (e.g., a child may be more sensitive to touch at the end of a long day rather than in the morning). Conversely, some children are slow to register input because of a high threshold but can rapidly become overloaded by accumulated sensation. Both of these tendencies makes it essential that any changes in the amount or type of sensory input provided to the child be done slowly and conservatively.

It is essential to observe the child closely after sensory experiences for autonomic signs of distress (e.g., yawning, hiccuping, sighing, irregular respiration, color change, sweating, motor agitation, startling, pupil dilation) or changes in sleep/wake patterns (Als, 1986). If the child demonstrates autonomic signs of distress, the examiner should stop the activities immediately and determine the cause for the child's reaction. Consultation with a knowledgeable therapist is helpful for determining an appropriate course of action for the future.

Variability in a child's daily performance is common. At any time, the consistency of a child's behavior can be influenced by many factors, such as the degree of environmental stimulation, the child's current emotional state, general level of arousal, coping skills, accumulated sensory build-up, and the availability of a familiar caregiver. Children with sensory processing problems are more often variable than predictable in their performance day by day. Therefore, any assessment must allow for repeated observations over time.

Stereotypic and repetitive sensory-based behaviors serve different functions, based on the child's current sensory threshold (Anzalone & Williamson, 2000). A child who is hyperreactive at a given moment (i.e., with a low threshold for sensory input) may use hand-flapping to gain selective focus and to screen out the rest of the visual environment. The outcome can be calming and organizing. The child who is hyporeactive (i.e., with a high threshold for sensory input) may use this same behavior to increase arousal and activation. A third child may use hand-flapping to discharge tension. Practitioners must use their knowledge of sensory processing to understand these stereotypical mannerisms and rituals. Behavioral techniques that do not consider sensory needs may result in stereotypies that resurface in a different form. Inappropriate behavioral intervention would involve intrusive, highly adult-directed

discrete trials when a child has major problems in sensory modulation. In such cases, it is a therapeutic error to interpret gaze avoidance or tactile defensiveness as willfully noncompliant behavior.

The examiner should not over-structure the assessment environment. The assessment process should provide the child with opportunities for choice, initiation, creativity, and flexible problem solving. During part of the time, the examiner needs to step back and avoid controlling the environmental conditions or initiating interactions. Direction from the examiner, although necessary for certain types of testing, can inhibit the child from expressing individual differences during qualitative observation.

Sensory Processing

It is important to evaluate two components of sensory processing as part of the assessment (Ayres, 1972; Fisher, Murray, & Bundy, 1991). First is sensory modulation, which is the ability to register, orient, and initially react to sensory stimuli. Second is the actual perception and discrimination of that input. Perception is the interpretation of sensory input in light of prior experiences and learning. Important to both modulation and perceptual discrimination are the sensory modalities and properties inherent in the stimuli themselves. Sensory modalities include the environmental senses (vision, hearing, smell, taste) and the body senses (vestibular, proprioception, touch). Proprioception is sensation from the muscles and joints that provide information about the posture and movement of the body. Vestibular receptors in the inner ear are responsive to movement of the body in relation to gravity.

When assessing sensory processing, it is essential to evaluate the child within the environment. The examiner must evaluate the situational demands, goodness-of-fit between the child and the environment, and the sensory properties of the environment (Schaaf & Anzalone, in press). Such sensory properties include intensity and duration. Intensity refers to how powerful or arousing the stimulus is. For example, light touch is more intense than firm touch, and touch on the face is more intense than on the arm. Duration encompasses both the length of the actual stimulus (e.g., how long a sound persists) and the lasting effect of that stimulus within the central nervous system (e.g., rapid spinning resulting in motion sickness or a prolonged increase in activity level). Since each child experiences sensory input in a unique way, an individualized approach to assessment is indicated. The examiner must evaluate both the stimulus (i.e., the objective sensory input) and the sensation (i.e., a specific child's subjective appraisal of that input). Sensation is influenced by the task demands and the child's prior sensory experiences, current state of arousal, and affective state. For example, a light touch perceived as pleasant by one child might be considered threatening or painful by another.

The assessment process considers the behavioral expression of sensory processing in terms of the child's self-regulation of arousal, attention, affect, and action (Williamson & Anzalone, 1997). The child's sensory status moderates, and is moderated by, the child's state of arousal. Arousal is a child's level of alertness and the ability to maintain and transition between different sleep and wake states. The sensory status also influences the child's attention, which is the ability to focus selectively on a desired stimulus or task. Affect, which is the emotional component of behavior, is also influenced by sensory input through either the emotional response to a specific input (e.g., fearfulness in response to unexpected light touch) or

through a global effect on behavior (e.g., the excitement of a child who has just gotten off a swing). Finally, action, which is the ability to engage in adaptive goal-directed behavior, is dependent upon sensory integration.

A child's ability to self regulate these processes depends upon the child's initial registration of sensory stimuli. Registration is the point at which novel sensory information is initially detected and the central nervous system activated. This point is considered the sensory threshold. Some children have a low threshold that results in hyperreactivity or sensory defensiveness. Their behavior is frequently characterized by high arousal, an inability to focus attention, negative or fearful affect, and impulsive or defensive action. Other children have a threshold that is very high, causing them to be hyporeactive to sensory input. Their state of arousal is usually decreased with a prolonged latency or an inability to attain focussed attention. Affect is typically flat, with a restricted expression of emotion that may interfere with social engagement. Their action tends to be passive and sedentary.

Perceptual discrimination is based upon the child's sensory modulation and higher order cognitive processes. The primary perceptual functions to be assessed in young children include visual, auditory, and tactile discrimination. Sample higher order perceptual skills include visual or auditory figure ground perception, visual-spatial relations, auditory memory, tactile localization, and stereognosis. Assessment of these functions is beyond the scope of this chapter, but is discussed in the clinical literature (e.g., Lezak, 1995; Schneck, 1996; Wetherby & Prizant, 2000).

Children with autistic spectrum disorders have sensory modulation problems present in two primary patterns: hyperreactive and hyporeactive. The profiles of each of these patterns provide a helpful framework for understanding the behavioral patterns of these children. A specific child, however, may have a combination of symptoms and not fit clearly into any one category (Anzalone & Williamson, 2000).

Hyperreactivity

Children with *hyperreactivity* tend to have a low sensory threshold and a bias toward a sympathetic nervous system reaction. (Sympathetic responses are those that indicate activation of the central nervous system, such as increased heart rate and respiration.) These children have a restricted range of optimal arousal. Their arousal level tends to be high with a narrow, rigid control of sensory input. It is important to note that the observable behavioral arousal is not always the same as physiological arousal as reflected by measures such as heart rate and respiration. Some hyperreactive children may appear to be non-responsive or under- aroused when, in fact, they are physiologically over-aroused (e.g., they may have either high levels of cortisol or elevated heart rate while appearing behaviorally inactive) (Miller & McIntosh, 1998; Porges, McCabe, & Yongue, 1982; Wilbarger & Wilbarger, 1991). In some children, this sensory overload becomes so threatening that they respond with an involuntary behavioral and physiological shutdown.

Children with hyperreactivity may overfocus their attention on detail (Kinsbourne, 1983). This phenomenon serves a gate-keeping or screening function, excluding a more generalized sensory awareness of the environment. The affective range of these children is usually limited, varying from disconnection to sensory input to negative withdrawal. An exception is the positive effect often associated with spinning of self or objects. Action in children with hyperreactivity tends to be narrowly focused, with limited elaboration and inflexibility of behavior

that often serves to control sensory input. Some of these children show little or no initiation of engagement. Others demonstrate repetitive actions; still others display surprising competence in very specific skills. Children with hyperreactivity may be very concerned about becoming disorganized and develop rigid routines, compulsions, and stereotypic patterns that help them maintain self-control. All these behaviors can be seen as adaptive at some level, as they are ways in which the children are trying to monitor and manage their registration and interpretation of sensory input so that they can maintain a level of comfort. These behaviors often interfere with interaction rather than foster it. Certain types of everyday sensation are actually painful for these children. The sound of a door slamming, unexpected laughter on a television soundtrack, or thunder can be so uncomfortable that the children will do everything they can to avoid experiencing the sensation again. Their rigid, controlling behaviors and rituals are understandable attempts to limit noxious sensory input, or at least to make the input predictable.

Hyporeactivity

Children with *hyporeactivity* tend to have a high sensory threshold; that is, they require a lot of sensory input to achieve arousal and activation. These children often have not registered novel sensory input; thus, they only have minimal information on which to base any interpretation. They do not learn from the environment because they have not noticed it. Their state of arousal is usually low or unmodulated. Attention is unfocussed or narrowly targeted to a specific type of sensory seeking to meet inner needs. Affect may be flat or uninvested, but may brighten with vestibular input. Action tends to be passive, aimless, and wandering. However, some children with hyporeactivity may have an insatiable craving for a preferred type of sensory input and may seek it out in order to be "fueled." Spinning (rotary vestibular activity) is a favorite type of stimulation. Frequently, children with bland, disconnected affects become delighted once they start to spin. It should be noted that the sensory input that is the most arousing for these children is not necessarily the most organizing.

There are two important caveats in understanding the sensory modulation profiles of children with autistic spectrum disorders. First, a child who appears flat and unavailable may not be hyporeactive. As previously mentioned, some of these children are actually physiologically hyperreactive, and their behavioral shutdown is the opposite of their internal state. During an assessment, the examiner can differentiate between these two profiles by systematically decreasing sensory input, providing organizing activity, and observing behavioral responses over time. With decreased sensory input, the child who is truly hyperreactive will become calmer and more attentive, whereas the truly hyporeactive child may become more lethargic. Second, not all sensory seeking behaviors are associated with hyporeactivity. Some children with hyperreactivity or sensory defensiveness may engage in sensory seeking as a way to modulate their reactions to sensation (i.e., discharging tension or refocusing attention to organize themselves).

Mixed Patterns

A child with autism or pervasive developmental disorder (PDD) can have a *mixed pattern* of being hypersensitive in certain modalities (often auditory or tactile) and hyposensitive in others (frequently proprioceptive or vestibular). Likewise, a child may have variability of responses within a single sensory modality (e.g., a child may be hyperreactive to high-frequency sounds and

hyporeactive to low-frequency sounds). A child can also be inconsistent over time in responding to the same stimulus. Variability among and within sensory systems is frequently linked to the child's shifting state of arousal, attention, and previous sensory experiences.

Some children have jumbling or distortion of sensory input and do not fit into the described clinical profiles. There is an erratic fluctuation in the registration of sensory input, somewhat like a volume switch being turned up and down repeatedly. For example, these children may hear only parts of words (e.g., the first part, the last part, or no consonants) or find that auditory or visual signals are intermeshed. Some adults with autism report seeing vibrations around a television set when it is on (Grandin, 1995; Williams, 1994).

Assessment of Sensory Processing

As previously described, sensory processing encompasses sensory modulation and perception. Sensory modulation precedes the more cognitive component of perception. This discussion focuses primarily on sensory modulation—the ability to register and orient to sensory stimuli. Assessment of sensory processing includes three complementary strategies: qualitative observation; parent interview; and, possibly, the administration of standardized instruments. Observation and parent interview are particularly important for screening, for enabling the practitioner to identify potential problems as well as the need for more in-depth assessment. A complete evaluation may require the skills of an occupational therapist with specialized training in sensory processing.

Qualitative Observation

Observation is the primary mode the examiner uses to identify problems and plan interventions for children who have difficulties in sensory processing. Examiners depend less on standardized instruments because they do not reliably capture individual differences in this aspect of performance since sensory processing is so variable and dependent upon a child's prior experiences. In designing qualitative observations of performance, it is helpful for the examiner to contrast behavior in structured and unstructured situations. Unstructured situations may include individual free play, gross motor exploration, and activities of daily living. Structured tasks may include observation during formal evaluations and adult-controlled situations. The examiner should observe the child's performance in relation to the sensory demands of the environment (e.g., a child's increased arousal and impulsivity would be interpreted differently in a disorganized setting versus a quiet one).

Observation of the Child. The practitioner observes the child's reactivity during engagement in a variety of tasks as well as the child's global behavioral organization. Observation focuses on the influence of sensory input and its impact on the child's self-regulation of arousal, attention, affect, and action. Since the child's reactivity to sensory input is cumulative, the examiner should observe the child's behavior over time. For instance, a child may exhibit a temper tantrum in the late morning that is a result of sensory buildup over the course of 3 hours in a childcare center. Variability in performance is expected in these children and the assessment should document the range of response. The examiner should pay special attention to the sensory conditions that support optimal performance.

The following list provides questions that an examiner can use to focus observation on relevant factors related to sensory-based behavioral organization in the child.

Arousal
- What is the child's state of alertness and how does it change in response to different sensory experiences?
- Is the child able to transition smoothly between different states of alertness?
- Is the child able to sustain levels of energy and activity that support successful task engagement?
- Does the child have a narrow or wide range of optimal arousal?
- Does the child have a range of coping strategies that enable him to modulate sensory reactivity and arousal?

Attention
- Is the child able to maintain selective focus on relevant stimuli?
- Is the child able to shift attention between two or more targets or modalities?
- Is the duration of the child's attention span comparable to other children of the same age?
- When attending to tasks, does the child seem to be using more effort than other children of the same age?
- Does the child prefer or avoid certain sensory modalities?

Affect
- Does the child have an organized range of emotional expression?
- Is there a predominant emotional tone in the child (e.g., fearfulness, anxiety, defiance, or withdrawal)?
- Is the child available for social interaction with peers and adults?
- Will the child interact socially with peers and adults?
- Does the child have a playful disposition that reflects ease in the situation and supports learning and engagement?

Action

- Is the child able to formulate goals for play behavior that are appropriate to his or her developmental skills and environmental opportunities?
- Is the child able to solve problems encountered during exploration or play with creativity, flexibility, and persistence?
- Is the child's behavior characterized by consistent approach or avoidance of specific materials or tasks?
- Does the child have adequate motor planning and coordination for age-appropriate tasks?

Observation of the Context. In addition to observing the arousal, attention, affect and action of the child as they relate to sensory modulation, the examiner also has to examine the characteristics of the physical and social environments. It is the interaction of the child and the environment that produces the sensory-related behavior. The examiner should simultaneously observe the child and the context in order to determine the goodness-of-fit between the two elements (Williamson, 1993; Zeitlin & Williamson, 1994). Without an understanding of this connection, the practitioner can make incorrect clinical assumptions. For example, a child may demonstrate defensive behaviors such as gagging, spitting up, and facial grimacing during feedings. These behaviors could be interpreted as hypersensitivity in the oral area. However, closer examination of the environmental context reveals that the caregiver is feeding the child too quickly, which elicits the aversive reaction. The difficulty is not sensory-based, but rather an indication of inappropriate feeding technique. Therefore, the context in which a child is functioning contributes to an understanding of the sensory processing of the child. The examiner

needs to appreciate the sensory attributes of the environment and how well they match the child's capacity for self-regulation and organization. A chapter appendix provides an observational form to assess the sensory-based characteristics of a school environment (Hanft & Place, 1996). The following questions can help focus observation on critical aspects of the physical and social environments.

Context

- What sensory input characterizes the physical and social environments (e.g., visual, auditory, tactile, proprioceptive, vestibular)?
- What are the sensory properties of the identified sensory systems (e.g., rate, intensity, and duration)?
- Does the environment require the child to form a response by organizing information simultaneously from different sensory systems?
- What is the quality of the physical environment in terms of temperature, lighting, noise, space, and related properties?
- What are the social characteristics of the situation (e.g., adult or peer, individualized or group, verbal or nonverbal, child- or adult-directed)?
- What are the specific environments, situations, or individuals that are particularly organizing for the child?
- Does the environment provide a routine that is reasonably predictable, consistent, and structured?

Parent Interview and Questionnaires. The parent interview supplements the examiner's observation of the child and context in providing important information regarding the child's ability to modulate sensory input in a variety of situations. The practitioner gathers information from the parents about the child's "sensory diet" (Wilbarger, 1995;

Williams & Shellenberger, 1996). The sensory diet is the profile of naturally occurring activities that occur throughout the day that provide sensory input and influence the child's regulation of arousal, attention, affect, and action. The profile provides data about the child's sensory tolerances and preferences as they are reflected in daily activity. It also identifies periods of behavioral organization and disorganization during the day and relates it to ongoing sensory experiences and environmental demands. Some situations that provide valuable insight into sensory modulation are bathing, mealtimes, disruptions in typical routines, and preferences in clothing or play. The following questions may generate a productive discussion with the parent or caregiver regarding a child's sensory processing and how it influences child and family functioning. These questions are designed to provide a starting point for an interview. They should be used selectively based on the presenting needs of the child and family.

Parent/Caregiver Observations
- What is a typical day like?
- What types of sensory activities does your child like and dislike?
- How does your child manage transitions and changes in daily routines?
- Is there a predictable time of day or type of activity when your child is most or least organized?
- Are your child's activities of daily living and self-care tasks limited by sensory or motor problems (e.g., does not tolerate textured foods, fearful during bathing)?
- Does your child have habits and routines that support daily functioning?
- How does your child respond to affectionate physical touch or handling?
- Does your child initiate exploration of novel as well as familiar situations?
- Does your child enjoy playing with other children?

The examiner can supplement semi-structured interviews with standardized questionnaires regarding the child's sensory and self-regulatory performance. The Infant Toddler Symptom Checklist (DeGangi & Poisson, 1995) addresses such areas as self regulation, attention, sleeping, eating, dressing, bathing, movement, language, vision, and emotional functioning in children between 7 and 30 months of age. The Sensorimotor History Questionnaire for Preschoolers (DeGangi & Balzer-Martin, in press) is a 51-item questionnaire that has been validated as a screening tool for 3-to 4-year-olds (see chapter appendix). This questionnaire categorizes behavior in terms of self-regulation, sensory processing of touch, sensory processing of movement, emotional maturity, and motor maturity. The Sensory Profile (Dunn, 2000 is a parent questionnaire appropriate for assessing sensory processing of children 3 to 10 years of age. Its 125 items address different sensory systems, activity level, movement, and emotional-social functioning. This questionnaire has been extensively studied with normative and clinical populations (Dunn & Brown, 1997; Dunn & Westman, 1997; Kientz & Dunn, 1997). The Short Sensory Profile (McIntosh, Miller, & Shyu, 2000) is an abbreviated version of the Sensory Profile with sound psychometric properties. The Short Sensory Profile has only 38 items in 7 subscales: tactile sensitivity, taste/smell sensitivity, under-responsive/seeks sensation, auditory filtering, visual/auditory sensitivity, low energy/weak, and movement sensitivity. The Functional Behavior Assessment for Children with Sensory Integrative Dysfunction (Cook, 1991) provides a way to use parent interviews to gather data regarding sensory-related activities of daily living.

Standardized Instruments. In addition to observation and parent interview, an examiner can use standardized instruments to assess sensory modulation. Table 1 describes the relatively few standardized tools that are available. The Test of Sensory Functions in Infants (DeGangi & Greenspan, 1989) is a diagnostic, criterion-referenced test administered by professionals trained in child development and sensory processing. It is designed to assess infants and toddlers with regulatory disorders, developmental delay, and those at risk for learning disorders. The Early Coping Inventory (Zeitlin, Williamson, & Szczepanski, 1988) assesses the coping style of children 4 to 36 months of age. The coping behaviors of the children are observed over time in a variety of situations. This psychometrically sound tool is particularly sensitive to measuring sensory-based self-regulation and adaptation. The Sensory Integration and Praxis Tests (Ayres, 1989) are a diagnostic, norm-referenced test battery designed for school-aged children who are relatively high

functioning. Sensory modulation is not directly measured on this instrument but can be inferred from qualitative observation. This battery requires extensive formal training for reliable administration and is dependent on the child having receptive language skills at the 4-year-old age level. It is typically not used for children with autistic spectrum disorders.

PRAXIS

Praxis is the ability to plan and sequence unfamiliar actions. It evolves from the interaction between the child and the environment and reflects the quality of sensory integration (Ayres,1985; Cermak, 1991). Praxis consists of three different components: (1) ideation, (2) motor planning, and (3) execution. *Ideation* is the ability to formulate a goal for action. It is the cognitive step of recognizing the multiple ways that toys, objects, or one's body can be used in play and learning

Table 1. Standardized Instruments for Assessing Sensory Processing

Name of Test	Age Range	Comments	Source
Test of Sensory Functions in Infants	4–18 months	Subtests include reactivity to tactile deep pressure and vestibular stimulation, adaptive motor functions, visual-tactile integration, and ocular-motor control.	DeGangi, G. A., & Greenspan, S. I. (1989) Western Psychological Corporation 12031 Wilshire Blvd. Los Angeles, CA 90025
Early Coping Inventory	4–36 months	The instrument addresses sensorimotor organization, reactivity, and self initiation as the child copes with daily living.	Zeitlin, S., Williamson, G. G., & Szczepanski, M., (1988) Scholastic Testing Service 480 Meyer Road Bensonville, IL 60106
Sensory Integration & Praxis Tests	4 years, 6 months– 8 years, 11 months	12 subtests assess sensory and perceptual function in visual perceptual, visual, vestibular and postural, and somatosensory domains.	Ayres, A. J. (1989) Western Psychological Services 12031 Wilshire Blvd. Los Angeles, CA 90025

situations. For example, the child appreciates that there are a number of ways to play with a toy truck. *Motor planning* involves figuring out how to get one's body to carry out the goal for action. This step of planning and sequencing of motor tasks is based on the child's body scheme; that is, an internal sensory awareness of body parts, how they fit together, and how they move through space. Motor planning is active problem solving and reflects an inner, sensory awareness of one's physical self. *Execution* is the actual performance of the planned action. It involves gross and fine motor coordination to accomplish the task.

Children with dyspraxia may have difficulty with any one or a combination of these three components. A lack of ideation is noted if the child is unable to formulate new goals specific to situational demands. The child does not have an idea of what to do or is rigid or inflexible in goal formulation. With a deficit in motor planning, the child knows the purpose of the object or task but cannot organize motor patterns to interact effectively with the environment or solve the problem. Children may tend to be inactive or play in a limited, perseverative pattern (e.g., lining up toys). Children with autistic spectrum disorders tend to have a primary deficit in ideation and a secondary one in motor planning. Impairment in execution is relatively less common in children with autism.

Children with dyspraxia are typically clumsy with a poor body scheme. They do not know where their body is in space and have difficulty judging their relationship to objects and people. As a result, they are accident-prone and tend to stumble, bump into furniture or others, and break toys. They are generally poor in athletics. Since these children have difficulty in sequencing daily activities, they tend to be disorganized and disheveled looking. Due to their inflexibility

in activity, they may perseverate and tend to prefer the familiar. Self-esteem is often poor as a result of frustration and repeated failure. They may be judged at times as manipulative and controlling. These behaviors reflect the child's use of language to compensate for the dyspraxia (e.g., distracting and redirecting attention away from the motor disorder). Problems in sequencing can include language, in which case organizational and educational deficits are generally present.

Observation of Praxis

The major means of assessing praxis is through observation of the child during novel gross and fine motor tasks. It is often observed that the child uses visual monitoring of movements to accomplish the skill. The examiner must provide a range of activities that require the control of large muscles as well as fine manipulation. Since children with dyspraxia often rely on familiar, over-learned activities, it is essential that any observation of praxis provide unexpected, flexible, and novel situations that challenge the child's ability to problem solve motor tasks. Observation focuses on *how* the child plans and sequences these tasks. The examiner should screen for the following behaviors during several observation periods.

Dyspraxia Indicators
- Inflexibility—perseverates on one aspect of the task and has difficulty in making transitions
- Lack of sensorimotor exploration
- Limited complexity of play
- Restricted problem solving of new tasks
- Low frustration tolerance
- Presence of "crash" solutions to terminate demanding activities (e.g., knocking down or throwing)

- Lack of organization in performance of activities
- Clothes in disarray and/or unfastened
- Poor quality of fine motor skills
- Poor temporal awareness and sequencing of daily living tasks
- Avoidance of group activities and peer play
- Preference for adult one-to-one interaction

A diagnosis of dyspraxia is not achieved with one observation but evolves over time. The examiner has to observe the child in numerous settings under diverse conditions to determine the nature of the problem. Is the breakdown in task engagement due to a sensory-motor deficit or other factors such as distractibility or impulsivity? Is this a sensory processing/practice deficit or primarily an issue of motor strength and coordination? Is the difficulty due to ideation, motor planning, and/or execution?

Assessment of Praxis with Standardized Instruments

As with sensory processing, there are few standardized instruments that are available for screening and assessment of praxis (see Table 2). Observation and clinical judgment are the most important factors in determining when praxis contributes to a performance deficit. For screening purposes, the Miller Assessment of Preschoolers (Miller, 1982) is a norm-referenced test that provides a few items directly addressing a child's motor planning. More formal standardized instruments for older children are the Sensory Integration and Praxis Tests (Ayres, 1989). This battery has specific tests that measure different components of praxis (e.g., postural praxis, sequencing praxis, oral praxis, constructional praxis, praxis on verbal command). As noted previously, this test is complex and requires certification through a formal training program.

MOTOR PERFORMANCE

Motor performance in the young child involves four interdependent components: neuromotor processes, and gross motor, fine motor, and oral-motor development. *Neuromotor processes* involve the underlying musculoskeletal elements that support movement, such as muscle tone and joint range of motion. *Gross motor* function incorporates those movements, postures, and skills of the large

Table 2. Standardized Instruments for Assessing Praxis

Name of Test	Age Range	Comments	Source
Miller Assessment of Preschoolers	2 years, 9 months – 5 years, 8 months	Developmental screening test that includes praxis items (imitation of postures and solving a maze).	Miller, L. J. (1982) Psychological Corporation 555 Academic Court San Antonio, TX 78204
Sensory Integration & Praxis Tests	4 years, 6 months – 8 years, 11 months	12 subtests assess sensory and perceptual function in visual perceptual, visual, vestibular and postural, and somatosensory domains.	Ayres, (1989) Western Psychological Services 12031 Wilshire Blvd. Los Angeles, CA 90025

muscles, whereas *fine motor* function is dependent on the small muscles of the arms and hands. *Oral-motor* function is based upon actions of the facial musculature for speech and eating. Table 3 provides further descriptions of each of these four components of motor performance.

There is more to assessment of motor performance than establishing the presence or absence of milestones and determining a

Table 3. The Four Components of Motor Performance

Component	Description
Neuromotor Processes	
Muscle tone	Muscle tension, ranging from hyper-to hypotonic, for maintaining posture and position of arms/legs for specific tasks
Range of motion	Extent of movement of each body joint, particularly arms, legs, trunk, and head
Postural stability and mobility	Holding positions and moving body parts to accomplish task (e.g., stabilize trunk and shoulders to squeeze toy with hands)
Symmetry	Use of both sides of the body in simultaneous or reciprocal action appropriate to the task at hand
Quality of movement	Degree to which child's actions are fluid and coordinated
Gross Motor Function	
Physical postures	Assuming and changing basic body positions for the task at hand (e.g., prone, supine, 4-point, sit, kneel, stand)
Physical skills	Actions dependent on large muscle movement (e.g., jumping, hopping, throwing a ball)
Functional mobility	Patterns of locomotion to move self from one point to another (e.g., rolling, crawling, creeping, walking, running)
Fine Motor Function	
Reach, grasp, and manipulation	Use of the arm/hand to secure, hold, and handle objects, toys, and utensils
Hand preference and bilateral coordination	Using two hands together, for stability and skilled manipulation (e.g., manipulatory exploration, using a fork, buttoning, writing with a pencil)
Visual-motor coordination	Coordination of visual perceptual information with action to guide the hand in skilled tasks
Oral-Motor Function	
Actions of the tongue, lips, cheeks	Coordination of sucking, swallowing, breathing, chewing, biting for eating, speaking, and self-exploratory play

developmental age. The *quality* of the child's motor performance is also a concern (e.g., a child's reach can be smooth and direct or tremulous). Many standardized tests provide a quantitative measure of the child's performance but fail to capture this qualitative aspect. It is often necessary for the practitioner to supplement findings with a clinical description of observations. Subtle differences in motor performance are important to note since they are often associated with early signs of behavioral and learning difficulties (e.g., low muscle tone and poor balance reactions are often seen in children who later exhibit learning or language disabilities).

A related issue is the need to evaluate the child's performance in terms of mobility and stability rather than as a compilation of motor skills. A child must be able to move part of the body with the active support of the rest of the body in order to develop gross and fine motor skills such as crawling, coloring, or buttoning. For example, in order to crawl, a child must move one hand and knee while the other hand and knee support the body weight. In the fine motor arena, this interplay between stability and mobility is equally important. For example, in order to color with a crayon, a child must be able to sit up and keep the head and shoulder steady (stability) while moving the wrist and fingers (mobility). This issue is critical since many children have inadequate stability to support functional movements (e.g., the preschool child who slouches in the chair during tabletop activities). Through the assessment, the examiner determines the adequacy of the child's mobility and stability functions during different motor tasks. The examiner always assesses motor performance in context and how the child organizes posture and movement to meet changing environmental demands.

Assessment of Neuromotor Processes

Assessment of neuromotor processes in young children focuses on muscle tone, range of motion, postural stability and mobility, symmetry, and quality of movement (DeMyer,1994; Piper & Darrah, 1994). These underlying neuromotor processes influence how a child assumes and maintains the positions needed to participate in play, self-help, and learning activities. Occupational and physical therapists have expertise in evaluating neuromotor processes using clinical observation and criterion-referenced scales. Other professionals can screen children to determine the need for an in-depth assessment of neuromotor functions. The following questions can guide the screening. A "yes" response to a number of these questions indicates the need for a comprehensive assessment. Concern is greatest if these risk indicators interfere with the child's acquisition of developmental skills.

Neuromotor Deficit Indicators

- Compared to peers, does the child have problems maintaining his or her posture during activity? Subtle examples of possible delays in neuromotor processes include leaning on the table for support, holding onto the wall to kick a ball, or lying on the floor instead of sitting during circle time.
- Compared to peers, is the child's muscle tone in the trunk and limbs too stiff or loose, resulting in restricted or floppy movement?
- Under the age of 3 years, does the child use one hand exclusively in play and self-help tasks? This may indicate a neglect of one body side or unusual muscle tone during a period when children are developing bilateral skills.

- Does the child fatigue easily and demonstrate poor endurance, especially during activities and gross motor play?

Table 4 lists criterion-referenced instruments useful for in-depth assessment of neuromotor processes. These tools require training to achieve reliability in administration and scoring. They are helpful for the early identification of emerging motor problems and soft neurological signs before the establishment of clear motor deficits or a definitive medical diagnosis. Understanding the

neuromotor processes helps one to appreciate the reasons for a developmental delay or functional limitation in motor performance.

Assessment of Gross Motor Function

Gross motor skills affect how children coordinate their body positions, move fluidly from one location to another, and interact with people and objects. Assessment of gross motor skills focuses primarily on physical posture and skills as well as functional mobility and stability (Alexander, Boehm &

Table 4. Measures of Neuromotor Processes

Name of Test	Age Range	Comments	Source
Test of Infant Motor Performance	32 weeks gestation– 4 months	Assesses the influence of postural control on head, trunk, arm, and leg movements	Campbell, S., Osten, E., Kolobe, T. & Fisher, A. (1993). Development of the Test of Infant Motor Performance. In C. Granger, G. Gresham (Eds.), *New developments in functional Assessment.* Philadelphia: W. B. Saunders
Alberta Infant Motor Scale	0–18 months	Observational and naturalistic assessment of ability within prone, supine, sitting, and standing positions	Piper, M., Darrah, J. (1994). *Motor assessment of the developing infant.* Philadelphia: W. B. Saunders.
Movement Assessment of Infants	0–12 months	Assesses muscle tone, reflexes, automatic reactions, and voluntary movement	Infant Movement Research PO Box 4631 Rolling Bay, WA
The Infanib	0–18 months	Consists of 20 items in 5 categories: spasticity, head and trunk, vestibular function, legs, French angles	Therapy Skill Builders 555 Academic Court San Antonio, TX 78204-2498
DeGangi-Berk Test of Sensory Integration	3–5 years	Measures three vestibular-based functions: postural control, bilateral motor integration and reflex integration	Western Psychological Services 12031 Wilshire Blvd. Los Angeles, CA 90025

Cupps, 1993; Bly, 1994). Table 5 identifies measures of gross motor function commonly used by occupational and physical therapists. There also are global developmental assessments that include major sections addressing gross motor development that are used by interdisciplinary professionals, but which are not referenced in this discussion.

Assessment of Fine Motor Function

Fine motor skills affect how children use their eyes and hands to manipulate objects, tools, and toys to engage in self-help and play activities, such as eating with a spoon, buttoning clothing, turning the pages of a book, and combing a doll's hair. Fine visual-motor skill

Table 5. Measures of Gross Motor Function

Name of Test	Age Range	Comments	Source
Gross Motor Function Measure	General	Assessment of motor function in five dimensions: lying/rolling; sitting; crawling/kneeling; standing; walking, running, jumping	Dianne Russell Dept. of Clinical Epidemiology & Biostatistics, Bldg. 74 Chedoke Campus McMaster University of Hamilton, Ontario Canada LSN 325
Peabody Developmental Motor Scales (PDMS) (revision underway)	0-83 months	Two scales measure gross motor skills (reflexes, balance, non-locomotor, locomotor, receipt/ propulsion of objects) and fine motor skills (grasping, hand use, eye-hand coordination and, manual dexterity)	DLM Teaching Resources One DLM Park Allen, TX 75002
Bruininks-Oseretsky Test of Motor Proficiency (BOTMP)	4 years, 6 months– 14 years, 6 months	Fine, gross, and visual-motor sections yield information in standard scores and age equivalents	American Guidance Service Circle Pines, MN 55014
Functional Independence measure for Children (WEEFIM)	6 months– 7 years	Measures function in order to determine extent of care needed in: self-care, sphincter management, mobility, locomotion, communication, social cognition	Center for Functional Research U.B. Foundation Activities 82 Farber Hall SUNY – South Campus Buffalo, NY 14214
Pediatric Evaluation of Disability Inventory (PEDI)	6 months– 7.5 years	Assesses functional abilities and performance in three domains: self-care, mobility, and social function	PEDI Research Group Dept. of Rehab Medicine New England Medical Center #75 K/R750 Washington St. Boston, MA 02111
School Function Assessment (SFA)	Grades K-6	Measures a student's performance of functional tasks (including eating, mobility, tool use and manipulation) that support participation in an elementary school program	Therapy Skill Builders 555 Academic Court San Antonio, TX 78204

Table 6. Measures of Fine Motor Function

Name of Test	Age Range	Comments	Source
Developmental Test of Visual Motor Integration (revised, 1997)	2 years, 9 months– 19 years, 8 months	Looks at integration of visual perception and motor control; yields age equivalents, percentile ranking, and standard scores	Modern Curriculum Press 13900 Prospect Road Cleveland, OH 44136
Test of Visual Motor Skills (1986)	2–13 years	Measures ability to copy 26 different designs. Yields motor ages, standard scores, percentiles, and stanine scores	Children's Hospital of San Francisco Publications Dept. OPR-110 PO Box 3805 San Francisco, CA 94119
Developmental Test of Visual Perception (2nd ed.)	4–10 years	Subtests measure visual perceptual ability with two conditions: motor-reduced or motor-enhanced. Provides age equivalents, percentiles, and composite quotients	Western Psychological Services 12031 Wilshire Blvd. Los Angeles, CA 90025

Note: See also the following tests, as reviewed in the previous section on assessing fine motor function: Peabody Developmental Motor Scales (PDMS), Bruininks-Oseretsky Test of Motor Proficiency (BOTMP), Functional Independence Measure for Children (WEEFIM), Pediatric Evaluation of Disability Inventory (PEDI), and School Function Assessment (SFA).

is also a factor in manual communication through gestures, sign language, drawing, and painting. Assessment of fine motor skills focuses particularly on reach, grasp, hand preference, bilateral coordination, manipulation, and visual-motor control (Henderson & Pehoski, 1995).

Table 6 identifies measures of fine motor function commonly used by occupational therapists and educators. In addition to these, there also are comprehensive developmental assessments that include major sections on fine motor development.

Assessment of Oral-Motor Function

Oral motor skills include the coordination of sucking, swallowing, breathing, chewing, and articulation. Assessment of oral motor development in young children focuses on the sensory and motor actions of the tongue, lips, cheeks, and respiratory system (Morris & Klein, 1987; Wolf & Glass, 1992; Oetter, Richter & Frick, 1988). Assessment of oral motor functions must be completed by professionals with specific training in this area, such as an occupational therapist or speech/language pathologist. Table 7 identifies measures of oral motor functional development commonly used by these practitioners. Other professionals can screen for the need for a comprehensive assessment by observing the child and answering the following questions. A "yes" response to more than one question indicates cause for a more comprehensive assessment.

Oral-Motor Assessment Indicators

- Compared to same-age peers, does the child have problems with speech or eating?
- Is there consistent or excessive drooling present, given the child's developmental age?
- When eating, does the child reject food based on texture or demand a bland or specific diet?
- Compared to same-age peers, does the child display excessive mouthing of toys, objects, clothing or furnishings?
- Are there significant disturbances in the parent/infant bond concerning the issue of feeding?

SUMMARY

In summary, this chapter addressed screening and assessment related to sensory processing, praxis, and motor performance. Qualitative observation and parental interviews were emphasized due to their importance in understanding the nature of the child's sensorimotor functioning. A dynamic process-oriented approach to assessment enables the clinician to capture subtle individual differences in performance. A primary concern is assessing the child within the context of environmental challenges and in the performance of functional tasks. The critical outcome of sensory and motor processes is to support functional participation in all aspects of daily life and not merely the achievement of developmental milestones. ∎

Table 7. Measures of Oral-Motor Function

Name of Test	Age Range	Comments	Source
Clinical Feeding Evaluation of Infants	0-3 years	Clinical observations of the state of affect; motor control; oral-motor structures; suck, swallow, breathe; physiological control	Wolf, L., & Glass, R. (1992). *Feeding and swallowing disorders in infancy.* San Antonio. TX: Therapy Skill Builders
Pre-feeding skills	Early years	Nonstandardized qualitative assessment of structural and functional oral motor coordination and skills in the context of feeding	Morris. S., & Klein, M. (1987). *Pre-feeding skills.* San Antonio, AZ: Therapy Skill Builders
Neonatal oral-motor assessment scale	Neonate	Examines tongue and jaw movements during both nutritive and non-nutritive sucking	Braun, M. & Palmer, M. (1985). A pilot study of oral motor dysfunction in "at-risk" infants. *Physical and Occupational Therapy in Pediatrics, 5,* 13-25.

Note: Also see the following tests reviewed in the section on assessing gross motor functions: Functional Independence Measure for Children (WEEFIM), Pediatric Evaluation of Disability Inventory (PEDI), and School Function Assessment (SFA)

REFERENCES

Alexander, R., Boehme, R., & Cupps, B. (1993). *Normal development of functional motor skills: The first year of life.* San Antonio, TX: Therapy Skill Builders.

Als, H. (1986). A synactive model of neonatal behavioral organization: Framework for the assessment of neurobehavioral development in the premature infant and for support of infants and parents in the neonatal intensive care environment. *Physical & Occupational Therapy in Pediatrics, 6,* 3-53.

Anzalone, M. E., & Williamson, G. G. (2000). Sensory processing and motor performance in autistic spectrum disorders. In A. Wetherby & B. Prizant (Eds.), *Communication and language issues in autism and pervasive developmental disabilities: A transactional developmental perspective.* Baltimore, MD: Paul H. Brookes.

Ayres, A. J. (1972). *Sensory integration and learning disabilities.* Los Angeles: Western Psychological Services.

Ayres, A. J. (1985). *Developmental dyspraxia and adult onset apraxia.* Torrance, CA: Sensory Integration International.

Ayres, A. J., 1989. *Sensory integration and praxis tests.* Los Angeles, CA: Western Psychological Corporation.

Bly, L. (1994). *Motor skills acquisition in the first year.* San Antonio, AZ: Therapy Skill Builders.

Braun, M., & Palmer, M. (1985). A pilot study of oral motor dysfunction in "at risk" infants. *Physical and Occupational Therapy in Pediatrics, 5,* 13-25,

Campbell, S., Osten, E., Kolobe, T. & Fisher, A. (1993). Development of the Test of Infant Motor Performance. In C. Granger, G. Gresham (Eds.), *New Developments in Functional Assessment.* Philadelphia: W. B. Saunders.

Cermak, S. A. (1991). Somatodyspraxia. In A.G. Fisher, E.A. Murray & A. C. Bundy (Eds.*), Sensory integration: Theory and practice* (pp. 137-171). Philadelphia: F. A. Davis.

Cook, D. (1991). The assessment process. In W. Dunn (Ed.), *Pediatric service delivery* (pp. 35-74). Thorofare, NJ: Slack.

Coster, W. J. (1998). Occupation-centered assessment of children. *American Journal of Occupational Therapy, 52,* 337-344.

DeGangi, G. A., & Balzer-Martin, L. A. (in press). The sensorimotor history questionnaire for preschoolers. *Journal of Developmental and Learning Disorders, 2.*

DeGangi, G. A., & Greenspan, S. I. (1989). *Test of sensory functions in infants.* Los Angeles: Western Psychological Services.

DeGangi, G. A., & Poisson, S. (1995). *Infant and toddler symptom checklist.* Tucson, AZ: Therapy Skill Builders.

DeMyer, W. E. (1994*). Technique of the neurologic examination: A programmed text* (4th ed.). New York: McGraw Hill.

Dunn, W. (2000). *The sensory profile examiner's manual.* San Antonio, TX: Psychological Corporation.

Dunn, W., & Brown, C. (1997). Factor analysis on the sensory profile from a national sample of children without disabilities. *American Journal of Occupational Therapy, 51,* 490-495.

Dunn, W. & Westman, (1997). The sensory profile: The performance of a national sample of children without disabilities. *American Journal of Occupational Therapy, 51,* 25-34.

Fisher, A.G., Murray, E. A., & Bundy, A. C. (Eds.) (1991). *Sensory integration: Theory and practice.* Philadelphia: F.A. Davis Co.

Grandin, T. (1995). *Thinking in pictures.* New York: Doubleday.

Greenspan, S. I., & Meisels, S. J. (1996). Toward a new vision for the developmental assessment of infants and young children. In S. J. Meisels & E. Fenichel (Eds.), *New visions for the developmental assessment of infants and young children* (pp. 11-26). Washington, D.C.: Zero-To-Three.

Hanft, B. E. & Place, P. A. (1996). *The consulting therapist: A guide for OTs and PTs in schools.* San Antonio: Therapy Skill Builders.

Henderson, A., & Pehoski, C. (1995). *Hand function in the child: Foundations for remediation.* St. Louis, MO: Mosby.

Kientz, M. A., & Dunn, W. (1997). A comparison of the performance of children with and without autism on the sensory profile. *American Journal of Occupational Therapy, 51,* 530-537.

Kinsboume, M. (1983). Toward a model of attention deficit disorder. In M. Perlmutter (Ed.), *The Minnesota Symposium on Child Psychology, Vol. 16: Development and policy concerning children with special needs.* Hillsdale, NJ: Erlbaum.

Lezak, M. D. (1995). *Neuropschological assessment* (3rd ed.). New York: Oxford University Press.

McIntosh, D. N., Miller, L. J., & Shyu, V. (2000). Development and validation of the Short Sensory Profile. In W. Dunn (Ed.), *The sensory profile examiner's manual.* San Antonio, TX: Psychological Corporation.

Miller, L. J. (1988). *Miller assessment of preschoolers.* San Antonio, TX: Psychological Corporation.

Miller, L. J., & McIntosh, D. N. (1998). The diagnosis, treatment and etiology of sensory modulation disorder. *American Occupational Therapy Association Sensory Integration Special Interest Section Quarterly, 21,* 1-3.

Morris, S., & Klein, M. (1987). *Pre-feeding skills.* San Antonio, TX: Therapy Skill Builders.

Oetter, P., Richter, E., & Frick, S. (1988). *M.O.R.E.: Integrating the mouth with sensory and postural functions.* Oak Park Heights, MN: Professional Developmental Programs.

Piper, M., & Darrah J. (1994). *Motor assessment of the developing infant.* Philadelphia: W.B. Saunders.

Porges, S. W., McCabe, P. M., & Yongue, B. G. (1982). Respiratory-heart rate interactions: Psychophysiological implications for pathophysiology and behavior. In J. Cacioppo, & R. Petty (Eds.), *Perspectives in cardiovascular psychophysiology* (pp. 223-264). New York: Guilford Press.

Schaaf, R. C., & Anzalone, M. E. (in press). Sensory integration with high risk infants and young children. In E. Blanche, S. Smith-Roley, & R. Schaaf (Eds.), *Sensory integration and developmental disabilities.* San Antonio, TX: Therapy Skill Builders.

Schneck, C. M. (1996). Visual Perception. In J. Case-Smith, A. S. Allen, & P. N. Pratt (Eds.), *Occupational therapy for children* (3rd ed.). St. Louis, MO: Mosby.

Wetherby, A., & Prizant, B. (Eds.) (2000). *Communication and language issues in autism and pervasive developmental disabilities: A transactional developmental perspective.* Baltimore, MD: Paul H. Brookes.

Wilbarger, P. (1995). The sensory diet: Activity programs based on sensory processing theory. *American Occupational Therapy Association Sensory-Integration Special Interest Section Quarterly, 18(2),* 1-4.

Wilbarger, P., & Wilbarger, J. L. (1991). *Sensory defensiveness in children aged 2-12: An intervention guide for parents and other caretakers.* Santa Barbara, CA: Avanti Education Programs.

Williams, D. (1994). *Somebody somewhere.* New York: Times Books.

Williams, M. S., & Shellenberger, S. (1996). *How does your engine run?: A leaders' guide to the Alert program for self-regulation.* Albuquerque, NM: Therapy Works.

Williamson, G. G., & Anzalone, M. E., (1997). Sensory integration: A key component of the evaluation and treatment of young children with severe difficulties in relating and communicating. *Zero-To-Three, 17,* 29-36.

Williamson, G.G. (1993). Coping frame of reference. In P. Kramer & J. Hinojosa (Eds.). *Frames of reference for pediatric occupational therapy.* Baltimore, MD: Williams and Wilkins.

Wolf, L., & Glass, R. (1992). *Feeding and swallowing disorders in infancy.* San Antonio, TX: Therapy Skill Builders.

Zeitlin, S. & Williamson, G.G., Szczepanski, M. (1988). *Early coping inventory.* Bensenville, IL: Scholastic Testing Service.

Zeitlin, S., & Williamson, G. G. (1994). *Coping in young children: Early intervention practices to enhance adaptive behavior and resilience.* Baltimore: Paul H. Brookes.

Appendix A

OBSERVATIONAL FORM FOR ASSESSING THE
SENSORY-BASED CHARACTERISTICS OF A SCHOOL ENVIRONMENT

School Observation: Environment*

Student observed:_____ Age:_____ Date: _____

Activity:_____ Environment observed: _____

The following questions help identify environmental factors that facilitate or interfere with learning. Observe all relevant spaces of the student's environment, such as classrooms, gym, cafeteria, bathrooms, playground, and hallways.

Observation of the General Environment

Room Arrangement	Observations
1. Room size and shape adequate for task?	Yes No
2. Furniture/equipment arrangement?	Diagram room on blank sheet
3. Varied space available?	Intimate 6″–18″ Personal 1½′ – 4′ Social 4′–12′
4. Space for personal belongings?	Describe:
5. Active and quiet spots?	Yes No

Traffic Patterns	
1. Clearly defined pathways?	Yes No
2. All areas and materials accessible?	Yes No
3. Any architectural barriers?	Yes No
4. Time and distance student covers:	Describe:

Routines	
1. Adequate structured/unstructured time?	Yes No
2. Toileting, drinks, snack?	As needed Scheduled

*Materials created by Barbara Hanft and Patricia Place.

145

Observation of the Sensory Environment

Auditory	Observations
1. Sounds in and out of observed setting?	Describe:
2. Unique acoustical features?	Carpet Cinder block Other

Visual	
1. Adequate light?	Yes No Source: _____ Natural _____ Fixtures
2. How is color used?	Highlight Guide Background Other:
3. Intense glare on materials?	Yes No
4. Unique visual features?	Describe:

Tactile/Kinesthetic	
1. Flooring	Tile _____ % Carpet _____ % Other _____ %
2. Use of textures in furniture/materials?	Describe:
3. Light touch from others?	Describe:
4. Unique tactile features?	Describe:

Movement	
1. What movement/breaks are permitted?	Describe:
2. Who moves through this space and how efficiently?	Describe:
3. Unique movement features?	Describe:

Observation of a Particular Learning Environment

Intent of Space	Observations
1. What is this space intended to facilitate?	Learning, resting, playing? Fine motor, gross motor, language, academic, social, self-help? Independent, cooperative? Intent unclear?
2. Clear boundaries?	Yes No
3. Enough space?	Yes No
4. Necessary materials easily accessible?	Yes No
5. Materials/furniture enhance performance?	Yes No
6. Time student is seated and/or in same position?	Time: _____ Seated _____ Same position

Recommendations for improving student performance:

Appendix B

SENSORIMOTOR HISTORY QUESTIONNAIRE FOR PRESCHOOLERS[1]

Sensorimotor History Questionnaire for Preschoolers[1]

Name of Child: _____

Gender: ❑ M ❑ F

Date Completed: _____

Birthdate: _____Age:_____

Completed By: _____

DIRECTIONS: The questionnaire may be administered by a parent, teacher, or therapist familiar with the child's functioning in the areas measured by this questionnaire. The questionnaire has been validated on 3- and 4-year-olds but may be administered to 5-year-olds as well. Sum the scores for each subscale, then enter the scores in the boxes at the bottom of the page. Children showing suspect performance in any one or more areas involving sensory processing or motor planning should be referred to an occupation therapist for further testing of sensory integration and motor skills. Children showing suspect performance in the general behaviors and emotional areas should be referred to a clinical psychologist or early intervention professional familiar with testing and treating problems in these areas.

Subscale	Normal	At-Risk
A. Self-Regulation: • Activity level and attention	0-2	3-6
B. Sensory Processing of Touch	0-2	3-9
C. Sensory Processing of Movement: • Underreactivity • Overreactivity	0-2 0	3-4 1-7
D. Emotional Maturity	0-2	3-10
E. Motor Maturity: • Motor planning and coordination	0-3	4-15

A. Self-Regulation (Activity Level and Attention)

Is your child: YES (1)   NO (0)
  1. Frequently irritable?   YES (1)   NO (0)
  2. Frequently clingy?   YES (1)   NO (0)
  3. Overly active and hard to calm down?   YES (1)   NO (0)
  4. Overly excited by sights, sounds, etc.?   YES (1)   NO (0)
  5. Distracted by sights and sounds?   YES (1)   NO (0)
  6. Restless and fidgety during times when quiet
      concentration is required?   YES (1)   NO (0)

                                                            TOTAL:_____

B. Sensory Processing of Touch

Does your child:
  1. Dislike being bathed or having his
      hands, face, or hair washed?   YES (1)   NO (0)
  2. Complain that other people "bump" into him?   YES (1)   NO (0)
  3. Dislike textured foods (chewy, crunchy)
      and avoid new food textures?   YES (1)   NO (0)
  4. Prefer certain clothing and complain about
      tags in clothing or that some clothes are
      too tight or itchy?   YES (1)   NO (0)
  5. Frequently bump or push other children
      and may play too rough?   YES (1)   NO (0)
  6. Prefer as little clothing as possible or
      prefer long sleeves and pants, even in
      warm weather?   YES (1)   NO (0)
  7. Seem excessively ticklish?   YES (1)   NO (0)
  8. **Overreact** or **underreact** to physically
      painful experiences? (Circle which one)   YES (1)   NO (0)
  9. Tend to withdraw from a group or
      seem irritable in close quarters?   YES (1)   NO (0)

                                                            TOTAL:_____

C. Sensory Processing of Movement

The first part of this section pertains to children who are underreactive to movement stimulation, the second part to children who are very sensitive or intolerant of movement in space.
Does your child:
  1. Prefer fast-moving carnival or playground
      rides or spinning equipment, but does not
      become dizzy or seems less dizzy than others?   YES (1)   NO (0)
  2. Frequently ride on the merry-go-round
      where others run around to keep the
      platform turning?   YES (1)   NO (0)

3. Especially like movement experiences at
    home such as bouncing on furniture,
    using a rocking chair, or being turned
    in a swivel chair?   YES (1)   NO (0)
4. Enjoy getting into an upside-down position?   YES (1)   NO (0)

                                                    TOTAL:_____

Does your child:
1. Tend to avoid swings or slides or use
    them with hesitation?   YES (1)   NO (0)
2. Seem afraid to let his feet leave the ground
    (getting up on a chair, jumping games) and
    prefer to be very close to the ground in play? YES (1)   NO (0)
3. Fall down often and have difficulty with
    balance (e.g., when climbing stairs)   YES (1)   NO (0)
4. Fearful of heights or climbing?   YES (1)   NO (0)
5. Enjoy movement that she initiates but does
    not like to be moved by others, particularly
    if the movement is unexpected?   YES (1)   NO (0)
6. Dislike trying new movement activities
    or has difficulty learning them?   YES (1)   NO (0)
7. Tend to get motion sickness in a car,
    airplane, or elevator?   YES (1)   NO (0)

                                                    TOTAL:_____

D. Emotional Maturity
Does your child:
1. Play pretend games with dolls, cars, etc.,
    with sequences or plots to the game (e.g., the
    doll gets up, gets dressed, eats breakfast)?   YES (0)   NO (1)
2. Engage you in games that he makes up
    or wants to play?   YES (0)   NO (1)
3. Seek you out for affection and play pretend
    games during which she will take care of a doll? YES (0)   NO (1)
4. Play pretend games that involve assertiveness,
    exploration, or aggression (car races, soldiers
    fighting, or a trip to grandma's house)?   YES (0)   NO (1)
5. Understand rules such as to wait for you to
    say it is safe to cross the street?   YES (0)   NO (1)
6. Understand that there are consequences to his
    behavior (if he behaves nicely, you are pleased;
    if naughty, he will be punished)?   YES (0)   NO (1)

7. Have difficulty getting over a temper
   tantrum (take longer than 10 minutes)?   YES (1)   NO (0)
8. Have difficulty in playing with peers?   YES (1)   NO (0)
9. Dislike changes in routine and prefer things
   to stay the same everyday?   YES (1)   NO (0)
10. Seem unaware of dangers and take too
    many risks, often getting hurt?   YES (1)   NO (0)

TOTAL:_____

E. Motor Maturity (Motor Planning and Coordination)
Does your child:
1. Use two hands for tasks that require two
   hands, such as holding down the paper while
   drawing or holding the cup while pouring?   YES (0)   NO (1)
2. Have difficulty getting dressed?   YES (1)   NO (0)
3. Avoid trying new play activities and prefer
   to play games that she is confident at?   YES (1)   NO (0)
4. Have difficulty using his hands in manipulating
   toys and managing fasteners
   (stringing beads, buttons, snaps)?   YES (1)   NO (0)
5. Seem clumsy and bump into things easily?   YES (1)   NO (0)
6. Have trouble catching a ball with two hands?   YES (1)   NO (0)
7. Have difficulty with large muscle activities
   such as riding a tricycle or jumping on two feet? YES (1)   NO (0)
8. Sit with a slouch or partly on and off the chair?   YES (1)   NO (0)
9. Have difficulty sitting still in a chair and seem
   to move very quickly (runs instead of walks)?   YES (1)   NO (0)
10. Feel "loose" or "floppy" when you lift him up
    or move his limbs to help him get dressed?   YES (1)   NO (0)
11. Have difficulty turning knobs or handles
    that require some pressure?   YES (1)   NO (0)
12. Have a loose grasp on objects such as a
    pencil, scissors, or things that she is carrying? YES (1)   NO (0)
13. Have a rather tight, tense grasp on objects?   YES (1)   NO (0)
14. Spontaneously choose to do activities
    involving use of "tools," such as crayons,
    markers, or scissors?   YES (0)   NO (1)
15. Eat in a sloppy manner?   YES (1)   NO (0)

TOTAL:_____

[1] Reprinted with permission from DeGangi, G. A., & Balzer-Martin, L. A. (in press). The sensorimotor
history questionnaire for preschoolers. *Journal of Developmental and Learning Disorders, 2.*

—◀ 9 ▶—

Screening, Evaluating, and Assessing Children with Sensorimotor Concerns and Linking Findings to Intervention Planning: Strategies for Pediatric Occupational and Physical Therapists

Toby M. Long, Ph.D., P.T., and Kirsten M. Sippel, M.P.P., P.T.

As noted in Chapter 8 (this volume) by Williamson, Anzalone, and Hanft, pediatric physical therapists and occupational therapists have traditionally measured the skills of young children and provided intervention to them in three areas of development: sensory processing, praxis, and motor performance, each of which contain specific elements (see Table 1).

In the past, therapists have used evaluation, assessment, or screening findings to

Table 1. Elements of Sensorimotor Development

Areas	Elements
Sensory processing	Modulation
	Perception
	Discrimination
Praxis	Ideation
	Motor planning
	Execution
Motor performance	Neuromotor
	Fine motor
	Gross motor
	Oral motor

make decisions regarding the status of a child and to develop intervention plans. Often these decisions were made independently of findings from other professionals or without parental input. However, during the last 20 years, there have been significant changes in how therapists view their role in the measurement and intervention process. Three factors have influenced these changes.

First, public policy and legislative initiatives have required therapists and other professionals to reassess basic methods of collecting developmental or behavioral information. The passage of Part B (PL 94-142) of the Individuals with Disabilities Education Act (IDEA) in 1975 required therapists working in educational systems to serve children within an educational framework, work in a multidisciplinary team, and recognize the inter-relatedness of motor skills to other areas of development. In 1986, Part H[1] of IDEA (PL 99-457) expanded services to

---

[1]The 1997 Reauthorization of IDEA realigned the Act: Part H is now called Part C. In further discussion in this chapter, the early intervention component of IDEA is referred to as Part C.

infants and young children and mandated that services be delivered in a family-centered manner. Therapists broadened their systems and strategies of gathering information about a child's performance and providing services to include collaboration with the family and other team members. Contemporary evaluation and assessment strategies, as well as intervention, how support collaboration among team members and the family, integration of findings across domains and environments, and the reporting of findings in a family-centered, culturally sensitive manner.

Second, research during the last 20 years has clearly indicated that the areas of development typically measured in a young child (e.g., behavior, motor, language, and cognition) are interdependent (Greenspan & Meisels, 1993). Biological, cultural, and environmental variables are recognized to support, facilitate, or impede the development of infants and young children. For therapy to be meaningful, therapists must not only be knowledgeable in how neuromotor development occurs but also in how it may be affected by sociocultural and environmental parameters. For example, muscle tone in a developing child may be affected if a caregiver does not encourage independent movement or holds or positions a child in certain ways (Cintas, 1995). Additionally, cognitive skills are enhanced if a child moves independently within the environment (Berenthal, Campos, & Barrett, 1984).

The third factor that has influenced the measurement process, the development of measurement instruments, and therapeutic intervention is the application of the dynamic systems perspective of motor development (Case-Smith, 1996; Piper, 1993). Traditional measurement instruments used by therapists are based on the neuromaturational theory of motor development advanced by McGraw (1945) and Gesell (1945). Early therapeutic

strategies also used the neuromaturational theory as a framework. The neuromaturational theory is based on the assumption that, as the central nervous system matures, motor development will proceed in a hierarchial fashion. Accordingly, development occurs in a cephalocaudal and proximal-distal direction at a specific rate. As the infant develops, higher centers of the central nervous system inhibit lower centers so that voluntary movements can occur when reflexes are integrated.

Dynamic systems theory views the development of motor skills as emerging from the interactions of many subsystems within a specific task (Heriza, 1991). These subsystems include the musculoskeletal system (joint mobility, muscle strength, and static postural alignment), movement patterns (motor milestones, reflexes and reactions, coordination, balance, and endurance), functional performance, sensation (visual, vestibular, proprioceptive, auditory, and tactile), and perception. According to Heriza (1991), an assessment following a dynamic system paradigm should identify age-appropriate tasks, transition periods, the subsystems impacting movement, and contextual variations.

Chapter 8 provided a review of many tools available to pediatric physical therapists and occupational therapists to gather information regarding a child's sensorimotor development. The components of sensory processing, praxis, and motor development also are described. The authors have stressed the need to include parental interview and child observation as part of a comprehensive assessment strategy. The purpose of this present chapter is to provide a framework that will assist therapists in choosing the most appropriate measurement model and instrument for children with sensorimotor and sensory-processing concerns. Additionally, intervention models and approaches will be reviewed.

THE MEASUREMENT PROCESS

This chapter presents a general discussion of the similarities and differences among the processes of screening, assessment, and evaluation, followed by descriptions of five models used by therapists to gather information for clinical decision making. Additionally, several measurement instruments are described. These instruments were chosen because of their unique contributions to the processes of (a) identifying infants and toddlers who may have a developmental problem, (b) predicting which infants will continue to demonstrate problems throughout childhood, or (c) documenting change in the acquisition of developmental or functional skills or change in the performance of existing skills. A chapter appendix lists several additional instruments not discussed here or in Chapter 8 that are also available to therapists.

Purpose of Measurement

Measurement is the process of describing characteristics of an individual by gathering information in an organized manner. A variety of methods are used to gather information, including (a) interviewing parents and other primary caregivers, teachers, and health professionals involved in the care of a child, (b) observing the child in natural settings, and (c) direct testing of the child. Measurement is conducted for seven purposes, as shown in Table 2. The procedures, strategies, and types of tests chosen as measurement tools will be driven by the purpose of measurement and what type of information is needed.

The IDEA defines evaluation, assessment, and screening as they relate to early intervention and educational programs (IDEA, 1997). The *screening process* is used to detect if a child's behavior or skill development is at a level that places the child at risk for a

Table 2. The Purposes of Measurement	
Purpose	**Strategy**
Identify risk	Screening
Diagnose	Evaluation
Determine eligibility	Evaluation
Plan intervention	Assessment
Determine change in functioning	Assessment
Determine efficacy of intervention	Assessment
Research	Evaluation

developmental problem, concern, or delay. The screening process should be brief and the test used should be easy to administer by a variety of people (physicians, therapists, nurses, teachers, and in some cases, parents). To increase the likelihood that screening takes place on a regular and consistent basis, the procedure should be designed to be used in pediatricians' offices, classrooms, and community-based health and social service agencies, or on an out-patient basis. Additionally, screening instruments should be reliable and accurate (Gilbaide, 1995).

The *evaluation process* is more complex. Evaluations are used to help make a diagnosis, identify atypical development, or determine eligibility for services. Instruments used as part of an evaluation process are usually norm-referenced, standardized tools. Many of the tests measure a single developmental area, such as motor or language (Taylor, 1993), but others are comprehensive developmental scales covering more than one area of development. Evaluation methods include what Kirshner & Guyatt (1985) refer to as a "discriminative index." A discriminative index distinguishes between individuals or groups on specific dimensions, such as the acquisition of developmental milestones. Discriminative measures are often used to determine if a child's behavior is typical for her age and are used to determine eligibility for services. Many of the tools traditionally used by therapists, such as the Bayley Scales of Infant Development-II and the Peabody Developmental Motor Scales, fall into this category.

Physical and occupational therapists are most often involved in the *assessment process*. Assessments often use comprehensive tools to delineate strengths and needs, develop appropriate intervention plans and strategies, and determine change in individual children. An assessment is most meaningful when it represents the child's typical performance (Shelton, 1989). Thus, the assessment process should gain information regarding the child's abilities and behaviors across domains and environments (Cicchetti & Wagner, 1990). Assessments use a variety of methods to gather information. Norm-referenced and criterion-referenced instruments are commonly used. The assessment process also gains valuable information through ecological and performance appraisals (portfolios). The emphasis in an ecological approach to assessment is on documenting the child's success in participating in activities and routines across domains and environments. The assessment is conducted in the child's natural environment; thus, the skills demonstrated also reflect the context of performance. Judgment-based assessments document the parents' and caregivers' perceptions of a child's performance. According to Kirshner and Guyatt (1985), an assessment can be "evaluative." An evaluative strategy is one that measures the magnitude of change in an individual over time on a specific dimension. The overall purpose of an assessment is to describe a child's strengths and needs to help design appropriate, individualized therapeutic intervention plans.

Approaches to Measuring Skills

In addition to classifying testing instruments according to their purpose, tools available to therapists can be classified according to how the information is obtained: informally, formally, or ecologically. *Informal* strategies gather information in a less structured format. Facility or therapist-made checklists, developmental skill level forms, and interviews are examples of instruments that obtain information informally. Informal measurement strategies are easy to administer, are flexible to meet a family's needs and schedules, and will often obtain information on the typical performance of the child. The information provided can be gathered by observation or through caregiver report. Due to the flexibility inherent in the informal classification, rigorous testing procedures that increase reliability and validity are often missing. However, using informal procedures initially will establish rapport with the family and delineate parental concerns.

Therapists are most familiar with *formal* measurement strategies. Norm-referenced, criterion-referenced, and curriculum-based measurement instruments are included in the formal classification. Formal strategies are most often used to discriminate those children who are showing atypical development or delays. Two advantages of formal instruments include an established criteria, and standardized administration and scoring procedures that increase the reliability, validity, and accuracy of the instrument. A commonly cited limitation of formal instruments is the lack of familiarity between the examiner and the child, which may limit the child's willingness or ability to demonstrate his capabilities (Greenspan & Meisels, 1993). Additionally, most formal tests do not take into consideration the context of performance. The Bayley Scales of Infant Development-II (Bayley, 1993) is an example of a formal, discriminative tool.

Ecologically based or naturalistic strategies are becoming more accepted by professionals as accurate methods to gather information regarding a child's behavioral repertoire. Ecologically based measurement strategies are designed to determine a child's ability to perform a functional activity rather than the child's capability to perform a skill. Ecologically based procedures take into consideration the physical, social, and psychological environment in which a task is performed. An ecological or naturalistic assessment provides qualitative and quantitative information about the child. Observing the child within the environment in which a skill needs to be performed increases the likelihood that the therapist will gain meaningful information. Also, naturalistic assessments provide opportunities for self-initiation, choice, and problem solving by the child. (See Williamson, Anzalone & Hanft, Chapter 8, this volume.) These capacities often are not observed during structured, formal testing. Evaluation or assessment strategies such as the Alberta Infant Motor Scale (AIMS) (Piper & Darrah, 1993), the Toddler and Infant Motor Development (TIME) (Miller & Roid, 1994), the Functional Outcome Assessment Grid (Campbell, 1993), and the School Function Assessment (SFA) (Coster, Deeney, Haltiwanger, & Haley, 1998) are consistent with the ecological classification, incorporating observation, family participation, and task-specific activities into the evaluation or assessment format. The ecologically based strategy is consistent with the contemporary view of motor development, recognizing the importance of context, task, and family or caregiver participation (Heriza, 1993; Gentile, 1987; Lyons, 1984). The naturalistic process emphasizes adaptive behavior and yields a description of a child's repertoire of behavior across skill domains. This type of measurement approach can be linked directly to program planning and is used primarily for assessment purposes.

Models of Measurement

This section discusses five models used to gather information about a child's sensorimotor performance. The bottom-up model is primarily used for evaluation purposes. Three of the models—top-down, routines-based, and arena—are more applicable for assessment procedures. The fifth model—the judgement-based approach—is used for both assessment and evaluation.

The Bottom-Up Model

Traditionally, therapists rely on a bottom-up perspective (see Figure 1a) to gather information about a child's motor performance (Campbell, 1993). The bottom-up perspective is a diagnostic prescriptive model where deficits are delineated in specific areas and a program is designed to remediate those deficits. This model is most appropriate for (a) evaluation, and (b) when designing interventions targeting impairments such as decreased joint range of motion or muscle weakness. This model is less helpful when designing functionally oriented intervention plans needed in early intervention and educational programs.

The Top-Down Model

As noted previously, assessment procedures are most often used for program planning. Therapeutic programs for children are functionally oriented and are geared to the accomplishment of outcomes. In the top-down model (see Figure 1b), desired outcomes guide the assessment process. Desired outcomes are statements that describe what the team (parents, caregivers, and professionals) would like to see happen with a child. Outcomes can be general ("I'd like to see Anna move around") or specific ("Ryan needs to walk from the bus to the classroom"). Assessment procedures that operationalize the top-down approach answer the following specific questions (Campbell, 1993):

- What environmental factors and/or performance components are interfering with or facilitating a child's performance of the desired outcome?
- Into what specific objectives can the outcome be divided to minimize the immediate and long-term negative effects of identified interferers?
- What intervention approaches, models, and strategies will be used to promote immediate and long-term attainment of the desired outcome?

Currently, there are only a few tools available that operationalize the top-down approach. Thus, research related to the rigor of these tools is lacking.

The Routines-Based Model

As part of the family-centered intervention planning process, McWilliam (1992) promoted the routines-based model of assessment. Consistent with the top-down approach, a routines-based assessment model judges the capabilities of the child within everyday routines and activities. A routines-based assessment identifies those factors (child-specific and environmental) that interfere with or promote the performance of a specific functional task within a specific routine. For example, a therapist would assess a child's stair-climbing ability while the child is ascending stairs to go to his bedroom to take a nap or descending stairs to the basement playroom to obtain a toy, and would assess how a child scoops with a spoon during snack time. The use of routines to assess

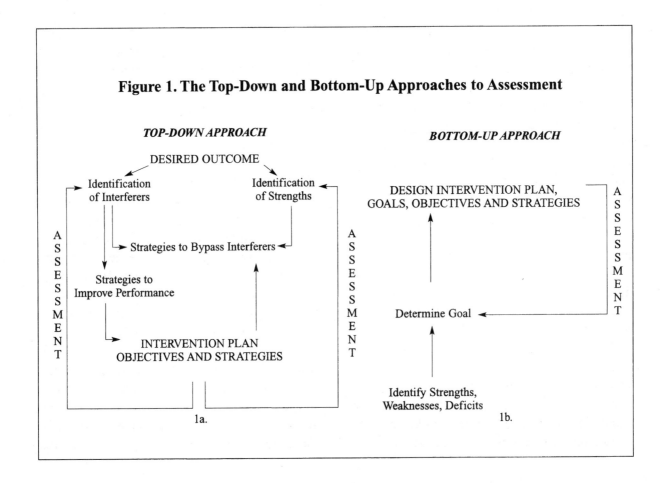

Figure 1. The Top-Down and Bottom-Up Approaches to Assessment

behaviors is helpful for program planning because:

- Routines are meaningful to parents and caregivers
- The use of routines promotes the delineation of functional outcomes and intervention strategies
- Observation of a child across domains, contexts, and environments is most efficient when it involves naturally occurring routines

As noted in the top-down approach, the routines-based approach has strong clinical significance but lacks research supporting its use.

Arena Assessment

The arena assessment, primarily used in early intervention, is the simultaneous observation of a child by specialists in various disciplines. The purposes of an arena assessment are to:

- Obtain an integrated, holistic view of the child
- Determine the interrelationship of skills across domains
- Decrease handling of the infant/toddler by multiple professionals
- Decrease repetitive questioning of the family

The arena assessment consists of five components (see Box 1) (Foley, 1990).

The arena assessment can streamline case management and promote integrated service delivery. The arena assessment, however, can be time consuming. In order for all members of the team to gain the information they need, preassessment planning is needed. Also, the model requires a great deal of collaboration among team members.

Box 1. Components of an Arena Assessment

Team: Multidisciplinary team where members are determined from the desired outcomes. Team membership will vary across children depending on purpose of assessment.

Facilitator: The individual team member who interacts with the child. The facilitator is usually determined by the team based on the needs of child, purpose of assessment, and family desires.

Process: The process is family driven and naturalistic. Although the process may vary depending on the needs of the child and family, it should obtain information on the physical, social-emotional, and psychoeducational capacities of the child.

Staffing: A working meeting in which the team (which may include the family) synthesizes and analyzes the information gained from the assessment.

Outcome: A thorough arena assessment should yield a qualitative and quantitative description of the child, delineating strengths and needs.

Judgment-Based Assessment

The judgment-based assessment format enables therapists to obtain task-specific information about a child from those individuals who observe the child's performance on a regular basis. Thus, asking parents and caregivers to fill out a form or answer a series of questions regarding the child's behavior would yield information that parents and caregivers (a) find meaningful, and (b) consider typical behavior for the child.

Measurement Instruments

In Chapter 8, Williamson, Anzalone, and Hanft discuss many tests used to directly evaluate or assess children on motor performance, sensory processing, and praxis. To avoid redundancy, the following section discusses only those tools that are specific to neuromotor and/or functional performance, and that are designed specifically to assist with program planning and documenting change over time. Additionally, all these tests have been specifically designed to capture a unique aspect of performance administered in a manner consistent with contemporary views of motor development, motor performance, and functional outcome.

Alberta Infant Motor Scale

The Alberta Infant Motor Scale (AIMS) (Piper & Darrah, 1993) was designed to identify infants up to 18 months of age who have gross motor delays. It can be used as a screening tool or as part of an assessment to measure gross motor skill maturation over time. The authors of the AIMS clearly indicate that the test should not be used for older children with known disabilities who are functioning below the 18-months-old level or to monitor progress of therapy in children with known disabilities. The AIMS is a criterion-referenced, standardized instrument with strong psychometric characteristics. The AIMS can be administered by a variety of health care professionals who have a background in infant motor development. Although scoring and interpretation are facilitated by detailed drawings in the manual and on the score sheet, use of the test requires extensive knowledge in normal and abnormal motor development. Test administration involves the observation of 58 items, divided among four positions: prone, supine, sitting, and standing. Within each position, three components of movement are evaluated: weightbearing, posture, and anti-gravity movements. Minimal handling of the child is required, and parents are encouraged to be the primary facilitators. Test administration typically requires 20 to 30 minutes to complete, but it can take as little as 10 to 15 minutes.

The AIMS is a practical tool and is efficient when performed by an experienced clinician. It yields information of clinical relevance to occupational therapists and physical therapists. The AIMS is unique in that it is one of the few tools that emphasize the *observation* of motor performance. This provides the child the opportunity to be evaluated in more natural environments, such as the home. It also allows the therapist to gather information on the child's typical motor performance.

Functional Outcomes Assessment Grid

The Functional Outcomes Assessment Grid (FOAG) (Campbell, 1993) is used by an interdisciplinary team to develop goals for children with disabilities in direct relation to the functional outcomes determined by the team, monitor change over time, and determine appropriate level of service. It is appropriate for all children with disabilities, regardless of their ages. The FOAG is based on the American Occupational Therapy Association's document, *Uniform Terminology for Occupational Therapy, 2nd Edition* (1994). Individualized observation of functional skill performance is conducted to determine which components (physical, environmental, behavioral, and sensory) are impacting positively or negatively on a child's performance of a skill. Each component is scored on a 5-point scale, from no problems to significant problems that impact on, or prevent, skill performance. Those factors that impact significantly on performance of team-established outcomes are targeted for intervention. The FOAG operationalizes the top-down model of measurement as well as the routines-based model. It is highly useful for assessing children with complex needs whose development is known to be atypical and whose disability affects a broad spectrum of functional skills. It is most helpful when used as a collaborative team decision-making tool, facilitating integrated service provision. The FOAG directly links assessment to program planning and is individualized to meet the unique needs of the child.

Pediatric Evaluation of Disability Inventory

The Pediatric Evaluation of Disability Inventory (PEDI) (Haley, Coster, Ludlow, Haltiwarger, & Andrellas, 1992) determines functional capabilities and performance, monitors progress in functional skill performance, and evaluates therapeutic or rehabilitative program outcomes in children with disabilities. It can be used with children with and without disabilities who are from 6 months to 7.5 years of age. The PEDI is a norm-reference test with strong psychometric characteristics. The test is divided into subtests focusing on the three functional skills of self-care, mobility, and social function. Also, environmental modification and amount of caregiver assistance are systematically recorded. Information can be obtained through parent report, structured interview, or professional observation of a child's functional behavior. The PEDI is a reliable and valid assessment of functional performance in children with significant cognitive and physical disabilities.

School Function Assessment

The School Function Assessment (SFA) (Coster et al., 1998) is specifically designed to be used within the educational environment to assess function and to guide program planning for students with disabilities in kindergarten through grade six. Teachers and other providers of services in the educational environment judge a child's performance on nonacademic tasks divided among those areas assessing level of participation, amount of task assistance or modification, and level of performance in cognitive or physical tasks. The SFA is a criterion-referenced test, and it specifically links assessment results to the development of an Individual Education Program (IEP). It uses a judgment-based format to gather information on the typical performance of a child from the variety of individuals involved in the student's education. It yields detailed information across domains and environments and, thus, requires collaboration from those that know the student well.

Toddler and Infant Motor Evaluation

The Toddler and Infant Motor Evaluation (TIME) (Miller & Roid, 1994) was developed to measure functional movements in an infant as observed in the infant's natural environment. The TIME was designed to be used with children 4 to 42 months of age with suspected motor dysfunction, and to identify those with mild to severe motor problems. It identifies patterns of movements, evaluates motor development over time, and assists in intervention planning and treatment efficacy research. The TIME is divided into eight subtests: five of the subtests have been standardized and norm-referenced. The test records the child's spontaneous movements in various positions, the child's sequence of movements, and any abnormal movements. The parents interact with, handle, and position the child according to the examiner's instructions and guidance. The TIME can be used as a comprehensive motor evaluation or assessment tool. As an evaluation tool, the TIME can be used to identify a child with a motor dysfunction. Repeated measures can be taken with the TIME, thus making it useful for assessing motor development over time as well as assessing treatment efficacy and/or motor maturation. The TIME is a valuable clinical tool. It is a tool that incorporates dynamic systems theory in the assessment of motor functions and development. It links a child's function, quality of movement, and motor skills. The TIME is comprehensive and detailed, providing excellent visual descriptors of the motor components that are being assessed. It primarily uses naturalistic observation to gather data, recognizing the importance of evaluating typical movements as they are impacted by the child's environment.

Test of Sensory Functions in Infants

The Test of Sensory Functions in Infants (TSFI) (Degangi & Greenspan, 1988) was developed to screen and quantify sensory processing and reactivity in infants. The test includes five subdomains of sensory processing: reactivity to tactile deep-pressure, adaptive motor responses, visual-tactile integration, ocular-motor control, and reactivity to vestibular stimulation. Infants between 4 and 18 months of age can be screened using the TSFI. This criterion-referenced test is most accurate in identifying infants between 10 and 18 months of age without sensory processing disorders or with sensory dysfunction. This age range is appropriate because definitive sensory processing dysfunction does not emerge until late in the first to second years of life.

The TSFI was designed to identify infants with sensory dysfunction. It can also be used with infants who have a known regulatory disorder or developmental delay. Because limited normative data are available, total test scores are used to make screening decisions. The individual subtests, however, can be used in conjunction with other standardized developmental and neuromotor tests when making diagnostic decisions and recommendations (DeGangi & Greenspan, 1988). Abnormal or

at-risk scores on the TSFI indicate that a child has potential problems in sensory processing and should be referred for further evaluation or assessment.

The TSFI is the first test developed to screen infants for early sensory processing problems. Although additional data are needed in order to use the test as a diagnostic tool, individual subtests and test items can provide useful clinical information.

LINKING ASSESSMENT FINDINGS TO INTERVENTION PLANNING

Linking assessment findings to a specific intervention plan for a child with a neuromotor or sensorimotor dysfunction is a complex process. Use of traditional methods to gather information has often resulted in planning interventions for children with disabilities that are intensive, isolated, and deficit-based. Strategies based on a neuromaturational framework have dominated therapeutic intervention during the last three decades. Contemporary practice, however, is outcome oriented, with strategies that emphasize functional relevance. Planning intervention that is outcome oriented has four components. The first component is *assessment*. Through assessment strategies, the therapist determines what is facilitating or interfering with the child's acquisition of a specified outcome. Next, the therapist—in collaboration with the team—determines whether the focus of *intervention* should be remediation, prevention, promotion, compensation, or alteration. Third, the therapist determines the *model of service delivery,* which can be direct, monitoring, or consultation. Finally, the therapist determines the *type of strategy* that would best meet the child's needs. Because children with disabilities in sensorimotor or neuromotor skills have complex problems, a combination of approaches, service delivery models, and strategies are most often used.

The purpose of intervention is fourfold. Therapists use a wide variety of strategies to (1) promote active movement, (2) promote functional skills, (3) prevent impairment, and (4) foster the integration of the child into society.

Most of the traditional strategies used by therapists (see Box 2) require direct, one-to-one application, which often take place in segregated settings such as clinics or assigned rooms in early intervention or educational programs. Although many of these strategies are useful in preparing a child for movement by relaxing tight muscles, strengthening weak muscles, or promoting motor milestone development, when used in isolation they have not been shown to increase function any more than nontherapeutic strategies (Warren and Horn, 1996). Additionally, generalization of skills practiced, facilitated, or learned during therapy has not been demonstrated using the traditional model of service provision.

Frames of Reference

A frame of reference often guides a therapist's selection of strategies used to treat children with sensorimotor dysfunction. The following discussion describes three broad frames of reference that therapists employ: neuromaturational, motor learning, and dynamical systems.

Neuromaturational

The traditional frame of reference used by most therapists is neuromaturational. Neuromaturational theory is based on the work of individuals such as Gesell (1945) and Shirley (1931). This theory promotes the concept that as a child grows and his central nervous system matures, skills or patterns of movement will unfold in a predictable, hier-

archial manner. Treatment strategies based on this theory attempt to promote skills in children by following the sequence of skill development documented in developmental scales. This theory assumes that skills will unfold naturally in a normally developing central nervous system. As the nervous system matures, adaptive behaviors and skills will become increasingly complex. An emphasis of treatment using this model is the promotion of central nervous system maturation. The analysis of reflex integration, facilitation of equilibrium and righting reactions, and promotion of the components of motor skills are integral to strategies developed from the neuromaturational model.

Learning-Based

Although strategies based on the neuromaturational model continue to be the most commonly used, the learning-based models are often integrated into a holistic treatment program. The learning-based models may be arrayed along a continuum from strict behaviorism as promoted by Skinner to the more widely accepted schema theory promoted by Schmidt (1975). Most therapists readily employ basic learning theory strategies, such as providing multimodal feedback, arranging the environment to promote skill performance, and repeating actions to increase the likelihood that the behavior will be retained. The schema theory proposes that motor development emerges from a set of "rules" used by the individual to evaluate, correct, and update memory traces for a movement. General motor programs are responsible for organizing the fundamental components of the movement. In order for the general motor program to produce a movement, recall and recognition schema are used. Recall and recognition schemas are memories of the relationships between past movement (recall) and sensory (recognition) patterns and the movement

Box 2. Strategies Used by Physical and Occupational Therapists*

Neurodevelopment Treatment (NDT): Direct handling of children. Specifically designed for young children with cerebral palsy to facilitate normal patterns of movement.

Myofascial Release (MFR): Specific techniques performed by a therapist to release the binding down of the fascia. Goal of MFR is to change structure to allow functional change. Promotes structural change techniques followed by functional activities. Little to no scientific research to determine effectiveness.

Craniosacral Therapy (CS): Therapist applies gentle pressure through the craniosacral system to promote movement of cerebral spinal fluid and rhythm. Gentle, noninvasive manipulative technique. Used for variety of conditions and promoted for use with infants including newborns to diminish effects of birth trauma. Little to no research on effectiveness.

Massage: Variety of specific tactile techniques from gentle laying of the hands to more vigorous Swedish and Indian techniques. Used for a variety of children, including babies born prematurely. Research has shown a variety of physiologic benefits including gastrointestinal functioning, improved blood and lymphatic circulation, and weight gain in preterm infants. Also shown are improvements in decreasing tactile sensitivity, parent-infant bonding, calming, comforting, and respiration.

Strength Training: Strength training using standard progressive-resistive exercise protocols may relate to improvement in function. Sound research on strength in children with cerebral palsy, but minimal research investigating the effects of strength in children without other developmental disabilities, such as sensorimotor dysfunction.

Mobilization: Based on concept that immobility affects all systems necessary to produce movement. Is indicated if extra-articular connective tissue abnormally restricts joint motion. Little research done with children to indicate effectiveness.

Sensory Integration (SI): Used with children with mild to moderate sensory processing dysfunction. Treatment uses specific tactile, vestibular, and proprioceptive activities to promote adaptive responses. Goal is to improve the ability of the central nervous system to process and integrate sensory inputs.

Conductive Education (CE): Intensive programming using rhythmic intention and sequenced facilitation to enhance organization and production of intentional movement within educational and life tasks. Performed by a specially trained and certified conductor. Research from the Peto Institute in Hungary is quite positive.

Movement Opportunities via Education (MOVE): Comprehensive, activity-based curriculum for children with severe neuromotor dysfunction. Teaches basic functional motor skills. Process designed to have children acquire skills necessary for sitting, standing, and walking. Team works on same set of skills so that skills are reinforced and consistent.

*These are only a selection of strategies used by therapists. Therapists also use, for example, assistive technology, splinting, bracing, remediation, and teaching of specific skills.

desired. In schema theory, the development of fundamental movement patterns is emphasized to generate the ability to develop more sophisticated patterns. For example, once the motor pattern for walking is established, individuals expand that pattern to walk on various terrains and at various speeds. Schema theory contends that children with disabilities may have difficulty initiating a movement, completing the movement with accuracy or precision, or stopping a movement because of a lack in recall or recognition schemas.

Children with sensorimotor dysfunction typically have problems in accurately producing a movement or controlling the execution of a movement. In schema theory, this would be due to poorly established recognition patterns. Schema theory promotes a use of practice that has clear implications for the treatment of children with sensorimotor dysfunction. Specifically, schema theory predicts that (a) variable practice of a skill or action promotes the establishment of a schema, and (b) varied practice works as well as repeated practice in promoting accurate performance of a novel action. Thus, treatment for learning motor patterns and schemas would be more effective if the child practices and repeats skills in various situations, under changing conditions. The integration of therapeutic strategies into daily caregiving routines operationalizes this concept. Daily caregiving routines ensure that a skill is practiced within a meaningful context for the child. Performing activities within the context where they will be used and are needed increases the likelihood that the child will be interested and motivated in performing the task.

Dynamical Systems

The dynamical systems theory (Heriza, 1991; Thelan, 1990) is the newest theory to emerge in the physical and occupational therapy literature as a way to explain how development and motor change take place. The dynamical system theory proposes that a functional movement emerges from the interaction of a variety of subsystems with the environment. In the case of motor skills, these subsystems include sensory, neurological, musculoskeletal, emotional, psychological, and other variables. Thus, depending on the task, any one of these variables can create a barrier to the accomplishment of the task or be a facilitator of task development. In neuromaturational theory, the development of skills is explained as a sequence of skills that build on one another and emerge in stages. The dynamical systems perspective, however, proposes that a change in behavior occurs as a consequence of a change in one or more of the variables that can impact the skill. Also, the dynamical system perspective emphasizes that change in motor behavior most likely will take place during times of transition. Treatment based on this perspective focuses on analyzing the variables that are preventing or promoting a specific skill; changing the combination of inputs, contexts, and tasks that are important to produce a specific task; and timing treatment to coincide with periods of transition. Intense therapeutic input during these periods of transition is suggested as the most effective treatment strategy to produce changes in motor skill acquisition. Because the dynamical system perspective emphasizes the interaction of multiple systems with the environment, the importance of family and caregiver interactions with the child cannot be overemphasized.

Approaches to Intervention

As with assessment practices, contemporary intervention theory encourages therapists to reassess practices and approaches to intervention. Dunn, Brown, and McGuigan (1994) describe five approaches available to therapists. These approaches allow therapists to design intervention strategies that target the specific needs of the child and the desired outcomes of the family. The approaches also provide a framework for the therapists to determine the intent of the intervention. Depending on the needs of the child, a therapist will most often use a variety of approaches and expect to change approaches as the needs of the child change.

Remedial

The remedial (or restoration) approach is the most familiar to therapists and is the basis for many of the more popular treatment strategies. Based on the traditional medical model of intervention, the remedial approach enables therapists to identify performance deficits and to seek to resolve them by facilitating age-appropriate sensorimotor capabilities. This approach may be appropriate for some children; however, using only an approach that encourages "average" development and "typical" movements may prevent other children from developing functional skills.

Compensation

The compensation approach is often used with older children, especially those with orthopedic disabilities or significant neuromotor dysfunction such as spastic type of quadriplegia. The purpose of the compensation approach is to use assistive technology, adaptive equipment, or other devices to allow a child to perform a skill that the child is not capable of performing or has yet to master. Compensation strategies also are used to prevent further impairment or disability as they are often used to bypass a barrier to the performance of a desired outcome. With young children, compensations are most often used in combination with other approaches. Compensation strategies also are used to promote development. For example, providing a

child who has minimal or no expressive language with an alternative communication system (e.g., sign, gestures, or a communication board) will promote the child's receptive language development by providing him with the ability to communicate interactively.

Promotion

The promotion approach creates naturally occurring activities and routines to promote skill development. This approach is typically used in community-based activity programs designed for all children, and which are often based on the *Developmentally Appropriate Practice Guidelines* (Bredekamp and Copple, 1997). The environment and activities are designed to facilitate developmental skill acquisition. This approach is well suited for children with global developmental delays or weaknesses in specific skill performance areas. Enriched, stimulating childcare programs use the promotion approach and can easily integrate children with delays into the program. Other programs such as tumbling, dance, or library story time utilize a promotion approach.

Prevention

The purpose of the prevention approach is to prevent the development of secondary impairments or disabilities in children with known difficulties. For example, proper positioning of an infant with cerebral palsy is used to help prevent trunk malalignment, which the child has a high risk of developing. Encouraging small-object manipulation or coloring for toddlers and preschoolers who shy away from these activities may prevent them from developing visual-motor or handwriting problems later on.

Alteration

The remedial approach emphasizes the facilitation of skills not yet acquired by a child.

The alteration approach, on the other hand, emphasizes the development of skills that are most functional for a child by providing the child with an alternative environment in which to foster skill development and use. The alteration approach requires that the therapist and team weigh the importance of changing a child's aberrant behavior or the lack of skill against any given activity or environment. For example, Andrew is a child with sensory-processing deficits who becomes behaviorally disruptive when in a highly sensory-charged environment. His intervention team, however, has identified his poor language skills as the most immediate concern. Since Andrew's behavior can interfere with his ability to benefit from the language enrichment offered to him, his team has several options. The team members can decide to teach Andrew behaviors that are age appropriate (remedial approach) within the sensory-charged environment; they can change the environment by decreasing sensory stimulation (compensation approach); or they may decide to move Andrew to a minimal-sensory environment (alteration approach). Although the first two options may be appropriate and necessary, it may be more functional to find a better environmental match for Andrew so that his intervention can focus on his language development, which is the identified area of concern.

Models of Service Provision

In addition to identifying the various approaches to intervention needed by a child, therapists also must decide on the most effective and efficient service delivery model. As noted above, the traditional intervention model—the remedial approach—promotes direct one-to-one therapeutic interventions. Contemporary practice, however, promotes the use of three models of service provision: direct, monitoring, and consultation (Dunn &

Campbell, 1991). These models allow the therapist to design a comprehensive intervention plan that takes into account the outcomes developed by the team, the individual strengths and needs of the child, family priorities, the environment, and other support factors.

Direct

Therapists most often use a direct service model of intervention. In this model, therapists provide one-to-one therapy, usually in a segregated setting (e.g., a clinic, a specially designed room within a childcare or educational program, or in a separate space within a classroom). Usually, the purpose of direct service is to provide intensive, remedial intervention to a child. Therapists use direct therapy to provide specialized therapeutic intervention strategies. Strategies are used to teach specific skills, introduce new behaviors to the child, change maladaptive behaviors, or to increase a child's tolerance to sensorimotor experiences.

Recent changes in research, legislative mandates, and societal attitudes about children with disabilities are creating a shift away from the provision of direct service to all children to an integrated service delivery program. Integrated programming is defined as:
- Specialized instruction
- Individualized to meet the unique strengths and needs of a child, within a naturally occurring environment
- With other children without disabilities
- Within the context that the skill is required (McWilliam, 1996)

Research comparing the benefits of integrated and direct service delivery has indicated little difference in the enhancement of skills in individual children (McWilliam, 1996). However, other benefits have been related to integrated therapy models. (See Advantages to Integrated Therapy, Box 3.)

Although changes in standardized testing scores were the same following interventions based on integrated or direct service delivery models, Cole, Harris, Eland, and Mills (1989) found that teachers preferred the integrated model. In teaching a child with severe motoric involvement how to use a microswitch, Giangreco (1986) found performance improved more during integrated programming than when teaching was conducted in isolation.

Obviously, more research needs to be done in this area, especially with children with various needs and conditions. It is clear, however, that the field is moving rapidly to develop programs that provide integrated therapy. In order to provide effective treatment within an integrated model, therapists require skills in putting into operation two additional service delivery models: monitoring and consultation.

Monitoring

Monitoring is a method to ensure that therapeutic strategies become infused into naturally occurring activities and are carried out throughout the day. Therapists monitor programming when they create and supervise the delivery of a plan that is carried out by someone else (Dunn, 1996). Monitoring can be used alone or in combination with direct service and consultation. Monitoring service provision may be as time consuming as direct service, especially initially. Therapists are required to ensure that any program or activity taught to another person is being carried out appropriately. Thus, monitoring requires therapists to
- Design the activities
- Teach the provider specific methods of integrating therapeutic strategies into existing routines
- Observe the provider performing the activities
- Adapt and update the activity as necessary

Box 3. Advantages to Integrated Therapy

- Active participation is enhanced because service to children is provided in a familiar, comfortable, nonthreatening setting.

- Developmentally appropriate, naturally occurring settings are enriching and therapeutic.

- Natural environments provide routine cues and opportunities to provide therapeutic tasks within context.

- Functional behavior is supported because the child's actions reinforced within the natural context and by peers.

- Generalization of skills is enhanced because learning is taking place within the environment in which the skills are expected.

- Normalization is valued and enhanced. All children recognize that each child has strengths and needs and that specialized services can be beneficial to all.

- Supervise the implementation, and *be responsible for documenting* the child's performance

Monitoring is beneficial because (a) it increases the amount of time a child is benefiting from a therapeutic strategy, (b) the strategy will promote generalization because it is being conducted within a naturally occurring activity, and (c) it provides continuous, ongoing reinforcement of the desired behavior.

Consultation

Monitoring service delivery requires that the therapist design the activities and therapeutic strategies that will be used by others to promote needed therapeutic skills. In consultation, the consulting therapist assists another therapist in meeting jointly identified goals. The consulting therapist contributes her expertise to help solve a problem or dilemma for another provider of service to a child. Hanft and Place (1996) promote the use of collaborative consultation as the preferred method of consultation. Collaborative consultation is an interactive process in which various team members work together to generate creative solutions to a problem. As the field moves toward integrated, discipline-free program plans, collaborative consultation will help teams put into effect the plan for the child, within the structure of an inclusive setting. Collaborative consultation is also used within the traditional model of direct service delivery. Effective consultation has three critical elements: dynamic interaction among the team members, respect, and a belief that the consultation will help achieve a common goal. Consultative service provision accepts that children with disabilities present with complex problems and issues that can only be helped by creative use of the expertise provided by all team members. Collaborative consultants must free themselves from discipline-bound perspectives and be open to combining various systems and approaches to assist the child and family. Ideally, the solution to a specific challenge reflects a variety of approaches. Table 3 illustrates the use of the five service provision approaches and three models of service.

EFFECTIVENESS OF SPECIFIC MOTOR INTERVENTION

The effectiveness of therapeutic input for children with neuromotor and sensorimotor disorders has been of particular interest for the last 30 years. Generally, research that assessed specific developmental skill improvement has shown that therapeutic

intervention had little effect on motor development. However, research has documented other nonmotor benefits for children receiving specific therapeutic intervention and when studies use a single-subject design. One of the earliest studies assessing the benefits of physical therapy for children with cerebral palsy (Wright & Nicholson, 1973) indicated that, although neuromotor performance was not necessarily enhanced by intervention, nonmotor benefits such as family competency, child happiness, sociability, and confidence were seen. Thus, there has been a recent emphasis on examining broader issues in development and functional capacity in children with known disabilities. Additionally, early research into the benefits of therapy for children with motor disabilities has indicated that therapy only minimally affected impairments in children with significant motor dysfunction (Shonkoff & Hauser-Cram, 1987). Based on this limited research base, physical and occupational therapists are encouraged to examine disability or the inability to perform a functional activity rather than to examine individual impairments.

Types of Intervention

For purposes of this section, the term "intervention" is limited to specific approaches used by therapists that purport to influence the neuromotor and sensorimotor processes to improve function, reach targeted outcomes, or promote developmental skill acquisition. Functional outcomes include performance on tasks related to developmentally appropriate tasks, interaction within the environment, and purposeful activity. Functional outcomes deemphasize change measured on standardized, norm-referenced tests of developmental skills. Functional outcomes include nonmotor benefits, such as decreased need for assistance by caregivers,

Table 3. Examples of Service Provision Approaches and Models

Service provision models	Service Provision Approaches				
	Remediate	Compensate	Alter	Prevent	Promote
Direct	Facilitate neck extensor muscles so child can look at friends when playing	Fabricate a splint to enable the child to hold the cup at snack time	Select a community preschool based on the level of noise the child can manage	Facilitate weight bearing during infancy to prevent possible delays in walking	Provide a play program for the community for all children to attend
Monitoring	Supervise the teacher's aide to facilitate tone for reaching during a game	Supervise a feeding program that minimizes the time for eating and enables socialization	Work with parents to identify which community locations will be best for their family outings	Create a "positions alternatives" chart for the aides to prevent skin breakdowns	Oversee the development of a morning preschool routine that optimizes early development possibilities
Consultation	Teach classroom staff how to incorporate enhanced sensory input into play routines during free time	Provide the team with information from skilled observations that enables them to select the best play partner for a child	Work with parents to identify which community locations will be best for their family outings	Teach a parent a range-of-motion sequence to prevent deformities	Assist the child care provider to develop a comprehensive curriculum

Adapted with permission from Dunn, W. (1996). Occupational Therapy. In R. A. McWilliam (Ed.), *Rethinking pull-out services in early intervention: A professional resource* (pp. 267–313). Baltimore: Paul H. Brookes.

caregivers' sense of competence and confidence in caring for the child, and other related improvements.

Although many types of intervention were listed previously in Box 2, the most common form of intervention used with children with primary neuromotor deficits such as cerebral palsy is a neurofacilitation type. The most common intervention of this type is neurodevelopmental treatment (NDT). Intervention for children with primary sensorimotor deficits, such as those on the autistic spectrum, is considered sensorimotor intervention, the most common being sensory integration. Contemporary practice promotes a more task-oriented approach based on the systems or motor-learning perspective. This approach is less diagnosis (or deficit) dependent, and is consistent with the emphasis on functional outcomes rather than on facilitation of developmental milestones.

The following discussion reviews research published in the 1990s and which is related to intervention in the neurodevelopmental, sensorimotor, and task-oriented approaches. Readers interested in prior studies are referred to 1980s reviews of meta-analysis (Ottenbacher, Biocca, DeCremer, Gevelinger, Jedovic, & Johnson, 1986; Ottenbacher & Peterson, 1985; Shonkoff & Hauser-Cram, 1987) and qualitative reviews (Harris, 1987, 1988).

Neurodevelopmental Treatment

Recent randomized, controlled trials (Law et al., 1991; Palmer, 1990) examining the benefits of NDT produced results that are consistent with previous studies. Studies that utilized a group experimental design found little definitive support that NDT is any more beneficial than other types of intervention (such as general stimulation) in enhancing the attainment of developmental skills (Palisano, 1991). However, families whose children received this type of intervention were found to be more emotional and verbally responsive to their children and more confident in caregiving (Palmer et al., 1990). In this era of family-centered care and recognition of the importance of parent-child interactions, these findings support intervention. These findings are especially important for children with disabilities such as cerebral palsy. Studies utilizing a single-subject design, however, are more supportive of NDT in improving specific motor skills in children with cerebral palsy. Unlike traditional group designs, the single-subject design is concerned with individual performance on specific tasks, unique to the individual being treated. Embrey, Yates, and Mott (1990) found that improvement in specific components of gait could be seen in children receiving intensive intervention. Generalization of this single-subject design is limited, but the design shows promise as a strategy to indicate improvement in children whose disabilities make it difficult to identify them as a homogenous group.

The difficulty in establishing the efficacy of NDT is multifaceted. One primary problem is that NDT is an approach to treatment, rather than a series of activities. This approach, based on neurophysiological principles, is individualized to meet the needs of a specific child and is modified based on the response of that child. Thus, an assessment of the techniques is very difficult. Unlike medication or a specific surgical procedure, specific treatment techniques vary from therapist to therapist, further complicating the analysis of the approach. As noted, most studies examining the effectiveness of the NDT approach have used developmental skill acquisition tests or checklists to determine outcome. These tools may not be responsive to the changes produced by using NDT. Alternative measurement instruments, such as the Gross Motor Function Measure (Russell et al., 1993), the TIME (Miller & Roid, 1994), or the use of goal attainment scaling (Ottenbacher & Cusick, 1989), may prove more helpful in determining if NDT can produce change over time in children with complex neuromotor dysfunction.

Learning-Based Models

Although there is only limited research on the learning-based (or task-oriented) approach used with children, available evidence indicates that this approach may be more useful in changing functional skills in children with significant motor disabilities. Horn, Warren, and Jones (1995) showed that developing activities targeting specific behaviors was successful in supporting the attainment of those functional behaviors. There also seemed to be a generalization effect in that movements not targeted, but assessed, improved. The benefits of this approach may be due to the principles of motor learning on which it is grounded (Larin, 1994). Motor learning indicates that motor performance is enhanced when children are afforded opportunities to experience and actively practice specific activities or tasks. The theoretical basis of the motor learning approaches provides evidence that should encourage therapists to examine the effects of integrating these principles into the development of motor skills, performance, and function.

Sensory Integration

Children with mild to moderate problems having a sensorimotor basis, such as dyspraxia or sensory-processing disorder, often receive sensory integration (SI). According to Ayres (1979), the theory of SI can be used to explain the relationship between sensory processing and behavior. For example, impaired sensory processing in children with autism has been linked to dysfunction in relating,

arousal, interactions with others, and goal-directed play (Greenspan & Weider, 1997; Koomar & Bundy, 1991). It is these relationships that provide support for the use of SI with children with autism, as well as other significant disabilities. According to the theoretical constructs, children who receive sensory integration should improve in the following areas (Parham and Malloux, 1996):

- Adaptive responses
- Self-confidence and self-esteem
- Motor skills
- Daily living skills and personal-social skills
- Cognition, language, and academic performance

As with NDT, there is little empirical evidence of the effectiveness of SI or other strategies with a sensory component commonly used by therapists for children with a variety of conditions (Ottenbacher, 1991; Vargas & Camilli, 1999). Also similar to NDT, the literature regarding SI demonstrates the many challenges faced in reaching any consensus as to its effectiveness. Children across studies vary, outcome measures do not focus on the same information, and there is little control of the exact treatment techniques employed. Another unique limitation is that SI is a complex construct that theoretically is presented as a whole. In reductionist-type research, the SI construct must be broken down into individual component pieces. Consequently, research is evaluating the effectiveness of each component of sensory stimulation rather than the overall construct of SI (Ottenbacher, 1991). Additionally, most of the research on SI has studied children with learning disabilities although many more children have sensory-processing disorders, which may be amenable to the effects of SI.

However, even with these limitations, support exists for activities that are considered sensory integrative. Humphries, Wright,

Snider, and McDougall (1992) found that children with learning disabilities who received SI showed improved motor planning. Using a single-subject, multiple-baseline design, Case-Smith and Bryan (1999) showed that preschoolers with autism improved on specific, individualized activities to gain mastery in play and engagement. As with NDT, there appears to be accepted, theoretical support for treatment based on sensory integrative principles, with minimal empirical evidence. Because the SI treatment approach is so widely used by occupational therapists (Watling, Dietz, Kanny, & Mclaughlin, 1999; Case-Smith & Miller, 1999) it is of utmost importance that research be conducted to assess its attributes, effectiveness, and overall benefits to children with complex sensorimotor considerations and their families.

IMPLICATIONS

Children with developmental disabilities often have significant problems related to motor performance, even when their primary diagnosis is not motor-based. Motor planning, sensory processing, and motor delays are all seen in children on the autism spectrum or with mental retardation, learning disabilities, language processing difficulties, or other similar diagnoses. This is especially true in young infants because the lack of attainment in motor milestones is often the area initially seen as problematic. Consequently, physical and occupational therapists become the professionals who frequently provide the initial intervention. As early interventionists, they are in an ideal position to effect functional change by applying strategies based on sound theoretical principles in a functional manner.

Research on the effectiveness of intervention with children with significant sensorimotor disabilities is more successful when functional skills are targeted. According to

Wolery (1996), functional skills include those behaviors that are:
1. Useful
2. Enable the child to be more independent
3. Foster learning more complex skills
4. Allow a child to live in a less restrictive environment
5. Enable the child to be cared for more easily

Infusing NDT, SI, and the learning-based system approach into daily caregiving routines and embedding strategies into natural environments increase the likelihood that children will obtain and retain functional behaviors. Although limited, there are some initial research findings that lend support to this service delivery model. McWilliam, Tocci, and Harbin (1995) found that when parents of children who were receiving direct, individualized, clinic-based therapy were asked what they valued most from the sessions, the parents said it was the information they received from the therapists. These same parents, however, were not comfortable in discussing what they felt their child could do at home as a result of the therapy. These findings indicate that families value the information therapists provide and use this information in caring for their children. They are unsure, however, what functional change is directly linked to a specific intervention.

Clearly, research is needed to determine the effectiveness of these treatment strategies. Research should include a variety of strategies that focus on a variety of areas. Although widely accepted as appropriate theoretical constructs, the basis of the theoretical perspectives of various intervention approaches should be examined to validate their usefulness in explaining sensorimotor and/or neuromotor dysfunction. This recommendation is especially relevant for the theoretical bases of NDT and SI. Both of these approaches and their treatment techniques were developed from a neuromaturational view of development. Assessing their validity in light of the contemporary motor-learning and control theories, as well as in light of the systems perspective, may be helpful in establishing sound research hypotheses.

Clinical research examining the effectiveness of specific techniques must clearly describe the techniques and the intervention procedure. Because of the variation in treatment, concluding that an approach is effective or ineffective is misleading. Specific techniques may be more advantageous than others for certain populations of children. Additionally, the outcomes sought through treatment must be clearly defined in functional, measurable terms. Improvements in processing ability or postural control are goals that have little direct meaning to the child's daily caregiving. To be functional, outcomes should have a direct relationship to Wolery's five areas.

Finally, measurement tools need to be responsive to the changes seen during therapeutic intervention. Too often, standardized developmental tools have been used to determine change over time in children with known disabilities. As these tools were not developed to detect these kinds of changes, their value is limited. Use of functional tools such as the FOAG, the PEDI, or the SFA (as previously described) may prove more beneficial. Intervention outcome is linked directly to tasks on these systems; thus, relevance to the treatment strategies may be clearly identified.

SUMMARY

Significant changes in therapeutic interventions provided to children with sensorimotor dysfunction have occurred during the past 20 years. These changes have primarily occurred in methods of gathering information about a child's functional status and delivering

appropriate, functionally oriented services. Therapists are revising traditional service delivery models to reflect the growing emphasis on providing integrated therapeutic services within inclusive settings. The physical and occupational therapists' expertise in neuromotor development, the effects of sensorimotor skills on function and other developmental areas, and the therapists' ability to task analyze all contribute to contemporary service delivery. In recognition of the overlap among service providers, integrated, discipline-free programming is becoming more common.

This chapter outlined models of information-gathering that therapists use to evaluate and assess infants and young children. It also reviewed several recently published measurement tools used by pediatric physical and occupational therapists. Instruments are used as one component of the measurement process to (a) screen children for potential developmental concerns, (b) evaluate children to determine diagnosis or eligibility for services, or (c) assess children to plan therapeutic intervention or to determine the effects of intervention.

Therapists should be aware of the purpose of each tool and the information they would like to gain from the tool prior to selecting an instrument. Therapists may need to use a variety of tools and strategies to meet their screening, evaluation, or assessment objectives.

In addition to the measurement instrument used to gather information, a comprehensive measurement strategy should encompass the principles developed by ZERO TO THREE, National Center for Infant, Toddlers, and Families (Greenspan & Meisels, ZERO TO THREE Work Groups on Developmental Assessment, 1996) (see Chart 1).

These principles recognize that the development of infants and young children is complex and requires an appreciation of the child's abilities within a functional context. The therapist needs to appreciate that

---

Chart 1. Principles of Assessment

1. Assessment must be based on an integrated developmental model.

2. Assessment involves multiple sources of information and multiple components.

3. An assessment should follow a sequence.

4. The child's relationship and interactions with his or her most trusted caregiver should form the cornerstone of an assessment.

5. An understanding of the sequence and timetables in typical development is essential as a framework for the interpretation of developmental differences among infants and toddlers.

6. Assessment should emphasize attention to the child's level and pattern of ongoing experience and to functional capacities, which represent an integration of emotional and cognitive abilities.

7. The assessment process should identify the child's current competencies and strengths as well as the competencies that will constitute developmental progression in a continuous growth model of development.

8. Assessment is a collaborative process.

9. The process of assessment should always be viewed as the first step in a potential intervention process.

10. Reassessment of a child's developmental status should occur in the context of day-to-day family and/or early intervention activities.

From Greenspan & Meisels with the ZERO TO THREE Work Groups on Developmental Assessment (1996). In S. J. Meisels & E. Fenichel (Eds.) *New visions for the developmental assessment of infants and young children.* Washington, D.C.: ZERO TO THREE, National Center for Infants, Toddlers, and Families.

---

the assessment or evaluation of neuromotor development can be influenced by the interaction of the child with significant others, the environment, and the infant's own neurobehavioral state. This is especially critical when establishing intervention priorities, outcomes, goals, and strategies. Collaboration with other professionals, family members, and caregivers of the child will increase the likelihood that the therapist's findings will reflect the child's capabilities across environments and her current capacities and strengths, as well as identify barriers to optimal development. Individualized assessment of a child's neuromotor skills should capture the child's movement patterns, components of movement, and the use of movement within a functional activity, as well as the

child's sensory processing and developmental skills acquisition.

The chapter also discussed treatment of children with sensorimotor dysfunction. An emphasis was placed on service delivery approaches and models reflecting the evolving context of service delivery for all children. These models and approaches allow the therapist to develop a variety of treatment strategies that best meet a child's needs and reflect evolving frameworks on sensorimotor development and behavioral change. ∎

Acknowledgments

The authors would like to thank Elaine Anderson, M.P.H., P.T., for her assistance in the preparation of this manuscript.

REFERENCES

Alyward, G. (1993). *Bayley infant neurodevelopmental screener.* San Antonio, TX: Psychological Corporation.

American Occupational Therapy Association. (1994). *Uniform technology for occupational therapy: Application to practice.* Rockville, MD: American Occupational Therapy Association.

Ayres, J. (1979). *Sensory integration and the child.* Los Angeles: Western Psychological Services.

Bayley, N. (1993). *Bayley scales of infant development-II.* San Antonio, TX: Psychological Corporation.

Berenthal, B., Campos, J., & Barrett, K. (1984). Self-produced locomotion: An organizer of emotional, cognitive, and social development. In R. Ende and R. Herman (Eds.), *Continuities and discontinuities in development* (pp. 175-209). New York: Plenum.

Bredekamp, S., & Copple, C. (Eds.) (1997). *Developmentally appropriate practice in early childhood programs, revised edition.* Washington, D.C.: National Association for the Education of Young Children.

Bricker, D. (1993). *Assessment, evaluation and programming systems for infants and children.* Baltimore: Paul H. Brookes.

Bricker, D., Squires, J., & Mounts, L. (1995). *Ages and stages questionnaires.* Baltimore: Paul H. Brookes.

Campbell, P. H. (1993). *Administration guide: Functional outcome assessment grid.* Philadelphia: Temple University Center for Research in Human Development and Education.

Case-Smith, J. (1996). Analysis of current motor development theory and recently published infant motor assessments. *Infants and Young Children, 9,* 29-41.

Case-Smith, J., & Bryan, T. (1999). The effects of occupational therapy with sensory integration emphasis on preschool-age children with autism. *American Journal of Occupational Therapy, 53,* 489-497.

Case-Smith, J., & Miller, H. (1999). Occupational therapy with children with pervasive developmental disorders. *American Journal of Occupational Therapy, 53,* 506-513.

Chandler, L. S., Swanson, M.W., & Andrews, M. S. (1980). *Movement assessment of infants.* Rolling Bay, WI: Infant Movement Research.

Cicchetti, D., & Wagner, S. (1990). Alternative assessment strategies for the evaluation of infants and toddlers: An organizational perspective. In S. J. Meisels & J. P. Shonkoff (Eds.), *Handbook of early childhood intervention.* New York: Cambridge University Press.

Cintas, H. L. (1995). Cross-cultural similarities and differences in development and the impact on parental expectations on motor behavior. *Pediatric Physical Therapy, 7,* 103-111.

Cole, K., Harris, S., Eland, S., & Mills, P. (1989). Comparison of two service delivery models: In-class and out-of-class therapy approaches. *Pediatric Physical Therapy, 1,* 49-54.

Coster, W., Deeney, T., Haltiwanger, J., & Haley, S. (1998). *School function assessment.* San Antonio, TX: Therapy Skill Builders.

DeGangi, G., & Greenspan, S. I. (1988). The development of sensory functions in infants. *Physical and Occupational Therapy in Pediatrics, 8,* 21-33.

DeGangi, G., & Greenspan, S. (1989). *Test of sensory functions in infants.* Los Angeles: Western Psychological Services.

Dunn, W. (1996). Occupational therapy. In R.A. McWilliam (Ed.), *Rethinking pull-out services in early intervention, (pp. 267-313)*. Baltimore: Paul H. Brookes.

Dunn, W., Brown, T., & McGuigan, A. (1994). The ecology of human performance: A framework for considering the effect of context. *American Journal of Occupational Therapy, 48*(7), 595-607.

Dunn, W. & Campbell, P. H. (1991). Designing pediatric service provision. In W. Dunn (Ed.), P*ediatric occupational therapy* (pp. 130-159). Thorofare, NJ: Slack.

Embrey, D. G., Yates, L., & Mott, D. H. (1990). Effects of neurodevelopmental treatment and orthoses on knee flexion during gait: A single-subject design. *Physical Therapy, 70,* 626-637.

Foley, G.M. (1990). Portrait of the arena evaluation: Assessment in the transdisciplinary approach. In F. D. Gibbs and D. M. Titi (Eds.), *Interdisciplinary assessment of infants: A guide for early intervention professionals.* Baltimore: Paul H. Brookes.

Folio, M. & Fewell, R. (1983). *Peabody developmental motor scale.* Allen, TX: DLM Teaching Resources.

Gentile, A. M. (1987). Skill acquisition: Action, movement, and neuromotor processes. In J. H. Carr, & R. B. Shepard (Eds.), *Movement science: Foundations for physical therapy in rehabilitation.* Rockville, MD: Aspen Systems.

Gesell, A. (1945). *The embryology of behavior: The beginnings of the human mind.* Philadelphia: J. B. Lippincott.

Giangreco, M. F. (1986). Effects of integrated therapy: A pilot study. *Journal of the Association for Persons with Severe Disabilities, 11*(3), 205-208.

Greenspan, S. I., & Meisels, S. (1993). *Toward a new vision for the developmental assessment of infants and young children.* Arlington, VA: ZERO TO THREE, National Center for Clinical Infant Programs.

Greenspan, S. I., & Meisels, S. J., with the Zero-to-Three Work Group on Developmental Assessment (1996). In S. J. Meisels and E. Fenichel (Eds.), *New visions for the developmental assessment of infants and young children.* Washington, D.C.: ZERO TO THREE, National Center for Infants, Toddlers, and Families.

Greenspan, S. I., & Weider, S. (1997). An integrated developmental approach to interventions for young children with severe difficulties in relating and communicating. *Zero to Three, 17*(5), 5-8.

Haley, S., Coster, W. J., Ludlow, I. H., Haltiwanger, J. T., & Andrellas, P. (1992). *Pediatric evaluation of disability inventory.* Boston: PEDI Research Group, Department of Rehabilitation Medicine, New England Medical Center Hospital.

Hanft, B., & Place, P. (1996). *The consulting therapist: A guide for OTs and PTs in the school.* San Antonio, TX: Therapy Skill Builders.

Harris, S. (1988). Early intervention: Does developmental therapy make a difference? *Topics in Early Childhood Special Education, 7,* 20-32.

Harris, S. (1987). Early intervention for children with motor handicaps. In M. J. Guralnick & F. C. Bennett (Eds.), *The effectiveness of early intervention for at-risk and handicapped children* (pp. 175-212). Orlando, FL: Academic Press.

Heriza, C. (1991). Motor development: Traditional and contemporary theories. In M. J. Lester (Ed.), *Contemporary management of motor control problems: Proceedings of the II Step Conference.* Alexandria, VA: Foundation for Physical Therapy.

Horn, E. M., Warren, S. F., & Jones, H. A. (1995). An experimental analysis of a neurobehavioral intervention. *Developmental Medicine and Child Neurology, 37,* 697-714.

Humphries, T., Wright, M., Snider, L., & McDougall, B. (1992). A comparison of the effectiveness of sensory integrative therapy and perceptual-motor training in treating children with learning disabilities. *Developmental and Behavioral Pediatrics, 13*(1), 31-40.

Johnson-Martin, N. M., Jens, K. A., Attermeier, S. M., & Hacker, B. J. (1991). *The Carolina curriculum for infants and toddlers with special needs.* (2nd ed.) Baltimore: Paul H. Brookes.

Kirshner, B., & Guyatt, G. (1985). A methodological framework for assessing health indices. *Journal of Chronic Diseases, 38,* 27-36.

Koomar, J., & Bundy, A. (1991). The art and science of creating direct intervention from theory. In A. G. Fisher, E. A. Murray, & A. C. Bundy (Eds.), *Sensory integration: Theory and practice* (pp. 251-317). Philadelphia: F. A. Davis.

Larin, H. (1994). Motor learning: Theories and strategies for the practitioner. In S. Campbell (Ed.), *Physical therapy for children* (pp. 157-182). Philadelphia: W. B. Saunders.

Law, M., Cadman, D., Rosenbaum, P., Walters, S., Russell, D., & DeMateo, C. (1991). Neurodevelopmental therapy and upper extremity casting for children with cerebral palsy. *Developmental Medicine and Child Neurology, 33,* 379-387.

Lyons, B. G. (1984). Defining a child's zone of proximal development: Evaluation process for treatment planning. *American Journal of Occupational Therapy, 38,* 446-451.

McGraw, M. B. (1945). *The neuromuscular maturation of the human infant.* New York: Hafner Press.

McWilliam, R. (1996). How to provide integrated therapy. In R. A. McWilliam (Ed.), *Rethinking pull-out services in early intervention* (pp. 147-184). Baltimore: Paul H. Brookes.

McWilliam, R. A. (1992). *Family centered intervention planning: A routines based approach.* San Antonio, TX: Therapy Skill Builders.

McWilliam, R. A., Tocci, L., & Harbin, G. L. (1995). *Services are child-oriented and families want them that way.* Chapel Hill: Early Childhood Research Institute on Service Utilization, Frank Porter Graham Child Development Center, University of North Carolina.

Miller, L. J., & Roid, G. H. (1994). *The TIME: Toddler and infant motor evaluation.* Tucson, AZ: Therapy Skill Builders.

Newborg, J., Stock, J. R., & Wnek, L. (1984). *Battelle developmental inventory.* Allen, TX: DLM Teaching Resources.

Ottenbacher, K. (1991). Research in sensory integration: Empirical perceptions and progress. In A. G. Fisher, E. A. Murray, & A. C. Bundy (Eds.), *Sensory integration: Theory & practice* (pp. 385-399). Philadelphia: F. A. Davis.

Ottenbacher, K., Biocca, Z., DeCremer, G., Gevelinger, M., Jedovic, K. B., & Johnson, M. B. (1986). Quantitative analysis of the effectiveness of pediatric therapy: Emphasis on neurodevelopmental treatment approach. *Physical Therapy, 66,* 1095-1101.

Ottenbacher, K., & Cusick, A. (1989). Goal attainment scaling as a method of clinical service evaluation. *American Journal of Occupational Therapy, 44,* 519-525.

Ottenbacher, K., & Peterson, P. (1985). The efficacy of early intervention programs for

Chapter 9. Screening, Evaluating, and Assessing Children with Sensorimotor Concerns and Linking
Findings to Intervention Planning: Strategies for Pediatric Occupational and Physical Therapists

211

children with organic impairment: A quantitative review. *Evaluation and Program Planning, 8,* 135-146.

Palisano, R. (1991). Research on the effectiveness of neurodevelopmental treatment. *Pediatrics Physical Therapy, 3,* 143-148.

Palmer, F. B., Shapiro, B. S., Wachtel, R. C., Allen, M. C., Hiller, J. E., Harryman, S. F., Mosher, B. S., Meinert, C. L., & Capute, A. J. (1990). Infant stimulation curriculum for infants with cerebral palsy: Effects on infant temperament, parent-infant interaction, and home environment. *Pediatrics, 85* (Suppl.), 411-415.

Parham, L. D., & Malloux, Z. (1996). Sensory integration. In J. Case-Smith, A. S. Allen, & P. N. Pratt (Eds.), *Occupational Therapy for Children* (3rd ed.) (pp. 307-356). St. Louis, MO: Mosby.

Piper, M. (1993). Theoretical foundations for physical therapy assessment in early infancy. In I. J. Wilhelm (Ed.), *Physical therapy assessment in early infancy.* New York: Churchill Livingstone.

Piper, M., & Darrah, J. (1993). *Motor assessment of the developing infant.* Philadelphia: W. B. Saunders.

Russell, D., Rosenbaum, P., Garland, C., Hardy, S., Lane, M., Plews, M., McGavin, H., Cadman, D., & Jarvis, S. (1993). *Gross motor function measure.* Hamilton, Ontario: Children's Developmental Rehabilitation Program at Chedoke-McMaster Hospitals.

Schmidt, R. A. (1975). A schema theory of discrete motor skill learning. *Psychological Review, 82,* 225-260.

Shelton, T. (1989). The assessment of cognition/intelligence in infancy. *Infants and Young Children: An Interdisciplinary Journal of Special Care Practice, 1,* 10-25.

Shirley, M. M. (1931). *The first two years: A study of twenty-five babies. Vol. 1: Postural and locomotor development.* Minneapolis, MN: University of Minnesota Press.

Shonkoff, J. P., & Hauser-Cram, P. (1987). Early intervention for disabled infants and their families. *Pediatrics, 80,* 650-658.

Taylor, R. L. (1993). Instruments for the screening, evaluation, and assessment of infants and toddlers. In D. M. Bryant & M. A. Graham (Eds.), *Implementing early intervention: From research to effective practice.* New York: Guilford.

Thelan, E. (1990). Coupling perception and action in the development of skill: A dynamic approach. In H. Block and B.T. Berenthal (Eds.), *Sensorimotor organization and development in infancy and early childhood* (pp. 39-56). Dordrecht, Netherlands: Kluwer Academic.

Vargas, S., & Camilli, G. (1999). A meta-analysis of research on sensory integration treatment. *American Journal of Occupational Therapy, 53,* 189-198.

Warren, S. F., & Horn, E. (1996) Generalization issues in providing integrated services. In R. A. McWilliam (Ed.), *Rethinking pull out services in early intervention: A professional resource* (pp. 121-143). Baltimore: Paul H. Brookes.

Watling, R., Dietz, J., Kanny, E. M., & Mclaughlin, J. F. (1999). Current practice of occupational therapy for children with autism. *American Journal of Occupational Therapy, 53,* 498-505.

Wolery, M. (1996). Early childhood special and general education. In R. A. McWilliam (Ed.), *Rethinking pull out services in early intervention: A professional resource* (pp. 182-215). Baltimore: Paul H. Brookes.

Wright, T., & Nicholson, J. (1973). Physiotherapy for the spastic child: An evaluation. *Developmental Medicine and Child Neurology, 15,* 146-163.

Appendix

ADDITIONAL MEASUREMENT INSTRUMENTS USED BY PEDIATRIC PHYSICAL THERAPISTS AND OCCUPATIONAL THERAPISTS

Name	Purpose	Areas Assessed	Age Range	Clinical Relevance
Ages and Stages Questionnaires, (Squires, J., & Bricker, D., 1999)	• Determine development through parental report	• Communication • Gross motor • Fine motor • Adaptive • Personal-social	4-60 months	• Cost effective monitoring system for high risk infants
Assessment, Evaluation and Programming System for Infants and Children (Bricker, D., 1993)	• Determine level of functioning • Develop intervention plans • Monitor effects of intervention	• Fine motor • Gross motor • Adaptive • Cognition • Social • Communication	1 month to 3 years	• Administered during naturally occurring events, routines, and activities • Direct link to programming • Allows for observation or direct testing • Takes into consideration task adaptations/ modifications
Batelle Developmental Inventory (Newborg, L., Stock, J. R., & Wnek, L., 1984)	• Determine level of development • Determine eligibility for educational intervention	• Personal-social • Adaptive • Motor • Communication • Cognition	1 month to 9 years	• Includes adaptations for children with disabilities • Screening component • Limited number of items in each domain
Bayley Scales of Infant Development-II (Bayley, N., 1993)	• Determine level of development • Determine eligibility for early intervention	• Cognition • Motor • Behavior	1-42 months	• Predictive value is moderate • Most widely used tool in infant research *Continued*

Name	Purpose	Areas Assessed	Age Range	Clinical Relevance
Bayley Infant Neurodevelopmental Screener (Alyward, G., 1993)	• Screen for potential delay or neurological impairments	• Neurologic • Receptive • Expressive • Cognitive	3-24 months	• Incorporates neuromotor items into developmental scale • Takes into consideration caregiver report • Especially relevant for NICU follow-up
The Carolina Curriculum for Infants and Toddlers with Special Needs (2nd ed.) (Johnson-Martin, N. M., Jens, K. A., Attermeier, S. N. & Hacker, B. J., 1991)	• Determine level of performance across dimensions	• Cognition • Communication • Gross motor • Fine motor • Self-help	0-36 months	• Criterion-referenced • Curriculum cross-referenced to measurement instrument
Movement Assessment of Infants (MAI), (Chandler, L. S., Swanson, M.W., & Andrews, M. S., 1980)	• Provide a uniform approach to the evaluation of high risk infants	• Muscle tone • Reflexes • Automatic • Reactions • Volitional movement	0-12 months	• Lengthy, great deal of handling of the infant • Risk profile for 4-month-old
Peabody Developmental Motor Scales (Folio, M., & Fewell, R., 2000)	• Determine developmental level	• Reflexes • Gross motor • Fine motor	0-72 months	• Scoring allows crediting of emerging skills • Activity cards available but of limited use

10

An Integrated Intervention Approach to Treating Infants and Young Children with Regulatory, Sensory Processing, and Interactional Problems[1]

Georgia A. DeGangi, Ph.D., O.T.R., F.A.O.T.A.

A variety of developmental therapies that therapists typically use to address constitutional and maturational problems in infants and young children are associated with regulatory difficulties involving sleep and eating problems, sensory reactivity, poor motor planning, and high irritability. These developmental therapies include (1) sensory integration therapy (Ayres 1972, 1979) to address the infant's sensory processing problems; (2) developmental therapy that emphasizes skills in communication, play, cognition, and movement; and (3) parent guidance approaches that integrate behavioral and developmental techniques to address sleep, mood regulation, eating, and attentional problems (DeGangi, Craft, & Castellan, 1991; DeGangi, 2000).

Many infants and children with regulatory and developmental problems also have problems with social interactions, which are observed first in how the child interacts with family members and, later, with peers (Greenspan, 1992, 1997). When the problem is considered severe enough, a mental health professional provides services. Regulatory and regulatory-related relational problems may be addressed through (1) infant psychotherapy approaches that focus on dyadic parent-child interactions (Fraiberg, 1980; Greenspan, 1992, 1997; Greenspan & Salmon, 1995; Greenspan & Wieder, 1998); (2) directive interactional guidance such as that developed by MacDonough (1989); or (3) supportive counseling. The way in which these approaches are used vary greatly depending upon the presenting concerns, the population being treated, and the theoretical framework adopted by the treating therapists.

In this chapter, an integrated model of treatment is advocated to address both the child's constitutional problems and how these problems impact the family and the parent-child dyad. This expanded model of treatment includes:

- *Parent guidance* that focuses on management of sleep, feeding, and behaviors in the home environment.
- *Child-centered interactions* (i.e, "floor time," [Greenspan & Wieder, 1998])

[1] This chapter focuses on circumscribed self-regulation, sensory procesing, and motor-planning challenges. For many children with significant problems in relating, communicating, and thinking, these strategies will need to be considered in the context of a comprehensive program, as described in Chapter 4.

activity that fosters healthy parent-child interactions within the context of play.

- *Sensory integration therapy* techniques that promote organized attention, adaptive behaviors, and normalized responses to sensory experiences.

The parent guidance, child-centered activity, and sensory integration therapy techniques are blended together in treatment, with primary emphasis on meeting the immediate needs of both the parent and child.

This chapter describes this family-centered approach. It presents the elements of parent guidance, using examples of typical problems. Child-centered activity—or floor time—and sensory integration therapy techniques are discussed in their application to infants and children with sensory, emotional, and attentional deficits. Research examining the effectiveness of the child-centered activity approach is presented. Lastly, the chapter includes a detailed case example that incorporates the various elements of the treatment approach and modifications that may be needed depending upon the presenting problems.

THE FAMILY-CENTERED APPROACH: ADDRESSING THE CONCERNS OF PARENTS

Legislation and current research on family involvement in a child's therapy program point to the value of a family-centered approach to intervention. In this approach, play is increasingly recognized by professionals as an important medium through which parents can address the special needs of their child. Play is viewed as the arena in which children learn and practice new skills with the people most important to them (Schaaf & Mulrooney, 1989). Research suggests that when parents realize a sense of empowerment in making decisions, their stress and depression may be reduced and

their sense of competence increased (Friedrich, Cohen, & Wilturner, 1988). Clinicians become consultants to the parents in this collaborative model of helping, and the parents' abilities are met with respect and confidence (Dunst, Trivett, Davis, & Cornwell, 1988).

Children who are fussy, irritable, and demanding are extremely challenging for parents. Oftentimes, parents cope by developing interaction patterns of under- or over-stimulation. For example, parents who must often soothe and regulate their distressed child may find that they tend to retreat or "shrink from interaction" when their child is happy and content so as not to "rock the boat." In the case of the highly distractible child who appears to seek constant novelty, the parents may exacerbate the problem by presenting many activities or toys to their child to try to keep the child happy.

The family-centered approach recognizes the stress that coping with a difficult child places on the family. The parents often experience sleep deprivation and, as a result, they have little reserve for coping with an irritable child. Many times, parents report that babysitters cannot cope with the child's difficult behaviors, which compounds feelings of entrapment. Marital tension may be heightened as the parents feel overwhelmed by the problems of the fussy and difficult child or make accommodations that interfere with their own relationship (i.e., infant sleeping in parents' bed). In some cases, the father becomes peripheral to the family, working long hours to avoid a hectic home life and a constantly screaming infant. The danger of child abuse is very real.

An adequate support system is necessary to help a family cope with a difficult situation. More and more parents have no extended family in their geographic area. As a result, they have no one to help them or to

Chapter 10. An Integrated Intervention Approach to Treating Infants and Young Children with
Regulatory, Sensory Processing, and Interactional Problems

217

provide respite. Parent-baby groups have become an alternative support system for many families; however, many fussy babies cannot tolerate being in a playgroup situation, thus removing this option for the parent. Additionally, many parents take their children to baby gym or swim classes; however, these activities are often too stimulating for the regulatory-disordered child. As a result, many parents feel even more isolated and removed from the typical activities in which parents engage with their children. Sometimes, parents who try such options feel stigmatized by other parents because their child appears so out of control.

Depression is frequently a side effect of coping with the demands of parenting the fussy baby. Many mothers report feelings of inadequacy when normal parenting skills do not seem to work with their child. First-time parents often confuse their child's constitutional difficulties with their own parental inexperience, which exacerbates depression or feelings of helplessness. These feelings are compounded when the infant rejects being held and cuddled because of hypersensitivities to touch. Sometimes the parents learn to avoid sensorimotor activities that provoke their child's hypersensitive responses. For example, if the child dislikes swings and playground equipment because of extreme fearfulness of movement in space, a protective mother may guide her child away from movement activities. In some cases the parents may experience similar hypersensitivities, which compounds their responses to their infant who has similar constitutional difficulties.

In summary, a family-centered approach focuses on parental concerns, family stresses in coping with the difficult child, adaptive and maladaptive parent-child interaction patterns, and parental depression or marital conflicts that may be secondary to the child's constitutional difficulties. These issues may

be addressed directly through parent guidance and the child-centered activity.

Parent Guidance

Approaches for infants and children with the range of developmental disorders involve a blend of behavioral management, supportive counseling, practical management techniques, sensorimotor activities, and developmental therapy to address specific constitutional problems (DeGangi et al., 1991). Parent guidance is an important component of the therapy process. It provides parents with emotional support in coping with their difficult child and is useful in developing effective strategies to set limits, manage the child's sleep, teach self-calming, and handle feeding problems. Although parent guidance is individualized, a variety of self-help books is often used to help parents in managing specific problems such as sleep or dietary problems (Carey & McDevitt, 1995; Daws, 1989; Greenspan, 1999; Greenspan & Salmon, 1995; Sears, 1985; Rapp, 1986; Turecki & Tonner, 1985). Although the relationship between food allergies and behaviors is controversial, the possibility of food allergies should be explored for those children who do not respond to behavioral management techniques. For example, it was recently reported that a significant number of infants who did not respond to behavioral techniques for sleeplessness did respond to a hypoallergenic diet that eliminated all milk products (Kahn, Mozin, Rebuffat, Sottiaux, & Muller, 1989).

Sleep problems are addressed by a combination of methods, including developing appropriate sleep-wake routines (Ferber, 1984). Since sleep problems are often accompanied by separation anxiety, separation games are practiced (e.g., chase games, peek-a-boo). Techniques to console the irritable child include addressing the child's sensory hypersensitivities, developing the child's own capacity to self-calm, and reducing parental anxieties when crying occurs. Techniques for managing temper tantrums and helping the child to accept limits focus not only on the child's difficulties in expressing frustration and negative affect, but on helping parents develop a consistent plan in approaching the child's behaviors. Management of feeding problems focuses on inhibiting tactile hypersensitivities of the face and mouth, expanding the child's repertoire of foods, and addressing behavioral feeding problems such as refusal to eat and food throwing. Attentional problems are addressed by structuring the environment, reducing the child's hyper-arousal through sensory inhibition, and facilitating sustained attention by helping the child to elaborate on play. In addition, problems with communication and play are addressed through structured intervention by explicitly teaching parents how to promote face-to-face engagement, reciprocal interactions, two-way communication, and gestural or vocal signaling.

When therapy is initiated, the clinician seeks to help the parents understand their child's behaviors and how they as parents respond when the behaviors occur. The clinician discusses what techniques the parents have already tried to determine which ones may or may not have worked. Sometimes it becomes apparent that parental inexperience or mismanagement of behaviors exacerbates the child's regulatory difficulties. When this appears to be the case, it is important for the therapist to be supportive and nonjudgmental. It is also important for the therapist to determine if discrepancies exist between the ways in which the father and the mother manage their child's difficult behaviors.

Parent guidance takes the form of a working dialogue with the parents to develop the best match between the parents' concerns, the family lifestyle, and management techniques.

Major emphasis is placed on developing problem-solving strategies from which the parents often develop insights about their child and themselves. For example, some parents may realize that they are over-controlling and cannot tolerate their child's overly active and loud behaviors. It is important to help such parents understand what underlies their child's difficulties and to help them develop strategies to help their child organize his behaviors before they become uncontrollable, yet at the same time provide him with opportunities for normal active exploration. Parent guidance blends the principles of behavioral management, supportive therapy, practical management techniques, brief psychodynamic therapy, family therapy principles, and sensory integration treatment.

Sensory Integration Therapy Approach

The family-centered approach addresses the constitutional problems of the children by incorporating the principles of sensory integration therapy (Ayres, 1972, 1979; Fisher, Murray, & Bundy, 1991). Concepts from sensory-integration therapy are integrated into functional activities, modifications of the environment, and play interactions with others. Sensory integration treatment techniques often involve desensitizing hyperreactivities; increasing the underreactive child's sensory awareness; organizing sustained attention; facilitating organized, purposeful activity; and promoting self-calming and modulation of arousal states through specific sensory inputs. The major principle underlying sensory integration therapy is the improvement of the child's ability to organize and process sensory input during self-directed, purposeful activities. The child's interest and motivation guide how the various sensory integration tasks are provided.

Chapter 10. An Integrated Intervention Approach to Treating Infants and Young Children with
Regulatory, Sensory Processing, and Interactional Problems

219

Sensory integration therapy provides a foundation for children experiencing sensory processing and attentional deficits. This therapy is provided within the contexts of the child-centered activity and parent guidance. Specific treatment techniques for desensitizing the hyperreactive child, organizing sustained attention and purposeful activity, and promoting self-calming and modulation of arousal states are derived from the sensory integration treatment approach. The next section describes the basic tenants of this philosophical approach.

The underlying premise of sensory integration theory is that the ability of the central nervous system to take in, sort out, and interrelate information received from the environment is necessary for purposeful, goal-directed responses. The major principle underlying sensory integration treatment is the improvement of an individual's ability to organize and process sensory input provided during meaningful events, thus allowing for an adaptive response to the environment. A child's ability to actively experience sensations while simultaneously engaging in self-directed, purposeful motor activity is essential to intervention. Sensory integration therapy facilitates an individual's ability to make adaptive responses to environmental stimuli, and these responses facilitate organization in the central nervous system by providing sensory feedback about a goal-directed event.

Self-directed and self-initiated actions differentially enhance central nervous system function and maturation (Kandel & Schwartz, 1985). In essence, approaches such as the child-centered activity allow a child to develop automatic functions of better self-organization and control. The child learns to develop appropriate motor responses to different sensory events based upon neural feedback and central nervous system organization (Clark, Mailloux, & Parham, 1985).

When children experience sensory integration dysfunction, they frequently benefit from occupational therapy input. The therapist works with the child and family to integrate sensory integration principles into the child's everyday living and play experiences. This is done by modifying daily routines, functional activities, play materials, and the manner in which important persons in the child's life interact with the child. It often includes making changes in the way in which the home environment is structured (e.g., reducing noise stimulation, providing small, enclosed spaces). The therapist often provides individualized sensory input to address specific atypical sensory responses. For example, the therapist may brush the child's skin with a surgical brush in specific ways to desensitize the child's tactile hypersensitivities, or she may introduce certain types of movement on suspended equipment (e.g., spinning) to normalize the child's responses to vestibular stimulation. These directed sensory integration techniques are very helpful in normalizing the child's sensory responses, but should be provided by a trained occupational therapist.

The sensory integration therapy approach advocated for use in the integrated therapy approach described in this chapter focuses on how principles from sensory integration therapy can be used to address the child's constitutional difficulties. This is done within the context of everyday activities and interactions with others. For example, when tactile hypersensitivities are present, activities are used that involve firm deep-pressure (e.g., mother and child wrapping up together in a big comforter), proprioception (e.g., embracing the child with firm contact with primary input on the child's back), and providing textured objects that will help organize the child's exploration. If a child is fearful of leaving the ground because of gravitational insecurity, low-to-ground equipment such as an inner tube filled with interesting toys is introduced. Motor-planning activities are encouraged by focusing on how movement can be sequenced in play and through transitions in activities. The case study presented at the end of this chapter more fully depicts how the sensory integration approach is integrated into the child's treatment program.

Child-Centered Activity: Floor Time

Description of the Floor Time Approach

Addressing the emotional and interactional aspects of the parent-child difficulties that exist between the child and the parents is central for treatment. Floor time was developed by Greenspan (1979, 1989, 1992, 1997, 1999; Greenspan & Lourie, 1981; Greenspan & Salmon, 1995; Greenspan & Wieder, 1998), to foster growth in the context of integrating the different realms of the child's experiences (i.e., physical, emotional, and interactive/family). This approach focuses on using the inner resources of the child and parent. Using an experiential model, floor time is a form of infant psychotherapy that is adapted to the sensorimotor phase of development (DeGangi, 2000). The theoretical approach underlying floor time therapy is based on ego psychology as described by Greenspan (1979) and an object-relations theoretical framework (Winnicott, 1960). In this child-centered approach, infant psychotherapy focuses on the dynamics of the parent-infant interaction and parent insights concerning their relationship with their child or issues from their past, as well as the emotional needs of parent and child during interactions (Lieberman & Pawl, 1993).

Others have also applied principles of infant psychotherapy to the sensorimotor phase of development (Mahrer, Levinson, &

Fine, 1976; Ostrov, Dowling, Wesner, & Johnson, 1982.) Wesner, Dowling, and Johnson (1982) described an approach which they term "Watch, Wait, and Wonder (WWW)" that is similar to Greenspan's floor time. In the WWW approach, the infant initiates all interactions and the parents seek to discover what it is that their infant is seeking and needing from them and the environment. In this process, the parents may become attuned to the child's constitutional and emotional needs, how the child wishes to communicate and interact, and the quality of their parent-child relationship. Helping parents recognize their projective identifications with their child is considered an important aspect of the treatment process. The WWW approach has been used successfully with mentally retarded and developmentally delayed children (Mahoney, 1988; Mahoney & Powell, 1988). It also has been used as a method to focus on unresolved relational conflicts of the mother involving the mother's projective identification with her infant (Muir, 1992).

Floor time focuses on improving the developmental capacities of the child within the context of the parent-child relationship. Relevant stages of emotional development outlined by Greenspan (1989, 1992) are used to help guide this process. These stages include engagement and disengagement with objects and persons; organized, intentional signaling and communication on verbal and gestural levels; representational elaboration of shared meanings; and symbolic differentiation of affective-thematic experiences. In this child-centered approach, constitutional problems of the child such as irritability, sensory hypersensitivities, inattention, and other problems of self-regulation are addressed through the medium of play with the parent. Insights gained by parents about their relationship with their child or issues from their own past are addressed as they pertain to parenting and fostering the child's healthy emotional development and regulatory capacities.

In floor time, the parent is taught to provide daily sessions of focused, nonjudgmental attention. The frequency and duration of the intervention will vary depending upon the child's and the family's needs. During this time, the child is the initiator of all play and the parent is the interested observer and facilitator, elaborating and expanding upon the child's own activity in whatever way the child seeks or needs from the parent (e.g., to imitate, admire, or facilitate). The parent is nonintrusive and nondirective in his or her interactions with the child. In this approach, the parent is instructed to "watch, wait, and wonder" what the child is seeking and needing both from the parent and the environment, then respond accordingly (Wesner, Dowling, & Johnson, 1982).

The child's attention span and activity level dictate the direction that the play takes rather than an imposed structure or specific task demand presented by the parent. In this way, the child needs to refine his ability to attend and give affective signals while the parent learns to become a more sensitive responder. If the child's gestural or vocal signals are nondifferentiated, the parent may reflect their nonspecificity by imitating, then waiting until the child can again signal what he wants. The environment is organized to make available toys and materials that promote sensorimotor development and emotional themes in a safe area where there are no prohibitions or interruptions. For example, if a child has tactile hypersensitivities, textured toys and heavy objects are placed in the room together with other play materials. If the child has feeding problems, dolls and feeding utensils and mediums such as corn, dried beans, or water are set out. In general, the toys are childproof and developmentally

appropriate. For example, for a 6- to 12-month-old, the play materials may be tableware, blocks, dolls, and tactile materials such as Koosh balls, whereas toys for a toddler may be toy telephones, a cradle with a doll, toy trains and cars, and blocks and balls. Extrinsic reinforcement, such as praise, is deemphasized. Instead, the parent reflects on the child's expressiveness by expanding on facial gestures, affect, or language cues. The parent is given permission to be an observer of the child and to respond to the child's cues. The medium of play offers parents space to ponder the nature of their relationship with their child and minimizes the need to do to, or for, their child.

During the time that the parent and child engage, the therapist acts as an attentive observer, modeling how to be a nonjudgmental observer of the parent-child relationship. In essence, the therapist provides for the parent what the parent provides for the child. Throughout the process, the therapist tries to convey a sense of respect for the caregiver's parenting ability. In challenging cases, the therapist may need to be more directive in helping the parent to follow the floor time structure. This issue is discussed more fully in a later section.

During therapy sessions, floor time is practiced for 20 minutes followed by a discussion between therapist and parent about the process. For some parents, 20 minutes is too long for them to tolerate this type of play with their child, in which case floor time is attempted for as long as the parent is able. The parents may be asked what they observed about their child. In addition, they may be asked questions about what it was like for them to play with their infant in this special way and how they felt during the playtime. The therapist's role is supportive, while seeking to help clarify and reflect on the parent's responses to the child and what the child's behaviors might serve for the child. This process is important in order to address how the parents have adapted to the child's regulatory problems and to help parents become more aware of how the child might perceive their cues. Parental stress, depression, feelings of incompetence or displeasure with parenting, connections with the past (e.g., how parented), feelings elicited by the child's behavior, and family dynamics (including the impact of the child on marital relations) may be topics that emerge. If a parent is resistant to exploring personal issues and prefers to focus solely on the child, the therapist is respectful of this wish. The therapist may gently raise concerns about how the child's behaviors affect the parents and family.

Unlike more structured therapy approaches, floor time is a *process-oriented* model rather than a technique to be mastered. Some parents need considerable help in allowing their child to take the lead. They may have difficulty resisting the temptation to teach their child new skills, particularly when they are worried about lags in development. The therapist seeks to help the parents gain insights about their child's regulatory problems through what is expressed in the play context.

The underpinnings of this approach lie in the view that play— rather than direct instruction and skills training—is the medium by which a child learns, and that children learn best when actively engaged in the presence of a loving parent. As the child becomes the initiator of an interaction, intrinsic motivation and active participation in interactions and explorations are enhanced. The child experiences the parents' encouragement to act on her interests, which enhances the child's feelings of success, competence, and control. As a result, the child learns to develop internal control, and to engage in explorations with her environment and in interactions with others.

Through the medium of child-centered activity, parents become more sensitized to their child's behavioral style, developmental needs, and interests. For a child with significant sensory disturbances, this learning has far-reaching implications. For example, the infant with tactile hypersensitivities may avoid handling textured objects, reject new food textures, and experience physical discomfort when touched by others. Because of the underlying tactile hypersensitivities, the infant may exhibit difficulties in manipulating small objects in feeding and in playing with peers. During treatment, the mother may set out several types of textured toys (e.g., a large bin of styrofoam chips with many interesting toy figures buried inside the bin) during the time designated for child-centered activity. She waits and watches the child as he approaches the materials, facilitating exploration by taking turns. In this way, the child learns to explore the materials on his own terms, taking in only as much tactile information as his nervous system can handle. Aggressive behaviors may be channeled appropriately by providing the child with toys such as heavy push carts that he can lift and move or large Nerf balls and bats that he can throw and hit. These types of activities also serve to desensitize the child's overly sensitive tactile system.

The child-centered activity approach, or floor time, has been applied by individuals in several disciplines to accomplish different goals. Speech and language therapists have used this approach to achieve balanced interactions between an adult and child through turn-taking. For example, a child initiates an action, and the adult imitates the action or vocalization or responds by continuing the child's topic. This turn-taking exchange may continue for a number of turns with variations in responses with each turn. It not only serves

Chapter 10. An Integrated Intervention Approach to Treating Infants and Young Children with Regulatory, Sensory Processing, and Interactional Problems

223

to facilitate communication, but also increases a child's attention to tasks.

Because the focus of the approach is on mastery for both parent and child, it is a highly positive and reinforcing experience for both parent and child. Preconceived notions that a child must be taught in order to learn are challenged, particularly for the parents who perceives that their child is less competent than her peers. The parents' difficulties are not considered detrimental to the treatment process; however, they must be addressed. Some parents may not be able to embrace this approach. Parents with obsessive or rigid parenting styles may find the more reflective and responsive style of child-centered activity difficult. If these parents can master floor time techniques, it may help them develop less rigid patterns of interaction and allow them to expand their repertoire of parent behaviors that will later enhance mental health. The child-centered activity is a natural foundation for developing listening skills.

Goals of Floor Time

Floor time has different goals for the parent and the child.

The ultimate goals of floor time for a child are to:
- Provide the child with focused, nonjudgmental attention from the parent.
- Facilitate self-initiation and problem-solving by the child.
- Develop intentionality, motivation, curiosity, and exploration.
- Promote sustained and focused attention.
- Refine the child's signal giving.
- Enhance mastery of sensorimotor developmental challenges through the context of play.
- Broaden the repertoire of parent-infant interactions.

- Develop a secure and joyful attachment between parent and child.
- Enhance flexibility and range in interactive capacities.

The goals of floor time for a parent are to:
- Develop better signal reading of their child's cues and needs.
- Become more responsive or attuned to their child, allowing the child to take the lead in the interaction.
- Develop a sense of parental competence as a facilitator rather than as a director of their child's activity.
- Take pleasure in their child in a totally nonprohibitive setting.
- Appreciate their child's intrinsic drive for mastery and the various ways in which it is manifested.
- Change their internal image of each other to that of a competent parent and a competent child.

Through the child-centered therapy process, parents who have felt overwhelmed by their child's difficulties may begin to acquire new ways of interacting and enjoying their child at home. By working through the parent-child relationship, the child's emotional and developmental competence is enhanced.

Instructions On How to Teach Floor Time

Instructions that a therapist may use in guiding a parent to learn floor time follow.

Instructions for Floor Time

1. *Set aside 20 minutes/day when there are no interruptions.* Be sure to do the play during a time when you and your child are well rested and you don't have other things to worry about, such as something cooking on the stove or the doorbell ring-

ing. Take the telephone off the hook or put the answering machine on. Be sure that your child's physical needs such as toileting, and feeding are met so that you won't need to stop the play to take care of these needs. Put things out of reach that you don't want your child to play with (e.g., business papers or fragile objects). Use an area that is childproof and where there are no prohibitions or limits that you might have to set.

2. *If you can, put out two sets of toys so that you can join in play with your child* (i.e., two toy telephones, several trucks and blocks). Select toys that allow your child to explore and try new things, and that are more open-ended in nature. Avoid toys that require teaching or that are highly structured, such as board games, puzzles, or coloring. Your therapist will help you in picking out the best toys for playtime.

3. *Let your child know that he or she is getting "special time" with you.* Get on the floor with your child unless you are uncomfortable getting down to, or up from, the floor. Try to stay close to your child so that she can see your face and you can see what she is doing.

4. *Let your child take the lead and initiate what happens.* Anything that your child does is acceptable, except for hurting himself or you or destroying toys and materials. If your child wants to throw toys, put out soft things that are okay to throw, like foam balls or bean bags. Play with your child however he wants to play. Discover what he wants from you during this time. Does he want you to admire him? To imitate him? Try out what you think he wants from you and watch his reaction. See if your child starts to notice you and begin to interact more. Respond

to what your child is doing, but don't take over the play.

5. *Watch, wait, and wonder about what your child is doing.* Think about what your child is getting out of doing a particular activity. Enter her world and reflect on what her experience of it and you might be. Observing your child is the first step to providing a foundation of good listening.

6. *Watch what your child seeks in play with you and try to pick materials each play time that allow for those kinds of interactions.* For example, if your child likes to bang and push toys, pick things that may be banged and pushed.

7. *Avoid cleaning up toys that your child seems to be finished with until special time is over.* Your child may return to those toys to play some more. Only clean up if your therapist suggests that your child is becoming overstimulated by a variety of materials and needs less stimulation.

8. *Interact with, and/or talk with your child about what she's doing without leading the play or guiding what should happen next.* For example, you may copy or describe what she did ("What a big bounce you made with that ball!" "Look how you like to run!"). With older, verbal children, you may ask questions about what is happening (i.e., "Why is the baby doll crying?" "What is the monster thinking of doing now?"). It's useful to help your child bridge play ideas, particularly if your child begins an activity, then moves onto the next play topic, leaving a play idea hanging (i.e., "What happened to the dinosaur? I thought he wanted some food to eat.").

9. *Have fun! This is very important!* Try to enjoy playing with your child during special time. If you find it boring, find the

Chapter 10. An Integrated Intervention Approach to Treating Infants and Young Children with
Regulatory, Sensory Processing, and Interactional Problems

225

balance that will make the play fun and interesting for both of you.

10. *Remember that special time is not a teaching time.* Try to avoid praising your child or setting limits while you play. You want the motivation and pleasure of doing things together and exploring the world to come from within the child rather than because you are encouraging these through praise or reinforcement. There is no right or wrong way to play with toys.

11. *Sometimes, special time elicits uncomfortable feelings or strong reactions in parents: reflect on what the play is eliciting in yourself.* These reactions are useful to talk about with your therapist, so that you may understand what they mean for you and your relationship with your child. Should you feel overwhelmed by feelings, try to be less involved and play the role of the interested observer. You may even want to take notes on what you notice about your child and shorten the play time to 5 to 10 minutes if that is all you feel you can do. The important thing is that you are giving your child focused, nonjudgmental attention and the joy of interacting with you.

12. *When special time is over, make it clear to your child that it is time to end.* If your child shows frustration because it is difficult to end special time, empathize with him and help him express his frustration (e.g., a gentle hand on his back or a statement, "Wouldn't it be wonderful if we could do this all day long! I wish we could, but now it's time to stop and do something else."). If your child should become tired during the playtime, end it earlier. Clean up the toys and transition to some other activity, such as having a snack or reading a book.

13. *Try to do special time every day.* This is particularly important during times when

there are other stressors in the child's or family's life.

14. *If there are other siblings, try to set aside time for focused interaction with them as well.*

15. *Take at least 20 minutes a day for yourself to rest, relax, and do something just for you.* Taking time to catch up on household chores, food shopping, or other work activities doesn't count as time for you. This is your time to restore yourself.

Role of Therapist in Floor Time

The role of the therapist is to be a facilitator of the parent-child relationship. Although the therapist's role varies depending upon what each dyad or family brings to the process, the therapist should try to avoid too much direct teaching or directing of the process. More direction may be necessary for children with more significant developmental challenges (e.g., autism or pervasive developmental disorder). There are instances when the therapist needs to coach or reassure the parent, or modify the approach to be most effective. For example, when parents have difficulty allowing their child to take the lead or they are overstimulating the child (e.g., too verbal, too active, or anticontingent to infant's response), the therapist may need to help the parents tune into the child's cues. In such cases, the therapist may cue the parent by making comments such as, "Let's see what she's doing here" or "It looks like she's changed the play topic to something else. Let's watch and see what she wants to do now." The therapist may also offer more direction when the child's developmental needs are especially challenging.

Therapeutic Challenges in the Application of Floor Time

There are a number of challenges that arise in doing floor time. Lieberman and Pawl

(1993) describe some common therapeutic mistakes in working through the parent-child relationship. Some of the challenges they describe include the therapist who may become so involved in the parents' experience that the baby's contribution is overlooked, or the therapist who colludes with the parent in maltreating the child, or the therapist who over-identifies with the child's experience and finds it difficult to become empathically attuned to the parents' experience.

Another challenges to the therapeutic process is that some parents cannot see the value of doing this type of therapy, particularly when their child is demanding and won't respond to limits. They may make comments such as, "Won't this make him even more demanding of me if we give him more time?" It is useful to explain that during floor time, the child learns how to exert control in a healthy, adaptive way while getting her emotional needs for attention met, thus making it easier for the child to accept limits at other times of the day. When accepting limits is an issue, it is useful to practice limit setting after doing floor time by cleaning up the toys and then embarking on an activity that may evoke conflict, such as having the child sit at the table for a meal or walk to the car without running into the street. All the while, the therapist should work with the parent and child on how to balance limits and share control.

Debriefing Parents About the Process

In the first few sessions, it is often useful to question parents about the experience of playing with their child. Some questions that may be useful are: "What have you noticed this week about your child?" "What do you think was happening when your child did x (or wanted you to do x)?" "How did you feel when you and your child were doing x together?" or "How easy or difficult was it

for you to do this play with your child?" As the caregivers become more comfortable with the process and in talking with the therapist about their reactions, the therapist can further explore their feelings and projections from the past. The therapist may ask things such as, "How did you play as a child with your parents?" "Does playing with your child remind you in any way of your experiences with your own parents?" It is not necessary that the parents make connections with their own past or feelings and reactions to their child in order for floor time to be successful, although insights are useful to the process. As the therapy process unfolds, the parents may talk more about the observations they made about their child while they were engaged in playtime at home. They may also discuss how they might have been surprised when their child responded quite differently than they had expected.

It is important for the therapist to avoid intellectualizing the play experience by focusing too much on questions about why the child did something or asking the parent too many questions about what happened. Some parents may express emotions such as feeling rejected by their child if the child turns his back to them. The therapist may normalize those feelings by expressing that many parents feel the same way when similar things happen to them. Empathizing with their position in a nonjudgmental way is very important. Some parents become preoccupied with their reactions to their child, or need to talk at length about themselves and their own past. When this occurs, the therapist may wish to refocus the attention on what happened that day between the parent and the child. It is often useful for a parent to receive individual counseling concerning his or her personal needs, rather than drawing attention away from the parent-child relationship during these sessions.

Sometimes the parents expresses feelings of being resentful or angry towards their child, or feeling depleted when they give their child full attention during play. It is important for the therapist to acknowledge these feelings, nurturing the parents so that they feel less depleted. It is often useful to spend the first few sessions attending to the parents' needs, listening to them, and acknowledging how they feel in a nonjudgmental way. As the parents feel more "filled up" by the therapist's focused attention, it may then be possible to try floor time in small doses. In some cases, a parent may need to play with the toys himself because he did not get to play as a child. The therapist should set out two sets of toys, one for the parent and one for the child. In addition to allowing a parent time to play, the therapist may nurture him further by providing a snack to "feed" both parent and child.

As the therapist and the parents process the experience of what happened in the session, it is useful for them to focus on positive interchanges. Parents with regulatory disordered children often need help in seeing the positive aspects of their relationship with their child. For example, the therapist might comment, "You looked like you were really enjoying each other when you were playing together in the pup tent." The therapist should be careful when sharing observations, so as not to interject her own interpretations or projections about the process. Such interjections create a dynamic between the therapist and a parent whereby the therapist is the "wise therapist" who expresses opinions about the parent and child. It is better for the therapist to validate the parents' own discoveries and learning process by eliciting the parents own interpretations and by helping to bridge the parents' feelings and reactions with what is actually happening in the relationship. Comments made by the therapist

may be, "I wonder what you were experiencing when x wanted you to hide?" or "Did you notice that x seemed to watch you more when you did x?"

The next section describes research investigating the effectiveness of child-centered activity, followed by a case example.

RESEARCH EXAMINING THE EFFECTIVENESS OF TREATMENT APPROACHES

There is a paucity of research investigating the outcome of therapy approaches for infants and toddlers with regulatory disorders. Because valid diagnostic criteria for young children are lacking, few systematic studies have been conducted. When infants are used as subjects, normal maturation often confounds the effects of therapy over time. In addition, outcome measures are often based on therapist ratings rather than on objective and valid observations. These methodological problems have confounded or negatively affected the results of many studies (Weisz & Weiss, 1993).

There also are few studies examining the benefits of interventions suitable for children with regulatory disorders, or the effectiveness of floor time and other child-centered therapies. This section describes research that analyzed variations of child-centered therapy. They include mother-infant psychotherapy, infant-led intervention, and the "Watch, Wait, and Wonder (WWW)" technique. These approaches emphasize the importance of the parent-infant relationship and its organizing effects in fostering the child's emotional development. The differences in these approaches are described earlier in this chapter.

Cramer and his collages (1990) compared the Fraiberg (1980) method of mother-infant psychotherapy with noninterpretive interactional guidance (MacDonough, 1989) with infants under 30 months of age showing behavioral disturbances. They found no differences in the two approaches; however, short-term gains were reported in symptom relief or removal and there were more harmonious mother-child interactions and better projective identification in as few as 10 treatment sessions provided once weekly.

Using a methodology that focused on the quality of attachment, Lieberman, Weston, and Pawl (1991) found that anxiously attached dyads receiving infant-parent psychotherapy improved in maternal empathy, the security of the infant's attachment, and the mother-child partnership. They found that the mother's emotional connection with the therapist significantly correlated with the mother's empathy towards her infant. Mothers who were more able to use the parent-infant psychotherapy to explore their own feelings towards themselves and their children were more empathic and more engaged with their toddlers at outcome than those who did not develop insights. In addition, their children showed more secure attachment, more reciprocity, and less anger and avoidance towards their mothers.

The infant-led psychotherapy (e.g., WWW) and traditional psychotherapy were compared in a study with 67 clinically referred infants and their mothers (Cohen et al., 1999). Treatment was provided once a week for 5 months. Dyads receiving the WWW approach showed more organized or secure attachment relationships and greater gains in cognitive development and emotion regulation than did infants in the psychotherapy group. Mothers in the WWW group also reported greater parent satisfaction and competence and a decrease in depression compared to mothers in the psychotherapy group. Both methods of treatment helped in reducing the infant's presenting problems, decreasing parent stress, and reducing maternal intrusiveness.

DeGangi and Greenspan (1997) conducted a study that compared the relative benefits of a child-centered (i.e., floor time) infant psychotherapy approach and a structured, developmental parent-guidance approach in the treatment of irritability and inattention. The intent of contrasting these two interventions was to examine the contributions and roles of the parent and the child in addressing the child's self-regulatory needs. In particular, the study examined how the child's locus of control (internally initiated versus externally directed) would impact regulatory capacities and function. Subjects consisted of 24 infants between the ages of 14 and 30 months who had disorders of regulation, including high irritability, sensory hypersensitivities, and a short attention span. There were three groups of eight subjects, matched for age and symptoms. Twenty-four subjects had irritability and 21 had attentional problems. Subjects receiving treatment were given a pretest, six one-hour per week sessions of either intervention A or B, and a retest 4 months after intervention. Subjects in the no-treatment group were retested between 4 and 6 months after initial testing. Formalized assessment procedures of development, attention, and self-regulation were used to systemize the change that might occur over time.

The results showed that child-centered therapy was more effective than structured therapy or no treatment in treating inattention and irritability. Seventy-five percent of subjects receiving child-centered therapy resolved in their attentional problems, in contrast to 37.5% of subjects receiving structured therapy and 0% of subjects receiving no treatment. For irritability, 57% of subjects resolved in their irritability after child-centered therapy, 28% after structured therapy, and 0% after no treatment. An important finding of this study was that

Chapter 10. An Integrated Intervention Approach to Treating Infants and Young Children with
Regulatory, Sensory Processing, and Interactional Problems

229

children with regulatory problems could make progress in resolving problems related to inattention and irritability in 6 weeks of intervention using a child-centered therapy approach. Since these basic skills of self-regulation (e.g., organizing attention and regulating mood) were responsive to short-term intervention using child-centered therapy, it suggests that therapies focusing on the relationship between parent and child are more useful than interventions that stress concrete developmental skills.

A second prospective study involved 39 infants with regulatory disorders (e.g., high irritability and sensory processing problems during infancy), who were retested at 3 years of age. Subjects were not randomly selected for the treatment or no-treatment group nor were they matched for type of problem or developmental capacities. Subjects who had received parent-child psychotherapy showed less behavioral and emotional problems than did the untreated group. This finding is especially interesting in light of the fact that the treated group evidenced more severe and continuing motor and sensory problems and, therefore, may have been more challenging than untreated subjects at 3 years of age (DeGangi, Sickel, Wiener, & Kaplan, 1996). Parents of infants with motor and sensory problems are more likely to seek treatment than will parents whose children only evidence emotional challenges at an early age. In a study examining the effects of infant temperamental traits and early home-based intervention on psychiatric symptoms in adolescence, it was found that early intervention focusing on the parent-child relationship helped to protect subjects from developing psychiatric symptoms in adolescence (Teerikangas, Aronen, Martin, & Huttunen, 1998). These studies point to the importance of improving the parent-child relationship in

preventing long-term emotional and behavioral problems in children at risk.

CASE EXAMPLE:
Julie, a Toddler With
Chronic Irritability

This last section presents a case example that exemplifies the treatment approach described in this chapter; that is, an approach that works with a child's motor and sensory challenges in the context of an integrated model of intervention.

Julie was a 26-month-old child who was referred by her early intervention program because of her constant irritability. Although she had attended the program three mornings a week for a year, her inability to separate from her mother was interfering with her ability to partake in various educational and therapeutic activities. Her mother—Mrs. T.—was interviewed at her school program because she was reluctant to go to a professional whom she did not know and because she felt more comfortable in the school setting. Her husband did not participate in this interview because of his heavy work schedule.

Presenting Concern

Mrs. T. described Julie as being an unhappy child since birth. She wanted to be held most of the time and demanded adult company constantly, seldom playing by herself. Once upset, Julie was difficult to console. She had no favorite toy and seemed to need consoling from an adult. Being held and rocked, riding in the car, and being offered the pacifier were the only things that calmed Julie. When not inconsolable, Julie would constantly tug at her mother's hand or whine for attention. It was very difficult for her mother to know what Julie wanted because her daughter had no spoken words and very limited gestures. Julie could point, but only in a general direction rather than to a specific object or person. Mrs. T. expressed concerns about spoiling her and not knowing when or when not to give in to Julie's demands.

Mrs. T. found Julie's whining and crying very difficult to handle, especially as she has two other children, a 7-year-old and a 7-month-old, who both need her attention as well. She felt frustrated that nothing she did seemed to work for very long. She described a typical scenario when she would first talk nicely to Julie, then sternly, and then scream and shout at her, followed by spanking. The mother stated that she never physically abused Julie beyond the spanking. The early intervention program staff had not observed any bruises or injuries; however, they had observed Mrs. T. yell and spank Julie at school and were concerned.

Pregnancy History

Julie was born full-term and there were no problems during the pregnancy or any neonatal complications. The parents had been trying to have a baby for many years. After the first child, the mother had a miscarriage and was then treated with fertility drugs to help her conceive again. After delivering Julie, the mother experienced a postpartum depression that lasted for about 3 months. She described it as feeling like the "third world war." She did not see a doctor or take medication for it because seeking medical help for depression was incompatible with her family's background. Both parents had looked forward to this child but, instead, felt very disappointed.

Developmental History

Julie was developmentally delayed in all areas of development, functioning approximately one year behind in all areas. She walked at 16 months and had motor difficulties. Her greatest problem was communication, with her expressive language skills falling at the 9-month-old level. She spoke no words, and used only gestures to indicate needs. Initially, there were feeding difficulties with choking and vomiting, but these had resolved. A complete neurological work-up revealed no cause for the developmental delay. There was no history of learning, behavioral, or other developmental problems in the family.

Family History

In addition to the parents and three children, Mrs. T.'s mother lived in their house. Mrs. T. felt that she had a great deal of stress in her life. Both she and her husband worked very hard and had little time alone together or for themselves. She was worried about Julie's future, and was eager to obtain some guidance on ways to help Julie become a happier child.

Diagnostic Impressions

On the Test of Attention in Infants, Julie showed poor attention for visual, auditory, and tactile events. She had little understanding of cause and effect, and tended to watch the toys for long periods of time without understanding how to play with them. On the Test of Sensory Functions in Infants, Julie was hypersensitive to touch. She was able to explore textured toys, but she had difficulty planning and organizing motor actions such as removing a furry mitt placed on her foot. In addition, Julie was sensitive to movement when rough-housed gently.

Chapter 10. An Integrated Intervention Approach to Treating Infants and Young Children with Regulatory, Sensory Processing, and Interactional Problems

231

Observations of mother-child interactions revealed that Julie had difficulty initiating reciprocal interactions with her mother. She would fill and dump toys, but not stay with any one toy long enough to show a preference. There was no symbolic play.

Overall, Julie was a child with multiple developmental delays and chronic irritability. Her predominant problems included poor communication, hypersensitivities to movement and touch, poor sustained attention, delayed play skills, and an inability to separate from her mother, on whom she relied for any soothing. At the time of the assessment, it was difficult to determine what was underlying the irritability. Was she overstimulated because of her sensory hypersensitivities? Was she frustrated because she could not communicate what she wanted? Was it an inability to self-soothe? Or, was it a problem in organizing herself for purposeful activity?

Regardless of the cause of Julie's irritability, a negative dynamic was occurring between mother and child. Mrs. T. reacted in a very negative way to Julie's constant need for her attention and the child's whining. This mother was overworked and felt unduly burdened by Julie's overwhelming needs. Although Mrs. T. stated that she suffered postpartum depression only temporarily after Julie was born, she appeared to be depressed when interviewed and during the assessment process. Although Mrs. T.'s mother was helpful in cooking for the household, Mrs. T. bore all of the responsibilities for child-rearing. Mr. T. worked long hours and was not involved in Julie's early intervention program. There was a lack of support from Mrs. T.'s family in terms of understanding her feelings and worries about Julie. Therefore, it was important that the intervention program provide support to Mrs. T. so that she would be able to help Julie. She needed to feel that she had an important role in helping Julie,

while not feeling as if she was having more demands and pressures placed upon her.

The Treatment Plan for Selected Concerns

The treatment plan developed for Julie follows.

1. **Irritability and self-regulation**
   a. Develop strategies that Julie could use to help herself self-soothe when distressed, other than demanding attention from her mother.
   b. Help mother to redirect Julie when the child is distressed or irritable, supporting Julie's capacity to self-organize in a positive way.
   c. Help Julie develop the capacity to read and give signals when attempting to communicate her desires and needs.

2. **Sensory processing and attention**
   a. Desensitize Julie's responses to touch and movement.
   b. Find sensory activities that Julie could use to help her focus attention and self-soothe.
   c. Develop strategies for managing the environment that help Julie to focus attention.

3. **Parent-child interactions**
   a. Facilitate Julie's ability to self-initiate play schemes.
   b. Foster Julie's motivation to explore the environment.
   c. Help Julie to engage in reciprocal interactions with her mother, using simple sensorimotor activities.
   d. Encourage the mother to provide focused, nonjudgmental attention on Julie for short periods of time.

e. Through play experiences, provide the mother with opportunities to observe Julie's skills and abilities rather than only having an experience of Julie as a demanding and irritable child with many needs.

4. **Parent support**
   a. Provide support to mother in a non-judgmental way, allowing her to express feelings about herself, her relationship with Julie, and Julie's demanding behavior and developmental problems.
   b. Help the mother find ways to restore her energy by doing things for herself as well as for her children and other family members so that she may feel more available to meet their many demands.

The Treatment Program

Julie and her mother were part of the research project (described earlier in this chapter) that provided only a limited intervention program: 12 weeks of intervention on a once-a-week basis. Nonetheless, her response to the intervention was instructive. (See chapter 3 for a description of a comprehensive intervention program.) Julie's treatment began with six weeks of structured intervention, followed by child-centered activity for another six weeks. The therapists in this case were two clinical developmental psychologists, one with a background in special education and the other with expertise as an occupational therapist. Mrs. T. attended all sessions. The father was not involved in the therapeutic program due to his long work hours.

As treatment began, the therapists had to confront several challenges that affected the treatment process. Mother had an unrealistic view of Julie's problems, thinking that her daughter would be fully normal if only she would talk and get better balance. Mother was also very intrusive with Julie, constantly trying to teach her new skills because she felt that Julie "had a lot of catching up to do." Her style was often frantic, so that Julie could not respond or self-initiate any responses. Mother was also feeling overwhelmed and depressed. It was very important that the therapists address the mother's needs in a way that she would find supportive and nurturing.

Session One

During the first session, Julie had difficulty transitioning from the waiting room to the play room. She was extremely fussy, and would not explore the room on her own. She spent the session in her mother's lap or by her mother's side. Mrs. T. talked about how stressed she felt that Julie needed her constant attention. Mother began talking about her many concerns for Julie: her poor attention to tasks and people, feeding problems, night wakings, immature play skills with mouthing and banging toys, no verbal and little gestural communication, and no ability to self-soothe.

The therapists tried several activities during this session to help Julie and mother engage in reciprocal interactions. The goals were to help Julie focus her attention on the task or her mother, to initiate exploration with the activity, and then to respond to her mother's cues in a reciprocal manner. Linear vestibular movement (e.g., rocking in a rocking chair) while providing firm deep pressure (holding Julie securely in mother's lap) were used to help soothe and calm both mother and child. The following list describes the activities tried during the initial clinical session, which the therapists wrote down and encouraged the mother to repeat at home.

Chapter 10. An Integrated Intervention Approach to Treating Infants and Young Children with Regulatory, Sensory Processing, and Interactional Problems

233

Recommended Home Activities

1. Find a quiet time to sit with Julie. Put out only a few toys. You may want to put on quiet, rhythmic music in the background. Start out soothed and calm. Slowly rock Julie on your lap.
2. Have Julie sitt on your lap while you rock. Have a blanket, dried beans, corn, or uncooked macaroni in a bowl. Play with the materials first to capture Julie's attention.
3. Next, try letting Julie take the first step. Imitate her, then let her take another turn. It should be like a circle—Julie does, you do, Julie plays more—all in the same activity.
4. Make up a game with your body, such as stamping your feet to the music or playing peek-a-boo. Have some fun.

During these activities, the therapists noted that there was little pleasure in the interaction between the mother and child. Mrs. T. was highly intrusive. She would not allow Julie to take a turn or wait for Julie's responses to occur. Mrs. T. seemed adverse to having Julie sit on her lap, but this became more palatable if there was a pillow between her and Julie. The therapists were very soothing and calm, praising Mrs. T. for trying the suggested activities. They focused the session on discussing Mrs. T.'s concerns, and on working with the dyad to establish attention and engagement through gentle rocking, tactile stimulation with textured objects, and soft rhythmic music. The therapists tried to think of activities that calmed both mother and child because they both seemed to need this. Suggestions were made to the mother to modify her verbal input to Julie, relying less on words and more on gesture and intonation. Finally, the therapists worked with the mother on following Julie's lead, and opening and closing circles of communication. They found the mother to be a very likeable, high-

ly motivated, and energetic woman who easily engaged with them. She appeared enthusiastic about the treatment.

Session Two

Mrs. T.'s concerns were similar to those she expressed the first week, although she felt Julie was using more gestures. During the second session, the therapists continued to help Julie acclimate and focus as she sat next to her mother or was rocked and held as they listened to music on the tape player. The therapists encouraged Mrs. T. to be more passive in her interactions while Julie took more initiative during sensory play with tactile materials (i.e., Koosh balls, corn, furry rug). They talked with Mrs. T. about allowing herself to be a secure home base while Julie explored a little on her own. The therapists discussed how this approach was different than teaching Julie specific skills. The take-home suggestions from this session follow.

Recommended Home Activities

1. Put a pillow on your lap, then encourage Julie to sit with you, giving her "pillow-hugs" while you watch a video together.
2. Play with water, using brushes. Paint her feet and hands with the water and brush. You might put a doll in the bathtub so that Julie might paint the doll with the brush too.
3. Continue playing with the corn and the dried beans.
4. Always let Julie take the lead. Make a circle of communication: Julie starts, Mom joins in, Julie takes another turn, then Mom joins again. Always let Julie end the turn so that she can close off the circle of communication.
5. Try music and rocking for soothing.

During these activities, the therapists noticed that the mother's need to play with the toys was as strong as the child's. The therapists speculated to themselves that Mrs. T.

might have had a deprived childhood and needed to revisit the experience of play for herself. They were very aware that they were re-parenting Mrs. T., providing her with aspects of nurturance that she may not have had early in life.

At the end of the session, Mrs. T. confided that she felt burnt-out, and that she had difficulty getting any time for herself to refuel physically and emotionally. The therapists encouraged her to spend some time alone each day, just for herself. Mrs. T. was able to say that she felt anxious about taking time for herself. Because there was so much to do at home, she felt guilty whenever she tried to take time to relax. The therapists again emphasized the importance of her needing to refuel so that she would be more available for her family.

Session Three

Mrs. T. reported some positive changes. She was faithfully doing "quiet play" with Julie, 20 minutes a day. She talked of her concerns about Julie's stubbornness, short attention span, and inability to play independently. She wondered how Julie would adjust to a Kindergarten routine in a few years. In this session, Julie was more organized and focused. The mediums used included water play and vestibular stimulation on a large bolster (e.g., rocking and bouncing). Julie also engaged in very nice reciprocal play with her mother using a tunnel to play peek-a-boo.

Session Four

During this week, the therapists noticed that Julie was able to organize several sequences of behavior with one toy, thus showing the beginnings of more elaborated play. She tolerated the swing nicely and engaged with her mother around music and movement. The therapists worked with the

mother on reading Julie's nonverbal cues and on reducing her own verbal barrage, being very careful to be nurturing towards the mother as they gave her feedback.

Mrs. T. opened up about her own exhaustion and depression. She felt that she must maintain a facade, a "happy face" on the outside in order to get through the day. Additionally, she felt conflicted by the competing demands of her three children, taking little time for herself. The therapists strongly encouraged her to take time out for herself, as they had before.

Session Five

Julie's mother entered this session feeling very positive about her daughter's progress. She felt that Julie was more organized, was communicating more purposefully, and was better able to sustain some independent play. During "quiet play" at home, Julie was focusing on some fine-motor tasks, using keys which her mother had encouraged her to use. The therapists strongly reinforced the good work both were doing, and stressed how important mother was to Julie's growth. The work in this session focused on oral-motor and feeding skills—using yogurt and crunchy granola, and on vestibular activity on the swing and inner tube. Julie initiated play and Mrs. T. was able to engage her in a reciprocal game around bouncing on the inner tube. Julie seemed to focus her attention better when deep proprioceptive input was provided (e.g., pressing on her hips while bouncing on the ball). The therapists counseled Mrs. T. to try this and other movement activities at home. She appeared very motivated to follow their recommendations. The activities that she was to try included the following:

Recommended Home Activities

1. Try rocking and singing with Julie on your lap. Use a little pillow to put on Julie's stomach or back if she likes this.

Chapter 10. An Integrated Intervention Approach to Treating Infants and Young Children with
Regulatory, Sensory Processing, and Interactional Problems

235

2. Put out dried beans and macaroni in a box for Julie to explore. Let her take her shoes off to put her feet in the box. Also try playdoh.
3. Pull Julie in a wagon. At the playground, encourage her to swing.
4. After movement activities such as swinging, encourage Julie to sit down and do fine-motor activities.
5. After her bath, pat Julie with the towel. Use lotion on her body, applying with firm pressure. Watch how she acts. If she pulls away, it means that she is not processing the touch in a positive way.

Session Six

Mrs. T. brought the maternal grandmother and the 12-month-old brother to the session. Julie was very unfocused with the overload of stimulation and was unable to play in the bath of plastic balls. Her play was very fleeting. Eventually, she organized herself to sit in a nest of pillows and listen to rhythmic, rocking music.

Despite feeling more positive about Julie's progress following the earlier sessions, Mrs. T came into this session expressing a good deal of frustration with Julie's slow progress. She continued to have an unrealistic picture of Julie's abilities, expressing relief in her belief that Julie was not mentally retarded or emotionally disturbed. Again, Mrs. T. felt depleted and the therapists encouraged her to take refueling breaks for herself.

Child-Centered Play Intervention

The child-centered play therapy was introduced after the first six sessions of the structured program. When the child-centered therapy began, Mrs. T. was suspicious about whether this type of intervention would work. She felt that Julie must be taught different skills, and she did not think that giving Julie the initiative in the play would work, although the therapists had been teaching the mother this strategy all along. However, because Mrs. T. had developed a strong therapeutic alliance with her therapists, she was willing to try this therapy.

Session Seven

During the first session of child-centered therapy, Julie initiated a lot of proprioceptive stimulation, stamping her feet, butting mother with her head, and bouncing while sitting on the inner tube in a fairly well-organized sequence. Her play was immature, but focused. Julie appeared to need to be grounded by the tactile play with her mother to help her focus her attention. Despite mother's worries that were expressed prior to the play, there was positive affect between mother and daughter. Mrs. T. seemed fairly relaxed with the child-centered play, although she needed to restrain herself from structuring turns and making verbal demands. Written notes provided to the mother about child-centered therapy included the following:

Child-Centered Therapy Activities
1. Find toys that make noise or music, such as a tape recorder or the pop-up tunes toy.
2. Use toys that Julie can pound, hit, or bang, such as a pounding bench with hammer or a chair to push.
3. Give her places where she can sit inside, such as a nest of pillows.
4. Let Julie take the lead, but stay next to her.
5. Give her all your attention for a concentrated time—up to 15 minutes if you can.
6. Julie likes seeing what she can make you do—sit down, now run with her, now jump. Go with it.
7. Let Julie do most of the work to show you what she wants.

Mrs. T. appeared to be dealing more with the reality of Julie's delays. The early intervention program staff had been discussing a Fall placement for Julie at a school for children with significant communication disorders and cognitive delays. Mrs. T. was concerned about Julie's diagnosis and what the future would hold for her. At a personal level, Mrs. T. discussed how isolated she felt from her peers, how different her experience of mothering was from that of her friends, and how her friends were unable to empathize with her. In addition, Julie had been ill with a skin irritation and a fever. Mrs. T. had been feeling very tired. The therapists suggested that she set a schedule that included special time for herself, free of distractions. The therapists delayed the child-centered therapy with mother and child until after Mrs. T. had time to discuss her many concerns.

Later during processing, and after mother practiced the child-centered therapy, Mrs. T. discussed tensions in her role and relationship with own mother, who was very critical of her. There was a very strong work ethic in the family that placed very high demands on the mother to meet all the needs of her children and husband. Mrs. T. stated that even if she had time for herself, she would feel guilty about it. In addition, she felt that her mother was critical of the way in which she parented her children.

Session Eight

During the eighth session, Julie appeared regressed in her play, unable to engage with objects or sequenced activities. The therapists mainly focused on trying to engage the mother in the therapeutic process and on helping her understand that Julie needed to be the initiator of the play. With this guidance, Mrs. T. was able to respond appropriately to Julie without being overly intrusive, and the affective engagement in the dyad was very positive.

Mrs. T. expressed doubts about the child-centered therapy. Julie seemed to be going "backwards" in her view since she was not teaching her daughter specific skills during therapy. Mrs. T. reported that special time at home consisted of her putting out toys that were good for Julie's cognitive level, but that Julie showed little interest in them. At the same time, Mrs. T. was feeling exhausted. She did take one hour for herself, but admitted that she felt guilty asking for relief from her husband since this was frowned upon by her mother. The therapists reinforced the need for her to get respite and to have some pleasure in her own life.

Session Nine

The play was consistent with the play of previous weeks in that Julie craved tactile grounding in order to focus. Julie spent time flitting from the inner tube to the big box enclosure to rocking activities. Julie was especially interested in pulling her mother's hand and tugging her mother along as she moved about her environment. Her mother responded by trying to fend off Julie's demands, stating, "What do you want?" The therapists' presence in the room at this point was somewhat counterproductive in that Mrs. T. wanted to talk about her concerns, which took her away from Julie. The therapists suggested the possibility that Mrs. T. finding someone to talk with privately as a future option. During the actual treatment session, the therapists found that it was better to allow Mrs. T. to practice the child-centered therapy while they went into the observation booth for about 15 minutes.

Mrs. T. was able to respond to the therapists' suggestions that she learn to separate her needs from Julie's. She acknowledged that she was loosening up on her usual involvement with the oldest child's schoolwork and in doing things constantly for Julie. There was a birthday party for the young

Chapter 10. An Integrated Intervention Approach to Treating Infants and Young Children with
Regulatory, Sensory Processing, and Interactional Problems

237

baby, in whom mother took great pleasure. She talked about how she and her husband were enjoying the time they had begun take for themselves after their long work day. All of these changes were occurring under the critical eye of her mother, who referred to Mrs. T. as being selfish. At the same time, Mrs. T. was worrying about not setting enough limits on Julie, particularly her high need for constant attention.

Session Ten

Mrs. T. came in looking very attractive and upbeat. She reported that Julie seemed better able to play by herself and able to separate more easily from her. The therapists continued to reinforce the idea that a big dose of child-centered play with mother could go a long way towards Julie's independence in other contexts. The therapists again contrasted the difference between structured teaching and child-initiated activity. In Julie's case, she had an essential need for both types of interventions due to the seriousness of her delays. Julie continued with her sensory play while attempting to control her mother's involvement with her activities, pulling and tugging her mother to come along with her. The dyadic play was positive and well modulated; mother was responsive and nonintrusive.

Interestingly, the early intervention staff from Julie's center had called during the week to discuss Julie's wonderful progress. They no longer found Julie to be irritable and demanding, and found that she could join into circle time, snack, and other activities without any difficulty. She was showing increased gestures, intentional communication, fewer problems with hypersensitivities to touch and movement activities, and better focused attention. They asked what techniques the therapists were using that were working so well.

Session Eleven

By session eleven, the therapists noticed that Julie's mood regulation was better, with less whining and more autonomy. After some reminders about letting Julie take the lead, the dyadic play went well. Mother needed repeated reminders to allow the play to be child-initiated: this was not something that came naturally to her. Julie engaged in the same tactile-proprioceptive activities of previous weeks, but had better organized sequences of play. There was very positive affect between mother and child.

Mrs. T. reported major changes in the family's sleeping arrangements. Julie was now sleeping in the older sister's bedroom and the baby was in a separate room. Although this had not been shared with the therapists before, Julie had been sleeping in the parent's bed. Mrs. T. stated that she and her husband now slept alone together ("I'm back with my husband and now we're having special time!"). At home, Julie was apparently observing and imitating her 1-year-old brother and experimenting more on her own. Mother described herself as standing by while Julie did things for herself.

Session Twelve

During the last session, Julie engaged in considerable tactile-proprioceptive play, laughing and smiling as her mother followed along with her. During this play, Julie gestured with signs while vocalizing with a few new words that she had just attained (i.e., "up" and "more"). Her sequences of play were intentional and organized. It was clear what Julie was wanting to do in her play. In addition, she was able to use the sensory play to help organize her attention for a focused fine-motor task. Julie indicated that she wanted to sit in a chair with a table in front of her. She pointed to the puzzle, signed "more," and clapped as her mother placed the puzzle on the table for her. She then proceeded to work at this task for at least 10 minutes.

The therapists reinforced Mrs. T.'s observation that Julie was happier when mother could give her a dose of full attention, even if only briefly. Julie was now able to play independently for 10 minutes at a time. Mother was in the throes of planning for Julie's Fall school placement, getting financial support, negotiating with her husband on the best plans for Julie, and accepting the fact that Julie was a "special needs" child. The therapists discussed termination of their work together. They also emphasized again that Mrs. T. needed to find support for herself when Julie moved into another setting. The therapists reviewed with Mrs. T. the activities that Julie liked and needed. In addition, they stressed the important role that she played in facilitating the changes that could be observed in Julie's behavior. Her playing with Julie, giving focused attention while Julie took the lead, and letting Julie show the mother what she wanted were important to the progress that Julie had made.

Conclusion of Treatment

By the conclusion of the therapy program, many of Julie's problems had resolved. Sleep and feeding problems were no longer a concern. Chronic irritability had diminished significantly. This second improvement appeared related to Julie's capacity to refine her gestures and vocalizations to communicate her needs, her ability to play by herself for short periods of time, and her mother's changed perception of Julie as a child who *could* master new skills. Julie's difficulties with separating from mother had improved when Mrs. T. had set aside playtime with Julie to fulfill her needs for focused, one-to-one attention. Julie was more animated and happier and was more able to play by herself

at home. Her mother found her to be far less clingy and needy, although Julie remained fairly demanding, requiring help to play with objects for any sustained period of time. Julie showed more organization and range in her variety of play skills. She was beginning to develop autonomy and had her own opinions about toy and activity preferences. Attentional skills had improved dramatically, particularly when tactile-proprioceptive or movement activities had been used prior to tasks that required focused cognitive, language, or perceptual thinking.

The success of the therapy program appeared strongly related to the mother's strong therapeutic alliance with the therapists. She became very comfortable with them, sharing her thoughts and feelings. The therapists emphasized the importance of mother's role in facilitating Julie's development through her interactions with Julie. Mrs. T. put a great deal of effort into practicing the various activities at home with Julie. Even when she was suspicious that the child-centered therapy was not going to help her with Julie, she gave it a try with the therapists' encouragement. After a few weeks, she began to see many changes in Julie and in her family life. The mother's depression improved and she was more able to meet her own personal needs, as well as those of her family.

It was fortuitous that structured therapy was first in the sequence in the research project for this child because, in hindsight, this mother needed explicit directions about how to interact with Julie. Once the dyad was on course and "cooking together," it became possible to help guide the mother in finding ways to help Julie through the interactions using a child-centered therapy approach. Mrs. T. began to understand the process of reading Julie's cues and responding in ways that Julie needed. It was important for the parent to learn how to internalize this process of reading the child's cues and finding what would help both of them.

Although Julie was a child with ongoing developmental needs who would probably require long-term educational and therapeutic services, this short-term therapy program helped to get this mother and child on a positive developmental trajectory. It was important for Julie and her mother to connect as a dyad so that they could engage with one another in a pleasurable exchange. As the mother gave Julie more focused attention, Julie could switch her efforts from demanding her mother's attention to expanding her gestures to communicate her intents. Through the interactions with her mother, Julie was able to develop the core processes of sensory processing, basic communication, attention, and emotional regulation that underlie many skills that she needed to develop.

CONCLUSION

This chapter presented an integrated therapeutic model designed for infants and children with constitutional and related relational problems and their parents. Within this child- and family-centered intervention approach, a combination of parent guidance, child-centered activity, and sensory integration therapy techniques address the complex needs of the child with sensory and motor problems. Parent guidance techniques provide parents with specific management techniques to handle their child's sleep and feeding problems and irritability. Child-centered activity (i.e., floor time—a form of infant psychotherapy) is applied to enhance parent-child interactions and facilitate self-initiation, sustained attention, purposeful behavior, and communication in the child. Sensory integration therapy techniques are integrated within the context of parent guidance and child-centered activity to normalize the child's responses to sensory stimulation, modulate arousal and state control, and promote organized, adaptive responses during play and everyday activities. Preliminary research suggests that these approaches are useful in addressing the problems of infants with regulatory disorders. Further research is needed to examine the effectiveness of the specific treatment approaches and the value of an integrated treatment model for children with developmental needs. ■

REFERENCES

Ayres, A. J. (1972). *Sensory integration and learning disorders*. Los Angeles: Western Psychological Services.

Ayres, A. J. (1979). *Sensory integration and the child*. Los Angeles: Western Psychological Services.

Carey, W. B. & McDevitt, S. C. (1995). *Coping with children's difficult temperament*. New York: Basic Books.

Clark, F. A., Mailloux, S., & Parham, D. (1985). Sensory integration and learning disabilities. In P. N. Pratt & A. S. Allen (Eds.), *Occupational therapy for children*. New York: C.V. Mosby.

Cohen, N. J., Muir, E., Lojkasek, M., Muir, R., Parker, C. J., Barwick, M., & Brown, M. (1997). Watch, Wait, and Wonder: Testing the effectiveness of a new approach to mother-infant psychotherapy. *Infant Mental Health Journal, 20*(4), 429-451.

Cramer, B., Robert-Tissot, C., Stern, D. N., Serpa-Rusconi, S., DeMuralt, M., Besson, G., Palacio-Espasa, F., Bachmann, J., Knauer, D., Berney, C., & D'Arcis, U. (1990). Outcome evaluation in brief mother-infant psychotherapy: A preliminary report. *Infant Mental Health Journal, 11*(3), 278-300.

Daws, D. (1989). *Through the night: Helping parents and sleepless infants*. London, England: Free Association Books.

DeGangi, G.A. (2000). *Pediatric disorders of regulation in affect and behavior: A therapist's guide to assessment and treatment*. New York: Academic Press.

DeGangi, G. A., Craft, P., & Castellan, J. (1991). Treatment of sensory, emotional, and attentional problems in regulatory disordered infants. *Infants and Young Children, 3*(3), 9-19.

DeGangi, G. A., & Greenspan, S. I. (1997). The effectiveness of short-term interventions in treatment of inattention and irritability in toddlers. *Journal of Developmental and Learning Disorders, 1*(2), 277-298.

DeGangi, G. A., Sickel, R. Z., Wiener, A. S. & Kaplan, E. P. (1996). Fussy babies: to treat or not to treat? *British Journal of Occupational Therapy, 59*(10), 457-464.

Dunst, C. J, Trivette, C. M., Davis, M., & Cornwell, J. (1988). Enabling and empowering families of children with health impairments. *Children's Health Care: Journal of the Association for the Care of Children's Health, 17*, 71-81.

Ferber, R. (1984). Diagnosis and treatment of sleep disorders in children. *Pediatric Basics, 39*, 7-14.

Fisher, A. G., Murray, E. A., & Bundy, A. C. (1991). *Sensory integration: Theory and practice*. Philadelphia: F. A. Davis.

Fraiberg, S. (1980). *Clinical studies in infant mental health: The first year of life*. New York: Basic Books.

Friedrich, W. N., Cohen, D. S., & Wilturner, L. T. (1988). Specific beliefs as moderator variables in maternal coping with mental retardation. *Children's Health Care: Journal of the Association for the Care of Children's Health, 17*, 40-44.

Greenspan, S. (1979). Intelligence and adaptation: An integration of psychoanalytic and Piagetian developmental psychology. *Psychological Issues*. Monogr. 47/48. New York: International Universities Press.

Greenspan, S. I. (1981). *Psychopathology and adaptation in infancy and early childhood: Principles of clinical diagnosis and preventive intervention*. New York: International Universities Press.

Greenspan, S. I. (1989). *The development of the ego*. Madison, CT: International Universities Press.

Greenspan, S. I. (1992). *Infancy and early childhood: The practice of clinical assessment and intervention with emotional and developmental challenges.* Madison, CT: International Universities Press.

Greenspan, S. I. (1997*). Developmentally based psychotherapy.* Madison, CT: International Universities Press.

Greenspan, S. I. (with Lewis, N.). (1999). *Building healthy minds: The six experiences that create intelligence and emotional growth in babies and young children.* Reading, MA: Perseus Books.

Greenspan, S. I. & Greenspan, N. T. (1989). *The essential partnership.* New York: Viking Press.

Greenspan, S. I., & Salmon, J. (1995). *The challenging child: Understanding, raising, and enjoying the five "difficult" types of children.* Reading, MA: Addison Wesley Longman.

Greenspan, S. I., & Wieder, S. (1998). *The child with special needs: Intellectual and emotional growth.* Reading, MA: Addison Wesley Longman.

Greenspan, S. I., & Lourie, R. S. (1981). Developmental structuralist approach to the classification of adaptive and pathologic personality organizations: Application to infancy and early childhood. *American Journal of Psychiatry, 138*(6).

Kahn, A., Mozin, M. J., Rebuffat, E., Sottiaux, M., & Muller, M. F. (1989). Milk intolerance in children with persistent sleeplessness. *Pediatrics, 84*, 595-603.

Kandel, E. R., & Schwartz, J. H. (1985). *Principles of neural science* (2nd ed.). New York: Elsevier.

Lieberman, A. F., & Pawl, J. H. (1993). Infant-parent psychotherapy. In C. H. Zeanah (Ed.), *Handbook of infant mental health* (pp. 427-442). New York: Guilford Press.

Lieberman, A. F., Weston, D. R., & Pawl, J. H. (1991). Preventive intervention and outcome with anxiously attached dyads. *Child Development, 62(1)*: 199-209.

Mahoney, G. (1988). Enhancing the developmental competency of handicapped infants. In K. Marfo (Ed.), *Parent-child interaction and developmental disabilities: Theory, research, and intervention.* Westport, CT: Praeger.

Mahoney, G., & Powell, A. (1988). Modifying parent-child interaction: Enhancing the development of handicapped children. *Journal of Special Education, 22*, 82-96.

Mahrer, A. R., Levinson, J. R., & Fine, S. (1976). Infant psychotherapy: Theory, research, and practice. *Psychotherapy Theory, Research and Practice, 13*, 131-140.

MacDonough, S. (1989). *Interaction guidance: A technique for treating early relationships.* Paper presented at the Fourth World Congress of Infant Psychiatry and Allied Disciplines, Lugano, Switzerland.

Muir, E. (1992). Watching, waiting, and wondering: Applying psychoanalytic principals to mother-infant intervention. *Infant Mental Health Journal, 13(4)*, 319-328.

Ostrov, K., Dowling, J., Wesner, D. O., & Johnson, F. K. (1982). Maternal styles in infant psychotherapy: Treatment and research implications. *Infant Mental Health Journal, 3*, 162-173.

Rapp, D. (1986). *The impossible child.* Tacoma, WA: Sciences Press.

Schaaf, R. C., & Mulrooney, L. L. (1989). Occupational therapy in early intervention: A family-centered approach. *American Journal of Occupational Therapy, 43*, 745-754.

Sears, W. (1985). *The fussy baby.* Franklin Park, IL: LeLeche League International.

Teerikangas, O. M., Aronen, E. T., Martin, R. P., & Huttunen, M. O. (1998). Effects of infant temperament and early intervention on the psychiatric symptoms of adolescents.

Journal of the American Academy of Child and Adolescent Psychiatry, 37(10), 1070-1076.

Turecki, S., & Tonner, L. (1985). *The difficult child.* New York: Bantam Books.

Weisz, J. R., & Weiss, B. (1993). Effects of psychotherapy with children and adolescents. *Developmental Clinical Psychology and Psychiatry* (Vol. 27). Newbury Park, CA: Sage.

Wesner, D., Dowling, J., & Johnson, F. K. (1982). What is maternal-infant intervention? The role of infant psychotherapy. *Psychiatry, 45*, 307-315.

Winnicott, D. W. (1960). The theory of the parent-infant relationship. In D. W. Winnicott (Ed.), *The maturational processes and the facilitating environment* (pp. 37-55). London: Hogarth.

≈ 11 ➤

An Ophthalmologist's Approach to Visual Processing/Learning Differences

Harold Paul Koller, M.D., F.A.A.P., F.A.A.O.

In the past, most ophthalmologists read or were told that treatment of the disorders affecting children with dyslexia and other learning disabilities fell outside the field of ophthalmology because the brain, and not the eyes, is the main organ active in the process of thinking and learning (Hartstein, 1971; Hartstein & Gable, 1984; Miller, 1988). Because dyslexia, for example, implied an inability to understand the written word, the definitive diagnosis and therapy was in the hands of the educators and clinical psychologists, not the ophthalmologist. The role of an ophthalmologist, thus, was to rule out disease as the first step in determining the reason for a learning difference before referring the child back to the pediatrician or family doctor for further evaluation and referral.

This limited role for ophthalmologists in treating children with learning disorders is now being displaced by a move toward an interdisciplinary approach. The ophthalmologist is often the first expert to whom the pediatrician refers a child suspected of having a learning disorder. Educating ophthalmologists in the medical and nonmedical conditions and situations that could affect learning in a child or older individual will help ensure that a patient receives appropriate, effective, and timely remedial treatment.

The first step in educating ophthalmologists is to introduce psychiatry, educational and neuropsychology, physical and occupational therapy, and educational science in all its forms relating to learning differences in children and adults to the ophthalmology community (Koller & Goldberg, 1999). (An appendix to this chapter outlines briefly what an ophthalmologist in general practice should know about learning disorders.) The second is to make the diagnosis and treatment of children more efficient by developing a system for classifying disorders that is oriented toward ophthalmologists. This chapter describes such a classification system for learning disorders. It then goes on to describe causes and treatment of medically based ophthalmic problems affecting learning, as well as other conditions affecting learning that are not purely ophthalmic but which ophthalmologists can help diagnose (Koller, 1999a).

AN OPHTHALMOLOGIST'S CLASSIFICATION APPROACH TO LEARNING DISORDERS

Children with learning disabilities can be classified into two main groups: (1) those with purely medically and surgically treated ophthalmic disorders that temporarily or chronically affect learning efficiency in school (DSM-IV: Axis III – general medical conditions), and (2) those with conditions not purely ophthalmic that traditionally have fallen into the243 fields of the cognitive sciences and education (DSM-IV: Axis I). The second group of conditions can be subdivided into the four traditional types of learning differences: (1) developmental speech and language disorders, (2) nonverbal learning disorders, (3) attention disorders, and (4) pervasive developmental disorders (PDD). Many of these have observable ophthalmologic findings. The social reasons for deficient learning in school, such as dysfunctional family environment, poor instruction, foreign first language, and severe psychiatric disease are not directly associated with eye abnormalities (DSM-II and IV). The next section discusses the causes and treatment of disorders within the first main group; that is, medical conditions that temporarily or chronically affect learning.

Ophthalmic Causes of Learning Difficulties

There are several purely ophthalmic causes of temporary or chronic learning difficulties. Many times these conditions cause intermittent blurry vision in school and at home, itchy eyes, redness, foreign body sensation, various visual phenomena, double vision, tearing, light sensitivity (photophobia), and ocular pain and headache. All of these symptoms can affect children's concentration in the classroom and at home and their ability to learn efficiently (Koller, 1997). The main categories of ophthalmic causes affecting learning are refractive errors, strabismus and amblyopia, nystagmus, systemic diseases affecting the eyes, local ocular diseases, and neuro-ophthalmic disorders.

Refractive errors are optical refractive imperfections due to the size and shape of the focusing structures of the eyeball (globe) itself. Refractive status is inherited, with the eyeballs of children shaped like the eyeballs of their parents. A nearsighted eye (myopia) is longer, and the light is focused in front of the retina. A farsighted (hyperopia) eye is shorter, and the light is abnormally focused in back of the retina, not on it. An astigmatic eye is one in which the cornea in front or the lens in the middle of the eye is misshapen microscopically like a lemon or football, more curved in one direction than the other, 90 degrees away. A blurry image results from all three refractive abnormalities (Reinecke, 1965). A corrective spectacle lens is necessary to refocus the light rays coming from the objects observed to create a sharp focused image on the retina, which is then transmitted to the brain so a person can interpret what is seen clearly.

Strabismus is the condition of misaligned eyes in which the eyes are not aimed in the same visual direction. The eyes may be divergent (exotropia or walleyes), convergent (esotropia or crossed eyes), or vertically apart (hypertropia). They also can be cyclotropic, or misaligned around an anterior-posterior axis through the pupil, which can cause significant visual confusion and image "tilt" or torsion. Most acquired strabismus can cause double vision (diplopia), which is most annoying to school-aged children. Less frequently, the sudden onset of strabismus with diplopia in a school-aged child or younger may be of paralytic etiology as a result of a virus infection, or even a brain tumor. The paralysis in the latter case is due to one of the three cranial nerves innervating the six extra-ocular muscles in each eye being affected. A thorough medical evaluation is mandatory (Parks, 1975).

Treatment for exotropia is usually surgical, although for small deviations and those less severe cases in which the eyes go out more at near (convergence insufficiency) than in the distance (divergence excess), eye exercises in the form of classic orthoptics or optometric vision training is quite acceptable. The idea is to train diplopia awareness to improve fusional convergence amplitudes. This enables the individual to see and focus singly over a broader area of viewing and for a longer duration (Bedrossian, 1969). Treatment for nonparalytic esotropia (the eyes are crossed in but move normally in all directions and to the extreme gaze positions) is usually surgical or optical (eyeglasses) if there is excessive farsightedness. In such a case, the eyes over-focus and turn in too much. The hyperopic power of the glasses assumes the focusing function and, when the lenses are worn, the eyes do not have to focus to see clearly and the eyes remain straight. If the eyes turn in more at near than in the distance, bifocal eyeglasses are required to cause more focusing relaxation close up. There are cases, however, involving both esotropia mechanisms that require both glasses and, for the portion of deviation not controlled by the eyeglasses alone, surgery. If left untreated, the weaker eye may develop suppression in order to avoid double vision and become amblyopic. Paralytic as well as restrictive esotropia patients often present with face turns to preserve use of their eyes together away from the side of the paralyzed eye muscle. This can sometimes interfere with efficient reading. Treatment is often surgical.

Hypertropia or vertical strabismus comes in a variety of forms but often it presents to the pediatrician or ophthalmologist as a head tilt, chin depression, elevation or face turn, or combinations of these abnormal head postures. These can all interfere with normal navigation as well as with reading and learning. The treatment is usually surgical. One common such condition is congenital fourth nerve palsy; head tilt is the presenting sign. One should also be aware of the so-called

"A" and "V" syndromes in which the eyes go "in" or "out" more in one gaze than in another. For example, a "V"-pattern esotropia is one in which the eyes go in more when looking down than when looking up, which could cause double vision when reading. Treatment is either with bifocal eyeglasses or surgery if spectacles are ineffective.

Amblyopia is the term applied to diminished vision without an obvious physical or structural abnormality present to account for the vision loss (Simon & Calhoun, 1998). It is called "organic amblyopia" when the vision loss is due to a structural defect such as an abnormal optic nerve. The lay term for amblyopia is "lazy eye," which people often confuse with strabismus or "a weak eye muscle." A more appropriate term for amblyopia would be "lazy vision." There are three types of amblyopia: (1) refractive, due to the eyes having different refractive errors and focusing ability; (2) strabismic, in which the eyes are not aimed at the same object, causing diplopia to occur; and (3) occlusion amblyopia, in which one eye has unclear or opaque media inhibiting light from being clearly transmitted from the environment to the retina, such as a cataract.

For vision to develop normally, both eyes must be in focus, see clearly, be aligned straight ahead, and maintain coordinated eye movements in all fields of gaze. If this does not take place, the lateral geniculate body in the brain develops ganglion cell degeneration and a subsequent decrease in visual acuity. The cause of this in the refractive type is one blurred retinal image in the affected eye and one clear image in the more normal eye. The brain automatically shuts off the blurry image and the cells in the lateral geniculate body atrophy. Giving these patients the correct eyeglasses and covering the better eye with a patch to cause the cells to regenerate is the best therapy. The earlier this is done, the easier it is for the cells to regenerate and the better the results. The brain becomes less plastic after age six and often does not respond to occlusion therapy after puberty. In the strabismic type, eyeglasses or surgery to eliminate the malalignment of the eyes, preceded and followed by occlusion therapy over the better eye, is the best treatment. In occlusion amblyopia, surgical therapy to remove the cause of the obstruction is performed first, followed by appropriate optical correction. A contact lens, or intraocular lens in the case of a unilateral cataract in a child, is currently the best therapy. Amblyopia is reversible if diagnosed early. However, treating school-aged children is frequently a challenge due to peer ridicule and the child's lack of compliance with eye patching. Schoolwork and learning can be affected because the patch covers the better eye. Alternatives to patching include cycloplegic eyedrops, such as atropine and cyclopentolate, to blur the vision in the better seeing eye as well as oral levodopa. L-dopamine seems to improve amblyopic vision in some individuals, even after adolescence, although this drug is not yet in widespread use in the United States (Leguire, Rogers et al., 1998).

Nystagmus is repetitive movements of the eyes, usually horizontally to-and-fro with a fast jerk in one direction (Reinecke, 1997). The movement may be only horizontal or vertical and rarely torsional, but more often it is a mixture. Nystagmus is typically stable in any specific field of gaze, which is termed the "null point." There are many types of nystagmus based on description of the pattern and on the etiology. Examples include vestibular nystagmus, latent and manifest latent nystagmus, amaurotic or "blind" nystagmus (which is more a searching, than jerking movement), and idiopathic infantile nystagmus. The latter is seen in patients with albinism and various retinal disorders.

Occlusion amblyopia can cause deprivation nystagmus, which decreases or is entirely eliminated when the obstacle to normal focusing is removed. Many types of nystagmus are associated with less than normal vision and often a null point exists in one field of gaze, causing a head tilt or face turn in order to achieve optimal visual acuity that exists in the field of least nystagmus activity. Treatment in some cases is surgical in order to move both eyes and the null point away from the extreme gaze position of the null zone and to the primary straight-ahead position. Reading can be labored for children and adults with nystagmus, and learning is therefore sometimes compromised.

Systemic disease affecting the eye and disrupting normal visual learning processes most commonly include (1) juvenile rheumatoid arthritis; (2) metabolic and endocrine disorders, such as juvenile diabetes or pituitary disorders; (3) blood dyscrasias affecting the eye and brain, such as leukemia; and (4) metastatic neoplastic disease to the eye and/or brain, such as neuroblastoma. All of these diseases are treated medically and surgically, as required. Disruption of schooling often occurs for significant periods of time in the more serious cases. Learning is thus secondarily compromised even if no basic learning disorder was present before the child became ill. If the brain becomes structurally involved in the disease process, the various learning centers can be directly affected, causing a possible permanent learning disorder.

Local ocular causes of decreased vision include:

- Ocular media opacities, such as opaque corneal lesions and cataracts.
- Congenital and infantile glaucoma (high intraocular pressure frequently causing legal or complete blindness).

- Significant unilateral and bilateral ocular trauma causing moderate to severe vision loss, such as rupture of the globe after falling on a sharp object.
- Ocular and adnexal neoplasms with secondary disfigurement and/or vision loss, such as retinoblastoma and rhabdomyosarcoma of the muscles of the globe or eyelids.
- Severe chronic ocular infections, such as Herpes Simplex Virus–I, with vision loss affecting the cornea.
- Congenital and degenerative retinal or optic nerve diseases affecting the macula or optic nerve, such as toxoplasmosis and optic nerve hypoplasia (small, poorly functioning optic nerve).

These are frequently seriously urgent conditions, often requiring surgery, chemotherapy, or other medical treatments to cure or control. Schooling and learning invariably suffer (Miller, 1988).

Neuro-ophthalmic causes of temporary or intermittent learning impairment and inefficiency include two broad categories frequently seen in the pediatric ophthalmologist's office: (1) primary brain diseases and tumors causing personality and behavior changes and (2) the vast variety of vascularly mediated pediatric migraine syndromes.

Classic migraine involves a vascular-mediated headache, often preceded by various visual auras, photophobia, and nausea. It is usually followed by the desire to sleep, after which the headache often is gone. Children frequently present with a variation termed "acephalgic migraine." Headaches are not usually a part of the presenting symptom complex. This fact often confuses the parents and many professional caregivers who expect migraine to always be a headache. Children who complain of blurry vision in school but who are found to have a normal eye evaluation may merely be experiencing the pediatric equivalent of adult, constricting visual fields and the typical "scintillating scotoma." These aura are often termed "ophthalmic migraine" when headache symptoms are minimal or absent in adults. Children have a number of associated signs and symptoms of pediatric migraine. These para-migraine entities include infantile colic, lactose intolerance, sleep disturbances (including night terrors and nightmares), and motion sickness. They also include frequent febrile seizures; unexplained abdominal discomfort; allergic predisposition; unusual sensitivity to light (photophobia), noise, and smell; and a type-A personality resistant to change with occasional obsessive/compulsive behavior. Para-migraine entities may also be characterized by various other visual phenomena, such as micropsia (things looking smaller or farther away), macropsia (things looking larger or closer), and metamorphopsia (things looking distorted, as in a fun house mirror). The classic description of the latter is the so-called "Alice in Wonderland" syndrome.

Children complaining of any of these symptoms, either as a single symptom or in combination, sometimes are not believed or are misunderstood, leading to a misdiagnosis or no diagnosis at all. A pediatric examiner must ask the parents of children with learning differences and difficulty with schoolwork if these symptoms occur to ascertain whether or not para-migraine complaints exist. A pediatric neurologist is best for advising these families about acephalgic pediatric migraine therapy. More severe pediatric vascular migraine can result in the syndrome of ophthalmoplegic migraine, which is manifested by paralysis of one or more extraocular muscles with resultant strabismus and diplopia. In these cases, a pediatric ophthalmologist should be consulted. More serious conditions such as a brain tumor must be ruled out. A migraine predisposition must be considered in any child with a learning problem. Migraine is definitely familial and inherited in a multi-factorial mode with various family members having different combinations of symptoms (O'Hara & Koller, 1998).

The following section discusses conditions that are not purely ophthalmic, but some of which may have ophthalmologic findings. These include receptive language disorders, a nonverbal learning disorder, and some pervasive developmental disorders.

COGNITIVE AND EDUCATIONAL CLASSIFICATIONS IN LEARNING DISORDERS

Speech and Language Disorders

Articulation and expressive language disorders (Koller, 1999b) can be grossly diagnosed by taking a history of the child from the parents and observing the child speaking or not speaking while seated in the exam chair. If the parents have not yet sought professional help, the child can be referred back to the pediatrician, an ear, nose, and throat specialist, or a speech and language pathologist for further evaluation and therapy with the primary care physician's knowledge and consent. The ophthalmologist is not directly involved in the specific diagnosis or treatment of children with these disorders.

Receptive language disorders, in contrast, involve visual processing and perception and should be more thoroughly analyzed by the pediatric ophthalmologist. Realizing that developmental dyslexia is now thought to be a result of a genetically inherited deficiency (Shaywitz, 1998) in cerebral phonetic analysis, the ophthalmologist can deduce the likely presence of dyslexia from the family history and by asking the child a few questions about simple words, such as "cat" and "bat," in an attempt to

bring out the inability of such children to identify the components of "bat" as "bu," "aah," and "teh." A history of letter reversals in school and difficulty reading may not really point to a receptive language disorder alone because nonverbal learning disorders and attention disorders can also cause these symptoms in certain instances. Early preschool identifying characteristics include unusual difficulty learning numbers, letters, and colors without evidence of eye disease. The ophthalmologist should refer these children to a knowledgeable neuropsychologist or speech and language pathologist for further testing to identify all the specific language disorders existing in each individual case and then to recommend diagnosis-specific therapy. A licensed reading teacher and a homework tutor may both be required, with additional therapy and monitoring by the speech and language pathologist and the neuropsychologist as necessary.

Auditory processing disorders are in the realm of ear, nose, and throat specialists, as well as speech and language pathologists, and should be referred to those professionals for appropriate, specific diagnoses and therapy (Welsch, 1980; Welsch & Healey, 1982). A tutor is often helpful to teach auditory interpretation and attention in the classroom environment. Auditory processing disorders are receptive language dysfunctions and the "hearing" equivalent of "visual" developmental dyslexia. One remedial method in reading disorders is to have the child simultaneously listen to a recording of the written text while following the printed material in the book in the presence of a reading instructor. This therapy is effective if only visual or auditory processing is abnormal, not if the child suffers from both disorders.

Nonverbal Learning Disorders

Appropriate diagnostic studies establish this all-too-often missed learning disorder.

The ophthalmologist can suspect a nonverbal learning disorder (NVLD) by giving the young patient a simple visual memory test in the office. It takes only 1 to 2 minutes to perform. (See Figure 1.) NVLD is thought to be associated with right hemisphere white matter dysfunction (Bannatyne, 1974; Foss, 1991; Johnson & Myklebust, 1967). The frontal lobe may also be involved. The main deficits of this disorder include visual-spatial perception, visual memory, psychomotor coordination, complex tactile-perceptual skills, reasoning, concept formation, mathematical abilities, and psychological/behavioral difficulties.

Well-developed verbal and reading skills, however, are frequently observed in these children and adults. Occupational therapy is the treatment path that is most efficient for individuals with NVLD. At times, therapy must be coordinated with a homework tutor, reading specialist, and/or a physical therapist if other, more complex aspects of NVLD are identified. Numerous treatment strategies have been tried over the years but utilizing current repetitive, standard rehabilitation science techniques seem, at present, to be best.

It is in this category of learning differences that some optometric vision training techniques appear to be effective. These techniques are partially based on occupational and physical therapy principles as well as standard rehabilitation science. Adults, after

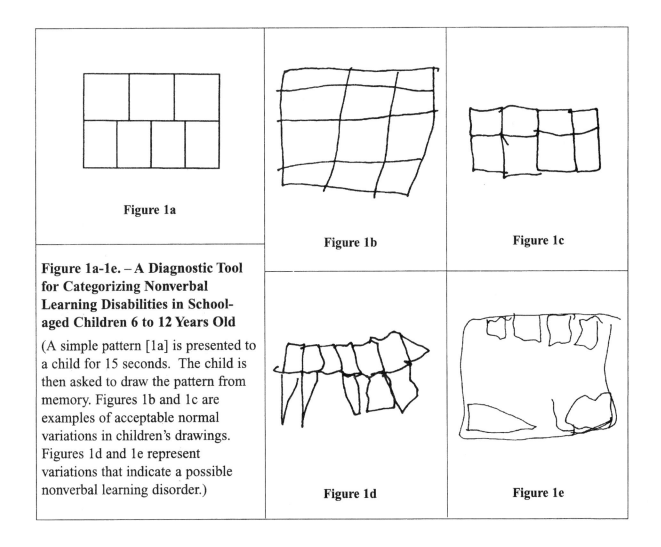

Figure 1a

Figure 1b

Figure 1c

Figure 1a-1e. – A Diagnostic Tool for Categorizing Nonverbal Learning Disabilities in School-aged Children 6 to 12 Years Old

(A simple pattern [1a] is presented to a child for 15 seconds. The child is then asked to draw the pattern from memory. Figures 1b and 1c are examples of acceptable normal variations in children's drawings. Figures 1d and 1e represent variations that indicate a possible nonverbal learning disorder.)

Figure 1d

Figure 1e

strokes, as well as all-aged individuals after accidental closed head trauma, are taught to utilize the uninjured functioning parts of their brain to compensate for loss of normal use of an injured or damaged brain area, despite the fact that the area of the brain assuming the new function was never intended to do so. Stroke patients thus learn to read, write, talk, and navigate once again despite permanent brain damage to the area previously programmed to maintain those particular functions. A similar model exists for children with naturally occurring brain dysfunction, such as the one for nonverbal learning disabled individuals. These children are born with inefficient or inadequate brain programming and processing. Laterality training, eye movement coordination strategies to help create smooth pursuits (saccades), and hand-eye coordination exercises all help improve, to some extent at least, performance of those functions. To what direct extent learning itself, in a classroom or at home, is enhanced in all cases has yet to be shown via evidence-based science using a masked or double masked controlled study. Published studies reviewed by the author to date are anecdotal or retrospective/prospective reviews of measurement parameters or performance, often while other remedial methods are carried out simultaneously (Atzmon et al., 1993).

Piaget's theory stating that "intelligence is the most important instrument of learning" and that environmental interaction is equally important has been used as the basis for utilizing games and play as a medium to enhance the process of thinking and learning. This was tried in a West Virginia school setting by Furth and Wachs more than 25 years ago (Furth & Wachs, 1974). Developmental optometry has adopted some of Piaget's theory for vision training. The idea is to think before you can actually learn a fact or concept.

Some optometric exercises (Scheiman, 1994) are designed to improve developmental visual information processing. The first goal of therapy is to develop the patient's motor-awareness ability by performing isolated, simultaneous, and sequential movements involving both sides of the body. The treating optometrist wishes to develop motor memory of the differences between the right and left sides of the body. This is typically accomplished using balance activities, ball bouncing, chalkboard squares, and other gross eye-hand coordination activities such as beanbag tossing or ball playing. The second goal of therapy is to develop the patient's motor-planning ability. This is accomplished using numerous other techniques, including jumping jacks, the Randolf shuffle, and slap-tap, among others. These strategies seem to work by repetitive, positive psychological reinforcement and one-on-one patient-therapist interaction as much as by direct influence on the cerebral academic learning process itself. Since NVLD involve higher cognitive learning centers in which abstract thinking, visual memory, and spatial recognition are the main deficits, repetitive training makes it possible for a child to learn to perform certain tasks more efficiently. "Practice make perfect" is a commonly accepted theme. If a child with NVLD is taught by optometric techniques to enhance motor memory, motor awareness, and motor integration—and this improvement can be transferred to the academic arena—then the claimed benefits of optometric vision training can be realized. Those who profess benefits from vision training in cases of speech and language disorders, attention disorders, and pervasive developmental disorders (including classic autism) are simply not reporting the other therapies for these individuals being carried out simultaneously by other professionals, including pediatric neurologists, psychiatrists, psychologists, language therapists, occupational therapists, physical therapists, educators, and pediatricians. NVLD account for less than 15% of all learning disabled individuals (Koller, 1999b). Vision therapy is but one of many interdisciplinary interventions necessary for these individuals.

Attention Deficit/ Hyperactivity Disorders

The diagnosis of attention deficit/hyperactivity disorders (ADD/ADHD) is established by the criteria listed in the DSM-IV, with behavior repeated over time. Some controversy still exists concerning the real existence and definition of these two diagnoses as a separate category of learning disorders (Carey, 1999). The pediatric neurologist, pediatric developmental specialist, family pediatrician or physician, or psychiatrist usually provides treatment. It is necessary for the ophthalmologist to identify the behavior by listening and observing while the child is in the examination chair and referring appropriately. Pharmacological therapy is the treatment of choice, with ancillary remediation from homework tutors, certified reading specialists, and, occasionally, occupational therapists. Teaching a child to concentrate quite often appears to be easier when the patient is on stimulant therapy such as Ritalin or Adderal. Nonetheless, many pediatric neurologists and pediatric developmental specialists now prefer to reserve drug therapy for more persistent cases.

The Committee on Quality Improvement (Subcommittee on Attention Deficit/Hyperactivity Disorder) of the American Academy of Pediatrics (2000) recently published its clinical practice guidelines, *Diagnosis and Evaluation of the Child with Attention Deficit/Hyperactivity Disorder,* which emphasizes to pediatricians the DSM-IV criteria for diagnosing ADHD and observing the typical behaviors in more than one setting, location, and situation over time. Research involving the study of academically efficient individuals with ADHD compared to those afflicted who are scholastically inefficient was suggested.

Pervasive Developmental Disorders

The ophthalmologist can frequently identify an individual with Asperger's syndrome or Rett syndrome by history and observation of the patient's behavior in the examination chair. Lack of eye contact is often the initial complaint and reason for referral to the ophthalmologist (Koller & Goldberg, 1999). Lack of social relatedness and peer interaction is obtained by the ophthalmologist from the family and patient history. The history can also provide information concerning an intense area of interest or other behavior peculiar to individuals with autistic spectrum disorders. Definitive diagnosis and treatment should be in the hands of a qualified psychiatrist and knowledgeable pediatricians, as well as occupational and physical therapists, who are well schooled in diagnosing and treating children with pervasive developmental or autistic spectrum disorders (PDD/AS) (Greenspan & Wieder, 1998). The role of the ophthalmologist is to suspect the diagnosis and refer appropriately, noting the high index of suspicion.

"Vision training" techniques have yet to be shown to directly influence the main deficits of autistic individuals. However, some vision training techniques and occupational therapy are appropriate for nonverbal learning disorders that are part of an autistic individual's component disabilities. Since the autistic spectrum involves people with difficulties in social relatedness and social skills, use of language for communicative purposes, and a limited but intense range of interest, many different professionals must become involved in ongoing therapy. Any eye abnormality present should be corrected by the ophthalmologist, just as an appropriate specialist should treat any medical condition. If the patient is sufficiently functioning and can concentrate on occupational and/or vision therapy tasks, these tasks should be provided for those component disorders the PDD/AS patient manifests. There is much to be learned in the future from studying these remedial methods with evidence-based science. Optometrists, ophthalmologists, occupational therapists, and speech and language pathologists should work together to bring about this research.

OTHER DISORDERS AFFECTING LEARNING

Other disorders affecting learning that an ophthalmologist frequently sees include Tourette syndrome and some purely mental disorders such as anxiety disorder, oppositional defiant disorders, and personality disorders (Axis-I). Idiopathic sleep disorders can also affect learning, as can social and family dysfunction or poor school instruction (Axis-IV). All these conditions can be suspected from a social and family history taken by an ophthalmologist in the office. Tourette syndrome is often treated by a pediatric neurologist or psychiatrist, whereas a pediatric psychiatrist most effectively handles the other conditions mentioned.

Several serious genetic disorders are frequently associated with learning differences, including familial dysautonomia (Reilly-Day syndrome) (Groom, Kay, & Corrent, 1997) and mitochondrial cytopathy (Phillips & Newman, 1997). Both these conditions involve multiple systems within the body. The brain is a high oxygen/energy uptake organ and the mitochondria are the oxygen generators of our cells. Any disease of the mitochondria affects most organ systems. The autonomic nervous system is almost nonfunctional in familial dysautonomia, and brain processing is also affected. Much more

research in the area of mitochondrial (not nuclear) inheritance must be done to correlate learning disabilities with these conditions. Familial dysautonomia may also be a partial mitochondrial disorder, as might many other types of learning differences and disabilities.

CONCLUSION

As noted previously, having the ophthalmologist aware of all of the medical and nonmedical conditions and situations that could affect learning in a child or older individual increases the potential for a child with learning disabilities to receive appropriate, effective, and timely remedial treatment. It is important for one professional to take the responsibility of coordinating all the specialists actually involved in the care of any patient with a learning difference. It doesn't matter what that person's specialty is, so long as he or she is knowledgeable in the general field and has the motivation, passion, and resources necessary to coordinate the efforts of numerous physicians, psychologists, educators, and allied health professionals, such as occupational therapists, physical therapists, optometrists, and speech and language therapists. Social workers and attorneys often are involved, too. Given the desire, an ophthalmologist can assume this task easily. The ophthalmologist is often the first expert to whom the pediatrician or family physician refers the child suspected of having a learning difference. However, the pediatric psychiatrist, neurologist, or developmental specialist could be equally effective. True multidisciplinary science and coordination of effort is mandatory if optimal benefit is to be achieved for all individuals with learning disorders. ■

REFERENCES

American Academy of Pediatrics (2000). Clinical practice guideline: Diagnosis and evaluation of the child with attention deficit/hyperactivity disorder. *Pediatrics, 105*(5), 1158-1170.

Atzmon, C. O. et al. (1993). A randomized prospective masked and matched comparative study of orthoptic treatment versus conventional reading and tutoring treatment for reading disabilities in 62 children (including pro and con editorial comments by Drs. Hardenbergh and Cibis Tongue). *Binocular Vision & Eye Muscle Surgery Quarterly, 8*(2), 91-106.

Bannatyne, A. (1974). Diagnosis: A note on recategorization of the WISC scaled scores. *Journal of Learning Disabilities. 7,* 272-274.

Bedrossian, E. H. (1969). *The surgical and nonsurgical management of strabismus.* Springfield, IL: Charles C. Thomas.

Carey, W. B. (1999). (in commentaries). Problems in diagnosing attention and activity. *Pediatrics, 103*(3), 664-667

Foss, J. M. (1991). Nonverbal learning disabilities and remedial interventions. *Annals of Dyslexia, 41,* 129-131.

Furth, H. G., & Wachs, H. (1974). *Thinking goes to school, (Piaget's theory in practice).* Toronto: Oxford University Press.

Gable, J. L. (1984). *Visual disorders in the handicapped child.* San Mateo, CA: Macel Dekker.

Greenspan, S. I., & Weider, S. (1998). *The child with special needs.* Reading, MA: Perseus Books.

Groom, M., Kay, M. D., & Corrent, G. F. (1997). Optic neuropathy in familial dysautonomia, *Journal of Ophthalmology, 17*(2), 101-102.

Hartstein, J. (1971). *Current concepts in dyslexia.* St. Louis, MO: Mosby.

Johnson, D., & Myklebust, H. R. (1967). Nonverbal disorders of learning. In *Learning Disabilities Educational Principles and Practices.* New York: Grune and Stratton.

Koller, H. P. (1997). How does vision affect learning? *Journal of Ophthalmic Nursing & Technology, 16* (Vol. I), 7-11.

Koller, H. P. (1999a). Visual perception and learning differences: An ophthalmologist's view. *American Orthoptic Journal, 49.*

Koller, H. P. (1999b). How does vision affect learning? *Journal of Ophthalmic Nursing & Technology, 18*(1), 12-18.

Koller, H. P., & Goldberg, K. B. (1999). A Guide to visual and perceptual learning disabilities, *Current concepts in ophthalmology,* 24-28. Pennsylvania Academy of Ophthalmology.

Leguire, L. E., Rogers, G. L., et al. (1998) Occlusion & Levodopa-Carbidopa Treatment for Childhood Amblyopia. *Journal of AAPOS, 2*(5), 257-264.

Miller, N. R. (1998). Neuro-Ophthalmologic Topographic Diagnosis of Tumors and Related Conditions. In Walsh & Hoyt (Eds.), *Clinical Neuro-Ophthalmology* (pp. 1137-1242).

O'Hara, M. A., & Koller, H. P. (1998). Migraine in a pediatric ophthalmology practice. *Journal of Pediatric Ophthalmology & Strabismus, 35,* 203-208.

Parks, M. M. (1975). *Ocular motility and strabismus.* Hagerstown, MD: Harper & Row.

Phillips, P. H., & Newman, N. J. (1997). Mitochondrial diseases in pediatric ophthalmology. *Journal of AAPOS, 1*(2), 115-122.

Reinecke, R. D. (1965). *Refraction: A programmed text.* New York: Appleton Century-Crofts.

Reinecke, R. D. (1997). Idiopathic infantile nystagmus: Diagnosis & treatment. *Journal of AAPOS, 1,* 67-82.

Scheiman, M. M., & Rouse, M. W. (1994). *Optometric management learning-related vision problems.* St. Louis, MO: Mosby.

Shaywitz, S. E. (1998). Dyslexia: Current concepts. *New England Journal of Medicine, 338*(1), 307-312.

Simon, J. W., & Calhoun J. H. (1998). *Amblyopia: A child's eyes.* Gainesville, FL: Triad.

Welsh, L. W., Welsh, J. J., & Healey, M. P. (1980). Central auditory testing and dyslexia. *Laryngoscope, XC*(6), 972-984.

Welsh, L. W. et al. (1982). Cortical, subcortical, and brainstem dysfunction: A correlation in dyslexic children. *American Journal of Otolaryngology, Rhinolaryngology and Laryngology, 9*(3), 310-315.

Appendix

VISUAL PERCEPTION AND LEARNING DIFFERENCES IN PEDIATRIC OPHTHALMOLOGY:
What the Ophthalmologist Needs to Know about Learning Disabilities in Clinical Practice

I. **Ophthalmic Causes of Temporary Learning Impairment and Inefficiency**
   A. Strabismus, amblyopia, and refractive errors
      1. Decompensated accommodative esotropia with secondary diplopia
      2. Secondary ocular cranial nerve palsies (n. III, IV, VI)
      3. Uncorrected congenital vertical strabismus with abnormal face and head positions
      4. Bilateral very high ametropias, such as bilateral amblyopia of high hyperopia
      5. Bilateral occlusion amblyopia, such as after congenital cataract surgery
      6. Associated untreated "A" and "V" syndromes
      7. Convergence insufficiency exotropia/phoria in certain individuals
   B. Nystragmus of moderate to severe degree causing significant vision loss
   C. Pediatric ocular diseases that can affect learning via visual and emotional effects
      1. Severe juvenile rheumatoid arthritis and related ocular inflammations
      2. Congenital glaucoma with vision loss
      3. Congenital cataracts and major corneal opacities with vision loss and nystragmus
      4. Significant unilateral and/or bilateral ocular trauma with vision loss
      5. Ocular and adnexal neoplasms with secondary disfigurement and vision loss
      6. Severe chronic ocular infections such as HSV-I with vision loss
      7. Congenital and degenerative retinal diseases affecting the macula

II. **Neuro-ophthalmic Causes of Temporary or Intermittent Learning Impairment and Inefficiency**
   A. Brain tumors causing a change in personality and behavior in a pediatric patient
   B. Migraine syndromes
      1. Acephalgic pediatric migraine with visual disturbances and variable vision in school
      2. Ophthalmic migraine in childhood
      3. Ophthalmoplegic migraine
      4. Classic migraine in the older student
   C. Optic nerve disease with significant visual impairment

III. **Systemic Diseases Associated with Vision and Neurologic Dysfunctions Potentially Affecting Learning**
   A. Metabolic and endocrinic disorders
   B. Blood dyscrasias affecting the eye and brain
   C. Metastatic neoplastic disease to the eye and/or brain

IV. The Ophthalmologist's Role in Examining a Child and Advising the Family of a Defect in visual processing and/or learning is to rule out the presence of eye disease or related systemic disorder and to refer the pediatric patient to the proper professionals for more definitive diagnoses and subsequent treatment(s). In order to effectively do this, a classification of non-ophthalmic learning disorders will now be outlined.

A. Learning disabilities (differences)
1. Developmental speech and language based disorders (epidemiology)
   a. Articulation disorders
   b. Expressive language disorders
   c. Receptive
      (1) Dyslexia—phonologic processing disorder
         (a) genetics
         (b) pathophysiology
         (b) remediation
         (d) early preschool identifying characteristics
      (2) Other receptive language disorders
2. Nonverbal learning disabilities (epidemiology)
   a. Definition
   b. Characteristics and affected areas of learning
      (1) visual-spatial perception
      (2) visual memory
      (3) psychomotor coordination
      (4) complex tactile-perceptual skills
      (5) reasoning
      (6) concept formation
      (7) mathematical abilities
      (8) psychological behavioral difficulties
      (9) good verbal and reading skills
   c. Early identification traits
   d. Differential diagnosis
   e. Methods of treatment. What exactly is optometric vision training?
   f. Rationale of therapy based on the traditional closed head trauma/stroke rehabilitation model
3. Attention deficit hyperactivity disorder (epidemiology)
   a. Definition
   b. Characteristics (DSM-IV) and diagnostic criteria observable during an eye exam
      (1) squirms in seat, fidgets with hand and/or feet
      (2) unable to remain seated when required to do so
      (3) easily distracted
      (4) blurts out answers before a question is finished
      (5) difficulty following instructions
      (6) unable to sustain attention in work activities
      (7) interrupts or intrudes on others

           (8)   does not appear to listen

           (9)   loses items for tasks such as toys, pencils, and books

           (10) often engages in dangerous activities without considering the consequences

      c. Subclassification

           (1)   inattention

           (2)   impulsivity

           (3)   hyperactivity

      d. Differential diagnosis

           (1)   Tourette's syndrome

           (2)   conduct disorder

           (3)   oppositional defiant disorder

           (4)   other tic disorders

      e. Treatment and community support

           (1)   pediatric neurologist

           (2)   pediatric developmental specialist

           (3)   pediatric psychiatrist

           (4)   special education teacher or tutor

           (5)   various support groups

   4. Pervasive developmental disorders/autistic spectrum disorders (PDD/ASD)

      a. Definition

      b. Characteristics: defects in social relatedness and language/communication skills

      c. Subclassifications

           (1)   Asperger's syndrome (chief eye symptom is "lack of eye contact")

           (2)   Rett syndrome

           (3)   classic autism

           (4)   unclassified PDD/ASD

      d. Referral and treatment options

      e. Micro and primary dyskinetic strabismus as a presenting sign of PDD

      f. Hyperlexia

V. Patient Support Groups for Learning Disabled (LD) Individuals

A. CHADD (Children and Adults with ADD)

B. CEC (Children's Educational Counsel)

C. ASLHA (American Speech, Language and Hearing Association)

D. LDAA (Learning Disabilities Association of America)

E. PERC (Parents Educational Resource Center)

F. The Orten Dyslexia Society

G. AHA (American Hyperlexia Association)

H. HALO (Health Achievement Learning Opportunities Centers)

VI. Role of the Pediatric and Comprehensive Ophthalmologist Concerning Individuals with Learning Disabilities

A. Identify and treat any eye or eye-related systemic disease or abnormality.

B. By observation and careful history, identify which broad category of learning differences the patient likely has and convey that impression to the pediatrician, the family, and any other interested parties. These children have often been through many psychological tests, tutoring, and other attempts at remediation without a definitive diagnosis or combination of diagnoses. Suggest a comprehensive neuropsychologic/ educational evaluation from a qualified, credentialed neuropsychologist when all interested parties agree.

C. Help the family by giving them a direction in which to proceed so that the child with non-ocular learning differences can start to achieve his full potential. Not every individual with learning disabilities requires every possible specialist. These professionals include:

1. Pediatric neurologist
2. Pediatric psychiatrist
3. Pediatric developmental specialist
4. Pediatric endocrinologist
5. Pediatric geneticist
6. Pediatric otolaryngologist
7. Pediatric ophthalmologist
8. Speech and language pathologist (audiologist)
9. Neuropsychologist
10. Educational psychologist
11. Educator with special education credentials
12. Reading tutor
13. Physical therapist
14. Occupational therapist
15. Pediatric social worker
16. School placement expert (educator)
17. Disabilities attorney
18. Family physician or general pediatrician

D. A specialized attorney is often beneficial for helping families receive federal LD benefits to which they are entitled under the terms of the Individuals with Disabilities Education Act (IDEA) and Americans with Disabilities Act (ADA).

E. When the answer the question, "Is the child's reading and/or learning problem in school due to his eyes?" is "No," the ophthalmologist must explain why it is not and offer a positive and constructive method to direct those families toward obtaining the proper and appropriate care. The public still believes that eye specialists are knowledgeable in the field of visual perception as well as visual function.

Part Four:

Home, School, and Family Approaches

◄ 12 ►

Developmentally Appropriate Interactions and Practices

Stanley I. Greenspan, M.D., and Serena Wieder, Ph.D.

Chapter 4 describes developmentally appropriate interactions and practices recommended for all children so that they can master the challenges of the particular stage of development through which they are passing. As described, however, children with special needs present special challenges to this general recommendation. Their processing challenges and functional developmental difficulties make it very difficult for therapists to create developmentally appropriate interactions. For example, how does a therapist create appropriate interactions for a preschooler who is avoiding human interaction by running away from people as soon as they come near? How does a therapist interact with a child who only wants to line up his toys or rub a spot on the floor over and over? What is the best tactic for comforting a child who is so oversensitive to sound and touch that she withdraws from the human world? Therapists must deal with these and other special challenges to implement developmentally appropriate practices and interactions for children with special needs.

In order to systematically develop appropriate strategies for the child with special needs, it is important to assess the child's functional developmental levels (attention, engagement, nonverbal reciprocal gesturing, complex problem solving, creative use of ideas, and abstract and logical thinking) and processing profile (auditory, visual-spatial, motor planning and sequencing, and sensory modulation). This assessment enables the construction of patterns of interactions tailored to each child's unique profile.

These patterns of interaction, however, must be available throughout the child's waking hours. Making them available only during therapy sessions will not be sufficient. For example, if a child is allowed to be self-absorbed and perseverative for 80% of his day and is developmentally appropriate for only 20%, most of his learning will be maladaptive rather than adaptive. On the other hand, if individually tailored interaction patterns are an integral part of all of his daily activities, he has an opportunity to learn adaptively throughout the day.

There are three types of developmentally appropriate interactions and practices that need to be part of the child's daily routine:

1. *Spontaneous interactions during which the caregiver follows the child's lead and helps her elaborate,* often referred to as floor time.

2. *Semistructured, problem-solving interactions,* during which specific learning objectives are worked on through the creation of dynamic challenges that the child wants to solve.

3. *Motor, sensory, perceptual-motor, and visual-spatial physical activities* to strengthen important processing foundations.

This chapter describes each of the three types of developmentally appropriate interactions in more detail. First, however, a description of the "generic" interactive processes that should be a part of all three types of developmentally appropriate practices is necessary. In essence, in every interaction with a child, the parents, caregivers, and educators should promote attention, engagement, a continuous flow of two-way communication with gestures and, when possible, ideas. At the same time, adults must tailor these interactions to the child's functional developmental level (e.g., fostering engagement or the elaboration of ideas) and individual processing differences (e.g., emphasizing visual-spatial or auditory processing, or being especially soothing with a sensitive child or animated with an underreactive child). These developmentally appropriate interactions, which meet the child at his functional developmental level in the context of his processing differences, are referred to as "floor time."

GENERIC PROCESSES COMMON TO ALL DEVELOPMENTALLY APPROPRIATE INTERACTIONS

Until a child is well into her school years, parents and caregivers will frequently interact with her when she is down on the floor, where she feels most comfortable and is surrounded by her toys and playthings. When interacting eye-to-eye with a child, the adult generates a sense of equality that encourages the child to

engage, take initiative, and act more assertively. Parents and caregivers also operate in a child's realm when they playfully make funny faces while changing a diaper, chatting at the dinner table together, visiting the supermarket, or going for a walk outside. Thus, the generic processes can occur anywhere and at any time the child and her caregiver are interacting in a way that mobilizes the child's interests, initiatives, gestures, and ideas. The foci of the generic processes follow. (In this discussion, the term "partner" means the therapist, parent, caregiver, or any other person engaged in floor time activities with the child.)

- *Engage and let the child set the emotional tone.* Partners can be very animated, using hand gestures and various facial expressions, as they encourage the child to choose any activity for them to do together. With a child operating at early developmental levels, partners can join in on whatever the child is doing at that moment, such as clapping, making noises, or wandering around the room. Attempting to capture the child's rhythm, intensity, and interests creates an important foundation for the initial sense of engagement and the interactions that will build on it.

- *Open and close circles of communication.* As partners follow a child's lead and build on his interests and overtures, they should inspire him to build on what has been done or said in turn. For example, if a child moves his toy car and the partner moves another car parallel to it or says "Where are we going?" or "Can my dolly have a ride in your car?," the partner is opening a communication circle. If the child gestures or verbalizes in response, building on his behavior by saying "We go to house!" or simply bangs his car into the partner's car while giving a knowing look, he is closing that circle of communication. Even when a child responds with a simple "No" or "Shh!" or by turning away, he is closing the circle of communication. The goal is to facilitate a continuous flow of circles in both unstructured and semi-structured interaction. Sometimes these circles will involve only the simplest back-and-forth gestures, such as looking, smiling, or pointing.

One way to extend constructive interactions with a child is to help a child reach a goal. For example, a child might be looking longingly, and pointing, at a toy fire engine placed beyond his reach. The partner can retrieve the toy, turn to the child, gesture, and ask "Want it?" When the child responds with a big smile and reaches for the toy, the partner has helped the child reach a goal as well as extended the interaction.

• *Use playful obstruction to expand circles of communication.* Sometimes, it may be necessary to expand play or conversation with a child by interacting in a playfully obstructive manner. For example, if a child avoids her partner during floor time, the partner might try positioning herself between the child and whatever is absorbing all the child's attention. Alternatively, the partner can assume the role of a moving, talking fence that the child needs to climb over or under to reach her favorite toy or simply to continue wandering around the room.

• *Increase the emotional range.* In creating developmentally appropriate interactions, it is helpful to look for opportunities to extend the child's gestural interactions or add a new twist or plot line that builds on a child's interests. In this way, over time, a child will become engaged in all the marvelously varied themes of life: closeness and dependency; assertiveness, initiative, and curiosity; aggression, anger, and limit setting; and pleasure and excitement. These experiences

will help the child develop a full range of emotions.

Many times, a child will avoid or neglect certain types of interactions, despite a person's best efforts to foster a supportive floor time environment. When this occurs, it is appropriate to gently challenge the child in those emotional areas that she seems inclined to bypass. For example, a child may be wonderfully easygoing, but a little passive in asserting herself and claiming her own toys during playgroup. A partner could encourage the child to be more assertive by doing something as simple as moving her favorite stuffed animal away from her group of animals. In so doing, the partner should appear impish, rather than malicious, and move the toy away very slowly and deliberately, in a smiling, nonthreatening manner. The child may very well assert herself and come after her prized toy!

If a child's interactions involve pretend play and use of words, but the interactions focus disproportionately on themes of anger and aggression, the partner should not interfere with the dramatic flow by stopping the action or by asking a verbal child questions such as "Why is (the character) so mad?" or "Why doesn't (the character) behave nicely?" Instead, it would be appropriate for the partner to join in the action, slow it down if it's getting too active, and elaborate on the emotion through his (the partner's) own actions. For example, if the child is banging the doll, the partner might begin banging a doll, but gradually turn the action toward slow, interactive banging. If the child is verbal, the partner might comment, "Gee, he really wants to bop those bad guys. He's going to destroy them in a hundred different ways. I bet he must have a good reason for that!" By acknowledging both the depth of anger that the child is portraying, and the fact that he must have good reason for it, the partner is empathetically engaged with him rather than promoting his own agenda. It is this kind of empathy that eventually helps a child learn to be empathic and kind.

The imaginative and verbal expression of feelings usually helps a child learn to understand and regulate them. A child tends to act out strong feelings (such as anger) that aren't acknowledged, either directly through aggression, or indirectly through an opposite response, such as being overly inhibited or fearful. Acknowledgment of a child's feelings does not imply that a person approves of a child acting them out in reality. In fact, recognizing a child's "pretend" agenda will help the child use ideas rather than actions. It will also strengthen a partner's ability to discuss and set relevant limits on aggressive behavior if it should emerge at school or at home during nonpretend times.

By broadening a child's emotional themes, floor time interactions supplement discipline. When a child is misbehaving, pretend drama can sometimes help reveal what the child is feeling. Surprisingly, acknowledgment of a child's negative, angry feelings may eventually help him introduce positive themes into his dramas. Most children have a balance of feelings. If the partner conveys an empathetic message that it is acceptable for the child to explore aggressive themes during play, the child will begin to explore dependency, love, and concern, too. However, if a child senses that his ideas are not understood, his frustration may cause him to polarize his feelings and opt for aggressive themes. Preverbal

children can often explore aggressive intentions through their actions, for example, by banging a car. When a partner joins in empathetically (e.g., by also banging a car) and then slows the action down and explores other options, it is possible to convey understanding, regulation, coping, and alternatives to the child.

- *Expand the range of processing capacities.* While a child is engaged with sounds, sights, touches, and movements, partners can make a conscious effort to appeal to her different processing and motor-planning capacities. In this way, the child's "mental team"—that is, all her emerging capacities—learn to simultaneously work together under the direction of an emotionally meaningful goal. For example, during a floor time session in which the child is moving a toy trolley, a partner can introduce some visual and spatial elements into the noisy play by having a house suddenly cover the trolley. This action may inspire the child to search for the disappearing trolley, thus adding a visual-spatial processing activity to her motor activity and stimulating her emotional interest in finding the toy. In a similar manner, spatial play during floor time—such as building block towers and forts—can also promote a child's ability to broaden the range of her processing and motor capacities.

THE THREE TYPES OF DEVELOPMENTALLY APPROPRIATE INTERACTIONS AND PRACTICES

The generic processes just described are basic to all three types of developmentally appropriate interactions and practices that are part of a comprehensive home and school program. Detailed discussions of all three types follow.

Spontaneous,
Follow-the-Child's-Lead Floor Time

In the preceding section, the term "floor time" referred to the process, or concept, through which therapists, parents, and other caregivers make a special effort to tailor interactions to meet the child at his unique functional developmental level and within the context of his processing differences. In this section, "Floor Time" is a specific practice that incorporates this process. Floor Time sessions focus on having partners follow the child's lead to encourage the child's initiative and purposeful behavior, deepening engagement, lengthening mutual attention, and developing symbolic capacities. The length of the sessions will depend on how long it takes the child to "warm up" and become fully engaged as well as how long it takes the child to create and expand on new gestures and/or ideas. Daily opportunities for 6 to 8 or more sessions lasting between 20 and 45 minutes each are often recommended.

Basic Principles of Floor Time

There are several basic principles of Floor Time:
- *Follow the child's lead.*
- *Join in at the child's developmental level and build on her natural interests.* Through your own affect and action, woo the child into engaging with you (go for the gleam in her eye).
- *Open and close circles of communication* (i.e., build on the child's interest and then inspire the child to, in turn, build on what you have done or said).
- *Create a play environment* with rattles, balls, dolls, action figures, cars, trucks, schools, etc. *that will provide a vehicle for the child's natural interests and facilitate opening and closing circles of communication* (e.g., some children do better with a few

selected toys whereas others interact more with many toys). Avoid very structured games that reduce creative interaction.
- Extend the circles of communication.
- Interact constructively to help the child reach his own goals (e.g., hold up the truck he wants so he can reach for it).
- Interact playfully, but obstructively, as needed (when the child is avoiding interaction, position yourself between the child and what he wants to do to encourage him to interact with you (e.g., hide the child's car in your hand so he is inspired to search for it, or build a little fence around the child with your arms so that he needs to duck under, push up, or say "out" in order to return to moving around the room).
- *Broaden the child's range of interactive experience.*
  - Broaden the thematic and/or emotional range.
  - Enjoy and engage in play dealing with the different themes of life: closeness and dependency; assertiveness, initiative, and curiosity; aggression and limit-setting; and pleasure and excitement.
  - Challenge the child to engage in neglected or avoided types of interactions (e.g., for a passive child who avoids taking the initiative, slowly and smilingly move away the toy the child is playing with, thereby challenging the child to take the initiative and come after it).
- *Broaden the range of processing and motor capacities used in interactions.*
  - Engage the child with sound and/or words, vision, touch, and movement (e.g., while playing with cars, make racing sounds or discuss where the

cars are going; look for the house or school the cars are going to visit).

— Challenge the child to employ under-used or avoided processing capacities (e.g., if the child moves her car alongside yours, but ignores your sounds and words and doesn't make sounds on her own, block the child's car with your car and challenge her to make a noise or say "go" to get your car to move out of the way. For a child who moves her car in only one direction, construct various barriers that encourage her to move the car in different directions).

- *Tailor your interactions to the child's individual differences in auditory processing, visual-spatial processing, motor planning and sequencing, and sensory modulation.*
  - Profile the child's individual differences, based on observation and history.
  - Work with the individual differences. Utilize natural strengths for interaction (e.g., visual experiences for the child with relatively strong visual-spatial capacities). Gradually remediate vulnerabilities (e.g., provide extra practice in listening to and using sounds and words for the child who has a receptive language or auditory processing challenge. Be extra soothing for the sensory-overreactive child and/or extra compelling and animated for the sensory-underreactive child).
- *Simultaneously attempt to mobilize the six functional developmental levels* (attention, engagement, gestures, complex preverbal problem-solving, using ideas, and connecting ideas for thinking). Younger children or children with developmental challenges will master the later levels as they develop.

Mobilizing the Six Functional Developmental Levels During Floor Time

During Floor Time, therapists and caregivers use developmentally appropriate interactions to mobilize the six functional developmental levels. Strategies for accomplishing this at each level follow.

1. **Shared attention**
   - Use the child's individual sensory and motor profile to draw him into shared attention (e.g., more visual experiences for the child who especially enjoys looking).
   - Harness all the available senses, as well as motor capacities and affects (e.g., combine highly enjoyable activities with interactions that involve vision, hearing, touch, and movement).
   - Use both constructive and playfully obstructive strategies (e.g., dance or run together with the active child; build a fence with your arms around the child who likes to avoid or run away).
   - Stretch the child's capacity for shared attention by increasing the interactive circles of communication rather than by trying to get the child to focus on a particular object or toy.

2. **Engagement**
   - Follow the child's lead in order to engage her in interactions that bring her pleasure and joy.
   - Build on these pleasurable and enjoyable interactions.
   - Join in the child's rhythm in terms of affect, visual, auditory/vocal, and motor movements.
   - Become part of physical objects that bring the child pleasure (e.g., put the car he is fascinated with on your head

and let him roll it on your head as though it were a mountain).

- Attempt to deepen the warmth and pleasure by giving priority to her comfort and closeness (soothing, rhythmic activities or sensory-organizing ones may be helpful).
- If necessary, use a little bit of playful obstruction to entice him to focus on you. (Engagement involves a range of emotions, from pleasure and warmth to annoyance and assertiveness.)

3. **Two-way, purposeful interactions with gestures**
   - Be very animated and attempt to exchange subtle facial expressions, sounds, and other gestures (i.e., entice her into a rapid back-and-forth rhythm).
   - Go for the "gleam in his eye" (e.g., use animated exchanges to entice him to enter into an alert, aware, involved back-and-forth pattern).
   - Open and close circles of communication by building on her natural interests, inspiring her to respond to what you do. Keep it going as long as you can.
   - Treat everything she does as purposeful to harness circles of communication (e.g., flapping hands could be the basis for an interactive flap-your-hands dance or for a game of waving at each other).
   - Encourage initiative by avoiding doing things for him or to him.
   - Support initiative by challenging him to do things to you (e.g., when roughhousing, get him to jump on you, push you down, or climb up to your shoulders. This is in contrast to your doing things with him, such as picking him

up and swinging him, which do not support his initiative.)

- Help her go in the direction she wants to by initially making her goal easier to achieve, such as by moving the desired ball closer to her.
- Help him be purposeful by creating a goal where none may appear to exist (e.g., if he is moving his car around in a back-and-forth motion, you might stand behind the schoolhouse and claim to need a delivery).
- Over time, build obstacles between her and her desired goal to increase the number of circles of communication (e.g., block her access to the door or turn the doorknob the wrong way).
- As needed, be playfully obstructive (build fences around him if he is aimless; get between him and his goals when he is repetitive or perseverative, such as getting stuck behind the door he's opening and closing).

4. **Two-way, purposeful problem-solving interactions**
   - Extend circles of communication by creating extra steps (e.g., play dumb so he has to show you how to open the door, or exclaim and gesture that you first need a delivery at the hospital when he is moving the car toward the school).
   - Extend circles of communication by being playfully obstructive and creating interesting barriers or obstacles to his goals.
   - Work up to a continuous flow of circles (e.g., some children will gradually go from three circles, to five, to ten, etc.; others will enter into a continuous flow of 30-plus circles quickly).
   - Challenge her to close circles of communication (e.g., if she is moving her

car, but is ignoring your request for your dolly go for a ride in it, block her car with your hand. Gesture in an animated fashion for her to give the dolly a ride.)

- Combine affect with action and interaction (i.e., always be animated and show affect through voice and facial expressions while creating interactions).
- Increase the interactive range, including affects and emotions (e.g., if he is just hugging a doll, become a trouble-making wolf so that the child becomes challenged to increase his assertiveness and knock the wolf away).
- Increase interactive range in different processing areas, including:
  - Visual-spatial (e.g., play games such as chase, hide-and-seek, or treasure-hunting).
  - Motor planning and sequencing (e.g., organize obstacle courses and search games where the child has to complete two or three actions before he can open the latch to find the cookie).
  - Perceptual motor (e.g., engage in looking/doing interactions such as rolling, throwing, and/or kicking Nerf balls back and forth, or making her reach for desired objects on a moving string [while crossing the midline]).
  - Auditory processing and language (e.g., use sounds and, when possible, words to communicate [e.g., use animated, compelling vocal tones to attract his attention or to indicate safety, danger, approval, disapproval, or excitement]).
  - Imitation (e.g., draw her into copycat interactions where she is

shown how to reach for or get something she wants, or to imitate a sound that will get her something she wants).

5. **Elaborating ideas**
   - Encourage the use of ideas in both imaginative play (e.g., hugging the dolls) and realistic verbal interactions (e.g., "open" the door).
   - Build ideas by using affect or intent (e.g., "want juice!" rather than labeling juice in a picture).
   - W(ords)A(ffect)A(ction)–Always combine words or ideas together with affect and action.
   - Chit-chat using words; talk constantly.
   - Encourage imagination by incorporating familiar interactions in pretend play (e.g., feeding, hugging, or kissing dolls).
   - Jump into a drama that he has begun. Become a character and ham it up. Communicate mostly as the character rather than as yourself.
   - Sometimes, alternate between being a character in a drama of her choosing and a narrator or commentator.
   - Periodically, summarize and encourage him to move the drama along by asking a question or presenting a challenge.
   - Entice her into long dialogues.
   - Create challenges where ideas or words are necessary (e.g., "up," because the desired action figure is up on the shelf). Keep extending the dialogue.
   - Encourage the use of all types of ideas (symbolic expression) (e.g., pictures, signs, complex spatial designs [building a city], and acting out roles oneself).

6. **Building bridges between ideas (emotional thinking)**

- Close all symbolic circles in both pretend play and reality-based dialogues (e.g., challenge him to always respond to what you are saying and doing, just as you respond to what he is saying and doing).
- Challenge her to connect different ideas or subplots in a drama.
- Whenever he seems confused, introduces something out of context, or if something seems fragmented or piecemeal in his thinking, challenge him to make sense and be logical. Let him, not you, supply the missing pieces of logic (e.g., "I'm confused. We were having a tea party and now we're flying to the moon? What happened?")
- Be patient and summarize the confusing elements. If she is not able to build bridges between her own ideas, provide some multiple-choice possibilities. Avoid supplying the answer or taking control of the discussion.
- Challenge with "wh" questions, such as "what," "where," "when," "who," and "why."
- When he ignores or avoids responding to "wh" questions, such as "What did you like at school today?," throw out some silly possibilities to stimulate thinking (e.g., "Did the elephant visit your class today?" or "Did you see your boyfriend [or girlfriend] in class?").
- Explore reasons for actions or feelings (e.g., "Why are you attacking me?").
- Use multiple choice as needed, always putting the likely answer first and the unlikely one second.

- Have your character in the pretend play create unexpected situations to challenge her to move toward creativity and new solutions. Use humor, conflict, and novelty.
- Challenge him to broaden the emotional range in his dramas (e.g., encourage play that includes caring as well as assertiveness and aggression).
- Encourage reflection on feelings in both pretend dramas and reality discussions (e.g., "Why do you want to go outside?" or "What's the reason for the attack?").
- Gradually increase the complexity of reflective thinking (e.g., challenge the child to give different reasons or motives for actions or consider different views—"How does Sally feel after Mary took her toy?" and "How does Mary feel?").
- Challenge the child to give opinions rather than facts (e.g., "What color do you like best and why?" rather than "Which color is this?").
- Engage in debates and negotiations, rather than simply stating rules (except where the rule is absolutely essential).
- Encourage choices and discussions of choices.
- Encourage and challenge the child into a back-and-forth use of ideas— the more, the better. This is more important than correct grammer.
- Increase spatial thinking (e.g., treasure hunt games or junior architect games, such as laying out a whole city for the action-figure drama).
- Encourage motor-planning and sequencing capacities (e.g., obstacle courses, drawings diagrams for a tea party).
- Encourage understanding and mastery of time concepts by challenging the child to use the past, present, and

future (e.g., "What are the space monsters going to do tomorrow?" or "Yesterday we went to the zoo. What would you like to do tomorrow?").

- Encourage understanding and use of quantity concepts (e.g., how many cookies should each doll at the tea party have?).
- Pre-academic or early academic work, complex problem solving, and social skills should be based on providing an understanding of basic concepts (i.e., connecting ideas) through emotional interactions. For example:
  - In math, negotiate using candies, cookies, or coins to learn adding or subtracting. Keep the numbers small to avoid rote memory responses. Eventually, work on visualizing the objects and doing the calculations using images.
  - In reading, visualize or picture what is being read (whether the parent or child reads it) and then act it out and/or discuss it. Embellish the ideas further.
  - In writing, initially use flexible spelling and word choice and focus on interactive, creative stories and communicating needs or opinions. Later, work on correct spelling and grammar rules.
  - For problem-solving and social skills, work on anticipating by visualizing what may happen later or tomorrow, including positive and negative situations. "Picture" the situations, feelings involved, typical solutions, and alternative ones.
  - In both pretend and reality-based conversations, challenge the child toward higher levels of abstraction by shifting back and forth

between the details (the trees) and the big picture (the forest). For example, periodically wonder how all the things the child has been talking about fit together.

- Gradually expand the child's range of experiences (without overload or over-stimulation) because emotionally based experiences are the basis for creative, logical, and abstract thought.
- Challenge the child to symbolize auditory, visual-spatial, tactile, motor-planning, and affective capacities in combinations (e.g., building a city [visual-spatial, motor planning, tactile] with different dramas being acted out [auditory-verbal, thematic, imaginative] involving creative, affective interests being played out in a pattern of integrated thinking).

Semistructured Problem Solving

Semistructured problem solving is the second of the three types of developmentally appropriate interactions that should be part of every child's comprehensive home and school program.

Basic Principles of Semistructured Problem Solving

Semistructured problem solving involves a shared agenda, where the caregiver can teach a child something new by setting up challenges for the child to solve. The challenges can be structured learning activities that are meaningful and relevant to the child's experiences, or they can be spontaneous challenges, such as when the child has to solve a problem or confront something different in his environment to get something he desires. The caregiver can create a new problem-solving challenge whenever it becomes evident the child may want something. Because problem-solving interactions involve creating challenges that motivate the child, semistructured problem solving is similar to following the child's lead, which builds on the child's interests and motivations. In problem-solving interactions, however, the caregiver helps to create these interests and motivations.

Problem solving can take different forms and require multiple interactions, such as expressing a new word(s) or gesture, learning a new concept, manipulating an object (motor planning), sequencing a series of steps to obtain an objective, or negotiating a turn or trade. For example, putting a child's favorite toy outside the door and challenging her to say "open" will help her learn what "open" is and to say the word "open" when she is feeling a strong desire (affect) to open the door. Purposeful gestures, words, concepts, and the use of pictures and signs can all be taught through problem-solving interactions (e.g., the child uses pictures, signs, and, gradually, words to convey "open," "juice," or "more").

The amount of time spent on semistructured problem solving will vary depending on the developmental level of the child, how purposeful he is, and specific areas of need, such as the need to increase gestural communication, language and concepts, or motor planning. Semistructured problem-solving interactions may occur from 3 to 6 times a day, for 15 minutes or more each time. Those children requiring more semistructure may have as many as five to eight sessions a day.

Problem solving interactions can occur during daily routines, with enough time allowed for extended interactions. Problem solving also can be added to activities such as finger plays and songs (e.g., "If you're happy and you know it" or "Simon Says"); social games (e.g., musical chairs, duck-duck-goose, hot or cold?); listening-auditory games ("Telephone," "Who, What, Where am I?," "Treasure Hunt-Blue's Clues"); board games (e.g., Barnyard Bingo, Memory, Mystery Garden, Connect Four); and book-picture telling. The key is to challenge the child to solve a problem generated by the game.

For children who are unable to imitate, more structured learning and behavioral approaches (such as TEACCH, Discrete Trial, and special education) can be implemented to teach imitation, motor planning, and problem-solving patterns. Once a child can imitate and problem solve, dynamic challenges should be used to teach new skills.

Each functional developmental level involves characteristic patterns of interaction and underlying processing abilities. Developmentally appropriate practices that involve semistructured problem-solving tasks and specific therapeutic interactions can, therefore, be geared to each functional level and underlying processing capacities. The following outline describes how semistructured problem-solving activities can be oriented to each functional developmental level and related processing abilities. This outline also includes comments on the different therapies that can be used in a semistructured problem-solving manner and that should be part of the plan that the therapeutic team develops.

Semistructured Interactions for Mastering The Functional Developmental Levels

Foster shared attention and engagement by creating interactions that:

- Mobilize pleasure and joy.
- Sustain a state of shared attention and engagement, in which the child wants to relate to another person.

Fostering attention and engagement also involves the infant's or child's ability *to use her interest and growing pleasure in others* to give purpose (or function) to processing capacities and vice versa (i.e., improving processing capacities enables the child to attend and engage more fully). This includes creating interactions that enable the child to:

- Engage in pleasurable experiences with caregivers and express the affects of joy, curiosity, and emotional interest.
- Modulate sensation in all the senses (i.e., cope with and not be compromised by sensory hyper- or hyporeactivity).
- Comprehend information through each sensory pathway (e.g., sights, sounds).
- Integrate information from the different senses.
- Begin to plan and sequence motor patterns or behavior (e.g., look and/or reach).

Specific interventions have been developed to strengthen these core processing capacities. In addition to spontaneous interactions, these interventions can be implemented through semistructured activities by different members of the therapeutic team in collaboration with the home and school. Specific therapeutic interventions include:

- Physical therapy for muscle tone and motor capacities.
- Sensory integration oriented occupational therapy for sensory modulation, processing, and motor planning.
- Speech therapy for auditory processing and oral motor functioning.
- Spatial and perceptual-motor approaches for visual-spatial and perceptual-motor capacities.

Foster intentionality, two-way affective signaling, communication, and multiple problem-solving interactions (a continuous flow of circles of communication) by creating interactions that enable a child to:

- Be purposeful, even if she appears aimless or repetitive (e.g., lining up toys).

Build on what the child is doing through your response, and inspire the child to close the circle by building on that response. Keep the process of opening and closing circles going as long as possible.

- Incorporate a range of emotional interactions (e.g., for closeness, hugs; for curiosity, searching).
- Increase the complexity of interactions and problem-solving challenges (e.g., going from simple peek-a-boo type interactions to searching for hidden objects and imitating motor gestures and sounds).

In addition, use the child's *emotional intent* through problem-solving interactions to harness the following processing capacities, which in turn will support higher levels of intentional communication. Create interactions that enable the child to:

- Connect affect (i.e., intent, motivation, desire) to motor-planning and sequencing capacities to give direction and purpose to behavior beyond that needed to meet simple needs.
- Connect intent to sensory processing channels (e.g., touch, vision, hearing) to give functional meaning to experiences and objects.
- Strengthen perceptual-motor capacities and gradually increase distal perceptual-motor capacities in relation to proximal ones. Initially, touch and close-in sounds and sights will help a child look or reach. Over time, sights and sounds at greater distances will provide a signal for looking, listening, and/or doing. As needed, distal modes can be connected to proximal ones (e.g., when a child ignores sound from across room, increase it's saliency and, if needed, combine it with gentle touch or playful interference with the child's activity of the moment).

- Increase motor planning and sequencing, including imitation (e.g., from banging a block to putting it on a car to copying sounds).
- Increase sensory processing, including discrimination, by gradually increasing complexity of sensory input as part of the problem-solving interactions (e.g., from simple sounds or words to more complex ones; simple shapes and pictures to more complex ones; and simple motor and spatial challenges, such as obstacle courses, to more complex ones). Use proximal modes (touch, vibration) to support distal modes (sounds, sights) and vice versa. For example, help the child feel and look at a shape. For a child who hears but ignores sounds, see if sound vibration (making sounds on maxillary bone) helps him focus on the sounds.
- Piece islands of experience into patterns by increasing the number and complexity of circles of communication for every interaction.
- Construct patterns with each processing capacity (e.g., motor patterns, spatial patterns, recognition of sounds and words).
- Integrate patterns across all processing areas (e.g., forming a pattern of the sights, sounds, and emotions that make up "Daddy"). Play games that involve looking, listening, doing, vocalizing, and spatial problem solving.
- Begin to form patterns with regard to time (i.e., expectations of what comes next); space (object found in the each room); motor planning and sequencing (e.g., getting a chair to get a toy); and emotional expectations (expectations of fun, such as roughhousing when Dad comes home). Integrate preverbal emotional, sensory, and behavioral patterns of self and others (e.g., piecing together different experiences of "Dad" or "Mom" or

"me") through longer and more complex emotional interactions with Dad, Mom, and me.

For most developmental disorders, a child needs to strengthen a number of these processing capacities. Specific therapies to work with these areas are most effective when they occur in semistructured, emotionally based learning situations. As indicated earlier, challenges are learning situations where the child wants to master a problem (e.g., to get to his favorite toy, a child has to get a person to help). Therapies include:

- Physical therapy for motor capacities.
- Sensory-integration occupational therapy for sensory modulation and processing and motor planning.
- Speech for auditory processing, oral-motor capacities, articulation, and preverbal communication.
- Miller Method for visual-spatial processing, motor planning, and areas of cognition.
- Perceptual-motor and visual-spatial approaches for motor planning, perceptual-motor patterns, and visual-spatial problem solving.

Foster the formation and use of meaningful ideas, and build bridges between ideas for logical thinking by creating interactions that enable the child to:

- Invest the act of communicating with pleasure and mastery by using it for fun, getting needs met, and solving solvable problems.
- Apply and use sounds, words, pictures, or other symbols in all aspects of emotionally based problem-solving interactions (e.g., negotiations to meet needs and using words for "Juice!" or "Open door!").
- Engage in pretend play (feeding the doll) and in imaginative dialogues in which

drama is the product of the interactive use of ideas.

- Interact using actions and ideas in all thematic areas (dependency and love as well as assertiveness and curiosity).
- Open and close many symbolic circles (e.g., long, opinion-oriented discussions or debates).
- Extend long chains of symbolic circles into abstract thinking, including negotiating emotional causality ("I am mad because...") and concepts of time ("I want it now!"), space ("Here, not there"), self and non-self ("This is mine!"), and reality/fantasy ("This is only pretend").

Developmentally appropriate practices geared to symbolic elaboration and bridge-building between ideas will foster the ability to think creatively and logically. The processing capacities that support attention, engagement, intentional communication, and problem-solving interactions will also foster thinking skills. The following processing capacities will further enhance thinking and vice versa. Create interactions that help the child to practice:

- Auditory/verbal comprehension (i.e., understanding words and sentences).
- Visual-spatial symbolic elaborations, including understanding the dimensions of space and related quantity concepts (e.g., creative building of a house with different rooms for different activities).
- Multistep problem solving, motor planning and sequencing.
- Verbal and spatial sequences ("if/then" and picture sequences).
- Affect and behavior regulation and modulation.
- The capacity to visualize verbal ideas, verbalize visual images, and visualize action and motor patterns (e.g., treasure hunt games).

- The integration of affect (wish) with emerging concepts of space, time, classification, sequencing, and causality.
- Part/whole relationship thinking, including big-picture thinking (forest for the trees).

The specific interventions that can work with these processing problems are most effective when the interventions are carried out in semistructured, emotionally meaningful learning interactions. These learning situations need to present a challenge where a child has a strong, modulated affect necessitating a need to master the challenge (e.g., a debate over staying up 15 minutes later or playing treasure hunt to find a favorite toy). Specific therapeutic interventions include:

- Speech therapy for auditory processing, articulation, elaborating, verbalizing ideas, and verbal reasoning.
- Sensory integration occupational therapy for motor planning and sequencing and behavior and affect modulation.
- Miller Method for visual-spatial reasoning, related cognitive capacities, verbal reasoning, sequencing, and motor planning (see Miller & Eller-Miller, Chapter 19, this volume).
- Perceptual motor interventions for visual-spatial reasoning, motor planning, and sequencing (see Wachs, Chapters 20; Youssefi & Youssefi, Chapter 21, this volume).
- Mediated learning and instrumental enrichment for visual-spatial reasoning and verbal reasoning and related higher-level concepts (see Chapter 22, Feuerstein, this volume).
- Lindamood-Bell Learning Process (Lindamood & Lindamood, 1998), the Miller Method (Miller & Miller, 1992), and various computer programs for auditory processing, reading, and math

skills (see Lindamood & Lindamood, Chapter 23; Bell, Chapter 25, this volume).

Motor, Sensory, and Preceptual-Motor Activities and Visual-Spatial Activities

This group of activities constitutes the third type of developmentally appropriate interactions that should be part of every child's comprehensive home and school program.

Basic Principles of Activities

These activities are geared to the child's individual differences and regulatory patterns. They build basic processing capacities and provide the support that helps children become engaged, attentive, and regulated during interactions with others. For example, children who are underreactive and have low muscle tone will benefit from proprioceptive activities (e.g., jumping on the trampoline) or vestibular activities (e.g., swinging) to increase arousal, attention, and intentionality. Other children need calming and organizing activities, which build awareness of their bodies in space, require bilateral movements, and reduce tactile defensiveness. Some children try to find their own supportive "solutions," which become evident in such behaviors as constant running and jumping or lying on the floor.

To understand a child's regulatory profile and organize a home program, it is useful to organize specific recommendations from all therapists working with these processing areas. These activities can be used to help a child get ready for Floor Time and semistructured activities, reorganize, and increase arousal or calm down and focus, as well as to strengthen the child's basic processing abilities.

The amount of time children should participate in these activities depends on their individual needs, but usually involves from 3 or more hours of 15- to 20-minute sessions interspersed throughout the day. For children at early developmental levels who need to become more fully engaged and purposeful, these activities may occur very frequently because they are "fun" and increase the children's pleasurable interactions with others. These activities also increase communication because children can be taught to gesture or use picture communication to indicate what they want (e.g., more or less, slower or faster). These activities can also be used for problem-solving interactions and sequencing (e.g., obstacle courses and other motor-planning activities).

At the more advanced developmental levels, the activities may focus on practicing specific abilities, such as visual pursuit and motor planning (e.g., flashlight games, bilateral drawing activities, construction). The activities can also be integrated with symbolic ideation, such as "flying to outer space" on the swing, "steering clear of sharks and pirates" on the platform swing, pretending to be Peter Pan fighting Captain Hook with Nerf swords (eye-hand coordination), going on jungle safaris in search of wild animals, or constructing forts.

At all levels, children may benefit from activities that support processing capacities. These activities may overlap with some of the semistructured activities described previously.

The basic areas of functioning that should be addressed include:

- *Sensory and motor modulation and integration* (e.g., start-stop activities, running and changing direction, red light-green light, jumping on a mattress or trampoline, spinning, swinging, and gentle roughhousing to wrestling, as well as musical chairs where the music tempo changes from slow to medium to fast).

- *Perceptual-motor challenges* (e.g., looking/doing games and activities involving destinations, such as throwing and catching a ball or reaching for a desired object moving on a string to the left, right, and across the midline; kicking and hitting a big Nerf ball; using the balance beams, playing dodge ball, or flashlight tracking and drawing. Fine motor and graphomotor activities include pencil and paper mazes, dot-to-dot, copying designs, Legos, Light Brights, cutting and pasting, and painting and coloring).

- *Visual-spatial processing activities* (e.g., treasure hunts, obstacle courses, hide-and-seek, "what's missing?" and games such as Connect Four, Othello, Guess Who, and junior architect games).

- *Tactile discrimination* (e.g., finding objects hidden in different textured materials, such as rice, beans, or bird seed; finger painting in pudding, paints, or shaving cream; or identifying objects and toys hidden in a pillow case [for this activity, add verbal clues or ask for a category]).

For additional information, see Miller & Eller-Miller, Chapter 19, on the Miller Method; Wachs, Chapter 20, on visual-spatial thinking; and Youseffi & Youseffi, Chapter 21, on sensory-motor integration, this volume.

Developmentally Appropriate Interactions with Peers

It is vital for the child to practice her emerging abilities through interactions with peers as well as with caregivers. Play with another child should be started as soon as a child is fully engaged and interactive and is beginning to master, or has mastered,

imitation and problem-solving interactions. Parents should provide mediation to encourage engagement and interaction between the children. The best playmates are those who are interactive and verbal and can reach out and encourage, as well as model for, the child with special needs. Play dates should be increased to three to four times a week as soon as possible.

It is also important for all involved to recognize the considerable demands of a developmentally appropriate, home-based program. Other family members and people (e.g., graduate students and volunteers) should be trained in the methods and principles of floor time and be scheduled in to help implement the program.

SEQUENCE OF PROGRESS WITH DEVELOPMENTALLY APPROPRIATE INTERACTIONS AND PRACTICES

Developmentally appropriate interactions (i.e., floor time) guide the work of parents, caregivers, and the therapeutic team. Other members of the team, such as speech and occupational therapists, should follow the principles of floor time so that their work also helps the child mobilize the six developmental levels, as well as helps the child achieve the specific goals of their therapeutic field. The primary goal of developmentally appropriate interactions is to enable children to form a sense of themselves as intentional, interactive individuals and to develop cognitive language and social capacities from this basic sense of intentionality.

Children with autism or other non-progressive disorders of relating and communicating often lack the most basic foundation for interpersonal experiences (that is, they are often not interactive in the purposeful way that ordinary 8-month-olds are). Therefore, much of the experience that they might use to abstract a sense of their own self is not available to them. Developmentally appropriate interactions and practices based on the Developmental, Individual Differences, Relationship-based (DIR) model mobilizes the child's emerging functional-emotional developmental capacities, which together form a sense of self characterized by the capacities to engage, be purposeful, and think. (See Chapter 4 for further discussion of this model.) Developmentally appropriate interactions are based on the thesis that affective interaction can harness cognitive and emotional growth (Carew, 1980; Feuerstein, Rand, Hoffman, & Miller, 1979; Feuerstein et al., 1981; Greenspan, 1979a & b, 1989, 1997; Klein, Wieder, & Greenspan, 1987).

The earliest therapeutic goal is often geared to the first steps in the developmental progression, that is, to foster focus and concentration (shared attention), engagement with the human world, and two-way intentional communication.

As described earlier, as parents and therapists foster focus and engagement, they must pay attention to the child's regulatory profile. For example, if he is overreactive to sound, talking to him in a normal loud voice may lead him to become more aimless and more withdrawn. If he is overreactive to sights, bright lights and even very animated facial expressions may overwhelm him. On the other hand, if he is underreactive to sensations of sound and visual-spatial input, talking in a strong voice and using animated facial expressions in a well-lit room may help him attend. Similarly, in terms of his receptive language skills, if he is already at the point where he can decode a complex rhythm, making interesting sounds in complex patterns may be helpful. On the other hand, if he can decode only very simple, two-sequence rhythms and sometimes understands a single word here and there, using single words (not as symbolic communication, but as gestural

communication) and using simple patterns of sound may help him engage.

Some children remain relatively better focused in motion, such as being swung. Certain movement rhythms may be more effective than others. For some children, fast rhythms, such as one swing per second, may be ideal. For others, slow rhythms, similar to the breathing rate (one swing every 4, 5, or 6 seconds) may be ideal. Different kinds of tactile input, such as firm pressure on the back, arms, or legs, may foster concentration and focus. Large-motor movement and joint compressing (e.g., jumping on the bed or any trampoline-like motion) may also foster attending. Each infant and child is unique.

It is especially difficult to foster a sense of intimacy in children with special needs. In helping a child attend and engage, it is critically important to take advantage of a child's own natural interests. It is most helpful to follow the child's lead and look for opportunities for that visceral sense of pleasure and intimacy that leads a child to want to relate to the human world.

Intimacy is further supported when a person helps a child form simple and then more complex gestural communications. For example, the father of a very withdrawn child was only verbalizing to his child. The therapist suggested that he try simple gestural interactions first. The father gently put his hand on a toy car that his son was exploring, and pointed to a particular part as though to say, "What's that?" But in pointing, the father actually moved the car, so the son felt the car moving in his hands and noticed, without upset, his father's involvement. The son took the car back, but looked at where the father had touched it with his fingers. This more physical, gestural communication seemed to initiate at least a faint circle of communication: The son's interest in the car and the father's pointing to a spot on the car and moving it a little opened a circle of communication. The son's looking at that particular spot and taking the car back closed a circle of communication. *These opening and closing circles of communication* create a foundation for subsequent communication.

Building on this minimal interaction, the father got another car and started moving it back and forth in imitation of his son's actions. The father moved his car toward his son's car but did not crash into it. The son initially responded by pulling his car out of the way, but then he mimicked his father by moving his car fast toward his father's car. The two had now closed three or four circles in a row and had begun a real interaction.

After gestural interaction becomes complex with, for example, the father hiding his son's car and his son pointing, searching, and vocalizing to find it, the father can foster the movement from gestures to symbols. Since the father and son were using the car for simple and complex gestures, the father started to say "fast," when he moved the car rapidly, and "slow" when he moved it slowly. After four or five repetitions, the boy boomed his car into his father's car and said the word "fast," although he did not pronounce it quite clearly. The father beamed. He was amazed that his son could learn a new word and use it appropriately so quickly.

Although the child quickly learned a symbol in the preceding case, most children require a long, slow process with lots of preliminary work at presymbolic levels. Words and symbols are more easily learned, however, if they are related to the child's actual experiences and built on the child's affective gestures. Words in isolation or as imposed labels have little meaning for the child.

A major challenge to developing intentionality is a child's tendency to perseverate. One child might only open and close a door; another might only bang blocks together. The key is to transform the perseveration into an interaction by using the child's intense motivation to her advantage to get gestural circles of communication opened and closed. For example, a therapist can get "stuck" in the child's way, or have his hands "caught" between the child's blocks, always being gentle and playful as the child tries to move the therapist out of the way (like a cat and mouse game). As gestural interactions occur, behavior becomes purposeful and affective. The therapist should modulate the child's feelings of annoyance and help soothe and comfort as well, though often a child finds "playful obstruction" amusing.

As the child becomes more purposeful, she can imitate gestures and sounds more readily and can copy feeding a doll or kissing a bear. With continuing challenges to be intentional, she copies complex patterns and imitates sounds and words, often gradually beginning to use words and "pretend" on her own.

Another challenge as the child moves toward more representational or symbolic elaboration is to help the child differentiate her experiences. She needs to learn cause-and-effect communication at the level of ideas and to make connections between various representations or ideas. Since most children with pervasive developmental problems have difficulty with receptive language (that is, auditory processing), and some also have difficulty with visual-spatial processing, it is much easier for them to pay attention to their own ideas rather than to the ideas of others. The way a child categorizes her experiences at the level of symbols or representations, however, is through feedback. The parent becomes the representative of what is outside the child and the foundation for reality. The clinician's or parent's ability to enter the child's symbolic world becomes the critical vehicle for fostering emotional differentiation and higher levels of abstract and logical thinking. For example, during pretend play, when a child ignores the therapist's inquiry about who sits where at the tea party, the therapist must bring the child back to the comment or question until the child closes the symbolic circle. The adult might "play dumb" and bring the child back to the point of confusion. For example, when the child has the puppet biting the head off the cat, the parent might say, "Ouch, you hurt me." Then, if the child looks at the tree outside, the parent might ask, "I see the tree you are looking at, but what about the cat? What about his ouch?" If the child then says, "I'll give another ouch," and bites the cat with the puppet, the child has closed the symbolic circle of communication. If the parent then says, as the child goes back to the tree, "Do you want to talk about the tree or the cat?" and the child says, "Let's look at the tree," the child has closed yet another circle and also created a logical bridge from one set of ideas to another.

As the parent or therapist helps the child create such bridges, always following the child's lead, the child becomes more representationally differentiated. But if the caregiver either lets the child march to his own drummer or remain fragmented, progress may not occur. The caregiver, therefore, must enter the child's symbolic world through the back-and-forth exchange of ideas. This exchange should include debates and opinions, rather than facts, in both pretend play and logical conversations. Interacting with emotionally meaningful symbols becomes the critical vehicle for fostering emotional differentiation and higher levels of abstract and logical thinking. For this reason, relating to the child when he is experiencing strong affects and following is lead is critical. As the child connects his behavior or words to underlying affects, he gives them purpose and meaning.

In contrast, there is often a temptation to script dialogue for the child because it is believed that children with pervasive developmental disorders find it especially difficult to shift from concrete modes of thinking to more abstract ones. That is, they do not easily generalize from one experience to other similar experiences. The child, however, can only learn to abstract and generalize by connecting more and more affectively meaningful experiences to the concepts, words, and behavior she is using. Imaginative play and emotionally meaningful negotiations, not memorized scripts, are the essential building blocks of higher-level social and cognitive abilities.

The stages of therapeutic progress will vary from child to child and are discussed more fully elsewhere (Greenspan, 1992; Greenspan and Wieder, 1997). It is essential, however, for therapists to recognize that a child must first master missing foundation pieces, such as a continuous flow of two-way, gestural communication, before the child can begin negotiating more advanced levels of relating and thinking.

CONCLUSION

This chapter described the three types of developmentally appropriate interactions and practices required by children with special needs. As discussed, children with special needs, because of their processing challenges, require caregivers, therapists, and educators to meet them at their functional developmental level in the context of their individual differences. Understanding their world makes it possible to help them enjoy meaningful relating and communicating.

Parents and families will find some of the developmentally appropriate interactions more natural than others. Some will find engaging easy, whereas others will fight their own feelings of rejection. Some will foster purposefulness and assertiveness without hesitation, whereas others will wrestle with conflicts over issues of control. Some will support all types of ideas, whereas others will be more comfortable with some themes (e.g., love) than others (e.g., anger). Family challenges can bring parents closer together or lead to conflicts. Many families will benefit from the various types of support and help that are available (see Shanok, Chapter 14, this volume, on family functioning). ■

REFERENCES

Carew, J. V. (1980). Experience and the development of intelligence in young children at home and in day care. Monograph. *Society for Research in Child Development, 45* (607), 1-115.

Feuerstein, R., Rand, Y., Hoffman, M., & Miller, R. (1979). Cognitive modifiability in retarded adolescents: Effects of instrumental enrichment. *American Journal of Mental Deficiency, 83*(6), 539-550.

Feuerstein, R., Miller, R., Hoffman, M., Rand, Y., Mintsker, Y., Morgens, R., & Jensen, M. R. (1981). Cognitive modifiability in adolescence: Cognitive structure and the effects of intervention. *Journal of Special Education, 150*(2), 269-287.

Greenspan, S. I. (1979a). Intelligence and adaptation: An integration of psychoanalytic and Piagetian developmental psychology. *Psychological Issues* (Monograph 47/68). New York: International Universities Press.

Greenspan, S. I. (1979b). Psychopathology and adaptation in infancy and early childhood: Principles of clinical diagnosis and preventive intervention. *Clinical Infant Reports, No. 1.* New York: International Universities Press.

Greenspan, S. I. (1989). *The development of the ego: Implications for personality theory, psychopathology, and the psychotherapeutic process.* Madison, CT: International Universities Press.

Greenspan, S. I. (1992). *Infancy and early childhood: The practice of clinical assessment and intervention with emotional and developmental challenges.* Madison, CT: International Universities Press.

Greenspan, S. I. (1997). *The growth of the mind and the endangered origins of intelligence.* Reading, MA: Addison Wesley Longman.

Greenspan, S. I., & Wieder, S. (1997). Developmental patterns and outcomes in infants and children with disorders in relating and communicating: A chart review of 200 cases of children with autistic spectrum diagnoses. *The Journal of Developmental and Learning Disorders, 1,* 87-141.

Greenspan, S. I., & Wieder, S. (1998). *The child with special needs: Intellectual and emotional growth.* Reading, MA: Addison Wesley Longman.

Klein, P. S., Wieder, S., & Greenspan, S. I. (1987). A theoretical overview and empirical study of mediated learning experience: Prediction of preschool performance from mother-infant interaction patterns. *Infant Mental Health Journal, 892,* 110-129.

Lindamood, P., & Lindamood, P. (1998). *The Lindamood™ Phoneme Sequencing (LiPS™) Program (formerly the A.D.D. Program).* Austin, TX: PRO-ED.

Miller, A., & Miller, E. (1992). *A new way with autistic and other children with pervasive developmental disorder* (Monograph). Boston, MA: Language and Cognitive Center.

◄ 13 ►

Educational Guidelines for Preschool Children with Disorders in Relating and Communicating

Serena Wieder, Ph.D., and Barbara Kalmanson, Ph.D.

Educate each child according to his ways. (Proverbs 22:6)

THE CHALLENGE

The challenge to create and implement effective educational programs for preschool children with disorders of relating and communicating is more compelling than ever given the apparent increase in the number of children diagnosed with these disorders in recent years. These disorders include pervasive developmental disorders (PDD), autistic spectrum disorders (ASD), multisystem developmental disorders, and severe regulatory disorders. There is a confusing array of possible educational approaches to use, and selecting the approach that will be most effective is a daunting task. The purpose of these guidelines is to conceptualize a comprehensive model and theory on which to select and build individualized educational programs for preschool children with special needs so that each child develops the best possible foundation for lifelong learning and functioning. The model proposed in this chapter is the DIR model. DIR stands for a child's **D**evelopmental capacities that integrate the most essential cognitive and affective processes; **I**ndividual differences in motor, auditory, visual-spatial, and other sensory processing capacities, and **R**elationships that are part of the child/caregiver and family interaction patterns. (See Chapter 3 for further discussion.)

Education is one of the central components of individual intervention programs, including the DIR model. Services may be provided directly by education personnel in regular and special education schools, in home-based programs, or through some combination of home, school, and related services in the continuum of inclusion services. Because educational services are both mandated and funded by law from birth, they provide essential resources to families. Congress provided the legislation for educational services more than 20 years ago and continues to be the impetus for raising standards and producing outcomes. In this chapter, the current educational law will be reviewed, followed by a presentation of educational guidelines, Individual Education Plan (IEP) models, and case illustrations.

THE LAW

More than 20 years ago, the PL 94.142 mandated that the educational system provide services from birth to all children with disabilities and significant developmental delays. Since then, numerous cases have challenged the law, leading to revised policies and the eventual passage of amendments to the Individual Disability Education Act (IDEA) of 1997, which set minimum standards for the states to provide educational services to all children from birth through age 21. Under the Medical Disability Act (504), IDEA mandates the provision of services in education to every child from birth to age 3 (Part C), ages 3 to 21 (Part B), and ages 3-9 (Developmental Delay). The law further mandates that service will be at the level necessary for the child to *benefit*. This law defines autism as a disability that excludes emotional disturbance.

The 1997 amendments brought significant changes to the law. The statute became *outcome driven,* in that educational programs must not only provide services but must also demonstrate educational benefits and progress. The statute requires access to the *least restrictive environment*, which means that children with special needs must have access to the general curriculum for academic studies as well as to extracurricular and other school activities. Schools must therefore provide these children with the *supplementary services they need to enter and progress* through the general curriculum. Children must receive the opportunity to benefit from the educational program with the help of related services, supplementary aides, and technology that provide benefits. The *presumption of inclusion* has acquired many meanings, from full to partial inclusion. Congress authorized a continuum of services as long as the child benefits and services are provided in the least restrictive environment. The law also requires that *teachers be appropriately and adequately trained* to teach within the least restrictive environment. In fact, Part D of the law designates state improvement grants for training.

The law also puts increased emphasis on the *family as a member of the IEP team,* with full participation in the decision-making

process. This provides parents with the opportunity to include high standards. Parents can also ensure that their child's program is individually suited to her educational needs and that she is not simply being fit into a program. In addition, access to *due process* ensures fairness in dealing with each child's individual needs, with access to records, hearings, and other information. Requiring *educational benefit* to each child establishes a goal of moving the child forward relative to himself without comparison to others. The law defines four areas of benefit: academic, behavioral, developmental, and emotional. Therefore, it is very important that the IEP set goals high enough to ensure that the child will progress (i.e., raising the bar) rather than identifying goals the child has already or has almost achieved (i.e., dumbing down the IEP). Since the burden of proof is on the parent to prove the child is not making progress, it is crucial for parents to have access to information and experts who know their child in order to develop and evaluate appropriate IEP goals.[1]

The 1997 amendments to the IDEA added some very important provisions that are not yet well disseminated. Most important, by mandating a team-based, decision-making process which includes parents, the law has created ways in which parents can identify options for their children that the schools may or may not be offering. This

---

[1]IDEA also has provisions for discipline and requires the development of functional assessment and Positive Behavioral Intervention and Support Plan (PBIS) for children who are removed from a program 10 or more days for disciplinary reasons. Nondisciplinary evaluations (NDE) can be provided to determine whether a disability exists and to help develop the IEP for the least restrictive environment. But at this time, the functional assessment and PBIS are triggered by disciplinary problems and come too late; that is, after serious problems have occurred rather than preventively. This provision is not usually used for preschoolers.

means that parents can ask to be part of the ongoing team working with their child in the school. The law does not define what specific approaches should be utilized, so schools can offer whatever they like unless families direct them to address their individual goals in the IEP.

Many challenges lie ahead in serving this population, including insufficient numbers of qualified teachers and training programs available to implement state-of-the-art programs and evaluate teaching skills and outcomes. The current law, however, can be used to improve education for children with disorders in relating and communicating. Later sections will present IEP models as a guide to educators and parents.

PAST APPROACHES

Given the important mandates of the IDEA, the field of special education had to quickly develop programs for large numbers of children. Many choices about the structure of programs had to be made, including hours, where to house these programs, which children to group together, the size of classes, student to teacher ratios, which curriculum to use, which related services to offer, and sources of funding. Needless to say, programs and services varied widely. Historically, educational programs began in restrictive, special education schools and slowly moved to special programs in community-based settings, followed by the recent continuum of inclusion services in the least restricted environments; that is, with typical children in local schools.

When preschool education was first mandated, typical preschool-aged children were not receiving public funding and were not attending public school. Consequently, children with special needs were often grouped together without the benefit of typical peer

models with whom they could interact and learn. These groups were both categorical; for example, there were classes for children with autism or PDD, or non-categorical classes for children with any kind of disability, including language delay, Down syndrome, cerebral palsy, mental retardation, and autism.

While the private sector began to accept some children with special needs, it was not until recently that public schools began to house Head Start and daycare programs, making typical children available for integration. It was at this point that schools began to develop a continuum of inclusion services. In some cases, a few typical children entered the special education classes—a process known as reverse mainstreaming—whereas in other cases children with special needs entered classes of typical children. The point was to provide opportunities to learn from and interact with typical peers who could reach out and model language and interactive play behaviors for children with special needs. Inclusion efforts also brought a more developmental perspective to early special education. Undoubtedly, the continuum of inclusion services is an important advance for most children with special needs, but it is still in its fledgling state.

THE MISSING GUIDE TO EDUCATION

The field of special education has generally lacked a theory to guide its goals and practice. In many cases, approaches to the education of older children were adapted for younger children, often leading to curricula based on rote learning and splinter skills and using structured approaches in groups. Efforts were made to adapt various curricula to children with special needs, but few special education programs were directed by a unified theory within a developmental perspective. Until recently, children with special needs were placed in classes with other children with special needs, without the benefit of typical peers.

Emerging approaches began to provide one-on-one instruction following a prescribed course, recognizing specific strengths, such as visual learning, and using visual strategies to help children learn to organize and to function independently. For example, TEACCH (Treatment and Education of Autistic and Related Communication Handicapped Children) emphasized solitary purposeful work, structuring the environment, structuring the tasks, and providing visual strategies to master a series of curriculum-driven tasks (skills) on a one-on-one basis. TEACCH also took a long-term perspective, helping children learn to work independently with the goal being adult independent living. Where possible, children were included with typical peers.

Using operant conditioning reinforcement techniques, ABA (Applied Behavioral Analysis) utilized a behavior modification system of discrete trials that used one-on-one instruction to develop language, cognitive, and social skills. Later, other techniques were added to support generalization and social interactions, including participation in typical preschool settings with aides. Behavioral programs, however, insufficiently considered individual differences and developmentally appropriate practices aimed at achieving functional developmental capacities, putting little emphasis on the child's emotional and higher-level cognitive capacities for abstract thinking. Although they employ various techniques to teach skills, special education and ABA models have not had a unifying developmental theory to guide the broad overall goals and instructional approaches necessary to achieve the basic developmental capacities to learn, including self-regulation, self-initiative, interpersonal reciprocity, and symbolic-abstract

thinking. Yet, these are the core deficits of ASD. Few programs address these core deficits directly, measuring them neither at entry or at outcome, but relying on such outcome measures as academic and cognitive scores or school placement, both of which may be defined differently in every school district.

That is not to say that many techniques have not been valuable in helping certain children. The TEACCH program has many strengths, especially its focus on strengthening the child's capacity for planning and sequencing actions, using visual cues, and, when possible, imagery (Schopler, 1997). The TEACCH program, however, needs to be integrated with a broad functional developmental model, as will be described later. A few other examples include the Picture Exchange Communication System (PECS) (Bondy, 1994), discrete trials (Lovaas, 1987), pivotal response interactions (Koegel, 1999; Schreibman, 1996), and augmentative communication approaches, as well as other efforts that cull from these approaches at the preschool level (Rogers, 1996). However, to be truly helpful, the specific techniques used must be based on a child's unique profile and only be a selective part, at a point in time, of a comprehensive functional developmental program.

More often than not, children have been placed in programs utilizing these techniques, and the techniques have become the program for the child, without addressing the full range of developmental capacities the child should be achieving or how individual differences affect the child's learning and functioning. The result is that children are often being put into programs rather than programs being designed for the individual needs of children.

The DIR guidelines that follow define the basic principles and hierarchical goals of an education program and present a comprehensive model program. It is based on the DIR model of functional developmental capacities described in Chapter 3 of this volume and Greenspan and Wieder (1998).

DIR PRINCIPLES FOR EDUCATIONAL PROGRAMS

The hierarchy of educational goals for children with developmental challenges follow:

1. To improve the child's functional developmental capacities to relate, communicate, and think (not to memorize rote content or splinter skills).
2. To strengthen and integrate underlying processing abilities.
3. To develop the specific cognitive processes that support higher levels of thinking and problem solving (e.g., to become logical and able to abstract as steps one and two are developed).
4. To expand the emotional range of experience to support initiative, intentionality, reciprocity, flexibility, curiosity, organization, cooperative learning, and exploration, first through mediation and then independently.
5. To acquire the specific knowledge and tools necessary for learning academic content (e.g., to read, write, do math, and perform related skills).
6. To expand emotional availability to respond to increasingly complex and independent learning situations.
7. To convey the centrality of affective connections to others and the logic of caring for others that leads to a social, interactive, rule-based society.

Ideally, upon entering school, most children are prepared for step five and have already developed the first four goals that make it possible. Children with developmental challenges, however, need educational programs explicitly designed to establish the first four foundation steps before focusing on content.

The Essential Underlying Premises

The philosophical underpinnings of programs specifically designed for children with developmental challenges follow.

- Affect plays a central role in all learning. The child has to invest affectively. It is affect that will help the child initiate actions, respond to others, generate ideas, find meaning, and symbolize experience.
- Individual differences are the norm, and variations in learning capacities are expected.
- The child has to bring different processing skills across modalities in order to learn.
- Process is more important than content.
- The child must apply his thinking to multiple contexts.
- The child must be challenged to keep reaching toward higher levels of interactions, problem solving, symbolic thinking, and abstraction.
- Relationships and pleasure are essential for learning to be meaningful and progressive.

Specific Features of Educational Programs That Can Carry Out These Goals

- *Children learn best through interaction and active learning processes and materials.* There is general agreement on this as seen in such wide-ranging models from DIR, Feuerstein's Mediated Learning Experience (1997), Klein's MISC program (1996), to TEACCH (Schopler, 1997) and ABA behavioral models (Maurice et al., 1996).
- *Children learn best through affective involvement and emotionally meaningful*

interactions. This view is shared by Feuerstein and Klein but it is *not* incorporated in most behavioral approaches. Programs should ensure that each child is an active, participating learner as evidenced by initiating and maintaining ongoing interactions; for example, by following a child's lead when she identifies what is meaningful to her and expanding on her intentions to support a *continuous flow of interactions.* When a child tends to be aimless or avoidant, specific approaches based on affect cues, playful obstruction, and problem solving will encourage the child to initiate a solution. Strengthening interaction to allow mediation will help a child expand her range and needs. When meaningful connections are not emphasized, a child learns to comply with external demands but lacks the internalization that leads to self-initiation, empathy, and abstract thinking.

- *Children learn best when they utilize multiple processing capacities simultaneously and have different ways to learn.* This is similar to concepts of multiple intelligence that recognize different kinds of intelligence. The question is not how smart is this child, but how is this child smart? The key is to bring different kinds of learning together simultaneously. The more ways different kinds of processing can be brought to bear on the same concept, the better the mastery. This is especially important for children with special needs who are compromised in certain processing areas and therefore have very uneven learning. The more opportunities the child has to use processes simultaneously, the more these pathways organize and develop. Open-ended, semistructured, and structured approaches can be used to support processing.

- *Children should not skip steps in the hierarchy of goals but should go back to foundation pieces.* Thinking builds on each of the steps. It is the memorizing of discrete facts or actions that can remain devoid of thinking, relying on rote memory and splinter skills. To integrate and digest learning, a child must establish or strengthen mastery of each foundation piece before proceeding. A child who is not yet capable of mutual attention and engagement, as seen by avoidant or fleeting behavior, should first learn to engage before attempting to move onto symbolic play, even though he may evidence presymbolic capacities. Symbolic play with toys must move from crashing the cars or feeding the baby to motivated stories with a beginning, middle, and end. Activities such as circle time need to be evaluated for component requirements, and each child should be assessed for his ability to meet them. For example, can the child sustain attention, engage in distal communication, and maintain trunk stability and balance for extended sitting? Similarly, a child should be capable of building bridges between ideas and holding conversations in order to be able to participate in a circle discussion encouraging understanding of motives and abstract thinking.

The educational goals outlined above are based on four interrelated premises essential for their implementation. The first is the understanding of individual differences. The second is the central role affect plays in processing and learning. The third is the importance of process over content. The fourth is the critical role of relationships in learning.

Individual Differences

Education must take into account individual differences in processing information and in regulating attention and engagement, which are the prerequisites for learning (Greenspan & Wieder, 1999). When the ability to process information (i.e., to take in and comprehend what is perceived through various senses and give it meaning) is impeded, it is necessary to create specific interactive experiences in a supportive educational environment to ensure the child's success. For example, a child who has low muscle tone and is usually underaroused needs and may seek continuous central nervous system stimulation to maintain sufficient arousal in the classroom to sustain attention for passive learning tasks or seat work. This child may need to have access to a small trampoline in the hallway, sit on a flotation cushion or large therapy ball instead of a chair, or chew gum in class to sustain arousal and attention. A child who is internally preoccupied with body states or his own thoughts may need his conversational partners to touch him, initiate eye contact, or give a verbal warning to alert him to an imminent interaction; for example, "Hey Joey, I want to ask you something!" as an entry into the interaction.

The Role of Affect

Affect makes the connections that make actions (behavior) and symbols (words and imaginative play) meaningful. The young child does not engage in cognitive processes without the link to emotions, which creates the intent or desire that directs actions, orchestrates problem solving, and develops the ability to think and create new ideas. For example, a child may memorize a song or story but not use words meaningfully until he desires something or objects to something being done to her. Or, a child might line up his cars in a row but not know what to do

next to use the car meaningfully until he can connect to his desire to go to some destination with the car. He may then drive his car to the ice-cream store. Affect generates the intentions and ideas, and opens the child to higher levels of analytic and reflective thinking. The process of helping a child learn needs a way to appeal to his emotions, meet him at his developmental level, and consider his individual differences. Providing playful interactions is the vehicle for learning and finding meaning. What is most helpful is what is derived from the child's spontaneous affects.

Process and Content

Process is the "how" of learning, while content is the "what" of learning. Most important is the process. Basic emotional and cognitive processes, as well as capacities for execution (motor planning), must be identified and evaluated in order to establish the hierarchy of educational goals for each child. Emotional processes include intentionality, initiative, reciprocity, curiosity, exploration, desire, pleasure, tolerance for delay, frustration, anger, and other affects that connect symbols and actions. Cognitive processes refer to different types of nonverbal and verbal thinking and organization, including cause and effect, deductive, inductive, inferential, and other abstract reasoning. Depending on the child's individual profile, these processes can be supported through nonverbal (visual-spatial, tactile, kinesthetic) and auditory verbal sequences.

Relationships

Further, education is not random but mediated through relationships and affective interactions with the child. The educator uses her relationship with the child to expand, facilitate, and scaffold upon the different ways the child can learn. It is the educator who follows the child's lead to expand learning based on what the child initiates, and creates environments or selects experiences within which the child can begin to discover meanings through exploration and problem solving, all of which serve to help the child learn. In essence, every adult interacting with a child is an educator, facilitating the child's comprehension and communication through interactions that expand the child's abilities.

For example, a parent begins to help her child learn to walk only when the child begins to pull to a stand or cruise along the furniture. The reward is the joint pleasure in their interactions and the child's accomplishments.

THE DIR DEVELOPMENTAL PROFILE

The four components just described are part of the comprehensive assessment used to assess each child when concerns are identified. They also are used during the ongoing course of intervention with the child and family. (See Shanok, Chapter 14; Greenspan & Wieder, Chapter 15, this volume) on comprehensive assessment and work with families, as well as the following case examples, which illustrate the use of developmental and sensory profiles.)

Program Principles and Best Practices

For each child, individual goals must be identified that ensure that the child will learn to think, relate, and communicate at different developmental levels. To this end, certain principles and best practices must guide educational programming.

A number of principles are essential for the delivery of appropriate educational services, including:

- *Programs should be designed for children, rather than fitting children into programs.* This means having the flexibility to take

into account each child's individual differences in sensory processing and regulation, rather than designing programs for specific categories of disabilities.

- *Programs should be comprehensive, providing a full range of educational services,* including a continuum of inclusion service delivery options and special education, as well as therapeutic services— speech, occupational, physical, vision, music, art, and sensorimotor.

- *Programs should provide teachers trained to work with children with special needs individually,* as well as with typical children in small groups and with parents.

- *Programs should provide teacher training, supervision, and mentoring* as an ongoing developmental process so that teachers are informed about new and effective intervention strategies. Programs should also provide support to teachers' efforts to provide flexible interventions for children, sensitive interventions with parents, inclusion for students, and team coordination.

- *Programs should include peers with whom children with special needs can interact;* that is, role models for communication and play with flexible formation of groups as the child progresses through developmental levels.

- *Programs should be flexible and adaptive to children's needs at all times.* Children may show variability day to day or hour to hour, and programs must be flexible enough to help each child maintain the most alert and responsive state possible. This may mean calming some children down and helping them reorganize when overwhelmed or distressed, or helping other children become more alert and tuned in if underreactive or withdrawn. Programs require flexibility to meet each child's needs at any moment.

- *Programs should include parents in the education process as active participants* interacting with their children. Families may also want counseling, group support, and other avenues of learning and basic support available. For some families, this will require that parents also have access to transportation services for children. Service providers from multiple agencies will need to coordinate their approaches for families to enable them to benefit from interdisciplinary efforts.

- *Programs should not be provided solely on the basis of a diagnosis.* There is a wide range of individual differences among children identified as having ASD or PDD, pragmatic language disorders, multisystem developmental disorders (MSDD), or regulatory disorders. Early identification of challenges is critical, and intervention should be provided as soon as concerns arise, even before diagnosis. Federal law has mandated services to all children demonstrating developmental delay without requiring specific diagnosis. This allows the possibility of providing intensive intervention and makes diagnosis an ongoing process, including how the child responds to intervention, without the risk of diagnosis as a condition for receiving services. When late diagnosis occurs, a child might be deprived of intensive services, which are best when started as early as possible. In fact, two worrisome trends are now apparent. One pushes children into specific behavioral models for autistic children; the other assigns them to noncategorical placements in which children with a wide range of differences receive the same educational program.

- *Programs should embrace the IDEA, revision PL 94-142.*

THE DIR COMPREHENSIVE INTERVENTION MODEL

Whereas other educational models for children with special needs often rely on structure, ritual, and repetition to help the child learn by making the environment and course of day very predictable, the DIR comprehensive model includes individualized educational programming as one of several intervention components. All components are based on the premise that learning is facilitated by interactive relationships. The child becomes intentional and capable of generalizing and abstracting information for future use through the continuous flow of interactions. The affective connections between the adult and child assist the child in making the link between perception and experience, which turns action into learning that can be used again by bringing learning under the child's intentional and functional control. Before focusing on specific educational programs, the DIR model will be described.

The DIR model includes the following components:

- *Home-based, developmentally appropriate interactions and practices,* also known as "floor time." Five levels of interaction may be utilized:
  1. *Spontaneous follow-the-lead floor time.* These sessions encourage the child's initiative and purposeful behavior, deepening engagement, lengthening mutual attention, and developing symbolic capacities through conversations and pretend play. It is recommended that up to 8 sessions a day be devoted to this effort.
  2. *Semistructured problem solving.* These sessions involve setting up problem-solving challenges in order for the child to learn something new. These challenges may be encountered informally

throughout the course of the day when the child desires something or encounters changes in expectations, which trigger the affect to motivate new learning and help the child experience new competencies. Solving problems may require new language, concepts, motor planning or sequencing, and motor skills. Semistructured learning also includes learning the ritualized social interactions and play of early childhood, such as duck-duck-goose, Simon Says, musical chairs, Indian Chief, red light-green light, and others. Other games focus on auditory or visual processing (e.g., Telephone, Treasure Hunt, board games, and books).

3. *Structured teaching strategies,* such as TEACCH, the Miller Method, ABA and other related interventions, may be necessary for children with more severe challenges who need support to sequence daily living skills, learn to imitate, and practice problem-solving strategies. Once a child can imitate, communicate gesturally, and problem solve, dynamic challenges should be utilized for new skills.

4. *Sensorimotor, sensory integration, and visual-spatial activities.* These activities are geared to the child's individual differences and regulatory system. They may initially be used to help children become more regulated, attentive, and engaged, and move onto development of various skills, as guided by occupational, physical, oral-motor, sensorimotor, and visual cognitive therapists (see Table of Contents for related chapters.).

5. *Play dates* with one child or small groups of children who provide good peer models.

  The amount of time to devote to each of the home components will vary from child to child and should be carefully planned in consideration of the additional support by extended family members, students, and others who can be trained to implement the program. It is self-evident, however, that there is little, if any, tolerance for children being isolated and not interacting with others to learn.

- *Speech and oral-motor therapy*—three or more individual/group sessions per week, plus a home program.
- *Occupational, physical, sensorimotor, visual-cognitive therapies*—two or more individual/group sessions per week, plus a home program and sensory diet.
- *Biomedical interventions,* including nutrition.
- *Consideration of new technologies designed to improve processing abilities.*
- *Educational programs*—these include the continuum of school (and in some cases home-based) educational programs, as described in the next section.

Implementing Preschool Educational Programs in Inclusion Settings

  The term "education" is used here to describe learning in a school setting with other children, both typical and with special needs. It is important for children with special needs to be with children who are communicative and can model social interaction and symbolic play experiences. Educational settings should provide programs for typical and special-needs children in a flexible setting where ratios can be adapted to fit both the individual needs of the child and the learning experiences at hand. With flexible organization, these ratios will allow children to have one-on-one educator support when needed, as well as any number of typical peers for specific activities when needed. For example, a small school might have three or four preschool groups, with six to eight children in each group. Larger public schools might reorganize into small-school modules to have the same flexibility and may bring in typical children at the preschool level.

The basic experiences to consider for educational programs are described in the next section, followed by suggested guidelines on group size, staff ratios, and settings.

Learning Experiences/Process and Content

All modalities of learning should be available for children, such as centers with visual-spatial problem-solving materials and sensory materials, as well as movement, pictures/ books, music, and especially symbolic play and dress-up areas. The environment should invite exploration and have materials out and available to attract and entice children to initiate, discover, and experiment. The environment should also be changed periodically to encourage flexibility, exploration, and problem solving. The environment should have many visible play options the child can encounter and/or observe other children using for play. Children should be encouraged to explore all areas. Even the child who feels secure only with his cars and trucks may find them parked in unexpected places.

Early learning should follow each child's lead, and new avenues should be encouraged indirectly by changing the environment, linking familiar experiences to new ones, and problem solving around desired objects and activities. This will also encourage the use of language and concepts critical for communication of specific needs and desires. Once a child has learned to play with certain

materials interactively with an adult, another child should be brought in to play with them. The goal shifts to both children working together on a task, such as completing two puzzles in which the pieces have been jumbled together or repairing the cars that have crashed with the new tool kit.

Materials should relate to developmental levels, with increasing challenges based on each child's abilities. Many children will have uneven abilities and should be able to move ahead in their areas of strength (e.g., visual-spatial, motor planning, symbolic play through gestures that even precede language) while auditory processing improves. Other children will move ahead verbally and start expressing their ideas but will not have strong enough motor planning to use many figures or actions. Some children will be highly sensitive to the level of auditory and visual stimulation in the environment, requiring modifications to their environment to match the sensory level they can handle. The environment should become increasingly complex as they are ready for more varied or intense stimulation.

School activities should also be *developmentally appropriate*. For example, while typical children may enjoy circle time at some point, children with special needs should not be required to join until they can participate actively and with comprehension, supported by augmentation and priming, and in modalities in which they can interact, such as music, cooking, or sensory integration activities. When circle activities are primarily language-based, the child with special needs should be capable of building bridges between ideas expressed verbally in order to be able to participate in discussions. Time spent on ritualized learning, such as the calendar and weather, should wait until the child finds this information meaningful and can personalize it to his experiences.

School Participation

As children progress and are able to benefit from attending school, it is often the case that some will not benefit equally from every activity in the existing program. It is therefore important to design some classroom activities that exercise the child's needs at her developmental level so that she can participate and learn in the group by interacting with good models, whereas other needs can be met through one-on-one learning. As the child progresses, additional activities related to overlapping needs of the individual child and the group can be added. Instead of just considering which classroom activities the child may fit into and pulling the child out of the classroom for individualized learning at other times, or having the child in a home program and attending selected activities in school, more efforts should be made to design activities that allow the child to participate and learn successfully in the group

Ratio, Group Size, Group Membership

Developmental level, individual differences, and the experience/activity all need to be taken into account simultaneously in order to make decisions about school placement. Flexibility to shift ratios, group composition, group size, and membership as needed is essential. Designing an educational program capable of the full range and flexibility of programming is challenging but critical during early intervention. Table 1 lists the kinds of group settings needed for children at different developmental levels.

INDIVIDUALIZED EDUCATIONAL PLAN (IEP) MODELS

The IEP provides the best opportunity for parents, educators, and therapists to identify the specific goals, approaches, and imple-

mentation methods for each child. The IEP depends on collaboration and has mandated requirements for joint agreement and timetables for assessment, review, and modifications. The most significant aspect of the IEP now is that parents can use the IEP to indicate their goals and to hold the educational program accountable for meeting all those goals. Traditionally, separate goals were written by teachers and therapists for various developmental areas, such as speech and language, fine and gross motor, social and emotional, and cognitive. Attempts were made not only to specify the goal but to quantify the percentage of times the child met the criterion for each goal. Goals often became so specific or fragmented that it was difficult to see how they related to who the identified child was and his actual functional capacities.

Before presenting model IEPs, it is important to discuss the essential goals of the IEP in evaluating the fidelity of the child's program relative to the IEP.

Does the IEP Benefit the Child?

Various approaches, including variations in style, categories, and specificity may be used to write the child's IEP, and it would not be possible to address all these differences here. Instead, this section provides a checklist to guide the evaluation of the IEP and suggest possible areas for inclusion. As indicated at the beginning of this chapter, it is very important for parents to exercise their rights to be members of the IEP team and to develop goals to ensure high-standard, comprehensive programming that will benefit the child. The IEP will not only determine the specific services provided, but also serve as the measure of outcome.

Key questions to ask when evaluating an IEP follow.

Table 1. Types of Settings Needed for Different Developmental Levels

Developmental Level	Ratio	Group Size	Composition
Until child is consistently engaged and interactive with one adult, 1:1 interaction is necessary to help the child develop mutual attention, reciprocal interaction, and continuous communication.[a]	1:1	N/A	N/A
Once the child is interactive with adults, small-group experiences for sensorimotor experiences can proceed. Typical peer models can encourage imitation and interaction. Child should begin with 1:1 support with one, two, or three typical children.	1:1	4	Inclusive[b]
As child moves from one developmental level to the next, one-on-one support should be provided (e.g., floor time for beginning symbolic play). Once underway, mediation with one other typical child can be added.	1:1	2	Inclusive
Once child is interactive with one other child, group size can be slowly expanded for sensorimotor play-ground/gym activities and games or center work. Child should first work with one other child on cooperative tasks and then expand.	1:1	4-6	Inclusive
Once child is symbolic and verbal, he may engage in both 1:1 and 2:1 interactive symbolic play sessions. Group composition can now be larger to encourage child to play with different children and themes.	1:2	4-6	Inclusive
When some social skills are in place, the ratio of teacher to child with special needs can be increased to 1:2 in a larger group composition. Children at this level can be grouped with other children with special needs who are more interactive and ahead developmentally. Using flexible groupings, all children can have the experience of being the more and the less advanced player.	1:3	8-10	Inclusive

[a] When more structure is needed, the Miller method, TEACCH, ABA, or other similar approaches for imitation or pivotal response may be utilized to prepare children for learning in groups.

[b] "Inclusive" refers to including typical children to interact with the child with special needs. Group size may vary depending on the activity and includes other teachers and therapists along with the one-on-one teacher. More than one child with special needs can be involved as long as they have individual support. Once the child is participating actively and cooperatively with another child or children, the one-on-one support can be reduced. To prepare the child for success, it is recommended that he be primed for new activities before joining the group.

- *Does the IEP match the amount of time needed to meet the priorities identified for each goal?* It is important to identify priorities for the child and check whether adequate time and intensity will be spent on these goals to really help the child progress. For example, if social interaction is a goal, is sufficient daily time spent on mediated "play dates" at school with another child or with a small group or "circle of friends?" Are social games taught? Are opportunities created for interaction with typical peers during potential activities, such as speech or occupational therapy, drama, cooking, or a reading or game club? If symbolic play is a priority, how much time and in how many ways is this goal implemented? Make a list of the goals and the corresponding time indicated to evaluate how good the match is and what other goals might need to be integrated into or deleted from the priorities at this time. For example, learning the calendar or weather could be incorporated into the schedule of "play dates," and planning activities could relate to the weather rather than to separate activities. This would also make the learning personal and relevant to the child's experience.

- *Does the IEP include goals specific to the child's functional developmental capacities and are they designed to help the child move from one developmental level to another?* (See specific goals for the six functional developmental levels.) For example, does the IEP identify the increasing number of circles of communication (or indicate time spent in a continuous flow of engagement through interactions) under the goal of two-way interactions with gestures and words? Does the IEP indicate the duration of time for a conversation the child should

engage in on various topics? Or, does the IEP specify the levels of symbolic play, such as creating ideas to building bridges between ideas, in which a story unfolds with a beginning, a middle, and an end and which expresses an increasing range of emotions?

- *Does the IEP provide developmentally appropriate goals and activities?*

- *Does the IEP provide appropriate and adequate individual therapies, including speech, oral-motor, occupational and physical therapy, and cognitive treatment?* It is important to question any general limits the school system imposes (or only "offers") and to relate the frequency and duration of therapies to the individual priorities and severity of the child's condition. These related services are required as part of a child's educational program and include individual as well as class-based treatment. The frequency and duration of each session should be specified and implementation should be monitored. The plan should also clarify whether administrative paperwork and meetings are part of the time indicated for direct therapy. Parents should seek consultation if it is unclear how much therapy time the child needs.

- *Does the IEP provide augmentative communication support in a timely fashion with appropriate training of teachers and parents* to *help the child use these supports at school and at home?* For example, does the IEP take advantage of voice output devices, computer software (e.g., Boardmaker, Away We Go, Earobics, or Info-Speech), sensory integration equipment, and other technical and environmental support in the classroom to enhance the child's visual and auditory capacities to learn?

- *Does the IEP provide for frequent parent-team meetings to evaluate progress, make modifications, discuss problems, and allow for parent participation in the class when desired, in addition to ongoing observations?* It is important to have flexibility in the program as well as a relationship with the child's team, which includes the parents as ongoing participants. Parents as classroom volunteers can improve the teacher:child ratio, bridge the learning between home and school and school and home, and bring special talents and skills to their child's class, to name just a few benefits.

- *Does the IEP provide home programs, training and guidance, and materials for activities at home?* For example, does it include a sensory diet and how to use sensory integration activities to help a child calm down or become stimulated as needed? Does the sensory diet also include oral-motor exercises to implement during daily eating and toothbrushing routines, or cognitive games, social games, a preliteracy program, or pragmatic speech activities to practice? The child's school program should be complemented by a home program to provide the intensity and interaction needed to optimize benefits.

- *Does the IEP raise the bar?* Parents and the team are responsible for ensuring that the standards or expectations in the child's IEP are relatively high enough to establish advancing goals. It is a good idea for the team to compare the last IEP with the current one and note the changes. The team should check if the identified goals are ones that the child has already achieved or is very close to achieving, as well as verify that the child has demonstrated achievement for any goal that has been checked as having been achieved or given high ratings.

GOALS RELATED TO THE SIX FUNCTIONAL DEVELOPMENTAL LEVELS

Different school systems organize and describe IEP goals in various ways. This section suggests goals for each developmental level that can be incorporated into the child's IEP. These goals are organized with the idea of helping children move from one level to another. In some systems, goals may appear under such major instructional headings as language and communication, cognition, social-emotional, sensory processing, self-regulation, or visual-motor/motor planning. In the following list, they are organized by core functional developmental capacities. Under each heading, specific long- and short-term objectives follow, including quantitative criteria for each goal.

The list reviews goals that can be included under one or another heading used by schools and provides a format for the statement of goals for the IEP. Chapter 3 of this volume includes examples of developmentally appropriate ways to implement these goals. The chapters on communication, occupational and physical therapy, vision, motor planning, and executive functions (neuropsychology) also include specific goals that can be adapted in these areas.

There are several ways to quantify both the amount of time and the expected outcomes for each goal. Although the quantitative criteria for the goals are not specified and would need to be added, goals can be established in terms that:

- *Indicate change in the percentage of response.* For example, for a child who may be closing the circle of communication 30% of the time, the specific goal would be to close circles 50% of the time at the next time interval.

- *Indicate change in the number of responses.* For example, if a child is opening and closing 20 circles, the next goal would be 50 circles or that the child will respond 3 out of 5 times.

- *Indicate the time interval designated for that goal:* for example, over a 1-week time period or during the next 3 months.
- *Indicate the amount of time to be spent on the goal,* such as 10-minute periods, 8 times a day.
- *Consider the use of the functional emotional assessment scale (FEAS) measures,* which have established reliability and provide specific examples for each level. The FEAS could be scored at pre- and post-intervention intervals.

Other important features to identify for each goal relate to spontaneity, unscripted and without direct prompting (e.g., saying or doing something without the instruction to "say" or "do"), and generalization across contexts and people. These goals may be quantified in terms that:

- *Indicate the context in which the child will demonstrate each developmental capacity,* such as at school, on the playground, or at home.
- *Indicate whether the child will demonstrate the developmental capacity spontaneously* (nonscripted) or with natural prompts, such as questions during interactions.
- *Indicate whether the child will demonstrate the developmental capacity independently.*
- References to adults include parents, teachers, aides, and therapists. As indicated in Box 1, parents are included in both home and school activities as well as during meetings and IEP sessions.

CASE STUDIES OF THREE CHILDREN AND THEIR IEPS

The case studies that follow provide examples of a range of children working on different developmental levels in a variety of educational settings. These studies illustrate how to make decisions about a child's individual needs in the context of his typical day at home, in therapies, and in an educational program. They also represent the three primary contexts in which the DIR comprehensive model is implemented. The IEP goals and objectives are constructed to address the child's individual needs and stretch the child to work toward the next developmental level. The IEPs also illustrate different styles and formats to serve as models for various school programs.

Each child's program has three major components that constitute the DIR comprehensive approach at home, in therapies, and in school-based educational programs. The first component promotes engagement and spontaneous interactions in multiple floor time sessions as well as through interactions throughout the day that encourage relating, communicating, problem solving, symbolic play, and symbolic thinking. The second component provides semistructured problem solving and ritualized social games, as well as structured activities such as the Miller method (see Miller & Eller-Miller, Chapter 19, this volume) TEACCH, behavioral interventions, and augmentative communication when indicated. These activities depend on the child's individual profile and current capacities to think and learn. The third component provides sensory integration and sensorimotor interventions that promote the child's organization and attention to support interactions and learning.

The particular formats for IEPs vary by schools and districts, but the intention to specify goals and objectives is universal. All IEP goals are based on the primary goal of establishing a foundation (structure) for learning based on the core capacities for engagement, two-way communication, and affect.

Box 1. Goals Related to the Six Functional Developmental Levels

I. Shared Attention

- Child will sustain shared attention with a special adult in sensorimotor interactive play using the child's preferred and pleasurable sensory and motor modalities, such as movement, looking, touching, or listening.
- Child will regulate his sensory system in order to sustain shared attention with support.
- Child will regulate his sensory system in order to sustain shared attention independently.
- Child will increase shared attention by increasing the interactive circles of gestural communication, resulting in a continuous flow of interactions between child and adult rather than trying to focus on a particular object or toy.
- Child will sustain shared attention with a peer in interaction.
- Child will sustain shared attention in a group.
- Child will sustain shared attention independently across contexts.

II. Engagement

- Child will form relationships with special adults through pleasurable and enjoyable interactions.
- Child will sustain engagement in reciprocal social interactions with special adults that bring pleasure and joy.
- Child will sustain engagement in reciprocal social interactions when annoyed and protesting.
- Child will increase sustained engagement by increasing the circles of communication.
- Child will increase sustained engagement through a wider range of emotions, such as jealousy or fear.
- Child will sustain engagement with a peer with adult mediation.
- Child will sustain engagement with a peer "expert player."
- Child will sustain engagement within group interactions.

III. Two-Way Purposeful Interactions

- Child will interact in a back-and-forth rhythm in animated exchanges using facial expressions, sounds, and other gestures.
- Child will initiate purposeful interactions around desires (open circles) and will close circles following adult's response to her initiative.
- Child will increase number of purposeful interactions around desires for sensorimotor activities, to go somewhere, to obtain objects, or in response to adult strategies to expand the number of circles; for example, the adult will pose obstacles, play "dumb," or create extra steps to reach desired goal.
- Child will increase number of purposeful interactions using imitation.
- Child will increase number of purposeful interactions using simple gestures, such as reaching, taking, pulling, or pointing.
- Child will increase number of purposeful interactions across widening range of emotions, such as dependency, assertiveness, and jealousy.
- Child will increase purposeful interactions in various processing areas, including visual-spatial, motor planning, perceptual motor, auditory processing, and language.
- Child will sustain purposeful interactions with a peer with adult mediation.
- Child will sustain purposeful interactions with a peer "expert player."
- Child will initiate purposeful interactions with a peer spontaneously.
- Child will sustain purposeful interactions within group interactions.

IV. Complex Problem-Solving Gestures

- Child will express communicative intent through gestures or words to get what he wants.
- Child will sequence (motor plan) in order to execute an idea, such as a desire for a cookie, to pull a chair over to a cabinet, climb up, open cabinet, open container, get cookies and smile at mom.
- Child will sequence (motor plan) in order to execute a desire; for example, in order to play with dad who is reading the paper on the couch, the child will climb up, bounce on dad, and pull him onto the floor to play.

Continued

Box 1. *Continued*

V. Creating Emotional Ideas–Representational Capacity and Elaboration

All the goals at levels V and VI assume that the child is creating ideas while playing interactively and spontaneously with another adult, child, or group. Some children may create ideas but prefer to play alone or act out all the roles themselves. These levels are not fully reached until the child is fully interactive based on previous levels of established shared attention, engagement, and two-way communication.

- Child will initiate the use of realistic ideas in interactive imaginative play, such as by hugging the dolls.
- Child will initiate the use of ideas using realistic verbal interactions.
- Child will express ideas derived from her affect or intent, such as saying "Play outside!" when she wants to go outside.
- Child will express ideas derived from her affect by combining words and reality-based actions, such as sequence pretending to be hurt and going to the doctor to get better.
- Child will engage in conversations to express ideas.
- Child will elaborate on ideas through increasing verbal and symbolic play sequences, such as getting hurt in a crash, going to the doctor, being examined, and going home.
- Child will create imaginary (not reality-based) ideas using magical thinking/powers.
- Child will assume different roles and act as the character in role-play.
- Child will predict how others will feel or act in certain situations.
- Child will respond to other's feelings appropriately.
- Child will demonstrate confidence to resolve conflicts that come up in social situations, such as waiting, trading toys, taking turns, playing together, asserting self to retrieve his toy, joining in, or defending others.
- Child will assume multiple roles and use figures to represent characters.
- Child will expand ideas to include a wide range of themes and feelings.

VI. Building Bridges Between Ideas–Abstract Thinking

- Child will close all symbolic circles in both pretend play and reality-based dialogues.
- Child will respond to "Wh" questions, including who, what, where, when, and why.
- Child will debate, negotiate, and make choices when deciding what to play, what to do, where to go, and who goes first.
- Child will connect ideas in logical ways that make sense (not fragment, change topic, or become tangential).
- Child will integrate concepts of time in ideas.
- Child will integrate concepts of space in ideas.
- Child will integrate concepts of quantity in ideas and problem solving.
- Child will explain reasons for feelings and actions.
- Child will compare and contrast ideas, preferences, and other people's views.
- Child will give opinions, selecting appropriate dimensions for views.
- Child will create dramas with a beginning, middle, and end.
- Child will identify motives of other people or characters' actions and understand different points of view and feelings.
- Child will predict feelings and actions of other characters.
- Child will recognize complex intents, such as deception, sarcasm, and conflict.
- Child will reflect on feelings in both pretend dramas and conversations taking place in reality.
- Child will expand to full range of emotional themes, including conflict, aggression, and morality.
- Child will reach higher levels of abstraction and will be able to see details as well as the big picture (trees and the forest).
- Child will recognize strengths and weaknesses in self and others.

Each case begins with a brief developmental profile. A typical day for each child is then described. A sample IEP follows each description to show how the goals and objectives are constructed and implemented. The sample IEPs include classroom goals and objectives but not the specific objectives of the occupational therapist (OT) or speech and language therapist.

Child 1: Henry

Henry was referred for intervention at 2 years, 9 months of age, after his preschool teachers noted that he was not forming relationships with the adults or children. Henry had already been receiving speech and language therapy 3 times a week for 9 months, because his parents had acted on an early concern about Henry's failure to develop expressive language. Now, at 4½ years old, Henry is a tall, sturdy-looking boy with brown hair and dark eyes, who appears friendly but guarded. Sometimes he gets very excitable, whereas at other times he is more passive. He eats and sleeps well.

Developmental Profile
Shared attention is achieved at all levels. Henry is able to integrate attention across sensory modalities to sustain his attention and activity level in multiple interactions. He can stay with an interactive game on the playground best if most of the cues for transition are visual and with assistance when cues are predominantly auditory. Henry is independent across contexts if he is motivated by the content and the expectations are for less than 20 minutes in a large group. He sustains attention at circle time best when seated in proximity to the teacher, he has previewed the story, or a favorite of his is read to the group, and the expectation for sustained attention is about 20 minutes.

Henry is capable of *engagement* in interactions led by him for periods of time up to an hour or longer, but his staying power for reciprocal engagement is significantly compromised when he has to adjust to an adult or peer taking the lead. Henry can develop an intricate imaginary plot and follow through without significant distraction in a play session with an adult who joins him and promotes his ideas. He is more likely to lose track of the plot or disengage from peer interaction in play when he is required to follow the lead of other children. This is in part due to his difficulties with auditory processing. He is not yet confident in his real social situations about resolving conflicts or negotiating turns. He either becomes overly excited and drifts from the interaction or becomes more passive, waiting for other children to assert themselves.

Two-way purposeful interactions flow smoothly when Henry's interactions with adults deal with pleasure, dependency, curiosity, and other positive emotions. These interactions currently break down when he is engaged in managing the negative range of emotions, such as jealousy, envy, annoyance, and disappointment. Henry will spontaneously initiate interactions with peers or in groups, but not with the regularity or follow through expected at his age. For example, he will greet a child from his class that he meets by chance in town, but he may require an adult to help him notice that the child has seen him. After the greeting, he becomes awkward and dependent on the adult to assist him in taking the next steps to maintain the conversation. On his own, he may withdraw or make a comment that is too adult for the situation. He has little confidence in his ability to negotiate independently with peers in social situations. Henry is most likely to withdraw and mumble to himself if left to his own devices when another child is assertive with him in a game.

Complex problem-solving gestures are frequent and spontaneous but limited by challenges in motor planning and visual-motor coordination. For example, Henry may decide that a character in his fantasy needs a black mask. He can assemble materials for creating the mask—paper, scissors, markers, and tape—but will become dependent on others to draw and cut. He is, however, able to describe the shape of the eyes he wants cut out or the size of the face.

Representational capacities include realistic and imaginary ideas. Henry expresses a wider range of affect through play than in his real life interactions. He will take the role of an angry bad guy but will not easily express anger with strong affect in a real interaction with an adult or peer. He will independently assume the role of one character in play. Abilities to switch roles or predict the feelings or behavior of others are emerging. In pretend play scenarios, Henry's *symbolic capacities* include creating emotional ideas focused on magical powers. He loves to be a wizard, a good witch, or the magical hero from computer games. With adult facilitation, he will try out more than one role and predict the feelings of characters, although his range of themes and emotions is restricted. He tends to focus on feelings of being stuck or trapped and working out escape strategies. He has moved from feeling helplessly trapped and hopeless in a visual-spatially confusing world to seeking alternative strategies for escape using multisensory problem-solving techniques. Henry is beginning to *build bridges between ideas for abstract thinking* in space, time, and quantity. He answers "Wh" questions intermittently and creates dramas with a beginning, middle, and end with adult facilitation. Henry is beginning to use adult facilitation to negotiate with others and to take their ideas into account while generating his own opinions. An adult may suggest that Henry does not like the idea that the pirates set sail, and encourage him to tell the others that he wants the pirates to get stuck in the deep dark cave. With help, Henry can offer the idea and acknowledge his friends' wish to sail across the sea, an activity that could take place after they escape from the cave.

Sensory Developmental Profile

Auditory processing: Henry's *expressive language* is more available and flexible (since he knows what he wants to say) than his receptive abilities, which are affected by a time lag in his processing and difficulties with multipart communications or following multiple sequences given in oral directions. Despite his extensive vocabulary, he has a limited ability to sustain a spontaneous conversation that takes the other persons' communications into account during a back-and-forth exchange. For example, on the playground, his peers may have suggested transforming from Disney characters into Star Wars characters and be off initiating a new scenario on another planet while Henry is still processing the idea and beginning to cope with feelings of being left behind.

Sensory reactivity is a challenging area. Henry is very excitable. He is challenged to maintain an optimal level of arousal to maximize his capacity to sustain focus without becoming overstimulated. His excitement is often seen in motor-overflow activity, such as chewing his shirt or wringing his hands.

Motor planning and visual-motor coordination also are areas of concern. For example, in setting up action figures on a table, Henry is likely to repeatedly knock over most of the setup while adding something new to it. He is awkward in his tool use and is just beginning to be willing to draw.

Visual-spatial processing, such as memory and comprehension of visual materials, is strong. He has a good memory for everything he sees, and comprehends visual information well. His visual-spatial thinking and organization is less well developed, and figure-ground discrimination is weak. He is apt to try to fill the table space with many more objects than the space can accommodate while losing track of the salient object.

Affective processing: Henry has made rapid and significant progress in his interest in the interpersonal world. He is now highly motivated to relate to others and can sustain interactions with those who are capable of tuning in to him. He is capable of *connecting affects to intentions* in his imaginary play but is less able to recognize the connections in other people's intentions. He will report that the creature is upset and depressed because he is feeling as though he will never find his way out of the dungeon, but he can not adjust his response to another child based on his affective expression. *Problem solving* is an intense area of interest for him.

Rate of Progress

Henry's rate of progress is very promising. Within the past year, he has become highly motivated interpersonally, seeking out peers at school and in his neighborhood. When Henry first began a DIR intervention, he had almost no intentional communication. He had learned vocabulary and some scripted language for making requests, but he had no spontaneous language or flexibility in his use of known words. Henry's sensory reactivity was not yet recognized, and many behaviors were seen as inappropriate and thought to be volitional. Henry had no symbolic play. Now, through the use of floor time sessions and sensory processing-oriented occupational

therapy, as well as continued speech and language therapy, Henry has become increasingly spontaneous in his use of language during conversations and more symbolic in his play. His excitability was treated as a sensory issue, and most of the behaviors previously interpreted as inappropriate have been transformed. Henry's parents are very hopeful about their son's progress following DIR intervention. His interactive, communicative, and thinking capacities are so improved that his parents are now considering sending him to a regular preschool.

Current Intervention Program

Henry's current intensive, comprehensive intervention program includes the following:

- Four to six sessions of "floor time" per day.
- Four days per week of 3 hours per day of preschool with typically developing children.
- Three times per week of individual speech and language therapy.
- Two times per week of occupational therapy (OT) with a sensory-processing emphasis.
- Two times per week of family DIR psychotherapy.
- One time per week of therapeutic creative drama class.
- One time per week of art class.

Henry's parents selected a full-inclusion setting because he was able to connect with, and was interested in relating to, the other children and the teachers. His verbal skills had become adequate to communicate with the children. Both parents and service providers expect Henry to make significant advances in his relational and symbolic capacities through his interactions with peers. With the assistance of an aide, he could follow the daily routines of the class and participate in all the activities.

A Typical Day

Henry's day begins with an early morning one-on-one speech and language session focused on encouraging Henry to generate spontaneous language about pictures chosen by the therapist from Henry's favorite books. In this semistructured setting, he is able to acquire skills in verbal description, self-initiated generation of language, and the pragmatic ability to comprehend what information his conversational partner will need in order to sustain reciprocity. After speech, he has a snack with his mother, often purchased from a local store where the clerk is eager to have Henry ask for what he wants, make friendly comments, and pay for his food. This gives Henry a real-life experience utilizing the skills he just practiced at speech, as well as an experience he can use to expand his symbolic play. On other days, he and his Mom might stop for gas or take the bus, always creating opportunities to learn more about how the world works. These experiences are essential for encouraging incidental learning.

Mom and Henry go home to meet his occupational therapist, who spends half her home visit working on fine motor skills, building with blocks and Duplo, and drawing at an easel. In order to use drawing as an activity to also build symbolic thinking, his therapist encourages Henry to draw a picture of his house and family by using the shapes he has been learning. The second half of her time is used for sensory integration activities. Today, they jump on the trampoline the parents bought for the yard and try out taking Henry on roller skates up and down the driveway. These sensory activities prepare Henry's central nervous system to be in the optimal state of arousal and attention for his upcoming day at school. After OT, Henry's Mom extends the fine motor activity by having him grate cheese and peel carrots for their lunch. She has learned from the occupational therapist

that chewing crunchy carrots is another avenue for sensory input. This activity also provides opportunities to problem solve and sequence, because Henry must locate all he needs, open different packages or containers, figure out why the cheese is kept in the refrigerator, and decide on what size and how many pieces he wants. These simple tasks provide him with the chance to make choices, give opinions, manipulate objects, use reasoning, and learn in rapid back-and-forth, one-on-one conversation.

After lunch, Mom and Henry have a spontaneous floor time session. Henry announces his intention to play restaurant. This game is a new favorite for Henry and his mother, following a successful experience at a real restaurant. Henry sets the table, but has trouble not overcrowding the table with plates and utensils. Many things fall, and Henry plays the polite waiter who apologizes and returns with pretend clean settings. His mother is the understanding and patient patron. Henry takes Mom's order and begins to show his new-found capacity to use humor to cope with frustration. He turns from being passive to being active by pretending to frustrate his Mom's attempts to order. Each food she orders is no longer available. "I'm afraid we're out of that just now. Please choose something else," he says with a smirk at his cleverness. With Mom's coaching, Henry shifts between the role of waiter and chef. He creates new ideas but stays focused on a long list of foods and the feelings of frustration and disappointment for Mom—two feelings Henry must work on for himself. The play story has a potential beginning, middle, and end, but the ending has to be mediated by his mother because, otherwise, Henry could perseverate indefinitely on the "joke" he has been playing on her. Nonetheless, he was able to anticipate her feelings in the context of the story and begin to speculate on the feelings of the chef and waiter. His descriptions, however, are still limited and restricted in range and complexity.

Following their playtime, Mom watches as Henry prepares for school by using visual communication strategies (photos of objects on a velcro strip) to identify what has to go in his backpack. Henry beams as he puts the last picture of the item he needs into the attached envelope indicating he put everything in his backpack. This approach has reduced the prompting he needed in the past and has allowed him to become more independent in following a sequence. They then go to school, talking about the ideas he played with or counting the stoplights on the way. The combination of sensory- and relationship-based activities all morning have primed Henry in his body organization and symbolic thinking to make the most of his time with peers.

Henry attends a private, 3-hour, prekindergarten program held in the afternoon with 13 typically developing children about 6 months younger than he is. The class size, with two teachers and an additional aide as well, afford Henry and the other children optimal opportunities for peer connections and adult support. Although he was eligible for a preschool, special-education day class, his parents and intervention team felt that he would benefit most from one-on-one interventions with specialists and typical play opportunities with peers. Henry is a good candidate for full inclusion because he is highly motivated to make friends and has acquired sufficient capacity to sustain interpersonal communication, to organize his body, and to respond to the requests of others.

His preschool was selected carefully for qualities that reflected the developmental, individualized, relationship-based approach to education. The staff at this school embraces a philosophy of adapting to the individual needs of all their students. The curriculum is organized around a mixture of unstructured and semistructured learning opportunities, with play at the heart of the program. Social interactions are available in every form, from nonverbal chase games to sophisticated symbolic play. Important for Henry is the staff's understanding of sensorimotor organization as the cornerstone for attention and self-regulation. Therefore, they do not hesitate to individualize sensory experiences throughout the day for all of the children. Teachers value their relationships with students as an important avenue to learning in all domains. Philosophically, they use their relationships with children directly, not just as facilitators or organizers of the children's day.

The school also includes Henry's parents in their frequent team meetings and encourages participation in various class activities. Because of Henry's identified special needs, the teachers meet with the parents every month and with the whole intervention team four to six times a year as needed.

When they arrive at school, Henry and Mom are met by Janie, his one-on-one aide, who flexibly facilitates his interactions with the children. She uses a brief verbal prompt to mediate his greetings to two boys who are waiting for him at the gate. Henry begins the school day outside and usually digs in the sand and plays chase with two other active boys. Beginning the day with large-motor activity and an opportunity to connect with peers through active, nonverbal play places the least demand on Henry's developmental vulnerabilities and optimizes his social connection to peers from the outset of the day. Henry has learned to sit on the bench with the other children to get ready to go inside. Janie stands about 3 feet behind the bench ready to help out, observing and chatting with the other children, available in case Henry has trouble calming himself enough to sit down, but not hovering or drawing unnecessary attention to Henry's special needs.

Inside, Henry needs Janie's hand on his shoulders to help him settle down to quieter activities. This small, interpersonal sensory input is sufficient to help Henry adjust to the quieter, indoor setting. He sits on the rug for circle time. When he starts to "wobble"—lose trunk control—Janie puts a heavy sand-bag across his legs to help him stabilize. Everyone is aware that wobbling is not voli-tional, naughty behavior or an attempt to draw the teacher's attention from the group activity but a reflection of Henry's current capacity to sustain trunk control over a peri-od of time. The importance of having senso-ry integration equipment available for flexible use throughout the day is recognized as a way to help Henry not miss opportuni-ties—in this case, to develop listening skills in a group. Now Henry is able to listen to the story read to the children. From the begin-ning, he is positioned near the teacher and the book so that he will feel closer to the com-munication source. His teachers know that Henry is still working on auditory processing of more distal communications and that his proximity to them assists him in processing the meaning of the story and in sustained lis-tening. By inviting Henry to sit near her at the outset, there is no special attention drawn to his disability or a chance of his feeling criticized for his behavior by changing his seat midway through the story. The children are praised for their patience in listening to their friends' ideas about the story before it is Henry's turn to painstakingly generate his comment about a favorite picture.

After story time, the children choose an area for playing. Henry is encouraged by the classroom teacher to choose something other than the computer (always his first choice), and he is able to choose the house-play area. Again, the teacher is casual in her approach

to Henry's special needs in front of the other children. She merely reminds him that he used the computer yesterday and she would like all of the children to try different things. With information from Henry's speech thera-pist about processing time, she waits for him to select an alternative. If he is not able to choose something or gets struck on the com-puter idea, she knows to make her offer more concrete, perhaps by offering two choices.

Janie becomes a bit more active in help-ing Henry choose a role, dress up, and com-prehend his friends' directions. Henry is able to follow the symbolic thinking of his peers and to generate his own ideas, but he needs Janie to help slow the interpersonal process so that he can digest all that is being said. He also needs mediation to facilitate the motor planning and coordination required in remov-ing his sweatshirt and putting on the dress-up clothes. Janie makes a point of assisting other children with ties or buckles as well so that everyone has an experience of her as the adult available to help. The school's approach is to assume that all children have individual special needs and that these can be accom-modated or adapted to throughout the day.

Henry assumes the role of "Dad" and gets the tie and briefcase, but he doesn't know where to go to leave for work or how fast the day can go by so he can return home. Janie helps him stay in the game by coaching him through many phone calls to his "wife" from his office at work. This game helps Henry develop motor, communication, and symbolic thinking capacities. Janie takes advantage of the game to develop all the children's capaci-ties for symbolic thought and linking feelings to actions. She asks them all why the "baby" is crying when Dad leaves for work. Then she asks them how they can reassure "baby." How could Dad stay in contact with his wife even when he is far away at work? What is it like for Dad not to be home when everyone else is home? During cleanup, Henry does not know where to put items, and the things he hangs up fall off the hooks. He becomes frustrated and starts to make funny noises, but Janie steps in and actively helps Henry find out from children where things go and ask friends to "hook" things for him. She coaches him but does not take over, preserving his sense of competence by helping him use his relationships with his peers for assistance.

Next, Henry is the pouring helper at snack. He asks each child at his table if he or she wants water, waits for an answer, and pours water into a cup for each one of them. This is a special job that is rotated among the children. It is a semistructured way to practice both communication and motor skills. It encourages the children to remain active and participate in grown-up tasks rather than to make them passive snack recipients, which encourages withdrawal. Henry is so excited he wrings his hands and bounces in his seat. Janie substitutes a therapy ball for his chair, and two other children request and receive balls, too. This is another example of flexibly attending to the children's sensory needs to support development in other domains. Henry cannot organize himself to eat, but he drinks water and bounces on his ball as he tries to interact with the others. He does say a few things to other children, frequently prompted by Janie. For example, Janie might say, "Henry, did you hear Max? He wants to ask you a question." (This alerts Henry that a question, which calls for a contingent response, is coming his way. He sits up and looks toward Max, giving the nonverbal cue of readiness.) Janie has learned to support Henry in learning communication skills whenever opportunities arise in the natural course of the day.

The children go outside briefly after snack, and Henry engages in a pretend game of pirates, mostly involving a chase after he steals the golden treasure. However, after a couple of hours at school, Henry's outside chase games have the added symbolic meaning connected with the story that unfolds about the pirates. His practice and comfort with school enable him to play at a higher symbolic level. On his way inside, he and Jake are given smocks and assigned to the cooking table. Henry and Jake have a two-way conversation about cooking pudding and speculate about whether they will be able to fingerpaint with it once it is prepared. Henry stumbles in front of Jake while trying to pull out his chair and sit down and nearly knocks Jake over. Henry apologizes for being so rude, and Janie softens it by suggesting Henry had no intention to fall on Jake, which Jake accepts. Inevitably, Henry's visual-motor issues create awkward moments for him, but Janie tries to intervene in ways that prevent other children from misinterpreting Henry's intentions.

Two girls and the teacher join the boys, now seated, and they all listen to directions, which are numbered with accompanying pictures. The teacher explains the four-part cooking sequence with illustrations, returns to showing picture 1, and asks the children what to do first. She knows that Henry will be better able to sequence events if they are presented visually as well as auditorily. She also recognizes the benefit of the visuals for all the children. Henry blurts out the answer, not waiting to be called on. The teacher appreciates the answer and announces which child will go next. Henry chews on his lower lip in an effort to control the impulse to say the answer when it is no longer his turn. Once the pudding is made, the children are invited to ask a friend to taste and fingerpaint with them. Henry chooses a very shy girl, who he hopes will allow him to eat the most and control their paper. The activity is a success and Henry has a sustained two-way conversation with Amy while painting. He is confused during clean-up because the sequence of events is unclear and there are no picture directions. (Janie makes a mental note about how a picture sequence for clean-up procedures will help Henry, and she draws the contrast to the cooking project in her conversation with the teacher after school.) Janie steps in and reviews the first thing to do, providing each next step as the prior is accomplished.

Singing songs in a group before the children say goodbye for the day goes well because the teacher, seeing that several children are aroused, has them stand and dance instead of sitting in a circle. Again, she makes a flexible adaptation to the curriculum based on the children's sensorimotor needs. For the last song, she has them hold hands in a circle and come closer and spread apart, giving them a concrete experience of themselves as an emotionally connected group before departing. Henry forgets to stop at his cubby on his way out the door so Janie asks if there is anything he is leaving at school that he might want. (She is carefully cueing him at a level that supports his own thinking and problem solving rather than doing it for him.) Henry returns and retrieves his sweatshirt and snack bag and walks to the gate where Mom is waiting. Mom offers a big hug and begins with an open-ended question about the day. When there is no response, she wonders aloud if that is chocolate on his chin, which prompts Henry to tell about the pudding. Today he will not have a friend come over after school, but he usually has three or four play dates each week.

Henry has a playtime with Dad when he arrives home from work. Their play evolves from Henry's enthusiastic greeting of Dad. He jumps up on him, and Dad circles them around slowly, then faster. Henry calls Dad "motorboat" and Dad leaves his briefcase in the hall and says he has to start up the motor

by pulling the starter rope. He loosens his tie and enlists Henry to start the motor by pulling his tie off. After a few moments of moving through the house making motor noises, they pull up to the bank in the playroom and have an adventure walk through the dark forest. Dad points out the stuffed animals as if they were real and they either hide, move away carefully, or come to pet them, depending on Henry's idea.

Dad takes Henry's lead as the journey unfolds, then offers ideas related to Henry's to help him expand, though only a few ideas are picked up by Henry. Dad encourages Henry to talk about how they feel encountering the different beasts, and Henry responds mostly with fear, which allows them to solve the problem of how to avoid being eaten by the animals. Dad encourages multiple solutions. Like his play with Mom, the theme has a beginning and a repetitive middle. If it were not for Dad, the trip home on the boat would have been forgotten as a logical end. In this context, Henry can connect emotion to intention and create emotional ideas, but the sequential nature of the story is lost in repetitions. Henry still needs to be in command of the mission with assistant Dad at his side as they anticipate what will happen next and join forces. The strength of their relationship helps Henry forge ahead into new territory as he begins to build bridges between his ideas. At the family dinner that follows, they describe their adventure and talk about their problems and feelings, as well as their victories. Then Henry has a bath, and a story read with Dad. High-interest stories with sufficient pictures are selected to encourage discussion of the ideas and problems, predicting what will happen, picturing the next scene, and reflecting on feelings. Then Henry has a kiss and cuddle with Mom before going to sleep. Even Henry's family time is kept within a familiar routine, especially as he transitions to bedtime, a time of day that requires him to calm himself and fall asleep.

Indications of Progress

Box 2 describes Henry's IEP. By following this plan, Henry achieved all of his goals during the school year, although he still needs adult mediation to manage problem solving with peers when strong emotions of disappointment or jealousy are present. He is sometimes so immersed in his fantasy world of symbolic play that he often needs an adult reminder to shift attention to a mundane task at hand. For example, he may go to his room to dress for school and be found by his mother enacting a scenario in which his sock is a sword. But this time, he is wondering whether to be the good guy or the bad guy. Henry also enjoys conversations with adults and peers. He is curious and is asking more

questions to better understand his environment and how others feel. He is helpful and kind toward peers, which makes him well liked even if he is occasionally slow to follow a friend's idea or process the communication to shift attention to another topic. Henry is generally organized in his body and able to modulate excitement.

Case 2: Denny

Denny has just turned age 3 and is beginning to attend a preschool special-day class in the public school setting. Denny's parents suspected developmental issues for some time before his pediatrician referred the family for a comprehensive assessment. When Denny was about $2\frac{1}{2}$ years old, he was formally assessed at a Child Development Center and was diagnosed with an ASD. He

---

Box 2. Henry's Individual Education Plan

All goals listed below include a foundation of engagement, continuous two-way communication, and affect-based cued interactions to achieve the specific goals that follow.

INSTRUCTIONAL AREA: Communication

- *Annual Goal* (a goal that can reasonably be expected to be accomplished within one school year, 9/99-6/2000): Henry will expand his functional use of language.

  1. Given a structured group setting, Henry will initiate social greetings and phrases to adults and peers four times a day over a one-week period as measured by a teacher observation log:
     a. with mediated verbal prompts
     b. with nonverbal gestural prompts
     c. independently without prompts

  2. Given an unstructured play setting in a group, Henry will express wants and needs verbally with peers two times a day over a one-week period as measured by an observation log completed by the teacher and the speech/language therapist:
     a. with mediated verbal prompts
     b. with mediated nonverbal prompts
     c. independently without prompts

  3. In an unstructured play activity of Henry's preference, Henry will sustain an interaction using verbal/nonverbal communication with a peer for 15 minutes, demonstrating comprehension of his play partners' informational needs:
     a. with adult mediation
     b. independently

Continued

Box 2. *Continued*

4. Given an unstructured play activity, Henry will verbalize ideas for actions/activities three times a day during a one-week period, as measured by a teacher observation log:
    a. given adult choices and prompts
    b. independently

5. During daily classroom activities, Henry will request help/assistance from appropriate staff when needed.
    a. with adult mediation
    b. independently

INSTRUCTIONAL AREA: Sensory Processing and Self-Regulation

- *Annual Goal:* Henry will improve sensory processing and regulation needed for learning and social interaction.

    1. Henry will transition from active to more quiet classroom activities appropriately (without excessive vocalizations or physical activity) two times a day over a one-week time period as measured by teacher/observation log:
        a. with adult-mediated prompts (verbal, pictures, modeling)
        b. independently

    2. Given appropriate activities/equipment, Henry will elicit staff aid to control/modulate level of emotional arousal (under stressful and/or exciting situations) as needed two times in a one-week period as measured by teacher/occupational therapist observation log:
        a. with adult prompts
        b. independently

    3. Given novel movement and sensory activities outside of daily routine, Henry will choose to participate in such activities with adult support for a 15-minute time period.

INSTRUCTIONAL AREA: Motor Planning/Visual Motor Coordination

- *Annual Goal:* Henry will improve motor planning skills required for learning and play activities at his age level.

    1. Given novel 3- to 5-step movement activities (games, obstacle course, dress-up, set table) within peer activities, Henry will successfully complete the activities three out of five trials as measured by the occupational therapist and teachers:
        a. with adult assistance
        b. independently

    2. Henry will successfully and independently complete the following daily-living classroom activities:
        a. hanging coat and backpack on pegs
        b. put away three out of five toys in proper location
        c. lay out lunch supplies
        d. serve other children snack/drinks
        e. sit with the group in circle and outside
        f. wait in line to enter/exit the classroom

    3. Henry will enact ideas in play that contain a beginning, a middle, and an ending once a day for a one-week period:
        a. with adult mediation
        b. independently, *with peer interaction*

Continued

Box 2. *Continued*

4. Henry will use at least one of the following tools at school daily for 5 minutes: markers, paintbrush, fork, pencil, crayon, toothbrush:
   a. with adult mediation
   b. independently
   c. by voluntary choice

INSTRUCTIONAL AREA: Cognition

- *Annual Goal:* Henry will improve abstract thinking skills within play and dialogue.

1. Henry will talk about feelings three times within a one-week period within a dialogue with adult giving mediation in situations involving the following emotions:
   a. disappointment
   b. jealousy
   c. fear
   d. joy/surprise
   e. aggression

2. Henry will answer simple "why" questions within high-affect situations in three out of five trials, as measured by staff in a one-week period:
   a. given adult mediation, pictures, gestures as needed
   b. independently

3. Given a problem involving an emotion of disappointment, jealousy, or fear within a preferred pretend play activity, Henry will find an alternative outcome to resolve the problem in three out of five trials over a one-week period with adult assistance.

4. Given a problem in the classroom with peers involving a high-affect level of disappointment, jealousy, or fear, Henry will attempt to resolve the problem using adult assistance in three out of five naturally occurring situations over a one-month period as noted in teacher/staff observation log.

5. Henry will expand use of emotional themes within his preferred play activities (disappointment, fear, anger, sadness, joy, surprise, jealousy, aggression) to include use of each of the above emotions at least once during a month-long period. Criterion for expansion is use of at least five circles of communication around each emotional theme:
   a. with adult facilitation or suggestion during play
   b. independently during play

6. Henry will anticipate the feelings and behavior of peers in pretend play, linking feelings to actions, using adult assistance, once a day in naturally occurring settings:
   a. with adult suggestion/mediation
   b. with nonverbal adult cue

7. Henry will expand understanding of concepts of time in pretend play activities by demonstrating logical/appropriate sequence of events as well as delays in each of five teacher-determined play activities. Examples follow:
   a. going to school, waiting for bus, time delay before reaching school, arrival
   b. parents coming home from work
   c. ordering, paying, and waiting for food at a fast-food restaurant
   d. waiting to use the bathroom
   e. going to a playground, waiting to use the swing or other play equipment

began to receive DIR psychotherapy with a private therapist and was referred to the school district for the special education services that were about to start. The psychotherapist helped the family immediately assemble an intervention team to begin an intervention the family could manage. Despite multiple studies and interventions, Denny continues to have a serious sleep disorder that has affected his developmental progress and his family's functioning. Both parents are well-educated professionals with full-time employment. His mother, who is self-employed, has had a hard time sustaining her professional practice due to the many nights of lost sleep combined with all of Denny's appointments. His father has used all his sick leave, and his employer graciously allowed his colleagues to donate their sick leave time to him. The family is exhausted.

Developmental Levels

Shared attention is reliably achieved with a special adult in sensorimotor play using movement, visual stimulation, and touch. He enjoys swinging, sitting in a parent's lap, bouncing or riding on Dad's back, and holding hands and jumping on the trampoline. Once Denny makes the connection and is sufficiently aroused, he will sustain shared attention for quieter activities for up to 10 minutes, using visual and sensory stimulation such as simple puzzles or computer games.

Engagement is sustained with preferred adults in pleasurable and protest interactions involving emotions of joy, fear, anger, or frustration. Denny can spend 30 minutes on the swing playing stop-and-go with a parent. He will work at insisting upon finding and securing a particular cereal he wants that he knows is "hidden" in his parents' closet. He seeks physical comfort from a parent when afraid; for example, if they encounter a large dog on the street, he will lead his parents and gesture to get away from the animal.

Two-way purposeful interactions can occur when Denny is not overtired or overwhelmed and if the interaction involves strong personal desires, uses photographs or pictures, gestures, and facial expressions, and takes place with a preferred adult. Denny will exchange photos or bring adults to objects he desires and gesture back and forth to find the object, put it where he wants it, open it, and arrange it for use.

Complex gestural problem solving is an area of strength for Denny. He expresses communicative intent nonverbally; for example, he will find Dad's jacket and car keys, pull Dad to the car, and gesture with the key to unlock it. He understands and sequences actions he can learn visually. Denny will pull a chair to the kitchen counter, climb up, open the correct cupboard to find noodle soup, accurately make his selection, prepare the package for the microwave, program the microwave, cook the soup, wait for the timer, prepare a bowl and spoon, pour, and eat. Denny uses his visual strengths to achieve his desires.

Representational capacity is present in Denny's use of picture symbols to communicate. He is able to represent sequences in picture, but does not yet represent in play.

Sensory/Developmental Profile

Auditory processing is difficult for Denny but impossible to test accurately. Because it is so hard to get consistent responses, developmental baselines have not been established. Denny is nonverbal. His hearing acuity tests as normal, though he has an early history of ear infections and a successful placement of tubes in early toddlerhood. At times, Denny shows almost no response to verbal input, but he will respond quickly to the same request made visually with photos or pictures.

Sensory reactivity is extremely uneven. Denny has many sensory sensitivities to auditory, tactile, and visual input. His responses are irregular; sometimes he appears hypersensitive and withdraws by running away from noise or jumping excitedly at loud music. At other times, he seems to crave sensation, especially by jumping and rocking. He has extraordinary balance skills and uses no judgment about safety in attempting death-defying feats of balance that amaze and frighten his caregivers, such as climbing to high, precarious ledges or balancing on one foot from a high bar intended to be grasped by the hand. He has little safety or social judgment in general and must be supervised around the clock. (He has thrown himself through windows.) Total supervision is a challenge because, despite multiple studies and interventions, Denny continues to have significant sleep issues—he is awake for extended periods of time throughout the night. Eating is also a challenge with Denny because he only eats about four foods. Remarkably, Denny is successfully toilet trained. He watched his two older brothers and he was "taught" by them.

Visual-spatial processing is a strength. Denny knows and remembers locations of objects and important peoples' homes or offices. Visual gross motor skills are remarkable, while fine motor skills are very uneven. He can use the computer but resists using a fork or marker. In combination with proprioceptive and vestibular stimulation, he knows how to judge distance and depth in balance and climbing.

Communication is best when it is primarily visually based with gesture and photographs. Denny seems to lack the ability to sequence oral-motor movements to articulate intelligible words. Occasional words such as "dog" or "Mom" are heard, then seem to disappear. He has learned a few signs to indicate desires but does not attend to signs as well as to pictures. His ability to

sign is unlikely to become elaborated because of motor-planning challenges. Because his wishes are still instrumental and concrete, there are few requests he cannot make understood. Denny's receptive language for familiar ritualized communications is good, but much of his comprehension is dependent on routine and visual cues.

Rate of progress in Denny's overall development is disappointing and worrisome to his parents. They had hoped that he would be more verbal by age 3 and had not anticipated Denny's oral-motor difficulties. Because he is such a daredevil, they had assumed his motor system was a developmental strength. It is difficult to determine the extent to which his progress is impeded by his serious sleep disorder and other regulatory issues. Despite multiple environmental and medical interventions, Denny continues to have difficulties both falling asleep and remaining asleep through the night. The long, wakeful periods in the night are stressful for the whole family and have affected everyone's ability to be attentive and engaged throughout the day. Denny's parents expected to resolve the sleep issue by his third birthday.

Embracing the DIR model was essential in restoring their hopes and expectations, recognizing how important it is for Denny to learn within relationships as well as in semistructured approaches. Denny's school program adds a semistructured approach to teaching and helps Denny develop a regular routine. A more organized routine during the day may aid the development of regular sleep/wake cycles. In the following example, the teacher uses sensory activities to extend attention and focus by alternating large-movement activity with seated activity and by incorporating sensory stimulation into the seated learning sessions.

Current Intervention Program

Intervention consists of the following:

- Four to six floor time sessions per day at home, with either a parent or the child-care provider, supplemented with extensive physical activity recommended by the occupational therapist .

- Three hours a week of speech and language therapy (including oral-motor therapy) in the home.

- Implementation of augmentative communication approaches at home.

- One hour a week of occupational therapy with a sensory-processing emphasis.

- One hour a week of DIR family psychotherapy.

- Denny is currently placed in a special education preschool 5 days a week, 4 hours per day, through the school district. He receives speech therapy in class and OT at the school site. Children from the typical kindergarten are brought in to interact with the children.

- Two to three play dates a week.

A Typical Day

It is hard to say when Denny's day begins. He is frequently awake with a parent between 2 a.m. and 5 a.m., finally falling back asleep so that he cannot be awakened for a school bus that arrives at 7:45 a.m. or for school that begins at 8:20 a.m. In the early hours, Denny's parents try activities that might put him back to sleep, such as looking at books, massage suggested by the occupational therapist, or singing. When these fail, one parent may rise with him and use the quiet time in the house for floor time play. Today, Dad takes Denny down two flights of stairs to play so that the others will not be awakened. They jump on the trampoline and sing along with his favorite tapes.

Dad chases Denny around the doorways and through the rooms, creating a hide-and-seek chase game that has social anticipation and a moment of surprise. These games foster shared attention and engagement. Denny indicates hunger by pulling Dad to the pantry and looking up at the top shelf where his favorite cereal is kept out of reach so that he will need to interact with an adult to have some. Dad extends the circles of communication between them by playing dumb using facial expression and gesture, but Denny goes to the picture board and brings Dad the picture of the cereal box he wants. Dad continues to extend the interaction by finding out if Denny wants one or two bowls, or a red or blue bowl, by holding out choices and allowing Denny to use gesture to state preference, which he does.

After eating, Dad tries once again to go back to sleep with Denny and is successful, snuggling on a futon bed in the playroom. One parent typically rises with the two older brothers and gets them to school while the other sleeps with Denny and eventually gets him ready and to school by car. Denny is always late to his new class, where the teacher is very empathic with the sleep problem. The classroom is located in a public elementary school across town. Denny's parents selected this class because the teacher has a strong background in sensorimotor integration, is committed to a developmentally based curriculum, and uses play as a primary mode for young children to learn. The room is set up with round tables for selected activities, area rugs for motor play, individual tutoring booths for structured learning, and a house-play area with big pillows for resting. The school district has already placed eight children in the class, which the teacher feels is too many. She has three assistants, which she feels is necessary. Given the level of the children's development and their unpredictability, she feels the rule should be one adult for each child.

Some days Denny goes back to sleep on the pillows and will not be roused. Most days he arrives in time for music, an activity of motion and songs specially selected for Denny and two classmates. Pictures are used to give Denny a choice about which songs to play. The goal is to create an optimal level of arousal with the music and movement to encourage Denny to vocalize. The same music is repeated frequently and, when it becomes familiar, he does hum along with perfect pitch. The speech-and-language therapist who joins Denny for this activity stays at his eye level and exaggeratedly enunciates the words for him. Today, Denny requests the "wheels on the bus" by giving the school bus photo to the therapist and saying "bu." Because his providers want him to understand the agency and power of his communication, no one praises him for speaking. Rather, they just begin the song as a contingent interaction. The therapist quickly takes out photos to symbolize each verse, and Denny chooses which comes next at the end of each verse. Because he laughs and smiles at the babies on the bus saying "waa,waa,waa," the therapist repeats this verse and pauses for Denny to make the "waa" sound, which he does, to everyone's delight. The therapist repeats the verse because he senses Denny's pleasure and caught the gleam in his eye; he is using the pictures and music to capitalize on any indications that Denny is affectively connected to him and to the activity.

Following music, Denny's teacher takes him by the hand and leads him to the tutoring cubicle. Quiet, focused activities are alternated with active events to optimize Denny's state of readiness and cooperation. Even during these seated one-on-one tasks, the teacher rubs Denny's palms, compresses his elbow joints, and blows on his hair. These sensory experiences help Denny maintain attention to tasks of the teacher's choosing. The teacher follows a modified TEACCH curriculum and

works with Denny to add the element of social interaction and interpersonal communication to the tasks. In a few minutes, Denny completes puzzles, a prewriting task, a sorting task, and a matching task. To sustain his interest in the matching task, the teacher adds number cookies for oral stimulation, reinforcement, and to gratify his current interest in numbers.

During recess, the teacher has arranged for each child in her class to be met at the door by a special friend, preidentified from the regular kindergarten class. Although her class is the only preschool on the site, she has created special peer friends from the kindergarten by having those children choose someone in her class they want to know. Denny is a great climber and balances in high places, which drew a daredevil boy to become his playmate. His friend has good judgment about safety and knows the playground rules well. He shakes his head vehemently "no" when Denny heads for a forbidden wall and pulls him to the balance beams. The classroom aides are watching and praising Denny and his buddy for knowing where to go. The kindergarten children cannot be counted on to stick with the avoidant children or to always show the best judgment, so the teacher makes sure all the assistants are watching and are nearby during recess. She gives them breaks during the structured class times when she can watch more children herself and ensure their safety.

After recess, two kindergarten children join Denny and another girl for an integrated play group. Since the preschoolers are still developmentally young and nonverbal, the teacher plans an activity that is sensory, motor-based, and fun for all. First, they stir and knead dough for bread. Then they build tents with chairs and sheets and find each other hiding beneath. The preschoolers walk their friends to the kindergarten class with an aide, stopping to look at, and name, pictures of the children up on the hall bulletin board. On the way to class, they take a bathroom break.

Back in class Denny and two others make a circle, holding hands with the teacher as they sit on the rug. Denny bolts away, running up and down the length of the room screaming and flapping his hands wildly. The teacher receives him in her arms and checks him to be sure he isn't hurt, then tries to seat him next to her, but he bolts again. She asks an aide who just returned with a child from the bathroom to take Denny to the trampoline and then bring him back to the circle. Denny jumps and the aide counts to 20—a familiar routine—then he jumps into her arms, and she sits him at circle between her legs, but only for a moment because someone else now needs to jump. The teacher uses the trampoline when she sees that the children are seeking sensory stimulation from running or jumping. This way, she addresses their sensory needs without having the running, screaming child disrupt or distract everyone in the room. After long discussions with the principal and support from all the parents, the administration agreed to allow her a small trampoline in an adjoining room that also houses a copier, a refrigerator, and other school equipment.

The teacher is trying to engage the children in identifying body parts by putting stickers and bean bags on them and having them remove the items. She sees that Denny and another child are becoming fussy, so she abandons the project and brings out a snack. This teacher has learned that when she is not engaging the children in a game, she needs to rethink its presentation. For example, do they need more preparation, should it be a one-on-one game first, is it visual enough, does it meet sensory needs, or was it presented at an inappropriate time of day? She does not try to make the

children complete the task if everyone is frustrated. Rather, she waits for a better time.

At snack, each child has favorite foods placed in several types of see-through containers they are learning to manipulate, including plastic zipper bags and lidded plastic or glass containers. Denny requests his food by giving a photo of that food to the teacher. She gives him the appropriate container, and he works on the fine motor skill involved in getting to the treat. The treats and containers are individualized for each child's needs, both fine motor and oral-motor. All the children are engaged now, and she works with them, as do the aides, in saying the name of the food, signing for more, or requesting a taste from a friend, as is appropriate for each child. Every activity is multisensory and has multiple objectives. Even snack time is a fine motor, oral-motor, social, and communication event.

After snack, Denny is led by the hand with another child to a corner with pillows for a modified circle time. The teacher arranges typical circle time activities for one adult with two children. These children are stretching to sustain relatedness and availability to learn in interaction with one or two people. They are not developmentally ready for a large-group activity, though in a small group they can prepare for the types of activities that usually take place during circle time. They look outside to see the weather and put a photo on a bulletin board that most closely matches the day. Today is gray and sunless. Then they each take a photo of themselves and take turns placing it in the window of a big drawing of a school bus. Some of the other children's photos are already in place because they had circle time earlier, so the aide names the other children and points to them in the room. Now Denny chooses a book, and each child sits beside the aide while she points to pictures and talks about the story in simple language. At the end of the story, she gives each child some different things to smell—a flower, coffee beans, spices, or lotion on their arms—then shows them their faces in the mirror and points to her nose. "We smell with our nose," she is saying. They each do some smelling, and she shows them their noses in the mirror. When circle time is over, the teacher lights a candle and the children blow it out, a ritual that marks the end of circle time as well as practices blowing for oral-motor development.

Denny is taken to OT by the aide. The occupational therapist works in a carpeted room set up as a gym. Today, Denny is joined by his special friend from kindergarten, whom they pick up on the way. The aide says she'll be back in a few minutes with Sam. The occupational therapist works on motor imitation by having the friend copy every move Denny makes. Then she gives the friend a toy that makes a "pop" and has him do it first. She gives one to Denny, and he imitates his friend. When she can't tell who is imitating whom, she adds more items—bubbles, a snapper, a clicker, and a flashlight—until Denny is following his friend's lead in making things happen. Denny gets to his sensory threshold quickly, however, and bolts, throwing a toy. The therapist puts Denny on the swing and the friend pushes, then he climbs on with Denny and models requests for a push. The aide arrives with Sam, drops him off, and returns to class with Denny.

The aide plays in the dress-up corner with Denny, reinforcing the names of the body parts the teacher intended to work on earlier. Denny is joined by another child in the class, and the assistant helps them try on clothes, name body parts, and begin to symbolize the roles the clothing suggests. For example, Denny with a briefcase and hat is told he looks like "Daddy." The children look at

themselves in the mirror. The aide tries to bring in a doll to represent a baby and offers Denny a bottle. Denny first tries to drink from it himself but then he puts it to the doll's mouth and smiles when the aide makes sucking noises. Denny is just learning that one object can represent another. The aide uses dress-up and doll play to work on these emerging ideas for symbolic play.

The bus monitor opens the door and announces that Denny's bus has arrived. The children in his class live in different sections of the city so, to minimize the length of the ride, the bus routes are arranged by class and neighborhood. Not everyone's bus arrives at the same moment, which has the advantage that the teacher can individualize each separation but the drawback that it brings uneven closure to the day. This is one of the compromises the teacher makes because the transportation system is so cumbersome. Denny is taken to the bus by the teacher, who gives him a photo of his parents in front of their house. She waves good-bye and belts him in. The teacher has taken on this task because Denny becomes agitated at this major transition and can upset the driver by screaming and kicking. If the teacher is with him and he has his photos, Denny is more accepting of the transition because he has her reassurance and the visual information about where he is being taken. It is important to remember that visually oriented, nonverbal children need visual prompts for all information, not just for structured tasks in the classroom.

Denny falls asleep on the bus and must be carried off by the childcare person, who greets him at his home. Both parents are at work, and his brothers will be home shortly. Nate, his caregiver, tries to arouse him with drink, food, and tickles, but in the end allows him to sleep about an hour, then tries to arouse him again. The pediatrician hopes that if he cannot sleep during the day, he will sleep at night. So far this idea has not worked. Nate takes Denny to a special play-room (really the living room given over to play equipment), and Denny starts by jumping on the trampoline. Nate hands Denny balls, which he accepts and throws at Nate. This begins a jumping-and-throwing game, which has Denny laughing, and the gleam in his eyes appears. Nate keeps it going and adds Denny's brother to the game when he gets home. A playtime develops between Nate and the two brothers, with running, chasing, tickling, jumping, and throwing and lots of engagement, with gesture and facial expression for communication. Nate ends the game to take the two boys to pick up their brother at soccer practice.

As they walk down the street to the playground, Denny bolts ahead repeatedly, so Nate turns the walk into a race/chase game. When they arrive at the playground, Nate gives Denny chewing gum in the wrapper. He knows this will occupy Denny for a few minutes while he reunites with this brother and listens to the report about the practice. On the way home, the boys take turns kicking the ball to the brother, who runs down the sidewalk to receive it. At the house, Nate gives the boys a bath, a very social time with all three in the tub together. Then Denny's brothers take him to the computer and try to keep him engaged with one of his CDs while Nate handles some dinner preparation. Other days Denny will join Nate and helps him find things they need, as well as mixing, pouring, and cooking. This has encouraged Denny to experiment with new foods as well as provided opportunities for communication and fun.

When Mom arrives home, she sits with the boys and hears about their day. Denny drapes himself over her back, arms around her shoulders, and she rocks and strokes him while she talks with the other two boys. Dad arrives and the family sits down to dinner in the dining room. This is a brief event during which Denny barely makes contact with a chair but does circle round for physical contact with Mom and Dad. Following dinner the parents leave everything on the table for later and attend to the boys. They alternate participating in play and supervising a bit of homework for the oldest. The two older brothers go to bed with stories and cuddles. Denny is encouraged to participate but tonight, as on many other nights, he has his own agenda, so one parent follows his lead. Tonight they play on an indoor swing in the basement. (It is a piece of equipment the occupational therapist recommended for the home.) After the brothers are in bed, one parent attends to chores while the other plays with Denny until they are tired and need to try to sleep themselves. Denny has a soothing massage and is put in a toddler bed in the parent's room with cuddling and a story. The lights are turned off everywhere in the house (a signal to Denny that everyone is sleeping), and the parents hope that Denny will fall asleep within the hour.

Indications of Progress

Box 3 displays Denny's IEP. By the end of the first year year, Denny takes pleasure in interacting with people and has doubled the period of time he sustains engagement with adults or with a peer, with facilitation. He has learned that it is more fun to "play" with others, and both initiates and persists, insistent on getting his way. His interest in others has led to expanded symbolic play. Denny has begun to use toys to express ideas, although he would rather be in a role himself. He enjoys dress-up and puppets, which reduce the motor-planning challenges. Denny can pretend where he wants to go and what he wants to do based on real-life experiences. He appears to remember many details, which he can enact to demonstrate his understanding and improved reasoning.

Daily life has also become more enjoyable as Denny spontaneously and independently communicates his desires with the use of augmentative communication pictures. He also can sequence pictures of events to create complex requests. Although Denny now attempts to vocalize choices, his intelligibility is poor. He still requires pictures to communicate his intentions. But every connection to his voice is valuable. He will reciprocate vocally in song or play using sounds and attempts at words. Denny's sensory diet has enabled him to extend attention to seated tasks through completion, and both structured and semi-structured learning has improved.

Denny's parents are very pleased with Denny's progress in his engagement and affectionate play with them and his brothers. They are also pleased to hear of his progress in school and how much further up the learning curve he had advanced. Although they still wish he talked, they are encouraged by how communicative he can be with gestures and pictures. Of course, they want a good night's sleep but realize the number of nights he sleeps through is increasing in general, despite periods of night-waking. His improved engagement, desire to interact, and "clever" problem solving have alleviated many of their fears, and they now join him with more

---

Box 3. Denny's Individual Education Plan

All goals include establishing a foundation of engagement, continuous two-way communication, and affect.

ANNUAL GOAL: Improve functional developmental capacities

- *Objective:* Denny will sustain shared attention to a sensorimotor activity of his choosing for 20 minutes:
  a. mediated by an adult
  b. mediated by an adult with a peer
  c. initiated by Denny
  d. independently across contexts (with a peer; in a small group)

- *Objective:* Denny will sustain mutual engagement with an adult or peer for the duration of a sensory-motor activity lasting up to 15 minutes:
  a. using gaze to regulate interaction
  b. using gesture to regulate interaction
  c. showing emotional involvement in facial expression
  d. showing pleasure
  e. showing protest

- *Objective:* Denny will initiate interaction and show intention through gesture, facial expression, vocalization, in at least three naturally occurring events throughout the school day:
  a. to meet felt needs
  b. for pleasurable activity
  c. to protest
  d. to sustain two-way interaction

- *Objective:* Denny will imitate an adult or peer to create five purposeful interactions within an activity:
  a. using sensory motor equipment and gross-motor activity
  b. using sensory experiences and fine-motor activity
  c. using objects for representational/symbolic activity

Continued

Box 3. *Continued*

GOAL: Strengthen processing capacities and improve integration across modalities

* *Objective:* Vocalizations will increase over baseline when Denny engages in activities that arouse him using music and movement:
    a. humming/singing
    b. vocalizing choice
    c. reciprocating verbally with adult or peer

* *Objective:* Attention to seated pre-academic tasks will increase with oral stimulation and joint compression:
    a. integrate visual-motor capacities
    b. oral directions to visual pointing or picture choosing response
    c. visual prompt to oral or motor response

GOAL: Improve problem-solving capacities

* *Objective:* Denny will demonstrate knowledge of three-part temporal sequences to solve an adult-selected visual-motor problem:
    a. lead adult to desired object; manipulate setup of object for use; engage in appropriate use of object; communicate pleasure or satisfaction to adult
    b. increase independence in problem solving; complete without prompts or cues from adult.
    c. use vocalizations to express intention/anticipation

GOAL: Improve symbolic thinking

* *Objective:* Denny will show realistic routines from daily living in imaginative play with an adult:
    a. self-care routines–pretend to comb hair, get dressed, brush teeth, take a bath
    b. enact common household activities–talk on the phone, stir food in a pot, answer the door

* *Objective:* Denny will demonstrate understanding that one object can represent another by:
    a. Using pictorial representation by showing photos of objects to make requests for the actual object
    b. Showing identification with roles by using dress-up props and house play materials with appropriate intention and affect
    c. Using toys such as cars and trucks on pretend roads (line drawings), make a house with blocks, or make a tent with a sheet
    d. Showing a number symbol to correspond with a number of objects

* *Objective:* Denny will classify and sort objects according to category:
    a. with adult assistance in naming object and category
    b. with nonverbal independent choices

---

energy and excitement, recognizing how important affects and joy are for his learning.

Case 3: Mariah

Mariah, age 2 years, 9 months, was first referred for intervention at 16 months of age to an Early Intervention Toddler Program operated by her local school district because her family and pediatrician were concerned about global delays in her development. She was assessed by the district team as eligible for their early intervention services. By age 18 months, she was receiving a 30-hour per week, home-based behavioral intervention in which tutors consulted with behavior therapists, an occupational therapist, and a speech and language pathologist. Through this intervention, Mariah learned some scripted language and compliance routines but was still unrelated and passive. Her family recently learned about the DIR approach and sought out a more relationship-based intervention.

Developmental Levels

Shared attention can be sustained around activities that provide firm tactile pressure, such as rub downs with lotion or towels. Mariah can also be offered favorite foods with strong flavors, such as bacon, to gain shared attention.

Engagement with significant adults is seen fleetingly in pleasurable interactions, usually involving touch and singing. More sustained engagement can be observed in battles over limiting Mariah's access to her obsessions. If Mom withholds Mariah's music tapes, Mariah will work hard protesting, with vocal communications of screaming and hissing, and with gestures, such as waving her arms, stamping her feet, or throwing herself to the floor. She will use facial expressions to communicate anger and disgust. Mariah does not initiate interpersonal interaction nor does she show spontaneous exploration or interest in play. In a room filled with toys, Mariah sits blankly on the couch and stares into space.

Two-way purposeful interaction is observed only in her pulling, gesturing, or screaming to regain possession of her tape recorder. The only self-initiated activity is an obsessive, repetitive listening to particular musical phrases on a children's audiotape. This activity has become a battle between Mariah and Mom for control of the tape player, because Mom is concerned about the self-stimulatory aspects of this interest and her

disconnection from others as she engages in the listening. However, Mariah is very purposeful in her demands to have the recorder.

Complex problem-solving gestures are present when Mariah is highly motivated and the solution doesn't involve much motor planning. For example, she can desire cookies, go to the diaper bag, pull it open, search for the cookie bag, pull it out, and bring it to her Mom or tear it open, usually with her teeth.

Representational capacities are limited. No one has seen Mariah spontaneously imitate others, although with many repetitions she does learn simple routines. There is some recall of learned verbal requests, but not even presymbolic use of toys or pretend play. Photo or picture communication devices have not yet been tried but are a likely area of representational capacity.

Sensory Developmental Profile

Auditory processing is uneven, with lag time in her responses, even to highly motivating activities. Mom can show Mariah a favorite food and call to her to come and get it. While waiting an extended time for Mariah to initiate movement across the room, Mom assumes her daughter's disinterest and begins to put the food away. Her obsession with repeating specific phrases from her audiotapes is a sign of her attempts to control input and perhaps treat herself. The family is exploring auditory-processing assessments and interventions because this is recognized as an area of great need.

Sensory reactivity varies. Mariah is seen as an underreactive child who requires firm touch, strong flavors, big movement, and high affect to stimulate her responsiveness to her environment. She is most responsive to firm tactile pressure on her arms and legs. She shows no evidence of registration of gentle touch. Mariah likes bacon and red hots, whereas she is indifferent to typical foods of early childhood, such as rice, noodles, or bread. On the other hand, she shows signs of high reactivity to certain sounds and to light. She will squint and turn away from the outdoors on a sunny day, or cover her ears at the sound of a motorcycle on the street.

Motor planning and visual motor coordination are areas of concern. Mariah can execute a sequential motor plan to retrieve something she desires, either by climbing or seeking the object put out of sight. However, her repertoire is limited, and her coordination and balance are poor. She may successfully drag a chair to a counter but may tumble off it as she climbs up. She may attempt to open a ziplock bag but quickly give up and bite through it as a strategy for access to the contents.

Visual-spatial processing is uneven. Mariah is able to retrieve objects from recall of prior location, but she may step too wide or too narrow to reach a surface she is climbing. At this point, it is difficult to differentiate her visual abilities from her motor issues. Her search techniques still are limited to looking in the last place where an item was found.

Affective processing tends to be low. Mariah appears to register strong affects of both pleasure and protest, especially if she receives them in opposition to her own intentions. Mostly, however, she is passive and flat in her affective expression and remains unaroused by her environment. She shows no evidence of spontaneous self-expression, either verbally or through gesture and facial expression. But she does respond with strong affective communication if her favorite things are removed or withheld.

Rate of progress has been slow. Although Mariah has made a few gains in learning simple routines and some vocalizations, her family is very concerned about the lack of progress in her spontaneous self-expression and relatedness. Here is an opportunity to integrate floor time

and applied behavioral analysis (ABA). Floor time will be used to support Mariah's as yet untapped capacity to initiate interactions that support her connectedness to others. Some of the actions she initiates may be learned through imitation practice drills in her ABA sessions. Through floor time, Mariah can learn to spontaneously use some of the language she has learned through ABA, in the naturally occurring context of play. Mariah also will learn to solve problems she is motivated to tackle during floor time sessions. The kinds of motor sequences and visual-spatial tasks involved in solving such problems can be coordinated with both occupational therapy and ABA so that she is shaping her motor skills to enable her to be successful at her problem-solving attempts. The challenge to her team is to coordinate these efforts by creating a communication system that allows for new ideas to be initiated as well as follow through with step-by-step awareness of progress.

Current Intervention Program

Mariah's comprehensive intervention program consists of the following:
- Six to eight floor time sessions daily
- 10 hours of ABA at home
- 3 days a week at a special education preschool with a parent, as well as home visits biweekly
- Speech, occupational, and physical therapy at preschool

Mariah and her parents are just beginning a 3-day per week DIR-oriented preschool program to supplement 10 hours per week of continued home-based behavioral intervention (ABA). The parents worked with other families in their school district to encourage the district to offer a relationship-based intervention as an alternative or as a supplement to the district's behavioral orientation. The preschool program will provide family-based services either in a center or in the home for eight families. Mariah and her parents will participate at the center 3 days per week and have one home visit every other week. The center program includes early childhood special educators with a special interest in DIR, a speech-and-language therapist, occupational and physical therapist, a school psychologist, and a nurse. The professional staff has been learning to work together in a DIR approach and will continue to work with a mentor for the academic year.

Mariah's parents are completely dependent upon the school district services for their intervention program. They have a strong commitment to personally provide six to eight floor time sessions with Mariah at home. The mentor working with the school staff has agreed to help the parents learn to use tasks from the 10 hours of home-based behavioral intervention in their floor time sessions. The ABA tutors will supply the DIR preschool with all the objectives and data on trials for each week. The DIR mentor will then work with the staff and parents to understand how to weave in opportunities for spontaneous practice through play during floor time sessions using similar materials and prompting/facilitating statements. For example, a receptive language exercise in which Mariah follows a command to shake a toy can be followed up in a floor time session with rattles, maracas, and other shaking toys to make music or a parade. This offers Mariah a chance to lead the shaking and have Mom imitate her.

Similarly, the DIR staff will inform the ABA providers of the activities they are working on with Mariah, especially in the areas of self-initiated activity and sensory diet issues that help Mariah sustain attention and focus. For example, the DIR staff found that Mariah loves to jump and is very engaged with them when they play jumping games. She uses gaze to regulate interaction and gestures and verbalizes to invite staff to play jumping games with her. Working with the occupational therapist, everyone learns that jumping helps Mariah organize her orientation in space and improves her focus on visual-motor activities. ABA tutors begin to use jumping off the couch as a reward just before they present a visual-motor task, such as a puzzle.

A Typical Day

Mariah is awakened by the strong smell of bacon cooking in the kitchen next to her bedroom. Her mother has learned to wake her this way because it helps prevent a struggle with Mariah in making the slow transition from sleep to wakefulness. By the time she serves the breakfast to the family of five (Mariah has two stepsisters who are teenagers), Mariah is tugging on her mother's pant leg, requesting bacon. Mariah is placed in an adaptive seat and strapped in to keep her at the table, preventing loss of balance and having her wander away. Mom holds all the bacon and toast, giving Mariah small pieces after coaxing her to make a verbal request, which she does. "Want" is clear but the "b" and "t" for bacon or toast are indistinguishable, so Mom holds up one of each and lets Mariah's gestures indicate preference. She is working with her team to integrate the ABA and DIR models of intervention. Mom has learned from the DIR program to use choices and gestured responses as complete communications, but she also ritualizes the meal to make it more predictable for Mariah. Mom reports that Mariah has been more willing to participate in such interactions since she (the mother) has learned to embed them in naturally occurring events, such as breakfast, and to offer choices and encourage Mariah to show her preference. The teens leave with their boom box blaring, and Mariah grimaces and screams until they are out of range. Because time is short, Mom quickly dresses herself and Mariah for school and takes her to the center. She wonders when she will be able to use visual communication strategies to encourage Mariah to dress more independently. Mom worries that she should make time for Mariah to be involved in dressing herself, and makes a mental note to add dressing to her list of requests for the occupational therapist. (The therapist will also teach the behavioral tutors routines for teaching Mariah to dress so that some part of her sessions can be used for practice.)

The school classroom looks more like a family room in the home of a large family, with couches and rocking chairs, area rugs, and baskets with toys, as well as well-stocked cabinets. One area is set up as a makeshift kitchen with a sink, a microwave, a toaster oven, a table, and chairs. Because the parents are attending the school with their children, the room is made comfortable for adults. All sources of sensory irritation have been reduced. The carpet is made of natural fibers and the fluorescent lighting has been removed. The parent group has decided to focus on healthy eating with an attempt to eliminate additives, sugar, casein, and wheat. Mariah's parents both work, so they have divided the time with her at school, each coming half the hours. They have successfully used the Parental Leave Act to secure the time to participate in the class with their daughter.

The teacher greets Mariah and Mom, while other staff greet other families. They go to a corner of the room that has a rocker and a table with sensory toys on it. The teacher coaches Mom to let Mariah explore the materials freely and to follow her lead. Mom resists the urge to prompt Mariah and tell her what to do. This period of time was designed to encourage initiative in her daughter. The

teachers will watch Mariah's spontaneous behavior to discover whether it is inhibited by difficulties with motor planning, coordination, or sequencing and report back to the ABA tutors so that incrementally shaped trials can be developed for tutoring sessions to support Mariah's spontaneous interests.

For now, the teacher talks with Mom about the goal of helping Mariah initiate for herself so that she will become less passive. Rather than telling Mariah what to do, Mom tries to find out what interests Mariah. Mariah begins to push at some play dough, so Mom pushes at it too. Spontaneously, Mariah looks up at Mom and their eyes meet. Mom is thrilled with this spontaneous gaze and offers Mariah some play dough. Mom rolls the play dough in her hand and makes a ball. She gives the ball to her daughter, and Mariah accepts it. Mariah then gives her Mom the play dough she has been holding. The teacher helps Mom see that Mariah has just closed a circle of communication by reciprocating her mother's gesture. Mom understands that no command to give the dough had been made and that this interaction has been spontaneous on her daughter's part. Mom takes the dough from her, and Mariah pushes her mother's hand, which Mom responds to as a request to make another ball. Mariah is initiating around play, opening and closing circles of communication.

Soon Mom is making balls from the dough her daughter gives her and giving it back to her daughter, who is arranging the balls in a line. Mom worries about the line but the teacher focuses Mom on the reciprocal nature and spontaneous eye contact in their interaction. Lining-up is discussed as something to work on once engagement can be sustained. The teacher talks to the mother privately about how they won't focus directly on eliminating the perseverative or rigid behaviors because she believes that, right now, Mariah needs to feel as though she has some control in her environment. Therefore, they will focus on the pleasure of interaction and help Mariah find a repertoire of new behaviors that she can take pleasure in, master, and control. As her sensory needs are addressed and her repertoire enlarges, the rigid, self-stimulatory behaviors will fade. Mom sighs with relief and recalls some terrible battles with Mariah when she tried to extinguish her daughter's self-stimulatory behaviors. Mom wonders how this will be coordinated with the behavioralists. The teacher explains that they will gently reorient Mariah to attend to the task they have in mind for her. If they are unsuccessful, they will use a sensory break suggested by the occupational therapist to reorganize Mariah for the next set of trials. The DIR and behavioral models will integrate their orientations, using the discrete trials primarily to teach imitation and shape motor planning and visual-motor organization.

The teacher suggests that Mariah might like a snack and talks with Mom about how transitions are made at home. Mom points out how dependent she is on routines to keep Mariah from becoming upset. After some exploration, the teacher discovers that Mariah makes transitions best when she can see what is going to happen. The teacher introduces the idea of using photographs to help explain the next event. She takes a photo of Mariah with Mom and the play dough to use the next day. She brings Mariah a photo of snacks on the table and Mariah goes calmly to the table, leaving the dough behind. The teacher makes a note to integrate visual materials into Mariah's total program, both in the DIR preschool for practicing sequences and during her one-on-one structured learning.

The speech therapist is at the snack table, talking to several parents about his observations of the children's oral-motor needs. He can use his observations of the children while they bite and chew to help the parents understand why their children's speech is not yet clear. Based on oral-motor needs, he suggests different kinds of snacks for each child. Mariah's Mom is familiar with using food as a reward, and she begins to withhold the snack until Mariah vocalizes as Mom instructs. The speech therapist talks with Mom about the importance of wooing Mariah to vocalize by creating the right level of stimulation and affect in the environment. He helps Mom pretend to eat and make satisfying 'mmm' sounds and then to offer the snack to Mariah. She accepts and puts her lips together, watching Mom's face as she takes the food. The therapist helps Mom see what Mariah is doing spontaneously to learn the "m" sound. Mom is especially interested in the difference between wooing her child and making demands. The speech therapist helps Mom with the fine line between the two and notes that wooing includes keeping the interaction pleasurable and fun for the child, using the affective connection to entice the child to sustain engagement in the process, and avoiding stressing the child so that she becomes disorganized. He clarifies the similarity in these objectives for intervention in both the DIR and ABA approaches.

Mom and Mariah go into a big gym to meet with the occupational therapist, who invites Mariah to explore. She climbs into a lycra swing and closes it over her. Mom wants to uncover her and the therapist talks with Mom about how much new stimulation Mariah has been exposed to today and encourages Mom to make a little game of peek-a-boo in the swing. This is a more gentle entry into interaction and a way that enables Mariah to take some initiative and reciprocate voluntarily to Mom's invitation. By the time they are ready to leave, Mariah is uncovering herself and peeking out at Mom with a big smile. The therapist talks with Mom about the purpose children may have in protecting themselves or maintaining a feeling of self-organization when they engage in behavior that seems inappropriate or not optimal for social-skill development. The occupational therapist thinks with Mom about the sensory processing meaning of her child's behavior and then decides how to approach the child to bring her back into interaction without disorganizing her. The therapist will discuss this understanding of the child's sensory needs at the team meeting coming up this week.

Mom and Mariah leave the first day at the new school with hope renewed. Mariah had spontaneously initiated social contact with Mom just for fun several times. Already the repertoire of her interests had increased, and she had not spent a passive moment all morning.

Indications of Progress

Box 4 describes Mariah's IEP. By the end of the year, Mariah was able to engage in meaningful affective interactions with her parents and teachers. She could initiate interactions to make requests as well as to just have fun. Mariah has a growing repertoire of words she learned through her behavioral intervention that she was using spontaneously in interactions with her family and teachers. Her Mom reported that she was reciprocating for so many circles of communication that she had stopped counting. Both the DIR and ABA practitioners learned from each other. The DIR practitioners were more appreciative of structure and gave many choices within a reliable routine for the school day. They learned the value of shaping play and interaction for small increments of change that support the child's experience of success. The ABA practitioners came to appreciate the individual needs of the sensory system and to make adjustments to

"feed" Mariah's sensory cravings. They were taken with the power of wooing the child as part of the system of positive reinforcement and adopted a style of keeping interactions going rather than stopping them in order to provide praise or reinforcers. In addition, they played with Mariah during breaks rather than sending her off alone.

Mariah's parents are thrilled with the new positive mood of their daughter. They saw her as more connected to them, more responsive, active, and self-initiating. They felt more competent as her parents, knowing how to think about what was inhibiting her responsiveness or causing her withdrawal. As her parents, they felt they had many more strategies at hand to handle unpredictable situations as well as engineer life for smoother days and nights. They were relieved that they could now attend gatherings of their extended families or at their church with Mariah. The family could now spend pleasurable time together at home and in their community.

SUMMARY

The educational models and the three cases, in particular, illustrate the wide range of educational interventions needed in comprehensive programs in order to achieve effective outcomes just during the course of one year. As these children strengthen and expand developmental capacities, they will be able to reach the next levels, because they have been provided with foundation skills for learning. Each child will progress at different rates relative to his or her unique strengths and weaknesses but each child should keep moving forward with continued, comprehensive educational programs.

The answer to what programs do work and for whom cannot be simply answered. It has been extremely difficult to evaluate program effectiveness. In order to compare

---

Box 4. Mariah's Individual Education Plan

GOAL: Improve Mariah's interest in and capacity for reciprocal social engagement.

- *Objective:* Mariah will sustain engagement in sensorimotor interactive play with a special adult for 10-minute periods 2 times per day at school and 5 to 6 times per day at home. Mariah will show engagement:
  a. By facial expression–smiles, wide eyes, upturned mouth–and through gesture (takes adult hand, signs or motions for more, pulls adult to object of desire).
  b. By verbal expression–laughing, cooing, words–and by showing that she is reciprocally involved with the adult in an activity, such as water play, play dough, putting lotion on her skin, pulling stickers off her clothing, chase and tickle games, and variations of peek-a-boo.
  c. By her seeking out the adult, showing anticipation of the next interpersonal exchange, offering objects or herself (e.g., takes a cup to pour water, puts arm toward adult for more lotion).

- *Objective:* Facilitated by an adult, Mariah will sustain engagement with a peer "expert player" for 10-minute periods 3 times per day.
  a. Mariah will make an ongoing relationship with one peer carefully selected for his/her interest in Mariah. Mariah will show interest in interaction with the peer as with the adult (above) in activities of high interest to her, such as sensory play, music, and snacking.
  b. At snack time, Mariah can be in charge and gesture to invite her friend to the table. She can inquire if her friend wants juice and pour for her from a small pitcher with which she can succeed. Mariah can give out cookies at her friend's request.
  c. Symbolic links can be made with circle cookies that roll or mini-bagels that can be held up as eyeglasses. Snack can segue into water play by washing the snack dishes and cups, dividing up jobs such as squirting soap, making bubbles in the water, scrubbing, and drying. Such activities teach sequencing of events, fine motor skills, motor planning, and the target, reciprocal sustained engagement.

GOAL: Improve Mariah's spontaneous interpersonal communication.

- *Objective:* Use moments of high affective motivation to elicit spontaneous verbal and nonverbal circles of communication with Mariah 20 or more times per day as they occur in the natural environment or as can be elicited with nonverbal temptations.
  a. During snack time, place a favorite snack in a container that is challenging for Mariah to open so that she will need assistance (and also benefit from practice with a fine motor skill). Provide support by offering adult proximity and gestural and verbal interest, such as "Need help?" or "What do you want?"
  b. Wait for Mariah to initiate, even by pushing the container toward the adult, and keep the circles of interaction going as long as is tolerable and fun for her. For example, do not just open the container and hand it to her after one gesture. Play dumb and silly. "Oh, this, how nice, a hat?" and put the container on your head. Visual humor and silliness are usually the key to keeping her engaged without introducing disorganizing frustration.

GOAL: Improve Mariah's comprehension of interpersonal communication.

- *Objective:* Mariah will connect learning of language to meaningful experiences through an activity-based approach to learning throughout the day.
  a. Mariah will learn the intentions and meanings of verbal communications through the manipulation of objects and the consequences of her requests and actions. For example, say you are teaching the concepts of "big" and "little." Mariah wants a piece of bacon from her lunch box. The adult asks, "Do you want a big piece or a little piece?" Mariah hears "little" last and repeats "little piece," even though she really wants it all. She doesn't have the comprehension for words related to size yet and still echoes the last thing she hears. Now, the adult gives her a small piece torn off the end of the strip and says, "Here is a little piece." Mariah's disappointment is evident by the

Continued

Box 4. *Continued*

expression on her face and her gesture to reach for the rest of the bacon. The adult empathizes, "You didn't mean little piece, you want the *big* piece." After several rounds of this kind of exchange, Mariah asks consistently for the big piece, and the adults expect that she has reached a new level of understanding. This approach is carried out with various things she wants throughout the day, such as the big crayon, the little bubbles, the big paintbrush. In this way, the concepts of "big" and "little" start to take on experiential meaning.

GOAL: Improve the quality of unstructured interactions within the family.

- *Objective:* Through the family-focused center and home-based program, assist Mariah's parents in developing mutually gratifying ways of relating to Mariah that support family cohesion and pleasurable interaction.
  a. Help parents work together on Mariah's behalf and develop a shared language for understanding her difficulties.
  b. Facilitate parents' discussion of their perspectives about how to help her and how to be with her at home.
  c. Develop mutually gratifying patterns of relating that use invitation and wooing, supporting positive feeling and sustained interpersonal engagement.
  d. Assist parents in the classroom to recognize and participate in successful social activities with Mariah.
  e. Meet with parents bimonthly to share ideas about how to engage Mariah in the less structured household activities. Teachers can offer opportunities for practice in the classroom, for example, someone comes to the door and the teacher has to greet them. What can Mariah do? What does the teacher do with Mariah before she attends to the person at the door?

The above goals and objectives are designed to support the development of Mariah's spontaneous self-expression, reciprocal engagement with adults and peers, and capacity for self-initiation. They are goals designed to ameliorate the core developmental issues in autism. These interactive, relationship-based interventions should not be implemented only in a complementary fashion with discrete trial training during which the focus of the goals is on compliance and prompted discrete-trial demonstration. Rather, these instructions are essential for the generalization and spontaneous use of what is learned through behavioral reinforcement.

---

educational programs or curricula and the degree to which they contribute to individual outcomes, both child and program characteristics need to be considered. Today, children falling under the autistic spectrum umbrella have very wide variations. To know which children are being addressed requires more than matching age, IQ measures, or even symptom lists, as is frequently done in outcome studies. Instead, multidimensional profiles and functional capacities are needed to identify the children in meaningful ways, with relevant measures of primary deficits in relating and communicating at entry and outcome (Greenspan & Wieder, 1997).

In order to compare educational approaches, it is necessary to identify the various elements of the educational models as well as their various operative elements, including intensity, quality, and skill of the providers; related services; and family interactions. Research designs that could take all these variables into account do not yet exist, and existing studies on program outcomes make claims that are questionable if not misleading. Programs often select certain children for study rather than sample from different groups. The study often is based on what is easy to measure or teach without considering all the real variables that are part of the child's intervention, in addition to the educational program, including other therapies or family approaches. Such research challenges make it clear that some questions are not going to be easily answered because it is not possible to control so many variables.

The challenge of evaluating program outcomes remains daunting. Data-driven programs, such as ABA and special education approaches, have not fulfilled their expectations. To date, there is little or no large-scale evidence supporting the effectiveness of these models, although large-scale funding continues to be poured into these programs—with limited results. Children often receive additional services beyond the educational programs offered at school. In addition, within educational programs, additional interventions such as speech and occupational therapies may be added to address specific processing deficits involved in developmental disorders.

While pursuing more effective approaches and measures based on functional capacities and educational gains, standards of practice can protect individual intervention and program integrity. One problem with program outcomes is that programs distribute their resources according to criteria that do not necessarily reflect the individual needs of each child. For example, a nonverbal child with auditory processing and oral-motor difficulties may be in the same class as a child with pragmatic language issues. They both receive the same 30 minutes per week of speech-and-language therapy in a group, even though each child really needs daily individual therapy. The program may not have the personnel or funding needed to provide the appropriate services and program outcomes would mask individual results because what was needed was not provided or integrated into the group.

Using the model of clinical trials may still be useful if it starts with cases based on developmental profiles that capture the functional capacities of children as the baseline for research, with children and their individual progress clearly identified. Informative research design utilizes a theoretical model from which a hierarchy of goals are evaluated. Evaluation is based on individual, multidimensional profiles of children receiving comprehensive interventions.

Until more and better research can be conducted, it is important to evaluate outcomes based on each individual child's functioning, for whom appropriate baseline evaluations have been conducted so that each child is evaluated relative to his or her progress. The program should be evaluated on the basis of how well it fits the individual child's needs reflected by his or her rate of progress.

Educators may still be debating the core philosophical issue about whether special education is intended to find special techniques for teaching ordinary school skills, such as reading, writing, and arithmetic to children, or whether the intention is to cure or ameliorate the disability to the fullest extent possible by whatever means are effective. This comes up often with PDD and autism because the social deficit is so central. But many disagree about whether the purpose of school is just to learn or to learn and to discover how to make friends and relate to others. It is in the latter area that some goals, such as staying on task, completing work independently, or compliance, are seen as developing school-related skills by many districts.

The DIR approach does not separate goals of academic success and social success but approaches the child from the perspective of achieving both. Attempts to separate the two are unsound because the same developmental foundations are involved in both. The hierarchy leading to reading comprehension, thoughtful writing, and mastery of history, science, English, and math begins with the abilities to attend, engage with others, communicate purposefully, use symbols creatively and logically, and think. On the other hand, mastery of the essential academic and social foundations of attending, relating, communicating, and thinking opens the door to higher-level abstract thinking capacities and lifelong new learning. Without mastering these foundations, a child will be limited to fragmented, rote memory skills, such as reading without comprehension, counting without under-standing, or solving problems, communicating, and thinking in only a fragmented, scripted, and concrete manner. True comprehension of English, history, or science will not be possible.

In this chapter, DIR educational guidelines have been proposed as a comprehensive model that embraces traditional, school-related goals only when a foundation of core developmental capacities to relate socially, communicate interactively, and to think is part of the work focus. Individualized approaches are then used to keep each child moving forward.   ■

REFERENCES

Bondy, A., & Frost, L. (1994). The picture exchange communication system. *Focus on Autistic Behavior, 9,* 1-19.

Feuerstein, R., Feuerstein, R., & Schur, Y. (1997). Process as content in education of exceptional children. In A., Kozulin (Ed.), *The ontogony of cognitive modifiability.* Jerusalem: ICELP.

Greenspan, S. I., & Wieder, S. (1997). Developmental patterns and outcomes in infants and children with disorders in relating and communicating: A chart review of 200 cases of children with autism spectrum disorders. *Journal of Developmental and Learning Disorders, 1*(1), 87-141.

Greenspan, S. I., & Wieder, S. (1998). *The child with special needs: Encouraging intellectual and emotional growth.* Reading, MA: Addison Wesley Longman.

Greenspan, S. I., & Wieder, S. (1999). A functional developmental approach to autism spectrum disorders. *Journal of the Association for Persons with Severe Handicaps, 24,* 147-161.

Klein, P. (1996). Enhancing learning potential and literacy in young children. In P. Klein (Ed.), *Early intervention cross-cultural experiences with mediational approach.* New York: Garland.

Koegel, L. K., Koegel, R. L., Harrower, J. K., & Carter, C. M. (1999). Pivotal response intervention I: Overview of approach. *Journal of the Association for Persons with Severe Handicaps, 24,* 174-185.

Lovaas, O. I. (1987). Behavioral treatment and normal educational and intellectual functioning in young autistic children. *Journal of Consulting and Clinical Psychology, 55*(1), 3-9.

Maurice, C., Green, G., & Luce, S. C. (Eds.) (1996). *Behavioral intervention for young children with autism: A manual for parents and professionals.* Austin, TX: PRO-ED.

Miller, A., & Miller, E. (1992). A new way with autistic and other children with pervasive developmental disorder. Boston, MA: Language and Cognitive Center.

Rogers, S. (1996). Brief report: Early intervention in autism. *Journal of Autism and Developmental Disorders, 26,* 243-246.

Schopler, E. (1997). Implementation of TEACCH philosophy. In D. J. Cohen & F. R. Volkmar (Eds.), *Handbook of autism and pervasive developmental disorders* (2nd ed.) (pp. 920-933). New York: Wiley and Sons.

Schreibman, L. (1997). Theoretical perspectives on behavioral intervention for individuals with autism. In D. J. Cohen, & F. R. Volkmar (Eds.), *Handbook of autism and pervasive developmental disorders* (2nd ed.) (pp. 920-933). New York: Wiley and Sons.

◄ 14 ►

The Action is in the Interaction: Clinical Practice Guidelines for Work with Parents of Children with Developmental Disorders[i, ii]

Rebecca Shahmoon-Shanok, M.S.W., Ph.D.[iii]

What is good for parents is good for their children. What is good for their children is good for parents. Aiming for both stimulates good outcomes. The invisible but powerful thread is relationship.

PARENTS AS "CENTRAL ORGANIZERS" FOR THEIR CHILD

All children need parents to keep them safe, to notice and respond to their needs and achievements and—gradually and over time—to bring them into the human community through interactive relationships, which include love, shared attention, evolving communication, and the burgeoning of symbols, of narrative, and of values. Indeed, the primary social institution responsible for children is their family, with their parents in the lead and at the heart. Families render humans human. Recent research and clinical experience demonstrate that such primary reciprocal attachments support, mediate, modify, and organize a child's genetic, central nervous system endowment to a far more significant degree than previously understood in areas as fundamental to later adaptation and achievement as cognitive and emotional intelligence, language, personality, and relational style (cf. Ainsworth et al., 1978; Greenspan, 1997;

Schore, 1994; Siegel, 1999; Sroufe, 1983). It is, therefore, in society's best interests that parents function optimally—or at least satisfactorily—during their children's developing years.

Children spend many, many hours in the context of their family life. Those with relational and communicative challenges have a harder time than typically developing youngsters in engaging others constructively, even within their own families. Their parents also are often at a loss in knowing how to constructively fill their children's time and get them through simple daily requirements. Parents may resort to television and videotapes to help their children get through the day, rationalizing that they are at least learning something when memorizing bits of scripts or songs. Parents may give up when their children engage in perseverative or self-stimulating behavior.

As Stanley Greenspan (this volume) has noted, most parents are happier, more productive, less stressed, and more apt to view themselves as competent, resourceful parents, able to meet their child's needs when they can involve their child—by themselves and/or through others—in a rich, interactive, home-based program. "In fact, these interactions at home can become the most important factor in (children's) growth" (Greenspan & Wieder, Chapter 12, this volume). This same observation holds true for parents! To become—and feel like—a capable parent, an individual finally *needs* to interact productively with her child.

And just as parents of typically developing children are their first and most profoundly effective teachers, parents of children with developmental, communicative, and relational disorders are as well. As pediatrician and psychoanalyst D.W. Winnicott quipped decades ago, "There's no such a thing as a baby," by which he meant that it is nonsense to consider the development of a young child outside the context of the adults who surround him night and day. A parent (or two) is, quite literally, the center of the child's emotional, social, and learning world. This happens spontaneously during everyday playtimes, feedings, bathtimes, and bedtimes (Shahmoon-Shanok, 1997b). Although the needs of these children may be masked by their avoidance of human contact, young children with serious relational and communicative challenges urgently require meaningful interactions with their parents. Paradoxically, their challenges prevent them from making their needs—and how to respond to those needs—known to parents.

When a child has severe difficulties relating and communicating, these obstacles affect not only the child's development. They also bear upon the parent's sense of self *and* the *relationship* between the child and his parents. Children with developmental disorders are compromised not only because of *constitutional* challenges but also because of

relational challenges (which usually stem from constitutional challenges and ensuing mismatches). Clinical or educational practice that addresses only the child's symptoms and behavior, rather than the underlying processes, must be revised to address the *context;* that is, mutual regulatory processes with intimate caregivers. Every element in a system reverberates—or not—with the others; when one element is stuck, it constrains the others (Sameroff & Friese, 1990; Shanok, 1981, 1987, 1990). As evidence mounts that children with difficult temperaments are more vulnerable to and modifiable by parental influences (Thompson, 1999), it becomes more evidently critical that the field of early intervention integrate a range of services to help parents cultivate growth-promoting relationships between themselves and their children. Therefore, working with the individual needs of parents is crucial to treating their children.

Special Challenges for Parents of Children with Special Needs

Children with special profiles have a profound, ongoing reliance on their parents as primary loved ones, as intermediaries, and as advocates. Yet, to be able to meet the particular needs of a child with a developmental disorder, parents must meet the following six profound challenges, which go well beyond the usual, already heavy demands of parenting young children.

1. *Parents must come to recognize the precipitous risks of their child's disability,* even as they cope with deep feelings of disbelief, loss, grief, confusion, isolation, helplessness, fear for the future, and "why me" anger.

2. *Parents must overcome the sense of mystification, distance, and rejection* inherent in their child's idiosyncratic,

Chapter 14. The Action is in the Interaction: Clinical practice Guidelines for
Work with Parents of Children with Developmental Disorders

335

perseverative, and impoverished range of behaviors and interactions.

3. Instead, *parents must learn to notice, observe, and read their child's odd and frustrating behaviors as individual differences*—meaningful signals explained by specific sensory processing and perceptual-motor capacities and challenges—in order to cross the bridge their child cannot yet cross, to meet and draw the child over and into interactive relationships.

4. *Parents need to recognize themselves as the central, organizing, and contingent force on behalf of their child*, even within the professional context of various assessments and interventions.

5. *Parents must recognize, welcome, and respond contingently to their child's increasingly complex functional communicative, cognitive, and emotional levels* (Greenspan & Wieder, 1998)—a complex challenge with children who tend to pull for sameness. For parents, this means recognizing that just when they become accustomed to dealing with one level, they must shift to another to keep up with and/or to stimulate their child's incipient growth.

6. *Parents must become knowledgeable, effective, and engaged advocates for their child* within a complex and grossly uneven maze of assessments and services.

In order to overcome these challenges, virtually all parents of children with a developmental disorder need facilitating partnerships with the professionals who serve their children. They may be so uncertain that they can generatively parent this child that they may need help to discern that their child favors them above others and that *they* have the central role to play in his improvement. Given facilitative partnership, some—perhaps even many—parents are able to meet at least the majority of these challenges.

However, the range of individual differences is as great among parents as among their children. With personally tailored supports, many more parents could become the significant resource that their children need them to be. When it is noted that, on the one hand, early parenthood is itself a time of enormous vulnerability, transition, and potential growth, and, on the other hand, that no professional, no matter how deeply committed or involved, can substitute for the profound impact parents have on their child, the magnitude of significance—and of potential—to parental inclusion may be grasped.

With the 1996 passage by the United States Congress of the Individual with Disabilities Education Act (IDEA), the field of treatment for children with disabilities took a significant step in the direction of parents by mandating the Individualized Family Service Plan (IFSP). However, the field has not yet focused on how to engage and respond to the enormous range of parents, nor has it attended to the differentiated, comprehensive spectrum of services and education needed to support not only parents but the staff who potentially could work with them.

Consequently, some professionals who work with challenging young children still conceive of *themselves* as the central rehabilitative agent for the child, even though it is *parents* who are their children's first, most significant, and life-long teachers. The contribution of parents is underscored by a quantitative analysis of early intervention programs serving disabled children and their families that found that "programs that ... targeted their efforts on *parents and children together* appeared to be the most effective" (Shonkoff and Hauser-Dram, 1987, p. 650, italics added). When the early intervention field recognizes that, for children with difficulties in relating and communicating, it is not only the child who needs assistance but, by definition, also the relationship between parents and child that must be supported, the focus of treatment becomes liberated. Clinicians may then see that the needs of parents and children are felicitously intermeshed in that parents need—and children need their parents—to reclaim their role as fundamental teachers. The less experienced or mature the parents and the younger or more challenged the child, the more attention this area will require. But all parents benefit from a developmentally sensitive alliance for how to "read" their child so that their child may become engaged with them.

Just as the recognition of each child's unique needs is placed in a developmental-relational understanding of typical childhood, so, too, must the understanding of each parent's needs be placed within an understanding of adulthood. The next section, "Parenthood and Parenting as a Marker of Adult Development," briefly describes the nature of adulthood and the developmental-relational facets of parenthood within that context. The chapter then goes on to address the following major topics:

- Parents and professionals as complementary, reciprocal, yet asymmetrical partners.
- Evaluating and working with a child conveys meaning to parents.
- Establishing and maintaining relationships with a range of parents.
- Developmentally appropriate practices and interactions: Using the concepts of relationship, individual differences, and development to understand parents, organize information, and intervene generatively.

PARENTHOOD AND PARENTING AS A MARKER OF ADULT DEVELOPMENT

Although development continues to occur in the adult years, it is different from development occurring in childhood. In contrast to the burgeoning maturational forces of childhood and adolescence and to the decline of late life, adulthood is freer of an age-related timetable. Parenthood may begin anywhere within a period of 35 or more years for women and an even longer span for men. Rather than the sequential emphasis that typifies the unfolding earlier life stages, adulthood is instead characterized by increased layering and complexity among aspects of the self and between the self and the social world (Seligman & Shanok, 1996, 1995a, 1995b; Shanok, 1981, 1987, 1990, 1993). Context is a critical thread in this rich fabric. Picture, for instance, parenting a baby dearly desired following several miscarriages in contrast with parenting a baby conceived in error.

Yet, whereas parenthood is intrinsic to a mother's development as a woman and a father's as a man, it is only one among several other marker processes, all of which affect the capacities for identity and intimacy in that person. Nonetheless, parenthood does *mark* adult development. But, although it is interconnected in a cogwheeled manner to the child's development, parenthood is not *itself* a developmental stage for the adult (cf. Benedek, 1959; Galinsky, 1981). Imagine, for example, how different an experience it is to become a parent at age 15 compared with becoming one at 45.

Visualize the daily care a small child requires: Parent*hood* is a role, a career, a defining activity. Parent*ing* is an intimate, evolving, and demanding relationship of enduring impact. Parent*hood* profoundly affects the experience of, and structures for, identity. Parent*ing* influences the capacities for and evolution of intimacy processes (Shanok, 1987, 1990, 1993). People become parents through experience, by "doing and being" (Musik, 1993).

It is in the nature of parenthood that, especially when a child is young, the parent's

sense of well-being is inextricably tied not
only to how she judges her child to be faring
(cf. Galinsky, 1981; Shanok, 1987, 1990,
1993; Stern, 1995) but also to how she judges
herself to be doing as that particular child's
parent. Parents *need* to feel that they are
ample resources for understanding and caring
for their young child. Indeed, there is likely
no greater wound to a parent's fledgling sense
of competence as a parent, and of relatedness
as *this* child's parent, than to see and feel the
child losing developmental ground and turning away from their relationship, all the while
not knowing how to help him.

As a marker process, becoming a parent
is, by definition, a long transitional period of
great openness and, thus, of both potential
and vulnerability. What new mother doesn't
recall being deeply upset, angry, or both by
an ill-chosen remark from a stranger about
her child? When that new mother *knows*
there is something wrong with her child, and
the stranger is a professional whom she
believes understands far more about such
topics than she does, the power to support or
to undermine confidence and functioning is
greatly intensified.

Thus, it is with abiding awareness of the
power to potentiate or disequilibriate that any
professional who evaluates or intervenes with
a child must work. Indeed, it is not sufficient
to evaluate and/or to treat a *child*. Concurrently, care and attention to the emotional
state and attitudes, the resources, and the
dilemmas of the adults responsible for that
child are also required. When parents are able
to function resourcefully and effectively with
and on behalf of their child with special needs,
that caring, careful professional attention can
remain informal and in the background, at
least until the first components of the child's
program—which should always include parents as much as is feasible—are underway.

Still, professionals need to bear in mind
that the fact of having a young child with
special needs forces parents to cede some of
their rightful centrality to virtual strangers.
Parents become caught in a paradox: Their
autonomy and authority is eroded while their
child's particular challenges heighten and
lengthen his dependency upon them.
Supporting a dawning sense of satisfying
centrality within parents is a critical, if often
poorly understood, piece of the clinician's
role *on behalf of the children*, parents, and
families they serve. Bearing in mind that the
parents' sense of self and capacities for relationship are being *marked* by the overall
experience of parenting this child, and that
these, in turn, profoundly affect the moment-
to-moment availability of parents to the child,
the professional must respect the parents'
central roles and help them build on the
child's strengths.

To illustrate how a child with developmental challenges may affect not only a parent's identity as a parent but also that person's
very capacity *to* parent that child, consider
the following case vignette. It has been
selected to highlight the importance of working *within* the relational interface between
parent and child—for the sake of the parent
and on behalf of the child.

"Working with Ezekiel's family was difficult both because this child was hard to
understand and because his parents (Phil and
Roz), and especially the father, found it very
hard to accept how reactive Ezekiel was to a
range of stimuli. Early in my work with the
family, the father, an outwardly jolly and confident fellow, began to relax enough to find
words to reveal that he felt rejected by
Ezekiel every day. I asked Phil to describe the
scenes in detail, as though they were a movie
which I could not see. What would happen
routinely, I gathered, was that Ezekiel and his
mother would usually be together in his room

at the time that Phil, a big bear of a guy, would arrive home from work. Eager to see his family, he would burst in with 'Hullo's' and 'How are ya's?' He would frequently bring a big gift in a (noisy) bag. Ezekiel would resolutely avoid looking in his father's direction. Phil believed that Zeke was not ready to give up cozy time with Roz, and that, in fact, he *preferred* mom. This hurt Phil, who tended to give up trying to make contact with his son for the rest of the evening. 'I'm not important to Zeke,' he would surmise. 'Roz can do it better. I'll (*turn off the pain by*) watch(*ing*) TV.'

Because the early intervention program Ezekiel had been attending had not offered Phil and Roz details about their son's processing and sensory system in ways they could comprehend and identify with, Phil found it difficult to believe that Zeke's behavior could represent his effort to cope with too much stimulation coming at him at once. It was also quite painful to Phil to imagine that Ezekiel had unique sensitivities. Insulting as it was to believe that Zeke preferred his mother, given his own demanding father, that was easier for Phil to bear than to recognize the vulnerability of his boy.

I proposed to Phil and Roz that Phil try this approach for a week: He would bring nothing into the room when he arrived home and, in fact, he would himself linger very quietly in the doorway. Only once Ezekiel appeared to register his father's presence, could Poppa gently smile and wave—no big, fast movements, no sounds. 'Let the first move for further contact come from Zeke,' I suggested, to give Phil a visible benchmark before taking another action.

Although he was doubtful, Phil agreed to try this approach. Even I was surprised at how well and how quickly the strategy worked. On the first evening, Phil silently leaned in the doorway for about one full minute, he told me later. Ezekiel looked up, looked away momentarily, looked up again, looked away, a hint of a smile beginning to tug at one corner of his lips. With his head still averted, he murmured in a low voice, 'Pop,' and smiled slightly. Utilizing enormous restraint, Phil remained where he was, quietly beginning to beam. His wish then came true: Ezekiel gazed at him, looked away, got up, sidled haltingly over to Phil and, at last, hugged his legs. This experience with his child contributed to a turning point in Phil's relationship with Zeke, in my relationship and work with Phil, and in Roz's sense that she could count on her husband as a father. Phil was so happy to garner his son's attention, he became better able to consider and be sympathetic to Zeke's sensory profile (Shahmoon-Shanok, 1997b)."

Relationships hold the potential to help people grow and change. By reinterpreting the reasons for Zeke's behavior and suggesting an alternative approach to try, the therapist enabled Phil and Zeke to have an interaction far more satisfying for both of them. Such experiences add up over time to mark each individual involved.

A central tenet of this chapter is that all children, and especially those with severe difficulties in relating and communicating, actually become differentiated socially, emotionally, and cognitively in everyday, ongoing, nuanced interaction with their parent(s). Another central point is that, with their children's special needs as profound inspiration, parents' relationships with professionals can similarly have a deep effect on their own growth as parents, as adults, as a couple, and on their abilities to affect and help their children. As parents begin to believe that they can relate to their child and help him unfold, wholesome developmental forces are unlocked, liberated to energize all that comes next. People find out who they are in their

Chapter 14. The Action is in the Interaction: Clinical Practice Guidelines for
Work with Parents of Children with Developmental Disorders

339

every day, every hour experiences with each other. When Phil found that Zeke would welcome him if only his son was not overwhelmed, Phil was learning that he could provide what was needed, and that he was ample as a father. He could then bounce back to be with his highly sensitive son and Roz could feel partnered. Just as children come to know who they are by their hour-by-hour experience with others so, too, do their parents. As has been said, the action is in the interaction.

PARENTS AND PROFESSIONALS AS PARTNERS

In designating the IFSP as a requirement, Congress pushed the field of early intervention into taking a significant step forward by recognizing parents as significant partners. What the legislation did not do, however, was to address the *nature* of this "partnership." In fact, parents and professionals each bring something quite different to the association. Although parents and professionals are complementary and reciprocal partners, they are not identical helpmates. The next three sub-sections explore the complexity of this relationship.

An Asymmetrical Balance

It is probably not surprising that so much anxiety often surrounds individualized family service planning. Embedded in the requirement for IFSPs lurks a set of unacknowledged and somewhat unrealistic factors confounding parents and professionals at this point in time. These factors are interrelated. The first is that parents and professionals are equal—they are not. The "we-are-equal" stance ignores the tensions built into any relationship between people whose perspectives, roles, and power differ greatly, even when they are working toward a common goal. The second confounding factor is that the professionals in this field

come from many different professional traditions and orientations, with differing views and levels of preparation for work with parents. The third confounder flows from the silent expectation that all parent/professional partnerships should be identical; that is, professionals should work with all parents in similar ways.

These factors ignore the fact that the range of parents who have a child with regulatory, communication, and/or relationship challenges is as diverse as any "group" could be. Actually, they are not a group at all, but rather individuals or couples with greatly varying circumstances, capacities, and even children. Yet many disciplines have little or no training that focuses on work with parents in general, let alone on recognizing their differences and individualizing the work. Other disciplines emphasize some aspects of parent work (such as psychotherapy) at the expense of others (such as home-based intervention or learning how to play resourcefully with their challenging child). Many programs offer little or no in-service training to support their staff in this critical area. It is not surprising, then, that many professionals report "flying by the seat of their pants" and feeling deeply awkward about the manifest expectation for "partnership" dictated by IFSPs. In this, they sense at the outset that it is not possible to partner everyone the same way, and that it is overly simplistic to "partner" people who may also see themselves as stakeholders, consumers, advocates, or clients.

Mental health professionals may know more than others about how to navigate through the levels and complexities of "many hat" work with adults. Yet individual parents and family advocates are sometimes wary of this group of professionals. They are concerned that these practitioners are likely to treat parents of children with challenges as though the *parents* have an emotional or mental disorder. They maintain, quite rightly, that having a child with a disability does not imply that the parents, or the family, is compromised.

Still, it is clear that any family whose child has severe difficulties in relating and communicating is living with significant stressors, perhaps particularly when they are in the process of discovery and decision making. Beyond that, there are many circumstances in family life, such as the birth of a baby, a move from one home to another, or parental unemployment, that must be considered and thoughtfully factored into the ways of working with that family. Marital strains are common in families with young children and are more likely when a child has unusual difficulties. Enduring factors, such as parents' personalities and their relationships with their families of origin, also need to be considered in order for intervention to be appropriately subtle, rich, and responsive (see Box 1, shown later in this chapter). Just as recognizing individual differences among children improves intervention, appreciating the individual differences among parents also immeasurably enriches clinical work. IFSPs should be just that: Individualized—and responsive to the *parents'* needs, strengths, challenges, *and* preferences, not just to their child's.

Shifting Leadership

Parents sometimes feel that professionals hold all the power while, paradoxically, professionals often feel the converse. In our society, ultimate responsibility for child-rearing decisions rests with parents.

Still, parents of children with challenges often rely on professionals when making nitty-gritty decisions and in developing day-to-day care. When trust develops, power is shared—a relief to both sides. It is useful to recognize the shifting nature of leadership in robust, trusting parent-professional partnerships. Sometimes parents are in the lead, as when

they decide to select a program, take their child out of a treatment program for a vacation, or hire an auxiliary practitioner. Sometimes, the professional is (temporarily) in the lead, as when she coaches parents in play skills, helps them set limits with their child, assists with a referral to a new therapist or program, or uses her general knowledge of development as a framework for helping the parents know what is realistic to expect from any young child. For example, first-time parents whose child has severe difficulties in relating and communicating may be relieved to learn that some of their child's challenging behavior is "normal." The professional might offer guidance in setting limits when a toddler is tired, saying, "No child Benny's age could be expected to stop by himself. All young children need help pulling away from activities, especially when they are wound up. One boy I know simmers down when you pick him up decisively but soothingly. How about trying that with Ben when he gets overtired?" Professionals (and parents) can learn to lead and follow, follow and lead.

Most professionals regard the care of a child as a precious trust. They base their recommendations on deep emotional concern for the child's wellbeing as well as on observations and overall experience. They may become especially aware of their feelings when they find themselves in disagreement with parents about the care of the child.

Embracing the perspective of each parent while also recognizing her own, the reflective practitioner can usually facilitate the making of rich, nuanced decisions by consensus. In the case of a hyperactive, driven boy, for instance, suppose that one parent wants to try dietary alterations, the other thinks applied behavioral analysis (ABA) would be best, while the therapist, based on her experiences with other, similar children, is convinced that the child would improve with medication.

Chapter 14. The Action is in the Interaction: Clinical Practice Guidelines for
Work with Parents of Children with Developmental Disorders

341

Thoughtful discussions with each participant respecting the other's perspective, could yield a prioritized plan, one that would systematically and quickly get further information about each option while also beginning a trial of the safest, least invasive alternative first, all with the goal of identifying the best fit for the particular child at this time.

The professional's role as a partner with parents is best attained by:

- *Realizing that it is the professional who sets the tone for collaboration*, especially at the beginning.
- *Meeting parents with respect.*
- *Welcoming parents into the program* and encouraging them to participate in decisions about their children's care (Bredekamp and Copple, 1997).
- *Establishing frequent, open, yet tactful and supportive, two-way communication with parents.*
- *Studying and understanding the parent's own personality, historical and current context and developmental factors* (discussed later in this chapter).
- *Offering an individualized program to parents*, based on their particular needs.
- *Seeing the parent-child and parent-therapist relationship as units of observation, assessment, and intervention.*
- *Becoming self-aware by recognizing and taking responsibility for their own emotions and predilections.*
- *Discovering flexibility and responsivity in the relationships with parents and child* at both staff and programmatic levels.
- *Holding mixed identifications or "co-identifications"* with *both* child and parent(s).
- *Recognizing the power of parallel process* (that is, for example, realizing that to join parents and support *their* intent almost always strengthens the parents' ability to do the same for their child).

- *Noticing implicit parental concerns and clarifying the scope and agenda of the work together so that it may shift and deepen over time.*
- *Openly negotiating differences of opinion*, using clear guidelines to agree about setting priorities, and making decisions about what to try first, next, and so forth.

When professionals can meet these challenges, they will very rarely, if ever, feel thwarted by parents. Parental "resistance" is bypassed when therapists stay with, and build shared attention around, the parents' intent. The result builds an alliance through which an open, collaborative learning process moves the parent, the practitioner, and the team forward.

Teamwork

Teamwork is a critical, if grossly underestimated, element of service from the point of view of the child's integration. Some programs function as though a team is automatically a team because it is made up of people who are assigned to the same case. Parents, however, may find themselves caught between appointments and competing priorities, often carrying the burden of ferrying messages back and forth between practitioners. In some home-based programs, practitioners have never even met each other. Growth-promoting team development does not just happen—it requires attention and cultivation. Before several practitioners, each of whom comes from another professional tradition, join cooperatively together as a *team* with deeply understood, shared goals for particular children and families, they must:

- Have regularly occurring times to talk.
- Describe, view videotapes or watch each other's practice, then think and talk together some more.

- Become dedicated to cross-fertilization and collaborative learning, building insight and generic knowledge from each discipline's perspective.
- Become ready to utilize observation and knowledge coming from another perspective within their *own* work with child and family.

Other purposes of team meetings include:
- Supporting parents as they plan, distinguish between, select, and advocate for various approaches and programs.
- Individualizing work with parents and getting clear on roles vis-a-vis parents.
- Promoting integration of parent and child work.
- Collaborating on timing: The team should help to answer "When do you do what, and how do you decide?"
- Quickly studying what is occurring and intervening deliberately when a child plateaus or begins to lose ground.
- To share what does and does not work with the child and family in an effort to speed the child's learning curve and foster progress.
- Shifting practice as the child improves, amplifying alternative approaches, or finishing up one approach/modality or another and moving on.

Center-based programs lend themselves most easily to collaboration because everyone working with a child and family is in one place and knows each other. But whether the treatment is center-based, home-based, practitioner's office-based, or some mixture of these elements, frequent 1- to 2-hour meeting times are key to practitioners becoming a team. Furthermore, only a rich, multifaceted approach based on birth-to-three developmental knowledge and staffing patterns will serve the variety and complexity of families

and children who seek early intervention services for young and older children with special needs. An interdisciplinary group of birth-to-three leaders working closely together over time to identify best practices across disciplines identified four requisites to acceptable practice: (1) a framework of concepts common to all disciplines, (2) ongoing observation, (3) reflective supervision, and (4) collegiality (Fenichel & Eggbeer, 1990). These considerations, carried through with respect, allow difficult concerns to emerge and receive the best of shared thinking.

Teams and Parents

Teams should include parents if they want to be involved. However, parents are not simply another discipline on a team, similar to an occupational therapist or a social worker. They were neither trained for their job nor did they ask for this type of assignment. Yet parents, by definition, have the most at stake. For them, this is a lifetime commitment, a life-long endeavor grounded in their love for their child and their dreams for their family. Furthermore, because what happens to their child in his relationship with them and in their home are, in critical ways, the most significant elements of any treatment approach, shared consideration of their participation in the team's work must be active and ongoing. It may shift, ebb, and flow depending on circumstances, their propensities and personalities, and team needs. The critical element is that their participation is discussed periodically in an atmosphere of open communication.

This can get sticky for practitioners when they need to work through disagreements with each other or when they feel the need to discuss the parents themselves and their own reactions to them. Practitioners realize that parents may be partners, but they are not

Chapter 14. The Action is in the Interaction: Clinical Practice Guidelines for
Work with Parents of Children with Developmental Disorders

343

exactly colleagues. In fact, parents are *both* partners and, to varying degrees, clients, at least in the sense that what they had been doing for their particular child was not all that he needed. Sometimes, other jointly identified purposes may emerge for which the parent wants or needs assistance. But whatever the needs and strengths of parents, they are the experts on the history, minutiae, and emotional flavor that make up their child's day-to-day life. Their critical role and knowledge of their child cannot be overexaggerated; they are the experts in areas at least as salient as any that the professionals represent. When treated with abiding respect and empathy, most parents accept—even welcome—that the team will sometimes meet without them present, particularly when they feel secure that private aspects of their own lives and histories will not be shared and that they will hear the highlights of the team's deliberations and have ample opportunities to integrate their views.

In any case, parents should have regular and frequent access to all the interventionists who work with their child. But they also need an integrative, overarching person for themselves, someone with whom to build a more intimate relationship over time, for the purposes of working with and through their emotions about the specific interactive capacities needed to best reach their child. They need this

- for their child,
- for their own identity development as parents, and
- for the *relationship* with their child and with other key people in their lives, relationships that may be buffeted by the stresses and demands of the child and his special needs.

Often, this special professional for parents becomes the team leader, the convener, and the central organizer of all the people who work with the child, the person who helps everyone concentrate on the particular profile of the child in the context of his parents' developmental and relational capacities. Since home activity and relationship-building is a critical, though sometimes neglected, aspect of the child's treatment, this person is the one who helps the parents and the professional team organize and carry through a rich, home-based program no matter what center-based services he receives, no matter the age of the child.

The following example demonstrates what can begin to happen in terms of team development when practitioners working with the same child begin to meet together, facilitated by a leader who tries to think across disciplines.

Dale Shipley (age 4) was just turning 21 months old when his parents sought a Developmental, Individual Difference, Relationship-based (DIR) mental health consultation.[iv] He was a sweet, low-tone child, who was just beginning to walk and say single words. Born 7 weeks premature and at a low birth weight, Dale was identified for early intervention during follow-up when he was 7 months old because he was not progessing adequately. He had been receiving an intensive, mostly home-based program since then. Greg and Gail, his parents, are serious-minded, devoted parents who have focused their efforts on constructing a full program for him. They struggled with feelings of depression and guilt.

Gail and Greg were particularly concerned about Dale's apparent lack of curiosity; he did not investigate by taking things out of drawers or closet floors, for example. They also questioned about how to set limits, because Dale sometimes hit them when they restricted him or, more often, just limply acquiesced. A question emerged following the DIR therapist's observational home visit about moving Dale out of W-sitting, as the parents had been instructed to do by his occupational and physical therapists (OT and PT), without discussion of alternatives. However, as soon as Dale legs were moved, his play was disrupted because poor pelvic control compromised the use of his upper body.

The Shipley's also felt unsure about how to play with him, were upset at being asked to leave his intervention sessions more often than before, and raised questions about one physical therapist, who insisted that Dale be held in place as she worked on his lower trunk and legs. Indeed, the parents had argued painfully with each other over this latter practice. They had taken him to a physical therapy session together, and the therapist asked that they hold Dale in place while she worked on his legs. Dale objected, but the father held fast despite his crying. The mother, who had endured many medical procedures herself as a child, felt frantic watching this and finally demanded that they stop, which they did. She was furious with her husband for having gone along with the therapist. In retrospect, he also felt badly about the incident and had questions about the therapist's approach.

Although some of the professionals had been working with Dale for just over a year, no meeting between them had yet been held. The first team meeting—organized by Gail and held at the DIR psychotherapist's suggestion—began with each practitioner describing what he or she was doing with Dale. Many questions coming from a general developmental, relational perspective were raised by the DIR therapist about what was being said. As the meeting progressed, discussion became increasingly animated and elaborated. This was a good sign, the first step toward building a team.

One topic of concern to all was Dale's attention span. His attention to one activity usually lasted for only 1 or 2 minutes, and his play often consisted of taking out each item in a box, holding it up for the adult to label, and then with an "aw-ga" ("all gone"), putting everything back in the box, shutting it, and putting it away. Given the fact that Dale tended to be distractible, several of the therapists mentioned that they were asking him to put each thing away before going on to the next activity. What had not been thought about prior to the meeting was the fact that Dale was not going far enough with the playthings that he did use. Although putting toys away before going on to the next thing might reduce his distractibility, there might be other approaches that could accomplish the same objective, such as having a more affectively lively interchange about whatever he played with or did. Furthermore, putting one thing away before taking out another would seem to constrict Dale's chances to discover that islands of interest could be linked one to another. For example, if the people figures were put away before the blocks were taken out, then the idea that he could use people figures *with* blocks by, for example, using a block as a bed, would be less likely to occur to him later down the developmental line.

The goal of this first meeting was to facilitate a good discussion, such as that just described. Talk that gets questions of concern onto the table and engages everyone reflectively begins to build knowledge about each other's thinking and, eventually, trust. There was so much to talk about that everyone agreed to meet again in 3 weeks, although some team members had been reluctant to put aside the time to meet the first time. The newly forming team also thought it was important to raise the possibility with Greg and Gail of meeting occasionally without them so that the practitioners could openly discuss their views about parental presence in Dale's sessions. They agreed that the notes taken by the DIR therapist on questions

Chapter 14. The Action is in the Interaction: Clinical Practice Guidelines for
Work with Parents of Children with Developmental Disorders

345

raised (Figure 1) would be distributed at the next meeting for further discussion, and additional questions could be integrated later on as well. The ability to accept and tolerate a certain tension inherent in different viewpoints emerging is key to teambuilding.

A constituency in the field of disabilities believes that professional *training* should be available to parents. Having parents as active participants in their child's treatment is, in fact, an apprenticeship of sorts. Some parents find their calling in the process and may flourish as advocates, support group leaders or, if they already work in an allied field such as speech/language, pediatrics or psychology, may turn their practice toward early intervention work. For them, their passionate, new sub-specialty becomes a gift of enhanced meaning and commitment given to them by their child. Parents should certainly be invited and encouraged to read widely, to attend conferences, courses, and even training programs, if they wish. Yet care needs to be taken not to press parents to do things that demoralize them or are simply too much. The most essential element of staff training is case discussion. Similarly, regular and frequent discussion of their child, their interactions with him, and their sense of their own participation is the crucial element of work with parents, always in the context of their own capacities, inclinations, and needs.

CHILD ASSESSMENT AND INTERVENTION CONVEYS MEANING TO PARENTS

Parents bring their child to a professional for expert advice. The professional's demeanor, words, and emphasis have a huge impact on how they feel and what they will do with and for their child. *The assessment of a child is always an intervention for his parents.* How parents come to define what is hindering the appropriate unfolding

of their child's development has great impact upon how they handle him and how they feel when they interact with him. In turn, these qualitative differences in parents' behavior and emotions influence how their child responds. This is true even for children who are very difficult to engage. Therefore, *how parents understand their child's problem is crucial* to the eventual outcome. Once parents understand their child's particular profile and absorb more about how to reach him, they can once again regain their rightful and powerful position as the central organizing agents on his behalf. Reaching this goal is so critical that it is essential to recognize their own and their child's strengths, even while acknowledging the work that lies ahead for everyone.

However, the initial contacts that most parents have with early intervention personnel are centered on an evaluation of the *child*. Often, in the process, parents (and child) encounter several specialists who offer little feedback, instead of seeing one thoughtful professional who establishes a relationship with them, who guides them through a process that concentrates on expeditiously bringing assistance to their child, and who reaches out to *them* with interest, increasing specificity, clarity, and support.

Establishing Eligibility Within a Mandated Time Period vs. an Integrated Evaluation

Professionals need to bear in mind that establishing eligibility for early intervention services is not the same thing as conducting a complete, integrated evaluation. In many jurisdictions, a child's development must be shown to be below certain norms before the child can qualify for services. As a result, securing the services that a child needs may involve emphasizing his deficiencies. It is crucial to help parents understand this so that the assessment

Figure 1. Notes of Questions Raised at an Actual Team Meeting about a Child with a Mild Regulatory Disorder, Low Tone, and Delayed Motor and Language Development

---

Team Meeting #1: Dale Shipley   **Date:**
                                                                     Age: 23 months

Present: Greg and Gail Shipley (parents); Jill Roth (PT); Melanie Allen (OT); Michelle Carr (OT); Jill
                 Toniada (speech); Barbara Andrus (speech); Rebecca Shahmoon-Shanok (DIR psychothera-
                 pist for parents and child)

Absent: Tina Henderson (PT)

The following major questions were raised during the course of each practitioner's description of her work with Dale:

1. How do each of us learn to integrate aspects of what the others are doing in our own work with Dale such that the demand for integration doesn't fall to him and, secondarily, to his parents?

2. How can we really share what we're doing with him, beyond the general/specific descriptions that each practitioner offers (e.g., observation of each other's work or videotapes)?

3. How can we come to recognize Dale's usual day-to-day capacities, as well as the fleetingly glimpsed next level capacities across developmental lines, so that we can set up his human and physical environment in such a way that he can more readily practice those dawning capacities and come to know himself as that capable person?

4. How can we assist Gail and Greg to really know and practice the approaches and capacities that each therapist offers Dale so that Dale will have as full a home program as possible with the people who are closest to him?

5. How can we work with him best, maximizing his intent (and supporting appropriate social-emotional development), when we recognize that his intent may include, for example, seeking his mother (who is asked to leave) during a particular session?

6. How can we help Dale go deeper and elaborate his play sequences to promote richer and more nuanced discovery, and, gradually, representational play?

7. How can we help Dale attend for longer periods and link islands of interest, one to another?

8. A question was briefly raised about how Dale can support himself to do an activity when he is taken out of or is requested to move from W-sitting. (When requested, Dale usually does straighten out his legs.) Reference was made to his doing activities while kneeling, standing, or sitting on a small chair at table position. There was also an allusion to some sort of back or prop to help position him when he's sitting on the floor, but we didn't get to a clear recommendation yet.

The decision was made to meet again in 3 weeks and that, in the meantime, each of us will try to video-tape parts of sessions in order to facilitate our cross-sharing.

Reflections: Questions and thoughts and plans that came to me after the meeting to be discussed with the team:

1. Does Dale cross midline and what can we do to help him develop and hone those capacities?

2. Following Gail's description of Dale watching/studying children going down the slide in the park and his

Continued

Chapter 14. The Action is in the Interaction: Clinical Practice Guidelines for
Work with Parents of Children with Developmental Disorders

347

Figure 1. *Continued*

ability to then copy them and go down the slide, like them, on his stomach and feet first, the question occurs: "What sensorimotor acts does Dale need to *see* in order to maximize his capacities?" (i.e., it seems like his motor planning is a strength). Bearing in mind that we want to develop *his* intent in this area, not his opposition, how can we take advantage of this developmental capacity?

3. As I contemplated the discussions of the meeting, it dawned on me that, while the OT's and PT's were focused on motor function, perhaps one of the reasons that Dale does not go further with various toys is avoiding or not aware of their sensory properties. He is not exploring: for example, banging them, mouthing them, smelling them, or touching them with various parts of his body. This suggests that he would be assisted by an expansion of *sensory based* play invitations. As has been said, learning is much more than labels, colors, numbers, and days of the week. I think that we should try to develop a very, very rich home-based sensory world for Dale and will explore this with Gail and Greg, as well as with the newly forming team next time.

4. It is important for me to explore with Gail and Greg how they would feel about a meeting of the team without them present.

process does not devastate their capacity to believe in a future for their child.

Professionals must reframe what they have been trained to think of as levels of deficit and instead concentrate on the fleetingly glimpsed, higher developmental levels that the child evidences. It is these fledgling promises that require nourishment. They are what challenged children need their parents to observe and aim for in order to motivate the children into developmentally in-tune interaction, one tiny step at a time.

Thus, the child's behavior and interactions with his most trusted caregiver(s) should form the cornerstone of assessment. Extending the developmental model described in *New Visions for the Developmental Assessment of Infants and Young Children* (Greenspan, Meisels et al., 1996), a growth-promoting assessment of a child will be guided by the following interrelated sequence:

1. *Establish an alliance with parents*, listening to their views of their child's strengths and challenges and discussing the issues to be explored in the assessment.

2. *Within this dawning alliance, obtain a developmental history of the child and a preliminary picture of the family's*

experience. The alliance comes first; the details are secondary. Some details may only emerge over time (see Box 1 in a later section in this chapter), as part of an ongoing relationship and working alliance. The key is to be responsive to the needs of the parents' explicit and implicit concerns.

3. *Observe the child in the context of unstructured play with parent(s)* or other familiar caregivers, preferably in a setting familiar to them. Observation of the child with his family can readily be done in conjunction with step 2 above. Most parents are relieved if, after seeing their child, the therapist maintains a positive, strength-based stance within the context of the dawning alliance.

4. *Remember that the parent-child, parent-parent, and parent-therapist relationships are essential units of observation, not just the child.*

5. *If needed, gently coach parents in interactions with the child to help them elicit the child's highest developmental levels.* Once the child has become accustomed to the therapist's presence, the therapist may also try to help the child interact and/or play directly with him. The idea is to glimpse

higher-order, incipient capacities in the child and help parents see how they can mobilize them. This is an intervention-centered assessment (Thomas, Benham, & Guskin, 2000; Shahmoon-Shanok, 2000) that can immediately initiate a significant component of the intervention program.

6. *Call for specific assessments of individual functions in the child only as needed,* within the context of a rationale specific to the particular child and the therapist's relationship with the parents. Similarly, target any medical tests to respond to particular questions.

7. *Be mindful of both explicit and implicit parental needs, concerns, strengths, and challenges,* tactfully articulating and elevating them for shared consideration and treatment planning.

8. Using a developmental model as a framework for integrating the data obtained from parents' reports, direct observation, and any other sources, *discuss findings with parents in the context of the alliance,* with the potential for beginning (or continuing) an intervention program, if needed.

Establishing Eligibility Within a Mandated Time Period vs. Prompt Intervention

In order to secure services for children in a reasonable amount of time, many jurisdictions limit the number of days the assessment phase can take, yet mandate that specific, specialty assessments all take place within the time limit. These simultaneous pressures often result in children and families being impersonally exposed to one assessor after another, each from a different discipline, within a short period of time, sometimes even on the same day. What is sacrificed by this approach is the opportunity to build an *integrated* picture of the *child within his rela-*

tional context and at his best. What is all too often simultaneously lost is the opportunity to begin building a generative relationship with his parents. This is unfortunate because such a beginning would likely yield more attuned interactions of parent with child which, in turn, might begin to exercise the child's fledgling relational capacities.

Instead, the assessment phase should be as brief as possible, which is to say that the earlier the treatment program can begin, the better. It is often not necessary to have each discipline's evaluation finished—or even begun—before a *provisional* diagnosis and one or two components of a treatment plan can begin. In fact, a provisional diagnosis for a child with developmental challenges is not difficult to make. It is often possible for an experienced practitioner to offer provisional impressions as well as generative guidance within an extended first or second contact. Thus, an intervention-centered assessment can begin assistance to child and parent almost immediately. The child's responses to the intervention and enhanced parental responsiveness inform next steps and help to clarify the diagnosis.

A word on diagnosis: Driven by considerations of public funding and insurance eligibility as the field is currently, reaching a diagnosis is sometimes reified as an end, as if the label itself would offer answers. In fact, diagnoses *are* critical in medical conditions in which discovering the correct pathological entity is requisite to finding the specific, appropriate treatment. Accurate diagnostic labels for agreed-upon entities are also necessary across cohorts for research to become meaningful. And whenever it is suspected that a child's developmental disorder is part of an active medical condition such as epilepsy, or a genetic abnormality with various risk factors such as tuberous sclerosis, the search for an accurate diagnosis is critical. Nevertheless,

Chapter 14. The Action is in the Interaction: Clinical Practice Guidelines for
Work with Parents of Children with Developmental Disorders

349

even in such cases the intervention program for the developmental disorder must be specifically informed by abiding scrutiny of the child's developmental, relational, and individualized sensory, motor, and processing profile, and how these shift over time. Since it is those particulars that inform professionals and parents about how to reach and engage the child relationally, they are the key to bringing him into the interactive, communicative, and learning world.

For many young children with developmentally significant functional impairments, the "impairment, in itself, should serve as a criterion for initiating appropriate intervention" (Greenspan & Wieder, Chapter 12). Often, the most significant *initial* interventions will be supportive coaching with parent and child to get shared attention and gestural interaction within their relationship moving, as well as occupational therapy with a heavy, sensory-integration emphasis. The information yielded by those interventions provides a rich picture, which can then direct the selection of further specific assessments. Speech/language and educational approaches can often begin just a little later and be layered in responsively, based on what is being learned about the child, the parent(s), and their relationship.

It is very unfortunate that many jurisdictions currently confuse subspecialty assessments with evaluation per se. They require all such assessments to be completed before treatment can begin and they further insist that only individuals who will *not* be treating the child and the family can assess. This usually tips the process toward a direction in which several different practitioners automatically evaluate the child outside an integrated context of the individual-in-family profile and outside of a supportive relationship-building process with parents. Going straight to specific interventions without attending to the parent or the child-parent relationship

either ignores or takes for granted necessary and critical fundamental levels of service. Yet for children with severe multisystem, autistic spectrum disorders, it is those basic levels that need strengthening first and foremost. Only upon a sturdy, substantial foundation can the upper levels be securely built.

Thus, continuity and relationship-building are requisite for thoughtful assessment to become effective intervention (and vice versa). The making of a diagnosis per se can—should—wait until effective intervention has begun to support the child, parents, and the relationship between them. Since labels tend to stick, a diagnostic determination should be made only in a favorable context, through which the child's better levels can be glimpsed. By then, the thoughtful practitioner will have helped parents begin to know their child's particular profile of strengths and challenges. In this context, parents are more likely to experience the diagnosis as a summarizing term rather than as a verdict. When funding considerations require a diagnostic label such as autism to secure services, professionals can acknowledge this with parents and then set out together to disprove it.

When work with a child and family *must* be limited to assessment, professionals should put forth every effort to make personal and meaningful their introduction to the family of the intervention program or practitioner. This step, so hard to achieve in these times of over-large caseloads, involves both assessors and intervenors. Recognizing how difficult a transition from one to the other may be for parents may inspire professionals to sustain their efforts to achieve such connections.

Setting the Tone of Partnership

Whether work with the child and family continues from the assessment phase through intervention or not, it is critical to bear in mind that from the very first contact, each professional's observations, ways of listening, ways of coaching, and ways of explaining the child's difficulty make a difference for families who are likely to be groping for some sense of an unfolding future for their child. Given parental anxiety during initial contacts, it is the professionals who set the tone for how they will work together. By acknowledging relative strengths, by discerning points of contact with their child (fragile as those may be), and by concentrating on next developmental steps, a growth-promoting partnership, and intervention plans, a practitioner—in any discipline—can offer some promise of a working future to parents and, through them, to their child.

Also during the initial phases of contact, the relationship potential between the professional and the parents on behalf of the child mandates consideration. Too frequently, this is given only passing attention in either the assessment or intervention phases of work with a family. Sometimes it is not even formally noted or discussed unless or until it becomes problematic. But, especially for children who struggle with developmental challenges, how the adults involved feel and think about each other is of significance to both the treatment process and the outcome. Not only should this potential be carefully considered but the *development of mutual respect and trust between parents and practitioner needs to be placed as a highest priority, equal in stature, even during the assessment phase, to assessment and diagnosis*. With most parents, the practitioner can openly discuss the potential for a relationship between them as a way of understanding more about parental expectations, preferences, and needs and also as concrete evidence that the practitioner and parents are forming a partnership and open exchange on behalf of the child.

For the mother or father of a child with special needs to function competently on behalf of their child, each parent must become open to utilizing professional resources for their child, for her- or himself, and sometimes for the family, while simultaneously experiencing the centrality of her or his position for the child. When professionals recognize this dual challenge, it becomes obvious that they have a fundamental responsibility to support these capacities over time. In order to fulfill this responsibility, reflective professionals will want to understand each *particular* parent within his or her unique developmental-relational-communal context.

A generative question that practitioners can ask themselves is, "How is this set of experiences *marking* this mother, this father, this family?" Having a child with special needs is a process that marks parents either for better or worse in terms of their sense of themselves and their capacities to be resourceful and relationally aware. When this question is pursued openly and empathetically, the vast majority of parents are responsive to—and deeply appreciative of—the care being offered. Parents want—even need—to be heard, understood, and treated with respect: They need their professional partner to recognize what the challenge of this child is like for them in the context of their life at this point in time.

When professionals manifest this basic investment while they help parents to see what *they*, as parents, can do for and with their child, when they are able to support parents' search for ways to meet and become resourceful in dealing with their challenging child, then they support parents in their search for their better selves in the face of enormous challenge. In this way, parents feel partnered and can work with the professionals to build and pursue the next therapeutic steps for their child. Furthermore, when professionals find this individualized

Chapter 14. The Action is in the Interaction: Clinical Practice Guidelines for
Work with Parents of Children with Developmental Disorders

351

footing, they find it easier to frame recommendations in the specialized, responsive ways that particular parents can understand and appreciate. Finally, when professionals reach out with the empathic interest described, they become able to discover which of the many parents are able to function optimally on behalf of their children with ongoing professional collaboration, and which parents may need additional, specialized interventions themselves.

In order to accomplish this kind of meaningful, individual- and couple-specific partnership, one professional should become the overall, responsive, resource-coordinator-integrator for parents and child. That key practitioner should work closely with parents to help them prioritize and build the intervention program their child needs as well as the supports they need to function optimally. Naturally, needs change over time, and as the key practitioner works closely with the parents, he learns how to respond resourcefully to shifts in their and/or their child's organization. The section that follows addresses some of the generic *content* knowledge necessary for any practitioner working with parents of young children with special needs. In order to learn how to work in these enhanced ways, *process* knowledge needs to be cultivated by practitioners through on-the-job reflective practice (cf. Fenichel & Eggbeer, 1990; Gilkerson et al., 1995; Gilkerson & Shahmoon-Shanok, 2000; Shanok; 1992, Shanok & Gilkerson et al., 1995).

ESTABLISHING AND MAINTAINING RELATIONSHIPS WITH DIVERSE PARENTS

As a rainbow of researchers, theoreticians, and poets have observed, "The child resides within the (hu)man." Thus, what has been learned about children's development and about how to build relationships with them can also be applied to work with adults (cf. Greenspan, 1997b; Greenspan & Wieder, 1987). Understanding and using developmental perspectives with parents enriches the practitioner's potential with them.

In work with all parents and children, there are many intertwining and parallel relational factors. Prominent among them are:

- The development of the person/parent within his or her relationship with the child
- The emergence of recollections, attitudes, and patterns, conscious and unconscious, from the parent's own early experience (Benedek, 1959; 1995b; Seligman & Shanok, 1995a; 1996; Shanok, 1987; 1993), sometimes called "internal representations," or "transference," or "internal working model" when these emerge in a current relationship
- The development of the person/parent within his or her evolving relationship with the professional.

Furthermore, there are stages to the development of any relationship (cf. Greenspan & Wieder, 1984), and developmental levels predominating within any individual. Each relationship can, itself, become a unit of observation, care, and growth. Indeed, relational forces are all in dynamic, cogwheeling relationship with one another; any influence on one constituent force affects the others. Looked at in this way, the idea that a parent's relationship with the professional can have significant influence on the parent and on the unfolding parent/child relationship may be glimpsed. Parents need *individualized* consideration and planning, simply because each one has a different history and set of perceptions, as well as widely varying abilities, sensitivities, and transferences to both child and professional.

Thus, not only do parents vary, but their children are also very different from each other, even if their "diagnosis" is the same. Furthermore, parental abilities to work with others in handling such an intimate responsibility vary widely. Just as "child-centered" intervention is now recognized as insufficient, so, too, "family-centered" intervention that only provides support, information, and guidance about their child's developmental needs is not enough. Even a two-or-three-size-fits-all programmatic approach cannot make the most of relational opportunities. Rather, responsive work, which begins and continues where *both* the parents *and* the child "are," is far more likely to support and mobilize the range of different parents on behalf of, and at least equally important, *with* their child.

Reaching the "Hard-to-Reach"

Parents of children with developmental disorders are as widely diverse a lot as the general population. They meet us with varying degrees of relational and communicative capacities themselves and with very different internal and contextual resources. It stands to reason that a segment of them would be hard to reach for a vast array of reasons. The idea of "holding so that others can hold" or "nurturing the nurturer" is considered fundamental to all work with parents of very young children (cf. Bronfenbrenner, 1979). It is perhaps even more critical in work with any parents whose child has severe difficulties in relating and communicating and who, for whatever reasons, are having difficulties engaging either with their child or with the team. This is especially true early on in intervention, before their child begins to consistently give back reassuring, interrelated feedback.

Depending on their capacities and preferences, avoidant parents should be offered regular contacts in their home, office, coffee shop, or on the phone—anything that works for them. They require time they can count on with an empathetic, deeply interested, optimistic and (occasionally, when crucially important) authoritative professional, time in which the entire focus can be on them and their child. Strength-centeredness and acceptance of such parents are key.

The knowledge and practice base emerging from community-based outreach work must be integrated into early intervention. Practitioners need to support one another when they find themselves feeling that they are selling something that the parents do not know they need, let alone want. Responsive creativity also can make the margin of difference in reaching a parent or not. In one project with very poor teenage moms and their challenging children, the "way in" to reluctant parenthood was through a support group that got off the ground with a focus on hair styling. As the young women fixed each other's hair, conversation drifted (and was *then* facilitated by the professional) to their children.

This parallels what children with difficulties in relating and communicating need from their parents. And again, it mirrors what some parents need from their program or practitioner. Consider another example: The director of an early intervention program serving young foster care children and their families brought the following topic for discussion to a professional seminar on leadership. Her agency a school-based program for young children with developmental challenges, invited biological parents to observe and participate in their children's classrooms on a daily basis. But, because the teenage mothers were very disruptive—talking among themselves, chewing gum loudly, moving around the room but not paying attention to the children, and going in and out of the room "just to have a cigarette"—she and her staff felt that they had to set strict limits on the times during which the young mothers could visit their children's classrooms. Using the leadership seminar discussion as a way to step back and reflect, the director was quickly able to see that, while she and her staff had wanted to be inviting and helpful to the biological parents by setting an open-door policy, they had been so focused on services *to the children* that they had ignored the needs of the biological parents who, by definition, are parents with challenges. The parent's negative expectations of relationships, based in all likelihood on powerful past experiences, made them skittish and, paradoxically, invited rejection, the opposite of what they needed. The program would have to find a way to build trust, to violate these young parents negative, anxiety-ridden expectations to succeed in constructive outreach.

After much shared discussion with her staff, they decided to offer a support group to the parents, complete with food and beverages, every day just prior to their entry into the children's classrooms. They reasoned that, if they attended to the parents, then perhaps the parents could better pay attention to their children, and indeed, the support group did the trick: It transformed these needy parents' behaviors such that many were able to participate and observe more appropriately in the classroom. In addition, within 2 or 3 months of support group attendance, several parents became more involved and asked for individual appointments "for themselves."

Just as adults naturally modify their approach to fit particular children, professionals must become thoughtful about how to approach parents, always aware that, inadvertently, they may put parents off. A good rule of thumb is that when parents do not show up or if they "behave badly," it is time to step back and reflect upon practice with resourceful colleagues. Parents' "lack of interest" or problematic attitude almost always conveys something about how the program is not yet connecting with them. Growth-promoting work with parents flows from *their* needs and concerns, from where *their* initiative is activated. Shared obser-

vations and then shared views develop over time. Working toward an alliance that has pleasurable components and can survive negative feelings is critical to long-term partnerships.

Co-identifications, Time, and Reflection

More than other types of psychotherapy or even child guidance work, this work is, in fact, child-centered. This point may seem to contradict the call for sensitive, relationally alive work with parents fueled by recognition of their many individual differences. There is a tension between children's and parents' needs, to be sure. But a young child's threatened development is in no small measure experienced as a threat to the parent's own sense of self; it provides a major impetus for parents to place the child's needs above their own, as if the child's needs *were* their own. "Best practice" requires that professionals not only evade the "contradiction" but also recognize and even embrace the tension inherent in identifying with each family member and in building family-specific relationships. What is good for children is good for their parents. What is good for parents is good for their children. Aiming for both stimulates good outcomes. The invisible but powerful thread is relationship.

All small children are a far more constant responsibility than could be imagined before they arrive, and children with special needs require far, far more than their typically developing peers. The level of demand on parents can be excruciating. Professionals need to be mindful of how overwhelming the task demands can be for parents with children with severe difficulties in relating and communicating.

Becoming fully engaged with a family requires time—time for the professional to become saturated with observations, details, and nuances about the child *and his relational context*. Especially in the first several stages of assessment and intervention, parents and children with severe difficulties relating and communicating should be seen *together*. This enables the professional to focus on the current strengths of the parent-child relationship, on how to help their relationship and communication become more lively and resourceful, and on how to enable the parents' own interactions with their child to support and extend whatever treatment is recommended.

It is also essential to see parents without their child regularly, predictably, and often enough to exchange information and develop shared perceptions, to reflect, to take stock, and to plan. Just as with children, parents need a supportive context. Not infrequently, the support that anxious or depleted parents experience in their own sessions liberates them to return to their child refueled. Sometimes, the sessions may involve talking about mutual frustrations with uneven or inadequate service systems. At other times, a parent may need to sort out memories and child-directed impulses based on the past. Or, parents may need to sort out subjective feelings of discouragement in the light of more encouraging objective reality. That is, sometimes parents may feel that they are not accomplishing enough and worry about the future. If the professional recognizes that they are, in fact, doing a great deal and that the child's developmental trajectory has already "taken off," then she can offer much-needed reassurance.

Guidance and coaching must be based on specific observations and interactions between parent and child, that the parent and the professional have witnessed together. Most parents and key caregivers are highly motivated: With sensitive, developmentally geared assistance, they can learn to observe, read, and respond to their child contingently, drawing their child into the relational, learning world.

Working with parents and children together and then reflecting with parents regularly without the child present allows the professional and parents to build a durable, insightful, resourceful relationship. Allowing time for sharing and thinking together makes for a partnership that can withstand differences and navigate through uncharted waters.

TOWARDS DEVELOPMENTALLY APPROPRIATE PRACTICE: APPLYING THE CONCEPTS OF RELATIONSHIP, INDIVIDUAL DIFFERENCE, AND DEVELOPMENT TO *PARENTS*

At the beginning of the 1900s, theorists such as Sigmund Freud, George Herbert Mead, and Harry Stack Sullivan began to recognize that personality—enduring ways of behaving, perceiving, and thinking about oneself and others—arises through early social interactions, beginning with the first relationships in earliest childhood. The patterns of those mutually regulated (or disregulated) early encounters (cf. Schore, 1994; Tronick, 1998) become the largely subconscious template through which current attitudes, interactions, behaviors, and expectations are governed. Over time, practitioners can recognize a parent's particular patterns and often find ways of acknowledging them. These patterns become the basis upon which the practitioner and parent come to set, and shift, their agenda or contract with each other. It is helpful to become aware of each parent's:

- Strengths and risk factors.
- Developmental levels and internal representations.

Chapter 14. The Action is in the Interaction: Clinical Practice Guidelines for
Work with Parents of Children with Developmental Disorders

355

- Social capacities, especially vis-à-vis the child; that is, the effect of this child on the parent now and the effect of each treatment resource for the child on the parent.

Knowledge and familiarity build a shared and sympathetic perspective between practitioner and parent, and boosts the likelihood that a practitioner will understand a parent's predilections and hesitations. Yet, whereas many parents readily respond with openness and trust, others take time to build the trust that comes before openness. Pulling together impressions of a parent's individual style, her developmental and relational level and capacities offers the reward of increasingly targeted practice. All practicioners serving a child should have general familiarity with these parental factors, while one person will hold major responsibility for seeing them regularly, and understanding and connecting with them.

Most parents will readily reveal personal details when they feel the interest of the professional and trust her intent. For *each* parent, information learned can be aggregated and organized, as shown in Box 1. This box includes important areas to notice and what to inquire of parents. This information usually becomes available in the course of meaningful discussions with parents over time. With this rich and nuanced picture in hand, developmentally appropriate interventions for parents can be planned. To accomplish this, programs and professionals must move toward providing interventions for *parents* based on their individual capacities and styles.

Unfortunately, in many programs, no one professional is designated to be "the parent person" for a particular family. All too often, even when there is such a designee, resources and knowledge to support more individualized work with parents are slim. Critical needs of both child and parent tend to be ignored.

Figure 2 compares intervention pyramids for both children with special needs and their parents. Although parents are requisite at every level of the Intervention Pyramid for Children, current evaluation and service programs nevertheless tend to cluster their offerings exclusively around specific interventions for the child; that is, they congregate at the uppermost section even of the child pyramid. By definition, the child's foundational levels remain weak and uneven while the engagement and intimacy the child desperately needs from the parents to build mutual regulation and repair (Tronick, 1986) are neglected.

As can be seen in the Intervention Pyramid for Parents, there are similar developmental and relational considerations for adults; in fact, they have striking parallels. Yet, most often, oferrings for parents in early intervention programs are add-ons, not the developmentally based, comprehensive, integrated layers required. When working appropriately, each of the four levels of interventive support within each pyramid would be seamlessly interwoven, with the basic levels providing the ongoing foundation for the others. Just as children need additional supports at the basic levels, so do many parents, given their levels of stress and/or their own pre-existing vulnerabilities.

When individual guidance or group support sessions are offered to parents in most early intervention programs, they are offered as program components rather than as an individualized, responsive, and tailor-made plan. How can these programs provide something meaningful enough—verbally and generally—about interactions that are preverbal, gestural, and specific? What is needed for contact to be effective is knowledge of each parent's individual functional developmental capacities, including their educational, social, economic, and cultural resources (as shown in Figure 2) as well as the specific, developmentally and relationally targeted needs of their

Box 1. Organization of Family Information[1]

- **History**
  - Where, when, and with whom did the parent grow up
  - Cultural beliefs, customs, aspirations, and support systems
  - Educational level and experience of self at school
  - Socioeconomic factors
  - How do they characterize their key relationships and memories of
    - Parents   • Grandparents   • Siblings
    - Is there a psychiatric history/oddness on either side of the family?
  - Work history
  - Impressions of *how* each parent tells life story (e.g., continuities, coherence, gaps, confusions, affect)
  - Circumstances of conception, pregancy, and birth
  - For whom was the designated child named? Does child remind the parent of anyone?

- **Current situation**
  - Housing
    - With whom they live
  - Current work situation
  - Financial resources, challenges, and attitudes
  - Familial/marital strengths and stressors
  - Descriptions and ages of other children
  - Next of kin and extended family—strengths and stressors
  - Social network-friendship base
  - Spiritual beliefs and practices
  - Attitudes toward and subjective experience of each key person in their lives, especially the designated child
  - Where is this parent in the emotional and adaptive process of encountering the child's significant challenges?
  - How does each parent respond to/feel about various symptoms and strengths of the child?
  - Cogwheeling between developmental needs of various family members
  - Does this parent (or other of their family of origin members) report over- or under- responsivity to stimuli? That is, what is this parent's sensory profile?

- **Impressions**
  - Where is this parent developmentally?
  - What distinguishes this parent from others? What are his/her strengths, vulnerabilities, particularities and life view?
  - Where is this parent relationally
    - In general?   • With child?   • With spouse?   • With key practitioner?
    - What do we know about this parents internal representations and inner life?
  - Coherence, confusion, and gaps in this parent's narrative (cf. Main, 1993; Main & Goldwyn, 1984)
  - Summarize your impressions of the child as a marker experience for this parent in the context of other resources and stresses in his/her life

[1]**This outline is not meant to be a semistructured interview**. Instead, it is a series of sections with which to sort, aggregate, and organize information gathered over time about *each* parent. (Other sections may be added to the outline for additional information about particular parents and their families.)

Chapter 14. The Action is in the Interaction: Clinical Practice Guidelines for
Work with Parents of Children with Developmental Disorders

357

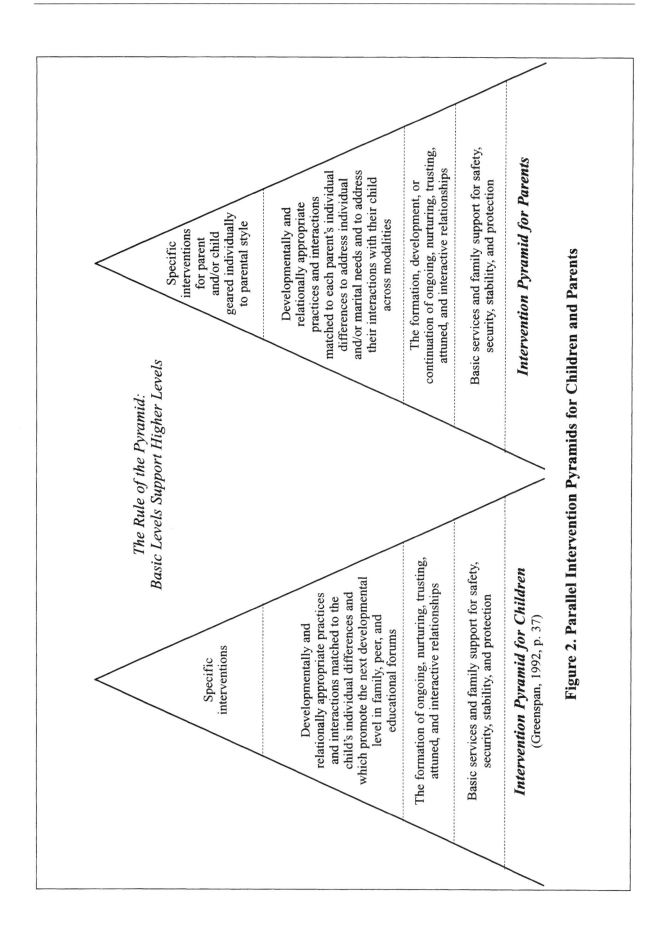

Figure 2. Parallel Intervention Pyramids for Children and Parents

child. It is these factors that should drive the *plan* (i.e., the type and frequency of interventions) for each parent and for parent(s) and child together.

In situations when either the parent her- or himself has challenges, intervening developmentally with a parent can make a margin of difference for parent and child. As was said at a recent conference, "Where the patient (in this case, parent) is evidencing significant deficit in any of the developmental levels, we must engage and challenge the (parent) at the earliest level of deficit and make that level the primary focus of treatment until that level is mastered. Then the next level is addressed and so on. Obviously, addressing one level does not mean that other higher levels of development are not engaged at the same time—it is a matter of emphasis. In other words, successful (developmental) psychotherapy addresses and remediates developmental deficits in a systematic and progressive manner" (Mann, November 1999).

Figure 3 illustrates developmental levels in the therapeutic process with parents. A relationally oriented mental health professional may be critical in moving parents up the developmental ladder.

Resources That Should be Available to Parents/Caregivers

Parents are society's agents for the care and raising of its young. Yet parents are a widely differing bunch, with diverse histories, profiles, resources, and needs. As they care for their children, parents must have choices in order to discover what will work for their child and their family. Parents of children with special needs also require choices. In fact, with greater demands placed upon them compared with those on parents of typically developing children, they need more choices, as well as a

more responsive communal infrastructure surrounding them than do others. And, for those who arrive at the therapist's door not fully knowing what could be helpful to them, parents also benefit from personally tailored supports and information so that they may become active participants in what they receive. Along complementary lines, professionals require an array of selections with which to constructively buoy the parents with whom they work. The interventions offered must be based on individual differences in the parents' surrounding ecological matrix and on their functional-developmental-relational capacities.

Integral to the intervention pyramid for parents is the recognition that *basic levels support next higher levels, and that each family must be fully considered level by level in order to help them help their children.* This requires that the field of early intervention move toward a state-of-the-art interweaving of supportive and, sometimes, insight-oriented psychotherapy, as well as experientially based adult education. Bearing in mind the developmental level and ecological context of each parent, programs and practitioners must consider each level on the comprehensive continuum of services (see the right side of Figure 4) necessary to reach parents and determine at what level to focus the interventions. The continuum begins with the most disadvantaged, wary, or preoccupied parents.

"Difficult" Parent or Child-Centered Program?

The reasons for which parents come to be considered difficult or disinterested by practitioners fall into three major categories: their own histories-profiles, an inadequate or otherwise mismatched response to parental needs by practitioners-program, or some mix of the two. Some parents, for reasons stemming from their own histories and/or reactivi-

Chapter 14. The Action is in the Interaction: Clinical Practice Guidelines for
Work with Parents of Children with Developmental Disorders

359

Ladder of Functional Developmental Levels	Regularity and Stability	Attachment	Process
VI. Emotional thinking	Comes regularly	Comfort with being known, with good and bad aspects exposed	• New patterns become more solid; can start to separate from the therapist without losing new patterns in spite of sadness • Can understand how her maladaptive patterns interfere and can make changes
V. Emotional ideas	Misses some sessions, but returns	Communicates difficult emotions	• Can see patterns in many different contexts and can see how present patterns developed out of past relationships • Can talk about still more complex patterns of feeling and behaving in relationships
IV. Complex communication	Makes it to some appointments	Uses relationship to communicate, not just to get needs met	• Self observing function in relation to more complex feelings, including contradictory feelings such as anger and love • Self-observing function—not only of behaviors, but also feelings
III. Two-way communication	Comes to center	Emotional interest in, attaches to therapist as a unique individual	• Can focus on the relationships in which these behaviors take place • Beginning to report on patterns of behavior, but no understanding of reasons
II. Intimacy/attachment/relationship	Acceptance of visits	Tolerates therapist	• Can communicate some things, such as needs and wants
I. Self-regulation and interest in the world	Refusal of visits	Concrete services	• Cannot communicate

Figure 3. The Developmental Ladder and Levels of the Therapeutic Process with Children and Adults
(Greenspan, 1992)

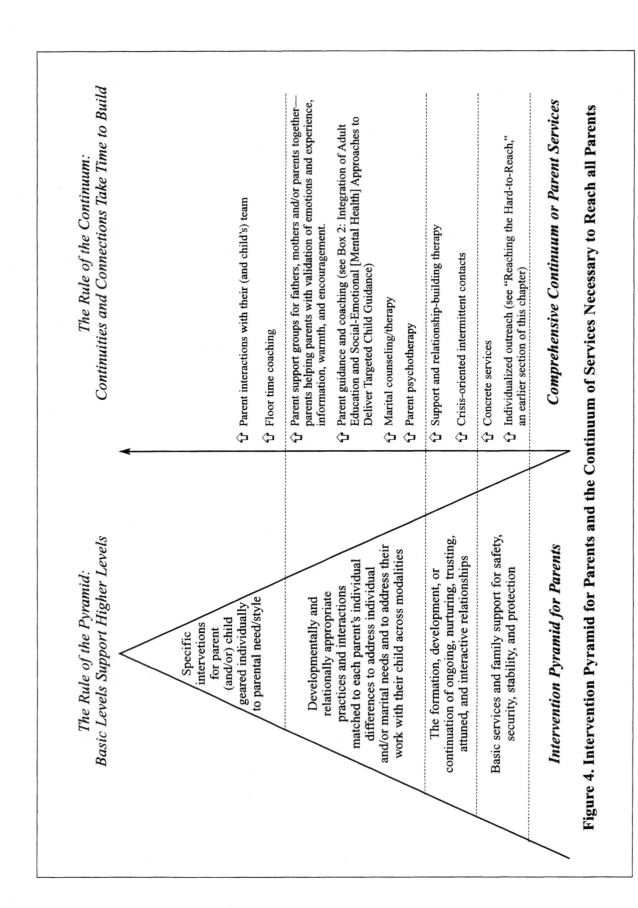

Figure 4. Intervention Pyramid for Parents and the Continuum of Services Necessary to Reach all Parents

Chapter 14. The Action is in the Interaction: Clinical Practice Guidelines for
Work with Parents of Children with Developmental Disorders

361

ties, may find it difficult to engage in regular collaboration. A parent may be "stuck," but with sensitive outreach, the marker process of having a needy child could become a motivation for new growth. These are parents whose own life experiences have left them mistrustful, resistant, disorganized, or overwhelmed, as briefly discussed earlier in the section called "Reaching the Hard-to-Reach." It is essential for the practitioners involved to talk with each other, sympathetically considering different approaches to outreach depending on what the *reasons* for a parent's avoidance may be. Just as children need their parents to woo them up the developmental ladder so, too, do some parents need professionals to do the same with them.

All too often, a program gives up on a parent who "never comes to meetings, let alone to appointments." Practitioners end up believing that parents may not care enough about their child or that they haven't accepted the child's disorder when, in fact, the reasons for noncompliance are likely to be far more complex. Outreach is an exercise in caring and extending developmentally based invitations over time—sometimes over a long time. If there is no one on the team who has experience with resourceful outreach, this is an area where generative consultation and staff training are indicated. What the parents need is sensitive, individualized outreach, with careful attention given to the levels of the developing therapeutic relationship (Greenspan, 1997) and an understanding of the parents' own perspective. Developmentally appropriate practices and interactions are based upon a recognition of individual differences and an increasing awareness of the state, mood, and intention of the parent on the part of the professional.

It is always crucial to stay connected with what parents are looking for and how parents view the professional's role, as well as the tra-

jectory of events and interactions that led up to the present one. When the parents of a severely delayed toddler reached the third intake social worker who asked them how they *felt*, the mother blurted out, "I *feel* like hitting you in the head! What I *want* are services for my child, not a discussion of how I *feel*. What I feel is that he needs services—NOW!" Although there is increasing recognition that parents' emotions are important, practitioners do not always know how to gain access to them. In-service training can target this area. Becoming aware of both manifest and latent elements boosts a practitioner's ability to meet parents "where they are." As it happened, the particular mother in this example is an exceptionally competent, warm, and related person and a very strong advocate for her child. She was not avoiding her feelings. She was simply fed up and needed the social workers to join her in addressing "first things first." Her emotional connection with her son had to be addressed first by providing services to him, which would make room for deepening the work with her a little later.

What might have appeared to be a difficult mom was, in fact, a frustrated mother-lioness, roaring to protect her young. She had already accepted her child's challenges and the fact that she had to work with others to help him. She was past ready to move ahead. A responsive social worker could use this mother's outburst to shift gears, welcoming it as a terrific opportunity to empathize with her frustration and to move the acquisition of child services along.

Mismatches are more likely between parents and practitioners of different cultures, ethnicities, and classes. Talking openly with parents about their views, reflecting with staff members, and consultation may all help minimize misattributions.

When several parents in a program do not participate or when practitioners experience the "we"/"they" phenomenon—as in, *we* hold events/make appointments, *they* don't show up—professionals should see this as an unequivocal announcement that there is a problem with the program. Discussing how to revise the program with a resourceful, trusted professional or a parent experienced with a range of parents can be a breath of fresh air for parents and professionals alike. Often, parent-facilitated support groups provide a lively, deep-feeling forum within which many ideas for improved parent-professional relations emerge. But flexible, responsive, self-aware, and thoughtful practitioners are needed for wholesome changes in programs to evolve.

The early intervention program for young children in foster care described earlier in this chapter illustrates how even situations that look nearly hopeless can be turned around. Well-intended personnel were about to abandon open visits in the classroom by disruptive and demanding birth parents. When helped to think about these parents as people having their own significant needs, the staff decided not to rescind the open visits but, instead, to hold a support group prior to the classroom visits, with refreshments provided. Before long, the program personnel not only found the birth parents more responsive, and even helpful, in the children's classes, but several parents used the support group as a stepping stone to individual, psychotherapeutically oriented intervention and/or skills training, such as, for example, studying for their high school equivalency exam.

In a privately run suburban speech/language and occupational therapy program, staff complained that they never glimpsed parents because their children arrived for sessions with nannies and au pairs. At a single meeting with an experienced consultant, open discussion revealed that the intake practices of these professionals—which left parents sitting in the waiting area—sent a clear message to parents that this place delivered services for *children*, not for *them*. Recognizing this, the staff could have accepted the status quo. Fortunately, they had become increasingly aware of the relational basis for wholesome growth in young children and realized that they wanted the presence of parents. Over time, the director and her key supervisors pursued training and further consultation, which yielded revised, relationally sensitive practices from a family's first visit onward.

Each of these vignettes, one from the south Bronx and the other from a wealthy Connecticut suburb, exemplifies the principle that early intervention program staff will work successfully with parents to the degree that they become aware of parental needs and concerns, on the one hand, and of their own latent messages, on the other.

Mission Integration: Charting New Directions

State-of-the-art practice with parents of children who have special needs requires a generic base of knowledge coming from across, and integrating, several fields. It is time that practitioners, programs, policymakers, and managed-care companies recognize that this knowledge base is growing rapidly and requires life-long learning and growth. This implies that while a good professional education and internship are necessary, they are not sufficient.

The single word "integration" refers to several challenges faced by parents and their children and the professionals dedicated to helping them. The first challenge is to note and integrate with the strengths that a parent brings. Some strengths are obvious from the outset; some emerge over time. Some are

Chapter 14. The Action is in the Interaction: Clinical Practice Guidelines for
Work with Parents of Children with Developmental Disorders

363

known to the parent, but only become mani-fest to the practitioner able to draw a parent out. Still others are discovered by the parent in the process of trying to meaningfully par-ent a special needs/hard-to-read-and-reach child. Practitioners able to follow both mani-fest and latent emotional content are able to play midwife to these parental discoveries, to cultivate them in their inception, by seeing and meeting them contingently.

To meet their children where they are, virtually all parents need to learn a great deal about topics ranging from typical unfolding development to:
– the complex meanings and layers of
   sensory processing,
– their own child's profile,
– ways of encouraging and limiting the
   child effectively, to
– service delivery options.

Thus, a second integrative challenge is that of education—how to offer parents the knowledge they need, when they need it, and in a form which they can use. *Targeted child guidance* can be very helpful for many parents who cope fairly well (see Box 2). They feel and function better as they become more effective on behalf of their child. Some of the knowledge coming from coached dyadic sessions is content knowledge, but much of it is process—doing and being—knowledge. In order for both kinds of knowl-edge to be synthesized and, thus, made usable, they need to be tailored to the partic-ular parent, the particular child, and their par-ticular relationship—what comes alive and grows, or does not, between them. Because several early intervention professions, such as education, speech, and occupational and physical therapy, do not prepare their practi-tioners to work with parents, mental health workers are often best able to do that tailor-ing. They are only effective, however, if they

integrate a strength-centered perspective and learn a great deal from their body-based col-leagues about individual differences in devel-opment.

The work is far more *in vivo* than the laid back, patient-does-most-of-the-talking-in-office type of work for which most mental health professionals were prepared. The process is less about interpretation or resist-ance, although experience with those domains of practice can provide productive guidance. It is more like life-space (Redl, 1966), community-based work (Shahmoon-Shanok, 2000), or kitchen-table psychothera-py (Fraiberg, Adelson, & Shapiro, 1975) in that it is not all talk and may, in fact, occur on-the-spot or in places of the parents' choosing. A lot of this work is preverbal, gestural, behavioral, interactive, and play-based, tailored to draw the person into relationship and communication.

Together, early intervention profession-als must develop a generic foundation of developmental and relational knowledge that can be geared to the individual parent and child. The material necessary for professionals to serve parents and their children adequately is both *content knowledge* (for example, the material contained in this chapter) and *process knowledge* (the "being and doing"—interac-tional, what-we-do-spontaneously-when-we're-with-someone knowledge that is absorbed in a reflectively supervised apprenticeship). There is no better forum for learning than ongoing, long-term, specific-child-and-family oriented in-service training with trustworthy teachers over time. The kind of training, in which strengths are cherished and vulnerabilities are partnered (Shanok, 1992, p. 40), enhances awareness and self-awareness so that practi-tioners are enabled to use their own profes-sional knowledge base with increasing sensitivity and connection to the feelings and relational capacities of parents (and children).

Box 2. Integration of Adult Education and Social-Emotional Approaches to Deliver *Targeted* Child Guidance[1]

I.   Ask each parent what they enjoy with their child and (help parents) build variations and continuities from there. Help them by meeting them where they are and noticing what *they* bring to their child. To find meaning, satisfaction and hope within the demands and resources of the child and the program, they must feel engaged and effective.

II. Observe each parent with their child over time.

III. Woo parents and other key figures (grandparents, babysitters, siblings, inclusion aides) *for* the child by helping them to:
   • Imagine the particulars of their child's sensory processing and arousal profile.
   • Understand how this profile affects the in-flow and output of signals to and from him.
   • Appreciate the fundamental role of (their) relationship in his learning.

IV. Coach parents and others in developmentally appropriate floor time play using knowledge coming from all team members.

V.   See children *with* their parents and other key figures to support their abilities to woo their child into communicative relationship and play by:
   • Observing.
   • Recognizing and understanding their child's evolving developmental and relational profile.
   • Reading and responding to his weak signals.
   • Meeting their child at his developmental level and building from *his* intentionality, the affective key to learning.
   • Drawing their child into an interactional, joyful relationship.
   • Building the child's capacities for floor time circles of communication by strategically following and building from the child's intent and pleasure, using high affect and/or a sense of playfulness, as the child can tolerate.

VI. Recognize with parents both the content *and* process elements of developing knowledge.

VII. Notice with parents what bubbles up for them in their recollections and associations.

[1]Targeted child guidance means guidance *tailored* to the particular parent, the particular child, and their particular relationship.

Another point about integration is that, since individuation grows out of attachment and not out of separation, children with challenges need to have essentially achieved the first four steps on the Developmental Ladder (see Figure 3) before it makes sense to work toward greater individuation (cf. Ainsworth, 1978; Sroufe, 1993). Hence, parents should be included in child sessions unless there is an important reason not to; for example, if they are disruptive or self-absorbed during periods when they are overwhelmed. When the child has already achieved a good deal and is finally ready to move towards greater individuation, then separations in digestible doses can become part of the work. But even when the child is developmentally ready to move towards greater autonomy, attention needs to be given to a particular parent's own styles of, and desires for, connecting and disengaging. Professionals are there to assist the dyad, not to dare, provoke, or pressure either child or parent to hurry separation along. Nuanced awareness of cultural differences is particularly significant here.

In many jurisdictions, there is an arbitrary shift from one set of providers to another when a child reaches age 3. This shift seriously undermines parents who need people who know their children intimately and over time, people who share the history of this crisis, this marker process, in their lives. The age cut-off also undermines the professionals who work with children and families, forcing their practice into a revolving door operation, their emotions and dedication blunted with each arbitrary turn. And, for children whose main challenges include relationship, interaction, communication, and integration, this abrupt age-based dislocation can only be termed ridiculous.

Parent involvement is necessary for a developmentally appropriate family-based program for every child. This includes in home floor time play— how to make the most of playing together developmentally—as well as a sensory integration motor program. It also includes the routines, expectations, and limits—depending on the age and capacity of the child and on the style of the parents—of interactions that occur at bathtime, bedtime, and mealtime. It is important that professionals learn to work with parents to develop shared attention over day-to-day details, mutually enlarging the picture of the child, each from their own perspectives.

Each of the professionals involved with a child can come closer to responding to the parents' needs. For example, parents are often desperate to have two-way interaction and, later, a conversation with their child. Professionals can join their intent. Occupational therapists, for instance, can teach parents about constitutional, maturational variations in terms of their child's particular strengths and challenges and about how to provide a sensory diet that helps a child down-regulate for hyperarousal or up-regulate for hypoarousal. Indeed, while parents or caregivers are providing children with appropriate sensory exercise, reciprocity of affect and increasingly long chains of interaction become possible. This helps children connect their heightened intent with motor planning and sequencing so that they enjoy a behavioral outcome that matches their intent. There is no greater reward than that for the child and, when parents have a hand in facilitating it, for parents.

In addition, occupational therapists have a vital role in helping parents understand how they can provide for their children's basic needs by supporting their in-flow and out-flow filtering capacities. Occupational therapists also have a critical role on the team, helping all the adults understand the particular child's sensory, processing, and motor-planning profile, as well as his challenges, in practical ways so that he can be helped to function at his highest levels more consistently across all his therapies.

Speech/language practitioners also can build upon the parents' growing desire to have reciprocal exchanges with their children by helping parents:

- Observe and notice their child's intent
- Slow down
- Use simple words or phrases
- Stay contingent to the child's interests
- Offer support
- Build joint attention
- Slow down some more
- Offer lots of clear cues
- Stay on the (child's) topic (S. Gerber, July 1999)

The dyadic, floor time, communication- and strength-savvy psychotherapist can help parents recognize even weak signals emerging from their child. One severely compromised, low-tone, bland, and pale-faced 2$\frac{1}{2}$-year-old boy, for example, manifested precious few shifts in facial expression in the course of a 90-minute dyadic assessment session. He did, however, evidence mild distress upon falling, and fleeting anxiety crossed his face as he stumbled against and made eye-to-eye contact with the seated therapist. The father seemed to see both encounters, yet ignored each one. The therapist quietly inquired, "Did you see that?" He responded, "My father would walk away when I hurt myself." Brief discussion and an on-the-spot acceptance of his own childhood feelings were followed by a few sentences about the need—especially the need of hypo-registering, weak signal senders—that signals be validated.

This brief interchange helped this father offer gentle, complementary affects. Thus, the next time his son registered an aversive reaction, the father quietly mirrored, gestured and said, "Ooh ... I see that banging your finger hurt ... ooh-ooh ... that's my boy ... okay

now" in time and pace with the child. The therapist helped the father see that his son's response—leaning into the father's lap and appearing *more* hurt for a long moment—as dawning progress. The child was distinguishing his sensation within the relational field: Sensation was becoming emotion, and emotion was becoming signal. And signals are, of course, communication. A hint of the mutual regulation familiar in typical early development (Tronick, 1986) can also be glimpsed in this example.

The issue addressed in the foregoing example—that practitioners and parents often ignore manifestations of a child's sensations, emotions, and intentionality that the child experiences—is a critical challenge for the field. The disorders professionals are trying to correct have to do with *relating* and *communicating*. In typical development, babies and young toddlers experience sensations—say, stomach distress—which are "read" by the caregiver familiar with his eat-sleep-poop schedule and his repertoire of sounds and behaviors. When projected into a caring relational field, the sensations are, in effect, *elevated* to the status of signal by the signal reader. It is not a mirroring of the child, exactly. Rather, initial, two-way communication begins as mirroring-empathizing, as if to say, "Ooh-ooh, looks like that hurt" (or "was it fun?") and becomes, "I'll join with you on this so that you come to know what you feel. Only then will we move on." It is an amplification of the child's signals by contingent attunement. These interactions, repeated hundreds of times a day over many days, become the very basis for communication and relationship. Children with challenges need even more, not less, practice than their typically developing counterparts, especially with their closest caregivers. Therapists can and must help parents move their responses into slower motion: as in "Oh, you got hurt.

Chapter 14. The Action is in the Interaction: Clinical Practice Guidelines for
Work with Parents of Children with Developmental Disorders
367

I see that this happened, that it registered on you. I emphathize and can stick with you while it is processed further. Only *then*, when it is processed further, will I help you move on." The response should not be "Let us cheerfully move on right away!" because the child is having trouble proessing the experience appropriately in the first place and conveying something about it in the second (cf. Fonagy & Target, 1998).

All practitioners would do well to note that people learn most effectively and thoroughly not by hearing or even by watching, but by doing, then reflecting on what they did, and then doing again. Facts, descriptive material, and theory boost and organize learning, but nothing can substitute for *experiential* knowledge. This is the idea behind supervised internships and field placements. Why should parental learning be any different? Thus, it is not sufficient to discuss general approaches with parents, nor is it enough to have them sitting to one side observing. Rather, parents have to be active in the child's therapies for them to really develop their potential for their child.

Jointly watched videotapes of child and parent or child and therapist, discussed together, can also become an asset in what should become a mutual learning and growing process. Practitioners may sometimes be surprised at how much there is to take in from observing a child with a parent. Certain approaches, such as comforting the child, may be adopted, adapted, or built upon.

SUMMARY

This chapter has briefly described the potential inherent in moving the state of the field toward the state of the art by meeting the needs of parents so that *they* can meet the needs of *their* children. Policymakers must move to fund varied options for parents as

well as reflexive supervision and other forms of care-based training for staff. Still, there are many actions that programs and practitioners can take to push forward in these directions. With concentrated work and concerted attention, programs and professionals can:

- *Remember that intervention begins at the first moment of contact and assessment never ends until the case is closed.*
- *Learn how to conduct outreach effectively* by making their approaches more individualized.
- *Designate one key person from the staff to serve the particular family.*
- *Engage in in-service meetings* that emphasizes social-emotional, developmental, and transactional themes as well as cross-disciplinary fertilization, case-by-case.
- *Help parents become active partners* in therapeutic sessions for children rather than being passive viewers or being excluded altogether.
- *Work with parents with regularity* and address their developmental level and both latent and manifest themes.

All the professions can also help parents recognize that baby steps do build incrementally over time. While it is sometimes difficult to believe that tiny baby steps can get anywhere, in most cases they do, so that children with significant challenges often become related and capable of sharing pleasure and fun. As one deeply dedicated mother of a child with special needs noted, "We measure miles in millimeters."

Developmental disorders are not only constitutional challenges residing in the child; they become *relationship* disorders. Because all children depend on their primary relationships for cognitive, social, emotional and identity development, practitioners must attend as much to the child's relationship with parent(s) as to the child. By placing the child's deep needs for the parents' love—and by placing the parents' deep needs for the child's love—both on center stage, therapists can nudge the spotlight away from symptoms and deficits and place it where it belongs: On the circular, back-and-forth transactions which, over time, become relationship and communication and which, simultaneously, nurture the developing emotional and cognitive intelligence of the child.

Virtually all parents of children with special needs require support, partnership, and substantial new skills and knowledge learned in the context of their particular child. Most parents also need assistance with difficult feelings. And some parents have a range of other needs, from concrete services, to crisis intervention, marital counseling, and psychotherapy, all of which need to be closely linked to the work with the child. Attuned, individually geared work with parents is likely to bolster their growing abilities to be attuned, engaged, and individualized with their children. Even as the child is being helped to function better during therapies, the parent is being assisted to more closely respond to the child's shifting states and capacities. Some interventions noted in this chapter respond primarily to the child's needs, whereas others respond to the parents' needs. A family is a dynamic system—what benefits one transactionally supports the other. Indeed, the action *is* in the interaction. ∎

Notes

[i]Parts of this chapter were previously published in Shanok, R. (1997a). Giving back future's promise: Working resourcefully with parents of children with severe disorders of relating and communicating. *Zero to Three, 17*(5), 37-48. The author acknowledges ZERO TO THREE, the National Center for Infants, Toddlers, and Families (formerly the National Center for Clinical Infant Programs) with profound appreciation. With the inspiration and leadership provided by its first president, Stanley Greenspan, M.D., ZERO TO THREE became the pioneering national forum for transdisciplinary exchange and network-building on the issues addressed in this chapter.

[ii]Throughout this chapter, for simplicity, all children are referred to as "he," and all therapists as "she."

[iii]As a set of guidelines, this chapter represents what *should* be in place for parents within every program that serves children who have developmental challenges. As such, it is a call to policymakers to provide the necessary funding, not only for the services themselves, but also for in-service training to support staffs as they move in these directions. At the same time, shifts can be initiated to improve interventions with parents through democratic program leadership with an engaged, mission-expanding staff. While discussion of program-based shifts per se lie beyond the scope of this chapter, some guidance about how to move toward the relationship-based, reflective practice that supports fine parent work may be gleaned from Gilkerson and Shahmoon-Shanok (2000) and from Shanok and Gilkerson et al. (1995).

[iv]All names and identifying details of children, families, and practitioners in these and other examples have been concealed, except for those of the author.

Chapter 14. The Action is in the Interaction: Clinical Practice Guidelines for
Work with Parents of Children with Developmental Disorders

369

REFERENCES

Ainsworth, M. D. S., Blehar, M. D., Waters, S., & Wall, S. (1978). *Patterns of attachment: A psychological study of the strange situation.* Hillsdale, NJ: Erlbaum.

Benedek, T. (1959). Parenthood as a developmental phase: Contribution to libido theory. *Journal of the American Psychoanalytic Association, 7,* 389-417.

Bredekamp, S. & Copple, C. (Eds.) (1997). *Developmentally appropriate practice in early childhood programs.* (Rev. ed.) Washington, D.C.: National Association for the Education of Young Children.

Bronfenbrenner, U. (1979). *The ecology of human development: Experiments by nature and design.* Cambridge, MA: Harvard University Press.

Fenichel, E. S. & Eggbeer, L. with the TASK Advisory Board (1990). *Preparing practitioners to work with infants, toddlers and their families.* Washington, D.C.: National Center for Clinical Infant Programs (now ZERO TO THREE: National Center for Infants, Toddlers and Families).

Fonagy, P. & Target, M. (1998). Mentalization and the changing aims of child psychoanalysis. *Psychoanalytic Dialogues, 8*(1), 87-115.

Fraiberg, S. H., Adelson, E., & Shapiro, V. (1975). Ghosts in the nursery: A psychoanalytic approach to the problem of impaired infant-mother relationships. *Journal of the American Academy of Child Psychiatry, 14,* 387-422.

Galinsky, E. (1981). *Between generations: The six stages of parenthood.* New York: Quadrangle/New York Times Book Co.

Gerber, S. (July, 1999). Comments made at a meeting of the Training and Certification Workgroup, Interdisciplinary Council of Developmental and Learning Disorders, Annapolis, MD.

Gilkerson, L., & Shahmoon-Shanok, R. (2000). Relationships for growth: Cultivating reflective practice in infant, toddler and preschool programs. In J. Osofsky and H. Fitzgerald (Eds.), *WAIMH Handbook of Infant Mental Health, Vol. II: Early intervention, evaluation and assessment.* New York: Wiley and Sons.

Greenspan, S. I. (1992). *Infancy and early childhood: The practice of clinical assessment and intervention with emotional and developmental challenges.* Madison, CT: International Universities Press.

Greenspan, S. I. (1997a). *The growth of the mind and the endangered origins of intelligence.* Reading, MA: Addison Wesley Longman

Greenspan, S. I. (1997b): *Developmentally based psychotherapy.* Madison, CT: International Universities Press.

Greenspan, S. I. & Meisels, S. J., with the ZERO TO THREE Work Group on Developmental Assessment (1996). Toward a new vision for the developmental assessment of infants and young children. In S. J. Meisels & E. Fenichel (Eds.), *New visions for the developmental assessment of infants and young children.* (Chap.1). Washington, D.C.: ZERO TO THREE: National Center for Infants, Toddlers and Families.

Greenspan, S. I., & Wieder, S. (1984). Dimensions and levels of the therapeutic process. *Psychology, 21*(1), 5-23. Reprinted (1987) in S. I. Greenspan, S. Wieder, R. Lieberman, R. Nover, R. Lourie, & M. Robinson (Eds.), *Infants in multirisk families: Case studies in preventive intervention* (Clinical Infant Report No. 3). New York: International Universities Press.

Greenspan, S. I., & Wieder, S. (1998). *The child with special needs*. Reading, MA: Addison Wesley Longman.

Main, M. (1993). Discoveries, prediction, and recent studies in attachment: Implications for psychoanalysis. In T. Shapiro & R. N. Emde (Eds.), *Research in psychoanalysis: Process, development, outcome* (pp. 209-244). Madison, CT: International Universities Press.

Main, M., & Goldwyn, R. (1984). Predicting rejection of their infant from mother's representation of her own experience; Implications for the abused and abusing intergenerational cycle. *Child Abuse and Neglect, 8,* 203-217.

Mann, H. (1999). Developmental therapy and mirroring. Presentation at Invited Session, Interdisciplinary Council of Developmental and Learning Disorders, McLean, VA, November 11, 1999.

Musick, J. (1993). *Young, poor and pregnant: The psychology of teenage motherhood.* New Haven: Yale University Press.

Redl, F. (1966). *When we deal with children.* New York: Free Press.

Sameroff, A. J., & Fiese, B. H. (1990). Transactional regulation and early intervention. In S. J. Meisels & J. P. Shonkoff (Eds.), *Handbook of early childhood intervention.* New York: Cambridge University Press.

Schore, A. N. (1994). *Affect regulation and the origin of the self: The neurobiology of emotional development.* Hillsdale, NJ: Erlbaum.

Seligman, S., & Shanok, R. S. (1996). Erikson, our contemporary: His anticipation of an intersubjective perspective. *Psychoanalysis and Contemporary Thought, 19*(2). Reprinted in R. S. Wallerstein & L. Goldberger (Eds.) (1998). *Ideas and identities: The life and work of Erik Erikson.* Madison, CT: International Universities Press.

Seligman, S., & Shanok, R. S. (1995a). Subjectivity, complexity and the social world: Erikson's identity concept and contemporary relational theories. *Psychoanalytic Dialogues 5*(4), 537-565.

Seligman, S., & Shanok, R. S. (1995b). Psychoanalytic theories, subjective experience, and clinical perspectives: Reply to Wallerstein, Sander & Altman. *Psychoanalytic Dialogues 5*(4), 605-613.

Shahmoon-Shanok, R. (1997a). Multisystem developmental disorder (MSDD), pattern B. *DC: Zero to Three casebook,* 335-358. Washington, D.C., ZERO TO THREE: National Center for Infants, Toddlers and Families.

Shahmoon-Shanok, R. (1997b). Giving back future's promise: Working resourcefully with parents of children who have severe disorders of relating and communicating. *Zero to Three, 17*(5), 37-48.

Shahmoon-Shanok, R. (2000). Infant mental health perspectives on peer play psychotherapy for symptomatic, at-risk and disordered young children. In J. Osofsky & H. Fitzgerald (Eds.), *The WAIMH Handbook of infant mental health, Vol. IV: Infant mental health in groups at high risk.* New York: Wiley and Sons.

Shanok, R. S. (1981). *Motherhood, womanhood and the life cycle.* Unpublished Master's Thesis, Clinical Psychology Program, Teachers College, Columbia University.

Shanok, R. S. (1987). *Identity and intimacy issues in middle class married women during the marker processes of pregnancy, adoption and Ph.D. work.* Unpublished Doctoral Dissertation, Clinical Psychology Program, Teachers College, Columbia University.

Shanok, R. S. (1990). Parenthood: A process marking identity and intimacy capacities. *Zero to Three, XI*(2), 1-9 & 11-12.

Shanok, R. S. (1992). The supervisory relationship: Integrator, resource and guide. In E. Fenichel (Ed.), *Learning through supervision and mentorship to support the development*

Chapter 14. The Action is in the Interaction: Clinical Practice Guidelines for
Work with Parents of Children with Developmental Disorders

371

of infants, toddlers and their families: A source book (pp. 37-41). Washington, D.C.: ZERO TO THREE: National Center for Clinical Infant Programs (now ZERO TO THREE: National Center for Infants, Toddlers and Families). (pp. 37-41).

Shanok, R. S. (1993). Towards an inclusive adult developmental theory: Epigenesis reconsidered. In G. Pollock & S. Greenspan (Eds.) *The course of life, Vol 5: Adulthood* (pp. 243-259). Madison, CT: International Universities Press.

Shanok, R. S., & Gilkerson, L., with Eggbeer, L., & Fenichel, E. (1995). *Reflective supervision: A relationship for learning.* (Discussion guide and videotape). Washington, D.C.: ZERO TO THREE: National Center for Infants, Toddlers and Families.

Shonkoff, J. P. & Hauser-Cram, P. (1987). Early intervention for disabled infants and their families: A quantitative analysis. *Pediatrics, 80*(5), 650-658.

Siegel, D. J. (1999). *The developing mind.* New York: Guilford Press.

Sroufe, C. A. (1983). Infant-caregiver attachment and patterns of adaptation in preschool: The roots of maladaption and competence. In M. Perlmulter (Ed.), *The*

Minnesota symposia on child psychology (Vol. 16) (pp. 41-84). Hillsdale, NJ: Erlbaum.

Stern, D. (1995). *The motherhood constellation.* New York: Basic Books.

Thomas, J., Benham, A., & Guskin, K. A. (2000). Intervention-centered assessment: Opportunity for early and preventive intervention. In J. Osofsky & H. Fitzgerald (Eds.), *WAIMH Handbook of infant mental health, Vol. II, Early intervention, evaluation and assessment.* New York: Wiley and Sons.

Thompson, R. (1999). Plenary address for a session entitled *Temperament: Who has it and why should we care?* Delivered at the ZERO TO THREE National Training Institute, Anaheim, CA, December 1999.

Tronick, E. Z. (1986). Interactive mismatch and repair: Challenges to the coping infant. *Zero to Three,* Vol. VI(3), 1-6. Washington, D.C.: National Center for Clinical Infant Programs (now ZERO TO THREE: National Center for Infants, Toddlers and Families).

Tronick, E. Z. (1998). Dyadically expanded states of consciousness and the process of therapeutic change. *Infant Mental Health Journal, 19*(3), 290-299.

Part Five:

Clinical Evaluation Process: Classification and Biomedical Evaluation and Intervention

◀15▶

Developmentally Based Approach to the Evaluation Process[1]

Stanley I. Greenspan, M.D., and Serena Wieder, Ph.D.

Infants and young children are very direct. An 8-month-old or 3-year-old doesn't disguise his true feelings; he is either engaged and related or aloof and withdrawn. There are, however, many factors influencing a child's behavior and many aspects of development that relate to one another. For example, an aloof and withdrawn child will be influenced by his own physical tendencies (e.g., auditory processing problems and/or over- or under-sensitivity to sound or touch), as well as his relationship with his caregiver and by the dynamics within his own family. He will also be influenced by the relationships between the different aspects of his development, including his sensory, motor, language, cognitive, affective, and interpersonal capacities.

The evaluation of emotional and developmental disorders in infants and young children, therefore, requires the clinician to take into account all facets of the child's experience. A model that looks at how constitutional-maturational (i.e., regulatory), family, and interactive factors work together as the child progresses through each developmental phase is necessary.

It is also necessary to distinguish this developmentally based evaluation model from other approaches. This developmentally based evaluation model is grounded on a theoretical framework of functional developmental capacities and processing abilities that unfold as the infant grows and interacts with others. Using this model requires a clinician to assess each child's relative strengths as well as challenges as they simultaneously impact functional capacities at each developmental level. The assessment provided by using this model contrasts with that of the typical deficit model, through which teams using standardized instruments, and often working in a single-session arena style, independently evaluate the developmental domains of fine motor, gross motor, speech, language, and social skills. The deficit model typically presents assessment results in terms of deficits within each developmental domain, with general recommendations, and frequently omits critical areas of interactive relationships and emotional functioning.

The following model is distinguished by its emphasis on multiple observations and

[1]Adapted from The *Assessment and Diagnosis of Infant Disorders: Developmental Level, Individual Differences and Relationship-based Interactions* (Greenspan & Wieder, 1999); *Infancy and Early Childhood: The Practice of Clinical Assessment and Intervention with Emotional and Developmental Challenges* (Greenspan, 1992); *The Child with Special Needs: Intellectual and Emotional Growth* (Greenspan, & Wieder, 1998), and *The Clinical Interview of the Child* (Greenspan, 1981).

in-depth interviews over time in both the natural environments and in child-centered settings. In the developmental functional approach, the evaluations go beyond the assessment of skills to the assessment of functioning within relationships. Standardized tools are used for strategic purposes rather than as the core assessment. The evaluations always include multiple observations of the child and parent/caregiver in interactions and play, as well as their interactions with the evaluator, whose relationship with the family affects the evaluation, interpretation, and implementation of the intervention plan.

THE BASIC MODEL

The basic developmental model guiding the evaluation process, which was also described in earlier chapters, needs to be re-emphasized in the context of the evaluation process. This model can be visualized with the child's (or infant's) constitutional-maturational patterns on one side and the child's environment—including caregivers, family, community, and culture—on the other side. Both of these sets of factors operate through the child-caregiver relationship, which can be pictured in the middle. These factors and the child-caregiver relationship, in turn, contribute to the organization of experience at each of six different developmental levels, which may be pictured just beneath the child-caregiver relationship (see Figure 1).

Each developmental level involves different tasks or goals. The relative effect of the constitutional-maturational, environmental, or interactive variables will, therefore, depend on and can be understood only in the context of the developmental level to which they relate. Thus, influencing variables are best understood as distinct and different

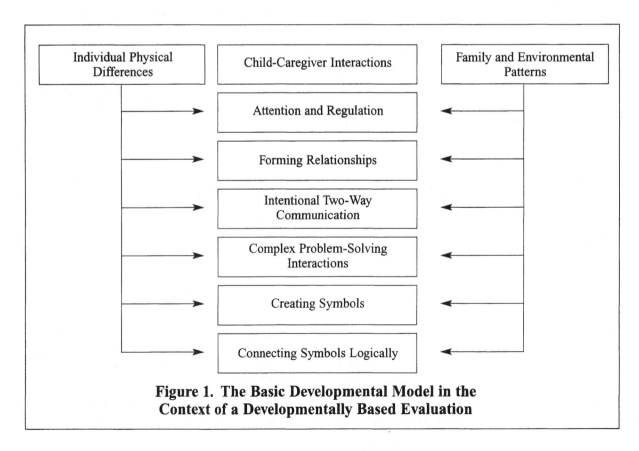

Figure 1. The Basic Developmental Model in the Context of a Developmentally Based Evaluation

influences on the six distinct developmental and experiential levels and not, in the traditional sense, as general influences on development or behavior. For example, as a child is beginning to engage in a relationship, her mother's tendency to be very intellectual and to prefer talking over holding may make it relatively harder for the child to become deeply engaged in emotional terms. If, constitutionally, the child has slightly lower than average muscle tone and is hyposensitive to touch and sound, her mother's intellectual and slightly aloof style may be doubly challenging because neither the mother nor the child is able to take the initiative in engaging the other.

Functional Developmental Levels

In this model, there are six functional developmental levels. They include the child's ability to accomplish the following:

1. *Attend to multisensory affective experience* and, at the same time, organize a calm, regulated state and experience pleasure.
2. *Engage* with and evidence affective preference and pleasure for a caregiver.
3. *Initiate and respond to two-way, presymbolic gestural communication.*
4. *Organize chains of two-way communication* (opening and closing many circles of communication in a row), maintain communication across space, integrate affective polarities, and synthesize an emerging prerepresentational organization of self and other.
5. *Represent (symbolize) affective experience* (e.g., pretend play or functional use of language), which calls for higher level auditory and verbal sequencing ability.
6. *Create representational (symbolic) categories and gradually build conceptual bridges between these categories.* This ability creates the foundation for such

basic personality functions as reality testing, impulse control, self-other representational differentiation, affect labeling and discrimination, stable mood, and a sense of time and space that enables logical planning. This ability rests not only on complex auditory and verbal processing abilities, but on visual-spatial abstracting capacities as well.

The theoretical, clinical, and empirical rationale for these developmental levels is discussed in *The Development of the Ego* (Greenspan, 1989) and *Intelligence and Adaptation* (Greenspan, 1979).

To make a developmental assessment of the functional level, the clinician should evaluate each of the six developmental levels in terms of whether or not the child has successfully negotiated the level, and whether there is a deficit at any level that the child has not successfully negotiated. A *defic*it occurs when the level has not been mastered at all. Sometimes a child may have successfully negotiated a level, but not for the full range of emotional themes. For example, a toddler may use two-way gestural communication to negotiate assertiveness and exploration by pointing at a certain toy and vocalizing for a parent to play with him. The same child may either withdraw or cry in a disorganized way when he wishes for increased closeness and dependency instead of, for example, reaching out to be picked up or coming over and initiating a cuddle. This behavior would indicate that a child has a *constriction* at that level. Sometimes a child is able to negotiate a level with one parent and not the other, with one sibling and not another, or with one substitute caregiver but not another. If it should reasonably be expected that a particular relationship is secure and stable enough to support a certain developmental level, but that level is not evident in that relationship, then the child has a constriction at that level as well.

If the child has reached a developmental level, but the slightest stress, such as being tired, having a mild illness (e.g., a cold), or playing with a new peer leads to a loss of that level, then the child has an *instability* at that level.

A child may have a deficit, constriction, or instability at more than one level. Also, a child may have a deficit at one level and a constriction or instability at another. Therefore, the clinician should make a judgment based on how fully each child has negotiated each developmental level. It is also useful for the clinician to indicate which areas or relationships are not incorporated into each developmental level. Consider the following areas of expected emotional range: dependency (closeness, pleasure, assertiveness [exploration], curiosity, anger, empathy [for children over 3½ years]); stable forms of love; self-limit-setting (for children over 18 months); interest and collaboration with peers (for children over 2 years); participation in a peer group (for children over 2½ years); and the ability to deal with competition and rivalry (for children over 3½ years). A Functional Emotional Developmental Scale was developed for research purposes and includes reliability and validity studies (DeGangi & Greenspan, 2000; Greenspan, 1992).

Constitutional-Maturational Patterns

A child's constitutional-maturational characteristics are the result of genetic, prenatal, perinatal, and maturational variations and/or deficits. These characteristics can be observed as part of the following patterns:

- Sensory reactivity, including hypo- and hyperreactivity in each sensory modality (tactile, auditory, visual, vestibular, and olfactory).
- Sensory processing in each sensory modality (e.g., the capacity to decode sequences, configurations, or abstract patterns).
- Sensory-affective reactivity and processing in each modality (e.g., the ability to process and react to degrees of affective intensity in a stable manner).
- Muscle tone.
- Motor planning and sequencing.

An instrument to clinically assess aspects of sensory functions in a reliable manner has been developed and is available (DeGangi and Greenspan, 1988, 1989a,b).

Sensory reactivity (hypo- or hyper-) and sensory processing can be observed clinically. Is the child hyper- or hyposensitive to touch or sound? How does the child react in terms of vision and movement in space? In each sensory modality, does the 4-month-old "process" a complicated pattern of information input or only a simple one? Does the 4½-year-old have a receptive language problem and is, therefore, unable to sequence words she hears together or follow complex directions? Is the 3-year-old an early comprehender and talker, but slower in visual-spatial processing?

If spatial patterns are poorly comprehended, a child may be facile with words and sensitive to every emotional nuance, but have no context. Such children have difficulty seeing the "forest" and get lost in the "trees." In the clinician's office, this child may forget where the door is or have a hard time picturing that mother is only a few feet away in the waiting room. In addition to lacking straightforward "pictures" of spatial relationship (i.e., how to get to the playground), such a child may also have difficulty with "seeing" the emotional big picture. If the mother is angry, the child may think the earth is opening up and he is falling in because he cannot comprehend that his mother was nice before and she will probably be nice again.

A child with a lag in the visual-spatial area may become overwhelmed by the affect of the moment. This reaction is often intensified when the child also has precocious auditory-verbal skills. The child, in a sense, overloads and does not have the ability to see how it all fits together. Thus, at a minimum, it is necessary for the clinician to have a sense of how the child reacts in each sensory modality, how the child processes information in each modality, and—particularly as the child gets older—a sense of the child's auditory-verbal processing skills in comparison to visual-spatial processing skills.

It is also necessary for the clinician to look at the motor system, including muscle tone, motor planning (fine and gross), and postural control. Observing how a child sits, crawls, or runs; maintains posture; holds a crayon; hops, scribbles, or draws; and makes rapid alternating movements will provide a picture of the child's motor system. Her security in regulating and controlling her body plays an important role in how she uses gestures to communicate and her ability to regulate dependency (being close or far away), aggression ("Can I control my hand that wants to hit?"), and an overall physical sense of self. Other constitutional and maturational variables have to do with movement in space, attention, and dealing with transitions.

Parent and Family Contributions

In addition to constitutional and maturational factors, it is important to describe the family contribution in terms of each developmental level. If a family system is aloof, it may not negotiate engagement well; if a family system is intrusive, it may overwhelm or overstimulate a baby. Obviously, if a baby is already overly sensitive to touch or sound, the caregiver's intrusiveness will be all the more difficult for the child to handle. We see, therefore, the interaction between the maturational pattern and the family pattern.

A family system may throw so many meanings at a child that the child is unable to organize a sense of reality. Categories of me/not me may become confused, because one day a feeling is yours, the next day it is the mother's, the next day it is the father's, the day after it is little brother's; anger may turn into dependency, and vice versa. If meanings shift too quickly, a child may be unable to reach the fourth level–emotional thinking. A child with difficulties in auditory-verbal sequencing will have an especially difficult time (Greenspan, 1989).

The couple is a unit in itself. How do husband and wife operate, not only with each other, but in negotiating on behalf of the children in terms of the developmental processes? A couple with marital problems could still successfully negotiate shared attention, engagement, two-way communication, shared meanings, and emotional thinking with their children. But the marital difficulties could disrupt any one or a number of these developmental processes.

Each parent is also an individual. How does each personality operate vis-à-vis these processes? While it may be desirable to have a general mental health diagnosis for each caregiver, one also needs to functionally observe which of these levels each caregiver can naturally and easily support. Is the parent engaged, warm, and interactive (a good reader of cues)? Is he or she oriented toward symbolic meanings (verbalizing meanings) and engaging in pretend play, and can the caregiver organize feelings and thoughts, or does one or the other get lost between reality and fantasy? Are there limitations, in terms of these levels, and if so, what are they?

Each parent also has specific fantasies that may be projected onto the children and interfere with any of the levels. Does a mother see her motorically active, distractible, labile baby as a menace and therefore overcontrol, overintrude, or withdraw? Her fantasy may govern her behavior. Does a father, whose son has low muscle tone, see his boy as passive and inept, and therefore pull away from him or impatiently "rev" him up?

In working only with the parent-child interaction, and not the parent's fantasy, a therapist may be dealing with only the tip of the iceberg. The father may be worried that he has a overly passive son, or the mother may be worried that she has a monster for a daughter (who reminds her of her cognitively delayed sister). All these feelings may be "cooking," and they can drive the parent-child interactions.

THE PROCESS OF CLINICAL ASSESSMENT

Each clinician has a personal way of conducting an evaluation. However, any assessment should (1) encompass certain baseline data, (2) organize data by indicating how each factor contributes to the child's ability to develop, and (3) suggest methods of treatment. A comprehensive assessment usually involves the following elements: presenting "complaints," developmental history, family patterns, child and parent sessions, additional consultations, and formulation. Chart 1 presents a brief outline of a formal assessment, followed by a discussion of selected elements.

Presenting "Complaints" (Overall Picture)

Therapists frequently spend an entire session on the presenting "complaints" or overall picture, which includes the development of the "problems," the child's (or infant's) and his

family's current functioning, and preliminary observation of the child both with the caregiver(s), or, in the case of a child over 3 years old, without them as well.

We will usually suggest that the parents bring the child with them to the first session. Even though we spend most of the time talking to the parents, we have our eyes on the child and we watch spontaneous interactions between them. If a verbal child is involved, we will have the parents leave the child at home the first time, if possible, so the parents can talk more freely.

We begin by asking the parents, "How can I help?" We encourage the parents to elaborate about the child's problem, whether it has to do with sleeping, eating, or being too aggressive or too withdrawn. If we ask a question, it is usually to clarify something they have said, such as, "Can you give me some examples of that?" "How is this different now from what it was 6 months ago, and when wasn't it a problem?" We try to find out when the problem started, how it evolved, and its nature and scope. For example, if a $2\frac{1}{2}$-year-old is aggressive with peers, we want to know whether it is with all peers or only certain children. We are interested in what precipitated the problem and what may be contributing to it. Was there a change within the family, such as the father getting a new job? Was there marital tension? Were new developmental abilities emerging which paradoxically were stressful to the child?

When the parents say, "Well, I think we have told you everything about the problem," then we will ask, "Is there more to tell about Johnny or Susie that would help fill out the picture?" We find it much more helpful to ask open-ended questions than to ask specific questions about cognitive, language, or motor development at this point. We can gather together more relevant information when the parents elaborate spontaneously. Parents also

Chart 1. Formal Assessment

I.   **Review of current challenges and functioning,** including
  • Each functional developmental capacity (e.g., from attention and engagement to thinking)
  • Each processing capacity (e.g., auditory, motor planning and sequencing, visual-spatial, and sensory modulation)
  • In relevant contexts (e.g., at home with caregivers and siblings, with peers, in educational settings)

II.   **History,** including history of the preceding review items, beginning with prenatal development

III.   **Two or more observational sessions of child-caregiver interactions** with coaching and/or in interactions with clinician (each session should be 45 minutes or more). These observational sessions should provide the basis for forming a hypothesis about the child's functional emotional developmental capacities, individual processing and motor planning differences, and interactive and family patterns

IV.   **Family and caregiver functioning**

V.   **Biomedical evaluations** (e.g., as needed, EEG, metabolic work-up, genetic studies, and nutrition)

VI.   **Speech and language evaluation**

VII.   **Evaluation of motor and sensory processing,** including
  • Motor planning
  • Sensory modulation
  • Perceptual-motor capacities
  • Visual-spatial capacities

VIII. **Evaluation of cognitive functions,** including neuro-psychological and educational assessments

IX.   **Mental health evaluations of family members, family patterns, and family needs**

NOTE: The evaluations listed in under Roman numerals V– IX should be carried out only to answer specific questions which arise from the history, review of challenges, and current functioning and observations of the child-caregiver interaction patterns and family functioning reveal their own feelings and private family matters if the therapist is empathetic in helping them describe their child. Therefore, we strive to be unstructured; ask facilitating, elaborative questions rather than yes-or-no or defining questions; and never be in a hurry to fill out a checklist.

We use the initial session to establish rapport with the family and child to begin a collaborative process. Our experience is that the developmental process discussed earlier in relation to the child—mutual attention, engagement, gestural communication, shared meanings, and the categorizing and connecting of meanings—may occur between an empathetic clinician and the parents. How the clinician relates to the parents reflects how they will be encouraged to relate to their baby. If the therapist asks hurried questions, with yes-or-no answers, he or she sets up an untherapeutic model. It usually takes parents a long time to decide to come for help; they should be able to tell their story without being hurried or criticized.

As part of this presenting picture, we find it is important to learn about all the areas of the child's current functioning. If the primary focus is initially on aggression and distractibility, we wants to know the child's other age-expected capacities. We consider if the child is at the age-appropriate developmental level and if so, the full range of emotional inclinations. Is the 8-month-old capable of reciprocal cause-and-effect interchanges? Is a 4-month-old wooing and engaging? Is a $2^1/_2$-year-old exhibiting symbolic or representational capacities? Does the child do pretend play? Does she use language functionally? How does the child negotiate needs? At each of these levels, how is the child dealing with dependency, pleasure, assertiveness, anger, and so forth?

Toward the end of the first session, we may fill in more gaps by asking questions about

sensory, language, cognitive, and fine and gross motor functioning. Usually, we have a sense of these capacities and patterns from anecdotes and more general descriptions of behavior. We listen for indications of the child's ability to retain information, if she does or does not follow commands, her word retrieval and word association skills, her fine and gross motor skills, and her motor-planning skills.

Some clinicians write down what parents say right after the session; others write during the session. Taking notes need not be an interference if the clinician stops throughout to make good contact. We take detailed notes during the first 15 or 20 minutes because we want as much information as we can get in the parents' words.

By the end of the first session, we have a sense of where the child is developmentally. We also have a sense of the range of emotional themes the child can deal with at his developmental level, as well as an awareness of the support, or lack of support, the child gets from his fine and gross motor, speech and language, and cognitive abilities. We also form an impression of the support the child gets from his parents. We observe how the parents communicate and organize their thinking, the quality of their engagement, their emotional availability, and their interest in the child. We have a good sense of their relative comfort or discomfort with each emotional theme. In general, we use the initial meeting to observe how the parents attend, engage, intentionally communicate, construct and organize ideas, and are able or not able to incorporate a range of emotional themes into their ideas as they relate to their child and to us as the therapists.

Developmental History

In the second session, we construct a developmental history for the child.

(However, sometimes martial or other family problems burst out during the first session. The parents may be at each other's throats; the mother and/or the father may be extremely depressed. In such cases, the focus of the second session is on the individual parent problems, as well as family functioning.)

We will usually start the session in an unstructured manner, allowing parents to describe how their child's development unfolded and what they think is important. We encourage them to alternate between what the baby or child was like at different stages and what they felt was going on as a family and as individuals in each of those stages. We try to start with how (or if) the couple planned for the child and progress through the pregnancy and delivery. Next, we cover the six developmental stages previously described to organize a developmental history.

Family Patterns

The next session focuses in greater depth on the functioning of the caregiver and family at each developmental phase. For example, the mother may say that she was a little depressed or angry, or that there were marital problems at different stages in the child's development.

Sometimes clinicians who are only beginning to work with infants and families feel reluctant to talk to the parents about any difficulties in the marriage. However, we use an open and supportive approach to elicit relevant information. We might ask, "What can you tell me about yourselves as people, as a married couple, as a family?" We are also interested in concrete details of a history of mental illness, learning disabilities, or special developmental patterns in either of the parents' families.

Some families will not hesitate to discuss marital difficulties or other problems.

Sometimes there will be discussion of how the "problem child" relates to the father and mother in terms of "power struggles." If they describe a pattern, for example, between mother and child or father and child, we are likely to ask, "Does that same pattern operate in other family relationships—between mother and father, for example?" Is the pattern a carryover from a parent's own family? By following the couple's lead, we try to develop a picture of the marriage, careers of one or both parents, relationships with other children and between all the children, the parents' relationships with their own families of origin, and friendships and community ties.

Sometimes the family as a whole functions in a very fragmented, presymbolic way. They gesture, "behave at" each other, overwhelm each other, or withdraw from one another, but they do not share any meanings with one another. Nothing is negotiated at a symbolic level. Even though each individual may be capable of functioning on a symbolic level, something about the family dynamics cancels out that ability. In this context, we want to know how the family handles dependency, excitement, and sexuality, as well as anger, assertiveness, empathy, and love.

For each unit of the family—the parents, each parent-child relationship, and the family as a whole—we want to find out how the different emotional themes were dealt with at different developmental levels.

Child (or Infant) and Caregiver Sessions

We focus the next two sessions on the child. Many clinicians may prefer to observe the child before exploring family patterns. Sequence is not critical. We conduct the session differently with an older child (a 3- or 4-year-old, for example) than with an infant. With an infant, we may ask the parent to play with the baby to "show me how you like to be with or play with your baby or child." The parent may ask, "What do you want me to do?" "Anything you like," is our response. We offer the use of the toys in the office or tell them they may bring a special toy from home.

We watch as each parent plays with the child in an unstructured way for about 15 or 20 minutes We are looking for the developmental level, the range of emotional themes at each level, and the use of and support that the child is able to derive from motor, language, sensory, and cognitive skills. We are also watching for the parents' ability to support or undermine the developmental level, the range in that level, and the use of sensory, language, and motor systems. After we watch the mother and father separately, we watch the three of them together to see how they interact as a group because sometimes the group situation is more challenging. Later, we will join them to do some coaching and/or start to play with the child (briefly in the first session and for a longer period in the second session).

During this time, we want to see the child interacting at her highest developmental level, as well as how she relates to a new person whom she knows only slightly. In addition, we want to determine how to bring out the highest developmental level at which the child can function. For example, if a child is withdrawn or self-absorbed and repetitively moving a truck, we will suggest joining her play, trying to move the truck together, put up a fence (one's hands) or take another car and, with great joy and enthusiasm, announce "Here I come!" to entice the child into interaction. Sometimes marching or jumping with an aimless child or lying next to a passive, withdrawn child and offering a back rub or tickle will draw the child in. If a child shows signs of symbolic functioning and the parents do not support symbolic functioning (i.e., in

their 3-year-old), we will try, through coaching or directing, to initiate pretend play. If an 8-month-old is being overstimulated, we will try to introduce cause-and-effect interactions. If a 4-month-old looks withdrawn, we'll try to flirt to pull him in. We will try to calm down a fussy 5-month-old by using visual or vocal support, gentle tactile pressure, and a change of positions. We will work hands-on with an infant to explore tactile sensitivity, muscle tone, motor planning, and preference for patterns of movement in space.

We learn a great deal through observation. By way of example, we might offer a doll to a child moving a train to see if he gives it a ride—suggesting symbolic capacities—or playfully obstruct the path of a child aimlessly wandering around the room to see if he ducks under our arms or smiles or simply turns and wanders away. We also might say to a child who is moving a train, "Oh boy, I can see that you know how to make this train go!" The child may put a doll on the train, make the doll a conductor, and add a passenger. The passenger may have a baby while the train is going through a tunnel, while, at the same time, a doctor makes sure the baby is all right. A 3-year-old who generates such a "drama" is sophisticated cognitively and evidences a rich fantasy life.

With children who can connect ideas together (e.g., hold a back-and-forth conversation), and depending on the child's comfort in being separated from his caregiver, we may reverse the sequence. We may have the first session with the child alone to explore how he or she engages, attends, initiates intentional two-way communication, problem solves, and shares and categorizes meanings.

During this time alone, a $3^1/_2$-year-old may stand in the middle of the room and look us over, while we look at him. If we don't try to control the situation too quickly and can tolerate 10 or 15 seconds of ambiguity, the child may become more self-absorbed and aimless or he may start to play, ask us a question about the toys, or talk about his family. What the child does with behavior or has to say without us saying too much ("Do you want to play with the toys?") can be very valuable. A child may look around and say, "I heard there were toys here. Where are they?" Such a statement indicates an organized, intentional child who has figured out why he is there and acts on his understanding. Another child may look puzzled and withdrawn and repetitively bang a block

Some 4-year-olds will talk to us throughout the session. We might have an almost adult-to-adult kind of dialogue about school or home, nightmares or worries, or just a chat about anything, as one might have with a neighbor. Other children will behave aggressively and want to jump on us or wrestle. They become too familiar too quickly.

We observe the way the child relates to us; that is, the quality of engagement—overly familiar, overly cautious, or warm. We look for how intentional she is in the use of gestures and how well she sizes up the situation and us (without words). We try to determine her emotional range and her way of dealing with anxiety (e.g., does she become aggressive or withdrawn?). We also note, during interaction with a child, the child's physical status, her speech, receptive language, visual-spatial problem-solving skills (e.g., can she search for a toy), gross and fine motor skills, and general state of health and mood. In general, we want to systematically describe the child's ability to attend, engage, initiate and be purposeful with affects and motor gestures, open and close many communication circles to problem solve, create ideas (pretend play), and converse and think logically.

The next step is to learn what is on the child's mind. If the child is symbolic, we look at the content of the play and dialogue, as well as the sequence of themes that emerge from them. Often, observing how a child shifts from one activity or theme to another (e.g., aggression to protectiveness or exploration to repetition) will provide some initial hypotheses. Our role as therapist is to be reasonably warm, supportive, and skillful in engaging the child and helping him evidence and elaborate upon his capacities.

Formulation

After learning about the child's current functioning and history and observing the child and family first hand, we should have a convergence of impressions. If a picture is not emerging, we may need to spend another session or two developing the history or observing further.

We ask ourselves a number of questions related to the child's assessment to determine how high up in the developmental progression the child has gone in terms of:
1. Attending and regulating
2. Engaging
3. Organizing two-way intentional communication
4. Engaging in preverbal problem-solving chains
5. Sharing symbolic meanings
6. Connecting symbols logically (or emotional thinking)

We evaluate how well a child has mastered the earlier phases and, if the child has not fully mastered a level, what are the unresolved issues? For example, does a child still have challenges in terms of his attentional capacities, the quality of engagement, and/or his intentional abilities?

Determining the developmental level tells us how the child organizes experience. To use a metaphor, it provides a picture of the "stage" upon which a child plays out his "drama." The presenting symptoms—nightmares, waking up at night, refusal to eat, as well as other concerns and inclinations—make up the "drama." The "stage" may be age-appropriate. For example, a 4-year-old who can categorize representational experience has a drama of being aggressive to other children, but this drama is being played out on a stage that is age-appropriate. This child has the capacity to comprehend the nature of his aggression and use "ideas" to figure out her behavior.

On the other hand, there may be major deficits in the stage (i.e., attending, being intentional, representing experience, or differentiating experience). If there are flaws in the stage, we want to pinpoint the nature of those flaws. For example, if a child is not engaged with other people, she may be perseverative and self-stimulatory because she can't interact or she may be aggressive because she basically has no sense of other people's feelings. She may not even see people as human. Alternatively, another child may be aggressive because he cannot represent feelings and, therefore, acts them out. Still another child may represent and differentiate his feelings, but have conflicts about his dependency needs.

We also look at the range of experience organized at a particular developmental level. If a child is at an age-appropriate developmental level, does he accommodate such things as dependency, assertiveness, curiosity, sexuality, and aggression at that level? On the other hand, even if a child is at the right developmental level, the stage may be narrow. In other words, he might be only at that developmental stage when it applies to assertiveness, but not when it applies to dependency. When it comes to excitement, he may function at a much lower level. We also look at the stability of the developmental organization: Does even a little stress lead to a loss of function or are the functions stable?

To continue the metaphor, if the child has major problems stemming from earlier developmental issues, we will say there are defects in the stage. If the stage is solid (no defects), it is either very flexible and wide or very narrow and constricted (e.g., it will tolerate a drama of assertiveness, but it will not tolerate a drama of intimacy or excitement). In addition, a stage is stable or unstable.

Next, we want to know about the contributing factors. One set of factors relates to observations about family functioning; the other set of factors relates to the assessment of the child's individual processing differences (i.e., sensory reactivity, processing, and motor planning). The child-caregiver interactions are the mediating factors. The developmental formulation or profile describes: (1) the child's functional developmental level; (2) the contributing processing profile (e.g., sensory reactivity auditory and visual-spatial and motor-planning difficulties); and (3) the contributing family patterns (e.g., high energy, overloading, and confusing family pattern), as well as the observed interaction patterns of each of the significant caregivers and the types of interactions that would be hypothesized to enable the child to move up the developmental ladder and decrease her processing difficulties.

SUMMARY

In this chapter we have outlined the practical clinical steps involved in conducting a comprehensive developmentally based evaluation. This discussion will hopefully complement the material presented in Chapters 3 and 4. ■

REFERENCES

DeGangi, G., & Greenspan, S. I. (1988). The development of sensory functioning in infants. *Journal of Physical and Occupational Therapy in Pediatrics, 8*(3).

DeGangi, G., & Greenspan, S. I. (1989a). The assessment of sensory functioning in infants. *Journal of Physical and Occupational Therapy in Pediatrics, 9,* 21-33.

DeGangi, G., & Greenspan, S. I. (1989b). *Test of sensory functions in infants.* Los Angeles, CA: Western Psychological Services.

DeGangi, G., & Greenspan, S. I. (in press, 2000). *The functional emotional assessment scale: Revised version and reliability studies.* Bethesda, MD: Interdisciplinary Council on Developmental and Learning Disorders.

Greenspan, S. I. (1979). Intelligence and adaptation: An integration of psychoanalytic and Piagetian developmental psychology. *Psychological Issues* (Monograph 47/68). New York: International Universities Press.

Greenspan, S. I. (1981). *The clinical interview of the child.* (2nd ed.). Washington, D.C.: American Psychiatric Press.

Greenspan, S. I. (1989). *The development of the ego: Implications for personality theory, psychopathology, and the psychotherapeutic process.* Madison, CT: International Universities Press.

Greenspan, S. I. (1992). *Infancy and early childhood: The practice of clinical assessment and intervention with emotional and developmental challenges.* Madison, CT: International Universities Press.

Greenspan, S. I., & Wieder, S. (1998). *The child with special needs: Intellectual and emotional growth.* Reading, MA: Addison Wesley Longman.

Greenspan, S. I., & Wieder, S. (1999). The assessment and diagnosis of infant disorders: Developmental level, individual differences and relationship based interactions. In J. Osofsky, & H. Fitzgerald (Eds.), *World Association for Infant Mental Health handbook of infant mental health: Vol. 2: Intervention, evaluation, and treatment.* New York: Wiley.

◄ 16 ►

Developmentally Based Approach to the Classification of Infant and Early Childhood Disorders

*Stanley I. Greenspan, M.D., Serena Wieder, Ph.D.,
and Andrew Zimmerman, M.D.*

(Introduction prepared by Stanley Greenspan and Serena Wieder)

Diagnostic classification approaches often operate on a number of levels, including descriptions of (1) patterns and symptoms, (2) functional adaptive and maladaptive processes (often related to symptoms), and (3) etiological pathways and mechanisms. Classification approaches based more on functional processes and etiological pathways offer potential guidance for interventions and future research. Classification involving meaningful subgroups that capture the unique developmental profiles of individual children also may be especially useful in guiding intervention and research. In fact, when planning interventions for disorders involving many functional components (e.g., language, motor, and social), it is critical that the intervention be based on each child's developmental profile.

For most complex developmental disorders, however, there are no definitive, etiologically based diagnostic tests. Furthermore, no category can completely capture each child's unique pattern. Diagnosis is, therefore, an approximation, at best. Nonetheless, a diagnostic classification system can facilitate research and be useful for various

administrative purposes. Such a system is most helpful when it is based not only on symptoms, but also on functional developmental processes and, when possible, etiological mechanisms.

Descriptive symptom- and process-oriented diagnoses for infancy and early childhood disorders fit into three general categories. These categories are: *interactive disorders*, which include problems related to infant-caregiver patterns; *regulatory disorders,* which include constitutional and maturational deficits; and *disorders of relating and communicating,* which include disorders stemming from multiproblem or multisystem pervasive developmental difficulties (Greenspan, 1992). All the DC 0-3 disorders, as well as most of the DMS-IV infant and early childhood mental health disorders, fall within these three categories.

The Diagnostic Classification 0-3, developed by the Diagnostic Classification Task Force established by ZERO TO THREE, the National Center for Infants, Toddlers, and Families, incorporates all three general categories (DC 0-3, 1994). This multidisciplinary task force met for almost 8 years to develop a systematic, developmentally based approach to the classification of mental health and developmental difficulties emerging during a child's first 4 years of life.

INTERACTIVE DISORDERS

Interactive disorders are characterized by a particular child-caregiver interaction or by the way the child perceives and experiences his emotional world (Greenspan, 1992). With difficulties that are a part of the infant-caregiver interaction pattern, there are only minimal contributions, if any, from constitutional-maturational differences. There are no significant irregularities, delays, or dysfunctions in core areas of functioning, such as motor, sensory, language, and cognition. In other words, the primary difficulty is in the interactions between the child and the caregiver.

The caregiver's own personality, fantasies, and intentions; the child's own emerging organization of experience; and the way these come together through the interactions form the basis for understanding the nature of the difficulty and for devising an intervention. Symptoms in this category include anxiety, fears, behavioral control problems, and sleeping and eating difficulties. Because interactive disorders involve symptoms stemming from interactive patterns, this category also includes situational reactions of a transient nature, such as a child's response to a mother returning to work. It also includes certain responses to trauma when the response does not involve multiple aspects of development.

For the interactive disorders, the primary diagnosis may include:
- Traumatic stress disorder
- Disorders of affect
- Anxiety disorders
- Mood disorders: prolonged bereavement/ grief reaction and depression

- Mixed disorder of emotional expressiveness
- Childhood gender identity disorder
- Reactive attachment deprivation/maltreatment disorder
- Adjustment disorders

REGULATORY DISORDERS

Regulatory disorders involve infants and young children who have significant and clearly demonstrable constitutional and maturational deficits (Greenspan, 1989, 1992). Regulatory disorders also have an interactive component. In this type of disorder, sensory over- or underreactivity, sensory processing, or muscle tone and motor-planning difficulties, as well as the child-caregiver interaction, the caregiver's personality and fantasies, and the family dynamics contribute to the problem. These disorders include attentional and behavioral problems, such as irritability, aggression, distractibility, poor frustration tolerance, tantrums, and sleeping and eating difficulties.

The regulatory disorders include four types:
- Hypersensitive: fearful and cautious
- Underreactive: (a) withdrawn, self-absorbed, and difficult to engage, and (b) underreactive, stimulus craving
- Hypersensitive: defiant, negative, and stubborn
- Inattentive and disorganized, with poor motor planning

In addition, sleep behavior and eating behavior disorders, so common in the early years, are included as separate classifications when there are no known sensory reactivity or sensory processing difficulties.

It may be argued that all infants and children have unique constitutional and maturational variations, including children with interactive disorders, when the focus is on the infant-caregiver interaction. The distinction for the regulatory disorders, however, is that constitutional and maturational factors are not just present as individual differences, but are a *significant* part of the child's problem. Therefore, for regulatory disorders, a clinician wants to understand individual differences as more than just part of the nature of the infant-caregiver interaction patterns. A clinician wants to make the constitutional and maturational factors a major focus in their own right, alongside the interaction patterns and the family dynamics. Here, where possible, a clinician will need to utilize intervention strategies that help the infant strengthen or organize in a more adaptive way her constitutional and maturational variations. The clinician will also seek to understand how the infant's constitutional and maturational variations are a stimulus for the parents' particular fantasies, and how the infant's constitutional and maturational variations bring out certain maladaptive personality dynamics in the caregivers, parents, or family as a unit.

DISORDERS OF RELATING AND COMMUNICATING

The third category of disorders involves problems in multiple aspects of a child's development, including social relationships and language and cognitive, motor, and sensory functioning. This category includes multisystem developmental disorders (MSDD) and the DSM-IV category of pervasive developmental disorders (PDD) (i.e., ASD). The main distinction between MSDD and PDD is that children with MSDD reveal capacities or potential for engagement and closeness in relating but may show difficulties in relating and communicating *secondary* to sensory processing, regulatory, and motor-planning difficulties. These children are quite responsive

to comprehensive intervention and become relatively quickly engaged and interactive.

Before describing this third group of disorders, it is important to note that another type of disorder that involves multiple aspects of development can occur when an environmental stress or trauma leads to a global disruption in multiple areas of functioning. For example, when an infant evidences a failure-to-thrive syndrome, the infant's motor, cognitive, language, affective, and physical growth may slow down or cease altogether. Persistent types of neglect or abuse may produce a similar global disruption in functioning.

In addition, it is important to distinguish how regulatory disorders differ from MSDD or PDD. Regulatory disorders involve processing capacities but do not derail overall relating and communicating, whereas MSDD or PDD do. Developmental disorders also involve regulatory difficulties in terms of significant constitutional and maturational variations. Disorders of relating and communicating often involve difficulties in the interactive patterns and caregiver and family dynamics. Even with the most flexible and adaptive parents, the infant or young child's developmental challenges, which combine regulatory problems and significant delays and dysfunctions, create difficulties in the infant-caregiver interaction or in the family dynamics. The nature of the challenge the child presents, and the lack of expectable feedback due to language, sensory modulation, visual-spatial, and motor processing difficulties, almost always places a significant stress on the interaction patterns and the family dynamics. Most families and most caregivers seem prepared for certain types of communication patterns with their infants and young children. When these biologically expectable interaction patterns are not forthcoming, special approaches are often needed.

The degree of the family contribution will vary considerably depending on the infant or child and the family's or caregiver's pre-existing patterns. Interventions must, therefore, focus simultaneously on the family dynamics, infant-caregiver interaction patterns, the child's regulatory patterns, and the child's developmental delays and dysfunctions in core areas, such as motor, language, cognition, and sensory functions.

In summary, the three types of disorders are (1) interactive, (2) regulatory, and (3) problems in relating and communicating, including MSDD and PDD. The *DC-0-3* Classification Task Force is currently conducting reliability and validity studies of this classification system. (For further discussions of evaluation/diagnostic challenges and related intervention strategies, see DC-0-3, 1994; Greenspan, 1992; Greenspan & Salmon, 1995; Greenspan & Wieder, 1998). The next section of this chapter proposes an expanded conceptualization for the third category: problems in relating and communicating, including MSDD and PDD.

CLASSIFICATION APPROACHES FOR DISORDERS OF RELATING AND COMMUNICATING

A number of challenges confront efforts to classify complex developmental disorders that derail a child's ability to relate to others, to communicate, and to think. Each child tends to have a unique functional profile. Often, the differences in functional profiles are greater than the similarities that are the basis for children sharing a diagnosis. Furthermore, children from different diagnostic groups may have similar functional profiles.

When these observations are coupled with the lack of a clearly identified etiological pathway for many complex developmental disorders, including ASD, there is an apparent

need to look again at classification approaches for complex developmental disorders. Two directions for improving classification need to be explored. One is to take a step back and describe complex developmental disorders in terms of early verifiable neurological and observable characteristics and refrain from going beyond biological and clinical data. The other is to explore descriptions of clinical subtypes based on functional profiles and responses to intervention. The next two sections explore both of these avenues: first, by looking at a very broad designation of neurodevelopmental disorders and, second, by examining clinical categories based on functional developmental profiles.

Classification of Neurodevelopmental Disorders
(Prepared by Andrew W. Zimmerman, M.D.)

The main objective of a practical and functional classification of neurodevelopmental disorders as a common ground for communication among different disciplines should be to help differentiate how these disorders lend themselves to rehabilitation, to the facilitation of developmental processes, and to medical evaluations and treatments. It is equally important that classification should flexibly incorporate the rapidly expanding knowledge of the genetics and neurobiology of these disorders.

Time-dependency in the evolution of neurodevelopmental disorders frequently distinguishes them with respect to their clinical and biological characteristics as well as to their responsiveness to therapies. Time is, therefore, a critical element in development, to which other variables relate in type and degree. Normal brain development depends on complex synergistic interactions among multiple genes, cell types, and their functions that follow sequential time-dependent patterns. Physical and environmental inputs are also essential for normal brain development and are likely to be synergistic with cellular activities during critical time periods. Physical changes may occur within the normally developing brain as a result of defined insults that occur at specific times (e.g., prenatal strokes, perinatal asphyxia, and infections). Genetic abnormalities may have variable expression over time (e.g., Down syndrome, autism, and Tay-Sachs disease). Sensory or emotional deprivations may themselves lead to cellular abnormalities undermining the individual child's inherent plasticity and capacity for repair in the developing nervous system.

This classification of neurodevelopmental disorders includes three types: static, static-dyssynergic and progressive. Some disorders, such as the epilepsies, mental retardation, and autistic disorders, may be included in more than one group.

Static Disorders

(not moving or progressing)

Static disorders include cerebral palsy and other static encephalopathies. These disorders result from specific insults to the developing central nervous system, usually before or around the time of a child's birth. Symptoms are non-progressive in that patients do not deteriorate. Development may be delayed but follows expected patterns and responses to therapies. Congenital anomalies (e.g., spina bifida, hydrocephalus) may fluctuate due to changing symptoms but are usually static with respect to development. Uncomplicated or medically controlled epilepsy remains static with respect to development (i.e., it progresses sequentially over time). Many forms of idiopathic mental retardation (of unknown cause) remain static, although the co-occurrence of epilepsy or a psychiatric disorder may transiently make patients appear to be "progressive." Genetic syndromes may be "static" if their developmental progress remains stable over time.

Static-Dyssynergic Disorders

(dys=abnormal; synergy=to work together)

This group includes ASD (autism and PDD). These disorders vary widely among individuals with respect to symptoms, course, and responses to therapies. As with static disorders, patients with static-dyssynergic disorders also do not deteriorate, despite limited periods of regression. Children with these disorders, however, show signs of atypical development (dyssynergy) among brain networks or abnormal synaptic development by age 3. Many families (40%-60%) report language and social regression in children between 18 and 24 months of age. Development of the disorders fluctuates over time and may progress unevenly within and among areas such as language and socialization. Although these disorders are multigenic (i.e., associated with several or more abnormal genes), other "single gene" (chromosomal) disorders (e.g., Down syndrome or fragile X syndrome) or "static" disorders (e.g., congenital rubella) also may be associated with autistic symptoms that evolve over time. Specific subtypes of autism (e.g., a hypothesized bipolar subtype) may receive further clinical and genetic definition and treatment in the future.

The varied timing of brain development, as well as the marked differences among cortical functions and abnormal behaviors, characterizes the dyssynergic disorders. The varied and complex patterns of maldevelopment observed in these patients imply that multiple genes, external causes, and neural pathways may be involved. Behavioral and language therapies for these disorders rely on the assumption that organizing and increasing sensory inputs during critical periods as early as possible, and in individually specific ways, improves outcomes. Outcome studies to date are consistent with this concept, and suggest that plasticity within the developing central nervous system can be used to modify dysfunctional pathways in these disorders. Possible medical treatments (e.g., corticosteroids, serotonin-modifying agents) may likewise show maximum benefit when started early in the course. Further study of the neurobiology of these disorders is necessary in order to learn how they differ from normal with respect to time sequences in cellular and neurochemical patterns (as well as other factors) in the developing cortex.

Progressive Disorders

(Med: becoming more severe)

The genetically determined neurodegenerative diseases (e.g., Tay-Sachs, Leigh's, and metachromatic leukodystrophy) show continuous regression in previously acquired functions due to flaws in critical cellular systems. Persons with these disorders do not improve functionally—but may stabilize and benefit in quality of life—with behavioral and other therapies. In most of the disorders, medical interventions are limited to diagnosis and supportive care or prenatal genetic diagnoses. Rett syndrome is a genetic disorder in girls that is similar to autism, especially its abnormal, but more widespread, development of the fine structure of the cortex (neuropil). Girls with Rett syndrome also show rapid early regression, but then stabilize for long periods. Unlike most children with autism, however, the girls' symptoms can slowly worsen over time.

In conclusion, neurodevelopmental disorders can be classified according to their clinical characteristics with respect to the time course as each evolves. This approach should facilitate therapeutic interventions with individual patients and their families, as well as support research on therapies and outcomes.

Clinical Groups for Non-Progressive Neurodevelopmental Disorders
(Prepared by Stanley I. Greenspan and Serena Wieder)

The information needed to begin classifying groups within the two non-progressive neurodevelopmental disorders just described—static and dyssynergic—now exists. In the 5 years since the publication of *Diagnostic Classification 0-3* (DC-0-3, 1994), and the 7 years since Greenspan (1992) proposed multisystem developmental disorders in *Infancy and Early Childhood*, clinicians have collected additional diagnostic, treatment, and outcome data on several hundred more children with severe disorders of relating, communicating, and thinking. This extensive clinical information enables clinicians to divide non-progressive disorders into several broad groups that can capture a child's developmental capacities, such as the degree to which a child can communicate, as well as the child's underlying processing differences (e.g., the child's relative strengths in visual-spatial or auditory processing). Reconceptualization of the existing classification system (including MSDD and PDD), therefore, can incorporate relevant developmental dimensions, including:

- *The child's ability to connect affect* (intent) with sequences of behavior and/or symbols. The affect serves as a signaling system telling the motor system what to do and allows the child to initiate, be spontaneous, and engage in meaningful gestures and symbolic acts.
- *The child's functional developmental level of presymbolic and early symbolic capacities*—the child's ability to engage in complex problem solving through gestures and early expression of ideas.
- *The child's engagement with others,* as evidenced by mutual or shared attention and mutual pleasure.

- *Motor planning*—the child's ability to initiate action, both imitate or have an idea, plan how to execute it, and then sequence the steps necessary to do or express what he wants or is thinking.
- *Auditory-verbal processing*—memory and comprehension, including receptive understanding (e.g., semantics, reasoning, and logic) and expression (e.g., retrieval and pragmatics).
- *Visual-spatial processing*—memory and comprehension, including part-whole discrimination, organization, tracking, directional stability, time sense, and visual-motor (e.g., construction and sequencing).
- *Sensory reactivity and regulation*—sensory registration, orientation, interpretation, and responding or reacting (under and overreactive or well-modulated) in different sensory modalities.
- *Symbolic thinking and rate of progress*— the rate the child climbs the symbolic ladder to becoming an imaginative, representational, and abstract thinker, the better the rate of progress.

The following section offers a classification of neurodevelopmental disorders of relating, communicating, and thinking, based on a child's presenting profile and the child's potential for early response to a comprehensive, developmentally based intervention program. This proposed classification is based on constructing developmental profiles implementing a comprehensive intervention program and following a large number of children and families (Greenspan, 1992; Greenspan & Wieder, 1997, 1998). It is an initial clinical descriptive effort that will hopefully create a framework for further research. It identifies four broad groups, some of which divide into smaller subtypes. Children within each group and subtype are described with respect to the preceding developmental dimensions. This section includes some case studies to help illustrate the characteristics and responses typical of children within each group.

Group I

Children whose presenting profile places them within this group tend to make very rapid progress, often moving within 2 to 3 years from patterns of perseveration, self-stimulation, and self-absorption to warm, emotionally pleasurable engagement, spontaneous use of language, and abstract levels of symbolic play, with healthy peer relationships and solid academic skills.

The overall group evidences the following identifying criteria, with four subtypes defined by unique patterns of processing differences.

Identifying Criteria

Children within Group I:
- Evidence difficulty connecting affect (or intent) to motor planning and sequencing as well as to symbol formation; therefore, behavior tends to be repetitive, self-stimulatory, fragmented, or lacks clear meaning or purpose.
- Either partially have, or within the first few months of intervention acquire, the ability to engage in preverbal, gestural problem-solving interactions with caregivers (e.g., taking a caregiver by the hand, leading her to the toy room, and showing her the desired toy).
- Either partially have, or within the first few months of intervention acquire, the capacity for warm engagement with positive affect, as evidenced by affectionate behavior with smiles and looks of delights at primary caregivers.
- Possess relatively strong motor planning (e.g., child can sequence three or more motor actions, including sounds or words,

though not at an age appropriate level, such as taking a car in and out of the garage, making car noises, and moving the car around the house).

- Either have, or within the first few months of intervention acquire, solid imitative skills for motor actions and/or sounds and/or words (e.g., can imitate actions, such as "touch your nose" or "touch your head," as well as simple sounds and words, such as "up" or "go"). The children use this skill to progress, over time, toward early stages of imaginative play.

Additional Characteristics

Children within Group I also display:

- Hypersensitivity to sensation, such as touch and sound. Although the children are often underreactive to movement and, occasionally, to pain, the overall tendency of the children is to be overreactive.
- Relatively strong or weak visual-spatial processing.
- Relatively mild to moderate auditory processing impairment with good progress once intervention begins.
- All the children in this group progress into imaginative play quickly, climbing the symbolic ladder from pretending real life experiences to representational play, and are able to build logical bridges between ideas and become abstract thinkers.

Sequence of Progress

Children within Group I often show rapid improvement in engagement, purposeful gesturing, range of affect expressed, and shared attention with caregivers and, over time, with peers. They also rapidly improve in imitative skills because of their better motor planning abilities, leading to language and imaginative play sequences. During the first year or two of intervention, many of the children become

excited about their emerging language skills and enter a stage of hyper-ideation where they talk about everything, but in a very fragmented (free-associative) manner. Over time, they learn to be more logical as the environment challenges them to build bridges between their ideas. During the early stage of becoming more logical, they tend to continue some preoccupations and perseverative tendencies with special interests, topics of conversation, or playthings (e.g., roads, cars, certain types of visual displays). During this early stage, some children have profile descriptions similar to that of Asperger's syndrome. However, when interventions emphasize creative interactions and dialogues (e.g., using their interests as a take-off for creative interactions), these children gradually become more spontaneous, flexible, creative, and empathetic. Over time, they progress to higher and higher levels of abstract reasoning and social skills.

Subgroups Patterns Within Group I

There are four different patterns within Group I. Children within these subgroups meet all the basic identifying criteria for the basic group, but display different, unique patterns of processing capacities.

Group I-A: *Relatively strong auditory, visual-spatial and motor-planning capacities, and a tendency toward overreactivity to sensation.*

Children within Group I-A make the most rapid progress. Over time, and possibly by the time they enter school, these children may even evidence precocious academic skills (e.g., abstract thinking, reading, or arithmetic). This subgroup has:

- A tendency toward relatively strong short-term auditory memory and expressive abilities (e.g., may recite the alphabet and numbers, fill in the blanks to songs and stories, and when older, memorize scripts from TV shows or books).

- Relatively strong visual-spatial memory skills (e.g., knows where things are, good sense of direction, good at puzzles, recognizes letters and shapes).
- A tendency to be more reactive to sensation and emotional states, showing more intense joy as well as frustration. These children develop better modulation over time.

Group I-B*: Relatively strong auditory processing but weaker visual-spatial and motor-planning capacities, with a tendency to be underreactive.*

While also making rapid progress, children in this group evidence:
- A tendency to remain more fragmented in their thinking and may have a harder time learning math (especially word problems), interpreting the meaning of what they read, and "seeing the forest for the trees" intellectually and socially.
- Relatively strong short-term auditory memory.
- Relatively weaker visual-spatial memory and processing capacities than children in Group I-A.
- Relatively weaker motor planning abilities than children in Group I-A.
- A tendency to be more underreactive with some sensory hypersensitivity. They have a longer fuse, but also tends to process information more slowly.

Group I-C*: Relatively stronger visual-spatial and motor-planning capacities but weaker auditory processing, and a tendency toward sensory underreactivity.*

Children within Group I-C make solid, consistent progress, but not quite as rapidly as those in Groups I-A and I-B above. They evidence:
- A tendency to take a longer time to progress, especially in learning to use

words, but they can use symbolic toys as a language to express many ideas. Group I-C children do not tend to evidence a dramatic hyper-ideation learning phase since language develops more slowly, but they are able to elaborate and sequence ideas through the use of toys and gestures, aided by their better motor-planning abilities.
- Relatively stronger visual-spatial memory and processing.
- Relatively weaker auditory processing and memory/retrieval.
- A tendency toward sensory underreactivity, but may get more emotional, especially when their weaker auditory processing and poor verbal communication leave them frustrated or frightened.

Group I-D*: Relatively strong auditory, verbal, and visual-spatial memory but relatively weaker verbal and visual-spatial comprehension and motor planning, and a tendency to be overreactive and become overloaded.*

Children in Group I-D tend to make consistent progress with good rote verbal skills, but have a narrower range of ideas. These children do not usually go through the hyper-ideation phase and have a weaker ability for higher-level processing of auditory and visual information. These children have:
- A narrower range of acceptable emotions. Unless the environment can be more soothing and interactive, they tend to be more rigid and anxious.
- Become more easily overloaded without the resources to comprehend and integrate. Consequently, these children resort to constrictions and rigidity and are more anxious and fearful because of their oversensitivity, with more challenges with reality testing. This subtype has many

similarities to what others have described as Asperger's syndrome.

- Both auditory and visual-spatial memory as relative strengths.
- Relatively weaker auditory and visual-spatial comprehension.
- Relatively weaker motor planning.
- A tendency to be more overreactive, especially to unexpected sensation or events, but also to be underreactive in some modalities. They may have reduced muscle tone.

Group I Case Illustration

Two-and-a-half-year-old David presented with self-absorption, perseveration, and self-stimulation, no peer play, and lack of eye contact and pleasure in relating to his parents. During his evaluation, David spent most of his time reciting numbers in a rote sequence, spinning and jumping around aimlessly and randomly, and lining up toys and cars, while making self-stimulatory sounds. David, however, showed strengths in his ability to indicate what he wanted when extremely motivated; occasional displays of affection; the capacity to imitate actions, sounds, and words; and the ability to recognize pictures and shapes.

With a comprehensive program, David quickly became more engaged and began imitating some pretend-oriented sequences. He gradually began using his language purposefully and creatively. He then went through the sequence of progress described previously and, at present, is in a regular school, where he excels in reading and English as well as in math. He has a number of close friends, a sense of humor, and insights into other people's feelings. His remaining challenges are with fine-motor sequencing (penmanship) and his tendency to become somewhat anxious and argumentative when in a competitive situation.

Group II

Children in Group II have greater challenges than those in Group I. They make slower, but consistent, progress with each hurdle requiring a great deal of time-consuming work. Typically, these children can initially engage a little bit, be partially purposeful, and intermittently do some problem solving. However, they take much longer to become consistent, preverbal problem-solvers and to learn to use imitation as a basis for language and imaginative play. When they achieve these milestones, they do not generally go through a stage of hyper-ideation and rapid learning, but rather move through each new capacity very gradually. Although many children in this group still make progress, most are not able to participate in all the activities of a regular classroom with a large class size, as are the children in Group I. They can benefit, however, from appropriately staffed inclusion or integrated programs, or from special needs language-based classrooms where the other children are interactive and verbal.

Identifying Criteria
Children within Group II:
- Evidence difficulty connecting affect (or intent) to motor planning and sequencing as well as to symbol formation; therefore, their behavior tends to be repetitive, self-stimulatory, fragmented, or lack clear meaning or purpose.
- Can be partially purposeful, often oriented to basic needs, but do not have solid mastery of preverbal, gestural problem-solving capacities (i.e., cannot do 20+ circles of problem-solving interaction and communication in a row).
- Possess an intermittent, but not full, capacity to engage with caregivers. These children initially rely more on sensorimotor

stimulation and, when self-absorbed or avoidant, need to be wooed and pursued.

- Have motor-planning skills that tend to be limited to two or fewer sequential actions (e.g., putting the car in the garage and taking it out, rolling the car toward a single destination).
- Do not yet evidence spontaneous imitative skills, other than perhaps some occasional ability to copy a familiar motor pattern, such as building with blocks, or setting up or drawing a scene that they memorized.
- Possess relatively limited auditory processing capacities, through which they can verbally express what they want better than they can understand what others say. They have a greater reliance on the use of scripts.

Group II children also tend to be characterized by the following, which are not, necessarily, early identifying criteria:

- Mixed reactivity to sensation with a tendency toward being underreactive and self-absorbed and/or underreactive and craving (as well as mixtures of the two), with some children tending to be more reactive.
- Relative degrees of compromise in visual-spatial processing but may have good visual memory and, sooner or later, may learn to read but with weak comprehension skills.

Sequence of Progress

Children within Group II have the capacity to become joyfully engaged, but may require wooing and persistent pursuit. They also have the capacity to move from simple, purposeful gestures to complex problem-solving, preverbal interactions and, eventually, use of imitation as the basis for learning words and becoming involved in pretend play. They learn primarily through what they

see and may get very immersed in videos and books (before being encouraged to do more interactive work). They also may borrow scripts and scenes to begin to embark on symbolic play as well. However, mastery of each of these steps, from engagement to using simple and then complex gestures and on to using words and ideas, tends to be very gradual. Children in this group may evidence a wide range of patterns of progress in the transition from preverbal gesturing to use of ideas. Some children in this group take a long time to progress beyond intermittent need-based, short, verbal phrases. Some of the children who are not able to develop imitative skills readily benefit from more semistructured challenges to imitate actions, sounds, and words. This work, however, must be part of a comprehensive program. As the children in this group develop language, their mastery of each step from creative elaboration to logical discussion is a gradual and time-consuming process. The children in this group can easily become mired in the use of more fragmented, concrete, and early types of logic and have great difficulty—in comparison to the children in Group I—in progressing to more abstract and creative thinking. Some children learn to read before they are fluent and conversant. Peer relationships are both possible and desired, but Group II children develop relationships very gradually in conjunction with advances in their functional thinking capacities. These children benefit from semistructured, sensorimotor games before they move on to symbolic levels in play. Their capacities for experiencing warmth and pleasure with other children often precede their ability to interact and communicate creatively. Nonetheless, with continued work, these children will continue to progress.

Subgroup Patterns Within Group II

Group II divides into two different patterns, both of which meet all the general criteria for the group.

Group II-A*: Relatively strong visual-spatial memory, relatively weak visual processing, auditory processing, and motor-planning capacities, with a tendency toward overreactivity.*

Children within Group II-A are more easily engaged and spontaneous. They tend to have:

- Moderate compromises in auditory processing (very difficult to respond to the words of others) but develop language, retrieve often-used phrases, and borrow fragments of scripts from books and videos, which they use for symbolic play. Although their language develops slowly and tends to be descriptive of what is seen or associative, these children slowly become more logical and able to reason. The children within this subtype also speak more spontaneously, which is related to their more reactive and often demanding nature.
- Moderate compromises in visual-spatial processing (easily lost, poor sense of direction, can't find things), but possess visual memory as a relative strength.
- Moderate compromises in auditory processing.
- Moderate compromises in motor planning.
- More reactivity and to be intermittently sensation seeking.

Group II-B*: Relatively strong visual-spatial memory, while other visual-spatial processing is moderately impaired. Moderate to severe auditory processing and motor-planning problems. Group II-B differs from Group II-A in that Group II-B children are underreactive with overreactivity to certain sounds.*

Children within Group II-B tend to be more self-absorbed and avoidant, requiring more encouragement to speak. They tend to have:

- Moderate compromises in auditory processing, but they do learn to speak, with greater difficulty in understanding the unpredictable speech of others. They have retrieval difficulties and rely on often-repeated phrases and scripts. The early conversations of these children tend to be short and repetitive.
- More underreactivity. They also tend to be more self-absorbed than children in Group II-A and have to be wooed to respond. They benefit from visual communication strategies, and often learn to read sooner than to speak fluently or spontaneously.
- Moderate compromises in visual-spatial processing (easily lost, poor sense of direction, can't find things) but their visual memory is a relative strength.
- Moderate to severe compromises in auditory processing.
- Moderate to severe difficulties with motor planning and low muscle tone.
- Hypersensitivity and overreactivity to sensation, with some sensation-seeking behavior.

Group II Case Illustration

Three-year-old Joey presented with a great deal of avoidant behavior, always moving away from his caregivers and having only fleeting eye contact. He frequently engaged in very simple perseverative and self-stimulatory behavior, such as rapidly turning the pages of his books or pushing his Thomas® train round and round the track. Joey could purposefully reach for his juice or take a block from his parents, but he was not able to negotiate complex preverbal interactions or, for that matter, imitate sounds or words.

Four years after his program began, Joey (6½) now shows abilities to relate with real pleasure and joy, use complex gestures to lead his parents places, and describe what he wants in sentences, such as "Give me juice now!" Joey can respond to simple questions ("What do you want to do?" "Play with my trains!"), and have short sequences of back-and-forth communication with four or five exchanges of short phrases. He is also able to engage in early imaginative play, having his action figures fly around the room with great joy and delight. He is not yet able to consistently answer "why" questions. He also is able to play with peers only with some adult involvement and when there is action or a structured game. However, he continues to make progress at a consistent but slow pace. Interestingly, Joey only occasionally displays perseverative, self-stimulatory patterns.

Group III

Children in this group have moderate to severe auditory and visual-spatial processing, with more severe motor planning that impedes purposeful communication and problem solving. They are capable of intermittent problem solving interactions, but cannot sustain their interactions. They are intermittently engaged in purposeful activities, with much self-absorption and/or aimless behavior. It is this "in-and-out" quality, with presymbolic "islands" of problem solving, that characterizes this group. Their islands may involve the use of words, pictures, signs, and other two- to three-step gestures or actions to communicate their basic needs. Some children will use toys as if they were real as long as they are the actors (e.g., they will eat pretend foods or feed a life-size baby doll) but they do not usually represent themselves or others through figures. Some

children with severe oral-motor dyspraxia will not speak more than a few ritualized words, if at all, but they may evidence preverbal communication through a few signs, or picture communication, or through the use of a favorite toy. Some children learn to recognize logos and may read words.

Identifying Criteria

Children within Group III evidence:

*   Very intermittent purposefulness at the presymbolic level, which is seen in islands of problem solving. Group III children cannot sustain interactions; that is, they cannot complete more than four or five circles of problem-solving interactions.
*   Very intermittent capacity to engage with caregivers, and usually engage as a result of sensorimotor stimulation. These children tend to break off into aimless, self-absorbed, or avoidant behavior.
*   Relatively strong auditory processing, which enables them to say a few words or phrases when in need or desiring something. Their receptive language is relatively stronger when it consists of often-used phrases in routines and/or accompanied by visual support and context. Their more severe motor planning, oral-motor and/or visual-spatial challenges make it difficult for them to convey just what they understand receptively.
*   Very limited motor planning, with most actions limited to two or three sequential actions that are often repeated again and again. Group III children often seek hand-over-hand assistance for actions.
*   Very weak imitation skills. Group III children do not imitate spontaneously and learn only through tremendous repetition.
*   Relatively weak visual-spatial processing (e.g., disorganized, poor discrimination, poor searching, easily lost).
*   Relatively strong visual memory.

- Mixed reactivity to sensation, with a tendency toward being underreactive and self-absorbed and/or underreactive and craving (as well as mixtures of the two), with some children tending to be more passive and with low muscle tone.

Sequence of Progress

Group III children tend to progress slowly, given the severity of their processing difficulties and their intermittent engagement and problem solving. The key to intervention is to "bring them in" to more sustained pleasurable interactions through persistent pursuit and by playing simple games, such as peek-a-boo, hide and seek, chase, tickling, horsy rides and other sensorimotor fun activities. More consistent engagement will create more motivation and lead to more interactive problem solving. The heightened affect inherent in having a "problem," such as getting a parent to do more roughhousing, finding a treasured Thomas® toy train, or getting more cookies, will motivate the child to process more information or input, be it visual or auditory. For example, the child will learn the sequence needed to get shoes, coat, key, and Mom's purse in order to go outside. Once engaged, the caregiver's affect cueing will help the child expand her perceptions as well as sustain her attention to the input. The child's desire or objections will then motivate her to go beyond her motor-planning constraints and respond in some form. With more sustained engagement and interactions, children in this group also can become more responsive to complex imitation, visual communication strategies, and practiced learning. They can go on to early levels of symbolic play.

Group III Case Illustration

Sarah ran in looking for her Winnie the Pooh and climbed up on the stool in front of the shelves, but she could not move the little figures in the basket around to search for her beloved character. The next moment, she pulled the basket off the shelf and all the figures fell out. She then looked in the next basket without bothering to look at the fallen figures on the floor. Her mom intervened before Sarah could drop the second basket and offered to help. Sarah echoed, "Help!" and grabbed her mother's hands and put them in the basket. Her mother had to point to Winnie before Sarah actually saw the figure. Sarah grabbed it and ran off to lie on the couch. Mom then brought Tigger over to say hello. Sarah grabbed Tigger and ran to the other side of the room. She held her figures tightly and turned away when Mom came over again. Mom then took Eeyore and started to sing "Ring around the rosie..." moving her figure up and down. This time, Sarah looked and filled in "down" to "all fall down," but she then moved rapidly away and went over to the mirror. Sarah's pattern of flight and avoidance after getting what she wanted, followed by not knowing what to do next, was quite typical.

Sarah's intervention program began when she was 3 years old. She slowly learned the labels for things she wanted and to protest. She recognized and could express familiar phrases like "come and eat," "go out," and "bathtime." She became quite engaged with sensorimotor play and loved to be swung and tickled. She even began to play imaginatively with toys, first dipping her toes into the water of the play pool and then letting Winnie "jump" in. She began to imitate more words and actions. She also tried to solve problems to get her figures, but only when she was very motivated or very angry, and usually only after energetic sensorimotor play pulled her in. Her expressive language expanded to include more and more phrases indicating what she wanted, but her weak receptive processing made it difficult for her to answer any questions. She relied on visual and affect cues to understand what was said to her. This transferred to puppet play and even simple role play as a cook or doctor. Sarah's problem solving also progressed very slowly because of her very poor motor planning, but she became more easily engaged and more responsive to semistructured and structured approaches to learning. Between ages 4 and 5, she learned to count and identify colors, and loved to paint and cut with scissors. By age 6½, Sarah demonstrated some pre-academic abilities, and was able to read some sight words. She now enjoys being with other children and joins the crowd running around, hiding, and chasing, but she does not yet play interactively, although she has learned the various social rituals, such as greeting, sharing, and protesting. Sarah can also spontaneously communicate "feel happy" with a big smile, and "feel mad" with a frown.

Group IV

Children in this group are characterized by significant challenges in being purposeful, which are related to their very severe motor-planning problems, as well as by significant auditory and visual-spatial processing difficulties. Children in Group IV fall into two subgroups. Both subgroups differ from Group III in that children have more severe challenges in all processing areas, especially motor planning (including oral-motor dyspraxia). As a consequence, children within the Group IV subgroups progress very unevenly, and slowly, having the most difficulty in developing intentional problem-solving patterns, expressive language, and motor planning. Over time, with continuing therapeutic work, they become engaged and partially interactive through gestures and action games.

Group IV-A Identifying Criteria

Children within Group IV-A evidence:

- An intermittent capacity to engage with caregivers. Initially, they tend to be very avoidant, with great difficulty in understanding what others want of them and being purposeful. They wander around aimlessly or lie down passively, with intermittent bursts of sensory-seeking behavior.
- Severe motor planning, which impedes sequences of more than one or two steps. Group IV-A children usually initiate actions to have their basic needs met. They are very dependent on adult actions to obtain what they want, although they are very persistent in communicating their desires through simple and, eventually, more complex gestures.
- Limited imitation abilities, usually restricted to single-step actions, such as pushing, pulling, or throwing an object.
- Relatively strong visual-spatial processing with moderate compromises; stronger visual memory, but weaker organization and visual-motor abilities (easily lost, poor sense of direction, can't find things, poor discrimination).
- Severe auditory processing difficulties. These children may learn some need-based words but rely on visual cues to understand what others say. Some children with more severe oral-motor dyspraxia do not speak but do have a narrow range of meaningful visual symbolic schemas (such as cars or trains) that they may enjoy and use repeatedly. Some children do eventually learn to say or sign some words through much practice and repetition.

Children within Group IV-A also:

- Show a wide range of reactivity. They tend to be primarily over- or underreactive to sensation, with a greater tendency to be avoidant rather than self-absorbed.

- Participate in presymbolic play when toys relating to real life experiences (e.g., baby doll, slide, pool, school bus) are readily in sight and modeled, but do not usually find or organize the toys themselves. (Structure and visual communication strategies are very helpful in learning pre-academic and adaptive skills.) They may learn to enjoy simple puzzles and cause-and-effect toys.
- Evidence symbolic understanding, as shown by their attachments to video and TV figures and their desires for specific books and videos. However, their very poor motor planning impedes purposeful play.

Group IV-A Sequence of Progress

With persistent pursuit, these children can become more engaged, enjoy being around their families, and become better problem solvers to get what they want. Because of severe motor planning difficulties, they do not often initiate purposeful steps, but can readily undo what they do not want and then have difficulty knowing what to do next. They often resort to the repetition of ideas (e.g., simple sequences with favorite toys, such as pushing a toy train on tracks through the tunnel). They may learn words (usually through ritualized phrases), songs, and filling-in-the-blank. Eventually, they retrieve the words for highly desired objects or objections while in high-affect states. Some children show visual-spatial learning on semistructured tasks, such as matching, pointing to pictures, and assembling easy puzzles, but they cannot sequence actions to express ideas independently. They function at a presymbolic level. Other children are unable to retain even repetitive learning, but do best when work focuses on their natural interests (e.g., to go outside, get food, play horsey). Some children with a relatively

strong visual-spatial capacity read logos or words, but their receptive understanding remains highly dependent on visual cues and context. With work on experiencing pleasure and consistent engagement, these children can diminish frustration, self-destruction, and aggression and can increase their adaptation to surroundings and their expectations. Over time, some children evidence unexpected strengths, moving on to presymbolic problem solving and increased rate of learning.

Group IV-A Case Illustration

Harold was able to progress only very slowly to imitating sounds and words, even with an intensive program organized to facilitate imitation. He could say one or two words spontaneously when angry or insistent on getting something, but otherwise he had to be prompted and pushed to speak. Every utterance was extremely difficult for him, and he would sometimes stare at a caregiver's mouth to try and form the same movements. His severe dyspraxia also interfered with his evidencing pretend play, although from the different facial expressions and the gleam in his eye when he engaged in playful interactions with his parents, it appeared he was playing little "tricks." He sometimes held onto toy objects, such as a Nerf® sword or magic wand, and used them in ritualized ways, but he could not use toys to sequence new ideas. He could engage and even initiate sensorimotor interactions during which he expressed pleasure and affection. Although games with his brother had to be orchestrated, he did enjoy running around the schoolyard and the pool with other children.

In the second year of intervention, Harold was able to interact and communicate with three or four back-and-forth exchanges about what he wanted, such as pulling his dad over to the refrigerator and finding the hotdogs. He could even retrieve a few words at such moments (e.g., "Hotdog" "What else?" "French fries"). Harold became more consistently engaged over time, with islands of presymbolic ability, and he became more aware of what was going on around him. He no longer wandered aimlessly and would pick up trucks to push or select other cause-and-effect toys and simple puzzles. He let others join him but invariably turned the interaction into sensori-motor play, which brought him great pleasure. His pre-academic progress was also very slow, even with lots of structure, repetition, and practice, but he did make progress in learning to complete "work" and self-care.

Group IV-B Identifying Criteria

Children in Group IV-B tend to evidence patterns of regression and/or more overt neurological involvement (e.g., persistent seizures). Children within this subgroup usually begin with enormous challenges and make very limited progress, no progress at all, or vacillate between a little progress and regression. Group IV-B children display:

- Fleeting to intermittent engagement. They tend to have severe processing challenges in all areas and yet, at the same time, can become more engaged and happier and, in learning this, to become partially purposeful in solving problems when they want something.

- Fleeting to intermittent purposeful behavior related to very strong needs. It is hard for this group to progress consistently into complex preverbal problem-solving strategies or into the use of ideas, words, or complex spatial problem solving. During times of progress, their developmental abilities may improve to the level of children in Group IV-A or Group III.

- Severe motor planning difficulties. These children may intermittently use cause-and-effect toys brought to them (e.g., a simple pop-up toy) but they often only engage in repetitive touching, banging, or self-stimulation. They frequently have severe oral-motor dyspraxia and have little or no imitative ability.

- Extremely limited auditory processing capacity.

- Extremely limited visual-spatial processing.

- A tendency to be underreactive to sensation. These children often evidence low muscle tone and passivity. They may also evidence more overt neurological symptoms.

Group IV-B Sequence of Progress

With a comprehensive program, these children can become more engaged and happier. Over time, they can learn to be intermittently purposeful, engaged, and involved in preverbal, gestural problem solving, but are unable to develop symbolic capacities. With structure, visual communication strategies, repetition and practice, they can develop basic adaptive skills for home and school. They will often find it difficult to move into complex, preverbal problem solving.

Group IV-B Case Illustration

Margaret had severe perinatal complications and evidenced low muscle tone from shortly after birth. She achieved her motor milestones very slowly, sitting up at 9 months, crawling at 12 months, and walking, with some asymmetry noted, at 17 months. Other than showing some pleasure in cuddling during the first year and some purposeful mouthing towards the end of the first year, she did not progress into consistent, purposeful interaction or complex, preverbal problem solving. At the time of the first visit, she tended to perseverate by rubbing a favorite spot on the carpet and by staring towards the light, but could smile and show some fleeting pleasure with sensory-based play.

With a comprehensive program, Margaret has progressed slightly. She has become more robustly engaged, with deeper smiles and pleasure, and more purposeful reaching. She engages in some exchange of facial expressions, which she sometimes uses to indicate preferences. At present, however, she has not progressed into complex, behavioral problem-solving interactions. Margaret has recently begun evidencing a seizure disorder, for which she has been placed on medications.

FROM ASSESSMENT TO FEEDBACK TO INTERVENTION

As noted earlier, classification approaches involving meaningful subgroups that capture the unique developmental profiles of individual children may be especially useful in guiding intervention as well as research. Given the approach described in this chapter and throughout this book, it is evident that intervention begins from the moment a parent calls and is asked what his or her concerns are. This approach assumes that every evaluation, assessment, or diagnostic session is an intervention and that parents are partners in this effort. It also assumes that the assessment process has a significant impact on the family and must be conducted sensitively and thoughtfully.

The evaluator needs to consider several factors during the course of the assessment before moving on to diagnosis and planning. How a family experiences the assessment, as well as how they interact with each other and the evaluator during the course of multiple sessions, establishes guidelines for the session when the evaluator will discuss his diagnosis with the family and they must mutually concur on an intervention plan. Factors the evaluator should consider follow.

- *How well did the parents engage with the clinician in the process of the evaluation?* Did the parents initiate the evaluation or did others encourage them to pursue it? Was rapport and trust established? How readily were the problems and family background discussed? What was the response to suggestions, coaching, and other inquiries? What was the family's experience of prior intervention or services?

- *Was the evaluation a therapeutic experience for the family and the child?* Did the evaluation lead to an evolving understanding of the problems, the effects of current environmental factors, and the past and present dynamics? Was there a change in the interaction patterns between family members and with the child? How did the family learn best? In what ways did the family experience the evaluation as helpful? What changes were most evident in the course of the evaluation? Did the parents express ideas about what they wanted to do or their priorities and resources?

- *How does the nature of the difficulties or diagnosis and the prognosis shape the feedback?* Are further medical or developmental assessments indicated? If so, should intervention be delayed until the additional information is obtained, or should parts of the intervention plan proceed?

By the time the family meets with the evaluator to discuss the diagnosis and plan the intervention, a base has been established for moving forward. The evaluator would begin the session by addressing the family's remaining questions and thoughts. The evaluator would then focus the discussion on the Developmental, Individual Differences, Relationship-based (DIR) model elements which were assessed during the evaluation by using the DIR model (see

Chapter 3, this volume). First, the evaluator would present a developmental profile of the child based on functional developmental capacities that highlight the child's strengths as well as challenges. To build agreement, the evaluator would refer to many of the joint observations and rapport shared during the assessment. Second, the evaluator would describe the child's individual differences, outlining the unique ways and relative strengths and weaknesses in the way the child comprehends and regulates sensory input as well as in motor planning and execution. Third, the evaluator would share impressions of the family's relationships and functioning, including the relationships with the child, others in the family, and between the parents, all within the context of the family's culture and environment.

The evaluator and the family are now ready to use the diagnostic feedback to discuss an intervention plan. Every intervention plan must have the parents at the center, both in the interventions they will try to provide their child as well as in the management of the "case," even when they are provided with case management assistance in seeking and coordinating services. The evaluator would begin the discussion with recommendations for an optimal intervention plan. Although the family may be unable to adopt the optimal plan, the plan provides the family with a basis for finding resources, determining priorities, and implementing the best available plan, even if they carry out different interventions in stages. It is important for both the evaluator and the family not to compromise prematurely the interventions that should occur. They must also leave open the possibilities of change and growth in the child, especially if an appropriate, comprehensive intervention plan is put in place.

There are times when an evaluation will turn into ongoing intervention, such as when it is possible for the evaluator to continue working with the family. At such times, an evaluator may want to deviate from the preceding recommendations, especially when this would protect the trust and emerging relationship with a high-risk or fragile parent. By continuing with a family, the evaluator has the flexibility to modify the intervention plan as indicated, delaying some steps and bringing in other therapists during the early stages of intervention. Transferring a child and family to another therapist, however, will require the evaluator to carefully weigh and time the effect this will have on the family.

After discussing the diagnosis and interventions with the family, the evaluator will have to consider what information should follow, including formal comprehensive reports, specific reports pertaining to obtaining services, and audio or videotape feedback. The range of information provided will vary considerably in different settings and according to what each case may warrant. Families should have access to the reports, and they should be apprised of any issues of confidentially, including the opportunities for selectively releasing information.

CONCLUSION

This chapter presented a developmentally based approach to classifying infant and early childhood disorders. This classification system uses a multidimensional approach to diagnosis, taking simultaneously into account (1) the developmental level, (2) individual differences in constitutional and maturational factors, and (3) relationships within the family and its environment. Utilizing these developmental dimensions makes it possible to identify clinical subtypes as well as individual development profiles. This chapter described in detail several proposed subtypes. Clinicians and researchers can test and refine these developmental dimensions and the subtypes as well as use them to guide further investigation. Most important, the functional developmental approach to assessment and diagnosis can enable clinicians to construct intervention plans that are more individualized and appropriate to the needs of each unique child and family. ■

REFERENCES

DC-0-3, Diagnostic Classification Task Force, Stanley Greenspan, M.D., Chair, Serena Wieder, Ph.D., Co-chair and Editor (1994). *Diagnostic classification: 0-3: Diagnostic classification of mental health and developmental disorders of infancy and early childhood.* Arlington, VA: ZERO TO THREE, the National Center for Clinical Infant Programs.

Greenspan, S. I. (1989). *The development of the ego: Implications for personality theory, psychopathology, and the psychotherapeutic process.* Madison, CT: International Universities Press.

Greenspan, S. I. (1992). *Infancy and early childhood: The practice of clinical assessment and intervention with emotional and developmental challenges.* Madison, CT: International Universities Press.

Greenspan, S. I., & Salmon, J. (1995). *The challenging child: Understanding, raising, and enjoying the five "difficult" types of children.* Reading, MA: Addison Wesley Longman.

Greenspan, S. I., & Wieder, S. (1998). *The child with special needs: Intellectual and emotional growth.* Reading, MA: Addison Wesley Longman.

◄ 17 ►

Medical Evaluation Of The Child With Autistic Spectrum Disorder

Ricki G. Robinson, M.D., M.P.H.

The role of the physician in the evaluation of the child with an autistic spectrum disorder (ASD) is guided by a multistep process. The first step includes the screening of all children to identify those with symptoms that may be indicative of a child on the autistic spectrum. The goal is to identify these children as early as possible. The next step is the evaluation of the child who is suspect of having a spectrum disorder in order to make a diagnosis. The third step involves the laboratory evaluation of the child who has been given a diagnosis of ASD to ascertain if there are any other medical conditions associated with this disorder and to collect baseline studies that may help direct treatment protocols. When a child does fit on the autistic spectrum, the fourth step is development of a treatment plan. It is the responsibility of a "team leader" to develop an appropriate treatment plan that is unique to the needs of the particular child and to ensure that the multidisciplinary team is functioning appropriately for the child and the family. The physician may participate as the team leader or as a team member. In either case, evaluation and management of medical protocols, including appropriate medication trials, is the physician's responsibility.

This chapter discusses each step in this evaluation process and the appropriate qualifications for the medical personnel. It is

important to note that the state of the science in the field of autism has not yet produced the replicable data necessary for comprehensive, verifiable practice guidelines. This chapter reflects not only on recent consensus statements (CAN Consensus Group, 1998), practice parameters (Bernet et al., 1999), and evidence-based guidelines (Filipek et al., 1999) using information currently available but also on clinical experience and judgment recorded by members of the Interdisciplinary Council of Development and Learning (ICDL). These guidelines are likely to be modified as results of more studies become available.

STEP ONE: INITIAL SCREENING

The initial screening of all children to identify those on the autistic spectrum occurs at the level of the primary health care provider (e.g. pediatrician, family practitioner, or nurse practitioner.)

It is imperative that physicians and other health care providers understand their key role in recognizing a child's potential difficulties and making appropriate referrals so that the child can begin to benefit from services. Recent research indicates that the children with autism who are identified earliest and receive subsequent treatment intervention may have the best prognosis (Greenspan

& Wieder, 1998; McEachin, Smith & Lovaas, 1993). It may be anticipated that early medical interventions that enhance the growth of the developing cortex (neuropil) may also have greater effects when given early, rather than late, in the child's course of treatment. In light of these findings, early identification of children with disorders of relating and communicating, including autistic spectrum disorders, is a primary goal of the ICDL. Certainly by the age of 18 months, those children who have not yet developed age-appropriate skills in relating and communicating need to be identified.

This task is particularly challenging for several reasons. When a child is young, parents—especially parents of their first child—may not realize that the child should have, or has not, acquired these skills. The parents may not even be willing to accept the fact that their young child has not yet acquired these skills. In addition, the physician may not recognize these subtle changes in the child's ability to relate and communicate because of the short amount of time usually allotted to well-child visits. This situation is especially likely if the parents themselves are not recognizing any possible delays in development and, therefore, are not bringing their concerns to the physician's attention.

In order to ensure early identification, both parents and professionals need to acquire an increased awareness of the possibility of development of these symptoms in the young child. Key clinical milestones to observe in a child include:

- *The child's ability for warm, joyful relating.*
- *The child's ability for engaging in a continuous back-and-forth pattern of emotional and gestural cueing.*

- *The child's ability to engage with a caregiver in an intentional, complex, reciprocal interaction pattern* in order to solve a problem, such as taking a parent to the door to help open it or pushing a caregiver to the refrigerator and pointing to the desired food.

If, by 18 months of age, the child is unable to demonstrate by both history and observation the above milestones, the child should have a complete evaluation to rule out a pervasive developmental disorder (PDD).

A standard screening device that can help distinguish between potentially autistic and nonautistic behavior and identify most children at risk also would be beneficial to early identification. The Checklist for Autism in Toddlers (CHAT) successfully identifies autism in many children. (Baron-Cohen, Allen, & Gillberg, 1992; Baron-Cohen et al., 1996). In Britain, this 3-minute screening tool, which is used at the 18-month well-baby exam, has been shown to predict 90% of children who will develop autism, PDD, or other developmental delay syndromes. The CHAT uses a questionnaire and an observation to elicit abnormalities in development of the child's joint attention and pretend play. A normal CHAT, however, does not rule out a developmental disorder. Therefore, a suspicion by the parent or clinician of poorly developed verbal or nonverbal communication skills and delay along the social-emotional continuum at any age should always trigger appropriate referral for formal evaluation. In addition, abnormal performance on the CHAT requires further assessment for possible ASD. It may be that abnormal CHATs are recorded for many children who end up developing normally or who have developmental delay for other reasons.

In conclusion, children must be followed and observed through routine well-care visits for their attainment of skills along the social-emotional continuum as described by Greenspan (1992). The child should be referred *immediately* for a step-two evaluation when there is suspicion by the parent or clinician that a child has a delay in (1) receptive and expressive language skills, (2) joint attention and engagement, (3) two-way communication skills, and/or (4) imaginative play, or if there is (5) an abnormal CHAT or a failure on other appropriate developmental screening tests in these areas (Filipek et al., 1999), or (6) a loss of language at anytime.

STEP TWO: NEURODEVELOPMENTAL REFERRAL

The step-two evaluation should be performed by a physician who understands the underlying characteristics and pathophysiology of ASD and who has experience in developing appropriate treatment programs for affected children. This evaluation will generally fall in the domain of a developmental pediatrician, a pediatric neurologist, or a child psychiatrist. The responsibility of this specialist is to (1) make the diagnosis, (2) use appropriate diagnostic tools together with other members of the diagnostic and treatment team to evaluate the child's baseline pathophysiologic parameters, (3) order an appropriate medical evaluation to rule out other associated medical conditions, and (4) put together a multidisciplinary treatment plan. This plan will then be followed closely and monitored over time so that it can remain unique, flexible, and dynamic in response to the needs of the child.

The primary role of the specialist physician is to make a diagnosis; however, there is a caveat here. If the child is delayed in any of the parameters discussed, this child will, in any case, need some type of early intervention. It

has been shown that in most cases, a 6-month delay occurs from the time the child presents with abnormal symptomatology to the beginning of an early intervention program (Greenspan & Wieder, 1998). Therefore, extensive diagnostic evaluations should be conducted concurrently with the initiation of the treatment program. The ICDL recommends that treatment begin as *soon as possible*, even while these other diagnostic evaluations are still being performed.

The specialist evaluation should include the following critical components:

- *Family histories,* with probes for history of autism, mental retardation, fragile X syndrome, tuberous sclerosis complex, and affective disorder.
- *Developmental and medical history,* with special emphasis on history of regression and specific developmental level attainment.
- *Physical and neurologic examination,* including longitudinal measurements of head circumference; notice of neurocutaneous abnormalities requiring a Wood's-lamp examination, dysmorphic features, reflexes and cranial nerves; and a thorough observation of muscle mass and tone, gait, posture, facial movement (including presence or absence of a Moebius mouth) and generalized movement abilities (given recent description of very early onset of abnormal motor movements in this group of children) (Teitelbaum, Nye, Fryman, & Maurer, 1998).
- *Functional/emotional developmental level assessment* to include:
- Observation of child-caregiver interaction patterns for 20 to 30 minutes or longer on at least two separate occasions.
- Clinician-child interaction designed to elicit the child's highest level of functioning.

- Observation and exploration of family interaction patterns including, if possible, parents and siblings.
- Construction of a developmental profile of the child's emotional, interactive, cognitive, language, motor, and sensory patterns based on the preceding components of evaluation and assessment.
- *Use of a standardized diagnostic instrument* based on the DSM-IVR definitions of ASD (American Psychiatric Association, 1994), which may be helpful in distinguishing children with autism or PDD from other developmental difficulties. Examples include the Childhood Autism Rating Scale (CARS) (Schopler, Reichler, DeVillis, & Daly, 1980; Schopler, Reichler, & Rodden-Renner, 1988), Autism Diagnostic Interview-Revised (ADI-R) (Lord, Rutter, & LeCouteur, 1994), and the Autism Diagnostic Observation Scale (ADOS) (DiLavore, Lord, & Rutter, 1995). The specialist physician will be familiar with the proper use and choice of these instruments as well as with how to tailor the testing to the needs of the child and the clinical setting. For example, the rigorous diagnostic inclusion criteria for a research study might require completion of the ADI-R, whereas those in a clinical setting may find use of a CARS more practical for initial diagnosis and long-term followup.
- *Evaluations by other members of the multidisciplinary diagnostic team,* which will be critical to the determination of the child's complete functional profile and may include (but are not limited to) the following disciplines (see the Table of Contents for related chapters in *The ICDL Clinical Practice Guidelines*):
- Speech and language
- Auditory functioning

- Pediatric occupational therapy
- Educational/cognitive abilities
- Visual-motor capacities
- Neuropsychiatric evaluations

STEP THREE: MEDICAL TESTING PROCEDURES

The ICDL recommends consideration of the following procedures as part of the complete medical evaluation, to be performed under the supervision of the appropriate specialist. The selection of the specific tests will be directed by the results of the history and the physical examination.

Audiologic evaluation: The hearing evaluation should be behavioral in focus and include formal, pure tone audiometry performed by an experienced pediatric audiologist. Brainstem auditory-evoked potentials are necessary only if the initial test is equivocal, suboptimal, or suggests central nervous system abnormality.

Electroencephalography: A significant number of children with autism and related disorders may have abnormal electroencephalograms (EEG's) and epileptiform activity and/or epilepsy (Tuchman & Rapin, 1997; Tuchman, 1994; Volkmar & Nelson, 1990; Tuchman, Jayakar, Yaylali, & Villalobos, 1998; Chez, Buchanan, Zucker, & May, 1997). It has been shown that EEG recording during all four stages of sleep may be necessary to identify these abnormalities. Prolonged EEG studies are significantly more likely to identify abnormalities in children with ASD than are routine one-hour studies. Epileptiform abnormalities have been found in only 27% of routine one-hour sleep EEG studies as compared with 60% of prolonged overnight EEG studies (Tuchman et al., 1998). In addition, there is a high rate of epileptiform activity when measured in an overnight study in children with ASD and a history of clinical regression (Chez et al., 1997). Therefore, an extended sleep-deprived EEG with adequate sampling of all four stages of sleep is recommended if the child has evidence of clinical seizures, history of regression in social and communicative functions, or any suspicion that clinical or subclinical epilepsy may be present. Whether the recording is conducted for 4 hours, overnight, or for a complete 24-hour period is not currently specified because the optimal time length is not known. However, many children will require overnight or 24-hour EEG's to obtain all stages of sleep (CAN Consensus Group, 1998).

Metabolic screening tests: Metabolic lab tests are indicated for those children who present with both autism and other signs of metabolic disease (e.g., lethargy, cyclic vomiting, failure to thrive, early seizures, dysmorphic or coarse features, severe or profound mental retardation). Metabolic tests are also used to evaluate rare disorders that are difficult to detect and which occur in less than 5% of children with ASD. Autism has been associated with several inborn errors of metabolism, primarily phenylketonuria (PKU). The following may be considered in the metabolic assessment: (1) quantitative amino acids, (2) urine organic acids, (3) uric acid and calcium in a 24-hour urine, (4) thyroid studies, (5) lactate, pyruvate and carnitine, and (6) lead levels, especially if pica is present.

Genetic testing: Population-based studies suggest that between 5% and 12% of children with autism have underlying medical or genetic conditions (Cohen & Volkmar, 1997). Both DNA fragile X testing and high-resolution cytogenetic studies should therefore be considered (Wing, 1996; Gillberg & Wahlstrom, 1985). These are indicated if there is associated mental retardation in the family or patient, or if dysmorphic features are present in the child. Karyotyping should

be at high resolution with particular attention noted for possible duplications of 15q 11-13 (Cook et al., 1997). Families need to be aware that absence of a positive genetic test does not exclude a genetic basis for autism. As ongoing research develops, these and other cytogenic tests may require reevaluation for inclusion in the assessment.

Structural neuroimaging: (Brain CT or MRI): The use of neuroanatomic imaging studies, such as the magnetic resonance imaging (MRI), in the primary diagnostic workup of children with autism is indicated only for those whose neurologic examination, EEG, or other clinical indicators suggest a focal lesion (CAN Consensus Group, 1998; Filipek et al., 1999).

Functional neuroimaging: Tests in this category, including single photo emission tomography (SPECT), position emission tomography (PET), magnetoencephalography (MEG), or magnetic resonance spectroscopy (MRS), are valuable research tools in this field. At the present time, however, they are not indicated for the primary diagnostic evaluation of autism.

Other laboratory tests: Children with autism may have an increased incidence of certain infections such as otitis media (Konstantareas & Homatidis, 1987). Altered immune parameters have also been demonstrated in some cases (Warren et al., 1996; Van Gent, Heijnen, & Treffers, 1997). In addition, a higher instance of allergies has been reported in this population. Recently, abnormal gastrointestinal dysfunction has been reported in a subset of children with autism (D'Eufemia, Celli, Finocciaro, Pacifico, Viozzi, & Zaccagnini, 1996; Horvath et al., 1998; Wakefield et al., 1998). However, there is not yet clear evidence to suggest that immune or gastrointestinal abnormalities cause (or that their treatments can reverse) the changes in the brain in autism. According to the current standards of care, medical evaluation should be directed toward the detection and treatment of any disorder that may contribute to discomfort and behavioral dysfunction. It also is emphasized that a child with autism is susceptible to any of the diseases of childhood. The treating physician should maintain a high index of suspicion for infection or other medical problems in the child, especially during episodes of regression or exacerbation.

STEP FOUR: THE TREATMENT PLAN

For a child who is on the autistic spectrum, the ICDL advocates the use of a multidisciplinary, integrated team to provide an intensive, relationship-based therapeutic plan, with specialty treatment usually conducted one-on-one. This plan is unique to each individual and delivered in a dynamic, flexible manner that is keyed to the interactive social-emotional, cognitive, sensory, and motor patterns of the child (Greenspan & Wieder, 1998). In addition, the plan must be family oriented because the family will play a significant role in the implementation of the treatment strategies. The plan must also be service coordinated (e.g., between regional centers, schools, and insurance companies) in order to garner both the human and financial resources required to implement an inclusive treatment plan. The plan can be home-based, school-based, or a combination of both, depending on the unique characteristics and challenges of the child. However, one role of the physician (including both the primary care and specialist) is to aid the parents in getting through the maze of finding the best human resources and to get health plans and public agencies to help finance these often expensive treatment plans. The team members may include, but are not limited to, clinicians from speech, occupational therapy,

nutrition, medicine, psychology, education, advocacy, and social work.

The role of the physician in the treatment plan involves:

- Leadership and involvement with the multidisciplinary team just discussed.
- Treatment of coexisting medical problems.
- Treatment of target behavior symptoms with medications as necessary.
- Ongoing monitoring and longitudinal followup coordination with the multidisciplinary team.

The role of the multidisciplinary team, as well as the assessment of functional abilities of the child over time, is discussed elsewhere in *The ICDL Clinical Practice Guidelines.*

It is imperative that all coexisting medical problems be addressed fully for the child. Some common clinical presentations include the following: If allergies coexist, elimination of appropriate allergens from the child's environment can markedly improve the child's capacity for attention and learning in the therapeutic setting. Attention to treatment of coexisting gastrointestinal abnormalities, such as constipation or obstipation with overflow diarrhea (Wakefield et al., 1998) or reflex esophagitis and disaccharide malabsorption (Horvath et al., 1999), could also markedly change a child's chronic pain level and might lead to improved learning capacity. In addition, sleep disorders have recently been described in a subset of children with autistic spectrum disorders (Thirumalai, Robinson, & Shubin, 1999). This association clearly could affect daily behavior and autistic symptoms and deserves medical evaluation and appropriate treatment.

There are three general categories of medications that may be helpful in treating target behavior symptoms in children with autism. These include:

- Drugs that affect neurotransmitters (e.g., selective serotonin reuptake inhibitors or SSRIs).
- Drugs that stabilize mood and treat epilepsy (or, presumably, EEG abnormalities) (e.g., "anticonvulsants").
- Hormonal or growth factors (e.g., steroids).

These medications have not proven to be curative, but they can help ease target symptom behaviors that may be interfering with development and learning. The aim of medication therapy, therefore, is to optimize functioning for the child. The various drug choices are best implemented through a drug trial where target behaviors are first identified and followed in as blind a manner as possible to overcome placebo effects.

As always, with the use of any pharmacologic agent, care should be taken in the selection and administration of medications. The profile of side effects and risk must be weighed against the potential benefits of course, and vary depending on the agent used and the target symptom identified. Use of simple charting techniques often helps parents and personnel working with the children to quantify and identify the symptomatology being observed over time. It is important to never lose sight of the overall goal of optimizing the child's functioning in therapeutic, educational, and social settings by monitoring the child's adjustment and engagement. For many of the medications used to alter target symptoms in children on the autistic spectrum, studies of large numbers of individuals who are affected have not been completed, although a body of clinical use with some of these medications is growing. In most cases, use of these medications is extrapolated from the adult literature using indications from the

pathophysiology. The ICDL suggests that usage of psychopharmacology may be recommended if the clinician monitors the children closely and in a trial format to optimize the efficacy and to avoid side effects. Typical target symptoms that may be evaluated for modulation with drugs that affect neurotransmitters include obsessive/compulsive ritualized behaviors, hyperactivity/inattention, tics, sleep disorders, anxiety, and aggressive or self-injurious behaviors.

There are several categories of psychopharmacologic drugs that can help address some of these target symptoms. The category with increasing clinical experience is the SSRIs. These medications are potent inhibitors of the serotonin transporter and include medication such as fluoxetine and fluvoxamine. The SSRIs can be used in autism to reduce the frequency and intensity of repetitive, ritualized behaviors, including motor stereotypes and more classic compulsive rituals. In addition, other autistic symptoms have been noted to improve on these drug trials, including improvement in eye contact, social initiation and responsivity, decreased withdrawal, and expanded repertoire of interests. In some children, behavior may improve with a decrease in tantrums, aggression, and self-injurious behavior. Parents also describe improvements in initiating, shifting, and sustaining attention with more connectedness to the environment and less internal preoccupation. All these improvements can result in a child wanting to be more a part of the group, less aloof, and more available to the therapeutic interventions. There is general consensus that the SSRIs should be administered in as low a dosage as possible and then titrated up slowly so that a narrow range of effect versus side effect can be maintained. For example, since the drug Prozac comes in a liquid form, it can be started at 1 mg to 2 mg per day and gradually increased, as needed, to help modulate target symptoms. Clinical experience has shown that many children achieve the best results on doses of less than 3 mg to 5 mg per day. Typical side effects from medications in this group include hyperactivity, sleeplessness, aggressiveness, and possible appetite changes. Imipramine and clomipramine (nonselective serotonin reuptake inhibitor tryciclic drugs), if used, have potential side effects consisting of cardiac arrhythmias. EKG monitoring should accompany the use of these drugs.

Other categories of psychopharmacologic drugs that may be useful for autism include neuroleptics, antidepressants, lithium, anxiolytics, and stimulant medications. Anticonvulsants have a place in the treatment protocol if the child has a diagnosed seizure disorder. Children diagnosed with regressive epileptic aphasia have been reported to respond to treatment with anticonvulsants (e.g., Depakote sprinkles) and/or steroids (e.g., prednisone) (Chez, Buchanan, Zucker, & May et al., 1998; Stefanatos, 1995). In these cases, use of these medications should be supervised by a specialist with experience in this field because these treatments have major side effect risk profiles that may offset any potential benefits.

The discussion of pharmacology is necessarily brief for the purpose of this chapter. For more extensive information, the practitioner is referred to several useful references on the subject (McDougle, 1997; Zimmerman, Bonfardin, & Myers, 2000 [in press]). It cannot be overemphasized, however, that medication trials are just one part of the multimodal, integrated treatment plan advocated by the ICDL in the guidelines.

CONCLUSIONS AND COMMENTS

Implementation of biomedical evaluations and interventions for children with disorders in relating and communication,

including ASD, can be especially challenging. One reason is that, at present, therapists lack a clear understanding of the causes and biological pathways involved in these disorders. In fact, it is likely that there are a number of different causes and pathways (e.g., genetic, autoimmune, environmental toxins) that influence development at various stages pre- and postnatally, resulting in different types of disorders in relating and communicating, including different subtypes of ASD. For example, different disorders, such as fragile X syndrome, fetal alcohol syndrome, tuberous sclerosis, congenital hypotonia, undiagnosed hearing loss, and prenatal rubella exposure, can all be associated with increased likelihood of symptoms of self-absorption, aimless behavior, lack of language, perseveration, and self-stimulation, all of which are common autistic symptoms. This suggests that there are many different pathways to these types of symptoms.

Therefore, the current state of knowledge suggests the possibility of multiple pathways leading to shared dysfunctions or expressions of symptoms. A few final common pathways may express a variety of different underlying biological patterns, much like a fever is an expression of many different biological processes. In addition, for certain children, etiological and mediating factors may be cumulative. For example, a variety of genetic vulnerabilities may be associated with a number of cumulative environmental challenges leading to disordered functioning. Furthermore, there are many different subtypes of disorders in relating and communicating, including many subtypes of ASD. It is likely that a number of subtypes have not yet been clearly described.

Research findings may, therefore, be particularly difficult to interpret. It may appear that a particular underlying biological pattern is not meaningful, when in fact it is relevant for a particular subtype that has not yet been tested out. For example, many clinicians and researchers have recently separated out the group of children who regress in the second or third year life after having had some appropriate functioning in the first year of life. But in all likelihood, there are many subtypes among the group of children who regress as well as among the children who have an earlier, insidious onset.

Therefore, determining appropriate biomedical evaluations and interventions for each individual child is particularly challenging. An intervention that may be helpful for one child may not be helpful for another. Similarly, a research finding that may be relevant for one child may not be for another. The clinician and parents must, therefore, attempt to use current research and clinical experience to determine what is likely to be most helpful for a given child and the family, given their individual differences. In this challenging context, there are a few guidelines that may be worth emphasizing.

Parents and clinicians need to be cautious about two courses of action. First, they need to be cautious about uncritically jumping on the bandwagon of an intervention that does not have systematic case study support and definitive studies in progress. At the same time, however, they need to investigate promising interventions. Even if one or two studies on a general population have not shown results, the intervention may be potentially helpful for a certain pattern or subgroup. In other words, a few positive or negative studies on a general population of children often cannot answer the question about what may be useful for a particular child.

In exploring biomedical interventions, it is also very important to balance potential risks and benefits. Interventions that have no known risks may be easier to explore than ones that have clear risks associated with them. For example, if a particular intervention is promising and there are reasons to believe it may be helpful with a specific child's unique profile, it is often possible to try the intervention and observe the child both on and off the intervention to ascertain its helpfulness. In contrast, one would be more reluctant to conduct such a trial if the risks were significant.

At present, there are no definitive, proven biomedical interventions, in and of themselves, that can significantly alter the course of severe disorders of relating and communication, including ASD. There are, however, a number of approaches that, at times, can be helpful when included in a comprehensive program and when tailored to a child's unique profile. Selected psychopharmacological approaches, as described previously, are an example. There are also exploratory approaches that have not yet been well researched. Some involve a limited number of studies, with some suggesting potential helpfulness and others suggesting no clear value. Some very promising approaches simply have not yet been studied systematically at all.

The lack of definitive biomedical treatment and insufficiently studied exploratory interventions often lead to a number of reactions. Some clinicians respond very cautiously, waiting for definitive research. Others respond in a more exploratory way, trying to figure out what will likely be helpful for a child with a unique profile (i.e., subtype). Some children may present with a pattern that suggests a particular exploratory approach (e.g., a history of severe allergic phenomena). Other children may present with a unique history, such as negative reactions to medications, leading to a less exploratory biomedical attitude. Each clinician and family must, therefore, work together to consider the options for a particular child, weighing potential risks and benefits, and taking into account the child and family's unique characteristics. In order to determine what's likely to be most helpful, however, clinicians and parents should be aware of the options available.

It is beyond the scope of this chapter and the guidelines to review all the well-researched and lesser-researched biomedical interventions. However, in this context, some of these emerging ideas and appropriate references include (but are not limited to) the following: The role of casein (milk) and gluten (wheat) proteins in the pathogenesis of autistic behavior (Reichelt, Ekrem, & Scot, 1990); the benefit of vitamin B6 in the treatment of target symptoms (Rimland, 1994); the possible link of autism to autoimmune mechanisms (Warren, Singh, Averett et al., 1996) for some individuals—especially those with positive family histories of other autoimmune diseases (Zimmerman, 1999); the possible association of GI dysfunction and brain functioning, especially with recently described "autistic enterocolitis" in a subset of children with autism (Wakefield et al., 1998), as well as reflux esophagitis and disaccharide malabsorption and relationship of symptom change, especially diarrhea with secretin treatment (Horvath et al., 1998; Horvath, Papadimitriou, Rabsztyn, Drachenberg, & Tildon, 1999). There are a number of resources available that can provide

further information on these subjects, including those written for parents (Gerlach, 1998; Seroussi, 2000) as well as protocols and guidelines for clinicians (Bernet, 1999; Filipek et al., 1999; CAN Consensus Group, 1998; Baker & Pangborn, 1999).

With increasing research support from government agencies and parent support groups, such as Cure Autism Now (CAN http//www.canfoundation.org) and the National Alliance for Autism Research (NAAR http//www.naar.org), the future holds the promise of more diagnosis and treatment modalities for individuals with ASD. Clearly, identification of underlying core neurobiological deficits of the autistic spectrum will lead to development of the most appropriate medical treatment. Future revisions to *The ICDL Clinical Practice Guidelines* will continue to update this progress. In the meantime, it must be emphasized that the role of the health care professional is to have the highest index of suspicion if social and language delays exist in any child and to make the earliest possible referral for evaluation. If this occurs, a multidisciplinary intervention program as discussed in these guidelines can then begin immediately, as this is the child's greatest hope for improved outcomes. ■

REFERENCES

American Psychiatric Association (1994). *Diagnostic and statistical manual of mental disorders* (4th ed.) Washington, D.C.: American Psychiatric Press.

Baker, S., & Pangborn, J. (1999). *Biomedical assessment options for children with autism and related problems – a consensus report of the Defeat Autism Now!* (DAN!) *Conference,* Autism Research Institute, San Diego, CA.

Baron-Cohen, S., Allen, J., & Gillberg, C. (1992). Can autism be detected at 18 months? The needle, the haystack, and the CHAT. *British Journal of Psychiatry, 161,* 839-843.

Baron-Cohen, S., Cox, A., Baird, G, Swettenham, J., Nightingale, N., Morgan, K., Drew, A., & Charman, T. (1996). Psychological markers in the detection of autism in infancy in a large population. *British Journal of Psychiatry, 168,* 158-163.

Bernet, W. et al., (1999). Practice parameters for the assessment and treatment of children, adolescents, and adults with autism and other pervasive developmental disorders. *Journal of the American Academy of Child and Adolescent Psychiatry* (Suppl. 38), 532-554.

CAN Consensus Group (1998). Autism screening and diagnostic evaluation: CAN consensus statement. *CNS Spectrums, 3,* 40-49.

Chez, M., Buchanan, C., Zucker, M., & May, B. (1997). Value of 24-hour EEG versus routine EEG in detecting occult epileptic activity in children with pervasive developmental delay. *Annals of Neurology, 42,* 509.

Chez, M., Buchanan, C. et al., (1998). Practical treatment with pulse dose corticosteroids in pervasive developmental delay or autistic patients with abnormal epileptiform sleep EEG and language delays. *New Developments in Child Neurology,* 695-698.

Cohen, D., Volkmar, F. (Eds.) (1997). *Handbook of autism and pervasive developmental disorders* (2nd ed.). New York: Wiley.

Cook, E., Jr., Courchesne, R., Cox, N., Lord, C., Gonen, D., Guter, S., Lincoln, A., Nix, K., Haas, R., Leventhal, B., & Courchesne, E. (1998). Linkage – disequilibrium mapping of autistic disorder with 15q 11-13 markers. *Americal Journal of Human Genetics, 62,* 1077-1083.

D'Eufemia, P., Celli, M., Finocciaro, R., Pacifico, L., Viozzi, L., & Zaccagnini, M. (1996). Abnormal intestinal permeability in children with autism. *Acta Pediatrica, 85,* 1076-1079.

DiLavore, P., Lord, C., & Rutler, M. (1995). The pre-linguistic autism diagnostic observation schedule. *Journal of Autism and Developmental Disorders, 25,* 355-379.

Filipek, P., Accardo, P., Baranek, G., Cook, E., Dawson, G., Gordon, B., Gravel, G., Johnson, C., Kallen, R., Levy, S., Minshew, N., Prizant, B., Rapin, I., Rogers, S., Stone, W., Teplin, S., Tuchman, R., & Volkmar, F. (1999). The screening and diagnosis of autistic spectrum disorders. *Journal of Autism and Developmental Disorders, 29,* 439-484.

Gerlach, E. (1998). *Autism treatment guide.* Eugene, OR: Four Leaf Press.

Gillberg, C., & Wahlstrom, J. (1985). Chromosome abnormalities in infantile autism and other childhood psychoses: A population study of 66 cases. *Developmental Medicine and Child Neurology, 27,* 293-304.

Greenspan, S. I. (1992). *Infancy and early childhood: The practice of clinical assessment and intervention with emotional and developmental challenges.* Madison, CT: International Universities Press.

Greenspan, S., & Wieder, S. (1997). Developmental patterns and outcomes in infants and children with disorders in relating and communicating: A chart review of 200 cases of children with autistic spectrum diagnoses. *Journal of Developmental and Learning Disorders, 1,* 87-141.

Greenspan, S. I., & Wieder, S. (1998). *The child with special needs.* Reading, MA: Addison Wesley, Longman.

Horvath, K., Stefanatos, G., Sokolski, K., Wachtel, R., Nabors, L., & Tilder, J. T. (1998). Improved social and language skills after secretin administration in patients with autistic spectrum disorders. *Journal of the Association for Academic Minority Physicians, 9,* 9-15.

Horvath, K. Papadimitriou, J., Rabsztyn, A., Drachenberg, C., & Tildon, J. (1999). Gastrointestinal abnormalities in children with autistic disorder. *The Journal of Pediatrics, 135,* 559-63.

Konstantareas, M. M., & Homatidis, S. (1987). Ear infections in autistic and normal children. *Journal of Autism and Developmental Disorders, 17,* 585-594.

Lord, C., Rutter, M., & LeCouteur, A. (1994). Autism diagnostic interview: A revised version of a diagnostic interview for caregivers of individuals with possible pervasive developmental disorders. *Journal of Autism and Developmental Disorders, 24,* 659-685.

McDougle, C. S. (1997). *Psychopharmacology: Handbook of autism and pervasive developmental delay* (2nd ed.). New York: Wiley.

McEachin, J. J., Smith, T., & Lovaas, O. I. (1993). Long-term outcome for children with autism who received early intensive behavioral treatment. *American Journal of Mental Retardation, 97,* 373-391.

Reichelt, K., Ekrem, J., & Scot, H. (1990). Gluten, milk proteins and autism: Dietary intervention effects on behavior and peptide secretion. *Journal of Applied Nutrition, 42,* 1-11.

Rimland, B. (1994). *Studies of high dosage vitamin B6 in autistic children and adults: 1965-1994.* San Diego, CA: Autism Research Institute.

Schopler, E., Reichler, R., DeVellis, R., & Daly, K. (1980). Toward objective classification of childhood autism: Childhood autism rating scale (CARS). *Journal of Autism and Developmental Disorders, 10,* 91.

Schopler, E., Reichler, R., & Roden-Renner, B. (1988). *The childhood autism rating scale (CARS).* Los Angeles, CA: Western Psychological Services.

Seroussi, K. (2000). *Unraveling the mystery of autism and pervasive developmental disorder.* New York: Simon and Schuster.

Stefanatos, G. A. (1995). Case study: Corticosteroid treatment of language regression in pervasive developmental disorder. *Journal of the American Academy of Child and Adolescent Psychiatry, 34,* 1107-1111.

Teitelbaum, P., Teitelbaum, O., Nye, J., Fryman, J., & Maurer, R. G. (1998). Movement analysis in infancy may be useful for early diagnosis in autism. *Proceedings of the National Academy of Sciences of the United States of America, 95*(23), 13982-13987.

Thirumalai, S., Robinson, R., & Shubin, R. (1999). Sleep disorders in children with autism. *Neurology* (Suppl. 52), A78-79.

Tuchman, R. F. (1994). Epilepsy, language, and behavior: Clinical models in childhood. *Journal of Child Neurology, 9,* 95-102.

Tuchman, R. F., & Rapin, I. (1997). Regression in pervasive developmental disorders: Seizures and epileptiform electroencephalogram correlates. *Pediatrics, 99,* 560-566.

Tuchman, R., Jayakar, P., Yaylali, I., & Villalobos, R. (1998). Seizures and EEG findings in children with autistm spectrum disorder. *CNS Spectrums, 3,* 61-70.

Van Gent, T., Heijnen, C. J., & Treffers, P. D. (1997). Autism and the immune system. *Journal of Child Psychology and Psychiatry, 38,* 337-349.

Volkmar, F. R., & Nelson, D. S. (1999). Seizure disorders in autism. *Journal of the American Academy of Child and Adolescent Psychiatry, 29,* 127-129.

Wakefield, A. J., Murch, S., Anthony, A., Linnell, J., Casson, D., Malik, M., et al (1998). Ileal-lymphoid-modular hyperplasia, non-specific colitis, and pervasive developmental disorder in children. *Lancet, 351,* 637-41.

Warren, R. P., Singh, V. K., Averett, R. E., et al., (1996). Immunogenetic studies in autism and related disorders. *Molecular and Chemical Neuropathology, 28,* 77-81.

Wing, L. (1996). Autistic spectrum disorders. *British Medical Journal, 312,* 327-328.

Zimmerman, A. (1999). The immune system in autism. *The Journal of Development and Learning Disorders, 3,* 3-15.

Zimmerman, A. W., Bonfardin, B., & Myers, S. M. (2000). Neuropharmacological therapy in autism. In P. Accardo, (Ed.), *Autism: Clinical and research issues.* Timonium, MD: York Press.

— 18 —

Neuropsychological Assessment of Developmental and Learning Disorders

Lois M. Black, Ph.D., and Gerry A. Stefanatos, D.Phil.

INTRODUCTION

Neuropsychological assessment plays an important role in the diagnosis and treatment of children with developmental and learning disorders. A neuropsychological evaluation can provide critical information regarding the integrity of the central nervous system and give a detailed picture of a child's neurocognitive functioning[i] across a wide range of abilities. Notably, neuropsychological assessment can contribute to a functional developmental approach by elaborating upon a child's unique profile of strengths and weaknesses and the particular component skills and processing deficiencies that may be contributing to developmental, learning, and social-emotional adaptation or difficulty. Neuropsychological assessment can help distinguish neurogenic (brain-based) from psychogenic (psychological) conditions, sort out how problems in one domain of functioning may impact on another, and guide educational, remedial, and psychotherapeutic interventions. Neuropsychological assessment can also be used for monitoring progress or deterioration over time, and for refining our understanding of the diversity and commonalities that may be inherent to a given developmental disorder across children.

In what follows, a summary description of what is involved in neuropsychological evaluations of children with developmental or learning disorders will be offered. The chapter will review some basic issues in child neuropsychological assessment, offer some guiding principles and procedures for the assessment process, and give an overview of a format for a comprehensive assessment.

To be noted is that the evaluation approach to be sketched here is not a conventional one: For one, as neuropsychological, it uses knowledge of brain-behavior relationships to orient its assessment and interpretation procedures. Moreover, it goes beyond a primary focus on standardized procedures, structured tests, and quantitative levels of performance that may characterize more traditional psychometric approaches in psychological or educational testing. These may fall short of capturing who the child with a developmental or learning disorder may inherently be because not exploratory nor flexible enough, nor focused sufficiently on the dynamic process of how the child learns and the ways in which he can and cannot demonstrate what he knows. An evaluation must, importantly, capture the impact that any handicapping condition may have on the child's ability to participate in the assessment process, perform on any test, or function adequately in life. For many children, especially those with disorders in relating and communicating, a more therapeutic, flexible, and clinically insightful approach must also be adopted in order to woo the child into performing in a way commensurate with what he can do, or in order to find out what strategies will work to enhance functional developmental capacities, adaptation, and learning. In addition, the approach outlined here is an integrative one: It integrates neuropsychological assessment with clinical understanding of the child's inner world, as well as family and school system issues, in order to provide a more powerful diagnostic procedure that can also disclose the possible interweaving of both psychological and neuropsychological issues in the subjective experience and behavior of the child.

The aim of this chapter is to provide an overview of an approach to neuropsychological evaluation that can serve as a guide to assessing children with *a wide range of developmental and learning problems*. Its focus is not limited to children with the more severe disorders, such as autism or pervasive developmental disorders (PDD) (see, for example, Lord, 1997; Sparrow et al, 1997). Yet, the principles to be reviewed here can be applied to assessment of children who show overt, severe difficulties as well as more hidden ones. For young children on the spectrum of disorders in relating and communicating, these guidelines may be particularly relevant for those children who show characteristics (e.g., mild to moderate processing difficulties, intermittent symbolic capacities) similar to a subgroup of children identified as making rapid progress over time and showing eventually more subtle problems (Type I Disorder in relating and communicating, Greenspan & Wieder, 1997, 1999). Neither is this chapter meant to be a detailed treatment of the various issues and approaches to

developmental neuropsychological assessment currently in practice, for which there are a number of resources. (Baron, Fennell, & Voeller, 1995; Bernstein & Waber, 1990, Fennell & Bauer, 1997; Fletcher & Taylor, 1984; Gaddes, 1985; Hynd & Obrzut, 1981; Hynd & Willis, 1988; Obrzut & Hynd, 1991; Pennington, 1991; Reynolds & Fletcher-Janzen, 1997; Rourke, Bakker, Fisk, & Strang, 1983; Rourke, Fisk, & Strang, 1986; Spreen, Risser, & Edgell, 1995; Stefanatos & Black, 1997; Teeter & Semrud-Clikeman, 1997; Vanderploeg, 1994; Wilson, 1987, 1992). Rather, it will briefly highlight some issues distinctive to child neuropsychology and focus on an assessment approach that emphasizes especially the importance of seeking out ways to capture a child's inherent abilities so as to best promote a child's cognitive and emotional development.

A summary of when, generally, to seek a neuropsychological evaluation is contained in Chart 1.

A NEUROPSYCHOLOGICAL APPROACH TO EVALUATION: ISSUES DISTINCTIVE TO DEVELOPMENTAL NEUROPSYCHOLOGY

What is Neuropsychological Assessment?

Neuropsychological assessment is distinguished from other forms of assessment primarily by its attempt to understand a child's behavioral and psychological functioning in terms of brain-behavior relationships. In contrast to psychological assessment of a child's intellectual and personality functioning, a neuropsychological evaluation bases its exploration and interpretation of a broad range of functions—spanning reasoning, attention, language, memory, visual, sensory-perceptual,

Chart 1.
When to Seek a Neuropsychological Evaluation

- When it is unclear whether or to what extent overt emotional, behavioral, or learning problems have a basis in CNS dysfunction.
- When greater specificity in a child's unique profile of strengths and weaknesses is sought for therapeutic, educational, or remedial planning.
- When a baseline understanding of the child's functioning is needed to monitor growth and progress or the effectiveness of therapeutic interventions (e.g., biomedical, social, remedial).
- When there is a complicated condition that gives rise to differing opinions and a clearer differential diagnosis is sought.
- When a more active brain process or neurological condition may be suspected and needs to be ruled out.

motor, as well as affective and personality functioning—on a theory and model of the developing brain and on an understanding of brain-behavior relationships. A principle goal of a neuropsychological evaluation is to determine the extent to which a child's possible difficulties in, for example, thinking, attending, talking, listening, remembering, learning, or even in emotional lability or behavioral disturbances, may form a *pattern of impairment related to central nervous system (CNS) dysfunction*. When coupled with clinical understanding of psychological dynamics in child and family, neuropsychological assessment can also contribute to uncovering how neuropsychological dysfunction may become exacerbated by or implicated in psychological conflict (Black, 1995, 1997).

Neuropsychological interpretation of a child's functional difficulties rests on the integration of data obtained from performances on formal and informal tests, clinical observations, and history (including the child's developmental, medical, educational, social, and cultural history), with what is known about the pathophysiology, brain basis, and neuropsychological profiles of different neurologically based developmental conditions.

Although an understanding of brain development and brain-behavior relationships may set it apart, many of its assessment principles and procedures may, nevertheless, overlap with good psychological assessment practice. Thus, the guidelines proposed here are considered applicable to good practice in psychological assessment more generally. Neuropsychological assessment, as put forward here, rests fundamentally on an hypothesis-testing approach that incorporates principles of dynamic learning into its core assessment procedures, understands the multifactorial nature of complex tests and behavior, and is inherently comprehensive and integrative in its approach to understanding the whole child in the context of his environment.

Understanding Brain-Behavior Relationships, Brain Maturation, and Brain Plasticity

Child neuropsychology has emerged as a distinct area within the field of clinical neuropsychology largely as a consequence of the recognition that brain-behavior relationships in children differ in many ways from those established in adults. The developmental context of child neuropsychology requires that attention be paid to normal brain maturation and its correlation with the changing complex processes that develop over childhood, as well as to the changing environmental demands placed upon children as they grow.

It also requires an understanding of sensitive periods, brain plasticity, and the dynamic changes that may result from neural dysfunction and repair at various stages of development (Broman & Fletcher, 1999; Dawson & Fisher, 1994; Elman et al., 1998; Gunnar & Nelson, 1992; Johnson, 1997; Kolb, 1995; Spreen, Risser, & Edgell, 1995; Stiles, Bates, Thal, Trauner, & Reilly, 1998).

Recent Developments in Understanding Different Developmental and Learning Disorders

There has been an impressive refinement of theory and practice in child neuropsychology especially during the last 10 years, which has witnessed a wealth of research and cross-fertilization of information across disciplines during the 1990's "decade of the brain." Developments in understanding brain maturation and the dynamic relationship between brain development, behavior, and the environment have begun to be woven into its theoretical framework and assessment principles (Bernstein & Waber, 1990; Dawson & Fischer, 1994; Spreen et al., 1995; Taylor & Schatschneider, 1992). Technological advances in brain imaging techniques, such as volumetric and functional Magnetic Resonance Imaging [MRI], Position Emission Tomography [PET], Single Photon Emission Computer Tomography [SPECT], Brain Electrical Activity Mapping [BEAM], EEG Coherence Studies, Magnetic Source Imaging [MIS] and event-related brain potentials (ERP), have enabled documentation of neuroanatomical abnormalities and substrates of many different disorders and facilitated understanding of brain development and brain functioning even in very young infants and children (e.g., see Bell and Fox, 1994; Chugani, 1994; Dawson, 1994; Duffy, 1994; Gunnar & Nelson, 1992; Huttenlocher, 1994;

Molfese & Molfese, 1994; Thatcher, 1994). Refined quantitative and statistical techniques, informed by continuing growth in the neuropsychological understanding of different childhood conditions, have generated ways of capturing the heterogeneity inherent in different developmental and learning disorders through subtyping paradigms (Hooper & Willis, 1989, Rourke, 1985, 1991; van Santen, Black, Wilson, & Riscucci, 1994). Research into neurocognitive profiles associated with various neurological syndromes and psychiatric conditions has increased awareness of the possible overlap, co-mobidity, and continuum of conditions previously thought of as diverse, while enhancing conceptualization and differential diagnosis of distinct disorders.[ii]

Evidence through neuroimaging, autopsy, and neuropsychological research studies, has been providing ample testimony to the role that CNS dysfunction plays in developmental and learning disorders, and has begun to specify areas and systems of the brain that may be involved. Thus, for example, in contrast to early characterizations of autism and related disorders as forms of "psychotic withdrawal" attributed to problematic parenting, present day neuroscientific research has been disclosing possible involvement of different brain areas. These areas include, among others, medial temporal lobe abnormalities in cell density and size in the limbic system's hippocampus and amygdala (Bauman & Kemper, 1994; Kemper & Bauman, 1998); cerebellar and brainstem hypoplasias (Bauman & Kemper, 1994; Courchesne, 1989; Courchesne, Yeung-Courchesne, Press, Hesselink, & Jernigan, 1988; Courchesne et al., 1994a, 1994b; Courchesne, Yeung-Courchesne, Townsend, & Saitoh, 1994; Bailey et al.,1998); excess white matter in temporal and posterior parietal-occipital regions (Filipek, 1996; Filipek et al., 1992), and, generally, involvement of multiple brain systems, with subcortical-cortical reciprocal influences (Dawson & Levy, 1989). From these studies and others, Waterhouse, Fein, and Modahl (1996), for example, have concluded that dysfunction in multiple overlapping neural mechanisms can explain certain observed behavioral dysfunctions in autism; in particular, problems in cross-modal sensory integration, impaired affective understanding, asociality, as well as problems in extended selective attention, fluid shifting of attention, effective working memory, ability to process complex stimuli, and other skills necessary for normal interaction, language acquisition, and play. (See also Zimmerman and Gordon, Chapter 27, "Neuromechanisms in Autism," this volume). *Neuropsychology's understanding of brain-behavior relationships grows as does its ability to identify the constellation of functional issues that fundamentally define a disorder with enhanced information about underlying neural mechanisms.*

Evidence for the neurogenic basis of reading and other types of learning disabilities has also been advancing and offsetting earlier misunderstandings of learning disabled children as "lazy," "stupid," or "lacking motivation." For example, dyslexia, understood as a specific reading disorder, has been related to the absence of normal asymmetry of the planum temporale, and to the presence of neuronal ectopias in the molecular layer of the left perisylvian cortex (Galaburda et al., 1989; Galaburda, 1991, 1993).[iii] This neural picture may help explain the functional difficulties in auditory and phonological processing experienced by many children with reading disabilities and provide a rationale for certain targeted remedial approaches. Developmental language disorders, for which there are different identified subtypes, have been shown to relate to many different areas of CNS involvement (Jernigan, Hesselink, Sowell, & Tallal, 1991). Studies of attention

deficit disorder give evidence for involvement of frontal-striatal circuitry (Casey et al., 1997; Castellanos, Giedd, & Eckberg, 1994; Castellanos et al., 1996; Filipek, 1997; Giedd & Castellanos, 1997; Heilman, Voeller, & Nadeau, 1991; Lou, Henriksen, & Bruhn, 1984; Lou, Henriksen, Bruhn, Borner, & Nielsen, 1989; Mirsky, 1996; Mirsky, Anthony, Duncan, Oherin, & Kellam, 1991; Mirsky, Fantie, & Tatman, 1995; Swanson & Castellanos, 1998; Zametkin, 1990) as well as cross-hemisphere fibers of the corpus callosum and smaller right frontal regions (Giedd et al., 1994; Hynd, Semrud-Clikeman, Lorys, Novey, & Eliopulus, 1990; Hynd et al., 1991a, 1991b; Semrud-Clikeman et al., 1994). *The implications of these studies for neuropsychological assessment are that behavioral measures can then be developed and used which tap into the functions known to relate to the different neural systems identified, thus contributing to more sensitive means for differential diagnosis of developmental and learning disorders.*

A Model of Brain-Behavior Relationships

A fundamental assumption in developmental neuropsychology, then, is that the overt behavioral difficulties involved in different developmental and learning disorders result from dysfunction of specific areas and systems of the brain. According to some models of cerebral function (Das & Varnhagen, 1986; Geshwind & Galaburda, 1987; Goldberg, 1995; Luria, 1973, 1980; Mesulam, 1985), the brain is considered to be a highly differentiated organ comprised of numerous systems or neural networks that are specialized to mediate a particular "domain" of behaviors while acting in a dynamic, integrated way. These neural systems subserve different roles in the acquisition, organization, and use of information. Anatomically distinguishable networks have been identified that mediate particular aspects of behavior such as language expression and comprehension, spatial abilities, memory, attention, and emotional processing. For example, for right-handed individuals, an area in the frontal lobe of the left cerebral hemisphere is thought critical to processes for oral word production, and an area of the left posterior temporal lobe is thought critical to processes involved in language comprehension. Frontal or anterior cortical regions have been associated with goal-directed and regulatory behavior, as well as aspects of attention. Other aspects of attention seem to be mediated by diverse areas such as, for example, the brain stem, portions of the limbic system, basal ganglia, superior temporal and inferior parietal cortices, and cerebellum (Akshoomoff, Courchesne, & Townsend., 1997; Castellanos, Giedd, & Eckberg, 1994; Castellanos et al., 1996; Denckla, 1994, 1996; Denckla & Reiss, 1997; Furster, 1989; Heilman et al., 1991; Mirsky, 1996; Mirsky et al., 1991, 1995).

Different networks or systems are thought to be distributed over different neural axes that define the functional parameters of the CNS. These include the anterior-posterior, lateral (left hemisphere-right hemisphere), and cortical-subcortical axes. Complex fiber networks interconnect different regions within and between different axes. All behavior is assumed to be then a function of the dynamic interaction among interconnected systems and subsystems. Dysfunction in particular cortical areas is assumed to result in difficulties in domains of behavior thought to be mediated, directly or indirectly, by those areas or interconnected systems.

Child Developmental Disorders vs. Adult Acquired Disorders: The Role of Brain Plasticity

Developmental and learning disorders are considered to represent congenital and static CNS dysfunction as opposed to acquired and progressive conditions. Despite the specific brain systems being identified for various conditions, it is generally thought that children with developmental and learning disorders may not have outright "deficits" on neuropsychological testing such as can be found, for example, in focal brain lesions caused in adults by a stroke or tumor. Instead, with *developmental disabilities and learning disorders, a more diffuse* (involving multiple brain areas) *and sometimes subtle picture of CNS involvement is often present.* Neuropsychological dysfunction in children can be hidden from view because overlaid by other issues or compensated for in various ways.

This is especially the case given the plasticity of the brain. Brain plasticity refers to the ability of the immature nervous system to change or reorganize in response to trauma or experience. The concept arose out of observations that damage to the cortex early in life often resulted in far more limited impairment than when sustained later in development. One of the processes thought to mediate neural plasticity is that uncommitted or undercommitted areas of the brain that have an exuberance of synaptic connections and resources can subsume functions that would normally have been subserved by the damaged area (Huttenlocher, 1990, 1994). Thus, when there is overt damage to specific areas of the brain, alternative neural pathways can be stimulated and reorganization may occur so that affected functions may be taken over by other areas (Burnstine, Greenough, & Tees, 1984). This can result in "alternative pathways" or "atypical circuitry" (Goldman-Rakic, Isseroff, Schwartz, & Bugbee, 1983). Changes in the organization of a brain system may sometimes, however, go on to affect, in a dynamic way, yet other functions, and as a consequence compensating areas themselves may become less efficient. For example, localized damage to the left inferior frontal cortex, which would impair speech production in adults, results in a brief period of disruption in children followed by substantial recovery (Aram & Eisele, 1992; Bates, 1999; Dennis, 1988; Stiles et al., 1998). This recovery of function is thought to be mediated, at least in part, by reorganization of language either intrahemispherically or in the contralateral hemisphere (Bates, Vicari, & Trauner, 1999; Rasmussen & Milner, 1977). Moreover, in some cases where there is reorganization of language to the right hemisphere, diminished right hemisphere functions, such as weakened visual-spatial skills, can result (Nass, Peterson, & Kork, 1989; Teuber & Rudel, 1962). Establishment of alternative pathways may also describe what is happening when strategies for reading used by reading disabled subjects are studied: For example, Frank Wood and his colleagues (Wood, Felton, Plowers, & Naylor, 1991), using a measure of cerebral blood flow detection, showed that during a task requiring processing of auditory verbal stimuli (e.g, words heard had to be analyzed as to the number of sounds in them), there was activation at Wernicke's area in the temporal region of the left hemisphere in normal subjects, but less activation in this area in reading disabled subjects and, instead, excessive activation in the area of the angular gyrus. This, it was interpreted, could imply either an altered connectivity with structurally displaced location of axons in dyslexics, or their use of a less efficient compensatory strategy because of disturbed connections.[iv] Once brain systems have fully matured, compromise by a lesion may not result in significant reorganization, and an individual may likely experience more permanent changes in affected skills.

Various brain regions become functional at different times in development and, until the region is functional, the effect of an early lesion may not be evident. The age at which a CNS disturbance occurs is thus also important, as is knowledge of brain maturation timetables as to when particular brain systems mature. The notion that it is "better to have your brain injuries early," referred to as the Kennard Principle after Margaret Kennard who described such effects in the motor system (Kennard, 1942), has expressed the resiliency of the young brain to compensate for early injuries. Since formulated, this principle has been expanded to include a more indepth understanding that sometimes deficits can be delayed or reemerge or result in anomalous behavior later on, depending on timing and brain location (Kolb, 1995). If, for example, an insult (which can either be acquired or genetically targeted to unfold) is to a region that has not yet matured, one may see behavioral disturbances only then when the anatomic substrate becomes critical for some neuropsychological function. This is what is called "growing into a deficit." The phenomenon of "growing into a deficit" has been suggested, for example, as one of a number of possible explanations for the regression in functioning sometimes seen in cases of autistic spectrum disorders in children at around age 19 to 22 months.[v] It is at this age, it is reasoned, that the functions specific to the maturation of the limbic system's amygdala and hippocampus, considered to be affected in autistic individuals, become developmentally important. At around this age, the normal developing child develops representational memory, flexible accommodation schemes, and the ability to learn in novel situations, functions in part attributable to the maturing amygdala and hippocampus. Things might start to fall apart, it has been speculated, at a time when these brain areas, found to be too small with too densely packed cells and with reduced complexity of dendritic arbors in autistic subjects, are supposed to mature and subserve age-appropriate functions (Bachelevier, 1994, 1997; Bauman, 1997; Kemper & Bauman, 1998; Overman, 1990). Similar factors may also determine late onset of other neurologic conditions that may have their origin much earlier in the perinatal period. For example, temporal lobe epilepsy may sometimes result from high forceps delivery, although seizures do not emerge until early adolescence.

Given continuing mylenation and brain maturation during childhood, and the positive effects on brain growth that can result from experiential learning and optimal conditions (Greenough & Black, 1992; Nelson, 1999), including appropriate and timely remediation, functional difficulties can also be compensated for and a child can "grow out of a deficit" as well. Thus, in children who have nonverbal learning disabilities (NLD), graphomotor functions may greatly improve in later childhood (Rourke, 1989). Visual-spatial and organizational difficulties may become ameliorated with hormonal changes and the onset of puberty (Bernstein, 1991; Stiles et al., 1998). In children with language and reading disorders, auditory processing, language comprehension, and reading inefficiencies may subside with directed remediation (Alexander, Anderson, Heilman, Voeller, & Torgeson, 1991; Baaker & Vinke, 1985; Bell, 1991b; Howard, 1986; Korkman & Peltomaa, 1993; Lindamood, & Lindamood, 1997; Lovett et al., 1994; Merzenich et al., 1996; Tallal, 1996.).

The absence of focal deficits and the phenomenon of neural plasticity all imply what Martha Denckla has called a "pastel" version of symptomatology in children (Denckla, 1979a). Child neuropsychological assessment of developmental conditions is thus different from assessment of adult conditions. This is reflected in some of its principles and procedures, which are aimed at assessing

sometimes subtle and "relatively inefficient" areas of functioning across a broad range of skill areas (Black, 1989; van Santen et al., 1994; Wilson, 1987) As will be seen, sometimes these inefficiencies reveal themselves in relatively weak rather than deficit scores; in compensatory efforts, successful or not; and in less than optimal coping strategies, which can increase emotional issues, processing time, lead to certain types of errors, or affect adequate functioning in other domains.

A Process-Oriented Approach to Child Neuropsychological Assessment

There are different approaches to child neuropsychological assessment. The one to be described here is not a fixed battery approach (e.g., Halstead-Reitan Battery) (Golden, 1980; Reitan & Wolfson, 1985; Russell, 1994), which uses a fixed number and grouping of tests, with interpretations made on the basis of quantitative analyses. A battery approach relies on data derived mainly from standardized tests, and uses algorithms, pattern analysis, and indices made up of scores from groups of tests, rather than individual subtests, in order to identify brain impairment, laterality of impairment, and empirical patterns typical of different diagnostic conditions. The approach to be described here is also not a clinical-inferential approach that makes use mainly of clinical experience and qualitative analyses without the use of any standardized tests.

Rather, the approach outlined here is a process-oriented, flexible approach that makes use of both quantitative and qualitative data, uses knowledge of brain-behavior relationships, information about performances of children with a variety of developmental and neurological disorders, and an understanding of the dynamic interplay between neural and behavioral systems and the environment to guide its assessment and neuropsychological interpretations (see Bernstein & Waber, 1990; Wilson & Risucci, 1986; Wilson, 1992). A process-oriented approach (see Bauer, 1994; Kaplan, 1990; Luria, 1973, 1980; Wilson, 1986, 1987, 1992), rests on a few core features, which will be described in greater detail in what follows. Briefly sketched, they include the key principle that observing and reporting *the way in which a problem or task is solved* may be as useful and sometimes even more important for understanding neuropsychological functioning *than any actual score* achieved. Thus observations and considerations of *how* a performance is accomplished, *rather than merely what* a child scored, become critical (Wilson, 1992).[vi] A process approach will look to the processing requirements of different tasks, their input and output demands, and to the nature of the child's handicaps, and continually, in a reiterative hypothesis-testing manner, find increasingly "process-pure" ways to determine what is impacting on performance. This will also involve, for example, testing of limits, modifying standardized procedures, and including strategies for enhanced learning to get at what is holding a child back or what will facilitate a child's performance. As one child neuropsychologist, Barbara Wilson, has put it, "such an approach requires that the question be: 'What needs to be assessed?' rather than 'What test to use?'" If the question about the child can be specified, then an appropriate way of "measuring" it can be found, whether one uses a standardized test or improvised procedure (Wilson, 1987).

THE ASSESSMENT PROCESS

Neuropsychological Functions and Domains of Assessment

The list of neuropsychological functions listed in Chart 2 stems from areas known to be affected in developmental disabilities of various kinds as well as in neurological conditions. *They are skills that relate to different systems and subsystems in the brain with a neuropsychological evaluation seeking to find out whether consistent, known behavioral clusters or patterns of functioning within and between these different areas are conjointly affected.* This list gives examples of functions assessed; it is not exhaustive. The functions listed have been developed as a result of knowledge of brain-behavior relationships, empirical and subtype studies of specific disorders, and are built up and amended with ongoing research. (Also included in Chart 2 are more overarching domains, such as overall cognitive functioning, academic functioning, and personality functioning.)

Some examples of measures which can be used for assessing functioning in the different domains are contained in a chapter appendix. The measures chosen are restricted to young children ages 2 to 10.

Some Guiding Principles and Procedures of Child Neuropsychological Assessment

Some key principles and strategies that orient our approach to assessment include understanding the need for:

- Breadth of Assessment (range of functions assessed)
- Depth of Assessment (developmental history and view of the child over time and in different contexts)
- Formal and Informal Assessment Procedures
- Use of Standardized Tests: Advantages and Disadvantages
- Criteria for Choosing Appropriate Measures
- Task Analysis of Complex Behaviors

Chart 2. Neuropsychological Functions and Domains of Assessment

- **Organizational and Executive Functions and Attention**
  - Vigilance and selective attention
  - Mental tracking and cognitive flexibility
  - Organized systematic functioning (e.g., visual search; planning vs. acting impulsively; problem solving; cause-and-effect reasoning).
  - Initiating, sustaining, and shifting of attention; inhibiting distractions
  - Dynamic motor coordination and integration
  - Motor persistence and modulation
  - Alertness and arousal

- **Language-Related Functions**
  - Auditory processing (e.g., auditory discrimination, analysis, sound blending)
  - Phonological production and speech
  - Auditory cognitive functions
    - Language comprehension
    - Expressive language

- **Memory Functions**
  - Verbal memory
  - Visual memory
  - Memory and learning

- **Visual-Related Functions**
  - Visual-perceptual functions
  - Visual-spatial functions
  - Visual cognitive functions

- **Sensory Perceptual Functions**
  - Auditory, visual, tactile perception
  - Finger agnosia and stereognosis

- **Motor Functions**
  - Fine and gross motor coordination
  - Graphomotor functions
  - Praxis

- **Affect Sensitivity**
  - Visual, vocal, contextual affect processing

- **Overall Cognitive Functioning**
  (e.g. performances on "intelligence" measures, including analysis of the impact that neuropsychological dysfunction and/or emotional issues may be having on resulting scores)

- **Academic Functioning**
  (e.g., performances on spelling, reading [word attack, word identification, reading comprehension], mathematics, and writing measures, including analysis of the impact that specific neuropsychological weaknesses and/or emotional issues may be having on resulting scores)

- **Social-Emotional/Personality Functioning**
  (e.g. performances on projective measures, standardized questionnaires, clinical observations)

- Testing of Limits and Modification of Test Procedures
- Reiterative Hypothesis-Testing Strategies
- Determining Cognitive Potential and Establishing a Neuropsychological Profile of Strengths and Weaknesses
- Neuropsychological Integration and Interpretation of the Data
- Diagnostic Formulation and Recommendations

The following sections attempt to review these critical components of the assessment process.

Breadth of an Assessment

An assessment should have sufficient "breadth;" that is, coverage of the range of functions targeted for evaluation, as outlined in Chart 2. A neuropsychological evaluation typically covers such a broad range of skills in order to assess for CNS integrity and to disclose *patterns of impairment* typical of a disability. Besides the fact that all neural axes and functional systems need to be explored in order to do this (e.g., the anterior-posterior axis; the lateral, left-right axis; the cortical-subcortical axis) (Bernstein & Waber, 1990; Luria, 1973), which necessitates completeness and balance in the range of functions looked at, breadth of assessment is necessary in developmental and learning conditions for a number of reasons:

First, a developmental disability is rarely identified by *one core deficit*, but, as mentioned, usually entails more *diffuse CNS involvement*, that is, involves more than one focal brain area. Breadth of assessment is necessary then to be able to discern such diffuse CNS dysfunction.

Second, the overt manifestation of a given disability may be very different in different children. This may reflect the etiological diversity of many developmental conditions

as well as the inherent variation across individuals, possibly due to the interweaving of genetics, environment, and maturation. For this reason, as well as because of the effects of plasticity as described earlier, neuropsychological assessment will often recognize the *heterogeneity* involved in different developmental and learning disorders. Research into the neuropsychological profiles of different subtypes of developmental disorders captures this heterogeneity. Subtypes, which are shorthand descriptions of the different possible neuropsychological profiles characteristic of a given disorder, have been proposed, for example, for reading disorders (Baaker, 1979, 1992; Denckla, 1979b; Mattis, French, & Rapin, 1975; Petrauskas & Rourke, 1979; Shaywitz et al., 1996), arithmetic disabilities (Keller & Sutton, 1991; Rourke, 1993), childhood language disorders (Aram & Nation, 1975; Black, 1989; Rapin & Allen, 1983; Rapin, Allen, & Dunn, 1992; van Santen et al., 1994; Wilson & Risucci, 1986), attention deficit disorders (Hynd et al., 1991b; Mirsky, 1996; Mirsky et al., 1991, 1995; Pennington, 1991), and pervasive developmental disorders (Klin, Volkmar, Sparow, Cicchetti, & Rourke, 1995). Each subtype of a developmental or learning disorder can be described in terms of its own characteristic *pattern of neuropsychological assets and deficits.*

Neuropsychological subtyping in developmental language disorders (DLD), for example, also makes clear that there is more affected in a language disorder than simply language-related functions. It is, in fact, the presence or absence of memory impairments, nonverbal visual-spatial and visual-cognitive impairments, or even affective processing deficits and emotional difficulties that can differentiate one subtype of DLD from another (Black, 1989; Rapin, 1996; van Santen et al., 1994; Wilson, 1986).

Thus, breadth of assessment is necessary for evaluating the distinctive patterns of impairment that characterize a disorder, and which may distinguish it from other disorders. A neuropsychological evaluation of a child with a DLD, in contrast to a language evaluation, would assess not merely expressive and receptive aspects of language functioning, but nonverbal cognitive, memory, organizational, attentional, perceptual, and motor functions. Important diagnostic information is thereby obtained, including greater insight into the child's nonverbal cognitive potential and information critical for identifying membership in a specific neuropsychological subtype group. A developmental language disorder otherwise hidden from view, or possibly confused with another disability, may then be identified (Black, 1997). Furthermore, since specific vulnerabilities and prognostic outcomes are also correlated with specific subtypes of DLD (Wilson & Risucci, 1988), such differential diagnosis, made real by the breadth of an assessment, also allows for long-term planning and remediation. Open channels and strengths, also disclosed because of the breadth of an assessment, can help generate specific compensatory and remedial recommendations for the individual child.

Thus, breadth of assessment is necessary because the goals of an evaluation include discerning *patterns of impairment* suggestive of a specific developmental or learning disorder, distinguishing one type of developmental disorder from another, and finding open channels and strengths for remediation.

Third, breadth of assessment is also necessary because most presenting problems, such as difficulties in listening, understanding, expressing oneself, and reading, are themselves inherently complex. The neuropsychologist uses a task analytic approach to understand higher cortical functions such as

these (Luria, 1973, 1980). Activities such as reading involve, from the neuropsychological perspective, a myriad of component skills. To understand why a complex skill may be deficient, one must be able to hone in on each of the component skills in order to find out what is contributing to the difficulty. Some of the component skills in reading, as an example, can include auditory processing skills (e.g., discrimination, analysis, and blending of sounds, and maintenance of sequences of sounds in memory—all a part of phonemic awareness), visual-perceptual discrimination of letters, association of letters with sounds, visual scanning, speed of processing, and comprehension of semantically and syntactically complex language. These correspond to multiple brain areas and systems, including cortical temporal, frontal, parietal, and occipital regions, as well as subcortical areas. There is a one-to-many relationship here of reading, as the index problem, to the many different component processes and possible neural substrates. There is also the possibility of there being a many-to-one relationship, where many different behaviors can be affected given one affected brain region.

The brain acts in an integrated way, linking up many highly differentiated systems and subsystems to eventuate in a higher cortical process or a complex behavior. A neuropsychological assessment will want to span the functions attributable to many different areas and systems to understand what is behind a deficient performance or a dysfunctional behavior. The intent of the assessment in evaluating for a developmental or learning disorder is to disclose the impaired component skills that lead to the complex skill breaking down. Breadth of assessment is necessary, then, because in neuropsychological evaluation one is engaged in differential understanding of complex presenting issues which may depend upon different and inter-related brain systems.

Depth of Assessment

Neuropsychological assessment necessarily has "depth" in the sense that it includes past, present, and future information in its attempts to neuropsychologically interpret the data. "Depth" reflects on the evaluation's fundamentally developmental and integrative orientation.

Depth means that it is inherently developmental, incorporating knowledge of brain development as well as developmental expectations across all functions—motor, language, cognitive. The child's brain continues to mature and to be vulnerable to different environmental influences and demands made upon it at different developmental stages and ages. Signs of impairment, as discussed earlier, may emerge, submerge, and re-emerge later on in the life cycle in different forms, not only in response to genetic unfolding, brain maturation, and plasticity but also in response to environmental stress or support. This opens up interpretative challenges; it also allows a future-oriented perspective to the evaluation, and opens up opportunities, as well, for making recommendations to intervene in the child-environment system.

Depth also includes knowledge of the child's personal history and developmental growth. The presence of risk factors such as prenatal, perinatal, and neonatal conditions, medical history, developmental milestones, as well as family and social-emotional factors, can provide a framework for raising hypotheses, in particular about possible etiology and other factors contributing to current problems.

The child's place within the family system and larger environmental context is important to know, especially in light of the impact that early manifestations of disabilities may have on interpersonal interactions which can, in turn, influence, exacerbate or mask neuropsychological underpinnings of a disability (Black, 1995, 1997). Thus, depth

will also include obtaining information about the child as seen in different contexts over time, understanding how others (parents, caretakers, teachers, therapists) have perceived and currently perceive the child, and how the child behaves in different settings. Integrative understanding here includes thinking through what impact the demands and interpretations made by others, at home and at school, may have on the child's experience and behavior.

Incorporating information across time and context provides a framework for understanding factors that have contributed to, are sustaining, or alleviating for current problems.

Formal and Informal Assessment Procedures

Neuropsychological assessment procedures include both formal and informal methods that are intended to tap into the targeted skill areas, whether or not a normed test is available. Again, fundamental to a process-oriented approach is that one searches for ways of understanding that and why a particular function or cluster of functions is impaired: Once one knows what the diagnostic question is, once one knows what brain areas or correlated functions need to be explored, one can then find measures or devise ways of assessment, whether one uses a standardized test, improvised procedure, or informed observation. Neuropsychology has a long tradition of using both formal and informal procedures to assess behavioral and psychological functioning. It is indebted in this approach to the endeavors of Aleksandr Luria, a pioneer in the field, who documented and devised innumerable non-standardized ways of tapping into higher cortical functions in brain-damaged patients and, by doing so, contributed to the core fundamental understanding of brain-behavior relationships (Luria, 1973, 1980).

In current practice in the assessment of childhood developmental disorders, an understanding of what neuropsychological functions need to be explored and what consistent patterns of impairment are to be expected if a brain-based condition is present are continually being updated and extended through ongoing research. Formal, standardized, normed test measures do not necessarily keep apace with these developments, nor tap into the functions that need to be assessed at all ages. Moreover, which tests to choose and how well or how confounded they are in assessing any particular function may have to be analyzed each time with each individual child (see the following section, "Task Analysis").

The choice of measures then is guided by brain-behavior relationships and how well a given measure can tap into a targeted skill, whether the procedure for doing so is a normed test or not. For example, in assessing for possible weaknesses in cross-hemisphere or intra-hemisphere white fiber connections, which may be affected in neurodevelopmental conditions such as attentional deficit disorders (Hynd et al., 1991a) or nonverbal learning disabilities (Rourke, 1989) (as well as in frank neurological conditions such as agenesis of the corpus callosum), one could use formal measures that test, for example, the efficiency of bilateral integration using both hands in simultaneous placement of pegs as on the Purdue Pegboard Test; or one could use informal measures which look at the *quality* of bilateral integration as, for example, in dynamic praxis tests (e.g., flipping one's hands in a smooth alternating sequence), catching a ball, bi-manually manipulating objects, or crossing midline. Using both quantitative data and qualitative observations, moreover, can increase the evidence for and certainty of any conclusions drawn.

As another example, if one were looking to see whether a young child of 3 or 4 had attention-related and executive function difficulties, one might have a hard time coming up with many standardized measures which would tap into such functions for this particular age group (see chapter appendix). Yet, assessing attention and executive functions would be a critical part of evaluating for whether a child was experiencing a brain-based developmental condition, and is especially important to assess in the preschool years because underlying frontal cortex matures especially rapidly in synaptic density and branching at that time (Chugani, 1994; Huttenlocher, 1979, 1997; Thatcher, 1997). Critical to know would be what is involved in attention and executive functions, especially for children of this age. Understanding the constellation of possible signs and behaviors associated with the underlying interconnected neural systems involved (e.g., frontal-striatal circuitry) would serve to guide the search for multiple pieces of evidence and help determine whether a consistent *pattern of performances* was present, implicating a neurogenic impairment. In this way, one could devise ways of looking as supplements to the few formal measures available.

Example of Using Both Formal and Informal Procedures to Assess Organizational and Executive Functions in the Preschool Child

The overarching principle to remember is that it is the targeted function or behavioral cluster to be assessed that guides the search for which measures to use, not just age-appropriate available tests. The assessment procedures chosen are guided by knowledge of brain-behavior relationships and the search for multiple pieces of evidence to rule in or rule out whether a function is impaired. The following will describe what is involved in assessing organizational and executive functions in the preschool-aged child in order to exemplify how assessment can proceed using both formal and informal methods.

First, there needs to be an understanding of what is involved in the behavioral cluster of attentional, organizational, and executive functions. Briefly defined, these are skills concerned with the regulation and organization of behavior and thinking at all levels, automatic and reflective—from automatic regulation of smooth, modulated motor movements to more "executive" functions of being able to organize play or language, methodically problem-solve, use a plan of action to guide behavior or think in a cause-and-effect way (Furster, 1989). Involved, too, are working memory or mental tracking of different trains of thought or input, as well as flexible shifting and sustaining of attention. Problems in self-control, self-modulation, motor persistence, and "defective response inhibition" are also characteristic of children who have problems here (Barkley, 1997; Heilman et al., 1991; Lyon & Krasnegor, 1996). Such children are unable to automatically use an external cue, such as a verbal command, to regulate behavior so that, for example, a command *not* to respond to a certain thing or *not* to behave in a certain way will, instead, elicit that very response. Children who show difficulties here may also show noncompliant tendencies and appear self-directed, stubborn, have "strong personalities," or be outright oppositional. They may also show perseverative behaviors, obsessive preoccupations, or rigid adherence to routines. Emotional lability is also associated with difficulties in frontal lobe functioning, with problems in affect regulation and extended negative mood states.

Thus, in looking to assess whether attentional and executive functions were affected in a 3- or 4-year-old one could analyze performances, whether on tests or in any context, to see if a consistent pattern, including

the above and related features, was present (see also Chart 2). In order to assess "defective response inhibition," for example, one could give a simple test of "competing programs," an informal procedure without norms that asks the child, for example, to put up one finger every time the examiner puts up two and put up two fingers every time the examiner puts up one. On this apparently simple test, a child who has problematic response inhibition (and is likely to appear impulsive) and shows difficulties with using a verbal rule to regulate behavior, will have a difficult time following the task at all, or may simply imitate what is visually presented rather than keep the complex verbal rule in mind. One can then observe whether such a child responds similarly to other verbal rules, whether in the testing situation or in real life. For example, given the command to pick up only one peg at a time on a pegboard task, such a child may consistently "forget" and pick up more than one peg, despite the finger dexterity to be able to do so; or told by his parents not to do something, he will consistently do that very thing, despite his ability to comprehend the message, and so appear noncompliant.

More generally, in assessing for organizational difficulties, one could look at *how* systematically and organized the child approached tasks and look at functioning at different levels and across different modalities—motor, visual, auditory. For example, motorically, one could informally look at how smooth, coordinated, or well-modulated a child's movements were. One could observe whether a child showed impulsive, jerky or tremulous movements; or difficulties sustaining a motor act.[vii] One could observe whether the child showed a lack of modulation in voice and motor control when focus and concentration were taxed. For example, one could observe how a child may scream out responses under time pressure when asked to quickly name things around the room or jump haphazardly and bang into things when asked to stand on one foot. Formally, there are some tests or scales that could be used at this age range (e.g., individual tasks on the Miller Assessment for Preschoolers [MAP], PEET [age 3] PEER [age 4]; or McCarthy Motor Coordination Scale), but cut-off scores or domain scores are often all that are available rather than individual scores, and observations and interpretations of performances remain critical (also because more general motor coordination difficulties may be confounding the scores). (For a reference list of all standardized tests mentioned, also in what follows, see the chapter appendix.)

One could also make informal observations while the child was performing on formal tests: Motorically, one could look at how systematic and organized a child's approach was while putting blocks away or placing pegs in a pegboard (e.g., while performing on WPPSI-R Animal Pegs or the Bayley's Pegboard). Visually, one could look at how organized the child's visual search for a hidden or targeted figure was and thereby how successful the child was in search and cancellation tasks (e.g., on the ITPA Visual Closure Test or on NEPSY Visual Attention). Verbally, one could read a story and ask a child to relate back what was remembered and see whether the child could organize his thoughts into words in a way commensurate with his comprehension and memory (e.g., on McCarthy Verbal Memory II). On all these tests, one could get scores, too, but the observations and the quality of responses would be significant in themselves, especially for confirming the interpretation of organizational difficulties as affecting low scores achieved.

One could proceed in a similar way to higher levels of functioning and look at whether organizational problems were evident

in the child's play, problem-solving, and cognitive style. For example, one could observe how spontaneously the child categorizes, structures, or organizes his play, or sets up a coherent and elaborate sequence of activities in an age-appropriate way. Or, does a random quality infect the child's play with schemes appearing disorganized, repetitive, or with little elaboration? One could also ask about the child's thinking and problem solving. Does the child use an intended result to plan actions or incorporate known consequences into the way he behaves? Formal testing can use, for example WPPSI-R Mazes to tap into planning skills. But, informally, one can see planning skills in any problem-solving task, in the methodical stop-and-think approach, rather than trial-and-error procedures, when a child is asked to put shapes in a formboard, get an object out of reach, or figure out how an unfamiliar mechanical toy works. In everyday life, one can ask if the child understands punishments and rewards, cause and effect, and can use them to guide his behavior.

One can also observe how flexible and naturally methodical the child is and focus on whether his cognitive and personality style is also consistent with such a neurogenic picture. Does the child show a tendency to be either overly impulsive and distractible, or, at the other extreme, overly rigid and compulsive? Children with frontal lobe dysfunction can show both these extremes. It seems that the very problems that underlie organizational and attentional difficulties may also co-determine defensive style and personality. The child who is highly distractible and unable to plan and guide actions in accord with rules or anticipated consequences can show a propensity to be impulsive in dealing with emotionally laden issues and to use, for example, avoidance, denial, or blaming others. A child sensitive to experienced disorganization, and loss of attentional focus as beyond his control (in an ego-dystonic way) may well opt for over-control and an obsessive and inflexible style.

One would want to answer all these questions, combining test performances and scores with observations and an understanding of the child's functioning in everyday life, in order to be able to determine whether a consistent pattern of difficulties was present, implicating executive and organizational dysfunction.

What applies to the use of formal and informal measures for assessing attentional and executive functions is also applicable when assessing other neuropsychological functions: Once one knows what brain areas or correlated functions need to be explored, one can then find measures or devise ways of assessment, whether one uses a standardized test, improvised procedure, or observations. Importantly, the use of both quantitative and qualitative data increases the evidence and likelihood that a clinical judgment is justified with regard to whether an area of functioning is truly impaired or not.

Standardized Tests: Advantages and Disadvantages

An important advantage of using formal, normed tests, however, is the ability to generate a *more precise picture of intra-individual differences* in the child, which can be crucial for disclosing patterns of relative inefficiencies and a characteristic neuropsychological profile known to be reflective of a disorder.

It is known that standardized tests are intended to provide a systematic and precise means of obtaining information about the child's functioning in different skill areas: Standardized administration and scoring procedures are designed to maximize reproducibility of performances at different times and places and across examiners. Tests, constructed with regard to reliability and validity

requirements, and normed on matched peers across diverse, but representative population parameters allow for performances to be reported in standard scores and percentile rankings. Thus a means is set up whereby a child can be reliably compared to others in his peer group, with a percentile ranking allowing one to know where in the normal distribution the child stands on a specific test. (For example, a ranking at the 65th percentile means that the child is performing in the average range, with 35% of all other children his age doing as well or better than him.) A standard score, such as a percentile ranking, allows, in other words, for one to appraise a child's performance with regard to other children and so determine whether, in relation to normally developing peers, a child's performance is adequate or not, strong or weak. (A performance in the borderline (by convention between the 9th and 2nd percentile) or deficit (less than the 2nd percentile) range is a weak performance absolutely. A score in the superior (from the 91st to 97th percentile) to very superior (the 98th percentile and above) range is a strong performance absolutely.)

More important, percentile scores allow one to compare the child's own performances in different areas of functioning with each other. It thus critically allows intra-individual comparisons to be made so that one can determine whether a score for a given child is weak relative to other performances of which he is capable. For example, a child may be of superior cognitive abilities, performing at the 95th percentile. For such a child, even a score in the average range on a particular measure (e.g., at the 50th percentile) may be considered "relatively inefficient" and index a critical weakness. Thus, performances on formal tests allow one to more precisely build up a profile of strengths and weaknesses for an individual child that reflect not only absolute levels of the child's standing in regard to peers, but the child's different levels of functioning relative to each other, using his own capacities as the internal standard of comparison (see the following section, "Determining Cognitive Potential and Establishing a Neuropsychological Profile of Strengths and Weaknesses" for further discussion).[viii]

It is important, however, to keep in mind the disadvantages to the use of standardized tests. These include the lack of measures for assessing various critical neuropsychological functions for specific ages, as described above; or, the lack of specifically sensitive tests, with many tests requiring multiple functions to do them, or having multiple subparts to them, so that the meaning of scores is dubious without interpretation. Because of the multifactorial nature of so many tests, it becomes, in fact, important when reporting standardized scores to simultaneously clarify and interpret the meaning of those scores for a particular child—to include not merely the score, but its significance as a reliable descriptor for particular skills (see the following section, "Task Analysis of Complex Behaviors").

There is also a more general caveat about the use of standardized tests: No matter how standardized procedures are meant to be, a host of nonspecific variables that have to do with the particular situation, examiner, or child intervene and affect performances, most often in nonobvious and nondocumented ways. These nonspecific variables can influence scores to a great extent. For example, with very young children, the differential affects of the unfamiliar, stressful testing situation itself are not frequently enough understood nor incorporated into efforts to woo the child into performing in a way commensurate with what he can do. Even less frequently are the child's emotional reactions to challenging tests used to qualify and clarify low performances obtained, or prompt searches to find other ways of eliciting information.

There are also problems with regard to normative data. Some tests are being republished with changes and new norms (for example, the Stanford-Binet, 4th edition, WISC III, Bayley, Leiter). Care must be taken to understand differences in content and norms when children are retested and not to misinterpret lower scores on newly normed measures to mean a decrement in functioning. Norms for some tests may also cover too wide an age range (e.g., over one year) without regard to critical growth that may take place within that time frame, so that scores can be inflated for an older child in the age span and depressed for a younger child. The quality of the normative data must be evaluated: Too few numbers of subjects in a validation study and/or too large a range of performances may make scores for an individual child less reliable. Also, importantly, there is a real lack of normative data obtained on special populations with which comparisons can be made more directly. Because of this, information from a given test is less informative, diagnostically and predictively, and could be misleading if an individual's performance is not interpreted accurately, since the influence of handicapping conditions on test performances are unaccounted for in national norms.

Criteria for Choosing Appropriate Measures

The most desirable measure is one from which a standard score such as a percentile ranking can be derived, measures a circumscribed skill area in as pure a way as possible, and whose input and output demands are so defined that they that can be easily weighted in performance outcome. Also to consider are the reliability and validity of a test, especially its construct validity and correlation with other known measures, and the quality of the existing normative data. The most important criterion for choosing a measure, however, is whether and how well it taps into the targeted neuropsychological function being explored.

Composite measures can be misleading, in particular composite IQ scores, but also broad "domain" scores, which may be even more confounded than individual subtests by the areas of neuropsychological dysfunction that one is striving to disclose. If using a composite test, one should be sought that has norms for individual subtests with a clear factorial make-up rather than one which reports only overarching scores on broad scales.

Measures used can be drawn from the entire repertoire of assessment instruments and procedures, whether these be psychological, cognitive, language, neurological, motor, or visual measures. It is the goal of detecting patterns reflecting involvement of different systems and subsystems of the brain that guides the choice of measures. It is perhaps erroneous to characterize an individual test as "neuropsychological" (a term usually reserved for measures having a history of use in neuropsychological research and evaluation); rather, it is tests or observations that are interpreted neuropsychologically.[ix]

Task Analysis of Complex Behaviors

A key principle of neuropsychological assessment is *task analysis of complex behaviors*. As mentioned, this involves analyzing or breaking down human activities, whether attending, comprehending, or reading, for example, and understanding the basic component skills that make them up. It also involves understanding the diverse and highly specialized areas of the brain as together, in a dynamic way, being responsible for such complex skills.

Even what looks to be an apparently simple motor coordination difficulty, exemplified by a child who shows a tendency to fall or to bang into things may have a number of

brain areas at its base: For example, the cerebellum for muscle tone and coordination; the basal ganglia for the integration of sensory messages; subcortical-cortical loops for impulsivity and planning problems; the frontal lobe for kinetic, sequenced flow of the motor act; the motor strip for motor weakness; the parietal lobe for visual-spatial difficulties or for a kinesthetic-based dyspraxia; the occipital lobe for visual disturbances; and so on. Neuropsychological assessment will focus on examining other skills that would also be affected if the given area of the brain was responsible, and would thus attempt to isolate as best as possible, through task analysis of behaviors and reiterative hypothesis testing, what systems were involved.

Task analysis is also an integral part of interpreting a child's performance on different tests because of the multifactorial nature of so many tests. Although the most desirable measure is one that can tap into a particular neuropsychological function as purely as possible, most tests in the available repertoire of measures do not tap into one skill, but rather demand the use of multiple skills. Moreover, even when a measure is considered to primarily assess a particular function, when evaluating a child with suspected neuropsychological dysfunction, it may be that the child's areas of weakness—which may reflect skills required by a test but not considered essential or part of the test's primary factorial structure—are what impact adversely on performance. In other words, because of interference by the child's areas of neuropsychological dysfunction, the targeted skill that the test is purported to measure may not be what ends up getting measured, at least not solely.[x] This phenomenon makes it particularly important during a neuropsychological assessment of a child with a developmental or learning disorder to analyze a child's performance on a given measure over and beyond any score achieved.

For example, it may be misleading to think that a test such as "Block Design" on the Wechsler scales assesses only visual-spatial abilities, or visual-motor coordination, which are the typical functions conventionally affixed to scores on this measure. Ideally, if all other systems were intact, it may primarily assess the functions it is known for, but executing the task requires a number of different component skills, and a number of different brain systems: For example, it could include visual-spatial apprehension of the gestalt, analysis of how the complex design is made up of individual blocks, ability to shift back and forth between analytic and synthetic reasoning skills, mental rotation of the blocks, planning and organizing the reconstruction of the design, fine motor agility to manipulate the blocks, visual-motor coordination to follow through with placing the blocks, sustained attention to the task, speed of performance, visual double-checking, and self-checking. If a child scores poorly on such a test, it becomes important to ask which of the possible component skills involved was making him fall down. Rather than visual-spatial ability (right hemisphere), it may be a child's faulty organizational skills, or weak analytic abilities (left hemisphere), or weak ability to quickly shift back and forth and use both analytic and synthetic strategies (weak inter-hemispheric fibers), or lack of differentiated finger agility to turn over the blocks, or the presence of a dysmetric or poor motoric aim so that the child is slowed down and feels too uncomfortable with the task to try his best—and, because a very sensitive child with esteem issues, he becomes self-directed and spaces out.

Many tests have such complex demands intrinsic to them, which need to be analyzed and uncovered during the evaluation. For example, if a child of almost 8 with a math disability does very poorly (5th percentile) on the Stanford-Binet, 4th edition, Quantitative subtest, one would think that the score needs no interpretation, but is simply indicative of the very disability that the child is known to have. However, analyzing the task demands and the child's performance reveals a number of problems. On this task, large dice with dots on them are used and the child is asked to match the number of dots, add the dots, and then to recognize a number pattern in them. At times, very lengthy verbal instructions are given to explain the switches in task demands. The task also uses pictures to support questions of addition, subtraction, measurement, and to query about mathematics-related language (i.e., spatial prepositions such as "between"). When this child's performance was analyzed, he was found to have considerable difficulties counting the dots on the dice because he would lose the 1:1 correspondence. He also had difficulty switching sets and, when instructions became wordy, tended to perseverate on an earlier task demand. And, he had difficulties processing the language of spatial concepts. Thus, a number of weaknesses appeared to interfere with his performance, including attention and executive function weaknesses (difficulty switching sets), language-related issues (comprehension), modulation issues (when trying to match the pace of counting with dots counted), and possibly visual scanning difficulties. The child also did not use any strategies to help himself on this task. He did not use a finger as an aid when visually scanning or counting; he did not verbally rehearse questions to help himself process task demand. In fact, when the test was re-administered in testing the limits, some of these strategies were provided along with more simplified language instructions. Under these circumstances, the child was able to do many of the items previously failed, with potential performance in the average range [40th percentile]. In this case, task analysis of the demands of the test and of the child's performance allowed one to discover a number of weaknesses that were all contributing to a poor score and, most likely, feeding into the child's school-related math disability. It also allowed one to isolate those areas that needed remedial attention in order to help the child do better.

Especially, then, when assessing a child with suspected neuropsychological dysfunction, it is important to ask not merely *what* a child scores but, importantly, *how* he achieved that score or performance. It is the *how* that reveals what component skills are making him fall down, or what avenues of compensation he may naturally bring to bear or can be taught to use.

Testing of Limits, Modifications of Test Procedures

Thus, neuropsychological assessment involves modifications of tests and standardized procedures in order to: (1) test hypotheses about dysfunctional areas impacting on the child's performances; (2) test strategies that may work to help the child; and (3) elicit the child's optimal performance potential.

Testing the limits is an accepted practice in psychological assessment. It entails relaxing standardized administration and scoring procedures, crediting items passed beyond the official ceiling cut-off, relaxing time constraints, and returning to missed items after a test is completed in order to explore weaknesses and provide compensatory strategies. Scores reported as a result of testing the limits can be reported as "potential" scores, and given in addition to scores based on standardized procedures. Such "potential" scores begin to show what a child is inherently capable of, were adjustments made to accommodate and compensate for his disability.

In neuropsychological assessment, where the explicit goals of the assessment include diagnostic disclosure of areas of neuropsychological dysfunction along with remedial recommendations to help a child function more optimally, testing of limits and modifications of procedures becomes an essential core component of the assessment process.

Impaired performances present opportunities then to explore what is holding a child back and what possible strategies can come to the child's aid to enable him to do better. Take, for example, a child who is suspected as having weak analytic and organizational skills on the Block Design task (e.g., possibly a child with a developmental language disorder in addition to attentional issues, but who has otherwise good spatial orientation). In testing the limits, the child can be shown how to explicitly analyze a design as made up of four blocks, and how to work methodically and piecemeal to reconstitute the design. Improved performance would indicate not only confirmation of the suspected weaknesses as negatively impacting on performance, but a chance for the child to try out for himself what strategies will work. Such modifications of procedures can engage the child in a learning process, in which he may be encouraged to see how, more generally, he might benefit from slowing down, analyzing things, and approaching things more methodically one step at a time, and that there are ways of getting around sensed weaknesses. In this way, testing may itself begin to be therapeutic.

As another example, take a child who does very poorly on a short-term visual memory task such as Bead Memory on the Stanford-Binet, 4th edition. On Bead Memory, the child is asked to reproduce a patterned sequence of differently colored and shaped beads shown briefly. The task also requires good mental tracking and executive function skills in that various aspects of the bead presentation (e.g., color, shape, sequence) have to be remembered and held in working memory simultaneously. The child who does poorly here may have a difficult time keeping track of all these things at the same time. Once he may get the colors but miss out on the shape; the next time he may get the colors and shapes, but miss out on the sequence. A child with visual memory difficulties, and difficulties shifting between left and right hemisphere strategies, may also not spontaneously use any verbalizing, visualizing, or other strategies to help him remember. From other tests, it may be discovered that such a child does better on visual memory tasks when representational material is used, such as material that pulls for language mediation (e.g., as on the WRAML Pictorial Memory test where a scene, such as beach scene, is briefly shown and the child is then asked to recognize elements that have been added or changed); and that he has, more generally, better language than visual-related skills, better verbal memory than visual memory. For such a child, testing the limits on the Bead Memory task can include giving him several strategies which play on the strengths he is not spontaneously using. He can be told to help himself by verbally rehearsing the names of the colors and shapes under his breath; he can be encouraged to imagine a visual image, like a lamp, that the bead pattern may resemble; he can be told that there are three aspects of the beads that he has to remember. Through such strategies, which include verbalizing, visualizing, and a metacognitive strategy that allows him to grasp the demands of the task as a whole, his performance may improve. Remedial recommendations can then be directly informed by such explorations with the child.

Making adjustments to standardized procedures is important when evaluating children with various handicapping conditions. A child who cannot point to a picture because of lack of differentiated finger movements can be given a "magic wand" to use; a child who has a very slowed response time may be tested under relaxed timing constraints; a child who cannot process complex language spoken too quickly may be given simplified instructions spoken slowly and supplemented with gestures; a child who has poor methodical visual scanning and checking of options because of an attentional disorder can be aided by pointing out options for him and reminding him to carefully look at each one. The divergence from standardized procedures after a test is administered must be consciously undertaken and duly noted. But, the goal of obtaining information essential to understanding the child's inherent abilities and weaknesses and how best to promote his optimal development necessitates it.

Reiterative Hypothesis-Testing Strategies

Both convergent and divergent evidence is used to confirm hypotheses about which specific skills may be affected and, eventually, about what the differential diagnosis may be. An evaluation can itself be a reiterative hypothesis-raising and testing process throughout all its phases, taken in abstraction, from the initial interview and review of history, to the selection of measures, interpretation of performances, choice of new measures, until and through the final phase when all data across domains of inquiry and different contexts is integrated, and diagnosis and recommendations are reached.

This section will discuss some strategies for ruling in or ruling out when a skill area may be affected, given the multifactorial nature of tests, the complexity of behavior, and the need for task analysis. As mentioned, one chooses measures partly based on how "purely" they can assess a given function. One also does so according to how well they may compliment additional measures so that the targeted skills contributing to the child's problems may be more systematically isolated and identified. Particular attention is paid throughout this process to understanding what the input and output demands of each test are, and how readily or not a given child may be able to respond to a set of implicit or explicit task expectations. How this hypothesis-testing process works can best be demonstrated by an example.

Hypothesis Testing While Exploring Visual Memory Skills: The Case of Harry

As an example, suppose the targeted skill to be explored is visual memory. We want to keep in mind whether a given measure assesses the targeted function reliably at the developmental age that we want, and what else is required beyond the targeted function that may also impact on performance. For young children, there are a number of visual memory measures available that make use of either representational (e.g., meaningful, familiar objects) or nonrepresentational materials (e.g., geometric figures, abstract designs). Representational materials can pull for language mediation, such as naming and verbal rehearsal strategies, and so can elicit left-hemisphere participation to enhance memory. Nonrepresentational material may pull more for visual-spatial cognition and right-hemisphere participation. Measures may also include a sequencing component, where the visual material to be remembered must be remembered in the order in which it was presented, which may require good organizational and related skills in addition to memory. One would thus want to select a number of measures that separate out these individual aspects involved so as to make clear what skill(s) are actually down if a child happens to do poorly. Visual-memory capacities are typically attributed to the medial

temporal lobe of the right hemisphere. Thus, one would also want to look for other indices that other functions, subserved by the same or interconnected brain areas, were affected or, on the contrary, intact. Furthermore, visual memory may itself be weak secondarily to or in conjunction with weaknesses in visual-related perceptual and visual-spatial skills.

As a case example, take a child of 8, Harry, who performs in the above average range overall on the Stanford-Binet, 4th edition (S-B) intelligence test (IQ=114, 81st percentile) but does relatively weakly, although still in the average range, on the S-B visual-memory tasks (e.g., S-B Bead Memory, 27th percentile; S-B Memory for Objects, 27th percentile). Does Harry have a visual memory impairment? On the basis of the scores, one could *hypothesize* a visual memory weakness, especially because of a striking discrepancy between these performances and his strongest scores on auditory cognitive measures, which are in the superior range (i.e., S-B Vocabulary, 92nd percentile), and in contrast to verbal-memory performances, which are also in the superior range (S-B Memory for Sentences, 92nd percentile; S-B Memory for Digits, 95th percentile). But, is it visual memory that is lowering Harry's performances? We know from an analysis of requirements on the two S-B visual-memory tasks that sequencing is part of task demand on both subtests. Additionally, on S-B Bead Memory, mental tracking and frustration tolerance (while awaiting the time delay before duplicating the visual bead pattern) are also involved. We wonder, then, if these aspects of task demand are contributing to Harry's low scores. We also know that verbal mediation can be used on both tasks and so wonder whether scores are modified up or down because of this.

Because review of Harry's errors does show sequencing problems, we cross-check our queries regarding sequencing with how well or poorly Harry does on other attentional, organizational, and sequencing tasks. We find that he, in fact, shows rather pronounced difficulties in these functions. Behaviorally, Harry could appear very absorbed and concentrated, but he could also show at times attentional lapses, with distractibility to internal thoughts, and a sometimes disinhibited tendency to bound out of his chair or lie on the floor. On a test of sustained, vigilant attention, the CPT (Vigil), Harry does very poorly (<1st percentile). He also shows problematic shifting of attention (e.g., Underlining Tests, overall 13th percentile; Rapid Automatized Naming [RAN], 15th percentile to 50th percentile) with an observed tendency to become obsessively preoccupied with certain thoughts and a compulsive-like style at times when responding. For example, he would repeatedly bang the table in exactly the same way each time he gave an answer. He shows problems in planning and sequencing; for example, when asked to put numbers on a clock face, he accumulated them all on one side, and he still had not mastered, even at age 8, certain rote sequences, such as naming the months of the year. Thus, it appeared reasonable to consider, on the basis of these formal and informal measures, that the attentional and sequencing demands on the S-B visual memory tasks may have, in fact, been stressful for Harry and contributed to relatively low performances.

But, this is still not evidence enough to rule out or rule in a visual-memory impairment. More evidence is needed—convergent or divergent—from other test performances, informal observations, and what is known about Harry's functioning in every day life to draw any firm conclusions. Other visual-memory measures are therefore given. On the WRAML Visual Learning Test, where there are no sequencing demands, Harry's performance is, in fact, deficient (2nd percentile). On this test, abstract visual designs distributed around a board are briefly shown and the child has to remember exactly where he saw each one, given four trials and opportunities to learn their exact placement. Here, even after repeated trials, Harry is unable to remember where on the board a particular abstract design was seen. He also becomes very distraught on this test because of the negative feedback built into it, with his participation dampened more and more as he is made aware of his errors and shown, per standardized administration, that the correct designs are elsewhere than he thought. Even though his score may be lower than ability because of this emotional reaction and consequent inability to profit from any repeated exposures, this deficient performance supports the hypothesis of a visual-memory impairment. Additional memory measures are given that make use of both representational and nonrepresentational materials.

Harry is found to do consistently better, although still relatively weakly compared to his vocabulary knowledge and verbal memory scores, whenever representational materials are used. When asked to remember familiar objects without any sequencing demands, such as details of a familiar scene like a picture of a grocery store on the WRAML Pictorial Memory test, Harry's enthusiasm and motivation for the task are high, and he is observed to actively rehearse the names of what he sees under his breath while viewing the pictures (37th percentile). It is now thought that Harry's weak, but still much better, performances on tests using representational material, including the ones from the S-B, are due to his using a left-hemisphere strategy, and his good verbal abilities, to compensate for what is considered, now with greater certainty, a visual-memory problem. On other visual-memory measures using nonrepresentational material, performances are all found, in fact, to be very weak. When asked to reproduce complex abstract designs after a time delay, Harry gives back much detail, but in a very fragmented way, with poor recollection of the exact placement of the details and of their interrelationships (e.g., WRAML Design Memory, 5th percentile; REY Complex Figure Test, delayed recall, 3rd percentile). Although Harry also has some fine motor and graphomotor difficulties that impact on his performances here, observations about the quality of his performance support the interpretation of his low scores. The over-attention to details reproduced in a fragmented way is congruent with what is known about error style on drawings when there is right hemisphere involvement.

Harry's visual-perceptual skills are adequate (DTVP-2 Position in Space, 50th percentile), and cannot account for the degree of difficulty he shows. He does show relative weaknesses in visual-spatial organization (poor right/left orientation on another, weak WISC III Object Assembly, 9th percentile; weak Benton Judgment of Line Orientation, 13th percentile), which indicate that poor memory for visual-spatial material may itself be twinned to more overarching visual-spatial difficulties. Additional information from other contexts, especially school, emphasizes Harry's tendency to avoid looking at people, with his teachers complaining of "poor eye contact." On a test of facial memory, in fact, he also does very poorly (TOMAL Facial Memory, 2nd percentile). Other relevant features in his presentation and history include an overly pronounced sing-song quality to his voice, poor social relations, and awkward, sometimes inappropriate behavior with peers. On tests of affect sensitivity, Harry shows weak ability to discriminate emotions in people's faces, in their vocal intonation, and in different contexts. Many of these weaknesses

are consistent with dysfunction in related right-hemisphere brain systems.

In sum, in this case, one obtains multiple pieces of convergent evidence to support the hypothesis of visual-memory weakness, set in yet starker relief by the child's areas of strength, and possibly aggravated by the child's more general visual-spatial, organizational, and attentional weaknesses. At the same time, it raises the broader hypothesis that the constellation of problems that the child shows may point to a nonverbal learning disability (NLD) or, perhaps, Asperger's syndrome, which would be further explored through examining whether the child's profile of neuropsychological strengths and weaknesses was similar to the paradigmatic profile *pattern* of neuropsychological assets and deficits known to be associated with these disorders (Klin et al., 1995; Rourke, 1989).

Determining Cognitive Potential and a Neuropsychological Profile of Strengths and Weaknesses

The concept of "cognitive potential" is somewhat elusive and hard to define. Yet, it plays an important role in neuropsychological practice.

As mentioned, overall scores on standard IQ measures may be misleading in determining the actual or inherent ability level of the child. The very areas of neuropsychological dysfunction that we are trying to isolate and understand may be adversely impacting on overall scores so that they may not be reliable indices of the abilities they purportedly measure, but, rather, reflections of the ways in which the child's disability interferes with his optimal functioning. Yet, it is essential that an assessment be able to document what a child's cognitive level and inherent ability potential may be. This is important not merely to enlighten those in the child's environment for the purposes of education and intervention, but because it is indispensable for determining the child's own areas of strength and weakness. Determining inherent cognitive ability in a child with a developmental or learning disorder is important for establishing an intra-individual comparison standard against which to judge the child's own performances.

Oftentimes, learning disability guidelines put forward by state education departments for placement and special education services refer to discrepancy formulae between a child's performances on academic measures and his IQ scores. Again, this can be quite misleading *because IQ scores may be reflective of the very same component skill inefficiencies that are bringing down academic performances* (see also Fletcher, 1992). Especially for children who are very bright, and who score in the average range in areas of weakness or at grade level on academic tests, this can prevent recognition of disabilities and appropriate intervention. Also, for children who are functioning at a lower cognitive level, a more sensitive means of determining when a performance indexes an impairment is desirable. Instead of overall IQ, then, for some children, another index or way of estimating cognitive ability level may be needed.

How does one determine what the intra-individual comparison standard should be, or how does one get at inherent cognitive ability? Unfortunately, there are no standard guidelines for doing so. In neuropsychology, both normative (derived from an appropriate population-normed measure) and individual (derived from the particular person being assessed) comparison standards are used (Lezak, 1995). When there is an acquired or traumatic brain condition, the intra-individual comparison standard is an estimate of premorbid (i.e., prior to the trauma) intellectual functioning. These estimates can include,

for example, a vocabulary score as a good "hold" test for original intellectual endowment, or any "best performance," whether that be the highest score or set of scores on testing, or scores derived from premorbid achievement (Lezak, 1995). In developmental conditions, the intra-individual comparison standard may be, likewise, an estimate derived, for example, from the child's best performance on one or more reliable, cognitively weighted tests or subtests that are thought to accurately represent the child's ability. The standard might also be some quantitative parameter computed from his mean performance across such a group of measures (van Santen et al., 1994), or a score extrapolated from testing the limits on one or a number of different core cognitive tests.

Once one establishes an intra-individual standard to use, there is still the question of determining when a score should be considered a weakness indicative of neuropsychological dysfunction. Because in developmental conditions one may find a "pastel" version of symptomatology, there may not be outright deficits (scores <1st percentile to 2nd percentile)—which would signal impairment based on absolute level derived from population norms. Rather, one frequently finds "relative inefficiencies." But, how do you know when a score is "relatively inefficient?" And, furthermore, when is such a score interpreted as representing an area of neuropsychological dysfunction? Although there are purely statistical criteria for determining when scores are "significantly discrepant" from each other (see Kaufman, 1976; Sattler, 1988), oftentimes these are applied to comparisons between subtests on composite measures and not to comparisons across measures (Chapman & Chapman, 1973, 1978). A rule of thumb derived from such statistical procedures, however, and often used clinically and in research, is that scores should be at least

1 to 1½ standard deviations from each other to signal a possible significant discrepancy. (Given the lack of equivalent reliability and validity of scores across measures, and given the fact that most measures are multifactorial and may be confounded by different functions, smaller and/or larger discrepancies may also be significant. Task analysis for deciding whether a given score adequately represents a targeted neuropsychological function is, of course, presupposed in making any of these score comparisons.) Nevertheless, even then one hasn't arrived at a neuropsychologically meaningful discrepancy. The clinical judgmental process for deciding on whether a score is a "relative inefficiency" and represents an area of neuropsychological dysfunction includes looking at a number of factors simultaneously: How discrepant a score is from the intra-individual comparison standard, how discrepant a score is from the absolute standard reflected in age-expected norms; and, importantly, whether the performance in question is an expected weakness given a known neuropsychological profile pattern for a given disability (Black, 1989; van Santen et al., 1994). A comparison of a child's individual profile of strengths and weaknesses with ideal, paradigmatic patterns reflective of a known disorder, or with a constellation of inefficiencies known to reflect brain dysfunction, is integrally a part of judging whether a given score or cluster of scores represents a neuropsychologically meaningful weakness.

Such an approach can help uncover hidden disabilities or establish in greater relief a child's profile of strengths and weaknesses. For example, in the previous case of Harry, his scores on some memory tests, which were in the average range, would not be considered inherently weak were it not for the comparison to his own cognitive abilities; and they were yet more strikingly set off when his very superior vocabulary score and verbal memory scores were used as the standard of comparison. The severity of Harry's deficits was, in fact, clear because of the enormous discrepancy between scores, especially those derived from more extended assessment to test hypotheses. And, they were seen as neuropsychologically meaningful because they formed part of a consistent pattern of weaknesses reflective of a known neuropsychological disorder. But, in many cases of developmental and learning disorders, problems are often more subtle or hidden: Many children perform in the low-average or average ranges, or perform fairly uniformly across many measures including on standard intelligence measures, even though some of these performances may reflect areas of considerable neuropsychological dysfunction. If their inherent cognitive potential is never sought out, if they are given only a limited battery of tests, and their scores on these are taken at face value rather than analyzed and interpreted, misdiagnosis and misunderstanding may easily result.

Searching for Cognitive Potential and Establishing a Neuropsychological Profile of Strength and Weaknesses: The case of Debbie

The case of Debbie, age 5, exemplifies the importance of searching for cognitive potential during an evaluation. Debbie was thought of as very "low functioning," possibly retarded, by her parents and teachers, and possibly on the pervasive developmental disorder spectrum. (Her older brother of 9 had been diagnosed with autism many years before.) At age 5, Debbie was not yet talking in coherent or intelligible sentences, was prone to rigid, over-controlling patterns of behavior, and showed "autistic features," such as flapping her hands and social withdrawal. Imperative in the assessment of

Debbie was the search for her open channels and strengths and how to facilitate them. Once optimal potential was elicited, a profile of strengths and weaknesses could be established. In the assessment process, the uncovering and addressing of Debbie's emotional coping strategies, along with modification of standardized procedures, helped reveal those strengths.

On the Stanford-Binet, 4th edition, administered and scored in a standardized way, Debbie performed in the borderline range (overall composite score 77, 8th percentile). Attentional issues, self-protective distractibility, refusals, and massive language difficulties all inhibited, however, her test-taking ability. When scoring and administration criteria were relaxed in testing the limits, performance potential across both verbal and nonverbal tasks was in the average range [composite 93, 33rd percentile]. (Brackets [ ] are used to denote "potential" scores obtained by testing the limits.) Differences and gains were most apparent in nonverbal and memory domains. It was here that attentional issues and inability to cue into complicated verbal instructions clearly inhibited her ability to show what she was truly capable of. For example, she refused to continue a test which moved from using a simple formboard to using blocks with design patterns (S-B Pattern Analysis): It was the *shift* in task demand, inherent to the subtest, that made her balk and refuse to go on despite all forms of encouragement. Readministration in another session of just the patterned blocks, saw her performance jump from a borderline level (8th percentile) to a solidly average level [65th percentile]. In fact, her score could have been superior [92nd percentile], were her attentional issues and lack of persistence, seen in the considerable intra-test scatter present, not interfering even on this administration. When Debbie was given nonverbal rather than standardized overly complex verbal instructions on a visual analogical reasoning task, she also performed well, with her score moving from borderline (8th percentile) to the above average range (S-B Matrices [81st percentile]). Thus, Debbie's visual-cognitive reasoning abilities, given testing of limits, were estimated to be at least above average rather than borderline, as standardized administration had yielded.

Because of an understanding of what was holding her back as well as glimpses into her visual-reasoning strengths, another nonverbal cognitive measure was administered, the Leiter, in order to provide confirmation of the hypothesis of above average nonverbal abilities. On the Leiter, no verbal demands are made at all: There are no verbal instructions, and no verbal responses are needed. Nor are there any internal shifts in task demands or expectations. Furthermore, a certain routine is set up where materials are presented and can be removed in a rhythmic, consistent manner. This was concordant with Debbie's own self-comforting strategies and need for routine and redundancy—a need which possibly had its roots in her language deficiencies and inability to feel secure in knowing what was expected of her, and not, as some had suspected, as part of an "autistic" need for sameness. Debbie easily caught on to task demand on the Leiter and did appear, in fact, comforted by the rhythm of the routine of its standardized administration. Her ability to concentrate and actively participate notably improved, her affect was more positive, and her interpersonal demeanor much more friendly, cooperative, and interactive. Debbie scored solidly above average on the Leiter, even using standardized procedures (IQ=113, 80th percentile; mental age = 5.9 years).

Once the circumstances under which Debbie could excel became clear, other performances could be elicited that tapped more capably into her abilities. One such area was on imitative tasks, such as visual-cognitive, motor praxis measures: For example, when asked to imitate a series of complicated body or hand movements, or when asked to gesture her way through her understanding of the use of objects (e.g., ITPA Manual Expression, 92nd percentile; KABC Hand Movements, 99th percentile). With inherent cognitive potential revealed, the severity of Debbie's weaknesses on language-related tasks became that much more striking, both receptively and expressively. Debbie's neuropsychological profile of strengths and weaknesses exemplified a very severe developmental language disorder, most likely of the phonological syntactic type, with clear strengths in most visual-related areas.

In the final interpretation, Debbie's lack of verbal skills masked easy access by others to her cognitive strengths. Furthermore, some of her unusual features, worrisome to the family and others, could have stemmed in part from her use of her excellent visual cognitive and imitative skills to emulate behaviors of her older autistic brother and to "fit in" to a family system which had been belabored and depressed by both children's needs. Once strengths were disclosed, the parents could renew their investment in their daughter, seen on her own individual trajectory. The search for cognitive potential allowed one to more accurately disclose Debbie's profile of strengths and weaknesses, aided in differential diagnosis, and significantly informed intervention to foster the child's developmental growth.

Integration and Interpretation of the Data

The above principles and procedures have been described in abstraction from what usually takes place as an integrated and dynamic process during the evaluation. In the final analysis, all data are interpreted as to their meaningfulness in an ongoing, hypothesis-testing, deliberative procedure which culminates in (1) identifying the child's neurocognitive profile as fitting a particular diagnostic condition; (2) summarizing the various contributions to the child's general adaptation as well as difficulties; and (3) elaborating upon recommendations for intervention. Throughout the evaluation, an active integration and weighing of information is done on the backdrop of what is known about brain-behavior relationships, brain maturation in typical and atypical populations, different childhood neurological, neuropsychiatric, and developmental conditions, and general expectations for development of language, motor, and cognitive functions in childhood.

The data of the evaluation that needs to be integrated and interpreted encompasses:

- The background history of the child, which includes developmental, medical, school, family, and cultural history.
- The compendium of qualitative and quantitative data resulting from administering formal and informal assessment measures, with attention given to observations of the child during all phases of the assessment process, especially to the child's errors, problem-solving approaches, compensatory strategies, and reactions under pressure.
- An understanding of the child's personality, social relations, and coping strategies, also as seen by significant others and in interactions with others during the evaluation.
- An understanding of the different demands, stresses, and supports provided the child in different contexts, at home and at school.

Integration of data is, in other words, across the breadth and the depth of the evaluation.

Review of background history lays the foundation for raising initial hypotheses related to diagnostic questions. It sets the framework for questions about the possible etiological roots of the child's problems, about the child's developmental course and rate of progress, and about the history of stress and support that may also be part of the dynamic interplay of factors contributing to the child's issues. Understanding prenatal, perinatal, and neonatal risk factors, for example, can begin to reveal whether there were early events which could have predisposed the child to constitutional vulnerabilities. For example, maternal condition during pregnancy (e.g. nutrition and stress, presence of medical conditions such as toxemia, gestational diabetes, need for medications, or use of drugs), and difficulties during and immediately following delivery (e.g., difficult labor, presence of distress signs such as meconium, low apgars) may have neurodevelopmental sequelae. A history of similar types of problems as the child's in the immediate and extended family can raise questions about genetic predisposition and the maturational unfolding of related difficulties. It can also raise questions about how other affected family members have dealt with problems and therefore what attitudes they consciously or unconsciously bring to bear toward the child. Medical history may reveal problems that are known to have repercussions associated with neuropsychological dysfunction (e.g., metabolic or hormonal problems, a history of severe otitis media, exposure to lead or other toxins). Early infancy difficulties such as problems establishing a routine sleep-wake pattern, early colic or fussiness, or feeding problems may signal neuropsychological vulnerabilities that continue in different forms later on. For example, problems in early feeding may be a result of difficulties in the smooth sequencing of suck and swallow

patterns which can reappear as more general organizational and sequencing difficulties later. Whether the child has met normal developmental milestones provides information about which systems may be affected and about early experiences of the child and family with the child's atypical development. Educational history is, of course, important for understanding how the child has met various demands placed upon him outside the home, about specific academic successes and failures, and about his social interactions with peers.

Information about the child's personality is obtained from the assessment process as well as from parents and other significant people in the child's life. This can be done on hand of standardized questionnaires, observations of interactions with parents, and possibly with peers in a classroom setting, as well as by formal, projective personality assessment and analysis of the interactive dynamics set up between child and evaluator. Personality measures, such as drawings (e.g., House-Tree-Person, Kinetic Family Drawing), the Rorschach, and story-telling projective measures (e.g., the CAT or TAT) can be important vehicles for disclosing emotional difficulties that may be present, including anxieties, depressive affect, aggressive ideation, difficulties in self-esteem regulation, experience of heightened vulnerability and loss of self-control, and the lack of a coherent sense of self. The child's subjective view of himself and others can be interpreted from responses on projectives, especially when combined with other information from history, observations, and testing. The child's ability to solve social problems, to understand the motives, feelings, and intentions of others, and to reach conclusions about appropriate behavior can be interpreted, for example, from the child's stories, or from other instruments (e.g., Test of Problem Solving

[TOPS]); or from explicit tasks set up to explore the child's understanding of other minds (Baron-Cohen, 1991; Happe, 1994). Projectives are an important vehicle for helping to distinguish neurogenic and psychogenic conditions. The first principle for such a differential is whether a consistent pattern of neuropsychological impairment is present, indicating a neurogenic condition. Projectives, however, can serve to further distinguish between those emotional difficulties that may be sequelae to and consistent with neuropsychological dysfunction from those whose intensity and character set them apart as primary concerns in their own right, and feeding into the child's difficulties. For example, a child may respond in a very tangential and hard-to-follow manner in stories told to ambiguous pictures on the TAT—a measure known to elicit depressive and aggressive themes and the child's attitudes and defensive coping style in face of them. The tendency to become verbally incoherent or sidetracked would have very different psychological import depending on whether evidence was also found that the child showed a language disorder with organizational difficulties affecting language formulation. A child who shows breakdowns in reality testing because of lack of conformity of his percepts with those conventionally seen by children his age on the Rorschach will be viewed very differently if he has visual-perceptual and visual-memory difficulties than if not.

Importantly, the final interpretation of the data should include an understanding of the child's particular coping style and personal ways, adaptive or not, of accommodating to various neuropsychological skill inefficiencies. In many cases of developmental and learning disorders, there is a strong concomitance with emotional and behavioral difficulties (Beitchman, 1985; Beitchman, Cohen, Konstantareas, & Tannock, 1996; Beitchman,

Nair, Clegg, Ferguson, & Patel, 1986; Black, 1989; Cantwell & Baker, 1991; Rourke, 1989). Neuropsychological dysfunction can itself masquerade as an emotional or behavioral problem and be hidden from view, or it can feed into and be inextricably interwoven with psychological conflict. The experience of inefficiencies and discrepancies in abilities are inevitably given meaning and explanation by the child, taken up into his sense of self, and played out in fantasy and behavior. This often takes place, moreover, alongside and in response to interpretations made by significant others in the child's environment about those behaviors, whether at home or at school. This can set up a powerful framework of interpretation and misinterpretation, by both the child and others, which may feed into and perpetuate the child's emotional difficulties and hinder understanding and redressing of his core problems. The task of a comprehensive neuropsychological evaluation then also includes "unbuilding" to find the disability in the child and its possible exacerbation or implication in psychological conflict also within the child-world system.

For this reason, information about the child's behavior in contexts other than the testing situation, and the attitudes, supports, or stresses on the child that come from the broader environment also form a critical part of the data to be integrated and evaluated.

Diagnostic Formulation and Recommendations

The final diagnostic formulation made on the basis of all the data should include whether there is a developmental or learning disorder and its specific characterization. If another neurological syndrome or condition is uncovered, this would be specified in terms of whether there was evidence for a static vs. an active process, diffuse vs. circumscribed deficits, long-term vs. acute condition. A summary statement of the child's current cognitive level and an estimate of inherent cognitive potential, however elusive, should be made along with specification of the major areas of strength and weakness found. Included, too, should be the nature of any emotional difficulties or complex interweaving of neurocognitive and emotional factors found. The final summary should describe, importantly, the child's key strengths and open channels that serve adaptation now and can enhance development in the future.

Recommendations resulting from the neuropsychological evaluation address those aspects of the child's functioning and the child-world system (including family and school) that may be hindering the child's optimal adaptation, while actively supporting those aspects that can be counted on to further promote it (see Bernstein & Waber, 1990). Recommendations can be remedial, therapeutic, and sometimes prophylactic given a forward trajectory into the child-world system of expectations. Recommendations are offered as suggestions for consideration and can pertain to:

- *A supportive educational placement for the child,* with description of the specific setting, structure, number of children, and teaching style most conducive to the child's development (e.g., ratio of teachers to children; small group learning, hands-on experiences, minimal distractions and background noise, visual supplements in the classroom, access to computers, augmentative communication, aided language stimulation). The child's neuropsychological profile of skills and general cognitive level of performance play an important role in delineating the child's learning style and needs, and the specific classroom characteristics that will best match them.
- *Type and frequency of specific therapeutic services* (e.g., occupational therapy,

physical therapy, language therapy, psychotherapy, reading remediation).

- *The need for other specialized evaluations* (e.g., medical, genetic, neurological, opthalmological, audiological, language, motor) or psychiatric consideration of psychopharmacological intervention (e.g., to address motor tics, anxieties, attentional deficits, impulsivity, hyperactivity).
- *Specific remedial suggestions that address the child's areas of neuropsychological dysfunction.* This is an area that should be elaborated upon extensively, in light of the detailed understanding of the child's neuropsychological profile gained from the evaluation, and on the basis of strategies tried out to enhance performances during testing of limits. Even seemingly small suggestions may be of significant benefit to the child: For example, having a child with visual search problems use a finger to help scan pictures or text, or suggesting that visual materials in school be presented in large, uncluttered formats so that the child does not disorganize and become distracted; or suggesting that a child who has serious organizational difficulties use her love of color and coloring to sustain her focus on a project and more actively process and encode the material. Remediation, generally, can be targeted at either the weaknesses directly or at strategies to help the child compensate. For example, a child found to have inefficient auditory-processing difficulties, with problems in sound discrimination and sound sequencing (e.g., problems in phonemic awareness), may profit from direct remediation of weaknesses through a program such as the Lindamood Phonemic Sequencing (LiPS) Program (Lindamood & Lindamood, 1998; also see Lindamood & Lindamood, Chapter 23, this volume, for further discussion).

This is a program which ties articulatory processes to expanding phonemic awareness, and may reinforce improvement in auditory processing through the oral-motor feedback also provided and the consequent activation of interconnecting fiber networks in the brain (Heilman, Voller, & Alexander, 1996). A child who has spelling problems because of difficulties in phonemic awareness may be encouraged to use possible strengths, such as good visual memory, and focus on encoding and recalling the "look" of a word. A child who has verbal-memory and language-comprehension difficulties, but good visual-related skills and a rich imagination, may be taught to capitalize on his strengths to compensate for weaknesses: He can be encouraged to rely on visualizing strategies to enhance verbal recall (i.e. "seeing" the numbers or message), and to similarly use strong visualizing and imaginative skills to enhance language comprehension (e.g., see Nanci Bell's program of Visualizing and Verbalizing for Language Comprehension and Thinking (V/V) (Bell, 1991a; Bell, Chapter 25, this volume). Such a child would also profit, more generally, from visual prompts and hands-on experiences in the classroom to supplement language communication and direction. Children who have problems in visualizing, and in weak integration skills (because of, perhaps, weak inter- and intra-hemispheric connections as with, for example, white matter disease or NLD), may also profit from direct remedial work on visualizing skills through such a program as V/V as well. Young children who have multiple challenges, with, for example, severe language disorders affecting both expressive and receptive communication, and possibly severe motor praxis difficulties too, may profit from augmentative communication strategies and "aided language stimulation" to open up their interest in and ability to process information in the world around them (see Goosens, Crain, & Elder, 1994).

- *Specific suggestions for psychotherapeutic intervention with the child and/or family.* These are informed by knowledge of the child's neuropsychological profile as well as the possible interweaving of neuropsychological dysfunction with the child's emotional and behavioral issues. As an example, psychotherapy may be recommended for a child, Nick, who appears depressed, has social problems, seems uninterested in making friends, and retreats into an overactive and isolative fantasy life. Found on evaluation to have a nonverbal learning disability, Nick also showed associated problems in affect perception and inability to readily take the perspective of another or have insight into another's feelings and intents. A highly verbal child, when telling stories on projectives, Nick ended up elaborately relating tales about his internal fantasy world, which appeared peopled by mechanical-like figures who fragmented, transformed into different shapes, and went on different death-defying adventures. Recommended for such a child could be a psychotherapeutic approach that would also be remedial since here the child's neurocognitive issues are certainly impacting on his interactional problems and his feelings of fragmentation, lifelessness, depression, and need for transformation. Other specific recommendations might then entail inclusion in a small, psychotherapeutic social-skills group with other children, where specific training in understanding and using facial expressions, gestures, posture, and prosody to express specific feelings and intentions could be combined with role playing and dramatic enactment of appropriate behavior in different social situations. Another possibility could include having the child write down the stories that preoccupy and isolate him from others, and have others in the group or family add to them and act them out with him. Individual psychotherapy could address more directly, through talk or through play, the child's self-concept, understanding of self in relationship to others, and problems in esteem regulation, while helping him to develop more self-satisfying and competent ways of fulfilling his social needs. In other words, individualized psychotherapeutic recommendations could be developed for a child that would address important aspects of the child's neuropsychological profile as these are related to emotional difficulties.

Recommendations could also be generated for work within the family, in particular for addressing possible misreadings and long-term misunderstandings that the parent(s) or other members of the family may have made about the child's issues. The medium for intervention with the child can then become work within the family and/or school system to support more realistic understanding of the child's strengths and weaknesses, to promote more effective coping and compensating strategies, and to address ways of either modifying demands placed on the child or helping the child meet future cognitive, academic, and social expectations.

SUGGESTED FORMAT FOR A NEUROPSYCHOLOGICAL EVALUATION

A comprehensive neuropsychological evaluation, as described here, which integrates understanding of the child's emotional functioning and behavior in different contexts, can take the following general format:

Background History and Previous Evaluations

Before the initial session, background information about the child is collected and reviewed in order to guide inquiries during the initial session with the parents and raise hypotheses about the child's functioning during the evaluation.

The parents are asked to complete a comprehensive developmental history questionnaire, which covers questions about the pregnancy, and the child's developmental, medical, school, family, and social history. Also included are questions about the family's concerns, the child's assets and weaknesses, other caretakers responsible for the child, and life events that may have critically impacted on the child or family. These questions will be taken up again in the context of meeting(s) with the parents.

The parents are asked to distribute school questionnaires to the child's teachers and/or therapists and have them returned directly. These questionnaires elicit information that can begin to set in relief how the child is seen in contexts other than the home. Questions asked pertain to the teacher's or therapist's views of any social, emotional, or academic problems the child has, how the child is different from other children in the class, the child's strengths and weaknesses in learning and in coping, the structure and setting of the classroom, strategies that have been found to work well for the child, and other types of helpful information.

Copies of any relevant previous evaluations, such as neurological, audiological, language, psychological, or motor evaluations, as well as relevant educational and school records are also requested. In addition, if there are particular concerns about the child's emotional functioning or attention-related issues, standardized questionnaires (such as the Achenbach Child Behavior Checklist, Conners, or McCarney Scales) are sent to both parents as well as teachers, to see whether perceptions of the child vary between people and in different contexts.

Clinical Interview with Parents

The clinical interview with the parents is held, without the child present, in order to complete questions about background history and to more fully understand the parents' concerns and viewpoints about the child. The clinical interview with the parents is used, importantly, to begin to understand what kinds of interpretations and possible misinterpretations each of the parents may have attributed to the child's behavior, as well as to understand family and marital dynamics. Some clinically revealing questions ask, for example, about parental fantasies and hopes before the child was born, parental "theories" about what is wrong with the child, what the parents worst fears for the child are, and how each of them sees the child as like or unlike the other parent. These types of questions also can elicit some of the deeper fantasies and fears as well as possible projections and defenses that may be orienting, even if not consciously, for each of the parent's interactions with the child. They start to bring into focus, as well, what the child may be experiencing and responding to in the family. The initial contact with the parents also allows an alliance to be built up with them based on

fuller knowledge of their own concerns and struggles. This alliance is important for later findings and discussions and for intervening into the system on behalf of the child and family's well-being.

Observations of Interactions

Especially for young children, ages 1 to 6, assessment of the child begins with observation of the family during a free-play session in the office, where each of the parents are encouraged to interact and play with the child as usual. For very young children, or children with separation issues, parent(s) may remain with the child during the course of the evaluation, with observations of interactions continuing.

An observational visit to the school may also be useful, especially if a disparity in viewpoints between family and school has been noted or if, for example, many of the child's behavioral issues occur in the school setting. Such a visit can also illustrate how the child behaves when other than family demands or supports are placed upon him, and how the child interacts with other children and other adults. For older children with learning problems, a visit to the school can be very illuminating about the structure of the classroom, teaching style, curriculum content, and academic expectations. It can also be very useful for understanding what further possibilities exist for incorporating later on specific remedial recommendations.

Assessment Sessions with Child

A series of more formal neuropsychological assessment sessions are then scheduled. The number and length of such sessions depend on the age and constraints of the child, the complexity of the case, the hypotheses raised, and what is needed to answer them. Very young children cannot be expected to go through testing that is longer than about 1 to

1½ hours. Older children can sometimes be scheduled for 3 hours or more or even for a whole-day session with breaks. The therapeutic needs of the child, which can include helping a child accommodate to the assessment process, as well as the assessment goal of finding strategies to elicit optimal performance, can lengthen the evaluation and number of sessions. The number of hours involved in an assessment can range anywhere from 3 to 15 or more.

Discussion of Findings

Findings are discussed with the parents usually over one or two sessions. If more follow-through and explanation are needed, additional sessions are scheduled, since the parents' processing of the evaluation's findings and recommendations are critical to the evaluation's effectiveness. It is during these feedback sessions that the child's behaviors may begin to be seen in a new light and that long-standing family dynamics may begin to be addressed. It is also a time for jointly considering how and where to intervene into the system, at home or at school. The parents may be encouraged to think through situations at home that exemplify some of the areas where neuropsychological dysfunction has fed, for example, into resistant, frustrating, or oppositional behavior or, on the other hand, into withdrawal and seclusion by the child. Specific ideas can then be generated together as to how the family may begin to address the child's issues at home. Fears and fantasies and other viewpoints of the parents, discussed during the initial interview, can be raised again and worked through in light of the evaluation. Pragmatic reassurances and steps that can be taken to follow through on enabling recommendations to move forward, especially with regard to school and different therapies, are also discussed. At the end of the first findings discussion, the parents are given a full written report which fully documents all of the child's performances and interpretations made.

Findings may also be discussed with the older school-aged child. Although discussion must be aimed at a level, complexity, and amount that the child is able to process, the child can be given a broad understanding of areas of strength and weakness, and of special talents. Especially, when specific component skills have been identified as interfering with certain academic subjects or functioning in everyday life, some insight into these, and strategies to use to manage problems, may start the remedial process off. Children with learning disorders, who may have the not so secret fear that they are stupid or crazy, may especially benefit from an emphasis on inherent cognitive strengths, with reminders of tests taken and successful strategies used. This approach can be a good dose of much needed esteem-enhancing support. Importantly, a discussion of findings with the child may begin to help circumscribe the weaknesses that may have started to spill over, because unknown and unchecked, into other areas of the child's life.

SUMMARY

In sum, developmental neuropsychological evaluation bases its exploration and interpretation of a broad range of neurocognitive functions on an understanding of brain maturation, brain-behavior relationships, and the dynamic interplay between neural systems, behavior, and the environment. The approach proposed for neuropsychological evaluation of developmental and learning disorders is a process-oriented, hypothesis-testing approach that incorporates principles of dynamic learning into its core assessment procedures, attempts to elicit the child's optimal performance potential, understands that the multifactorial nature of tests and the complexity of behavior requires analysis of performance, and is inherently comprehensive and integrative in its attempts to understand the child in the context of his experiences and the world around him. ∎

Notes

[i]Terminological clarification of "neurocognitive" and "cognitive" might be helpful: The term "neurocognitive" in neuropsychology refers to the broad, supraordinate domain that forms the focus of its study and encompasses all functions related to cortical and subcortical structures. The term "cognitive" may be used synonymously with "neurocognitive;" or "cognitive" may also refer, in a more delimited way, to reasoning, thinking, or problem-solving skills, whether mediated verbally or nonverbally. Although perhaps not truly separate from other functions, such as language, visual, or memory functions, because building upon them and mediated by them, "cognitive" functioning may, nevertheless be separable from functioning in any one particular domain while still not being equivalent to the broad supraordinate "neurocognitive" domain. Different neuropsychological constructs may be used to denote components of a child's more cognitively weighted abilities; for example, one may focus on a child's "auditory-cognitive" skills or "visual-cognitive" skills, or imaginative, integrative, or abstract reasoning capacities. In all these cases, weight is given to the more conceptual and complex requirements of the child's functioning when denoting an ability as "cognitive." "Cognitive" in this latter sense is perhaps more congruent with the general understanding of the term "cognitive" and its use in other disciplines, such as developmental psychology. In this chapter, "cognitive" is used in this latter, more commonly understood sense and the term "neurocognitive" is reserved for the more over-arching term.

[ii]For example, there is now documented overlap of cases of Tourette's syndrome, ADHD and obsessive-compulsive disorder (OCD), sometimes characterized within the notion of a broad "basal ganglia syndrome" as well as by "Pandas." (Palumbo, Maughan, & Kurlan, 1997; Swedo, Leonard, & Kiessling, 1994,; Swedo et al., 1998). Although ADHD is comorbid with a number of disorders, it can and should be reliably distinguished from other conditions, such as anxiety and conduct disorders.

As another example, Rourke (1989, 1995) identified the syndrome of nonverbal learning disabilities (NLD)(a term first coined by Mykelbust,1975). Children with NLD have arithmetic disabilities and show a particular neuropsychological profile pattern: They evidence neuropsychological weaknesses in visual-perceptual, psychomotor, tactile-perceptual, visual-spatial, and organizational skills; have difficulties in concept formation, adapting to novel information, and have social-emotional problems; and they show strengths in psycholinguistic abilities and rote verbal memory. This characteristic neuropsychological profile of NLD is thought by Rourke to be related to disturbances of the white matter of the brain. It has now been shown that there are numerous neurological and neurodevelopmental conditions in which the NLD pattern is exemplified, including early hyprocephalus (Fletcher, Francis, Thompson, & Brookshire, 1992); Asperger's syndrome (Klin, Volkmar, Sparrow, Cicchetti, & Rourke, 1995); Williams Syndrome (Bellugi, Sabo, & Vaid, 1988), de Lange syndrome (Stefanatos & Musikoff, 1994); callosal agensis (Casey, Del Datto, & Rourke, 1990); Turner's syndrome (Ross, Stefanatos, Roeltgen, Kushner & Cutler, 1995); congenital hypothyroidism (Rovet, 1993); and traumatic brain injury (Fletcher & Levin, 1988).

[iii]Dyslexics show larger right plana and so symmetrical plana rather than normal asymmetry of left plana greater than right. Neuronal ectopias are brain cells that are inappropriately placed and form disorganized circuits in the molecular layers of a brain region. The ectopias identified are most likely attributable to faulty pruning of neurons during the last trimester of prenatal brain development, whether this be due to genetic or environmental causes.

Difficulties when required to rapidly process visual information, also possibly involved in reading, have been related to a magnocellular defect in the lateral geniculate nucleus of the thalamus (responsible for processing fast, low contrast information, motion perception, and stabilization of images during eye movements) (Livingston, Rosen, Drislane, & Galaburda, 1991; Galaburda & Livingston, 1993).

[iv]More recently, Simos, Brier, Apouridakis, & Papanico-Laou (1999) have shown, using the spatial and temporal analysis possible with MEG, that dyslexic subjects will switch from a left hemisphere strategy when distinguising voiced or unvoiced consonants ('e.g., 'b' vs 'd' or 'p' vs 'k') to a right hemisphere strategy. Normal subjects maintain a left hemisphere strategy over time.

[v]Early regression among PDD children may also be a result of subclinical epileptiform activity, or possibly some auto-immune process that may be environmentally triggered, or due to some as yet unidentified process (see Stefanatos, Grover, & Geller, 1995; Stefanatos, Kolros, Rabinovitch, & Stone, 1998; Tuchman & Rapin, 1997; Chez, Buchanan, Field-Chez, Loeffel, & Hammer, 1998; Connolly et al.,1997, 1999; Swedo, Leonard, & Kiessling, 1994; Swedo et al., 1998; Warren, Odell, Meciulis, Burger, & Warren, 1996; Warren et al., 1997; Zimmerman, Potter, Stakkestao, & Frye, 1995; Zimmerman, 1999).

[vi]As Barbara Wilson (1992) says "…it is as important to understand how a child arrived at a given score as it is to know the score itself. Ten children who obtain the same test scores may have arrived at them in ten different ways. It is most important to have some understanding of what those ways are." She has said this in a myriad of ways and its wisdom infuses her approach to assessment and teaching.

[vii]Difficulties sustaining a motor act are known as "motor impersistence" and involves such things as not being able to maintain standing on one foot or sustaining quick repetitive finger movements. Norms are available for children 5-10 years on the PANESS, developed by Martha Denckla (1974, 1985) (see also Gardner, 1979, pp.100-109), but not for younger chil-

dren, although general age expectations are known for younger children (see, for example, Bayley motor scale; McCarthy, leg coordination subtest; Carolina Curriculum). Motor impersistence has been correlated with attentional disorders (Heilman et al., 1991) and considered reflective of behaviors that may serve as signs of neostriatum involvement, or of prefrontal-subcortical circuitry (Denckla & Reiss, 1997; Giedd, 1996; Giedd et al., 1994).

[viii]For these inter-test comparisons to be meaningful, all tests involved must have adequate levels of reliability because otherwise spurious individual differences can easily occur.

[ix]There may be claims that a test is "neuropsychological" only because of its history of being used, or being similar to other tests that have been used, for assessing specific neuropsychological functions in children and adults with different acquired and congenital neurological conditions (e.g., the NEPSY is composed of such types of tests). But, it is the interpretation of a test performance rather than the test itself that characterizes the assessment as a neuropsychological assessment.

[x]That such skills are not recognized in any of the factor loadings for a test may be due to the absence of special populations in test validation and norming studies.

REFERENCES

Alexander, A., Anderson, H., Heilman, K., Voeller, K., & Torgeson, J. (1991). Phonological awareness training and remediation of analytic decoding deficits in a group of severe dyslexics. *Annals of Dyslexia, 41*, 193-206.

Aram, D. M., & Eisele, J. A. (1992). Plasticity in recovery of higher cognitive functions following early brain injury. In I. Rapin & S. J. Segalowitz (Eds.), *Handbook of neuropsychology, Vol. 6: Child Neuropsychology* (pp. 73-92). Amsterdam: Elsevier Press.

Aram, D. M. & Nation, J. E. (1975). Patterns of language behavior in children with developmental language disorders. *Journal of Speech and Hearing Research, 18*, 229-241.

Akshoomoff, N. A., Courchesne, E., and Townsend, J. (1997). Attention coordination and anticipatory control: The role of the cerebellum in attention. In J. D. Schmahmann (Ed.), *The cerebellum and cognition*. New York: Academic Press.

Bachevalier, J. (1994). The contribution of medial temporal lobe structures in infantile autism: A neurobehavioral study in primates. In M. L. Bauman and T. L. Kemper (Eds.), *The neurobiology of autism* (pp. 146-169). Baltimore: Johns Hopkins University Press.

Bachevalier, J. (1997). *Research on the underlying central nervous system mechanisms associated with disorders of communication, relating, and learning.* Paper presented at the November 14, 1997 conference of the Interdisciplinary Council on Developmental and Learning Disorders, Rockville, MD.

Bailey, A., Luthert, P., Dean, A., Harding, B., Janota, I., Montgomery, M. Rutter, M., & Lantos, P. (1998). A clinicopathological study of autism. *Brain, 121*, 889-905.

Bakker, D. (1979). Hemispheric differences and reading strategies: Two dyslexias? *Bulletin of the Orton Society, 29*, 84-100.

Bakker, D. J. (1992). Neuropsychological classification and treatment of dyslexia. *Journal of Learning Disabilities, 25*, 102-109.

Bakker, D., & Vinke, J. (1985). Effects of hemisphere-specific stimulation on brain activity and reading in dyslexics. *Journal of Clinical and Experimental Neuropsychology, 7*, 505-525.

Barkley, R. A. (1997). *ADHD and the nature of self-control.* New York: Guilford Press

Baron, I., Fennell, E., & Voeller, K. (1995). *Pediatric neuropsychology in the medical setting.* New York: Oxford University Press.

Baron-Cohen, S. (1991). The theory of mind deficit in autism: How specific is it? *British Journal of Developmental Psychology, 9*, 301-314.

Bates, E. (1999). Plasticity, localization, and language development. In S. H. Broman and J. M. Fletcher (Eds.), *The changing nervous system: Neurobehavioral consequences of early brain disorders.* New York: Oxford University Press.

Bates, E., Vicari, S., & Trauner, D. (1999). Neural mediation of language development: Perspectives from lesion studies of infants and children. In H. Tager-Flusberg (Ed.), *Neurodevelopmental disorders* (pp. 533-581), Cambridge, MA: MIT Press.

Bauer, R. M. (1994). The flexible battery approach to neuropsychological assessment. In R. D. Vanderploeg (Ed.), *Clinicians guide to neuropsychological assessment* (pp. 259-290). Hillsdale, NJ: Erlbaum.

Bauman, M. L. (1997). *Research on the underlying central nervous system mechanisms associated with disorders of communication, relating, and learning.* Paper presented at the November 14, 1997 conference of the Interdisciplinary Council on Developmental and Learning Disorders, Rockville, MD.

Bauman, M. L., & Kemper, T. L. (1994). Neuroanatomic observations of the brain in autism. In M. L. Bauman and T. L. Kemper (Eds.), *The neurobiology of autism* (pp. 119-145). Baltimore: John Hopkins University Press.

Beitchman, J. H. (1985). Speech and language impairment and psychiatric risk: Toward a model of neurodevelopmental immaturity. *Psychiatric Clinics of North America, 9,* 721-735.

Beitchman, J. H., Cohen, N. J., Konstantareas, M. M., & Tannock, R. (Eds.) (1996). *Language, learning and behavior disorders: Developmental, biological, and clinical perspectives.* New York: Cambridge University Press.

Beitchman, J. H., Nair, R., Clegg, M., Ferguson, B., & Patel, P. G. (1986). Prevalence of psychiatric disorders in children with speech and language disorders. *Journal of the American Academy of Child Psychiatry, 25,* 528-535.

Bell, M. A., & Fox, N. A. (1994). Brain development over the first year of life: Relations between electroencephalographic frequency and coherence and cognitive and affective behaviors. In G. A. Dawson & K.W. Fisher (Eds.), *Human behavior and the developing brain* (pp. 314-345). New York: Guilford Press.

Bell, N. (1991a). *Visualizing and verbalizing for language comprehension and thinking.* (revised edition). San Luis Obispo, CA: Gander Educational Publishing (Originally published in 1986).

Bell, N. (1991b). Gestalt imagery: A critical factor in language comprehension. *Annals of Dyslexia, 41,* 246-260.

Bellugi, U., Sabo, H., & Vaid, J. (1988). Spatial deficits in children with Williams syndrome. In J. Styles-Davis, M. Kritchevsky, & U. Bellugi (Eds.), *Spatial cognition: Brain bases and development* (pp. 173-298). Hillsdale, NJ: Erlbaum.

Bernstein, J. H. (1991). *Child neuropsychology: Cognitive development and disorder.* Paper presented at the New York Neuropsychology Group/New York Academy of Sciences, April 6, 1991.

Bernstein, J. H., & Waber, D. P. (1990). Developmental neuropsychological assessment: The systemic approach. In: A. A. Boulton, G. B. Baker, & M. Hiscock (Eds.), *Neuromethods, Vol. 17, Neuropsychology* (pp. 311-371). Clifton: Humana Press.

Black, L. M. (1989). Subtypes of language disordered children at risk for social-emotional problems. *Dissertation Abstracts International,* No. 8910782. Ann Arbor, MI: University of Michigan.

Black, L. M. (1995). The interweaving of neuropsychological dysfunction and psychological conflict. *Zero to Three, National Center for Clinical Infant Programs,* 15(4), 26-35.

Black, L. M. (1997). Regulatory disorders: Type I: Hypersensitive–fearful and cautious. In *DC: 0-3 casebook* (pp.195-232). Washington, D.C.: ZERO TO THREE: National Center for Infants, Toddlers, and Families.

Broman, S., & Fletcher, J. (Eds.) (1999). *The changing nervous system: Neurobehavioral consequences of early brain disorders.* New York: Oxford University Press.

Burnstine, T. H., Greenough, W. T., & Tees, R. C. (1984). Intermodal compensation following damage or deprivation: A review of behavioral and neural evidence. In R. C. Almi & S. Finger (Eds.), *Early brain damage, Vol. 1: Research orientation and clinical observations* (pp. 3-34). Orlando: Academic Press.

Cantwell, D. P., & Baker, L. (1991). *Psychiatric developmental disorders in children with communication disorder.* Washington, D.C.: American Psychiatric Press.

Casey, B. J., Castellanos, F. X., Giedd, J. N., Marsh, W. L., Hamburger, S. D., Schubert, A. B., Vauss, V. C., Vaituzis, A. C., Dickstein, D. P., Sarfaltic, S. E., & Rapoport, J. L. (1997). Implication of right frontostriatal circuitry in response inhibition and attention deficit/hyperactivity disorder. *Journal of the American Academy of Child and Adolescent Psychiatry, 36,* 374-383.

Casey, J. E., Del Dotto, J. E., & Rourke, B. P. (1990). An empirical investigation of the NLD syndrome in a case of agenesis of the corpus callosum. *Journal of Clinical and Experimental Neuropsychology, 12,* 29.

Castellanos, F. X. (1997). Toward a pathophysiology of attention deficit hyperactivity disorder. *Clinical Pediatrics, 36,* 381-393.

Castellanos, F. X., Giedd, J. N., & Eckberg, P. (1994). Quantitative morphology of the caudate nucleus in attention deficit hyperactivity disorder. *American Journal of Psychiatry, 151,* 1791-1795.

Castellanos, F. X., Giedd, J. N., Marsh, W. L., Hamburger, S. D., Vaituzis, A. C., Dickstein, D. P., Sarfatti, S. E., Vauss, Y. C., Snell, J. W., Lange, N., Kaysen, D., Krain, A. L., Ritchie, G. F., Rajapaske, J. C., & Rapoport, J. L. (1996). Quantitative brain magnetic resonance imaging in attention deficit hyperactivity disorder. *Archives of General Psychiatry, 53,* 607-616.

Chapman, L. J., & Chapman, J. P. (1973). Problems in the measurement of cognitive deficit. *Psychological Bulletin, 79,* 380-385.

Chapman, L. J., & Chapman, J. P. (1978). The measurement of differential deficit. *Journal of Psychiatric Research, 14,* 303-311.

Chez, M. G., Buchanan, C., Field-Chez, M., Loeffel, M. F., & Hammer, M. S. (1998).

Treatment of electroencephalographic epileptiform activity on overnight EEG studies in children with pervasive developmental disorder or autism: Defining similarities to the Landau-Kleffner syndrome. *The Journal of Developmental and Learning Disorders, 2*(2), 217-230.

Chugani, H. T. (1994). Development of regional brain glucose metabolism in relation to behavior and plasticity. In G. Dawson & K. Fischer (Eds.), *Human behavior and the developing brain* (pp. 153-175). New York: Guilford Press.

Connolly, A. M., Chez, M. G., Pestronik, A., Arnold, S., Mehta, S., Buchanan, C., Zucker, M., & Deuel, R. K. (1997). Serum antibodies to human temporal lobe cortex in children with epilepsy and language dysfunction. *Annals of Neurology, 42,* 490.

Connolly, A. M., Chez, M. G., Pestronik, A., Arnold, S., Mehta, S., Buchanan, C., Zucker, M., & Deuel, R. K. (1999). Serum antibodies to brain in Landau-Kleffner variant, autism, and other neurologic disorders. *Journal of Pediatrics, 5.*

Courchesne, E. (1989). Neuroanatomical systems involved in infantile autism. The implications of cerebellar abnormalities. In G. Dawson (Ed.), *Autism: Nature, diagnosis and treatment,* (pp. 119-143). New York: Guilford Press.

Courchesne, E., Saitoh, O., Yeung-Courchesne, R., Press, G. A., Lincoln, A. J., Haas, R. H., & Schreibman, L. (1994a). Abnormalities of cerebellar vermal lobules VI and VII in patients with infantile autism: Identification of hypoplastic and hyperplastic subgroups by MR imaging. *American Journal of Roentgenology, 162,* 123-130.

Courchesne, E., Townsend, J. P., Akshoomoff, N. A., Yeung-Courchesne, R., Press, G. A., Murakami, J. W., Lincoln, A. J., James, H. E., Saitoh, O., Egaas, B., Haas, R. H., &

Schreibman, L. (1994b). A new finding: Impairment in shifting attention in autistic and cerebellar patients. In S. H. Broman and J. Graffman (Eds.), *Atypical cognitive deficits in developmental disorders: Implications for brain function.* Hillsdale, NJ: Erlbaum.

Courchesne, E., Townsend, J., & Saitoh, O. (1994). The brain in infantile autism: Posterior fossa structures are abnormal. *Neurology, 44,* 214-223.

Courchesne, E., Yeung-Courchesne, R., Press, G. A., Hesselink, J. R., & Jernigan, T. L. (1988). Hypoplasia of cerebellar vermal lobules VI and VII in autism. *New England Journal of Medicine, 318,* 1349-1354.

Das, J. P., & Varnhagen, C. K. (1986). Neuropsychological functioning and cognitive processing. In J. E. Obruzt & G. W. Hynd (Eds.), *Child neuropsychology, Vol. 1: Theory and research* (pp. 117-140). New York: Academic Press.

Dawson, G. (1994). Development of emotional expression and emotion regulation in infancy: Contributions of the frontal lobe. In G. Dawson & K. Fischer (Eds.), *Human behavior and the developing brain.* New York: Guilford Press.

Dawson, G., & Fischer, K. (1994). *Human behavior and the developing brain.* New York: Guilford Press.

Dawson, G., & Levy, A. (1989). Reciprocal subcortical-cortical influences in autism. The role of attentional mechanisms. In G. Dawson (Ed.), *Autism: Nature, diagnosis and treatment,* (pp. 144-173). New York: Guilford Press.

Denckla, M. B. (1974). Development of motor coordination in normal children. *Developmental Medicine and Child Neurology, 16,* 729-741.

Denckla, M. B. (1979a). Minimal brain dysfunction. In J. Chall & A. Mirsky (Eds.),

Education and the brain (pp. 223-268). Chicago, IL: University of Chicago Press.

Denckla, M. B. (1979b). Childhood learning disorders. In K. M. Heilman & E. Valenstein (Eds.), *Clinical neuropsychology.* New York: Oxford University Press.

Denckla, M. B. (1985). Revised neurological examination for subtle signs (PANESS). *Psychopharmacology Bulletin, 21,* 773-800.

Denckla, M. B. (1994). Measurement of executive function. In G. R. Lyon (Ed.), *Frames of reference for the assessment of learning disabilities* (pp. 117-142). Baltimore: Paul H. Brookes.

Denckla, M. B. (1996). A theory and model of executive function: A neuropsychological perspective. In G. R. Lyon & N. A. Krasnegor (Eds.), *Attention, memory, and executive function* (pp. 263-278). Baltimore: Paul H. Brooks.

Denckla, M. B., & Reiss, A. L. (1997). Prefrontal-subcortical circuits in developmental disorders. In N. A. Krasnegor, G. R. Lyon, & P. S. Goldman-Rakic (Eds.), *Development of the prefrontal cortex: Evolution, neurobiology, and behavior* (pp. 283-293). Baltimore: Paul H. Brookes.

Dennis, M. (1988). Language and the young damaged brain. In M. Dennis, E. Kaplan, M. I. Posner, D. G. Stein, & R. F. Thompson (Eds.), *Clinical neuropsychology and brain function: Research, measurement, and practice.* Washington D.C.: American Psychological Association Press.

Duffy, F. H. (1994). The role of quantified electroencephalography in psychological research. In G. Dawson & K. Fischer (Eds.), *Human behavior and the developing brain* (pp. 93-133). New York: Guilford Press.

Elman, J., Bates, E., Johnson, M., Karmiloff-Smith, A., Parisi, D., & Plunkett, K. (Eds.) (1998). Brain development. In *Rethinking Innateness: A connectionist perspective on development* (Chap. 5). Cambridge, MA: MIT Press/Bradford Books.

Fennell, E. B., & Bauer, R. M. (1997). Models of inference in evaluating brain-behavior relationships in children. In C. R. Reynolds, & E. Fletcher-Jansen (Eds.), *Handbook of child clinical neuropsychology* (2nd ed.) (pp. 204-215). New York: Plenum Press.

Filipek, P. A. (1996). Brief Report: Neuroimaging in autism: The state of the science 1995. *Journal of Autism and Developmental Disorders, 26*(2), 211-215.

Filipek, P. A., Richelme, C., Kennedy, D. N., Rademacher, J. Pitcher, D. A., Zidel, S. Y., & Caviness, V. S. (1992). Morphometric analysis of the brain in developmental language disorders and autism. *Annals of Neurology, 32,* 475.

Filipek, P. A., Semrud-Clikeman, M., Steingard, R. J., Renshaw, P. F., Kennedy, D. N., & Biederman, J. (1997). Volumetric MRI analysis comparing subjects having attention-deficit hyperactivity disorder with normal controls. *Neurology, 48,* 589-601.

Fletcher, J. M. (1992). The validity of distinguishing children with language and learning disabilities according to discrepancies with IQ. *Journal of learning Disabilities, 25*(9), 546-548.

Fletcher, J. M., Francis, D. J., Thompson, N. M., & Brookshire, B. L. (1992). Verbal and nonverbal skill discrepancies in hydrocephalic children. *Journal of Clinical and Experimental Neuropsychology, 14,* 593.

Fletcher, J. M., & Levin, H. S. (1988). Neurobehavioral effects of brain injury in children. In D. K. Routh (Ed.), *Handbook of pediatric psychology* (pp. 258-295). New York: Guilford Press.

Fletcher, J. M., & Taylor, H. G. (1984). Neuropsychological approaches to children: Towards a developmental neuropsychology.

Journal of Clinical Neuropsychology, 6(1), 39-56.

Furster, J. (1989). *The prefrontal cortex: Anatomy, physiology, and neuropsychology of the frontal lobe.* New York: Raven Press.

Gaddes, W. H. (1985). *Learning disabilities and brain function.* New York: Springer-Verlag.

Galaburda, A. M. (1991). Anatomy of dyslexia. In D. D. Duane & D. B. Gray (Eds.), *The reading brain: The biological basis of dyslexia,* (pp. 119-132). Parkton, MD: York Press.

Galaburda, A. M. (1993). Neurology of developmental dyslexia. *Current Opinion in Neurobiology, 3,* 237-242.

Galaburda, A., & Livingston, M. (1993). Evidence for a magnocellular defect in developmental dyslexia. *Annals of the New York Academy of Sciences, 682,* 70-82.

Galaburda, A. M., Rosen, G. D., & Sherman, G. F. (1989). The neural origin of developmental dyslexia: Implications for medicine, neurology, and cognition. In A. M. Galaburda (Ed.), *From reading to neurons* (pp. 376-388). Cambridge: MIT Press.

Galaburda, A. M., Sherman, G. F., Rosen, G. D., Aboitiz, F., & Geschwind, N. (1985). Developmental dyslexia: Four consecutive patients with cortical anomalies. *Annals of Neurology, 18,* 222-233.

Gardner, R. A. (1979). *The objective diagnosis of minimal brain dysfunction.* Creskill, NJ: Creative Therapeutics.

Geschwind, N., & Galaburda, A. M. (1987). *Cerebral lateralization: Biological mechanisms, associations, and pathology.* Cambridge: MIT Press.

Giedd, J. N. (1996). *Neuroimaging of ADHD.* Paper presented at the New York Neuropsychology Group conference: Adult Attention Deficit Disorder: Brain Mechanisms and Life Outcomes, New York, New York, April 20, 1996.

Giedd, J. N., & Castellanos, F. X. (1997). Developmental disorders. In K. R. R. Krishnan & P. M. Doraiswamy (Eds.), *Brain imaging in clinical psychiatry*. Durham, NC: Duke University Press.

Giedd, J. N., Castellanos, F. X., Casey, B. J, Kozuch, A. C., King, S., Hamburger, D., & Rapoport, J. L. (1994). Quantitative morphology of the corpus collosum in attention deficit hyperactivity disorder. *American Journal of Psychiatry, 151,* 665-669.

Goldberg, E. (1995). Rise and fall of modular orthodoxy. *Journal of Clinical and Experimental Neuropsychology, 17*(2), 193-208.

Golden, C. J. (1980). *Manual for the Luria-Nebraska neuropsychological test battery*. Los Angeles: Western Psychological Services.

Goldman-Rakic, P. S. (1987). Development of cortical circuitry and cognitive function. *Child Development, 58,* 642-691.

Goldman-Rakic, P. S., Isseroff, A., Schwartz, M. L., & Bugbee, N. M. (1983). The neurobiology of cognitive development. In P. H. Mussen (Ed.), *Handbook of child psychology: Biology and infancy development* (pp. 281-344). New York: Wiley & Sons.

Goosens, C., Crain, S. S., & Elder, P. S. (1994). *Engineering the preschool environment for interactive symbolic communication. 18 months to 5 years developmentally* (Rev. ed.). Birmingham, AL: Southeast Augmentative Communication.

Greenough, W. T., & Lack, J. E. (1992). Induction of brain structure by experience: Substrates for cognitive development. In M. R. Gunner & C. A. Nelson (Eds.), *Developmental behavioral neuroscience, Minnesota symposia on child psychology* (Vol. 24). (pp. 155-200). Hillsdale, NJ: Erlbaum.

Greenspan, S. I. (1992). *Infancy and early childhood: The practice of clinical assessment and intervention with emotional and developmental challenges*. Madison, CT: International Universities Press.

Greenspan, S.I., and Wieder, S. (1997). Developmental patterns and outcomes in infants and children with disorders in relating and communicating: A chart review of 200 cases of children with autistic spectrum diagnoses. *The Journal of Developmental and Learning Disorders, 1*(1), 87-141.

Greenspan, S. I., & Wieder, S. (1998). The child with special needs. Reading, MA: Addison Wesley Longman.

Greenspan, S. I., & Wieder, S. (1999). A functional developmental approach to autistic spectrum disorders. *Journal of the Association for Persons with Severe Handicaps*.

Gunnar, M. R., & Nelson, C. A. (Eds.) (1992). *Developmental behavioral neuroscience, Minnesota symposia on child psychology* (Vol. 24). Hillsdale, NJ: Erlbaum.

Happe, F. G. E. (1994). An advanced test of theory of mind: Understanding of handicapped, and normal children and adults. *Journal of Autism and Developmental Disorders, 24,* 129-54.

Heilman, K. M., Voeller, K., & Alexander, A. (1996). Developmental dyslexia: A motor-articulatory feedback hypothesis. *Annals of Neurology, 39,* 407-412.

Heilman, K. M., Voeller, K., & Nadeau, S. E. (1991). A possible pathophysiologic substrate of attention deficit hyperactivity disorder. *Journal of Child Neurology 6,* (Suppl. S76-81).

Hooper, S. R., & Willis, W. G. (1989). *Learning disability subtyping: Neuropsychological foundations, conceptual models, and issues in clinical differentiation*. New York: Springer Verlag.

Howard, M. (1986). Effects of pre-reading training in auditory conceptualization on subsequent reading achievement. Ph.D. dissertation. Brigham Young University.

Huttonlocher, P. R. (1979). Synaptic density in human frontal cortex: Developmental changes and effects of aging. *Brain Research, 163*, 195-205.

Huttenlocher, P. R. (1990). Morphometric study of human cerebral cortex development. *Neuropyschologia, 28*, 517-527.

Huttenlocher, P. (1994). Synaptogenesis in human cerebral cortex. In G. Dawson, & K. Fischer (Eds.), *Human behavior and the developing brain* (pp. 137-152). New York: Guilford Press.

Huttenlocher, P. (1997). Developmental anatomy of prefrontal cortex. In N. A. Krasnegor, G. R. Lyon, & P. S. Goldman-Rakic (Eds.), *Development of the prefrontal cortex* (pp. 69-84). Baltimore, MD: Paul H. Brookes.

Hynd, G. W., Lorys, A. R., Semrund-Clikeman, M., Nieves, N., Huettner, M., & Lahey, B. B. (1991b). Attention deficit disorder without hyperactivity: A distinct behavioral and neurocognitive syndrome. *Journal of Child Neurology, 6* (Suppl. S37-S43).

Hynd, G. W., & Obrzut, J. E. (Eds.) (1981*). Neuropsychological assessment and the school-age child: Issues and procedures.* New York: Grune & Stratton.

Hynd, G. W., Semrud-Clikeman, M., Lorys, A. R., Novey, E. S., & Eliopulus, D. (1990). Brain morphology in developmental dyslexia and attention deficit disorder/hyperactivity. *Archives of Neurology, 47*, 919-926.

Hynd, G. W., Semrud-Clikeman, M., Lorys, A. R., Novey, E. S., Eliopulos, D., & Lyytinen, H. (1991a). Corpus callosum morphology in attention deficit hyperactivity disorder: Morphometric analysis of MRI. *Journal of Learning Disabilities, 24*(3), 141-146.

Hynd, G. W., & Willis, W. G. (1988). *Pediatric neuropsychology.* Orlando, Florida: Grune & Stratton.

Jernigan, T. L., Hesselink, J. R, Sowell, E., & Tallal, P. A. (1991). Cerebral structure on magnetic resonance imaging in language- and learning-impaired children. *Archives of Neurology, 48*, 539-545.

Johnson, M. H. (1997). *Developmental cognitive neuroscience.* Cambridge, MA: Blackwell.

Kaplan, E. (1990). The process approach to neuropsychological assessment of psychiatric patients. *Journal of Neuropsychiatry, 2*, 72-87.

Kaufman, A. S. (1976a). A new approach to the interpretation of test scatter in the WISC-R. *Journal of Learning Disabilities, 9*, 160-168.

Kaufman, A. S. (1976b). Do normal children have "flat" ability profiles? *Psychology in the Schools, 15*, 284-285.

Keller, C. E., & Sutton, J. P. (1991). Specific mathematics disorders. In J. E. Obrzut & G. W. Hynd (Eds.), *Neuropsychological foundations of learning disabilities* (pp. 549-572). San Diego, CA: Academic Press.

Kemper, T. L., & Bauman, M. (1998). Neuropathology of infantile autism. *Journal of Neuropathology and Experimental Neurology, 57*(7), 645-652.

Kennard, M. A. (1942). Cortical reorganization of motor function: Studies on a series of monkeys of various ages from infancy to maturity. *Archives of Neurology and Psychiatry, 47*, 227-240.

Klin, A., Volkmar, F. R., Sparrow, S. S., Cicchetti, D. V., & Rourke, B. P. (1995). Validity and neuropsychological characterization of Asperger syndrome: Convergance with nonverbal learning disabilities syndrome. *Journal of Child Psychology and Psychiatry, 36*, 1127-1140.

Kolb, B. (1995). *Brain plasticity and behavior*. Hillsdale, NJ: Erlbaum.

Korkman, M., & Peltomaa, A. K. (1993). Preventive treatment of dyslexia by a preschool training program for children with language impairments. *Journal of Clinical Child Psychology, 22*(2), 277-287.

Lezak, M. (1995). *Neuropsychological assessment* (3rd Ed.). New York: Oxford University Press.

Lindamood, P., Bell, N., & Lindamood, P. (1997). Sensory-cognitive factors in the controversy over reading instruction. *The Journal of Developmental and Learning Disorders, 1*(1), 143-182.

Lindamood, P., & Lindamood, P. (1998). *The Lindamood phoneme sequencing (LiPS) program* (formerly the Auditory Discrimination in Depth (ADD) Program; originally published 1969). Austin, TX: PRO-ED.

Livingston, M. S., Rosen, G. D., Drislane, F. W., & Galaburda, A. M. (1991). Physiological and anatomical evidence for a magnocellular defect in developmental dyslexia. *Proceedings of the National Academy of Sciences, 88*, 7943-7947.

Lord, C. (1997). Diagnostic instruments in autism spectrum disorders. In D. J. Cohen and F. R. Volkmar (Eds.), *Handbook of autism and pervasive developmental disorders* (pp. 460-483). New York: Wiley & Sons.

Lou, H. C., Henriksen, L., & Bruhn, P. (1984). Focal cerebral hypoperfusion in children with dysphasia and/or attention deficit disorder. *Archives of Neurology, 41*, 825-829.

Lou, H. C., Henriksen, L., Bruhn, P., Borner, H., & Nielsen, J. B. (1989). Striatal dysfunction in attention deficit and hyperkinetic disorder. *Archives of Neurology, 46*, 48-51.

Lovett, M. W., Borden, T., DeLuca, T., Lacerenza, L., Benson, N. J., & Brackstone, D. (1994). Treating the core deficits of developmental dyslexia: Evidence of transfer of learning after phonological -and strategy-based reading training programs. *Developmental Psychology, 30*(6), 805-822.

Luria, A. R. (1973). *The working brain.* New York: Basic Books.

Luria, A. R. (1980). *Higher cortical functions in man* (2nd edition). New York: Basic Books.

Lyon, G. R., & Krasnegor, N. A. (1996). *Attention, memory, and executive function.* Baltimore, MD: Paul H. Brookes.

Mattis, S., French, J. H., & Rapin, I. (1975). Dyslexia in children and young adults: Three independent neuropsychological syndromes. *Developmental Medicine and Child Neurology, 17*, 150-163.

Mesulam, M. M. (1985). *Principles of behavioral neurology.* New York: F. A. Davis.

Merzenich, M. M., Jenkins, W. M., Johnston, P., Schreiner, C., Miller, S. L., & Tallal, P. (1996). Temporal processing deficits of language-learning impaired children ameliorated by training. *Science, 271*, 77-81.

Mirsky, A. (1996). Disorders of attention. A neuropsychological perspective In G. R. Lyon & N. A. Krasnegor (Eds.), *Attention, memory, and executive function* (pp. 71-96). Baltimore, MD: Paul H. Brooks.

Mirsky, A. F., Anthony, B. J., Duncan, C. C., Oherin, M. B., & Kellam, S. G. (1991). Analysis of elements of attention: A neuropsychological approach. *Neuropsychology Review, 2*, 109-145.

Mirsky, A. F., Fantie, B. D., & Tatman, J. E. (1995). Assessment of attention across the lifespan. In R. L. Mapou, & J. Spector (Eds.), *Clinical neuropsychological assessment: A cognitive approach* (pp. 17-48). New York: Plenum Press.

Molfese, D. L., & Molfese, V. J. (1994). Short-term and long-term developmental outcomes. In G. Dawson, & K. W. Fischer (Eds.),

Human behavior and the developing brain (pp. 493-517). New York: Guilford Press.

Myklebust, H. R. (1975). Nonverbal learning disabilities: Assessment and intervention. In H. R. Myklebust (Ed.), *Progress in learning disabilities: Vol. 3* (pp. 85-121). New York: Guilford Press.

Nass, R., Peterson, H. D., & Koch, D. (1989). Differential effects of congenital left and right brain injury on intelligence. *Brain and Cognition, 9,* 258-266.

Nelson, C. (1999). The neurobiological bases of early intervention. In S. J. Meisels & J. P. Shonkoff (Eds.), *Handbook of early childhood intervention* (2nd ed.). Cambridge, MA: Cambridge University Press.

Obrzut, J. E., & Hynd, G. W. (1991). *Neuropsychological foundations of learning disabilities: A handbook of issues, methods, and practice.* New York: Academic Press.

Overman, W. H. (1990). Performance on traditional matching to sample, nonmatching to sample, and object discrimination tasks by 12 to 32 month-old children: A developmental progression. In A. Diamond (Ed.), *The development and neural bases of higher cognitive functions: Annals of the New York Academy of Sciences* (pp. 365-383). New York: New York Academy of Sciences.

Palumbo, D., Maughan, A., & Kurlan, R. (1997). Tourette syndrome is only one of several causes of a developmental basal ganglia syndrome. *Archives of Neurology, 54,* 475-483.

Pennington, B. (1991). *Diagnosing learning disorders.* New York: Guilford.

Petrauskas, R. J., & Rourke, B. P. (1979). Identification of subtypes of retarded readers: A neuropsychological, multivariate approach. *Journal of Clinical Neuropsychology, 1,* 17-37.

Rapin, I. (Ed.) (1996). *Preschool children with inadequate communication.* London: Mac Keith Press.

Rapin, I., & Allen, D. A. (1983). Developmental language disorders: Nosologic considerations. In U. Kirk (Ed.), *Neuropsychology of language, reading, and spelling.* New York: Academic Press.

Rapin, I., Allen, D. A., & Dunn, M. A. (1992). Developmental language disorders. In I. Rapin & S. J. Segalowitz (Eds.), *Handbook of neuropsychology, 7.* Amsterdam: Elsevier Press.

Rasmussen, T., & Milner, B. (1977). The role of early left brain injury in determining lateralization of cerebral speech functions. *Annals of the New York Academy of Sciences, 299,* 355-369.

Reitan, R. M., & Wolfson, D. (1985). *The Halstead-Reitan neuropsychological test battery: Theory and clinical interpretation.* Tucson, AZ: Neuropsychology Press.

Reynolds, C. R., & Fletcher-Janzen, E. (1997*). Handbook of clinical child neuropsychology* (2nd ed.). New York: Plenum Press.

Ross, J., Stefanatos, G. A., Roeltgen, D., Kushner, H., & Cutler, G. (1995). Ulrich-Turner Syndrome: Neurodevelopmental changes from childhood through adolescence. *American Journal of Medical Genetics, 58,* 74-82.

Rourke, B. P. (Ed.), (1985). *Neuropsychology of learning disabilities. Essentials of subtype analysis.* New York: Guilford Press.

Rourke, B. P. (1989). *Nonverbal learning disabilities. The syndrome and the model.* New York: Guilford Press.

Rourke, B. P. (Ed.) (1991). *Neuropsychological validation of learning disability subtypes.* New York: Guilford Press.

Rourke, B. P. (1993). Arithmetic disabilities, specific and otherwise: A neuropsychological perspective. *Journal of Learning Disabilities, 26*(4), 214-226.

Rourke, B. P. (1995). *Syndrome of nonverbal learning disabilities: Neurodevelopmental manifestations.* New York: Guilford Press.

Rourke, B. P., Bakker, D. J., Fisk, J. L., & Strang, J. D. (1983). *Child neuropsychology.* New York: Guilford Press.

Rourke, B. P., Fisk, J. L., & Strang, J. D. (1986). *Neuropsychological assessment in children.* New York: Guilford Press.

Rovet, J. F. (1993). The nonverbal learning disability syndrome in congenital hypothyroidism. *Journal of Clinical and Experimental Neuropsychology, 15,* 41.

Russell, E. W. (1994). The cognitive-metric, fixed battery approach to neuropsychological assessment. In R. D. Vanderploeg (Ed.), *Clinician's guide to neuropsychological assessment* (pp. 211-258). Hillsdale, NJ: Erlbaum.

Sattler, J. M. (1988). *Assessment of children* (3rd ed.). San Diego, CA: Jerome Sattler.

Semrud-Clikeman, M., Filipek, P. A., Biederman, J., Steingard, R., Kennedy, D., Renshaw, P., & Bekken, K. (1994). Attention-deficit hyperactivity disorder: Magnetic resonance imaging morphometric analysis of the corpus collosum. *Journal of the American Academy of Child and Adolescent Psychiatry, 33,* 875.

Shaywitz, B. A., Shaywitz, S. E., Pugh, K. R., Skudlarski, P., Fulbright, R. K., Constable, R. T., Fletcher, J. M., Liberman, A. M., Shankweiler, D. P., Katz, L., Bronen, R. A., Marchione, K., Lacadie, C., & Gore, J. C. (1996). The functional organization of the brain for reading and reading disability (dyslexia). *The Neuroscientist, 2*(4), 245-255.

Simos, P. G., Breier, G., Zpouridakis, G., & Papanico-Laou, A. C. (1999). MEG correlates of categorical perception of temporal cues for voicing in humans. *Journal of the International Neuropsychological Society, 5*(2), 135.

Sparrow, S., Marans, W., Klin, A., Carter, A., Volkmar, F. R., & Cohen, D. J. (1997). Developmentally based assessments. In D. J. Cohen & F. R. Volkmar (Eds.), *Handbook of autism and pervasive developmental disorders* (pp. 411-447). New York: Wiley & Sons.

Spreen, O., Risser, A. H., & Edgell, D. (1995). *Developmental neuropsychology.* New York: Oxford University Press.

Stefanatos, G. A., & Black, L. M. (1997). Contributions of neuropsychological assessment to the diagnosis and treatment of developmental and learning disorders. *The Journal of Developmental and Learning Disorders, 1*(1), 9-59.

Stefanatos, G. A., Grover, W., & Geller, E. (1995). Corticosteroid treatment of language regression in pervasive developmental disorder. *Journal of the Academy of Child and Adolescent Psychiatry, 34*(8),1107-1111.

Stefanatos, G. A., Kolros, P., Rabinovitch, H., & Stone, J. J. (1998). Acquired epileptiform aphasia (Landau-Kleffner Syndrome): Current concepts and controversies. *The Journal of Developmental and Learning Disorders, 2*(1), 3-50.

Stefanatos, G. A., & Musikoff, H. (1994). Specific neurocognitive deficits in cornelia de lange syndrome. *Developmental and Behavioral Pediatrics, 15*(1), 39-43.

Stiles, J., Bates, E. A., Thal, D., Trauner, D., & Reilly, J. (1998). Linguistic, cognitive, and affective development in children with pre- and perinatal focal brain injury: A ten-year overview from the San Diego longitudinal project. In C. Rovee-Collier (Ed.), *Advances in infancy research* (pp. 131-163). Norwood, NJ: Ablex.

Swanson, J., & Castellanos, X. (1998). *Biological bases of attention deficit hyperactivity disorder: Neuroanatomy, genetics, and pathophysiology.* Proceedings of NIH Consensus Development Conference, November 16-18, 1998.

Swedo, S. E., Leonard, H. L., & Kiessling, L. S. (1994). Speculations on antineuronal antibody-mediated neuropsychiatric disorders of childhood. *Pediatrics, 93,* 323-326.

Swedo, S. E., Leonard, H., Garvey, M., Mittleman, B., Allen, A. J., Perlmutter, S., Zamkoff, J. Dubbert, B. K., & Lougee, L. (1998). Pediatric autoimmune neuropsychiatric disorders associated with streptococcal infections: Clinical description of the first 50 cases. *American Journal of Psychiatry, 155*(2), 264-271.

Tallal, P., Miller, S., Bedi, G., Byma, G., Wang, X., Nagarajan, S., Schreiner, C., Jenkins, W., & Merzenich, W. (1996). Language comprehension in language-learning impaired children improved with acoustically modified speech. *Science, 271*, 81-84.

Taylor, H. G., & Schatschneider, C. (1992). Child neuropsychological assessment: A test of basic assumptions. *Clinical Neuropsychology, 6*, 259-275.

Teeter, P. A., & Semrud-Clikeman, M. (1997). *Child Neuropsychology: Assessment and interventions for neurodevelopmental disorders.* Needham Heights, MA: Allyn & Bacon.

Teuber, H-L., & Rudel, R. G. (1962). Behavior after cerebral lesions in children and adults. *Developmental Medicine and Child Neurology, 4*, 3-20.

Thatcher, R. W. (1994). Cyclic cortical reorganization: Origins of human cognitive development. In G. Dawson & K. Fischer (Eds.), *Human behavior and the developing brain.* New York: Guilford Press.

Thatcher, R. W. (1997). Human frontal lobe development: A theory of cyclical cortical reorganization. In N. A. Krasnegor, G. R. Lyon, & P. S. Goldman-Rakic (Eds.), *Development of the prefrontal cortex* (pp. 85-116). Baltimore, MD: Paul H. Brookes.

Tuchman, R. F., & Rapin, I. (1997). Regression in pervasive developmental disorders: Seizures and epileptiform electroencephalogram correlates. *Pediatrics, 99*(4), 560-566.

van Santen, J. P., Black, L. M., Wilson, B.C., & Riscucci, D.A. (1994). Modeling clinical judgment: A reanalysis of data from Wilson and Riscucci (1986). *Brain and Language, 46*, 469-481.

Vanderploeg, R. D. (Ed.) (1994). *Clinicians guide to neuropsychological assessment.* Hillsdale, NJ: Erlbaum.

Warren, R. P., Odell, J. D., Warren, W. L. et al. (1997). Brief report: Immunoglobulin a deficiency in a subset of autistic subjects. *Journal of Autism and Developmental Disorders, 27*, 187-192.

Warren, R. P., Odell, J. D., Maciulis, R. A., Burger, & Warren, W. L. (1996). Immune and immunogenetic studies in autism and related disorders. *Molecular Chemistry and Neuropathology,* May-Aug. (28), 77-81.

Waterhouse, L., Fein, D., & Modahl, C. (1996). Neurofunctional mechanisms in autism. *Psychological Review, 103*(3), 457-489.

Wilson, B. C. (1986). Neuropsychological assessment of preschool children. In S. Filskov & T. Boll (Eds.), *Handbook of clinical neuropsychology: Vol. 2.* (pp. 121-171). New York: Wiley & Sons.

Wilson, B. C. (1987). Neuropsychological assessment. In V. B. Van Hasselt & M. Hersen (Eds.), *Psychological evaluation of the developmentally and physically disabled.* New York: Plenum.

Wilson, B. C. (1992). Neuropsychological assessment of the preschool child. In I. Rapin, & S. J. Segalowitz (Eds.), *Handbook of neuropsychology: Vol. 6.* Amsterdam: Elsevier Press.

Wilson, B. C., & Riscucci, D. A. (1986). A model for clinical-quantitative classification: Generation 1. Application to language disordered preschool children. *Brain and Language, 27*, 281.

Wilson, B. C., & Riscucci, D. A. (1988). The early identification of developmental language disorders and the prediction of the acquisition of reading skills. In R. L. Masland & M. W. Masland (Eds.), *Pre-school prevention of reading failure* (pp. 187-203). Parkton, MD: York Press.

Wood, F., Felton, R., Flowers, L., & Naylor, C. (1991). Neurobehavioral definition of dyslexia. In D. D. Duane, & D. B. Gray (Eds.), *The reading brain: The biological basis of dyslexia* (pp. 1-26). Parkton, MD: York Press.

Zametkin, A. J., Nordahl, T. E., Gross, M., King, A. C., Semple, W. E., Rumsey, J., Hamburger, S., & Cohen, D. J. (1990).

Cerebral glucose metabolism in adults with hyperactivity of childhood onset. *New England Journal of Medicine, 323*(20), 1361-1366.

Zimmerman, A. W. (1999). The immune system in autism. *Journal of Developmental and Learning Disorders.*

Zimmerman, A. W., Polter, N. T., Stakkestao, A., & Frye, V. H. (1995). Serum immunoglobulins and autoimmune profiles in children with autism. *Annals of Neurology, 38*, 528.

Appendix

STANDARDIZED MEASURES FOR CHILDREN AGES 2 THROUGH 10

This list is a sampling of standardized tests available for children ages 2 through 10 years. Measures are listed with regard to the age range of available norms and according to the primary function or domain that a test is purported to measure. Given the multifactorial nature of tests, however, what a test actually measures needs to be determined, as described in this chapter, by careful analysis of the demands of each test, its input and output demands, and by understanding *how* a given child achieves or fails to achieve a score; that is, through analysis of the child's performance, through modification of procedures, reiterative hypothesis testing, and integration and understanding of other data, including observations and informal assessment procedures.

There is considerable overlap and even redundancy between measures listed in each domain. The decision as to which test(s) to choose depends on the hypotheses raised about a given child, task analysis of the test, the test's reliability, validity, and normative data, and other criteria.

Overall Cognitive Functioning

Some tests may contain a separate "cognitive domain;" some may have different cognitive indices reflecting verbal and nonverbal domains; some may be primarily nonverbal. Composite measures (e.g., Stanford-Binet, WISC) may be made up of individually normed subtests that tap heavily into, for example, language, motor, and memory functions, which can be used independently to give an indication of the child's functioning in these areas. Table A-1 lists tests available for testing overall cognitive functioning.

Table A-1. Tests of Overall Cognitive Functioning

Test	Age Range of Norms (in years)
Bayley Scales of Infant Development	0 to 4 (48 mo.)
Columbia Mental Maturity Scale (CMMS)	3.6 to 7.11
Differential Ability Scales (DAS)	2.6 to 17.11
Hiskey-Nebraska Test of Learning Aptitude (H-N)	3.0 to 16.0
Kaufman Assessment Battery for Children (K-ABC)	2.6 to 12.6
Leiter (Arthur adaptation)	3.0 to 7.11
Leiter-R	2.0 to 20.11
McCarthy Scales of Children's Abilities	2.6 to 8.7
Miller Assessment for Preschoolers (MAP)	2.9 to 5.2
Mullen Scales of Early Learning	0 to 5.8 (68 mo.)
Pictorial Test of Intelligence (PTI)	3 to 8
Ravens Colored Progressive Matrices	5.6 to 11.6
Stanford-Binet, revised 4th edition. (S-B)	2.6 to adult
Test of Nonverbal Intelligence (TONI-2)	5 to adult
Wechsler Intelligence Scale for Children (WISC-III)	6.0 to 16.11
Wechsler Preschool & Primary Scale of Intelligence (WPPSI-R)	3.0 to 7.3

Attention, Organization, and Executive Functions

This group taps into a seemingly disparate set of functions that include, for example, working memory or mental tracking, flexible shifting of attention, sustained attention, organizational and sequencing skills as these affect planning, motor movements, visual search, problem solving, reasoning, language formulation, and other functions. (See chapter for description of what an evaluation of these functions may mean for a preschool-aged child.) Table A-2 lists tests available for testing attention, organization, and executive functions. Tables A-3 through A-9 list tests available for testing other functions.

Table A-2. Tests of Attention, Organization, and Executive Functions

Test	Age Range of Norms (in years)
Computerized Performance Test (CPT) (e.g., Conners', IVA, TOVA, Vigil,)	6.0 to adult
ITPA Visual Closure Test	2.4 to 10.3
K-ABC Hand Movements	2.6 to 12.6
Matching Familiar Figures Test	5 to 12
NEPSY Visual Attention, Statue	3.0 to 5.0
NEPSY Tower, Auditory Attention, Visual Attention	5.0 to 12.11
PANESS (Denckla)	5.0 to 10.0
Purdue Pegboard (bilateral coordination)	2.6 to 16
Rapid Automatized Naming (RAN) (Denckla)	5 to 13

Rey-Osterrieth Complex Figure Test	5 to adult
Trail Making Test (Halstead-Reitan) (A vs. B)	8 to 15
Underlining Tests	5 to 15
Verbal Fluency Tests:	
California Verbal Learning Test (CAVLT-2)	6.6 to 17
CELF-R Word Associations	5.0 to 16.11
McCarthy Verbal Fluency	2.6 to 9
NEPSY Verbal Fluency	3.0 to 12.11
Controlled Oral Word Association: FAS, Categories	6 to 13
Wisconsin Card Sorting Test	6 to adult
WISC-III Symbol Search, Coding, Mazes	6.0 to 16.11
WPPSI-R Mazes, Animal Pegs	3.0 to 7.3

Table A-3. Tests of Auditory Processing and Language-Related Functions

Test	Age Range of Norms (in years)
Auditory Processing	
Comprehensive Test of Phonological Processing (CTOPP)	5.0 to 24.11
GFW Auditory Discrimination	3.8 to 65
GFW Sound Symbol Tests	3.9 to 18.11
Lindamood Auditory Conceptualization Test (LAC)	5 to 18
NEPSY Phonological Processing	3.0 to 12.11
The Phonological Awareness Test	5 to 9
Wepman Auditory Discrimination	5 to 8
WRAML Sound Symbol	5.0 to 17.11
Language-Related Functions	
Phonological production and speech articulation:	
(buccalingual tests, oromotor exam, articulation screening)	
Goldman-Fristoe Test of Articulation	2.0 to 16
MAP Tongue Movements	2.9 to 5.2
NEPSY Oromotor Sequences	3.0 to 12.11
Auditory cognitive functions, receptive language emphasis:	
CELF/Preschool, receptive language tests	3.0 to 6.11
CELF-R or CELF-III, receptive language tests	5.0 to 16.11
DAS Verbal Comprehension	2.6 to 5.11
DAS Similarities, Word Definitions	6.0 to 17.11
ITPA Auditory Reception, Auditory Association	2.4 to 10.3
K-ABC Riddles	2.6 to 12.6
McCarthy Opposite Analogies, Verbal Memory II	2.6 to 8.7
Menyuk Syntactic Comprehension	5 to 12
NEPSY Comprehension of Instructions	3.0 to 12.11
Peabody Picture Vocabulary Test (PPVT-R)	1.9 to 18
PEER Complex Sentences	4 to 6
Receptive One Word Picture Vocabulary Test (ROWPVT)	2.11 to 11
Reynell Developmental Language Scales, receptive tests	1 to 7

	Age Range
S-B Comprehension, Vocabulary	2.6 to adult
Test of Auditory Comprehension of Language-revised (TACL-R)	3.9 to 11
Test of Language Competence (TLC)	5.0 to 18.11
Token Test	3 to 10
WISC-III Comprehension, Similarities, Vocabulary	6.0 to 16.11
WPPSI-R Comprehension, Similarities, Vocabulary	3.0 to 7
Zimmerman Preschool Language Scale	1 to 7

Expressive language emphasis
(includes tests of fluency and word retrieval):

Boston Naming Test	5.0 to 13
California Auditory Verbal Learning Test (CAVLT-2)	6.6 to 17
CELF Preschool, expressive language tests	3.0 to 6.11
CELF-R or CELF-III, expressive language tests	5.0 to 16.11
DAS Naming Vocabulary	2.6 to 8.11
DAS Word Definitions	6.0 to 17.11
Expressive One Word Picture Vocabulary Test (EOWPVT)	2.11 to 11
ITPA Auditory Association, Grammatic Closure	2.4 to 10.3
McCarthy Verbal Memory II, Verbal Fluency	2.6 to 8.7
NEPSY Verbal Fluency	3.0 to 12.11
Rapid Automatized Naming (RAN)	5 to 13
S-B Absurdities, Vocabulary, Comprehension	2.6 to adult
Test of Language Competence (TLC)	5.0 to 18.11
Test of Word Finding (TWF)	6.6 to 12.11
WISC-III Vocabulary, Similarities, Comprehension	6.0 to 16.11
WPPSI-R Vocabulary, Similarities, Comprehension	3.0 to 7

Table 4. Tests of Memory Functions

Test	Age Range of Norms (in years)
Overall:	
Test of Memory and Learning (TOMAL)	5.0 to 19.11
Wide Range Assessment of Memory and Learning (WRAML)	5.0 to 17.11
Verbal memory:	
(for word retrieval, see also Language Functions, expressive emphasis)	
CALVT-2	6.6 to 17
McCarthy Numerical Memory (digits), McCarthy Auditory Memory I (words) & II (story)	2.6 to 8.7
NEPSY Narrative Memory	3.0 to 12.11
NEPSY List Learning	7.0 to 12.11
S-B Digits, Sentence Memory	2.6 to adult
TOMAL, verbal memory subtests	5.0 to 19.11
Token Test IV	3 to 10
WRAML, verbal memory and verbal learning subtests	5.0 to 17.11

Visual memory:

Benton Visual Retention Test	7 to 13
DAS Recall of Designs	6.0 to 17.11
Hiskey-Nebraska Visual Attention Span	3.0 to 15
ITPA Visual Sequential Memory	2.4 to 10.3
NEPSY Memory for Faces	5.0 to 12.11
PTI Immediate Recall	3 to 8
Rey-Osterrieth Complex Figure Test	5 to adult
S-B Bead Memory	2.6 to adult
S-B Memory for Objects	5.0 to adult
TOMAL, nonverbal memory subtests	5.0 to 19.11
WRAML, visual memory and visual learning subtests	5 to 17.11

Table A-5. Tests of Visual-Related Functions

Test	Age Range of Norms (in years)
Visual-Related Functions	
Visual-perceptual/discrimination:	
Embedded Figures Test	6 to 13
Hiskey-Nebraska Picture Identification	3.0 to 16.0
PTI Form Discrimination	2.6 to 9
Test of Visual-Perceptual Skills (non-motor) (TVPS)	4.0 to 12.11
Visual-spatial processing, constructional and reasoning skills:	
Benton Judgment of Line Orientation	7 to 14
DAS Block Building	2.6 to 4.11
DAS Pattern Construction	3.0 to 17.11
Hooper Visual Organization Test	5 to 13
Jordan Left-Right Reversal Test	5.0 to 12.6
McCarthy Block Building, Puzzles	2.6 to 8.7
McCarthy Right-Left Orientation	5.0 to 8.7
NEPSY Route Finding, Arrows	5.0 to 12.11
Reversals Frequency Test	5.0 to 15.9
Right-Left Orientation Test (Benton & Spreen)	8 to 15
S-B Pattern Analysis	2.6 to adult
WISC-III Object Assembly, Block Design	6.0 to 16.11
WPPSI-R Object Assembly, Block Design	3.0 to 7
WRAVMA Visual-Spatial Matching	3.0 to 17.11
Visual-cognitive reasoning skills:	
Benton Test of Facial Recognition	6 to 14
DAS Picture Similarities	2.6 to 7.11
DAS Matrices	6.0 to 17.11
ITPA Visual Reception, Visual Association, Manual Expression	2.4 to 10.3
Leiter	2 to 20.11
PTI Similarities	3 to 8

Ravens Coloured Progressive Matrices	5.6 to 11.6
Ravens Standard Progressive Matrices	6.6 to 16.6
S-B Matrices	5.0 to adult
Test of Problem Solving (TOPS)	6 to 11
TONI-2	5.0 to adult
WPPSI-R Picture Completion	3.0 to 7
WISC-III Picture Arrangement	6.0 to 16.11

Table A-6. Tests of Sensory-Perceptual Functions

Test	Age Range of Norms (in years)
Benton Finger Localization	6 to 12
Benton Tactile Form Perception	8 to 14
MAP Stereognosis, Finger Localization	2.9 to 5.2
NEPSY Finger Discrimination	5.0 to 12.11
PEER Graphesthesia, Stereognosis	4 to 6
PEET, Intersensory Integration	3 to 4
Tactual Performance Test (Reitan)	5 to 13
Tests for Sensory-Perceptual Disturbances (Reitan-Klove) (e.g., sensory imperception (tactile, visual, auditory), finger-tip number writing, tactile finger recognition)	5 to 14

Table A-7. Tests of Motor Functions

Test	Age Range of Norms (in years)
Overall (laterality, hand grasp, motor tone, muscle strength, motor coordination, fine motor):	
Purdue Pegboard	2-1/2 to 16
Graphomotor and visual-motor:	
Beery VMI	4.0 to 17.11
Bender Gestalt Test	5.0 to 10.11
DAS Copying	3.6 to 7.11
McCarthy Drawings, Geometric Design	2.6 to 9
NEPSY Visuomotor Precision	3.0 to 12.11
WPPSI-R Geometric Design	3.0 to 7
Wide Range Assessment of Visual Motor Abilities (WRAVMA)	3.0 to 17.11
Motor coordination, motor impersistence, and praxis:	
Bayley, Motor Scale	0 to 4 (48 mo.)
ITPA Manual Expression	2.4 to 10.3
McCarthy Imitation, Leg Coordination, Arm Coordination	2.6 to 8.7
MAP Imitation of Postures, Hand-to-Nose, Romberg, Foundations, Coordination	2.9 to 5.2

Mullen, Motor Scale	0 to 5.8 (68 mo.)
NEPSY Imitating Hand Positions, Oromotor Sequences	3.0 to 12.11
NEPSY Fingertip Tapping, Manual Motor Sequences	5.0 to 12.11
PANESS (Denckla)	5.0 to 10
PEER, Gross Motor	4 to 6
PEET, Gross Motor	3 to 4
Sensory Integration and Praxis Tests	4.0 to 8.11

Table A-8. Tests of Achievement

Test	Age Range of Norms (in years)
DAS Early Number Concepts, Matching Letter-Like Forms (pre-academic)	2.6 to 7.11
DAS Basic Number Skills, Spelling, Word Reading	6.0 to 17.11
Gray Oral Reading Test -3 (GORT-3)	7.0 to 16.11
Wide Range Achievement Test 3 (WRAT-3)	5.0 to adult
Woodcock Reading Mastery Tests	5 to adult
Wechsler Individual Achievement Test (WIAT)	5 to 19
KeyMath Revised	K to grade 9 (5 to 14 yrs.)
PEER, Preacademic Learning	4 to 6
Test of Written Language (TOWL)	7.6 to 17.11
Test of Written Spelling (TWS)	5.5 to 15

Table A-9. Tests of Personality Functioning

Test	Age Range of Norms (in years)
Projective Techniques:	Preschool to adult
Children's Apperception Test (CAT, CAT-S)	
House-Tree-Person	
Kinetic Family Drawings	
Rorschach	
Sentence Completion	
Thematic Apperception Test (TAT)	
Standardized Questionnaires	
Child Behavior Checklist (CBCL), Parent and Teacher forms	2 to 18
Personality Inventory for Children (PIC)	3 to 16
Conners' Rating Scales-Revised (CRS-R), Parent and Teacher forms	3 to 17
McCarney Attention Deficit Disorders Evaluation Scale (ADDES)	4 to 20
Parenting Stress Index	
Vineland Adaptive Behavior Scales	0 to 18.11

TEST REFERENCES

References for most of the tests mentioned in the appendix follow. Some tests may not be available through regular publishing companies. Descriptions and norms may be obtained in articles or book chapters or sometimes in unpublished manuscripts. For an overview of measures and norms available for children, refer to O. Spreen & E. Strauss (1998). **A Compendium of neuropsychological tests** (2nd ed.). New York: Oxford University Press.

Abidin, R. R. (1995). *Parenting stress index (3rd ed.).* Odessa, FL: Psychological Assessment Resources.

Achenbach, T. M (1991a). *Manual for the child behavior checklist/4-18 and 1991 profile.* Burlington, VT: University of Vermont, Dept. of Psychiatry.

Achenbach, T. M. (1991b). *Manual for the teacher's report form and 1991 profile.* Burlington, VT: University of Vermont, Dept. of Psychiatry.

Achenbach, T. M. (1992). *Manual for the child behavior checklist and profile/2-3 and 1992 profile.* Burlington, VT: University of Vermont, Dept. of Psychiatry.

Adams, W., & Sheslow, D. (1995). *Wide range assessment of visual motor abilities (WRAVMA).* Wilmington, DE: Wide Range.

Ayres, A. J. (1991). *Sensory integration and praxis tests: Manual.* Los Angeles, CA: Western Psychological Services.

Bayley, N. (1993). *Bayley scales of infant development (2nd ed.).* San Antonio, TX: Psychological Corporation.

Bender, L. (1946). *Bender motor gestalt test. Cards and manual of instructions.* American Orthopsychiatric Association.

Beery, K. E. (1989). *The developmental test of visual-motor integration (VMI) (3rd rev.).* Cleveland, OH: Modern Curriculum Press.

Beery, K. E. (1997). *The developmental test of visual-motor integration (VMI) (4th ed.).* Austin, TX: PRO-ED.

Bellak, L., & Bellak, S. S. (1965, 1988). *Children's apperception test (human figures) (CAT).* Larchmont, NY: C.P.S.

Bellak, L., & Bellak, S. S. (1952, 1988). *Supplement to the children's apperception test (animal figures) (CAT-S).* Larchmont, NY: C.P.S.

Benton, A. L. (1974). *Revised visual retention test (4th ed.).* San Antonio, TX: Psychological Corporation.

Benton, A. L., Sivan, A. B., Hamsher, K., Varney, N. R., & Spreen, O. (1994). *Contributions to neuropsychological assessment. A clinical manual (2nd ed.).* New York: Oxford University Press. (Benton tests; e.g. Judgment of Line Orientation, Facial Recognition, Finger Localization, etc.)

Benton, A. L., & Spreen, O. (1969). *Right-left orientation test, Victoria form.* Neurosensory Center Publication No.163. Victoria, BC: Neuropsychology Laboratory, University of Victoria.

Bernstein, J. H., & Waber, D. P. (1996). *Developmental scoring system for the Rey-Osterrieth complex figure.* Odessa, FL: Psychological Assessment Resources.

Blackman, J. A., Levine, M. D., & Markowitz, M. (1986). *Pediatric extended examination at three (PEET).* Cambridge, MA: Educators Publishing Service.

Brown, L., Sherbenou, R. J., & Johnsen, S. K. *Test of nonverbal intelligence (2nd ed.) (TONI-2).* Austin, TX: PRO-ED.

Buck, J. N. (1978). *The house-tree person technique (Revised Manual).* Los Angeles, CA: Western Psychological Services.

Burgemeister, B. B., Blum, L. H., & Lorge, I. (1972). *Columbia mental maturity scale (CMMS)*. Harcourt Brace Jovanovich: Psychological Corporation.

Carrow-Woolfolk, E. (1985). *Test for auditory comprehension of language (Rev.) (TACL-R)*. Allen, TX: DLM Teaching Resources.

Conners, C. K., & Multi-Health Systems Staff. (1995). *Conners' continuous performance test.* North Tonawanda, NY: Multi-Health Systems.

Conners, C. K. (1997). *Conners' rating scales (Rev.).* North Tonawanda, NY: Multi-Health Systems.

Connolly, A. J. (1988). *Key math, revised: A diagnostic inventory of essential mathematics.* Circle Pines, MN: American Guidance Service.

Delis, D. C., Kramer, J., Kaplan, E., & Ober, B. A. (1994). *California verbal learning test (children's version) (CAVLT-2).* San Antonio, TX: Psychological Corporation.

Denckla, M. B. (1974). Rapid "automatized" naming of pictured objects, colors, letters, and numbers by normal children (RAN). *Cortex 10,* 186-202.

Denckla, M. B. (1985). Revised neurological examination for subtle signs (PANESS). *Psychopharmacology Bulletin 21,* 773-800.

DiSimoni, F. (1978). *The token test for children.* Austin, TX: DLM Teaching Resources.

Dunn, L. M., & Dunn, L. M. (1981). *Peabody picture vocabulary rest (Rev.) (PPVT-R).* Circle Pines, MN: American Guidance Service.

Elliot, C. D. (1990). *Differential ability scales (DAS).* San Antonio, TX: Psychological Corporation.

French, J. L. (1964). *Pictorial test of intelligence.* Boston, MA: Houghton Mifflin Company.

Gardner, M. F. (1982). *Test of visual-perceptual skills (non-motor) (TVPS).* Burlingame, CA: Psychological and Educational Publications.

Gardner, M. F. (1985). *Receptive one-word picture vocabulary test (ROWPVT).* Novato, CA: Academic Therapy Publications.

Gardner, M. F. (1990). *Expressive one-word picture vocabulary test (Rev.) (EOWPVT).* Novato, CA: Academic Therapy Publications.

Gardner, R. A. (1978). *Reversals frequency test.* Creskill, NJ: Creative Therapeutics.

Gardner, R. A., & Broman, M. (1979). The Purdue pegboard: Normative data on 1334 school children. *Journal of Clinical Child Psychology, 8,* 156-162.

German, D. J. (1989). *Test of word finding.* Allen, TX: DLM Teaching Resources.

Goldman, R., & Fristoe, M. (1986). *Goldman-Fristoe test of articulation.* Circle Pines, MN: American Guidance Service.

Goldman, R., Fristoe, M., & Woodcock, R. W. (1974). *Auditory skills test battery. GFW sound symbol tests.* Circle Pines, MN: American Guidance Service.

Goldman, R., Fristoe, M., & Woodcock, R. W. (1970). *GFW test of auditory discrimination.* Circle Pines, MN: American Guidance Service.

Greenberg, L. (1990). *Test of variables of attention 5.01.* St. Paul, MN: Attention Technology.

Hammill, D. D., & Larsen, S. C. (1988). *Test of written language (TOWL-2).* Austin, TX: PRO-ED.

Heaton, R, Chelune, G. J., Talley, J. L., Kay, C. G., & Curtis, G. (1993). *Wisconsin card sorting test.(WCST) (manual revised and expanded).* Odessa, FL: Psychological Assessment Resources.

Hiskey, M. S. (1955). *Hiskey-Nebraska test of learning aptitude (H-N).* Lincoln, NE: College View Printers.

Hooper, H. E. (1983). *Hooper visual organization test.* Los Angeles, CA: Western Psychological Services.

Jordan, B. T. (1990). *Jordan left-right reversal test*. Los Angeles, CA: Western Psychological Services.

Kaplan, E. F., Goodglass, H., & Weintraub, S. (1983). *The Boston naming test (2nd ed.)*. Philadelphia, PA: Lea & Febiger.

Kaufman, A. S., & Kaufman, N. L. (1983). *Kaufman assessment battery for children (K-ABC)*. Circle Pines, MN: American Guidance Service.

Kirk, S. A., McCarthy, J. J., & Kirk, W. D. (1968). *Illinois test of psycholinguistic abilities (ITPA)*. Los Angeles, CA: Western Psychological Services.

Kirk, U. (1992). Evidence for early acquisition of visual organization ability: A developmental study. *The Clinical Neuropsychologist, 6,* 171-177. (child norms for Hooper Visual Organization Test)

Koppitz, E. (1974). *The Bender gestalt: Research and application*.

Korkman, M., Kirk, U., & Kemp, S. (1998). *NEPSY*. San Antonio, TX: Psychological Corporation.

Lachar, D. (1984). *Personality inventory for children (PIC) (Revised format manual supplement)*. Los Angeles, CA: Western Psychological Services.

Logos, C. J. (1973). *Bender visual-motor gestalt test: Children's scoring booklet (norms)*. Los Angeles, CA: Western Psychological Services.

Leiter, R. G. (1979). *Leiter international performance scale*. Wood Dale, IL: Stoelting Co.

Levine, M., & Schneider, E. A. (1988). *Pediatric examination of educational readiness (PEER)*. Cambridge, MA: Educators Publishing Service.

Levine, N. L. (1982). *Leiter international performance scale: A handbook*. Los Angeles, CA: Western Psychological Services. (Leiter and Arthur Adaptation Norms)

Lindamood, C. H., & Lindamood, P. C. (1979). *Lindamood auditory conceptualization test (LAC)*. Chicago, IL: Riverside.

McCarthy, D. (1972). *McCarthy scales of children's abilities*. San Antonio, TX: Psychological Corporation.

Miller, L. J. (1988). *Miller assessment for preschoolers (MAP)*. San Antonio, TX: Psychological Corporation.

Mullen, E. M. (1995). *Mullen scales of early learning*. Circle Pines, MN: American Guidance Service.

Murray, H. A. (1971). *Thematic apperception test (TAT)*.

Raven, J. C., Court, J. H., & Raven, J. (1986, 1988). *Manual for Raven's Progressive Matrices and Vocabulary Scales, Section 1: General Overview; Section 2: Coloured Progressive Matrices; Section 3: Standard Progressive Matrices*. London: H. K. Lewis & Co., Ltd. (available from The Psychological Corporation)

Reitan, R. M. (1984). *Aphasia and sensory-perceptual deficits in children*. Tucson, AZ: Neuropsychology Press.

Reitan, R. M., & Wolfson, D. (1985). *The Halstead-Reitan neuropsychological test battery*. Tucson, AZ: Neuropsychology Press. (The Trail Making Test, Tactual Performance Test, Sensory-Perceptual Tests can be obtained from Reitan Neuropsychology Laboratory, Tucson, AZ.)

Reitan, R. M., & Wolfson, D. (1995). Category test and trail making test as measures of frontal lobe functions. *Clinical Neuropsychologist, 9,* 50-56.

Reynell, J. K., & Gruber, C. P. (1990). *Reynell developmental language scales*. Los Angeles, CA: Western Psychological Services.

Reynolds, C. R., & Bigler, E. D. (1994). *Test of memory and learning (TOMAL)*. Austin, TX: PRO-ED.

Reynolds, W.M. (1993). *Wepman's auditory discrimination test (2nd ed.).* Los Angeles, CA: Western Psychological Services.

Robertson, C., & Salter, W. (1997). *The phonological awareness test.* East Moline, IL: LinguiSystems.

Roid, G., & Miller, L. (1997). *Leiter international performance scale-Revised.* Wood Dale, IL: Stoelting.

Rorschach, H. (1948). *Psychodiagnostics-plates.* New York: Grune & Stratton Inc.

Rourke, B., & Gates, R. D. (1980). *The underlining test: Preliminary norms.* Windsor, Ontario: Authors.

Salkind, N. J. *The development of norms for the matching familiar figures test (MFF),* unpublished manuscript.

Semel, E., Wiig, E. H., & Secord, W. (1987, 1995). *Clinical evaluation of language fundamentals (Revised) (CELF-R); Clinical evaluation of language fundamentals (3rd ed.) (CELF-III).* San Antonio, TX: The Psychological Corporation.

Sheslow, D., & Adams, W. (1990). *Wide range assessment of memory and learning (WRAML).* Los Angeles, CA: Western Psychological Services.

Sparrow, S. S., Balla, D. A., & Cicchetti, D. V. (1984). *Vineland adaptive behavior scales.* Circle Pines, MN: American Guidance Service.

Spreen, O., & Benton, A. L. (1969). *Embedded figures test.* Victoria, BC: Neuropsychological Laboratory, University of Victoria.

Spreen, O., & Strauss, E. (1998). Rey-Osterrieth complex figure test. In: *A compendium of neuropsychological tests (2nd ed.)* (pp. 341-363). New York: Oxford University Press.

Spreen, O., & Strauss, E. (1998). Visual, visuomotor, and auditory tests: Trail making tests. In *A compendium of neuropsy-chological tests (2nd ed.)* (pp. 533-547). New York: Oxford University Press.

Spreen, O., & Strauss, E. (1998). Language tests: Controlled oral word association (COWA). In *A compendium of neuropsy-chological tests (2nd ed.)* (pp.447-464) New York: Oxford University Press.

Tiffin, J. (1968). *Purdue pegboard.* (Available from Lafayette Instrument Co., Lafayette, IN).

Thorndike, R. L., Hagen, E. P., & Sattler, J. M. (1986). *Stanford-Binet intelligence scale (4th ed.).* Chicago, IL: Riverside.

Wagner, R., Torgesen, J., & Rashotte, C. (1999). *Comprehensive test of phonologi-cal processing (CTOPP).* Austin, TX: PRO-ED.

Wechsler, D. (1989). *Wechsler preschool and primary scale of intelligence (Rev.) (WPPSI-R).* San Antonio, TX: Psycho-logical Corporation.

Wechsler, D. (1991). *Wechsler intelligence scale for children (3rd ed.) (WISC-III).* San Antonio, TX: Psychological Corporation.

Wechsler individual achievement test (WIAT) (1992). San Antonio, TX: Psychological Corporation.

Wiederholt, J. L., & Bryant, B. R. (1992) *Gray oral reading tests (3rd ed.) (GORT-3).* Austin, TX: PRO-ED.

Wiig, E. H., & Secord, W. (1989). *Test of lan-guage competence-expanded edition (TLC).* San Antonio, TX: Psychological Corporation.

Wiig, E. H., Secord, W., & Semel, E. (1992) *Clinical evaluation of language fundamen-tals - CELF-preschool.* San Antonio, TX: Psychological Corporation.

Wilkinson, G. S. (1993). *WRAT-3 administa-tion manual.* Delaware: Wide Range. (Available through The Psychological Corporation, San Antonio, TX).

Wilson, B. C., Iacovello, J. M., Wilson, J. J., & Risucci, D. (1982). Purdue pegboard performance of normal preschool children. *Journal of Clinical Neuropsychology, 4,* 19-26.

Wirt, D., Lachar, D., Klinedinst, J. K., & Seat, P. D. (1984). *Mutlitdimensional description of child personality: A manual for the personality inventory for children (PIC) (Rev.).* Los Angeles, CA: Western Psychological Services.

Woodcock, R. W. (1987). *Woodcock reading mastery tests (Rev.) (WRMT-R).* Circle Pines, MN: American Guidance Service.

Yeates, K. O. (1994). Comparison of developmental norms for the Boston naming test. *The Clinical Neuropsychologist, 8,* 91-98.

Zachman, L., Hisingh, R., Barrett, M., Orman, J., & LoGiudice, C. (1984) *Test of problem solving (TOPS).* East Moline, IL: LinguiSystems.

Zimmerman, I. L., Steiner, V. G., & Pond, R. E. (1992). *Preschool language scale-3 (PLS-3).* San Antonio, TX: Psychological Corporation.

Part Six:

Innovative Models that Work with Especially Challenging Functional Developmental Capacities

—◀ 19 ▶—

The Miller Method®:
A Cognitive-Developmental Systems Approach for Children with Body Organization, Social, and Communication Issues[1]

Arnold Miller, Ph.D., and Eileen Eller-Miller, M.A., C.C.C.-S.L.P.

WHAT IS THE MILLER METHOD®?

The Miller Method is an integrated approach that addresses problems of body organization, social interaction, and communication in school, clinic, and home settings as presented by children on the autistic spectrum as well as those with significant challenges in learning or communication. Integrated means that, in this approach, each person working with the child—while focusing on one aspect of the child's functioning—also addresses other areas of concern. It is also a coordinated program in that each person working with the child is in close touch with and contributes to others working with that child. It is an action-oriented program, which assumes that children learn best when they move and make direct physical contact with things and people. It also assumes that children learn best when they are taught or treated by those who understand that they require a combination of both support and demand. Greenspan and Wieder (2000) refer to the present approach as "semistructured," in that the people working with a child are guided both by the initiatives of the child and by certain

developmentally organized interventions introduced by teachers and therapists.

The Miller Method is guided by a cognitive-developmental systems theory with links to the work of Piaget (1948, 1954, 1962), von Bertallanfy (1968), Vygotsky (1962), Werner (1948), and Werner and Kaplan (1963) and is adapted to the needs of children with severe developmental challenges. It was developed by the authors during the last 40 years (Miller, 1963, 1968, 1991; Miller & Eller-Miller, 1989; and Miller & Miller, 1968, 1971, 1973). Current outcome research includes studies by Cook (1998), Messier (1971), Miller and Miller (1973), and Warr-Leeper, Henry, and Lomas (1999).

The approach is cognitive because it deals with the manner in which children organize their behavior, develop concepts of time and space, problem solve, and form

---

[1]The Miller Method is currently in practice at schools and clinics within six States as well as in Canada and other countries, under videoconferencing consultation arrangements with the Language and Cognitive Development Center in Boston, Massachusetts. For additional information, contact the Language and Cognitive Development Center at (800) 218-5232 or through its website: www.millermethod.org.

relationships with people. It is developmental because it deals with the ability of children to shift from action stages of functioning to communication and representation of reality through various symbolic forms. It also is a systems approach because it views the formation and use of systems as indispensable to the entire array of human performance.

The goals of the Miller Method are to:

- Assess the child's capacity to interact with people and objects, adapt to change, and learn from experience.
- Build the child's awareness of her own body as it relates to objects and people.
- Guide children from closed, disconnected, or scattered ways of being into functional, social, and communicative exchanges.
- Provide the necessary transitions from concrete to more abstract symbolic functioning.

Unique Aspects of the Miller Method®

Among the novel features of the Miller Method are its pragmatic use of two major strategies. The first is the exploitation for developmental gains of the aberrant systems, or "part systems," the children bring. The assumption behind this strategy is that all organized behaviors—even those that are aberrant—have within them the potential for developmental gain. For example, atypical behavior systems of children with disorders (e.g., lining up things, flicking light switches, or flushing toilets) can often be transformed into functional, interactive behaviors.

The second major strategy is the systematic introduction of developmentally relevant spheres (repetitive activities concerned with objects and people) to repair developmental lags and restore developmental progressions. For example, children who have never experienced picking up and dropping objects or who have not learned that they can push over

an object with their hands or with a stick can be taught to do so in a way that helps fill in a developmental gap by establishing, often for the first time, their ability to act on and influence objects and events in their surroundings.

Another important strategy is having the therapist narrate, with signs and spoken words, what the children are doing *while* they are doing it. We find that such narration helps the children relate the words and signs to their own actions. As this happens, they seem to become more aware of themselves and to begin to develop the inner speech so important in communicating both with themselves and with others.

This process is facilitated by elevating the children $2^{1}/_{2}$ feet above the ground on an Elevated Square or similar structure. Elevating the children seems to enhance not only word-sign guidance of behavior but also to induce an awareness of body/self and others, more focused and organized planning of behavior sequences, and better social-emotional contact. It also provides a framework in which the children can more readily be taught to transition without distress from one engaging object or event to another. In addition to work on the Elevated Square and other such structures, special programs are introduced during the day to help children develop both spoken and written language. These programs are described later in this chapter.

DEFINING CENTRAL CONCEPTS

Before discussing assessment and intervention, it is desirable to define and discuss the concept of systems and the various roles that systems play in the economy of both typical children and those with disorders.

Systems

Systems are organized, coherent "chunks" of behavior that are, initially, quite repetitive.

Chapter 19. The Miller Method®: A Cognitive-Developmental Systems Approach for
Children with Body Organization, Social, and Communication Issues

491

They involve the child acting with the body on or with some object, event, or person in a predictable manner. A 10-month-old baby repetitively involved in picking up and dropping everything on the food tray is involved in a system, as is the 15-month-old toddler repeatedly filling and emptying a sand bucket. There are also interactive systems, such as when the 12-month-old plays peek-a-boo with her mother, an 18-month-old child realizes that after the ball is rolled to her she is to roll it back, or when the small child holds up his arms to communicate a desire to be picked up. Systems also are involved in symbolic play, such as when children begin to feed their dolls in the manner in which they themselves are fed. When children are able to indicate objects by pointing, gestures, or words, these gesture/word relations to various objects, events, or people are systems that may be regularly reactivated by the sight of particular referents.

Systems vary in their complexity from the simplest one-component systems such as pick up/drop, which are referred to as *minisystems*, to more complex, multistep systems leading to a particular goal. The latter are referred to as *integrative* systems as, for example, when a child learns to climb up steps to go down a slide or to open a cupboard door to get something inside. Children who are able to address previously developed (internalized) systems in new ways (*spontaneous expansions*) have a basis for problem solving and creative thought and play.

The hallmark of all systems is the investment the child has in maintaining or continuing them. This investment becomes apparent when a particular system is interrupted. For example, a 15-month-old child involved in a system of putting on and taking off a series of bracelets on her arm became very distressed when a bracelet was taken—crying, pointing at the desired bracelet and even trying to say the word—in an effort to have it replaced on

her arm to restore the interrupted system. As discussed later, the careful interruption of systems is an important technique for helping children initiate actions or words to help repair their "broken" systems.

Interrupting systems is also used to motivate a child. For example, one child who at first refused to use a rake to get a disc that was out of reach did so when the therapist proceeded as follows. First, the therapist helped the child establish a disc-in-bottle system by having the child repeatedly put discs in the slit on top of a bottle until the child did this completely on his own. Then, the therapist interrupted this system by placing the disc out of the child's reach while placing the rake between the child and the disc. At this point, the child immediately used the rake to bring the disk closer so that he could restore the interrupted system by continuing to place the disks in the slit on top of the bottle.

Unlike typical children, those on the autistic spectrum as well as those with other developmental issues show system aberrations that interfere with their performance and development: They may, for example, tend to become so overinvolved with things and events that they are unable to detach from them, as does the child who perseveratively flicks on and off light switches or television sets. Alternatively, these children may be so uninvolved or disconnected from things and people around them, that there is little basis for building or sustaining relations with either things or people. This means that before such children can progress, careful attention must be given to their system problems.

Steps in the Early Formation, Maintenance, and Expansion of Systems

For children with disorders to develop, it is important that many different kinds of systems form, expand, and, increasingly, come under their control. There is a progression in the manner in which systems are formed. At first, system formation is driven by the external properties of objects, events, and people, with the child reactive to the process. Later, the formation, expansion, and combination of systems come increasingly under the child's active control as the child uses previously developed systems in the service of various ends. The following sections outline the progressive steps of forming, maintaining, and expanding systems.

Orienting

Systems begin to form as a salient sound, motion, or a particular property of an object, event, or person induces the child to "'turn toward," or orient, toward the source of the stimuli (Goldstein, 1940; Pavlov, 1927; Sokolov, 1963). Orienting has been shown to make the stimulus that the child is turning toward more salient for the reacting child. However, even at this initial phase of system formation, aberrations are evident among many developmentally challenged children. For example, some children with disorders are so driven that they orient to any stimuli that they see, hear, or feel in a way that keeps them helplessly reacting to so many stimuli that they have difficulty with the next step in system formation—engagement.

Engagement

Once a child orients toward a salient stimulus, the next step in system formation entails the child moving toward and becoming physically and emotionally involved or engaged with the stimulus properties of the object, event, or person in his immediate surroundings. In cognitive-developmental systems theory, orienting plus engagement provides the precondition for the formation of systems which, in turn, provides the

framework for not only making functional and emotional contact with things and people but for maintaining and expanding that contact. However, engagement by itself does not ensure the development of a system.

From Engagement to System Formation

Engagement is to system formation as a casual encounter between one person asking another for the current time is to a life-long friendship between the two people. The initial brief encounter (engagement) is a necessary prerequisite for a relationship (system) to develop between people or objects, but such a relationship may or may not develop from the initial encounter. The system develops only through a more prolonged and repetitive engagement with an object, event, or person.

For example, a 16-month-old girl who stumbles over a bucket half filled with sand is momentarily *engaged* with that bucket. However, she has not formed a system with that bucket until she repetitively addresses it in any of a variety of ways: Having stumbled over it, she may form a system by repeatedly kicking the bucket across the sand or by repeatedly filling and emptying the bucket, and so forth. Once her behavior with the bucket follows a predictable pattern she has transformed her initial engagement with the bucket into a system. At that point, her behavior is internalized as a way of being with that object.

The decisive indication that an internalized system has developed occurs when, following interruption of the child's system by removing her bucket or preventing her from acting on or with it, the child becomes *compensatorily* driven to maintain or restore action with that object by reaching for the bucket, yelling, pointing, and otherwise indicating her urgent need to continue that system. When interruption of an activity *does*

Chapter 19. The Miller Method®: A Cognitive-Developmental Systems Approach for
Children with Body Organization, Social, and Communication Issues

493

not induce a child to continue or restore that activity, a system has not yet developed.

However, if systems are to move beyond mere rituals, there must be both a means of recalling or reactivating them when they have not been used for a time *and* a means of extending their influence to other aspects of a child's surroundings. Two principles—*inclusion* and *extension*—suggest how this occurs.

The Inclusion Principle

This principle states, "Whenever the child, engaged by a stimulating object or event, is concurrently stimulated by a background aspect of the situation, that background aspect soon becomes part of the total, engaging system which emerges. Subsequently, when only the background aspect appears (partial interruption), the child compensatorily behaves as he/she had toward the originally engaging object" (Miller & Eller-Miller, 1989).

For example, if while an infant is nursing at the breast (nursing system), the mother simultaneously croons and strokes the infant's cheek, then subsequently, in the absence of the breast, the mother's crooning or cheek-stroking, by itself, will elicit vigorous sucking by the infant. In a similar fashion, a small child who has not previously responded to the term "Push!" or to a pushing gesture will do so if, while the child is pushing a wagon (pushing-wagon system), the child repeatedly hears the therapist saying, "Push ... push ... push!" accompanied by pushing gestures. As this occurs, both word and gesture soon become included within the child's pushing-wagon system so that when the therapist later introduces either word or push-gesture in the presence of the wagon (partial interruption), the child feels compelled to push the wagon to complete the system.

The following outline summarizes the steps involved in system formation and expansion via the inclusion principle:

1. **Orienting**
   Child orients (turns toward) the introduction of a large object (a wagon) within her visual field.

2. **Engagement to system forming**
   Child approaches and pushes the wagon, which moves and then stops in a way that induces him to push it again and again until a pushing-wagon system forms.

3. **Inclusion process**
   a. *Introducing new parts to the system.* Therapist uses words and gestures to introduce the word "push" while the child is repeatedly pushing the wagon. At first, the child orients toward the sounds and gestures (indicating that she still experiences them as separate from her pushing-wagon system).
   b. *Assimilating new parts to the system.* As the spoken word and gesture continue to accompany the pushing-wagon system, the child no longer orients toward them as if they were separate entities but experiences them as part of the pushing-wagon system. In other words, the child now experienced it as a pushing-wagon + "push" (word) + (gesture) system.

4. **Partial interruption**
   Later, when *only* the spoken word or gesture part of the system is introduced (partially interrupted system), the child compensatorily searches for a wagon or other moveable objects to push.

The Extension Principle

The extension principle comes into play when the child has already developed some gestures, utterances (natural signs), or spoken words that are closely related to a particular referent located in the child's immediate surroundings. This principle explains how the familiar meanings attached to these expressive systems become extended to an initially neutral entity, which then becomes part of the child's expressive system. This occurs by the child's expressive system acting upon the neutral property.

The principle states, "Whenever a system with which the child is engaged acts upon a new property of an object or event, that property becomes an extended part of the original system. The child then maintains the integrity of the newly extended system when it is interrupted just as with the original system" (Miller & Eller-Miller, 1989).

Two examples illustrate the operation of the extension principle. In one, the child has established the natural sign "ch ch" to refer to his small train. Subsequently, the parent introduces the term "train." The child responds by saying, "ch ch train," clearly extending the rhythmic "ch ch" cadence to include the new term. In the second example, a 2-year-old child sees a bird land on the fork of a branch and begin pecking on it. The child points and exclaims, "Bird!" (word "bird" plus bird-pecking-on-forked-branch system). Abruptly, the bird disappears (interruption) behind the fork in the branch. Nevertheless, the child continues to point at the forked branch (where the bird had been pecking) and to exclaim, "Bird!" On subsequent occasions when the child passes that forked branch, the child points at the branch and says "Bird!" even though no bird is present.

Because the bird had acted upon the forked branch, it had assumed bird significance for the child. In other words, the "bird

system" had been extended for this child to include not only the bird but the forked branch on which the bird had been pecking. However, the bird valence of the forked branch only became evident when the bird disappeared behind it (interruption) and left only the forked branch part of the system, which the child continued to designate as "bird." This extension principle, as illustrated later in this chapter, plays an important role in the transfer of meaning from spoken words to the arbitrary forms of printed words in the Symbol Accentuation Reading Program (Miller & Eller-Miller, 1989).

Executive Function

The system expansions discussed so far have largely depended on external events driving the system. Early in a child's life, such externally driven expansions are the primary mode by which systems are expanded. They entail minimal intention or initiative on the part of the child. Gradually, however, this reactive mode of expanding systems is accompanied by a new mode whereby the child deliberately forms systems as well as new combinations of systems based on an inner plan. This emerging capacity is referred to as the development of *executive function*.

Early examples of executive function may be noted as a child decides that he no longer wishes to go down the slide in the sitting position but prefers, instead, to slide down on side, back, stomach, etc. These *spontaneous expansions* of the slide system are possible because of the newly emerging executive function. It appears that executive function is only possible when children have developed sufficient awareness of their bodies to self consciously direct them in different ways. When this occurs, they find that they have the ability to choose one system over another, to alter systems, or to combine previously developed systems in new ways. Perhaps the best known

Chapter 19. The Miller Method®: A Cognitive-Developmental Systems Approach for
Children with Body Organization, Social, and Communication Issues

495

indication that executive function is well established occurs when the typical 2-year-old responds to her mother's request to do something with a defiant "No!"—a statement that marks both awareness of self and other as well as the notion of choice.

The failure of this shift to fully occur among developmentally challenged children accounts for many of the dramatic differences in behavior between typical and compromised development. The following examples of children's activities with blocks during an unstructured period contrasts the functioning of a 3-year-old who has developed executive function with the functioning of two children on the autistic spectrum who demonstrate little or none of this capacity.

Children With and Without the Capacity for Executive Functioning

- *Jack, a typical 3-year-old with capacity for executive function.* As soon as Jack received the pile of assorted blocks, he began to build a connected structure of ramps and towers. He picked up each block, examined it, selected a place for it in the block structure, and inserted it carefully. Needing a block of a particular size, he scanned the blocks and spotted an appropriate one near the foot of the observing adult about 6 feet away. He looked at the adult, pointed at the block, and exclaimed, "Block, please!" After receiving the block, he smiled at the adult, added the block to his structure, and took another block. Next, while making "rmm" car sounds, he "drove" his block up the ramp and around the block towers. Finished with car-block play, he got up and set off for something else to do.

- *Damon, a 3-year-old boy on the autistic spectrum with minimal capacity for executive function.* Damon, seeing the pile of

blocks, immediately began to build a connected structure. But, unlike Jack's construction, his structure consisted only of a row of rectangular blocks carefully placed so that each block abutted the previous one. Curved or triangular blocks were not attended, and he did not make the sounds that other children made as they played.

Damon worked with rapid intensity, regularly scrambling from the end of the row of blocks to get another block so that he could continue extending the structure. At no time did Damon acknowledge the existence of the adult seated nearby. When the adult tried to hand him a block, Damon rapidly turned his body so that his back was between the adult and the blocks. When the adult removed one block from the row, Damon screamed, then frantically sought another block to close the gap in the structure. Damon continued to extend the row of blocks until it reached the wall. Confronted by the wall, he made a right angle with the next block and continued placing blocks along the wall until there were no more blocks. Then he began rocking back and forth while twiddling his fingers in front of his eyes. Except for his scream when the adult altered his block structure, he uttered no sound.

- *Brian, a 3-year-old boy on the autistic spectrum who demonstrates little or no executive function.* Presented the blocks, Brian was momentarily drawn to the clattering sound they made when they were placed in front of him. What Brian saw and heard, however, seemed quite disconnected from what his hands were doing. Even though he picked up a block, it soon slid from his hands, forgotten, as he was "caught" by the movement and sound the adult made as she seated herself in a near-by chair. When the adult offered him another block, he seemed not to notice it because he was now turned toward the sound of a bus starting up outside the building. At no time did Brian spontaneously explore his surroundings or examine the manner in which blocks stacked or things worked. Instead, time and again, he turned toward or began to move toward a stimulating object or event only to be diverted by another new stimulus, which "drove" his behavior.

An Analysis of the Children's Executive Functioning and System-Forming Ability

Although both Jack and Damon produced systems, their systems differed dramatically. Jack, the typical child, had a complex, integrative system composed of towers, ramps, and cars. As Jack played with the blocks, it became evident that he experienced himself as the executive or master-builder *with an inner plan* to which both the blocks and the adult contributed. This allowed him to form a complex, integrative system with the blocks (towers and ramps) that he could exploit in different ways. He could, for example, turn a block into a car and move it, car-like, up and down the ramps. He could also turn from the main block structure to request a block from an adult and turn back to his structure without losing touch with his goal. In carrying through his plan, Jack demonstrated that he could integrate several smaller systems into a larger one.

In sharp contrast, Damon, the autistic child with a *closed-system disorder*, had a single, minisystem composed of lining up blocks. Damon's system was not driven by any inner plan but by the way each block abutted the next one. He changed the structure only when the physical barrier of the wall

required such a change. This change, however, came about not through any executive decision on Damon's part, but because the wall required the change. Finally, there was no decision to stop connecting blocks; Damon stopped when he ran out of blocks. When this occurred, he had no means of directing himself to a new activity. Apparently, the only means he had of filling the void left by the end of the block-connecting system was rocking and hand twiddling.

For Brian, the observing adult seemed to exist only momentarily as the adult moved and made sounds. Brian's constant tendency to be driven by transient stimuli (sudden sound or motion) interfered with the prospect of a deeper relationship with either people or objects. Brian oriented but seemed unable to become physically engaged with the stimuli. Because of his "drivenness," Brian formed only fleeting contact with objects and events as he was driven from one source of stimulation to another—never lighting long enough to physically engage the stimulating source. The unfortunate outcome is that he failed to develop either coherent systems or the executive capacity required to explore their properties. In short, like Damon, Brian lacked the executive functioning to guide his own behavior, but unlike Damon, he also lacked coherent, compelling systems.

The different ways the children related to the observing adult illuminates the extent to which they dominated or were dominated by their systems. Jack, needing a block to complete his block structure and seeing a block near the adult, was able to turn toward the adult and ask her for the block. In doing this, Jack creatively brought together the world of relationships with people with his world of objects. The situation was very different for Damon: for him, the observing adult did not exist except as a momentary threat (when removing a block from his lined-up blocks) to the integrity of the structure being built. Clearly, he lacked the executive function required to draw upon relationships with people. Stated differently, his closed-system tendency precluded people from being part of his system.

After children make the shift to executive function, their relation to the systems they have formed changes radically. *Systems previously triggered only by properties of the environment are now at the disposal of the executive capacity of the child.* The distinction between systems that dominate the behavior of children and those which children dominate is evident in the comparison of Jack, who has made the shift to executive function, with Damon and Brian, who have not.

Closed-System and System-Forming Disorders

There are two broad system dispositions among children having autistic spectrum as well as those with other developmental disorders: *closed-system disorders* (Miller, 1991; Miller & Eller-Miller, 1989) and system-forming disorders. Both kinds of *system disorders* are divided into Type A and B forms to indicate the nature and limitations of their systems and the extent to which executive function plays a role.

Type A of the *closed-system disorders* refers to those children, like Damon, who become so involved with one or two action-object systems that they are unable to notice or respond to any stimuli unrelated to the system with which they are engaged. These are the children who are so unresponsive to being called that parents often have the children's hearing checked. They are also unable to scan their environment, tending to "live" quite close to their bodies. Not surprisingly, these children have great difficulty shifting from one object or event to another. Equally

important, children with Type A closed-system disorders tend to prohibit parents or others from entering and participating within their object or event systems. In other words, having only minimal executive function, these children are quite dominated by their few systems. Clearly, children with such closed systems are restricted in their social interactions and ability to communicate with others about things and events in the immediate environment.

Children with Type B closed-system disorders share some but not all dispositions with Type A closed-system children. Similarly, they resist having people enter their systems. However, unlike Type A children, Type B children are able to demonstrate executive functioning in a circumscribed domain composed of action-object systems. In contrast to Type A children who tend to remain engaged with one or two objects from which they cannot extricate themselves, Type B children have sufficient executive function to scan their surroundings and to move without difficulty from one object or event system to another. However, their executive functioning does not yet permit them to allow people to participate in their systems. In other words, they have *child-object* systems but not *child-object-person systems*. Should a person attempt to enter one of their systems, the children show the same kind of resistant behavior (although to a lesser degree) found with Type A children with closed-system disorders.

Children with *system-forming disorders* are very different from those with closed-system disorders. Children with system-forming disorders have great difficulty forming any systems. Brian (described earlier), with his tendency to be "driven" by every salient stimulus, falls into a Type B system-forming disorder. Children such as Brian are repeatedly driven to orient toward stimuli from objects and events but fail to engage them physically.

However, there is another group of children, designated Type A system-forming disorder, whose difficulty forming systems stems largely from their poor sensory-motor coordination. Such a child may orient toward a particular salient object or event but have difficulty relating his body to that object or event in a way that forms either mini- or multistep integrative systems.

It is interesting to note that children with Type A system-forming disorders can, with proper intervention, learn to form integrative systems, such as climbing up steps to slide down a slide. The problem is that the child's sensory-motor coordination is often so sluggish that by the time the child has climbed the stairs and slid down, she has completely lost contact with the location of the stairs and so, having slid down, continues straight ahead. Failing to return to the stairs, the child at first cannot repeat and "own" that system without continuing physical support. However, with many repetitions and rapid pacing, the child *will* begin to anticipate the various parts of the step-slide system. Nevertheless, the rigid, circumscribed quality of the integrative systems, which these children achieve through repetition, is very different from the creative and complex integrative systems achieved by the typical child, such as Jack. Because Jack had achieved executive functioning, he could creatively combine systems following his inner plan. In contrast, children with Type A system-forming disorders, who lack executive function, can form integrative systems only in a rigid, unvarying manner by virtue of having been repeatedly led by a therapist through the system until it "takes."

While children with both Type A and Type B system-forming disorders have difficulty forming coherent systems with objects and events in their surroundings, their challenges come from different sources. Type B children are "too sensorily driven" by various stimuli to readily form systems, whereas Type A children have physical coordination problems that interfere with the sequencing and motor planning they need to form their systems. (See Table 1).

Finally, there is a developmental sequence in the formation of systems. Least developed are children such as Brian, whose drivenness

Table 1. Contrasting Children with Closed-System and System-Forming Disorders

Disorder	Children	
	Type A	Type B
Closed system	Minimal executive functioning and few systems. Poor shifting/scanning. People excluded from systems.	Executive functioning with many object systems. Ability to shift from one to another system. People excluded from systems.
System-forming	Minimal executive functioning. Poor sensory-motor coordination limits system forming.	Little executive functioning. Salient properties of many sources induce repeated orienting, but not engagement.

results in aborted system formation and an almost total lack of executive function. More developed, but still compromised, are those closed-system, Type B children whose modest executive function enables them to shift from one closed system to another but who still exclude people from their systems. Most developed are children such as Jack, who have the executive capacity to creatively assemble a variety of minisystems into an integrative system (involving people) that they can modify as they choose in accord with their inner plans. Table 1 captures the major distinctions between the two types of disorder and their subcategories.

ASSESSMENT

Before therapists can intervene effectively, they need to assess the nature of each child's system functioning. The following sections explore different assessment strategies.

Assessing the Children

One of the goals of the Miller Method is to assess each child's capacity to interact with people and objects, adapt to change, and learn from experience. An Umwelt assessment was developed to determine how best to intervene with children on the autistic spectrum (Miller & Eller-Miller, 1989). An

Umwelt (Uexküll, 1934) refers to the "world around one." Consequently, in performing an Umwelt assessment for a particular child, we try to determine the nature of the systems the child brings to a new situation by first examining his behavior in unstructured situations where he has access to both people and a variety of objects, but where the adults are passive. We also examine the child's ability to become engaged in new systems that the examiner introduces. Recently, influenced by the work of Greenspan and Wieder (1998), we have been paying more attention to affectively driven systems between the child and others. Now, just as we examine the child's resourcefulness in coping with objects via detours or by using tools, we seek to determine the child's emotional resourcefulness in initiating and maintaining ongoing interactive systems supported by the adult.

This means that we now examine three kinds of interaction with a particular child: (1) the child's response to unstructured situations (adults passive); (2) the child's ability to maintain an interactive system with the examiner when the examiner actively builds on the child's initiatives, and so forth; and (3) the child's ability to accept and participate in examiner-initiated systems. Table 2 captures the three different ways of examining the child.

Each of the adult stances is important in determining how well a child can cope with

Table 2. General Strategies Used During the Umwelt Assessment		
Assessment Strategies	**Adult Stance**	**Child's Task**
Unstructured	Passive	Child to initiate without support.
Child-initiated	Interactive	Child initiates and cyclically builds on adult's response to his or her initiatives.
Adult-initiated	Active	Child to accept adult-initiated interaction and expansions.

people and things in her immediate surround-ings. The child who, during the unstructured period, can—without support—initiate actions toward people and things in unfamiliar sur-roundings demonstrates a repertoire of organ-ized behaviors (systems) that enable her to engage with people or objects. In this condi-tion, the relative emphasis on people or objects, and the quality of interaction or exploration (if it exists at all) tells much about the coping resources available to that child. On the other hand, child-driven interactions tell more about the emotional capacity of the child to initiate and to sustain more prolonged interactive systems with the examiner (Greenspan & Wieder, 1998). How well the child can sustain shared attention and involve-ment with the adult is an important indication of the relationship potential of the child.

However, since many circumstances, such as school, entail teaching the child from the adult's and not the child's agenda, it is also important to determine how well the child can accept adult-driven interactions. How the child responds to an adult setting up, expanding, and directing shifts from one sys-tem to another provides important clues about how well the child will learn in school-related or similar situations. Further, the importance of therapist- or teacher-initiated systems (called spheres) lies in their potential for remedying serious developmental lags.

Different tasks from the Umwelt assess-ment help clarify the unique way in which

each child with disorders experiences reality as well as her adaptive potential. The follow-ing example indicates how one of the Umwelt tasks throws light on a child's abili-ty to interact with both a person and an object in a simple game.

Assessing the Capacity to Interact with a Person and an Object: The Swinging Ball Task

Figure 1 illustrates the manner in which the examiner assesses the child's ability to form an interactive system involving an object and another person.

Figure 1a represents a child enjoying a repetitive pushing-game (a child-object-adult system) in which adult and child push a swing-ing ball back and forth. The dotted lines to both ball and adult indicate that the child's system includes awareness of both the ball and the adult. Figure 1b, reflects a more limited child-object system that includes the ball, (which the child pushes whenever it arrives) but does not include the adult. Figure 1c shows an even more circumscribed system. Here, the child fails to react even when the ball bumps into him, which infers that the child lacks that object system.

Typical children as young as 2 years of age will behave interactively with ball and person as illustrated in Figure 1a. Children with closed-system disorders will interact with the ball but not with the person, as shown in Figure 1b. Children with system-

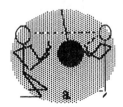 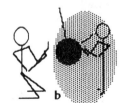 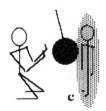

Figure 1a, b, c. Assessing a Child's Ability to Form an Interactive System:
a. Child-object-adult   b. Child-object   c. No object system

Chapter 19. The Miller Method®: A Cognitive-Developmental Systems Approach for
Children with Body Organization, Social, and Communication Issues

501

forming disorders may respond as shown in Figure 1c because they have difficulty coordinating with the ball's trajectory.

Assessing the Capacity to Adapt to Change: Stacking Cups and Bowls

Successfully coping with surroundings requires the child to adjust her approach to changing circumstances. To get at this capacity during the Umwelt assessment, the child is required to stack cups and bowls in different ways. The task is graduated from simple stacking of cups (then bowls) with their openings facing upwards to those involving progressively more complex adjustments. At the most complex stacking level, the child is required to alternately stack cups and bowls, with the cup presented upside-down over the bowl and the bowl presented right-side-up over the right-side-up cups (Figure 2).

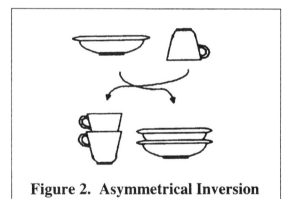

Figure 2. Asymmetrical Inversion

The final sequence tests the child's ability to shift from a stacking mindset to one in which he is required to place a cup in each of six bowls spread out in front of the him (Figure 3). Closed-system Type A children typically show such a strong perseverative tendency that they persist in stacking the cups given them—instead of placing a cup in each bowl—even after the examiner has modeled placing one or two cups in the bowls in front of them. Often, we will repeat the set-up in

Figure 3. Breaking the Stacking Set

Figure 3 with additional cues to determine how close a child is to making the shift from one kind of organization (vertical stacking) to another (lateral).

Problem Solving and Learning from Experience: The Elevated "Swiss Cheese" Board

The next two tasks examine, although in different ways, the child's ability not only to adjust to changing circumstances but to learn from the experience. One task examines the child's response to the elevated "Swiss Cheese" Board (Figure 4); another, called "Croupier" (Figure 5), examines the child's manner of coping with progressively more demanding tasks involving the use of rakes and obstacles to gain a desired object.

Figure 4. "Swiss Cheese" Board

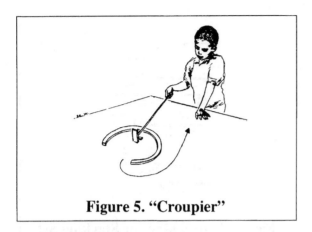

Figure 5. "Croupier"

The ability to learn from experience comes into play when the child on the "Swiss Cheese" Board inadvertently steps in a hole (care being taken that the child does not fall). Then, as the child continues to cross the board, we are able to determine whether or not the child now avoids the holes by stepping over them. In the rake-obstacle task, we seek to determine if the child—shown pulling a desired object toward himself—can learn to push it away from himself through the gap and then toward himself. Often we will test the limits by placing the desired object closer and closer to the gap to determine at what point the child will understand the need to first push the object away before it can be brought closer. Once the child pushes the object away, we return the next object to the center of the horseshoe ring to determine if the child has generalized this understanding to the new object given or will revert to the original, unsuccessful effort to bring the object toward himself.

INTERVENTIONS

Before a child can achieve executive control of his own systems, he must first achieve a certain awareness of his body and the distinction between his body and that of others, as well as the object or event system with which his body is engaged at a particular moment. If there is little or no awareness of the body or body-self as a separate entity independent of what the body is engaged with, then the child becomes so captured by the ongoing body-object system in play at that time that he cannot spontaneously detach from the ongoing system. Only as the child develops the notion that his body and its parts have an existence independent of the object or event system with which he is engaged can the executive function emerge (which makes possible a child's spontaneous expansion of his systems). In other words, body-world polarity is a prerequisite for executive function.

Among typical children, this capacity emerges gradually in the course of the first 2 years of development. For example, by 6 months of age, the child has achieved sufficient differentiation between her body and others to demonstrate a clear preference for her mother over others. Between 6 and 9 months of age, the child is able to relate to (establish systems with) either a person or an object. By 9 or 10 months of age, the child can relate to another around an object (child-object-person system) as evident in the ability to give an object to a caregiver on request (Trevarthen & Hubley, 1979). And, of course, by 24 months of age, the child becomes self-consciously aware of her ability to accept or refuse requests.

Children whose development has been compromised often fail to achieve these basic body-object-other capacities. For example, they may not differentiate between one person and another, and they may not be able to give an object on request. They remain fixed in a "single track" involvement with a particular property of an object or event and show striking difficulties in relating their bodies to people and objects in their surroundings.

The following section details some ways in which these difficulties become apparent.

Body-world problems may become apparent with child-object systems, child-person systems, and child-object-person systems. For example, picking up and dropping an object or flicking a light switch on and off are *child-object* systems, while peek-a-boo and chase games are *child-person* systems. On the other hand, rolling a ball back and forth with mom or dad is a *child-object-person* system that combines both object and people worlds. The problem for developmentally challenged children stems from the unusual way they form or fail to form systems in the world of objects and the world of people and their difficulty in forming systems that combine the two worlds.

Strategies for Developing Body-World Awareness

Strategies for developing body-world awareness include "rough and tumble" activity, mutual face-touching, estabilization, deep pressure, swinging, elevation, and introducing causal systems. One goal of these strategies is to guide children from closed, disconnected, or scattered ways of being into functional, social, and communicative exchanges.

An Intervention Case Example: Damon

Damon, the 3-year-old described earlier, is a child on the autistic spectrum with a closed-system disorder, Type A. His various problem areas are:
1. Poor human contact (won't look at people) or include them in his systems.
2. Perseverative tendency—has great difficulty shifting from one action-object system to another.
3. Does not seem to hear or follow directions ("word deaf").
4. Does not communicate his needs except by pulling the adult toward the desired object.
5. Does not participate in "make-believe" play.

The following illustrates the treatment approach Damon received at the Language and Cognitive Development Center (LCDC), in Boston, MA. Although children at LCDC participate in both school classes (limited to six children with three teachers), as well as individual therapies guided by the Center's orientation (cognitive-developmental systems therapy, speech/language therapy, movement and occupational therapies as well as manual arts), for clarity, this discussion relates only to the child's work in cognitive-developmental systems therapy. (A chapter appendix outlines a typical daily curriculum for nonverbal or limited verbal children.) The word "we" refers to all the therapists at the Center who worked with Damon.

Improving Damon's Human Contact

We begin each 45-minute therapy session with about 5 to 10 minutes of big-body work. This entails a combination of pleasurable "rough and tumble" activity, guided bouncing on a trampoline, and swinging him in a sheet. We follow this activity by gentle, mutual face touching coupled with subtle destabilizing (i.e., tugging him front and back and left to right in a way which makes it necessary for him to constantly "right" himself).

Our experience with these procedures is that—when introduced carefully—they result in the child smiling or laughing and in improved eye contact. Then, when certain big body systems (jumping, swinging, "rough and tumble") are abruptly interrupted, the child often indicates by natural signs a wish to continue the activity.

Working with Damon's Perseverative Tendency and Difficulty Following Directions

Following the big body work just described, we introduce Damon to the Elevated Square. Before describing work on the Square, it is important to understand why we used it.

The Elevated Square

The Elevated Square we have designed (see Figure 6) is about 5 feet by 8 feet, with boards about 14 inches wide. The structure is 2½ feet high, which places most 3- to 6-year-old children at or near eye level with most adults. The short side pieces of the square are removable, making it possible for the therapist to stand in the middle in easy reach of the child. Removing the side pieces also creates the conditions in which the child must make a detour in order to get to a person on the opposite side. The steps used with the Elevated Square are attached to each other with Velcro and—because they are designed to fit snugly in the channels of the Elevated Square—are readily used as obstacles or small platforms placed around the square so that the child can respond to "Up!," "Down!," and "Around!," as well as "Get up!" and "Sit down!" Finally, there are stations at each corner of the square, which can be adjusted to the child's height to provide the best possible conditions for effective eye-hand coordination with the various tasks placed on these stations. The last piece of equipment is the slide, which connects to the Square but can be readily removed.

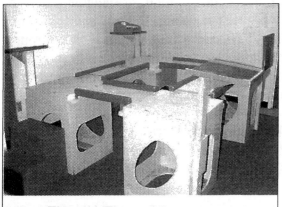

Figure 6. Elevated Square

Placing the child on the Elevated Square effectively limits the child's options for movement because of the constraints the Square places on movement. The Square serves different purposes for different kinds of children. For easily "scattered" children with system-forming disorders, the Square provides the external organization the children desperately require in order to function. However, for children with closed-system disorders, such as Damon, the Square provides the framework in which they can be taught to expand their systems, learn to move from one system to another, and to include people within these systems. Contributing to these changes is the enhanced awareness of body and other that the elevation seems to induce. This changed state is evident not only in the improved eye contact almost immediately evident but in the finding that many children who toe-walk on the ground walk with their feet firmly grounded when elevated.

Working the Short and the Long Sides

Once Damon climbs the steps that places him on top of the Square, we begin a systematic process of both expanding his systems and including people within them. First, a parent is placed at one end of the short side of the Square and a therapist on the other side. The parent is instructed to say "Come!" while using the manual sign (beckoning). The vector of the board, coupled with the parent calling and with the therapist's support, quickly allows Damon to move to his mother. She then briefly hugs him, does mutual face-touching with him, turns him around and directs him toward the therapist, who also says and signs "Come!" Once Damon is responding to "Come!" appropriately, the same procedure is used on the long side of the Square. This continues until Damon can respond to "Come" from mother and therapist from both the short and long distances on the Square.

Chapter 19. The Miller Method®: A Cognitive-Developmental Systems Approach for
Children with Body Organization, Social, and Communication Issues

505

Once Damon develops the appropriate response to a command while on the Square, the next step is for his parents to help him expand his response to their settings. The goal is to get Damon to generalize "Come!" to first short and then longer distances on the ground at both the LCDC and at home until he responds from various distances to everyone in his family.

Turning the Corners

Turning the corners may be difficult for Damon because it requires a sudden shift of direction. However, turning corners to get to a person just around the corner of the Square is an important part of understanding how the body must adjust to changing circumstances. When turning the corner is mastered at one location on the Square, Damon generalizes the skill by performing it at other locations. Successfully coping with corners as well as short and long sides of the Square enables Damon to become quite comfortable working on the Square.

Understanding Detours

Next, Damon is shown how detours work. This is taught by placing Damon on the short side of the Square and removing the short piece. His mother stands on the opposite side and calls and beckons as before. Eventually, Damon, seeing the gap, looks around the Square and then navigates around it until he gets to his mother. In doing so, he demonstrates a beginning understanding of how detours work. He then has to perform detours with others calling him across the gap from both directions and using both short and long sides of the Square.

Using Multispheres to Cope with Damon's Perseverative Tendency

One of Damon's most serious difficulties is his tendency to perseverate with a task, such as lining up blocks, to the exclusion of all else. Once he becomes comfortable with the Elevated Square, we address this issue by setting up a multisphere arrangement designed to reduce Damon's perseverative tendency and to make it possible for him to transition without distress from one system to another.

A sphere is any activity that we introduce repetitively with the expectation that the child will "take it over" and transform it into an internalized system. Therefore, a multisphere setup is one in which the child learns to cope with two, three, or four different spheres. The rationale for the multisphere procedure is that the child perseverates because (a) he lacks knowledge of how to detach from the action-object system, and (b) because the child has no sense of the system's continuing existence once it is left (the "out of sight/out of mind" phenomenon). Based on this rationale, our procedures are designed to teach the child that he can detach from a compelling system and still return to it. The assumption is that by demonstrating this to the child, then the child's perseverative impulse will be attenuated. We do this by first engaging the child in a particular action-object system and then interrupting it by leading the child to a second, then a third, and then a fourth system and repeating the process as follows.

After the child becomes engaged with A—the first sphere (for example, pouring water over a water wheel) —we interrupt this sphere at the point of *maximal tension* (the point at which the child most needs to continue the activity). When this is done, the child experiences—in Lewinian (1935) terms—*a tension state* related to the need to continue that activity. By maintaining that tension state while having the child become engaged with B—a second, entirely different sphere (sending marbles down a zigzag ramp) —the first sphere continues to remain "alive" for the child even while the child becomes engaged by the second sphere. (It is this duality of experience that begins to make it possible for the child to relate and soon easily shift from one sphere or station to another.) After a number of cycles involving two (AB), then three (ABC, hanging up cups), and four (ABCD, cutting clay) spheres, the child begins to demonstrate by glancing at the different spheres a sense of *possible* relations between them. After a few sessions, he is no longer distressed when one sphere is interrupted because he understands that he will soon return to it.

But merely being able to shift clockwise from A to B to C to D spheres—although important—is not sufficient for Damon to cope flexibly with his surroundings. At this point, we begin to vary the stations. In other words, after A, Damon expects to move from A to B. Instead, Damon—clearly unhappy—is guided past Station B to Station C. This process is continued over a number of sessions until Damon can tolerate shifts from one station to another in all possible combinations—ACBD, DBAC, and so on.

Once Damon can cope with shifting in all possible combinations on the Elevated Square, stations are shifted to the ground. Here, without the support of the Square, Damon generalizes his new ability to shift to various stations set up on the ground. After Damon masters this sequence, he is placed in a position where he can scan all the stations. He is then asked to choose which one he wishes to go to. When he can express a preference for one system over another by pointing, sign, or word, we have evidence of the emergence of new executive functioning.

Developing Damon's Language

Receptive Language

Damon, as described earlier, is "word deaf," which means that it is not possible to guide his behavior solely by using words. He will do better when spoken words are paired with signs, as do most nonverbal children on the autistic spectrum (Konstantareas, 1984; Konstantareas, Oxman, & Webster, 1977; Miller & Miller, 1973).

To increase Damon's capacity to respond to spoken words, we follow the principle of inclusion described earlier under "Defining Central Concepts." By repeating the appropriate word while Damon is performing the relevant action, he soon includes both word and manual sign as part of his action system. We use this technique with the words "Up!," "Down!," "Push!," "Pull!," and "Around!," followed by "Pick up!," "Drop!," "Pour!" and many others. For example, as Damon steps up on the block in his path, we say "Up!" while pointing upward. We continue in similar fashion with Damon's *pushing* and *pulling* actions. Each time that Damon performs the action we also *narrate* what he is doing by saying, "Damon is pushing (going up, down, etc.)."

We support Damon's behavior by using a vocal tone that expresses the delight we feel at the child's performance. We find this affective narration to be far more relevant to the development of the child's receptive language than using the term "Good job!," with its doubtful meaning to the child.

In developing receptive language, we find it important to gain a clear sense of the extent to which the child is guided by just the spoken word in contrast to the word in context. In doing so, we:
- Determine if the child can give an object to us when it is right in front of us and we tap an extended hand while saying, "Give!"
- Determine if the child can retrieve a designated object in plain sight some 8 to 10 feet away.
- Determine if the child can bring a familiar object (out of sight) from an adjacent room after we designate that object.

Chapter 19. The Miller Method®: A Cognitive-Developmental Systems Approach for Children with Body Organization, Social, and Communication Issues

507

- Determine if the child can bring a familiar object (out of sight) from an *unusual* location in another room (e.g., "Bring shoe on kitchen table!").
- Place two familiar objects, one in front of the other, directly in front of the child. We then ask the child for the object farthest from him. The child who is word-guided will succeed; the child who is still guided more by context will incorrectly select the closest object to the examiner (Vygotsky, 1962).

Developing Expressive Language from Systems

Before expressive language can develop to any extent, a child such as Damon must first solve the problem of including people within his systems. This is because communication requires the ability to relate to another around a third entity, such as an object, event or person that becomes the "conversation piece." Often, we see children able to relate to their parents *or* to objects but not to both at the same time

The capacity for communication is developing when reciprocal games (such as the swinging ball) become possible or at the earliest level, when the small child at 9 or 10 months of age finds it possible to give an object on request (Trevarthen & Hubley, 1979).

A second important precursor of communication is the child's understanding that her actions are influential. In other words, that she can cause things to happen first with hands, then with tools that extend the reach of hands, then by gestures that simulate actions, and finally by spoken words. All the action systems developed on the Elevated Square and on the ground provide a basis for eliciting expressive signs and words from Damon and others like him. However, before the action system can be used in this way it is desirable to expand all the systems so that

they are not limited to one context. To do this we make certain that Damon performs an activity with different *people*, in different *locations*, with different *objects*, presented in different *positions*.[2]

It is also desirable to expand from simple minisystems to more complex integrative systems. Once this is accomplished, we can systematically begin to interrupt the system at different points to elicit the signs and words that previously have been introduced with the system. For example, suppose Damon has to *pick up* a box to get a marble to send *down* a ramp. We stop the marble midway down the ramp, inducing Damon to say or sign, "Go!" After such integrative setups are repeated several times, we can then selectively stall (interrupt) at key places to elicit the signs or words the child needs to produce to have the system continue. For example, by preventing the child from lifting the box, the child must sign or say, "Pick up!" Or, after repeatedly opening a box with the word and sign for "open," we interrupt the system by holding the box closed and, in doing so, elicit from the child the word or sign "Open!"

Another important strategy used when the child is responding very well to the sign and word "Come!" entails having the child sit on a box in the middle of the short end of the Square with a therapist behind him, while the mother stands at the other end of the Square (opened to accommodate her). Then, we help the child make the *come* sign, beckoning the mother to move toward him. Mother is instructed to take one step each time her child makes the *come* sign. Often, suddenly, the child becomes aware of the influential nature

---

[2] We are indebted to Dr. Louise Ross for the acronym "PLOP" to remind staff to perform **P**osition, **L**ocation, **O**bject, and **P**erson expansions with each developing system.

of his *come* sign and will repeat it rapidly to bring mother swiftly toward him. The contagious excitement that goes with this often elicits the vocalized word, "Come!"

Supplementing the work on the Elevated Square is work with the Sign and Spoken Language Program (SSLP), which presents real-life situations of children running, jumping, and performing other activities interspersed with signs that closely resemble these activities. Children sitting around the television monitor are guided in the use of signs in the context of the videos. They then have the opportunity to use the signs with teachers, parents, and the other children. An example of one such sign from the SSLP may be seen in Figure 7.

Teaching Order for Developing Communication Using the Miller Method

The following outline summarizes the manner in which we work to help the children learn to communicate:

1. *Teaching action words related to self and others.*
   (a) Begin receptively by having the child learn to respond to certain imperative signed and

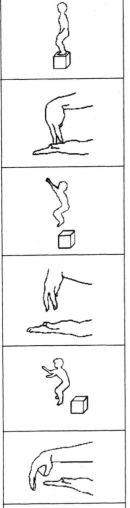

Figure 7. Videotape sequencing of a child jumping and the signs for "jump."

spoken directions: "Come!," "Stop!," "Get up!," and "Sit down!" The child's capacity to respond immediately to "Come!" and "Stop!" can be a matter of survival.

   (b) Transform receptive sign-words to expressive. After the child understands two or three action sign-words, we help the child use them expressively with others. It is desirable to do this early on so that the child learns that not only do these sign-words compel her to respond, they also can be used to "compel" a response in others. If a child is having trouble using signs expressively (and it does not seem to be a motor-based problem), it may be because the child does not yet understand the influential power of signs. Introducing more causal experiences can be helpful. Parents should be encouraged to find dramatic cause-and-effect toys and to work with their child in using them. Providing the child with many opportunities to experience the self as agent can prepare the way for the child to use sign-words to effect a desired response in others.

2. *Teaching objects and the sign-words that designate them.* The child must learn to designate objects both close to his body and at a distance. To achieve the latter, the child must learn how to scan; that is, to distinguish the desired object from an array of competitive objects and stimuli.
   (a) Begin by using engaging objects close to the child's body. Engage the child with objects that lead to action-object systems and use sounds and intonation both to draw the child's attention to the object and to enrich

Chapter 19. The Miller Method®: A Cognitive-Developmental Systems Approach for
Children with Body Organization, Social, and Communication Issues

509

the action-object system (e.g., "Rrrm-car" or "Car-rrrm").

Narrate the sequence while and just after the child performs the activity; fo example, "Damon sends car down!" We teach the child to differentiate sequences: Car-down-ramp vs. ball in bucket vs. ring on pole, and so forth. Having differentiated one sign-word-action sequence from another, the child can follow spoken and signed directions appropriately.

Have the child use sign-words to designate different people. Each person working with the child should have their own unique sign paired with their name. The child should also have access to a full-face, 8-by-11 inch picture of each person to assist the child with recall in the person's absence and to help with syntax development.

(b) Teach objects, and the sign/words that designate them, away from the child's body. The strategy is aimed at getting the child to differentiate a distant object from its surrounding field by pointing at it, touching it with a long stick, snaring it, or by squirting water at it with a squirt bottle. The use of sticks or squirting may be thought of as preliminary steps toward perceptually "holding" the object by pointing and, eventually, by designating it via sign-word or picture.

In teaching objects at a distance, we use objects that already have been part of minisystems. By removing an object from a well-established system, we induce an interrupted system that can only be completed by the child acquiring the object part of that system. For example, if the child has been pumping water into a cup, then the cup should be one of the distant objects.

(c) At home, parents or caregivers should use the same principle of narration and interrupted systems to develop object awareness and designation. For example, the spoon required to eat dessert may be located on the wall, a missing shoe can be located on top of a bureau and so forth. We have parents do scavenger hunts with their child. The parents should help their child find various objects (a rusty bolt, a hairpin, a washer, or empty candy box), point at and name them, put them in a sack or other container, and bring them home. At home, they should pour out the contents on a table, examine them together, talk about them, and mount them on boards for future reference.

(d) The parents should perform adjunct procedures for building vocabulary. The parents can videotape their child in action. For example, as he loads a wagon or wheelbarrow, pulls/pushes it to another site, and dumps out the cargo; climbs monkey bars or swings on a swing; pushes a cart in the grocery store; or rides a tricycle. They can narrate what the child is doing, interrupting periodically to see if the child contributes a sign or word. If possible, they should encourage the child to simulate the videotaped activity with miniature toys.

3. *Moving the child toward the naming insight* (Miller & Eller-Miller, 1989). Although we cannot guarantee that a child will achieve the notion that each thing has its name and that the name is actually a category for all things that have those particular properties, we can facilitate the likelihood of the child gaining this insight. One way of doing this is to teach

the critical properties of certain objects on the Elevated Square.

For example, to teach the properties of cup, at one station we have the child place cups on hooks (accenting the handle of the cup); at a second station, we have the child stack cups (accenting their contours); and at a third station, we have the child pour water in and then out of a series of cups (accenting their water-holding property). In a similar fashion, we can teach that a ball is an object that can be thrown, caught, bounced, rolled, placed in a container, and so forth. Each varied use of the object is, of course, accompanied by its sign and name. As children learn the multiple properties of each object subsumed under a unique name, they internalize the criteria for that object to be generalized. In other words, even if a cup or ball has unusual characteristics, if the essential properties are present they may be able to identify it as belonging to the cup or ball category. When children can do this with a number of common objects, they often achieve the generalization that each thing has its own name.

4. *Developing syntax.* It is often a challenge to help children who have single signs or spoken words move toward functional syntax. Recently, we have developed effective procedures for achieving this with the help of sign-morphs and pictures. The sign-morphs are cards that, when held at a certain angle, produce an action sign in motion. By tilting the card, the child sees the manual sign for "push" in action, the sign for "jump" seems to jump, the "break" sign makes a breaking motion, and so forth. Since the children are already familiar with these signs from the SSLP and from daily use in class and in therapy sessions, it is not difficult for

them to correctly identify the signs. Then, to teach subject plus verb sequences, we pair a full-face picture of the child with the sign-morph and require the child to perform the appropriate action.

(a) For example, a picture of Damon plus sign-morph for "jump" requires Damon to jump. Then pictures of mother, teacher, or therapist are substituted and placed next to the sign-morph so that Damon expects others to perform the action. We followed this procedure with a range of sign-morphs until the notion is well established that changing the picture next to the sign-morph induces that person to perform the action.

(b) Once the child fully understands subject plus verb sequences (step one), we shift the emphasis to sign-morph plus noun (step two). For example, we follow the sign-morph for "pour" with either a picture of water or rice. The child demonstrates her understanding of the verb plus noun relation by selecting and pouring the correct material from the bottle.

(c) The final step in this process is when the child understands subject plus verb plus noun sentences. We teach this by combining strategies from steps one and two. Once the children have internalized this assisted procedure for developing syntax, we find that many can eventually use it spontaneously without picture or sign-morph support.

Providing the Necessary Transitions from Concrete to Symbolic Functioning

Many children with developmental issues—but particularly children on the autistic spectrum—require assistance to achieve

Chapter 19. The Miller Method®: A Cognitive-Developmental Systems Approach for
Children with Body Organization, Social, and Communication Issues

511

symbolic functioning. Often, for example, there is little evidence of symbolic play, as was the case with Damon. However, we can encourage such play by providing a careful transition from a real-life experience a child has just had to a comparable play experience that relates directly to the real-life situation. We find that we can often induce symbolic play by first having a child perform certain acts on the Elevated Square and then introducing the child to a miniature Elevated Square with dolls. Observing the miniature Square, a number of children have spontaneously moved a doll figure in the same way they have just moved on the large Elevated Square.

Similar transitions may be made for those children who have learned to speak in two- to three-word sentences but who seem stymied when they first confront the arbitrary forms of printed words and are asked by teachers and parents to attribute specific object meanings to these forms. Just as some children have difficulty with the shift from object to picture, so others have difficulty with the shift from picture to printed word. Assisting children with this transition requires another set of strategies.

We derived these strategies from the observation that, unlike the iconic relation between picture and object, the forms of printed words do not resemble their referents. Therefore, before many children can understand that a printed word may convey the meaning of an object to which it bears no resemblance, they require an interim means of investing printed words with object meaning. In a series of experiments, we demonstrated that children previously unable to find meaning in printed words could do so when provided a transition from picture to printed word (Miller & Miller, 1968, 1971). This was first accomplished by having pictures of objects fused with the printed word on one side of a flash card that could be flipped to

the other side, revealing the word in its conventional form (Figure 8). Subsequently, even very delayed children could recognize the meaning of the printed word.

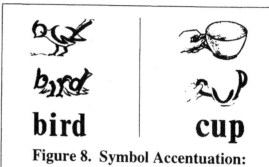

**Figure 8. Symbol Accentuation:
Picture-to-Word Transition**

These procedures have been developed further in the Symbol Accentuation Reading Program (Miller, 1968/1996) so that, with the help of animation to make the transition from picture to printed words and from mouth movements to letters (Figure 9), many children with disorders who were previously unable to read and write have learned to do so.

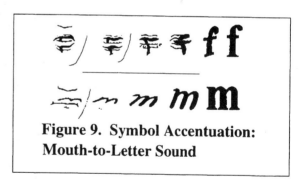

**Figure 9. Symbol Accentuation:
Mouth-to-Letter Sound**

SUMMARY

This chapter described the Miller Method in detail, including its basic concepts and its principles of assessment and intervention. It also presented a case study of a 3-year-old boy on the autistic spectrum to illustrate how this method can be used to improve poor human contact, decrease perseverative tendencies, develop receptive and expressive language, and engage a child in symbolic functioning (or "pretend play"). Our experience suggests that there are five general factors that play a role in determining how successful the Miller Method will be for a child. These are:

1. *The child's age* (younger children tend to do better than older);

2. *Neurological status* (those without cortical insult or seizure disorders do better);

3. *The child's relationship with his parents* (those with a bond with at least one parent do better than those who have no such bond);

4. *System characteristics* (those with closed-system disorders progress more rapidly than those with system-forming disorders); and

5. *Support demand stance* (parents with a high support/high demand stance have children who progress more rapidly than those who have high support/low demand stance).

Beyond these general impressions, we find that highly motivated families who "live" the program by implementing it in their homes and who form a close alliance with the therapeutic staff frequently have children who make unexpectedly strong gains. ■

Chapter 19. The Miller Method®: A Cognitive-Developmental Systems Approach for
Children with Body Organization, Social, and Communication Issues

513

REFERENCES

Cook, C. (1998). The Miller Method: A case study illustrating use of the approach with children with autism in an interdisciplinary setting. *Journal of Developmental and Learning Disorders, 2*, 231-264.

Goldstein, K. (1939). *The organism: A holistic approach to biology.* New York: American Book.

Greenspan, S. I. (1998). Personal Communication.

Greenspan, S. I., & Wieder, S. (1998). *The child with special needs: Encouraging intellectual and emotional growth.* Reading, MA: Addison Wesley Longman.

Greenspan, S. I., & Wieder, S. (2000). Developmentally appropriate interactions and practices. In S. I. Greenspan (Ed.) *The Interdisciplinary Council on Developmental and Learning Disorders' clinical practice guidelines* (Chap. 12). Bethesda, MD: Interdisciplinary Council on Developmental and Learning Disorders.

Konstantareas, M. M., Oxman, J., & Webster, C. D. (1977). Simultaneous communication with autistic and other severely dysfunctional nonverbal children. *Journal of Communication Disorders, 10*, 267-282

Konstantareas, M. M. (1984). Sign language as a communication prosthesis with language-impaired children. *Journal of Autism and Developmental Disorders, 17*(1), 115-131.

Lewin, K. (1935). *Dynamic theory of personality.* New York: McGraw-Hill.

Messier, L. P. (1970). *Effects of reading instruction by symbol accentuation on disadvantaged children.* Unpublished doctoral dissertation, Boston University, Boston.

Miller, A. (1963). Verbal satiation and the role of concurrent activity. *Journal of Abnormal and Social Psychology, 3*, 206-212.

Miller, A. (1968). Symbol Accentuation: Outgrowth of theory and experiment (symposium paper). In the *Proceedings of the First International Congress for the Scientific Study of Mental Deficiency, Montpellier, France* (pp. 766-772). Surrey, England: Michael Jackson Publishers.

Miller, A. (1991). Cognitive-developmental systems theory in pervasive developmental disorders. In J. Beitchman & M. Konsstantareas (Eds.), *Psychiatric clinics of North America (Vol. 14): Pervasive developmental disorders* (pp. 141-161). Saunders Press.

Miller, A., & Miller, E. E. (1968). Symbol accentuation: The perceptual transfer of meaning from spoken to written words. *American Journal of Mental Deficiency, 73*, 200-208.

Miller, A., & Miller, E. E. (1971). Symbol accentuation: Single-track functioning and early reading. *American Journal of Mental Deficiency*, 110-117.

Miller, A., & Miller, E. E. (1973). Cognitive-developmental training with elevated boards and sign language. *Journal of Autism and Childhood Schizophrenia, 3*, 65-85.

Miller, A., & Eller-Miller, E., (1989). *From ritual to repertoire: A cognitive-developmental systems approach with behavior-disordered children.* New York: Wiley & Sons.

Pavlov, I. P. (1927). *Conditional reflexes: An investigation of the psychological activity of the cerebral cortex.* Oxford: Oxford University Press.

Piaget, J. (1948). *Language and thought of the child.* London: Routledge and Kegan Paul.

Piaget, J. (1954). *The construction of reality in the child.* New York: Basic Books.

Piaget, J. (1962). *Play, dreams and imitation in childhood.* New York: Norton.

Sokolov, Y. N. (1963). *Perception and the conditioned reflex.* New York: MacMillan.

Trevarthen, C., & Hubley, P. (1979). Secondary intersubjectivity: Confidence, confiding, and acts of meaning in the first year of life. In A. Locke (Ed.), *Action, gesture, and symbol* (pp. 83-229). London: Academic Press.

Uexkull, J. von (1934, 1957). A stroll through the worlds of animals and men. In Claire Schiller (Ed.), *Instinctive behavior*. New York: International Universities Press.

von Bertalanffy, L. (1968). *Organismic psychology and systems theory*. Clark University Press with Barre Publishers.

Vygotsky, L. S. (1962). *Thought and language*. Cambridge, MA: The MIT Press.

Warr-Leeper, G. A., Henry, S. L., & Lomas, T. C. (in press). The effects of Miller Method intervention on functional communication: Multiple case studies for children with severe communication disorders and hearing impairments. Submitted for publication in the *Journal of Developmental and Learning Disorders*.

Werner, H. (1948). *Comparative psychology of mental development*. Chicago: Follett.

Werner, H., & Kaplan, B. (1963). *Symbol formation: An organismic developmental approach to language and the expression of thought*. New York: Wiley & Sons.

Chapter 19. The Miller Method®: A Cognitive-Developmental Systems Approach for
Children with Body Organization, Social, and Communication Issues

515

Appendix

LANGUAGE AND COGNITIVE DEVELOPMENT CENTER TYPICAL DAILY CURRICULUM FOR NONVERBAL OR LIMITED-VERBAL CHILDREN

Time	Activity	Areas Developed
8:30 am	*Orienting:* Handing over the child Massage/compression with voice modulation Rough-and-tumble and selective tickling Narrating and predicting imminent events Reciprocal touching, exploration and part naming Tableau calendar for structured transitions	Interaction Body awareness Body awareness Communication Interaction Interaction
9:00 am	*From One-on-One to Group:* Circle spheres- contagious activity with teachers and children. ("This is the way we pat our head [rub nose, run, walk, jump, fall, stamp feet]," etc.)	Interaction Body awareness Communication
9:30 am	*Sign and Spoken Language Program:* Training Film I (action signs/words: *walk, run, jump, fall, come, go, stop*, etc–receptive and expressive). Generalizing action concepts to other settings.	Communication Interaction
10:00 am	Toileting/washing	Coping
10:20 am	*Snack Time:* Child uses signs/words *give, pour, eat, cookie, drink, spoon, fork*, etc., for desired objects/events	Coping Communication
10:40 am	*Elevated Board Spheres:* Using Bridge or Template Tunnel and combined board structures including Grand Central sphere. Using multiple orienting to revitalize an inert system.	Body efficacy/awareness Interaction Coping
	Reciprocal Spheres:	
11:15 am	Using Traveler with terms *push, open, pick up, close*	Interact/communication
11:45 am	Reciprocal ball pushing sphere	
12:00	Lunch	Interaction
12:30 pm	Rest Period	
1:00 pm	*Cooperative Building Spheres:* Boards to build large and small Velcro house Cooperative repair of Broken Table and Chair	Coping Coping Interaction
1:30 pm	*C-D Art Program:* Repetitive circles, lines and dots as minispheres and integrative spheres	Representation
2:00 pm	*Symbolic Play Spheres:* Using Elevated board replicas (small) with dolls	Representation

All children in this category will spend at least 30 minutes each day working on elevated board structures as part of a class of five or six children with three teachers. In addition, each child in the non- or limited-verbal category is scheduled for 45 minutes each week with a therapist and a parent in cognitive-developmental systems therapy, which typically involves work on the Elevated Square. Children also have access to speech and language therapy, occupational therapy, movement therapy, adaptive physical education, and manual arts during the course of the week.

◄ 20 ►

Visual-Spatial Thinking

Harry Wachs, O.D.

THE THEORETICAL BASIS OF VISUAL-COGNITIVE INTELLIGENCE

Jean Piaget and Hans Furth subdivided intelligence into three categories: (1) biological intelligence (Furth's term), (2) sensorimotor intelligence, and (3) operational intelligence (Furth, 1986).[1] Biological intelligence is prewired in utero and is manifest after birth in the form of developmental reflexes. Sensorimotor intelligence can be referred to as "action knowing," and continues throughout adult life. When Piaget discovered object permanence (which occurs developmentally in a child around 2 years of age and involves the ability to do things at a mental level—"in the child's head"—rather than solely to know them through physical action), he became more fascinated and involved with what he termed operational intelligence. Although Piaget delved very little into sensorimotor intelligence beyond object permanence, he did not imply that sensorimotor intelligence stopped at object permanence. Operational intelligence can be described as reasoning or thinking by a child, which usually starts around age 2 and matures around ages 5 to 7, but continues to be embellished throughout life.

To these three categories, Furth and I added a fourth—*body and sense thinking*—to describe sensorimotor development in a child

between the ages of approximately 2 and 7 years of age (Furth & Wachs, 1974). Extending Piaget's theory from object permanence through concrete operations—the period when a person can use reasoning to tap sensorimotor intelligence—the term describes the child's ability to apply reasoning to sensorimotor experiences once the child can mentally manipulate his or her visual-spatial world. During this period, the child's action knowing can be enhanced by reasoning or operatory thought.

Piaget's theory can be applied to all individuals, impaired or nonimpaired. Its application includes the autistic spectrum, from pervasive developmental disorder (PDD) to severe autism, as well as attention deficit disorder (ADD) and the more common learning disabilities (LD) and dyslexia (Wachs, 1980, Vol. 2, pp. 51-78). In my research on the application of Piagetian theory, I have worked with children from Europe, Asia, and North and South America, as well as with many indigenous groups—Africans, South American Indians, Bedouins, Aborigines, Eskimos, Native Americans, mestizos, and hill tribes in Thailand—with similar results on sensorimotor and body and sense thinking tasks.

---

[1]The term "operational" describes intelligence, whereas the act of doing something operational is described as "operatory."

The word "intelligence" is often misused in common speech, as in statements like "Scott is intelligent" or "Cathy is not very intelligent." In fact, "intelligent" should not be used to describe a person, but rather what a person does or is involved in. "Scott is doing this intelligently" would be a better use of the word.

This chapter deals with visual and spatial intelligence and spans the child's development from birth to approximately age 7. All the developmental visual-cognitive hallmarks are stages of growth and should not be misconstrued as age-related norms (Wachs & Vaughn, 1977). Some children with special needs have difficulty developing intellectually, even up to the level of an average 7-year-old. A negative outcome, however, should not be assumed, as I have seen many children develop far beyond their prognoses. A distorted body does not necessarily imply a distorted mind.[2]

Furth and I have coordinated our work to follow the general principles of Piaget's constructivist theory in both diagnosis and intervention. For all children, especially those with special needs, we assign tasks chosen from a repertoire of probes and interventions designed to diagnose, elicit, and foster cognitive understanding. All our probes and interventions are hierarchically based. They are not designed solely to achieve the "right answer" from the child, but rather to lead the child to construct cognitive understanding by developmentally raising or lowering the demands of the tasks.

The following brief outline lays out our developmental approach for developing the visual-spatial aspects of body and sense intelligence:

I. General Movement
- Reflexes (e.g., obligatory arm movements when head or feet move)

- Mental map of body (e.g., awareness of joints and body dimensions)
- Integration of body sections (e.g., creeping-crawling, "angels in the snow")
- Integration of body axes (e.g., rolling, bimanual circles on chalkboard)
- Rhythm (e.g., moving or tapping body parts to the accompaniment of a metronome)
- Coordinated actions (e.g., skipping, hopping, jumping rope)

II. Discriminative Movement
- Fingers (e.g., crumpling or tearing paper)
- Eyes (e.g., focusing, tracking, fixating on an object)
- Lip, tongue, and vocal chords (e.g., tongue motility, making funny faces, gargling)

III. Visual Thinking
A. *Matching* (e.g., household items, blocks, pegs)
  - Coincident (reconstructing a given model with some part of each block touching other blocks)
  - Separated (matching items spread apart)
  - Negative space (placing items in spaces purposely not filled in)
  - Recalling (reconstructing a given model in a distant part of the room)

B. *Transposition* (coordinated with body axes)
  - Horizontal (toward and away)
  - Vertical (right and left)
  - Transverse (rotations)

---

[2] In this context, see Furth, H. (1991). Life's essential: The story of mind over body. *Human Development,* for a discussion of the 1989 memoirs of Ruth Sienkiewicz-Mercer.

- Analysis (determining how a given design was transposed)
- Positions (constructing from a different viewpoint; that is, north, south, northeast, etc.)

"Vision" is another misused word. A parent who says, "My child's vision is 20/20," really should be saying, "My child's *sight* is 20/20." The difference is tremendous. We look with our eyes (looking); we see with our brains (sight); and we understand with our minds (vision). Here is where Piagetian theory is so valuable. Piaget's theory of constructivism holds that knowledge is not neurally constructed; instead, neural connections are built through mental constructs. In other words, the retina and the brain are used to construct, not evoke, new knowledge.

Piaget's theory of sensorimotor intelligence lays the foundation for visual intelligence. The determining factor for visual intelligence is not what passes through the eye but rather what a person can understand from a particular visual experience and eventually coordinate with other aspects of body and sense thinking. Thus, a partially sighted child may have well-developed visual intelligence and a child with acute 20/20 sight may have poorly developed visual intelligence. The foundation for visual intelligence is developed through sensorimotor intelligence in the first few years of a child's life, even during the neonatal period when the child is nonmobile. This does not imply that visual intelligence cannot be developed in the movement-impaired child, but rather that the more developed the child's movement (or sensorimotor) intelligence, the better the opportunity for the child to develop visual intelligence. In addition, even in the nonmotorically impaired child, a lack of movement intelligence development could confuse and inhibit the development of visual intelligence. My experience has shown that most children with cerebral palsy have inadequate

visual intelligence, and also that many children with inadequate visual intelligence have inadequate movement intelligence, despite being neurologically intact (Fraiberg, 1977).

DEVELOPMENTAL REFLEXES

For biological intelligence, Furth uses the phrase "biological knowledge" to describe the intelligence the child is born with. Modern neuroscientists refer to this knowledge as "pre-wiring," observable in the many developmental reflexes in a healthy, intact newborn (Goddard, 1996). Clinical experience has shown that the existence of these primitive reflexes can inhibit sensorimotor function and that removal of the reflex obligatory responses actually can aid the efficiency of such sensorimotor functions as ocular motility and general body motility.

British neuropsychologist Peter Blythe has made an exhaustive study on the diagnosis and treatment of such reflexes sustained beyond their useful years (Blythe, 1990; personal communications with H. Wachs, 1995-1999). His work shows that children who retain primitive reflexes often show the following dysfunctional traits (this list is not all-inclusive and does not imply that primitive reflexes are the sole factors involved):

- Rigidity of movement
- Poor handwriting
- Gaps in athletic performance, especially in throwing or catching
- Clumsiness
- Bumping into things
- Dis-coordination
- Poor ocular tracking
- Poor rhythm
- Difficulty in showing usual expected response to intervention procedures

Though I have not been trained in Blythe's methods, I have incorporated three

Tables 1A. Primitive Reflexes Adopted into Vision and Conceptual Development Theory

Table 1A. Feet

Observed Reflex	Diagnostic Procedure	Clinical Picture, if Sustained	Clinical Picture, if Reabsorbed
FEET (exact origin still undetermined, possibly caused by the amphibian, labyrinthine, or Moro reflex)	Stand erect, hands hanging by side. Turn feet inward in "pigeon-toed" position, then outward in "Charley Chaplin" position.	With feet pointing inward, the child thrusts elbows and arms backward in "scarecrow" position, hands rotated with palms facing away from body. With feet pointing outward, the child moves elbows toward body and rotates hands so that palms face forward. Thus any movement of feet triggers an obligatory movement of arms. This could be very confusing and disturbing, especially to an already confused child.	The child does not move arms in either feet position, even when marching in place.

NOTE: Some individuals have such severe gaps in sensorimotor development that they are unable to rotate their feet in either one direction or both directions. These individuals require specific therapy procedures (see treatment section for more information). Other individuals show no reflexive arm movement until asked to turn their feet in or out while marching in place and swinging their arms accordingly. The sustained reflex inhibits and sometimes actually stops the arm movements. I am presently treating a young Mennonite child in rural Maryland who is so reflex-bound that every time she attempts to turn her feet inward, even when seated, her left arm shoots straight up in the air. How can she possibly participate successfully in daily activities at home and in school?

Table 1B. Asymmetric and Symmetric Tonic Neck Reflexes

Observed Reflex	Diagnostic Procedure	Clinical Picture, if Sustained	Clinical Picture, if Reabsorbed
Asymmetric Tonic Neck Reflex (ATNR)*	With hands and knees on the floor in a creeping position and head hanging downward, rotate head right and left.	Elbow on opposite body side of head rotation bends; i.e., rotate head to right and left elbow bends, etc. Occasionally only one side is affected.	Neither elbow bends.
Symmetric Tonic Neck Reflex (STNR)**	Ask child to get down on hands and knees (or place child in creeping position), and to drop head downward. Repeat, alternately raising and lowering head. This could cause poor posture, with all its visceral and skeletal problems, or dysfunctional results when working at a desk or reading in a chair.	Sitting back on heels indicates retention of STNR. Collapse (flex) of elbows and/or humping of back when head is lowered (and collapse of back when head is raised) indicate existence of STNR. Elbows collapse Back sags Back arches Sitting on heels	Back stays straight; elbows do not bend.

* An occupational therapist (OT) told me that she felt the ATNR was responsible for some auto accidents. The driver's head turned to the right caused flexion of the left arm and the resultant swerving of the car.
** Imagine trying to learn to swim, ski, or play a sport if your symmetric tonic neck reflex is severe and inhibitory.

of the primitive reflexes identified by him and some of his teachings in my therapy procedures. Tables 1A and 1B list the identifying features (diagnostic procedure) of each reflex and its clinical picture if sustained or reabsorbed as a result of therapy.

Treatment for Children Who Retain Primitive Reflexes

My approach to therapy for children who retain the reflexes just described is twofold. I have the child (1) work through sensorimotor experiences that in normal development precede cessation of the reflex and (2) participate in sensorimotor experiences that contradict the obligatory movements of the reflex in question.

For step 1, my therapists and I use such early sensorimotor experiences as rolling, crawling and "starfish." Starfish is a simulated in utero procedure borrowed from Peter Blythe in which the child, in a sitting position, first crosses the right leg over the left leg and the right arm over the left arm, with body and head leaning forward. The child maintains this position for a count of ten. The child then thrusts both arms and legs apart and leans body and head backward, again for a count of ten. The child repeats this two-step procedure several times, alternating right over left and left over right (Blythe, 1990).

For step 2, we use animal walks (e.g., bear walk, crab walk, duck walk, inchworm, crawling on the belly) to contradict the FEET and ATNR reflexes. In each of these actions, the hands and feet must coordinate, though they each play an independent but supportive role in the activity. The wall walk and feet-in-and-out have also proved helpful in eliminating the FEET reflex. In the wall walk, the child stands more than an arm's length from a wall, the distance forcing a stretch to reach the wall. With feet stationary, the child walks both hands up

and down the wall, as high and as low as possible. The wall-walking procedures can be made more complex by having the child

- place hands alternately on either side of a vertical line,
- move hands rhythmically to a metronome,
- turn hands and feet outward and inward opposite to the assumed position of the feet reflex, and
- turn the head right and left opposite to the ATNR.

For treatment to eliminate the symmetric tonic neck reflex, I use two procedures adopted from yoga practice. In the "turtle," the child sits erect on heels with toes bent under, hands resting on thighs, and back straight. After staying in this position for a count of five, the child leans forward and, supported by the arms, straightens toes (toenails toward the floor) and again sits back on heels with arms resting in the lap for a count of five. The child then grasps the back of the neck with both hands and tucks the head downward between knees, again for a count of five. This is repeated several times. In the yoga technique of "cat and cow," the child—on hands and knees—tucks head down and between arms while arching the back upward, and then bends head backward and arches back downward. This, too, is repeated several times. Eventually, the child performs this procedure rapidly and vigorously.

Readers can add to these examples of treatment activities or use them to build procedures of their own. After the child is free from obligatory reflex movement, the therapist can employ procedures to construct sensorimotor knowledge that will eventually lead to the child's spatial knowledge of the construction of his own body. This is known as endogenous spatial constructs, and is analogous to the knowledge of a car's construction that is required by a person to parallel park the car (Furth & Wachs, 1974, pp. 71-110).

SENSORIMOTOR

My format for addressing sensorimotor growth and endogenous spatial constructs leading to exogenous spatial constructs follows a proven hierarchical developmental plan:

1. Developmental absorption of primitive reflexes
2. Mental map of the body
3. Integration of body sections
4. Rhythm
5. Coordination of body axes
6. Coordination of body actions

Occupational therapy procedures are a valuable adjunct to movement development prior to the body and sense activities just listed. Occupational therapy should be used for children with vestibular (balance) needs and lack of motility or muscle joint adequacy (Furth & Wachs, 1974, pp. 94-107). Perceptual-motor procedures are also a valuable adjunct at the level of coordinated actions. Ocular, digital, and oral discriminative movements also play important roles in spatial constructs in that each has a component of right-left, up-down, and forwards-backwards. This discussion, however, relates only to ocular discriminative movement.

Before discussing interventions for sensorimotor growth, it is necessary to clarify the major difference between development and externally imposed learning. Development implies new mental constructs leading to Piaget's object concepts (mental awareness of an item in the absence of that item) (Ginsberg & Opper, 1979). Externally imposed learning could be conceptual if it were based on solid mental constructs, or solely content learned if the child did not have the prior mental constructs to understand that which was being taught. Children with special needs are particularly prone to such memorized or rote learning. Excessive content learning can actually thwart development and make intervention more difficult because such rote learning encourages the child to memorize and not search for understanding.

The following traits can be observed in children with gaps in sensorimotor development:

- Clumsiness
- Bumping into things
- Inability to ride a bicycle
- Inability to skip
- Poor performance in sports
- Inability to catch or throw, or awkwardness or poor institution of these actions
- Poor handwriting
- Tendency to lose place when reading or when switching fixation from far to near
- Carsickness, especially in the back of a car
- Preference for verbal or manual activities
- Difficulty using scissors
- Difficulty staying within borders—coloring or walking
- Difficulty drawing geometric forms
- Moving of head rather than eyes
- Inability to maintain personal space

The next section briefly discusses probes and interventions for gaps in body and sense thinking, which could well be the cause of the preceding traits.

GENERAL MOVEMENT

Mental Map of Body

The body is a physical construction in which the person resides. The person, or the self, is that unique property that characterizes one as an individual. At death, the person leaves; but the body, as a construction, remains. The person has to develop an understanding of the width, height, and breadth of the body, as well as its hinges and rotary components. Mobility through space requires knowledge of the extensions and limitations of the spatial components of the body, just as parallel parking requires knowledge of the extensions and limitations of the spatial components of a vehicle. Any dysfunctional movement warrants suspicion of an inadequate mental map of the body. A therapist can determine if a child has an adequate mental map of the body through the following probes (Furth & Wachs, 1974, pp. 77-83).

Mental Map of Body Probes

Body lifts. The child lies prone (face down) on the floor, feet extended and arms at sides on the floor. The therapist touches each of the child's limb individually; then two limbs of the same side of the body; then two limbs on opposite sides of the body; then three; then in sequence; then in sequence asking for a response in reverse order; then touching specific parts such as shoulder or elbows; and so on. If the child does not respond while in a prone position, the therapist starts with the child in a supine position (face up), but switches the child to a prone position as soon as possible.

Observations:
- Does the child move only the limb that is touched?
- When the lower leg is touched, does the child lift the whole leg?
- When the elbow is touched, does the child raise the whole arm?
- When the head is touched, does the torso remain stationary?
- Does the child move several parts before deciding on the proper part to move?

Dimensions. The child stands facing the therapist, who is about 6 feet away. The therapist holds a pole (or thick dowel) horizontally and perpendicular to the vertical axis of

the child, and asks the child to indicate, either verbally or through gestures, whether the pole should be raised or lowered until it is the same height from the floor as the specified body parts of the child (e.g., eyes, knees, shoulders). This procedure is performed sideways—right and left—as well as frontward. In another task, the therapist asks the child to estimate how far to walk forward or sideways to be at arm's length or foot's length from a wall. At that point the child, with eyes shut, extends a limb to check body judgment. The therapist uses similar techniques to elicit a response for torso dimensions, height, and movements required to get under a stick. Various other tasks can be assigned to encourage body spatial judgment.

Observations:
- Is the child unable to make a judgment? (If so, the therapist works closer to the child, or moves rather than asking the child to move.)
- Does the child seem to be confused, guessing rather than making judgments? (If so, the therapist has the child walk under the stick, try to touch the stick while seated, or walk between two chairs while varying the spatial requirements.)

Joints. The therapist moves a pole or stick toward various parts of the child's body, and the child stands "glued" to one spot and bends the body at the joints to avoid being touched by the stick. Another adult can first demonstrate (but not teach!) how to avoid the stick.

Observations:
- Does the child bend only at the waist?
- Does the child have to move feet from the "glued" spot?
- Are there any joints that seem confusing to the child?

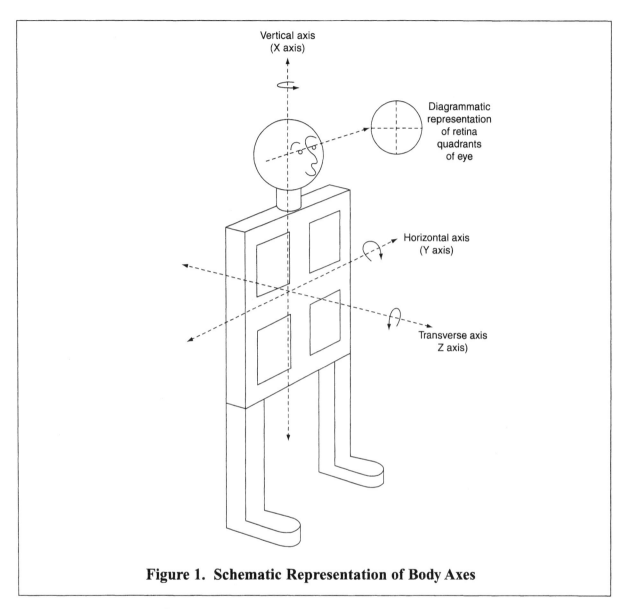

Figure 1. Schematic Representation of Body Axes

Integration of Body Sections and Axes

The body, which is the container and vehicle of the person in all of us, is divided into a right and left half and an upper and lower half. These sections rotate around three axes—vertical, horizontal, and transverse. The axes remain constant in all body positions. The person inside must manipulate the body (the container) for effective, efficient movement. The midline of the body, which lies along the vertical axis, is the longitudinal center of the container and the spatial reference center for the inside person's orientation in space and self (see Figure 1). The ear is thus further from "the person" than the nose. The eye can focus more easily on an object held temporally than on an object held nasally under binocular exposure because the object held nasally is closer to the person's center of reference.

The three axes interact to develop endogenous spatial coordinates and are our internal reference for three-dimensional space. Thus an object moving from right to left moves toward us until it reaches our body's midline, where it begins to move away from us. As evidence, try this simple exercise. Keep both your eyes shut. Hold your right hand level with your face but off to your right. Slowly move your right hand toward the left. As you cross your body's center line, you will feel that your arm and hand have shifted direction and are moving away from your body—even though they are still moving in the same direction, leftward.

The construction of this internal directional focus depends on physiological readiness and psychological awareness and motivation. To properly establish an internal directional focus, the child must develop integration and coordination of all sections of the body and coordinate all this mentally through vision, hearing, smell, and touch. Once this is established, the child is ready to develop efficient exogenous spatial coordinates, or a knowledge of the three-dimensional space of the child's external world. A child who has difficulty imitating simple body positions that involve right and left arm, or a child who is unable to walk cross-legged backward along a line on the floor, has not yet developed adequate endogenous spatial coordinates. These are usually developed around 6 years of age—prior to school entry in the United States—and are the foundation of the right-left concept important to academics.

Most children with reversal difficulties fall into the nondeveloped endogenous and exogenous visual-spatial category (Fraiberg, 1977, pp. 5, 78, 157-159, 197; Furth & Wachs, 1974, pp. 86). (Endogenous is *internal*; exogenous can be described as a baby's ability to project an internal model of space through visual, auditory, and manual appreciation of spatial relationships in its *external* world) A therapist can determine adequate integration of body sections through the following probes.

Integration of Body Section Probes

Static imitative movement. The child and the therapist (or parent) stand facing each other about 10 feet apart. The therapist raises his own right hand and instructs the child to imagine standing alongside the therapist and to raise the same hand as the therapist has raised. Keeping that hand raised, the child moves alongside the therapist and observes whether they both have the same arms raised. If not, the child is told to "fix it." The child then returns to the original position—facing the therapist from 10 feet away. The therapist again asks the child if the raised arm is the same arm as the therapist has raised.

Observations:

• Does the child then mirror the therapist (e.g., uses the left arm to imitate the therapist's right arm)? If so, no further probe is necessary—the child has not developed adequate visual-spatial knowledge.

• If the child successfully imitates the therapist, the therapist models several right-left positions but does not cross hands over the midline. The therapist's final modeling is to put the right hand on nose and left hand on right ear. This position requires a crossover of the central body locus.

Observations:

• Can the child imitate the positions modeled by the therapist? The child's successful imitation of this position indicates basic development of endogenous-exogenous, visual-spatial knowledge. An inability to imitate the position indicates that the child has not yet developed this visual-spatial knowledge.

Cross-legged walk-on-line. The therapist places a strip of tape approximately ten feet long on the floor, and demonstrates walking forward cross-legged (right foot forward over left foot, then left foot forward over right), until the entire tape is traversed. Then the

therapist instructs the child to do the same walk backward (placing the left foot backward and behind the right foot, etc.)
Observations:
- Does the child have an inability to perform the action backward? This indicates inadequate endogenous spatial development.
- Does the child have an inability to perform the action forward? This indicates a severe lack of endogenous spatial development.

Skipping. The therapist asks for and/or demonstrates skipping, having the child skip at least 20 feet (in a circle, if space is limited).
Observations:
- The child may not skip at all. (My research with Orinoco children of the Waika tribe in Venezuela revealed that skipping is not part of their culture, nor are hopping or jumping up and landing on both feet simultaneously. On the other hand, Zulu children in South Africa skip well at age three. Children in the Western world usually skip by approximately six years of age.) Skipping cannot, *and should not* be taught. Step-hop is not skipping. A sighted child who has the necessary motoric constructs will skip by observing others.

"Angels in the snow," crawling on the belly, creeping on hands and knees, human ball roll, and rolling (Furth & Wachs, 1974, pp. 84-107) all involve sensorimotor knowledge of how body halves can work together for purposeful movement. Any physical challenge that requires basic understanding of how to coordinate right and left as well as top and bottom of body sections can be used. The key is *not to teach*. Tasks can be demonstrated but not taught. If the child is unable to perform the task, the demands and complexity of the task should be simplified, but not taught.

RHYTHM

Rhythm adds a temporal component to body and sense thinking. Though often categorized as an auditory function, rhythm is really internal timing with an auditory, visual, and tactile component. In half a century of clinical experience, I have seen very few children in need who have adequate, if any, rhythm constructs. The following three probes can be used to test rhythm constructs.

Rhythm Probes

Accompanying tapping (observed). The therapist taps rhythmically in steady beats on a table in front of the child. The child accompanies the therapist's tapping. Both child and therapist are observing.

Accompanying tapping (hidden). The child accompanies the therapist's tapping while the tapping instrument is hidden from the child.

Recall tapping. The therapist taps rhythmically and stops. The child recalls the rhythm and taps accordingly.
Observations:
- A well-developed 3-year-old can accompany rhythmic taps—hidden or visible.
- A well-developed 4-year-old can recall a simple rhythm pattern.
- By age 6, a well-developed child can maintain rhythm under various conditions with hands and feet, stopping one limb and reversing the cycle in time to the beat of a metronome.

Rhythm Interventions

Body support. The therapist stands behind the child and taps on the child's shoulder to the beat of a metronome set at about 100 beats per minute. The child taps on a table to the accompanying sound of the metronome and the therapist's tapping. The therapist gradually ceases tapping on the child's shoulder as the child's tapping on the table becomes more efficient.

Rhythm light. The child observes as the therapist flashes a light rhythmically to the beat of a metronome. This adds an additional signal to the child to reinforce the child's rhythmic response.

Puppet. The child sits in a chair with hands on the table and feet flat on the floor. To the beat of a metronome (started slowly at 100 beats per minute) the child taps, in a circular pattern, right hand, right foot, left foot, left hand, right hand and maintains this pattern. The therapist decides when the circle should be reversed—clockwise and counterclockwise. An advanced step is to ask the child to stop one limb and maintain the beat. Thus, the right hand stops but the child maintains the beat as though the right hand were moving. Eventually, two limbs can be stopped. The therapist can also ask the child to reverse the circular pattern—clockwise and counterclockwise. Another advanced procedure is "simultaneous same" (right hand, right foot, then left hand, left foot) and "not same" (right hand, left foot, then left hand, right foot). Again, stopping of limbs adds complexity. As the child improves, the speed of the metronome can be varied.

Sitting spider. This activity is similar to the Puppet, but the child sits on the floor with hands on the floor, hips and feet flat on the floor, and knees bent and raised. The same procedure is used as in the Puppet, that is, circular, same/not same, stopping of limbs, and reversing circular motion clockwise and counterclockwise.

Creeping. (Furth & Wachs, 1974, pp. 90-91). On hands and knees, the child creeps "simultaneous same" and "not same" on the therapist's

command to various rhythmic beats of the metronome. Complexity can be added by placing signs printed with an "R" (for right hand) and "L" (for left hand) on the floor in varying sequences. If the child has no knowledge of the symbols, the therapist can just put blank cards on the floor or designate the hand that is to touch that card with a pattern (e.g., a red dot) and draw the same symbol on the child's hand.

Coordination of Body Actions

Coordination of body actions is a very high phase of sensorimotor intelligence. At this point, the child's sensorimotor development is fairly well established. Too early involvement in coordinated action activities can mask, or even thwart, development of the basic sensorimotor foundation for well-developed sensorimotor intelligence. Jumping rope, sports, gymnastics, rope and monkey bar activities, and walking rails and balance boards are all physical skill activities that require total body coordination.

OCULAR SENSORIMOTOR DISCRIMINATIVE MOVEMENT

The four basic movements of ocular sensorimotor intelligence are:
- Tracking
- Fixation
- Focus
- Convergence

Tracking is the ability to sustain fixation on a moving object. An intact, well-developed 4-year-old child should have adequate tracking. A 3-year-old can fixate, or move the eyes to point to a specific exogenous spatial object. Focusing is the ability to see an exogenous object clearly, and is not well developed until a child is 4 or 5 years old. Convergence is the ability to bifixate (point each eye at) an object as that object moves toward the eyes. A well-developed 3-year-old should be able to converge on a target held 2 inches from the eyes. An intellectually healthy, well-developed 5-year-old can perform adequately in all these areas (Furth & Wachs, 1974, pp. 71-110). The following probes can be used to test the basic movements of ocular-sensorimotor intelligence.

Tracking Probes

The therapist asks the child to fixate (look at, point their eyes at) a penlight or other attention-getting object while the therapist moves the object horizontally, right to left and back to the right. Observing the ocular movement and, if possible, reflection of the object in the center of the child's eyes, the therapist then moves the target up and down vertically, with the child fixating the target. The therapist follows this with irregular, reverse motion movement of the target while the child tries to fixate and follow the target. *Observations:*

- Is the child able to fixate on even a stationary target?
- Does the child move the head rather than the eyes?
- Does the child lose fixation?
- Do the child's eyes cross in the attempt to follow the target?
- Does the child track horizontally but not vertically?
- Does one eye stop while the other continues tracking?
- Does the child track if the therapist uses slow, steady motion, but lose fixation when the tracking pattern is irregular?

Tracking Interventions

Pen stab. The child holds the top cover of a felt tip pen. The therapist holds the pen itself and moves it in various directions at various heights while the child tries to put the cover on it.[3]

Paper stab. The therapist draws a bull's-eye target on a piece of paper and ascribes various scores to the rings on the bull's eye (the center area has the highest score and the area outside the bull's eye has a minus score). The paper is moved on the table with the bull's eye in view, and the child uses a felt tip pen to stab at the bull's eye as in a game of darts. After a specified number of stabs, the therapist adds up the score . The child tries to better the recorded score during the next session.

Washer or ball stab. The therapist suspends a metal or wooden washer (or other device with a hole in the center) from a rope. The child tries to stab the hole in the washer with a pencil or stick as the washer swings to and fro (Furth & Wachs, 1974, pp. 111-128).

Fixation

Tracking is dynamic fixation. Since a person who has difficulty tracking has difficulty fixing, the probes for tracking will also indicate the adequacy of fixation.

Focus

Focusing requires optometric evaluation. Asking a child whether she sees something clearly is far too subjective to indicate adequate focusing. However, looking far to near and back to far, and having to identify the target used, is the treatment of choice.

Convergence

Convergence is the ability to turn each eye inward to bifixate a near vision target. A well-developed 3-year-old should be able to converge on a target held 1 inch from the

---

[3]Dr. Arnold Sherman, O.D., of New York, first invented this simple procedure.

eyes. Two basic probes can determine the adequacy of convergence.

Convergence Probes

First, the therapist brings a fixation object forward from over the child's head to approximately 1 inch in front of the bridge of the child's nose while the child bifixates the target. Second, the therapist holds the fixation object from above about 8 inches from, and aligned with, the bridge of the child's nose, and then moves the object toward the child while the child tries to bifixate on the target.

Observations:

- Do the child's eyes remain looking straight ahead—no convergence?
- Does one eye fixate the target while the other remains looking straight ahead, turns in, or turns out?
- Does the child try to fixate by thrusting the head forward rather than converging the eyes?

Convergence Intervention

Convergence is a complex function and often requires professional intervention. If not, the simple procedure called "push-ups" can be used. The therapist has the child bifixate a target while moving the target toward and away from the child. If this does not help, the parents should enlist the aid of a visual-cognitive or developmental optometrist.

VISUAL THINKING

Visual thinking is making sense out of the sense of sight. As described earlier, the eye's role is to change photic energy into neural energy. When this energy is transmitted to the brain, a child with the requisite mental construct will either understand the photic event or develop a new scheme to enhance knowledge of that photic event. Visual thinking is involved in all performance testing as well as academic and intelligence testing. Visual thinking also is involved in mathematical thinking, especially in geometry. Visual thinking is involved in viewing and understanding molecular structures in organic chemistry. In short, visual thinking is visual intelligence.

To explore visual thinking, the therapist can best do probes using parquetry blocks, pegs, form boards, and sticks (Furth & Wachs, 1974). Most children in need start by matching patterns of blocks placed before them. Some can only stack blocks. The following outline illustrates a hierarchy of actions using parquetry blocks. At any step, time can be introduced as a factor (e.g., speed, time limits, tachistoscope). A minimal clue also can be introduced, such as blurring the child's vision, camouflaging the model with overlays, and partially hiding or partially forming the model. The therapist should avoid developmentally inappropriate strategies.

A Hierarchy for Demonstrating Visual Thinking

This hierarchy (Furth & Wachs, 1974, pp. 286-287; Wachs & Vaughan, 1977, pp. 8-10) is not sacrosanct. The progression does apply generally but not totally universally. Some individuals (both child and adult) may be able to use strategies and appear to achieve a higher function but still not be conceptually solid on a lower function (Wachs & Vaughan, 1974).

A. Same/not same

A tenet basic to both learning and development is recognition of the conflict between known and unknown elements (Furth & Wachs, 1974; Wachs & Vaughan, 1977). This conflict provides the impetus for inquiry and eventual understanding. To probe a child's ability to distinguish between what is known and not known, the therapist asks the child to differentiate one color, size, or shape of block from another.

B. Stack blocks

The child is asked to duplicate the therapist's model by placing one block upon another in a balanced position, matching either the broad side or the narrow side of the blocks. (See Figure 2.)

C. Build a bridge

The therapist makes a model by placing blocks at least one pencil width apart and spanning them with another block, and then asks the child to duplicate the model. (See Figure 2).

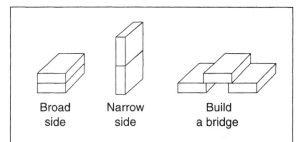

Broad   Narrow   Build
side   side   a bridge

Figure 2. Illustration of Stacking Blocks and Building a Block Bridge

D. Actual match (blocks to blocks)

The therapist asks the child to reproduce a model arrangement of blocks. The reproduction should be such that the model, when placed on top of the reproduction, fits exactly. Various configurations of blocks can be made.

1. **Parallel square** - the central block (square) placed so that the sides of the square are parallel to the sides of the table. (Figure 3 illustrates the following variations on the parallel square.)

    a. <u>Juxtaposition</u> - The sides of all blocks are coincident (the whole side of one touches the whole side of the

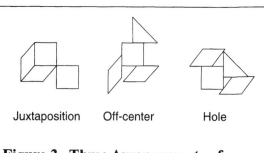

Juxtaposition   Off-center   Hole

Figure 3. Three Arrangements of Blocks Around a Parallel Square

other). The ultimate number of blocks is five—preferably two squares, one triangle, and two diamonds. The following procedures are designed to build same/not same awareness:
    – take away
    – add on
    – substitute

    b. <u>Off-center</u> – The blocks are placed so that the edge of any block only meets half the edge of the central block.

    c. <u>Hole</u> – The blocks are placed so that their edges only partially meet the edges of the central block, thus creating holes (or spaces) between blocks.

2. **Tilted square** - The central square is tilted so that the corners, rather than the sides, point to the sides of the table. The substeps are the same as those for the Parallel Square.

3. **Separation** - This activity can either be simple (i.e., blocks edges are parallel, but the blocks do not touch) or advanced (i.e., blocks edges are not parallel nor do the blocks touch). (See Figure 4.) Separation involves the following elements:
    – add-on
    – take away
    – substitute

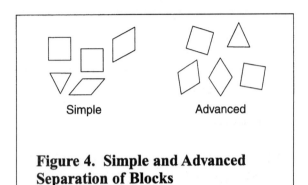

Figure 4. Simple and Advanced Separation of Blocks

4. **Recall** - The therapist presents a model, either in another room or apart and unseen in the same room. The child assembles a reconstruction of the model from memory. The therapist encourages repeat viewing until the child completes the replica, and then the therapist places the model on top of the replica to give the child visual feedback.

E. **Transposition**

This is the introduction to exogenous visual-spatial concepts. Flipping and rotation of blocks are simulations of the rotation around the three body axes: vertical (through the head down), horizontal (through the hips side to side), and transverse (through the navel and out the back). Knowledge of how to manipulate the body around these various axes provides our endogenous spatial concepts.

Figure 5 illustrates transposition according to the following hierarchy of axes.

1. **Hierarchy of axes -**
   a. Horizontal
   b. Vertical
   c. Transverse
      – side-to-side
      – corner-to-corner
      – corner-to-side
      – side-to-corner

2. **Hierarchy of block assembly** - Using three blocks, the therapist can instruct the child to assemble the blocks according to the following hierarchy of increasing complexity. Figure 6 illustrates the final two levels of this hierarchy.

1. Parallel basic - center square parallel to the sides of the table and the sides of the other two blocks coincident with the sides of the square.

2. Parallel advanced - center square parallel, and only one of the other two blocks coincident with the square.

3. Tilted basic - center square tilted and the other two blocks' sides coincident with a side of the square.

4. Tilted advanced - only one of the other two blocks coincident with the square.

5. Individual placement – the therapist presents the child with the blocks one

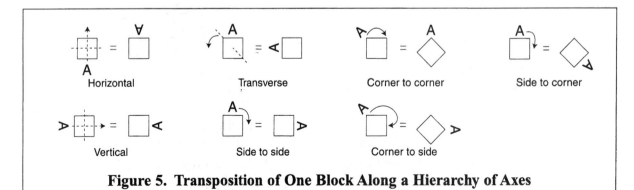

Figure 5. Transposition of One Block Along a Hierarchy of Axes

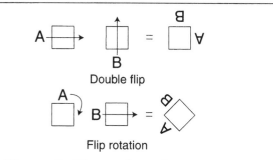

Figure 6. Illustration of a Double Flip and Flip Rotation of Blocks

at time, with the central block last. The above hierarchy is maintained, and the child or person is not to reposition the blocks until the final one is placed on the table.

6. Double flip – the therapist asks the child to flip the blocks in two directions simultaneously.

7. Flip rotation - transverse axis rotation combined with a horizontal or vertical flip.

The hierarchy of block assembly, as well as the transverse axis complexity, is maintained for both the Double Flip and the Flip Rotation.

F. Positions

The therapist's blocks remain stationary in the center of the table. The child replicates the design as it would be viewed from any of the four cardinal positions of the table (north, east, south, west), as well as from the corners of the table. In previous actions, the blocks were moved and the child was stationary; here, the child moves and the blocks remain static.

G. Analysis

The model *and* the transposed replica are both presented to the child who must determine the type of transposition (e.g., horizontal flip, double flip, flip side-to-side or

toward and away, rotate from corner to side or side to corner of sheet) required to transpose the model into the replica (that is, how the model was flipped or rotated to create the replica).

H. Pictures Around the Room

The therapist places a drawing of a three-, four-, or five-piece block design in various positions around the room, and then a blank card before the child. The child is asked to duplicate the designs.

I. Outline

The therapist traces the outline of a three- or four-block design (with blocks placed either horizontally or vertically) onto a card and asks the child to visualize the component parts of the outline and construct the design alongside (not on) the card. Basic to this is placing the blocks *on* the card within the outline.

J. Positional Hierarchy (from basic to complex)

1. Coincidence
2. Off-center
3. Hole

K. Hierarchy of Media Complexity

Within each of the following elements, there is a hierarchy; that is, chips are juxtaposed, then overlap; pegs are in sequence, then in random order lying flat and diagonal. Any medium lends itself to both matching and transposition tasks.

1. Cuisenaire rods
2. Cubes or chips
3. Parquetry blocks
4. Pegs
5. Dot patterns (4 or 5 missing dots)
6. Geometric designs

7. KOHS blocks or other multicolored cubes (the position of color or block adds another dimension)

CONCLUSION

I have made no attempt to be all-inclusive in this chapter, as a full explanation of visual-cognitive development would require many pages of text. Instead, I have tried to introduce optometric, visual-cognitive therapy in the hopes of encouraging parents of children in need to seek the help of a visual-cognitive optometrist. The consequences of well-developed visual thinking are manifold. Academic subjects such as geometry (a visual mathematics), biology (with its visually presented experiments), geography (requiring the visualization of graphically presented symbols), and organic chemistry (demanding visual organization of molecular structures) are some of the visually dependent tasks students are required to perform. Such vocations as architectural design, engineering, surgery, dentistry, sculpture, and painting are visually dependent. The congenitally totally blind person can learn to do many things that sighted people can do, but are restricted when the activity is solely visually demanding, as in dentistry or restoration of a painting.

My research has shown that mathematical thinking is very visually dependent. A small study I conducted at West York School District in Pennsylvania demonstrated that second-grade pupils who scored high in state-level math competency tests had well-developed visual thinking, visual-logic, and numerical literacy, whereas children who scored poorly were inadequate in these functions. Because mathematics is a visual-related child, the use of manipulatives to teach math in normal and remedial settings has long been the method of choice.

In essence, visual-spatial knowledge plays a major role in our intellectual growth and everyday existence. Children have a right to every opportunity to develop this knowledge to their fullest capacity. This tenet guides the work of visual-cognitive optometry, which is a necessary link in the chain of total development.

CASE STUDIES

Case One

M. was 11 years old when I met him. His father was a teacher in rural Maryland, and his mother a college-educated homemaker. M. had received occupational therapy and countless hours of remedial reading. He had also been seen by several outstanding opthamologists. He was a large boy, affable and cooperative. His verbal ability was superior, and all previous mentors and testers had assured his parents that he was of superior intellect. Nevertheless, M. still could not read. He had trouble even with the words "the" and "and." The boy's most serious problem was his lack of development in ocular sensorimotor schemes. He measured slight hyperopia (far-sightedness) and had severe esophoria (overfocus) bordering on intermittent esotropia (crossed eyes). M. could not see near objects clearly, and glasses alone could not solve his problem. He was so uncomfortable trying to perform near vision tasks that he had simply stopped trying by the time I met him. One helpful "eye doctor" had actually suggested that M. learn Braille. M. also had developmental gaps in general movement as well as operatory thought. I worked with M. in my home office for about one hour weekly for nearly a year. Since M.'s most serious problem concerned his poor ocular sensorimotor schemes, I first concentrated on developing his skills in tracking, fixation, focus, and convergence. We then worked on general movement to improve his mental map of his body and on visual thinking to help him make sense out of what he could now see. M. did not complete as much of the visual-cognitive therapy as I would have liked, but he did complete enough of the sensorimotor (ocular and body as well as visual thinking) therapy to begin reading. His reading proficiency was sufficient to enable him to finish high school in the upper part of his class and attend college. The last I heard, M. had moved up in the corporate world to a position as assistant director of a major museum in Washington, D.C. From an illiterate, "pseudo-blind" school failure, this boy became a literate, successful person.

Case Two

Y. first came to my office when she was almost 8 years of age. Her early developmental milestones were severely delayed. She had received speech therapy and special education in her native Middle Eastern country, but she spoke very few words and was extremely withdrawn. All testing had resulted in a clinical developmental age of 3 to 4 years. When I first met her, Y. did not respond to anything. She would not, or could not, interact in any way. Her social and societal dysfunction, together with her major cognitive deficits, had resulted in a guarded and unfavorable prognosis.

Upon testing, I found her visual acuity to be 20/20 at distance and near, but she had considerable sensorimotor confusion when attempting near vision fixation. She was under such stress and visual confusion at near that she actually crossed her eyes from the distress of near vision binocular fixation. I prescribed glasses with special lenses to relieve her near vision distress. When I

offered to work with Y., her parents moved to Washington, D.C., and were totally cooperative and consistent, both with her therapy in our office and with other therapies in the Washington area. Treatment continued for a 3-year period. I worked with Y. on an optometric, visual-cognitive regime consisting of general body and ocular sensorimotor development as well as very basic body and sense thinking. I paid special attention to Y.'s receptive-expressive language, having her stay focused on a task, and improving her ability to follow verbal and gestural instructions. For example, I had Y. place inch cubes (or other objects) on designated locations, as well as walk to specific locations or mark specific locations on a chalk board or table top. To do this, I had to ascertain her level of development in each task on each day as it varied quite often. I then presented each task at a slightly more challenging complexity, being certain that the new task was not too high for Y. to comprehend. As Y. grew cognitively and new tasks became more complex in minute steps, I introduced new aspects of intelligence. Other therapists addressed her speech, her neuro-physiology, and her special education needs. The family lived in Washington, D. C. from September to June every year and returned home for the summers, during which they maintained a home therapy program.

The results of these efforts have been outstanding. Y. is now a gregarious and talkative girl, attends a local public school, and reads adequately. Her eyes are straight and her parents are delighted. At 11 years old, Y. functions at about age 8. She may never perform at an age-appropriate level, but her prognosis for a normal, intellectually competent adult life is now excellent.   ■

REFERENCES

Blythe, P. (1990). *A physical basis for panic disorder.* Paper presented at the 4th International Conference on Neurological Dysfunction in Children and Adults, Guernsey, Channel Islands, UK (September).

Fraiberg, S. (1977). *Insights from the blind.* Boston: Basic Books.

Furth, H. (1991). Life's essential: The story of mind over body. *Human Development.* Basel, Switzerland: S. Karger AG.

Furth, H. (1986). *Piaget for teachers.* Washington, D.C.: C.A.E. (Originally published by Englewood Cliffs, NJ: Prentice Hall, 1970).

Furth, H. & Wachs, H. (1974). *Thinking goes to school; Piaget's theory in practice.* New York: Oxford University Press.

Ginsberg, H. & Opper, S. (1979). *Piaget's theory of intellectual development.* Englewood Cliffs, NJ: Prentice-Hall.

Goddard, S. (1996). *A teacher's window into the child's mind.* Eugene, OR: Fern Ridge Press.

Wachs, H. (1980). Piaget's theory in special education. In B. Keogh (Ed.), *Advances in Special Education, Vol. II* (pp. 51-78). Columbus, OH: JAI Press.

Wachs, H. & Vaughn, L. J. (1984). *The Wachs analysis of cognitive structures.* Huntingtown, MD: Huntingfields. (Originally published by Los Angeles: Western Psychological Services, 1977).

◄ 21 ►

Sensory-Motor Integration: A Perceptual-Motor Approach for Enhancing Motor Planning in Children with Special Needs

Parviz Youssefi, Ed.D, and Arousha Youssefi

Sensory-Motor Integration (SMI) is a multifaceted approach developed by the authors to enhance the quality of movement and motor planning for children with special needs. This chapter describes the SMI approach as well as its methods of assessment and intervention. This material is intended to serve as a guide for parents and professionals who seek new methodology for instructing movement in children with special needs.

SMI can be best described as a multisensory approach to addressing learning needs of children who have been diagnosed primarily with developmental delays, autistic spectrum disorders, hypotonia/motor delays, and apraxia, among other diverse clinical diagnoses related to early childhood development. By incorporating visual- and audio-motor perception, kinesthetic awareness, laterality, directionality, haptic perception, and vestibular stimulation, SMI enables children with special needs to sequentially and successfully acquire motor capabilities and motor planning.

The goals of the SMI approach are to:
- Enhance the child's quality of movement and motor planning.
- Expose the child to a multisensory milieu that will strengthens his relationship with the world around him.

- Incorporate perceptual-motor activities to improve visual-motor, audio-motor, and spatial awareness.

To achieve these goals, SMI builds upon two basic concepts: a child (1) learns to move, and (2) learns through movement. The fundamental difference between these two concepts is very important. *Learning to move* involves continuous development in a child's ability to use the body effectively and joyfully, with increasing evidence of control and quality in movement. It involves the growing ability to move in a variety of ways, in expected and unexpected situations, and in increasingly complex tasks. *Learning through movement* implies using movement as a means to an end, but the end is not necessarily the end of improvement in the ability of the child to move effectively. It is a means through which a child may learn more about herself and about her environment. It is not enough to assume that movement control and skill development will automatically occur for all children simply by virtue of having experienced a movement task: the challenge is far greater than this. To imply that a child *may not* improve and extend the range of quality in her movement as she tries to express feeling through movement is not to say that she *will not*. The learning environment must make it possible. Consequently, it is essential for therapists to know what they hope to accomplish both *in* and *through* movement as they plan for this learning environment. In other words, to know what is possible, therapists must know the child and know movement.

MOVEMENT: THE BASICS

A number of clinicians have observed the importance of movement to the larger goal of integrating different mental processes. For example, it has been observed that, through movement, individuals have greater access to thoughts and emotions and can better translate them into a language of action. It is this expression that creates intelligence and individuality. Hannaford (1995) hypothesized that "Every time we move in an organized manner, full brain activation and integration occurs, and the door to learning naturally opens." Recent research has suggested that two areas of the brain—the basal ganglia and the cerebellum—which are associated solely with control of muscle movement, are also critical to coordinating thought. These areas are connected to the frontal lobe, where subsequent motor planning and reaction time occur (Humphries, 1990).

Neuropsychological functions relate to movement and are extremely important in how the child will feel about himself emotionally, as well as interact with, and learn from, his social world. For example, problems in motor planning and sequencing (stringing together a set of motor responses) not only lead to frustration and lowered self esteem in a child, but may also impair a child's further brain and social-emotional development, including:

- *Play with parents and peers.* When a child cannot maintain reciprocal motor responses with others in a play game, the

result is dysynchrony, or the child being "out of sync."
- *Exploration of the environment,* which leads to a sense of one's body and a sense of self, and the ability to distinguish reality from one's imagination.
- *Mastery of separation anxiety,* and control over his body environment.

Furthermore, these children frequently have temperaments that are immature, demanding, needy, oppositional, and defiant. These qualities, in addition to the child's movement difficulties, will further strain the child's relationship with her parents, who may already have their own stresses, such as marital problems or financial difficulties. Parents may then respond negatively, leading to a vicious cycle of constant tension and negative interactions between child and parent. The consequences of this negativity may be seen in temper tantrums, emotional outbursts, control and power struggles, and other adversarial behaviors. By the age of 2 or 3, children can begin to manifest the beginning of certain developmental pathways, placing them at risk for specific problems later in development. An awareness of these patterns allows a therapist to intercede with early identification of at-risk children, early treatment interventions, and—very importantly—prevention. There is conclusive evidence that school programs for preschoolers with learning disabilities are working by preventing future learning failures.

The SMI approach stresses the importance of a multisensory approach that stimulates two or more sensory apparatus each time a child attends a therapeutic session. The typical SMI candidate ordinarily exhibits several of the following characteristics: low muscle tone, delayed speech, poor motor planning, poor body awareness, and a fear of heights.

Chapter 21. Sensory-Motor Integration: A Perceptua-Motor Approach for
Enhancing Motor Planning in Children with Special Needs

539

SMI attempts, in each therapeutic session, to encourage the child to perform activities that she has not been able to accomplish elsewhere. We allow her to engage in activities that demand rapid and frequent left brain-right brain communication, and make certain the child is exposed to situations where she is able to express herself freely and creatively, stimulating many new avenues of the nervous system. Activities that involve height, speed, excitement, courage, and revolution activate many different parts of the cerebral cortex, causing never-before-stimulated parts of the brain to " wake up!" (Youssefi, 1987).

The critical link between brain activity and movement has been a curiosity to scientists for many years. Scientists have long recognized that children who skip the critically important crawling stage may exhibit learning difficulties in the future school years. The motor act of crawling activates development of the corpus callosum. Performing cross lateral movements, like crawling, stimulates both sides of the body to function in unison. With equal stimulation of the two hemispheres, the senses actively access the neural pathways, which allow both sides of the body to move together in an integrated fashion for more efficient movement (Hannaford, 1995).

THE IMPORTANCE OF THE INDIVIDUALISTIC SENSORY-MOTOR INTEGRATION APPROACH

In addressing the children's mental health needs as well as their physical and emotional well being, SMI creates an environment for learning that addresses the specific learning deficiencies of each individual child. SMI, in conjunction with other essential developmental therapies, aids in sensory-motor processes such as reading, writing, language development, cognition, social awareness, kinesthetic awareness, and self-concept. The difference

between the SMI approach and other distinct therapeutic approaches lies primarily in the implementation and lesson planning procedures. It is based on the belief that children surmount insurmountable tasks through the knowledge of and exposure to multisensory activities that are designed specifically to meet individual needs.

It is imperative for children to be exposed to and explore each and every aspect of the sensory milieu in order to be proficient in their learning processes. Thirty years of experience with children with special needs and with movement has led to the formation of a few basic principles for SMI, which are:

- Children perform more efficient motor planning when given the opportunity to explore diverse movement settings.
- Children with special needs need to engage in integrated activities in order to improve multifaceted learning deficiencies.
- Affect-driven responses can be attributed to a child's interest and sensory-motor needs.
- Therapists involved in the child's treatment program play a critical role in motivation and encouragement.

FORGOTTEN PERCEPTUAL-MOTOR AND SENSORY EFFICIENCY THEORIES

Motor therapy specialists and perceptual-motor pioneers discovered many links between movement and learning. Unfortunately, their contributions and hypotheses have long been overlooked and unappreciated. The lack of demand for perceptual-motor theory and a lack of educational curriculum for the field has buried many important concepts and methodologies.

Research by many theorists supports the principles behind the integrated SMI approach. Raymond Barsch (1967) explored the educational needs of children whose problems in learning did not lend themselves to precise and neat categorization. Barsch's theory of "movigenics" depicted the origin of development of patterns and movement in man and the relationship of those movements to his learning efficiency. Barsch's primary concern was the developing child and his problems in achieving a mature adult status. The backbone of Barsch's "movigenics" was the concept that physical and cognitive movements are inseparable. Barsch based his theory on the concept that "Man moves. Man learns. He learns to move. He moves to learn." This concept helps to describe problems confronted by children in static classroom and learning environments. Barsch, therefore, linked the necessity of developing mature movement patterns to proper cognitive processes, which would lead to success in learning environments.

Newell Kephart further advanced the theory of perceptual-motor development and its impact on academic potential. In his now classic book, *The Slow Learner in the Classroom,* Kephart (1960) stated that in order for learning to take place effectively, perception and movement had to be coordinated—a process that occurred through a wide variety of sensory experiences and movement opportunities. As a result, movement and perception had to be integrated and function simultaneously (Arnheim & Sinclair, 1975).

Getman, an optometrist who believes visual perception could be developed through motor training, analyzed perceptual-motor development and its component parts. According to Getman, perception is a process through which an individual's sensory skills translate reaction to the environment into physical movement. An individual's perception of her environment serves as a blueprint for her subsequent motor tasks. Perception includes the integration of visual, auditory, and tactile functions.

The interdependence between perceptual and motor skills is a priority for the SMI methodology and for children's academic and social success (Youssefi, 1987). A child with special needs may inefficiently integrate these perceptual-motor skills. To address this need, Jean Ayres analyzed central nervous system processes and their impact on learning (Ayres, 1979). Her theories of sensory integration described how the child used the input of the eyes, ears, and body to acquire information from the outside environment to help make sense of it. According to Ayres, the brain must organize all sensations to learn in order to behave normally. Exposing children to tactile stimulation, vestibular stimulation, and motor activity stimulates and involves portions of the brain stem. With the information from the sensory system, a child can perceive and learn on a progressive level.

Bryant Cratty (1969) developed his concept of adaptive physical education to address the needs of children who required special services. Cratty stressed the importance of the motivational levels of children when learning in academic and nonacademic settings. Cratty believed a child's inability to perform motor tasks could lower his self-esteem as well as his acceptance by peers, which could adversely affect motor and cognitive processes (Arnheim & Sinclair, 1975).

The SMI methodology uses the frameworks established by these pioneers and others. It has, however, sought to systematize the work of various pioneers into a practical, individualized approach that can help children integrate the most critical motor and sensory processing capacities. With these concepts as background, the following section explores the SMI approach in detail.

Chapter 21. Sensory-Motor Integration: A Perceptua-Motor Approach for
Enhancing Motor Planning in Children with Special Needs

541

MOTOR DEVELOPMENT

The observable course of motor development in humans begins about 7½ weeks after conception when, for example, the fetus flexes its head laterally away from stimulation in the lip region. By week 8½, this isolated avoidance response has radiates into patterns of movements organized in space and time. Simple lip stimulation now elicits contra-lateral flexion of the neck and trunk, extension of the arms at the shoulders, and rotation of the pelvis away from the side of stimulation.

The earliest patterns of motor behavior appear to be genetically coded in the species; that is, humans have some initial organization or template that guides the pattern of new formations. In addition, there are some operational rules that lead to patterns of behavior. Variable changes in these patterns are accounted for by the particular conditions of individual experience (learning). The study of motor development is concerned with the factors that influence motor behavior, the design of experiences that will result in desirable changes in behavior, and the influence of this learning on the capacity of the individual for future development (Thomas, 1984).

As a child grows, expectation of more mature movements increases proportionally. Movement becomes symbolic of life and existence. Movement is the sole manner of the physical *expression* of intelligence. It is believed that movement as the important expressive aspect of the human personality has great potential for use in educational programs for the child with special needs. However, motor activity constitutes only a component of the human personality. Numerous distinct modalities accompanied by, or exclusive of, overt action are also brought into use as the human infant and adult deal with their worlds (Cratty, 1969).

Similar to building blocks, there are graduated levels of motor development and motor planning originating from fundamental sensory-motor development. Children should complete patterns at every stage of development before they can efficiently carry out a more complex pattern. If a child misses a critical developmental stage, if he lacks the link from one pattern to the next, he will show evidence of problematic motor performance. The following behaviors may be indicative of a disintegration of senses and of gaps in motor development:
- Poor coordination
- Poor awareness of time and space
- Poor visual judgement
- Clumsiness
- Poor rhythm
- Poor flexibility of movements
- Poor handwriting
- Difficulty maintaining balance
- Motion sickness
- Kinesthetic and tactile defensiveness
- Fear of velocity
- Fear of inversion
- Fear of heights

Fortunately, delayed reflexive activity, which is indicative of poor sensory-motor development, can be detected at an early stage. Within the first few months, a parent should be able to identify certain motor patterns their infant has displayed or skipped. Table 1 describes the expected movement pattern of a growing child.

To reach and enjoy full motor maturity, the infant must receive the constant stimulation that comes from experiencing a rich variety of stimuli. However, if the interactive environment has excessive visual or auditory stimuli, sensory overload will occur and hinders the natural course of development. Incorporating the sensory systems into learning has an enormous impact on delayed and

Table 1. Expected Movement Patterns of Growing Children

Age	Expected Movement Pattern
Newborn-12 weeks	• Predominately reflexive • Flexion of knee and hip when soles of feet are pricked • Head flexes laterally towards source of stimulation • Head is held erect and steady • Rolls front side to back • Reaches for hanging object
15 weeks	• Grasps hanging object • Rolls from back to side
7 months-8 months	• Sits alone • Transfers object from one hand to the other • Crawls purposefully to get from one place to the next • Homolateral pattern of crawling observed • Creeps on hands and knees • Cross-lateral pattern of creeping observed • Pulls up to a standing position
9 months	• Follows simple commands • Picks up food with hands and attempts to self-feed • Copies simple movements
11 months	• Stands alone • Grasps and releases object
12 months	• Walks alone • Uses hands and fingers to explore space (under, over, beneath, across) • Uses hands and fingers to push and pull objects • Changes directions
14 months	• Awareness of force distribution increases (stroking vs. striking) • Maneuvers efficiently about objects • Proficient pincer grasp
16 to 18 months	• Crawls up stairs efficiently • Plays "peek-a-boo"
24 months	• Runs • Spins about central axis by taking small steps in a circular pattern
32 months	• Bounces, with both feet simultaneously lifting off the ground • Slides sideward • Walks backwards • Runs and stops on verbal command • Premature under arm throw • Rolls down an incline • Performs inverted somersault • Jumps from a 12-inch elevation • Balances on 8-inch walking board • Proficient grasping and hanging
3 years	• Jumps from 18-inch elevation • Performs somersault on flat surface • Walks on balance beam with 12-inch elevation • Bounces efficiently on trampoline, maintaining balance • Throws object over arm • Dodges oncoming objects efficiently

Chapter 21. Sensory-Motor Integration: A Perceptua-Motor Approach for
Enhancing Motor Planning in Children with Special Needs

543

autistic spectrum children. Stimulation of the sensory system and motor performance is influenced both by physiological conditions and by the dynamics of the learning environment. Special education professionals suggest a variety of social and personal traits will be enhanced as a child interacts with his learning environment.

Essential to cognitive, social, emotional, and physical development is the interrelatedness of perceptual-motor processes, motor delays, hypotonicity, sensory-motor integration disorder, and audio-visual perception difficulties. The SMI approach to integrating higher neural functions maintains that certain elements of movement and perception are essential to establish a network of neural pathways that interrelate, and to enhance communication of the left and right brains. These elements improve limb articulation, dominance, depth perception, body and space awareness, balance, and general coordination (Arnheim & Sinclair, 1975). Locomotion, balance, non-locomotion, kinesthetic awareness, visual-motor perception, and audio-motor perception are areas of main intervention by a SMI therapist (see Table 2).

Table 2. Areas and Elements of Sensory-Motor Intervention

Area of Intervention	SMI Elements
Locomotion	• Rolling • Crawling • Creeping • Walking • Hopping
Balance	• Static balance • Dynamic balance • General balance
Nonlocomotor movements	• Throwing • Catching • Batting • Kicking
Kinesthetic awareness	• Laterality • Directionality • Body and space awareness • Haptic perception • Tactile perception • Airborne activities • Velocity modulation
Visual-motor perception	• Eye-hand coordination • Eye-foot coordination • Fine motor visual planning • Fine motor coordination
Audio-motor perception	• Following verbal commands • Beat discrimination • Coding and decoding auditory cues • Move to cadence
Physical fitness	• Static strength • Dynamic strength

CASE EXAMPLE: SMI IN PRACTICE

The following example presents the pre-evaluation, evaluation, and remediation procedures conducted for Sam, a 5½-year-old child diagnosed with autistic spectrum disorder.

Pre-Evaluation

Because SMI training is an educational, progressive intervention program, it is *most* beneficial to children who can at least minimally respond to an educational environment. Due to a child's natural tendency to enjoy movement, the child who does not make eye contact soon finds in SMI an avenue of interest through which the therapist can become a part of his world and engage him in reciprocity.

In Sam's case, he was told to walk next to the therapist and follow him to the other side of the room. Sam was hesitant at first, but then followed. When the therapist initiated a game of catch, Sam had no awareness of the object that was being thrown and was unable to continue the game.

Next, Sam was instructed to stand on an box elevated 2 feet off the ground. Sam was extremely uncomfortable with the situation. As Sam kicked and screamed, the therapists removed him from the box and his mother comforted him. Sam refused to detach himself from his mother after that point. Throughout the entire pre-evaluation procedure, he demonstrated extreme fear of heights and would not allow his mother to leave the room.

However, because Sam was able to follow simple directions and make minimal eye contact, he could benefit from SMI intervention.

Evaluation and Assessment

After the informative pre-evaluation, the child undergoes a full evaluation procedure, which is videotaped and later reviewed for detailed analysis. In a full evaluation, the child is separated from his caregiver and asked to perform certain skills based on the specifications of his age and diagnosis.

The following evaluation is a modified version of an SMI assessment, which was used with Sam. As with all children, Sam's movement skills were tested in several important areas. Directions for conducting each test, as well as observation questions, are included.

Locomotion

Log roll. Tell the child to roll like a pencil, either on a mat or down an incline.
Observations:
- Do the body parts move together in one line?

Crawl. Let child crawl under an object, telling him to "crawl like an alligator."
Observations:
- Look for homolateral body movement. Does the elbow meet the knee on one side while the other side of the body is straight?
- Does the head tilt to the side of the body that is flexed?

Bounce. Instruct the child to bounce, lifting both feet off the ground.
Observations:
- Do both feet leave the ground simultaneously?
- Is balance kept throughout bounce?
- Are arms down by his side or do they jerk?

Hop. Instruct the child to hop on designated spots, eight hops on each foot.
Observations:
- Is balance maintained easily?
- Does the child tire easily?
- Can the child perform hopping task with both feet?

Chapter 21. Sensory-Motor Integration: A Perceptua-Motor Approach for
Enhancing Motor Planning in Children with Special Needs

545

Slide. Demonstrate sliding. Instruct the child to follow.
Observations:
- Is head at midline?
- Are arms swinging easily?
- Is there planning of distance and direction?
- Are arms, head, and trunk involved in coordination?

Static and Dynamic Strength
Grasping. Instruct the child to hold onto a bar for 10 seconds.
Observations:
- Does the head stay in alignment?
- Does grasp appear weak?
- Is the child able to perform the task without assistance?

Leg lift. Instruct the child to lay on back and lift both legs 10 inches off the ground. Have the child hold legs off the ground for 10 seconds.
Observations:
- Are both feet easily held off the ground?
- Is contraction equally distributed?

Flexibility. Instruct the child to sit in a straddle position. Ask him to touch his elbows to the floor and/or forehead to the floor.
Observations:
- Does the child perform a straddle sit?
- Does the child perform task with straight legs?
- Do elbows reach the center?

Hamstring. Instruct the child to sit in a straddle position. Ask him to touch his elbows and/or forehead to the floor.
Observations:
- Does the child perform the task with straight legs?
- Do elbows reach the center?

Lower back. Instruct the child to perform an "L" shaped sit. Ask the child to touch his toes.

Observations:
- Does child perform "L" sit comfortably?
- Does the child touch toes with ease?
- Are knees kept straight?

Back. Instruct the child to lie down in a prone position and hold his ankles.
Observations:
- Does the child perform task with ease?
- Does his back contract to achieve an "arch up" position?

Balance
Balance board. Instruct the child to stand on balance board and try not to shift back and forth.
Observations:
- Does the child maintain balance?
- Is force distributed evenly from both feet?
- Does head remain at midline?
- Are both sides regulating weight shift?

Walking on 4-inch surface. Instruct the child to walk on a 4-inch-wide balance beam.
Observations:
- Does the child walk heel to toe?
- Do feet alternate?
- Does the child perform task with hesitation?

Walking on incline. Instruct the child to walk uphill on an incline.
Observations:
- Does the child utilize his whole foot?
- Is weight shift smooth?
- Is balance maintained easily?
- Do eyes follow path?
- Do legs provide adequate balance?

Walking down declined elevation. Instruct the child to walk down a 3-foot elevation.
Observations:
- Do legs provide adequate balance?
- Do eyes follow path?

- Is child running to avoid controlled posture?
- Is changing directions done with ease?
- Are feet alternating?

Non-Locomotion

Catching. Instruct the child to toss and catch large, medium, and small balls.
Observations:
- Do the eyes follow the object?
- Does the body move in space to receive the object?
- Does the body shift weight as needed?

Throwing. Instruct the child to throw a small ball to a target that is placed 5 feet from eye level.
Observations:
- Do the eyes follow the object?
- Are both sides involved in throwing?
- Which is the dominant arm?
- Are shoulder joints loose?
- Does the child step into the task?

Batting suspended ball. Instruct the child to strike the suspended ball with a large bat.
Observations:
- Do the eyes follow the object?
- Does the child strike the ball with at least 50% accuracy?
- Is balance maintained?
- Is there planning of distance and direction?
- Are arms, head, and trunk involved in coordination?

Visual-Motor Perception

GMS balancing tube. (This tube is similar to a builder's level, which has a bubble that moves left or right from a midpoint depending on slope. When the level is balanced, the bubble centers at the midline.) Instruct the child to hold the tube with both hands and try to roll the marble to the middle, between the red lines.

Observations:
- Does the child distribute force evenly throughout?
- Do the eyes follow the marble?
- Is motor planning adequate?

Balloon paddling. Instruct the child to keep the balloon from hitting the ground. Ask him to count how many times he can strike the balloon.
Observations:
- Do eyes follow the object?
- Are arms, head, and trunk involved in coordination?
- Is balance maintained easily?

Running through hoops. Instruct the child to walk through a series of hoops. If the child walks without difficulty, ask him to run.
Observations:
- Is running performed at an even speed?
- Is one foot placed in each hoop?
- Is running done while alternating feet?
- Does the child start and stop on command?

Tracing using a flashlight. Provide an elevated surface on which the child can stand. Instruct the child to trace the designated lines with a flashlight.
Observations:
- Do the eyes follow the light?
- Are wrists coordinated with arms and fingers?
- Is there planning of distance and direction?
- Is task performed with 50% accuracy?

Evaluation Results and Lesson Planning

Upon completion of the evaluation procedure, the videotape was reviewed and a lesson plan for Phase I of Sam's therapy was

Chapter 21. Sensory-Motor Integration: A Perceptua-Motor Approach for
Enhancing Motor Planning in Children with Special Needs

547

devised. The results of the evaluation, by assessed area, follow.

Locomotion

Sam, at $5\frac{1}{2}$, had the motor proficiency expected of a child at age 2 years, 3 months. The test of locomotor skills revealed his ineptness in large and small muscle control, a lack of communication between left brain and right brain functions, and the inability to produce effective motor-planning sequences.

Locomotion Intervention and Lead-Up

Drills. The following activities were selected to enhance Sam's ability to utilize his upper and lower extremities and improve locomotor skills.

Log roll. The child lies on his back with his shoulders positioned on a line, body fully extended, feet together, arms flat to the ground above his head. One therapist takes the left arm over the right arm in a crisscross manner, while a second therapist takes the left leg over the right leg in the same crisscross fashion, and proceeds to roll the child. Each time the child makes a full revolution of the body, he must become reoriented to the horizontal plane. The head first turns in the direction of the roll, followed by the hips. The trunk is twisted, the shoulders lifted, and one thigh rotated inward and over the other thigh. In this manner all segments of the body are aligned and maintained in good control. When the child is able to roll effectively in one direction, then rolling in the other direction should be attempted.

Crawl. Crawling is a natural extension of rolling. Like rolling, crawling provides the physically clumsy child with security because the body is fully in contact with a surface. The child moves along the floor in a prone position by various movements of the arms and legs. Each crawling task must be executed in the proper form before the next higher-level skill is attempted. Crawling is attempted in an amphibian fashion by moving the arm and leg on one side of the body in unison and then moving the limbs on the opposite side. The head should be turned toward the side on which the limbs are flexed. One therapist bends the child left arm, and bends the child's left leg so the elbow meets the knee. A second therapist holds the right arm and right leg, creating a straight line from the right hand to the right foot. One therapist counts "1-2-3" and manually alternates extended and bent positions.

Bouncing. The ability to propel the body upward from a supporting surface requires much strength, balance, and coordination. To efficiently produce the correct pattern of bouncing, the child must distribute force equally between the right and left sides of the body. Modification of bouncing can be performed on a trampoline or mini trampoline. If the child has no pattern of bouncing, a therapist must stand behind the child, hold his hips, and initiate the motor act of jumping.

Hop. The motor act of hopping requires static and dynamic balance, dynamic strength, and motor planning. The child must be able to stand on one foot to perform the act of hopping. Once he has mastered balancing on one foot, he will be able to proceed to the next level, hopping with support. A therapist stands behind the child, holding the child's left leg behind him and his right arm forward to initiate hop direction. As the therapist proceeds to walk forward, the child will reflexively want to maneuver forward, hence initiating the hopping task. Once the child has mastered this task, he will be able to perform hopping on an adaptive surface (e.g., springboard or minitramp).

Static and Dynamic Strength

The awkwardness in motor activity of children with special needs can be attributed to below-average motor fitness because motor ability and fitness are mutually dependent. Sam exhibited below-average muscle tone and tested at a proficiency level of a child of 3 years, 5 months. He had trouble maintaining balance and posture throughout the evaluation. Sam was only minimally able to perform static and dynamic strength activities. Sam could not sit in a chair without tiring, was unable to maintain his posture while walking, had no concept of hanging, and was completely unable to utilize fingers and wrists to hold a pencil. The following remediation procedures were devised to treat Sam's lack of static and dynamic strength.

Static and Dynamic Strength Intervention and Lead-up Drills

Arm hang. Arm hanging is used to determine the efficiency of grasping ability. An average 5^1/$_2$-year-old boy should be able to hang for 10 seconds or longer. A proficient arm hang suggests adequate strength of the shoulders, wrists, and forearm. The ability to hang from a bar, being suspended in the air without any support, involves regulation of the vestibular and proprioceptive systems.

The therapist starts with a stick, 4 inches in diameter, with two lines drawn where the child should place his hands. The therapist raises the stick up and down until the child begins to support his own weight. Once the child feels comfortable with the stick, the therapist leads him to a bar with a 4-foot elevation. He holds the child's feet until he is comfortable hanging without support, making certain that the child's grip is correct. The whole palm of the child's hand should be in contact with the bar.

Arch up. A modified pushup is a significant method for examining arm and shoulder strength and muscle endurance. The child assumes a prone position with fingers pointed laterally away from him; legs are extended and relaxed. The child should then straighten both arms simultaneously to produce a "seal-like" position.

Abdominal and trunk strength. To improve upper abdominal muscle strength and endurance, the child should perform abdominal curls. The child assumes a supine position with knees bent, feet flat on the mat and arms folded across chest. The child lifts his head up until his chin touches his chest, rolls both shoulders forward, and lifts his back from the mat so that he comes to a full sitting position. Since Sam was not interested in performing this drill, the therapists modified it to create a more interactive approach to "boring" sit-ups. The therapists laid 10 beanbag animals on the floor directly behind Sam's head. Sam would reach back and pick up a beanbag with both hands, and then sit up and shoot it in into a target. This allowed him to practice projectile management (throwing) while developing abdominal and trunk strength.

Flexibility

Flexibility refers to the capacity to move a particular joint in the body through its range of motion. A full range of motion of the hip flexor allows the child to crawl effectively; a full range of motion of the shoulders and wrists allows the child to explore the world of creative shapes and its relationship to body awareness. Sam exhibited extremely poor flexibility. The simple act of tying shoes was a motor disaster. When he sat on the floor to remove his shoes, his hands barely reached his toes. The position was extremely tiresome for Sam. After 2 minutes of reaching and struggling, he gave up and asked his mother for help. Crawling was problematic because of lack of flexibility in the lower trunk

Chapter 21. Sensory-Motor Integration: A Perceptua-Motor Approach for
Enhancing Motor Planning in Children with Special Needs

549

region. Consequently, activities to improve Sam's hamstring and trunk flexibility were of high priority.

Flexibility Intervention and Lead-Up Drills

Hamstring. The child sits on the mat with legs extended away from each other and toes pointed. The child tries to touch both elbows to the space created by the "v" shape position.

Balance

Balance is defined as the ability to maintain equilibrium while engaging in various locomotor and nonlocomotor activities. There are three basic categories of balance: (1) static balance—the ability to maintain a specific position for a given amount of time, (2) dynamic balance—the ability to control the body in motion, and (3) object balance— the ability to support some external objects without letting it fall.

Sam suffered from severe vestibular dysfunction as well as an excessive fear of elevated surfaces. Sam was unable to perform the simplest of balance tasks. When asked to walk across a balance beam with a 4-inch width, he walked with one foot leading the other, a behavior below his expected age proficiency. In fact, for static and dynamic balance, Sam tested at a 23 months of age level. The top priority for his lesson planning was to help him get over the fear of elevated surfaces and familiarize him with revolution and velocity.

Balance Intervention Implementation and Lead-Up Drills

Balance board. The therapist instructs the child to stand on a balance board and maintain his balance.

Level 1: The child may use the wall or a bar for support as the therapist stands behind the child and holds his knees. The child needs to have an idea of what the correct manner of balancing feels like.

Level 2: The child uses therapist as support.

Level 3: Child stands alone.

Level 4: Child stands on balance board while catching a medium-size ball.

Walking across a 4-inch-wide balance beam. The therapist should be positioned in such a way that he can easily give verbal directions and can spot the child when it is necessary. The child should hold all balance postures for 10 seconds.

While balancing on a 8-inch side of the balance beam, the therapist instructs the child to:
- stand heel to toe, right foot in front of left, hands placed on the waist,
- stand heel to toe, left foot in front of right, hands out to the side,
- stand on left foot with arms crossed,
- stand on right foot with arms crossed,
- walk along the balance beam heel to toe, and then
- walk backward heel to toe.

Walking up an incline. For this exercise, an elevated square is placed on a mat-covered surface, with one side of an 8-inch beam placed on the elevated square to create an uphill slope. The slope should be no more than 30 degrees from the floor.

Level 1: The child creeps up the beam to adapt to height of elevation.

Level 2: The child walks up the beam with one foot leading with support.

Level 3: The therapist places beanbag buddies at increasing higher levels to indicate how high child should go (e.g., "Sam, go up and say 'hi' to Mr. Alligator").

Level 4: Two therapists hold the child's hands and briskly walk him up the beam. (This helps the child walk with alternating feet.)

Level 5: The child goes up the incline by himself.

Walking down an elevated surface. Walking down an elevated surface involves tremendous strength as well as balance. The child must be able to control his speed as he walks down the beam. (Running down the beam is a good indicator of lack of visual-motor perception and static balance.) For this exercise, the therapist places a beam on an elevated surface to raise it 30 degrees from the ground, with the 8-inch side up. The therapist places dominoes or beanbag buddies on the beam about 1 foot apart from one another and asks the child to either count the dots on the dominoes or talk about the beanbag buddies as he steps over each object. This task will allow the child time to balance while he counts the dots or names the animals.

Nonlocomotor Skills

It is developmentally and socially important for a child to succeed in performing skills that consist of propelling and retrieving various objects. The child tends to receive a tremendous amount of self-gratification and praise from peers. Conversely, the child with special needs may lack the eye-hand or eye-foot coordination necessary for effectively managing objects in play. Nonlocomotor skills are motor tasks involving force application, reaction time, and visual judgment.

Sam had severe visual-motor impairment and subsequent focal failure. In addition to the lack of visual acuity, Sam had no concept of reciprocity and had no interest in engaging in any catching, throwing, or batting tasks. Towards the end of the evaluation, Sam began to engage in several bouts of catching and throwing. A main priority for lesson planning was to enhance his awareness of reciprocity and reaction time.

Nonlocomotor Intervention and Lead-Up Drills

Catching. Catching is a reflexive activity proficient in a child by the age of 3. It involves awareness of time, space, and use of legs to aid in the catching task. When using the skill of catching to improve visual-motor planning, the therapist should stress the fact that the eyes must remain open and watching the ball at all times. The thought of catching induces fear in many children. To minimize the anxiety as much as possible, a light plastic or rubber ball approximately 9 inches in diameter should be used at first.

Level 1: Place a hula hoop in front of the child. Ask him to toss the ball around eye level and let it drop into the hoop. The task is to toss the ball and have a designated area for it to drop in.

Level 2: Move the hula hoop 8 inches from the child's feet, and ask him to toss a medium-size ball, about 6 inches in diameter, and let it drop to the ground.

Level 3: Instruct the child to toss the medium-size ball and catch it.

Level 4: Instruct the child to toss a small ball, about 4 inches in diameter, and catch it.

Throwing. Throwing is a skill that involves the release of an object with one or both hands in one of three basic patterns: (1) underarm pattern, (2) side arm pattern, and (3) overarm pattern. It also is a motor act that demonstrates the physics principle of a summation of forces as the total force of all the muscles and levers in the body move in a sequential pattern. Since the object is controlled by the speed and direction of the hand doing the throwing, improving a child's throwing ability requires the therapist to consider methods for developing speed and controlling the direction of the hand movement. It is imperative that each child be afforded ample opportunity to handle a variety of projectiles. In Sam's case, the therapists used small balls that were projected toward a target.

Level 1: A child who has no throwing pattern should start with a large rubber ball, 9 inches in diameter. The therapist should

Chapter 21. Sensory-Motor Integration: A Perceptua-Motor Approach for
Enhancing Motor Planning in Children with Special Needs

551

start with underhand rolling. When object rolling is being taught, the child should lower his body by bending his knees with the back straight and head lifted.

Level 2: The child's hands are placed on opposite sides of the ball with palms facing each other and fingers apart and pointing down. The ball is held in front of the body. As his arms swing forward, the child should flex his knees and release the ball onto the ground by extending his elbows and wrists.

Level 3: The child uses two hands to throw the ball underhand.

Level 4: The child performs a two-hand chest pass.

Level 5: The therapist places the child's feet in a stride position, opposite to the dominant throwing hand. The therapist should hold the child's dominant hand behind the corresponding ear and then guide the child's arm forward to perform a throw into a target.

Visual-Motor Perception

One of the most important factors that links vision to movement is postural fitness. Posture is the primary pattern of movement on which all other patterns are based. Problematic visual perception may cause the child to exhibit poor and unstable posture. It is invariably found that children with movement problems are unable to integrate movement with vision. They also are unable to make accurate movements with their upper and lower extremities with adequate control.

Sam tested extremely below age level in the area of visual-motor perception. He constantly tripped over objects and bumped into obstacles that were in his way. His poor posture resulted in an extremely limited span of visual stimuli. He could only interact with the area immediately around him. Sam was able to make minimal eye contact; however, the therapist had to stand right in front of him and hold his chin for 10 seconds

before any eye contact was achieved. Sam had no scope of vision above that of his eye level. His lesson plan would surely include maximum visual-motor perception at a very basic level.

Visual-Motor Perception Intervention and Lead-Up Drills
Balloon paddling.

Level 1: The therapist allows the child to play with a balloon. The therapist instructs the child to try to keep the balloon off the ground as long as possible, counting each time the child hits the balloon. If the child cannot follow the balloon, the therapist must bat the balloon back and forth to the child until he can perform the task without help. The therapist instructs the child to keep his eyes on the balloon. This drill for increasing visual-motor perception allows the child to expand his visual field: for children who have difficulty "looking up," balloon paddling exposes them to the wonderful world of "up!"

Level 2: The therapist uses two paddles—one red and one yellow—and instructs the child to alternately hit the balloon once with the red and once with the yellow, while correctly saying "red, yellow, red, yellow" in time to the hits. This activity promotes verbal feedback and allows verbal processing to occur at the same speed as the action is proceeding. This task involves significant visual-motor planning.

Level 3: The therapist uses two paddles and two balloons and asks the child to keep the two balloons within reach.

Running through obstacles. If the child hits the hoops as he runs through them, the therapist uses the following lead-up drills:

Level 1: The therapist places colored dots on the ground and asks the child to walk across the "river" by way of the "stones." Telling the child to keep his feet dry and out of the water will help the child understand the concept of taking big steps.

Level 2: The therapist places the hoops around the colored dots and asks the child to walk across the river and not touch his foot to anything other than the dots.

Level 3: The therapist lays 10 hula hoops on a matted or carpeted surface and instructs the child to walk through the hoops without hitting the edges. If the child is placing two feet into each hoop, the therapist asks him to try to place only one foot in each hoop.

Level 4: If the child can walk through without touching the edges of the hoops, the therapist asks the child to run through. (By age $5^1/_2$, the normally developed child runs through with 90% accuracy.)

Flashlight tracing. Tracing shapes and lines with a flashlight improve handwriting and visual motor accuracy. Therapists try the following lead-up drills if the child is not proficient in tracing with a flashlight.

Level 1: The therapist draws a figure on a dark surface so that the child can stand on a elevated surface and be directly above the drawn figure. The child flashes the light at the start position and travels in between the drawn lines until he reaches the finishing line.

Level 2: The therapist draws a figure that incorporates the shapes of the alphabet, circles, half circles, straight lines, slanted lines, and zigzags. She traces the line and instructs the child to superimpose his light over the therapist's light. The two lights travel together until their lights reach the finish line.

Level 3: The therapist draws the same figures as in Level 2, but the child alone uses a light to trace the figure to the best of his ability. (A typical $5^1/_2$-year-old boy should be able to stay on the line for 90% of the figure.)

Audio-Motor Perception

Children with special needs usually have difficulty processing auditory information as a result of a dysfunctional vestibular apparatus or structural deformities, which occur in the ear. The SMI technique of integrating auditory and motor perception provides the child an opportunity to connect auditory organization to movement that he already knows. Thus, pattern recognition, force application, and reaction time improve tremendously.

Sam was a relatively average listener. He followed simple verbal commands; however, he could not react to them in an organized fashion.

Audio-Motor Perception Intervention and Lead-Up Drills

Drum activities. The therapist sits directly in front of the child and holds a buffalo drum, making sure the child imitates the position. The child tries to copy the therapist's rhythm.

Level 1: The child says how many beats the therapist is making (the therapist should not exceed 2 beats initially).

Level 2: The child copies the number of beats the therapist played.

Level 3: The child plays "soft like a mouse," then "loud like an elephant."

Level 4: The child plays two loud beats, followed immediately by two soft beats, creating a pattern of BAM-BAM-bum-bum.

Sound localization. This is the ability to determine the direction of sound. The following activities are lead-up drills to improve a child's sound localization.

Level 1: The therapist stands behind the child and rings a bell, twice on the right and then to the left. The child points to the direction from which the sound originates.

Level 2: The therapist blindfolds the child and asks him to follow the sound of the therapist's voice and try to catch him. "Where am I, Sam? Catch me!" Although the child

Chapter 21. Sensory-Motor Integration: A Perceptua-Motor Approach for
Enhancing Motor Planning in Children with Special Needs

553

should be challenged, the therapist should not allow the child to fail, but allow the child to catch him.

Agility, Speed, and Body Awareness

The child with special needs, whose problems include poor body perception, often has difficulty moving effectively in space. Bumping into obstacles and dropping things are indicative of poor body and space perception. Sam had marked trouble with body awareness. During the evaluation, Sam exhibited a lack of mental imagery and acquisition of body boundaries. He was unaware of his body in space, he did not want to be airborne. Sam was uncomfortable with velocity and height—he would tremble at the very thought of swinging or hanging.

Agility, Speed, and Body Awareness Intervention and Lead-Up Drills

Running through poles. This is a drill used to increase body and space awareness. Ten poles, each about 5 feet high, are placed on a carpeted area in a straight line. The child runs through the poles in a zigzag fashion (similar to how a slalom skier races). A drawn path gives the child a visual cue of where to go. There is always a start and a finish line.

Swinging in octagon. A suspended octagon should be placed 5 feet above a matted area. The child sits in the donut, holding the handles, legs straight in front of him (see Figure 1 for a picture of an octagon).

Level 1: The therapist swings the octagon back and forth.

Level 2: The therapist swings the octagon left and right.

Level 3: The therapist swings the octagon in a circular manner, first slowly, then gradually increasing the speed.

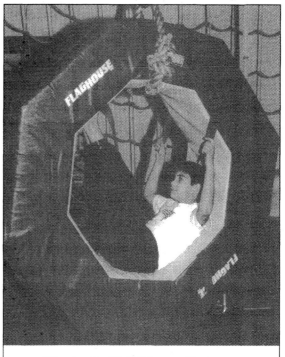

Figure 1. Child in an Octogon

Rolling in Octagon. Place the octagon on a matted area. The child lays on his back inside the octagon and holds onto the handles.

Level 1: The therapist holds the child inside the octagon as he rolls the octagon back and forth.

Level 2: The child lays on top of the octagon in a prone position. The therapist holds him by the legs and rock him back and forth, then left and right

Level 3: The child gets inside the octagon and hold his legs straight onto the walls of the octagon. The therapist rolls the child all the way around, holding one hand on his legs to push them to the walls of the octagon, and having one hand free to roll the octagon.

Laterality

Laterality is defined as internalizing the awareness of the difference between right and left. Sam had no awareness of right and left. His therapists started with very simple tasks to teach the concept of the right side of the body by utilizing many techniques, including the following one.

Laterality Lead-Up Drill
Visual awareness of left and right via balloon paddling. Using a soft paddle stick with protusions at each end, the therapist marks an "L" and an "R" to represent right and left protrusions. The therapist instructs the child to strike the balloon with the left and then with the right protrusions.

Multistepped Motor Planning

Since Sam exhibited poor balance and coordination, as well as poor visual-motor perception, multistepped motor-planning skills were not a part of his initial lesson planning. However, the following lead-up drills were introduced 6 months after his therapy began.

Multistepped Motor-Planning Intervention and Lead-Up Drills
Jumping Jacks.

Level 1: The child makes "angels in the snow," performing X and I positions.

Level 2: The therapist draws a picture of an X and a picture of an I on a wall where the child can stand directly in front of it. The child copies the pictures on the wall with his body position, first by making an X, then by making an I position.

Level 3: The child performs jumping jacks to a cadence of "X 2,3,4, I, 2,3,4."

Making knots. Using two pieces of rope (one 3 feet long and the other 2 feet long), the therapist wraps about 3 inches of each end with a different color of tape (e.g., red and gray).

Level 1: The child ties a knot with the 3-foot rope. The therapist observes the knotting pattern.

Level 2: Following a U-shape drawn on the floor with chalk, the child superimposes the U-shape with the 3-foot rope, keeping track of the red-taped end. The red end should represent the child's left hand. Next, the therapist draws two crossing lines in the

middle of the U-shape. The child superimposes the rope over the crossing lines, keeping the red-taped end on the top.

Level 3: Using a 2-foot piece of rope that is thinner in diameter than the 3-foot rope, the child performs the same task as described in Level 2, again placing the red-taped end over the gray. The child reaches and pulls the red-taped end to form a knot. This procedure is repeated eight times.

Finger-to-thumb taps
"a good morning ritual."

Level 1: The therapist places a sticker on the thumb of the child. The child touches every finger individually to the sticker: the thumb is saying "good morning" to all the fingers.

Level 2: With the sticker removed, the child taps his thumb to each of his fingers.

Advanced Multisensory Intervention Drill

The following activity requires proficient balance, coordination, audio-motor perception, projectile management, and visual-motor perception.

Rhythm response. The child stands on a balance board, holding a 9-inch diameter ball. The therapist stands directly behind the child, holding a drum. The child listens to the number of drum beats and tosses the ball according to the number of beats heard, while maintaining his balance. If the therapist hits the drum twice, the child will perform two tosses of the ball. The task requires the child to integrate the eyes, ears, and vestibular system with gross motor coordination and projectile management.

Sam's Progress with SMI

In the 2 years since Sam started his SMI training, he has made tremendous improvement in every aspect of his therapy. Sam now runs,

Chapter 21. Sensory-Motor Integration: A Perceptua-Motor Approach for
Enhancing Motor Planning in Children with Special Needs

555

jumps, flips, swings, and climbs up a 40-foot spider net! He completely integrates visual-motor and audio-motor perception while performing motor tasks and absolutely loves swinging—fast. Sam was selected as the case example for this chapter because he has made significant progress and provides readers a perfect opportunity to understand why. Sam speaks and asks questions, and greets his peers and the staff members with a warm smile every day. More important, he now enjoys the wonderful world of movement.

CONCLUSION

This chapter presents parents and professionals with a motor therapy program that uses the techniques of the SMI approach. The model presented is to be used in accordance with the concepts previously discussed, including:

- Academic tasks normally require skill in forming perception, symbol recognition, visual language development, and other motor-perceptual abilities.
- Practice and training aimed at helping children develop these skills can prevent or alleviate a certain proportion of learning problems.
- Children with learning disabilities often demonstrate inadequate development of perceptual-motor skills.
- Preparation for these tasks requires development of general coordination, physical balance, spatial relationships, eye-foot and eye-hand coordination, eye movement control, and sensory perception.

Just as children learn to walk and talk, they must learn to utilize their senses to fulfil motor and cognitive needs. They demand opportunities to examine things in their environment by looking, feeling, smelling, and sometimes tasting them. Through the manipulation of objects and gaining control of their body movements, children are using the sensory-motor process to learn and perform skills that require problem solving. They need to take things apart, discover how they work, and put them back together. They need to identify and relate to the various colors, shapes, sizes, textures, and noises around them. Thus, children learn to make a sensory impression and produce an appropriate motor response.

Information applicable to the development of motor skills, sensory processing, and perceptual proficiency comes from a variety of sources including psychology, neurology, anatomy, physiology, physical therapy, occupational therapy, and human development. The goal of the SMI approach is to identify those movement priorities in both objective and expressive functioning that will further abilities best allocated to the motor and perceptual framework, in the psychological, social, intellectual, and physical development of the child. Finally, the concept of SMI factors that make up the intricate system of motor planning should be interwoven with the acquisition of new skills and extended through movement with different environmental stimuli. ∎

REFERENCES

Arnheim, D. D., & Sinclair, W. A. (1975). *The clumsy child*. St. Louis, MO: Mosby.

Ayres, J. (1979). *Sensory integration and the child*. Los Angeles, CA: Western Psychological Services.

Barsch, R. H. (1967). *Achieving perceptual motor efficiency*. Washington, D.C.: Special Child Publications.

Braley W. T., Konicki G., & Leedy, C. (1968). *Daily sensory-motor training activities*. CA: Peek Publications.

Cratty, B. (1969). *Movement, perception and thought*. CA: Peek Publications.

Cratty, B., & Martin M. M. (1969). *Perceptual motor efficiency in children*. Philadelphia: Lea & Feibger.

Eckert, H. M. (1987). *Motor development*. IN: Benchmark Press.

Greenspan, S. I. (1995). *The challenging child*. Reading, MA: Addison Wesley Longman.

Hannaford, C. (1995). *Smart moves*. Arlington, VA: Great Ocean.

Humphries T. (1990). The efficacy of sensory integration therapy for children with learning disability. *The Journal of Developmental and Learning Disorders, 2*(2), 171-192.

Kephart, N. (1960). *The slow learner in the classroom*.

Thomas, J. R. (1984). *Motor development during childhood and adolescence*. MN: Burgess.

Tomatis, A. (1996). *The ear and language*. Canada: Moulin.

Stallings, L. (1983). *Motor skills*. Wm. C. Brown.

Youssefi, P. (1987). *Preparation of human development resources for improving the physical education programs suitable to the needs of students with disabilities*. Unpublished doctoral dissertation, George Washington University, Washington, D.C.

◄ 22 ►

Mediated Learning Experience, Instrumental Enrichment, and the Learning Propensity Assessment Device[1]

Reuven Feuerstein, Ph.D.
(with an Introduction by Serena Wieder)

INTRODUCTION

During the past 50 years, Reuven Feuerstein and his colleagues have pioneered a variety of approaches to enhance the cognitive abilities of children. Children with special needs have challenges to learning for many different reasons, but their learning difficulties have often been used to set limits on their potential, just as symptoms and other signs have often been used to limit expectations. As a result, many believe that little can be done to modify the course of life for children with autistic spectrum disorders or difficulties in relating and communicating, as well as those with Down, fragile X, and other syndromes. Feuerstein has long refuted this notion that signs, symptoms, and diagnostic labels lead to a condition of immutability. Instead, he believes that with appropriate mediation (i.e., interactive learning experiences) many children can learn to greater degrees than usually expected. Feuerstein has not only pioneered understanding of the basic conditions underlying learning disorders and defined the specific cognitive capacities necessary for learning, but also *how* to develop these capacities to allow each child to move forward through mediated learning experience.

The following chapter presents a brief overview of Feuerstein's theory and practice of enhancing cognitive functioning. The main part of the chapter focuses on specific techniques developed to enhance abstract thinking and problem-solving skills in children with cognitive challenges, including children with the syndromes mentioned previously. Because so much has been written about Mediated Learning Experience, Feuerstein's Instrumental Enrichment, and the Learning Propensity Assessment Device, this chapter will—by necessity—present the highlights in an outline and schematic fashion. More detailed descriptions, including a large number of research studies, are available on the website for The International Center for the Enhancement of Learning Potential at http://icelp.org.

---

[1] With the exception of the "Introduction" and the "Conclusions" section, this chapter has been adapted, with permission, from information available from the website for The International Center for the Enhancement of Learning Potential at http://icelp.org.

MEDIATED LEARING EXPERIENCE

Mediated Learning Experience (MLE) describes a special type of interaction between a learner and a person, whom we shall call a "mediator." A mediator is different from a teacher, as illustrated by Figures 1 and 2.

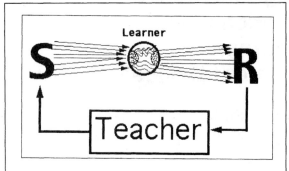

Figure 1. Schematic of Teacher-Learner Model

In this model, the teacher provides a suitable stimulus (e.g., homework, test, or assignment) and then observes the response of the learner to the stimulus. Based on the response, the teacher interacts with the learner (e.g., praise, criticism, encouragement, grade, new assignment) and the process is continued until either the teacher or the learner is satisfied or time runs out. Teachers develop their own repertoire of methods depending upon the size of the class, the apparent ability of the learner(s), and the subject matter.

In Feuerstein's method, the above figure is replaced by one in which a warm human being, indicated by the "H" in the diagram, intervenes in the process by placing himself or herself between the learner and the stimulus and between the learner and the response.

The "intentionality" of the mediator is different from that of a teacher. The mediator is not concerned with solving the problem at hand. Rather, the mediator is concerned with how the learner approaches solving the problem. The problem at hand is only an excuse to involve the mediator with the learner's thinking process.

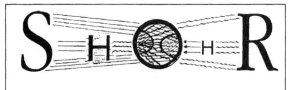

Figure 2. Schematic of Mediator-Learner Model

For the learner's thinking process to be successful, at least three important features must characterize the interaction: intentionality and reciprocity, mediation of meaning, and transcendence.

1. Intentionality and Reciprocity

Intentionality has been explained previously. The mediator concentrates on understanding and helping the learner understand how the learner is using his or her brain. Reciprocity refers to the need for the learner and the mediator to see each other at the "same level." That is, the teacher does not pretend to know the answer as to how the learner should be thinking.

2. Mediation of Meaning

The mediator interprets for the learner the significance of what the learner has accomplished. The mediator also mediates feelings of accomplishment. "Now that you have figured that out, you can probably use the same method on this harder problem." "Now I'll bet you see the advantage of having developed a strategy for solving the problem." "Did you notice how you went faster when you decided you could be flexible in your approach?" In various ways, the mediator causes the learner to reflect not just on the solution to the problem but also on how the solution was obtained and the generalizations that flow from it.

3. Transcendence

Human beings differ from the other species in the way they can transfer lessons learned from one experience to rules and methods to use in another situation. Indeed, this is what learning should be about, for if a person does not generalize from experience that person does not gain 30 years of experience, that person simply repeats one year 30 times. Transcendence means "bridging" between the experience and lessons learned in the current situation and new situations. "Where else in your life to you suppose it is important to have a strategy?" "How often has 'impulsivity' gotten you into difficulty in your family life?" "Where else do you find that you are imposing structure on what would otherwise be a confusing set of input information?" "When and where do you find it useful to categorize information?"

The above three criteria are essential in defining MLE. However, the mediator also pays close attention to other aspects of learning from experience, and mediates for other (affective) components of learning, including:

- Regulation and control of behavior
- Feelings of competency
- Sharing behavior
- Individuation/psychological differentiation
- Goal seeking/setting/achieving/monitoring
- Challenge: The search for novelty and complexity
- Awareness of the potential for change
- The search of optimistic alternatives
- Feeling of belonging

Cognitive Dysfunctions at the Three Problem-Solving Stages

In examining the approach of the learner in a problem-solving situation, it is helpful to the mediator to develop a mental image of the steps learners take in successful problem solving and in what can go wrong. Feuerstein and his associates have developed the following examples of cognitive dysfunctions at the three stages of problem solving.

Stage 1: Difficulties of the Learner During the Input Stage of Problem Solving

- Blurred and sweeping perception.
- Unplanned, impulsive, and unsystematic exploratory behavior.
- Lack of or impaired receptive verbal tools that affect discrimination, (e.g., objects, events, and relationships are not appropriately labeled).
- Lack of or impaired spatial orientation and lack of stable system of reference by which to establish topological and Euclidian organization of space.
- Lack of or impaired temporal concepts.
- Lack of or impaired conservation of constancy.
- Lack of or a deficient need for precision and accuracy in data gathering.
- Lack of capacity for considering two or more sources of information at once. (This is reflected in dealing with data in a piecemeal fashion rather than as a unit of facts that are organized.)

Stage 2: Difficulties of the Learner During the Elaboration Phase

- Inadequacy in the perception of the existence of a problem and its definition.
- Inability to select relevant as opposed to irrelevant cues in defining a problem.
- Lack of spontaneous comparative behavior or the limitation of its application by an inhibited need system.
- Narrowness of the mental field.
- Episodic grasp of reality.
- Lack of need for the establishment of relationships.
- Lack of need for and/or exercise of summative behavior.
- Lack of or impaired need for pursuing logical evidence.
- Lack of or impaired ability to use inferential or hypothetical (if) thinking.

- Lack of or impaired ability to use planning behavior.
- Non-elaboration of certain categories because the verbal concepts are not part of the individual verbal inventory on a receptive level, or because they are not mobilized at the expressive level.

Stage 3: Difficulties of the Learner During The Output Phase

- Egocentric communication modality.
- Blocking.
- Trial and error responses.
- Lack of or impaired verbal or other tools for adequately communicating elaborated responses.
- Lack of or impaired need for precision and accuracy in the communication of one's responses.
- Deficiency of visual transport.
- Impulsive, random, unplanned behavior.

Although MLE may be used with any situation in which the learner is challenged by a problem, there are some situations which are much easier to deal with than others. For example, in Feuerstein's Instrumental Enrichment, the problems have been designed to be attractive and fun to solve. They have also been designed to emphasize one or another of the potential dysfunctions listed earlier. Another example is in the Learning Propensity Assessment Device, in which the problems posed to the learner are aimed specifically at one or another of the above potential difficulties.

FEUERSTEIN'S INSTRUMENTAL ENRICHMENT

Feuerstein's Instrumental Enrichment Program (FIE) is a cognitive education program that was begun in the 1950s. The program has been successfully used in 70 countries as a tool for the enhancement of learning potential in specially challenged individuals and those in high-risk environments.

FIE is a classroom curriculum designed to enhance the cognitive functions necessary for academic learning and achievement. The fundamental assumption of the program, based on the theory and research pioneered by the author is that intelligence is dynamic and modifiable, not static or fixed. Thus the program seeks to correct deficiencies in fundamental thinking skills: provide students with the concepts, skills, strategies, operations and techniques necessary to function as independent learners; to diagnose; and to help students learn how to learn.

FIE materials are organized into instruments that comprise paper-and-pencil tasks aimed at such specific cognitive domains as analytic perception, orientation in space and time, comparative behavior, classification, and more. The FIE program is mediated by a certified FIE trainer and can be implemented in the classroom setting or as an individual tutoring and remedial teaching device. This program has received worldwide recognition and has been translated into 16 languages.

Mastery of the tasks in FIE is never a matter of rote learning or mere reproduction of a learned skill. It always involves the application of rules, principles, or strategies in a variety of tasks. Thus, FIE systematically reinforces the cognitive functions that enable learners to define problems, make connections and see relationships, motivate themselves, and improve their work habits.

FIE consists of fourteen instruments that focus on specific cognitive functions. Learning how to learn takes place through repetitionænot repetition of the FIE tasks themselves, but of the cognitive functions that enable individuals to think effectively. Tasks become increasingly complex and abstract, and the instruments reinforce cognitive functions in a cyclical manner. Deliberately free of specific subject matter, the FIE tasks are intended to be more readily transferable to all life situations. Through FIE, students develop the ability to apply their cognitive functions to any problem or thinking situation.

Samples from each of the 14 instruments in the FIE program follow. Each sample describes an instrument, provides a summary of the cognitive processes the instrument addresses, and presents a task from the instrument. The sample tasks have been chosen randomly from the sequence of tasks in each instrument and do not necessarily reflect the development of the program.

Instruments of FIE

Organization of Dots

Organization of Dots provides practice in projecting virtual relationships through tasks that require an individual to identify and outline given figures within a cloud of dots. The projection of a potential relationship requires that the learner search for meaning among otherwise separate phenomena. Through repeated practice and successful completion of progressively more difficult exercises, the instrument encourages task-intrinsic motivation and activates a variety of cognitive functions.

Cognitive Functions Developed
- Definition of the problem
- Selection of dots that are relevant to the figure that is sought
- Planning behavior
- Hypothetical thinking and use of logical evidence
- Summative behavior

Mediation of Sample Task
Mediation of challenge is indicated in the sample task shown in Figure 3, in which there are no given cues and the dots are numerous

and close together. Mediation of a feeling of competence is important as the students compare strategies of solution. As in all tasks in Organization of Dots, there must be regulation and control of behavior.

Sample Task
Spontaneous comparison of projected figure to the model.

Instructions: Connect the dots so that the geometric figures in the first frame appear in each of the following frames. The orientations of the figures may be different from the first frame. Some of the figures overlap.

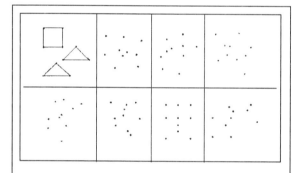

Figure 3. Sample Task in the Organization of Dots Instrument

Comparisons

The Comparisons instrument increases an individual's ability to differentiate between parameters of comparison and to develop the cognitive functions involved in comparative behavior. The instrument provides concepts, labels, and operations with which to describe similarities and differences. From Comparisons individuals learn to organize and integrate separate and distinct bits of information into coordinated and meaningful systems. The instrument helps build learners' feelings of competence and independence by enriching the repertoire of attributes by which they compare objects and events.

Cognitive Functions Developed

- Ability to keep in mind a great number of parameters during the process of elaboration.
- Making a plan that will take into account the complexity of the tasks.
- Use of hypothetical thinking and hypothesis testing to evaluate the alternative response.
- Selection of relevant cues and reference points.

Mediation of Sample Task

An opportunity for mediated regulation and control of impulsive behavior is provided in the sample tasks shown in Figure 4, in which an individual must discriminate among a number of given parameters. A feeling of competence is mediated to the students as strategies for the solution of the tasks are discussed. Goal-setting and goal-achieving behavior must also be mediated.

Sample Task

Instructions: Circle the word or words that describe what is common between the sample picture on the left and each of the pictures in the same row.

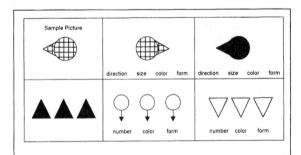

Figure 4. A Sample Task in the Comparisons Instrument

Orientation in Space-I

Orientation in Space-I addresses the poor articulation, differentiation, and representation of space that may result from an inability to detach oneself from one's own body position as a reference. It deals with a relative system of reference for localizing objects in space and in relation to one another. As a result of their experience with these tasks, learners discover why there are differing points of view in the perception of an object or an experience and how to give consideration to an opinion that is different from their own.

Cognitive Functions Developed

- Definition of problem when no instructions are given or when tasks vary from frame to frame.
- Hypothetical thinking: "If...then."
- Use of logic to solve tasks for which the information is not directly provided.
- Comparison as a strategy for checking one's work.
- Internalization of the relationship between the elements of the system of reference.

Mediation of Sample Task

Mediation of goal-seeking, goal-setting, goal-planning, and goal-achieving behavior is indicated in the sample task shown in Figure 5, which varies from frame to frame. Mediation of challenge is also indicated.

Sample Task

Instructions: Fill in what is missing so that each frame will contain an arrow, a dot, and an indication on which side of the arrow the dot is located.

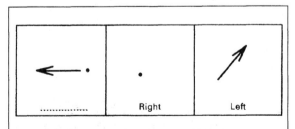

Figure 5. A Sample Task in Orientation in Space -I Instrument

Analytic Perception

Analytic Perception enhances one's ability to differentiate (divide a whole into its parts) and integrate (join parts into a whole). Adaptation to the world depends upon the flexibility to alternate between these two perceptual processes. As a result of their experiences with the tasks in this instrument, learners begin to differentiate between inner and outer sources of reference. They are then able to form and discriminately use internal referents to process information and to structure and restructure their varied life experiences.

Cognitive Functions Developed

- Spontaneous comparison to model.
- Establishment of relationship between parts, and between the parts and the model.
- Categorization of parts according to their shapes and colors.
- Visual transport of parts to the model.

Mediation of Sample Task

Mediation for intentionality, reciprocity, transcendence, and meaning are necessary in confronting the sample task in Figure 6. Sharing behavior is encouraged in comparing strategies and expression.

Sample Task

Instructions: In each of the exercises below you are given a model. Choose the box that

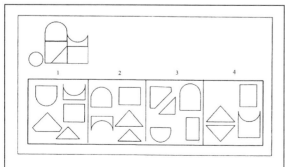

Figure 6. A Sample Task in the Analytic Perception Instrument

contains all the parts that make up the design, and write its number in the circle provided.

Illustrations

Illustrations presents a collection of situations in which a problem can be perceived and recognized. Learners attempt to offer an appropriate solution to the identified problem. This instrument mediates learner's ability to perceive details, use several sources of information, and exercise comparative behavior. Illustrations lends itself to the development of vocabulary and oral and written language; it is also highly useful for generating task-intrinsic motivation.

Cognitive Functions Developed

- Definition of the inferred problem.
- Use of relevant cues as a basis for inference.
- Use of comparative behavior.
- Use of summative behavior.
- Hypothetical thinking and use of logical evidence to support conclusions.
- Establishment of relationships between the individuals, objects, and events shown in the illustrations.

Mediation of Sample Task

Goal-seeking, goal-setting, goal-planning, and goal-achieving behavior must be mediated in the discussion of the plight of the piano movers in the sample task shown in Figure 7. Regulation and control of behavior should be mediated as playing a major role in ensuring time for planning and reflection. The meaning of the pictured event should be mediated and projected into various life situations.

Sample Task

Instructions: Examine the picture carefully. Is there a problem?

Figure 7. Sample Task in the Illustrations Instrument

Family Relations

The Family Relations instrument uses a system of relationships to link separate beings and categories and emphasizes the necessary and sufficient conditions for inclusion in and exclusion from categories. The exercises in Family Relations demand precise use of language in encoding and decoding relationships and require inferential thinking, analytic thinking, and deductive reasoning to justify conclusions based on logical evidence.

Cognitive Functions Developed

- Definition of problem in order to determine what one is being asked to do.
- Using only information that is relevant.
- Comparison between elements and relationships to determine similarities and differences.
- Enlarging the mental field by bearing in mind a number of discrete elements and the relationships among them.
- Hypothetical thinking and the use of logical evidence to justify one's conclusions.
- Overcoming an episodic grasp of reality by seeking the links and bonds that unite separate entities.

Mediation of Sample Task

Individuation and psychological differentiation, as well as sharing behavior, should be mediated in the sample tasks shown in Figure 8, which require taking a point of view other than one's own. Mediation of goal-planning and goal-achieving behavior is necessary in discussing the process by which the tasks are solved.

Sample Task

Instructions: Using the information in the genealogical map, answer the questions listed on the page.

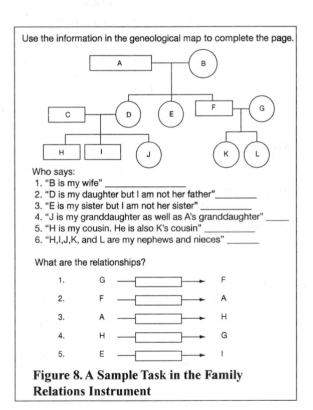

Figure 8. A Sample Task in the Family Relations Instrument

Categorization

Categorization is based on successful comparison, differentiation, and discrimination. This instrument helps individuals develop the flexibility and divergent thinking necessary for categorizing and recategorizing the same objects into different sets as the principles and parameters of categorization change with new needs and objectives. In categorizing, an individual moves from establishing relationships among concrete items to projecting relationships among concepts. This ability is essential to and basic for logical and verbal operations.

Cognitive Functions Developed
- Comparative behavior to ascertain similarities and differences
- Selection of relevant attributes
- Summative behavior
- Projection of relationships
- Determination of cognitive categories

Mediation of Sample Task

Mediation of goal-seeking, goal-planning, and goal-achieving behavior is indicated for the sample tasks shown in Figure 9. Mediation of challenge is elicited in the complex task at the bottom of Figure 9. Individuation is mediated in comparing two alternative solutions to the same task.

Sample Task

Instructions: Classify the cubes according to size and color. Fill in the headings and write the correct letter in each empty square.

Numerical Progressions

The Numerical Progressions instrument helps learners search for, deduce, and induce relationships between separate objects or events. Learners draw accurate conclusions regarding the cause of progressions as the instrument increases their ability to compare, infer, and reason deductively and inductively. This instrument mediates precision, discrimination, and a willingness to defer judgment until all of the elements have been worked out in determining a common rule for a progression.

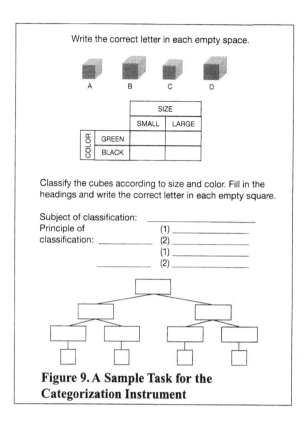

Figure 9. A Sample Task for the Categorization Instrument

Cognitive Functions Developed
- Use of relevant tacit cues like index (the place of a number in the progression).
- Projection of relationships between the elements of the progression.

Mediation of Sample Task

Mediation of challenge is essential for the very difficult, very complex, and novel sample tasks shown in Figure 10 (see next page). Mediation of intentionality, transcendence, and meaning is indicated in fostering an understanding of higher-order relationships.

Sample Task

Instructions: Fill in the progressions, the relationships between the numbers, and the relationship between the relationships.

Temporal Relations

The Temporal Relations instrument develops learner's ability to use temporal concepts to describe and order their experiences. An

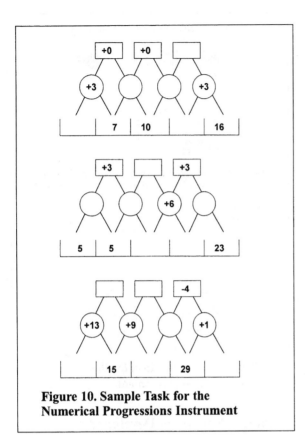

Figure 10. Sample Task for the Numerical Progressions Instrument

adequate orientation to time is important to relational thinking and is acquired through mediated learning experiences. Without an awareness of the continuity of time, its ordered succession, and of the rhythm of events, individuals make no use of their past to predict, anticipate, plan, and prioritize future events. The Temporal Relations instrument helps mediate temporal relationships and appropriate and precise use of temporal concepts and relationships.

Cognitive Functions Developed

• Comparison of the temporal characteristics of events
• Use of relevant cues
• Formulation of hypotheses

Mediation of Sample Task

Mediation of a feeling of competence is necessary in order to define the nature of the sample

tasks that follow and the relevance of the given information to its solution. Projection and control of behavior is mediated in restraining impulsivity in gathering and processing information.

Sample Task

Riddles:

1. Lucy has been in the United States for 2 years. Steve has been in the United States for 1 year. Is it possible to know which of the two is older? Why?
2. Terry runs 117 yards (107 meters) per minute. Harry runs 223 yards (214 meters) per minute. Is it possible to know who will win if they have a race? Why?
3. Maria's mother arrived in Canada 15 years ago. Maria's grandmother arrived 6 years ago. Who is older?
4. Mark and Lisa are new immigrants. Mark is 18 years old. Lisa is 16 years old. Which one has been in the country for a longer period of time?

Instructions

The Instructions instrument focuses on encoding and decoding verbal and written information. The difficulty in the tasks is not in the meaning of the words themselves, although learners may occasionally have problems with unfamiliar terms; the difficulty is rather with the significance of the words and with what they imply in context. Through the insights gained into the reasons for their successes and failures, learners are transformed into generators of information, able and willing to interpret and transmit complex instructions.

Cognitive Functions Developed

• Definition of the problem
• Comparison of completed drawing with verbal instructions
• Use of relevant cues to clarify ambiguities
• Hypothetical thinking and use of logical evidence to support hypotheses

Mediation of Sample Task

Mediated regulation and control of behavior is indicated until the instructions and picture have been completed and errors identified.

Sample Task

Instructions: Matching/not matching: On the left side of the page there is a description.

Beside the description there is a corresponding drawing. Look at the drawing and read the description. Check whether the description matches the drawing. If it does, circle the word MATCHING and go on to the next exercise. If it does not, circle the words NOT MATCHING, and write on the lines the correct description that will match the drawing. Figure 11 shows a sample task.

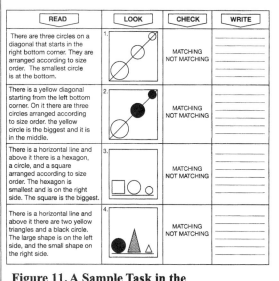

Figure 11. A Sample Task in the Instructions Instrument

Orientation in Space-II

Orientation in Space-II introduces and provides practice in the use of external, stable, and absolute systems of reference. Geographical concepts such as compass points, coordinates, and graphs are used to describe relationships and an object's orientation in space. Learners have to simultaneously apply the relative (internal) system of reference and the absolute (external) system of reference to describe and understand spatial relationships.

Cognitive Functions Developed

- Definition of the problem.
- Comparison of alternative solutions.
- Summing right and left turns and finding their equivalents in fractions of a circle.
- Projection and description of spatial relationships in terms of relative and absolute systems of reference.
- Hypothetical thinking in considering alternative solutions.
- Use of logic in the integration of two systems.

Mediation of Sample Task

An opportunity for the mediated regulation and control of behavior is provided in the sample tasks. The willingness to defer the response until the information has been decoded, gathered, and elaborated and the strategy planned is especially necessary in the last task. Figure 12 shows a sample task.

Sample Task

Instructions: Using the picture, fill in the blanks (see Figure 12 on following page).

Syllogisms

The Syllogisms instrument presents formal, propositional logic. In syllogistic reasoning, the integration of information from two premises about the relationship between terms yields the deduction of an unknown relationship. Through the tasks of Syllogisms, learners gain the ability to discriminate between valid and invalid conclusions and between possible and inevitable outcomes. The instrument fosters inferential and abstract thinking.

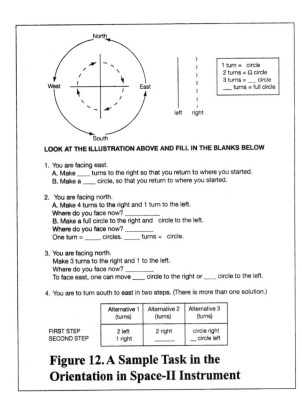

Figure 12. A Sample Task in the Orientation in Space-II Instrument

Cognitive Functions Developed

- Appropriate definition of problem.
- Spontaneous comparative behavior between attributes of a set and those of set members.
- Selection of relevant data for elaboration.
- Overcoming episodic grasp of reality by establishing relationships.
- Broadening of mental field to simultaneously elaborate information from several sources.
- Elaboration of cognitive categories on the basis of conceptual criteria.
- Use of summative behavior.
- Hypothetical thinking and search for logical evidence.

Mediation of Sample Task

Transcendence is reached through insight and generalization from the sample task into other areas of academic, vocational, and life experiences. Meaning is assigned to the logical processes that allow the mind to exceed the confines of the concrete experiences through inferential thinking. Goal-seeking, goal-setting, goal-planning, and goal-achieving behavior is mediated along with the mediation of regulated behavior and a feeling of competence. (See Figure 13).

Sample Task

Instructions: Using the drawing, answer the questions by writing the appropriate letters for each set in the parenthesis and by filling in the blanks.

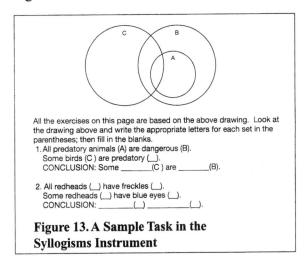

Figure 13. A Sample Task in the Syllogisms Instrument

Transitive Relations

The Transitive Relations instrument deals with relationships that exist in ordered sets, in which the differences between set members are described by the terms "greater than," "less than," and "equal to." This instrument helps learners recognize conditions that permit deductive and inductive reasoning. Through the tasks in Transitive Relations, learners demonstrate their ability to engage in inferential thinking based on logical implication and relational thinking.

Cognitive Functions Developed

- Definition of problem
- Selection of relevant information
- Comparison and categorization

- Hypothetical thinking
- Planned and systematic behavior

Mediation of Sample Task

Transcendence is reached through insight and generalization from the sample task into other areas of academic, vocational, and life experiences. Meaning is assigned to the logical processes that allow the mind to exceed the confines of the concrete experiences through inferential thinking. Goal-seeking, goal-setting, goal-planning, and goal-achieving behavior is mediated along with the mediation of regulated behavior and a feeling of competence. A feeling of optimism is mediated as students learn to induce conclusions about unknown relationships. (See Figure 14.)

Sample Task

Instructions: Complete the following problem. Four construction workers are building a building. Arthur and David together can put up two walls in one workday. Charles and Harold together can also put up two walls in one workday. Arthur does more work in one day than Charles does.

Substitute letters for the names:

Arthur _____ Charles _____

David _____ Harold _____

Using the signs (>, <), signify the relationship between the work rates:

Arthur	_____	David
Charles	_____	Harold
Arthur	_____	Charles
Charles	_____	David
David	_____	Harold
Arthur	_____	Harold

Figure 14. Sample Task in the Transitive Relations Instrument

---

Representational Stencil Design

Representational Stencil Design consists of tasks in which the student must mentally construct a design. The completion of the tasks requires a complex series of steps. The identification of the whole through its superimposed parts requires an active, mental construction with the help of inferences, and an anticipation and representation of the outcome. Answers are sought by affirmation, negation, and elimination of what is logically impossible. Learners must extrapolate from the known to the unknown and rely on logic to identify the constructions.

Cognitive Functions Developed
- Comparison
- Summative behavior
- Categorization
- Establishment of temporal and spatial relationships

Mediation of Sample Task

Challenge, competence, and optimism are mediated as students realize their ability and teachers expect them to perform this very difficult task. Regulation of impulsive behavior and representational goal-oriented cognitive behavior are key to the mediation offered by the teacher in the context of this instrument. (See Figure 15.)

Sample Task

Instructions: List the stencil numbers that make up the completed design in the right order.

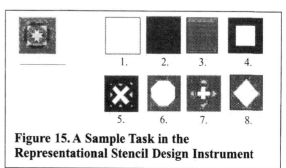

Figure 15. A Sample Task in the Representational Stencil Design Instrument

A DESCRIPTION OF THE LEARNING PROPENSITY ASSESSMENT DEVICE (LPAD)[2]

Process and Instruments

The Learning Propensity Assessment Devise (LPAD) is a series of tests or activities that (1) evaluate the way an individual learns, and (2) identify the development of cognitive functions. That is, the LPAD enables us to observe and record how a person learns, what kinds of teaching are required to respond more successfully, and how much of the observed learning is retained as new and more challenging tasks are presented. Through this approach, we can gain a picture of the way a person thinks, learns, and the possibilities for the development of their thinking and learning potential. The LPAD differs from traditional educational and psychological evaluation in that we gain information not from scores or single responses, but from observations of repeated responses to the tasks, and from teaching the subject how to solve problems and respond correctly (mediation).

Used in conjunction with standardized assessment, the LPAD adds a perspective on what kinds of interventions are needed and the individual's learning abilities and potential for growth. Another important feature of the LPAD instruments is their inclusion of all of the various important ways of processing and responding to informationæverbal, pictorial, numerical, figural, symbolic, graphicæand the ways in which the subject combines them to respond cognitively.

---

[2] This section on LPAD has been previously adapted from Feuerstein, Re., Falik, L. H., & Feuerstein, Ra. (1998). The Learning Propensity Assessment Device: An alternative approach to the assessment of learning potential. In R. J. Samuda, Re. Feuerstein, A. S. Kaufman, J. E. Lewis, & R. J. Sternberg (Eds.), *Advances in cross cultural assessment.* Thousand Oaks, CA: Sage.

An LPAD assessment consists of a battery of several instruments, chosen to allow the evaluator to observe as many as possible ways in which the learner responds. As the subject responds, the assessor gathers information, develops ideas about the learner's needs and functions, and uses these insights in choosing and analyzing performance in subsequent instruments. Therefore, the amount of time needed for the assessment and the number and range of instruments can vary a great deal.

The following is a brief description of each of the LPAD instruments used in this assessment.

Instruments Focusing on Perceptual-Motor Functions Organized by Cognitive Components

Organization of Dots

On this test, the subject looks at a model figure containing simple geometrical shapes, starting with squares and triangles, and increasing in complexity with subsequent task demands to include shapes composed of both regular and irregular curvilinear and rectilinear forms. The subject is then asked to "find" the model shapes in frames filled with unstructured, visually amorphous clouds of dots. The task is to draw lines to connect the dots to produce the shapes of the model, presented in many instances as overlapped, rotated, and superimposed in various ways. The subject must look for the relationships, plan and use information that must be internalized, and exercise eye-hand coordination to draw the connecting lines. As the subject completes the tasks the examiner observes and mediates the development and use of cognitive strategies such as planning, inferring, and regulating perceptual conflicts. The primary modality of the task is figural and graphomotor. Operations in this task include differentiation, segregation of overlapping figures, conservation of the figure across changes in its position, articulation of the field, and representation (interiorization). This instrument is based upon the original contributions of Andre Rey.

Complex Figure-Drawing Test

The Complex Figure Drawing Test is adapted from Rey (1941) and Osterrieth (1945). The subject is asked to copy the Rey/Osterreith complex geometric design by looking at the model. The subject must use organizational principles to create an efficient production in the face of the complexity of the task. The great number of units of information become reduced by organization and awareness of the succession of steps needed to internalize the multitude of details. During the first reproduction phase, only minimal orienting mediation is offered. Following the first reproduction, and after a 3- to 5-minute latency period, the subject is asked to reproduce the design from memory (without looking at the model). Following the memory phase, and based on observations of the subject's performance, a mediation phase is conducted where the examiner reviews with the subject aspects of his or her performance, identifies errors and inefficiencies, and teaches organizational and design aspects. After mediation the subject is asked to copy the design again from the stimulus model, and again from memory.

Assessment is directed toward the initial performance (e.g., organizational approach, accuracy of motor skills and structural details) in reproducing the design and changes in the second copy, and memory productions, following mediation. The task requires functioning in a figural and graphic modality and measures both short-term learning and the persistence of perceptual organization difficulties. The mental operations

involved in this test include discrimination, segregation of proximal elements, the articulation of a complex field, and reproduction, representation, differentiation, integration, and visual-motor coordination.

An additional phase is also available for this test, the Representational Organization of Complex Figures, in which the subject is presented with a template containing 10 designs, constructed in such a way that a central geometric figure is embedded in a set of adjacent or juxtaposed figures. The subject is asked to scan the first figure and indicate which part of the figure he or she would prefer to draw first, and the order in which all of the remaining parts would be drawn. The examiner then proceeds through the rest of the figures. No figure is actually drawnæthe subject merely indicates the parts and sequence in which they "would" be drawn. This phase is useful for those subjects who present persistent difficulties in organizational aspects of the CFD, and reveals the effects of mediation offered in earlier phases of the instrument. It removes from performance any difficulties the subject may have in the visual-motor modality.

Reversal Test

This instrument requires the subject to look at two figural designs contained in a frame and indicate whether they are the same or different. If different, the subject is asked to make a rapid mark, and move on to the next differentiation. There is no focused mediation on this instrument other than establishing a clear response expectation in the subject, which is done with several practice problems before the test is given. The subject responds rapidly, using visual tracking, without mediational intervention. The differentiations are based on reversals, part-whole relationships, and structural changes. The modality is figural with minimal motor performance required. While this instrument does not involve mediational intervention, it gives excellent cues regarding the development of lexic functions in the subject, and orients to mediational options in other instruments (as on Raven and Set Variations), and in the content areas of reading and mathematics (as regards the decoding aspects of numerical symbols). As this instrument has recently entered the LPAD battery, there is no corresponding section in the LPAD Examiner's Manual (Feuerstein, 1995) detailing its use. This test is based on the work of Edfeldt (1954).

Diffuse Attention Test (Lahy)

This instrument was developed by Lahy from the work of Zazzo (1964). It is used in the LPAD procedure to assess the subject's adaptability and flexibility, manifested in rapidity and precision on a task that requires visual scanning. The subject must maintain attention and focus on a visual/motor and repetitive process, learning a perceptual set, and either maintaining it over time or being able to learn a new set without interference from the prior learning. Three of the eight figures are designated as model figures, and are isolated at the top of each section of the test page which the subject "learns" to differentiate. The subject must then scan lines of 40 figures, comprising the eight figures presented in a random order, and mark the three model figures when they are perceived and identified. The stimulus field is thus perceptually quite dense, and requires the subject to scan carefully and work to maintain visual tracking and cognitive attention. There are two forms of this test, one having only one such array, and 24 lines of stimuli to scan. A second form has three sections, with three different sets of three-dimensional model figures, thus enabling the assessment of retroactive inhibition—the effect of learning one set

of differentiations on the subsequent performance on another set. Performance is observed in one-minute intervals, yielding scores of the proportion of correct and incorrect inclusions, and omissions, within the segments. No mediation is typically offered during the performance on the task, but the task can be practiced and mediated in a variety of ways after performance, and repeated after various practice experiences, to assess the changes with "over learning." The modality of this test is visual-motor and graphic. The operations included are limited to the identification of differentiated cues (an encoding process) and the "re-cognition" of the model.

Instruments Focusing on Memory, With a Learning Component

Positional Learning Test (5 x 25)

This test is adapted from the work of Andre Rey. The subject is shown a grid of 25 squares, organized in 5 rows and 5 columns, with 5 positions (corresponding to one for each row and column) designated and indicated by the examiner using an auditory verbal and motor modality (saying "here" and pointing). After a short (10-second) latency period, the subject is asked to reproduce the indicated positions by marking them on the same grid. The procedure is repeated, with minimal mediation, until the subject can reproduce the pattern correctly three times in succession. If the subject experiences difficulty, mediation is directed toward the apparent source of the errors, and to establishing strategies that the subject can use. After learning one pattern, the procedure is repeated similarly with different patterns, enabling the examiner to observe learning of new patterns in the presence of previously learned and potentially confounding patterns. The learning on this instrument reflects a visual-motor and graphic modality and requires the subject to use the operations of encoding, sequencing, and the reproduction of a perceived set of positions.

Plateaux Test

This instrument is also adapted from the work of Andre Rey. On this test, the subject is presented with a set of four plates, superimposed upon one another in the subject's view. Each plate contains nine buttons or pegs, arranged in three parallel columns or rows (a 3 x 3 design). Each plate has one peg that cannot be removed. The fixed peg is in a different position on each of the four plates. On the exploratory phase, the subject is asked to search for the fixed peg on the first plate by taking out the pegs and replacing them until the fixed one is located, and to identify its position. The subject is asked to repeat the process for the remaining three plates successively, being encouraged to develop strategies leading to learning the positions on each plate and discovering a generalizationærule or principleærelating to the pattern of fixed positions. After the subject has learned the four positions (making three errorless repetitions), the orientation of the plate is rotated and the subject is asked to identify the position of the fixed pegs following the rotation(s). A second, representational phase is undertaken when the subject is asked to draw the pattern of fixed pegs on paper, reflecting a two-dimensional transition and interiorization. This phase assesses the transition from the concrete position to the use of a memorized or internalized representation from a three dimensional experience to a graphical two dimensional planeæa substitution of learned reality. A third phase is introduced in order to learn about the plasticity and flexibility of the memorized data. In this phase the well established positions and their successions are successively rotated by 90, 180, and 270 degrees, and the examinee is required to represent schemati-

cally (on paper) the fixed peg in the new positions produced by the respective rotations. This phase represents a higher ordered cognitive operation than the simple reproduction of the positions and their initial graphic representations, reflecting the outcome of rotations requiring shifting of learned positions.

Associative Recall

Associative Recall is assessed through two tests: The Functional Reduction and Part-Whole and the 16-Word Memory Test. Descriptions of these tests follow.

1. Functional Reduction and Part-Whole

This test consists of two versions, similar in organization and objective but differing in stimulus presentation. The subject is shown a page that contains a row of 20 simple line drawings along the top row, selected for their familiarity to the subject and the unambiguity of their figural presentations. In the first row the objects are presented in their entirety, and the subject is asked to name them (a labeling phase). In the second row, on the Functional Reduction (FR) page drawings of functional substitutes are shown. On the Part-Whole (PW) page a salient feature of the object is presented. In the third and fourth rows, there is a further stimulus reduction and changes in order of presentation. The subject is asked to recall the original labeled object on the top row from a visual inspection of the reduced stimuli under the various conditions presented in the subsequent rows that are exposed, with the preceding rows concealed. The FR page is usually used with most subjects, and the PW page may be used when the examiner feels further mediation is needed for repetition or crystallization of the functions learned on the FR page, or when the subject's level of perceptual functioning suggests that restricting the task to a focus on structural details as the link to associate memory will yield more efficient and elaborative responses. Both pages also enable the assessment of immediate free recall and delayed free recall of the original 20 objects. The modality of this test is visual, auditory, motor and graphic. It requires the subject to use the operations of encoding, symbolization, and the discovery of functional relationships.

2. 16-Word Memory Test

This test consists to a group of 16 simple common words presented orally to the subject. The words are presented in a fixed but conceptually random order. The subject is asked to repeat as many as can be recalled following the presentation of the list and a latency period of approximately ten seconds. The subject is told that the process will be repeated several times. No mediation is offered for the first three or four repetitions. The examiner observes the subject's spontaneous recognition and inclusion in memory of the four categories into which the 16 words can be grouped. After approximately four repetitions, mediation is offered if needed to encourage the memory process, using a variety of cues, both mnemonic and cognitive, until the subject can recall all or a majority of the list using internalized memory functions and achieve accuracy and efficiency of response. The modalities of this test are auditory and verbal, and the mental operations require the reproduction of an auditory set of stimuli, internalized controls, organization, and both encoding and decoding (representationally) skills.

Instruments Involving Higher-Order Cognitive Processes and Mental Operations

Tri-Modal Analogies

This instrument is used with younger children and low-functioning individuals to establish analogical thinking, using figural,

pictorial, symbolic, and verbal modalities. The stimuli require the subject to mentally manipulate and elaborate, thus moving the learner into abstract mental operations without needing to rely on concrete manipulatives. As such, the stimuli are useful as a preliminary to working on the more abstract and complex Raven's and Set Variations tasks. The instrument is administered in a format similar to the Set Variations described shortly.

The subject is shown two stimuli, asked to consider the relationship between them, and then to look at a third stimulus. The subject is then asked to select from a number of alternatives a fourth choice that is consistent with the relationship existing in the first two.

The learner is required to use concepts of size, shape, number, and positional orientation to establish relationships and complete the analogy. The mediational opportunities in this instrument enable the teaching of orienting and superordinate concepts, and the analysis of errors can indicate areas of deficiency or fragility in concept formation or acquisition. The general progression of tasks is at a lower level (as regards necessary mental operations), but assesses similar processes as in the Raven's and Set Variations instruments described shortly.

This instrument has just entered the LPAD battery, but at the present time is not addressed in the Revised Examiner's Manual (Feuerstein, 1995). However, the reader is advised to study the sections on the Raven's and Set Variations instruments to develop a deeper understanding of, for example, the mediational suggestions, general goals and objectives, because there is a close consonance.

LPAD Matrices

The instruments used in the LPAD procedures are those of the published Ravens Colored (CPM) and Standard Progressive

Matrices (SPM) (1956; 1958). Set Variations B-8 to B-12 are based on Ravens CPM items 8 to 12. Set Variations I is based on items from the CPM levels A, Ab, and B. Set Variations II is based principles similar to SPM levels C, D, and E, but the items present greater novelty in the modality of presentation. The LPAD objective in the presentation of these problems to the examinee is to assess to what extent a rule and set of prerequisites acquired to solve a particular problem are adaptively used in variations of the task, and to what extent the learned elements of the original task become the facilitating factor in adaptation to the new task.

The Ravens instruments are administered according to LPAD procedures, using a "test-teach-retest" approach. The Set Variations instruments are constructed and administered on principles similar to those of Ravens, with a sample problem for each set of variations which receives intensive mediation, and then independent performance is observed on a series of problems similar to but also becoming progressively more difficult than the mediational example. The tasks require the learner to look at a series of designs, and complete the series by selecting a correct alternative from a number of choices. To choose the correct alternative, the subject must understand the relationship among the variables. The tasks progressively add variables and change the dimensions used to establish the relationships. What is assessed on these tasks is the subject's ability to think using analogies presented as figural (visual/perceptual) information, and his or her response to the teaching of strategies to solve the problem. The operations involved are those of perceptual closure and discrimination; and the generation of new information through synthesis, permutations and seriation, inferential thinking, analogical thinking, deductive reasoning, and relational thinking.

Representational Stencil Design Test (RSDT)

The RSDT is based on the Stencil Design Test of Grace Arthur (1930) but differs significantly in its structure and technique of application, primarily in its shift of the task away from the concrete, manipulative modality toward a representational, internalized modality. In the LPAD procedure, the design is constructed by the subject on a purely mental level. The instrument consists of 20 designs, which the subject must reconstruct representationally by referring to a page of model "solid" and "cut-out" stencils that must be mentally superimposed upon one another. The problems increase in level of difficulty (on dimensions of form, color, and structure) and are organized so that mastering simpler problems leads to the ability to successfully solve harder ones. The procedure of this test is to orient the subject to the Stencil page, offer a test page of problems, and then provide a training page to mediate various processes and strategies according to what is observed during performance on the test page. A parallel test is provided to be used following mediation. The instrument assesses the subject's ability to learn a complex task using internalized systems of organizing, and to use acquired learning to solve more complicated problems. Part of what is assessed in this instrument is how readily available the learner's inner (representational) processes are, and how easily and adaptively they are used in subsequent problems of increased complexity and abstraction. The modalities involved are figural, numerical, and verbal. The operations involved in successful mastery of the tasks are segregation, differentiation, representation, anticipation of transformation, encoding and decoding, and generalization.

Numerical Progressions

This test assesses the subject's capacity to understand and deal with relationships, identify them as rules, and apply them to building new information, using numerical and graphic modalities. The task presents progressions of numbers related to one another according to rules which must be deduced from the available information. At the end of a sequence of numbers the subject is asked to supply the two missing numbers. A correct response infers that the subject has understood how the numbers are related to one another. The format is that of a pretest, a learning phase, and two forms of a post-test. In the learning phase, the subject is encouraged to formulate and state the rule by which the answers were achieved. The examiner teaches relationships that are not understood and establishes strategies according to an analysis of needs (errors and performance on the pretest). Following mediation, a post-test is given to determine how well the subject has learned strategies for solving the problems. The parallel form of the post-test makes possible the assessment of the permanence and stability of what has been learned over time. The operations involved in this instrument are those of basic mathematics (addition, subtraction, multiplication, and division) and the more generalized mental operations of differentiation, segregation, inferential thinking, and deductive reasoning.

Organizer

This instrument presents the subject with a series of verbal statements consisting of sets of items which must be organized according to closed, logical systems. The task involves the subject placing the items (e.g., colors, objects, people) in positions relative to one another according to the determined attributes or conditions presented in the statements. A series of statements or premises is presented in each task. Each premise permits the extraction of only a part of the needed information required to determine a full and precise placement of the items. Thus, the subject must gather available information, develop and test hypotheses with succeeding information given, and generate information which is not immediately available in the given propositions. The tasks become more complex because of more units of information and the level of inference needed to solve them. What is assessed in this instrument is the subject's ability to gather new information through the use of inferential processes, formulate hypotheses and test them according to new information or assumptions generated, and apply strategies for discovering relationships. The instrument consists of pretest, learning, and test phases. The modality is verbal, with a numerical subcomponent. The operations involve decoding, encoding, representation, inferential thinking, transitive thinking, combinatorial skills, propositional reasoning, negation, with a heavy loading of mnemonic (memory) functions.

CONCLUSION

This chapter presented a brief overview of Mediated Learning Experience, Feuerstein's Instrumental Enrichment, and the Learning Propensity Assessment Device. Work with these models has been done with many different groups of children and their families. The principles described in this chapter are consistent with the emphasis throughout *The ICDL Clinical Practice Guidelines* to use an understanding of a child's developmental profile as a basis for creating individualized learning interactions. It is these individualized learning interactions that create the opportunity for growth. ■

REFERENCES

Arthur, G. A. (1930) *A point scale of performance tests: Clinical manual, Vol. I.* New York: Commonwealth Fund.

Feuerstein, R. (1995) *Revised LPAD examiner's manual.* Jerusalem, Israel: International Center for the Enhancement of Learning Potential.

Osterreith, P. A. (1945). Copie d'une figure complexe. Archives de Psychologie, 205-353.

Rey, A. (1959). *Test de copie d'use figure complexe.* Manual. Paris: Centre de Psychologie Applique.

Zazzo, R. (1964) *Le test de deuz barrages.* Neuchatel: Delachaux et Niestle.

—◄ 23 ►—

Speech-Language Development: Oral and Written

Patricia Lindamood, M.S., C.C.C.-S.L.P., and Phyllis Lindamood

The human brain comes wired for language. Under normal development, the brain has a broad-based ability to acquire receptive and expressive oral language followed later by written language. Whatever the particular language a child is born into, the child's brain acquires those specific phonemes and the syllable patterns through which they combine to form words. These phonemes and syllable patterns are thus the foundation for acquiring the morphology, grammar, syntax, and semantics through which the words then form the structure of the language. Under normal development, acquisition occurs simply by having the brain immersed in the auditory input of that language. Considering that there are more than 5,000 languages in the world, this attests to the brain's incredible flexibility and innate capacity for language.

Immersion in language, however, does not result in normal oral language development for an estimated 10% or more of the population; problems in written language development are much higher. The National Adult Literacy Survey (1993) indicated that 48% of the adult population lack written language skills sufficient for the normal requirements of life. This is in spite of those individuals having had opportunities for schooling, with some of them even having college degrees. This chapter provides an overview of what is known about normal oral and written language development, factors that can interfere with that development, current interventions that are proving effective in preventing or remediating speech-language and written language problems, and some questions in need of further investigation.

HIERARCHIES IN ORAL LANGUAGE ACQUISITION

Research and theory on language acquisition have largely dealt with English language learning. Contributions from crosslinguistic study of language acquisition and infant research are broadening our understandings. Although much is still unknown, infant research shows promise of helping to identify predictors of later problems, which could enable intervention to be mounted earlier for preventive action. David Lewkowicz and colleagues with the New York State Institute for Basic Research in Developmental Disabilities have been seeking better understanding of perceptual development in human infants in research spanning more than 20 years. Lewkowicz has particularly focused on how infants perceive the relationship between auditory and visual information within the general issue of intersensory integration. In his most recent work with faces and voices,

Lewkowicz (1999, in press) found that complex relationships are involved in whether infants attend to auditory or visual information, and depend on the specific nature of the information presented. Overall, infants are sensitive to the synchrony of auditory and visual inputs. Lewkowicz (2000) has recently proposed a theoretical model related to responsiveness to the four basic features of multimodal temporal experience; that is, temporal synchrony, duration, temporal rate, and rhythm. Lewkowicz's model proposes that responsiveness emerges in a sequential, hierarchical fashion during the first year of life and that responsiveness to one temporal feature builds on the previously acquired intersensory temporal processing skills. According to Lewkowicz (personal communication), "Much of the support for the model comes from our work showing that infants detect and respond to temporal synchrony relations very early in development, but that they do not begin to respond to intersensory temporal relations based on duration and rate until later in the first year of life." These findings suggest a probable benefit for speech-language development if we make it a point to hold our babies so they have the synchrony of visual input from our faces with the auditory input from our voices as we talk to them.

Slobin (1997) has also been researching speech and language development for more than 20 years. He has led the way in identifying additional universals in language development through crosslinguistic studies. Slobin's view of language acquisition has evolved. Initially skeptical regarding an innate structure for language, later he recognized "strongly inbuilt tendencies to analyze speech into certain types of units, and to systematize and interrelate and cross-classify these units in highly specific ways" (Slobin, 1985, p. 1244). His current view is that there are *"indications of accessibility hierarchies and individual differences which are based on independent cognitive or processing variables rather than on linguistic features across languages"* (Slobin, 1997, p. 452, italics added). We at Lindamood-Bell Learning Processes strongly agree with Slobin's current view. Our clinical and classroom experience and research definitely validate his position that it is not the linguistic features of languages that cause differences in how children access the hierarchies of developmental progression, but that the differences are due to individual variations in sensory or cognitive processing abilities. In approaching children with a wide range of special needs, including speech and language, Greenspan and Wieder (1997) have provided a Developmental, Individual Differences, Relationship-based (DIR) intervention model with this same basic philosophy: that individual differences in each child's functional developmental profile and the ability to interact with the sensory world, form emotional and interactive relationships with people, and cognitively connect to incoming sensory information are what should drive our intervention, not the child's chronological age (see Chapter 3 for further discussion of the DIR model). In their model, the age-appropriate interactions known as floor time set the tone for this philosophy of intervention. Floor time begins at the basis of communication; that is, emotional and interactive relationships between child, parents, and other caregivers.

PROGRESSIONS IN NORMAL SPEECH-LANGUAGE DEVELOPMENT

Vowels, Consonants, and Babbling

Under normal patterns of acquisition, there is a normal range of individual differences in how early speech-language emerges.

However, the development of spoken language follows a hierarchy of progression in its emergence, and that hierarchy is essentially the same across languages, regardless of the final form of the specific language. For example, in all languages, infants produce isolated vowel and consonant phonemes very early. The child, however, experiences several months of receptive language input before combining consonants and vowels together repetitively to produce simple syllables in the vocal play called babbling. Babbling, and the extension of this play with nonsense syllables into chants, rhymes, and songs by older children and adults, occurs in all known languages and tells us the human mind finds this play with syllables pleasurable. There is even a core of same-syllable configurations involving the same phonemes that occurs across many languages.

Single Words

Single words are the next step in the progression, and here the linguistic environment can have an effect. For example, nouns for names of people and things are stimulated and acquired first in English, but verbs are stimulated and acquired first in Japanese (Clancy, 1985) and in Mandarin Chinese (Tardif, 1996). Choi noted that verbs are acquired first in Korean, and reported a connection between language and cognition because her data indicated form-function relationships were attended to as early as first words (Slobin, 1997). The senior author of this chapter also observed this on the second morning of a car trip from New York to California. As her 9-month-old son awakened in a hotel room again, he looked around wonderingly and asked, "Bye-Bye?" His rising inflection clearly indicated he was asking whether he would be traveling again that day.

Interestingly, at 10 months of age, he began forcing the naming of things. When he saw something for which he didn't have a name, he would point and stare intently in its direction while making a radar-type blip sound. As we (his parents) named various things in the vicinity he was indicating, he would shake his head "No" and continue the sound until he was satisfied that he had a name for the object of his interest. Then the sound would stop. This naming demand may have been stimulated by our early efforts to introduce him to language. Starting when he was about 6 months of age, we had expressly given single words for things and actions so that he could experience the beginning and end of a word rather than having those features lost within the flow of a sentence. During his babbling period, we had also enjoyed an interaction with him that increased and varied his babbling. For example, after he said "ba,ba,ba" we repeated it, and then he said it again. When this interaction was set, we imitated the babbled pattern a second time but varied the final syllable as in "ba,ba,ga" or "ba,ba,da" to see if he would perceive and produce the change. He could and did, after a short transition period when he just accepted the second stimulation receptively for a period before he began to imitate the variation.

The progression from isolated sounds to the syllable play of babbling to meaningful single words will, of course, occur normally without the interactive stimulation just described. However, many real words in our language are composed of only two sounds: a vowel/consonant (VC), that is, eat, in, out, up, on; or a consonant/vowel (CV), that is, go, bye, see, pie, no, and so on. When imitative interaction is established during babbling with these simple syllables, it facilitates the early acquisition of a vocabulary of similarly structured real words and empowers children to become early active communicators in their world.

Jargon

Just before or during the period when single words are first beginning to emerge, standard descriptions of language development cite a *jargon period*. This is when children express long strings of syllables inflected in the normal rhythm and prosody of sentences. The jargon period is referred to as a necessary and normal stage in speech and language development, but it can be a frustrating period for parent and child. The child appears to be communicating an idea or a request, but the parent cannot understand it because no single word is discernible. There is a possibility, however, that this frustrating jargon period could be avoided and does not have to be a step in "normal" development. For example, when my child forced the extensive single-word naming, he acquired sufficient words to go easily into phrases and sentences, thereby bypassing the jargon period. On the basis of that experience, the same babbling intervention and extensive single-word naming were provided to two more sons and a daughter, and the same phenomenon occurred. None of them experienced a jargon period. They bypassed it and went from intelligible single words to intelligible phrases and sentences. Although this is only anecdotal information, it would appear a pilot study is warranted with a formal experimental and control group design to explore whether the effect of such intervention can be replicated and jargon bypassed. Data from intervention research indicate that environmental variables can influence infant vocalization and later phonological development (McReynolds, 1978).

Milestones

The following developmental milestones in speech-language acquisition were summarized by Berry (1969), although there can be wide individual variation. In general, the timing occurrence of Berry's milestones has not changed appreciably in the years since that initial analysis, judging by the work of Rescorla (1989). These milestones follow.

- With the single-word receptive and expressive vocabulary developing steadily in the period between 1 and 2 years, a child normally develops a minimum 50-word vocabulary and combining of words into phrases between 18 and 24 months.
- A child will normally progress to short sentences before 30 months of age. By 36 months, a child can structure sentences as questions, and most sentences involve three or more words. Speech is fairly intelligible, although inconsistent substitutions, omissions, and distortions of consonants will be common.
- Between 3 and 4 years of age, a child makes important gains in phoneme production and accurate articulation of consonants in various positions in words. Omissions and substitutions are significantly reduced, and speech is 90% or more intelligible.
- By 5 years of age, some children will still have problems articulating the consonants /f/, /v/, /th/, /l/, /r/ or /s/. But, since these errors generally do not make speech unintelligible, speech pathologists in school settings tend to wait to see whether maturation will take care of these problems before scheduling these children for speech therapy.
- Between 6 and 8 years of age, a child's speech becomes virtually 100% intelligible. However, about 10% of children may need some assistance in mastering those final, more complex phonemes or in some

aspect of language comprehension or expression. The average sentence involves about seven words, and any grammar irregularities are likely to be related to the child's cultural environment.

In spite of this positive picture for oral language becoming adequate for the bulk of the population during the course of normal development, two major concerns remain. First, the picture for written language development is far different, as cited previously. Also, research has shown clearly that early problems in articulation are predictive of later problems in written language acquisition and that lack of phoneme awareness is a factor in both (Mann, 1993). This suggests that phoneme awareness should be routinely stimulated as a preventive early in speech-language development. Preventive action should also be planned to avoid written language problems by helping all children to develop and consciously connect phoneme awareness to the logic of our alphabet system for success in spelling and reading (Lindamood, Bell, & Lindamood, 1997a). Preventive action is not a waste for those with a genetic predisposition to acquire phoneme awareness; it simply accelerates their development of spoken and written language skill and the benefits and pleasures it provides (Lindamood, Bell, & Lindamood, 1997b).

Second, when vocabulary and syntax are adequate, language comprehension and expression are often also assumed to be adequate. However, data from college and adult populations indicate that significant weakness in language comprehension can persist even into adulthood for significant numbers of individuals. For example, in a recent measure of performance of 60 freshmen Early Education majors on the Watson-Glaser Test of Critical Thinking, 50% of them ranked at the 20th percentile or below. In performance on the Watson-Glaser for 50 primary and

secondary classroom teachers, special education, resource, reading teachers, and speech pathologists, 28% ranked at the 25th percentile or below (Lindamood, Bell, & Lindamood, unpublished data). This should be of concern in these training programs because the weakness indicated can be identified and remediated.

PREVENTING ORAL SPEECH-LANGUAGE PROBLEMS

Vegetative Functions

Speech is an overlaid function. The basic functions of the mouth are vegetative and involve sucking, valving, swallowing, and, later, chewing. Thus, the motor coordination of vegetative functions is a base for the motor coordinations of speech. Preventive and remedial intervention should first give attention to the vegetative acts to be certain this base is functional. The mouth at rest should be closed, with the tongue in light contact with the roof of the mouth. If the jaw is slack and the mouth open, the tongue follows the jaw and is pulled away from its normal rest position. We swallow twice a minute. If the tongue is resting down and forward instead of up and in, this encourages a tongue-thrust position in swallowing. The tongue sucks and valves forward rather than taking its normal position against the roof of the mouth, where it forms a peripheral seal while a peristaltic action moves liquids and solids to the back of the mouth for swallowing. When babies are nursed, the mother's nipple flattens between the tongue and the roof of the mouth and facilitates this normal swallowing action. When babies are bottle-fed, long firm nipples that don't flatten can interfere with this normal pattern. The MAWS Feeding Bottle with its VARIFLO nipple and the AVENT Naturally have nipples designed to facilitate this normal sucking and swallowing pattern and are wise choices. They are both European products, but are available widely in the United States in stores selling baby goods. It is well to avoid the extended use of pacifiers and thumb-sucking because they also interfere with the tongue's normal rest position and action in sucking and swallowing and in speech. With well-coordinated vegetative functions, drooling is controlled, and the use of the tongue, lips, and mouth in articulatory action is facilitated.

Vocal Play

When sensory stimulation is begun by parents and other caregivers through early vocal play, an interactive relationship is established that can continue to develop and be enjoyed throughout the normal emergence and progression of language.

- *The rationale* is language emerges as a result of sensory stimuli. We see, hear, and feel and connect those experiences to form language.
- *The procedure* is to select and intensify the input of sensory stimuli basic to language.

Given the brain's innate tendency to imitate speech, vocal play with babies with individual consonants and vowels can be initiated very early. It is easy and fun to do and to observe their interest and response. For example, if babies are diapered on a counter or changing table, this is an ideal time for vocal play. The adult's face and mouth are above the baby and close enough to give an excellent view of tongue and mouth actions. Another good time is when giving babies a bath, or anytime there can be close physical contact for a few minutes without other distractions. To make tongue actions visible, caregivers should keep their mouth as open as possible. All manner of nonspeech sounds and mouth

actions can also be included, such as tongue clucking, lip smacking, lip pursing and blowing, tongue grooving, tongue protrusion, or tongue trilling. Babies only a few months old can imitate tongue trilling. The first indication that they are registering the tongue action is when their tongue tip rises and holds on their upper gum ridge. Some time after that they will produce a trill, matching the trilling input. Because the processing of speech sounds and the human voice occur in different parts of the brain than are involved in the processing of other acoustic signals, it is important to include individual vowel and consonant sounds, too. High and low tonal contrasts should also be offered.

For vocal play with vowels and consonants, the following categories and their labels are suggested from the Lindamood Phoneme Sequencing™ (LiPS™) program (Lindamood & Lindamood, 1998), formerly the Auditory Discrimination in Depth (ADD) program. When the LiPS™ program is used to remediate oral and written language problems with children who can answer questions, its categories are not told; they are discovered through Socratic questioning and problem-solving experiences in analyzing the oral-motor actions that produce individual speech sounds. In preventive stimulation with infants, however, the individual sounds are simply produced in a play routine, twice with exaggerated articulation while the baby is watching, and again after approximately a 3-second pause. No sound imitation occurs at first, but the baby's mouth begins mirroring the stimulus mouth shape. The sensory input provided must be experienced receptively for some time before the brain begins to interact with it. With children between 1 and 3 years of age, the labels for the categories are verbalized during stimulation (i.e., "Watch me make a lip popper - /p/!"). This directs the child's attention to the motor production features that distinguish the sounds. The child can also feel the difference between plosive and continuant air streams by having the child feel the air stream on the back of his or her hand.

Vowels

There are four vowel categories, which are labeled for mouth shape. They should be stimulated in the order presented, with the easier ones to imitate given first.
1. Round sounds
   - /OO/ (as in boot)
   - /OO/ (as in foot)
   - /OE/ (as in toe)
2. Open sounds
   - /O/ (as in odd)
   - /AW/ (as in paw)
3. Smile sounds
   - /EE/ (as in eek)
   - /I/ (as in it)
   - /E/ (as in Ed)
   - /AE/ (as in ape)
   - /A/ (as in at)
   - /U/ (as in up)

As imitation occurs on some of these, add the "Sliders," which involve sliding from one mouth shape to another.
4. Sliders
   - /IE/ (as in ice)
   - /UE/ (as in use)
   - /OI/ (as in oil)
   - /OW/ (as in owl)

Consonants

There are eleven categories of consonants. There are eight "quiet/noisy" pairs, in which each pair has the same mouth action but one sound is quiet (whispered) and the other is noisy (voiced). The whispered sound should be given first in each pair. There are also three other groups in this category for which some primary feature of the sounds is the same, and the label identifies that same-

ness. As with vowels, consonant sounds should be presented with exaggerated mouth actions.
- Quiet/Noisy Pairs:
  - Lip poppers: /p, b/
  - Tip tappers: /t, d/
  - Scrapers: /k, g/
  - Lip coolers: /f, v/
  - Tongue coolers: /th, th/
  - Skinny air: /s, z/
  - Fat air: /sh, zh/
  - Fat pushed air: /ch, j/
- Other Groups:
  - Nose sounds: /m, n, ng/
  - Wind sounds: /w, h, wh/
  - Lifters: /l, r/

Babbling

Babies babble spontaneously, producing repetitive CV syllables after enough play has occurred with isolated consonants and vowels. To increase the amount of babbling, feed back the syllables the baby has just produced. Pause to allow the baby to produce them again. To increase the variety of sounds used in babbling, feed back the sequence of syllables produced by the baby, but modify the last syllable. For example:

Baby: /ba,ba,ba/
Adult: /ba,ba,ba/
Baby: /ba,ba,ba/
Adult: /ba,ba,da/
Baby: (May just listen for a while before imitating changes.)

Some parents misinterpret participating in a baby's babbling as encouraging "baby talk." It is not. "Baby talk" is encouraging simplified mispronunciations of words (i.e., /boo/ for blue). Helping babies to extend and modify the babbling of syllables strengthens and enriches their experience with the building blocks of language.

Even deaf babies babble initially, but the babbling extinguishes after a period because they do not experience the stimulation of the auditory feedback. However, when mirrors are hung over their beds so that they get visual feedback from their mouth movements, they continue to babble longer. Because of the crucial importance of early intervention for deaf and hearing-impaired babies, a coalition of 20 organizations capped a 9-year effort and attained passage of the "Newborn and Infant Hearing Screening and Intervention Act" by Congress in November 1999. This landmark legislation specifies that three federal agencies will work together to develop, expand, and link statewide screening programs and intervention services so that every newborn in America will be screened for hearing loss and will have access to intervention (Boswell, 2000).

Single Words

Naming

As with the previous sensory input, babies need to experience naming input receptively for a period before they begin to name things in expressive output. Table 1 illustrates the differences between the receptive and expressive levels of naming. In naming, include single-word verbs and adjectives as well as nouns so children learn to name features and actions as well as things. For example, name the banana you are about to share, but also name what you do with it: peel, bite, chew. Use single words for what it is like: sweet, good. Also, use synonyms to

give exposure to more than one name for something. In this way, children are stimulated with single-word language that they soon use. This emphasis on providing stimulation with single words will not deprive children of exposure to the language they will use eventually because phrases and sentences are receptively stimulated whenever others are conversing around them. Exaggerate the final consonants in pronouncing words. Children perceive initial consonants earlier than final consonants unless the final consonants are given extra attention. When possible, hold objects being named next to your mouth to permit the child to synchronize the auditory and visual input. When saying words ending in the plosive sounds /p, b/, /t, d/, /k, g/, or /ch, j/, say the words against the child's hand so the exploded air can be felt, since it cannot be seen. Again, this permits a synchronized experience with the auditory and kinesthetic input and increases the sensory experience with the words.

Phrases and Sentences

In developing a child's phrases and sentences, use gesture to pantomime actions, size, shape, or movement when possible to provide visual images for the meaning of phrases and sentences. Synchronize these meaningful gestures with language. Verbalize about your activities: what you are doing, what you are noticing, what you are thinking. Table 2 illustrates the differences between the

Table 1. Receptive and Expressive Levels of Naming	
Receptive Level	**Expressive Level**
Hears own name, looks at self in mirror	Names self
Touches body part named	Names body parts
Points to people named	Names people
Points to objects named	Names objects
Does actions named	Names actions to manipulate environment

Table 2. Receptive and Expressive Levels in Phrase and Sentence Use	
Receptive Level	**Expressive Level**
Complies with noun/verb or noun phrase request	Uses noun/verb or noun phrase to manipulate environment
Complies with sentence request	Communicates with sentences

receptive and expressive levels in phrase and sentence use.

The suggested progression will assist the development of speech-language in three important ways. First, by starting at the sensory level to stimulate conscious awareness of the distinctive motor-kinesthetic, visual, and auditory features of phonemes, a child will develop phoneme awareness. Second, this progression also provides a strong support base for the later development of written language. Phoneme awareness has been documented in worldwide research as the best single predictor of success in acquiring written language skills (Shankweiler and Liberman, 1989). Third, stimulation of images for the meaning of words and the ideas expressed by language increases comprehension of oral and written language. Individuals with strong imagery for words have the benefit of dual coding of language (Paivio, 1996).

REMEDIATING DELAYED LANGUAGE DEVELOPMENT

Oral Language Delay

What if oral speech-language development is obviously delayed? It is not uncommon for pediatricians to tell parents who are concerned because their 3-year-old does not have intelligible speech to relax—that their child may just be a "late bloomer." There are many reasons to take preventive action instead, primarily because speech-language delay also causes problems in several other areas of development. Therefore, it would be highly desirable for pediatricians to lead in preventive action. Speech-language stimulation can be light and fun for both the person providing the stimulation and the one receiving it. Pediatricians could arrange with speech pathologists to teach parenting groups the art of enjoying vocal play with their babies, starting very early and then continuing through the progression of language development just described. From the field of behavioral psychology, the research of Hart and Risley (1996) strongly supports preventive action. In a $2^{1}/_{2}$-year longitudinal study, they observed 42 families for an hour each month to learn what typically went on in homes with 1- and 2-year-old children learning to talk. They report that the most important difference among the families was the amount of talking that went on within five categories of quality features: language diversity; proportional amounts of feedback tone providing encouragement and discouragement; emphasis on names, relations, and recall; an interactive style focused on asking rather than demanding; and responsiveness stressing the importance of the child's behavior during an interaction.

In extrapolating from their observational data, Hart and Risley found significant differences in the amount of talking related to socioeconomic status (SES) differences. In a 100-hour week, the average child in the professional families was provided with 215,000 words of language experience, whereas the average child in a working-class family was provided with 125,000. The average child in a welfare family was provided with 62,000 words of language experience. A reverse pattern emerged for SES differences related to children's hourly verbal encouragements versus discouragements from parents. In professional families, the average child accumulated "32 affirmatives and 5 prohibitions per hour, a ratio of 6 encouragements to 1 discouragement." In working-class families, the average child accumulated "12 affirmatives and 7 prohibitions per hour, a ratio of 2 encouragements to 1 discouragement." In welfare families, the average child received "5 affirmatives and 11 prohibitions per hour, a ratio of 1 encouragement to 2 discouragements" (Hart & Risley, 1996, p. 199). Extrapolating these weekly and hourly differences to estimate differences in children's cumulative verbal experiences makes it easy to understand why these differences "were strongly linked to differences at age 3 in rates of vocabulary growth, vocabulary use, and general accomplishments, and strongly linked to differences in school performance at age 9" (Hart & Risley, 1996, p. 193). Hart and Risley point out that daycare providers and parents need specific training if they are to help close the gap for lower SES children. It is clear from these data that it is vital to have well-planned and funded intervention to help parents and other caregivers understand the critical effect on children's speech-language development of the amount of time spent talking with them, the importance of an encouraging tone of voice, and why this input must begin in the infant years.

However, the number of single words that a child recognizes and uses is not in itself a guarantee of language comprehension when those words occur in sequence to express ideas, requests, and questions. The ability to create visual images for the gestalts being expressed by language is an additional processing level that must not be taken for granted. The problem is less likely to be recognized as a lack of imagery for language, and is often thought to be related to less intelligence or a problem in paying attention. Fortunately, in our experience we have found the ability to create visual imagery for language can be directly stimulated with special procedures, with life-enhancing effects. (See Bell, Chapter 25, this volume.)

Written Language Delay

What if written language development is delayed, not only in first and second grade when children are first learning to read, but through middle and secondary schools and into adulthood? Currently, the general guidelines that public schools work under require a child's reading skills to be 2 years or more below grade level before remedial services can be offered through Federal Title I funding. Compare this to a child having a physical illness. Would we require a child to be ill for 2 years before diagnosis and treatment could be provided? Research has shown that the lack of phoneme awareness is the primary cause of problems in learning to read, that it is a genetic tendency (DeFries, Fulkes, and Labuda, 1987), and that there is neurophysiological evidence that lack of phoneme awareness is related to brain structure and function differences. Given this information, is it reasonable then to require a child to endure this cause of an "illness" in learning to read for 2 years before treatment is officially considered appropriate? And, when medical treatment is offered to an ill child, would doctors offer the same treatment that did not work before? This is commonly the situation in educational settings when retention has been the solution to below-grade-level reading. Fresh thinking and action in the educational field are required to address reading difficulties.

Fortunately, more and more parents are becoming advocates for their children and are seeking out and demanding adequate intervention (Kantrowitz and Underwood, 1999). Unfortunately, when early intervention has not been provided or has not been successful, well-meaning but poorly informed educators, psychologists, and doctors may incorrectly advise parents that older students who are not reading well by middle-school age cannot be expected to overcome their problem. It is usually suggested that efforts must be directed instead toward making use of various compensatory strategies rather than pursuing intervention regarding the cause of the problem. Alternatively, individuals are often advised to pursue a livelihood that does not require reading. Is there such a thing today? On the basis of 30+ years of clinical and classroom experience, the author can say that age is not the issue in successful remediation of written language problems. The issue is that diagnosing and treating the cause(s) of the problem rather than the symptoms enables older as well as younger individuals to develop functional reading language skills.

What if it is the encoding/decoding aspect of written language that is delayed? As discussed earlier, lack of phoneme awareness can be predicted if encoding (spelling) and decoding (word attack and word recognition) are the problem. What if decoding is accurate, but comprehension of what is read is the problem? Lack of, or partial and indistinct images for the ideas expressed—a lack of concept imagery—is revealed when the problem is comprehension of written language rather than decoding. And again, the need can be addressed both developmentally and remedially.

Another way to describe these two problems is that they both involve difficulty with part/whole relationships, but from opposite directions. In lack of phoneme awareness, for example, the person perceives a spoken word as a whole and cannot accurately identify and sequence the individual parts that comprise it. In lack of concept imagery, the person gets bits and parts, but doesn't comprehend the wholeness or gestalt of the message. It is encouraging to report, however, that success can be expected in addressing these problems in part/whole relationships with special procedures.

INTERVENTION PROGRAMS

The brain only receives information through the senses, and two levels of sensory processing are important. The first level is speed and magnitude of processing. How soon and with what vigor does the brain register incoming sensory information? Electrophysiology measures provide some objective information about this, and more access to this level of measurement would provide information that could assist improvement in treatment procedures. The second level involves incoming information from the three primary senses (auditory, visual, and motor-kinesthetic). How does the brain consciously process and integrate information so that these three senses support and augment each other? How are these senses additionally integrated with language for the cognitive benefit of dual coding (Paivio, 1986)? Performance measures can provide information about this to determine the effectiveness of intervention procedures and programs.

Various interventions are effective in preventively and remedially developing this sensory processing and integration if they are used for the processing needs for which they were created. This is where the diagnostic evaluation makes its critical contribution. The battery of tests needs to be carefully chosen to provide a variety of performance information. When that information is appropriately interpreted, the diagnostic evaluation will indicate the areas of intervention that are needed.

The next section describes the Lindamood-Bell intervention programs. Other technologies that facilitate language and motor function will be described in Chapter 24.

Lindamood-Bell™ Sensory-Cognitive Programs

Lindamood-Bell have developed intervention programs for five areas of learning need identified during the 30 years they have been engaged in diagnosis, clinical and classroom intervention, and research. The following sections describe these areas of learning need and the progression of small processing steps that must be developed through intervention. There is an important difference between most language intervention programs (including the technology-based programs described in Lindamood, Chapter 24, this volume) and the Lindamood–Bell programs described here. The difference is the degree to which sensory information is brought to a *conscious* level from the auditory, visual, and motor-kinesthetic modalities, made concrete, and integrated with language in a dual-coding support system. This approach enables both children and adults to "own" the sensory information and its relationship with language, and assists them in accessing both to crosscheck information. This process supports thinking and reasoning about relationships between parts and wholes involved in learning tasks.

To understand the development, structure, and interrelationship of Lindamood-Bell™ sensory-cognitive programs, again we return to dual coding theory: "Cognition is proportional to the degree to which images and language are integrated" (Paivio, 1994).

Topping the array of research supporting this simple statement is a layer of our own experience as learners: for the things we know best, we have both sensory experience and rich and detailed mental imagery. This dual knowledge enables us to talk easily about our experiences, which enables us to think critically about them. That is how we know something and can reason about it even when the thing is not physically present: our images and language bring "it" into our central nervous system. For example, it is said that Native Americans in the far north have a very large number of words to describe snow. They have become aware of contrasts in the look, feel, sound, taste, and smell of snow that we more southern folks probably could not, at first, notice. They developed multisensory images of snow, they talked about and labeled their sensory awareness of differences in snow, and the labels captured and crystallized the sensory awareness. The sensory input/images triggered language, and the language strengthened the imagery. Noticing sensory contrast enables language, and language enables noticing. This reciprocal relationship between language and sensory-cognitive processing/imagery is the backbone of five sensory-cognitive programs developed at Lindamood-Bell Learning Processes®. Their descriptions follow.

Lindamood Phoneme Sequencing™ (LiPS™) Program

The discovery of the causal role of individual differences in phonemic awareness in producing differences in the development of reading skills is one of the most important findings in reading research during the last 20 years. As a result, however, educators must decipher the meaning of at least three now very familiar (but often misunderstood) phrases known as the PH terms: phonics, phonemic awareness, and phonetic or phonological processing. The differences among these concepts tend to confuse many who are trying to learn how best to help students. Does phonics develop phonemic awareness or phonetic processing? Or both? Or neither? Which is the cart and which is a horse? And what is the other one? It doesn't help that publishers have sprung into action adding PH words on their boxes and in their catalogs, sometimes without making any appreciable changes in program content.

A simple understanding of these terms is of considerable help in understanding how various programs that address phonemes, phonics, and phonetic processing compare. Phonemic awareness is a sensory-cognitive ability to think about and manipulate sounds within words; it is an oral language processing function. Phonics is instruction about how letters represent sounds in our language; it is written language instruction. Phonetic processing is the ability to decode written words, and requires both phonemic awareness and phonics knowledge. Students can learn phonics information (the letter "p" says /p/, an "e" at the end of the word usually makes a vowel say its name) without phonemic awareness; but without phonemic awareness, they cannot do phonetic processing. They cannot apply their phonics knowledge about sounds and letters for fluent and accurate phonetic processing unless they can detect phonemes within words. Without phonemic awareness, students cannot detect decoding errors unless a disruption in meaning clues an error. In addition, without phonemic awareness, students cannot self-correct even when meaning does clue an error because they cannot determine the nature of their error. So, phonemic awareness is the horse and it pulls several carts: phonetic processing in reading and spelling, rhyming, and other phoneme-manipulation tasks such as elision and substitution. (Another horse that pulls the phonetic processing cart—symbol imagery—will also be discussed later in this chapter and in Chapter 25.)

The PH-word concepts provide background for categorizing the LiPS™ Program. It is truly a phonemic awareness program that also includes phonics instruction and application of phonemic awareness to phonetic processing in both reading and spelling. Before addressing letter symbols, the LiPS™ program engages students in discovering the articulatory gestures that differentiate phonemes so that they can use oral-motor feedback to concretize, track, and prove the identity, number, and order of phonemes in words. Second, LiPS™ engages students in a variety of "phoneme tracking" experiences that directly require application of the newly developed awareness of articulatory feedback. Then, as they learn the symbols that represent phonemes, students have only a half step to take into reading and spelling. Having already begun to sequence phonemes at a very concrete level, such as with mouth pictures, it is quite easy for students to grasp the logic of the alphabetic principle and the use of letters for sequencing phonemes. Also, all the instruction is delivered in a "discovery" format through the use of questioning techniques that connect students to sensory experiences in order to form concepts. In summary, LiPS™ stretches from a prereading level where phonemic awareness is developed, into single syllable, multisyllable, and contextual reading levels in which phonemic awareness and orthographic expectancies are applied.

Steps in the LiPS™ Program

The following steps comprise the key elements of the LiPS™ Program.

1. *Setting the climate*: Students are helped to understand what they will be doing and

why—learning to *feel* as well as see and hear speech sounds in order to make reading and spelling easier.

2. *Consonants:* Students discover how each of the consonant sounds are articulated and use that sensory information to organize them into pairs and groups. Simple, high-imagery labels are attached to each category (e.g., lip poppers /p, b/, tongue lifters /l, r/) to enable teacher and students to communicate clearly about sounds within words in subsequent steps. For example, "When you say /clap/, what do you feel last?"

3. *Vowels:* Here, too, students discover how the sounds are articulated, and use that sensory information to organize the sounds into mouth shape categories such as Smile, Open, Round, and Sliders.

4. *Tracking*: As soon as students have awareness of the articulatory gestures for a few consonants and vowels, they need to begin using their oral-motor awareness to track the identity and order of phonemes in spoken words. They learn to use mouth pictures to show what they feel first in a word, and what comes right after that, and so on. Figures 1 and 2 are examples of mouth picture tracking.

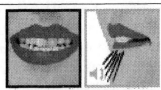

Figure 1. "Show me.../if/."

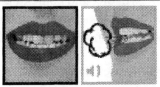

Figure 2. "That says/if/, now show me/it/."

Then, to move onward from this very concrete phoneme tracking, students use colored blocks to show sounds in the tracking task (see Figures 3 and 4).

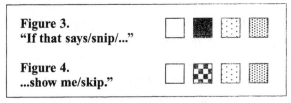

Figure 3. "If that says/snip/..."

Figure 4. ...show me/skip."

The labels (e.g., lip popper, tip tapper) are used as the teacher asks questions about what students feel and as students verbalize contrasts between words. Thus, phonemes are dual coded at each step with imagery and language.

5. *Decoding and spelling:* Tracking establishes a base for students to grasp the logic of coding speech sounds with letters. In decoding, "Since I see an 'L' right after the smile vowel, I will have to make my tongue do a lifter there." As phonetic processing emerges, orthographic expectancies are introduced so that students begin to integrate phonetic processing with an ability to predict how words will be spelled or read. Sight words also are stimulated so that students can progress simultaneously into fluent contextual reading and writing. Tracking, spelling, and reading are kept synchronized as work progresses through words with simple, complex, and multisyllable structures, in an age-appropriate format for the student.

The intensive, concrete, dual-coded processing stimulated in the LiPS™ Program makes it quite different from others labeled as phonemic awareness programs. Although various studies show training in phonemic awareness to be effective in helping students understand the alphabetic principle and develop independent word reading skills, research points to a common problem in that phonemic awareness training procedures may not be powerful enough to aid students who are most at-risk for the development of reading difficulties. For example, both Torgesen et al. (1992) and Lundberg (1988) found that a significant number (20%-30%) of the least able students were unable to profit from their phonemic awareness training procedures. These students are not "missed" if phonemic awareness stimulation is very concrete, with sensory experiences captured by language, as in the LiPS™ Program.

For example, Alexander, Heilman, Voeller, and Torgesen (1991) used LiPS™ (then called the ADD Program) with a group of severely reading-disabled students with an average age of 10 years, 9 months. They had been unable to benefit from either regular classroom instruction in reading or resource help with several different remedial programs. After 65 hours of clinical intervention, this group of 10 students improved from an average standard score of 77 on a measure of alphabetic reading skills to an average of 98.4 (standard score mean=100). The poorest reader in the group improved his standard score in reading from 62 to 92, which placed him in the average range. This group of students had begun treatment with an average score on a measure of phonological awareness of 57.9 (minimum score recommended for their grade=86), and had improved to an average score of 99.9 following treatment. Although these students had been unable to progress in reading instruction previously, their situation changed after the development of their phonemic awareness and its application to decoding. Dr. Joseph Torgesen, one of the principal investigators in this study, states that a subsequent report after follow-up testing during the next 2 years indicated "these students were continuing to gain in growth of sight word vocabulary and passage comprehension. To my knowledge, this is the first time we have observed a remedial study with older students severely impaired in reading ability documenting continued growth after the instructional intervention is over." (Personal communication with permission to quote.)

This significant effect for very at-risk students can also be seen in Lindamood-Bell™ clinical data on 76 students, randomly selected, who were seen individually for an average of 98 hours of LiPS™ combined with the Seeing Stars™ program (described later in this chapter). We routinely combine the two programs for students who have a severe lack of phoneme awareness because the Seeing Stars™ program develops students' ability to make mental images for sequences of letters. We have found the ability to create symbol imagery interacts with phoneme awareness, and results in more fluent decoding as well as better gains in spelling. The group, composed of 36% females and 64% males, ranged in age from 6 to 18 years, with a mean age of 10 years, 3 months. The average pre- and post-test gains in percentile rankings shown on the various measures indicated in Graphs 1A and 1B that follow were all significant at the p<.05 level.

Several preventive studies using LiPS™ to stimulate phonemic awareness and its application to reading and spelling in kindergarten and first grade have demonstrated strongly positive results. There are three primary reasons for its success. First, LiPS™ can stimulate phonemic awareness for *all* students in a classroom setting, with highly significant effects on word attack, word recognition, spelling, and reading comprehension. Second, stimulating a conscious processing base of phoneme awareness is productive for students who are not high-risk for reading difficulty as well as for those who are. And third, early phonemic awareness stimulation with LiPS™ produces advantages in written language skills that continue into high school (Lindamood, Bell, & Lindamood, 1997b). We

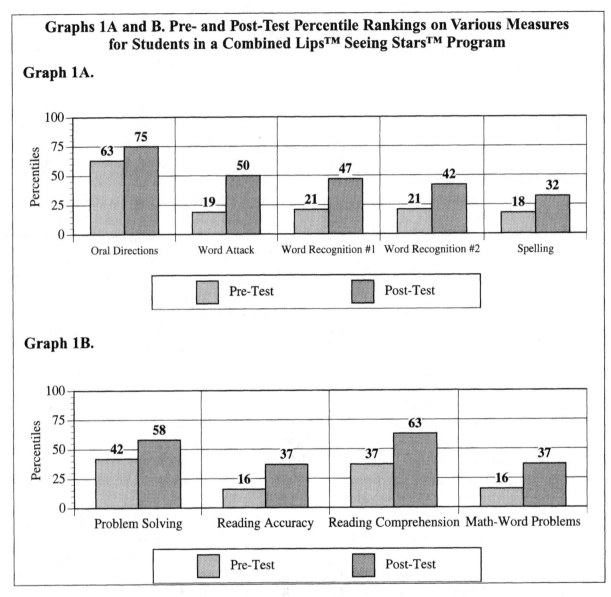

Graphs 1A and B. Pre- and Post-Test Percentile Rankings on Various Measures for Students in a Combined Lips™ Seeing Stars™ Program

Graph 1A.

Percentiles

Oral Directions	Word Attack	Word Recognition #1	Word Recognition #2	Spelling
63 / 75	19 / 50	21 / 47	21 / 42	18 / 32

Pre-Test   Post-Test

Graph 1B.

Percentiles

Problem Solving	Reading Accuracy	Reading Comprehension	Math-Word Problems
42 / 58	16 / 37	37 / 63	16 / 37

Pre-Test   Post-Test

are beginning to gather data on the effect on spelling and fluency in reading of combining the LiPS™ and Seeing Stars™ programs to focus on integrating stimulation of phoneme awareness and symbol imagery. Initial trends appear to indicate this is a productive approach, but more data are needed before we can publish findings. The concern is that significant gains in spelling and reading fluency have consistently been less predictable than decoding gains after development of phoneme awareness and sequencing. It will be a contribution to intervention if we are able to document that there can be a better effect in those two areas if we directly stimulate symbol imagery along with phoneme awareness.

Visualizing and Verbalizing for Language Comprehension and Thinking™ (V/V™)

In contrast to the LiPS™ Program, which stimulates accuracy and self-correction in decoding and spelling, the V/V™ Program stimulates concept imagery to develop language comprehension and higher-order thinking skills. Where LiPS™ develops students' ability to process the smallest parts of language, V/V™ develops students' ability to process gestalts of meaning, in which the whole is larger than the sum of the parts. The instructional procedures of the V/V™ Program are supported by dual coding theory; that is, visual imagery for language can produce powerful effects on the memorability and comprehensibility of sequentially presented material such as oral or written discourse. In the V/V™ Program, students are helped to discover that they can create visual images for single words, and can add more imagery to comprehend single sentences. They can then connect imagery for a first sentence to imagery for the next sentence and so on until a mental movie has captured an array of detail into a gestalt. The ability to create images is generally assumed in many comprehension programs, but the V/V™ Program actually helps students develop this ability where it is lacking (whether due to environmental or genetic influences, or both).

Many of the same discovery and questioning techniques that are employed in the LiPS™ Program are utilized by the V/V™ Program. This is because teachers cannot create sensory experiences for students by telling them information; teachers must ask questions that cause students to check and notice sensory experiences. Similar to the LiPS™ Program, the V/V™ process first addresses the sensory-cognitive function that underlies the skill students need to acquire. The horse in this case is concept imagery, which is the ability to create mental images for meaning of language, and the cart it pulls is language comprehension and expression. Vocabulary is also tightly related to imagery and comprehension, either as a second horse or second cart, depending on how it is conceptualized. Perhaps vocabulary should be pictured as the harness connecting the horse to the cart, connecting imagery to comprehension.

(For further discussion of the V/V™ process, see Bell, Chapter 25, this volume.)

Steps of V/V™ Program

The following steps make up the key elements of the V/V™ program.

1. *Setting the climate:* Answers the questions of, What is the teacher's job? What is the student's job?
2. *Picture to picture:* Develops students' ability to verbalize about given pictures before they verbalize their own mental images.
3. *Word imaging:* Develops detailed imagery for the meaning of single nouns.
4. *Sentence-by-sentence imaging:* Begins developing an imaged gestalt as detailed imagery is added and changed sentence by sentence through a paragraph.
5. *Sentence-by sentence-imaging with HOTS (Higher-Order Thinking Skills):* Begins stimulating students' ability to use imagery for main idea, inference, conclusion, and prediction.
6. *Multisentence imaging:* In steps 5 through 8, students gain experience in capturing increasingly larger amounts of language in their imagery.
7. *Paragraph imaging.*
8. *Paragraph-by-paragraph imaging.*
9. *Whole-page imaging.*

Graph 2 shows clinical data for 58 students, randomly selected, who were seen individually for an average of 96 hours of V/V™. The group, composed of 53% females and 47% males, ranged in age from 6 to 47 years, with a mean age of 14 years, 7 months. Pre-and post-test average percentile gains on all measures indicated were significant at the $p < .05$ level of confidence.

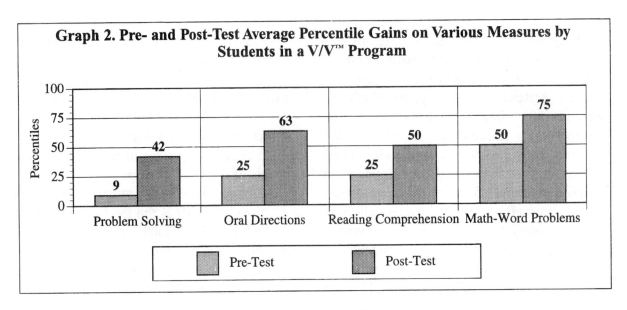

Graph 2. Pre- and Post-Test Average Percentile Gains on Various Measures by Students in a V/V™ Program

We have used V/V™ with many high-functioning autistic/autistic spectrum students. Although autistic students are often thought to have strength in visual processing and visual-spatial imagery, it is our clinical experience that there tends to be a significant weakness in connecting images to language and language to images. In other words, dual coding tends not to occur for autistic students. However, "tends not to occur" does not mean "will not occur" for students. In applying V/V™ with students in our clinics, it has been our experience that dual coding can be stimulated even for students on the autistic spectrum, with measurable improvement in language comprehension and expression.

Temple Grandin, a high-functioning autistic individual who is a professor of animal behavior and also a celebrated author, speaker, and researcher on autism, has analyzed her own problems with language. Her description of how she specifically has to assist herself to express her thoughts with language is remarkably similar to the imagery process Bell (2000) has developed, which has successfully assisted autistic as well as nonautistic individuals to improve their receptive and expressive language (see Bell, Chapter 25, this volume). Grandin

reports, "In my brain, words act as a narrator for the visual images in my imagination… When I am talking about something for the first time, I look at the visual images on the 'computer monitor' in my imagination, then the language part of me describes those images" (Grandin, 2000, p. 14). She describes this occurring as two separate steps for her, but believes they occur "merged into one seamless consciousness" for most people. Her assessment is striking because early in the V/V™ progression we see this two-step processing occur, but we also see the two-step process merging into one process as treatment is continued. The question in our minds is "Would this merging of images and language occur and become seamless for Grandin if we took her through the small steps of processing in the V/V™ Program that enable the merged processing to develop?"

Grandin also verifies our clinical observation that autistic spectrum individuals tend to give more attention to details or to parts and miss the big picture, the whole or gestalt. Grandin states, "I look at lots of little details and piece them together to make a concept." (Grandin, 2000, p. 18). She has figured out how to serve her comprehension needs by consciously making use of her inclination to give attention to details. However, autistic spectrum students in general need to be directly helped to discover they can do this to create an imaged gestalt for comprehension of spoken or written language.

Seeing Stars™: Symbol Imagery for Phonemic Awareness, Sight Words, and Spelling

Seeing Stars™ is Lindamood-Bell's "other" imagery program. Compared to Visualizing and Verbalizing™, it addresses what we call "the other side of the coin": not the ability to image the meaning of language but the ability to image the orthography of language, the letters and letter patterns of the written language. In her imagery chapter, Bell (Chapter 25, this volume) presents considerable evidence for the role of symbol imagery in phonemic awareness, spelling, word attack, word recognition, and fluency. She reports strong correlations between performance in these areas and imagery for letters in words. More important than the existence of symbol imagery as a sensory-cognitive process and its relationship to written language processing is that symbol imagery can be stimulated. Even more important, stimulating symbol imagery produces significant gains in phoneme awareness, decoding, spelling, and reading in context.

The steps of Seeing Stars™ stretch from imaging single letters, to imaging simple syllables (such as /if/, /fip/, and /cab/), to imaging complex syllables (such as /ask/ or /streak/), to imaging multisyllable words, to using imagery to learn specific sight words and spelling words, and on to applying symbol imagery to reading in context. Each step includes specific symbol imagery exercises such as naming requested letters (e.g., "What letter do you picture after the r?"), decoding the imaged word (e.g., "The word you're picturing says …?"),

and manipulating the image and decoding again (e.g., "Take out the T—what letters do you picture? So that says …?")

Classroom findings indicate that these steps are very appropriate for students just beginning to learn about sounds and letters because symbol imagery instruction strengthens phoneme awareness and phonics instruction. For example, after observing early indications of a future phonemic awareness problem in her own daughter at 2 and 3 years of age, Phyllis Lindamood offered articulatory stimulation coupled with symbol imagery stimulation (LiPS™ and Seeing Stars™) in a light and lively fashion. This could be quite manageable for many parents, and could prevent some early failure experiences for children, as it seems to have done for Phyllis's child.

Symbol imagery stimulation impacts far more than sound/symbol associations; we have shown its effects beyond phonics knowledge on phonemic awareness and phonetic processing. When teachers stimulate both articulatory feedback and symbol imagery for students, the students' grasp of the alphabetic principle is strong, and their reading and spelling performance is significantly strengthened. Students and teachers then have a very concrete sensory reference for the elusive phonemes within words (articulatory feedback) as well as a rapid visual-sensory reference (symbol imagery). Thus, when they need to, students can do slow and careful phonetic processing using articulatory feedback and, using symbol imagery, can shift to the faster processing that fluency requires. Even when teachers do not develop students' use of articulatory feedback to concretize phonemes, symbol imagery can serve a concretizing function that supports phonemic awareness and phonetic processing. (See Bell, Chapter 25, this volume, for more detail on symbol imagery.)

Steps of the Seeing Stars™ Program

The following steps are key elements of the Seeing Stars™ Program.

1. *Imaging letters:* Stimulating sound/letter relationships and imagery for consonants and vowels.
2. *Syllable cards:* Stimulating the ability to image a word from a model (a card with a word on it) and decoding/encoding for single-syllable words using orthographic expectancies.
3. *Syllable board:* Generating symbol imagery from a spoken word (whole to parts) or spoken letters (parts to whole). Students also get motor-kinesthetic input at this step as they finger-write on a hard surface.
4. *Imaging syllables with and without a chain:* Stimulating symbol imagery and decoding/encoding for single syllable words.
5. *Imaging sight words:* Establishing visual memory and instant recognition.
6. *Imaging spelling:* Establishing visual memory for orthographic expectancies and real-word spelling.
7. *Multisyllable reading, spelling, and imagery:* Decoding/encoding imaging of affixes, use of multisyllable syllable cards, multisyllable syllable board, and multisyllable reading and spelling of real and nonword lists.
8. *Contextual integration:* Applying word attack and word recognition skills to contextual reading, with symbol imagery to print-comparing stimulated for rapid self-correction.

Vanilla Vocabulary

Vocabulary development is, appropriately, a major concern for those trying to help students with learning difficulties. A good vocabulary does not result in good comprehension and reasoning, but a weak vocabulary will limit comprehension, reasoning, and communicating. Teachers at every grade level see this issue in action: students who can decode words that have no meaning for them, or the difficulties of teaching new concepts when students have terrible gaps in basic vocabulary. Although teachers may be well aware of their students' vocabulary needs, when asked how they help students develop vocabulary they typically talk about their frustrating search for tools and how little effect their efforts have.

It is the premise of the *Vanilla Vocabulary* program (Bell & Lindamood, 1993, 1998), that studying words—an unfamiliar word and more unfamiliar words to define it—often does not result in significant vocabulary growth because it does not result in dual coding. Unless words are tightly integrated with the sensory input of imagery, they tend not to become a part of one's functional vocabulary. Vocabulary drills often make individuals familiar with a word in terms of having heard it but do not stimulate enough imagery to enable use of the word in speaking or to gather complete meaning when listening and reading. Stimulating vocabulary with concept imagery (dual coding) is really quite straightforward with the structure that *Vanilla Vocabulary* provides. Beginning level (Book 1) and intermediate level (Book 2) words are defined by using high-imagery language to enable dual coding. For example, compare an "American Heritage School Dictionary" definition with a *Vanilla Vocabulary* definition:

- *Dictionary:* **illusion** – an appearance or impression that has no real basis, i.e., creating the illusion of depth in a painting.
- *Vanilla Vocabulary:* **illusion** – something that seems to be real, but is not. "The castle towers appeared higher than the clouds but it was only an illusion."

The *Vanilla Vocabulary* definition is created to provoke imagery. The high-imagery definition is followed by three simple, but high-imagery sentences for students to visualize using the new word. Many dictionaries do not provide sentences to further illustrate the meaning of words. It is not assumed that students will form an image just because *Vanilla Vocabulary* definitions and sentences are "high imagery." Teachers are directed to question students about what they are picturing, using choice and contrast to develop vivid, personal imagery. Then, students visualize and verbalize to create their own sentence using the target word. As students master the new vocabulary by visualizing and verbalizing, there are companion books intended for reading aloud which use the target words again in humorous, high-imagery stories titled *Ivan Sleeps Over* and *Ivan, King of the Neighborhood* (Bell & Lindamood, 1997).

On Cloud Nine™—Visualizing and Verbalizing for Math

While the sight words versus phonics versus whole language wars raged in the field of reading, the manipulatives versus memorization wars raged in math. Manipulatives have been used for years in teaching math (Stern & Stern, 1971), but many individuals who experienced success with this most concrete level failed in the shift to computation (Moore, 1990; National Council of Teachers of Mathematics, 1989; Papert, 1993). Some students could think logically in problem solving but couldn't seem to memorize the math facts that enable rapid processing. Others could memorize facts but couldn't seem to reason with those facts in word problems.

At Lindamood-Bell™, as we looked at students struggling with math, we saw the same critical sensory input/imagery/language link that had resulted in solutions for students with

decoding and comprehension problems. The missing link in the math wars seemed to be imagery: concept imagery and numeral imagery at a conscious level. Students who are not imaging do not leave behind the manipulatives and move on to mental imagery so that they are able to do mental manipulations with numbers. For individuals to grasp math concepts, reason with numbers, and compute accurately, concept imagery and numeral imagery are critical sensory-cognitive precursors.

The On Cloud Nine™ math program moves through the following three basic steps to develop mathematical reasoning and computation:
1. Using manipulatives to experience the realness of math.
2. Using imagery and language with those manipulatives to concretize the realness in the sensory system.
3. Using numeral imagery and concept imagery to apply computation to word problems.

The following specific steps illustrate how the program links sensory experience to language to concept imagery to numeral imagery. The goal is dual coding in math.

Steps of the On Cloud Nine™ Program

The steps of the On Cloud Nine™ Program begin with *setting the climate,* and proceed according to the increasing difficulty of number concepts, as follows:
1. *Imaging numerals*
2. *Imaging the number line*
3. *Addition family facts*
4. *Subtraction family facts*
5. *Word problems*
6. *Place value*
7. *Jumping*
8. *Carrying and borrowing*

9. *Multiplication*
10. *Division*
11. *Decimals*
12. *Fractions and a "step-ladder"*

Drawing With Language™

Because some individuals have adequate visual-motor processing, they easily think about and generate "drawings." (By "drawings," we mean anything where lines and space create a figure. A drawing is not just artistic pictures such as nudes and still lifes, but letters and numbers, maps, diagrams, geometric figures, and such.) But some individuals, especially young children, have difficulty processing visual-spatial relationships—the whole and the parts. These difficulties can persist beyond the developmental norm, causing individuals to have difficulty with print and handwriting, copying from the board, organizing work on the page, and interpreting graphically presented information. Based on the number of individuals referred to our clinics, those with weak visual-motor processing as the primary difficulty seem to comprise a smaller group than those with weak decoding or comprehension. Alternatively, perhaps educators and parents tend to view weak visual-motor processing as less of a problem and so are less concerned about it.

The fact that fewer students are referred for "difficulty in drawing" than for difficulty in reading does not diminish the very real and negative effects for students. Although individuals certainly vary in the fine motor coordination needed to grip a pencil and generate a line, this variation does not account for the difficulties regularly seen as weak visual-motor processing. For example, Cody, a high school student, made many "careless errors" in math due to numeral misalignment and poor legibility, and often lost his way in unfamiliar physical environments. He could form

single lines in any direction, but had extreme difficulty recalling and drawing lines in relationships in even fairly simple figures, such as that shown in Figure 5, the Detroit Test of Learning Aptitude, Design Reproduction Subtest. The stimulus figure is shown for a specific number of seconds, then removed and the individual draws the figure.

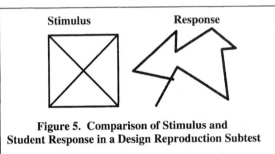

Figure 5. Comparison of Stimulus and Student Response in a Design Reproduction Subtest

In our clinics, we have found that connecting language to sensory input/imagery is as effective with visual-motor development as with the other sensory-cognitive functions we address. We see significant improvement for students such as Cody through what we call our Drawing with Language™ Program. This program stimulates an individual's ability to:
- *verbalize* the units and relationships involved in drawings, and
- *visualize* those units and relationships as a mental model from which to compare and reproduce them.

Steps of the Drawing with Language™ Program

The following steps are key elements of the Drawing with Language™ Program.
1. *Setting the climate*
2. *Collecting language for drawing*
3. *Learning three kinds of lines*
4. *Line-by-line production: verbalize-visualize-draw*
5. *Shapes*
6. *Designs and symbols*
7. *Drawings*
8. *Application*

In early steps, students learn to use language to create a mental image, compare what they drew to the model, and describe exactly how and where corrections need to be made. Although comparing a drawing and a model point by point can be a slow process, it is this ability to compare a stimulus and a response that results in self-correction. As verbalizing becomes more automatic and internalized, it becomes the inner language that the frontal cortex uses to direct the members of the orchestra—the visual and motor cortices. As visualizing becomes more automatic, imagery becomes the means of comparing drawing to model, a much more rapid process. As with other Lindamood-Bell™ programs, the goal is to address sensory-cognitive functions so that a person develops *independent* and, ultimately, *rapid and automatic* self-correction and accurate processing.

Programs and Technology

CD-ROMs are presently available for the LiPS™ and V/V™ programs, and the other programs are targeted for future CD-ROM support. Through careful planning, the technology contains interactions that border on artificial intelligence in providing feedback on error responses. This means technology can provide additional problem-solving practice that furthers the development of dual coding and rapid, automatic sensory-cognitive processing.

CONCLUSION

This chapter has presented issues in the prevention and remediation of problems in oral and written speech-language development. It also has included ways that can be used either preventively or remedially to approach problems in math and visual-spatial cognition because of the interactive roles of sensory processing and language in these areas of learning as well.

An over-arching theme in this chapter was the issue of parts/wholes relationships in sensory-cognitive processing. Our clinical experience at Lindamood-Bell™ makes us wonder if satisfying three conditions might enable us to teach virtually anyone virtually anything. These conditions are:

1. If we are able to identify, label, and experience the *units* involved concretely enough at the sensory level to bring them to consciousness.

2. If we use the labels, sensory information, and language to track and compare the *relationships* of the units.

3. If we think and reason together about how the units and relationships combine to create and form the *whole* that is greater than the sum of the parts.

A secondary theme in this chapter was the evidence that there is sufficient research to drive practice in some of these areas of learning needs. Does this mean we shouldn't explore the use of emerging preventive and remedial practices until definitive research is available on their efficacy? The answer to that question is "No." We can use emerging practices so long as they cannot harm children and there is a body of anecdotal support for their positive effect. Recent developments in technology are now making it possible for medical research and clinical practice to complement each other. Pilot findings from beginning efforts to look at brain functions pre- and post-Lindamood-Bell™ treatment indicate there may be information from fMRI and electrophysiology measures documenting that appropriate stimulation enables brain functions to become established or improved. These measures, analyzed in combination with performance measures, give hope of further progress in meeting the need for oral and written communication for more children and adults.

We will soon conduct research aimed at answering the many questions that remain relative to management of intervention. It is our expectation that sorting by age groupings, severity of processing deficits, intensity of treatment (4 or more hours of daily intervention compared to the more common 1 hour), and single areas of processing need compared to two or more will generate information that will lead to better prognosis and treatment recommendations.

Being (and feeling) competent in communicating through either oral or written language is a base upon which a person can manage the rest of life's demands. If we, as therapists, provide intervention in these areas we should never be satisfied with just our current efforts. Nor should we be isolated in our efforts. As discussed further in the next chapter, our goal should be to strive toward advances that we know may be possible through research on combining intervention programs—rather than through research that *compares* intervention programs. Such research should be with programs in our own field as well as with programs of other disciplines in the team effort needed. ∎

REFERENCES

Alexander, A., Anderson, H., Heilman, P. C., Voeller, K. S., & Torgesen, J. K. (1991). Phonological awareness training and remediation of analytic decoding deficits in a group of severe dyslexics. *Annals of Dyslexia, 41*, 193-206.

American Heritage School Dictionary (1972). New York: American Heritage.

Bell, N., & Lindamood, P. (1993). *Vanilla vocabulary, level 2*. San Luis Obispo, CA: Gander Educational.

Bell, N., & Lindamood, P. (1998). *Vanilla vocabulary, level 1*. San Luis Obispo, CA: Gander Educational.

Bell, N., & Lindamood, P. (1997). *Ivan sleeps over & Ivan king of the Neighborhood*. San Luis Obispo, CA: Gander Educational.

Berry, M. (1969). *Language disorders of children*. Englewood Cliffs, NJ: Prentice Hall.

Boswell, S. (2000). Congress funds newborn hearing screening. *ASHA Leader, 5*(1).

Clancy, P. (1985). The acquisition of Japanese. In D. I. Slobin (Ed.), *The crosslinguistic study of language acquisition: Vol. 1. The data* (pp. 373-524). Hillsdale, NJ: Erlbaum.

DeFries, J., Fulkes, D., & Labuda, M. (1998). Reading disability in twins: Evidence for a genetic etiology. *Nature, 329,* 537-539.

Grandin, T. (2000). My mind is a web browser: How people with autism think. *The Dana Forum on Brain Science, 2*(1), 13.

Greenspan, S. I., & Wieder, S. (1997). *The child with special needs: Encouraging intellectual and emotional growth*. New York: Perseus Books.

Hart, B., & Risley, T. (1996). *Meaningful differences in the everyday experience of young American children*. Baltimore, MD: Paul H. Brookes.

Kantrowitz, B., & Underwood, A. (1999). Dyslexia: New hope for kids who cannot read. *Newsweek*, November 22.

Lewkowicz, D. (1999). Infants' perception of the audible, visible, and bimodal attributes of talking and singing faces. In D. Massaro (Ed.), *Proceedings of the auditory-visual speech processing international conference*. Santa Cruz, CA.

Lewkowicz, D. (in press). Infants' perception of the audible, visible and bimodal attributes of multimodal syllables. *Child Development*.

Lewkowicz, D. (2000). Development of intersensory temporal perception: An epigenetic systems/limitations view. *Psychological Bulletin, 126,* 281-308.

Lindamood, P., & Lindamood, P. (1998). *Lindamood phoneme sequencing™ (LiPS™) program*. Austin, TX: PRO-ED.

Lindamood, P., Bell, N., & Lindamood, P. (1997a). Achieving competence in language and literacy by training in phonemic awareness, concept imagery, and comparator function. In C. Hulme & M. Snowling (Eds.), *Dyslexia: Biology, cognition, and intervention*. San Diego, CA: Singular.

Lindamood, P., Bell, N., & Lindamood, P. (1997b). Sensory-cognitive factors in the controversy over reading instruction. *The Journal of Developmental and Learning Disorders, 1,* 143-182.

Lundberg, I. (1998). Preschool prevention of reading failure: Does training in phonological awareness work? In R. L. Masland & M. W. Masland (Eds.), *Prevention of Reading Failure* (pp. 163-176). Parkton, MD: York Press.

Mann, V. (1993). Phoneme awareness and future reading ability. *Journal of Learning Disabilities, 26*(4), 259-269.

McReynolds, L. (1978). Behavioral and linguistic considerations in children's speech production. In J. F. Kavanagh, & W. Strange (Eds.), *Speech and language in the laboratory, school, and clinic.* Cambridge, MA: MIT Press.

Moore, D. (1990). Uncertainty. In L. Steen (Ed.), *On the shoulders of giants: New approaches to numeracy.* Washington, D.C.: National Academy Press.

National Center for Education Statistics. (1993). *National adult literacy survey.* Washington, D.C.: Author.

National Council of Teachers of Mathematics (NCTM) (1989). *Curriculum and evaluation standards of school mathematics.* Reston, VA.

Paivio, A. (1986). *Mental representations: A dual coding approach.* New York: Oxford University Press.

Paivio, A. (1994). *Dual coding theory.* Presentation at the National Lindamood-Bell Research and Training Conference, Sacramento, CA.

Paivio, A. (1996). *Dual coding: A factor in language processing.* Presentation at the National Lindamood-Bell Research and Training Conference, San Francisco, CA.

Papert, S. (1993). *The children's machine: Rethinking school in the age of the computer.* New York: Basic Books.

Rescorla, L. (1989). The language development survey: A screening tool for delayed language in toddlers. *Journal of Speech and Hearing Disorders, 54,* 587-599.

Shankweiler, D., & Lieberman, I. (1989). *Phonology and reading disability.* Ann Arbor, MI: University of Michigan Press.

Slobin, D. (1985). Crosslinguistic evidence for the language-making capacity. In D. I. Slobin (Ed.), *The crosslinguistic study of language acquisition: Vol. 2. Theoretical issue* (p. 1244). Hillsdale, NJ: Erlbaum.

Slobin, D. (1997). *The crosslinguistic study of language acquisition: Vol. 5.* Expanding the contexts (Beverly A. Goldfield, 1999). Applied *Psycholinguistics. Book Review, 20*(3).

Stern, C., & Stern M. (1971). *Children discover arithmetic.* New York: Harper & Row.

Tardif, T. (1996). Nouns are not always learned before verbs: Evidence from Mandarin speakers' early vocabularies. *Developmental Psychology, 32,* 492-504.

Torgesen, J., Morgen, S., & Davis, C. (1992). The effects of phonological awareness training on word learning in kindergarten children. *Journal of Educational Psychology, 84,* 364-370.

◄ 24 ►

Technologies to Facilitate Language, Sensory Processing, and Motor-Planning Capacities

Patricia Lindamood, M.S., C.C.C.-S.L.P.

The rapid development and availability of technology is enabling many computer-assisted sensory, motor, and language training programs to be produced. There are hundreds of such programs available, and examples of the three types are included in this chapter. This chapter describes the contribution of technology to the area of *augmentative and alternative communication*, with some programs suitable for home as well as professional use. This chapter also briefly discusses the language therapies *Fast ForWord®* and *4wd™*, *Earobics*, and *The Sentence Master Program*, as well as a motor-planning and timing program, the *Interactive Metronome®*. In addition, auditory processing approaches using music are discussed. The programs described all have web sites that can be accessed for further information.

AUGMENTATIVE AND ALTERNATIVE COMMUNICATION

The field of augmentative and alternative communication (AAC) has found that it can combine assistance from technology with its basic efforts, and can make speech-language and the ability to communicate more widely available to populations with very special needs in this area. The AAC services, with the assistance of very creatively engineered technology products, are enabling many children and adults to interact with their world in spite of having little or no oral expressive language. Because humans have a universal need to communicate, AAC emerged as a service concept internationally, with the first efforts occurring during the 1960s in Canada, Sweden, the United Kingdom, and the United States. The International Society of Augmentative and Alternative Communication (ISAAC) has chapters in 11 countries and members in more than 50 countries. An international conference is held every 2 years in a different location. The organization recognizes the need to be research-oriented, and it follows each conference with a research symposium. There is also a journal, titled *Augmentative and Alternative Communication*, published by Decker. Much of this current information about AAC was graciously provided by Dr. Sarah Blackstone, past president of ISAAC. She is currently an AAC consultant, and has a web site that gives information about AAC as well as information regarding her widely read newsletter, *Augmentative Communication News*.

AAC serves groups of individuals with varying degrees of need within three general categories:

1. Individuals whose poor ability to speak is secondary to a primary organic condition,

such as cerebral palsy, aphasia, apraxia, multiple sclerosis, and traumatic brain injury, and who typically exhibit a big gap between their adequate receptive language and their lack of expressive language.

2. Individuals who are autistic or within the autistic spectrum.

3. Individuals who are physically able, but are, nonetheless, unable to engage in symbolic representation due to developmental delay or unknown cognitive disabilities.

AAC goals are grounded in speech-language communication. It is an ongoing process for most clients, over a considerable period of time, and requires a *team* approach. It starts with an analysis of a client's most immediate needs *at this time* in regard to communication and an assessment of his or her future needs, with the ultimate goal being independence. The AAC process involves working step-by-step toward the highest degree of independence in communication that a person can achieve. A *multidisciplinary* provision of services is necessary in accomplishing this goal.

Historically, the first AAC efforts involved Language Boards with pictures or, if the person was able to read, printed words and phrases to which the person pointed. Depending on the disability, a person in a wheelchair could find these boards physically difficult to handle. Manual signs were also used to augment the effort to communicate, and are still in use to some extent. The inclusion of technology started in England and Scotland in the 1970s, when electronic devices began to become available. There are more than 100 products available that use both synthesized and digitized speech. Some have become very sophisticated and somewhat difficult to use, which has led to a sense

within the AAC community that these devices need to be made more user friendly. This improvement is most likely to occur through the Rehabilitation Engineering Research Centers (RERC) authorized by the Rehabilitation Act of 1973. The mandate of a RERC is to enhance opportunities for meeting the needs and addressing the barriers confronted by individuals with disabilities in all aspects of their lives. The Secretary of Education may make grants to public or private agencies to conduct research, demonstrations, and training activities related to rehabilitation technology, but the RERC must be operated in, or in collaboration with, an institute of higher education or a nonprofit organization. By most recent count, there are now RERC in 14 different locations.

For young children with cerebral palsy, Down syndrome, or autism, AAC serves as a bridge to speech-language communication. Its tools include manual gestures, signs, graphics, and print. These provide visible signs of communication that appear to stabilize beginning language input and enhance a child's ability to attend to it and acquire receptive language. Receptive language is the first level to be accomplished. Ultimately, however, AAC has a profound relationship with literacy. Until literacy is achieved, particularly the spelling aspect of literacy, the individuals are dependent on what someone else has put on their Language Board or in the technology device they are using.

For individuals who lack oral speech-language, or for whom the speed and ability to articulate oral language is extremely slow and burdensome, true independence in communication hinges upon their success in generating what they want to say in written language. For this reason, it is very important for AAC professionals to understand the role of phonemic awareness in literacy development, presented in the discussion of written language in

Chapter 23 in this volume. It has been reported that many individuals receiving AAC services are not literate, which severely limits their ability to use many of the technology devices or even a Language Board if it uses print. If these individuals have received traditional instruction in reading and spelling but have not been able to benefit from it, *a lack of phoneme awareness can be predicted.* If this is a need, it can and must be addressed, as phoneme awareness is a primary factor in literacy development. Age and intelligence do not guarantee the availability of this genetic tendency of phoneme awareness, but it can be developed by special procedures.

Practitioners in AAC have learned that the use of multiple systems is significantly more effective than the use of a single system. After a system for establishing or documenting some level of receptive language is successful, a current intervention of choice among AAC providers is The Picture Exchange Communication System (PECS). This system focuses on the initiation component of communication. In six phases of training, it integrates theoretical and fundamental teaching strategies from the fields of speech-language pathology and behavioral analysis. Its emphasis is on clarifying for family, residential-care providers, and educators the *how* of teaching initiation of communication rather than simply *what* to teach. The goal is the development of functional communication skills regardless of communication modality. PECS has been successful with individuals from preschool age to adults in a broad array of settings, and many preschoolers using PECS also begin developing speech. Training workshops for groups and programs are available both nationally and internationally, coordinated by Pyramid Educational Consultants.

Present research in AAC involves a federally funded, 5-year longitudinal study of the use of technology devices. Two groups in the study will receive AAC while using the devices, and one group will not use the devices. A pilot study found that devices help. Further research and sharing of experiences are needed to determine which individuals, with what types of abilities, benefit from what types of technology. The AAC goal is speech-language communication however it can best be accomplished, and the sense within the AAC community is that technology devices have their place as *one* of the many tools for individuals unable to speak. *Telerehabilitation* is a new element coming into play as the Internet is enabling expansion into distance access to AAC services. The issue of our aging population, the reality of strokes and other debilitating conditions that affect speech-language and the ability to communicate, and the fact that the Health Care Financing Administration (HCFA) is considering reimbursement through Medicare for AAC devices hold promise for impacting the expansion of AAC services and devices. What the future holds in full in respect to AAC and technology is yet to be seen.

LANGUAGE AND MOTOR PROGRAMS

There are a number of technologies that work on language functioning and a relatively new technology that works on motor-planning and sequencing capacities. The language technologies provide ways to exercise important language functions, especially receptive capacities. There are different theoretical rationales for the different approaches. Until there are comparative studies among the different technologies (and intensive speech-language therapy, employing the same number of hours as a particular technology) that can isolate the hypothesized mechanism of action, it will be difficult to know why a given technology may help. For example, improvement might be the result of a general practice effect or a specific process, such as initially slowing down auditory input.

It is also vital to emphasize that the spontaneous, meaningful use of language is the cornerstone of progress. Computer-based technologies should not be allowed to detract from interactive play and conversation or peer play. In fact, during times of intensive computer-based work, it is important to increase dynamic interactive play and conversation to maintain the child's engagement, interactive capacity, flexibility, and creativity.

Fast ForWord® and 4wd™

These two computer programs work with the auditory and language processing abilities of individuals who have receptive language problems. *Fast ForWord®* was developed for children whereas *4wd™*, which uses the same technology as *Fast ForWord®*, was developed for adolescents and adults. The approach is based on research which shows that, at the rate phonemes occur in normal speech, language learning impaired (LLI) persons have difficulty accurately distinguishing short-duration consonants such as /b/, /d/, /p/, /t/ and even short-duration vowels such as /e/, /i/ when they occur in proximity to other short-duration consonants. When these phonemes are electronically slowed down, and emphasized by increasing the intensity of the sounds, or when the time between the phonemes is lengthened, LLI persons may be able to perceive them more effectively. The programs start with phoneme segments that are electronically stretched and/or emphasized to the point where they become distinguishable for each student using the program. The programs also separate speech elements in time. Next, the programs repetitively adjust these rate, emphasis, and spacing ele-

ments until the brain's responses are trained and the ability to better process speech at the normal temporal rate is developed.

A number of research studies in this approach (Merzenich et al., 1996; Tallal et al., 1996; Tallal, Merzenich, Miller, & Jenkins, 1998) have been conducted, with encouraging results. It would be highly desirable to have additional, more specific information so comparisons can be drawn. For example, within the total number in the representative populations, how many students did not move into the average range on the various measures? In addition, there need to be comparative studies that contrast this approach with other similar approaches or with an equal number of hours of speech-language therapy.

Earobics

Earobics is an auditory-processing and phonics program with two levels: *Step 1, and Step 2*. The content is chosen and organized to teach phonemic awareness and auditory-processing skills. Using an interactive game format, *Step 1* provides 6 games with up to 114 levels of difficulty to be mastered within each game. This allows practice with each type of task presented. Acoustically modified speech, adaptive training, and careful control of learning variables are techniques given attention.

The *Earobics Clinician Version, Step 1*, provides professional users with the ability to customize the program for students through the selection of games and starting levels, the ability to skip or repeat levels, and the ability to keep records on each student, generate reports, and cite learning objectives for each activity in the Individual Educational Program (IEP) format required by many schools. There is also a *Home Version, Step1*, which does not include the customizing features of the *Clinician Version*. The *Earobics,*

Step 2, program continues building the phonemic and phonological awareness skills addressed in *Earobics, Step 1,* and provides practice in phonics activities and various auditory-processing skills. A clinical study with third- to fifth-graders identified as having central auditory processing disorder (CAPD) and/or as learning disabled based on language impairment (LI), and a public school study comparing *Earobics* effectiveness with two other programs are reported as completed, but analyses of the data are still in progress.

The Sentence Master

The Sentence Master is a linguistically based reading program that integrates computer activities and print materials to focus on developing automaticity in the reading of more than 350 frequently occurring *non-content* and *content* words. This program, designed by psychologist Marion Blank, is for children and adults who are at risk for reading difficulty or who have already had problems in reading. The program links diagnosis and intervention with structured materials and motivating rewards to address and overcome language deficits known to exist for the majority of poor readers; that is, problems with *naming, syntax*, and *comprehension*. Phoneme awareness development is not included, but Dr. Blank recognizes its contribution to decoding and recommends including a phoneme-awareness training program concurrently with her program for students who need it. Activities in the three areas of naming, syntax, and comprehension are included in each of the four levels of reading instruction.

No formal research on this approach is available at present, and this is needed. Sites using *The Sentence Master* could make an important contribution by organizing to collect data on program effectiveness with the different populations it serves.

Interactive Metronome® (IM) Motor Planning and Rhythmicity Program

The IM intervention has findings from several studies indicating that it appears to work on *underlying* processes involved in motor planning, sequencing, timing, and rhythmicity that support motor, cognitive, and learning processes. In the IM program, the participants complete seven movements by keeping pace with the metronome beep. Through the computer program, they receive feedback that enables them to establish a close connection between the metronome beat and then their own motor patterns. The movements include patting knees with both hands, clapping hands together, patting knees with alternating hands, patting knee with preferred hand, patting knee with the non-preferred hand, and toe-tapping the floor pad with alternating feet. In many types of learning and developmental challenges, motor planning and sequencing are involved in problem solving and other adaptive actions as well as in executive functions, such as organizing information and planning. In the past, it has only been possible to work with these capacities clinically.

In a recent study of the IM intervention, an attention deficit hyperactivity disorder (ADHD) population of 56 boys, ages 6 to 12, was randomly assigned to three groups and compared for findings on selected aspects of motor, attentional, and cognitive skills. The IM group received 15 hours of training, a placebo video group received an equal number of hours of training on selected nonviolent computer video games, and the other control group received no intervention. Each participant was pre- and post-tested with published tests in four areas of performance: attention and concentration; behavioral functioning; sensory and motor functioning; and academic and cognitive skills, including reading.

The IM group showed statistically significant improvements over both of the control groups in attention, language processing, reading, and the regulation of aggression. This study will be published in the *American Journal of Occupational Therapy* (Burpee et al., in press; Shaffer et al., in press). Other studies have suggested that IM is helpful for children with special needs and show correlations between IM performance and academic performance (Kuhlman & Schweinhart, in press; Stemmer, 1996). Current studies include work with different developmental and learning challenges and studies of IM performance as a diagnostic tool for categorizing types of motor-planning, sequencing, and timing differences in children and adults with developmental and learning challenges. Additional research on larger populations that look at patterns of improvement in relationship to severity of challenge and other clinical characteristics is needed.

AUDITORY PROCESSING THERAPIES USING MUSIC

Evidence is accumulating that when there is delay in speech-language development, various interventions can be offered at the *sensory* level that may help the emergence of relating and communicating behaviors. Music therapies are one type of sensory therapy being offered. Stimulation with classical music in highly structured experiences is provided in three of these interventions: the *Tomatis*, the *SAMONAS Sound Therapy*, and the *Berard Therapy*. These therapies are theorized to generally have a balancing or integrating effect between the left and right hemispheres and to improve comfort in the world of sound. At present, there is a problem in predicting which individuals may benefit from them, and there is insufficient formal research on their effectiveness, with some

conflicting reports (American Academy of Audiology, 1993). However, there are many anecdotal reports of gains and a number of studies involving a small number of subjects that suggest improvements in aspects of auditory processing and social communication (Bettison, 1996; Edelson et al., 1999; Gravel, 1994; Highfill & Cimorelli, 1994; Madell, 1997; Madell & Rose, 1994; Porges & Barzhenova, 1997; Rimland & Edelson, 1991; Rimland & Edelson, 1994; Rimland & Edelson, 1995; Veale, 1994; Woodward, 1994). It appears to be a promising area, and is in the process of being researched.

The Tomatis music therapy was developed in the 1950s by Dr. Alfred Tomatis, a French physician. It filters classical music through an Electronic Ear, initially blocking some high and low frequencies and then including them later. Input is first given to just one ear, then to the other, and later to both. Amplitude modulation of the signal is also used. Therapy is given in daily segments, in periods spaced over 2 to 3 months. The program is currently administered in more than 200 Tomatis centers worldwide. Its effect on a variety of problems are described in Tomatis' book, *The Conscious Ear*, and include voice and speech difficulties, developmental disturbances, and postural and social problems. Many parents are also reporting helpful clinical results, including improvement in reading, and efforts are being made to establish formal research.

SAMONAS is an acronym for *Spectral Activated Music of Optimal Natural Structure*. Ingo Steinbach, a German physicist, sound engineer, and musician, developed the intervention after years of studying the work of Dr. Tomatis. He discovered that, although the human ear can only process frequencies up to 15,000 Hz, the brain can detect frequencies above that. He developed special recording and playback techniques that provide these higher frequencies on his compact disks (CDs), which he believes challenge the brain to function at higher levels and enhance the therapeutic value of music by facilitating alertness and interest. The SAMONAS program uses classical music on all CDs, with the exception of one that uses the sounds of nature. Some of the CDs are only available to professional therapists, while most are available to parents or others along with extensive directions regarding their use.

The *Berard* approach was developed in the 1960s, by Dr. Guy Berard, a French otolaryngologist/audiologist. This approach was introduced in the United States in 1991, and is also called *Auditory Integrative Therapy (AIT)*. Berard worked with Tomatis and developed his own modifications. The first step of AIT involves a detailed audiogram: an individual is considered an appropriate program candidate if there are peaks of hypersensitivity or if there is hyposensitivity at certain frequencies. The individual takes another audiogram after 5 hours of listening to determine whether the auditory peaks are still present and whether new peaks have developed. A third audiogram is conducted after an individual completes the listening sessions. The listening sessions consist of two 30-minute sessions per day for 10 consecutive days, during which a person listens through headsets to ever-changing and unpredictable electronically altered music from an Audiokinetron device. Frick and Lawton-Shirley, occupational therapists, report on their web site that, in treating more than 300 children and adults, they have found persons with known vestibular dysfunctions to appear to make the greatest gains. There are also reports of some children increasing their sensitivities to sound rather than decreasing them. The American Academy of Pediatrics issued a policy statement in 1998 that, until further research information is available, AIT should be considered controversial, and pedi-

atricians should provide guidance and assistance in obtaining and reviewing information for families considering this treatment option.

Clearly, more research is needed on technologies working with auditory processing. Until there is definitive research available, all aspects of a child's presenting symptoms and functioning should be weighed, and each family and the child's clinicians must make a careful decision whether to try one of these approaches. Nevertheless, this is an emerging area of intervention to watch and consider on an individual basis while it is under study.

SUMMARY

In addition to the programs described in this chapter, many other programs are available that use technology to assist the development of language, sensory processing, and motor-planning abilities. Most of them have web sites on the Internet, and many offer free demonstration CDs. A factor to be concerned about in evaluating their benefits for a given individual is whether, in assessing response errors, the programs assist the individual in analyzing the *nature* of their errors, rather than simply counting the number of right responses. The goal should be self-correcting behavior. Determining the nature of errors enables children as well as adults to consciously monitor and attend to what *causes* their errors so that, ultimately, they do not commit the same errors again and have to be corrected afterward.

Another factor to keep in mind is that learning to learn is a complex process that is sensory-based. We must keep alert to the difference between activities that require *application* of a particular sensory or language processing capacity, and those that *develop* a capacity so that it is available to be applied. In this respect, it is evident that some technology-assisted programs are complementary.

Rather than thinking of these programs as being competitive and researching their individual effects in comparison to each other, perhaps we should be researching how they could be sequenced, or whether they should be used concomitantly, for the best results. Many individuals have lives that are "on hold" because their sensory and/or language *processing* needs have not been identified and/or addressed adequately. For their sake, we can not afford to approach program effectiveness research only from a competitive stance. Research on complementary use of certain programs might result in these individuals realizing their potential for communicating and learning sooner and more fully. ∎

REFERENCES

American Academy of Audiology. (1993). Position statement: Auditory integration training. *Audiology Today, 5*(4), 21.

Bettison, S. (1996). The long-term effects of auditory training on children with autism. *Journal of Autism and Developmental Disorders, 26,* 361-374.

Burpee, J., DeJean, V., Frick, S., Kawar, M., Koomar, J., & Murphy Fischer, D. (in press). Theoretical and Clinical Perspectives on the Interactive Metronome®: A view from occupational therapy practice. *American Journal of Occupational Therapy.*

Edelson, S., Arin, D., Bauman, M., Lukas, S., Rudy, J., Sholar, M., Rimland, B. (1999). Auditory Integration Training: A double-blind study of behavioural and electrophysiological effects in people with autism. *Focus on Autism and Other Developmental Disabilities, 14*(2), 73-81.

Gravel, J. S. (1994). Auditory integration training: Placing the burden of proof. *American Journal of Speech-Language Pathology, 3*(2), 25-29.

Highfill, M., & Cimorelli, J. (1994). *Positron emission tomography measure of modified auditory integration therapy: A case study.* Poster presented at the Annual Convention of the American Speech-Language-Hearing Association, New Orleans, LA, November.

Kuhlman, K. & Schweinhart, L.J. (in press). *Timing in child development.* Ypsilanti, MI: High/Scope Educational Research Foundation.

Madell, J. R. (1997). *New interventions to enhance auditory processing, language, reading, and learning.* Paper presented at the Interdisciplinary Council on Developmental and Learning Disorders' Approaches to Developmental and Learning Disorders

in Infants and Children: Theory & Practice, McLean, VA, November 14-16.

Madell, J., & Rose, D. E. (1994). Auditory integration training. *American Journal of Audiology,* March, 14-18.

Merzenich M. M., Jenkins, W. M., Johnston, P., Schreiner C., Miller, S. L., & Tallal, P. (1996). Temporal processing deficits of language-learning impaired children ameliorated by training. *Science, 271*(5245), 77-81.

Porges, S. W., & Bazhenova, O. V. (1997). Evolution and the autonomic nervous system: A neurological model of socio-emotional and communication disorders. Paper presented at the Interdisciplinary Council on Developmental and Learning Disorders' conference, *Approaches to Developmental and Learning Disorders in Infants and Children: Theory & Practice 1997,* McLean, VA, November.

Rimland, B., & Edelson, S. M. (1991). *Improving the auditory functioning of autistic persons: A comparison of the Berard auditory training approach with the Tomatis audio-psychophonology approach.* (Tech. Report No. 111). San Diego, CA: Autism Research Institute.

Rimland, B., & Edelson, S. M. (1994). The effects of auditory integration training on autism. *American Journal of Speech-Language Pathology, 3*(2),16-24.

Rimland, B., & Edelson, S. M. (1995). Brief report: a pilot study of auditory integration training in autism. *Journal of Autism and Developmental Disorders 25*(1), 61-70.

Shaffer, R. J., Jacokes, L. E., Cassily, J. F., Greenspan, S. I., Tuchman, R. F., & Stemmer, P. J. (in press). Effect of Interactive Metronome® (IM) training on children with ADHD. *American Journal of Occupational Therapy.*

Stemmer, P. M. (1996). *Improving student motor integration by use of an interactive metronome*. Study paper presented at the 1996 Annual Meeting of the American Educational Association, Chicago, IL.

Tallal, P., Miller. S. L., Bedi, G., Byma, G., Wang, X., Nagarajan, S. S., Schreiner, C., Jenkins, W. M., & Merzenich, M. M. (1996). Language comprehension in language-learning impaired children improved with acoustically modified speech. *Science, 271*(5245), 81-84.

Tallal, P., Merzenich, M. M., Miller, S., & Jenkins, W. (1998). Language learning impairments: Integrating basic science, technology, and remediation. *Experimental Brain Research, 123*(1-2): 201-209.

Veale, T. K. (1994). Auditory integration training: The use of a new listening therapy within our profession. *American Journal of Speech-Language Pathology, 3*(2), 12-15.

Woodward, D. (1994). Changes in unilateral and bilateral sound sensitivity as a result of AIT. *Sound Connection, 2*, 4.

Imagery and the Language Processing Spectrum

Nanci Bell, M.A.

If I can't picture it, I can't understand it. - Albert Einstein

Albert Einstein's achievements are milestones in the history of science and have become an integral part of the 20th century. No other modern physicist has altered and expanded our understanding of nature as significantly. Named "man of the century" by *Time Magazine,* Einstein's esteemed contributions were the result of his ability to think critically and creatively. He made his thinking concrete with a specific sensory system function—imagery. His statement, "If I can't picture it, I can't understand it," not only illuminates his genius, but also embodies a truth about language processing that may unlock some answers for children and adults with weakness on the language processing spectrum.

The language processing spectrum ranges from processing words (decoding and encoding print) to processing concepts (comprehending and expressing language). When there is weakness on the spectrum, labels such as "dyslexia" appear on the left and those such as "hyperlexia" appear on the right, extending into the label of autism. Figure 1 highlights the language processing spectrum.

As causes and solutions have been sought for children and adults with weaknesses on the spectrum, important knowledge has been

Language Processing
--→

Processing Words (Symbol Imagery) Dyslexia	*Processing Concepts* (Concept Imagery) Hyperlexia→Autism

Figure 1. The Language Processing Spectrum

gained. Researchers know that the sensory system is the issue—the heart of good language processing or the root of the problem. People can process language across the spectrum because they can receive and process sensory information, generally in the form of imagery. Strength in imagery results in language processing strength; weakness in imagery results in language processing weakness—words and concepts.

On the left side of the spectrum—the processing of words—a rather recent breakthrough has changed the lives of many dyslexics. We now know that in order to read and spell written language, the human sensory system needs to process sounds and letters within syllables, referred to as *phoneme awareness* and *symbol imagery*. However, during the years of searching for answers, the professional community was lost for awhile. Dyslexia was often viewed as an array of symptoms so disparate that, it was thought, they could not be related. Dyslexia was attributed to everything from misreading words to not being able to program a VCR. Rampant symptoms seemed unrelated. With the problem so extensive, uncovering a primary cause seemed both impossible and improbable. Statements such as "not everything works for everybody" and "not everybody is the same" worsened the problem. Too often, each dyslexic was viewed as unique rather than as sharing a simple, yet core, sensory weakness. After years of studying the problem, some organizations suggested that there was no cure for dyslexia. Compensation strategies were offered that didn't fix the problem. Learning to live with dyslexia was painful and gave little hope to the many that suffered.

Fortunately, however, persistent research provided answers and solutions. Stimulation at the sensory level—phonological awareness and symbol imagery—brought significant improvement in reading and spelling skills. Gains, seemingly impossible before, were made even with adult dyslexics. As a core sensory deficit was specified, treatment became specific rather than random. In addition to the research, the shortcomings of the "whole language" movement provided additional information about the importance of developing phonological processing. By failing to stimulate phoneme awareness, the whole language approach increased the incidence of poor reading and dyslexia increased. This failure provided a contrast and an additional lesson about the underlying sensory processing necessary for reading and spelling words. Unfortunately, while the professional community searched and debated, children and adults often were not given appropriate sensory stimulation.

Research and insight about the sensory system has since contributed to solving some issues on the left side of the spectrum. Because of a better understanding of the sensory system, improvements are now being made that were previously considered impossible. But what about the right side of the language processing spectrum? Has the volume of symptoms and their seeming disparity caused scientists to think that there may not be primary sensory causes, or contributors, to the range of symptoms and labels on the right side? If Einstein used imagery for his genius of thought, is imagery a primary sensory system factor related to weak comprehension, hyperlexia, and possibly even autism? Is imagery just imagery, or is there more than one type of imagery? Is the imagery for letters the same as the imagery for concepts? Is imagery a two-sided coin?

A TWO-SIDED SENSORY COIN: MARCUS AND HANNAH

There are two primary language processing deficits that cause individuals to perform below their potential: weak decoding/encoding of words and weak comprehension/expression of concepts. These two deficits are the two sides of the sensory processing coin. Each side uses imagery in a specific manner, opposite in nature from the other side. One side images and processes parts, while the other images and processes wholes.

The story of Marcus represents the side of the coin concerned with difficulty in processing concepts, the primary focus of this chapter. His symptoms stem from weakness in his sensory system, and are not disparate or disconnected. Hannah, Marcus's twin, represents the other side of the coin. The following case study, told in his mother's words, describes how Marcus functions.

Marcus's Story

"Our son, Marcus, is 9 years old now, and we have been everywhere for help. We don't know what to do. They are suggesting a special day school, but we are reluctant to make another change. Marcus has been in speech therapy since he was 4 years old. We've tried special therapy, special classes, summer programs, and medication. We just don't know what to do. Marcus is a sweet boy, but no one seems to be able to help him—or us.

"What? Oh, yes. He's been tested, repeatedly, by a variety of professionals. I have accumulated everything in a file that's about 4 inches thick. It began when he was a toddler because he wasn't developing language as well as his twin sister, Hannah.

"Yes. They first diagnosed Marcus as having a delay in speech development and more recently he was diagnosed as hyperlexic. He can read words, but he can't understand what he reads. Actually, remembering back, it seems that he could read before he could talk! He learned to read long before he went to school, and in first and second grade, he got really good marks in reading. It's just that he can't comprehend or understand what he reads…but he can read it.

"No, he doesn't seem to understand what he hears either. For example, at the dinner table, or in any conversation, he doesn't appear to get what is going on around him—but he is very easy to be with since he tends to entertain himself.

"What? Well, yes, he has a good oral vocabulary. He generally tests well in vocabulary. He seems to understand the meaning of individual words very well.

"His expressive language? Like how much does he talk? Well, no, he doesn't talk a lot, like his sister does, but he can talk. He has never had trouble saying words. He just doesn't talk a lot.

"Sequence? No, his expression doesn't seem sequential. It comes out 'out' of sequence. Sometimes he tells us things, but we have difficulty putting what he says together. He talks about the last thing first, or the middle thing last, and his language gets all messed up and he gets frustrated. And, sometimes it seems as if he is stuck on some detail, like a specific part in a movie he watched or a detail from a television show.

"What? No, he doesn't contribute much to conversation. Well, sometimes he does if it is about a very specific thing he is interested in. He has difficulty making friends and almost seems confused by social situations. It seems like he isn't getting what is going on around him. Sometimes we see him off by himself, just playing with a certain toy or a certain computer game. He is generally quiet. He does answer questions…though sometimes I have to repeat the questions to him quite a few times.

"No, he is not generally a behavior problem. His teachers say that he is pleasant, but sort of spacey. Do you know what I mean? Sometimes he just looks a little dazed when you're talking to him. I think he wants to have friends because I see him watching other children. I think he just doesn't know what to do or how to interact, and he ends up being alone.

"Yes, he has a lot of trouble following directions. He doesn't seem to pay attention to what you say to him, and he can't follow a stream of directions, especially with more than one or two things to do. It seems like what I say just goes in one ear and out the other. One physician thought he had attention deficit disorder, and we have been trying medication. He is a little better on medication, but it still hasn't fixed the problem. I keep thinking we're missing something.

"No, he doesn't get jokes easily. In fact, he is pretty serious most of the time.

"What? No, he never had difficulty with spelling! He can spell anything! His sister can't, however. His sister, Hannah, has recently been labeled learning disabled and put in a special class one hour a day. She is having trouble reading and spelling words. They think she may be dyslexic.

"Hannah? No, she has never had trouble understanding conversation. Hannah is talkative, friendly, and very social. She has lots of friends and tells us all the things that happened to her during the day. Pretty much just the opposite of Marcus.

"Yes, I read to both children when they were little, but Marcus didn't like it. Sometimes he looked at the pictures, but then he got bored and left. Yes, his sister liked to listen to stories. Yes. She definitely gets what she reads; she just has trouble reading the actual words. They seem to have exactly the opposite problem! Marcus can read the words but can't comprehend. Hannah can comprehend, but she can't read the words.

"Hmmm. Now that you ask, a few years ago a physician did suggest that Marcus might be autistic. It seems that some of the best and most caring professionals have given attention to Marcus, but nothing seems to really be helping him. We've tried everything.

"A few days ago, I took Marcus to a new professional who told me that if something didn't change by the time Marcus is 12… well, it is very likely it will never change. I came home, pulled the drapes, and spent the rest of the day crying on the couch for my son. I'm calling you for one more try."

Weak Concept Imagery: A Primary Deficit for Marcus

Marcus's weakness in processing language had not been diagnosed or addressed, even by age 9, despite care and concern from many qualified professionals. The symptoms

he exhibited were on the right side of the language processing spectrum and matched those of hyperlexia and high-functioning autism, perhaps Asperger's syndrome.

In response to his mother's concern, Marcus was given an extensive battery of diagnostic testing for language processing. During the testing, Marcus did not express himself easily, make eye contact well, relate to the tester, or appear to understand directions or conversation. Though his oral vocabulary was at the 75th percentile and he could read words at the tenth grade level, he performed at a 5-year-old mental age level in oral language comprehension and the 5th percentile in following oral directions. He scored above the 99th percentile in paragraph decoding, but below the 1st percentile in comprehension.

When asked what his favorite thing in school was, he didn't answer at first, then finally said, "What?" He appeared not to hear the language. The question was repeated and again he said, "What?" This time he appeared confused. Finally, the question was stated as simply as possible, "What do you like best in school?"

"Recess."

"What is the hardest thing in school?"

After a delay, Marcus replied, "Paying attention."

Marcus had a primary weakness in his sensory system—*weak concept imagery*. As he took language in, he did not have adequate imagery activity to make language stop, make language connect, or make language relate. Language entered adequately through the auditory channel but then faltered for lack of sensory activity in imagery.

Concept imagery is the ability to create imaged gestalts—wholes. Marcus's sensory system could not easily create mental representations for the whole, but he could easily create mental representations for parts.

Words seemed to go in one ear and out the other without the sensory mechanism of concept imagery to anchor and relate them. The side of his sensory coin that imaged and processed parts was functioning well, but the side that imaged and processed wholes was not.

Processing language—cognition—is a parts-whole issue. Some individuals, Einstein included, are able to *rapidly and automatically* create an imaged gestalt from what they read or hear. They can combine parts into a whole. Most important, with the imaged gestalt they can process language and think critically. From the gestalt, they can comprehend oral language, comprehend what they read, problem solve, think logically, think creatively, "get the big picture," move from concrete to abstract thinking, express themselves relevantly, make their point, get humor, read social situations, make inferences, draw conclusions, and pay attention. Referring to imagery's contribution to thought and problem solving, Einstein said that *imagination is more important than knowledge.*

Although the ability to create gestalt imagery is a basic and primary asset in the sensory system, there are many individuals who find concept imagery difficult, slow, partially accessible, situation-specific, or unavailable. These individuals, like Marcus, may process *parts* well. Many even appear to be stuck on parts—details—because their sensory system is able to image them rapidly and automatically. They can create images for parts—letters, isolated facts, names, and dates—and they can often read and spell words well. Their sensory system easily and rapidly gives them information about bits and pieces by easily and rapidly creating mental representations for parts of language, parts of conversations, parts of oral language, parts of directions, parts of written language, parts of movies, and parts of social situations.

Sometimes the parts seem to be overwhelming and consuming.

A part in a conversation or lecture is imaged and processed, then discussed, often irrelevantly. The point of a conversation is missed, but the parts are processed. The main idea is lost somewhere in an array of random parts. The critical thinking ability to draw a conclusion or make an inference is impaired because there is a limited gestalt, or whole, from which to process or think. Unrelated or unconnected imaged parts float around in a sensory-cognitive system, contributing to erroneous conclusions and inferences.

The random and unconnected imaged parts often bounce back in the form of random and unconnected language expression. As parts are taken in, they come back out. Parts are expressed. Bits and pieces that are imaged and processed are expressed. Language expression may not be sequential. With no imaged gestalt, written or oral language expression is an array of parts with the first, middle, and last out of sequence.

Social interaction and conclusions may suffer the same fate. Parts of social situations are processed. A part of a situation is misread and then reacted to, with limited understanding of "cause and effect." Personal interaction may be difficult. Language swirls around, parts are processed and parts are expressed. Social interaction with a language-filled environment is difficult if the primary, incoming sensory information is in "parts."

Weakness in concept imagery may range from mild to severe, with some individuals experiencing moderate difficulty comprehending and expressing language. Those individuals might have to study a little harder or read chapters a few more times. However, as the weakness in imaging gestalts becomes more severe, so do the symptoms. Labels such as hyperlexia, Asperger's syndrome, and autism begin to surface. Weak concept imagery is a primary sensory deficit for hyperlexia, and while it is not the only weakness related to autism, poor concept imagery may be a primary contributing factor. The right side of the language processing spectrum requires concept imagery function.

Marcus received 6 weeks of intensive concept imagery instruction (4 hours a day, 5 days a week) and improved from the 5th to the 75th percentile in following oral directions and from the 1st to the 50th percentile in reading comprehension. He also began to engage in conversation, interact socially, and understand humor.

SYMPTOMS OF WEAK CONCEPT IMAGERY

Understanding the range of weakness in concept imagery is important in order to understand the symptoms it presents. College students and educated adults may experience language processing weakness stemming from the same sensory system weakness as Marcus had. For example, Sam, a college graduate, experienced mild concept imagery weakness that had negative consequences for his chosen vocation. With good decoding and above average intelligence, Sam attempted to enter medical school; however, he was unable to pass the MCAT entrance test. His reading comprehension score was 4, but 8 was average. He waited a period of time and retook the test. Again he scored 4. Persistent and committed to becoming a physician, he sought help to improve his reading comprehension. During the diagnostic testing, in which he scored significantly below his potential in reading comprehension, Sam described his frustration throughout his schooling. He felt that he missed most of his academic course content, indicating that information seemed to go in— but out again. He likened his comprehension disability to an incomplete cognitive tool kit.

"I couldn't get [comprehend] things, but I'd look around me and others seemed to get things easily. I couldn't understand how they did it…and why I couldn't. It seemed like when I opened up my cognitive tool kit there was something missing."

Another student had a more serious weakness in concept imagery, though still not severe. Peter had good oral vocabulary and good decoding, but was on academic probation in college, despite having saved the difficult classes for his last years in college. He said, "There wasn't one thing I could do right in school. I couldn't easily get the lectures, and I didn't remember anything I read. It was very frustrating. I read each sentence three times and then went on to the next sentence and read it three times. It didn't make any sense put together…If I read the information enough times, I could remember it for maybe 30 seconds and then I had no clue." Peter dropped out of college.

Sam, Peter, and Marcus are examples of individuals with mild to severe concept imagery weakness, but there are a host of others, some milder and some more severe. The weakness moves on a continuum, a spectrum. As the sensory weakness becomes more severe, so do the symptoms.

The following behaviors are symptoms of weak concept imagery, based on a range of individuals, from young to old, with mild to severe weakness. The issue of a weak gestalt contributes to each symptom. At the time these symptoms were noted several years ago, the diagnosis of autism was not as prevalent.

Symptoms of Weak Concept Imagery

An individual with weak concept imagery has:

- *A tendency to process parts more than, or rather than, wholes.* Gets details rather than big pictures. Attends to facts more than concepts.

- *Difficulty with conceptual, critical, logical, and/or abstract thinking.* Gets stuck on details and parts. Enjoys facts rather than concepts. Appears to be a concrete thinker because is processing specific part-images.
- *Difficulty grasping oral language, whether stories, conversations, or lectures.* Is not interested in listening to stories, can't seem to pay attention. Misses the point of a lecture or conversation. Appears to process irrelevant or incidental parts of what is heard. Often asks and re-asks the same question. May be labeled as a poor listener or inattentive.
- *Weak reading comprehension.* Though oral vocabulary and decoding may be sufficient, may only get a few facts from what is read. Has trouble answering higher-order thinking questions, such as the main idea, a conclusion, an inference, and a prediction. Has to read sentences, paragraphs, and chapters more than once. May still not get the big picture or point, and may do poorly on tests that measure more than just facts.
- *Difficulty following directions, oral or written.* Gets confused with more than one or two directions. Language appears to go in one ear and out the other. Seems unable to pay attention to language or successfully engage in a social environment.
- *Weakness in expressing language orally.* Language expression is a random array of parts, facts, and details. Talks about irrelevant parts or issues. Tells stories out of sequence. Talks very little or talks a lot, but is scattered and disconnected.
- *Difficulty expressing language in writing.* Often writes in unrelated parts. Has "five essays in one." Does not connect thoughts and make a point, a whole. Does not begin with a topic, support the topic, and summarize the topic. Cannot easily answer a question due to missing the point of the question.
- *Difficulty understanding humor.* Misses the joke. Takes language literally and doesn't see the imagery in humor. May respond to physical humor, such as slipping on a banana, but can't comprehend language-based humor. Laughs at inappropriate times.
- *Difficulty reading social situations.* Attends to a part of an expression or situation. Based on a part, makes inappropriate expressions or takes inappropriate actions. Has difficulty understanding cause and effect.
- *Appears to find language and social interaction a confusing mix of disconnected parts.* Prefers own company. The world seems to be a puzzling, disconcerting, and meaningless array of parts.

CAUSES AND CONTRIBUTORS TO WEAK CONCEPT IMAGERY

Because more research, particularly brain research, is needed, theories about the specific cause of the sensory weakness in creating an imaged gestalt are still speculative, but they are based on substantial experience, clinical insight, and logic. As with other disorders, including dyslexia, heredity appears to be a factor. Children and adults with weak comprehension often have one or both parents exhibiting a similar deficiency. As the issue of imaging and processing a whole is explained, typically one parent acknowledges difficulty comprehending and expressing language. The more severe the concept imagery weakness, the more likely a parent experiences a similar problem or tells of someone else in the family with a similar issue. The familial reference may range from comprehension weakness to autism.

Environmental issues appear to contribute to an increased incidence in mild to moderate comprehension problems. For example, in a culture in which television is a primary source of entertainment, the sensory system may not be receiving enough imagery stimulation. This becomes of particular concern when noting the duality of coding for cognition, as in Paivio's theory.

Paivio's dual coding theory (1986) emphasized the critical role of imagery for cognition and stated that cognition is proportional to the extent that mental representations (imagery) and language are integrated. The increased cultural activity of television and video games may have a negative cognitive impact on one-half of the cognitive code—imagery. When someone listens to an old radio shows or story records, sound effects enhance the imagery of language. In contrast, when a person watches television, the mind is provided with images. Watching television may have an atrophying effect on imagery because the images are created for the viewer. Further impacting cognition, the time an individual spends watching television or playing video games may consume the time that individual might otherwise have spent reading, storytelling, or conversing: in other words, time that could have been used for stimulation of concept imagery and language expression.

Another concern currently being discussed is the environmental and medical use of chemicals called *neurotoxins*. For example, childhood vaccines are under investigation as contributors to language processing disorders and learning disabilities, including autism.

Whether the cause is a hereditary factor, environmentally induced, or both, the ability to image a gestalt appears to be a function unto itself. Although impaired phonological processing and impaired decoding, weak oral vocabulary, and reduced prior knowledge and

background experiences may contribute to weak concept imagery, these factors do not appear to be causal. As with Marcus, hyperlexics often have good decoding, oral vocabulary, and imagery for isolated words, but they are not able to comprehend concepts and answer higher-order thinking questions. The same applies to individuals considered to have poor reading comprehension but not given the label of hyperlexia. Many individuals with wide experiences and good education are not able to comprehend language effectively and efficiently. In contrast, many poor decoders, including severe dyslexics, are able to comprehend language and create images for concepts. If language is presented orally to these dyslexics, they appear brilliant in their ability to interpret and reason. Their imagery weakness is on the opposite side of the sensory coin and is similar to Hannah's— they can't image letters, which are the parts of words.

Weak oral vocabulary may interfere with concept imagery and comprehension; however, imagery plays a significant role in the development of appropriate vocabulary. Stimulating imagery for vocabulary aids in the storage and retrieval of meaning for isolated words. Smith, Stahl, and Neil (1987), after a study with 142 university students, stated, "The significant difference that occurred between the definition only and the definition and sentence and imagery groups supports Paivio's dual coding theory. In accord with Paivio's theory the visual image did provide an additional memory trace that improved long term memory for the vocabulary items in the study. This finding mirrors research spanning the years as far back as Kirkpatrick in 1894."

Deficits in prior knowledge and background experience may interfere with language comprehension, but instructional techniques designed to access prior knowledge, such as first discussing material, setting the scene, and teaching vocabulary, do not necessarily stimulate independent comprehension. Imagery is assumed. An individual needs to be able to set the scene with language by imaging and interacting with stored images to create and process the new concept. This interaction needs to be quick and easy—automatic. If it is labored and difficult, the whole may be lost and random parts prevail.

STIMULATION OF CONCEPT IMAGERY: THE VISUALIZING AND VERBALIZING™ PROGRAM

The firm "earth" of experience was the basis for the initial hypothesis of two types of imagery: concept imagery and symbol imagery. A clinical environment, laden with individuals of all ages and all types of language processing weakness, led to cognitive theory and the instructional procedures of the Visualizing and Verbalizing™ for Language Comprehension and Thinking (V/V™) program.

The first realization in applying theory to procedure was that individuals need to develop the ability to image a whole. The next was that imagery couldn't just be developed by a reminder or simple cue, such as, "Visualize what you read." For individuals with a sensory weakness of bringing parts to whole with imagery, specific steps and specific questions needed to be presented.

The steps of V/V™ are sequential and require the teacher or therapist to ask questions directed to the sensory system. Pribram (1971) said, "We cannot think about something of which we are not consciously aware, and we cannot be aware of something not perceived sufficiently at the sensory level to come to consciousness." *Therefore, teacher language must directly stimulate specific sensory-input.*

"What did you *hear?*" may not be specific enough to stimulate imagery. Such a question may direct the child to attend primarily to the sensory stimuli of the airplane whirring by or the tapping of the woodpecker on a nearby tree. But the question, "What did you *picture?*" directs the child's attention to the specific sensory information of imagery. The next sensory-directed question builds concept imagery by directing the child to continue picturing the same subject while extending it to action. "What did you *picture* the white horse doing—running or jumping?*" The language directs the student to compare the input of imagery to the input of language—stimulating the integration of verbal to nonverbal sensory stimuli.

The V/V™ procedure develops concept imagery with the smallest unit of language— a word—and extends the imagery to sentences, paragraphs, and pages of content. The specific steps follow.

Steps of V/V™

1. *Picture to Picture*

The goal is to develop fluent, detailed verbalization from a given picture (prior to requiring detailed verbalization of a *generated* image in the next step).

The individual describes simple, given pictures. *Structure words*—what, size, color, number, shape, where, when, background, movement, mood, perspective, and sound—are introduced to provide concrete descriptive elements. The choice and amount of structure words presented depends on the severity of the weakness or age of the individual. The teacher questions with "choice and contrast" to stimulate verbalization of the picture and directs the student to monitor and compare his verbalization. Not looking at the given picture, but imaging from the student's language, the teacher says, "What should I picture for the boy's pants? Does he have on blue pants or red pants? Are they long pants or short pants?" This reference to imagery in the question helps the student think about relevant and detailed verbalization—the goal of this step and the preparation for the next step.

2. *Word Imaging*

    The goal is to develop detailed visualizing and verbalizing (dual coding) for a single word.

    The individual describes a generated image for a single word, beginning with a personal image and extending it to a high-imagery known noun, such as "clown" or "cowboy." The structure words, introduced earlier, are used to provide detailed, vivid imagery. The teacher uses choice and contrast to ask sensory-driven questions to specifically develop imagery. "Are you picturing a white hat or a black hat on the cowboy? Does he have hair or no hair?"

3. *Phrase and Sentence Imaging*

    The goal is to extend the imagery and language from one word to a phrase and then to a single, simple sentence.

    As the steps overlap, the individual uses a specifically imaged known noun as the subject of a sentence to be imaged. For example, the clown that was imaged as a single word, with vivid images from the structure words and questioning, is now the imagery to which action, a verb, is attached. "Keep the same clown we just visualized, and now picture this, the clown jumped on the red ball." The extent of the imagery stimulation is dictated by the age and severity of the dysfunction (the sentence could have only one subject and one verb to image; that is, the clown

jumped, the clown cried, the clown laughed, the clown snorted).

4. *Sentence by Sentence Imaging*

    The goal is to extend the integration of imagery and language to a gestalt—sentence by sentence.

    The procedure begins receptively, from a short, self-contained paragraph, with each sentence read to the individual. As the individual visualizes and verbalizes each sentence, colored squares are placed sequentially in front of him to designate the imaged part (the sentence). Structure words are used to develop detailed imagery for the first sentence (the topic, or gestalt, sentence). At the completion of the paragraph, with approximately four to five colored squares representing the sentences, the individual gives a "picture summary." Touching each colored square, he says, "Here I saw..." At the completion of the picture summary, the colored squares are collected and put away. The student then gives a "word summary," using his imagery to paraphrase the paragraph.

5. *Sentence by Sentence with Higher-Order Thinking Skills (HOTS)*

    The goal is to develop critical thinking from the imaged gestalt developed in the previous step.

    The same sentence-by-sentence procedure of placing colored squares for the parts, verbalizing with a picture summary to sequentially summarize the imaged parts, and verbalizing with a word summary to paraphrase the whole is used to establish the cognitive base for interpretation. With the imaged whole as the base, the student is asked the main idea, conclusion, and inference questions. "What was the main thing you *pictured* from that paragraph? Did you *picture* elephants or fleas...and what did you picture about the elephant, how it eats, how it sleeps...?" "From all *your images*, why do you think the elephant might destroy a forest?" "What do you *picture* might happen if...?"

6. *Multiple Sentence, Paragraph, and Whole Page Imaging with HOTS*

The goal is to increase and extend the language input, either receptive or expressive, to develop the imaged gestalt and apply that cognitive base to critical thinking, problem solving, and interpretation.

The succeeding steps increase the language from which the individual visualizes and verbalizes, creating the gestalt. HOTS questions are included for every paragraph, and the material may become longer and denser, depending on the age and level of the student. The stimulation is from oral language as well as from language the student decodes.

The steps of V/V™ develop an individual's ability to bring parts to whole and think with an imaged gestalt. Once the gestalt is able to be imaged, it can be brought to a conscious level for problem solving, paragraph writing, comprehending and studying content, following directions, logical thinking exercises, mathematics, play, and interpreting and responding appropriately to social situations.

Dual Coding Theory and Visualizing and Verbalizing™

The V/V™ program was developed to meet language processing needs, but its importance and direct relationship to dual coding theory was noted later. Paivio (1979) states, "The most general assumption in dual coding theory is that there are two classes of

phenomena handled cognitively by separate subsystems, one specialized for the representation and processing of information concerning nonverbal objects and events, the other specialized for dealing with language." The nonverbal (symbolic) subsystem is referred to as the imagery system because its critical functions include the analysis of scenes and the generation of mental images. The language-specialized system is referred to as the verbal system. The V/V™ program stimulates and integrates the two systems of language and imagery and heads toward the imaged gestalt for cognition.

Paivio also (1986) writes, "Human cognition is unique in that it has become specialized for dealing simultaneously with language and with nonverbal objects and events. Moreover, the language system is peculiar in that it deals directly with linguistic input and output (in the form of speech or writing) while at the same time serving a symbolic function with respect to nonverbal objects, events, and behaviors. Any representational theory must accommodate this functional duality." The V/V™ Program stimulates language and imagery, integrating the two systems in a systematic, sequential format—accommodating the functional duality.

The simplicity of dual coding theory—the duality of verbal and nonverbal subsystems—is compatible with clinical experience when cognition is observed on the language processing spectrum. From dyslexia on the left to comprehension and expression on the right, the integration of imagery and language is at the core of successful processing. Imagery for parts—symbol imagery—integrates imagery and language for processing words. Imagery for wholes—concept imagery—integrates imagery and language for processing concepts, abstractions, and the big picture.

PARTS-WHOLE AND SYMPTOMS OF AUTISM

As discussed earlier, the more severe the concept imagery weakness, the more severe the symptoms, which may move onto the autistic spectrum. Although not the only weakness causing the symptoms of autism, it is likely that weak concept imagery is a primary contributing factor.

The integration of verbal and nonverbal processing is critical for children on the autistic spectrum. The nonverbal system of imagery provides sensory support for their language processing ability—with the imaging of concepts foremost. In noting language processing as a parts-whole issue, many of the symptoms on the autistic spectrum can be traced to weakness processing the whole.

The following well-accepted symptoms of autism can be separated into parts-whole processing strengths or weaknesses.

Ability to process parts contributes to strength in:
• Rote memory
• Mechanical tasks
• Acquisition of simple information
• Simple procedural tasks
• Simple associations
• Word recognition
• Spelling
• Rote computational tasks
• Short-term immediate repetition of oral material

Inability to process wholes contributes to weakness in:
• Complex information processing
• Concept formation
• Abstract and critical thinking
• Interpretive oral language comprehension
• Interpretive reading comprehension
• Complex memory for oral and written material
• Following complex oral/written directions
• Problem solving
• Analysis and synthesis of information
• Organizational strategies

With the parts-whole issue in mind, the specific type of imagery an autistic child may be able or unable to do needs to be identified. For example, is "visual thinking" thinking in parts, or is it thinking in wholes? Does "visual-spatial thinking" mean imagery for parts or imagery for wholes?

IMAGERY AND VISUALLY BASED MATERIAL

It is often noted that autistic children respond well to visually based material because it makes language and the physical environment concrete for them. Auditory input is supplemented with visual "back-up." The following section lists the benefits of using visually based material, such as cue cards, to supplement auditory information (Twachtman-Cullen 1998). Note that "visual imagery" can be substituted in each item, as shown, and that the stimulation of imagery can offer children an internal visual back-up system.

Strengths of Visually Based Material

• Visually based material is stable over time. *(Visual imagery is stable over time and internal for children, taken with them wherever they go.)*
• By supplementing the auditory channel with visual back-up, the individual has the benefit of two input channels. *(By supplementing the auditory channel with visual imagery, the individual can inte-*

grate verbal with nonverbal sensory information, anywhere at anytime.)

- Visual information is an "eye catcher" for capturing and maintaining attention. *(Visual imagery is the same eye-catcher, only internal, enabling the individual to attend and focus.)*

- Visual supplementation aids processing ability. *(Given that visual imagery is the nonverbal code for dual coding, visual imagery aids processing ability and is available to the individual anywhere at anytime.)*

- Visual information helps make concepts more understandable by making them concrete. *(Visual imagery makes concepts concrete with sensory information that can be internally manipulated, related, and processed.)*

- Visual information can increase understanding in general. *(Visual imagery for the gestalt enables individuals to process concepts, anywhere at anytime.)*

- Visual supports can be used to prompt individuals. *(Visual imagery can be used to prompt individuals through conscious questioning of imagery relative to the event or concept, or through the individuals' own internal "prompt," which allows them to contrast and compare with imagery.)*

- Visual supports can help minimize anxiety. *(Visual imagery for concepts helps minimize anxiety by making the world less a jumble of random parts. With the imaged gestalt, meaning can be derived from both oral and written language.)*

- Visual supports can render information more memorable. *(As research shows, imagery is related to memory and recall; hence, visual imagery renders information more memorable.)*

Although visual back-up is helpful and effective, visual imagery can be stimulated at a conscious level and then supplemented and eventually substituted for visual aids. As the imagery begins to reside within the child, independence is developed for crossover to all environmental situations.

Concept Imagery for Floor Time, Play, and Pragmatics

With an imaged gestalt developing from V/V™ stimulation, teachers and therapists can drive "the sensory" bus by asking specific imagery-related questions or giving specific imagery-related stimulation. The imagery stimulation, either in conjunction with adapted V/V™ or separate from V/V™ stimulation, is applicable for floor time (see Greenspan & Wieder, Chapter 12, this volume) and play activities.

During floor time and play, imagery can be specifically stimulated with questions that draw attention to mental representations for actions or events. Following the child's lead, imagery can be consciously activated as a connection to the play and the language. Even if imagery cannot be brought to a conscious level for the child, the reference to it causes stimulation in the sensory system and awareness of imagery as a cognitive tool. For example, while following the child's lead in a play activity, ask, "I'm picturing that the horse is going to fall off the wall. What are you picturing? Let's picture it, then do it." Use choice and contrast by asking, "Tell me how you picture him falling, on his head or tail? Now let's do it and check it."

Then reverse the stimulation and begin with a play action, followed by talk about the imagery of the action. For example, consciously connect imagery to memory by picturing an action that didn't happen yet. "That was fun. Let's see if we can picture it. I'm picturing that the horse fell on his tail. Is that what you pictured?" Repeat the play action to compare it to imagery. "Hmmm, let's check to see if what we pictured happened." Even if the child can't image easily, and is responding minimally to the language, it is important to connect the concrete activity of play to the concreteness of imagery, helping to move the child into symbolic play based on mental representation ability. The more absurd the play and imagery, the more contrast there is and the more likely the child will engage and begin to make the play-imagery-language connection.

As the play interaction progresses, extend the play-imagery-language stimulation to prediction and abstract thinking. Use imagery to make thought concrete. "If our big truck (a toy truck) runs into this little fence, what do you picture will happen to the fence? Okay, let's see if what you pictured really happens." Verify imagery with action, then use language to describe both.

Language such as, "What do you *think* will happen next?" or "What do you remember?" doesn't direct and specify attention to imagery. However, language such as, "What do you *picture* will happen next?" drives the sensory bus and directs the child to attend to the specific and more concrete sensory input of imagery. A young boy, labeled high-functioning autistic, made an illuminating comment, "What I like about V/V™ is that you don't have to think anymore."

Regarding pragmatics, the play-imagery-language interaction can be used in connection with V/V™ or separate from formal V/V™ stimulation. However, using imagery for pragmatics requires that the individual have the ability to image a whole. To meet this prerequisite, as a student is developing gestalt imagery through the steps of V/V™, the therapist can overlap concept imagery to have the student vicariously experience social situations, problem solve, and determine appropriate reactions. For example, the therapist can set up an imaged social situa-

tion, visualize the setting and the characters, and then create different actions and reactions. Imagery can be used to interpret the situation, the cause of the event, and the appropriate and/or inappropriate reactions or responses. From the imagery, conclusions, inferences, and predictions can be asked and answered. This imagery practice for social situations allows individuals to use the sensory input of concept imagery to monitor, self-correct, and become independent in a social situation without a parent or therapist present.

RESEARCH ON THE V/V PROGRAM

The effectiveness of using the V/V™ program for concept imagery stimulation has been consistently evident for many years in Lindamood-Bell clinical intervention. Significant gains have been noted in following oral directions, reading recall, reading comprehension, and visual-motor skills. The clinical population studied included students on the autistic spectrum, though usually not with what would be described as severe autism or a Type IV classification (Greenspan & Wieder, 2000).

What follows is a summary of the research on the V/V™ Program. Spanning nearly a 10-year period, the data to date note positive effects of V/V™ on language processing skills. While the data have remained consistent, continued research is needed to further understand and document the role of imagery in language processing skills, specifically for target populations with labels such as hyperlexia and autism.

The first reporting of V/V™ Program success was in 1991, when Bell measured statistically significant gains for 22 males and 23 females, ranging in age from 9 to 57, who had received V/V™ only stimulation. Although performing poorly in language comprehension, their performance on other diagnostic tests indicated a normal range for receptive and expressive oral vocabulary, phonemic awareness, word attack, and word recognition. After an average treatment time of 47.26 hours, with a range of 16 to 110 hours, all study participants noted significant improvement in comprehension. For example, pretesting of the group indicated a percentile mean for reading comprehension on the Gray Oral Reading Test, Revised (GORT-R), of 43.94 and a post-testing percentile mean of 75.55 (p<.001). A subgroup of 16 of the 45 individuals, who ranged in age from 15 to 57 years old, were given the Descriptive Tests of Language Skills of the College Board, Reading Comprehension subtest. Their percentile mean was 56.06 on the pretesting and 71.29 on the post-testing (p<.001).

The Lindamood-Bell™ clinical gains continue to verify that the V/V™ program produces statistically significant gains in language processing. With an N of 843, V/V™ program-only students from 1994 to 1998, including some identified on the autistic spectrum, had an average pretest score in the 15th percentile for reading comprehension on the Gray Oral Reading Test-3, (GORT-3). After an average of 72 hours of instruction, the post-test average was at the 37th percentile (p<.0001). For the same population and time, an N of 302 V/V™ program-only students achieved similar improvement in following oral directions. For example, the average pretest score in following oral directions was at the 37th percentile. After an average of 82 hours of instruction, the post-test results were at the 63rd percentile (p<.0001).

Lindamood-Bell™ school projects using the V/V™ program show gains similar to those seen in Lindamood-Bell™ clinics. For example, for the 1999-2000 school year, 96 students in the Pueblo School District,

Colorado, received V/V™ program-only instruction for an average of 62 hours. They performed at the 9th percentile in reading comprehension (GORT-3) on the pretest but at the 25th percentile on the post-test (p<.0001). They showed similar statistically significant results in following oral directions (p<.0001). Thirty-two students at the Corwin Middle School in Colorado, many of whom spoke English as a second language, progressed from the 9th to the 25th percentile (p<.0091) in reading comprehension (GORT-3) after 41 hours of V/V™ instruction. The same middle school children demonstrated similar gains in following oral directions, improving from the 16th to the 50th percentile (p<.0001).

Additional studies replicate the Lindamood-Bell™ clinical findings. A 1995 controlled study in the Long Beach, California, public schools involved an entire fourth-grade class for four months. Comparisons between the experimental group and the control group, which received no V/V™ stimulation, showed that the experimental group made significant improvement in following oral directions and reading comprehension. For example, although both groups were at approximately the 50th percentile in word recognition, both groups were at the low end of the normal range in reading comprehension—the 27th and 28th percentiles, respectively. Pre- and post-testing on the GORT-3 reading comprehension test showed that the control group improved from the 27th to the 34th percentile, whereas the experimental group, after approximately 40 hours of V/V™ program instruction, improved from the 28th to the 45th percentile (p< .036).

In a federal project study at Window Rock Elementary School on the Navajo Indian Reservation, Kimbrough (1991) studied the effects of the V/V™ program on language comprehension on a sample population of fourth- and fifth-graders. The criterion for student selection was a standard score of 3 or below (5 is average) from the Iowa Tests of Basic Skills (ITBS) Reading Comprehension subtest. The measured gains were based on National Curve Equivalent Scores (NCES), and not grade-level equivalent scores. The project students received V/V™ program instruction in small groups, for approximately 30 minutes a day for 5 weeks, for a total of 12 hours of intervention. The average gain in reading comprehension was 6.6 points on the NCES compared to the national average gain of 3 points. Kimbrough states, "In the past, my students have always averaged a gain of 2 to 3 NCES points. After doing V/V™ for 5 weeks, my students doubled their scores compared to years past."

Research from Truch (1996) reports using the V/V™ program with 66 subjects for 80 hours of instruction. Subjects were of different ages and ability levels. Overall, 60% were in the age group of 6-12, another 25% were between the ages of 13 and 17, and the remaining 15% were adults ages 18 and over. The majority met the traditional criteria for learning disabilities, and some met the criteria for attention deficit disorder. The average age was 21 years. After 80 hours of V/V™ instruction, the gains in comprehension on the GORT-3 were highly significant, with an average gain of four grade levels in reading comprehension. Word reading was not a factor in the initial weak reading comprehension score, and the influence of vocabulary as a covariant failed to reach statistical significance.

The Chance Program at Graceland College in Iowa used the V/V™ program in the 1988-89 school year study with 16 college students referred for reading comprehension problems and possible dropout potential. Following V/V™ instruction, their ranking on the Descriptive Tests of Language Skills of the College Board, Reading Comprehension subtest, improved from a mean percentile of 29.8 to 51.6 (p <.05), placing them well within the normal range of processing. On the Nelson-Denny Reading Comprehension Test, their mean percentile ranking improved from 13.3 to 33.1, again placing the students within the normal range of function, this time showing a significance at p<.001.

The number of students at Lindamood-Bell™ clinics who are specifically labeled autistic has increased only recently. Prior to the current understanding of autism and a subsequent increase in the number of children diagnosed with this disorder, some of the "V/V students" were probably severe enough to have had the label of high-functioning autism or Asperger's syndrome applied to their symptoms. Those students are included in the Lindamood-Bell™ clinical data and were referred to clinically as having a "severe V/V" profile. The V/V™ stimulation has been productive for developing language processing in individuals with that "severe V/V" label. However, while individual gains have been encouraging, modification of the V/V™ program for younger or more severely impaired autistic students is currently being studied.

HANNAH: SYMBOL IMAGERY AND DYSLEXIA

Although the focus of this chapter is on the relationship of imagery to the right side of the language processing spectrum, it is also important to understand imagery and the left side. Contrast aids perception. Briefly, symbol imagery—the ability to visualize the identity, number, and order of letters within words—is a neurological, sensory-cognitive function critical to literacy development. The research documenting difficulty in segmenting phonemes within spoken syllables has been extensive. This sensory processing problem has been called lack of auditory conceptual function, phonological awareness, and phoneme awareness by various researchers (Calfee, Lindamood, & Lindamood, 1973; Liberman & Shankweiler, 1985; Lundberg, Frost, & Peterson, 1988; Torgesen, Wagner, & Rashotte, 1996; Wagner, Torgesen, & Rashotte, 1994). However, the awareness of the segmental structure of words requires symbol imagery ability in order to process the internal parts.

The ability to image letters in words makes phonological processing concrete. The sensory-system function that moves phonological information to a concrete level is the ability to attach meaning to imaged letters so that they form words that also have meanings. When this function is not available rapidly and easily, dyslexia, in mild to severe forms, may occur. Recent research has noted that abnormalities in phonological processing are invariably present in dyslexia; however, deficits in visual processing are also commonly seen (Eden, 1999).

The relationship between imagery and reading skills has been considered important by a number of researchers for many years. The difference between good and poor readers on auditory discrimination tasks may arise not only from deficient auditory skills in poor readers, as is commonly thought, but also from the ability, as evidenced in good readers, of imaging written language symbols to improve their ability to discriminate sounds (Ehri, 1980).

A measure of phonemic awareness with an instrument as precise as the Lindamood Auditory Conceptualization (LAC) test is a contribution to the field of reading and to an understanding of the role of phonological processing. A new measure of symbol imagery appears to be making a similar

contribution. The Symbol Imagery test (Bell, 1999) documents the correlation between the ability to image letters within words and a student's function in phonemic awareness, word attack, word recognition, and spelling. For example, analyzing testings of 330 students on a range of standardized reading and spelling tests demonstrated that symbol imagery ability correlated with phoneme awareness at a .70 level, with word attack at .81, with word recognition at .85, with spelling at .84, and with passage reading at .82. The data further suggested that symbol imagery correlates higher than phoneme awareness to word attack, word recognition, spelling, and paragraph reading. For example, phoneme awareness, as measured on the LAC test, correlated with word attack at .72, with word recognition at .67, with spelling at .59, and with passage reading at .61.

Although the information on symbol imagery is an important contribution to understanding the sensory mechanism involved in the acquisition of literacy skills, it is also important to note that not all individuals have this function available to them. For example, Jacob, a 14-year-old dyslexic had undiagnosed difficulties with symbol imagery. Jacob was exceptionally bright, got A's on term papers that he dictated orally, had exceptionally high oral language comprehension, and "everyone wanted to work with him because he truly contributed to others' understanding." A few weeks after he began treatment to develop articulatory feedback to assist him in perceiving sounds within words, he reached a plateau in applying his phonological processing to reading and spelling. His mother a pediatrician, wrote:

"Jacob was finally moving forward, but something was still missing. After a couple of weeks, Kimberly called me and said she was planning on adding symbol imagery to Jacob's program. I honestly didn't know what that was until Jacob came home and asked, 'Mom, do you picture letters in your head, because I never have.' So, that's why the lists of sight words were a joke throughout school. He was 14 years old and didn't have a single sight word. That was why he had to sound out a word twice if it appeared again in the same sentence. Amidst all the files of information (imagery) crammed into his extensive memory, literature, people, events, geometry, there was not one single letter!"

Symbol imagery is processing parts and results in the ability to process words rapidly and automatically. To return to Hannah, she was like Jacob in that her weakness in this imaging skill caused a resultant weakness in reading and spelling words. As her symbol imagery was developed and applied to decoding and encoding single through multisyllable words, she began to self-correct rapidly and automatically during the reading and spelling tasks. Her reading fluency developed, as did her orthographic spelling skills.

Hannah's improvement is consistent with the clinical work at Lindamood-Bell™, which verifies the interrelationship of imagery to print decoding and encoding. The 1997-98 Lindamood-Bell™ clinical data for children in the 10- to 13-year age range who were trained in only the Seeing Stars™ Symbol Imagery program (see Lindamood & Lindamood, Chapter 23, this volume) showed significant mean percentile improvement for all standardized tests, with the greatest improvements in word attack, paragraph accuracy, and paragraph reading (combining rate and accuracy). For example, in word attack the students' mean percentile improved from 32 to 68 (p<.0001). In paragraph accuracy, their mean percentile improved from 37 to 63 (p<.0001). In

passage reading, their mean percentile improved from 25 to 50 (p<.0001).

A 1998-99 controlled study verified that dual coding with symbol imagery and language is applicable for reading and spelling words, as well as processing language concepts. The role of symbol imagery was researched in a Lindamood-Bell™ controlled study at an elementary school in Idaho, where only the stimulation of symbol imagery was examined. In second- and fifth-grade classrooms (an N of 32 and 26, respectively), the experimental group, receiving an average of 42.5 hours of small-group stimulation in the Seeing Stars Symbol Imagery program, had statistically significant gains in word attack, word recognition, and spelling. For example, in word attack, the second-grade experimental group had a mean standard score gain of 13.12, compared to the control group's mean standard score gain of 5.94 (p>.01). In word recognition, the experimental group had a standard score gain of 9.62, compared to the control group's mean standard score gain of 2.75 (p<.01). In spelling, the experimental group had a mean standard score gain of 9.56, compared to the control group's mean standard score gain of 3.25 (p< .01).

Comparison between the fifth-grade experimental group and control group showed similar gains by the group receiving Seeing Stars Symbol Imagery program instruction. In word attack, the experimental group had a mean standard score gain of 8.85, compared to the control group's mean standard score gain of 1.85 (p<.05). In word recognition, the experimental group had a mean standard score gain of 5.46, compared to the control group's mean standard score gain of .54 (p= .08). In spelling, the fifth-grade experimental group had a mean standard score gain of 4.92, compared to the control group's mean standard score gain of 3.25 (p = .05).

Symbol imagery is a sensory mechanism that places orthography for words in memory as well as enabling phonological processing at an automatic level. When individuals have an extensive sight word base and can quickly self-correct decoding errors, reading fluency is increased (Bell, 1997), and the left side of the language processing spectrum is intact.

A BRIEF HISTORICAL PERSPECTIVE OF IMAGERY

This chapter focuses on the relationship of imagery to parts-whole thinking and competence in language processing. Within this context, a brief examination of the historical perspective on imagery will be more illuminating. The following historical comments and research with imagery can be viewed from the perspective of parts-whole, symbol, and concept imagery theory.

Einstein wasn't alone in his reference to imagery as a primary sensory-cognitive function. References begin as far back as 348 BC, when Aristotle, in his contemplations on the ability to reason, theorized that *man cannot think without mental imagery*. His summation of memory concludes, "Thus, we have explained that memory or remembering is a state induced by mental images related as a likeness to that of which it is an image." Together with the statements from Aristotle and Einstein, there is compelling evidence and historical perspective that imagery is a primary factor in cognition, ranging from reading and spelling words to language comprehension and critical thinking.

A few hundred years before Aristotle, Simonides (556-468 BC) taught imagery as a system to improve memory. The great Greek and Roman orators used the system of imagery to enable them to speak for hours

without written notes. This critical role of imagery comprised the classical art of memory for thousands of years, and there was direct stimulation of imagery as a primary sensory function for memory and thinking. Then, modifications of Plato's thoughts, neo-Platonic ideas, began to gradually remove imagery from prominence. In the 11th and 12th centuries, memory systems again became useful for purposes of remembering and making memorable the central Christian ideas. Statements such as Thomas Aquinas's, "Man's mind cannot understand thoughts without images of them" were responsible for renewed interest in imagery as a cognitive function.

In more modern times, Jean Piaget (1936, cited by Bleasdale, 1983) wrote that "knowledge, structures, or schemata are acquired when the infant actively manipulates, touches, and interacts with the environment. As objects are manipulated, sensory-motor schemata are developed and changed to accommodate new information. Over time, schemata become internalized in the form of imaged thought." Perhaps weakness on the right side of the language processing spectrum is caused by an inability to take the last step in Piaget's thinking. Perhaps the breakdown is not in the sensory-motor stimulation of manipulating objects, but rather a breakdown at the sensory level of imagery—*internalizing the schemata in the form of imaged thought*. Perhaps the sensory function of creating images is not developed to a sufficient enough level so as to be able to create imagery from either kinesthetic or language experiences.

Seeming to answer the above question, Piaget further stated, "It is clear that imaginal representations are not formed with the same facility in each case, and that there is therefore a hierarchy of image levels, which may correspond to stages of development. The evolution of images is a kind of intermediate between that of the perceptions and that of the intelligence."

Proceeding chronologically to some of the more interesting research and commentary, Arnheim (1966) wrote, "Thinking is concerned with the objects and events of the world we know...when the objects are not physically present, they are represented indirectly by what we remember and know about them. In what shape do memory and knowledge deliver the needed facts? In the shape of memory images, we answer most simply. Experiences deposit images." But, for the child or adult for whom imagery is not fast, automatic, vivid, or conceptual, these experiences may not happen easily or automatically.

Arnheim quoted the psychologist Edward B. Titchener, "My mind, in its ordinary operations, is a fairly complete picture gallery, not of finished paintings, but of impressionist notes. Whenever I read or hear that somebody has done something modestly, or gravely, or proudly or humbly, or courteously, I see a visual hint of the modesty or pride or humility." The visual hint Titchner describes is a higher level of imaging that begins with imaging the concrete and moves to imaging the abstract.

Continuing in the 1960s, Paivio (1969) wrote extensively on the role of imagery in cognition. "As every psychologist knows, imagery once played a prominent role in the interpretation of associative meaning, mediation, and memory. It was widely regarded as the mental representative of meaning—or of concrete meaning at least. William James (1890), for example, suggested that the static meaning of concrete words consists of sensory images awakened."

The 1970s brought further illumination from Paivio (1971). He had been attempting to demonstrate the way in which imagery can affect the acquisition, transformation, or retrieval of different classes of information. His dual coding theory, discussed earlier, defined imagery as one of two types of cognitive code, the other code being a verbal one. Paivio suggested that linguistic competence and performance are based on a substrate of imagery. Imagery includes not only static representations but also dynamic representations of action sequences and relationships between objects and events. Pribram (1971) stated, "Recently the importance of the Image concept has started to be recognized: cognitive psychologists analyzing the process of verbal learning have been faced with a variety of Imaging processes which demand neurological underpinnings.... Neurological research, as well as insights derived from the information-processing sciences, have helped make understandable the machinery which gives rise to this elusive ghost-making process." He further hypothesized that "all thinking has, in addition to sign and symbol manipulation, a holographic component."

Also in the 1970s, Kosslyn (1976) conducted a developmental study on the effects and role of imagery in retrieving information from long-term memory. In two blocks of trials, first-graders, fourth-graders, and adults were asked to determine whether various animals are characterized by various properties, first upon the consultation of a visual image and then without imagery. He reported that imagery provided more opportunity for retrieval.

Additional evidence surfaced during the 1980s. For example, Linden and Wittrock (1981) stated, "Reading comprehension is the generation of meaning for written language... We found that reading comprehension can be facilitated by several different procedures that emphasize attention to the text and to the construction of verbal or imaginal elaborations." In a study comparing fourth-graders with a control group of students given equal time to learn with the same reading teacher, he noted, "the generation of verbal and imaginal relations or associations between the text and experience increased comprehension approximately by fifty percent."

Further research by Oliver (1982) was based on three experiments to determine if an instructional set for visual imagery would facilitate reading comprehension in elementary school children. He concluded, "These findings indicate that teachers should try to help children develop the metacognitive skill of visual imagery as a strategy for improving comprehension... Visualization enhances comprehension."

Kosslyn (1983) noted, "A number of great thinkers, most notably Albert Einstein, professed to rely heavily on imagery in their work. Consider these words of Einstein: 'The psychical entities which seem to serve as elements of thoughts are certain signs and more or less clear images which can be voluntarily reproduced... this combinatory play seems to be the essential feature in productive thought—before there is any connection with logical construction of words or other kinds of signs which can be communicated to others.'"

Long, Winograd, and Bridge (1989) further summarized, "Our results suggest that imagery may be involved in the reading process in a number of ways. First, imagery may increase the capacity of working memory during reading by assimilating details and propositions into chunks, which are carried along during reading. Second, imagery seems to be involved in making comparisons or analogies—that is, in matching schematic and textual information. Third, imagery seems to function as an organizational tool for coding and storing meaning gained from the reading."

As is evident, theories and research on the relationship of imagery to thinking have been held and proven repeatedly throughout history. The 1990s continued to produce supportive research to uphold the role of imagery in cognition and reading. For example, Bower and Morrow (1990) observed, "Readers or listeners construct mental models of the situation a writer or speaker is describing. This is the basis of language comprehension."

Another researcher, Sadoski (1992), continues, "Imaginative processes, including imagery and emotional responses, are necessary to breathe life into the reading experience." In researching dual coding theory, reading theory, and reading efficiency, Sadoski noted that imagery is directly related to reading comprehension, reading recall, and verbal expression. He validated Paivio's dual coding theory in numerous studies involving imagery, comprehensiveness, and recall by carefully proving that the more reading concepts are imaged, the better they are comprehended, the longer they are recalled, and the more interesting they are to the reader.

Kosslyn and Koenig (1992) reported that the best clues about what different parts of the brain are doing during reading come from Positron Emission Tomography (PET) studies. These PET studies indicated that even reading single words is a complex activity, which involves several different parts of the brain. In particular, they reported that reading has a visual component and an associate memory component. The visual component clearly appears to involve the preprocessing and pattern activation subsystem, given the locus of the activation, and the associative memory component appears to involve the categorical property look-up subsystem (imagery).

SUMMARY

It is seemingly simple to think of imagery as a primary sensory system function necessary for efficient language processing skills. However, the premise includes two important considerations: (1) the integration of imagery to language, nonverbal and verbal stimuli, is necessary for cognition, and (2) there are two subtypes of imagery—symbol and concept imagery—for parts-wholes processing. The imagery subtypes move from left to right on the language processing spectrum. Symbol imagery is a primary sensory mechanism for reading and spelling words. Concept imagery is a primary sensory mechanism for language comprehension, expression, and conceptual thinking.

Labels such as dyslexia, hyperlexia, and autism reflect weakness on the spectrum. Concept imagery is a primary weakness for hyperlexia; however, more research is needed to know the precise role concept imagery plays in autism. Conceptual thinking is a processing deficit for individuals on the autistic spectrum, hence it is important to look for a primary sensory weakness. While the behavioral complexity involved in conceptual thinking suggests that the mechanism of the process does not involve a single sensory or cognitive process, the inability to create mental representations that rapidly and automatically bring parts to whole is very likely a primary contributing factor in autism.

The V/V™ program was developed on the basis of clinical observation and experience, and without the knowledge of Paivio's dual coding theory on the duality of processing verbal and nonverbal stimuli for cognition. However, the V/V™ program accommodates Paivio's theory of duality. Similarly, it stimulates concept imagery. As the program develops an individual's ability to image gestalts, the therapist can apply the imagery to developing numerous other skills in the individual, such as conceptual thinking, critical thinking, problem solving, oral and written language comprehension and expression, pragmatics, floor time, and play. There are, however, further challenges ahead for program refinement. Although the V/V™ has produced documented changes in processing ability, the program may need modification to work most effectively with high-functioning autistic individuals as well as with more severely involved autistic children. The research and process of modifying V/V™ to this level is underway.

Important knowledge has been gained about the imagery connection to parts-wholes processing; however, there are still challenges to be met. For example, tests of imagery need to be further developed to document the relationship of language processing behaviors to imagery. The brain processing ability of children with the label of hyperlexia, Asperger's syndrome, and autism needs to be measured before and after imagery stimulation.

If the greatest thinkers of our time attribute their strength in cognitive ability to imagery, it is reasonable to think that weakness in cognitive ability is conversely related to weakness in imagery. Oliver Sacks said that language is the symbolic currency for which we exchange meaning. Understanding the role imagery plays in symbolizing meaning may contribute to our continuing effort to bring children from darkness into the light.   ∎

REFERENCES

Aristotle (1972). *Aristotle on memory.* Providence, RI: Brown University Press.

Arnheim, R. (1966). Image and thought. In G. Kepes (Ed.), *Sign, image, symbol.* New York: George Braziller.

Bell, N. (1986). *Visualizing and verbalizing for language comprehension and thinking.* San Luis Obispo, CA: Gander Educational.

Bell, N. (1991). Gestalt imagery: A critical factor in language comprehension. *Annals of Dyslexia, 4,* 246-260.

Bleasdale, F. (1983). Paivio's dual coding model of meaning revisited. In J. C. Yuille (Ed.), *Imagery, memory and cognition: Essays in honor of Allan Paivio.* Hillsdale, NJ: Erlbaum.

Bower, G. H., & Morrow, D. G. (1990). Mental models in narrative comprehension. *Science*: Jan., 44-48.

Calfee, R., Lindamood, C., & Lindamood, P. (1973). Acoustic-phonetic skills and reading—kindergarten through twelfth grade. *Journal of Educational Psychology, 64,* 293-298.

Eden, G. F. (1999). FMRI studies of remediation in developmental dyslexia. Grant Application for the Department of Health and Human Services.

Ehri, L. (1980). The role of orthographic images in learning printed words. In J. F. Kavanaugh and R. L. Venesky (Eds.), *Orthography, reading and dyslexia.* Baltimore: University Park Press.

Greenspan, S. I., & Wieder, S. (2000). Neurodevelopmental disorders of relating and communicating. The Infancy and Early Childhood Training Course, Arlington, VA, April.

Kimbrough, J. (in preparation). Project ROLL: Reaching out for lifelong literacy.

Kosslyn, S. M. (1976). Using imagery to retrieve semantic information: A developmental study. *Child Development, 47,* 434-444.

Kosslyn, S. M. (1983). *Ghosts in the mind's machine.* New York: W. W. Norton.

Kosslyn, S. M., & Koenig, O. (1992). *Wet mind, the new cognitive neuroscience.* New York: Free Press.

Liberman, I., & Shankweiler, D. (1985). Phonology and the problems of learning to read and write. *Remedial and Special Education, 6,* 8-17.

Lindamood, C. H., & Lindamood, P. C. (1979). *Lindamood auditory conceptualization test.* Austin, TX: PRO-ED

Lindamood, P., Bell, N., & Lindamood, P. (1997). Sensory-cognitive factors in the controversy over reading instruction. *The Journal of Developmental and Learning Disorders, 1,* 143-182.

Linden, M. A., & Wittrock, M. C. (1981). The teaching of reading comprehension according to the model of generative learning. *Reading Research Quarterly, 17,* 44-57.

Long, S. A., Winograd, P. N., & Bridge, C. A. (1989). The effects of reader and text characteristics on reports of imagery during and after reading. *Reading Research Quarterly, 19*(3), 353-372.

Lundberg, I., Frost, J., & Peterson, O. (1988). Effects of an extensive program for stimulating phonological awareness in preschool children. *Reading Research Quarterly, 23,* 263-284.

Oliver, M. E. (1982). Improving comprehension with mental imagery. Paper read at the *Annual Meeting of the Washington Organization for Reading Development of the International Reading Association,* Seattle, WA, March.

Piaget, J., & Inhelder, B. (1971). *Imagery and the child.* New York: Basic Books.

Paivio, A. (1969). Mental imagery in associative learning and memory. *Psychological Review, 76,* 241-263.

Paivio, A. (1979). *Imagery and verbal processes.* New York: Holt, Rinehart, and Winston. (Reprinted 1979, Hillsdale, NJ: Erlbaum.)

Paivio, A. (1986). *Mental representations: A dual coding approach.* New York: Oxford University Press.

Pribram, K. (1971). *Languages of the brain: Experimental paradoxes and principles in neuropsychology.* New York: Brandon House.

Sadoski, M. (1983). An exploratory study of the relationship between reported imagery and the comprehension and recall of a story. *Reading Research Quarterly, 19*(1), 110-123.

Smith, B. D., Stahl, N., & Neil, J. (1987). The effect of imagery instruction on vocabulary development. *Journal of College Reading and Learning, 20,* 131-137.

Torgesen, J., Wagner, B., & C. Rashotte, C. (1996). Approaches to the prevention and remediation of phonologically based reading disabilities. In B. Blachman (Ed.), *Cognitive and linguistic foundations of reading acquisition: Implications for intervention research.* Hillsdale, NJ: Erlbaum.

Truch, S. (In preparation). Stimulating basic recall using the visualizing-verbalizing program.

Twachtman-Cullen, D. (1998). *Maximizing the effectiveness of socio-communicative interactions in more able verbal children.* Paper read at the Child with Special Needs, Autism Preconference, Anaheim, CA, April.

Wagner, R. K., Torgesen, J. K., & Rashotte, C. A. (1994). The development of reading-related phonological processing abilities: New evidence of bi-directional causality from a latent variable longitudinal study. *Developmental Psychology, 30,* 73-87.

Chapter 26. Adolescents and Adults with Special Needs: The Developmental, Individual
Difference, Relationship-Based (DIR) Approach to Intervention

639

◄ 26 ►

Adolescents and Adults with Special Needs: The Developmental, Individual Differences, Relationship-Based (DIR) Approach to Intervention

Stanley I. Greenspan, M.D., and Henry Mann, M.D.

When working therapeutically with developmentally disabled adolescents and adults, there are many challenging issues. The biggest and most significant challenge is to move our thinking beyond the stereotype that children reach a plateau beyond which improvement can only be minimal.

In treating severely compromised older children, adolescents, and adults, many therapists give up trying to promote meaningful developmental progress. They teach only superficial skills and routines instead of trying to support and strengthen the patient's functional developmental and processing capacities. This limited treatment approach is based on myth and false belief—there are no data to support the idea that individuals at age 14 or 16 or 25 cannot make significant developmental progress. During this time, the nervous system is still developing. The brain continues to myelinate into the fifth and sixth decades. The frontal cortex areas of the brain that regulate sequencing, as well as parts of the brain that influence abstract thinking and concept building, keep myelinating into what we consider middle to old age. Judgment and wisdom improve during these years. While motor and memory skills degrade with age, our abstract thinking ability, our ability to see the big picture, to reflect, and to have insight improves with age.

In addition, there is the factor of exercise of a function. The popular saying, "Use it or lose it," describes this process. There has been a popularly held idea that certain math and memory abilities reach their peak in our late 20s and early 30s, but these notions were only based on examining limited or splinter skills and are not representative of later development as a whole.

There is another area in which we are being misled into limiting our expectations and our hopes for our patients. As many individuals grow and progress through school, they may have the sort of problems that lead them to be identified as mentally retarded. In part this happens because school systems use standardized testing protocols that may not be appropriate for a particular child's learning profile. Reliance on standardized testing at a point in time (rather then looking at change over time) can lead to an assumption that the child has a permanent and severe mental limitation that is not amenable to change. The label of "mental retardation" implies a permanent and severe developmental limitation. We believe that the diagnosis of mental retardation should be made only after a child has participated in an optimal program for at least 3 years and has not made intellectual and/or developmental progress. An optimal program for these children would include a strong emphasis on identifying and strengthening the individual's processing profile. Prematurely identifying a child as retarded carries with it a resignation to the status quo rather than fostering an approach that works with a child and family to see if it is possible to improve his processing capacities, including auditory, visual-spacial, motor planning, and affective.

It is often assumed that if a child has deficits across the spectrum of cognitive abilities tested this shows that the problems are more likely a part of a global cognitive deficit than specific processing differences. Sometimes however, children may have underlying processing problems, such as deficient motor planning and sequencing, which can affect functioning across the board. Severe motor planning dysfunctions can derail the development of other skills, such as verbal and visual-spatial, as well as compromise a child's capacity to participate in a test. In such cases, individuals who have an underlying condition that could improve with proper remediation are misdiagnosed as having an untreatable, chronic developmental limitation.

In addition, rather than a global cognitive deficit, many children have multiple processing deficits which can be worked with. If the child has processing problems in two or three pathways, we try to remediate those pathways. If a child has physical problems in different systems of the body, such as concurrent renal, pulmonary, and cardiac problems, we attempt to treat all the problem areas. Similarly, in our patients, the visual-spatial, auditory, and the motor-planning systems often all need to be treated. Each one of these areas may have many components to it, and there may be strengths or weaknesses within the different components. This approach is more demanding of us as diagnosticians and therapists, but it also allows us to bring hope for developmental progress to a population that has been previously designated as too chronically and permanently developmentally impaired to be helped to a significant degree. We lose sight of the fact that helping an adult go from aimless, nonverbal, self-injurious behavior to having the capacity to purposefully interact with others, take pleasure in relating, engage in problem-solving interactions (e.g., signaling to get food or a game), and even learn some signs or words is a huge gain. Even though the individual still has enormous limitations, the quality, meaning, and competency of his life have grown significantly.

Another problem that we have in working with older children, adolescents, and adults is their size. At an unconscious level, older and larger patients often do not generate in us the same sort of nurturing and protective feelings that affect and motivate us when we work with younger children. Our response to an angry and agitated adolescent is generally quite different than our response to a 3-year-old who is clearly anxious in a new situation and is acting in an angry manner. If we have a 3-year-old child who wants to go out into the snow with her shoes off, we attempt to educate and support the child and firmly help her make the correct decision. If we are dealing with a 17-year-old adolescent boy who angrily demands to go out into the snow with his shoes off, we have quite a different response. This sort of unconscious fear inevitably affects the staff of educational institutions, rehabilitation centers, and other institutions. Because of this mindset, the administration and staff may focus on limit setting, containment, and restraints rather than on fully engaging with their clients and bringing them to a higher developmental level.

EVALUATING AND TREATING ADOLESCENTS AND ADULTS WITH DEVELOPMENTAL DISABILITIES

In order to work effectively with older children and adults, we need to extend our Developmental, Individual Differences, Relationship-based (DIR) model into the adolescent and adult years and then tease out the principles of intervention that are especially pertinent. If not already familiar with the DIR model, the reader should review Chapters 3, 4, and 12 this volume, as well as *Infancy and Early Childhood: The Practice of Clinical Assessment and Intervention with Emotional and Developmental Challenges* (Greenspan, 1992), *The Child with Special Needs: Intellectual and Emotional Growth* (Greenspan & Wieder, 1998), and *The Growth of the Mind and the Endangered Origins of Intelligence* (Greenspan, 1997). Basic principles of applying the DIR model to adolescents and adults are delineated and described here within the context of a clinical case.

Jim: An Adult with Developmental Disabilities

A mother recently related to us her concerns about her 30-year-old son, Jim. The questions she asked about her adult son illustrate some of the issues and principles involved in evaluating and treating adolescents and adults with developmental disabilities. The mother was conversant with the functional developmental approach (i.e., the DIR model) She reported that when she began working with Jim about 10 years ago on the process of engagement, she found his abilities in the area of two-way communication to be quite minimal. He was mostly self-absorbed and had no spoken language. She said that when her son became frustrated or worried he would often scream. Initially, she

had interpreted his screaming as a communication to her that something was wrong and that he needed help from her. Later, she found out that he was having tremendous difficulty with word retrieval and had become overwhelmed with frustration. At a later point in his development, he was able to type "the words would not come, and all I could do was scream." Mother noted that she had started working with a typing program as part of increased engagements and gesturing when Jim was 20 years old and had pursued it actively during the following 10 years.

Mother reported that she could not get verbal responses. At the same time she was working with Jim on the typing program, she also worked with him on more gesturing and simple imitations of sounds and later words. Eventually, he learned to use some words (e.g., "No car" or "Buy cookie" or "Go sleep"). He had developed this new ability to verbalize very recently.

This young man's progression to simple verbal expressions illustrates that appropriate interventions can be initiated at any age and may lead to unexpected progress if they are pursued consistently. In this case, the young man had been actively working with his mother for 10 years, from age 20 to 30, before he began to use spoken words to communicate.

Mother described what it was like teaching him first to type and gradually to use some meaningful language. She attended a symposium related to the topic of using typing to teach language and began using it with her son. In order to help her son, who had low muscle tone, she needed to hold his forearm. Jim learned slowly and laboriously, but gradually he could type out one word at a time. She found that sometimes one word would appear within a large group of other letters. This gave her hope, and she continued to pursue her quest. Mother is currently working with facilitating Jim's transition to verbal expression by saying to him, "Now let's try and say it in words." The typing program may have provided mother with a goal and structure around which engaging and gesturing could occur.

Jim's mother described how she was dealing with his other developmental challenges. She was trying to help him learn to engage in pretend play, but found this difficult for several reasons. She, herself, was not comfortable with pretend play, but she was concerned that if she did not set the stage for pretend play her son would not initiate it. Her son's low muscle tone also interfered with his development of skills in pretend play. In addition, she reported that her son's ability to engage in pretend play was compromised by his difficulty with two-way communication. However, her son, who was almost completely self-absorbed, is now seeking out other people and says, "Come sit with me." When he played with his father recently, he began to engage in spontaneous pretend play on a very limited basis. He had not been able to do this prior to his recent usage of simple words to communicate.

Jim's mother reported that he loves music and listens to records and tapes. He would look through tapes and select his own music. She believes that he read labels as part of the selection process. Recently he was able to read some simple books to her. She has asked him many times how he learned to read. He says "myself."

Jim's mother has ongoing concerns about how to soothe her son. She had tried using a brushing technique recommended by sensory integration therapists and also found that he responded to the music on some of his favorite videos. Her most frequent problem continues to be dealing with his frustration about not being able to get out the words he is reaching for (at which point he often starts to scream). They are working on soothing and regulating interactions rather than on agitating ones.

At this point, it should be clear that this young man struggles with many of the same issues as does a 3- or 4-year-old child who is just becoming verbal and beginning to piece together several words, is still working on gestural communication, is still working on engagement, and has some splinter skills in the area of reading and word recognition. As he is learning to type and talk however, he is raising the possibility that he may have been perceiving more than he could communicate. This is not an unusual picture. The lesson to be drawn here is that we can use interventions with a 30-year-old man that would be comparable to what we might use with a 3- to 5-year-old child.

BASIC PRINCIPLES OF INTERVENTION

The first principle of intervention is to work with the basic building blocks in the context of the person's interests. Working with Jim would be somewhat different than working with a 3- to 5-year-old child because Jim has some adult interests. He likes different kinds of music; he is a little more set in his ways. He is not going to be as easily drawn in as would a young child. Nonetheless, we still need to work on the same building blocks, but with different, more age-appropriate interests and possibly more understanding and awareness than is obvious.

For example, if we were trying to work on pretend play with a teenager or a young adult who was embarrassed by getting down on the floor and pretending because he was aware that this is something that only little kids do, we would be faced with a dilemma. The patient needs the benefits of pretend play but, because of issues of pride and shame, is unwilling to participate. The solution to this dilemma might be to set up an improvisational theater setting, such as a home-based drama program. We might even encourage the teenager to participate in a class of other teenagers or adults with developmental challenges to do improvisational work. The very act of playing different role parts in acting allows us to learn to improvise and therefore to pretend and imagine. Integrating developmental therapy into an activity that would be considered age-appropriate rather than childish will allow such an individual to obtain the benefits of the treatment without having to feel shame and humiliation.

In working with Jim, we would recommend building on his interest in music as a way of beginning and stimulating imaginative play. One of his parents might listen to music with him and then begin to dramatize the music to see what the music brings to mind. Then, perhaps, they could create imagery with the music. If Jim were to select the music, he would select it to fit his mood. Therefore, his choice would be quite revealing. If he selected a vigorous marching piece or a soft and soothing piece, we would have some clue about his feelings at the moment. We might dramatize the music and the story with the use of dolls or cars or pictures.

The use of pictures might be particularly helpful here because they allow quick recognition and interaction and also support symbol formation. Because the expressive auditory channel is critically challenging for Jim, we want to give it as much usage as possible even while he is learning to use words. If Jim could sequence pictures that were imaginative, he would also strengthen the same process in his verbal sphere. He should be given the opportunity to select pictures related to his favorite interests by looking through books or magazines in which he already has an interest. Then the pictures could be cut out, and he could use them to tell a story. Another possibility would be to use a digital camera to take pictures of people, pets, and other things that are part of his everyday life. If he combined these pictures

with cutouts from magazines, then he would have a wide range of images from which to draw. Pictures might also be helpful to him if they were kept available for times when he was agitated and upset so that he could point to them quickly to indicate his concerns. The picture system would serve as an intermediary and part of the next step to verbalization. We might anticipate that Jim's visual skills are stronger than his oral language skills. The key is to use pictures not just to help him meet basic needs but also as part of a continuous flow of two-way communication in both pretend and reality-based situations.

The second principle in working with developmentally challenged individuals is that it is crucial to keep moving sequentially through the functional developmental capacities. Unfortunately, with many older children, adolescents, and young adults, we often stop working with them when they have reached the level of having a partially developed language system. However, much more is needed when the older child or adolescent still is unable to appreciate experiences and to make gradations of thought and feeling. The concrete child might say, "I like this, I don't like that, I want this, I don't want that." However, this is insufficient to help a child use language to learn to master complex feeling states and interactions. Children at this level are vulnerable to being impulsive or to having tantrums because they cannot understand relativity (i.e., shades of gray), time concepts, or quantity concepts, such as a little bit of this or a lot of that. These children think concretely and then do not learn to anticipate the future well enough to move into the stage in which they are capable of hypothetical reasoning, a characteristic of adolescence.

Techniques for introducing relativistic thinking might include the following. When the individual is feeling angry or upset, we might ask, "How upset? A little bit? A lot? A whole lot?" And then we might spread our hands to demonstrate the extent of the feeling. If we wanted to present a stronger visual image, we might blow up a balloon and ask him to show whether the feelings state relative to the size of the balloon is small, medium, or large.

If we were dealing with a person who was able to operate at a relativistic, gray-area thinking level but not able to anticipate the future very well, we could begin with questions such as, "If we do this now, what will this mean for the future?" In order to work at this level, we would need to make use of circumstances in the person's life and use a subject that she finds emotionally interesting. For example, if we wanted to discuss an event that is going to occur in the near future, we might ask someone to make choices between goods that they really want, such as, "Do you want a chocolate cookie or vanilla ice cream? One we can get in 5 minutes, and the other one we can get tomorrow." An exercise like this one allows us to teach the person to project into the future with two highly cherished emotional items, as well as teaching the person to think in terms of the future.

Then we might want to move to hypothetical thinking about possibilities, which is more difficult. An example of the questions might be used here are: "Do we take one cookie now or do we gamble and take a chance on maybe getting two ice creams later?" We can set up little games of chance around prized things that include the notion of probabilities as well as projections into the future. It must be clear that at this level of interaction we are teaching the person a way of thinking that is crucial to social and emotional self-regulation.

At this juncture, we need to ask a general question. Why is it that most adults who remain in special-needs programs rarely function above the 10- to 12-year-old age level in their general functional intellectual capabilities? We believe that the answer to this question has to do with the limitations of our general educational approach to these individuals. Many of them have the yet undeveloped capacity to progress far beyond the 10- to 12-year-old level of concrete thinking. Yet this capacity is not challenged because of the inadequacies in our understanding and our curriculums. We often end up working on very concrete solutions that reinforce concrete thinking rather than moving forward through the developmental levels in our treatment approach.

To review our approach to individuals such as Jim, we would encourage more of the work that his mother initiated in approaching him through the auditory receptive system and through facilitated writing, eventually progressing to the use of oral language. Pictures also should be introduced as part of the intervention. Once an individual is quite verbal or can communicate with written words or other symbols, there should be efforts at "gray area thinking" and learning to make gradations about feelings. In order to strengthen earlier developmental building blocks of engagement and gestural language, we would recommend looking for opportunities to engage in 20- to 30-minute floor time sessions focused on the individual's interests. For a person like Jim, who is interested in music, we would recommend to his mother that she take him to music stores and help him look at different choices of music and make selections. She should try to get him to negotiate around the selections, meaning that he should have to make choices between one CD and another.

There may be times when the individual wants absolutely to be alone, and there will be other times when he will gradually begin to accept his parent's offer to listen to music with him. The listening together may start simply with sitting quietly in the room with him. We would start strengthening basic shared attention and engagement by entering into his rhythm of life. This way, he will learn to share quiet time, relaxed time, and listening time, but through this, he will also begin to learn to interact more and to become more engaged.

Concurrently, we would take him out into the community, working with him on making choices, talking about his feelings, and interacting with others. The overall goal is to build gray area thinking as well as an ability to interact with others. Throughout this process, we need to remember that the work we are doing takes time and patience. It took Jim's mother approximately 10 years of patient work before Jim was ready to use oral language as well as written language.

The third general principle in working with older children and adults is the importance of creating emotionally meaningful learning contexts. For example, consider a typical situation of a child who has learned some speech and is able to answer "why" questions. The child also has some small ability in math and reading but is not able to master abstract concepts. Therefore, he has a very limited understanding of the world, which then persists into adolescence and adulthood. We now find ourselves dealing with a person who thinks concretely and does not understand issues such as justice, fairness, and unfairness, does not understand what taxes are, and cannot grasp other complex issues. We see this situation in children who come to us with autistic spectrum diagnoses, Asperger's syndrome, cognitive delays, or mental retardation. We see it in some individuals who simply have severe learning disabilities and processing problems. A common underlying factor in all these children is the presence of processing problems. We have found that one way to make progress is to create more emotionally meaningful learning contexts.

Consider the case of a young girl who was unable to understand the meaning of taxation. Her mother was certain that she would never learn to understand the concept. As a way of teaching her about taxation, we involved her in a role-play during which she was required to trade pieces of pizza for things that she needed, such as protection from her aggressive and intrusive brother. She was asked how much would she pay a policeman to protect her from her brother. She decided to pay two pieces of pizza to protect the remaining eight pieces. The two pieces became "the taxes" she was willing to pay the police, who would then protect her from pizza thieves. This role-play took about 15 minutes. After completing it, she was able to give other examples of the meaning of taxes. She understood that she would need to pay for cleaning the streets and for taking out books from the library, as well as to pay in advance for the services of the fire department. This girl was beginning to understand a difficult abstract concept. She was able to grasp this concept by using it in multiple emotionally significant contexts.

How does a child learn about justice? Justice is a vague and abstract notion. We are continually refining our sense of justice through being in situations that are fair and unfair. If we want to give a definition of justice to a child, we could give a dictionary definition, but this approach would not get us very far with most children. But if we create make-believe situations such as one in which all the family's cookies are going to a brother or sister and not to the individual we are working with, the child will quickly say, "That's unfair." "That's unjust." Through this scenario, the child begins to understand that when he gets to share, that is called justice. This is only one example, but an *emotionally meaningful one* that helps him grasp an abstract concept. Then the child can refine his understanding of the concept through other experiences. In order for this to happen, however, we need to have emotionally significant experiences that build on the word and concept. Every word and concept begins with its simple definition. More complicated and gradually acquired meanings unfold over time through more and more emotional experiences.

For example, concepts such as love or caring acquire more meaning throughout life. As we get older, we change our notion of these concepts. To a young child, love means caring, hugs, and kisses; to an adult, love means devotion, hugs, kisses, warmth, compassion, and empathy. To understand the complex concepts of life, we have to acquire more and more experience with them.

The concept of size, which has both physical and mathematical dimensions, expands and becomes more complex as we grow older. When we are very young, there is "big," and there is "little." As we have experience in play, we note that some things are very big, super big, or super little. The more experience we have, the more the continuum of big vs. little stretches out. We find that the more severe the processing problems, the stronger the emotional meaning of the learning experience has to be to try to break through. Unfortunately, we are geared to certain standard ways of teaching, and frequently we are not working with the individual in this kind of dynamic way. It is essential that we continually remind ourselves that the worse the processing deficits, the more important it is to work in an emotionally meaningful context.

The importance of finding an emotionally meaningful context for learning increases when we are attempting to deal with helping individuals establish gray area thinking and then hypothetical probabilistic thinking. The reason for this is that the concrete level of thinking comes much more easily and more

naturally. Simple "why" questions are relatively easy to answer compared to the challenges faced by an individual entering the gray, or hypothetical, thinking area. Here, without the strong motivation provided by an emotionally meaningful context, progress might be impossible. It is a crucial point in an individual's development to be able to think in these realms. Without this capacity, we cannot understand other people's motives, and we can only understand a very limited amount of academically important materials. An individual who has only learned memory-based reading and memory-based mathematics will have quite limited academic capacities because the ability to think has not been mastered.

In addition, we cannot work effectively with individuals with developmental problems—whether they are 5, 20, or 30 years old—without knowing which functional developmental capacities are missing. With each patient, we need a functional developmental road map. For example, if we are working on conceptual thinking, we need to know which concepts present a challenge for the individual, and then we need to develop emotionally meaningful ways to teach these concepts.

ADULTS WITH SEVERE DEVELOPMENTAL CHALLENGES

So far, we have been discussing some of the issues related to individuals with moderate to severe disabilities. We should consider another group, those individuals who cannot relate at all and whose behavior appears to be aimless, aggressive, and disorganized. These individuals often lack the capacity to put together a sequence of three or four gestures. If we can help such a person move from aimless activity to engagement and then on to some simple purposeful and reciprocal sequencing, we are producing a tremendous change in the quality of life, meaning, and

Chapter 26. Adolescents and Adults with Special Needs: The Developmental, Individual
Difference, Relationship-Based (DIR) Approach to Intervention

647

competency for that individual. Our next step should be to help that same individual reach a level where she can problem solve and participate in five or six interactive sequences so that, for example, she might be able to take us to the refrigerator and show us what she wants. Then we try to move that individual to function at the early symbolic level of development so that she can use a few pictures as words to communicate.

With individuals who have profound developmental problems, we may give up because of our own reaction to the person's developmental limitations. In such individuals, there is often no purposeful reciprocity. Because of that, they often display a great deal of aggression toward others and toward themselves, as well as much diffuse and aimless behavior. At this point, the caretakers of such a person have to either resort to physical restraint or the heavy use of medication. Unfortunately, although large doses of tranquilizers may help with behavior management, medication may also reduce an individual's cognitive capacities and his chance of making developmental progress.

Henry Mann's recent work with the functional developmental approach in an institutional setting with several individuals who have profound developmental delays and range in age from their mid 30s to late 50s shows promise. Two case studies follow that illustrate how this approach is being applied to chronically institutionalized individuals with severe developmental deficits.

Peter: A Mentally Retarded Adult

Peter is a 34-year-old profoundly retarded man who was institutionalized in the Connecticut division of the mental retardation system when he was 5 years old. Peter was the product of a normal pregnancy and delivery. He was identified as retarded because of his failure to develop language or any non-verbal communication skills. At the time he entered residential care, he had frequent uncontrollable rages and required full time one-on-one care. As Peter grew, so did his capacity for dangerous and aggressive attacks on other clients and staff. Over the course of many years, he was given large amounts of psychotropic and mood stabilizing medications, including Thorazine, Mellaril, Haldol, Prolixin, Lithium carbonate, and many others. Despite extremely high doses of medication, he did not seem to respond well. He needed a very high level of care until the introduction of Risperdol to his medical treatment. At that point, he was able to handle frustrating situations and changes in schedule without explosive reactions.

Peter was never able to function beyond the very earliest developmental stages. He could focus on various objects that might be of interest to him, such as cans of soda, pieces of paper, and pens, which would inevitably end up in his mouth. With the Risperdol, he was better able to regulate his mood to the extent that his decreasing intensity and frequency of rage reactions were indicative of such a change. There was no noticeable engagement with staff or others throughout his time in residential care. He also showed little or no evidence of purposeful, two-way communication. His day-to-day life consisted of being cared for and passively accepting directions. In addition, he also did not seem to understand higher-level problem-solving gestures or words.

When the DIR approach was initiated with Peter, he rapidly began to focus his attention on the interviewer. The technique used to engage his attention was simple imitation or mirroring of all his movements and sounds. This technique is one that mothers naturally use to engage their babies' attention in the first months of life. It was appropriate for Peter because the first therapeutic task was to engage his attention and then build on this to develop relating and finally some sort of purposeful interaction between him and the therapist.

In order to explore what might be helpful for Peter, he was seen for 20- to 30-minute sessions twice monthly. The infrequent sessions were because of the limitation of the therapist's schedule: it would have been helpful to see Peter more regularly. The goal was to learn how to engage him and to create opportunities for two-way communication and then to use these insights to work with the staff so that they could work with Peter on a daily basis. During this time, the task was engagement of attention and then creation of conditions that allowed for emotional engagement. Peter responded very quickly during the first floor time session and even reached a point where he leaned toward the therapist and almost touched heads with him. In the second session, he showed what was probably a reaction to the first meeting by coming into the interview room and turning his back to the therapist for nearly 10 minutes. Eventually, the staff persuaded him to come to the other side of the table and to sit next to the therapist. Peter looked away and during that time almost never allowed the therapist to engage his attention. Whenever it was clear to him that the therapist was attending to him, he dropped his gaze or turned his body.

The third floor time session showed almost the reverse. Peter came into the meeting making loud guttural sounds. The therapist responded with a similar sound and a friendly tone. For about 10 minutes, they sat next to each other making these sounds. There was no synchronicity on Peter's part, meaning that he did not build on the therapist's sounds, although his persistence and occasional look of real interest in this activity was a clear indication of fleeting involvement and engagement.

Over a series of sessions, Peter began to increase his repertoire of sounds to include short combinations of consonants and vowels in a somewhat rhythmic pattern, which the therapist imitated. He appeared to be extremely engaged and to be aware that the therapist was picking up on whatever he produced. During some sessions, he was openly interested in the therapist. He showed this by taking the therapist's eyeglasses or pens and putting them in his mouth and by moving close to the therapist.

During this time, a 2- or 3-minute period of intimacy was usually followed by withdrawal for an equivalent amount of time or longer. A "good session," in which there was a great deal of intimacy, was usually followed by a session in which there was some withdrawal and disconnection. However, over time, the periods of intimacy became longer, growing from about 20 seconds to 3 or 4 minutes. In one dramatic recent session, Peter included other staff in the floor time interaction and responded equally well to two staff members during the session. He exchanged looks, had some fleeting smiles, and exchanged objects.

During this time, it was noted that Peter was very sensitive to light touch and sound and could use visual-spatial problem solving (find things) much more effectively than verbal strategies (he never followed directions).

Currently, Peter has entered a treatment phase in which other staff members have begun daily floor time sessions with him, under supervision by the psychiatrist/therapist. Staff are careful not to intrude on his sensitive tactile or auditory systems and to use lots of gestural animation to appeal to his stronger visual problem-solving skills. They begin with some simple imitation of Peter's behavior to get interactions going. The staff has attended an in-service training program; they will make videotapes of their floor time sessions with Peter to be reviewed by the consulting psychiatrist. The staff now seem to be enthusiastic and fully engaged in learning about floor time whereas initially they were quite skeptical about this new way of communicating with their client. In a recent treatment session with one of the staff, Peter demonstrated his new ability for engagement by maintaining his attention on the staff person for the full length of a 20-minute period. Peter also has increased the complexity of his use of sounds. The typical floor time session with Peter now consists of the purposeful exchange of a wide range of sounds and variations in volume and some motor gestures such as giving or taking objects. The hope is that within several years Peter will extend his use of gestures and sounds to the beginnings of some words or symbolic gestures to communicate with others.

Peter's mood also has improved during the treatment period. Prior to treatment, Peter would have one to two months of extreme agitation each spring, during which he would become assaultive and aggressive, sleepless, and irritable. Since the beginning of the program and engagement, his seasonal problems appear to have abated. He still demonstrated a considerably increased amount of energy during the spring, but he did not have periods of agitation and depression. His overall mood has been happier, and he has shown more signs of engagement with others.

Alice: An Autistic, Mentally Retarded Adult

Our next case is Alice, a 59-year-old profoundly retarded woman who was placed in a large residential center when she was a child. Alice is a spastic quadriplegic who also has kyphoscoliosis. She has been withdrawn and avoidant of contact with others and has carried a diagnosis of autism since childhood.

During her time in various residential programs, she has never engaged with others. She has been nonverbal, gaze avoidant, and has shown a complete indifference to her surroundings, to staff, and to other clients. She has had frequent episodes of crying and whining that have appeared unrelated to any external circumstances.

Kim, a nurse's aide, showed an interest in learning the DIR approach as a way to communicate with autistic clients and asked to work with Alice about 1 year ago. She agreed to come with Alice to the semiweekly psychiatric clinics for training. During a 20-minute period at each clinic, Kim was supervised in how to initiate contact with Alice and how to engage her attention. The initial approach was simply to mirror all of Alice's gestures and sounds, which Kim learned fairly quickly. Within several clinics, she was able to very competently engage Alice's attention. As Kim worked in Alice's residential home, she was able, with her supervisor's support, to set aside three 30-minute periods per week for individual floor time with Alice.

Alice responded to these meetings by beginning to reach out for Kim and to make eye contact with her. After several months, Alice started to become attached to Kim. She showed signs of pleasure when Kim entered her room. She would reach out for Kim's hand and bring it close to her head to rub the side of her face. Alice, who had not been observed to smile or show signs of pleasure for many years, began to smile spontaneously. She reduced the frequency of her episodes of crying and whining. After several more months of regular floor time work, Alice started to reach out for other staff and to show signs of recognition of others. She also made eye contact with other staff.

With severely challenged adults, the key is to pay attention to the early functional developmental capacities of attention, engagement, and two-way purposeful interaction. Gains in these basic foundations can make an enormous difference to an individual's adaptation, including basic emotional, social, and cognitive capacities (e.g., to be purposeful rather than aimless). Of interest is that initially many of the residential staff that worked with Alice were quite skeptical and unsupportive of this approach. However, within 6 months they became more supportive and began to use some of the floor time techniques to engage Alice themselves. Other staff members have now asked to attend in-service training sessions, and several will be starting to work with other clients within the next few months.

The impact on the staff was quite significant. Prior to their experiencing the effect of a functional developmental approach on their retarded or autistic clients, they were unaware of any opportunities to improve their autistic clients' quality of life other than trying to make sure that their day-to-day lives were conflict-free and somewhat interesting. There were, however, many hours of aimless activity coupled with attempts at control. Once the staff saw that they could help their clients relate and be purposeful, and as they paid attention to the subtle signs of interaction, they worked more with their clients. Kim has experienced a large change in her self-confidence both in dealing with clients and other staff. One would expect that as further learning and practice of the developmental approach occurs, the staff's overall morale and level of engagement with all their clients may grow.

FACILITATING
PEER RELATIONSHIPS

Another basic principle in working with developmentally challenged adolescents and young adults is that we need to pay very close attention to the quality and extent of their ability to relate to their peers. Many of us have had the experience of helping children with the diagnosis of Asperger's syndrome who are verbal and academically skillful enough to be in a regular class but cannot interact appropriately with the other children. Therefore, they feel isolated and alienated. As a result, the child often becomes very sad and depressed. The child is aware enough to know that he wants to have friends and be part of a social group, but he is also keenly aware of his deficits and his lack of acceptance by others. Teenagers and adults with these developmental disabilities experience this same phenomenon. Ordinarily, if we were working with a child at a young age, we would start to encourage developing peer relationships as soon as the child had mastered gestural communication. The children who learn complex, preverbal, problem-solving gesturing and who strengthen this through ongoing social interactions become quite socially competent. Even if they have strong deficits in other areas, they have learned to engage other children and can play with them in a manner that is enjoyable both to themselves and to the other children. Children who cannot develop this capacity are viewed by themselves and by others as being "different." There is no substitute in this process for lots of practice with peer interaction.

A 15-year-old boy, Donald, was seen for therapy because of severe depression and withdrawal following the death of his grandfather. He had previously been seen in therapy by another therapist who had diagnosed him as having Asperger's syndrome and had treated him with a combination of antipsychotic and stimulant medication. The boy had been seen in a supportive therapy, but according to the therapist, was very difficult to engage and generally interacted with the therapist with very little emotion. Donald had adequate use of language and could learn his coursework with the support of special educa-

Chapter 26. Adolescents and Adults with Special Needs: The Developmental, Individual Difference, Relationship-Based (DIR) Approach to Intervention

651

tion classes and an individual tutor. Although he had auditory and tactile hypersensitivities in addition to low motor tone and problems with fine and gross motor coordination, the family had not been able to obtain adequate occupational and physical therapy services for him. Dr. Mann soon discovered that Donald's greatest concerns were the loss of his grandfather and his lack of peer relationships. Apparently, for several years prior to his grandfather's death, Donald had daily telephone conversations with his grandfather that lasted up to an hour and a half. His grandfather had, in fact, been attempting to fill in for the social contact that was otherwise completely lacking in Donald's life.

As part of the treatment plan, Dr. Mann saw Donald weekly or semiweekly for psychotherapy sessions and talked with him on the telephone 7 days a week for 5 to 10 minutes. As part of the regular weekly therapy sessions and the telephone conversations, the therapist offered Donald an opportunity to engage in role-playing. Donald welcomed this chance to do some "grown up" pretend and to participate in a more dynamic interactive learning experience than he had experienced in prior treatment programs. With Donald's guidance, one element that was especially helpful was when the therapist transformed himself into a personification of a somewhat aggressive, highly verbal, obnoxious, and playful adolescent. The content of the discussions was generally meaningless and irrelevant to the treatment. The substance of the conversations was to engage Donald and to educate him in the nonverbal ways of teenage boys both face-to-face and on the phone. After 4 months of this approach, Donald's initial extraordinarily flat and depressed affect changed. The pace, rhythm, and range of affect in his speech improved and began to approximate that of other adolescents his age. Within the next 5 months, he began, for the

first time in his life, to have some limited friendships, to have a girlfriend, and to start work in a volunteer position at a local hospital. The therapeutic relationship was encouraging these relationships and lots of "practice" with real peers on a daily basis.

In some communities, there are special programs designed to foster and develop social interactions. In Bethesda, Maryland, the Bethesda Academy for the Performing Arts has special groups for children with developmental challenges. In one troop, there are a number of children with Down syndrome and a number with nonspecific developmental delays. Some of them are on the autistic spectrum, and others have Asperger's syndrome. What they have in common is that they are all at least partially verbal. In some of the acting groups, they are integrated with other children who have no developmental challenges, and they work together to do their own productions. They usually write their own scripts and perform plays several times a year. While writing and performing their plays, they create a strong social network that is supportive and positive.

The acting is quite good because it is performance- and movement-based, with heavy use of visual imagery. Different people, depending on their ability level, play different roles. Some have very limited parts, and others are leaders; everyone seems to enjoy participating to the degree that they are able. It should be noted that drama is a particularly fruitful activity because it draws upon many functional developmental capacities (engaging, gesturing, pretending) and different kinds and levels of abilities, especially because a play requires that all of the participants, both onstage and off, have a close working relationship with each other.

Although some adults require medication, not infrequently medication is used as a substitute for the basic developmental building blocks of engagement: shared attention, reciprocity, and using ideas. Medication can be helpful as an adjunct to developmental work if the patient is overwhelmed by anxiety, depression, or fragmented thinking. It should be noted that medication could be uniquely helpful in assisting the child in beginning to regulate himself so that he can participate in therapy and even get through the day. Unfortunately, as we noted earlier in this chapter, adolescents and young adults who become easily frustrated, aggressive, or in any way threatening to their caretakers usually end up in a medication-based treatment in which the fundamentals of a developmentally based approach are left far behind, along with the individual.

THE STAGES OF LATER CHILDHOOD, ADOLESCENCE, AND ADULTHOOD

In considering the treatment of adolescents and adults, we need to think about the functional developmental stages that come after the basic first six stages. Many adults will have relative mastery of the early stages and have limitations in the more advanced ones. The first six are shared attention, engagement, simple purposeful movement and gestures, complex problem solving, continuous flow of reciprocal gestural interactions, and using ideas creatively and logically by building bridges between them. At the seventh level, which typically begins between the ages of 4 and 7, the child begins to get very expansive in his thinking and to go from simple logical thinking to triangular logical thinking. An example of triangular logical thinking is when a young boy figures out that if he wants to be friends with Johnny, the way to do that might be to become friends with either Sarah or Billy, who are already friends with Johnny. He decides to take this tack because

Johnny has already rebuffed him several times. In other words, he has learned that not all roads to Rome are linear or direct and that he can go a roundabout way and still get there.

At this stage in development, children begin to see three variables in interactions with each other as opposed to just two variables. The child dealing with two variables can answer the "why" questions, "Why do we feel happy or sad" with the answers, "Because we didn't do this" or "Because I did not think about that." The three-person system is much more sophisticated and one that is requisite for successful functioning in a family system, social group, or work setting. Without adequate understanding of the three-person system, the child cannot truly understand higher-level mathematics or life itself. Children who reach this level take a greatly expanded view of life and show an interest in all facets of their world. They become curious about their bodies, sex, anger, death, where their parents came from, and about anything else that even remotely touches their lives.

Along with an expanded interest in their world, children at this level also show more fears and anxieties at this stage, coinciding normally with the Oedipal phase of development that is associated both with anxieties and grandiosity. Working with adolescents and adults who begin to engage in triangular thinking for the first time may create some anxiety for therapists because now we are dealing with individuals who are showing an interest in their bodies and in sex and who suddenly become more manipulative. As individuals become more adept at navigating three-person relationships, we should expect—and even welcome—a certain amount of manipulativeness. Our role as parents or therapists is to support these individuals throughout this period and help them both to learn good judgment and to reduce their anxiety about their newfound assertiveness. We also need to help them keep

Chapter 26. Adolescents and Adults with Special Needs: The Developmental, Individual Difference, Relationship-Based (DIR) Approach to Intervention

653

their grandiosity and expansive thinking at a realistic and manageable level.

We call the eighth developmental level "playground politics," or proper, or "gray area" thinking. At this level, the child goes from simple triangular thinking to being able to see shades of gray. We can ask a child, "Gee, what's happening at school? What do you do well? What do other kids do well in?" The child will tell us, "Well, I'm the best at this, Johnny is the best at that, and Sally is the best at that. I'm number 4 at this and number 6 at that." The child is developing a relative sense of her place in the social hierarchy. At this time, she can also tell us whether she is a little angry or very angry or super angry or furious or very loving or super loving. She can now see things in shades of gray, which helps her see the world in relativistic terms.

Mastering this developmental level is obviously important, not only for the child's social and emotional world but also for her intellectual world. We cannot understand math or physics or interpret stories or understand history without understanding things in their relative contexts. This developmental milestone occurs as the child is also learning to understand the nature of peer relationships better. She is learning to reduce a tendency toward catastrophic thinking and reactions. For example, if she is not chosen to play on a team one day, instead of feeling totally rejected, she can say to herself, "Well, they are not nice to me today but maybe they will be a little nicer to me tomorrow," or, "I can be friends with Susan and that may change the way Samantha and her group feel about me." Reaching this level of relativistic thinking, which is essential to problem solving, typically occurs between the ages of 7 and 10, but many of the children whom we are concerned with may not arrive at this stage until their mid-teens or even later.

The next stage is one that we call "the two worlds inside me," during which the child goes from relativistic thinking to being able to hold onto an internal reality of a self-image with beliefs and values. He can then compare his peer-based relativistic world to those standards he is trying to create. A 7- or 8-year-old defines himself by his relationship with the peer group; that is, "I am good or bad by whether I was chosen for this or that game." In the middle latency years, a child's self-definition is very much a social and group-related one.

By 10 to 12 years of age, the child begins saying, "I'm a good person because I was nice to my brother and sister and because I did my homework. And, yeah, Sally was mean to me today at school, but I'm still a good person and she was just having a bad day." The 10- to 12-year-old can begin comparing these daily experiences against an internal standard, which the 7- or 8-year-old cannot do. We call that "the world inside me," or the ability to create two worlds. Obviously, this ability is crucial for internalizing values, having a conscience, and being able to regulate behavior. During this developmental period, we see what we call the "ego ideal," or conscience, becoming consolidated to some degree. Obviously, this is an important emotional, social, and intellectual stage of development because a person cannot really reflect to any significant degree unless he has an internal standard available for comparison.

Children then enter into the adolescent years. At this age, we see a flowering of all kinds of abilities and interests. Focus on the larger community and even television characters is increasing, friendship patterns are broadening, and awareness of conflicting values between "my" generation and others becomes an issue. But the biggest change, by far, is that the body is changing, and children are entering the area of sexuality in a more formal way. There is sexual interest; there is sexual acting out, masturbation, and interest in sexual relationships. Aggression is more dangerous at this time because the body is getting bigger, muscles are developing, and hormones are changing. Particularly in boys, there is much more testosterone, which affects the quality of their aggression.

Around this time, identities are forming. Adolescents ask, "What am I? Who am I going to be?" There is a lot of concern about humiliation around body image issues; the changing body can be very scary and frightening. We cannot describe all the aspects of adolescence, but from this discussion we should understand that adolescence is hard enough for a child who has no processing difficulties and who has mastered all the prior functional capacities. What about a child who is very, very concrete and just has the bare minimum of some verbal concepts, who can answer "why" questions but can not do gray area and triangular thinking? What about a child who cannot even answer "why" questions yet, but who can elaborate some simple phrases? What happens when these changes in the body, sexual interests, and level of aggression happen in children whose processing and functional capacities are weaker? If a person does not have strong visual-spatial processing, he or she cannot establish a body image very well. How does the adolescent cope with that? This is where the adults involved begin to have many concerns about the level of the person's propensity toward aggression or sexual acting out.

An overriding principle is that the experience of mastery of new stages and new skills is a very important source of self-esteem throughout these different developmental stages. This experience is one of the largest sources of self-esteem available to any of us. We are always trying to master new things. If we stop challenging children and do not provide them opportunities for new mastery, they feel worse about themselves. Children generally do not feel too inadequate if they

are making progress and mastering new things, even if they are far behind other kids. They may not feel wonderful, but they can feel pretty good about the fact that they are making progress. It is very, very important for us to create that experience for our children, ourselves, and for our patients. Consider the previous case of Jim, who has a strong interest in music. By putting together experiences in the area of music that increased Jim's knowledge and confidence, we could go a long way toward increasing his sense of self-esteem. Whether it is helping a child to learn to do magic, develop his sense of humor, or develop his artistic abilities, we are helping him develop strong sources of pleasure and identity.

The development of sexual interest and acting out is an extremely challenging situation for parents and therapists. A child may have adolescent urges but still function developmentally as a 5-, 6-, 7-, or even a 3-year-old. We need to deal with his sexual urges in the context of his functional developmental capacity. We may tell a simple "birds and bees" story to one child, whereas we may need to emphasize to another that, while individuals like to touch their bodies in different places, it is a private activity and there is a place and time to do it. We can work with a teenager with a few words to help him understand that we know that he likes doing this but also that this is something that goes on in the bathroom or the bedroom. For the child who is at the 7- or 8-year-old level but is physically a 15-year-old, we could use one of the books that have pictures and explanations about how the body works as a basis for some discussion, as we would ordinarily do with a 9- or 10-year-old. In addition, the notion of how to protect oneself from being exploited sexually or getting diseases is no different than any other discussion about self-protection. It should be addressed to the functional thinking level of the individual.

The key thing—and the hardest thing to do during the adolescent years—is to maintain a nurturing relationship with the adolescent or young adult, because he is larger physically and is moving on with his own different interests. Adolescents and adults are not as cuddly and warm as younger children. So we often find that parents, therapists, and other caregivers hold back nurturing, warmth, and intimacy. When this happens, the adolescent or adult does not have his dependency needs met by his parents and family. He then seeks to have his basic security and dependency needs met in other settings. When this occurs, we are more likely to see the creation of negative identities, such as involvement in substance abuse and other risk-taking activities, because the child is searching out an identity that brings him closeness with someone. With adolescents and adults who are functionally and developmentally compromised, there are ways other than cuddling to meet their dependency needs. These ways may be as simple as the phone calls made to Donald or listening to music with Jim. In other words, spending time with adolescents and adults and focusing with them on their interests will help meet their needs for warmth and intimacy.

Obviously, new challenges come up as developmentally compromised individuals move into adulthood. Whether a person lives at home or begins living independently, there is often some relative separation from parents, with other relationships taking over the parental function. Ordinarily, these relationships would be friendships or sexual relationships in which a young person looks to someone else to supply not only a new relationship but also what the parents were providing. However, these transitional relationships can be quite chaotic and often full of conflict because the adolescent is expecting so much from the other person. Unrealistically high expectations are why late adolescent and early adult relationships are often so difficult.

Children with developmental problems who have progressed to the adolescent years in a functional developmental sense will be ready for relationships, but they may not have all the tools they need. They may have processing problems, or they may easily regress into concrete modes of thinking or fragmented thinking. They are going to need more support. They may get more depressed, anxious, and fragmented than children without these problems, but they are clearly struggling with some important issues. We have to be aware of those issues in order to provide more support, either in therapy or through the family to help them have the "glue" they need to hold together during those times.

The issues of adulthood—having a family, middle age, the challenge of coming to grips with the past and the future, and the aging process—are especially relevant for individuals with milder developmental problems and those who have made good progress. These struggles need to be recognized because these individuals may need support, whether it is from the nuclear family or counseling. The better we are able to help the developmentally compromised child and young adult move into higher functional capacities, the more they will be able to experience new and meaningful challenges.

CONCLUSION

In this chapter, we have tried to emphasize that working with adolescents and adults involves the same principles as working with younger children. This work, however, involves meeting the adolescent or adult in the context of his unique interests and developmental profile and embarking on a continuing developmental journey. ∎

REFERENCES

Greenspan, S. I. (1992). *Infancy and early childhood: The practice of clinical assessment and intervention with emotional and developmental challenges.* Madison, CT: International Universities Press.

Greenspan, S. I. (1997). *The growth of the mind and the endangered origins of intelligence.* Reading, MA: Addison Wesley Longman.

Greenspan, S. I., & Wieder, S. (1998). *The child with special needs: Intellectual and emotional growth.* Reading, MA: Addison Wesley Longman.

Part Seven:

Neuroscience and Neuropsychological Foundations for Clinical Practice

— 27 —

Neural Mechanisms in Autism[1]

Andrew W. Zimmerman, M.D., and Barry Gordon, Ph.D., M.D.

Currently, there is no reliable evidence as to exactly what are the neural bases for autism. There are no accepted genetic markers, even though there are several candidates (Bailey, Palferman, Heavey, & Le Couteur, 1998; Folstein, Bisson, Santangelo, & Piven, 1998; Szatmari, Zwaigenbaum, & MacLean, 1998). It is also increasingly clear that autism is a heterogeneous disorder, even if it is genetic. There are no objective tests *in vivo* that are specific for the condition. There have been no structural, metabolic, or neuropathologic abnormalities that have been reliably linked to autistic features. There is no accepted animal model of the condition, although infant monkeys with selective brain lesions (Bachevalier, 1991; Bachevalier & Merjanian, 1994) show behavioral features suggestive of autism.

NEUROBIOLOGIC STUDIES

Although no neuropathologic features have been found yet to be characteristic of autism, a number of abnormalities have been reported. Bauman and Kemper (1994) found consistent neuronal changes ("too many, too small") in the hippocampus, amygdala, and other areas of the limbic system, as well as decreased Purkinje cells in the lateral cerebellum. More recently, Bailey et al., (1998) reported cerebellar, neocortical, and olivary (but not limbic) changes. These findings may reflect "developmental curtailment" of the cellular connections in the developing cortex (neuropil) that affects information processing and representational memory (in the hippocampal complex); recognition of facial gestures and cross-modal memory (amygdala); and shifting attention, language processing, and motor function (cerebellum). In spite of the limitations of traditional methods inherent in light microscopic studies of autism so far (Rapin & Katzman, 1998), and the paucity of postmortem tissue available for study, these studies have fostered a new era in neurobiological research in autism by other investigators who are using recently developed genetic, neurochemical, and morphological techniques.

Diverse Causes for Similar Defects of "Higher Cortical Functions"

Autism can be caused by a number of different insults and etiologies. These causes may be as diverse as viral infections, dysmorphic syndromes, or genetic abnormalities of intracellular metabolism. In any individual,

[1]Condensed with permission from a chapter in Pasquale Accardo (Ed.), Autism: Clinical and research issues. Towson, MD: York Press. (2000).

these would produce a fairly unique pattern at the neural level, even though their behavioral outcomes are more similar. There are some aspects of function in which it is possible to make a fairly direct correlation to neuroanatomy, particularly in the fully developed organism. The elementary sensory and motor systems are the best examples. However, higher cognitive abilities, by their very nature, are the product of a number of different underlying mental functions. Each of these functions may have very complex relationships to neural structures. These mental functions may not even be products of structures per se, as much as of their internal dynamics or the dynamics of other systems and structures. Moreover, many of the functions considered to be *higher* abilities are actually *chains* of abilities that unfold over time. The higher functions considered to be most important were unlikely to have sprung up full-blown in phylogeny. More likely, they have been cobbled together out of refined and rearranged combinations of other functions. Therefore, such functions may not have very direct brain correlations. The situation is even more complicated in the case of developmental disorders. Normal mental development proceeds through a cascade of many different processes, which tend to bootstrap each other. The interruption, or just simple delay, in any part of this sequence, can and often does have major effects on the final components and their assembly into a functional whole.

The genetic deficits of autism may be expressed in peculiar patterns that can be related to neurobiologic organization, but not to the functional organization of the nervous system. They also may be expressed at different times in the developing nervous system. Some of these effects may be visible at the time they occur, whereas some may take a long period of subsequent development to be expressed. It is still a reasonable strategy to look as early in development as possible for clues to the neurobiologic problems. A recent example is the study by Teitelbaum, Teitelbaum, Nye, Fryman, & Maurer (1998), which showed that movement disorders could be retrospectively detected in autistic children as early as ages 4 to 6 months. Of particular relevance to the issues raised here is that the movement disorders were expressed in different movements, and in different ways, among the different children.

Neural Networks

Neuropathological findings in the limbic system, cerebellum, and frontal cortex in autism suggest that disorders in these structures may be important contributors to the autism deficit. Variations in clinical expression among autism spectrum disorders may relate to different types of effects—as well as their distribution—in related structures, such as the basal ganglia (important for motor planning) and prefrontal cortex (motivation, executive functions) (see Figure 1). These regions may be dysfunctional by themselves (e.g., following closed-head injury, stroke, or encephalitis) or may become disconnected from their interactive partners within networks due to their failure to develop, modify, or prune their connections during development of the neuropil (Zilbovicius et al., 1995). For example, the basal ganglia (caudate and globus pallidus) and thalamus are essential subcortical integrating way-stations in networks with prefrontal and anterior cingulate cortex. Abnormalities in subcortical neurotransmission to or from the prefrontal cortex are likely to contribute to executive dysfunction, disinhibition and irritability, and apathy and inertia (Denckla & Reiss, 1997).

The capacity for repair of, or compensation for, brain lesions (plasticity) is maximal during the early years of development (Jacobson, 1991). Therapeutic programs in autism may take advantage of this potential for repair (Greenspan & Wieder, 1997; Lovaas, 1987). Although its biological basis is poorly understood, clinically effective repair may depend on the regulation of multiple neurotransmitters, growth, and other trophic factors in the brain while training programs are taking place. (Repair also may occur to some degree with or without training.) Compensation for defective way-station processes (e.g., hippocampal or cerebellar), or disconnection within networks, probably depends on correct forms of rerouting ("functional plasticity," see Fig.1). Plasticity is functional if it compensates for a disconnection between way-stations (e.g., between globus pallidus and thalamus). "Dysfunctional plasticity" (e.g., from caudate to thalamus) may reduce the efficiency of the repair or even negate its effects if the new route bypasses critical parts of the network (e.g, globus pallidus).

FUNDAMENTAL COGNITIVE AND BEHAVIORAL DEFICITS IN AUTISM

There have been a number of attempts to tease apart the cognitive and behavioral deficits that occur in autism, and to hopefully

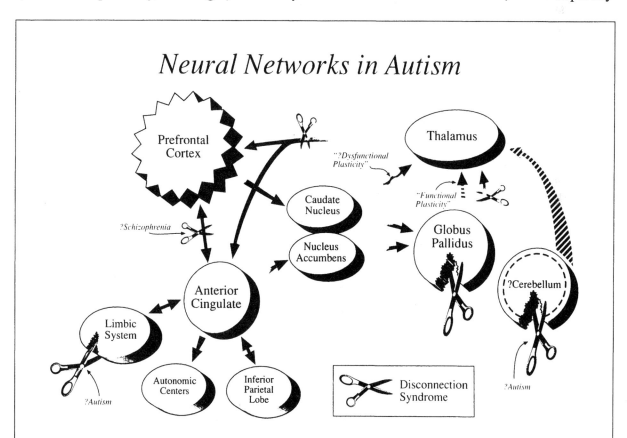

Figure 1. Putative Neural Networks in Autism. Solid arrows indicate direction of neural transmission, based on current information; large striped arrow depicts uncertain cerebellar effects. Large scissors depict cellular "lesions" in important structures that might contribute to network dysfunction or a "disconnection syndrome." Small scissors show potential sites for disconnection within networks and an example of "functional" (correct: globus pallidus to thalamus) or "dysfunctional" (aberrant) repair that might occur from bypassing the globus pallidus. In schizophrenia, a disconnection is thought to occur between the dorsolateral prefrontal area and the anterior cingulate cortex (Benes, F. M. (1993). Relationship of cingulate cortex to schizophrenia. In A. Vogt and M. Gabriel (Eds.), *The Neurobiology of cingulate cortex and limbic thalamus* (pp. 581-605). Boston: Birkhauser.

identify some as more fundamental than others (for reviews, see Bailey, Phillips, & Rutter, 1996; Happe & Frith, 1996; Rapin 1997; Rumsey, 1996; and Litrownik & McInnis, 1982). A recent example has been attention to the lack of a *theory of mind* in autism. Theory of mind was the term used by Premak & Woodruff (1978) to describe an individual's understanding of the motives, knowledge, and beliefs of others. Frith, Baron-Cohen, and others (Baron-Cohen, 1995; Baron-Cohen & Swettenham, 1997; Frith & Happe, 1994) have noted that autistic individuals do not seem to have such understanding, nor are they able to develop it. Consequently, these authors have posited that a deficit in the primitive functions that form the basis for having a theory of mind could be a major cause of the difficulties in autism. However, just what constitutes a theory of mind, who has it, and whether it is truly impaired in autism has been debated (see, for example, Povinelli & Preuss, 1995).

A different, perhaps more fundamental deficit should be entertained as being present in many persons with autism, particularly if they are low-functioning: a deficit in the ability to selectively manipulate sensory representations, concepts, and thoughts. This manipulatory deficit would be independent of the sensory representations, concepts, and thoughts themselves (although these may also be deficient). In basic terms, this is a problem with the *ability to imagine*. However, it is not a deficit in simple visual imagery; there is self-reported evidence that high-functioning persons with autism not only have visual imaginations but rely upon them (Grandin, 1997). Instead, what is referred to here is the ability to select elements of mental states and manipulate them. Normally, humans are able to focus on different aspects of an object or experience, and even seem to be able to break these aspects

away from the original experience and manipulate them separately. A person can see a red cup and separate out its redness from its shape. Persons with autism, however, are notorious for not being able to do this. They are notorious for context-dependence and for apparently focusing on the "wrong" features of everyday objects.

There is some evidence that, in normal individuals, this ability to select features from otherwise unitary representations is dependent upon the prefrontal cortex (Thompson-Schill, Esposito, Aguirre, & Farrah, 1997). A deficit in such functions would certainly fit with many of the other noted behavioral characteristics of persons with autism: their rigidity, repetitive behavior, and perservation; their lack of symbolic play; and, more elaborately, a theory of mind. Deacon (1997) and others have suggested that this type of mental manipulation, which is essentially symbolic, is one of the important mental prerequisites of humanness.

Within the subgroups of autism, much still needs to be explained. Each of the subgroups (described in Zimmerman & Gordon, 2000) is known to be associated with at least two paradoxes. One is that autistic individuals often have disproportionate mental abilities and skills, in addition to their obvious disabilities. The other paradox is that, despite the clear cognitive and behavioral abnormalities in each of the autistic categories, the underlying neural pathology still seems to resist a consistent description. Going back and reclassifying the pathology of autism into clinical subcategories does not yet result in a more coherent picture. According to published studies, even within these clinical subcategories, reported abnormalities may be present in some individuals and absent (or different) in others. The inability to find beneficial effects of any categorization scheme may simply reflect how conflated these categories have been in reported studies, and in the impossibility of reconstructing them from the published accounts. It is also very possible that some heterogeneity—in mental functions as well as in neuropathology—will prove to be a fundamental characteristic of each category of autism.

Behavioral Heterogeneity

One of the most striking features of autism is that that it is often accompanied by relative strengths in some areas of cognition, in addition to disabilities in others (Happe & Frith, 1996; O'Connor & Hermelin, 1989). Such patterns are well known in developmental disorders. In Williams sydrome, speech, surface language abilities, and (at times) musical ability, are typically far superior to visual-spatial abilities and to general cognitive abilities (Capirci, Sabbadini & Volterra, 1996; Tager-Flusberg, Boshart, & Baron-Cohen, 1998). Many of the developmental syndromes of mental retardation have relative preservation of visual-perceptual ability (Pulsifer, 1996). However, supranormal islands of ability are much rarer in other conditions compared to autism spectrum disorders (Happe & Frith, 1996). It has been claimed that 10% of the autistic population has "special abilities" (Rimland & Fein, 1988). The supranormal skills that have been described in both autistics and in individuals with other diagnoses include lightning calculation, calendar skills, list learning (Mottron, Belleville, Stip, & Morasse, 1998), visual memory, hyperlexia, puzzle construction, drawing ability, musical memory, and playing by ear and improvisation. (For more complete lists, see Happe & Frith, 1996; O'Connor & Hermelin, 1989.) Regardless of the exact proportion having such abilities, the overabundance of such skills demands some explanation and might even shed some light on the nature and neurobiology

of autism itself, as Frith (1989), O'Connor (1989), and others have suggested.

Not all of the apparently superior skills that have been reported are difficult to explain. Restricted attentional focus, repetitiveness, and the lack of competing thoughts or abilities (Frith, 1989) can certainly account for many apparent abilities. A recent study of atypical memory abilities in one individual (Mottron et al., 1998) is perhaps an example of how superior performance in one area may be accounted for, in some instances, by actual cognitive deficiencies in other areas.

However, there are other examples of apparently superior ability that seem to arise spontaneously (e.g., Selfe, 1977) and do not seem to be easily explained by the absence of normal mental impediments. These often seem to involve implicit learning of rules and patterns (Hermelin & O'Connor, 1986). They also often seem to be remarkably circumscribed. An individual who can do lightning calculations of dates may not even be able to multiply numbers (Happe & Frith, 1996). It may not be unreasonable to ask that any unified account of the neural basis for autism account for these abilities as well autism's documented disabilities.

NEURAL NETWORK THEORIES

It may be possible to unify both the behavioral heterogeneity—the abnormalities and the supernormalities—as well as the possible neural heterogeneity. To do so requires a digression into neural network theories. (It should be noted that Cohen 1994 raised many of the same hypotheses proposed here.) Neural network theories of cognitive processes posit that many mental operations are carried out through successive sets (layers) of neuronal processing elements. (For a brief overview, see Gordon, 1997.) With the proper input and training criteria, and the proper learning of rules, such networks have proven to be extremely adept at embodying rules and patterns that are implicit in the data presented to them. However, the accuracy of this extraction is very dependent upon the number of processing elements in the active learning layer (Baum & Hausler, 1989). If there are too few elements, then the network does not learn with very good accuracy: it, in fact, tends to over-generalize. If there are too many elements, then the network learns each specific situation presented to it and doesn't generalize enough. If some number of working elements leads to adequate performance, a somewhat greater number can result in truly superior performance in learning implicit rules and patterns, as long as it avoids becoming too specific.

This observation might be tied in to normal development, and to the abnormal development(s) that occur in autism, in the following way: the normal development of higher cerebral functions in a child's cortex appears to be driven by at least two major influences. One is predetermined connections: the other is activity and use. It has often been noted that the number of genes coding for the brain and neural tissue (~50,000) are insufficient to specify all the connections of the mature brain. Thus, the development of these connections must be guided in part by experience. Edelman (1987) and Intrator and Edelman (1997) have suggested that whether an uncommitted area develops connections with one region or another is based on the outcome of a competition for use. The developing child's brain normally has several primary sensory inputs, including vision, audition, and touch. These inputs are hardwired and fairly compelling. Such sensory inputs will do all they can to recruit whatever upstream neuronal processing resources are not yet committed.

Normally, the multiple influences on a child lead to a balance of forces, with the normal balance of lower and higher processing abilities (and neuroanatomic maps) as a result. The amount of neural tissue that is devoted to each higher function therefore represents a tradeoff between several forces: an attempt to optimize processing, the practical limits on optimization (because of lack of enough experience and training time), and competition with other functions for those same neuronal processing elements.

What if a developing brain had all those same forces at work, but for some reason some processing systems were impaired or delayed in their development? What if the systems in question were those involved in speech perception and speech production? Specific genetic deficits in speech production have been tentatively identified. It is conceivable that there are other deficits or combinations of deficits with more widespread effects on both speech production and speech perception. If the systems related to speech perception and speech production were developmentally impaired, then many higher abilities dependent upon appropriate auditory input and output would never develop properly. Whatever cerebral tissue would have been devoted to those higher functions would then be free to be incorporated into other processes (assuming the tissue itself was not too badly affected by the same defects). If vision were intact, then visual-related abilities would be expected to appropriate the extra cerebral tissue. The result would be a child's brain that was not capable of all of the normal functions of a child, but that was capable of performing some functions superlatively well. The brain would not be capable of those abilities that are related to speech and language capability, such as a long-term component of working memory (the part normally dependent upon an articulatory loop), and perhaps even such higher functions as the "inner voice" aspects of consciousness. It would, however, be extraordinarily good at wordless visual perception and analysis. Neuropathologically, such a brain might have only a few, apparently nonspecific, abnormalities. It would not have to have fewer neurons than normal. Autistic brains are, if anything, average or larger-than-average in size (Courchesne, Muller & Saitoh, 1999; Lainhart et al., 1997). It might be possible to detect additional territory devoted to visual-related functions, but perhaps not with current behavioral tasks and instrumentation. Autism may therefore represent disorders of activity-dependent plasticity during brain development that occur at several different levels: gene, synapse, neuron, network, and neuronal group.

Hypothesis of Activity-Dependent Plasticity

In broader outline, the hypothesis is this: Either because of genetics or external influences, several regions or neuronal networks of the developing brain are damaged or delayed in their development. Regions involved in social connection and those involved in speech and language seem to be particularly susceptible. (It is not too speculative to imagine that they have a functional linkage and perhaps, therefore, a genetic one as well.) There are two consequences of this primary pathology. Functions that require these inputs cannot develop fully. Functions that were not dependent upon these impaired routes can develop normally, and might well develop supranormally. They would develop supranormally if these functions were normally kept constrained by a competition for neural resources from the functions that were now impaired (with the competition being either in functional space or perhaps just through simple anatomic proximity).

This hypothesis has several testable consequences. There will be *forme frustes* of autistic disorder—in speech and language and in socialization—representing less extreme forms of the autistic pathology. These types of deficits should be familial. The domino effect on functions should be predictable after research establishes a better understanding of what functions depend upon other functions, in both development and in operation. Finally, it should be possible to identify some *in vivo* correlates of the extra neural tissue that has been adopted for processing (e.g., vision) in these individuals.

This hypothesis does not explain the primary cause or causes of the deficits. It would, however, help to explain why persons with autism tend to have the patterns of disabilities and abilities that they do, and why their neuropathology (in the broadest sense) has been so variable from individual to individual. It might also suggest ways in which functional retraining can try to ameliorate some of their disabilities or take advantage of their particular strengths.

CONCLUSION

The next stages of investigation of neural mechanisms in autism spectrum disorders should first focus on the selection of subjects and clinical definition of subsets. Although well-studied animal models are desirable, high-functioning subjects with autism are more likely to reveal the essential abnormalities in this very "human" disorder. Multiple investigative techniques, from cellular and neurochemical to cognitive neurophysiology, and quantitative and functional neuroimaging, will help to define the neural networks that contribute to autism. ∎

Acknowledgments

Preparation by Andrew W. Zimmerman was supported in part by the National Alliance for Autism Research and the East Tennessee Chapter, Autism Society of America. Barry Gordon was supported in part by the New York Community Trust—Hodgson Fund, the Hodgson Family, the Benjamin A. Miller Family Fund, and by gifts made in memory of Bernard Gordon.

The authors thank Martha Bridge Denckla, M.D., for her helpful discussions regarding neural pathways in autism, and James Marcum, who contributed to the artwork (Figure 1).

REFERENCES

Bachevalier, J. (1991). An animal model for childhood autism. In C. A. Tamminga and S. C. Schultz (Eds.), *Advances in neuropsychiatry and psychopharmacology* (pp. 129-140). New York: Raven Press.

Bachavalier, J., & Merjanian, P. (1994). The contribution of medial temporal lobe structures in infantile autism: A neurobehavioral study in primates. In M. L. Bauman and T. L. Kemper (Eds.), *The Neurobiology of autism.* Baltimore: Johns Hopkins University Press.

Bailey, A., Phillips, W., & Rutter, M. (1996). Autism: Towards an integration of clinical, genetic, neuropsychological, and neurobiological perspectives. *Journal of Child Psychology and Psychiatry, 37,* 89-126.

Bailey, A., Palferman, S., Heavey, L., & Le Couteur, A. (1998). Autism: The phenotype in relatives. *Journal of Autism and Developmental Disorders, 28,* 369-392.

Bailey, A., Luthert, P., Dean, A., Harding, B., Janota, I., Montgomery, M., Rutter, M., & Lantos, P. (1998). A clinicopathological study of autism. *Brain, 121,* 889-905.

Bailey, C. H., Bartsch, D., & Kandel, E. R. (1996). Toward a molecular definition of long-term memory storage. *Proceedings of the National Academy of Sciences of the United States of America, 93,* 13445-13452.

Baron-Cohen, S. (1995). *Mindblindness: An Essay on autism and theory of mind.* Cambridge, MA: MIT Press.

Baron-Cohen, S., & Swettenham, J. (1997). Theory of mind in autism: Its relationship to executive function and central coherence. In D. J. Cohen, & F. R. Volkmar (Eds.), *Handbook of autism and pervasive developmental disorders.* New York, NY: John Wiley & Sons.

Baum, E. B., & Hausler, D. (1989). *What sized net gives valid generalization? Neural Computation, 1,* 151-160.

Bauman, M. L., & Kemper, T. L. (1994). Neuroanatomic observations of the brain in autism. In M. L. Bauman, & T. L. Kemper (Eds.), *The neurobiology of autism.* Baltimore, MD: Johns Hopkins University Press.

Benes, F. M. (1993). Relationship of cingulate cortex to schizophrenia. In B. A. Vogt & M. Gabriel (Eds.), *The neurobiology of cingulate cortex and limbic thalamus* (pp. 581-605). Boston: Birkhauser.

Capirci, O., Sabbadini, L., & Volterra, V. (1996). Language development in Williams Syndrome: A case study. *Cognitive Neuropsychology 13,* 1017-1040.

Cohen, I. L. (1994). An artificial neural network analogue of learning in autism. *Biological Psychiatry, 36,* 5-20.

Courchesne, E., Muller, R. A., & Saitoh, O. (1999). Brain weight in autism: Normal in the majority of cases, megalencephalic in rare cases. *Neurology 52,* 1057-1059.

Deacon, T. (1997). *The symbolic species: The Co-evolution of language and the brain.* New York: W.W. Norton.

Denckla M. B., & Reiss, A. L. (1997). Prefrontal-subcortical circuits in developmental disorders. In N. A. Krasnegor, G. R. Lyon, & P. S. Goldman-Rakic (Eds.), *Development of the prefrontal cortex: Evolution, neurobiology and behavior.* Baltimore, MD: Paul H. Brookes.

Edelman, G. M. (1987). *Neural Darwinism: The theory of neuronal group selection.* New York: Basic Books.

Folstein, S. E., Bisson, E., Santangelo, S. L., & Piven, J. (1998). Finding specific genes that cause autism: a combination of approaches will be needed to maximize power. *Journal of Autism and Developmental Disorders, 28,* 439-445.

Frith, U., (1989). *Autism: Explaining the enigma*. Oxford: Blackwell.

Frith, U. and Happe, F. (1994). Autism: Beyond "theory of mind". *Cognition, 50*, 115-132.

Gordon, B. 1997. Models of naming. In. H. Goodglass & A. Wingfield (Eds.), *Anomia* (pp. 31-64). San Diego, CA: Academic Press.

Grandin, T. (1997). A personal perspective on autism. In D. J. Cohen and F. R. Volkmar (Eds.), *Handbook of autism and pervasive developmental disorders*. New York, NY: John Wiley and Sons.

Greenspan, S. I., & Wieder, S. (1997). Developmental patterns and outcomes in infants and children with disorders of relating and communicating: A chart review of 200 cases of children with autistic spectrum diagnoses. *The Journal of Developmental and Learning Disorders, 1*, 87-141.

Happe, F., & Frith, U. (1996). The neuropsychology of autism. *Brain, 119,*1377-1400.

Hermelin, B., & O'Connor, N. (1986). Idiot savant calendrical calculators: Rules and regularities. *Psychological Medicine, 16*, 885-893.

Intrator, N., & Edelman, S. (1997). Competitive learning in biological and artificial neural computation. *Trends in Cognitive Sciences, 1*, 268-272.

Jacobson, M. (1991). *Developmental Neurobiology* (3rd Ed.) New York, NY: Plenum Press.

Lainhart, J. E., Piven, J., Wzorek, M., Landa, R., Santangelo, S. L., Coon, H., & Folstein, S. E. (1997). Macrocephaly in children and adults with autism. *Journal of the American Academy of Child and Adolescent Psychiatry, 36*, 282-290.

Litrownik, A. J., & McInnis, E. T. (1982). Cognitive and perceptual deficits in autistic children: A model of information processing, critical review, and suggestions for the furture. In J. J. Steffen and P. Karoly (Eds.), *Autism and severe psychopathology, Vol. 2. Advances in child behavioral analysis and therapy* (pp. 103-155). Lexington, KY: Lexington Books.

Lovaas, O. I. (1987). Behavioral treatment and normal educational and intellectual functioning in young autistic children. *Journal of Autism and Developmental Disorders, 9*, 315-323.

Mottron, L., Belleville, S., Stip, E., & Morasse, K. (1998). Atypical memory performance in an autistic savant. *Memory, 6*, 593-607.

O'Connor, N., & Hermelin, B. (1989). The memory structure of autistic idiot-savant mnemonists. *British Journal of Psychology, 80*, 97-111.

Povinelli, D., & Preuss, T. (1995). Theory of mind: Evolutionary history of a cognitive specialization. *Trends in Neurosciences, 18*, 418-424.

Prior, M. R. (1987). Biological and neuropsychological approaches to childhood autism. *British Journal of Psychiatry, 150*, 8-17.

Pulsifer, M. B. (1996). The neuropsychology of mental retardation. *Journal of the International Neuropsychological Society, 2*, 159-176.

Rapin, I. (1997). Autism. *New England Journal of Medicine, 337*, 97-104.

Rapin, I., and Katzman, R. (1998). Neurobiology of autism. *Annals of Neurology, 43*, 7-14.

Rimland, B., and Fein, D. (1988). Special talents of autistic savants. In L. Obler and D. Fein (Eds.), *The exceptional brain: Neuropsychology of talent and special abilities* (pp. 474-492). New York: Guilford Publications.

Rumsey, J. M. (1996). Neuroimaging studies of autism. In G. R. Lyons & J. M. Rumsey (Eds.), *Neuroimaging: A Window to the neurological foundations of learning and behavior in children* (pp. 119-146). Baltimore, MD: Paul H. Brooks.

Selfe, L. (1977). *Nadia.* New York: Harcourt Brace Jovanovich.

Szatmari, P., Jones, M. B., Zwaigenbaum, L., and MacLean, J. E. (1998). Genetics of autism: Overview and new directions. *Journal of Autism and Developmental Disorders, 28,* 351-368.

Tager-Flusberg, H., Boshart, J., & Baron-Cohen, S. 1998. Reading the windows to the soul: Evidence of domain-specific sparing in Williams Syndrome. *Journal of Cognitive Neuroscience, 10,* 631-639.

Teitelbaum, P., Teitelbaum, O., Nye, J. Fryman, J., & Maurer, R. G. (1998). Movement analysis in infancy may be useful for early diagnosis of autism.

Proceedings of the National Academy of Sciences of the United States of America, 95(23), 13982-13987.

Thompson-Schill, S., D'Esposito, M., Aguirre, G.K., & Farrah, M. J. (1997). Role of the left inferior prefrontal cortex in retrieval of semantic knowledge: A reevaluation. *Proceedings of the National Academy of Sciences of the United States of America, 94,* 14792-14797.

Zilbovicius, M., Garreau, B., Samson, Y., Remy, P., Barth, C., Syrota, A., & Lelord, G. 1995. Delayed maturation of the frontal cortex in childhood autism. *American Journal of Psychiatry 152,* 248-252.

Zimmerman, A.W., and Gordon, B. (2000). In P. Accardo (Ed.), *Autism: Clinical and research issues.* Towson, MD: York Press.

—◀ 28 ▶—

Autism as a Disorder of Complex Information Processing[1]

Nancy J. Minshew, M.D., and Gerald Goldstein, M.D.

This chapter reviews the evidence leading to the proposal of the neurobehavioral model, or conceptual construct, of autism as a disorder of complex information processing that spares the visual-spatial system. This model is a multiple primary cognitive deficit model proposing that the pattern of deficits within and across cognitive domains in autism is a reflection of complex information processing demands.

NEUROBEHAVIORAL MODELS IN NEUROBIOLOGIC CONTEXT

Neurobehavioral models for autism are hypotheses about the cognitive basis of behavior and its neural representation in the brain. Numerous such models have been proposed for autism in the decades since a neurologic origin gained acceptance. These models, and the large body of research they arose from and led to, have resulted in major progress in the characterization of the neurocognitive basis of autism with several major consequences. First, this research has led to substantial improvements in diagnostic criteria, recognition of affected individuals, and treatment. Second, recent developments in the definition of structural and functional abnormalities of the brain have culminated in the recognition that the brain in autism

reflects the unique effects of disruption of the dynamics of brain development. A third milestone resulting from this research has been the recognition of partially affected family members and the resulting appreciation of autism as a family genetic disorder with multiple probable genetic loci. Collectively, these research contributions have led to the current conceptualization of the neurobiology of autism as originating with familial abnormalities in the genome that code for brain development. Multiple families of gene abnormalities are anticipated, reflecting various clinical phenomena. These gene abnormalities are expected to code for various abnormal mechanisms for brain development, which culminate in the structural and functional abnormalities of the brain seen in autism. These functional and structural abnormalities constitute the neural basis for the cognitive impairments underlying the behavior that defines autism (see Figure 1). The achievement of this conceptualization of the neurobiology of autism has been the product of decades of research and has made

---

[1]Previously published as: Minshew, N.J., & Goldstein, G. (1998). Autism as a disorder of complex information processing. *Mental Retardation and Developmental Disabilities Research Reviews, 4,* 129-136. Adapted by permission of Wiley-Liss, Inc., a subsidiary of John Wiley & Sons, Inc.

the long-term goal of developing corrective neurobiologic interventions for autism finally conceivable. The eventual attainment of this goal is dependent on achieving a detailed characterization of each of the elements in this neurobiologic chain of events. The continuing investigation of the cognitive and neural basis of autism in future research can be expected to play as significant a guiding role in reaching this goal as it did in making such a goal feasible.

Figure 1. Components of Cause

Autism: Components of Cause

Abnormalities in Genetic Code for Brain Development

↓

Abnormal Mechanisms of Brain Development

↓

Structural and Functional Abnormalities of Brain

↓

Cognitive and Neurologic Abnormalities

↓

Behavioral Syndrome

EVOLUTION IN NEUROBEHAVIORAL MODELS FOR AUTISM

The investigation of the cognitive and neural basis of autism has led to numerous neurobehavioral models in the 35 years since a neurologic origin for autism first gained acceptance (Rimland, 1964). These models reflect a stepwise series of progressively improving approximations of the underlying pathophysiology that resulted from research investigating important hypotheses about the neurocognitive basis of autism. Current neurobehavioral models are a composite reflection of the accumulated knowledge of decades of research as well as the considerable remaining unknowns about autism and about the normal human brain, cognition, and behavior. Neurobehavioral models are thus,

by definition, temporary conceptual constructs that organize existing findings into testable hypotheses for further investigation.

The earliest neurobehavioral models for autism emerged in the 1960s and 1970s and generally proposed a single primary deficit in an aspect of information acquisition as the cognitive basis for this behavioral syndrome. Therefore, the earliest models hypothesized deficits in sensory perception, brainstem attentional or arousal mechanisms, or associative memory. These models were ultimately abandoned when the previously demonstrated abnormalities in post-rotary nystagmus, brainstem auditory-evoked potentials, temporal horn ventricular size on imaging, and associative memory were found to be the result of the inclusion of a substantial number of autistic subjects with coexisting causes for these findings. Repetition of these studies with autistic subjects screened to exclude those with other disorders causing brain damage failed to provide evidence of abnormalities (Campbell, Rosenbloom, & Perry, 1982; Creasey et al., 1986; Courchesne & Lincoln, 1985; Courchesne, Hicks, & Lincoln et al., 1985; Damasio, Maurer, Damisio, & Chui, 1980; Dunn, 1989; Minshew & Goldstein, 1993; Ornitz, Atwell, Kaplan, & Westlake,1985; Ornitz, Sugiyama & deTraversay, 1993; Prior, Tress, Hoffman, & Bolt, 1984; Rumsey, Grimes, Pikus, Duara, & Ismond, 1984). However, even the latter studies provided little neuropsychologic evidence documenting the status of sensory perception, attention, and associative memory abilities in autism.

A second, shorter-lived group of neurobehavioral models emerged in the 1970s, proposing a left hemisphere-language acquisition defect or a lack of hemispheric specialization as the basis for autism (reviewed in Minshew, 1994). By the mid-1980s, however, neuropathologic (Bauman & Kemper, 1985) and neurophysiologic studies (reviewed in Minshew,

1991) had consistently demonstrated a bilaterally symmetric pattern of brain involvement in autism. In addition, evidence of right hemisphere language deficits involving prosody, gesture, and facial expression was emerging, highlighting the limitations of drawing conclusions about the brain localization for autism based on the localization of a single cognitive deficit.

In 1980, the first formal information processing model for autism was proposed. This model was based on the first report in autism of attenuation or absence of auditory P300 evoked potentials with sparing of visual P300 potentials, which led to the hypothesis of a selective auditory information processing defect (Novick, Kurtzberg, & Vaughan, 1979; Novick, Kurtzberg, Vaughan, & Simpson, 1980). In light of the intact behavioral performance of the subjects, Novick and colleagues (1980) proposed that the neurophysiologic abnormality reflected the reliance by parietal cortex on less efficient neural pathways for the processing of auditory information. The disparity observed between auditory and visual P300 potential abnormalities in autism was replicated by subsequent investigators (Dunn, 1989), and led to questions about the involvement of visual information processing and the posterior regions of the cerebral hemispheres. These neurophysiologic findings were among the first data demonstrating the central involvement in autism of information analysis and evaluation rather than of information acquisition. These data were also of major significance for providing documentation of the consistent and reliable conduction of sensory information to the cerebral cortex and of the consistency of sensory perception by individuals with autism (Minshew, Sweeny, & Bauman, 1997).

In the latter 1980s and early 1990s, several major cognitive findings were reported that led to a number of new neurobehavioral models. In 1988, a study of neuropsychologic functioning across domains in 10 autistic men with average group mean verbal and performance IQ scores documented a cognitive profile characterized by dramatic deficits in conceptual reasoning abilities, relatively intact language, memory, and motor abilities, and intact sensory perception and visual-spatial abilities (Rumsey & Hamburger, 1988). Based on this profile, Rumsey and Hamburger proposed a core deficit in a broad class of verbal and nonverbal conceptual reasoning abilities, but had difficulty relating this deficit conceptually to the behavioral syndrome of autism. Ozonoff, Pennington, and Rogers (1991) replicated this overall profile and accumulated evidence of executive function deficits, which led to their proposal of an influential executive dysfunction-frontal systems model for autism (Ozonoff, Pennington, & Rogers, 1991). In a second significant study, Ozonoff, McMahon, & Filloux (1994) investigated the specific cognitive components in autism responsible for executive dysfunction on the Wisconsin Card Sorting Test. They identified the cognitive flexibility component as the major source of impaired performance, and the inhibition of prepotent responses as making a modest contribution. Notably, they found that components related to shifting attention between different features of an object and to inhibiting responses failed to demonstrate impairments, leading Ozonoff and colleagues to propose that autistic individuals' perseverative focus of attention on details had a conceptual rather than a perceptual basis. This study was also significant for demonstrating that complex cognitive tasks received contributions from multiple component processes that could be separated with appropriate procedures and that the impaired performance of different neuropsychiatric populations could be traced to dysfunction of different components.

A second major recent contribution to neurobehavioral conceptualizations of autism was the recognition of "theory of mind" deficits as a major cognitive mechanism underlying the abnormal social behavior in autism. The identification of this cognitive ability and its impairment in autism demystified social behavior in autism and brought it clearly into the realm of cognitive psychology. It was also a milestone, and likely the first of many, for having identified a previously unsuspected cognitive ability responsible for an important aspect of human behavior (Tooby & Cosmides, 1995). The model proposed for theory of mind abilities in autism was also notable for highlighting the role of multiple cognitive abilities acting in concert in novel ways to subserve complex human behavior (Baron-Cohen, 1995). Thus, the impairment in the capacity for making inferences about the mental beliefs and knowledge of others was seen as functionally linked to deficits in the social use of eye contact. This model thus converged with reports on autism of deficits in the use of eye contact to achieve shared attention (Sigman, 1996), another newly recognized cognitive or neurologic function contributing to social behavior. These two newly recognized abilities provided clear examples of the many yet-to-be defined cognitive abilities that contribute to the complex cognitive and behavioral competencies impaired in autism, and of the likely need to reconceptualize the cognitive contributions to other impaired abilities in autism as new research findings are reported.

A third major influence on recent neurocognitive models for autism pertains to reports of attentional deficits. Deficits in attention have been proposed repeatedly throughout the course of autism research in an attempt to explain the autistic individual's intense focus on details, on the one hand, and a lack of interest in people, on the other.

Although recent research studies summarized previously have provided evidence for a conceptual basis for these abnormalities in behavior, deficits in attention continue to be reported and proposed as the primary cognitive basis for behavior in autism. Deficits in selective attention, attention to extra-personal space, and shifting attention have been among those recently proposed (Courchesne et al., 1993; Ornitz, 1988; Townsend & Courchesne, 1994). The first two of these deficits were inferred from neurophysiologic abnormalities in the absence of impairments in cognitive performance and imaging abnormalities involving the parietal lobe, respectively. The shifting attention deficit was documented with a cognitive paradigm, but the paradigm also had substantial executive function and working memory demands in addition to the demand for an attentional shift at the perceptual level. The multiple demands of this task made it impossible to determine the cognitive origin for the impaired performance in autism without investigating these contributions individually. A number of subsequent studies attempted to clarify the role of attentional processes in autism. Collectively, these studies examined the reflexive and voluntary or executive control of attention in individuals with autism of varying levels of ability (reviewed in Burack, Enns, & Johannes, 1997). These studies provided evidence that abnormalities in attentional focus in autism are related to the information processing aspects of the tasks and the voluntary or executive control of attention, and not to deficits in reflexive orienting abilities. These latter studies were also of major importance in highlighting the influence of developmental level or general ability level on the expression of deficits in autism, and the limitations of conclusions about core deficits that did not consider these influences.

Up to this point, neurobehavioral models for autism generally were single primary cognitive deficit models, proposing a clinically apparent deficit in a single cognitive domain or modality as underlying the social, communication, and odd nonsocial behavior in autism. By the early 1990s, however, substantive evidence of deficits in several higher-order cognitive abilities had emerged, posing a major question for the validity of single primary deficit models. As most of the cognitive and neuropsychologic studies in autism had focused on a single cognitive domain, their design precluded the identification of potential deficits in other domains and the consideration of their significance in the various neurobehavioral models.

PROFILE OF NEUROPSYCHOLOGIC FUNCTIONING IN AUTISM

Examination of cognitive functioning across domains within the same subject sample provided an obvious opportunity for addressing the issue of single versus multiple co-existing cognitive deficits in autism. It also provided an opportunity for observing the pattern of these deficits, which itself might contain additional important clues to the underlying neurobiology. One of the first studies to investigate neuropsychologic functioning across domains in a group of autistic subjects screened to exclude those with causes of brain dysfunction other than autism was that of Rumsey and Hamburger (1988). This study was viewed as remarkable for the demonstration of dramatic impairments in the reasoning domain that were not explainable by deficits in other domains. However, less noticed was the characterization of the language, memory, and motor domains as "relatively intact," whereas sensory perception and visual-spatial abilities were described as intact. Examination of the test

battery revealed only a few tests and mixed results in the language, memory, and motor domains, whereas there were a larger number and broader range of tests for the reasoning domain. The relatively intact domains reflected a combination of good performance on tests of simpler abilities and impairments on tests of more complex abilities, especially in the memory and language areas. A number of investigators subsequently replicated this profile, emphasizing the evidence for executive dysfunction but again relying on few tests in the language and memory domains, with the same mixed results.

One study attempted to address this issue by expanding the memory and language test battery and by separately considering simple and complex abilities at analysis (Minshew et al., 1992). This study of 15 nonmentally retarded individuals with autism revealed intact function on memory tests of simple associative processes and on language tests of basic skills such as word fluency, reading decoding, and spelling. Memory deficits were documented on delayed recall measures, suggesting that information encoding was not sufficiently supported by organizing strategies. Language deficits were documented on tests of higher-order abilities, such as comprehension of idioms, metaphors, and ambiguous sentences. This pattern of findings in the language and memory domains suggested the presence of a dissociation in autism between simple and complex abilities. The second major finding of this study was the absence of impairments on the Wisconsin Card Sorting Test (WCST). Deficits on this test had come to be viewed as a hallmark of the abstraction deficit in autism as a result of the extensive investigation of executive dysfunction based on this test. Instead, abstraction deficits were demonstrated on the Goldstein-Scheerer Object Sorting Test with a test of verbal reasoning and in the capacity to shift concepts. The absence of deficits on the WCST in this study was attributed to the higher level of function of the autistic subjects compared to prior studies. In these subjects, the deficit was better characterized by deficits on concept-formation tests than by rule-learning tests, such as the WCST. The third significant finding of this study was the presence of deficits on Part A, but not on Part B, of the Trail Making Test. Deficits on Part B are typically viewed as evidence of problems with executive function or shifting attention, as subserved by the frontal lobes. Part A has minimal cognitive demands and serves as practice for Part B; the major demand of part A is on psychomotor skills. The intact performance by the subjects with autism on Part B, but with impairments on Part A, suggested the presence of psychomotor slowing. Review of the Rumsey and Hamburger (1988) Trail Making Test data revealed that their subjects had exhibited greater deficits on Part A than on Part B, as well as exhibiting evidence of psychomotor slowing on a finger-tapping task.

Several of the findings from the preceding study were amplified in follow-up studies. Concept formation ability was investigated further with the Twenty Questions Procedure, which requires subjects to identify a preselected object from an array using a maximum of 20 questions. The most efficient strategy is to formulate constraint-seeking questions that involve characteristics shared by several objects, which can eliminate several alternatives at once and thus progressively narrow the possibilities to the target item. Four trials were administered in a study comparing the problem-solving skills of nonmentally retarded individuals with autism and matched control subjects. The autistic subjects solved significantly fewer of the four trials and used a significantly smaller number of constraint-seeking questions. Their impaired performance on this test of the

concept formation aspect of abstraction was contrasted with their intact performance on tests of the rule-learning aspect of abstraction, a less challenging aspect of abstraction. The mixed pattern of results in the language and memory area in the Minshew et al. study (1992) led to an in-depth examination of the language domain investigating the hypothesis of a dissociation between preserved simple abilities and impaired complex abilities (Minshew, Goldstein, Taylor, & Siegel, 1994; Minshew, Goldstein, & Siegel, 1995). In these studies, the simple language category was comprised of tests of mechanical skills, such as verbal fluency, mechanical reading, word recognition, spelling, phonetic analysis, and simple calculation. The complex language category included tests of interpretive abilities, such as reading comprehension, understanding of the metaphorical aspects of spoken and written language, and verbal reasoning. The performance of high-functioning subjects with autism was compared to that of normal community volunteers matched by age, gender, race, IQ, and socioeconomic status (SES). The results of the study indicated that the autistic subjects did as well and often better than control subjects on the tests of mechanical language skills, but significantly more poorly on tests of complex interpretive skills. These studies provided additional evidence suggesting that subjects with autism had selectively failed to acquire the higher-level interpretive language abilities expected on the basis of their age, verbal IQ score, and basic language skills.

EVIDENCE FOR A COMPLEX INFORMATION PROCESSING DISORDER

In light of these findings, a third study of the profile of neuropsychologic functioning was designed to further characterize the pattern within and across domains in a large group of rigorously defined subjects with autism and individually matched controls. The test battery was expanded and designed to address the neuropsychologic deficits hypothesized by various neurobehavioral models for autism, as well as to address the hypothesis of selective involvement of higher-order cognitive abilities related to generalized dysfunction of association cortex. The battery was composed of valid and reliable neuropsychologic tests assessing the major cognitive domains of attention, sensory perception, motor function, language, memory, reasoning, and visual-spatial abilities (see Table 1 in the chapter appendix, "Results of Neuropsychological Tests Assessing the Major Cognitive Domains.") The visual-spatial domain was included because its status was important in completing the profile of cognitive functioning in autism, although visual-spatial abilities have long been considered a strength of individuals with autism. A range of abilities was considered within each domain to address the various hypothesized deficits, and both verbal and visual modalities were assessed where appropriate. The large number of measures relevant to the assessment of simple and complex language and memory abilities in both the visual and auditory modalities required subdivision of these cognitive domains into simple and complex categories for separate analysis. In other domains, the number of tests was fewer and individual consideration of the tests within domains was relied upon to characterize the features related to deficits and intact abilities. Tests in each domain were considered as multivariate sets, and stepwise discriminate function analyses were used to evaluate the accuracy of each set in correctly classifying cases into autistic and control groups. Classification accuracy was assessed with Cohen's kappa, an index of strength of

agreement for nominal scales. Tests included and not included in the regression equations and their order of entry provided additional information on which tests had the most discriminatory power. Individual t-tests were computed to clarify performance on tests not included in the regression equations (see Table 2, chapter appendix).

Tests in the attention, sensory perception, simple memory, and visual-spatial domains did not yield satisfactory classification accuracy, providing evidence of intact basic information acquisition abilities and intact information processing in the visual-spatial domain. *Kappa* scores in the fair to good agreement range (0.40-0.75) were obtained for the motor, simple language, complex language, complex memory, and abstract reasoning domains. For the simple language category, the significant *kappa* score reflected superior performance by the subjects with autism relative to control subjects, in contrast to the motor, complex memory, complex language, and reasoning categories where the significant *kappas* reflected impairments.

Examination of tests entered and not entered into the regression equations, order of entry, and individual t-test results provided additional evidence about the nature of the deficit pattern. The attention domain was most notable for the absence of evidence of deficits. Only tests with a motor component—the letter and number cancellation tasks—were entered into the regression equation, and these failed to achieve significant classificatory accuracy. Performance on these two tests was notable for the low rate of errors by both subject groups and the absence of a predilection for any quadrant; thus, there was no support for a hypothesized deficit in attention to extra-personal space. In the motor domain, it was of note that discriminatory accuracy was achieved with the Grooved Pegboard Test and Trail Making Test, Part A, the two tests of skilled motor sequences. In contrast, there was no difference between subjects with autism and control subjects on the test of simple or isolated motor movements (Finger-tapping Test). T-tests revealed significantly poorer performance on Part A, but not Part B, of the Trail Making Test, which is consistent with prior observations and the assignment of Part A to the motor domain and Part B to the reasoning domain. In the complex language and complex memory domains, test entry was notable for including both verbal and visual tests, thus failing to support the hypothesis of a selective auditory processing deficit in autism. In the reasoning domain, the WCST and the Halstead Category Test (two tests of the rule-learning aspect of abstract reasoning) failed the tolerance test consistent with the previously reported findings in nonmentally retarded individuals with autism (Minshew et al., 1992). The first test passing the tolerance test for the reasoning domain was the Twenty Questions Procedure, which is a concept formation test. This was followed by the Picture Absurdities subtest of the Binet scales, which requires consideration of context and a conceptual framework in order to identify incongruities, and the Trail Making Test, Part B, which challenges working memory and shifting cognitive sets (executive function). The selection of these three tests suggests that the reasoning deficit in autism involves a broad range of conceptual abilities as previously proposed by Rumsey and Hamburger (1988), and that executive dysfunction or cognitive inflexibility might be too narrow to encompass the deficit.

The profile of cognitive functioning in these nonmentally retarded autistic adolescents and adults was therefore defined by deficits in concept formation, complex memory, complex language, and skilled motor abilities and by intact or superior function in

the attention, sensory perception, simple memory, simple language, rule-learning, and visual-spatial areas. The implications of these findings are several.

RESEARCH IMPLICATIONS

The characterization of the cognitive profile in terms of both deficits and intact abilities is significant, as it demonstrates the distinctions between autism and general mental retardation, on the one hand, and the developmental specific learning disabilities, on the other. The two-part characterization also demonstrates the selective impact of autism on higher-order abilities. Thus, the presence of age- and IQ-appropriate performance on tests of spelling, reading, arithmetic, and visual-spatial abilities distinguishes autism from the developmental specific learning disabilities and the nonverbal learning disability syndrome. The intact language, memory, arithmetic, rule-learning and visual-spatial abilities account for the attainment of IQ scores in the average range. The deficits in problem solving, concept formation, complex language and complex memory abilities explain the failure of the average IQ scores to be accurate predictors of adaptive behavior and function in society. This dissociation between intact and deficit skills also explains the clinical observation that abstraction, communication, and social abilities fall rapidly (or disproportionately) with declining IQ in the autistic population as compared to the nonautistic, mentally retarded population, and the lower adaptive function of mentally retarded individuals with autism compared to mentally retarded individuals without autism of the same general level ability.

In addition to demonstrating the selective impact of autism on higher-order cognitive abilities, the documented intact abilities fail to support neurobehavioral models that hypothesize clinically apparent deficits in sensory perception, attention at the perceptual level, and associative memory as the basis for autism. The integrity of these basic abilities also demonstrates that the deficits documented in concept formation, complex memory, complex language, and skilled motor abilities are not secondary to deficits in more elementary abilities.

A second unique feature of cognitive functioning in the subjects with autism was the pattern of intact simpler abilities in domains demonstrating deficits. Perhaps contrary to expectations, a deficit in the abstract reasoning domain, for example, did not mean that all abstraction was impaired. Rather, deficits in each domain involved the highest level abilities expected on the basis of an individual's age and IQ, while leaving simpler abilities intact or even enhanced. That is, in each domain, deficits appeared to correspond to the highest level tasks, thus depending on the most cognitively advanced abilities, whereas intact function appeared to correspond to the simplest or most basic skills. This pattern conformed to the neurophysiologic pattern reported for autism of impaired, late cognitive potentials and intact earlier potentials. Across domains, complexity also appeared to account for the predilection of deficits for those domains with the highest demands on information processing. The consistency of this pattern within and across domains and with the neurophysiologic pattern suggests that it reflects a neurobiologic feature or principle of brain structure and function.

As one way of probing the validity of this conceptualization or characterization of cognitive functioning in autism, the cognitive profile defined in this study was compared with that reported by Tallal for a disorder of early or simple information processing (Jernigan, Hesselink, Sowell, &

Tallal, 1991; Johnston, Stark, Mellits, & Tallal, 1981; Neville et al., 1993; Tallal & Piercy, 1973; Tallal et al., 1996). This comparison revealed that the cognitive profile in autism was the converse of that described by Tallal for children with developmental specific learning impairment (SLI). As in autism, the neuropsychologic profile in children with SLI involved multiple domains but included the attention domain as well as the sensory perception, motor, memory, and language domains. Unlike autism, the deficits involved the elementary or simple abilities; namely, basic attentional processes, sensory perception, elementary motor, simple memory, and simple language abilities. This profile was found to correspond to a disturbance in early information processing, resulting in the failure to acquire information dependent on the first 100 msec of information processing. In contrast, higher-order interpretative and reasoning skills were intact, and the children could sometimes use these abilities to fill in or infer missing information.

Evidence of a deficit in complex abilities in the motor domain also supports the neurobiologic validity of a complex information processing construct in autism. That is, the presence of a dissociation between simple and complex abilities in an area of minor clinical involvement would also suggest that the dissociation reflects a fundamental feature of the neurobiology. The coexistence of a similar pattern across domains suggests that the deficits are dependent on a common neural substrate or organizing principle of the brain.

In arriving at the characterization of the cognitive profile in autism as reflecting a complex information processing disorder, consideration was given to the ways that complexity is defined. Within cognitive theory, complexity is defined in several ways, including number of elements contained in the stimulus material as well as the multiplicity of cognitive processes involved in task performance. The latter definition involves emergent abilities that are not directly reducible to simpler elements of cognitive function (i.e., the reductionist fallacy). Thus, the cognitive capacity to comprehend extended blocks of language is not simply reducible to vocabulary and grammar skills, but requires another level of language abilities in order to comprehend the meanings beyond those implicit to vocabulary and the arrangement of words into sentences. The model proposed here does not distinguish between these definitions of complexity, particularly because they are related in the sense that, as the number of elements increases, there is typically an increase in the number of cognitive processes needed for task performance.

The application of a complexity construct to the cognitive profile in autism requires several constraints or specifications to accurately reflect the data from which it was derived. First, the data in this study define deficits by complexity within domains, not independent of domains; thus, the definition of complexity conveyed in this model is domain-related. That is, although any language skill might be viewed from a cognitive perspective as more complex than any motor skill, the deficits found do not conform to a cognitive ranking of relative complexity independent of domain. Rather, the deficit pattern appears to conform to the fact that different cognitive functions are represented by separate neurologic systems in the brain. Second, visual-spatial abilities involve complex information processing but were found to be intact; thus, the disorder of complex information processing in autism must be stipulated to spare the visual-spatial domain. Because the visual-spatial system is a separate neural system, it is reasonable to assume that this neural system could be spared through various neurobiologic mechanisms

without invalidating a complex information processing model for cognitive functioning in other domains. Third, this model was derived from the study of nonmentally retarded adolescents and adults with autism. If it is to be applied to younger or lower-functioning individuals with autism, it is clear that complexity in terms of cognitive function has to be conceptualized in relation to age and IQ. The specific expression of the complex information processing deficit is therefore going to float as a reflection of the age and general ability level of the individual.

Several key aspects of the clinical syndrome of autism were not assessed in this study because of the time-intensive nature of experimental measures or the lack of sufficiently challenging measures for nonmentally retarded individuals with autism. Consequently, the test battery did not assess social or nonverbal language abilities, although deficits in these abilities are implicit to the diagnosis of autism and were documented with the structured instruments used for diagnosis, which were the Autism Diagnostic Interview (LeCouteur et al., 1989; Lord, Rutter, & LeCouteur, 1994) and the Autism Diagnostic Observation Schedule (Lord, Rutter, & Goode, 1989). Nonetheless, the deficits in these areas can be conceptualized within a complex information-processing model. Theory of mind skills are therefore viewed as a higher-order inferential, cognitive ability. Similarly, the modulation of eye contact and facial expression for communication purposes and the comprehension and expression of satire, irony, and innuendo in prosody are likewise viewed as higher-order complex, information-processing skills. On the other hand, deficits were found in complex memory skills that are not obviously related to the clinical criteria for autism. The data supporting their presence is clear, so the issue is how such an impairment might relate to the clinical deficits. The evolution of theory of mind abilities in relation to autism provides a model for considering the existence of a previously unrecognized cognitive contribution to the clinical manifestations of autism (Baron-Cohen, 1995). The memory data from the present study provided evidence of intact rote memory for simple information in limited amounts but a reduced capacity for remembering information as its complexity increased. This reduced memory capacity applied to an increasing number of units of the same kind, such as words in a sequence and branch points in a maze, as well as to an increase in the intrinsic complexity of the material, as in the case of stories and the Rey-Osterreith complex figure (Minshew et al., 1996). Thus, these subjects with autism have difficulty remembering increasing amounts of information and discerning the intrinsic organizational structure of information that normally supports memory. Given that social interactions, communication, and problem-solving situations typically involve the presentation of large amounts of information, it would seem likely that a memory impairment of the type found would contribute to impaired function. As proposed by Toobes and Cosmides (1995) in their foreword to Baron-Cohen's book describing the evolution of the theory of mind data and construct in autism, there are many as-yet-undescribed cognitive abilities that are performed so automatically that their existence is not suspected. The theory of mind model described by Baron-Cohen further suggests that cognitive abilities also may act in concert in ways not currently described to support complex capabilities in humans, and that these interactions may also be disrupted in autism. Consistent with this, it has been proposed that the social and language systems must interact in order for communication to be related to a social context and that

these interactions are disrupted in autism. Such an interaction provides a cognitive and neural basis for the use of language for communication. Similarly, it is probable that the memory system interacts at a cognitive and neural systems level with the social, language, and reasoning systems to support the cognitive functions impaired in autism. Ultimately, these relationships will be explored and elucidated with experimental cognitive procedures and fMRI.

SUMMARY

In summary, this study of neuropsychologic functioning in autism provided evidence of the co-existence of deficits in multiple domains within a single-subject group, supporting a multiple primary cognitive deficit model for the cognitive basis of behavior in autism. No evidence was found of deficits in attention, sensory perception, or associative memory to support neurobehavioral theories hypothesizing clinically apparent deficits in these abilities as the basis of behavior in autism. Within affected domains, impairments consistently involved the most complex tasks dependent on higher-order abilities whereas intact or superior function was found on simpler abilities within the same domains. Across domains, complex information-processing demands also provided an explanation for the particular constellation of deficits that define autism; that is, those domains with the highest complex information-processing demands. The neuropsychologic profile for autism characterized in this study is consistent with the evoked potential pattern of abnormal late, endogenous potentials and preserved earlier potentials, and the converse of the neuropsychologic and neurophysiologic pattern described for a simple or early information-processing disorder. The presence of such a common denominator within and across domains would suggest that impairments are dependent on a common feature of neuronal organization. As such, there is likely to be a larger class than currently appreciated of yet-to-be-defined cognitive abilities impaired as a result of this disturbance in neuronal organization. Theory of mind abilities and the deficits in complex memory identified in this study are examples of the unknown features of the cognitive basis of autism to be defined in future research. Both of these impairments also highlight the emerging recognition of the importance of disruption in the interactions between different cognitive functions and neural systems as the basis for certain aspects of behavior in autism.   ∎

Acknowledgments

The authors gratefully acknowledge the commitment of the subjects and their families to the pursuit of research in autism as a way to a better future. They also acknowledge the dedicated and careful work of the research associates who completed all of the testing and of Evelyn Herbert who generously assisted parents and researchers alike. This research was supported by the National Institute of Neurologic Disorders and Stroke (NINDS) grant NS33355 and National Institute of Child Health and Human Development (NICHD) grant HD35469 to Nancy Minshew and the Department of Veterans Affairs.

REFERENCES

Baron-Cohen, S. (1995). *Mindblindness: An essay on autism and theory of mind.* Cambridge, MA: MIT Press.

Bauman, M. L., Kemper, T. L. (1985). Histoanatomic observations of the brain in early infantile autism. *Journal of Neurology, 35,* 866-874.

Burack, J. A., Enns, J. T., & Johannes, E. A. (1997). In D. J. Cohen and F. R. Volkmar (Eds.), *Attention and autism behavioral and electrophysiological evidence: Handbook of autism and pervasive developmental disorders (2nd ed.),* (pp. 226-247). New York: Wiley and Sons.

Campbell, M. S., Rosenbloom, S., & Perry, R. (1982). Computerized axial tomography in young autistic children. *American Journal of Psychiatry, 139,* 510-512.

Courchesne, E., Courchesne, R. Y., Hicks, G., & Lincoln, A. J. (1985). Functioning of the brain stem auditory pathway in non-retarded autistic individuals. *Electroencephalography and Clinical Neurophysiology, 6,* 491-501.

Courchesne, E., & Lincoln, A. J. (1985). Event-related brain potential correlates of the processing of Novel Visual and auditory information in autism. *Journal of Autism and Developmental Disorders, 15,* 55-76.

Courchesne, E., Townsend, J. P., Akshoomoff, N. A., Yeung-Courchesne, R., Press, G. A., Murakami, J. W., Lincoln, A. J., James, H. E., Saitoh, O., Egaas, B., Haas, R. H., & Schreibman, L. (1993). A new finding: Impairment in shifting attention in autistic and cerebellar patients. In S. H. Broman and J. Grafman (Eds.), *Atypical deficits in developmental disorders: Implications for brain function* (pp. 101-137). Hillsdale, Lawrence Erlbaum.

Creasy, J., Rumsey, J. M., Schwartz, M., Duara, R., Rapoport, J. L., & Rapoport, S. I. (1986). Brain morphometry in autistic men as measured by volumetric computed tomography. *Archives of Neurology, 43,* 669-672.

Damasio, H., Maurer, R. G., Damasio, A. R., Chui, H. C. (1980). Computerized tomographic scan findings in patients with autistic behavior. *Archives of Neurology, 37,* 504-510.

Dunn, M. (1989). Neurophysiologic observations in autism and implications for neurologic dysfunction. In C. Grillon, E. Courchesne & N. Akshoomoff (Eds.), Brainstem and middle latency auditory evoked potentials in autism and developmental language disorders. *Journal of Autism and Developmental Disorders, 19,* 255-269.

Jernigan, T. L., Hesselink, J. R., Sowell, E., & Tallal, P. A. (1991). Cerebral structure on magnetic resonance imaging in language and learning impaired children. *Archives of Neurology, 48,* 539-545.

Johnston, R. B., Stark, R. E., Mellits, E. D., & Tallal, P. (1981). Neurological status of language-impaired and normal children. *Annals of Neurology, 10,* 159-163.

LeCouteur, A., Rutter, M., Lord, C., Rios, P., Robertson, S., Holdgrafer, M., & McLennan, J. (1989). Autism diagnostic interview: A standardized investigator-based instrument. *Journal of Autism and Developmental Disorders, 19,* 363-387.

Lord, C., Rutter, M., & Goode, S. (1989). Autism diagnostic observation schedule: A standardized investigator-based instrument. *Journal of Autism and Developmental Disorders, 19,* 185-212.

Lord, C., Rutter, M., & LeCouteur, A. L. (1994). Autism diagnostic interview revised: A revised version of a diagnostic interview for caregivers of individuals with possible pervasive developmental disorders.

Journal of Autism and Developmental Disorders, 24, 659-685.

Minshew, N. J. (1991). Indices of neural function in autism: Clinical and biologic implications. *Pediatrics,* 774-780.

Minshew, N. J. (1993) *In vivo* brain chemistry of autism: 31P magnetic resonance spectroscopy studies. In: N. J. Minshew, & G. Goldstein (Eds.), Is autism an amnesic disorder?: Evidence from the California verbal learning test. *Neuropsychology 7(2),* 209-216.

Minshew, N. J., Goldstein, G., Muenz, L. R., & Payton, J. B. (1992). Neuropsychological functioning in nonmentally retarded autistic individuals. *Journal of Clinical and Experimental Neuropsychology, 14(5),* 740-761

Minshew, N. J., Goldstein, G., & Siegel, D. J. (1996). Designing instruction for the high functioning autistic individual. *Journal of Developmental and Physical Disabilities, 8,* 1-19.

Minshew, N. J., Goldstein, G., & Siegel, D. J. (1995). Speech and language in high functioning autistic individuals. *Neuropsychology, 9,* 255-261.

Minshew, N. J., Goldstein, G., Taylor, H. G., & Siegel, D. J. (1994). Academic achievement in high functioning autistic individuals. *Journal of Clinical and Experimental Neuropsychology, 16(2),* 261-270.

Minshew, N. J., Sweeney, J. A., & Bauman, M. L. (1997). Neurological aspects of autism. In D. J. Cohen & F. R. Volkmar (Eds.), Handbook of autism and pervasive developmental disorders (2nd ed.) (pp. 344-369). New York: Wiley & Sons.

Neville, J. N., Coffey, A. S., Holcomb, J. P., & Tallal, P. (1993). The neurobiology of sensory and language processing in language-impaired children. *Journal of Cognitive Neuroscience, 5,* 235-253.

Novick, B., Kurtzberg, D., & Vaughan, H. G., Jr. (1979). An electrophysiologic indication

of defective information storage in childhood autism. *Psychiatry Resource, 1,* 101-108.

Novick, B., Kurtzberg, D., Vaughan, H. G., Jr., & Simpson, R. (1980). An electrophysiologic indication of auditory processing defects in autism. *Psychiatry Resource, 3,* 107-114.

Ornitz, E. M. (1988). Autism: A disorder of directed attention. *Brain Dysfunction, 1,* 309-322.

Ornitz, E. M., Atwell, C. W., Kaplan, A. R., & Westlake, J. R. (1985). Brain-stem dysfunction in autism. *Archives of General Psychiatry, 42,* 1018-1025.

Ornitz, E. M., Sugiyama, T., & deTraversay, J. (1993). Startle modulation studies in autism. *Journal of Autism and Developmental Disorders, 23,* 619-637.

Ozonoff, S., Pennington, B. F., & Rogers, S. J. (1991). Executive function deficits in high-functioning autistic individuals: Relationship to theory of mind. *Journal of Child Psychology and Psychiatry, 32,* 1081-1105.

Ozonoff, S., Strayer, D. L., McMahon, W. M., & Filloux, F. (1994). Executive function abilities in autism and tourette syndrome: An information processing approach. *Journal of Child Psychology and Psychiatry, 35,* 1015-1032.

Prior, M. R., Tress, B., Hoffman, W. L., & Boldt, D. (1984). Computed tomographic study of children with classic autism. *Archives of Neurology, 41,* 482-484.

Rimland, B. (1964). Infantile autism: The syndrome and its implications for a neural theory of behavior. New York: Appleton-Century Crofts.

Rumsey, J. M., Grimes, A. M., Pikus, A. M., Duara, R., & Ismond, D. R. (1984). Auditory brainstem responses in pervasive developmental disorders. *Biological Psychiatry, 19,* 1403-1417.

Rumsey, J. M., & Hamburger, S. D. (1988). Neurophysiological findings in high-functioning men with infantile autism, residual state. *Journal of Clinical and Experimental Neuropsychology, 10,* 201-221.

Sigman, M. (1996). Behavioral research in childhood autism. In M. F. Lenzenweger & J. J. Haugaard (Eds.), *Frontiers of developmental psychology* (pp. 190-208). New York: Oxford University Press.

Tallal, P., Miller, S. L., Bedi, G., Byma, G., Wang, X., Srikantan, S. N., Schreiner, C., Jenkins, W. M., & Merzenich, M. M. (1996). Language comprehension in language-learning impaired children improved with acoustically modified speech. *Science, 271,* 81-84.

Tallal, P., & Piercy, M. (1973). Developmental aphasia: Impaired rate of non-verbal processing as a function of sensory modality. *Neuropsychologia, 11,* 389-398.

Tooby, J., & Cosmides, L. F. (1995). In S. Baron-Cohen (Ed.), *Mindblindness: An Essay on autism and theory of mind.* Cambridge, MA: MIT Press.

Townsend, J., & Courchesne, E. (1994). Parietal damage and narrow "spotlight" spatial attention. *Journal of Cognitive Neuroscience, 6,* 220-232.

Appendix

RESULTS OF NEUROPSYCHOLOGIC TESTS ASSESSING THE MAJOR COGNITIVE DOMAINS

Table A1. Discriminant Analysis Results By Domain and By Order of Entry

Domain	Tests Failing Tolerance Test	Tests Passing Tolerance Test	% Correct	% Jackknife	Kappa[1]
Attention	Serial Digit Learning; Digit Span; Continuous Performance	Letter Cancellation; Number Cancellation	66.7	66.7	.33
Sensory Perception	Luria-Nebraska Tactile Scale: Touch, Position, Finger Position and Stereognosis items	Finger Tip Writing; Luria-Nebraska Sharp/Dull Tactile Scale item	64.6	62.5	.29
Motor	Finger Tapping; Developmental Test of Visual Motor Integration	Grooved Pegboard; Trail Making A	75.8	75.8	.52[1]
Simple Language	WAIS-R Vocabulary	K-TEA Reading Decoding; K-TEA Spelling; WRMT-R Word Attack; Controlled Oral Word Association	71.2	66.7	.42[1]
Complex Language	WRMT-R Passage Comprehension; TLC- Metaphoric Expression	K-TEA Reading Comprehension; Verbal Absurdities; Token Test	72.7	65.2	.45[1]
Simple Memory	Paired Associates; 3 Word Short Term Memory; Maze Recall	CVLT Trial 1	65.2	65.2	.30
Complex Memory	Paired Associates-Delayed; CVLT Long Delay	NVSRT-Consistent Long Term Retrieval; WMS-R Logical Memory-Delayed Recall; Rey Figure-Delayed Recall	77.3	75.8	.55[1]
Reasoning	Category Test; Wisconsin Card Sort Test	20 Questions; Picture Absurdities; Trail Making B	75.8	72.7	.52[1]
Visual-Spatial	WAIS-R Picture Completion, Object Assembly	WAIS-R Block Design	56.1	56.1	.12

[1]Indicates a significiant between-group difference in performance.

Table A2. Psychometric Data Used for Discriminant Analysis

Tests Entered into Prediction Equations	Autistic Group		Control Group		
	M	**SD**	**M**	**SD**	**p**
Attention Domain					
WAIS-R Digit Span	9.88	3.81	10.52	2.46	.424
Serial Digit Learning-Correct Responses	16.52	8.17	17.42	7.91	.648
Continuous Performance Test-Mean Reaction Time Correct Responses	0.34	0.62	0.23	0.66	.487
Letter Cancellation-Omissions	1.09	1.63	0.45	1.00	.061
Number Cancellation-Omissions	3.27	4.03	4.39	5.38	.342
Sensory Perception Domain					
Luria-Nebraska Tactile Scale:					
Simple Touch Errors	0.29	0.55	0.17	0.48	.407
Stereognosis Errors	0.46	0.59	0.21	0.42	.096
Sharp-Dull Discrimination Errors	0.88	0.80	0.58	0.72	.189
Position Sense Errors	0.00	0.00	0.08	0.41	.328
Finger Position Errors	0.67	1.27	0.46	1.02	.535
* Halstead-Reitan: Fingertip Number Writing-Errors	5.38	4.30	2.79	2.84	.019*
Motor Domain					
Finger Tapping-Dominant Hand	44.27	13.78	45.19	16.24	.805
Developmental Test of Visual-Motor Integration-Total Points	15.42	32.43	22.18	31.69	.465
* Grooved Pegboard-Dominant Hand-Time in Seconds	86.73	18.30	70.67	16.03	.000*
* Trail Making A-Time in Seconds	31.52	15.81	20.45	7.99	.001*
Simple Language Domain					
Controlled Oral Word Association (FAS)-Number of Words	36.00	13.31	34.00	16.18	.586
WAIS-R Vocabulary	9.45	3.02	9.70	2.26	.713
K-TEA Spelling	102.58	16.93	100.91	11.50	.642
Woodcock Reading Mastery-Word Attack	107.24	11.55	103.52	15.53	.273
K-TEA Reading Decoding	97.48	13.60	102.79	10.19	.078

Continued

Table A2. *Continued*

Tests Entered into Prediction Equations	Autistic Group		Control Group		
	M	SD	M	SD	p
Complex Language Domain					
Token Test (number correct)	18.03	2.19	18.42	5.19	.690
* K-TEA Reading Comprehension	91.36	14.43	103.06	12.45	.001*
* Woodcock Reading Mastery-Passage Comprehension	92.27	15.04	104.27	14.34	.002*
* Test of Language Competence-Metaphoric Expression (scaled score)	6.85	3.25	9.42	3.70	.004*
* Binet Verbal Absurdities-Raw Score	9.30	3.64	12.48	3.97	.001*
Simple Memory Domain					
Maze 1 Recall (correct/incorrect)	0.42	0.61	0.52	0.57	.534
3 Word Short Term Memory-Number of Correct Sequences	3.24	3.04	2.91	3.15	.663
Paired-Associate Learning-Number Correct	42.55	23.13	48.76	24.21	.290
CVLT A List-Trial 1 Number Correct	4.50	3.90	6.30	3.90	.072
Complex Memory Domain					
Paired-Associates-Delayed Recall	16.00	7.46	17.45	6.13	.390
CVLT A List-Long Delay	7.00	5.49	9.00	5.55	.146
* WMS-R Logical Memory-Delayed Recall-Elements	5.58	5.79	8.45	6.02	.052*
* Nonverbal Selective Reminding-Consistent Long-term Retrieval	19.94	15.09	37.39	16.09	.000*
* Rey-Osterrieth Figure-Delayed Recall-Number of Elements	16.83	8.58	21.94	7.49	.012*
Reasoning Domain					
Halstead Category Test (errors)	46.24	28.71	40.73	22.46	.388
Wisconsin Card Sorting Test-Perseverative Errors	16.45	15.48	13.27	11.13	.342
Trail Making B (time in seconds)	65.48	37.19	52.42	23.31	.093
* Binet Picture Absurdities (raw score)	20.00	11.46	27.52	6.12	.002*
Questions (% constraint seeking)	35.49	23.82	56.08	14.02	.000*
Visual-Spatial Domain					
WAIS-R Picture Completion	8.76	2.22	9.21	2.27	.415
WAIS-R Object Assembly	9.88	3.63	9.73	2.88	.852
WAIS-R Block Design	10.79	3.25	9.70	2.14	.113
Rey-Osterrieth-copy score	31.30	4.80	33.09	3.75	.096

◄ **29** ►

Autism: Clinical Features and Neurobiological Observations[1]

Margaret L. Bauman, M.D.

Since its first description in 1943 (Kanner, 1943), autism has intrigued clinicians and scientists alike, largely because of its association with significant disturbances in cognition and behavior in the absence of obvious physical and brain dysmorphology. For many years, parenting and environmental factors were believed to be to blame for the social aloofness, obsessive need for sameness, perseverative and stereotypic behaviors, and impaired language that characterize this disorder. However, with the advent of improved neurobiological technology and with the awareness of the high incidence of seizures (Deykin & MacMahan, 1979) and abnormal electroencephalograms (Small, 1975) within the autistic population, evidence for neurological basis for the disorder began to mount.

In any consideration of the clinical deficits exhibited by autistic children, disturbances in language development are usually the first concern and are the symptom that most frequently brings the child to the attention of a physician (Rapin, 1991). Initially, some autistic children may appear deaf, failing to respond to being called by their name or to follow simple commands. Rapin and Allen (1987) have suggested that many (if not most) autistic children have impaired comprehension of language and that some may

exhibit a verbal-auditory agnosia or word-deafness (Rapin, Mattis, Rowan et al., 1977).

In the majority of autistic children, expressive language also is significantly delayed, and a significant proportion of these fail to develop any meaningful communication skills (Rutter, 1978). Approximately one-fifth of autistic children appear to develop language at the appropriate time, some of which development can seem to be precocious and associated with an exceptional vocabulary. However, these skills undergo regression, usually between 12 and 18 months of age, following which language development in these children is similar to that of autistic children whose verbal output was delayed from the beginning (Kurita, 1985).

Those children who eventually do develop language display a wide variation in the quantity and quality of communication patterns exhibited. Frequently, little spontaneous language is exhibited, and expressive output is obtained with the assistance of verbal or physical prompts. Some children will demonstrate rote patterns of counting, reciting the alphabet, or repeating scripts they have acquired from television, videotapes, books,

[1]Previously published as: Bauman, M. (1999). Autism: Clinical features and neurobiological observations. In H. Tager-Flusberg (Ed.), *Neurodevelopmental disorders* (pp. 383-399). Reprinted with permission from MIT Press, Cambridge, MA.

or parents with little understanding of their meaning. Echolalia may be present, and children perseveratively may repeat a word or the last several words of a sentence just heard. For those children who become fluent speakers, abnormalities of prosody or the melody and intonation of speech may substantially impair communicative intent. Their verbal output may have a sing-song or monotone quality, and they may have difficulty in modulating the volume of their voice. Some highly verbal autistic children may speak pedantically to others, particularly on a favorite topic, with little appreciation of the interest of the listener. Many of these children can appear to have little need of a conversational partner, and social language often is impaired. Typically, they have difficulty in maintaining a topic of conversation, particularly if it is a topic which they themselves have not chosen. They have difficulty with conversational turn taking, do not easily establish or use eye contact during communication, and typically interpret poorly the body language, tone of voice, or facial expression of others (Rapin, 1991).

Nonverbal communication also is impaired in autistic children. They rarely use a pointing response, nor do they exhibit joint attention. Rather than gesture, autistic children will lead the hand of an adult to a desired object or obtain the object themselves (Minshew & Payton, 1988).

Though it is now acknowledged that autistic individuals exhibit a wide range of intellectual abilities, estimates suggest that approximately 75% function within the retarded range [Diagnostic and Statistical Manual of Mental Disorders (fourth edition) (DSM-IV)]. Regardless of the level of function, the profile of cognitive development tends to be uneven (DSM-IV). Many are very concrete, and even very intelligent autistic individuals may experience difficulty with concept formation, reasoning, abstract thought, and insight (Rapin,

1991). Typically, autistic children tend to have better nonverbal than verbal skills and tend to be better visual learners than auditory learners (Rapin, 1991). They tend to have an exceptional memory for details and tend to overgeneralize rules. In contrast, autistic individuals often have difficulty with the processing of information related to the integration and generalization of concepts and the development of abstract thought (Minshew & Payton, 1988). Some autistic persons have shown superior skills for a narrow range of abilities, such as calendars, calculations, music, drawing, and rote verbal tasks, despite otherwise impaired cognitive abilities (Rapin, 1991).

During early childhood, the majority of autistic children demonstrate significant deficits in imaginary or symbolic play. In the high-functioning adult, this deficit may contribute to the inability to develop generic notions in regard to abstract concepts, such as justice, beauty, or jealousy (Grandin, 1995).

Along with language and cognitive impairments, social deficits are one of the most striking clinical manifestations of autism. During infancy, autistic children may be extremely passive babies requiring little attention, or they may be very irritable, difficult to feed, have irregular sleep patterns, and resist cuddling. As young children, they appear to be socially aloof, seemingly unaware of the presence or feelings of others. Alternatively, some autistic children can be overly and inappropriately affectionate, even with strangers. They can become excessively attached to and clingy with one parent and tolerate separation poorly. Autistic children do not know how to make friends or to engage others in their activities or play. They tend to be rigid and do not easily learn socially appropriate behavior, such as initial greetings. Some basic social skills can be taught, but only rarely do they become automatic and used with total ease. The extent to which socialization abilities are related to or interdigitate with either language or cognitive functioning remains unknown.

Nearly all autistic children appear to have difficulty with the regulation of attention (Dawson & Lew, 1989). Many are easily distractible and hyperactive, rarely giving any task or toy more than momentary interest. Alternatively, others may become hyperfocused and "lock into" a task of particular interest to them, such as the computer, lining up objects, or twirling string. In this case, shifting or transitioning their attention to another activity often is difficult and leads to disruptive behavior (Kinsbourne, 1991).

Although autistic children initially were believed to be motorically normal, more careful observation has found that many demonstrate a generalized hypotonia with hyperextensibility of some of the joints. Posture tends to be poor. Though most of these children meet their developmental gross motor milestones on time, a significant proportion walk late. Gait patterns may lack fluidity, and bilateral motor coordination for such skills as skipping and cutting with scissors may be executed poorly. Some children walk on their toes, but whether this practice is related to a dysfunctional motor pattern or to excessive sensitivity on the bottoms of the feet (or both) is unclear. Refined fine motor skills, such as buttoning, controlling a pencil, or tying shoes, often are exceedingly difficult and (in some cases) are never achieved. In addition, a deficit may be possible in the ability to imitate motor movements and automatically to execute skilled motor tasks or to perform these tasks in a demand situation, suggesting the presence of motor dyspraxia in these children (Rapin, 1991). Poorly executed oral-motor movements can be associated with drooling, poor articulation (resulting in reduced intelligibility), and difficulty in chewing. Repetitive and stereotypical motor movements are seen in approximately one-third of autistic children. Although the disorder frequently is termed "self-stimulatory" behavior, its etiology and functional significance remains a matter of debate.

Many autistic children appear to have difficulty in modulating the input of sensory information. Some appear to be particularly sensitive to auditory stimuli, such as mechanical noises, school bells, a baby's cry, or the subtle noises made by fluorescent lighting. Some are particularly sensitive to light touch, such as tags in their shirts, seams in their socks, haircuts, and new unwashed clothing that is perceived as scratchy. Alternatively, these same children may appear impervious to pain, failing to cry even when severely hurt. Some seek comfort from the sensation of pressure and may be found contentedly curled up between two mattresses in their bedroom. Occasionally, some autistic children also appear to be excessively sensitive to odors and others to food textures, which may result in restricted dietary intake.

NEUROPHYSIOLGOICAL STUDIES

Given the variety and complexity of symptoms with which the autistic child presents, some benefit derives from considering possible brain mechanisms that may underlie some of the clinical features of the disorder. Some of the earliest studies that attempted to address this question were neurophysiological investigations that demonstrated abnormal auditory-nerve and brainstem-evoked responses (Student & Schmer, 1978; Tanguay, Edwards, Buchwald, Schwofeld, & Allen, 1982) and rapid eye movement sleep patterns (Tanguay, Ornitz, Forsythe, & Ritvo, 1976). However, in retrospect, these abnormalities were found to be related primarily to the heterogeneity of the study population and to methodological factors. Subsequent investigations on well-documented autistic subjects have failed to confirm the original reports (Rumsey et al., 1984; Courchesne et al., 1985a).

P300 and negative component (Nc) have been the most common event-related potentials (ERPs) studied in autism. P300s are believed to originate from the modality-non-specific association cortex in the parietal lobes and are thought to be dependent on the intact connectivity between this cortical region and the hippocampus and limbic cortex (Wood et al., 1984). Nc is believed to originate from the frontal cortex. ERPs are of cortical origin and depend on the brain's intrinsic processing of sensory information, not on the stimulus.

Small or absent auditory P300s and visual P400s have been recorded in autistic subjects who were required to detect random missing stimuli from a regular series of auditory or visual stimuli (Novick, Kurtzberg, & Vaughan, 1979). Because the subjects were able to detect the missing stimuli, the authors suggested that the attenuated ERPs were related to a disturbance in information storage secondary to a dysfunction in the circuitry connecting the inferior parietal cortex with the entorhinal cortex and hippocampus, not to motivational or attentional factors. Further, cross-modulation studies involving both auditory and visual stimuli have suggested an impairment in information processing (Novick et al., 1979). This hypothesis was revised in 1980 when the same authors reported significantly smaller auditory P200 and P300 potentials in autistic subjects in response to pitch changes and deleted stimuli (Novick et al., 1980). It was noted that the depression in the late potentials occurred during tasks that required direct sequential comparison of auditory stimuli and was not limited to conditions in which a temporal interval must be registered. Based on these findings, the authors hypothesized that the abnormalities

were not related to a dysfunction in information storage as previously proposed but to a disturbance in the processing of auditory information and that the abnormality most likely was located in the parietal association cortex. Subsequently, Courchesne et al. (1985b) noted the absence of Nc to novel visual or auditory stimuli in autistic subjects, despite normal task performance and sustained attention, suggesting abnormalities involving the frontal cortex. Thus, evidence appears to point to neurophysiological abnormalities in the parietal and frontal association cortices in autism; they have been hypothesized to be related to inefficient cortical auditory processing or to dysfunctional cortical handling of selective attention (Minshew, 1991).

POSITRON EMISSION TOMOGRAPHY AND FUNCTIONAL IMAGING STUDIES

Relatively few positron emission tomographic (PET) studies have been reported in autism. In 1985, Rumsey et al. noted increased 2-fluoro-2-deoxy-D-glucose uptake throughout the cerebral cortex, hippocampus, thalamus, and basal ganglia in a series of adult high-functioning male autistic subjects. However, substantial overlap occurred in the data between the control and autistic groups in this study. When these data later were subjected to correlation analysis, reduced frontal-parietal intercorrelations were found in the autistic individuals and were hypothesized to be related to an imbalance in mutually inhibitory neuronal circuits associated with attention (Horwitz et al., 1988). Two additional studies have failed to show any statistically significant differences between the autistic and control subjects (De Volder et al., 1987; Herold et al., 1988). More recently, Chugani et al. (1996) studied serotonin synthesis with PET in 10 normal adults in comparison with

4 adult autistic subjects. The results of this study demonstrated significantly higher serotonin synthesis in normal female subjects as compared to male subjects and increased serotonin synthesis in the autistic subjects in comparison with that in controls. These preliminary findings are intriguing and warrant further investigation.

Using (31)P nuclear magnetic resonance spectroscopy, Minshew et al. (1994) reported a decrease in phosphocreatine and adenosine triphosphate levels, borderline decreased phosphomonoesters, and increased phosphodiesters in the dorsal prefrontal cortex in a group of high-functioning autistic adolescents and young adults, suggesting neuronal membrane alteration and altered energy metabolism in the frontal cortex The authors hypothesize that these preliminary findings may be reflective of inefficient information processing in autism.

IN VIVO NEUROANATOMY

The first imaging study to suggest a neuroanatomical basis for autism was a pneumoencephalographic study performed on 18 children who presented with retarded language development and autistic behavior (Hauser, Delong, & Rosman, 1975). Enlargement of the left temporal horn was noted in 15 cases, with some subjects showing enlargement of both temporal horns or mild enlargement of the lateral ventricles, more pronounced on the left. On the basis of these observations, the authors suggested that abnormalities involving the medial temporal lobe structures might play a role in the symptomatology of autism.

The introduction of computed tomography (CT) n the mid-1970s resulted in numerous attempts to further define brain abnormalities in autism. In 1979, Hier, Lemay, and Rosenberger reported a reversal of the normal left-right parietal-occipital asymmetry in 57% of the autistic subjects who were studied in comparison with mentally retarded and neurological control groups. On the basis of these findings, the failure of normal language development in autism was speculated possibly to be related to the morphological inferiority of the left hemisphere. However, subsequent CT studies failed to replicate these initial findings (Damasio et al., 1980; Tsai, Jacoby, & Steward, 1983; Rumsey et al., 1988). Further CT studies focused on observations of ventricular size (Jacobson et al., 1988; Rumsey et al., 1988) without documentation of consistent abnormalities.

With the emergence of magnetic resonance imaging (MRI) technology, in vivo morphometrical studies of the brain have focused on the analysis of specific brain regions. The major focus of these studies has been on the cerebellum (following the initial reports of Courchesne et al. in 1987 and 1988) and on a remeasurement of the same cases in 1989 (Murakami et al., 1989), indicating a selective hypoplasia of lobules VI and VII of the vermis on midsaggital images in autistic subjects. However, five well-designed subsequent studies have failed to replicate these findings (Ritvo & Garber, 1988; Holttum et al., 1992; Filipek et al., 1992; Kleiman, Neff, & Rosman, 1992; Piven et al., 1992). In 1994, Courchesne et al. reanalyzed data from previously published MRI vermal measurements in 78 autistic subjects. Although the majority of the patients were found to demonstrate hypoplasia of lobule VI and VII as originally reported, a small subgroup was noted to have hyperplasia of these same lobules. The authors concluded that, because of the presence of both vernal hypoplasia and hyperplasia and the averaging of these measurements, cerebellar midline abnormalities were not detected in several of the previously reported series. However, given that only a single midsaggital section was measured, they did not address the possibility that the shape and total volume of the cerebellum, age, intelligence quotient, and other factors unrelated to autism may be significant variables. Further studies involving large numbers of carefully matched subjects will be needed before the significance of cerebellar findings on MIR can be resolved.

Other areas of the brain also have been studied by MRI in autism, including the brainstem and more recently the parietal lobe and corpus callosum (Gaffney et al., 1988; Filipek et al., 1992; Piven et al., 1992). So far, the findings in these studies have been inconsistent, and their significance at this time is uncertain.

HISTOANATOMICAL OBSERVATIONS OF THE BRAIN

Relatively few neuropathological studies have been reported in autism. In large part, this has been due to the limited availability of post-mortem material for study and to the fact that, in most cases, the brains appear to be grossly normal, giving few clues to the location and nature of the neuropathology that underlies this disorder. On the basis of the clinical features of autism, and extrapolating from observations derived from clinical and animal research, a variety of candidate sites of abnormality have been hypothesized. These have included the basal ganglia (Vilensky, Damasio, & Maurer, 1981), the thalamus (Coleman, 1979), the vestibular system (Ornitz & Ritvo, 1968), and structures of the medial temporal lobe (Boucher & Warrington, 1976; Delong, 1978; Damasio & Maurer, 1978; Maurer & Damasio, 1982). Despite these considerations, early neuropathological studies failed to determine any consistent morphological abnormalities (Aarkrog, 1968;

Darby, 1976; Williams et al., 1980; Coleman et al., 1985).

Using the technique of whole-brain serial section (Yakovlev, 1970), the brains of nine well-documented autistic patients have been systematically studied in comparison with identically processed age-and sex-matched control material (Bauman & Kemper, 1995). All cases studied to date have shown no abnormalities of external brain structure or myelin. With the exception of the anterior cingulate gyrus, microscopical analysis of multiple cortical regions in all the autistic brains also have shown no abnormality of cortical lamination, neuronal size or number, or cellular migration consistent with the findings of Coleman et al. (1985). In addition, a systematic survey of the basal ganglia, thalamus, hypothalamus, and basal forebrain failed to delineate any differences from the controls.

Areas of the forebrain that were found to be abnormal were confined to the hippocampus, subiculum, entorhinal cortex, amygdala, mammillary body, anterior cingulate cortex, and septum. These structures are known to be related to each other by interconnecting circuits and make up a major portion of the limbic system of the brain. In comparison with controls, these areas showed reduced neuronal cell size and increased cell-packing density (number of neurons per unit volume), which appeared to be equal bilaterally. Using the rapid Golgi technique, pyramidal neurons of areas CAI and CA4 of the hippocampus showed reduced complexity and extent of dendritic arbors (Raymond, Bauman, & Kemper, 1996). In the amygdala, small cell size and increased cell-packing density was most pronounced medially in the cortical, medial, and central nuclei, whereas the lateral nucleus appeared to be comparable to controls. The exception to this profile was observed in the brain of a 12-year-old autistic boy with a history of serious behavioral disturbances but with documented average intelligence. In this case, the findings of small cell size and increased cell-packing density was less robust in the hippocampal complex, compared with that of more severely impaired subjects, but the entire amygdala was diffusely abnormal.

In the septum, reduced cell size and increased cell-packing density were similarly observed in the medial septal nucleus in all cases. However, a different pattern of abnormality was found in the nucleus of the vertical limb of the diagonal band of Broca (NDB). Compared with controls, unusually large but otherwise normal-appearing neurons, present in adequate numbers, were found in all the autistic patients younger than age 12. In contrast, these same neurons were noted to be small and markedly fewer in all the autistic patients older than age 22.

Outside of the forebrain, additional abnormalities in the autistic brains have been limited to the cerebellum and related inferior olive. In all cases, a marked reduction in the number of Purkinje cells was observed throughout the cerebellar hemispheres, most dramatically in the posterolateral neocerebellar cortex and adjacent archicerebellar cortex, with sparing of the vermis (Arin, Bauman, & Kemper, 1991; Bauman & Kemper, 1996). Abnormalities also have been found in the globose, emboliform, and fastigal nuclei located in the roof of the cerebellum which, like the findings in the septum, appear to differ with age. Small pale neurons that are reduced in number are seen in these nuclei in all the autistic patients older than age 22. However, in all the younger autistic subjects, these same neurons and those of the dentate nucleus are enlarged and present in adequate numbers (Bauman & Kemper, 1994).

No evidence of atrophy or cell loss was found in the principal inferior olivary nucleus of the brainstem in any of the autistic brains, areas known to be related to the abnormal regions of the cerebellum (Holmes & Stewart, 1908). Because of this close relationship, neuronal cell loss and atrophy of the inferior olive invariably have been noted in human neuropathology after the perinatal and postnatal loss of Purkinje cells (Norman, 1940; Greenfield, 1954). In the three oldest cases, the olivary neurons were small and pale but exhibited no evidence of cell loss. In all the younger subjects, these same neurons were enlarged but otherwise normal-appearing.

IMPLICATIONS OF LIMBIC SYSTEM ABNORMALITIES FOR AUTISM

Microscopical analysis of the brain in autism has shown abnormalities that have been confined consistently to the limbic system, the cerebellum, and the related inferior olive. The findings of decreased neuronal cell size and increased cell-packing density that characterize the limbic system are consistent with a pattern of developmental curtailment involving this circuitry. This concept is supported further by the presence of decreased complexity and extent of dendritic arbors observed in the pyramidal cells of the hippocampus.

Given its extensive network of interrelated circuits and widespread connections to other parts of the brain, abnormalities of the limbic system could disrupt significantly the function of the limbic and sensory association neocortex and the reticulate core of the brain. Lesions in experimental animals involving the structures of the medial temporal lobe have shown pronounced effects of emotion, behavior, motivation, and learning, many of which effects resemble the clinical features of autism. Purposeless hyperactivity, severe impairment in social relatedness, hyperexploratory behavior, and the inability to remember or recognize the significance of visually or manually examined objects have been observed in monkeys after bilateral surgical ablations of the medial temporal lobe (Kluver & Bucy, 1939). Similar behaviors have been noted after comparable neurosurgical lesions in humans (Terzian & Delle-Ore, 1955).

Selective lesions involving specific medial temporal lobe structures, introduced experimentally in adult animals, have provided further insight into the function of each of these individual regions. In the rat, bilateral ablations of the hippocampus produced hyperactive animals with stereotypical motor behavior and unusual responses to novel stimuli (Roberts, Dember, & Brodwick, 1962; Kimble, 1963). Similar surgical lesions in monkeys, confined to the amygdala, resulted in animals who exhibited loss of fear of normally aversive stimuli, compulsive indiscriminate examination of objects, and withdrawal from formerly socially rewarding situations (Mishkin & Aggleton, 1981). Further, these same animals showed a reduced ability to attach meaning to new environments based on past experience, resulting in poor adaptability to novel situations. When ablations were confined to the most medially located amygdalar structures (the central, medial, and cortical nuclei), the influence of familiarization on learning was reduced significantly (Vergnes, 1981). Further evidence for the importance of the amygdala for learning has been supplied by Murray and Mishkin (1985). In these studies, monkeys experienced a severe impairment of cross-modal associative memory after bilateral ablations of the amygdala. These animals failed to recognize visually an object that had been examined previously by taste or touch. These observations suggests that one of the major functions of the amygdala may be the integration and generalization of information that is processed by multiple sensory systems

in the brain, a skill that is typically difficult for autistic individuals.

In 1991, Squire and Zola-Morgan reconsidered the hypothesized relationship of medial temporal lobe structures to memory. They noted that the severe memory loss previously attributed to bilateral combined lesions of the amygdala and hippocampus was the result of inadvertent surgical damage to the cortical regions adjacent to the amygdala, not to the inclusion of the amygdala, as previously believed (Mishkin, 1978). Thus, it appears that structures involved in the medial temporal lobe memory system include the hippocampal formation and related entorhinal, perirhinal, and parahippocampal cortices and that the amygdala is not a component of this system.

Studies in human and nonhuman primates have suggested the presence of at least two memory systems: representational or associative memory, and procedural or habit memory (Mishkin & Appenzeller, 1987; Murray, 1990; Squire & Zola-Morgan, 1991). Representational memory is believed to involve all sensory modalities and mediates the processing of facts, experiences, and events and the integration and generalization of information that leads to higher-order cognition and learning. In contrast, habit memory is involved in skill learning and automatic connections between stimulus and response. The two systems are believed to be anatomically separate, representational memory depending on the hippocampus, amygdala, and areas related to them, whereas the anatomical substrate for habit memory is believed to reside in the striatum and neocortex of the cerebral hemispheres. Neuropathological studies of the brain in autism have shown no abnormalities of the striatum and, with the exception of the anterior cingulate cortex, the neocortex likewise is unremarkable. In contrast, the hippocampal complex, amygdala, entorhinal cortex, septum, and medial mammillary body have shown significant abnormalities. Thus, the substrate for representational memory appears to be selectively abnormal in the autistic brain, whereas the structures responsible for habit memory appear to be spared.

Though the effect of an early disturbance to the limbic system structures is unknown, likely curtailment of development and prenatally acquired lesions in these regions could disrupt or distort the acquisition and interpretation of information. Such a disturbance in the processing of information could lead to the disordered cognition, social interaction, and language characteristics of the autistic child. In contrast, the preservation of the habit memory system could account for the need for sameness and preoccupation with a narrow range of interests and activities and for the outstanding memory for rote information observed in some autistic individuals.

Studies have suggested that these two neural systems mature at different times in both human and nonhuman primates, the habit system being functional early in life, though the representational system develops later in childhood (Bachevalier & Mishkin, 1991; Overman et al., 1992). Given this pattern of cognitive maturation, possibly a developmentally dysfunctional neuronal circuitry involving the limbic system would have little impact during the first 1 to 2 years of life. However, with development, the effect of this dysfunctional circuitry gradually may become evident, leading to what appears to be social, language, and cognitive deterioration—features frequently reported as part of the early history of childhood autism.

IMPLICATIONS OF CEREBELLAR ABNORMALITIES

Areas of abnormality outside the forebrain in autism have been confined to the cerebellum

and related inferior olive. Marked reduction in the number and size of Purkinje cells has been noted, primarily in the posterior and inferior regions of the hemispheres, with sparing of the vermis and without the presence of significant gliosis. The absence of glial hyperplasia suggests that the lesions have been acquired early in development. Animal studies have shown a progressively decreasing glial response after cerebellar lesions at increasingly early ages (Brodal, 1940).

The preservation of the neurons of the inferior olive further support an early origin for the cerebellar abnormalities. Retrograde loss of olivary neurons regularly occurs after cerebellar lesions in immature postnatal and adult animals (Brodal, 1940) and neonatal (Norman, 1940) and adult humans (Homes & Stewart, 1908; Greenfield, 1954), presumably because of the close relationship of the olivary climbing-fiber axons to the Purkinje cell dendrites (Eccles, Ito, & Szentagothai, 1967).

In the fetal monkey, prior to establishing their definitive relationship with the Purkinje cells dendrites, the olivary climbing fibers have been shown to synapse in a transitory zone beneath the Purkinje cells called the *lamina desiccans* (Rakic, 1971). In the human fetus, this zone is no longer present after 30 to 32 weeks' gestation (Rakic & Sidman, 1970). Therefore, in the absence of retrograde cell loss in the olive in the presence of a marked reduction in the number of Purkinje cells, likely the cerebellar cortical lesions seen in autism have their onset at or before this time.

The relationship of the cerebellar findings to the clinical features of autism is unclear. Dysfunction of the cerebellum beginning before birth may be associated with few if any neurological symptoms (Norman, 1940; Adams, Corselis, & Duchen, 1984). Studies in adult animals have demonstrated both a pathway between the fastigial nucleus of the cerebellum and the amygdala and septal nuclei of the limbic system and a reciprocal connection between this nucleus and the hippocampus, suggesting that the cerebellum may play a role in the regulation of emotion and higher cortical thought (Heath & Harper, 1974; Heath et al., 1978). The cerebellum also has been implicated in the regulation of affective behavior (Berman, Berman, & Prescott, 1974) and in functional psychiatric disorders (Heath et al., 1979).

More recently, studies in animals and humans have suggested a role for the cerebellum in cognition, including mental imagery and anticipatory planning (Leiner, Leiner, & Dow, 1987) and in some aspects of language processing (Peterson et al., 1989). Further, the cerebellum has been implicated in the control of voluntary shift of selective attention between one sensory modality and another, for example, shifting between auditory and visual attention (Akshoomoff & Courchesne, 1992; Courchesne et al., 1994). Also, the cerebellum has been suggested to play a possible role in cognitive planning, a function independent of memory and most significant in novel situations (Grafman et al., 1992). More recently, studies in monkeys have established that the dorsolateral prefrontal cortex, believed to be involved in spatial working memory, is the target of output from the dentate nucleus of the cerebellum (Middleton & Strick, 1994). This relationship to the prefrontal cortex suggests that the cerebellum may be involved in the planning and timing of future behavior. Thus, a growing body of evidence suggests that the cerebellum is important in the regulation of the speed, consistency, and appropriateness of mental and cognitive processes and in the control of motor and sensory information and activity (Schmahmann, 1991). Therefore, it is likely the anatomical abnormalities observed

in the cerebellum in autism contribute to many of the atypical behaviors and disordered information-processing characteristic of the syndrome. However, the precise functional significance of these abnormalities, their relationship to the findings observed in the limbic system, and their impact on the specific features of autism remain to be elucidated.

CONCLUSION

Although science has made significant advances in our understanding of autism, particularly within the last 15 years, numerous challenges remain. Most now accept that autism is a disorder of neurological development probably occurring or beginning before birth. The most obvious anatomical abnormalities of the brain appear to be selective and appear to be confined to the limbic system and to the cerebellum and related inferior olive. Although now genetics appears possibly to play a significant etiological role, the pathogenic mechanisms for the disorder remain unknown. Future research undoubtedly will be directed toward elucidating the genetic profile associated with autism, thereby offering opportunities for prenatal and more precise and earlier postnatal diagnosis. Equally important will be the pursuit of in vivo functional imaging studies and neurochemical analysis of autopsy material, with a particular emphasis on the parts of the brain identified as being abnormal. Autism also is a disorder that offers the clinical investigator an unusual opportunity to study multiple aspects of atypical cognition, emotion, social awareness, language, and behavior from a developmental perspective, and likely, science ultimately may have a better understanding of normal development as the result of these present and future research efforts. ∎

REFERENCES

Aarkrog, T. (1968). Organic factors in infantile psychoses and borderline psychoses: Retrospective study of 45 cases subjected to pneumoencephalography. *Danish Medical Bulletin, 15*, 283-288.

Adams, J. H., Corselis, J. A. N., & Duchen, L. W. (1984). *Greenfield's neuropathology.* New York: Wiley.

Akshoomoff, N. A., & Courchesne, E. (1992). A new role for the cerebellum in cognitive operations. *Behavioral Neuroscience, 106*, 731-738.

Arin, D. M., Bauman, M. L., & Kemper, T. L. (1991). The distribution of Purkinje cell loss in the cerebellum in autism [abstract]. *Neurology, 41*, 307.

Bachevalier, J., & Mishkin, M. (1991). Effects of neonatal lesions of the amygdaloid complex or hippocampal formation on the development of visual recognition memory. *Society Neuroscience Abstract, 17*, 338.

Bauman, M. L., & Kemper, T. L. (1994). Neuroanatomic observations of the brain in autism. In M. L. Bauman & T. L. Kemper (Eds.), *The neurobiology of autism* (pp. 119-145). Baltimore, Johns Hopkins University Press.

Bauman, M. L., & Kemper, T. L. (1995). Neuroanatomic observations of the brain in autism. In J. Panksepp (Ed.), *Advances in biological psychiatry* (pp. 1-26). New York: JAI Press.

Bauman, M. L., & Kemper, T. L. (1996). Observations on the Purkinje cells in the cerebellar vermis in autism [abstract]. *Journal of Neuropathology and Experimental Neurology, 55*, 613.

Berman, A. J., Berman, D., & Prescott, J. W. (1974). The effect of cerebellar lesions on emotional behavior in the rhesus monkey. In I. S. Cooper, M. Kiklan, & R. S. Snyder (Eds.), *The cerebellum, epilepsy and behavior* (pp. 227-284). New York: Plenum.

Boucher, J., & Warrington, E. K. (1976). Memory deficits in early infantile autism: Some similarities to the amnestic syndrome. *British Journal of Psychology, 67*, 73-87.

Brodal, A. (1940). Modification of the Gudden method for study of cerebral localization. *Archives of Neurology and Psychiatry 43*, 46-58.

Chugani, D. C., Muzil, O., Chakraborty, P., et al. (1996). Brain serotonin synthesis measured with 11C alpha methyl-tryptophan positron emission tomography in normal and autistic subjects [abstract]. *Annals of Neurology, 40*, 296.

Coleman, M. (1979). Studies of autistic syndromes. In R. Katzman (Ed.), *Congenital and acquired cognitive disorders* (pp. 265-303). New York: Raven.

Coleman, P. D., Romano, J., Lapham, L., et al. (1985). Cell counts in cerebral cortex in an autistic patient. *Journal of Autism and Developmental Disorders, 15*, 245-255.

Courchesne, E., Courchesne, R. Y., Hicks, G., et al. (1985a). Functioning of the brain stem auditory pathway in non-retarded autistic individuals. *Electroencephalography and Clinical Neurophysiology, 51*, 491-501.

Courchesne, E., Hesselink, J. R., Jernigan, T. L., et al. (1987). Abnormal neuroanatomy in a non-retarded person with autism. *Archives of Neurology, 44*, 335-341.

Courchesne, E., Lincoln, A. J., Kilman, B. A., et al. (1985b). Event-related brain potential correlates of the processing of novel visual and auditory information in autism. *Journal of Autism and Developmental Disorders, 15*, 55-76.

Courchesne, E., Townsend, J., & Saitoh, O. (1994). The brain in infantile autism. *Neurology, 44*, 214-228.

Courchesne, E., Yeung-Courchesne, R., Press, G. A., et al. (1988). Hypoplasia of cerebellar vermal lobules VI and VII in autism. *New England Journal of Medicine, 318*, 1349-1454.

Darby, J. H. (1976). Neuropathological aspects of psychosis in childhood. *Journal of Autism and Childhood Schizophrenia, 6*, 339-352.

Dawson, G., & Lew, A. (1989). Arousal, attention, and socioemotional impairments of individuals with autism. In G. Dawson (Ed.), *Autism: Nature, diagnosis and treatment* (pp. 49-74). New York: Guilford.

Delong, G. R. (1978). A neuropsychological interpretation of infantile autism. In M. Rutter & E. Schopler (Eds.), *Autism*. New York: Plenum.

Damasio, A. R., & Maurer, R. G. (1978). A neurological model for childhood autism. *Archives of Neurology, 35*, 777-786.

Damasio, H., Maurer, R. G., Damasio, A. R., et al. (1980). Computerized tomographic scan findings in patients with autistic behavior. *Archives of Neurology, 37*, 504-510.

De Volder, A., Bol, A., Michel, C., et al. (1987). Brain glucose metabolism in children with the autistic syndrome: Positron tomography analysis. *Brain Development 9*, 581-587.

Deykin, E. Y., & MacMahon, B. (1979). The incidence of seizures among children with autistic symptoms. *American Journal of Psychiatry, 136*, 1312-1313.

Diagnostic and Statistical Manual of Mental Disorders (4th ed.) (1994). Washington, D.C.: American Psychiatric Association.

Eccles, J. C., Ito, M., & Szentagothai, J. (1967). *The cerebellum as a neural machine*. New York: Springer.

Filipek, P. A., Richelme, C., Kennedy, D. N., et al. (1992). Morphometric analysis of the brain in developmental language disorders and autism [abstract]. *Annals of Neurology, 32*, 475.

Gaffney, G. R., Kuperman, S. Tsai, L. Y., et al. (1988). Morphological evidence of brainstem involvement in infantile autism. *Biological Psychiatry, 24*, 578-586.

Grafman, J., Litvan, I., Massaquoi, S., et al. (1992). Cognitive planning deficit in patients with cerebellar atrophy. *Neurology, 42*, 1493-1496.

Grandin, T. (1995, November). *Autism: A personal perspective*. Paper presented at Current Trends in Autism, Boston, MA.

Greenfield, J. G. (1954). *The spino-cerebellar degenerations*. Springfield, IL: Charles C. Thomas.

Hauser, S. L., Delong, G. R., & Rosman, N. P. (1975). Pneumographic findings in the infantile autism syndrome. A correlation with temporal lobe disease. *Brain, 98*, 667-688.

Heath, R. G., Dempsey, C. W., Fontana, C. J., et al. (1978). Cerebellar stimulation: Effects on septal region, hippocampus and amygdala of cats and rats. *Biological Psychiatry, 113*, 501-529.

Heath, R. G., Franklin, D. E., & Shraberg, D. (1979). Gross pathology of the cerebellum in patients diagnosed and treated as functional psychiatric disorders. *Journal of Nervous and Mental Disorders, 167*, 585-592.

Heath, R. G., & Harper, J. W. (1974). Ascending projections of the cerebellar fastigial nucleus to the hippocampus, amygdala and other temporal lobe sites: Evoked potential and other histologic studies in monkeys and cats. *Experimental Neurology, 45*, 268-287.

Herold, S., Frackowiak, R. S. J., LeCourteur, A., et al. (1988). Cerebral blood flow and metabolism of oxygen and glucose in young autistic adults. *Psychological Medicine, 18*, 823-831.

Hier, D. B., LeMay, M., & Rosenberger, P. B. (1979). Autism and unfavorable left-right asymmetries of the brain. *Journal of Autism and Developmental Disorders, 9*, 153-159.

Holmes, G., & Steward, T. G. (1980). On the connection of the inferior olives with the cerebellum in man. *Brain, 31*, 125-137.

Holttum, J. R., Minshew, N. J., Sanders, R. S., et al. (1992). Magnetic resonance imaging of the posterior fossa in autism. *Biological Psychiatry, 32*, 1091-1101.

Horwitz, B., Rumsey, J. M., Grady, C., et al. (1988). The cerebral metabolic landscape in autism: Intercorrelations of regional glucose utilization. *Archives of Neurology, 45*, 749-755.

Jacobson, R., Lecouteur, A., Howlin, P., et al. (1988). Selective subcortical abnormalities in autism. *Psychological Medicine, 18*, 39-48.

Kanner, L. (1943). Autistic disturbances of affective contact. *Nervous Child, 2*, 217-250.

Kimble, D. P. (1963). The effects of bilateral hippocampal lesions in rats. *Journal of Physiological Psychology 56*, 273-283.

Kinsbourne, M. (1991). Overfocussing: An apparent subtype of attention deficit-hyperactivity disorder. *Pediatric and Adolescent Medicine 1*, 18-35.

Kleiman, M. D., Neff, S., & Rosman, N. P. (1992). The brain in infantile autism. *Neurology 42*, 753-760.

Kluver, H., & Bucy, P. (1939). Preliminary analysis of functions of the temporal lobes in monkeys. *Archives of Neurology and Psychiatry 42*, 979-1000.

Kurita, H. (1985). Infantile autism with speech loss before the age of thirty months. *Journal of Child Psychiatry, 24*(2), 191-196.

Leiner, H. C., Leiner, A. L., & Dow, R. S. (1987). Cerebellar learning loops in apes and humans. *Italian Journal of Neurological Science, 8*, 425-436.

Maurer, R. G., & Demasio, A. R. (1982). Childhood autism from the point of view of behavioral neurology. *Journal of Autism and Developmental Disorders, 12*, 195-205.

Middleton, F. A., & Strick, P. L. (1994). Anatomical evidence for cerebellar and basal ganglia involvement in higher cognitive function. *Science, 266*, 458-461.

Minshew, N. J. (1991). Indices of neural function in autism: Clinical and biologic implications. *Pediatrics, 87* (Suppl.), 774-780.

Minshew, N. J. (1994). In vivo brain chemistry of autism: 31P magnetic resonance spectroscopy studies. In M. L. Bauman & T. L. Kemper (Eds.), *The neurobiology of autism* (pp. 86-101). Baltimore: Johns Hopkins University Press.

Minshew, N. J., & Payton, J. B. (1988). New perspectives in autism: I. The clinical spectrum of autism. *Current Problems in Pediatrics, 18*(10), 567-610.

Mishkin, M. (1978). Memory in monkeys severely impaired by combined but not separate removal of amygdala and hippocampus. *Nature, 273*, 297-298.

Mishkin, M., & Aggleton, J. P. (1981). Multiple functional contributors of the amygdala in the monkey from the amygdaloid complex. In Y. Ben-Ari (Ed.), *The amygdaloid complex. INSERM symposium: No. 20* (pp. 409-419). Amsterdam: Elsevier-North Holland.

Mishkin, M., & Appenzeller, T. (1987). The anatomy of memory. *Scientific American, 256*, 80-89.

Murakami, J. W., Courchesne, E., Press, G. A., et al. (1989). Reduced cerebellar hemisphere size and its relationship to vermal hypoplasia in autism. *Archives of Neurology, 46*, 689-694.

Murray, E. A. (1990). Representational memory in non-human primates. In R. P. Kesner & D. S. Olton (Eds.), *Neurobiology of comparative cognition* (pp. 127-155). Hillsdale, NJ: Erlbaum.

Murray, E. A., & Mishkin, M. (1985). Amygdaloidectomy impairs crossmodal association in monkeys. *Science, 228*, 604-606.

Norman, R. M. (1940). Cerebellar atrophy associated with etat marbre of the basal ganglia. *Journal of Neurology and Psychiatry, 3*, 311-318.

Novick, B., Kurtzberg, D., & Vaughan, H. G. (1979). An electrophysiologic indication of defective information storage in childhood autism. *Psychiatry Research, 1*, 101-108.

Ornitz, E. M., & Ritvo, E. R. (1968). Neurophysiologic mechanisms underlying perceptual inconstancy in autistic and schizophrenic children. *Archives of General Psychiatry, 19*, 22-27.

Overman, W., Bachevalier, J., Turner, M., et al. (1992). Object recognition versus object discrimination: Comparison between human infants and infant monkeys. *Behavioral Neuroscience, 106*, 15-29.

Peterson, S. F., Fox, P. T., Posner, M. I., et al. (1989). Positron emission tomographic studies in the processing of single words. *Journal of Cognitive Neuroscience 1*, 153-170.

Piven, J., Nehme, E., Simon, J., et al. (1992). Magnetic resonance imaging in autism: Measurement of the cerebellum, pons and fourth ventricle. *Biological Psychiatry, 31*, 491-504.

Rakic, P. (1971). Neuron-glia relationship during granule cell migration in developing cerebellar cortex: A Golgi and electron microscopic study in macacus rhesus. *Journal of Comparative Neurology, 141*, 282-312.

Rakic, P., & Sidman, R. L. (1970). Histogenesis of the cortical layers in the human cerebellum particularly the lamina dissecans. *Journal of Comparative Neurology 139*, 473-500.

Rapin, I. (1991). Autistic children: Diagnosis and clinical features. *Pediatrics, 87* (Suppl.), 751-760.

Rapin, I., & Allen, D. A. (1987). Developmental dysphasia and autism in preschool children: Characteristics and subtypes. In *Proceedings of the first international symposium on specific speech and language disorders in children* (pp. 20-35). London, England: Association of All Speech Impaired Children.

Rapin, I., Mattis, S., Rowan, A. J., et al. (1977). Verbal auditory agnosia in children. *Developmental Medicine and Child Neurology, 19*, 192-207.

Raymond, G., Bauman, M. L., & Kemper, T. L. (1996). Hippocampus in autism: A Golgi analysis. *Acia Neuropathologica, 91*, 117-119.

Ritvo, E. R., & Garber, J. H. (1988). Cerebellar hypoplasia and autism [abstract]. *New England Journal of Medicine, 319*, 1152.

Roberts, W. W., Dember, W. N., & Brodwick, H. (1962). Alteration and exploration in rats with hippocampal lesions. *Journal of Comparative Psychiatry, 55*, 695-700.

Rumsey, J. M., Creasey, H., Stepanek, J. S., et al. (1988). Hemispheric asymmetries, fourth ventricular size and cerebellar morphology in autism. *Journal of Autism and Developmental Disorders, 18*, 127-137.

Rumsey, J. M., Duara, R., Grady, C., et al. (1985). Brain metabolism in autism. *Archives of General Psychiatry, 42*, 448-455.

Rumsey, J. M., Grimes, A. M., Pikus, A. M., et al. (1984). Auditory brainstem responses in pervasive developmental disorders. *Biological Psychiatry, 19*, 1403-1417.

Rutter, M. (1978). Diagnosis and definition of childhood autism. In M. Rutter & E. Schopler (Eds.), *Autism: A reappraisal of concepts and treatment* (pp. 1-25). New York: Plenum.

Schmahmann, J. D. (1991). An emerging concept: The cerebellar contribution to higher function. *Archives of Neurology, 48,* 1178-1187.

Small, J. G. (1975). EEG and neurophysiologic studies of early infantile autism. *Biological Psychiatry, 10*(4), 385-397.

Squire, L. R., & Zola-Morgan, S. (1991). The medial temporal lobe memory system. *Science, 253,* 1380-1386.

Student, M., & Schmer, H. (1978). Evidence from auditory nerve and brainstem evoked responses for an organic lesion in children with autistic traits. *Journal of Autism and Childhood Schizophrenia, 8,* 13-20.

Tanguay, P. E., Edwards, R. M., Buchwald, J., Schwofel, J., & Allen, V. (1982). Auditory brain stem evoked responses in autistic children. *Archives of General Psychiatry, 38,* 174-180.

Tanguay, P. E., Ornitz, E. M., Forsythe, A. B., & Ritvo, E. R. (1976). Rapid eye movement (REM) activity in normal and autistic children during REM sleep. *Journal of Autism and Childhood Schizophrenia, 6,* 275-288.

Terzian, H., & Delle-Ore, G. (1955). Syndrome of Kluver and Bucy reproduced in man by bilateral removal of the temporal lobes. *Neurology, 3,* 373-380.

Tsai, L. Y., Jacoby, O. G., & Steward, M. A. (1983). Morphological cerebral asymmetries in autistic children. *Biological Psychiatry, 18,* 317-327.

Vergnes, M. (1981). Effect of prior familiarization with mice on elicitation of mouse killing in rats: Role of the amygdala. In Y. Ben-Ari (Ed.), *The amygdaloid complex. INSERM symposium: No. 20* (pp. 293-304). Amsterdam: Elsevier-North Holland.

Vilensky, J. A., Demasio, A. R., & Maurer, R. G. (1981). Gait disturbances in patients with autistic behavior. *Archives of Neurology, 38,* 646-649.

Williams, R. S., Hauser, S. L., Purpura, D. P., et al. (1980). Autism and mental retardation. *Archives of Neurology, 37,* 749-753.

Wood, C. C., McCarthy, G., Squires, N. K., et al. (1984). Anatomical and physiological substrates of event related potentials: Two case studies. *Annals of the New York Academy of Science, 425,* 681-721.

Yakovlev, P. I. (1970). Whole brain serial sections. In C. G. Tedeschi (Ed.), *Neuropathology: Methods and diagnosis* (pp. 371-378). Boston: Little, Brown.

◄ 30 ►

The "BOLD" Approach:
A Multimodal Format for Understanding
Communication and Learning Disorders

Mark Rosenbloom, M.D., and Galina D. Kitchens, M.A.

Communication and learning disorders, similar to other disorders, are multiply determined and influenced by interacting and interdependent levels of genetic, physiological, social, and behavioral processes. The BOLD approach presents a multimodal format to identify, assess, treat, and guide research of these disorders. This approach takes into account the broad context of interlocking influences on communication and learning disorders, including **B**iological milieu, **O**riginal traits, **L**earned behaviors, and **D**erived behaviors (or BOLD). Although there has been an explosion of information, research, and analysis in the field of communication and learning disorders, there has been a lack of consistency in approach, presentation, and structure. The BOLD format was developed to address this lack by facilitating comparisons of ideas across disciplines and to expedite recommendations and evaluations of relevant research.

The BOLD format was developed by a physician and parent to synthesize, analyze, categorize, and interpret the vast array of emerging knowledge about communication and learning disorders. In developing this approach, its creator, Mark Rosenbloom, found it useful to (1) summarize current knowledge, (2) clarify research needs and directions, (3) evaluate a child by clearly delineating individual behaviors and looking for underlying determinants of these behaviors, and (4) identify, implement, and evaluate appropriate interventions. The purpose of this chapter is to introduce the concepts and uses of the BOLD format.

There are numerous categorical diagnostic labels, such as attention deficit hyperactivity disorder (ADHD), autistic spectrum disorders (ASD), pervasive developmental disorder (PDD), and dyslexia, as well as specific learning disorders. Innovative investigators may use these syndromes as a window to making new observations. Over-adherence to these formal syndromes as fixed categories with expected (but not fully identified) biological pathways, however, may lead the field to overlook the significance of multiple determinants and interlocking, systematic influences within each disorder. Such limitations often result in offering unitary treatment approaches to patients labeled with one of the preceding diagnoses. As discussed in other chapters of this book, a broader, functional approach is needed to include more eclectic intervention and more treatment options, and to accommodate individual needs of children who display unique patterns of functional deficits.

In Chapter 3, "Clinical Practice for Principles of Assessment and Intervention," it was pointed out that at the current level of knowledge and understanding, a fixed, syndrome-based approach overstates the current evidence with regard to communication and learning disorders. These disorders do not appear to have a single, fixed biological pathway. There is a tendency, however, to focus on specific behavior symptoms without sufficient attention to the full range of the underlying biological differences. In fact, the same behavior can often be caused by the opposite patterns. For example, one "autistic" child may bang his head as an attempt to drown out overwhelming sensory input. Another may engage in the same behavior in order to create sensation because he is afflicted with sensory deficits and wants to break through the extreme sensory insensitivity. Hypothetically, from a biological standpoint, the same behavior may be caused by a serotonin deficiency *or* a serotonin excess.

There is understandable pressure to go beyond existing data and oversimplify categorization of developmental and learning disorders with children who, at present, do not have identifiable fixed etiologies. The goal of the BOLD approach is to consider the multiple factors that influence communication and learning disorders with a focus on relating recent neuroscience research (see the prior two chapters) in the context of different biological levels (e.g., genetics, constitutional, and developmental patterns) with different levels of observed behavior (e.g., different levels of adaptation and maladaptation). It attempts to look relatively more microscopically at the interface between biology and experience as part of the overall Developmental-Individual differences-Relationship-based (DIR) model described in other chapters.

Research has indicated that communication and learning disorders result from complex dynamics between genetic and environmental factors (Folstein & Rutter, 1988; Troittier, Srivastava, & Walker, 1999). The BOLD approach may prove helpful in that it addresses the factors that serve as modifiers at each of four levels. These levels include: **B**iological milieu, **O**riginal or primary traits, **L**earned or secondary behaviors (simple "coping mechanisms") and **D**erived or tertiary behaviors. Interactions between a level and its modifiers result in changes at subsequent levels. Thus, the dynamic of environmental factors modifying the first level, biological milieu, leads to the second level of the model, original traits. Even though the second level is closely related to genetic composition, it is not purely genetic. Instead, various influences of the chemical and physical environment result in expression of particular genes. Likewise, the original traits level is modified by basic stimulus-response type interactions of the child with caregivers and others resulting in level three, learned behaviors. This level is represented by an array of "coping mechanisms," basic in nature and rudimentary in structure. Finally, the fourth level of the model, derived behaviors, results from a dynamic interplay between a child's learned behaviors (level three) and the response of the child's complex social environment to his or her learned behaviors. However, unlike the third level, derived behaviors go beyond basic coping mechanisms. They are highly complex, goal directed, and require higher processing. The interconnectedness among the four levels of the model stipulates a multimodal approach for organizing a large amount of information and for assessment and treatment. What follows is a more detailed description of each level of the model.

LEVEL ONE: BIOLOGICAL MILIEU

Genes, biochemistry, and fundamental structural components of the human body, along with their environmental influences, constitute the biological milieu level. This includes the central and peripheral nervous systems and their interface with all other body systems. Although certain aspects of this level may be predictable or preventable at earlier stages of development, the structural aspects of the biological milieu are commonly thought of as essentially unchangeable in standard forms of current therapy. As knowledge expands and technology improves, modifications of biological components are becoming more possible. However, once the medical evaluation is complete for any particular child and no correctable abnormalities have been found, therapists are likely to regard biological characteristics as unmodifiable. Specific biological components that need to be addressed in connection with communication and learning disorders include, at a minimum, the basic genetic structure, central and peripheral nervous systems, neurotransmitters, the immune system, and the digestive system.

A strong genetic component of communication and learning disorders has been consistently supported by research (Folstein, Bisson, Santangelo, & Piven, 1998; MacLean et al., 1999). A 60% to 91% concordance rate for autistic spectrum disorders was found among monozygotic twin pairs, while the concordance rate among dizygotic twins was significantly lower, between 3% and 5% (Bailey et al., 1995; Gillberg, 1998; Steffenburg, 1989). In 25% of cases, autism appeared to be associated with genetic disorders, such as fragile X syndrome. Although it has been speculated that more than one gene may be involved in the etiology of the developmental disorders, the exact genetic mechanisms have not been identified. However, some advances have been made in identifying the connection between certain autism markers of brain development (three markers of the c-Harvey-

ros oncogene) and homebox gene EN2, and between ADHD and the D^2 and D^4 dopamine receptors genes and the dopamine transporter gene (Faraone & Biederman, 1998; Trottier, Srivastava, & Walker, 1999). Investigations in this area continue and are expected to provide more important information about autism and other developmental disorders. Most researchers agree that genetic predisposition may be necessary but not sufficient to cause autism and that environmental insult plays an essential role in the development of the disorder (Folstein & Rutter, 1988; Trottier, Srivastava, & Walker, 1999). This notion will be addressed further in the discussion of biological milieu modifiers.

Research has further demonstrated an association between communication and learning disorders and certain structural abnormalities in the brain. Thus, intrinsic, neocortical dysfunction as well as structural anomalies in cerebellar hemispheres and vermian lobules, parietal lobe, and the posterior regions of the corpus callosum were found in association with autistic spectrum disorders (Minshew, Luna, & Sweeney, 1999; Saitoh & Courchesne, 1998). Structural anomalies were also detected in the corpus callosum and the midsagittal surface of dyslexic children (Robichon & Habib, 1998). Many children with autism display altered evoked-response potential and conduction time and about 50% have abnormal electroencephalograms (Trottier, Srivastava, & Walker, 1999). In addition, children with ADHD exhibited abnormalities in frontal cortex activation patterns (Baving, Laucht, & Schmidt, 1999; Faraone & Biederman, 1998; Zametkin et al., 1990). However, because virtually all of the studies in this area are correlational by nature, no definite conclusions can be made at this time about whether these abnormalities are causes or effects of the disorders.

Positron emission tomography (PET) studies have focused on examining brain function in addition to the simple brain structures. These studies demonstrated abnormalities in language and auditory functioning, such as reversed hemispheric dominance during verbal auditory stimulation, reduced activation of auditory cortex during acoustic stimulation, and reduced cerebellar activation during nonverbal auditory perception (Muller et al., 1999). Hypometabolic and neuronal migration anomalies were also detected in other areas of the brain (Schifter et al., 1994). In addition, individuals with ADHD exhibited working memory patterns that were different from those displayed by controls (Schwitzer et al., 2000). Neurochemical studies have investigated the role of neurotransmitters in communication and learning disorders. It appears that levels of glutamate, dopamine, serotonin, epinephrine, norepinephrine, and beta-endorphines are altered in autism, ADHD, and other developmental disorders (Carlson, 1998; Chugani et al., 1999; Leboyer et al., 1999; Vallone, Picetti, & Borrelli, 2000). In addition, alternative hypotheses implicate an overactive brain opioid system and changes in oxytocin neurotransmission (Trottier, Srivastava, & Walker, 1999).

The biological milieu is continuously influenced by physical environmental factors. For example, an association between autism and virus serology and brain autoantibody suggested that a virus-induced autoimmune response may play a causal role in autism (Singh, Lin, & Yang, 1998; Connolly et al., 1999). This hypothesis was further supported by an increased rate of autoimmune disorders found in relatives of children with autism (Comi, Zimmerman, Frye, Law, & Peeden, 1999). A number of research studies have focused on other relationships between various environmental events and communication and learning disorders (Barton & Volkmar, 1998; Bolte, 1998; Carlson, 1998; Kobayashi & Murata, 1998; Patzold, Richdale, & Tonge, 1998).

Factors that appear to be associated with and to influence these disorders are referred to in the BOLD format as modifiers. At the biological milieu level (level one), these include pregnancy variables, delivery, neonatal complications, diet, pollution, illness, medical interventions, and other insults as yet unidentified.

By examining obstetrical records, researchers of a number of studies have investigated various associations between pregnancy, delivery, neonatal experiences, and developmental disorders (including autistic spectrum disorders and ADHD) (Bolton et al., 1997; Lord, Mulloy, Wendelboe, & Schopler, 1991; Milberger, Biederman, Faraone, Guite, & Tsuang, 1997). In spite of some controversy, most researchers agree that the following events were significantly higher among individuals with communication and learning disorders in comparison to the general population: rates of prenatal, perinatal, and neonatal complications and insults (e.g., bleeding, smoking, illicit drug use, family problems, or viral infections during pregnancy), birth complications, use of anesthetics during delivery, low birth weight, and seizures at birth (Knobloch & Pasamanick, 1975; Milberger et al., 1997; Ticher, Ring, Barak, Elizur, & Weizman, 1996; Torrey, Hersh, & McCabe, 1975). Furthermore, an association was found between pregnancy and delivery complications and the development of tardive and withdrawal dyskinesia in children with autism who were treated with haloperidol (Armenteros, Adams, Campbell, & Eisenberg, 1995). Further research is needed to explore relationships between communication and learning disorders and such teratogenic factors as malnutrition, stress, prescribed and illicit drugs, various diseases, and radiation exposure. Despite the significant excess of total obstetric complications observed in connection with developmental disorders, no single event or combination of adversities could reasonably account for any large number of cases of a particular disorder (Deykin & MacMahon, 1980).

Diet may also modify, in various ways, the biological milieu in terms of developmental disorders. For example, some researchers suggest that abnormal levels of glutamate in children with autism may be dietary by origin, and dietary interventions have been demonstrated to be beneficial for children with ADHD (Boris & Mandel, 1994; Moreno-Fuenmayor, 1996). Ecological conditions, such as air, water, and ground pollution, have been considered in association with the etiology of autism (Sanua, 1986). Medical illnesses such as epileptic seizures and viral diseases, especially when experienced in early childhood, have also been found to be associated with developmental disorders (Kobayashi & Murata, 1998).

Of course, there are biological milieu modifiers that are intentional, such as surgery or medications directed toward symptom reduction of the communication and learning disorder. Studies suggest that more than 50% of patients are treated with one or more medications and that this treatment results in some symptom relief for many of them (Aman, Van Bourgondien, Wolford, & Sarphare, 1995). In addition, reduction in autistic symptoms was reported in patients who underwent epilepsy-related brain surgery (Gillberg, Uvebrant, Carlsson, Hedstrom & Silfvenius, 1996). It has also been suggested that some of the medical interventions not targeted at developmental disorders, such as antibiotics or vaccinations, may be affecting the biological milieu. Indeed, research indicates that a significant percentage of individuals with autism have a history of extensive antibiotic use. Inasmuch as oral antibiotics disrupt protective intestinal microbiota and create a favorable environment for colonization by opportunistic pathogens, it is feasible that some of these pathogens (e.g., Clostridium tetani) may result in production of neurotoxins that disrupt neurotransmission (Bolte, 1998). However, the literature remains controversial in reference to the hypothesized link between vaccines (particularly MMR) and developmental disorders (Boyles & Key, 1998; Duclos & Ward, 1998). Additional biological milieu modifiers are likely to be identified as research in this area continues.

As previously noted, biochemical interventions (medications) can be significant modifiers of level one, biological milieu, and can affect level two, original traits, as well as subsequent levels. Ideally, assessment and treatment of the communication and learning disorder should begin at level one in order to impact effectively upon original traits and address the "core" problem, especially if treatment involves biochemical interventions. Unfortunately, medications are often utilized without assessment at this primary level. Instead, they are utilized in response to symptoms at later levels. For example, Ritalin is often utilized to "control" problems at the later behavioral levels. This can result in other expressions of the primary problem, other problematic behaviors, or a compromising of a child's ability to learn appropriate behavior without the use of medication.

LEVEL TWO: ORIGINAL/PRIMARY TRAITS

Original or primary traits are the functional, operating, core determinants of the individual's behavior. They are the biologically based individual differences in terms of the child's motor, sensory, cognitive, and affective patterns. As noted previously, these traits are not purely genetic; they emerge as a result of interactions between one's genetic makeup and the immediate chemical and physical environment that promotes expression of some genes while hindering that of others.

Whether original traits are modifiable depends on a child's current developmental stage in the biological life cycle. The earlier an intervention occurs, the more likely it is to result in successful modification of original traits. While evaluating and treating communication and learning disorders, a number of original traits can be considered in terms of the child's strengths or weaknesses in respective areas. These traits include but are not limited to visual and auditory acuity and processing, sensory modulation, motor planning/sequencing and kinesthetic processing, affective processing, cognitive functioning, and memory processing.

Research literature highlights a number of differences in original traits that distinguish individuals with communication and learning disorders from the general population. Thus, abnormalities in visual acuity and processing were consistently detected among children with autism (Scharre & Creedon, 1992). A nonnegligible number of children with autism were also found to have peripheral hearing impairments (Kiln, 1993). For children with learning disabilities, hearing loss compounded a significant part of their communication and educational problems (Welsh, Welsh, & Healy, 1996). Stereotypical behaviors, specifically behavioral rigidities, often displayed by children with developmental disorders were found to be associated with tactile defensiveness (Baranek, Foster, & Berkson, 1997). Some anomalies in sensory processing and sensorimotor functioning were detected among children with autism as early as at 9-12 months of age (Baranek, 1999). Multichanneled sensory processing and remarkably detailed memory for past events were reported in high-functioning individuals with autism (Cesaroni & Garber, 1991). Children with autism showed reduced expression of positive affect while interacting with their family members (Joseph & Tager-Flusberg, 1997). Finally, children with

autism did not appear impaired on metamemory tasks but rarely made spontaneous use of memory strategies (Farrant, Boucher, & Blades, 1999).

A number of these and other anomalies in original traits can be referred directly to the biological characteristics described in the previous section. For example, neurological impairments within the brain stem, the cerebellum, the midbrain, and the frontal lobe could be associated with deficits in affective processing, sensory processing, motor planning, and cognitive flexibility (Huebner, 1992). More specifically, abnormal hippocampal system function leads to the disrupted integration of information known as canalesthesia. Abnormal amygdaloid system function disrupts affect association and results in impaired assignment of the affective significance to stimuli. Impaired oxytocin system function flattens social bonding and affiliativeness, and abnormal organization of temporal and parietal polysensory regions yields aberrant overprocessing of primary representations, leading to extended selective attention (Waterhouse, Fein, & Modahl, 1996).

Modifiers of original traits include sensory stimuli from the child's environment. The nature of the environmental stimuli will affect the child's ability to progress normally through subsequent developmental stages. A child with adequate ability to process the sounds, sights, movements, events, and circumstances impinging upon her senses from the surrounding environment will progress adequately unless the environmental stimuli are inadequate, depriving, excessive, threatening, overly harsh, erratic, unusual, or inconsistent. Developmental delay, or even a disorder, may then result. The child's ability to advance adaptively to the level of learned behaviors or derived behaviors may also be compromised inasmuch as there is diminished ability to respond appropriately to normal patterns of learning contingencies, modeling, and interaction. A child with inadequate processing abilities may, of course, also experience developmental delay or disorder even in a "normal" environment. A normal environment may be excessive or depriving for a child with abnormal processing abilities. Modifying the environment specifically to target abnormalities in processing may result in adequate compensations and allow for normal development. Of course, the interactions between environmental stimuli that are depriving or excessively harsh and sensory abilities that are inadequate place a child at highest risk for communication and learning disorders or delays, especially at particular critical stages of development.

LEVEL THREE: LEARNED/SECONDARY BEHAVIORS

Various types of learned behaviors emerge as a result of interaction between the child's original traits and rudimentary sensory environmental stimuli with caregivers, family members, peers and therapists, the media, the computer, and other visual, auditory, gustatory, olfactory, and tactile stimuli. These learned behaviors can best be described as basic "coping mechanisms." They are generally connected to spoken and written language (e.g., in children diagnosed with ASD, dyslexia, and specific learning disabilities), memory and attention (e.g., in children with ADHD and ASD), impulsivity (e.g., in children with ADHD, autism, and other developmental disorders), and social interactions (especially in children with ASD) (Berger & Posner, 2000; Hardan & Sahl, 1997; Jolliffe & Baron-Cohen, 1999).

All of the learned behaviors can be divided into three broad categories: executive developmental functions, adaptive coping behaviors, and maladaptive coping behaviors.

Executive functions are behaviors that serve to organize a series of events over a long period of time. They include prolongation, or a person's ability to hold and evaluate events in working memory; separation; regulation of affect based on his ability to distinguish facts from feelings; internalization of language; and reconstitution, which involves analysis and synthesis of events. The development of these functions are often impaired or delayed in children with learning and communication disorders (Pennington & Ozonoff, 1996). This leads to a number of problems, including deficient self-regulation of mood and behavior, impaired ability to organize and plan behavior over time, inability to direct behavior toward the future, and diminished social effectiveness and adaptability (Houghton et al., 1999; Pennington & Ozonoff, 1996; Vig & Jedrysek, 1995).

Some of the research on autism has posited an association between failure to learn adaptive social behavior and autistic children's lack of a "theory of mind" (Baron-Cohen, 1996; Happe, 1995, 1997). "Theory of mind" is a term used to describe one's understanding of the motives, knowledge, and beliefs of others. This includes understanding of the mental states of self and others, including wanting, feeling, believing, and thinking (Bartsch & Wellman, 1995; Baron-Cohen, Leslie, & Frith, 1985). Such understanding is achieved and usually inferred by normally developed individuals through the acquisition of the ability for affective signaling between an infant and her caregiver and such related skills as eye contact and joint attention (Greenspan, 1995, 1997). It has been proposed that children with communication and learning disorders may be delayed in acquiring abilities related to the theory of mind and that they may have problems generalizing these abilities due to a deficient sense of "self" and/or the absence of healthy social contexts and inadequate community contacts (Hadwin, Baron-Cohen, Howlin, & Hill, 1997; Sparrevohn & Howie, 1995). However, in many cases, such apparent delays or deficiencies may actually only signify insufficient means of assessment. Examples of a more appropriate assessment model will be presented later in this chapter.

As far as the adaptability of these learned behaviors or coping mechanisms, it may be suggested that if all the child's biological milieu, original traits, and their modifiers were known, the so-called "maladaptive" behaviors could be understood in terms of their origin and purpose. This would make them not only predictable but also elucidate how the behaviors may be attempts at adaptation. Unfortunately, syndrome diagnoses are often made based on limited information about learned behaviors and in the absence of a broader picture of levels one and two. However, since the same maladaptive coping behaviors may originate from different combinations of biological milieus, original traits, and their modifiers, such generalized diagnoses may be misleading in reference to the choice of interventions. In order for the intervention strategies to be successful, all levels must be considered.

Modifiers of learned behaviors include the responses of other people in the child's environment. For example, abnormal behaviors tend to evoke responses from parents, relatives, caregivers, teachers, and the community, which may modify the learned behaviors toward better adjustment or toward further abnormality. These responses from others to the developing child's learned behaviors will tend to modify them therapeutically in proportion to available knowledge about the child's specific biological milieu, environmental modifiers, and other levels of the model noted in earlier sections. In turn, learned behaviors may be modified negatively due to ignorance about the dynamics of these multilayered and interconnecting levels.

This may include professional interventions that over-focus on one dynamic or ignore important interacting variables. Some inappropriately interventions may include sole use of medications to control behavior, inappropriate rigid reliance upon any one-dimensional treatment strategy, isolating a child in a locked facility, or restricting him to a special needs environment where there are no "typical" children. Of course, the responses from people in a child's environment to his learned behaviors lead, in turn, to further responses from the child that are called "derived behaviors," or level four, of the BOLD model. These behaviors will be even more disruptive if responses, including interventions, toward abnormally learned behaviors are shortsighted, narrow, or otherwise inappropriate.

LEVEL FOUR: DERIVED BEHAVIORS

Derived behaviors are represented by children's responses to the initial reactions that their original traits and learned behaviors evoke in other people and society. These are multidimensional patterns of behaviors that are far more complex than the rudimentary coping mechanisms referred to at the third level. Because they can be particularly disruptive or dysfunctional, derived behaviors represent the most obvious, and usually the most alarming, symptoms of the learning and communication disorder. This is the level at which evaluation and diagnosis frequently occur, and the level likely to be targeted by treatment interventions. Unfortunately, derived behaviors are often so far removed from the biological milieu and original traits that it becomes very difficult, if not impossible, to properly assess a child solely at this fourth level and to implement appropriate intervention strategies. Examples of derived behaviors may be easily recognized as commonly assessed symptoms of numerous syndromes falling under the category of learning and communication disorders. These behaviors may include head-banging, rocking, spinning, continuous self-stimulation, and other stereotypical behaviors. Also, there may be aggressiveness toward others expressed in biting, kicking, head-butting, or spitting. Other problem behaviors may include idiosyncratic rituals and compulsions, inappropriate yelling out, continuous seeking out of attention by inappropriate acting out, severe temper tantrums, angry outbursts, social isolation, withdrawal, and lack of development of spoken language.

Modifiers of these behaviors include various intervention programs. A number of such programs have been developed (Rogers & Lewis, 1989; Schopler, Mesibov & Hearsey, 1995; Strain & Hoyson, 1988). Some programs are highly structured and have a behavioral orientation; others are multidisciplinary and have a relational focus (Campbell, Schopler, & Hallin, 1996; Greenspan & Wieder, 1998; Lovaas, 1981, 1987; Robinson, 1997; Wieder, 1992, 1996). Such programs work on modifying derived behaviors through a variety of means, including facilitating communication, decreasing inattention and irritability, improving cognitive and social skills, and promoting generalization and maintenance of new adaptive behaviors (Bondy & Peterson, 1990; DeGangi & Greenspan, 1997; Greenspan, 1992; Greenspan & Wieder, 1997, 1998; Olley, Robbins, & Morelli-Robbins, 1993; Stokes & Osnes, 1988).

Many intervention programs have traditionally remained self-contained by including only the population of children with communication and learning disorders, with no emphasis on providing them with opportunities to socialize with children from general populations. Research seems to indicate, however, that development of many of the maladaptive derived behaviors could be prevented by placing the children in an environment that includes adaptive peers (Bricker & Cripe, 1992; Fewell & Oelwein, 1990; Giangreco, Dennis, Coninger, Edleman, & Shattman, 1993). Such an environment may allow them to learn positive social roles and communication skills by observing and imitating their peers. Mesibov (1984) suggested that many children with communication and learning disorders exhibit social deficits due to the lack of friends and positive role models. This suggestion is confirmed by research findings that children with learning and communication disorders benefited from opportunities to interact with their more typically developed peers (Mahoney & Powell, 1992; Odom & McEvoy, 1988). Their gains were more significant than those of children in self-contained programs, and included increased social behavior as a result of being actively engaged in social interaction by their more typically developed peers. Also, children with learning and communication disorders gained enhanced development of language as well as improved cognitive, social, motor, and other age-appropriate skills (Mahoney, Robinson, & Powell, 1988; McHale, 1993; Peck, Odom, & Bricker, 1993; Roeyers, 1996; Strain & Kerr, 1981; Strain, Kerr, & Ragland, 1979; Yoder, Kaiser, & Alpert, 1991). Effective and creative curricula that ensure inclusion of both children with developmental disorders and their more typically developed peers are currently available (Jorgensen, 1997; Onosko & Jorgensen, 1997; Sizer, 1992).

USING THE BOLD APPROACH TO ENHANCE ASSESSMENT

As previously noted, the BOLD format was developed as a multimodal approach to communication and learning disorders. What follows is a breakdown of how this approach may enhance one of these applications; namely, the assessment of communication and learning disorders. Looking at the different levels contributing to a child's challenges may help in asking the additional questions that will reveal the different "contributors" to the child's behaviors.

A comprehensive, team-based approach to assessment can use the different levels as reminders of the different functions involved and the relationship among them. The biological milieu—that is, all relevant biological areas, including individual physical differences and possible modifiers of this level (e.g., birth complications, medical interventions)—is a basic level. Assessment may then proceed sequentially to original traits (functional developmental level) and corresponding modifiers (e.g., various sensory and environmental stimuli), then learned behaviors and modifiers (e.g., responses of caregivers), and, finally, derived behaviors and modifiers (e.g., therapeutic interventions an home, family, and school interactions).

Assessment of the biological milieu (level one) can rule out possible metabolic abnormalities, seizure activity, brain lesions, neurological disorders, immune disorders, and other likely influences on communication and learning disorders. The child's biochemical makeup, genetic structure, and central and peripheral nervous systems can be assessed by means of standard medical evaluations, pediatric neurological evaluations, metabolic/endocrine screenings, nutritional and genetic screenings, MRIs, PET scans, and EEGs.

Modifiers of the child's biological milieu, such as pregnancy complications, birth complications, medications, surgery, diet, and contaminants, can also be evaluated by these and other procedures. Assessments of the modifiers of the biological milieu are important because some modifiers, such as diet, medications, and pollutants, may be preventable or reversible. Moreover, such assessments may shed light on

different expressions of the same genetic structure, for example, as seen in identical twins.

Assessment of original traits (level two) should examine functional strengths and/or weaknesses in auditory reception and processing, visual-spatial perception, and processing, olfactory, gustatory, tactile, and other sensory input/processing modes, basic cognitive abilities, and memory. Specialists in pediatrics, ophthalmology, audiology, and other processing areas may rule out abnormalities in vision, hearing, perception, and sensorimotor processing. Psychological testing may rule out cognitive processing, memory deficits, and other complications.

As noted previously, a child's ability to advance adaptively to subsequent developmental levels may be compromised, even with normal original traits, if these traits (hearing, vision, and others) are abnormally modified by an environment that is depriving, excessive, threatening, or otherwise harsh. Thus, a child may unfortunately not experience normal patterns of learning contingencies, not respond to conditioning stimuli and reinforcement, nor be able to benefit normally from social modeling. Assessment of the status of the child's environment may include psychosocial histories, immediate observations of child-caregiver interactions, and on-site evaluations at the child's home or school.

Likewise, assessment of learned behaviors (level three) may include on-site observation of learning contingencies in the child's usual environment to rule out possible inadequate social interactions, parenting styles, or deficient preschool or academic conditioning. The child's developmental level of functioning (e.g., age appropriateness) is assessed at this level and may also include formal tests, such as psychological evaluations, behavior checklists, and tests for learning disabilities. Also included may be tests to rule out abnormalities in spoken and/or written communications, impulse control problems, attention deficits, low frustration tolerance, inability to postpone immediate gratification, deficits in mood regulation, faulty cognitive responses to stress that may influence affect (e.g., overgeneralizing or "catastrophizing"), empathy ("emotional quotient"), and social skills delays.

Assessment of modifiers of learned behaviors involves evaluations of others' reactions or interventions to the child's problematic learned behaviors. The responses of parents, relatives, peers, and the child's community to his learned behaviors may modify those behaviors therapeutically or even worsen them. It will be important to assess what kinds of informal and formal interventions have been applied or are currently in place. Of course, this can be done by taking a thorough history of previous clinical interventions and *in vivo* observations of the child in his natural environment at home, in school, at clinics, and in the community. Assessment may rule out responses or interventions that are ignorant of the interacting dynamics of the various levels affecting communication and learning disorders. Interventions or responses that are not comprehensive, overfocus on only one dynamic, or are too narrow or shallow may be uncovered.

Assessment of derived behaviors (level four) involves ascertaining the child's responses, in turn, to the interventions or reactions of others toward her learned behaviors. These responses of the child are often the alarming or stereotypical behaviors that are the hallmark of the communication and learning disorders, such as head-banging, chronic self-stimulation, rocking, spinning, aggressive outbursts, and withdrawal. Assessment of these may include matching the problem behavior to antecedent stimuli or triggers (e.g., child bangs head when intervention is isolation from peers). Also, assessment will ascertain and list the quantity or number of behaviors

and their type and severity. This may be done through direct observations, anecdotal reports from others, use of checklists, narrative descriptions, and other means.

Finally, assessment of modifiers of derived behaviors involves assessment of the interventions applied toward the most problematic behaviors. The interventions may be assessed in terms of observed effectiveness, short- or long-range effectiveness, whether they generate further problems, and whether they make use of multiple influencing variables. Assessment of modifiers of derived behaviors can identify whether interventions are unitary, multimodal, comprehensive, shortsighted, or too self-contained. The assessment may evaluate if interventions are increasing communication, attention, social interest, mood regulation, and cognitive skills, and whether interventions are making use of beneficial interactions with normal peers. At times, an intervention may over-focus on a particular behavior and undermine the more important relationship and positive feelings a child has with a caregiver, therapist, or teacher. Although the child may change specific behaviors, the results of missing the most important component of the intervention may show up in negative changes in the child's mood, flexibility, and overall thinking and problem-solving capacities.

As new research in the field of communication and learning disorders becomes available, the BOLD format may serve as a framework to channel and organize new knowledge on the understanding between different biological levels of organization (genetic, constitutional, and developmental) with various levels of observed behavior. As a multimodal approach, it may sort comprehensive new information for the purpose of meaningful synthesis with established knowledge and prompt new directions in research and intervention. ■

REFERENCES

Aman, M. G., Van Bourgondien, M. E., Wolford, P. L., & Sarphare, G. (1995). Psychotropic and anticonvulsant drugs in subject with autism: Prevalence and patterns of use. *Journal of the American Academy of Child and Adolescent Psychiatry, 34,* 1672-1681.

Armenteros, J. L., Adams, P. B., Campbell, M., & Eisenberg, Z. W. (1995). Haloperidol-related dyskinesias and pre- and perinatal complications in autistic children. *Psychopharmacological Bulletin, 31,* 363-369.

Bailey, A., Le Courteur, A., Gottesman, I., Bolton, P., Simonoff, E., Yuzda, E., & Rutter, M. (1995). Autism as a strong genetic disorder: Evidence from a British twin study. *Psychology and Medicine, 25,* 63-77.

Bailey. A., Palferman, S., Heavey, L., & LeCouteur, A (1998). Autism: The phenotype of relatives. *Journal of Autism and Developmental Disorders, 28*(5), 369-392.

Baranek, G. T. (1999). Autism during infancy: A retrospective video analysis of sensorimotor and social behaviors at 9-12 months of age. *Journal of Autism and Developmental Disorders, 29,* 213-224.

Baranek, G. T., Foster, L. G., & Berkson, G. (1997). Tactile defensiveness and stereotyped behaviors. *American Journal of Occupational Therapy, 51,* 91-95.

Baron-Cohen, S. (1996). *Mindblindness: An essay on autism and theory of mind.* Cambridge, MA: MIT Press.

Baron-Cohen, S., Leslie, A.M., & Frith, U. (1985). Does the autistic child have a "theory of mind?" *Cognition, 21,* 31-46.

Barton, M., & Volkmar, F. (1998). How commonly are known medical conditions associated with autism? *Journal of Autism and Developmental Disorders, 28*(4), 273-278.

Bartsch, K., & Wellman, H.M. (1995). *Children talk about the mind.* New York: Oxford University Press.

Baving, L., Laucht, M., & Schmidt, M. H. (1999). Atypical frontal brain activation in ADHD: Preschool and elementary school boys and girls. *Journal of the American Academy of Child and Adolescent Psychiatry, 38,* 1363-1371.

Berger, A., & Posner, M. I. (2000). Pathologies of brain attentional networks. *Neuroscience Behavioral Review, 24,* 3-5.

Bolte, E. R. (1998). Autism and clostridium tetani. *Medical Hypotheses, 51,* 133-144.

Bolton, P. F., Murphy, M., Macdonald, H., Whitlock, B., Pickles, A., & Rutter, M. (1997). Obstetric complications in autism: Consequences or causes of the condition? *Journal of the American Academy of Child and Adolescent Psychiatry, 36,* 272-281.

Bondy, A. S., & Peterson, S. (1990). *The point is not the point: Picture exchange communication system with young students with autism.* Paper presented at the Association for Behavioral Analysis Convention, Nashville, TN.

Boris, M., & Mandel, F. S. (1994). Foods and additives are common causes of the attention deficit hyperactive disorder in children. *Annals of Allergy, 72,* 462-468.

Boyles, S., & Key, S. W. (1998). No evidence for link between MMR vaccine and autism/bowel disease syndrome. *Tuberculosis and Airborne Disease Weekly,* May 18, 12.

Bricker, D. D., & Cripe, J. J. (1992). *Activity-based approach to early intervention.* Baltimore: Paul H. Brookes.

Campbell, M., Schopler, E., & Hallin, A. (1996). The treatment of autistic disorder. *Journal of the American Academy of Child and Adolescent Psychiatry, 28,* 200-206.

Carlsson, M. L. (1998). Hypothesis: Is infantile autism a hypglutamatergic disorder? Relevance of glutamate-serotonin interaction for pharmacotherapy. *Journal of Neural Transmission, 105,* 525-535.

Cessaroni L., & Garber, M. (1991). Exploring the experience of autism through firsthand accounts. *Journal of Autism and Developmental Disorders, 21,* 303-313.

Chugani, D. C., Muzik, O., Behen, M., Rothermel, R., Janissee, J. J., Lee, J., & Chugani, H.T. (1999). Developmental changes in brain serotonin synthesis capacity in autistic and nonautistic children. *Annals of Neurology, 45,* 287-295.

Comi, A. M., Zimmerman, A. W., Frye, V. H., Law, P. A., & Peeden, J. N. (1999). Familial clustering of autoimmune disorders and evaluation of medical risk factors in autism. *Journal of Child Neurology, 14,* 388-394.

Connolly, A. M., Chez, M. G., Pestronk, A., Arnold, S. T., Mehta, S., & Deuel, R. K. (1999). Serum autoantibodies to brain in Landau-Kleffner variant, autism, and other neurologic disorders. *Journal of Pediatrics, 134,* 607-613.

DeGangi, G. A., & Greenspan, S. I. (1997). The effectiveness of short-term interventions in treatment of inattention and irritability in toddlers. *Journal of Developmental and Learning Disorders, 1,* 277-298.

Deykin, E. Y. & MacMahon, B. (1980). Pregnancy, delivery, and neonatal complications among autistic children. *American Journal of Disabled Children, 134,* 860-864.

Duclos, P., & Ward, B. J. (1998). Measles vaccines: A review of adverse events. *Drug Safety, 19,* 435-454.

Faraone, S. V. & Biederman, J. (1998). Neurobiology of attention-deficit hyperactivity disorder. *Biological Psychiatry, 44,* 951-958.

Farrant, A., Boucher, J., & Blades, M. (1999). Metamemory in children with autism. *Child Development, 70,* 107-131.

Fewell & Oelwein (1990). The relationship between time in integrated environments and developmental gains in young children with special needs. *Topics in Early Childhood Special Education, 10,* 104-114.

Folstein, S. E., Bisson, E., Santangelo, S. L., & Paven, J. (1998). Finding specific genes that cause autism: A combination of approaches will be needed to maximize power. *Journal of Autism and Developmental Disorders, 28,* 439-445.

Folston, S. E. & Rutter, M. L. (1988). Autism: Familial aggregation and genetic implications. *Journal of Autism and Developmental Disorders, 45,* 357-362.

Giangreco, M. R., Dennis, R., Coninger, C., Edleman, S., & Shattman, R. (1993). "I've counted Jon:" Transformational experiences of teachers educating students with disabilities. *Exceptional Children, 59,* 359-372.

Gillberg, C. (1998). Chromosomal disorders and autism. *Journal of Autism and Developmental Disorders, 28,* 415-425.

Gillberg, C., Uvebrant, P., Carlsson, G., Hedstrom, A., & Silfvenius, H. (1996). Autism and epilepsy (and tuberous sclerosis?) in two pre-adolescent boys: Neuropsychiatric aspects before and after epilepsy surgery. *Journal of Intellect Disability Research, 40,* 75-81.

Greenspan, S. I. (1992). *Infancy and early childhood: The practice of clinical assessment and intervention with emotional and developmental challenges.* Madison, CT: International Universities Press.

Greenspan, S. I. (1995). Alternatives to behaviorism. *On Task with Autism Support and Advocacy in Pennsylvania, 3,* 1-17.

Greenspan, S. I., & Wieder, S. (1997). Developmental patterns and outcomes in infants and children with disorders in relating and communicating: A chart review of 200 cases of children with autistic spectrum diagnoses. *Journal of Developmental and Learning Disorders, 1*, 87-141.

Greenspan, S. I. & Wieder, S. (1998). *The child with special needs: Intellectual and emotional growth*. Reading, MA: Addison Wesley Longman.

Hadwin, J., Baron-Cohen, S., Howlin, P., & Hill, K. (1997). Does teaching theory of mind have an effect on the ability to develop conversation in children with autism? *Journal of Autism and Developmental Disorders, 27*, 519-538.

Happe, F. G. (1997). Central coherence and theory of mind in autism: Reading homographs in context. *British Journal of Developmental Psychology, 15*, 1-12.

Happe, F. G. (1995). The role of age and verbal ability in the theory of mind task performance of subjects with autism. *Child Development, 66*, 843-855.

Hardan, A. & Sahl, R. (1997). Psychopathology in children and adolescents with developmental disorder. *Research on Developmental Disabilities, 18*, 369-382.

Houghton, S., Douglas, G., West, J., Whiting, K., Wall, M., Langsford, S., Powell, L., & Carroll, A. (1999). Differential patterns of executive function in children with attention-deficit hyperactivity disorder according to gender and subtype. *Journal of Child Neurology, 14*, 801-805.

Hubner, R. A. (1992). Autistic disorder: A neuropsychological enigma. *American Journal of Occupational Therapy, 46*, 487-501.

Jolliffe, T., & Baron-Cohen, S. (1999). A test of central coherence theory: Linguistic processing in high-functioning adults with autism or Asperger syndrome: Is local coherence impaired? *Cognition, 71*, 149-185.

Jorgensen, Cheryl M., with Fisher D., & Roach V. (1997). *Curriculum and its impact on inclusion and the achievement of students with disabilities* (Issue Brief 2(2), July). Consortium on Inclusive Schooling Practices Publications.

Joseph, R. M., & Tager-Flusberg, H. (1997). An investigation of attention and affect in children with autism and Down syndrome. *Journal of Autism and Developmental Disorders, 27*, 385-396.

Klin, A. (1993). Auditory brainstem responses in autism: Brainstem dysfunction or peripheral hearing loss? *Journal of Autism and Developmental Disorders, 23*, 15-35.

Knobloch, H., & Pasamanick, B. (1975). Some etiologic and prognostic factors in early infantile autism and psychosis. *Pediatrics, 55*, 182-191.

Kobayashi, R. & Murata, T. (1998). Setback phenomenon in autism and long-term prognosis. *Actuarial Psychiatry Scandanavia, 98*, 296-303.

Leboyer, M., Phillipe, A., Bouvard, M., Guilloud-Bataille, M., Bondoux, D., Tabuteau, F., Feingold, J., Mouren-Simeoni, M. C., & Launay, J. M. (1999). Whole blood serotonin and plasma beta-endorphin in autistic probands and their first-degree relatives. *Biological Psychiatry, 45*, 158-163.

Lord, C., Mulloy, C., Wendelboe, M., & Schopler, E. (1991). Pre and perinatal factors in high-functioning females and males with autism. *Journal of Autism and Developmental Disorders, 21*, 197-209.

Lovaas, O. I. (1981). *Teaching developmentally disabled children*. Austin, TX: PRO-ED.

Lovaas, O. I. (1987). Behavioral treatment and normal educational and intellectual functioning in young autistic children. *Journal of Consulting and Clinical Psychology, 55*, 3-9.

MacLean, J. E., Szatmari, P., Jones, M. B., Bryson, S. E., Mahoney W. J., Bartolucci, G., & Tuff, L. (1999). Familial factors influence level of functioning in pervasive developmental disorder. *Journal of the American Academy of Child and Adolescent Psychiatry,* 38, 746-753.

Mahoney, G., & Powell, A. (1988). Modifying parent-child interaction: Enhancing the development of handicapped children. *Journal of Special Education, 22,* 82-96.

Mahoney, G., Robinson, C., & Powell, A. (1992). Focusing on parent-child interaction: The bridge to developmentally appropriate practices. *Topics in Early Childhood Special Education, 12,* 105-120.

McHale, S. (1983). Social interactions of autistic and non-handicapped children during free play. *American Journal of Orthopsychiatry, 52,* 81-91.

Mesibov, H. (1984). Social skills training with verbal autistic adolescents and adults: A program model. *Journal of Autism and Developmental Disorders 14,* 395-404.

Milberger, S., Biederman, J., Faraone, S. V., Guite, J., & Tsuang, M. T. (1997). Pregnancy, delivery and infancy complications and attention deficit hyperactivity disorder: Issued of gene-environment interaction. *Biological Psychiatry, 41,* 65-75.

Minshew, N. J., Luna, B., & Sweeney, J. A. (1999). Oculomotor evidence for neocortical systems but not cerebellar dysfunction in autism. *Neurology, 52,* 917-922.

Moreno-Fuenmayor, H., Borjas, L., Arrieta, A., Valera, V., & Socorro-Candanoza, L. (1996). Plasma excitatory amino acids in autism. *Investigacion Clinica, 37,* 113-128.

Muller, R. A., Behen, M. E., Rothermel, R. D., Chugani, D. C., Muzik, O., Mangner, T. J., & Chugani, H. T. (1999). Brain mapping language and auditory perception in high-functioning autistic adults: A PET study. *Journal of Autism and Developmental Disorders, 29,* 19-31.

Odom, S. L., & McEvoy, M. (1988). Integration of young children with handicaps and normally developing children. In S. Odom and M. Karnes (Eds.), *Early intervention for infants and children with handicaps: An empirical base.* Baltimore: Paul H. Brookes.

Olley, J., Robbins, F., & Morelli-Robbins, M. (1993). Current practices in early intervention for children with autism. In E. Schopler, M. Bourgondien, & M. Bristol (Eds.), *Preschool issues in autism.* New York and London: Plenum.

Onosko, J. & Jorgensen, C. (1998). Unit and lesson planning in the inclusive classroom: Maximizing learning opportunities for all students. In C. Jorgensens (Ed.), *Restructuring high schools to include all students: Taking inclusion to the next level.* Baltimore: Paul H. Brookes.

Patzold, L. M., Richdale, A. L., & Tonge, B. J. (1998). An investigation into sleep characteristics of children with autism and Asperger's disorder. *Journal of Pediatric Child Health, 34,* 528-533.

Peck, C.A., Odom, S. L., & Bricker D. D. (Eds.) (1993). *Integrating young children with disabilities into community programs.* Baltimore: Paul H. Brooks.

Pennington, B. F., & Ozonoff, S. (1996). Executive functions and developmental psychopathology. *Journal of Child Psychology and Psychiatry, 37,* 51-87.

Robichon, F., & Habib, M. (1998). Abnormal callosal morphology in male adult dyslexics: relationships to handedness and phonological abilities. *Brain Language, 62,* 127-146.

Roeyers, H. (1996). The influence of non-handicapped peers on the social interactions of children with a pervasive developmental disorder. *Journal of Autism and Developmental Disorders, 26,* 303-320.

Rogers, S. J., & Lewis, H. (1989). An effective day treatment model for children with pervasive developmental disorders. *Journal of the American Academy of Child and Adolescent Psychiatry, 28,* 207-214.

Saitoh, O. & Courchesen, E. (1998). Magnetic resonance imaging study of the brain in autism. *Psychiatric Clinical Neuroscience, 52,* 219-222.

Sanua, V. D. (1986). A comparative study of opinions of USA and European professionals on the etiology of infantile autism. *International Journal of Social Psychiatry 32,* 16-30.

Scharre, J. E., & Creedon, M. P. (1992). Assessment of visual functioning in autistic children. *Optometry and Visual Science, 69,* 433-439.

Schifter, T., Hoffman, J. M., Hatten, H. P., Hanson, M. W., Coleman, R. E., & DeLong, G. R. (1994). Neuroimaging in infantile autism. *Journal of Child Neurology, 9,* 155-161.

Schopler, E., Mesibov, G., & Hearsey, K. (1995). Structured teaching in TEACCH system. In E. Schopler & G. Mesibov (Eds.), *Learning and cognition in autism.* New York: Plenum.

Schweitzer, J. B., Faber, T. L., Grafton, S. T., Tune, L. E., Hoffman, J. M., & Kilts, C. D. (2000). Alterations in the functioning anatomy of working memory in adult attention deficit hyperactivity disorder. *American Journal of Psychiatry, 157,* 278-280.

Sing, V. K, Lin, S. X., & Yang, V. C. (1998). Serological association of measles virus and human herpesvirus-6 with brain antibodies in autism. *Clinical Immunology and Immunopathology, 89,*105-108.

Sizer, T. (1992). *Horace's school: Redesigning the American high school.* Boston: Houghton Mifflin.

Sparrevohn, R., & Howie, P. M. (1995). Theory of mind in children with autistic disorder: Evidence of developmental progression and the role of verbal ability.

Journal of Child Psychology and Psychiatry, 36, 249-263.

Steffenburg, S., Gillberg, C., Hellgren, L., Anderson, L., Gillber, I. C., Jakobsson, G., & Bohman, M. (1989). A twin study of autism in Denmark, Finland, Norway, and Sweden. *Journal of Child Psychology and Psychiatry, 30,* 405-416.

Stokes, T. F., & Osnes, P. G. (1988). The developing applied technology of generalization and maintenance. In Horner, R., Dunlap, D., & Koegel, R. L. (Eds.), *Generalization and maintenance.* Baltimore: Paul H. Brookes.

Strain, P. S., & Hoyson, M. (1988). *Follow-up of children in LEAP.* Paper presented at the meeting of the Autism Society of America, New Orleans, LA.

Strain, P. S., Kerr, M. M., & Ragland, E. U. (1979). Effects of peer-mediated social initiations and prompting/reinforcement procedures on the social behavior of autistic children. *Journal of Autism and Developmental Disorders, 9,* 41-54.

Ticher, A., Ring, A., Barak, Y., Elizur, A., & Weizman, A. (1996). Circannual pattern of autistic birth: Reanalysis in three ethnic groups. *Human Biology, 68,* 585-592.

Torrey, E. F., Hersh, S. P., & McCabe, K. D. (1975). Early childhood psychosis and bleeding during pregnancy. A prospective study of gravid women and their offspring. *Journal of Autism and Child Schizophrenia, 5,* 287-297.

Trottier, G., Srivastava, L., & Walker, C. D. (1999). Etiology of infantile autism: A review of recent advances in genetic and neurobiological research. *Journal of Psychiatry Neuroscience, 24,* 103-115.

Vallone, D., Picetti, R., & Borrelli, E. (2000). Structure and function of dopamine receptors. *Neuroscience Biobehavioral Review, 24,* 125-132.

Vig, S., & Jedrysek, E. (1995). Adaptive behavior of young urban children with developmental disabilities. *Mental Retardation, 33*, 90-98.

Waterhouse, L., Fein, D., & Modahl, C. (1996). Neurofunctional mechanisms in autism. *Psychological Review, 103*, 457-489.

Welsh, L. W., Welsh, J. J., & Healy, M. P. (1996). Learning disabilities and central auditory dysfunction. *Annals of Otolology, Rhinology, and Laryngology, 105*, 117-122.

Wieder, S. (1992). Opening the door: Approaches to engage children with multisystem developmental disorders. *Zero to Three, 14*, 10-15.

Wieder, S. (1996). Integrated treatment approaches for young children with multisystem developmental disorders. *Infants and Young Children, 8*, 24-34.

Yoder, P. J., Kaiser, A. P., & Alpert, C. L. (1991). An exploratory study of the interaction between language teaching methods and child characteristics. *Journal of Speech and Hearing Research*, 155-167.

Zametkin, A. J., Nordahl, T. E., Gross, M., King, A. C. Semple, W. E., Rumsey, J., Hamburger, S., & Cohen, R. M. (1990). Cerebral glucose metabolism in adults with hyperactivity of childhood onset. *New England Journal of Medicine, 323*, 1361-1366.

Part Eight:

Functional Developmental Approach to Intervention Research

— ◄ 31 ► —

Evaluating Effective Interventions for Children with Autism and Related Disorders: Widening the View and Changing the Perspective

Elizabeth Tsakiris, M.Ed., M.A.

INTRODUCTION

Intervention research reviews for autistic spectrum disorders typically consider only research on children with this syndrome. An alternative approach is to broaden the focus and consider intervention research on the many functional developmental deficits found in autistic spectrum disorders. This would include intervention research on speech and language, executive functions and motor planning, sensory processing (including sensory modulation and visual-spatial thinking), relationships (including symbolic play, caregiver-child interactions, and peer interactions), and surface behaviors. When such a broader review is carried out, the results suggest that there is considerable research support (i.e., clinical trial studies) for interventions with speech and language, executive functioning and motor planning, symbolic play, and child-caregiver and peer relationships.

Intervention for surface behaviors (i.e., behavioral approaches) involves a large number of studies, but many of them involve multiple-baseline designs with small numbers and with no control groups. None of them,

including Lovaas's longitudinal study (1987), sufficiently assesses the outcomes most relevant to autism (i.e., abstract thinking, the capacity for empathy and theory of mind, and the ability for affective reciprocity and relating with trust and intimacy). In addition, the major behavioral studies, including the Lovaas study, did not use a clinical trial methodology (i.e., random assignment), leaving the support for this area relatively weak.

In addition, there is less support for interventions on sensory modulation and visual-spatial thinking. But there is a great deal of support for the importance of these areas of functioning in autism and other developmental problems, supporting the view that the best available approaches need to be employed and more research implemented in these areas.

Reviewing the intervention research suggests that there is considerable support for working with many of the functional developmental deficits that characterize autism and other disorders involving problems in relating, thinking, and communicating. In fact, there is far more support for a comprehensive functional developmental approach to interventions for autism and other developmental problems than for circumscribed approaches that work only with selective cognitive skills, symptoms or surface behaviors (without attention to underlying processing or developmental deficits).

BACKGROUND

Autism intervention research reviews typically focus only on intervention research on children with autistic spectrum disorders. The research reviews are limited to this specific syndrome based on the assumption that the syndrome constitutes a unitary disorder with a sufficiently unique pattern of functional deficits to warrant a circumscribed research review. As discussed in Chapters 1 through 3, however, there is not sufficient evidence at present to consider autism as a unitary disorder, either neurobiologically or psychologically (Cohen & Volkmar, 1997). Interestingly, specific theories are often suggested to account for autistic patterns, such as Baron-Cohen's work on theory of mind (1994), Minshew's hypothesis about the autism deficit involving specific types of higher-level abstract thinking (making inferences) (1997, 1999), Zimmerman and Gordon's work on selected neurophysiological patterns (Chapter 27, this volume), and Bauman's work on neuroanatomical and chemical pathways (Chapter 29, this volume). Inevitably, these perspectives illuminate a particular facet of this complex problem. While developing a unifying framework is an ultimate goal, we need to consider these current findings.

Current evidence seems to favor multiple deficits involving multiple neurobiological and psychological mechanisms. The complex interweaving of these deficits and mechanisms in varying forms for each individual helps explain the unusually large heterogeneity of autism, and the wide spectrum of presentations of the disorder. What may be most unique about the patterns described under the autistic spectrum umbrella is the large number of functional developmental deficits involved (e.g., higher-level abstract thinking, empathy, affective reciprocity, functional language, sensory modulation, motor planning, emotional arousal and regulation, and the organization and attention involved in the executive processing of information) and the critical role of each in the development of the social competence that is generally deficient in autism (Casey, Bronson, Tivnan, Riley, & Spenciner, 1991; Guralnick, 1998; Klinger & Dawson, 1992).

Because the individual symptoms of autism vary so widely, breaking these characteristics down into specific common areas of deficits at a neuropsychological and functional developmental level can provide a stronger foundation to evaluate the effectiveness of the various interventions currently utilized to treat autistic spectrum disorders. A framework of common areas would enable more specific examination of what each intervention program addresses in terms of each deficit area as well as the soundness of educational and therapeutic strategies for remediating these common deficit areas (Rogers, 1998a, 1998b, 1998c). There is general agreement in medicine, education, psychology, speech-language, and occupational therapy that children with autism show varying degrees of deficits in the following areas:

- *Speech-language, communication, and auditory processing skills* (verbal and nonverbal communication, acquisition of language, processing, pragmatics and comprehension)
- *Executive cognitive functions and motor planning* (attending to, planning, prioritizing, sequencing, and integrating information from input to output in an organized manner)
- *Visual processing and visual-spatial skills*

- *Sensory reactivity and sensory modulation*
- *Affect and social/emotional skills*
  - Play skills
  - Parent and caregiver relationships
  - Peer relationships and social skills
- *Surface behaviors*
  - Deficit areas (behaviors needing to be increased, e.g., eye-gaze, attention, compliance)
  - Excess areas (behaviors needing to be decreased, e.g., self-stimulation, aggression, noncompliance, perseveration)

In looking at the intervention literature for autistic spectrum disorders, it is necessary to broaden the research base to include research in all of these neuropsychological and fundamental functional developmental areas that characterize autism.

In this broad research perspective, we are also looking at a focus on surface behavior as another type of functional deficit for research review. The justification is that, just as sensory modulation (i.e., the ability to regulate and modulate sensation) constitutes an underlying neurophysiologic parameter that can be worked with through appropriate interventions, surface behaviors such as perseverative behavior, self-stimulatory behavior, and other similar symptoms can be similarly worked with directly as a behavior rather than in relationship to underlying processing differences. In fact, this is the assumption and theoretical orientation of applied behavioral approaches (ABA), including ABA discrete trial interventions. Therefore, the research for working on the behavioral system directly through behavioral intervention can be examined in the same manner as research for working with different underlying processing capacities.

The multiple functional developmental deficits that characterize autistic spectrum problems can be approached in two ways. Interventions for these functional deficits

(e.g., speech-language therapy for auditory processing problems) can be reviewed only for children with autism, as is often done. Alternatively, a broader alternative can be considered. In this broader alternative, rather than limit the research reviewed to studies conducted on children with autism, the scope would be expanded to include studies conducted on children who demonstrate one or more of these neuropsychological or functional developmental deficits who are not on the autistic spectrum. For example, research on children with functional language deficits; problems with motor planning, executive functions, and their higher-level cognitive capacities; visual-spatial thinking; sensory modulation; and affective reciprocity would be relevant even when these deficits are part of cerebral palsy, Down syndrome, or specific learning disabilities because it is the functional deficits that the interventions work on rather than the "syndrome."

There is a strong tradition in medical research for this type of an approach. For example, a complex disorder such as diabetes involves problems in the cardiovascular, renal, and neurological systems. Research findings on nondiabetic individuals, but who also have similar cardiovascular, renal, or neurological challenges, are highly relevant to understanding the multiple functional problems seen in diabetes. Interventions for these different systems are often generic across different syndromes.

Within autism, the use of this approach has even more cogent rationales based on a number of "stumbling blocks" that have faced researchers in the field of autism. The most important of these is the unusual heterogeneity of the population, not only in intelligence levels but also in variety and degree of symptomatology present. While nonverbal IQs are frequently used as comparative measures, two children of the same age, sex, and nonverbal IQ could be dramatically different in their presentations of the disorder (i.e., one might engage in extensive hand-flapping, repeatedly stack blocks in play, and have no language, whereas another might echo lines from her favorite television shows and constantly try to climb high objects). Describing these children as equivalent would obviously be inaccurate. Newer paradigms stressing matching groups based on skills in information processing (Zelazo, 1997) and scores on play observation scales (Rogers & Lewis, 1989) show promise in remedying this deficit but have not yet gained widespread use, perhaps because they are so labor- and time-intensive. Alternatively, researchers have been studying smaller groups, unfortunately decreasing the validity of the study. Single-case studies, descriptive studies, and chart reviews, while allowing for specificity, have important limitations in comparison to experimental research standards due to their inability to compare equivalent groups as well as to have matched controls.

Research with populations of children with more defined syndromes and disabilities is not burdened with these challenges to the same degree as research with populations of autistic spectrum children. As a result, research from other, more well-defined etiological groups can provide valuable intervention-relevant insights. For example, the results of biobehavioral research in the attention-arousal systems for children with attention deficit disorder have been used to help increase the understanding of the derailed developmental patterns in many other disabilities that involve problems in attention (Spiker, 1990).

Using research from other etiological populations, combined with a focus on functional developmental areas, avoids another pitfall that research has fallen into in the field of autism—namely, the emphasis on program comparison. In general, outcome studies in autism have striven to measure the effects of intervention *programs* versus pinpointing specific strategies per se. The goal has been to conduct studies that measure the effects of intervention programs against control groups that did not receive the intervention or received a less intensive version of the same or different intervention. This is problematic.

We know that early childhood interventions have a cross-modal effect developmentally to make intervention as a whole better than no intervention (when IQ scores are used as the index of improvement) (Guralnick, 1998). However, this does not mean that social awareness, communicative intentions, conceptual development, and language improve simultaneously, nor that improvement in one area means improvement in another (Goldstein & Hockenberger, 1991). When research reviews in the field of autism emphasize program effectiveness and program comparison, focus on the individual child with autism with his unique pattern of deficits tends to be overlooked. Freeman, in his 1998 article "Guidelines for Evaluating Outcomes for Children with Autism," asserted that the field would not be able to develop appropriate interventions unless a focus was maintained on the individual child's needs and deficit areas. Only by moving beyond which approach is best for a heterogeneous disorder will we be able to answer the more important question of how to develop individualized interventions for a child who exhibits his own unique pattern of development and symptoms, regardless of IQ level (Freeman & Piazza, 1998).

Another limitation of program comparisons involves traditional pre- and post-design models as well as traditional strategies (e.g., t-test, ANOVA) that are frequently used in such clinical trial methodology. These research protocols are usually unable to model and measure changes in developmental growth during the course of intervention as they often only evaluate the level of an outcome behavior at a particular point (following the intervention.) (Rogosa & Willet, 1985). Thus, these designs cannot look at change throughout the course of the intervention (Muthen, 1994; Muthen et al., 1991, 1995). In the field of autism, and particularly for preschool children with autism, this information is important so that we can ascertain how much growth was attributed to the specific intervention and how much might be attributed to the ongoing course of developmental maturation. This could be done by accounting for typical developmental growth rates with the rate of change during the intervention. Although multiple-baseline designs can do this somewhat better, they can only focus on a few subjects. Thus, the generalization of these results to the population as a whole is limited.

Other issues also plague program comparison models. The findings in the developmental literature regarding speech and language strongly suggest that among typical as well as challenged children, "There may be considerable differences both in the way individuals learn language and in the extent to which specific aspects of language are susceptible to certain types of training" (Law, 1997). As language and communication are critical components of all early childhood programs, let alone those for children with autism, it is reasonable to suggest that the array of individual learning differences may even make program comparison research ultimately inaccurate, and particularly so in the extremely heterogeneous autism population. What may work for one child does not necessarily work for another, even if the children were identical in age and received equivalent interventions in terms of intensity and duration. The issue may have nothing to do with one intervention being better or worse than another. Rather, the issue may be one of appropriateness: how *much* of *what intervention* for *which deficit area*, works *to what degree*, for *what type of child*, and *when is the optimal time* for such services. This degree of specificity is what Guralnick (1998) refers to as the "second generation of research" that has yet to occur in the field of early intervention as a whole, let alone for children with autism and disorders of relating and communicating.

Translating and integrating the increasing bulk of developmental and biobehavioral information into highly individualized intervention strategies and curriculum is necessary before we can evaluate their success potential for an autistic child's individual needs. Organizing the enormous wealth of information to structure and execute interventions from a sound data base must occur as the first step in this regard. In an effort to provide a foundation for this "second generation of research" this chapter will examine the intervention research for the critical functional developmental deficits seen in children with autistic spectrum disorders from this wider perspective, using studies from both the field of autism as well as those focusing on children with other developmental deficits.

METHODOLOGICAL CHALLENGES

Funding sources not infrequently limit a family's ability to tailor a program to a child's unique profile, using the justification that they only consider intervention programs that have been evaluated with a clinical trial methodology (e.g., random assignment, equivalent groups, double-blind evaluations). As indicated, however, program evaluations are fraught with significant limitations. In addition, as will be discussed, the vast majority do not employ rigorous clinical trial methodologies, and, as this review will show, the result is often a funding source (i.e., school system/insurance company) going beyond the limitations of current data to justify a particular policy.

Before the second generation of research occurs to generate a wider range of interventions, it is imperative that families, clinicians, and educators have a literature base to aid them in making critical treatment decisions.

What kind of research base is necessary to initiate programs and strategies, yet still will not overstep the current data? Michael Rutter has eloquently stated that the essence of research, in any field, is "in the process of problem solving, and not in the mere provision of a set of factual answers" (Rutter, 1998). If the problem to solve is what interventions work best for what child with autism and his own unique symptoms, than the framework and perspective for evaluating research must be expanded beyond the factual answers presumed to be provided by the clinical trial methodology.

An important construct within such an expanded framework relates to the distinction between clinically *significant* and clinically *meaningful*. While results should be clinically significant (i.e., those that indicate a substantial change in the variables being measured, unrelated to any other variables), this alone is inadequate. For example, increases in receptive language scores on tests that were administered before and after an intervention under the identical conditions might yield score increases that are significantly higher than those of a similar group of children who did not receive any intervention. Such results would be seen as clinically significant and as an indication that the intervention was effective. However, if those children could not use their increased vocabulary in a reciprocal conversation, their functional use of language did not improve in a clinically meaningful way. In other words, increases

in rote use of language as an outcome measure may be clinically significant but not clinically meaningful. We need to begin to require that our studies discuss not only clinically significant results, but clinically meaningful results as well.

A focus on what is clinically meaningful in research will point out the limitations in many clinically significant studies that do not focus on clinically meaningful changes. It will also highlight the need to present a wider range of studies for consideration because, not infrequently, studies employing experimental designs may include significant degrees of clinically meaningful outcome measures. Anecdotal records, single-case studies, parent reports, and chart reviews become important elements of the knowledge base if they represent the current status of studies on clinically meaningful phenomena and changes. As Rutter stated in the 1998 Emanuel Miller Memorial Lecture, *Autism: Two-Way Interplay between Research and Clinical Work*, "Many key advances (in autism research) have been prompted by astute clinical observations, while some more extravagant research claims were given a more balanced perspective through the light of clinical experience."

In addition to the terms *clinically significant* and *clinically meaningful*, other terms to be utilized in this review are defined as follows:

- *Equivocal results:* Results that did not demonstrate evidence for use of an intervention nor evidence against the use of it.
- *Evidence for use:* Study demonstrates increase in desired behavior, trait, or construct measured as a direct result of the intervention utilized.
- *Evidence against use:* Study demonstrates negative effects on desired behavior, trait, or construct measured as a direct result of the intervention utilized or as side effects.

- *Experimental study (clinical trials)*: Outcome-based study looking at the cause-and-effect relationship between an intervention (independent variable) and a change in skill level or subject characteristic (dependent variable). A clinical trial must include random assignment to treatment groups for intervention as well as use of a control group. Variables must be held constant and controlled to prevent confounding influence of other factors to cause-and-effect relationship desired.

- *Quasi-experimental study (non-clinical trials)*: Outcome case study looking at cause-and-effect relationship between intervention and change in skill level or subject characteristics (dependent variable). It does not involve use of control group, and may not include random assignment to treatment groups.

- *Long-term gain:* Increase in skill level/ desired characteristic from a baseline level that is maintained at designated point in time after administration of an independent variable (e.g., skills in spontaneous request-making are still present 6 months after intervention was terminated at a higher rate than before intervention took place).

- *Short-term gain:* Increase in skill level/ desired characteristic from a baseline level immediately after administration of independent variable (e.g., use of intervention, service delivery model).

- *Meta-analysis:* A cumulative review of several studies that attempts to show the validity of an intervention through determining a statistical effect size or other measure of justification for the effectiveness/comparison of several studies in a related area.

- *Record/chart review:* A systematic review of subject history through treatment, school, medical records, questionnaires, and other data sources. Usually, subject characteristics of common interest are predetermined and defined prior to the review to enable comparison of subjects.

- *Research review:* A narrative review of a variety of research articles and studies on a given topic in an attempt to summarize the information and possibly to provide an informed judgement or opinion on it.

Based on the considerations described previously, it was decided to conduct this research review based on interventions for different functional areas regardless of the syndrome (e.g., autism, cerebral palsy, Down syndrome). Because such a review has not been conducted before in this format for these functional areas with challenged populations of children, studies during the past 15 years in each area were reviewed in detail using abstract or full-text format according to the criteria stated earlier. As research on autism has been reviewed in-depth previously in other sources, studies on populations in the autistic spectrum were sampled and summarized in a briefer and more narrative format within each functional area.

Searches for studies to be included in this review were conducted using ERIC, MED-LINE, PubMed, and a variety of other literature and data bases. Obtaining parent reports and anecdotal records and case studies was more difficult and required more literature-based research efforts as well as consultation with various agencies and advocacy groups involved in their respective areas. Although some published studies and reviews may have been inadvertently missed, the reader is assured that no such study or review was intentionally excluded from this review. Specific research studies reviewed for each of the functional areas can be found in subject area sections of a bibliography included as a chapter appendix. Citations for references cited in this chapter are located either in the "General References" section or in the related subject area section.

SPEECH-LANGUAGE AND COMMUNICATION

This area is important because language and communication deficits are core characteristics of autism, and the lack thereof are frequently the first reasons for referral of young children for diagnosis. The theoretical and descriptive research base in this area is enormous and well reviewed in other sources. For example, the research of Prizant (1983), Schuler and Prizant (1985), Wetherby & Prutting (1984), and Wetherby and Prizant (1992) analyzed and described from a developmental perspective the uneven emergence and patterns indicative of the particular communication and language patterns common to the wide spectrum of autism in relation to typical language development. This was done with detailed precision that laid the foundation for the design of many appropriate interventions ranging from prelinguistic communication skills to more complex conversation maintenance. It is a credit to the field of speech-language therapy that their research has maintained a focus on this continuum of skill level, from the most to the least severe deficits within the spectrum, and thus is applicable for a broad range of children with autism. Further theoretical work in linguistic dysfunction and its continuum has been summarized by others in the field (e.g., Beitchman & Inglis, 1991; Rapin & Dunn, 1997; Rapin & Allen, 1983; Baron-Cohen, Tager-Flusberg, & Cohen 1993).

To clarify the scope of the analysis to follow, it should be pointed out that theories espoused in the literature are generally incorporated by multiple disciplines and service providers as well as by specific programs, and not just by speech-language clinicians. For example, the TEACH program incorporates the Prizant and Wetherby theory of using visual-processing skills to teach language and communication. Bondy and Peterson's (1990) work with the Picture Exchange Communication system (PEC) is now a mainstay of most special education programs for children with autism nationwide, although its initial successful outcomes were first documented at the Delaware Autism Program in 1990. The Walden School program in Massachusetts incorporates the Natural Language Paradigm (Koegel, O'Dell, & Koegel, 1987; Williams, Koegel, & Egel, 1981) as well as discrete trial formats. Each of these program reviews indicates clinically significant pre- and post-test data outcomes in the areas of language and communication, and some give clinically meaningful data as well. Many other programs, including the University of Colorado Health Sciences Center, the Miller Language and Cognitive Development Center in Boston, and the Princeton Child Development Center, clearly give pre- and post-language/communication outcome data, but the have broader forms of instruction and intervention that are more programmatic in nature rather than being oriented to speech-language in particular. The majority of program review studies (including those listed previously) look at program effectiveness as a whole, with speech-language outcomes as only one of many variables. Because isolating the variables in such comprehensive programs that improved speech-language skills is difficult, if not impossible, they will not be further reviewed in this section.

Many research studies have also been conducted on the teaching of specific speech-language and communication skills to children with autism using behavioral methodology; for example, Charlop and Haymes (1994) and Donnellan and Kilman (1986). To avoid overlap with the "Surface Behavior" section of this chapter, this review of speech-language interventions in autism specifically targeted interventions and studies designed, supervised, and/or implemented by speech-language

Table 1. Speech-Language Communication Intervention Studies in Autism

Type of Study	Evidence for Intervention	Evidence Against Intervention	Short-Term Gains	Long-Term Gains	Clinically Significant	Clinically Meaningful
Case study	3	0	3	1	3	2
Single-subject designs (N < 1, but > 7)	6	0	6	0	6	4
Quasi-experimental design (non-clinical trials)	5	0	5	2	5	2
Experimental design (clinical trials)	1	0	1	1	1	1

clinicians, based on theories from the field of speech-language pathology and not solely on the behavioral literature. However, studies that used behavioral methods in combination with, or in the context of, other speech-language communication interventions were also included in this autism review.

The speech-language intervention literature in autism will be surveyed briefly, as this information is available in detail in other sources. In particular, the reader is referred to Schuler, Gonsier-Gerdin, and Wolfbergs' *The Efficacy of Speech and Language Intervention: Autism* (1990) for a more detailed review of this research. A summary of the 15 samples of this research can be seen in Table 1.

The subject number in these studies ranged from 1 to 60, with 10 of these studies having a size of less than 6 subjects. Topics covered in these studies include using sign language, pictures, promoting communicative eye-gaze and prelinguistic communication skills, peer mediation, imitation skills, integrated play settings, and maintaining attention during structured tasks. Studies also contrasted analog versus natural language teaching as well as developmental versus behavioral models. All of these studies focused on short-term gains, as well as the clinically significant results. A little more

than half of these had clinically meaningful results as well.

One of these studies warrants particular recognition in covering the variables utilized for evaluation in this chapter. This study used clinical trial methodology and included careful matching of 60 students diagnosed with autism and random assignment to one of 4 treatment groups (Yoder & Layton, 1988). The study included both long- and short-term gains, as well as clinically meaningful outcome of the retention of signs and words taught 3 months after treatment. Results were differential, but clinically significant in that high-verbal imitators did equally well in four treatment conditions—speech-alone, sign-alone, alternating sign-and-speech, and simultaneous sign-and-speech. Low-verbal imitators did poorest in speech-alone conditions and high-verbal imitators performed better than the low-verbal imitators in all conditions. Regardless of the condition or imitative ability, the words or signs learned were retained and utilized in real-life situations after 3 months of treatment. The results of this study have a direct impact on the instruction of individual children with autism and can be applied differentially, based on individual language and communication needs.

Our next review of the literature in speech-language and communication research was much broader. This was done in an effort to focus on those studies that targeted speech-language deficit areas that were similar to those for children on the autistic spectrum as described in DSM-IV and noted by leading researchers in the field, but presented in children who were not identified specifically with this disability at the time of the study. Diagnoses of the various subjects in these studies included specific language impairment, oral-motor dyspraxia, developmental dyspraxia, receptive and expressive language delays, mental retardation, and communication disorders. The studies did not focus on treatment of the disorders, but rather emphasized specific skill remediation, regardless of the diagnosed disability. The skill areas surveyed included:

- Expressive language delays
- Limited single-word vocabulary
- Weak comprehension of verbal language
- Limited/incorrect use of grammatical and linguistic structure
- Limited/incorrect use of language pragmatics
- Limited use of communicative actions and signals (verbal and nonverbal)
- Limited or absent social conversation with peers and/or adults

Studies focusing on these skill areas investigated the effects of a wide variety of strategies, service delivery models, and individual-child characteristics on the acquisition of these skills using standardized instruments and observational techniques to different degrees to determine short- and long-term gains.

Given the size of this review, studies looking at phonology and articulation were not included. Also omitted was the wealth of descriptive studies that compared and contrasted the characteristics of children with a variety of speech-language deficits with those of children with typical language levels and acquisition patterns. Although many of these were conducted using clinical methods and eventually led to the development of specific teaching strategies in the field, in the interest of scope and time, this review focused on studies that were experimental in nature. That is, studies were included that tried to determine a cause-and-effect relationship between the treatment, delivery model, child characteristic, and the change or lack of change in a specific skill area.

Between 1985 and 1999, 60 studies were reviewed, and fell into the descriptive categories displayed in Table 2. Many of the studies conducted covered more than one topic and thus are accounted for in several of the categories.

Table 2. Skills Categories in Speech-Language Outcome-Based Research

Topic	No. of Studies
Increasing single-word vocabulary (receptive and expressive)	11
Increasing communicative acts and range of intent (nonverbal and verbal)	14
General expressive language gains	14
Improvement in semantic, grammatical, linguistic, and pragmatic structures (expressive and receptive)	16
Improved social interactions	none
Effectiveness of various treatment strategies[a]	19
Effectiveness of various service delivery models[b]	12
Influence of individual child characteristics	15

[a]Strategies included milieu teaching, environmental arrangement, Mand, Mand model, incidental teaching, mediated instruction, direct instruction, specific curriculum sequelae response to child initiation, imitative modeling, Hanen, and combinations of all of these.

[b] Direct service in clinic, direct service in home, parent training and parent teaching, center-based services, inclusion-based services, small-group services, and combinations of all of these.

These studies were then categorized for evaluation purposes in Table 3.

Of the 33 quasi-experimental studies, none met the criteria for clinical trial research due to either the lack of a control group or the lack of random assignment to groups. Given the difficulties inherent in meeting these requirements, it is quite impressive that 21 articles did indeed surmount these methodological obstacles to be categorized as a true experimental design.

The majority of the reviewed studies dealt with strategies for improving expressive language or expressive means of communication. While outcomes measuring receptive language were usually included in most of the studies, the means to get these outcomes usually had an expressive output requirement.

An unexpected emphasis on the variety and type of different service delivery models was noted, regardless of what strategies were implemented. Service delivery models included home teaching by parents, training of parents combined with parent/staff teaching, clinic- or school-based instruction, and combinations of all of these. Five of the research studies specifically dealt with parent training, parent implementation, and delivery of strategies in the child's home.

Arguments regarding directive teaching styles versus more incidental ones that followed the child's lead and initiative were also studied frequently, as well as more behavioral versus interactive approaches. These are quite similar to the current issues in the field of autism for such diverse approaches.

Seventy percent of the surveyed studies demonstrated clinically significant results (statistically, $p<.05$ or better), usually for short-term gains. The results of these studies involved standardized test measures of quantification of defined behaviors taken before, after, and sometimes during the intervention.

Results were classified as *clinically meaningful* if they included observational measures of the child's increase in the designated skill area in unstructured settings outside of the teaching situation. These included, for example, observations and recording of language discourse in the home, in recreational settings, and with peers at playtime. Clinically meaningful results generally demonstrated the child's use of the designated skill (for example, three-word utterances) in noninstructional demand situations and contexts. For example, let us say that 3-word utterances were observed to increase in 3 separate 15-minute samples during a child's interactions with peers and adults in her playgroup, home, and day care. These results would be considered clinically meaningful differences that were seen in the amount of

Table 3. Speech-Language and Communication Research Summary

Type of Study	Evidence for Intervention	Evidence Against Intervention	Short-Term Gains	Long-Term Gains	Clinically Significant	Clinically Meaningful
Case study	1	0	1	1	0	0
Record/chart review	0	0	0		0	0
Quasi-experimental design (non-clinical trials)	33	2	32	3	24	23
Experimental design (clinical trials)	21	3	20	6	18	13

three-word utterances produced in such settings before and after intervention. Sixty percent of the speech language research reviewed included such criteria, providing support for many of the strategies generalizing to multiple and novel settings.

Lacking in this area of research were studies that looked at long-term gains and skill maintenance over time. This appeared difficult to determine because of the possibility of intervening variables, which may have served to maintain the skill over time as opposed to the intervention in isolation. Such information, however, is important, particularly given the cumulative nature of language development and the need to master and maintain a skill before learning more complex ones.

Two other intervention areas are rapidly emerging in the field of autism, as well as in other learning-and-relating challenges that merit attention. The first of these is auditory processing. Deficits in this skill area ultimately affect language comprehension and the ability to attend to listening tasks (including interpersonal conversations) for any extended time period. The basis for the importance of this area was in part established in a variety of neuroimaging studies that demonstrated central nervous system patterns associated with auditory processing and comprehension in relation to language and reading (see Bruneau, Dourneau, Garreau, Pourelot, & LeLord, 1992; Lyon, Reid, & Rumsey, 1996).

Because it is an emerging area, there are a number of different approaches that focus on auditory processing per se that are quite distinct, each one with its own research base. The strongest evidence (based on physiological measurements and neuroimaging studies) is seen in phonemic awareness instruction for improving not only language, but also reading and developmental spelling. Six quasi-experimental studies were located in this

area, all of which had both clinically significant and clinically meaningful results. (For a review of the state of the art as well as literature on phonemic awareness, see Lindamood & Lindamood, Chapter 23, this volume). There is also emerging support for acoustically modified environments and acoustic modification of speech as well (Tallal et al., 1996). Finally, augmentative communication is another emerging area to be noted. By changing the emphasis from language output to communication, augmentative systems enable children with autism to use their visual and other strengths to communicate with or without verbal language in real-life settings (see Lindamood, Chapter 24, this volume).

Discussion

Because speech-language and communication skills (and lack thereof) are among the defining features and earliest diagnostic indicators of children on the autistic spectrum, this is one of the most important functional developmental areas in this syndrome. The research base for this area shows an exceptionally strong empirical and qualitative foundation.

Of the studies, 21 met the criteria for true experimental designs using clinical trial methodology and 33 were quasi-experimental for etiological populations other than autism, with one case study. All of these studies researched constructs that were pertinent to children with autism and disorders of relating and communicating. The clinical significance of this work is supported by statistically significant results for 44 of these studies, and clinically meaningful results for 37. Future research in this area can be improved by examining long-term gains and skill maintenance over time.

As many of the interventions were successful for a wide variety of children, it is reasonable to expect that we can refer to them when dealing with a child with autism or pervasive developmental disorder whose language deficit area can be specifically identified.

EXECUTIVE COGNITIVE FUNCTIONS AND MOTOR PLANNING

In cognitive psychology, intelligence is no longer accepted as an isolated construct separate from the processes that enable children to learn. Specifically, higher-order processes are involved that integrate, organize, and sequence learning and social behaviors across tasks. Children with autistic spectrum disorders have particular difficulty attending to salient aspects of information and planning and organizing this information to respond to it appropriately. Problem solving, particularly social problem solving, is a hallmark deficit of autism, as well as unusual patterns of learning strengths and weaknesses that make "thinking" with full integration of all sensory and cognitive modalities atypical (Bauman & Kemper, 1994; Dawson, Warrenburg, & Fuller, 1982; Denckla, 1986; Huebner, 1992; and Rogers, 1996). This functional area is, therefore, very important to address.

A brief description of the history and constructs of executive function and motor planning is presented to help clarify the constructs reviewed. In the past decade alone, the field has undergone tremendous changes due to an influx of neuropsychological and corresponding neurological and physiological data. Indeed, the United States Congress declared the 1990s as the "Decade of the Brain." Based on Luria's work (1966 through 1980), the PASS theory of intelligence was developed and describes a theory based on Planning, Attention, Simultaneous, and Successive (PASS) information processing to conceptualize cognitive processes (Das, 1984; Das, Naglieri, & Kirby, 1994). These theories have been expanded to include additional constructs of self-regulation, regulation of affect, working memory, motor planning and sequencing, rhythmicity, and timing that all affect the broader constructs of planning and attention (Barkley, 1997; Denckla, Rudel, Chapman, & Krieger, 1985; Gillberg, 1989; Piek et al., 1999a, 1999b). During the past 20 years, confirmation of these constructs includes neurological data on brain differences between children with reading disabilities, conduct disorders, attention deficit disorders, and hyperactivity (Hynd, Hern, Voeller, & Marshall, 1991; Hynd et al., 1993; Hynd & Semrud-Clikeman, 1989; Morgan, Hynd, Riccio, & Hall, 1996).

The impact of this information upon education and therapy for children changed much of the basic framework on which previous interventions have been based. Even for preschool children, executive processing skills are now emerging as a factor that is separate from the field's, and the public's, traditional view of intelligence and assessments of intelligence (Casey, Bronson, Tivnan, Riley, & Spenciner, 1991). Executive functions are now viewed as clearly relevant to both nonsocial and social problem-solving tasks, and must be considered as part of any assessment and intervention system for children (Guralnick, 1993, 1998).

Motor planning and sequencing is a construct developed by the field of occupational therapy. It is a specific type of problem solving that describes a similar process involving sequential actions or motor acts. Praxis (i.e., motor planning) and motor control correlate with better mathematical skills, social behavior, and more frequent peer interactions, and these relationships strengthen with age (Parham, 1998).

One of the studies that documented the difficulties for typical, mentally retarded, and autistic children in motor planning analyzed the performance of each group on a simple task of reaching, grasping, and placing an object in a location (Hughes, 1996). The descriptive data indicated that the autistic subjects had more problems than the other groups in executing goal-directed motor acts, even in very simple situations, suggesting an independent and marked impairment in motor planning and control (and corresponding neurologic executive functions) as well as other action-outcome competencies (Losche, 1987). Others showed deficits in ball-catching and throwing skills, as well as lack of lateralization and consistency of handedness (Cornish & McManus, 1996).

Studies looking at specific intervention strategies under the heading "motor planning" are not as widespread as studies listed under the umbrella of executive functioning, with only 16 found (including case-study reports and compilations). Some of the motor-planning research was conducted under the umbrella of sensory integration therapies, and these studies are included in the "Sensory Reactivities" section of this chapter. Because both executive functioning and motor planing deal with a child's basic ability to plan and sequence actions and thoughts in order to problem solve, they will be looked at together.

Within the areas of executive functioning and motor planning and sequencing, studies were classified as clinically meaningful if they included measures of children's motor functioning and sequencing in real-life skill and play situations, as opposed to just test scores and observations in the therapy room or during the therapy session. Stacy Barnes (1996) documented individual progress of students in Linda Biadabe's MOVE curriculum, first on the movement skill itself, and then on the use of such skills in real-life situations in what is more of a multiple-study case format. Her case studies in California of severe and profoundly disabled children showed that her movement activities caused dramatic increases in attention, affect, and responsivity in her clients (Barnes, 1996). Freeman and Dennison described their use of movement, balance, laterality repatterning, and vision training (based on the theories of Paul Dennison's educational kinesiology theories) to work with a wide range of multiply challenged children. The authors documented case studies of several years of work with children with cerebral palsy, mental retardation, deafness, and blindness, as well as autism, showing their progress at home and school.

Shaffer et al. (in press) used a computer-based interactive metronome (IM) to improve motor planning and, as a consequence, sustained attention, focus, academic, and social skills with children with attention deficit disorder using an experimental pre- and post-test design. Unlike other interventions in the field, the IM was assessed for internal reliability and concurrent validity as a measure of motor performance on a sample population of 585 children ranging in age from 4 to 11 years old before it was utilized in treatment (Kuhlman & Schweinhart, 1999). The intervention groups in the Shaffer et al. study showed statistically significant improvements over control groups in areas of attention, motor control, language processing, reading, and the ability to regulate aggression. This clinically significant evidence was translated into clinically meaningful evidence by Burpee, Dejean, Frick, Kawar, and Murphy (in press) using clinical applications of the IM in an individual case study format to show longer-term changes as a result of the intervention. Stemmer (1997) improved the motor integration and writing skills of special education students using the IM.

Autism research for executive processing has not looked at interventions specifically. One exception is Zelazo's 1998 study that looked at remediating deficits in information processing for toddlers diagnosed with autism. Most of the other studies were descriptive in nature and compared aspects of executive functioning with control groups using traditional neuropsychological test instruments to look at frontal lobe processing, working memory, temporal memory, temporal-order functions, and short- and long-term recall (Benetto et al., 1996; Prior & Hoffman, 1990; and Russell & Jarrold, 1996).

Surveying the literature base outside of autism on interventions based on executive function theory of cognition and motor planning involved varying definitions of terms and use of constructs. A focus was kept on locating studies that attempted interventions to achieve outcomes versus descriptive reports of varying executive function characteristics in designated populations. Studies on adolescents and adults were excluded unless they involved long-term gain measurement for these groups from the time the children were younger.

The research revealed intervention research with a major emphasis on learning disabilities and attention difficulties. Outcomes with students with mental retardation were also located. Interventions reviewed included the following:

- Self-assessment for students
- Schema-based instruction
- Self-monitoring strategies
- Attention cueing
- Interspersion of known and unknown tasks
- Use of progressive and consistent time delays
- Transfer strategies
- Metalinguistic problem-solving strategies
- Transactional strategies
- Reciprocal teaching
- Emotional regulation
- Cognitive instruction
- Planning/process strategies
- Mediated learning
- Comprehension strategies
- Process-oriented problem solving
- Sequential movement rehearsal
- Laterality repatterning/balance training

A review of the literature studied is given in Table 4.

Of the 61 studies reviewed, all but 6 demonstrated support for the use of the intervention. The results of 72% of the studies reached a clinically significant level. In particular, evidence supports motor-learning and

Table 4. Executive Cognitive Functions and Motor Planning Research Summary

Type of Study	No.	Evidence for Intervention	Evidence Against Intervention	Equivocal Results	Short-Term Gains	Long-Term Gains	Clinically Significant	Clinically Meaningful
Case study	9	9	0	0	9	8	2	9
Parent report	3	3	0	1	3	0	1	0
Research reviews/ meta-analysis	6	5	0	1	6	1	4	1
Quasi-experimental design (non-clinical trials)	36	33	0	3	33	4	30	8
Experimental design (clinical trials)	7	6	0	1	5	2	6	3

perceptual-motor skill training to improve clumsiness, lack of coordination, perceptual-motor skills, and graphomotor skills in many children, and increased speed of motor gains in populations with Down syndrome (Shanz & Menendez, 1992).

Clinically meaningful results were ascertained if the children demonstrated the executive functioning and motor-planning skills mastered in solving problems in real life at play, home, school, and in social situations and not just on standardized test scores or observations of progress in the therapy room during a session. Close to 30% of the studies met this criterion. Long-term gains based on follow-up results 3 months to several years later (for case studies) were generally positive, even if few were noted.

Discussion

The review of literature in this area reveals 7 designs out of 61 that met criteria for true experimental designs. Six of these showed clinically significant results. Of the quasi-experimental cases, 36 of the 61 were clinically significant whereas 9 were clinically meaningful. Three studies showing equivocal results indicated that gains in motor treatment groups did not differ from other or no interventions.

It is possible that the inability to locate more parent reports or case studies resulted in a lack of clinically meaningful information. Perhaps such reports are included within books that describe motor and perceptual-motor learning techniques and thus could not be specifically accessed through the traditional means of literature searches used for this review.

The research base in the descriptive and theoretical literature regarding the constructs of executive functioning and motor planning is large, while the research base of the effec-

tiveness of interventions in this area is embryonic, but showing some positive trends in the areas of parent reports and case studies. Future research efforts are needed to focus on direct measurement of constructs such as improved attention span, alertness states, and use of body in space and in novel situations. Studies are needed on the ability of such interventions to improve the ease, efficiency, and precision of sequencing, processing, planning, and organizing of cognitive and motoric information.

The executive functioning and motor planning and sequencing research intervention base is promising, considering the relative novelty of this construct. The research emphasizes learning beyond a rote level, with an end goal of generalization and organization of the material that has been taught. Deficits in this capacity are a common problem for children with autism and other disorders of relating and communicating. These children frequently learn rote skills easily but can not apply them in a sequential, problem-solving manner in their play and social interactions without prompting. The importance of this functional developmental area in autism dovetails with the increasing knowledge base regarding executive function and motor-planning capacities.

Recent research regarding infants between the ages of 9 and 12 months who were later diagnosed with autism confirms deficits and differences in sensory-reactivity and motor skills for these children compared with other developmental delays and typical children (Baranek, 1999: Osterling & Dawson, 1994). Although deficits in motor planning and learning have not been commonly listed as one of the core characteristics of autism, the descriptive research in this review indicates clear differences between even the most basic goal-directed motor actions for children with autism versus other populations that may begin to be evident in infancy. This knowledge suggests that motor-planning skills may be one of the earliest "open windows" available for intervention, lending further support to the relevance of this functional area.

SENSORY REACTIVITY

The importance of this area is probably best found in the poignant and often painful narrative accounts of Barron (1992), Christopher and Christopher (1989), Grandin (1988, 1995), McDonnell (1993), McKean (1994), and Williams (1993, 1995)—all individuals with autism who describe in great detail their over- or underreactivity to sensory information. Differences within the autistic spectrum population itself in the areas of sensory processing and sensory reactivity were documented in a "Chart Review of 200 cases of Children with Autistic Spectrum Disorder" (Greenspan & Wieder, 1997). The importance of this area is reflected in the relationship between stereotyped behaviors (repetitive motor patterns, object manipulations, and behavioral rigidities) and tactile defensiveness found in research by Baranek and Berkson (1994) and Baranek, Foster, and Berkson (1997). They found the relationships in children with autism and/or mental retardation, using empirically precise methods and instruments. These findings lent empirical support to the theory that stereotypic behaviors were not just behaviorally based, and paved the way for increasing the use of occupational therapy techniques, which work with sensory processing, to work with developmental disabilities, especially autism. Furthermore, research with 9- to 12-month-old infants who were later diagnosed with autism found deficits and differences in sensory reactivity and motor skills for these children compared with other developmental

delays and typical children (Baranek, 1999; Osterling & Dawson, 1994).

Research reviewed in this area focused on studies looking at the therapies of sensory integration and vestibular movement therapy as administered by occupational therapists or treatment teams including occupational therapists. The bulk of literature in this area is descriptive in nature and is based on Ayres's work from 1965 to 1987, which factor-analyzed perceptual-motor and sensory deficits in children with disabilities compared to peers without disabilities. Since that time, this original analysis has met with much criticism (Arendt, MacLean, & Baumeister, 1988; Cummins, 1991; Hoehn & Baumeister, 1994). Simultaneously, information from the neuropsychological sciences and descriptive studies of children with autism and related disorders, as well as hyperactivity, learning disabilities, obsessive compulsive behaviors, and self-stimulatory behaviors, have lent theoretical support to Ayres's original ideas of sensory differences in children with disabilities, with some revisions to her theory (Ghez, Gordon, Ghilardi, & Sainburg, 1995; Lincoln, Courchesne, Harms, & Allen, 1995).

Since 1983, descriptive studies have attempted to quantify more precise sensory processing and integration deficits in children with attention deficit disorder, obsessive-compulsive behaviors, learning disabilities, and other developmental delays. Thirteen studies have specifically looked at the differences in sensory processing for children with autism compared to other populations, and clearly document differences. All these studies were descriptive versus strategy-oriented in nature and are cited in the reference section.

This analysis reviewed 34 studies that examined the effects of sensory integration and movement-based treatment on the constructs listed in Table 5 for populations of students with and without autism. Effects on the following outcome areas were noted.

Table 5. Skill Categories in Sensory Reactivity Research

Skill Category	No. of Studies
Play skills	2
Eye movements	2
Motor skills	11
Academic skills	8
Calming/self-organization	5
Self-stimulation	4
Perceptual processing	2

Of interest was the lack of outcome studies looking at the constructs of attention, arousal, and interaction, and under- and over-reactivity more specifically. Although gains in skills in these areas would be difficult to measure using standardized instruments, such measurement would be more in keeping with the short-term goals of occupational therapies. Rather, cause-and-effect studies tended to focus on the byproduct of improvement in these skill areas; that is, increased attention and less reactivity should result in better academic skill scores.

The intervention studies on the effectiveness of sensory integration therapies (including movement) and occupational therapy that were reviewed yield a puzzling picture (see Table 6). Twelve of the studies yielded results that were equivocal in nature; that is, gains in specific skill areas could not be attributed to the intervention itself because control groups and comparison groups receiving alternative treatments made the same gains. In these studies, there was not specific evidence against the use of the intervention but rather no data to definitively point to the intervention as the only cause of the change. The fact that three meta-analyses of several studies did show significant effect sizes for the outcomes measuring improvements in motor skills is encouraging, although no long-term gains were assessed in these same studies. Only two of the studies looked at long-term gains for their interventions.

The experimental studies reviewed showed gains in the areas of academic performance, perceptual processing, and perceptual-motor skills based on standardized test results. Only one of these studies, however, attempted to look at transfer of these skills in a different classroom setting and to different subject matter. The quasi-experimental studies did look at the ability to self-calm and organize as well as at academic, motor, and perceptual skills, providing evidence to support use of sensory integration strategies for deficits in this regard as well as in motor and perceptual processing. But five of these studies showed the same

Table 6. Sensory Reactivity Research Summary

Type of Study	No.	Evidence for Intervention	Evidence Against Intervention	Equivocal Results	Short-Term Gains	Long-Term Gains	Clinically Significant	Clinically Meaningful
Case study	7	7	1	0	5	0	0	8
Meta-analysis	3	1	0	3	2	0	3	0
Record/chart review	1	1	0	1	0	0	0	0
Quasi-experimental (non-clinical trials)	15	11	0	5	5	2	5	3
Experimental design (clinical trials)	8	4	0	3	4	0	4	1

skills were also acquired using alternative treatments and even by a no-treatment control group!

Case studies documented increases in language and play and decreases in self-stimulation behaviors (such as head-banging). The results of those reviewed in this analysis were all clinically meaningful in that the descriptive accounts described improvement in quality of life for the individuals treated as a result of the decreases/increases in areas treated. It is likely that a larger bank of anecdotal evidence from teachers and parents is available in sections of books, letters, and narrative accounts that are not directly accessible through a more traditional literature review format.

Case studies include the previously noted autobiographical accounts of Barron (1992), Christopher and Christopher (1989), Grandin (1988, 1995), McDonnell (1993), McKean (1994), and Williams (1993, 1995). These include narrative accounts of what sensory experience felt like to these individuals, and what techniques seemed to help them feel better and keep them more available for learning and interaction. These techniques included joint compression, massage, brushing, and several other sensory integration activities. Temple Grandin, now an accomplished animal behavior researcher, presented a paper before the National Institutes of Health requesting funding for more research for this area as well as for overall support for the field. Her paper kept reiterating that, despite the lack of clinically significant evidence, the issues of sensory over- and underreactivity interfered with her life, her work, and her overall health, as well as that of other autistic individuals she had met in her lifetime. She gave an impassioned account of the interventions she herself had developed and began experimenting with, as well as those from the occupational therapy literature.

A more recent attempt to measure the benchmark characteristics of autism (nonengaged behavior, inability to master goal-directed play, and low-interaction frequency) showed that these change as a result of sensory integration therapy (Case-Smith & Bryan, 1999). Checklists and videotaped observations were used to quantify the results using a single-subject format.

Even without clinically significant documentation of effectiveness, other leading methods of treatment have incorporated accommodations for sensory, attention, and arousal deficits. For example, the TEACCH curricula include an emphasis in their instructional formats, physical layouts, visual strategies, and schedules that reduces uncertainty and over-arousal. Roger's Denver Model program uses sensory input to optimize arousal levels for learning, to increase experiences of positive affect, and to stimulate child initiations. Rogers openly acknowledges her belief in these constructs and use of them, and describes them as being critical elements of her program (Rogers, 1998). At the same time, she acknowledges the lack, and ambiguity, of research results in this area, but justifies her use of the strategies as being grounded in neuropsychological theory and neurological research.

Newer approaches that involve "top down" processing, such as that used in cognitive rehabilitation techniques (Toglia, 1997), as well as technology to improve timing and rhythmicity related to motor planning and sequencing (Shaffer et al., in press), are also being implemented in conjunction with more traditional sensory integration therapies.

Discussion

Because variations in sensory reactivities are difficult to empirically document, it is easy to underestimate their importance.

However, the voluminous number of case studies, narrative accounts, and personal reports provide evidence on the significant impact of such reactivities.

Because sensory reactivity ultimately affects an individual's availability for relationship development as well as spontaneous and specific learning tasks, it is part of the foundation for acquiring many of the other functional developmental capacities. This makes it a very important and critical functional area to address.

Furthermore, neuropsychological constructs offer a strong theoretical support for occupational therapy constructs involving sensory modulation, attention, and body organization, including hyper- or hypo-arousal and sensory reactivity. Using brain scans, Courchesne, Townsend, Akshoornoff, and Saitoh (1994) have described the neurological deficits that result in impairment in shifting attention, arousal, and spatial orientation in individuals with autism.

While the research base for sensory integration interventions in children with other disabilities is limited and mixed, there are some studies (8 experimental and 15 quasi-experimental) supporting their use in improving motor skills, perceptual-motor skills, self-calming and organization, and play skills. The 12 studies in which clinically meaningful information did exist were largely narrative accounts describing increased attentiveness, calmness, and the ability to tolerate a larger variety of instructional and recreational environments after interventions.

A challenge for future research is to focus on outcomes that are specifically related to sensory reactivity as opposed to those that are the byproducts of normal sensory regulation. This would involve looking at attention levels, amounts of sustained attention under varying social and play circumstances, under- and over-arousal levels in children,

and problem-solving capacity. The newer, computer-based instruments looking at sustained attention, distractibility, perseverance, and other attention related traits may be useful for pre- and post-testing in these areas.

Even though the outcome research is limited, this is an area of enormous clinical importance, which requires more research. Many program models for children with autism (Walden, TEACH, LEAP, Princeton Child Development Institute) emphasize attending to the individual differences in the sensory reactivity areas as a critical intervention component. Therefore, the best available approaches should be considered while additional research is being carried out.

VISUAL AND VISUAL-SPATIAL PROCESSING

Closely related to executive functioning and motor-planning are sensory-processing capacities dealing with visual-spatial processing. There are a number of levels to visual-spatial processing:

- Recognizing visual patterns (e.g., identifying pictures or shapes).
- Remembering what is seen (reproducing a sequence of shapes such as a circle, square, rectangle, and diamond).
- Solving a basic visual-spatial problem, such as finding an object hidden in a room and/or playing treasure hunt with mom, dad, or peers.
- Perceptual-motor exercises that involve locating something in space (e.g., tracking a ball, finding words on a page).
- Visual-spatial problem-solving involving reproducing and transforming spatial configurations (e.g., copying basic shapes with blocks or drawings, transforming shapes [flipping a block design over in different planes]).
- Visual-spatial problem-solving involving conservation tasks, relativistic thinking,

and complex sequencing challenges (e.g., tall glass and short glass holding same amount of water, sequencing objects by size, color, weight, volume).

- Problem-solving involving figuring out sequencing patterns (e.g., number or shape sequences that require analyzing patterns).
- Part and whole problem solving (e.g., how the parts make up the whole and vice versa).

(See Wachs, Chapter 20, this volume, for a complete description of different types of visual-spatial challenges).

Many of these visual-spatial challenges involve sequencing and are mastered by performing motor acts with objects. Therefore, there is considerable overlap between the areas of visual-spatial processing and executive functions and motor planning. The research supports for the importance of, and working with, executive functioning and motor planning discussed earlier, therefore, also support the importance and usefulness of working with visual-spatial thinking.

Visual-spatial thinking, however, also needs to be discussed in its own right. It involves its own independent elements as well as overlapping elements with executive functioning and motor planning. There are individuals, for example, who can solve complex visual-spatial tasks as just described if someone else helps with the motor component (e.g., a child describing where to search for a toy or solving a complex conservation problem without motor actions). Visual-spatial thinking can be clearly assessed through neuropsychological test batteries and a variety of related procedures (see Black & Stefanatos, Chapter 18; Wachs, Chapter 20; Feuerstein, Chapter 22, this volume). It has been studied in a variety of ways in neuropsychological and neurobiological studies

(See Minshew & Goldstein, Chapter 28, this volume). In addition, visual-spatial processing problems are an important component of many learning problems and developmental disorders, including autistic spectrum disorders (e.g., Asperger's syndrome and many other autistic patterns (Greenspan & Wieder, 1997; Klin et al., 1999; Klin, Volkmar, Sparrow, Cicchetti, & Rourke, 1995; Schultz et al., 2000; also see Minshew & Goldstein, Chapter 28, this volume). It also appears to be an essential part of scientific, mathematical, and general analytical thinking in a variety of contexts (Furth & Wachs, 1974).

The literature on perceptual-motor activities involving visual tracking is sometimes confused with the larger category of visual-spatial processing. Perceptual-motor activities involved in tracking, however, are one part of perceptual-motor capacities which, in turn, are only a small part of a larger set of capacities involved in visual-spatial processing.

Visual-spatial processing is a relatively new area of intervention research, even though a number of clinicians have been working in it for many years (See Wachs, Chapter 20; Youssefi & Youssefi, Chapter 21; Feuerstein, Chapter 22, this volume). Therefore, reports about visual-spatial processing interventions are often clinical case descriptions, informal clinician networks, or are embedded in the category of executive functioning and motor planning discussed earlier.

Visual-spatial processing is a critical area of functioning, often impaired in many developmental and learning disorders, including autism. The innovative clinical techniques now available and being developed require more attention and systematic research efforts. In the meantime, visual-spatial processing needs to be worked with as part of a comprehensive program. It needs to be worked with either as part of a broad approach to motor planning and executive functioning or in its own right. At present, therefore, expert clinical opinion, together with available research, especially from the work on executive functioning and motor planning, will need to guide efforts in this area.

AFFECT AND SOCIAL-EMOTIONAL CAPACITIES

Play and Symbolic Play Skills

Deficits in symbolic play are listed in the DSM-IV (1995) as one of the core and diagnostic features of the autistic spectrum disorders. The importance of this functional deficit area is also indicated in a number of studies. When compared to subjects matched for mental age, autistic children displayed considerable deficiencies in these areas in studies by Ungerer and Sigman (1981) and Wing and her colleagues (1979). Greenspan and Weider (1997) described deficiencies in play in their chart review of 200 cases of children with autistic spectrum disorder. These deficiencies ranged from the total absence of any play and odd use of toys to the inability to be symbolic and generate more than one step of a sequential reenactment of a symbolic play sequence.

Yet while the importance of play in early childhood development has long been emphasized in education, psychology, and medicine, the outcomes-based research on this topic during the past 15 years is not as profuse as one might expect. Only 12 studies surveyed attempted to show the effects on various strategies of improving or increasing play skills in a specific manner, not only for children with disabilities but also for typical children. The majority of research on this topic was descriptive in nature, and not outcome-based. These studies hypothesized constructs that were demonstrated by showing a relationship between one construct and

another (e.g., the parallel between language ability and symbolic play skills). Those studies that did look at intervention outcomes affecting play fell into these categories:

- Behavioral interventions
- Pivotal response training
- Play therapy sessions (described for children with mental retardation)
- Effect of amount of maternal involvement available for play
- Increasing vocabulary levels to increase play levels
  - Child-chosen options for play versus adult-imposed options
- Effects of mixed-age grouping
- Effects of occupational therapy
- Social-skills training (As the overall objective of these studies was to improve peer relationships, a review of these studies is included in the "Peer Relationships" section of this chapter.)
  - Inclusive and mainstream settings for children with disabilities

Table 7 displays a summary of research related to play and symbolic play skills.

The majority of outcome based studies demonstrated evidence of use of various interventions, with close to 30% of these reaching clinically significant levels. Results demonstrate improved (e.g., higher levels of play, more complex play, use of more themes) in a setting other than the experimental one. Of the outcome studies reviewed, 68% could be classified as both clinically meaningful and clinically significant. Most of the studies, however, did not provide evidence for long-term gains or maintenance of play skills over time. Many programmatic interventions (e.g., Princeton Child Development Institute, TEACH, UCLA Intensive Behavioral Program, and Walden) include play as part of their programs, but do not measure play variables specifically enough outside of a general

Table 7. Play and Symbolic Play Skills Research Summary

Type of Study	No.	Evidence for Intervention	Evidence Against Intervention	Equivocal Results	Short-Term Gains	Long-Term Gains	Clinically Significant	Clinically Meaningful
Case study	5	5	0	0	1	3	0	1
Descriptive or correlation studies	15	7	0	1	4	3	9	7
Research reviews	2	2	0	1	1	1	1	1
Quasi-experimental (non-clinical trials)	12	10	0	2	9	2	7	8
Experimental design (clinical trials)	1	1	0	0	1	0	1	1

measure of program effectiveness to be included in this review.

Finally, as noted in other functional developmental deficit areas, there is a strong likelihood of case study and parent report evidence in narrative forms that may indicate at least qualitative improvement of play skills after various interventions. Such information is, unfortunately, not accessible at large through the search methods used for this review and thus was unintentionally left out. Samples of such accounts were utilized whenever located.

The descriptive studies reviewed largely examined the relationship of levels of play skills to language and prelinguistic language skills and, for the most part, confirmed theories regarding this relationship. Hierarchical levels of play corresponding to language levels were then usually formulated. Three studies looked at the play characteristics of children with Down syndrome, and one reviewed the characteristics of children with specific language impairment. If the strong relationship between speech-language competencies and play skills is as valid as the descriptive and theoretical research suggests, it is of interest that more research on play and language is not occurring for challenged children who do not have autism. The majority of other disabilities clearly fall into the category

of having language difficulties, delays, and deficits, which would ultimately impact their play skills.

In surveying this category of literature, it was noted that the outcome-based studies that looked at play skills for children with autism were as numerous as the outcome studies for both typical children and children with other disabilities (10 outcome-based studies and 11 descriptive studies).

Discussion

The importance of play as a functional deficit area in the autistic spectrum disorders is indicated by the fact that a deficit in symbolic play is one of the definitive diagnostic indicators in the classification of the disorder. Numerous descriptive literature reviews and studies also note not only the deficiencies in this area but also the qualitative characteristics that make the play of children with autism so different from other challenged as well as typical populations of children. In general, however, the field has expended more effort on describing this play as opposed to determining how to intervene with it.

Out of the 13 experimental and quasi-experimental designs located, only one met the criteria for a true clinical trial. Eight of these 13 studies were clinically significant and 9 were clinically meaningful.

Most programs for autism include play to varying degrees as part of an intervention package with general outcomes of program effectiveness. Much more outcome-based research, however, is needed on existing and new interventions working with symbolic play skills.

Parent/Caregiver Relationships

Qualitative impairment in social interaction is a core characteristic of autism. For infants, toddlers, and preschoolers (with and without disabilities), early development is embedded within a social context. During these early years, this context is largely defined by the interactions with the child's parents and caregivers (these terms will be used synonymously throughout this section), thus establishing the importance of this area as a functional deficit. To foster an environment that facilitates optimal developmental outcomes, child-caregiver interactions are a critical window through which to influence developmental outcomes of concern and to influence outcomes across several domains of functioning (McCollum & Hemmeter, 1998).

Both the autism literature and the child development literature have emphasized a number of constructs that highlight specific facets of interaction and relationships. These include reciprocity (Dawson & Galpert, 1990; Lewy & Dawson, 1992; Tanguay, 1999), shared attention (Mundy, Sigman, & Kasari, 1990), empathy and theory of mind (Baron-Cohen, 1994), and functional interactive use of language (Prizant & Wetherby, 1993). These constructs are incorporated into relationship-based interventions and more subtle outcome measures.

An overview of this area historically is given first to clarify the constructs in this area. The importance of attachment and bonding with the caregiver has been well-documented in the attachment literature by Bowlby (1978, 1982, 1984), Spitz (1972), Ainsworth (1962), and others, beginning in 1945 and continuing to the present. The first true statistical verification that infant's interact with others was seen in an extensive literature review and experiments by Carew (1980a, 1980b). Her work showed that interactions with others were important for a range of developmental capacities. This led theorists to hypothesize that the power of human interaction could impact abnormal development and its course positively and perhaps significantly. A more integrated approach to support human development began to gain favor, such as the model developed by the Peckham project in London in 1935. This project established health centers to serve as social, recreational, medical, and psychological resources for high-risk families. This was later replicated in the work of the South End Community Health Center in Boston.

Several significant studies were completed prior to 1985 that produced clinically significant results to set the stage for the increase in funding for education and social early intervention for the next decade. Two of these studies followed children into adulthood and reviewed the effects of early educational and family support interventions in high-risk families. The Perry Preschool project and the Carolina Abecedarian programs both showed enduring social and intellectual gains in children who received such early services. Analysis of these programs showed statistically significant positive gains in long-term follow-up, leading the National Education Consortium in 1992 to present such papers as "At Risk Does Not Mean Doomed" (Ramey & Ramey, 1992).

Other seminal work in this area include studies by Honig and Lally (1981) and Provence and Naylor (1983), which both showed clinically meaningful results inferring that providing support to families and opportunities for socialization and cognitive enrichment helped children do better in school and have fewer difficulties when they grew up.

The same effects of early and relationship-based interventions were seen not only in typical and high-risk children, but also with young children with disabilities as well. Important results with a Down syndrome population were described in studies led by Feuerstein (1980, 1981). He described an increase in cognitive abilities that remained 2 years after the intervention was completed. Most interesting in this research was the finding that the instruction involving more actual teaching time (300 hours of more instruction!) of specific content areas did not produce the same gains in cognitive ability scores as did the intervention of *individualized adult interaction* together with teaching of problem-solving skills strategies. Results lent support to the idea that teaching thinking skills within an emotionally based individual relationship was especially important. Without the relationship emphasis, the teaching was not as effective for a population with developmental challenges. For many years, the Son-Rise program has emphasized the importance of relationships and family support in working with children with autistic spectrum disorders (Kaufman, 1976). There are a number of detailed case narratives about this program. A parallel emphasis on different types of processing capacities and different types of outcome studies, including ones with clinical trial designs, however, are needed.

Sally Provence summarized the literature from 1980 to 1985 on long- and short-term results of early intervention programs, and noted the positive trend towards more comprehensive services to children versus approaches that focused primarily on cognitive areas. She recommended the use of broad measures of adaptation and social competence for measuring program effectiveness rather than cross-sectional IQ outcomes as the direction future research should head at that time.

Recent neuroscience research (Greenough & Black, 1992; Weiler, Hawrylak, & Greenough, 1995) further supports appropriate interactional experiences during the early years to foster central nervous system growth.

To complement the knowledge base in this area of parent-child interaction interventions for children with disabilities, the reader may wish to refer to the comprehensive work completed in this area by McCollum and Hemmeter in *The Effectiveness of Early Intervention* (Guralnick, 1998). The focus of this chapter is to take a comprehensive look at research strengths and weaknesses in this area.

In reviewing the research base in this area during the last 15 years, most of the studies surveyed covered the following topics and interventions:

- Following the child's lead
- Behavior modification techniques
- Contingent response training
- Floor time
- Types of adult utterances
- Combining structured with unstructured activities
- Naturalistic language
- Turn-taking
- Interactive matching of affect
- Therapeutic support/counseling to families

Outcomes reviewed in these studies included affect levels, amount of child initiations, amount of reciprocal parent-child interactions, types of child verbal/communicative acts, and increases in levels of symbolic play. The research summary of this area is given in Table 8.

Of the 27 articles reviewed, all but two demonstrated beneficial uses of the interventions surveyed. The issues of matching family

Table 8. Parent/Caregiver Research Summary

Type of Study	No.	Evidence for Intervention	Evidence Against Intervention	Equivocal Results	Short-Term Gains	Long-Term Gains	Clinically Significant	Clinically Meaningful
Case study reports	6	6	0	0	6	3	0	6
Descriptive studies/single-subject designs	7	6	0	1	7	0	4	5
Research review	2	2	0	1	2	2	2	0\
Quasi-experimental (non-clinical trials)	9	8	0	1	8	3	8	4
Experimental design (clinical trials)	3	3	0	0	2	0	1	0

and child characteristics and ethical considerations in using control groups obviously limited the number of true experimental clinical trial designs in this research area. However, the majority of this research was clinically significant when short-term gains were measured (p < .05). Long-term gains (in regard to changes in the children) were usually not adequately defined to draw conclusions that were as clinically significant as those seen in studies prior to 1985. Two exceptions to this were the studies by Greenspan et al. (1987) and Klein, Wieder, and Greenspan (1989). These studies looked at change over 4- and 2-year time periods, respectively, in multiple developmental and cognitive areas. Clinically meaningful results were determined if the outcomes measured were demonstrated in the home and measured under more than one circumstance when interventions were no longer taking place. Also included in this category were studies that measured outcomes in settings other than the home.

The study conducted by Klein, Wieder, and Greenspan with the Clinical Infant-Child Program of the National Institutes of Mental Health (1985) was particularly comprehensive. This 4-year longitudinal study noted previously provided counseling, teaching, and assistance in obtaining services for multi-risk families and included more than 200 children. Parents were trained in strategies of affect, social interaction, sensory-motor development, and cognition, and also given an ongoing emotional relationship in an attempt to reverse maladaptive developmental patterns. The approach was transactional and holistic as opposed to remedial, skill, or developmental-domain specific. Infants in the intensive intervention group showed a capacity to recover from early perinatal stress or developmental deviations, both from qualitative observations and statistical measures using relationship scales. Infants whose development had decompensated during the first 3 months of life (as demonstrated by chronic gaze aversion, lack of human attachment, and extreme affect lability) were able to achieve adaptive homeostatic and attachment capacities. This was done by helping parents make subtle changes in handling and approaches unique to the infant's sensory and processing style in their daily interactions and to eventually take over the treatment of their child.

Interestingly, the parent intervention research does not simply indicate that quantity of parent intervention sessions, or number of service providers correlates with positive outcomes. Intervention models that were associated with increased stress in mothers actually caused less improvement in development in a population of infants with developmental disabilities in low socioeconomic status (SES) families in a study by Brinker, Seifer, and Sameroff (1994).

Rather, the combination of quality and intensity of the intervention intersecting with the unique and changing characteristics of the child, the parent, and the resulting relationship characteristics tended to show the more robust research findings and clinically meaningful results.

In general, the research reviewed indicates that interaction strategies taught as content-bound skills were not as effective as context-bound skills taught as flexible processes based on the unique characteristics of the child's and the caregiver's ability to read and to adapt to these characteristics. This suggests that the intervention processes assume equal importance with the content, and are systematically selected to support specific content (Barrera, 1991; Rauh, Achenbach, Nurcombe, Howell & Teti, 1988). This involves defining characteristics and representative behaviors from within the context of the interactions between parent and child. Dyad research in this regard conducted by Landry and colleagues (1990, 1994) was particularly exemplary.

Discussion

The importance of parent/caregiver relationships as a functional deficit area is established not only by the core characteristic of impairment in social relatedness for autistic spectrum disorders but also by the literature across psychological, developmental, and psychiatric disciplines that have emphasized parent/caregiver relationships with the child as a foundation for social relationships and many emotional and problem-solving capacities.

Three experimental and 9 quasi-experimental designs yielded 9 clinically significant

results, and 4 clinically meaningful ones. Of the 27 articles reviewed, the most evidence for clinically meaningful results was seen in case-study reports, whereas the most clinically significant results were seen in the quasi-experimental studies.

Across all developmental challenges, research emphasized the avoidance of a one-size-fits-all approach to the child-parent dyad interaction, the need for integrated support to families, and the sensitivity to individual-child characteristics as the critical components in this intervention area. Many of the program evaluation studies that were not accessed specifically indicated that inclusion of the parent/caregiver relationships into an intervention seemed to be correlated with the most stable and enduring results of other treatment areas as well.

Although the construct of parent/caregiver relationships seems to be known across disciplines, much more research is needed in this area regarding interventions to improve these relationships. There has been insufficient research on interventions that work on relationships for children with autism and other developmental disorders. The role of parent/caregiver-child relationships for intervention with autistic spectrum disorders and other developmental problems, therefore, requires special emphasis.

The research support for interventions on parent/caregiver-child relationships and symbolic play, when coupled with the autism research on shared attention (Mundy & Crowson, 1997; Mundy et al., 1990), affective reciprocity (Lewy & Dawson, 1992; Tanguay, 1999), theory of mind (Baron-Cohen, 1994), functional language (Prizant & Wetherby, 1993), and abstract thinking (e.g., making inferences)(Minshew, 1997, 1999, in press), presents a substantial case for working with relationships at multiple functional developmental levels. These levels include shared attention, relating to others, reciprocal social interaction and social problem-solving, the creative and functional use of ideas (symbolic play), and logical and abstract thinking (see Chapters 3 and 4, this volume).

Peer Relationships

The inability to socially relate to other peers, and not just to adults, is one of the diagnostic indicators and core characteristics of children with autistic spectrum disorders. The importance of this functional deficit area is established not only by the DSM-IV definition of autism, but also because children's social competence in general, and peer-related social competence in particular, has emerged as a central issue in the treatment and education of children with disabilities (Guralnick, 1988). Much attention is being given to the difficulty with peer interactions that challenged children have because problems in this area extend well beyond what is expected, based on the child's overall developmental level (Guralnick & Groom, 1985, 1987, 1988; Lieber, Beckman, & Strong, 1993).

The research literature base over the past 15 years reflects this emphasis in the field, and mirrors the current educational reform movements towards more inclusive education models for children with disabilities. This review surveyed studies for all disabilities, including autism, that attempted to show the effects of interventions on the peer relationships of challenged children with more typical peers. While the preponderance of studies reviewed involved preschoolers, studies of elementary-age children were also utilized. The types of interventions utilized fell into the following categories, with several studies incorporating more than one intervention in their research (see Table 9).

Table 9. Interventions Surveyed by Peer Relationship Studies

Category	No. of Studies
Use of mainstream/inclusive settings	21
Social-skills training for challenged students	8
Training of typical peers in strategies/responses	6
Typical peer collaboration/mediation	6

A wide range of outcomes were evaluated, using both standardized and observational measures. These included the following:
- The amount/type of challenged child interactions typical peers
- The amount/type of typical peer interactions with challenged peers
- The type of play demonstrated by challenged peers
- Developmental progress in language, gross motor skills, comprehension, and cognition
- Social-competence measures
- Measures of teacher acceptance
- Amount of typical peer integration of challenged peers
- Generalization of all of the above skills to alternate settings

The research is summarized in Table 10. Of the studies reviewed, 78% had results that were clinically significant, even when measures taken were behavioral indices of incidents of observed interactions. Studies were determined to be clinically meaningful if measures of skill generalizations in settings other than the experimental ones were utilized and demonstrations of targeted skills were observed spontaneously, with no interventions. Fifty-seven percent of the studies included such information.

Long-term gains were not studied frequently but, when they were, they ranged

Table 10. Peer Relationship Intervention Research Summary

Type of Study	No.	Evidence for Intervention	Evidence Against Intervention	Equivocal Results	Short-Term Gains	Long-Term Gains	Clinically Significant	Clinically Meaningful
Single-subject design	5	4	1	2	5	2	3	5
Multiple-study review	1	1	0	1	1	0	1	1
Quasi-experimental (non-clinical trials)	29	24	2	7	28	6	22	14
Experimental design (clinical trials)	6	6	3	2	5	2	6	3

from 3 months to 1 year after the intervention was completed. While evidence against the use of the intervention was rare, the negative effects were interesting. One study noted better social interactions for children with higher-cognitive ability, but weaker social interactions for children with more limited ability in an integrated setting compared to a control group in a specialized setting. A decrease in measured gross motor skill development was noted in one integrated setting compared to a specialized one, possibly because of the lack of consistent physical and occupational therapy in the integrated setting. More challenged peer interaction with adults than with typical peers was noted in two of the studies in integrated settings.

Equivocal results centered on the limited differences in academic and developmental skill gains between challenged children in mainstreamed and specialized settings, despite gains in social competence measures and quantity of social interaction. Cognitive levels of play also did not tend to change in several of the studies as a result of the setting, although this was hypothesized.

The studies widely support the use of integrated settings for challenged children as well as the effectiveness of social-skills training for both typical and challenged peers. The literature demonstrates, however, that placement in such a setting is not sufficient in and of itself to improve peer relationships. The qualities of the setting (e.g., staff, program elements, and types of interactions facilitated are obviously of great importance). Placement in integrated settings had the largest effect sizes when adult mediation and teaching of specific skills occurred as a part of the program for both the challenged and typical peers. Particularly innovative strategies for social skills instruction for children with autism have been initiated by Carol Gray in her social stories (1994a, 1994b). Finally, the selection of setting and program intervention should be based on the individual profile of the child involved, and not just on a category of a disability. Because one intervention worked for one child with autism, there is no information that specifies which type of child with autism (in terms of his language, arousal levels, eye contact) would benefit the most from this intervention.

Discussion

The importance of peer relationships as a functional developmental area for intervention is seen not only in the diagnostic characteristic criteria for the autistic spectrum disorders but also in the general trend in educational programs that emphasizes social competence through inclusion with typical peers.

More than 60% of intervention studies were done using experimental and quasi-experimental designs, while most of the remaining surveyed research used single-subject designs. For many of the functional deficit areas surveyed in this chapter, a preponderance of traditional research designs over more narrative formats usually did not correlate with a large amount of clinically meaningful results. This was not true in the peer relationships area. Even with a lack of parent report and narrative case studies, 50% of these studies still yielded clinically meaningful results. Six of the studies were experimental in nature, with all 6 yielding clinically significant results and 3 showing clinically meaningful data. Twenty-nine of the 41 reviewed were classified as quasi-experimental—22 of these were clinically significant with 14 having clinically meaningful outcomes.

In general, the studies widely supported the use of integrated settings for challenged children, but emphasized that placement in such a setting was not sufficient to improve peer relationships without inclusion of adult mediation and specific skill instruction for both the challenged and typical peers. The studies also stressed the need for a "fit" between a program and a child, based on the child's individual profile, not just age or grade level.

Constructs that lay the foundation for social competence, such as shared understanding, emotional regulation, and information processing, were not generally researched with peer relationships, despite their strong theoretical base as foundations for such social skills and relatedness. It is likely that the understanding of processes rather than an attempt to "train" processes per se will be central in determining if peer relationship interventions will have long-term efficacy (Guralnick, 1998). Strategies for these interventions would benefit from research on the processes associated with being able to relate to others. The relationship of these constructs to executive functioning deficits (previously surveyed in this chapter) is postulated by many of the leading theorists (Barkley, 1993; Gilberg, 1998; Hynd et al., 1994). An interesting direction in research for the future could involve looking at the interaction of interventions in both the peer relationship and executive functions areas to see if one improves the other.

Interventions for improving peer relationships for children with characteristics in the autistic spectrum have experimental research validity. There is a need for interventions to be systematic and imbedded in a developmentally based framework and to look at long-term gains in skill maintenance. More case study formats, as well as parent and staff report narratives, are needed to give more qualitative and clinically meaningful information.

SURFACE BEHAVIORS: INTERVENTIONS FOCUSING ON CHANGING BEHAVIOR WITHOUT A FOCUS ON THE UNDERLYING PROCESSING DEFICITS

Surface behaviors can be viewed as an area of functioning, the same as language or motor planning. In general medicine, it is similar to considering the skin and dermatological functioning as a physical system, similar to kidney or cardiac functioning. To understand surface behavioral characteristics as a functional area, however, it is necessary to step back and look at the history of behaviorism in regards to the autistic spectrum, and its early importance.

Overview of Surface Behavior Intervention History

Prior to 1962, autism was viewed within the traditional medical model of disease. Literature regarding autism focused on identifying and/or curing the disease. Various studies showed that available psychological therapies were not effective in remediating autism (Havelkova, 1968; Kanner & Eisenberg, 1958; Rutter, 1966). Many children were labeled "incurable" and were institutionalized for the duration of their lives. This poor prognosis, combined with the advent of behaviorism, set the stage for some to view autism as a learning disorder instead of a disease. According to proponents of the behavioral approach, if the disease model had been able to provide an effective treatment paradigm, it is likely that the behavioral model would never have surfaced (Lovaas, 1979).

The shift from treating the disease, to identifying and treating the behaviors of autism (and their many manifestations), provided many families and professionals with a new sense of optimism and the focus in the field became the more tangible set of skills and behaviors. The public could not see a cure, but they could see when an autistic child learned to feed himself or say a word. The small successes provided by the studies at that time motivated treatment professionals, educators, and parents with specific behavioral goals.

Ferster (1961) was the first to present a theoretical construct regarding autism within a behavioral framework. He proposed that the behavioral problems of autistic children were based on a general deficiency in acquired reinforcers, and then conducted studies to show that such children could be taught simple tasks if reinforcers were significant or functional for them. When their behavior was explained by basic learning theory, it was a logical conclusion within the behavioral model that autistic children could be taught to comply with certain aspects of reality by rearranging the environmental consequences (Ferster & DeMyer, 1962). Several small case studies were reported that successfully used mild punishment and extinction to decrease self-injurious behaviors and teach basic imitation and beginning language skills (Hewitt, 1965; Metz, 1965; Wolf, Risley, & Mees, 1964). Although the studies presented no

data on whether treatment effects endured beyond the therapy, they had significance in the kinds of questions they began to ask about autistic children, as well as in the methodology and study designs employed.

Very few of the early studies in the immense body of behavioral literature ever mentioned a "recovery" from autism. Only the Lovaas studies from 1973 to 1987 made more ambitious claims. In the 79 studies reviewed for this chapter (excluding 6 research reviews), only 6 studies (including the Lovaas study) focused on the following broad outcomes at the end of the treatment interventions:

• Enrollment in regular education classes
• IQ score increases
• Language quotient gains
• Normal vs. abnormal developmental rates of learning
• Diagnosis of autism or pervasive developmental disorder

Rather, the mastery of specific skills and the decrease of designated aberrant behaviors were the major focuses of the behavioral research and literature. The number of studies according to treatment objective is shown in Table 11. A summary of all of the above studies in terms of variables reviewed in this article is given in Table 12.

Only 16% of the studies reviewed were experimental or quasi-experimental in nature and, of these, only 2 were experimental (i.e., involved clinical-trial methodology of random assignment and double-blind outcome assessment). While all of these studies showed clinically significant results in the broad outcome areas noted above, only five showed results that could be described as clinically meaningful. (As noted previously, the clinically meaningful outcomes are indicated when a skill targeted by the intervention is used and applied as it was intended to

Table 11. Treatment Objectives of Surface Behavior Interventions

Treatment Objective	No. of Studies
Initiating behaviors (verbal, language, and social)	6
Decreasing behaviors (echolalia, aggression, self-stimulation/ stereotypy, eating problems)	20
Increasing behaviors (verbal compliance, eye-gaze, verbal imitation, pointing)	4
Specific language skills (question-asking, increased vocabulary; object identification; linguistic formats)	6
Language use in general	7
Academic skills (number and letter identification, basic reading, vocabulary, basic math facts)	6
Sign language acquisition	3
Peer interaction behaviors (peer initiations to autistic children; increase in pivotal social response behaviors)	5
Functional life skills (toileting, dressing, shoe-tying)	2
Play skills (increase in appropriate toy play; increase in symbolic play)	4

be in real life, outside of the intervention setting and the therapist's presence.) The clinically meaningful outcomes in these studies included the following: the ability to tie shoes independently, increased verbal and nonverbal communication in novel settings, and increased amount of spontaneous language at home and at school.

The majority of clinically meaningful information was seen in the more narrative parent reports.

Within this format, clinically meaningful information was cited when the narratives did not note just a skill acquisition or mastery but rather gave an example of a generalized use of the skill spontaneously in a nontreatment setting. Some examples in the parent accounts included a child with autism telling a peer in a preschool that he liked the dinosaur he made, and another telling about his day to a grandmother on the phone.

Forty-eight percent of the total studies reviewed were multiple-baseline studies. This study format is unique to the behavioral literature. As opposed to comparing group performances between treatment and control groups, these studies measure the progress of single subjects at various stages of treatment depending on the design of the study (e.g.,

Table 12. Summary of Surface Behavior Studies

Type of Study	No.	Evidence for Intervention	Evidence Against Intervention	Equivocal Results	Short-Term Gains	Long-Term Gains	Clinically Significant	Clinically Meaningful
Parent reports/ narratives	7	7	0	0	7	7	0	7
Case study reports/ single subjects	16	16	0	0	16	1	13	3
Research reviews	6	4	2	0	5	1	5	0
Multiple-baseline comparison/ non-control group	38	35	1	2	36	7	35	11
Quasi-experimental (non-clinical trials)	10	6	0	1	6	6	10	4
Experimental design (clinical trials)	2	2	0	0	2	0	2	1

alternating, pre-post, time-delay). Twenty-seven of these studies had no comparison groups of children (i.e., the child's earlier performance was the basis for comparison). Eleven of the studies used some type of comparison with other children. In these studies, rates of change (or lack of) are compared against other subjects individually (and sometimes averaged with larger numbers of subjects) to determine treatment effectiveness. For example, a decrease in self-abusive behavior prior to a behavioral intervention, during, and after the intervention would be compared against a youngster with self-abusive behaviors who was having a different type of intervention during this time period. These studies often involved only a few subjects at a time. Overall, 29% of the multiple-baseline studies had some clinically meaningful findings. These outcomes included increased initiation of interactions with peers in a classroom setting, increased use of gestures with verbal settings, and a reduction in inappropriate vocalizations. This format permits a look at the effectiveness of an individual strategy in a narrow context, but can not be statistically generalized to a larger sample/population of children with autistic spectrum disorders because of the small size of the subject group.

Throughout the 1970s, 1980s, and much of the 1990s, applied behavior analysis (ABA) techniques were touted as the intervention of choice for working with children to change behaviors. This approach was especially appealing to a family coping with a child with a worrisome behavior, such as head-banging, because the immediate need to stop the behavior obviously takes precedent over all other concerns.

Lovaas's seminal work between 1973 through 1987 studied an intensive application of behavioral approaches to children with autism. His 1987 study asserted that 47% of his experimental group receiving intensive ABA treatment achieved normal intellectual and educational functioning, measured by normal IQ scores and first-grade performance in public schools (Lovaas, 1987). He referred to this group as "fully recovered." Five years later, McEachin, Smith, and Lovaas (1992) conducted a follow-up study of the experimental and control groups of children. The experimental group earned continued significantly higher scores in adaptive behavior measures, IQ tests, and on a personality inventory.

Later studies (Smith, Eikeseth, Klevstrand, & Lovaas, 1998) reported outcome data on children with intake IQs below 37, noting that none achieved normal functioning (defined by authors as IQ>85), although some children did make gains. Low IQ was seen to be associated with poor prognosis for most children in this study.

Preliminary data on six children participating in one of the Lovaas replication sites (at that time, the Bancroft Young Autism Project) was published in the summer of 1996 and showed limited success. All of these children received 2 years of treatment beginning at an age between 24 and 42 months. Treatment group IQ scores rose from a mean of 49 to 57 (for 3 children), while the IQ scores for the alternative control treatment group dropped from a mean of 57 to 37 (for 3 children). Adaptive behavior scales in the social area raised from a mean of 8 months to 20 months for the treatment group, and 10 to 12 months for the alternative treatment group. After 2 years, the 3 children in the treatment group were placed in regular education classes with aides, while control group children continued in special education classes. However, the treatment group children were still evidencing severe cognitive and language problems, as indicated by the mean IQ score of 57. It is also important to point out that mainstreaming with an aide may be helpful, but it is not a relevant indication of academic success for a child whose IQ is 57. It is not clear from these results what the individual IQ of each child was, and if one score skewed the average IQ score to be this low.

Other related outcome studies reviewed included the Anderson, Avery, DiPetro, Edwards, and Christian study (1987) at the May Institute in Massachusetts. This study, which did not use a comparison group, involved 114 children with autism receiving 15 to 25 hours per week of intensive behavioral teaching in their homes. Results showed increases: mental age and social age scores increased from range of 2 to 23 months, with language gains ranging from 3 to 18 months. Full language and cognitive and social functioning were generally not achieved. No children in the group were integrated full-time into regular education programs. The Murdoch Program study in Australia, involving 9 treatment and 5 comparison children (Birnbrauer & Leach, 1993), also studied an intensive home ABA model at close to 19 hours a week of programming. Gains were seen after 2 years for half of the treatment group, but even children with the best outcome did not achieve the level of functioning the Lovaas study claimed. Similar results were seen in the Sheinkopf and Siegel (1998) home-based intervention study of 10 treatment and 11 comparison children. While the highest IQ score gain was seen for an experimental group, as well as a decrease in symptom severity, all of the experimental group still met the criteria for diagnosis of autistic spectrum disorder after a year of treatment.

School and center-based behavioral interventions were studied at the Princeton Child Development Institute, (Fenske, Zalenski, Hall, Krantz, & Mclannahan, 1985). Results indicated 67% of children who enrolled before age 5 achieved some positive gains compared to just 1 out of 9 children who enrolled after the age of 5. Harris, Handleman, Kristoof, Bass, and Gordon (1990) used ABA methods in both a segregated classroom for children with autism as well as an integrated model with typically developing peers. Children in this group were higher functioning and older than those seen in other studies. On post-testing with the Stanford-Binet, children with autism achieved IQ gains, but the scores of all the children with autism were still well below those of their typical peers on both pre- and post-tests. Other studies also examined ABA methodology within integrated group program settings.

Overall, other behavioral studies have not produced results consistent with the Lovaas claims. They have, however, demonstrated that various forms of behavioral intervention are associated with selective gains. Long-term gains in the major deficit areas of autism—the capacity for empathy, abstract thinking, and relating with intimacy and trust to others—has not been demonstrated in either of these studies or the Lovaas study.

Limitations of the Behavioral Approach

There are two major limitations of the behavioral approaches. One involves working with isolated behavior with relative underemphasis of the whole dynamic system that comprises human functioning. A second is a tendency by many proponents of behavioral approaches to insufficiently deal with numerous methodological limitations pointed out by colleagues over a number of years and, instead, to go beyond the available data in making statements about treatment efficacy.

The last 15 years have seen neurobiological and psychological research that clearly implicates biochemical and genetic influences, as well as neuropsychological processes, in autistic behavior that are far more complex than the environmental variables tested in the early behavioral research (see Zimmerman & Gordon, Chapter 27; Minshew & Goldstein, Chapter 28; Bauman, Chapter 29, this volume). Recent behavioral scholars have attempted to account for the environmental aspects of isolated behaviors in an attempt to remediate this deficit (e.g., Carr & Durand, 1985; Carr et al., 1999). With increasing evidence of the biological and psychological characteristics of autism, the limitations of the behavioral research have emerged.

In general medicine, it has long been acknowledged that it is essential to consider the whole pattern; that is, the entire body system. For example, the side effects of treatment must be looked at when considering a course of treatment for an illness. A medication that is used to treat pneumonia should not also cause heart disease. Yet the ABA studies largely do not account for the increase or decrease in other constructs that are widely, if not universally, accepted as critical for human functioning. These include the capacity for intimacy, creativity, introspection, mood stability and regulation, attention, and relationships with others. Neuroimaging and other neurological assessments now indicate the corresponding physiological areas of the brain critical for these functions. Stopping head-banging is only treating a symptom of the disorder of autism; it is not addressing the multiple intricacies of neurological and emotional patterns and disregulations that are part of the problem. By their very nature, in addressing skills in isolation, the behavioral research is too incomplete to care for the child as a whole. As such, their skill remediation needs to be viewed as one possible aspect of a broader approach. Furthermore, when behaviors are dealt with in isolation, the side effects of the treatment on other skills—including the ability for abstract

thought, creativity, trust and intimacy, relating to others with warmth and joy, and mood regulation—are not known or even accounted for, positively or negatively, in the majority of the behavioral literature. Responsible and ethical treatment approaches must acknowledge and measure these side effects, particularly when the client may not be able to provide self-reports of these internal states.

The variables designated as "progress" within the behavioral literature are much easier to measure than the previously discussed constructs, which are more complex. Recent research (Baron-Cohen, Tager-Flusberg, & Cohen, 1993; Minshew, 1997, 1999, in press), however, has substantiated the importance of using more complex, difficult-to-measure outcome variables, not only in the social-emotional realm but also in the cognitive one. Studies by these individuals show that, when matched for IQ scores with normal and retarded individuals, those with autism tend to show selective difficulties in the mental processes associated with higher-level abstract thinking and emotional and social capacities. These include the ability to make inferences, interpret information, generate new ideas or perspectives, and empathize with and understand the feelings and perspectives of others. This information was not known when the behaviorists began to study their outcomes with some of the behaviors of autism. Now that it is known, it is curious that most behavioral studies still do not attempt to measure these constructs—particularly since they are viewed as the benchmark characteristics of the disorder. Similarly, deficits in the ability to relate to others with intimacy and trust and engage in reciprocal, affective interactions (Baranek, 1999; Dawson & Galpert, 1990; Lewy & Dawson, 1992; Osterling & Dawson, 1994; Tanguay, Robertson, & Derrick, 1998; Tanguay, 1999) are benchmark characteristics of the disorder (e.g., they are listed in DSM-IV), but are generally not sufficiently used in behavioral studies as outcome variables. There are a few notable exceptions in the behavioral research area that have begun to look at more complex social behavior, but still do not deal with some of the most important human capacities such as creative and abstract thought and a sense of self (Koegel, Koegel, Harrower, & Carter, 1999; Koegel, Koegel, Shoshan, & McNerny, 1999; Schreibman, 1996). These studies have creatively combined milieu-teaching procedures with behavioral methodology to focus on increasing motivation to produce generalized and spontaneous child initiations within a wide range of social situations. These researchers emphasize that treatment responsiveness varies greatly among children and that there is a need to study the child, family, and environment more closely to see how they interact with treatments. Schriebman (1996) has challenged the behavioral field to think "out of the box" of single target behaviors and focus on larger behavior aggregates that result in overall improvement in the quality of life for children with autism. She advocates striving for "social validation" of change that an outside observer could notice (i.e., a difference in the child with autism after an intervention time period that is above and beyond a simple increase in skills or decrease in behavior).

ABA research also has been criticized from additional methodological and statistical vantage points, despite the large quantity of studies. For example, the New York State Guidelines for Evaluating Programs for autism only recommended ABA or behavioral methods based on its review of the available research at that time. Surprisingly, the majority of the studies surveyed in that document do not involve a true clinical trial procedure using random sampling and group assignment, let alone equivalent groups. The conclusions in that report, therefore, went significantly beyond what the data could support. An analysis of the quantitative characteristics of the 54 studies reviewed in this document, as well as 15 additional studies, is shown in Table 13.

Of the 71 studies reviewed, 76% were individual case studies or used groups that had fewer than 5 subjects. Random assignment to treatment groups, or even choosing a random sample, was not a part of these studies. If traditional research standards are used for reviewing these studies, these factors and the use of such small groups ultimately decrease their validity. The other studies cited focused on circumscribed behaviors, were not sufficiently long-term, and did not demonstrate long-term gains in the deficit

Table 13. Quantitative Characteristics of Surface Behavior Studies

Total Number of Subjects	No.	Use of Non-Treatment Control Groups	Use of Comparison Treatment Groups	Use of Equivalent Matched Groups	Random Assignment into Groups/ Controls	Clearly Defined Representative Sample of Specific Child With Autism	Representative Sample of Full Autistic Spectrum
Single subject	20	0	0	0	0	0	0
1 to 4	34	4	0	0	0	4	0
5 to 10	8	2	1	0	0	1	0
10 to 20	6	1	3	0	0	1	0
20 +	3	3*	1	1	0	1	0

*In one study, crossover design of future treatment; group used as non-treatment; control group.

areas most relevant to autism; that is, the capacity for relating with intimacy and trust, engaging in reciprocal, affective interactions, being empathetic and understanding the feelings of others, and thinking creatively and abstractly.

However, it is Lovaas's research that is generally cited as the basis for funding ABA interventions for autistic spectrum disorders. His studies, however, evidence a number of methodological problems. The methodological issues around which Lovaas has been criticized center on three areas: bias in selection of subjects, inappropriate outcome measures, and an inadequate control group. These were later expanded in a series of criticisms by Gresham and MacMillan (1997, 1998) to also include concerns regarding treatment integrity as well as threats to internal and external validity. Gresham and MacMillan questioned whether the outcome data were related to the intensity of treatment rather than to any specific feature of the intervention itself.

Schopler and colleagues (1989) felt strongly that Lovaas's subjects were skewed toward relatively high-functioning children, and excluded children functioning not only in the profound, but also the mild to moderate ranges of cognitive deficits. Recent estimates suggest that at least 30% of autistic individuals have IQs within the mild to moderate range of mental retardation, 16% have scores in the severe mental retardation range, and half have scores in the average range, with only 5% having scores in the above-average range (Rosenblatt, 1993). The emphasis in autism/pervasive developmental disorder literature on obtaining given IQ scores as an entry criterion for various treatment studies thus makes generalizabilty of results to the wider range and truer representation of autistic children limited.

Lovaas's stated exclusion criteria only allowed children into the study who had or were in the processes of learning imitational communication skills. These children, therefore, had higher cognitive abilities than most typical children with autism. Most typical children with autism are not able to imitate when they first enter an intervention program. Most of the Lovaas intervention group, at the beginning, evidenced developmental capacities in the 14- to 18-month-old level of functional abilities, whereas the typical child presenting with autism often evidences developmental capacities at the 6- to 8-month-old level of functioning. In addition, children who were 40 to 46 months old were only admitted into the study if they demonstrated echolalia. Echolalia is commonly perceived as a characteristic of young children with autism who tend to have a better prognoses. Critics have stated that the study selected a group of children with relatively good prognoses and thus was not truly representative of autistic children as a whole (Schopler et al., 1989).

The issue of inadequate control groups has also been discussed. There was no random assignment to a treatment and control group, and families likely knew which group they were in by the intensity of the treatment program. Attempts at making the intensive treatment and control group comparable were fraught with a number of difficulties. Children who applied to enter the study earliest were assigned to the treatment group because the largest number of student trainers was available at that time. While other children did enter the treatment group later, it was only when the correct number of student trainers was available. Thus, initially, the control group consisted of children who met the criteria, but for whom no therapists could be found. The control group received a much less intense form of the treatment (10 hours per week). As all of the families in the intensive intervention group received and engaged in a 40- hour per week program, selection could not possibly be random in regards to the many personal and family variables that could restrict a family's abilities to participate in such an intense program. While Lovaas claims SES means were almost identical to the national average, the issues here are probably not the range or mean SES but the lack of information gauging the precise numbers of families in each SES category and descriptions of their life circumstances. The life circumstances issue became cogent because Lovaas had previously stated in his 1978 study that parents with restrictions of divorce, maternal employment, and personal and financial problems were counseled to other treatment and placements. Schopler (1989) suggested that Lovaas's own inconsistencies between the reports on his work in 1978 and 1987 appeared to more post-hoc analysis in nature than a true randomly controlled clinical trial.

Lovaas's claims for "recovery" of 47% of his experimental group were based on the children's placement in a regular education classroom and on the result of IQ measures (pre- and post-treatment) (Lovaas, Smith, & McEachin, 1989). The use of IQ as a measure of progress, let alone "recovery," from autism is seriously problematic.

The lack of validity of using IQ scores with children with autism has been noted in several research studies (Lincoln, Allen, & Kilman, 1995; Lord & Schopler, 1989; Lord, Schopler, & Revecki, 1982). These studies indicated that, while IQ scores for a speaking autistic child were likely to remain in the same range, the converse for a nonverbal child was not true. In fact, in one study, 50% of the nonverbal autistic 3-year-olds showed increases of more than 30 points when reassessed 5 to 8 years later.

Most important, as pointed out earlier, low IQ is not the distinguishing characteristic of autism and, while gains in IQ are welcome,

they do not indicate improvement in many of the most critical autistic patterns. Individuals with autism can have high IQ scores and have severe deficits in abstract thinking (e.g., making inferences), emotional regulation, social behavior, the capacity for empathy, and understanding feelings (Minshew, 1997; Baron-Cohen, Tager-Flusberg, & Cohen, 1993). When matched for IQ scores with nonautistic individuals, those with autism evidence these specific deficits in abstract thinking, empathy, social interaction, and emotional regulation. Therefore, it is these characteristics that are the hallmark of autism that must be improved in a successful intervention program. Also, IQ scores measure what has been learned as opposed to how easily or the manner in which something was learned. It does not measure the dynamic cognitive processes of how information is processed.

Lincoln et al. (1995) and Schriebman et al. (1981) hold that because children with autism frequently lack the skills necessary to function adaptively in certain contexts, it might actually be more valid to utilize alternative assessment techniques. Such techniques could incorporate the ability to gain from instruction—that is, the before and after abilities/skills that are associated with varying tasks that have been taught, rehearsed, and practiced.

It can also be hypothesized that part of the failure of children with autism to function adaptively across contexts is a failure to measure and design interventions that focus on the key characteristics of autism noted in more recent research, such as empathy, reciprocal interactions, and abstract thinking (Minshew, 1997; Baron-Cohen, Tager, Flusberg, & Cohen, 1993). Recovery from autism for a child with significant cognitive deficits might mean limited degrees of IQ increases, but dramatic improvement in social-interaction skills, communicative functions, play levels, and range of emotions, as well as a decrease in aberrant behavioral mannerisms. Schriebman et al. (1981) stresses that these types of changes in functioning must also be "socially valid;" that is, an outside observer could look at such children after an intervention and determine changes in the above areas.

Discussion

The "Surface Behavior" literature (without focusing on underlying processing deficits that may or may not contribute to the behavior) is an important area because of the degree and quantity of aberrant and maladaptive behaviors that can be seen in children with autistic spectrum disorders. Indeed, it is the interventions for these behaviors that provided the earliest assistance to families long before autism began to be understood better in terms of it range and underlying processing differences.

Contrary to the conclusion of the New York State Health Department, ABA discrete trial and behavioral methodologies do not have definitive scientific support and, in fact, face the same methodological challenges and weaknesses seen in the other functional deficit areas.

The majority of the behavioral studies reviewed have very small numbers of subjects, even though a lot of these studies (71) look at discrete behaviors in isolation and do not employ a clinical trial methodology. The eight larger-scale outcome studies (still relatively small groups with a size of 10 to 20) reviewed also did not use a true clinical trial procedure that included random assignment and grouping. More important, none of these studies included clinically meaningful data. This is because the larger-scale studies focused on such outcome variables as IQ scores and placement in regular education

and not on critical abstract thinking, emotional, and social skills.

The existing research base supports behavioral interventions for discrete behaviors in the short term without sufficient attention to "side effects," long-term outcomes, or the most important human capacities that are compromised in autism. These include such constructs as relating with others, reciprocal affective interactions, abstract and creative thinking, empathy and understanding of the feelings of others.

At the same time, however, the base of clinically meaningful information seen in the parent narratives should not be ignored. Interestingly, the information parents provided as meaningful and important in their children did not always dovetail with the goals and outcomes espoused by the behavioral studies. Thus, it is difficult to determine if these parent reports reflect change attributed to the behavioral intervention itself or to other variables, such as the relationship between therapist and child, occurring during the intervention (e.g., Catherine Maurice's poignant account of the time her daughter first pointed and looked back at her to show her a water fountain in the park). Practitioners should look closely at the constructs parents deemed to be meaningful in their accounts and consider quantifying and documenting this information more systematically to set new targets for behavior interventions.

In addition, it would be helpful at some point to obtain personal accounts from individuals who underwent intensive ABA programs and are now becoming young adults. As this information led to much clinically meaningful information for the sensory reactivity interventions (which were weak in clinically significant information), it would be interesting to see if the same applies to the surface behavior interventions (which are relatively strong in clinically significant information, but weak in clinically meaningful data). At the present time, the literature supports the consideration of behavioral interventions for selected and isolated behaviors for children who may require them as one part of a comprehensive program.

OVERALL CONCLUSIONS

As discussed earlier, this review characterized the studies along the dimensions of clinically significant and clinically meaningful. It also looked at studies that used a clinical trial methodology involving random assignments to a control group and appropriate objectivity in the evaluation process (e.g., individuals and evaluators not knowing which group they are assigned to), as well as other types of less definitive research designs. The strongest research support and the only that could be considered definitive would be a study that showed both clinically significant and clinically meaningful findings emerging from a clinical trial-like design. Using this standard to review the research analyses in the prior sections suggests that only a few functional developmental deficits have definitive research support for interventions. This includes speech and language interventions, relationship-based interventions, and circumscribed motor planning interventions. Other areas, including behavioral interventions (ABA discrete trials), do not have definitive research support, although there is support from less vigorous designs.

Therefore, if we only recommended interventions that have definitive research support behind them, we would advocate programs focused on speech and language, relationships—including child-caregiver and peer interactions—and selected sequencing and motor capacities. Focusing on these areas, while not comprehensive, is actually not a bad beginning and would constitute a more comprehensive approach than many children are presently receiving. Many children, for example, receive very little work on child-caregiver interactions and insufficient work on sequencing and motor planning or motor-based interventions.

There is, however, another criterion that needs to be applied to what is recommended for a comprehensive intervention program. It relates to the importance of a particular problem area; that is, the degree to which the problem itself requires the best approach available. In working with complex problems in the real world, clinicians do not have the luxury of ignoring critical problems, even in the absence of definitive research support for interventions for those problems. There are many medical problems, for example, which require the best treatment approaches available even though definitive evidence of efficacy for a treatment is lacking. In fact, only a small percentage of general medical practice is based on definitive, clinical trial supported treatments.

As a general rule, the more significant the problem area, the more compelling the case can be made for using the best interventions available as more research is being conducted. Often, these determinations, as indicated in Chapters 1 through 3 of this volume, are made by expert opinion, combining clinical experience with available research.

Therefore, a number of the functional developmental areas described in the research review that have some degree of research support behind them, including systematic case studies and quasi-experimental designs, require interventions based on this combination of clinical experience and available research. The areas of sensory reactivity and visual-spatial processing in particular are critically important and, therefore, require the best approaches available. As indicated, behavioral approaches are also in this category. Such approaches can be an important part of an overall program for children with severe motor planning problems who have difficulty executing initial motor sequences required in play and speech, including basic imitative skills. Using a behavioral approach to teach a child how to stack a three-block building, or clap hands, or sit down briefly in a small group can provide a foundation for skill competence that can then be expanded into relationship-based play and verbal and nonverbal communication with the interventions noted in the other functional developmental areas. Interestingly, Lovaas did not specifically mention this type of problem in his original study, and there are indications that children who appear lower functioning on standardized test scores due to these types of deficits were omitted from the study. There is not a great deal of efficacy data in the behavioral literature on this topic. Nonetheless, clinical experience suggests that very structured behavioral approaches, as well as structured developmental approaches (see McGee, Morrier, & Daly, 1999; Prizant & Rubin, 1999; Miller & Eller-Miller, Chapter 19, this volume), may be a helpful component of a program for this particular challenge.

Comprehensive, Functional Developmental Approach Versus More Circumscribed Approaches

When we combine analysis of available intervention research with research on the identification of the areas of functioning that require intervention, we observe the importance of a comprehensive approach to assessment and intervention that works with the core areas where there are functional developmental deficits (e.g., language). The alternative approach is to work only with circumscribed aspects of this larger pattern of problems, such as selected surface behaviors or selected cognitive skills (as is done in

many programs). There is, however, compelling evidence for the usefulness of interventions for multiple functional areas and evidence for the existence of other functional deficits that are part of the pattern of disordered functioning. It is, therefore, untenable to support a more circumscribed approach. This is especially true given the fact that research support for the more circumscribed approaches, such as those that focus on surface behaviors or circumscribed cognitive skills, do not have definitive, clinical trial research support behind them. In other words, it is good practice both from a humane point of view and from an analysis of current research and clinical experience to use a comprehensive developmental approach.

The support for a comprehensive approach includes interventions for the major areas of motor and sensory processing, including auditory processing and language, sensory modulation, and visual-spatial thinking, as well as motor planning and executive functioning. It also includes interventions for relationships, including child-caregiver and peer interactions and the functional developmental capacities that derive from relationships, including shared attention, engagement, affective and social reciprocity, social problem solving, the functional and creative use of ideas and symbolic play, and logical and abstract thought (including theory of mind).

Related to the comprehensive versus circumscribed approach debate is the issue of what school systems are willing to provide and what third-party reimbursers are willing to cover. Interestingly, as this research review has shown, there are many functional areas that have traditionally been supported by both educational systems and medical care for a variety of developmental disorders, even though definitive research evidence for efficacy is not yet available. A good example would be physical therapy for a child attempting to recover from a cerebral-vascular accident (e.g., post-surgery for an aneurysm). When it comes to autistic spectrum disorders, however, school systems and medical insurers are often reluctant to cover the full range of services required to work with the identified functional deficits. These parties will often cite lack of definitive efficacy studies. This selective use of such a rationale for one disorder and not other disorders or medical conditions constitutes a real bias against certain types of developmental problems. In light of this bias, and in light of the lack of definitive research support for more circumscribed approaches, it is especially important to employ a model for assessment and intervention that can delineate all the relevant areas of functional developmental deficits. Such a model facilitates both comprehensive, developmentally based assessment and intervention programs.   ■

GENERAL REFERENCES

Achenbach, T. M., Howell, C. T., Aoki, M. F., & Rauh, V. A. (1993). Nine-year outcome of the Vermont Intervention Program for Low Birth Weight Infants. *Pediatrics, 91,* 45-55.

Ainsworth, M. S. (1962). The effects of maternal deprivation: A review of findings and controversy in the context of research strategy. *WHO Public Health Paper, 14,* 97-165.

Ainsworth, M. S. (1997). The personal origins of attachment theory. An interview with Mary Salter Ainsworth. *Psychoanalytic Study of the Child, 52,* 386-405.

Anderson, S. R., Avery, D. L., DiPietro, E. K., Edwards, G. L., & Christian, W. P. (1987). Intensive home-based early intervention with autistic children. *Education and Treatment of Children, 10,* 352-366.

Arendt, R. E., MacLean, W. E., Jr., & Baumeister, A. A. (1988). Critique of sensory integration therapy and its application in mental retardation. *American Journal of Occupational Therapy, 92,* 401-411.

Aryes, A. J., & Mailloux, Z. K. (1981). Influence of sensory integration procedures on language development. *American Journal of Occupational Therapy, 35*(6), 383-390.

Aryes, A. J., & Mailloux, Z. K. (1983). Possible pubertal effect on therapeutic gains in an autistic girl. *American Journal of Occupational Therapy.*

Aryes, A. J., & Tickle, L. S. (1980). Hyperresponsivity to touch and vestibular stimuli as a predictor of positive response to sensory integration procedures by autistic children. *American Journal of Occupational Therapy, 34,* 375-381.

Baranek, G. T. (1998). Sensory processing in persons with autism and developmental disabilities: Considerations for research and clinical practice. *Sensory Integration Special Interest Section Quarterly, 21*(2), 1-4.

Baranek, G. T. (1999). Autism during infancy: A retrospective video analysis of sensory-motor and social behaviors at 9-12 months of age. *Journal of Autism and Developmental Disorders, 29*(3), 213-224.

Baranek, G. T., & Berkson, G. (1996). Tactile defensiveness in children with developmental disabilities: Responsiveness and habituation. *Journal of Autism and Developmental Disorders, 24*(4), 457-471.

Baranek, G. T., Foster, L. G., & Berkson, G. (1997). Sensory defensiveness in persons with developmental disabilities. *Occupational Therapy Journal of Research, 17,* 173-185.

Baranek, G., Foster, L., & Berkson, G. (1997). Tactile defensiveness and stereotyped behaviors. *Journal of Occupational Therapy, 51,* 91-95.

Barber, P. A., Turnbull, A. P., Behr, S. K., & Kerns, G. M. (1988). A family systems perspective on early childhood special education. In S. L. Odom & M. B. Karnes (Eds.), *Early intervention for infants and children with handicaps: An empirical base* (pp. 179-198). Baltimore: Paul H. Brookes.

Barkley, R. A. (1997). Attention-deficit/hyperactivity disorder, self-regulation, and time: Toward a more comprehensive theory. *Journal of Developmental and Behavioral Pediatics, 18,* 271-279.

Barkley, R. A. (1997). Behavioral inhibition, sustained attention, and executive functions: Constructing a unifying theory of ADHD. *Psychological Bulletin, 121,* 85-94.

Barnes, S. B. (1996). *Promoting motor skill development through the MOVE curriculum.* Paper presented at the 74th Annual International Convention of the Council for Exceptional Children, Orlando, FL, April.

Baron-Cohen, S. (1994). *Mindblindness: An essay on autism and theories of mind.* Cambridge, MA: MIT Press.

Baron-Cohen, S., Tager-Flusberg, H., & Cohen, D. (1993). *Understanding other minds: Perspectives from autism.* London: Oxford University Press.

Barrera, M. E. (1991). The transactional model of early home intervention: Application with developmentally delayed children and their families. In K. Marfo (Ed.), *Early intervention in transition: Current perspectives on programs for handicapped children* (pp.109-146). New York: Praeger.

Barrera, M., & Rosenbaum, P. (1986). The transactional model of early home intervention. *Infant Mental Health Journal, 7,* 112-131.

Barron, J. (1992). *There's a boy in here.* New York: Simon & Schuster.

Bauman, M. L., & Kemper, T. L. (1994). Neuroanatomic observations of the brain in autism. In M. L. Bauman & T. L. Kemper (Eds.), *The neurobiology of autism* (pp. 119-145). Baltimore: Johns Hopkins University Press.

Beitchman, J. H., & Inglis, A. (1991). The continuum of linguistic dysfunction from pervasive developmental disorders to dyslexia. *Psychiatric Clinics of North America, 14*(1).

Bell, M. A., & Fox, N. A. (1994). Brain development over the first year of life: Relations between EEG frequency and coherence and cognitive affective behaviors. G. Dawson & K. Fischer (Eds.), *Human behavior and the developing brain* (pp. 315-345). New York: Guilford.

Bennetto, L., Pennington, B. F., & Rogers, S. J. (1996). Intact and impaired memory functions in autism. *Child Development, 67,* 1816-1835.

Birnbrauer, J. S., & Leach, D. J. (1993). The Murdoch early intervention program after 2 years. *Behaviour Change, 10,* 63-74.

Blackman, S., & Goldstein, K. M. (1982). Cognitive styles and learning disabilities. *Journal of Learning Disabilities, 15,* 106-115.

Bondy, A. S. & Peterson, S. (1990). *The point is not to point: Picture Exchange communication system with young students with autism.* Paper presented at the Association for Behavior Analysis Convention. Nashville, TN.

Bonoclonna, P. (1981). Effects of a vestibular stimulation program on stereotypic rocking behavior. *American Journal of Occupational Therapy, 35,* 775-781.

Bowlby, J. (1977). The making and breaking of affectional bonds. II: Some principles of psychotherapy. The fiftieth Maudsley Lecture. *British Journal of Psychiatry, 130,* 421-431.

Bowlby, J. (1978). Attachment theory and its therapeutic implications. *Adolescent psychiatry, 6,* 5-33.

Bowlby, J. (1982). Attachment and loss: Retrospect and prospect. *American Journal of Orthopsychiatry, 52*(4), 664-678.

Bricker, D. (1993). Then, now, and the path between: A brief history of language intervention. In A. P. Kaiser & D. B. Gay (Eds.), *Enhancing children's communication: Research foundations for intervention: Vol. 2* (pp. 11-13).

Brinker, P. R., Seifer, R., & Sameroff, A. J. (1994). Relation among maternal stress, cognitive development, and early intervention in middle and low SES infants with developmental disabilities. *American Journal on Mental Retardation, 98,* 463-480.

Bristol, M., Cohen, D., Costello, J., Denckla, M., Eckberg, T., Kallen, R., Kraemer, H., Lord, C., Maurer, R., McIllvane, W., Minshew, N., Sigman, M., & Spence, A. (1996). State of the science in autism: Report to the National Institutes of Health. *Journal of Autism and Developmental Disorders, 26,* 121-154.

Bronfenbrenner, U. (1986). Ecology of the family as context for human development research perspectives. *Developmental Psychology, 22,* 723-742.

Bruneau, N., Dourneau, M. C., Garreau, B., Pourcelot, L., & Lelord, G. (1992). Blood flow response to auditory stimulations in normal, mentally retarded, and autistic children: A preliminary transcranial Doppler ultrasonographic study of the middle cerebral arteries. *Biological Psychiatry, 32*(8), 691-699.

Burack, J. A. (1994). Selective attention deficits in persons with autism.

Burpee, J., DeJean, V., Frick, S., Kawar, M., & Murphy, D. (in press). Theoretical and clinical perspectives on the Interactive Metronome® (IM): A view from clinical occupational therapy.

Carew, J. V. (1980a). Black beginnings: A longitudinal, videotaped observational study of the reading and development of infants in black families.

Carew, J. V. (1980b). Experience and the development of intelligence in young children at home and in day care. (Monograph). *Society for Research in Child Development, 45*(6/7), 1-115.

Carew, J. V., et al. (1975). Observed intellectual competence and tested intelligence: Their roots in the young child's transaction with his environment.

Carew, J. V., et al. (1980). Environment, experience, and intellectual development of young children in home care. *American Journal of Orthopsychiatry, 44*(5), 773-781.

Carr, E. G., & Durand, V. M. (1985). Reducing behavior problems through functional communication training. *Journal of Applied Behavioral Analysis, 18,* 111-126.

Carr, E. G., Horner, R. H., Turnbull, A. P., Marquis, J. G., Magito-McLaughlin, D., McAtee, M. L., Smith, C. E., Anderson-Ryan, K. A., Ruef, M. B., & Doolabh, A.

(1999). *Positive behavioral support for people with developmental disabilities* (Monograph series). Washington, D.C.: American Association on Mental Retardation.

Case-Smith, J., & Bryan, T. (1999). The effects of occupational therapy with sensory integration emphasis on preschool-aged children with autism. *American Journal of Occupational Therapy, 53,* 489-497.

Casey, M. B., Bronson, M. B., Tivnan, T., Riley, E., & Spinciner, L. (1991). Differentiating preschoolers' sequential planning agility from their general intelligence: A study of organization, systematic responding, and efficiency in young children. *Journal of Applied Developmental Psychology, 12,* 19-32.

Charlop, M. H., & Haymes, L. K. (1994). Speech and language acquisition and intervention: Behavior approaches. In J. Matson (Ed.), *Autism in children and adults: Etiology, assessment, and intervention* (pp. 213-240). Pacific Grove, CA: Brooks/Cole.

Chez, C., Gordon, J., Ghilardi, M. F., & Sainburg, R. (1995). Contributions of vision and proprioception to accuracy in limb movements. In M. S. Gazzaniga (Ed.), *The cognitive neurosciences* (pp. 548-564). Cambridge, MA: MIT Press.

Christopher, W., & Christopher, B. (1989). *Mixed blessings.* Nashville, TN: Abingdon Press.

Chugani, H. T., & Phelps, M. E. (1986). Maturational changes in cerebral function in infants determined by 18FDG positron emission tomography. *Science, 231,* 840-843.

Chugani, H. T., Phelps, M. E., & Mazziotta, J. C. (1994). Positron emission tomography study of the human brain function development. *Annals of Neurology, 22,* 487-497.

Cohen, D., & Volkmar, F. (Eds.) (1997). *Handbook of autism and pervasive devel-*

opmental disorders (2nd ed.). New York: Wiley & Sons.

Cohen, S. (1998). *Targeting autism: What we know, don't know and can do to help young children with autism and related disorders.* Los Angeles: University of California Press.

Comer, J. (1980). *School power: Implications of an intervention project.* New York: Free Press.

Cornish, K. M., & McManus, I. C. (1996). Hand preference and hand skill in children with autism. *Journal of Autism and Developmental Disorders, 26*(6), 597-609.

Courchesne, E., Townsend, J., Akshoomoff, N. A., & Saitoh, O. (1994). Impairment in shifting attention in autistic and cerebellar patients. *Behavioral Neuroscience, 108,* 848-865.

Cummins, R. A. (1991). Sensory integration and learning disabilities: Ayres' factor analyses reappraised. *Journal of Learning Disabilities, 24,* 160-168.

Das, J. P. (1984). Aspects of planning. In J. R. Kirby (Ed.), *Cognitive strategies and educational performance* (pp. 13-31). New York: Academic Press.

Das, J. P., Naglieri, J. A., & Kirby, J. R. (1994). *Assessment of cognitive processes: The PASS theory of intelligence.* New York: Allen and Bacon.

Dawson, G., & Galpert, I. (1986). A developmental model for facilitating the social behavior of autistic children. In E. Schopler & G. B. Mesibov (Eds.), *Social behavior in autism* (pp. 237-261). New York: Plenum Press.

Dawson, G., & Galpert, I. (1990). Mother's use of imitative play for facilitating social responsiveness and toy play in young autistic children. *Developmental Psychopathology, 2,* 151-162.

Dawson, G., & Lewy, A. (1989). Arousal, attention and the socioemotional impairments of individuals with autism. In G. Dawson (Ed.), *Autism: Nature, diagnosis,* and treatment (pp. 49-74). New York: Guilford Press.

Dawson, G., & Osterling, J. (1997). Early intervention in autism. In M. J. Guralnick (Ed.), *The effectiveness of early intervention* (pp. 307-326). Baltimore: Paul H. Brookes.

Dawson, G., Warrenburg, S., & Fuller, P. (1982). Cerebral lateralization in individuals diagnosed as autistic in early childhood. *Brain and Language, 15,* 353-368.

Denckla, M. B. (1986). New diagnostic criteria for autism and related behavioral disorders—guidelines for research protocols. *Journal of the American Academy of Child Psychiatry, 25*(2), 221-224.

Denckla, M. B., Rudel, R. G., Chapman, C., & Krieger, J. (1985). Motor proficiency in dyslexic children with and without attentional disorders. *Archives of Neurology, 42,* 228-231.

Donnellan, A. M., & Kilman, B. A. *Behavioral approaches to social skills development in autism: Strengths, misapplications, and alternatives.*

Douglass, L. (1999). *An evaluation of the effectiveness of early intervention on autistic children.* Master's Research Paper, Chicago State University, IL.

Eikeseth, S., & Lovaas, O. I. (1992). The autistic label and its potentially detrimental effect on the child's treatment. *Journal of Behavior Therapy and Experimental Psychiatry, 23,* 151-157.

Elliott, R., Hall, K., & Soper, H. (1991). Analog language teaching vs. natural language teaching: Generalization and retention of language learning for adults with autism and mental retardation. *Journal of Autism and Developmental Disorders, 21,* 433-447.

Feinberg, E., & Beyer, J. (1998). Creating public policy in a climate of clinical indeterminacy: Lovaas as the case example du jour. *Infants and Young Children, 10*(3), 54-66.

Fenske, E. C., Zalenski, S., Krantz, P. J., & McClannahan, L. E. (1985). Age at intervention and treatment outcome for autistic children in a comprehensive intervention program. *Analysis and Intervention in Developmental Disabilities, 5,* 49-58.

Ferster, C. B. (1961). Positive reinforcement and behavioral deficits of autistic children. *Child Development, 32,* 437-456.

Ferster, C. B., & DeMyer, M. K. (1962). A method for the experimental analysis of behavior of autistic children. *American Journal of Orthopsychiatry, 32, 89-98.*

Feuerstein, R., Rand, Y., Hoffman, M., & Miller, R. (1979). Cognitive modifiability in retarded adolescents: Effects of instrumental enrichment. *American Journal of Mental Deficiency, 83*(6), 539-550.

Feuerstein, R., Rand, Y., Hoffman, M., & Miller, R. (1979). *The dynamic assessment of retarded performers.* Baltimore: University Park Press.

Feuerstein, R., Rand, Y., Hoffman, M., & Miller, R. (1980). *Instrumental enrichment: An intervention program for cognitive modifiability.* Baltimore: University Park Press.

Feuerstein, R., Miller, R., Hoffman, M., Rand, Y., Mintsker, Y., Morgens, R., Jensen, M. R. (1981). Cognitive modifiability in adolescence: cognitive structure and the effects of intervention. *Journal of Special Education, 150*(2), 269-287.

Fewell, R. (1991). Individualized family service plans. *Topics in Early Childhood Special Education, 11*(3), 54-65.

Fillmore, L. W. (1979). Individual differences in second language acquisition. In G. S. Fillmore, D. Kempler, & W. S. Wong (Eds.), *Individual differences in language ability and language behavior.* New York: Academic Press.

Foxx, R. M. (1993). Sapid effects awaiting replication. *American Journal of Mental Retardation, 97*(4), 375-376.

Freeman, B. J. (1993). The syndrome of autism: Update and guidance for diagnosis. *Infants and Young Children, 6,* 1-11.

Freeman, B. J. (1998). Guidelines for evaluating intervention programs for children with autism. *Journal of Autism and Developmental Disorders, 27,* 641-652.

Freeman, B. J., Rahbar, B., Ritvo, E. R.; Bice, T. L., Yakota, A., & Ritvo, R. (1991). The stability of cognitive and behavioral parameters in autism: A 12-year prospective study. *Journal of the American Academy of Child and Adolescent Psychiatry, 30,* 479-482.

Freeman, B. J., Ritvo, E. R., Needleman, R., & Yakota, A. (1985). The stability of cognitive and linguistic parameters in autism: A five year study. *Journal of the American Academy of Child and Adolescent Psychiatry, 24,* 290-311.

Freeman, K. A., & Piazza, C. C. (1998). Combining stimulus fading, reinforcement, and extinction to treat food refusal. *Journal of Applied Behavior Analysis, 31*(4), 691-694.

Frith, U. (1989). *Autism.* Worchester, GB: Billing & Sons.

Frith, U. (1993). Autism. *Scientific American,* 108-114.

Furth, H. G., & Wachs, H. (1974). *Thinking goes to school: Piaget's theory in practice.* New York: Oxford University Press.

Gardner, H. (1983). *Frames of mind: The theory of multiple intelligences.* New York: Basic Books.

Ghez, C., Gordon, J., Ghilardi, M. F., & Sainburg, R. (1995). Contributions of vision and proprioception to accuracy in limb movements. In M. S. Gazzaniga (Ed.), *The cognitive neurosciences* (pp. 548-564). Cambridge, MA: MIT Press.

Gillberg, C. (1989). The role of endogeneous opiods in autism and possible relationships to clinical features. In L. Wing (Ed.), *Aspects of autism: Biological research* (pp. 31-37).

Gillberg, C. (1990). Autism and pervasive developmental disorder. *Journal of Child Psychiatry, 31*(1), 99-119.

Gillberg, C., & Coleman, M. (1992). *The biology of the autistic syndromes* (2nd ed.) New York: Cambridge University Press.

Gillberg, C., & Stefferburg, S. (1987). Outcome and prognostic factors in infantile autism and similar conditions: A population-based study of 46 cases followed through puberty. *Journal of Autism and Developmental Disorders, 17,* 273-287.

Goldstein, H., & Hockenberger, E. H. (1991). Significant progress in child language intervention: An 11-year retrospective. *Research on Developmental Disability, 12*(4), 401-424.

Grandin, T. (1988). My experiences as an autistic child and a review of selected literature. *Journal of Orthomolecular Psychiatry, 13*(3), 144-174.

Grandin, T. (1995). *Thinking in pictures.* New York: Doubleday.

Grandin, T., & Sarrano, M. (1986). *Emergence: Labeled autistic.* Novato, CA: Arena Press.

Gray, C. (1994a). *The new social story book.* Jenison MI: Jenison Public Schools.

Gray, C. (1994b). *The original social story book.* Jenison MI: Jenison Public Schools.

Green, G. (1990). Least restrictive use of reductive procedures: Guidelines and competencies. In A. C. Repp & N. N. Singh (Eds.), *Perspectives on the use of non-aversive and aversive interventions for persons with developmental disabilities* (pp. 479-493). DeKalb, IL: Sycamore Press.

Greenough, W. T., & Black, J. E. (1992). Induction of brain structure by experience: Substrates for cognitive development. *Developmental Behavioral Neuroscience, 24,* 155-299.

Greenspan, S. I. (1979). Intelligence and adaptation: An integration of psychoanalyt-ic and Piagetian developmental psychology. *Psychological Issues, 12(3/4)* (Monograph 47/48). New York: International Universities Press.

Greenspan, S. I. (1981). Psychopathology and adaptation in infancy and early childhood: Principles of clinical diagnosis and preventive intervention. *Clinical Infant Reports, 1.* New York: International Universities Press.

Greenspan, S. I. (1990). An intensive approach to a toddler with emotional, motor, and language delays: A case report. *Zero to Three, 11*(1), 20-26

Greenspan, S. I. (1992). *Infancy and early childhood: The practice of clinical assessment and intervention with emotional and developmental challenges.* Madison, CT: International Universities Press.

Greenspan, S. I. (1992). Reconsidering the diagnosis and treatment of very young children with autistic spectrum or pervasive developmental disorder. *Zero to Three, 13*(2), 1-9.

Greenspan, S. I. (1995). *The Infancy and Early Childhood Training Course* (Conducted in Bethesda, MD, April).

Greenspan, S. I. (1995). *The Infancy and Early Childhood Training Course* (Conducted in Arlington, VA, April).

Greenspan, S. I. (1996). *Developmentally Based Psychotherapy.* Madison, CT: International Universities Press.

Greenspan, S. I. (1996). *The growth of the mind and the endangered origins of intelligence.* Reading, MA: Addison Wesley Longman.

Greenspan, S. I., and DeGangi, G. (1997). The functional emotional assessment scale: Revised version and reliability studies.

Greenspan, S. I., & Lourie, R. S. (1981). Developmental structuralist approach to the classification of adaptive and pathologic personality organization: Infancy and early childhood. *American Journal of Psychiatry, 1380*(6), 725-734.

Greenspan, S. I., Lourie, R. S., & Nover, R. (1979). A developmental approach to the classification of psychopathology in infancy and early childhood. In J. Noshpitz (Ed.), *The basic handbook of child psychiatry: Vol. 2.* New York: Basic Books.

Greenspan, S. I., & Porges, S. W. (1984). Psychopathology in infancy and early childhood: Clinical perspectives on the organization of sensory and thematic experience. *Child Development, 55,* 49-70.

Greenspan, S. I., & Sharfstein, S. S. (1981). The efficacy of psychotherapy: Asking the right questions. *Archives of General Psychiatry, 38*(11), 1213-1219.

Greenspan, S. I., & Wieder, S. (1997). *Facilitating emotional and intellectual growth in infants and young children with special needs problems.* Reading, MA: Addison Wesley Longman.

Greenspan, S. I., & Wieder, S. (1997). *The child with special needs.* Cambridge, MA: Perseus Books.

Greenspan, S. I., & Wieder, S., Lieberman, A., Nover, R., Lourie, R., & Robinson, M. (1987). Infants in multirisk families: Case studies in preventive intervention. *Clinical infant report, No. 3.* New York: International Universities Press.

Greenspan, S. I., & Weider, S. (1999). A functional developmental approach to autism spectrum disorders. *Journal of the Association for Persons with Severe Handicaps (JASH), 24*(3), 147-161.

Gresham, F. M., & MacMillian, D. L. (1977). Autistic recovery? An analysis and critique of the empirical evidence on the Early Intervention Project. *Behavioral Disorders, 22,* 185-201.

Gresham, F. M., & MacMillian, D. L. (1998). Early Intervention Project: Can its claims be substantiated and its effects replicated?

Journal of Autism and Developmental Disorders, 28(1), 5-13.

Guess, D., & Carr, E. (1991). Emergence and maintenance of stereotypy and self-injury. *American Journal of Mental Retardation, 96*(3), 299-319.

Guralnick, M. J. (1990). Major accomplishments and future directions in early childhood mainstreaming. *Topics in Early Childhood Special Education, 10*(2), 1-16.

Guralnick, M. J. (1991). The next decade of research on the effectiveness of early intervention. *Exceptional Children, 58*(2), 174-183.

Guralnick, M. J. (Ed.) (1991). *The effectiveness of early intervention.* Baltimore, MD: Paul H. Brookes.

Guralnick, M. J. (1993). Developmentally appropriate practice in the assessment and intervention of children's peer relations. *Topics in Early Childhood Special Education, 13*(3), 334-371.

Guralnick, M. J. (1998). Effectiveness of early intervention for vulnerable children: A developmental perspective. *American Journal on Mental Retardation, January, 102*(4), 319-345.

Guralnick, M. J., & Groom, J. M. (1985). Correlates of peer-related social competence of developmentally delayed preschool children. *American Journal of Mental Deficiency, 90,* 140-150.

Guralnick, M. J., & Groom, J. M. (1987). Dyadic peer interactions on mildly delayed and nonhandicapped preschool children. *American Journal of Mental Deficiency, 92,* 178-193.

Guralnick, M. J., & Groom, J. M. (1988). Friendships of preschool children in mainstreamed play groups. *Developmental Psychology, 24,* 595-605.

Haas, R. H., Townsend, J., Courchesne, E., & Lincoln, A. J. (1996). Neurologic abnormalities in infantile autism. *Journal of Child Neuropsychology, 11,* 84-92.

Handen, B. (1993). Pharmacotherapy in mental retardation and autism. *School Psychology Review, 22*(2), 162-183.

Handleman, J. S., & Harris, S. L. (1994). the Douglass Developmental Disabilities Center. In S. L. Harris & J. Handleman (Eds.), *Preschool education programs for children with autism* (pp. 71-86). Austin, TX: PRO-ED.

Harris, S. L. (1975). Teaching language to non-verbal children with an emphasis on problems of generalization. *Psychological Bulletin, 82,* 565-580.

Harris, S. L., Handleman, J. S., Gordon, R., Kristoff, B., & Fuentes, F. (1991). Changes in cognitive and language functioning of preschool children with autism. *Journal of Autism and Developmental Disorders, 21,* 281-290.

Harris, S. L., Handleman, J. S., Kristoff, B., Bass, L., & Cordon, R. (1990). Changes in language development among autistic and peer children in segregated and integrated preschool settings. *Journal of Autism and Developmental Disorders, 20*(1), 23-31.

Havelkova, M. (1968). Follow-up study of seventy-one children diagnosed as psychotic in preschool age. *American Journal of Orthopsychiatry, 38,* 927-936.

Hazen, Black, and Fleming-Johnson (1984). Social acceptance. *Young Children, 39,* 26-36.

Heidemann, S., & Hewitt, D. (1992). *Pathways to play: Developing play skills in young children.* St. Paul, MN: Redleaf Press.

Hemmeter, M. L., & Kaiser, A. P. (1994). Enhanced milieu teaching: An analysis of the effects of parent-implemented language intervention. *Journal of Early Intervention, 18,* 155-167.

Hewitt, F. M. (1965). Teaching speech to an autistic child through operant conditioning. *American Journal of Orthopsychiatry, 35,* 927-936.

Hibbs, E. D., Findikoglu, M., Lieberman, A., Lourie, R., Nover, R., Wieder, S, Greenspan, S. I. (1987). In S. I. Greenspan, S. Weider, A. Liberman, R. Nova, R. S. Lourie, & M. Robinson (Eds.), *Infants in multi-risk families: Case studies in preventive intervention: Clinical Infant Reports, No. 3.* New York: International Universities Press.

Hobbs, N., Blalock, A., Chambliss, C. (1995). *The economic and social burdens associated with Lovaas treatment with childhood autism.* Unpublished master's thesis, Ursinus College, PA.

Hobson, R. P. (1991). Methodological issues for experiments on autistic individuals' perception and understanding of emotions. *Journal of Child Psychiatry and Psychology, 321,* 217-250.

Hobson, R. P., Ouston, J., & Lee, A. (1988). Emotion recognition in autism: Coordinating faces and voices. *Psychological Medicine, 18,* 911-923.

Hoehn, T., & Baumeister, A. (1994). A critique of the application of sensory integration therapy to children with learning disabilities. *Journal of Learning Disabilities, 27,* 338-350.

Hofheimer, J. A., Poisson, S. S., & Greenspan, S. I. (1981). *The reliability, validity, and generalizability of assessments of transactions between infants and their caregivers: A multicenter design.* Unpublished paper, Clinical Infant Development Programs, National Institutes of Mental Health.

Hofheimer, J. A., Poisson, S. S., Strauss, M. E., Eyler, F. D., & Greenspan, S. I. (1983). Perinatal and behavioral characteristics of neonates born to multi-risk families. *Journal of Developmental and Behavioral Pediatrics, 4*(3), 27-36.

Honig, A. S., & Lally, J. R. (1981). *Infant caregiving: A design for training.* Syracuse, NY: Syracuse University.

Hoy, M. P., & Retish, P. M. (1984). A comparison of two types of assessment reports. *Exceptional Children, 51,* 225-229.

Huebner, R. A. (1992). Autistic disorder: A neuropsychological enigma. *American Journal of Occupational Therapy, 46*(6), 487-501.

Hughes, C. (1996). Brief report: Planning problems in autism at the level of motor control. *Journal of Autism and Developmental Disorders, 26*(1), 99-107.

Hynd, G. W., Hern, K., Novey, E. S., Eliopulos, D., Marshall, R., Gonzalez, J. J., & Voeller, K. K. (1993). Attention deficit-hyperactivity disorder and asymmetry of the caudate nucleus. *Journal of Child Neurology, 6,* 339-347.

Hynd, G. W., Hern, K., Voeller, K. K., & Marshall, R. M. (1991). *School Psychology Review, 20*(2), 174-186.

Hynd, G. W., & Hooper, S. R. (1990). *Neurological basis of childhood psychopathology: Vol. 25: Developmental clinical psychology and psychiatry.* Newbury Park/London/New Delhi: Sage.

Hynd, G. W. & Semrud-Clikeman, M. (1989). Dyslexia and neurodevelopmental pathology: Relationships to cognition, intelligence, and reading skill acquisition. *Journal of Learning Disabilities, 22*(4), 204-216.

Jarrold, C., Boucher, J., & Smith P. K. (1994). Executive function deficits and the pretend play of children with autism: A research note. *Journal of Child Psychology and Psychiatry, 35,* 1473-1482.

Kanner, L. (1943). Autistic disturbances of affective contact. *Nervous Child, 2,* 217-250.

Kanner, L. (1971). Follow-up of eleven autistic children originally reported in 1943. *Journal of Autism and Child Schizophrenia, 1,* 119-145.

Kanner, L., & Eisenberg, L. (1958). Child psychiatry, mental deficiency. *American Journal of Psychiatry, 114*(7), 609-615.

Kazdin, A. E. (1982). *Single-case research designs.* New York: Oxford University Press.

Klein, P. S., Wieder, S., & Greenspan, S. I. (1989). A theoretical overview and empirical study of mediated learning experience: Prediction of preschool performance from mother-infant interaction patterns. *Infant Mental Health Journal, 8*(2), 110-129.

Klein, S., & Magill-Evans, J. (1998). Reliability of perceived confidence measures for young school-aged children. *Canadian Journal of Occupational Therapy, 65*(5), 293-298.

Klin, A., Sparrow, S. S., deBildt, A., Cicchetti, D. V., Cohen, D. J., & Volkmar, F. R. (1999). *Journal of Autism and Developmental Disorders, 29*(5), 385-393.

Klin, A., Volkmar, F. R., Sparrow, S. S., Cicchetti, D. V., & Rourke, B. P. (1995). Validity and neuropsychological characterization of Asperger syndrome: Convergnce with nonverbal learning disabilities syndrome. *Journal of Child Psychology and Psychiatry, 36*(7), 1127-1140.

Klinger, L. G., & Dawson, G. (1992). Facilitating early social and communicative development in children with autism. In S. Warren & J. Reichle (Eds.), *Communication and language intervention series: Vol. I. Causes and effects in communicating and language intervention* (pp. 167-186). Baltimore, MD: Paul H. Brookes.

Koegel, L. K., Koegel, R. L., Harrower, J., & Carter, C. M. (1999). Pivotal response intervention I: Overview of approach. *Journal of the Association of Persons with Severe Handicaps (JASH), 24*(3), 174-185.

Koegel, L. K., Koegel, R. L., Shoshan, Y., & McNerney, E. (1999). Pivotal response intervention II: Preliminary long-term outcome data. *Journal of the Association of Persons with Severe Handicaps (JASH), 24*(3), 186-198.

Koegel, R. L., Dyer, K., & Bell, L. K. (1987). The influence of child-preferred activities on autistic children's social behavior. *Journal of Applied Behavior Analysis, 20,* 243-252.

Koegel, R. L., Koegel, L. K., & O'Neill, R. (1989). Generalization in the treatment of autism. In L. V. McReynolds & J. E. Spradlin (Eds.), *Generalization strategies in the treatment of communication disorders* (pp. 116-131). Toronto: Decker.

Koegel, R. L., O'Dell, M., & Koegel, L. K. (1987) A natural language paradigm for teaching non-verbal autistic children. *Journal of Autism and Developmental Disorders, 17,* 187-199.

Kohen-Raz, R., Volkmar, F., & Cohen, D. J. (1992). Postural control in children with autism. *Brain Dysfunction, 4,* 419-429.

Krauss, M. W. (1998). Two generations of family research in early intervention. In M. Guralnick (Ed.), *The effectiveness of early intervention* (pp. 611-624). Baltimore, MD: Paul H. Brookes.

Kuhlman, K., & Schweinhart, L. J. (1999). *Timing in child development.* Ypsilanti, MI: High/Scope Educational Research Foundation.

Lally, J. R. (1995). The impact of child care policies and practices on infant/toddler identity formation. *Young Children, November,* 58-67.

Landry, S. H., & Chapieski, M. L. (1990). Joint attention of 6-month-old Down syndrome and preterm infants: I: Attention to toys and mothers. *American Journal on Mental Retardation, 94,* 488-498.

Landry, S. H., Garner, P. W., Pirie, D., & Swank, P. R. (1994). Effects of social context and mothers' requesting strategies on Down's syndrome children's social respon-siveness. *Developmental Psychology, 36,* 465-477.

Law, J. (1997). Evaluating intervention for language impaired children: A review of the literature. *European Journal of Disorders of Communication, 32,* (2 Spec. No.) 1-14.

Law, M., Polatajko, H, Schaffer, R., Miller, J., & Macnab, J. (1991). The effect of a sensory integration program on academic achievement, motor performance and self-esteem in children identified as learning disabled: Results of a clinical trial. *The Occupational Therapy Journal of Research, 11,* 155-176.

Lewy, A. L., & Dawson, G. (1992). Social stimulation and joint attention in young autistic children. *Journal of Abnormal Child Psychology, 20*(6), 555-566.

Lieber, J., & Beckman, P. J. (1991). The role of toys in individual and dyadic play among young children with handicaps. *Journal of Applied Developmental Psychology, 12,* 189-203.

Lieber, J., Beckman, P. J., & Strong, B. O. (1993). A longitudinal study of the social exchanges of young children with disabilities. *Journal of Early Intervention, 17,* 116-125.

Lincoln, A. J., Courchesne, E., Harms, L., & Allen, M. (1995). Sensory modulation of auditory stimuli in children with autism and receptive development language disorder: Event–related brain potential evidence. *Journal of Autism and Developmental Disorders, 25,* 521-539.

Losche, G. (1987). Sensorimotor and action development in autistic children from infancy to early childhood. ERIC No. ED294380.

Lovaas, O. I. (1979). Contrasting illness and behavioral models for the treatment of autistic children: A historical perspective. *Journal of Autism and Developmental Disorders, 98,* (4), 315-323.

Lovaas, O. I. (1987). Behavioral treatment and normal educational and intellectual functioning in young autistic children. *Journal of Consulting and Clinical Psychology, 55,* 3-9.

Lovaas, O. I., & Simmons, J. Q. (1969). Manipulation of self-destruction in three retarded children. *Journal of Applied Behavior Analysis, 2,* 143-157.

Lovaas, O. I., & Smith, T. (1988). Intensive behavioral treatment for young autistic children. In B. B. Lahey & A. E. Kazdin (Eds.), Advances in *clinical child psychology* (Vol. 11) (pp. 285-324). New York: Plenum Press.

Lovaas, O. I., & Smith, T. (1989). A comprehensive behavioral theory of autistic children: Paradigm for research and treatment. *Journal of Behavior Therapy and Experimental Psychiatry, 20,* 17-29.

Lovaas, O. I., Smith, T., and McEachin, J. J. (1989). Clarifying comments on the young autism study: Reply to Schopler, Short, and Mesibov. *Journal of the Academy of Applied Behavior Analysis, 18,* 3-16.

Luria, A. R. (1966). *Human brain and psychological processes.* New York: Harper & Row.

Luria, A. R. (1970). The functional organization of the brain. *Scientific American, 222,* 66-78.

Luria, A. R. (1973). *The working brain: An introduction to neuropsychology.* New York: Basic Books.

Luria, A. R. (1974). Language and brain: Towards the basic problems of neuro-linguistics. *Brain and Language, 1,* 1-14.

Luria, A. R. (1980). *Higher cortical functions in man* (2nd ed., rev.). New York: Basic Books.

Lyon, G., Reid, E., & Rumsey, J. (1996). *Neuroimaging: A window to the neurological foundations of learning and behavior in children.* Baltimore: Paul H. Brookes.

Mahoney, G., & Powell, A. (1988). Modifying parent-child interactions: Enhancing the development of handicapped children. *Journal of Special Education, 22,* 82-96.

Majuovana, J., & Prior, M. (1995). Comparison of Asperger syndrome and high functioning autistic children on a test of motor impairment. *Journal of Autism and Developmental Disorders, 25,* 23-41.

Marfo, K. (Ed.). (1988). *Parent-child interaction and developmental disabilities: Theory, research, and intervention.* New York: Praeger.

Markowitz, P. I. (1990). Fluoxetine treatment of self-injurious behavior in mentally retarded patients. *Journal of Clinical Psychopharmocology, 12,* 21-31.

Maurice, C. (1993). *Let me hear your voice.* New York: Knopf.

McArthur, D., & Adamson, L. B. (1996). Point attention in preverbal children: Autism and developmental language disorder. *Journal of Autism and Developmental Disorders, 26*(5).

McClannahan, L. E., & Krantz, P. J. (1993). On systems analysis in autism intervention programs. *Journal of Applied Behavior Analysis, 26,* 589-596.

McClannahan, L. E., & Krantz, P. J. (1994). The Princeton Child Development Institute. In S. L. Harris & J. S. Handleman (Eds.), *Preschool education programs for children with autism* (pp. 107-126). Austin, TX: PRO-ED.

McClannahan, L. E., Krantz, P. J., & McGee, G. G. (1982). Parents as therapists for autistic children: A model for effective parent training. *Analysis and Intervention in Developmental Disabilities, 2,* 223-252.

McEachin, J. J., Smith, T., & Lovaas, O. I. (1993). Long-term outcome for children with autism who received early intensive behavioral treatment. *American Journal of Mental Retardation, 4,* 359-372.

McCollum, J. A., & Bair, H. (1994). Research in parent-child interaction: Guidance to developmentally appropriate practice for young children with disabilities. In B. L. Mallory & R. S. New (Eds.), *Diversity and developmentally appropriate practices: Challenges for early childhood education* (pp. 84-106). New York: Teachers College.

McCollum, J. A., & Hemmeter, J. L. (1998). Parent-child interaction intervention: When children have disabilities. In M. Guralnick (Ed.), *The effectiveness of early intervention*. Baltimore: Paul H. Brookes.

McCollum, J. A., & Stayton, V. D. (1985). Infant/parent interaction: Studies and intervention guidelines based on the SIAI model. *Journal of the Division for Early Childhood, 10*, 124-135.

McCollum, J. A., & Yates, T. (1994). Dyad as focus, triad as means: A family–centered approach to supporting parent–child interactions. *Infants and Young Children, 6*(4), 54-63.

McDonnell, J. (1993). *News from the border.* New York: Ticknor & Fields.

McGee, G. G., & Gonzalez, L. (1990). Gentle teaching and the practice of human interdependence: A preliminary group study of fifteen persons with severe behavioral disorders and their caregivers. In A. C. Repp & N. N. Singh (Eds.) *Perspectives on the use of non-aversive and aversive interventions for people with developmental disabilities* (pp. 215-230). Sycamore, IL: Sycamore.

McGee, G. G., & Gonzalez, L. (1990). Gentle teaching and the practice of human interdependence: A preliminary group study of fifteen persons with severe behavior disorders and their caregivers. In A. C. Repp & N. N. Singh (Eds.), *Perspectives on the use of non-aversive and aversive interventions for people with developmental disabilities* (pp. 215-230). Sycamore IL: Sycamore.

McGee, G. G., & Izeman, S. (1988). *The Walden Learning Center.* Paper presented at the annual convention of the Autism Society of America, New Orleans, LA.

McKean, T. (1994). *Soon will come the light.* Arlington, TX: Future Education.

Mesibov, G. (1993). Treatment outcome is encouraging. *American Journal of Mental Retardation, 97*(4), 379-380.

Mesibov, G. B., Schopler, E., & Schaffer, B. (1989). Use of the childhood autism rating scale with autistic adolescents and adults. *Journal of the American Academy of Child and Adolescent Psychiatry, 28,* 538-541.

Metz, J. R. (1965). Conditioning generalization in autistic children. *Journal of Experimental Child Psychology, 77,* (115-126).

Miller, A. (1991). Cognitive developmental systems theory in pervasive developmental disorders. *Child Psychiatric Clinics of North America, 14*(1), 8-21.

Miller, A., & Miller, E. (1992). A new way with autistic and other children with pervasive developmental disorder (Monograph). Boston, MA: Language and Cognitive Center.

Miller, H. (1996). Eye contact and gaze aversion: Implications for persons with autism. *American Occupational Therapy Association Sensory Integration Special Interest Section Newsletter, 19*(2), 1-3.

Minshew, N. J. (1997). Autism and the pervasive developmental disorders: The clinical syndrome. In B. K. Shapiro, P. J. Accardo, & A. J. Capute (Eds.), *Behavior belongs in the brain: Neurobehavioral syndromes* (pp. 49-68). Baltimore, MD: York Press.

Minshew, N. (1999). Autism as a disorder of complex information processing and underdevelopment of neocortical systems. Paper presented at the Interdisciplinary Council on Developmental and Learning Disorders' Third Annual International Conference, *Autism and Disorders of*

Relating and Communicating, McLean, VA, November.

Minshew, N. J. (in press). The core deficit in autism and autism spectrum disorders. *Journal of Developmental and Learning Disorders.*

Minshew N., & Goldstein, G. (1998). Autism as a disorder of complex information processing. *Mental Retardation and Developmental Disabilities, 4*, 129-136.

Mirenda, P., & Donnellan, A. (1986). Effects of adult interaction style on conversational behavior in students with severe communication problems. *Language, Speech and Hearing Services in the Schools, 17*, 126-141.

Morgan, A. E., Hynd, G. W., Riccio, C. A., & Hall, J. Validity of DSM-IV ADHD Predominantly inattentive and combined types: Relationship to previous DSM diagnoses/subtype differences. *Journal of the American Academy of Child and Adolescent Psychiatry, 35*(3), 325-333.

Mouridsen, S. E. (1995). The Landau-Kleffner syndrome: A review. *European Child and Adolescent Psychiatry, 4*(4), 223-228.

Mundy, P., & Crowson, M. (1997). Joint attention and early social communication: Implications for research on intervention with autism. *Journal of Autism and Developmental Disorders, 27*(6), 653-76.

Mundy, P., Sigman, M., & Kasari, C. (1990). A longitudinal study of joint attention and language development in autistic children. *Journal of Autism and Developmental Disorders, 20*(1), 115-128.

Muthen, B. (1994). Latent variable modeling of longitudinal and multilevel data. Project 2.4, Quantitative models to monitor the status and progress of learning and performance and their antecedents. ED379322.

Muthen, B. O., & Nelson, G. (1991). Advances in multi-level psychometric models: Latent variable modeling of growth with missing data and multilevel data. Project 2.6: Analytic models to monitor status and progress of learning and performance and their antecedents.

Muthen, B., et al. (1995). Opportunities-to-learn effects on achievement: Analytical perspectives. *Educational Evaluation and Policy Analysis, 17*(3), 371-403.

Naglieri, J. A., & Das, J. P. (1990). Planning, attention, simultaneous, and successive (PASS) cognitive processes: A model of intelligence. *Journal of Psycho-educational Assessment, 8*, 303-337.

Odom, S. L., & Strain, P. (1986). A comparison of peer-interactions and teacher-antecedent intervention for promoting reciprocal social interactions of autistic preschoolers. *Journal of Applied Behavior Analysis, Spring: 19*(1), 59-71.

Olds, D. L. (1984). Case studies of factors interfering with nurse home visitors' promotion of positive caregiving methods in high-risk families. *Early Childhood Development and Care, 16*, 149-166.

Olley, J., Robbins, F., Morelli-Robbins, M. (1993). Current practices in early intervention for children with autism. In E. Schopler, M. Bourgondien, & M. Bristol (Eds.), *Preschool issues in autism* (pp. 223-245). New York/London: Plenum Press.

Ornitz, E. M. (1974). The modulation of sensory input and motor output in autistic children. *Journal of Autism and Developmental Disorders, 4*, 197-215.

Ornitz, E. M. (1988). Autism: A disorder of directed attention. *Brain Dysfunction, 1*, 309-322.

Ornitz, E. M. (1989). Autism at the interface between sensory processing and information processing, In G. Dawson (Ed.), *Autism: Nature, diagnosis and treatment* (pp. 174-207). New York: Guilford.

Osterling, J., & Dawson, G. (1994). Early recognition of children with autism: a study of first birthday home videotapes. *Journal of Autism and Developmental Disorders, 24*(3), 247-257.

Panskepp, J., Lensing, P., Leboyer, M., Bouvard, M. (1991). Naltrexone and other potential pharmacological treatments for autism. *Brain Dysfunction, 4,* 281-300.

Parham, L. (1998). The relationship of sensory integrative development to achievement in elementary students: Four-year longitudinal patterns. *Occupational Therapy Journal of Research, 18*(3), 105-127.

Pearse, I. H. (1979). *The quality of life: The Peckham approach to human ethnology.* Edinburgh: Scottish Academic Press.

Peck, C. (1985). Increasing opportunities for social control by children with autism and severe handicaps: Effects on student behavior and perceived classroom climate. *Journal of the Association for Persons with Severe Handicaps (JASH), 4,* 183-193.

Piek, J. P., Pitcher, T. M., & Hay, D. A. (1999a). Motor coordination and kinaesthesis in boys with attention deficit-hyperactivity disorder. *Developmental Medicine and Child Neurology, 41*(3), 159-165.

Piek, J. P., & Skinner, R. A. (1999b). Timing and force control during a sequential tapping task in children with and without motor coordination problems. *Journal of the International Neuropsychology Society, 5*(4), 320-329.

Piven, J., Harper, J., Palmer, P., & Arndt, S. (1996). Course of behavioral change in autism: A retrospective study of high-IQ adolescents and adults. *Journal of the American Academy of Child and Adolescent Psychiatry, 35*(4), 523-529.

Porges, S. W., & Bazhenova, O. V. (1997). *Evolution and the autonomic nervous system: A neurological model of socio-emotional and communication disorders.* Paper presented at the Interdisciplinary Council on Developmental and Learning Disorders conference, "Approaches to Developmental and Learning Disorders In Infants and Children: Theory & Practice," McLean, VA.

Powers, M. (1992). Early intervention for children with autism. In D. Berkell-Zager (Ed.), *Autism: Identification, education, and treatment.* Hillsdale, New Jersey: Erlbaum.

Prior, M., & Hoffman, W. Brief report: Neurosychological testing of autistic children through an exploration with frontal lobe tests. *Journal of Autism and Developmental Disorders, 20*(4), 581-590.

Prizant, B. M. (1982). Gestalt processing and gestalt language in autism. *Topics in Language Disorders, 3,* 16-23.

Prizant, B. M. (1983). Language acquisition and communicative behavior in autism: Towards an understanding of the "whole" of it. *Journal of Speech and Hearing Disorders, 48,* 296-307.

Prizant, B. M. (1987). Clinical implications of echolalic behavior in autism. In T. Layton (Ed.), *Language and treatment of autistic and developmentally disordered children.* Springfield, IL: Charles Thomas.

Prizant, B. M., Reichle, J., Barrett, C., Rice-Tetlie, R., & McQuarter, R. (1987). The effect of prior intervention to establish generalized requesting on the acquisition of object labels. *Augmentative and Alternative Communication, 3,* 3-10.

Prizant, B. M., Schuler, A. L., & Wetherby, A. M. (in press). Enhancing language and communication: Language approaches. In D. Cohen & F. Volkmar (Eds.), *Handbook of autism and pervasive developmental disorders* (2nd ed.) New York: Wiley.

Prizant, B. M., & Wetherby, A. M. (1985). Intentional communicative behavior of children with autism: Theoretical and applied issues. *Australian Journal of Human Communication Disorders, 13,* 21-58.

Prizant, B. M., & Wetherby, A. M. (1987). Communicative intent: A framework for understanding social-communicative behavior in autism. *Journal of the American Academy of Child and Adolescent Psychiatry, 26,* 472-479.

Prizant, B. M., & Wetherby, A. M. (1988). Providing services to children with autism (0-2 years) and their families. *Topics in Language Disorders, 9,* 1-23.

Prizant, B., & Wetherby, A. (1990). Toward and integrated view of early language and communication development and socio-emotional development. *Topics in Language Disorders, 10,* 1-16.

Prizant, B., & Wetherby, A. (1993). Communication assessment for young children. *Infants and Young Children, 5,* 20-34.

Provence, S., & Naylor, A. (1983). *Working with disadvantaged parents and their children: Scientific and practical issues.* New Haven: Yale University.

Py, Bernard (Ed.) (1994). Group interventions and interactions. *Proceedings of the Colloquium on Speech Therapy,* Neuchatel, Switzerland, September.

Ramey, C. T., & Campbell, F. A. (1984). Preventive education for high-risk children: Cognitive consequences of the Carolina Abecedarian Project. *American Journal of Mental Deficiency, 88,* 515-523.

Rapin, I. Allen, D. A. (1983) Developmental language disorders: Nosologic considerations. In U. Kirk (Ed.), *Neuropsychology of language, reading and spelling.* New York: Academic Press, 155-184.

Rapin, I., & Dunn, M. (1997). Language disorders in children with autism. *Seminars in Pediatric Neurology, 4*(2), 86-92.

Ratey, J. J., Sorrer, R., Mikkelsen, E., & Chmielinski, H. E. (1989). Buspirone therapy for maladaptive behavior and anxiety in developmentally disabled persons. *Journal of Clinical Psychiatry, 50*(10), 382-384.

Rauh, V. A., Achenbach, T. M., Nurcombe, B., Howell, C. T., & Teti, D. M. (1988). Minimizing adverse effects of low birthweight: Four-year results of an early intervention program. *Child Development, 59,* 544-553.

Resnick, M. B., Armstrong, S., & Carter, R. L. (1988). Developmental intervention program for high-risk premature infants: Effects on development and parent-infant interactions. *Journal of Developmental and Behavioral Pediatrics, 9,* 73-78.

Ricks, D. M., & Wing, L. (1976). Language, communication, and the use of symbols in normal and autistic children. In L. Wing (Ed.), *Early childhood autism: Clinical, social and educational aspects.* Oxford: Pergamon.

Rimland, B. (1964). *Infantile autism.* New York: Appleton-Century Crofts.

Rogers, S. J. (1996). Early intervention in autism. *Journal of Autism and Developmental Disorders, 26*(2).

Rogers, S. J. (1998a). An examination of the imitation deficit in autism. In J. Nadel & G. Butterworth (Eds.), *Imitation in Infancy.* Cambridge, UK: University of Cambridge Press.

Rogers, S. J. (1998b). Empirically supported comprehensive treatments for young children with autism. *Journal of Clinical Child Psychology, 27,* 168-179.

Rogers, S. J. (1998c). Neuropsychology of autism in young children and its implications for early intervention. *Mental Retardation and Developmental Disabilities Research Reviews, 4,* 104-112.

Rogers, S. J., Herbison, J. M., Lewis, H., Pantone, J., & Reis, K. (1988). An approach for enhancing symbolic, communicative, and interpersonal functioning of young children with autism and severe emotional handicaps. *Journal of the Division of Early Childhood, 10*(2), 135-145.

Rogers, S. J., & Lewis, H. (1989). An effective day treatment model for young children with pervasive developmental disorders. *Journal of the American Academy of Child and Adolescent Psychiatry, 28,* 207-214.

Rogers, S. J., Lewis, H. C., & Reis, K. (1987). An effective procedure for training early special education teams to implement a model problem. *Journal of the Division of Early Childhood, 11,* 180-188.

Rogers, J. M., Ozonoff, S., & Maslin-Cole, C. (1991). A comparative study of attachment behavior in young children with autism or other psychiatric disorders. *Journal of American Academy of Child and Adolescent Psychiatry, 30,* 483-488.

Rogers, S. J., & Pennington, B. F. (1991). A theoretical approach to the deficits in infantile autism. *Developmental Psychopathology, 3,* 137-162.

Rogosa, D., & Willett, J. B. (1985). Satisfying a simplex structure is simpler than it should be. *Journal of Educational Statistics, 10*(2), 99-107.

Rosenblatt, A. (1993). *Pervasive developmental disabilities.* Symposium conducted at Early Childhood Annual Division Training, Montgomery County Public Schools, Rockville, MD.

Rumsey, J. M., Rapoport, J. L., & Sceery, W. R. (1985). Autistic children as adults: Psychiatric social and behavioral outcomes. *Journal of the American Academy of Child and Adolescent Psychiatry, 24,* 465-473.

Russell, J., Jarrold C., & Henry, L. (1996). Working memory in children with autism and with moderate learning difficulties. *Journal of Child Psychology and Psychiatry, 37*(6), 673-686.

Rutter, M. (1966). Diagnosis: Psychotic children in adolescence and early life. In J. K. Wing (Ed.), *Early childhood autism: Clinical, educational, and social aspects.* London: Pergamon Press.

Rutter, M. (1983). Cognitive deficits in the pathogenesis of autism. *Journal of Child Psychology and Psychiatry, 24,* 513-531.

Rutter, M. (1998). *Autism: Two-way interplay between research and clinical work.* London: Institute of Psychiatry.

Rutter, M. (1998). Routes from research to clinical practice in child psychiatry: Retrospect and prospect. *Journal of Child Psychology and Psychiatry, 39*(6), 805-816.

Rutter, M., Greenfield, D., Lockyer, L. (1967). A five to fifteen year follow-up study of infantile psychosis: II. Social and behavioral outcomes. *British Journal of Psychiatry, 112,* 1183-1199.

Schopler, E. (1987). Specific and non-specific factors in the effectiveness of a treatment system. *American Psychologist, 42,* 262-267.

Schopler, E., & Mesibov, G. (1987). *Neurobiological issues in autism.* New York: Plenum Press.

Schopler, E., Mesibov, G., & Baker, A. (1982). Evaluation of treatment for autistic children and their parents. *Journal of the American Academy of Child and Adolescent Psychiatry, 21,* 262-267.

Schopler, E., Mesibov, G., & Hearsey, K. (1995). Structured teaching in the TEACH system. In E. Schopler & G. Mesibov (Eds.), *Learning and cognition in autism.* New York: Plenum Press.

Schopler, E., Short, A., & Mesibov, G. (1989). Relation of behavioral treatment to "normal functioning": Comments on Lovaas. *Journal of Consulting and Clinical Psychology, 57,* 162-164.

Schopler, E., Brehm, S., Kinsbourne, M., & Reichler, R. J. (1971). Effect of treatment structure on the development of autistic children. *Archives of General Psychiatry, 24,* 415-421.

Schriebman, L. (1988). *Autism.* Newbury Park, CA: Sage.

Schriebman, L. (1996). Brief report: The case for social and behavioral intervention research. *Journal of Autism and Developmental Disorders, 26*(2), 247.

Schriebman, L., Koegel, R. L., Mills, J. I., & Burke, J. G. (1981). The social validation of behavior therapy with autistic children. *Behavior Therapy, 12,* 610-624.

Schuler, A. L., Gonsier-Gerdin, J., & Wolfberg, P. (1990). The efficacy of speech and language intervention: An 11-year retrospective. *Research in Developmental Disabilities, 12,* 401-424.

Schuler, A. L., & Prizant, B. M. (1985). Echolalia in autism. In E. Schopler & G. Mesibov (Eds.) *Communication problems in autism.* New York: Plenum Press.

Schultz, R. T., Gautheir, I., Klin, A., Fulbright, R. K., Anderson, A. W., Volkmar, F., Skudlarski, P., Lacadie, C., Cohen, D. J., & Gore, J. C. (2000). Abnormal ventral temporal cortical activity during face discrimination among individuals with autism and Asperger syndrome. *Achieves of General Psychiatry, 57*(4), 331-340.

Shaffer, R. J., Jacokes, L. E., Cassily, J. F., Greenspan, S. I., Tuchman, R. F., & Stemmer P. J. (in press). Effect of Interactive Metronome® training on children with ADHD. *American Journal of Occupational Therapy.*

Shanz, M. T., & Menendez, F. J. (1993). Early motor training in Down's syndrome babies: Results of an intervention program. *Reports-Research* (143).

Sheinkopf, S., & Siegel, B. (1998). Home-based behavioral treatment for your autistic children. *Journal of Autism and Developmental Disorders.*

Sigman, M., & Ruskin, E. (1999). Continuity and change in the social competence of children with autism, Down syndrome and developmental delays. *Monographs of the Society for Research in Child Development, 64.*

Sigman, M., & Ungerer, J. A. (1984). Attachment behaviors in autistic children. *Journal of Autism and Developmental Disorders, 14*(3), 231-244.

Simpson, R. L. & Zionts, P. (1992). *Autism: Information and resources for parents, families, and professionals.* Austin, TX: PRO-ED.

Smilansky, S. (1968). *The effects of sociodramatic play on disadvantaged preschool children.* New York: Wiley & Sons.

Smith, T., Eikeseth, S., Klevstrand, M., & Lovaas, I. (1998). Intensive behavioral treatment for preschoolers with severe mental retardation and pervasive developmental disorder. *American Journal on Mental Retardation, 102*(3), 238-249.

Smith, T., & Lovaas, O. I. (1998). Intensive and early behavioral intervention with autism: The UCLA young autism project. *Infants and Young Children, 10*(3), 67-78.

Sparrow, S. S., Balla, D. A., Cicchetti, D. V. (1984). *Vineland Adaptive Behavior Scales.* American Guidance Service.

Sperry, L. A., Whaley, K. T., Shaw, E., & Brame, K. (1999). Services for young children with autism spectrum disorders: Voices of parents and providers. *Infants and Young Children, 11*(4), 17-33.

Sperry, R. W. (1985). Consciousness, personal identity, and the divided brain. In F. Benson & E. Zaidel (Eds.), *The dual brain* (pp. 11-27). New York: Guilford Press.

Spiker, D. (1990). Early intervention from a developmental perspective. In D. Cicchetti & M. Beeghly (Eds.), *Children with Down syndrome: A developmental perspective* (pp. 424-448). Cambridge: Cambridge University Press.

Spitz, R. A. (1972). *Journal of American Psychoanalysis Association, 20*(4), 721-735.

Stahmer, A. C. (1993). Teaching symbolic play to children with autism using pivotal response training: Effects on play, language and interaction. *Dissertation Abstracts International, 25*, 123-141.

Stahmer, A. C. (1995). Teaching symbolic play skills to children with autism using pivotal response training. *Journal of Autism and Developmental Disorders, 25*, 447-459.

Stahmer, A. C., & Schreibman, L. (1992). Teaching children with autism appropriate play in unsupervised environments using a self-management treatment package. *Journal of Applied Behavior Analysis, 25*, 123-141.

Stehli, A. (1992). *The sound of a miracle.* New York: Avon Books.

Stehli, A. (1995). *Dancing in the rain.* Westport, CT: Georgiana Organization.

Stemmer, P. M., Jr. (1997). *Improving student motor integration by use of an Interactive Metronome®.* Paper presented at the annual meeting of the American Educational Research Association, Chicago, IL, March.

Stokes, T. F., & Osnes, P. G. (1988). The developing applied technology of generalization and maintenance. In R. Horner, G. Dunlap, & R. L. Koegel (Eds.), *Generalization and maintenance* (pp. 5-19). Baltimore: Paul H. Brookes.

Strain, P. S., Cordisco, L. K. (1994). LEAP Preschool. In S. L. Harris & J. S. Handleman (Eds.), *Preschool education programs for children with autism* (pp. 225-244). Austin, TX: PRO-ED.

Strain, P. S., & Hoyson, M. (1988). *Follow-up of children in LEAP.* Paper presented at the meeting of the Autism Society of America, New Orleans, LA.

Strain, P. S., Hoyson, M., & Jamison, B. (1983). Normally developing preschoolers as intervention agents for autistic-like children: Effects on class, department, and social interaction. *Journal of the Division of Early Childhood, 9,* 105-119.

Szatmari, P., Barolucci, G., Bremmer, R., Bond, S., & Rich, S. (1989). A follow-up study of high-functioning autistic children. *Journal of Speech and Hearing Research, 24,* 420-429.

Tallal, P. , Miller, S. L., Bedi, G., Byna, G., Wang, X., Nagariajan, S. S., Schreiner, C., Jenkins, W. M., Merzenich, M. M. (1996). Language comprehension in language-learning impaired children improved with acoustically modified speech. *Science, 271*(5245): 81-84.

Tanguay, P. E. (1999). *The diagnostic assessment of autism using social communication domains.* Paper presented at the Interdisciplinary Council on Developmental and Learning Disorders' Third Annual International Conference, Autism and Disorders of Relating and Communicating, McLean, VA, November.

Tanguay, P. E., Robertson, J., & Derrick, A. (1998). A dimensional classification of autism spectrum disorder by social communication domains. *Journal of the American Academy of Child and Adolescent Psychiatry, 37*(3), 271.

Tiegerman & Primavera (1981). Object manipulation: An interactional strategy with autistic children. *Journal of Autism and Developmental Disorders, 11,* 427-438.

Tiegerman & Primavera (1984). Imitating the autistic child: Facilitating communicative gaze behavior. *Journal of Autism and Developmental Disorders 14,* 27-38.

Toglia, J. P. (1998). The multicontext treatment approach. In M. E. Neistadt & E. B. Crepeau (Eds.), *Willard and Spackman's occupational theory* (9th ed.) (pp. 557-559). Philadelphia: Lippincott.

Ungerer, J. A., & Sigman, M. (1981). Symbolic play and language comprehension in autistic children. *Journal of the*

American Academy of Child and Adolescent Psychiatry, 20(7), 31-43.

Venn, M. L., Wolery, M., & Graco, M. (1996). Effects of every-day and every-other day instruction. *Focus on Autism and Other Developmental Disabilities, 11*(1), 15-28.

Weiler, I. J., Hawrylak, N., Greemough, W. T. (1995). Morphogenesis in memory formation: Synaptic and cellular mechanisms. *Behavioural Brain Research, 66,* 1-6.

Western Psychology Services (1988). Childhood Autism Rating Scale (CARS). *Childhood autism.* Los Angeles: Western Psychology Services.

Wetherby, A., Koegel, R. L., & Mendel, M. (1981). Central auditory nervous system dysfunction in echolalic autistic individuals. *Journal of Speech and Hearing Research, 24,* 420-429.

Wetherby, A., & Prizant, B. (1992). Facilitating language and communication in autism: Assessment and intervention guidelines. In D. Berkell (Ed.), *Autism: Identification, education, and treatment* (pp. 107-133). Hillsdale, NJ: Erlbaum.

Wetherby, A. M., & Prizant, B. M. (1993). Profiling young children's communicative competence. In S. Warren & J. Reichle (Eds.), *Causes and effects in language disorders and intervention.* Baltimore: Paul H. Brookes.

Wetherby, A. M., & Prizant, B. M. (1993). Profiling young children's communication and symbolic abilities. *Journal of Childhood Communication Disorders, 15,* 23-32.

Wetherby, A. M., & Prizant, B. M. (1993). Communication and symbolic behavior scales-Standardized edition/Normed edition. Chicago, IL: Riverside.

Wetherby, A., & Prizant, B. (1993). Communication in preschool autistic children. In E. Schopler, M. Bourgondien, & G. Mesibov (Eds.), *Preschool issues in autism* (pp. 112-126). New York: Plenum.

Wetherby, A., & Prizant, B. (1995). *Communication and symbolic behavior scales.* Chicago: Riverside.

Wetherby, A. M., Prizant, B. M., & Schuler, A. L. (1997). Enhancing language and communication: Theoretical foundations. In D. Cohen & F. Volkmar (Eds.) *Handbook of autism and pervasive developmental disorders* (2nd ed.). New York: Wiley & Sons.

Wetherby, A., & Prutting, C. (1984). Profiles of communicative and cognitive social abilities in autistic children. *Journal of Speech and Hearing Research, 27,* 364-377.

Wetherby, A., & Zelazzo, P. R. (1997). Infant-toddler information processing treatment of children with pervasive developmental disorder and autism: Part II. *Infants and Young Children, 10*(2), 1-13.

Williams, D. (1993). *Nobody, nowhere.* New York: Avon.

Williams, D. (1995). *Somebody, somewhere.* New York: Avon.

Williams J. A., Koegel, R. L., & Egel, A. L. (1981). Response reinforcer relationships and improved learning in autistic children. *Journal of Applied Behavior Analysis, 14,* 53-60.

Williamson, G. (1988). Motor control as a resource for adaptive coping. *Zero to Three, 10*(1), 1-7.

Wing, L. (1979). Mentally retarded and autistic children in Camberwell. In L. Wing (Ed.), *Estimating needs for mental health care.* Berlin: Springer.

Winsler, A., DeLeon, J., Carlton, M., Barry, M., Jenkins, T., & Carter, K. (1997). *Components of self-regulation in the preschool years: Developmental stability, validity, and relationship to classroom behavior.* Paper presented at the Bienniel Meeting of the Society for Research in Child Development, Washington, D.C., April.

Wolf, M. M., Risley, T. R., & Mees, H. (1964). Application of operant procedures to the behavior problems of an autistic child. *Behavior Research and Therapy, 1,*305-312.

Yoder, P. J., & Davies, B. (1992). Do parental questions and topic continuations elicit replies from developmentally delayed children: A sequential analysis. *Journal of Speech and Hearing Research, 33*(3), 563-573.

Yoder, P. J., & Davies, B. (1992). Do children with developmental delays use more frequent and diverse language in verbal rou-tines? *American Journal on Mental Retardation, 97*(2), 197-203.

Yoder, P. J., & Davies, B. (1992). Greater intelligibility in verbal routines with young children with developmental delays. *Applied Psycholinguistics, 13*(1), 77-91.

Yoder, P. J., & Layton, T. L. (1988). Speech following sign language training in autistic children with minimal verbal language. *Journal of Autism and Developmental Disorders, 18*(2), 217-229.

Appendix

SUBJECT AREA BIBLIOGRAPHY

SPEECH-LANGUAGE AND COMMUNICATION

Alpert, C. L., & Kaiser, A. P. (1992). Training parents as milieu language teachers. *Journal of Early Intervention, 16*(1), 31-52.

American Academy of Audiology. (1993). Position statement: Auditory integration training. *Audiology Today, 5*(4), 21.

Arnold, K. S., Myette, B. M., & Castro, G. (1986). Relationships of language intervention efficacy to certain subject of characteristics in mentally retarded preschool children: A meta-analysis. *Education and Training of the Mentally Retarded, 123*, 108-116.

Baer, R. A., Williams, J. A., Osnes, P. G., & Stokes, T. F. (1985). Generalized verbal control and correspondence training. *Behavior Modification, 9*, 477-489.

Bambara, L. M., Warren, S. F., & Komisar, S. (1988). The individualized curriculum sequencing model: Effects on skill acquisition and generalization. *Journal of the Association for Persons with Severe Handicaps (JASH), 13*, 8-19.

Barnett, W. S., Escobar, C. M., & Ravsten, M. T. (1988). Parent and clinic early intervention for children with language handicaps: A cost analysis. *Journal of the Division for Early Childhood, 12*(4), 290-298.

Beitchman, J. H., & Inglis, A. (1991). The continuum of linguistic dysfunction from pervasive developmental disorders to dyslexia. *Psychiatric Clinics of North America, 14*(1).

Bettison, S. (1996). The long-term effects of auditory training on children with autism. *Journal of Autism and Developmental Disorders, 26,* 361-374.

Bondy, A. S. & Peterson, S. (1990). *The point is not to point: Picture Exchange communication system with young students with autism.* Paper presented at the Association for Behavior Analysis Convention. Nashville, TN.

Brown-Gorton, R., & Wolery, M. (1988). Teaching mothers to imitate their handicapped children: Effects on material mands. *Journal of Speech Education, 22,* 97-107.

Bruneau, N., Dourneau, M. C., Garreau, B., Pourcelot, L., & Lelord, G. (1992). Blood flow response to auditory stimulations in normal, mentally retarded, and autistic children: A preliminary transcranial Doppler ultrasonographic study of the middle cerebral arteries. *Biological Psychiatry, 32*(8), 691-699.

Bunce, B. H., Ruder, K. F., & Ruder, C. C. (1985). Using the miniature linguistic system in teaching syntax: Two case studies. *Journal of Speech and Hearing Disorders, 50,* 247-253.

Burpee, J., DeJean, V. Frick, S., Kawar, M., Koomar, J. & Murphy Fischer, D. (in press). Theoretical and clinical perspectives on the Interactive Metronome®: A view from occupational therapy practice. *American Journal of Occupational Therapy.*

Camarata, S. (1993). The application of naturalistic conversation training to speech production in children with speech disabilities. *Journal of Applied Behavior Analysis, 26,* 173-182.

Camarata, S. M., Nelson, K. E., & Camarata, M. N. (1994). Comparison of conversational-recasting and imitative procedures for training grammatical structures in children with specific language impairment. *Journal of Speech and Hearing Research, 37,* 1414-1423.

Charlop, M. H., & Haymes, L. K. (1994). Speech and language acquisition and intervention: Behavior approaches. In J. Matson (Ed.), *Autism in children and adults: Etiology, assessment, and intervention* (pp. 213-240). Pacific Grove, CA: Brooks/Cole.

Cole, K. N., & Dale, P. S. (1986). Direct language instruction and interactive language instruction with language delayed preschool children: A Comparison study. *Journal of Speech and Hearing Research, 29*(2), 206-217.

Cook, J., Urwin, S., & Kelly, K. (1989). Preschool language intervention: A follow-up of some within-group differences. *Child Care Health Development 15*(6), 381-400.

Cooper, J., Moodley, M., & Reynell, J. (1974). Intervention programmes for preschool children with delayed language development: A preliminary report. *British Journal of Disorders of Communication, 9,* 81-91.

Cooper, J., Moodley, M., & Reynell, J. (1979). The developmental programme: Results from a five year study. *British Journal of Disorders of Communication, 14,* 57-69.

Dawson, G., & Galpert, L. (1986). A developmental model for facilitating the social behavior of autistic children. In E. Shopler & G. B. Mesibov (Eds.), *Social behavior in autism* (pp. 237-261). New York: Plenum Press.

Dodd, B., McCormack, P., & Woodyart, G. (1994). Evaluation of an intervention program: Relation between children's phonology and parents' communicative behavior. *American Journal on Mental Retardation, 98*(5), 632-645.

Edelson, S., Arin, D., Bauman, M., Lukas, S., Rudy, J., Scholar, M., & Rimland, B. (1999). Auditory integration training: A double-blind study of behavioral and electrophysiological effects in people with autism. *Focus on Autism and Other Developmental Disabilities, 14*(2), 73-81.

Eiserman, W. D., McCoun, M., & Escobar, C. M. (1990). A cost-effectiveness analysis of two alternative program models for searching speech disordered preschoolers. *Journal of Early Childhood Intervention, 14*(4), 297-317.

Elliott, R., Hall, K., & Soper, H. (1991). Analog language teaching vs. natural language teaching: Generalization and retention of language learning for adults with autism and mental retardation. *Journal of Autism and Developmental Disorders, 21,* 433-447.

Engleman, S., & Osborn, J. (1976). *DISTAR Language I: An Instructional System.* Chicago: Science Research Associates.

Fenichel, E. (Ed). (1992). Infants and young children with pervasive developmental disorders. *Zero to Three, 13,* 42.

Fey, M. E., Cleave, P. L., Long, S. H., & Hughes, D. L. (1993). Two approaches to the facilitation of grammar in children with language impairment: An experimental evaluation. *Journal of Speech and Hearing Research, 36,* 141-157.

Foxx, R., Faw, G., McMorrow, M., Kyle, M., & Bittle, R. (1988). Replacing maladaptive speech with verbal labeling responses: An analysis of generalized responding. *Journal of Applied Behavior Analysis, 21*, 411-417.

Girolametto, L. E. (1988). Improving the social-conversational skills of developmentally delayed children: An intervention study. *Journal of Speech and Hearing Disorders, 53*, 156-157.

Girolametto, L., Verbry, M., & Tonnock, R. (1994). Improving joint engagement in parent-child interaction: An intervention study. *Journal of Early Intervention, 18*(2), 155-167.

Goldstein, H., Angelo, D., & Mousetis, L. (1987). Acquisition and extension of syntactic repertoires by severely mentally retarded youth. *Research in Developmental Disabilities, 8*, 549-574.

Goldstein, H., & Brown, W. (1989). Observational learning of receptive and expressive language by preschool children. *Education and Treatment of Children, 12*, 5-37.

Goldstein, H., & Ferrell, D. R. (1987). Augmenting communicative interaction between handicapped and nonhandicapped preschool children. *Journal of Speech and Hearing Disorders, 52*, 200-211.

Goldstein, H., & Hockenberger, E. H. (1991). Significant progress in child language intervention: An 11-year retrospective. *Research in Developmental Disability, 12*(4), 401-424.

Goldstein, H., & Mousetis, L. (1989). Generalized language learning by children with severe mental retardation: Effects of peer's expressive modeling. *Journal of Applied Behavior Analysis, 22*, 245-259.

Goldstein, H., & Wickstrom, S. (1986). Peer intervention effects on communication interaction among handicapped and non-handicapped preschoolers. *Journal of Applied Behavioral Analysis 19*, 209-214.

Gottwald, S. R., & Starkweather, C. W. (1995). Fluency intervention for preschoolers and their families in the public schools.

Language, Speech, and Hearing Services in Schools, 26(2), 117-126.

Gravel, J. S. (1994). Auditory integration training: Placing the burden of proof. *American Journal of Speech-Language Pathology, 3*(2), 25-29.

Guevremont, D. C., Osnes, P. G., & Stokes, T. F. (1986a). Preparation for effective self-regulation: The development of generalized verbal control. *Journal of Applied Behavior Analysis 19*, 215-219.

Haley, K. L., Camarata, S. M., & Nelson, K. E. (1994). Social valence in children with specific language impairment during imitation-based and conversation-based language intervention. *Journal of Speech and Hearing Research, 37*, 378-388.

Handleman, J. (1991). A specialized program for preschool children with autism. *Language, Speech, and Hearing Services in Schools, 22*(3), 107-110.

Haring, T. G., Blair, R., Lee, M., Breen, C., & Gaylord–Ross, R. (1986). Teaching social language to moderately handicapped students. *Journal of Applied Behavior Analysis, 19*, 159-171.

Haring, T. G., Neetz, J., Lovinger, L., Peek, C., & Semmel, M. (1987). Effects of four modified incidental teaching procedures to create opportunities for communication. *Journal of the Association for Persons with Severe Handicaps (JASH), 12*, 218-226.

Hart, B., & Risley, T. R. (1975). Incidental teaching of language in the preschool. *Journal of Applied Behavior Analysis 8*, 411-420.

Hemmeter, M. L., & Kaiser, A. P. (1994). Enhanced milieu teaching: Effects of parent-implemented language intervention. *Journal of Early Childhood Intervention, 18*(3), 269-289.

Hester, P. P., Kaiser, A. P., Alpert, C. L., & Whiteman, B. (in press). The generalized effects of training trainers to teach parents to implement milieu teaching. *Journal of Early Childhood Intervention.*

Highfill, M., & Cimorelli, J. (1994). *Positron emission tomography measure of modified auditory integration therapy: A case study.* Poster presented at the annual convention of the American Speech-Language-Hearing Association, New Orleans, LA, November.

Hoffman, P., Norris, J., & Monjure, J. (1990). Comparison of process targeting and language treatments for phonologically delayed preschool children. *Language, Speech, and Hearing Services in Schools, 21,* 102-109.

Hunt, P., Alwell M., & Goetz, L. (1988). Acquisition of conversation skills and the reduction of inappropriate social interaction behaviors. *Journal of the Association for the Persons with Severe Handicaps (JASH), 13,* 20-27.

Hunt, P., Goetz, L., Alwell, M., & Sailor, W. (1986). Using an interrupted behavior chain strategy to teach generalized communication responses. *Journal of the Association for Persons with Severe Handicaps, 11,* 196-204.

Huntley, R. M. C., Holt, K. S., Butterfill, A., & Latham, C. (1988). A follow-up study of language intervention programme. *British Journal of Disorders of Communication, 23,* 127-140.

Hupp, S. C. (1986). Use of multiple exemplars in object concept training: How many are sufficient? *Analysis & Intervention in Developmental Disabilities, 6,* 305-317.

James, S. D., & Egel, A. L. (1986). A direct prompting strategy for increasing reciprocal interactions between handicapped and nonhandicapped siblings. *Journal of Applied Behavior Analysis, 19,* 173-186.

Kaiser, A. P., Hendrickson, J. M., & Alpert, C. I. (1991). Milieu language teaching: A second look. *Advances in Mental Retardation and Developmental Disabilities, 4,* 463-492.

Kaiser, A. P., Ostrosky, M. M., & Alpert, C. L. (1993). Training teachers to use environmental arrangement and milieu teaching with nonvocal preschool children. *Journal of the Association for Persons with Severe Handicaps (JASH), 18*(3), 188-199.

Keller, M. F., & Bucher, B. (1979). Transfer between receptive and productive language in developmentally disabled children. *Journal of Applied Behavior Analysis, 12,* 311.

Kim, Y. T., & Lombardino, L. J. (1991). The efficacy of script contexts in language comprehension intervention with children who have mental retardation. *Journal of Speech and Hearing Research, 34,* 845-857.

Kouri, T. (1988). Effects of simultaneous communication in a child-directed treatment approach with preschoolers with disabilities. *Augmentative and Alternative Communication, 4*(4), 222-232.

Kuhlman, K., & Schweinhart, L. J. (in press). *Timing in child development.* Ypsilanti, MI: High/Scope Educational Research Foundation.

Law, J. (1997). Evaluating intervention for language impaired children: A review of the literature. *European Journal of Disorders of Communication, 32,* (2 Spec. No.) 1-14.

Leonard, L. B. (1986). Conversational replies of children with specific language impairment. *Journal of Speech and Hearing Research, 29,* 114-119.

Letts, C. A., & Reid, J. (1994). Using conversational data in the treatment of pragmatic disorder in children. *Child Language Teaching and Therapy, 10,* 1-22.

Losardo, A., & Bricker, D. (1994). Activity-based intervention and direct instruction: A comparison study. *American Journal on Mental Retardation, 98*(6), 744-765.

Luciano, C. M. (1986). Acquisition, maintenance, and generalization of productive intraverbal behavior thorough transfer of stimulus control procedures. *Applied Research in Mental Retardation 7*, 1-20.

Madell, J. R. (1997). *New interventions to enhance auditory processing, language, reading, and learning.* Paper presented at the Interdisciplinary Council on Developmental and Learning Disorders conference, Approaches to Developmental and Learning Disorders in Infants and Children: Theory and Practice, McLean, VA, November.

Mahoney, G., & Powell, A. (1988). Modifying parent-child interaction: Enhancing the development of handicapped children. *Journal of Special Education, 22*(1), 82-96.

McLean, J., & Snyder-McClean, L. (1987). Form and function of communicative behaviour among persons with severe developmental disabilities. *Australia and New Zealand Journal of Developmental Disabilities, 13*(2), 83-98.

McTear, M. F. (1985b). Pragmatic disorders: A case study of conversational disability. *British Journal of Disorders of Communication, 20*, 129-142.

Meline, T. (1986). Referential communication skills of learning disabled/language impaired children. *Applied Psycholinguistics, 7*, 129-140.

Merzenich, M. M., Jenkins, W. M., Johnston, P., Schreiner, C., Miller, S. L., & Tallal, P. (1996). Temporal processing deficits of language-learning impaired children ameliorated by training. *Science, 27*(5245), 77-81.

Mirenda, P., & Dattilo, J. (1987). Instructional techniques in alternative communication for students with severe intellectual handicaps. *Augmentative and Alternative Communication, 3*, 143-152.

Mirenda, P., & Donnellan, A. (1986). Effects of adult interaction style on conversational behavior in students with severe communi-

cation problems. *Language, Speech and Hearing Services in Schools, 17*, 126-141.

Norris, J. A., & Hoffman, P. R. (1990). Comparison of adult-initiated vs. child-initiated interaction styles with handicapped prelanguage children. *Language, Speech, and Hearing Services in Schools, 21*, 28-36.

Peck, C. (1985). Increasing opportunities for social control by children with autism and severe handicaps: Effects on student behavior and perceived classroom climate. *Journal of the Association for Persons with Severe Handicaps (JASH), 4*, 183-193.

Porges, S. W., & Bazhenova, O. V. (1997). *Evolution and the autonomic nervous system: A neurological model of socio-emotional and communication disorders.* Paper presented at the Interdisciplinary Council on Developmental and Learning Disorders conference, "Approaches to Developmental and Learning Disorders In Infants and Children: Theory & Practice," McLean, VA.

Prizant, B. M. (1982). Gestalt processing and gestalt language in autism. *Topics in Language Disorders, 3*, 16-23.

Prizant, B. M. (1987). Clinical implications of echolalic behavior in autism. In T. Layton (Ed.), *Language and treatment of autistic and developmentally disordered children.* Springfield, IL: Charles Thomas.

Prizant, B. M., Reichle, J., Barrett, C., Rice-Tetlie, R., & McQuarter, R. (1987). The effect of prior intervention to establish generalized requesting on the acquisition of object labels. *Augmentative and Alternative Communication, 3*, 3-10.

Prizant, B. M., Schuler, A. L., & Wetherby, A. M. (in press). Enhancing language and communication: Language approaches. In D. Cohen & F. Volkmar (Eds.), *Handbook of autism and pervasive developmental disorders* (2nd ed.) New York: Wiley & Sons.

Prizant, B. M., & Wetherby, A. M. (1985). Intentional communicative behavior of children with autism: Theoretical and applied issues. *Australian Journal of Human Communication Disorders, 13,* 21-58.

Prizant, B. M., & Wetherby, A. M. (1988). Providing services to children with autism (0-2 years) and their families. *Topics in Language Disorders, 9,* 1-23.

Rapin, I., & Dunn, M. (1997). Language disorders in children with autism. *Seminars in Pediatric Neurology, 4*(2), 86-92.

Rimland, B., & Edelson, S. M. (1991). *Improving the auditory functioning of autistic persons: A comparison of the Berand auditory training approach with the Tomatis audio-psychophonology approach.* (Tech. Report No. 111). San Diego, CA: Autism Research Institute.

Rimland B., & Edelson, S. M. (1994). The effects of auditory integration training on autism. *American Journal of Speech-Language Pathology, 3*(2), 16-24.

Rimland B., & Edelson, S. M. (1995). Brief report: A pilot study of auditory integration training in autism. *Journal of Autism and Developmental Disorders, 25*(1), 61-70.

Rogers-Warren, A., & Warren, S.F. (1980). Mands for verbalization: Facilitating the display of new trained language in children. *Behavior Modification, 4,* 361-382.

Salmon, D. J., Pear, J. J., & Kuhn, B. A. (1986). Generalization of object naming after training with picture cards and with objects. *Journal of Applied Behavior Analysis, 19,* 53-58.

Schuler, A. L., Gonsier-Gerdin, J., & Wolfberg, P. (1990). The efficacy of speech and language intervention: An 11-year retrospective. *Research in Developmental Disabilities, 12,* 401-424.

Schuler, A. L., & Prizant, B. M. (1985). Echolalia in autism. In E. Schopler & G.

Mesibov (Eds.) *Communication problems in autism.* New York: Plenum Press.

Schwartz, R. G., Chapman, K., Terrell, B. Y., Prelock, P., & Rowan, L. (1985). Facilitating word combination in language-impaired children through discourse structure. *Journal of Speech and Hearing Disorders, 50,* 31-39.

Schwartz, R. G., Leonard, L. B., & Neef, N. A. (1985). Lexical imitation and acquisition in language-impaired children. *Journal of Speech and Hearing Disorders, 50,* 141-149.

Seifert, H., & Schwartz, I. (1991). Treatment effectiveness of large group basic concept instruction with Head Start students. *Language, Speech and Hearing Services in Schools, 22,* 60-64.

Shaffer, R. J., Jacokes, L. E., Cassily, J. F., Greenspan, S. I., Tuchman, R. F., & Stemmer, P. J. (in press). Effect of Interactive Metronome® IM training on children with ADHD. *American Journal of Occupational Therapy.*

Silverman, K., Anderson, S. R., Marshall, A. M., & Baer, D. M. (1986). Establishing and generalizing audience control of new language repertoires. *Autism and Developmental Disabilities, 6,* 21-40.

Smedley, M. (1989). Semantic-pragmatic disorder: A description with some practical suggestions for teachers. *Child Language Teaching and Therapy, 5,* 174-190.

Snyder-McLean, L., & McLean, J. (1987). Children with language and communication disorders. In M. J. Gurainick & F. C. Bennett (Eds.), *The effectiveness of early intervention* (pp. 213-274). New York: Academic Press.

Sommer, K., Whitman, T., & Keogh, D. (1988). Teaching severely retarded persons to sign interactively through the use of behavioral script. *Research in Developmental Disabilities, 9,* 291-304.

Stehli, A. (1992). *The sound of a miracle.* New York: Avon Books.

Stremel, K., & Waryas, C. (1974). A behavioral psycholinguistic approach to language training. In L. McReynolds (Ed.), *Developing systematic procedures for training children's language.* ASHA Monograph 18.

Stemmer, P. M., Jr. (1997). *Improving student motor integration by use of an Interactive Metronome®.* Paper presented at the annual meeting of the American Educational Research Association, Chicago, IL, March.

Tallal, P., Miller, S. L., Bedi, G., Byma, G., Wang, X., Nagarajan, S. S., Schrei W. M., & Merzenich, M. M., Miller, S., & Jenkins, W. (1998). Language learning impairments: Integrating basic science, technology, and remediation. *Experimental Brain* (2), 210-219.

Tannock, R., Girolametto, L., & Siegel, L. S. (1992). Language intervention with children who have developmental delays: Effects of an interactive approach. *American Journal on Mental Retardation, 97*(2), 145-160.

Tiegerman & Primavera (1981). Object manipulation: An interactional strategy with autistic children. *Journal of Autism and Developmental Disorders, 11,* 427-438.

Tiegerman & Primavera (1984). Imitating the autistic child: Facilitating communicative gaze behavior. *Journal of Autism and Developmental Disorders, 14,* 27-38.

Veale, T. K. (1994). Auditory integration training: The use of a new listening therapy profession. *American Journal of Speech-Language Pathology, 3*(2), 12-15.

Warren, S. F. (1992). Facilitating basic vocabulary acquisition with milieu teaching procedures. *Journal of Early Intervention, 16*(3), 235-251.

Warren, S. F., & Bambara, L. M. (1989). An experimental analysis of milieu language intervention: Teaching the action-object form. *Journal of Speech and Hearing Disorders, 54,* 448-461.

Warren, S. F., & Gazdag, G. (1990). Facilitating early language development with milieu intervention procedures. *Journal of Early Intervention, 14*(1), 62-86.

Warren, S. F., Gazdag, G. E., Bambara, L. M., & Jones, H. A. (1994). Changes in the generativity and use of semantic relationships concurrent with milieu language intervention. *Journal of Speech and Hearing Research, 37,* 924-934.

Warren, S. F., & Kaiser, A. P. (1986). Generalization of treatment effects by young language-delayed children: A longitudinal analysis. *Journal of Speech and Hearing Disorders, 51,* 239-251.

Warren, S. F., McQuarter, R. M., & Rogers-Warren, A. (1984). The effects of teachers mands and models on the speech of unresponsive language-delayed children. *Journal of Speech and Hearing Research, 49,* 43-52.

Warren, S. F., Yoder, P. J., Gazdag, G. E., Kim, K., & Jones, H. A. (1993). Facilitating prelinguistic communication skills in young children with developmental delay. *Journal of Speech and Hearing Research, 36,* 86-97.

Weismer, S. E., & Murray-Branch, J. (1989). Modeling versus modeling plus evoked production training: A comparison of two language intervention methods. *Journal of Speech and Hearing Disorders, 54,* 269-281.

Weismer, S. E., Murrary-Branch, J., & Miller, J. F. (1993). Comparison of two methods for promoting productive vocabulary in late talkers. *Journal of Speech and Hearing Research, 36,* 1037-1050.

Weistuch, L., & Lewis, M. (1985). The language interaction intervention project.

Analysis and Intervention in Developmental Disabilities, 5, 97-106.

Weistuch, L., Lewis, M., & Sullivan, M.W. (1991). Project profile: Use of language interaction intervention in the preschools. *Journal of Early Intervention, 15*(3), 278-287.

Wetherby, A. M., Prizant, B. M. (1992). Facilitating language and communication in autism: Assessment and intervention guidelines. In D. Berkell (Ed.), *Autism: Identification, education, and treatment.* Hillsdale, NJ: Erlbaum.

Wetherby, A. M., Prizant, B. M. (1992). Profiling young children's communicative competence. In S. Warren & J. Reichle (Eds.), *Causes and effects in language disorders and intervention.* Baltimore: Paul H. Brookes.

Wetherby, A. M., Prizant, B. M. (1993). Profiling young children's communication and symbolic abilities. *Journal of Childhood Communication Disorders, 15,* 23-32.

Wetherby, A. M., Prizant, B. M. (1993). Communication and symbolic behavior scales-Standardized edition/Normed edition. Chicago, IL: Riverside.

Wetherby, A. M., Prizant, B. M., & Schuler, A. L. (1997). Enhancing language and communication: Theoretical foundations. In D. Cohen & F. Volkmar (Eds.) *Handbook of autism and pervasive developmental disorders* (2nd ed.)

Wetherby, A. M., & Rodriguez, G. P. (1992). Measurement of communicative intentions in normally developing children during structured and unstructured contexts. *Journal of Speech and Hearing Research, 35,* 130-138.

Whitehurst, G. J., Fischel, J. E., Arnold, D. S., & Lonigan, C. J. (1992). Evaluating outcomes with children with expressive lan-guage delay. In S. F. Warren & J. Reichle (Eds.), *Communication and language intervention series: Vol. 1. Causes and effects in communication and language intervention* (pp. 277-313). Baltimore: Paul H. Brookes.

Whitehurst, G. J., Fischel, J. F., Caulfield, M. B., DeBaryshe, B., & Valdez-Menchaca, M. (1989). In P. Zelazo & R. Barr (Eds.), *Challenges to developmental paradigms: Implications for theory, assessment, and treatment* (pp. 113-133). Hillsdale, NJ: Erlbaum.

Whitehurst, G. J., Fischel, J. E., Lonigan, C. J., Valdez-Menchaca, M. C., Arnold, D. S., & Smith, M. (1991). Treatment of early expressive language delay: If, when, and how. *Topics in Language Disorders, 11*(4), 55-68.

Wilcox, M. J., Kouri, T. A., & Caswell, S. B. (1991). Early language intervention: A comparison of classroom and individual treatment. *American Journal of Speech-Language Pathology, 1*(1), 49-62.

Williams, D. (1992). *Nobody, nowhere.* New York: Times Books.

Winslow, M., & Guitar, B. (1994). The effects of structured turn-taking on disfluencies: A case study. *Language, Speech, and Hearing Services in Schools, 25,* 251-257.

Wolfberg, P. J., & Schuler, A. L. (1993). Integrated play groups: A model for promoting the social and cognitive dimensions of play in children with autism. *Journal of Autism and Developmental Disorders, 23,* 467-489.

Woodward, D. (1994). Changes in unilateral and bilateral sound sensitivity as a result o *Sound Connection, 2,* 4.

Yoder, P. J., Kaiser, A. P., & Alpert, C. L. (1991). An exploratory study of the interaction between language teaching methods and child characteristics. *Journal of Speech and Hearing Research, 34,* 155-167.

Yoder, P. J., Kaiser, A. P., Alpert, C., & Fischer, R. (1993). Following the child's lead when teaching nouns to preschoolers with mental retardation. *Journal of Speech and Hearing Research 36,* 158-167.

Yoder, P., Kaiser, A., Goldstein, H., Alpert, C., Mousetis, L., Kaczamrek, L. & Fischer, R. (1995). An exploratory milieu teaching and responsive interaction in classroom application. *Journal of Early Intervention, 19,* 218-242.

Yoder, P. J., & Layton, T. L. (1988). Speech following sign language training in autistic children with minimal verbal language. *Journal of Autism and Developmental Disorders, 18*(2), 217-229.

Yoder, P. J., Warren, S. F., Kim, K., & Gazdag, G. E. (1994). Facilitating prelinguistic communication skills in young children with developmental delay: II: Systematic replication and extension. *Journal of Speech and Hearing Research, 37,* 841-851.

EXECUTIVE COGNITIVE FUNCTIONS AND MOTOR PLANNING

Ault, M. J., Gast, D. L., & Wolery, M. (1988). Comparison of progressive and constant time delay procedures in teaching community-sign word reading. *American Journal of Mental Retardation, 93*(1), 44-56.

Ault, M. J., Wolery, M., Doyle, P. M., & Gast, D. L. (1989). Review of comparative studies in instruction of students with moderate and severe handicaps. *Exceptional Children, 55,* 346-356.

Ault, M. J., Wolery, M., Gast, D. L., Doyle, P. M., & Martin, C. P. (1990). Comparison of predictable and unpredictable trial sequences during small group instruction. *Learning Disability Quarterly, 13,* 12-29.

Auxter, D. (1972). Evaluation of perceptual motor training programs. *Teaching Exceptional Children, 4*(2), 89-97.

Ballinger, E. (1996). *The learning gym: Fun-to-do activities for success at school.* Ventura, CA: Edu-Kinesthetics.

Barkley, R. A. (1997a). Attention-deficit/ hyperactivity disorder, self-regulation, and time: Toward a more comprehensive theory. *Journal of Developmental and Behavioral Pediatrics, 18,* 271-279.

Barkley, R. A. (1997b). Behavioral inhibition, sustained attention, and executive functions: Constructing a unifying theory of ADHD. *Psychological Bulletin, 121,* 85-94.

Barnes, S. B. (1996). *Promoting motor skill development through the MOVE curriculum.* Paper presented at the 74th Annual International Convention of the Council for Exceptional Children, Orlando, FL, April.

Bennetto, L., et al. (1996). Intact and impaired memory functions in autism. *Child Development, 67*(4), 1816-1835.

Black, L. M. (1995). The interweaving of neuropsychological dysfunction and psychological conflict. *Zero to Three,* Feb./March.

Bransford, J., Sherwood, R., Vye, N., & Rieser, J. (1986). Teaching thinking and problem solving: Research foundations. *American Psychologist, 41*(10), 1078-1089.

Burpee, J., DeJean, V., Frick, S., Kawar, M., & Murphy, D. (in press). Theoretical and clinical perspectives on the Interactive Metronome® (IM): A view from clinical occupational therapy.

Cassily, J. F. (1996, June). Methods and apparatus for measuring and enhancing neural motor coordination. *United States Patent: 5, 528,498.*

Conway, R. N., & Ashman, A. (1989). Teaching planning skills in the classroom: The development of an integrated model. *International Journal of Disability, Development and Education, 36,* 225-240.

Cormier, P., Carlson, J. S., & Das, J. (1990). Planning ability and cognitive performance: The compensatory effects of a dynamic assessment approach. *Learning and Individual Differences, 2, 1437-449.*

Cornish, K. M., & McManus, I. C. (1996). Hand preference and hand skill in children with autism. *Journal of Autism and Developmental Disorders, 26*(6), 597-609.

Covington, M. V. (1985). Strategic thinking and the fear of failure. In J. W. Segal, S. F. Chipman, & R. Glaser (Eds.), *Thinking and learning skills: Relating instruction to basic research* (Vol. 1) (pp. 389-416). Hillsdale, NJ: Erlbaum.

Das, J. P., Naglieri, J. A., & Kirby, J. R. (1994). *Assessment of cognitive processes: The PASS theory of intelligence.* New York: Allyn & Bacon.

Denckla, M. B., Rudel, R. G., Chapman, C., & Krieger, J. (1985). Motor proficiency in dyslexic children with and without attentional disorders. *Archives of Neurology, 42,* 228-231.

Dennison, P. E., & Dennison, G. E. (1986a). *Brain gym.* Ventura, CA: Edu-Kinesthetics.

Dennison, P. E., & Dennison, G. E. (1986b). *Personalized whole brain integration.* Ventura, CA: Edu-Kinesthetics.

Dennison, P. E., & Dennison, G. E. (1987). *Edu-K for kids.* Ventura, CA: Edu-Kinesthetics.

Dennison, P. E., & Dennison, G. E. (1989). *Brain gym teacher's edition.* Ventura, CA: Edu-Kinesthetics.

Dickerson, J. N. (1972). *A study of the effectiveness of a non-specialist in remediating visual-motor skills in a Title I school.* South Bend, IN: South Bend Community School Corp.

Doyle, P. M., Gast, D. L., Wolery, M., Ault, M. J., & Farmer, J. A. (1990). Use of constant time delay in small group instruction: A study of observational and incidental learning. *Journal of Special Education, 23,* 369-385.

Egel, P. (1998). Personal correspondence. Wirthlin Worldwide: July 1, 1998.

El-Dinary, P. B., Pressley, M., Coy-Ogan, L., & Schuder, T. (1996). *Teaching practices and challenges of transactional instruction of reading strategies.* Manuscript submitted for publication.

El-Dinary, P. B., & Schuder, T. (1993). Seven teachers' acceptance of transactional strategies instruction during their first year using it. *Elementary School Journal, 94,* 267-283.

Feuerstein, R., Rand, Y., Hoffman, M. B., & Miller, R. (1980). *Instrumental enrichment.* Baltimore, MD: University Park Press.

Gardner, H. (1985). *Frames of mind: The theory of multiple intelligences.* New York: Basic Books.

Garofalo, J. F. (1986). Simultaneous synthesis, behavior regulation and arithmetic performance. *Journal of Psychoeducational Assessment, 4,* 229-238.

Grandin, T., & Sarano, M. (1986). *Emergence: Labeled autistic.* Novato, CA: Arena.

Hamlett, K. W., Pellegrini, D. S., & Conners, C. K. (1987). An investigation of executive processes in the problem-solving of attention deficit disorder-hyperactive children. *Journal of Pediatric Psychology, 13,* 227-240.

Hannaford, C. (1995). *Smart moves: Why learning is not all in your head.* Arlington, VA: Great Ocean.

Hannaford, C. (1997). *The dominance factor: How knowing your dominant eye, ear, brain, hand, and foot can improve your learning.* Arlington, VA: Great Ocean.

Hartmann, T. (1993). *Attention deficit disorder: A different perception.* Novato, CA: Underwood-Miller.

Heath, E. J., & Early, F. (1971). Development of perceptual-motor skills: First things first: Building effective visual perception. *Academic Therapy Quarterly, 7*(2), 203-210.

Hellgren, L., Gillberg, C., Gillberg, I. C., & Enerskog, I. (1993). Children with deficits in attention, motor control and perception (DAMP) almost grown up: General health at 16 years. *Developmental Medicine and Child Neurology, 35,* 881-892.

Hellgren, L., Gillberg, I. C., Bagenholm, A., & Gillberg, C. (1994). Children with deficits in attention, motor control and perception (DAMP) almost grown up: Psychiatric and personality disorders at age 16 years. *Journal of Child Psychology and Psychiatry and Allied Disciplines, 35,* 1255-1271.

Huebner, R. A. (1992). Autistic disorder: A neuropsychological enigma. *American Journal of Occupational Therapy, 46*(6), 487-501.

Hughes, C. (1996). Brief report: Planning problems in autism at the level of motor control. *Journal of Autism and Developmental Disorders, 26*(1), 99-107.

Hynd, G. W., Hern, K. L., Novey, E. S., Eliopulos, D., Marshall, R., Gonzalez, J. J., & Voeller, K. K. (1993). Attention deficit-hyperactivity disorder and asymmetry of the caudate nucleus. *Journal of Child Neurology, 6,* 339-347.

Iannicelli, M. M., & McConnaughey, F. B. (1976). *A sensory based program model for pre-school handicapped children.* Paper presented at the Annual International Convention, The Council for Exceptional Children, Atlanta, GA, April.

Jitendra, A. K., & Hoff, K. (1996). The effects of schema-based instruction on mathematical word-problem-solving performance of students with learning disabilities. *Journal of Learning Disabilities, 29*(4), 422-431.

Kar, B. C., Dash, U. N., Das, J. P., & Carlson, J. S. (1992). Two experiments on the dynamic assessment of planning. *Learning and Individual Differences, 5,* 13-29

Koegel, L. K., & Koegel, R. L. (1986). The effects of interspersed maintenance tasks on academic performance in a severe childhood stroke victim. *Journal of Applied Behavior Analysis, 19,* 425-430.

Kuhlman, K., & Schweinhart, L. J. (1999). *Timing in child development.* Ypsilanti, MI: High/Scope Educational Research Foundation.

Laws, G., et al. (1996). The effects of a short training in the use of rehearsal strategy on memory for words and pictures in children with Down syndrome. *Down Syndrome: Research and Practice, 4*(2), 70-77.

Libkuman, T. M., & Otani, H. O. (in press). Training in timing and accuracy in golf. *Golf Research News.*

Luria, A. R. (1966). *Human brain and psychological processes.* New York: Harper & Row.

Luria, A. R. (1970). The functional organization of the brain. *Scientific American, 222,* 66-78.

Luria, A. R. (1973). *The working brain: An introduction to neuropsychology.* New York: Basic Books.

Luria, A. R. (1974). Language and brain: Towards the basic problems of neuro-linguistics. *Brain and Language, 1,* 1-14.

Luria, A. R. (1980). *Higher cortical functions in man* (2nd ed., rev.). New York: Basic Books.

Lyon, G., Reid, E., & Rumsey, J. (1996). *Neuroimaging: A window to the neurological foundations of learning and behavior in children.* Baltimore: Paul H. Brookes.

McGee, G. G., & Izeman, S. (1988). *The Walden Learning Center.* Paper presented at the annual convention of the Autism Society of America, New Orleans, LA.

Montague, M. (1997). Cognitive strategy instruction in mathematics for students with learning disabilities. *Journal of Learning Disabilities, 30*(2), 164-177.

Naglieri, J. A., & Das, J. P. (1990). Planning, attention, simultaneous, and successive (PASS) cognitive processes: A model of intelligence. *Journal of Psycho-educational Assessment, 8,* 303-337.

Naglieri, J. A., & Gottling, S. H. (1995). A cognitive education approach to the instruction for the learning disabled: An individual study. *Psychological Report, 76,* 1343-1354.

Naglieri, J. A., & Gottling, S. H. (1997). Mathematics instruction and PASS cognitive processes: An interaction study. *Journal of Learning Disabilities, 30*(5), 513-620.

Neuwirth, S. (1997). *Autism: Decade of the brain* (Report No. NIH-97-4023). Bethesda, MD: National Institutes of Mental Health.

O'Neill, M. E., et al. (1991). Study strategies and story recall in attention deficit disorder and reading disability. *Journal of Abnormal Child Psychology, 19*(6), 671-692.

Palincsar, A. S., & Brown, A. L. (1984). Reciprocal teaching of comprehension-fostering and monitoring activities. *Cognition and Instruction, 1,* 117-175.

Palincsar, A. S., et al. (1992). Fostering literacy learning in supportive contexts. *Journal of Learning Disabilities, 27*(6), 360-370.

Parham, L. (1998). The relationship of sensory integrative development to achievement in elementary students: Four-year longitudinal patterns. *Occupational Therapy Journal of Research, 18*(3), 105-127.

Parlow, S. E. (1991). *A closer look at motor overflow in dyslexic children.* Paper presented at the International Neuropsychological Society Conference, San Antonio, TX, February.

Pelligrino, J. W. (1985). Inductive reasoning ability. In R. J. Sternberg (Ed.), *Human abilities: An information-processing approach* (pp. 195-225). New York: W. H. Freeman.

Piek, J. P., Pitcher, T. M., & Hay, D. A. (1999). Motor coordination and kinaesthesis in boys with attention deficit-hyperactivity disorder. *Developmental Medicine and Child Neurology, 41*(3), 159-165.

Piek, J. P., & Skinner, R. A. (1999). Timing and force control during a sequential tapping task in children with and without motor coordination problems. *Journal of the International Neuropsychology Society, 5*(4), 320-329.

Pintrich, P. R., et al. (1994). Intra-individual differences in motivation and cognition in students with and without learning disabilities. *Journal of Learning Disabilities, 27*(6), 360-370.

Precious, C. J. (1985). *Efficiency study of two procedures: Constant and progressive time delay in teaching oral sight word reading.* Unpublished master's thesis, University of Kentucky, Lexington.

Pressley, M., & El-Dinary, P. B. (1997). What we know about translating comprehensive-strategies instruction research into practice. *Journal of Learning Disabilities, 30*(5), 486-488.

Pressley, M., El-Dinary, P. B., Gaskins, I., Schuder, T., Bergman, J. L., Almasi, J., & Brown, R. (1992). Beyond direct explanation: Transactional instruction of reading comprehension strategies. *Elementary School Journal, 92,* 511-554.

Prior, M., & Hoffman, W. Brief report: Neurosychological testing of autistic children through an exploration with frontal lobe tests. *Journal of Autism and Developmental Disorders, 20*(4), 581-590.

Reid, R. (1993). Implementing self-monitoring interventions in the classroom: Lessons from research. In R. B. Rutherford, Jr., & S. R. Maihur (Eds.), *Severe behavioral disorders of children and youth* (Vol. 16) (pp. 43-54). Reston, VA: Council for Children with Behavioral Disorders.

Rosner, J., et al. (1969). *The identification of children with perceptual-motor dysfunction: A study of perceptual-motor dysfunction among emotionally disturbed, educable mentally retarded and normal children in the Pittsburgh public schools.* Pittsburgh, PA: Pittsburgh Public Schools, Learning Research and Development Center.

Russell, J., Jarrold C., & Henry, L. (1996). Working memory in children with autism and with moderate learning difficulties. *Journal of Child Psychology and Psychiatry, 37*(6), 673-686.

Salend, S. J., & Meddaugh, D. (1985). Using a peer-ameliorated extinction procedure to decrease obscene language. *The Pointer, 30*(1), 8-11.

Schonfeld, I., Shaffer, D., & Barmack, J. (1989). Neurological soft signs and school achievement: The mediating effects of sustained attention. *Journal of Abnormal Child Psychology, 17,* 575-596.

Shaffer, R. J., Jacokes, L. E., Cassily, J. F., Greenspan, S. I., Tuchman, R. F., & Stemmer P. J. (in press). Effect of Interactive Metronome® training on children with ADHD. *American Journal of Occupational Therapy.*

Shanz, M. T., & Menendez, F. J. (1993). Early motor training in Down's syndrome babies: Results of an intervention program.

Stemmer, P. M., Jr. (1997). *Improving student motor integration by use of an Interactive Metronome*®. Paper presented at the annual meeting of the American Educational Research Association, Chicago, IL, March.

Swanson, H. L., et al. (1996). Learning disabled and average readers' working memory and comprehension: Does metacognition play a role? *British Journal of Educational Psychology, 66*(3), 333-355.

Toglia, J. P. (1998). The multicontext treatment approach. In M. E. Neistadt & E. B. Crepeau (Eds.), *Willard and Spackman's occupational theory* (9th ed.) (pp. 557-559). Philadelphia: Lippincott.

Welsh, M. C., et al. (1990). Neuropsychology of early-treated phenylketonuria: Specific executive function deficits. *Child Development, 61*(6), 1697-1713.

Winsler, A., DeLeon, J., Carlton, M., Barry, M., Jenkins, T., & Carter, K. (1997). *Components of self-regulation in the preschool years: Developmental stability, validity, and relationship to classroom behavior.* Paper presented at the Bienniel Meeting of the Society for Research in Child Development, Washington, D.C., April.

Vye, N. J., Burns, M. S., Delclos, V. R., & Branford, J. D. (in press). Dynamic assessment of intellectually handicapped children. In C. S. Lidz (Ed.), *Dynamic assessment: Foundations and fundamentals.* New York: Guilford Press.

Wolery, M., Ault, M. J., & Doyle, P. M. (1992). Teaching students with moderate and severe disabilities: *Use of response prompting strategies.* White Plains, NY: Longman.

Wolery, M., Ault, M. J., Doyle, P. M., Gast, D. L., & Griffen, A. K. (in press). Comparison of choral and individual responding during small group instruction. *Education and treatment of children.*

Wolery, M., Ault, M. J., Gast, D. L., Doyle, P. M., & Mills, B. M. (1990). Use of choral and individual attentional responses with constant time delay when teaching sight word reading. *Remedial and Special Education, 11,* 47-58.

Wolery, M., Cybriwsky, C. A., Gast, D. L., & Boyle-Gast, K. (1991). General and specific attentional responses: Acquisition and maintenance of target, observational, and related nontarget facts. *Exceptional Child, 57,* 462-474.

Wolery, M., Doyle, P. M., Ault, M. J., Gast, D. L., Meyer, S., & Stinson, D. (1991). Effects of presenting incidental information in consequent events on future learning. *Journal of Behavioral Education, 1,* 79-104.

Wolery, M., Holcombe, A., Cybriwsky, C., Doyle, P. M., Schuster, J. W., Ault, M. J., & Gast, D. L. (in press). Constant time delay with discrete responses: A review of effectiveness and demographic, procedural, and methodological parameters. Manuscript submitted for publication. *Research in Developmental Disabilities.*

Wolery, M., Holcombe, A., Werts, M. G., & Cipollone, R. (in press). Effects of simultaneous prompting and instructive feedback. *Early Education and Development.*

SENSORY REACTIVITY

Abrahamson, E. P., & Mitchell, J. R. (1990). Communication and sensorimotor functioning in children with autism. *Journal of Autism and Developmental Disorders, 20*(1), 75-85.

Arendt, R. E., MacLean, W. E., Jr., & Baumeister, A. A. (1988). Critique of sensory integration therapy and its application in mental retardation. *American Journal on Mental Retardation, 92,* 401-411.

Aryes, A. J., & Mailloux, Z. K. (1981). Influence of sensory integration procedures on language development. *American Journal of Occupational Therapy, 35*(6), 383-390.

Ayres, A. J., & Mailloux, Z. K. (1983). Possible pubertal effect on therapeutic gains in an autistic girl. *American Journal of Occupational Therapy, 37*(8), 535-540.

Ayres, A. J., & Tickle, L. S. (1980). Hyperresponsivity to touch and vestibular stimuli as a predictor of positive response to sensory integration procedures by autistic children. *American Journal of Occupational Therapy, 34,* 375-381.

Baranek, G. T. (1999). Autism during infancy: A retrospective video analysis of sensory-motor and social behaviors at 9-12 months of age. *Journal of Autism and Developmental Disorders, 29*(3), 213-24.

Baranek, G. T., & Berkson, G. (1994). Tactile defensiveness in children with developmental disabilities: Responsiveness and habituation. *Journal of Autism and Developmental Disorders, 24*(4), 457-71.

Baranek, G., Foster, L., & Berkson, G. (1998). Tactile defensiveness and stereotyped behaviors. *Journal of Occupational Therapy, 51*, 91-95.

Carte, E., Morrisson, D., Sublett, J., Uemura, A., & Setrakian, W. (1984). Sensory integration therapy: A trial of a specific neurodevelopmental therapy for the remediation of learning disabilities. *Journal of Developmental and Behavioral Pediatrics, 5*, 189-194.

Case-Smith, J., & Bryan, T. (1999). The effects of occupational therapy with sensory integration emphasis on preschool-aged children with autism. *American Journal of Occupational Therapy, 53*, 489-497.

Casey, M. B., Bronson, M. B., Tivnan, T., Riley, E., & Spenciner, L. (1991). Differentiating preschoolers' sequential planning agility from their general intelligence: A study of organization, systematic responding, and efficiency in young children. *Journal of Applied Developmental Psychology, 12*, 19-32.

Clark, F. A., Mailloux, Z., & Parham, D. (1985). Sensory integration and children with learning disabilities. In P. N. Clark & A. G. Allen (Eds.), *Occupational therapy for children* (pp. 359-405). St. Louis: Mosby.

Close, W., Carpenter, M., & Cibiri, S. (1986). An evaluation study on sensory motor therapy for profoundly retarded adults. *Canadian Journal of Occupational Therapy, 53*, 259-264.

Cook, D. G. (1990). A sensory approach to the treatment and management of children with autism. *Focus on Autistic Behavior, 5*(6), 2-19.

Cummins, R. A. (1991). Sensory integration and learning disabilities: Ayres' factor analyses reappraised. *Journal of Learning Disabilities, 24*, 160-168.

Densem, J. F., Nuthall, G. A., Bushnell, J., & Horn, J. (1989). Effectiveness of a sensory integrative therapy program for children with perceptual-motor deficits. *Journal of Learning Disabilities, 22*(4), 221-229.

Ghez, C., Gordon, J., Ghilardi, M. F., & Sainburg, R. (1995). Contributions of vision and proprioception to accuracy in limb movements. In M. S. Gazzaniga (Ed.), *The cognitive neurosciences* (pp.548-564). Cambridge, MA: MIT.

Gorman, P. (1997). Dysfunction in dual diagnosis: Mental retardation/mental illness and autism. *Occupational Therapy and Mental Health, 51*, 530-537.

Grimwood, L. M., & Rutherford, E. M. (1980). Sensory integrative therapy as an intervention procedure with grade "one risk" readers: A three year study. *Exceptional Child, 27*, 52-61.

Honomies, T., Wright, M., McDougall, B., & Vertes, J. (1996). The efficacy of sensory integration therapy for children with a learning disability. *Physical and Occupational Therapy in Pediatrics, 13*(13), 1-17.

Horowitz, L. J., Oosterveld, W. J., & Adrichem, R. (1993). Effectiveness of sensory integration on smooth pursuits and organization time in children. *Padiatrie und Grenzgebiete (Berlin) 31*(5), 331-344.

Huff, D. M., & Harris, S. C. (1987). Using sensorimotor integrative treatment with mentally retarded adults. *American Journal of Occupational Therapy, 41*, 227-231.

Humphries, T., Snider, L., & McDougall, B. (1992). A comparison of the effectiveness of sensory integrative therapy and perceptual–motor training in treating children with learning disabilities. *Journal of Developmental and Behavioral Pediatrics, 13*, 31-40.

Humphries, T. W., Snider, L., & McDougall, B. (1993). Clinical evaluation of the effectiveness of sensory integrative and perceptual motor therapy in improving sensory integrative function in children with learning disabilities. *Occupational Therapy Journal of Research, 13,* 163-183.

Humphries, T., Wright, M., McDougall, B., & Vertes, J. (1990). The efficacy of sensory integration therapy for children with a learning disability. *Physical and Occupational Therapy in Pediatrics, 10*(3), 1-17.

Kientz, M. A., & Dunn, W. (1997). A comparison of the performance of children with and without autism on the sensory profile. *American Journal of Occupational Therapy, 51,* 530-537. King, L. J. (1987). A sensory-integrative approach to the education of the autistic child. *Occupational Therapy in Health Care, 34,* 382-386.

Law, M., Polatajko, H., Schaffer, R., Miller, J., & Macnab, J. (1991). The effect of a sensory integration program on academic achievement, motor performance and self-esteem in children identified as learning disabled: Results of a clinical trial. *Occupational Therapy Journal of Research, 11,* 155-176.

Law, M., Polatajko, H. J., Schaffer, R., Miller, J., & Macnab, J. (1991). The impact of heterogeneity in a clinical trial: Motor outcomes after sensory integration therapy. *Occupational Therapy Journal of Research, 11,* 177-189.

Leary, P. M. (1997). Interventions for children with neurodevelopmental delay. *South African Medicine, 87*(12), 1680-1684.

Lincoln, A. J., Courchesne, E., Harms, L., & Allen, M. (1995). Sensory modulation of auditory stimuli in children with autism and receptive development language disorder: Event–related brain potential evidence. *Journal of Autism and Developmental Disorders, 25,* 521-539.

Morrison, D., & Sublett, J. (1986). The effects of sensory integration therapy on nystagmus duration, equilibrium reactions and visual-motor integration in reading in retarded children. *Child: Care, Health and Development, 12,* 99-110.

Nelson, D., Nitzberg, L. & Hollander, T. (1980). Visually monitored postrotary nystagmus in seven autistic children. *American Journal of Occupational Therapy, 34,* 382-386.

Oetter, P., Richter, E., & Frick, S. (1988). *M.O.R.E.: Integrating the mouth with sensory and postural functions.* Oak Park Heights, MN: Professional Developmental Programs.

Ottenbacher, K., & Short, M. A. (1985). Sensory integrative dysfunction in children: A review of theory and treatment. *Advances in Developmental and Behavioral Pediatrics, 6,* 287-329.

Polatajko, H., Kaplan, B., & Wilson, B. (1992). Sensory integration treatment for children with learning disabilities: Its status 20 years later. *Occupational Therapy Journal of Research, 12,* 323-341.

Polatajko, H., Law, M., Miller, J., Schaffer, R., & Macnab, J. (1991). The effect of a sensory integration program on academic achievement major performance and self-esteem in children identified as learning disabled: Results of a clinical trial. *Occupational Therapy Journal of Research, 11*(3), 155-176.

Porges, S. W., McCabe, P. M., & Yongue, B. G. (1982). Respiratory-heart rate interactions: Psychophysiological implications for pathophysiology and behavior. In J. Caccipio & R. Petty (Eds.), *Perspectives in cardiovascular psychophysiology.* New York: Guillford.

Price, A. (1980). Neurotherapy and specialization. *American Journal of Occupational Therapy, 34,* 809-881.

Scanlon, K. (1993). Art therapy with autistic children. *Pratt Institute Creative Arts Therapy Review.*

Schaaf, R. C. (1990). Play behavior and occupational therapy. *American Journal of Occupational Therapy, 44*(1), 68-75.

Schaaf, R. C. (In press). Sensory integration with high risk infants and young children. In E. Blanche, S. Smith-Roley, & R. Schaaf (Eds.), *Sensory integration and development disabilities.* San Antonio, TX: Therapy Skill Builders.

Schaffer, R. (1984). Sensory integration therapy with learning disabled children: A critical review. *Canadian Journal of Occupational Therapy, 51*, 73-77.

Schaffer, R., Law, M., Polatajko, H., & Miller, J. (1989). A study of children with learning disabilities or let's not throw the baby out with the bathwater. *Physical and Occupational Therapy in Pediatrics, 9*, 101-117.

Tickle-Degnen, L. (1988). Perspectives on the status of sensory integration theory. *American Journal of Occupational Therapy, 42*, 427-433.

Vargas, S., & Camili, G. (1999). A meta-analysis on sensory integration treatment. *American Journal of Occupational Therapy, 53*(2), 189-198.

Werry, J. S., Sealetti, R., & Mills, F. (1990). Sensory integration and teacher-judged learning problems: A controlled intervention trial. *Journal of Pediatric Child Health, 26*(1), 31-35.

Williamson, G. G., & Anzalone, M. E. (1997). Sensory integration: A key component of the evaluation and treatment of young children with severe difficulties in relating and communicating. *Zero to Three, 17*, 29-36.

Wilson, B. N., Kapian, B. J., Fellowes, S., Gruchy, C., & Faris, P. (1992). The efficacy of sensory integration treatment compared in tutoring. *Physical and Occupational Therapy in Pediatrics, 12*(1), 1-36.

Wolkowicz, R. (1998). Sensory integration with autistic children. *Canadian Journal of Occupational Therapy, 44*, 171-175.

Zeitlin, S., & Williamson, G. G. (1994). *Coping in young children: Early intervention practices to enhance behavior and resilience.* Baltimore: Paul H. Brookes.

Zisserman, L. (1992). The effects of deep pressure on self-stimulation behaviors in a child with autism and other disabilities. *American Journal of Occupational Therapy.*

Ziviani, J., Poulsen, A., & O'Brien, A. (1982). Effect of a sensory integrative/ neurodevelopmental programme on motor and academic performance of children with learning disabilities. *Australian Occupational Therapy Journal, 29*, 27-33.

AFFECT AND SOCIAL/EMOTIONAL CAPACITIES

Play and Symbolic Play Skills

Ariel, S. (1985). *Applying Chomsky's linguistic methodology to the clinical interpretation of symbolic play.* International Symposium, Netherlands Organization for Postgraduate Education in the Social Sciences International Symposium. Amsterdam, The Netherlands, September.

Bagleyu, D. M., & Chaille, C. (1996). Transforming play: An analysis of first-, third-, and fifth-graders' play. *Journal of Research in Childhood Education, 10*(2), 134-142.

Barkley, R. A. (1977). The effects of methylphenidate on various types of activity level and attention in hyperkinetic children. *Journal of Abnormal Child Psychology, 5*(4), 351-369.

Beeghly, M. (1989). Structural and affective dimensions of play development in young children with Down syndrome. *International Journal of Behavioral Development, 12*(2), 257-277.

Bergen, D. (1991). *Play as the vehicle for early intervention with at-risk infants and toddlers.* Annual Conference of the American Educational Research Association, Chicago, IL, April.

Bornstein, M. H., & Tamis-LeMonda, C. S. (1995). Parent-child symbolic play: Three theories in search of an effect. *Developmental Review, 15*(4), 382-400.

Casby, M. W. (1997). Symbolic play of children with language impairment: A critical review. *Journal of Speech, Language, and Hearing Research, 40*(3), 468-469.

Chang, P. Y., & Yawkey, T. D. (1998). Symbolic play and literacy learning: Classroom materials and teacher's roles. *Reading Improvement, 35*(4), 172-77.

Chapman, M. (1987). A longitudinal study of cognitive representation in symbolic play, self-recognition, and object permanence during the second year. *International Journal of Behavioral Development, 10*(2), 151-170.

Clark, P. M. (1989). Symbolic play and ideational fluency as aspects of the evolving divergent cognitive style in young children. *Early Childhood Development and Care, 51*, 77-88.

Corrigan, R. (1987). A developmental sequence of actor-object pretend play in young children. *Merrill–Palmer Quarterly, 33*(1), 87-106.

Dawson, G., & Glapert, I. (1990). Mother's use of imitative play for facilitating social responsiveness and toy play in young autistic children. *Developmental and Psychopathology, 2*, 151-162.

Doescher, S. M. (1991). Encouraging symbolic play in young children: A guide for developing creative and imaginative experiences.

Douglas, L. (1999). An evaluation of the effectiveness of early intervention on autistic children. Master's thesis, Chicago State University, IL.

Fallon, M. A., & Harris, M. B. (1989). Factors influencing the selection of toys for handicapped and normally developing preschool children. *Journal of Genetic Psychology, 150*(2), 125-134.

Fein, D. (1991). *Symbolic play development in autistic and language disordered children.* Annual Meeting of the International Neuropsychological Society, San Antonio, TX, February.

Fiese, B. H. (1990). Playful relationships: A contextual analysis of mother-toddler interaction and symbolic play. *Child Development, 61*(5), 1648-1656.

Flannery, K. A., & Watson, M. W. (1993). Are individual differences in fantasy play related to peer acceptance levels? *Journal of Genetic Psychology, 154*(3), 407-416.

Galsa, L. (1989). A short-term longitudinal study of preschoolers' emergent literacy. *Research in the Teaching of English, 23*(3), 292-309.

Girolametto, L. (1995). The effects of focused stimulation for promoting vocabulary in young children with delays: A pilot study. *Journal of Children's Communication Development, 17*(2), 39-49.

Gruen, R. J., Folkman, S., & Lazarus, R. S. (1988). Centrality and individual differences in the meaning of daily hassles.

Haring, T., & Lovinger, L. (1989). Promoting social interaction through teaching generalized play initiation responses to preschool children with autism. *Journal of the Association for Persons with Severe Handicaps (JASH), 14*(1), 58-67.

Hazen, Black, and Fleming-Johnson (1984). Social acceptance. *Young Children, 39,* 26-36.

Heidemann, S., & Hewitt, D. (1992). *Pathways to play: Developing play skills in young children.* St. Paul, MN: Redleaf Press.

Johnson, J. E., & Ershler, J. L. (1985). Social and cognitive play forms and toy use by nonhandicapped and handicapped preschoolers. *Topics in Early Childhood Special Education, 5*(3), 69-82.

Kennedy, M. D. (1991). Play-language relationships in young children with developmental delays: Implications for assessment. *Journal of Speech and Hearing Research, 34*(1), 112-122.

Kim, Y. T. (1989). Effects of symbolic play intervention with children who have mental retardation. *Mental Retardation, 27*(3), 159-165.

Lederberg, A. R. (1991). Social interaction among deaf preschoolers. The effects of language ability and age. *American Annual of Deafness, 136*(1), 53-59.

Li, A. K. F. (1985). Toward more elaborate pretend play. *Mental Retardation, 23*(3), 131-136.

Libby, S., Powell, S., Messer, D., & Jordan, R. (1998). Spontaneous play in children with autism: a reappraisal. *Journal of Autism and Developmental Disorder, 28*(6), 487-497.

Lifter, K. (1993). Teaching play activities to preschool children with disabilities: The importance of developmental considerations. *Journal of Early Intervention, 17*(2), 139-159.

Lucariello, J. (1987). Spinning fantasy: Themes, structure, and the knowledge base. *Child Development, 58*(2), 434-442.

Matousek, N., Edwards, J., Jackson, H. J., Rudd, R. P., & McMurray, N. E. (1992). Social skills training and negative symptoms. *Behavior Modification, 16*(1), 39-63.

Morrison, C. D., Bundy, A. C., & Fisher. A. G. (1991). The contribution of motor skills and playfulness to the play performance of preschoolers. *American Journal of Occupational Therapy, 45*(8), 687-694.

Nowak-Fabrytkowski, K. (1994). Can symbolic play prepare children for their future? *Early Childhood Development and Care, 102,* 63-71.

Ogura, T. (1987). *Symbolic play and early language development in normal children.* Biennial Meeting of the International Society for the Study of Behavioural Development, Tokyo, Japan, July.

Ogura, T. (1987). *The relationship between early language, cognitive and social development through a longitudinal study of autistic children.* Biennial Meeting of the

International Society for the Study of Behavioral Development, Tokyo, Japan, July.

Pellegrini, A. D. (1985). The relations between symbolic play and literate behavior: A review and critique of the empirical literature. *Review of Educational Research, 55*(1), 107-121.

Pellegrini, A. D. (1991). A longitudinal study of the predictive relations among symbolic play, linguistic verbs and early literacy. *Research in the Teaching of English, 25*(2), 219-235.

Pellegrini, A. D. (1998). Physical activity play: The nature and function of a neglected aspect of playing. *Child Development, 69*(3), 577-598.

Pellegrini, A. D., & Galda, L. (1993). Ten years after: A reexamination of symbolic play and literacy research. *Reading Research Quarterly, 28*(2), 162-175.

Py, Bernard (Ed.) (1994). Group interventions and interactions. *Proceedings of the Colloquium on Speech Therapy,* Neuchatel, Switzerland, September.

Restall, G., & Magill-Evans, J. (1994). Play and preschool children with autism. *American Journal of Occupational Therapy, 48*(2), 113-120.

Roth, F. P., & Clark, D. M. (1987). Symbolic play and social participation abilities of language-impaired and normally developing children. *Journal of Speech and Hearing Disorders, 52*(1), 17-29.

Saunders, I., Sayer, M., & Goodale, A. (1999). The relationship between playfulness and coping in preschool children: A pilot study. *American Journal of Occupational Therapy, 53*(2), 221-226.

Schrader, C. T. *Symbolic play as a curricular tool for early literacy development.*

Shore, C. (1986). Combinatorial play, conceptual development, and early multiword speech. *Developmental Psychology, 22*(2), 184-190.

Slade, A. (1987). A longitudinal study of maternal involvement and symbolic play during the toddler period. *Child Development, 58*(2), 367-375.

Smilansky, S. (1968). *The effects of sociodramatic play on disadvantaged preschool children.* New York: Wiley & Sons.

Stahmer, A. C. (1995). Teaching symbolic play skills to children with autism using pivotal response training. *Journal of Autism and Developmental Disorders, 25*(2), 123-141.

Stahmer, A. C., & Schreibman, L. (1992). Teaching children with autism appropriate play in unsupervised environments using self-management treatment package. *Journal of Applied Behavior Analysis, 25*(2), 447-459.

Stilson, S. R., & Harding, C. G. (1997). Early social context as it relates to symbolic play: A longitudinal investigation. *Merrill-Paler Quarterly, 43*(4), 682-693.

Strain, P. S. (1985). Social and nonsocial determinants of acceptability in handicapped preschool children. *Topics in Early Childhood Special Education Quarterly, 4*(4), 47-58.

Tamis-LeMonda, C. S., & Bornstein, M. H. (1991). Representation in the second year: Models of predictive validity of language and play.

Thorpe, D. M., Stahmer, A. C., & Schreibman, L. (1995). Effects of sociodramatic play training on children with autism. *Journal of Autism and Developmental Disorders, 25*(3), 265-282.

Umek, L. M., & Musek, P. L. (1997). Symbolic play in mixed-aged and same-age groups. *European Early Childhood Education Research Journal, 5*(2), 47-59.

Umek, L. M., & Marjanovic, L. P. (1996). *Social interaction and types of play in mixed-age and same-age groups in early childhood institutions.* European Conference on the Quality of Early Childhood Education, Lisbon, September.

Wehman, P., & Marchant, J. A. (1978). Improving free play skills of severely retarded children. *American Journal of Occupational Therapy, 32*(2), 100-104.

Yoder, P. J. (1995). Predicting children's response to prelinguistic communication intervention. *Journal of Early Childhood Intervention, 19*(1), 78-84.

Parent/Caregiver Relationships

Abidin, P. R. (1986). *Parenting stress index* (2nd ed.). Charlottesville, VA: Pediatric Psychology.

Bakeman, R., & Adamson, L. (1984). Coordinating attention to people and objects in mother-infant and peer-infant interaction. *Child Development, 55*, 1278-1289.

Barrera, M. E. (1991). The transactional model of early home intervention: Application with developmentally delayed children and their families. In K. Marfo (Ed.), *Early intervention in transition: Current perspectives on programs for handicapped children* (pp.109-146). New York: Praeger.

Barrera, M., & Rosenbaum, P. (1986). The transactional model of early home intervention. *Infant Mental Health Journal, 7*, 112-131.

Bayley, N. (1993). *Bayley scales of infant development* (2nd ed. manual). San Antonio, TX: Psychological Corporation.

Bell, R. Q. (1974). Contributions of human infants to caregiving and social interaction. In M. Lewis & L. A. Rosenblum (Eds.), *The effect of the infant on its caregiver* (pp.1-19). New York: Wiley.

Belsky, J., Goode, M., & Most, R. K. (1980). Maternal stimulation and infant exploratory competence: Cross-sectional, correla-

tional and experimental analyses. *Child Development, 51*, 1168-1178.

Berrueta-Clement, J. R., Schweinhart, L. J., Burnett, W. S., Epstein, A. S., & Weikart, D. P. (1984). *Changed lives: The effects of the Perry preschool program on youths through age nineteen.* Ypsilanti, MI: High Scope.

Boyce, G. C. (1993). The effectiveness of adding a parent involved component to an existing center-based program for children with disabilities and their families. *Early Education and Development, 4*(4), 327-345.

Bradley, R. H., & Brisby, J. (1990). Assessment of the home environment. In J. Johnson & J. Goldman (Eds.), *Developmental assessment in clinical child psychology: A handbook* (pp. 219-250). Elmsford, NY: Pergamon.

Brinker, P. R., Seifer, R., & Sameroff, A. J. (1994). Relation among maternal stress, cognitive development, and early intervention in middle and low SES infants with developmental disabilities. *American Journal on Mental Retardation, 98*, 463-480.

Bromwich, R. M. (1981). *Working with parents and infants: An interactional approach.* Baltimore, MD: University Park.

Bruner, J., & Sherwood, V. (1976). Peekaboo and the learning of rule structures. In J. S. Bruner, A. Jolly, & K. Sylva (Eds.), *Play: Its role in development and evolution* (pp. 277-285). New York: Basic Books.

Cardone, I. A., & Gilkerson, L. (1989). Family administered neonatal activities: An innovative component of family-centered care. *Zero to Three, 10*, 23-28.

Cicchetti, D. & Beeghly, M. (1990). An organizational approach to the study of Down syndrome: Contributions to an integrative theory of development. In D. Cicchetti & M. Beeghly (Eds.), *Children with Down syndrome: A developmental perspective* (pp.29-62). Cambridge, MA: Cambridge University.

Clarke-Stewart, K. A. (1973). Interactions between mothers and their young children: Characteristics and consequences. *Monographs of the Society for Research in Child Development, 38*(6-7) (Serial No. 153).

Denckla, M. B. (1986). New diagnostic criteria for autism and related behavioral disorders—guidelines for research protocols. *Journal of the American Academy of Child Psychiatry, 25*(2), 221-224.

Feldman, M. A. (1994). Parenting education for parents with intellectual disabilities: A review of outcome studies. *Research of Developmental Disabilities, 15*(4), 299-332.

Floyd, F. J., & Phillippe, K. A. (1993). Parental interactions with children with and without mental retardation: Behavior management, coerciveness, and positive exchange. *American Journal of Retardation, 97*(6), 673-684.

Girolametto, L. (1988). Improving the social-conversational skills of developmentally delayed children: An intervention study. *Journal of Speech and Hearing Disorders, 53*, 146-167.

Girolametto, L., Verby, M., & Tannock, R. (1994). Improving joint engagement in parent-child interaction: An intervention study. *Journal of Early Intervention, 18*, 155-167.

Greenspan, S. I., & Wieder, S., Lieberman, A., Nover, R., Lourie, R., & Robinson, M. (1987). Infants in multirisk families: Case studies in preventive intervention. *Clinical infant report, No. 3*. New York: International Universities Press.

Harrold, M., Lutzker, J. R., Campbell, R. V., & Touchette, P. E. (1992). Improving parent-child interactions for families of children with developmental disabilities. *Behavioral Therapy and Experimental Psychiatry, 23*(2), 89-100.

Helm, D. T., Kozloff, M. A. (1986). Research on parent training: Shortcomings and remedies. *Journal of Autism and Developmental Disorders, 16*(1), 1-22.

Hemmeter, M. L., & Kaiser, A. P. (1994). Enhanced milieu teaching: An analysis of the effects of parent-implemented language intervention. *Journal of Early Intervention, 18*, 155-167.

Honig, A. S., & Lally, J. R. (1981). *Infant caregiving: A design for training*. Syracuse, NY: Syracuse University.

Kalmanson, B., & Seligman, S. (1992). Family-provider relationships: The basis of all interventions. *Infants and Young Children, 4*(4), 46-52.

Kaufman, B. N. (1976). *Son-rise*. New York: Harper & Row.

Klein, P. S., Wieder, S., & Greenspan, S. I. (1989). A theoretical overview and empirical study of mediated learning experience: Prediction of preschool performance from mother-infant interaction patterns. *Infant Mental Health Journal, 8*(2), 110-129.

Knieps, L. J., Walden, T. A., & Baxter, A. (1994). Affective expressions of toddlers with and without Down syndrome in a social referencing context. *American Journal of Mental Retardation, 99*(3), 301-312.

Lally, J. R. (1995). The impact of child care policies and practices on infant/toddler identity formation. *Young Children, November*, 58-67.

Landry, S. H., & Chapieski, M. L. (1990). Joint attention of 6-month-old Down syndrome and preterm infants: I: Attention to toys and mothers. *American Journal on Mental Retardation, 94*, 488-498.

Landry, S. H., Garner, P. W., Pirie, D., & Swank, P. R. (1994). Effects of social context and mothers' requesting strategies on Down's syndrome children's social responsiveness. *Developmental Psychology, 36*, 465-477.

Lantzy, T. J., & Gable, R. A. (1989). Effects of parent training on the behavior problems in the home of preschool handicapped children. National Conference of the Council for Exceptional Children/Council for Children with Behavioral Disorders, Charlotte, SC, September.

Mahoney, G. (1988). Enhancing the developmental competence of handicapped infants. In K. Marfo (Ed.), *Parent–child interaction and developmental disabilities: Theory, research, and intervention* (pp. 145-162). New York: Praeger.

Marfo, K. (1991). The maternal directiveness theme in mother-child interaction research: Implications for early intervention. In K. Marfo (Ed.), *Early intervention in transition: Current perspectives on programs for handicapped children* (pp.177-203). New York: Praeger.

McCollum, J. A. (1984). Social interaction between parents and babies: Validation of an intervention procedure. *Child: Care, Health, and Development, 10,* 301-315.

McCollum, J. A. (1991). At the crossroad: Reviewing and rethinking interaction coaching. In K. Marfo (Ed.), *Early intervention in transition: Current perspectives on programs for handicapped children* (pp.137-176). New York: Praeger.

McCollum, J. A., & Bair, H. (1994). Research in parent-child interaction: Guidance to developmentally appropriate practice for young children with disabilities. In B. L. Mallory & R. S. New (Eds.), *Diversity and developmentally appropriate practices: Challenges for early childhood education* (pp. 84-106). New York: Teachers College.

McCollum, J. A., & Stayton, V. D. (1985). Infant/parent interaction: Studies and intervention guidelines based on the SIAI model. *Journal of the Division for Early Childhood, 10,* 124-135.

McCollum, J. A., & Yates, T. (1994). Dyad as focus, triad as means: A family–centered approach to supporting parent–child interactions. *Infants and Young Children, 6*(4), 54-63.

Moran, D. R., & Whitman, T. L. (1985). The multiple effects of a play-oriented parent training program for mothers of developmentally delayed children. *Analysis and Intervention in Developmental Disabilities, 5,* 73-96.

Olds, D. L. (1984). Case studies of factors interfering with nurse home visitors' promotion of positive caregiving methods in high-risk families. *Early Childhood Development and Care, 16,* 149-166.

Pearse, I. H. (1979). *The quality of life: The Peckham approach to human ethnology.* Edinburgh: Scottish Academic Press.

Provence, S., Naylor, A. (1983). *Working with disadvantaged parents and their children: Scientific and practical issues.* New Haven: Yale University.

Ramey, C. T., & Campbell, F. A. (1984). Preventive education for high-risk children: Cognitive consequences of the Carolina Abecedarian Project. *American Journal of Mental Deficiency, 88,* 515-523.

Roberts, R. N., & Barnes, M. L. (1992). Let momma show you how: Maternal-child interactions and their effects on children's cognitive performance. *Journal of Applied Developmental Psychology, 13,* 363-376.

Russell, D, & Matson, J. (1998). Fathers as intervention agents for their children with developmental disabilities. *Child & Family Behavior Therapy, 20*(3), 29-49.

Seifer, R., Clark, G. N., & Sameroff, A. J. (1991). Positive effects of interaction coaching on infants with developmental disabilities and their mothers. *American Journal on Mental Retardation, 96,* 1-11.

Stallibrass, A. (1982). Child development and education: The contribution of the

Peckham experiment. *Nutrition and Health, 1*, 45-52.

Stallibrass, A. (1984). *The Peckham experience: A hope for a healthier future.* London: Pioneer Health Centre, Ltd.

Tannock, R. (1988). Mother's directiveness in their interactions with their children with and without Down syndrome. *American Journal of Mental Retardation, 93*, 154-165.

Tannock, R., Girolametto, L., & Siegel, L. S. (1992). Language intervention with children who have developmental delays: Effects of an interactive approach. *American Journal on Mental Retardation, 97*(2), 145-160.

Telzrow, C. F. (1993). Commentary on comparative evaluation of early intervention alternatives. *Early Education and Development, 4*(4), 359-365.

Teti, D. M., & Gelfand, D. M. (1990). Behavioral competence among mothers of infants in the first year: The mediational role of the maternal self-efficacy. *Child Development, 62*, 918-929.

Turnbull, A. P., & Turnbull, H. R. (1982). Parent involvement in the education of handicapped children: A critique. *Mental Retardation, 20*, 115-122.

White, K. R., & Greenspan, S. I. (1987). An overview of the effectiveness of preventive early intervention programs. In J. D. Noshpitz, et al. (Eds.), *Basic handbook of child psychiatry.* New York: Basic Books.

Wiese, M. R., & Kramer, J. J. (1988). Parent training research: An analysis of the empirical literature 1975-1985. *Psychology in the Schools, 25*(3), 325-330.

Williams, B. W. (1992). Increasing the effectiveness of in–home behavior interventions. Annual Meeting of the American Association on Mental Retardation, New Orleans, LA, May.

Yoder, P. J., & Davies, B. (1990). *Do Parental questions and topic continuations elicit replies from developmentally delayed children? A sequential analysis.* Nashville: Vanderbilt University.

Peer Relationships

Bailey, D. B., Jr., McWilliam, R. A., Ware, W. B., & Buchinal, M. A. (1993). Social interactions of toddlers and preschoolers in same-age and mixed-aged play groups. *Journal of Applied Development Psychology, 14*, 261-276.

Bennerson, D. (1991). Increasing positive interpersonal interactions: A social intervention for students with learning disabilities in the regular classroom. Annual Conference of the Council for Exceptional Children, Atlanta, GA, April.

Brysse, V., & Bailey, D. B., Jr. (1993). Behavioral and developmental outcomes in young children with disabilities in integrated and segregated settings: A review of comparative studies. *Journal of Special Education, 23*, 434-461.

Chandler, L. K., Lubeck, R. C., & Fowler, S. A. (1992). Generalization and maintenance of preschool children's social skills: A critical review and analysis. *Journal of Applied Behavior Analysis, 35*, 415-429.

Craig, H. K., & Washington, J. A. (1993). Access behaviors of children with specific language impairment. *Journal of Speech and Hearing Research, 36*, 322-337.

DeKlyen, M., & Odom, S. L. (1989). Activity structure and social interactions with peers in developmentally integrated play groups. *Journal of Early Intervention, 13*, 342-352.

Dodge, K. A. (1991). Emotion and social information processing. In I. J. Garber & K. A. Dodge (Eds.), *The development of emotion regulation and dysregulation* (pp. 159-181). Cambridge: Cambridge University.

Fey, M. E., & Leonard, L. B. (1984). Partner age as a variable in the conversational performance of specifically language-impaired and normal-language children. *Journal of Speech and Hearing Research, 27*, 413-423.

Field, T., Roseman, S., DeStefano, L., & Knewler, J. H., III. (1981). Play behaviors of handicapped preschool children in the presence and absence of nonhandicapped peers. *Journal of Applied Developmental Psychology, 2*, 49-53.

Goldstein, H. (1997). Interaction among preschoolers with and without disabilities: Effects of across-the-day peer intervention. *Journal of Speech, Language, and Hearing Research, 40*(1), 33-48.

Goldstein, H. (1993). Use of peers as communication intervention agents. *Teaching Exceptional Children, 25*(2), 37-39.

Goldstein, H., & Cisar, C. L. (1992). Promoting interaction during sociodramatic play: Teaching scripts to typical preschoolers and classmates with handicaps. *Journal of Applied Behavioral Analysis, 25*, 265-280.

Goldstein, H. Kaczmarek, L., Pennington, R., & Schafer, K. (1992). Peer mediated intervention: Attending to, commenting on, and acknowledging the behavior of preschoolers with autism. *Journal of Applied Behavior Analysis, 25*, 289-305.

Goldstein, H., & Wickstrom, S. (1986). Peer intervention effects on communicative interaction among handicapped and non-handicapped preschoolers. *Journal of Applied Behavior Analysis, 19*, 209-214.

Gonzalez-Lopez, A., & Kamps, D. M. (1997). Social skills to increase social interactions between children with autism and their typical peers. *Focus on Autism and Other Developmental Disabilities, 12*(1), 2-14.

Grubbs, P. R., & Niemeyer, J. A. (1999). Promoting reciprocal social interactions in inclusive classrooms for young children. *Infants and Young Children, 11*(3), 9-18.

Guralnick, M. J. (1991). The next decade of research on the effectiveness of early intervention. *Exceptional Children, 58*(2), 174-183.

Guralnick, M. J., Connor, R. T., Hammond, M, Gottman, J. M., & Kinnish, K. (1996). Immediate effects on mainstreamed settings on the social interactions and social integration of preschool children. *American Journal on Mental Retardation, 100*(4), 359-377.

Guralnick, M. J., & Groom, J. M. (1985). Correlates of peer-related social competence of developmentally delayed preschool children. *American Journal of Mental Deficiency, 90*, 140-150.

Guralnick, M. J., & Groom, J. M. (1987). Dyadic peer interactions on mildly delayed and nonhandicapped preschool children. *American Journal of Mental Deficiency, 92*, 178-193.

Guralnick, M. J., & Groom, J. M. (1988). Friendships of preschool children in mainstreamed play groups. *Developmental Psychology, 24*, 595-605.

Guralnick, M. J., & Paul-Brown, D. (1989). Peer related communicative competence of preschool children: Developmental and adaptive characteristics. *Journal of Speech and Hearing Research, 32*, 930-943.

Haak, J. A. (1993). Establishing social skills for exceptional needs students and their nonhandicapped peers in the elementary classroom utilizing a social skills training program.

Hall, L. J., & Smith, K. L. (1996). The generalization of social skills by preferred peers with autism. *Journal of Intellectual and Developmental Disability, 25*(4), 313-330.

Haring, T. G., & Lovinger, L. (1989). Promoting social interaction through teaching generalized play initiation responses to preschool children with autism. *Journal of the Association for Persons with Severe Handicaps (JASH), 14*, 58-67.

Johnson, L. J., & Pugach, M. C. (1991). Peer collaboration: Accommodating students with mild learning and behavior problems. *Exceptional Children, 57*(5), 454-461.

Kohl, F. L., & Beckman, P. J. (1990). The effects of directed play on the frequency and length of reciprocal interactions with preschoolers having moderate handicaps. *Education and Training in Mental Retardation, 25,* 258-266.

Lieber, J., & Beckman, P. J. (1991). The role of toys in individual and dyadic play among young children with handicaps. *Journal of Applied Developmental Psychology, 12,* 189-203.

Lieber, J., Beckman, P. J., & Strong, B. O. (1993). A longitudinal study of the social exchanges of young children with disabilities. *Journal of Early Intervention, 17,* 116-125.

Lowenthal, B. (1996). Teaching social skills to preschoolers with special needs. *Childhood Education, 72*(3), 137-140.

McConnell, S. R., McEvoy, M. A., & Odom. S. L. (1992). Implementation of social competence interventions in early childhood special education classes: Current practices and future directions. In S. L. Odom, S. R. McConnell, & M. A. McEvoy (Eds.), *Social competence of young children with disabilities: Issues and strategies for intervention* (pp.277-306). Baltimore, MD: Paul H .Brookes.

McConnell, S. R., Sisson, L. A., Cort, A. A., & Strain, P. S. (1991). Effects of social skills training and contingency management on reciprocal interaction of preschool children with behavioral handicaps. *The Journal of Special Education, 24,* 473-495.

McGee, G. G., et al. (1986). An extension of incidental teaching procedures to reading instruction for autistic children. *Journal of Applied Behavior Analysis, 19*(2), 147-157.

McGee, G. G., et al. (1992). Promoting reciprocal interactions via peer incidental teach-ing. *Journal of Applied Behavior Analysis, 25*(1), 117-126.

McGee, G. G., Feldman, R. S., & Morrier, M. J. (1997). Benchmarks of social treatment for children with autism. *Journal of Autism and Developmental Disorders, 27*(4), 353-365.

McIntosh, R. (1989). Peer rejection is a stubborn thing: Increasing peer acceptance of rejected students with learning disabilities. Annual Convention of the Council for Exceptional Children, San Francisco, CA, April.

McMahon, C. M. (1996). Analysis of frequency and type of interactions in a peer-mediated social skills intervention: Instructional vs. social interactions. *Education and Training in Mental Retardation and Developmental Disabilities, 31*(4), 339-352.

Odom, S. K., Chandler, L. K., Ostrosky, M., McConnell, S. R., & Reaney, S. (1992). Fading teacher prompts from peer-initiation interventions for young children with disabilities. *Journal of Applied Behavior Analysis, 25,* 307-317.

Odom, S. L., McConnell, S. R., & Chandler, L. K. (1993). Acceptability and feasibility of classroom-based social interaction interventions for young children with disabilities. *Exceptional Children, 60,* 226-236.

Peterson, C. A., & McConnell, S. R. (1993). Factors affecting the impact of social interaction skills interventions in early childhood special education. *Topics in Early Childhood Special Education, 13,* 38-36.

Pierce, K., & Schreibman, L. (1995). Increasing complex social behaviors in children with autism: Effects of peer-implemented pivotal response training. *Journal of Applied Behavior Analysis, 28*(3), 285-295.

Rettig, M., Kallam, M., & McCarthy-Salm, K. (1993). The effect of social and isolate toys on the social interactions of preschool-aged children. *Education and Training in Mental Retardation, 28,* 252-256.

Shores, R. E. (1987). Overview of research on social interaction: A historical and personal perspective. *Behavioral Disorders, 12*, 233-241.

Storey, K., Danko, C. D., Ashworth, R., & Strain, P. (1994). Generalization of social skills intervention for preschoolers with social delays. *Education and Treatment of Children, 17*(1), 29-51.

Strain, P. (1983). Generalizations of autistic children's social behavior change: Effects of developmentally integrated and segregated settings. *Analysis and Intervention in Developmental Disabilities (Issues in Mainstreaming Developmentally Disabled Children) 3*(1), 23-34.

Strain, P. (1985). Normally developing preschoolers as intervention agents for autistic-like children: Effects on class deportment and social interaction. *Journal of the Division for Early Childhood, 9*(2), 105-15.

Strain, P. S., & Kohler, F. (1998). Peer-mediated social intervention for young children with autism. *Seminars in Speech and Language, 19*(4), 391-405.

Strain, P. S., & Kohler, F. W. (1991). Programmatic research on social interaction maintenance and generalization with severely handicapped preschoolers. Final Report.

Strain, P. S., Kohler, F. W., Storey, K., & Danko, C. (1994). Teaching preschoolers with autism to self-monitor their social interactions: An analysis of results in home and school settings. *Journal of Emotional and Behavioral Disorders, 2*, 78-88.

Strain, P. S., & Odom, S. L. (1986). Peer social initiations: Effective intervention for social skills development of exceptional children. *Exceptional Children, 52*(6), 543-551.

Strain, P. S., Wolery, M., & Izeman, S. (1998). Considerations for administrators in the design of service options for young children with autism and their families. *Young Exceptional Children, 1*(2), 8-16.

Swanson. H. L. (1996). Meta-analysis replication, social skills, and learning disabilities. *Journal of Special Education, 30*(2), 213-221.

Thompson, S. (1992). Proposed differentiated service model for community-based consultation organizations and the need for inter-ministerial integrated service plan for persons with autism in B.C. *British Columbia Journal of Special Education, 16*(2), 139-53.

Thorp, D. M., Stahmer, A. C., & Schreibman, L. (1995). Effects of sociodramatic play training on children with autism. *Journal of Autism & Developmental Disorders, 25*(3), 265-282.

Trapani, C., & Gettinger, M. (1989). Effects of social skills training and cross-age tutoring on academic achievement and social behaviors of boys with learning disabilities. *Journal of Research and Development in Education, 23*(1), 1-9.

Venn, M. L., Wolery, M., Werts, M. G., Morris, A., DeCesare, L. D., & Cuffs, M. S. (1993). Embedding instruction in art activities to teach preschoolers with disabilities to imitate their peers. *Early Childhood Research Quarterly, 8*, 277-294.

Venn, M. L., Wolery, M., Fleming, L. A., DeCesare, L. D., Morris, A., & Sigesmund, M. H. (1993). Effects of teaching preschool peers to use the mand-model procedure during snack activities. *American Journal of Speech-Language Pathology, 2*(1), 38-46.

Wiener, J., & Harris, P. J. (1997). Evaluation of an individualized, context-based social skills training program for children with learning disabilities. *Learning Disabilities Research and Practice, 12*(1), 40-53.

Wolfberg, P. J., & Schuler, A. L. (1993). Integrated play groups: A model for promoting the social and cognitive dimensions of play in children with autism. *Journal of Autism and Developmental Disorders, 23*, 467-48.

SURFACE BEHAVIORS

Anderson, S. R., Avery, D. L., DiPietro, E. K., Edwards, G. L., & Christian, W. P. (1987). Intensive home-based early intervention with autistic children. *Education and Treatment of Children, 10*, 352-366.

Bagnato, S. J. (1998). Do actions speak louder than words? The case of the disappearance of social communication oddities. *Seminars in Speech and Language, 19*(1), 31-38.

Barrera, R. D., Lobato-Barrera, D., & Sulzer-Azaroff, B. (1980). A simultaneous treatment comparison of three expressive language training programs with a mute autistic child. *Journal of Autism and Developmental Disorders, 10*(1), 21-37.

Barrera, R. D., & Sulzer-Azaroff, B. (1983). An alternating treatment comparison of oral and total communication training programs with echolalic autistic children. *Journal of Applied Behavior Analysis, 16*(4), 379-94.

Beisler, J. M., & Tsai, L. Y. (1983). A pragmatic approach to increase expressive language skills in young autistic children. *Journal of Autism and Developmental Disorders, 13*(3), 287-303.

Birnbrauer, J. S., & Leach, D. J. (1993). The Murdoch early intervention program after 2 years. *Behaviour Change, 10*, 63-74.

Carr, E. G., & Kemp, D. C. (1989). Functional equivalence of autistic leading and communicative pointing: Analysis and treatment. *Journal of Autism and Developmental Disorders, 19*(4), 561-578.

Cattell-Gordon, D., & Cattell-Gordon, D. (1998). The development of an effective applied behavioral analysis program for a young child with autism: A parent's perspective. *Infants and Young Children, 10*(3), 79-85.

Charlop-Christy, M. H., & Haymes, L. K. (1996). Using obsessions as reinforcers with and without mild reductive procedures to decrease inappropriate behaviors of children with autism. *Journal of Autism and Developmental Disorders, 26*(5), 527-546.

Cipani, E. (1998). Three behavioral functions of classroom noncompliance: Diagnostic and treatment implications. *Focus on Autism and Other Developmental Disabilities, 13*(2), 66-72.

Dunlap, G. (1984). Continuity of treatment: Toilet training in multiple community settings. *Journal of the Association for Persons with Severe Handicaps (JASH), 9*(2), 134-141.

Dunlap, G. (1984). The influence of task variation and maintenance tasks on the learning and affect of autistic children. *Journal of Experimental Child Psychology, 37*(1), 41-64.

Dunlap, G. (1995). Modifying activities to produce functional outcomes: Effects on the problem behaviors of students with disabilities. *Journal of the Association for Persons with Severe Handicaps (JASH), 20*(4), 248-258.

Durand, V. M. (1982). A behavioral/pharmacological intervention for the treatment of severe self-injurious behavior. *Journal of Autism and Developmental Disorders, 12*(3), 243-251.

Eikeseth, S., & Lovaas, O. I. (1992). The autistic label and its potentially detrimental effect on the child's treatment. *Journal of Behavior Therapy and Experimental Psychiatry, 23*, 151-157.

Fantuzzo, J. W., & Smith, C. S. (1983). Programmed generalization of dress efficiency across settings for a severely disturbed, autistic child. *Psychology Report, 53*(3) (Pt. 1), 871-879.

Fenske, E. C., Zalenski, S., Krantz, P. J., & McClannahan, L. E. (1985). Age at intervention and treatment outcome for autistic children in a comprehensive intervention program. *Analysis and Intervention in Developmental Disabilities, 5*, 49-58.

Fisher, W. W. (1996). On the reinforcing effects of the content of verbal attention. *Journal of Applied Behavior Analysis, 23*(2), 135-138.

Fisher, W. W., Lindauer, S. E., Alterson, C. J., & Thompson, R. H. (1998). Assessment and treatment of destructive behavior maintained by stereotypic object manipulation. *Journal of Applied Behavior Analysis, 31*(4), 513-527.

Ford, L. (1994). Facilitating desired behavior in the preschool child with autism: A case study. *Contemporary Education, 65*(3), 148-151.

Freeman, B. J., Rahbar, B., Ritvo, E. R., Bice, T. L., Yokota, A., & Rivto, R. (1991). The stability of cognitive and behavioral parameters in autism: A 12-year prospective study. *Journal of the American Academy of Child and Adolescent Psychiatry, 30*, 479-482.

Freeman, K. A., & Piazza, C. C. (1998). Combining stimulus fading, reinforcement, and extinction to treat food refusal. *Journal of Applied Behavior Analysis, 31*(4), 691-694.

Friman, P. C. (1984). Effects of punishment procedures in the self-stimulatory behavior of an autistic child. *Analysis and Intervention in Developmental Disabilities, 4*(1), 39-46.

Gena, A. (1996). Training and generalization of affective behavior displayed by youth with autism. *Journal of Applied Behavior Analysis, 29*(3), 291-304.

Godby, S., Gast, D. L., & Wolery, M. (1987). A comparison of time delay and system of least prompts in teaching object identification. *Research in Developmental Disabilities, 8*(2), 283-305.

Gordon, R., et al. (1986). The effects of contingent versus non-contingent running on the out of seat behavior of an autistic boy. *Child and Family Behavior Therapy, 8*(3), 37-44.

Green, G. (1990). Least restrictive use of reductive procedures: Guidelines and competencies. In A. C. Repp & N. N. Singh (Eds.), *Perspectives on the use of non-aversive and aversive interventions for persons with developmental disabilities* (pp. 479-493). DeKalb, IL: Sycamore Press.

Gresham, F. M., & MacMillian, D. L. (1998). Early Intervention Project: Can its claims be substantiated and its effects replicated? *Journal of Autism and Developmental Disorders, 28*(1), 5-13.

Hackler, J. (1986). Treatment of compulsive eating disorders in an autistic boy or girl by combining behavior therapy and pharmacotherapy: A case report. *Z. Kinder Jungendpsychiatry, 14*(3), 220-227.

Handleman, J. S., & Harris, S. L. (1980). Generalization from school to home with autistic children. *Journal of Autism and Developmental Disorders, 10*(3), 323-333.

Handleman, J. S., & Harris, S. L. (1994). The Douglas Developmental Disabilities Center. In S. L. Harris & J. Handleman (Eds.), *Preschool education programs for children with autism* (pp. 71-86). Austin, TX: PRO-ED.

Haring, T. G., Kennedy, C. H., Adams, M. J., & Pitts-Conway, V. (1987). Teaching generalization of purchasing skills across community settings to autistic youth using videotape modeling. *Journal of Applied Behavior Analysis, 20*(1), 89-96.

Harris, S. L., Handleman, J. S., Gordon, R., Kristoff, B., & Feuntes, F. (1991). Changes in cognitive and language functioning of preschool children with autism. *Journal of*

Autism and Developmental Disorders, 21, 281-290.

Holden, E. W. (1984). The treatment of self-injurious behavior in profoundly retarded autistic children. Annual Meeting of the Southeastern Psychological Association, New Orleans, March.

Howlin, P. A. (1981). The effectiveness of operant language training with autistic children. *Journal of Autism and Developmental Disorders, 11*(1), 89-105.

Howlin, P. A. (1981). The results of a home-based language training programme with autistic children. *British Journal of Disorders of Communication, 16*(2), 73-88.

Israel, M. L., Connolly, D. A., von Heyn, R. E., Rock, J. M., & Smith, P. W. (1993). Teaching severely self-abusive and aggressive autistic residents to exit to fire alarms. *Journal of Behavior and Therapy in Experimental Psychiatry, 24*(4), 343-355.

Kazdin, A. E. (1982). *Single-case research designs.* New York: Oxford University.

Koegel, L. K. (1992). Improving social skills and disruptive behavior in children with autism through self-management. *Journal of Applied Behavior Analysis, 25*(2), 341-353.

Koegel, L. K., Camarata, S. M., Valdez-Menchaca, M., Koegel, R. L. (1998). Setting generalization of question-asking by children with autism. *American Journal of the Mentally Retarded, 102*(4), 346-357.

Koegel, R. L. (1980). Behavioral contrast and generalization across settings in the treatment of autistic children. *Journal of Experimental Child Psychology, 30*(3), 422-437.

Koegel, R. L., & Frea, W. D. (1993). Treatment of social behavior in autism through the modification of pivotal social skills. *Journal of Applied Behavior Analysis, 26*(3), 369-377.

Koegel, R. L., O'Dell, M. C., & Koegel, L. K. (1987). A natural teaching paradigm for nonverbal autistic children. *Journal of Autism and Developmental Disorders, 17*(2), 187-200.

LaGrow, S. J., & Repp, A. C. (1984). Stereotypic responding: A review of intervention research. *American Journal of Mental Deficiencies, 88*(6), 595-609.

Luiselli, J. K., Suskin, L., & McPhee, D. F. (1981). Continuous and intermittent application of overcorrection in a self-injurious autistic child: Alternating treatments design analysis. *Journal of Behavior Therapy and Experimental Psychiatry, 12*(4), 355-358.

Luscre, D. M., & Center, D. B. (1996). Procedures for reducing dental fear in children with autism. *Journal of Autism and Developmental Disorders, 26*(5), 547-556.

Maag, J. W. (1986). Sensory extinction and overcorrection in suppressing self-stimulation: A preliminary comparison of efficacy and generalization. *Education and Treatment of Children, 9*(3), 189-201.

Mace, A. B., Shapiro, E. S., & Mace, F. C. (1998). Effects of warning stimuli for reinforcer withdrawal and task onset on self-injury. *Journal of Applied Behavior Analysis, 31*(4), 679-682.

Mason, S. A., & Iwata, B. A. (1990). Artifactual effects of sensory-integrative therapy on self-injurious behavior. *Journal of Applied Behavior Analysis, 23,* 361-370.

Matson, J. L. (1993). An evaluation of two methods for increasing self-initiated verbalizations in autistic children. *Journal of Applied Behavior Analysis, 26*(3), 389-398.

Matson, J. L. (1996). Behavioral treatment of autistic persons: A review of research from 1980 to the present. *Research in Developmental Disabilities, 17*(6), 433-465.

Maurice, C. (1993). *Let me hear your voice.* New York: Knopf.

McEntee, J. E., & Saunders, R. R. (1997). A response-restriction analysis of stereotypy in adolescents with mental retardation:

Implications for applied behavior analysis. *Journal of Applied Behavior Analysis, 30*(3), 485-506.

McEvoy, M. A., & Brady, M. P. (1988). Contingent access to play materials as an academic motivator for autistic and behavior disordered children. *Education and Treatment of Children, 11*(1), 5-18.

McMorrow, M. J., & Foxx, R. M. (1986). Some direct and generalized effects of replacing an autistic man's echolalia with correct responses to questions. *Journal of Applied Behavior Analysis, 19*(3), 289-297.

Nelson, D. L., Gerfenti, E., & Hollander, A. C. (1980). Extra prompts versus no extra prompts in self-care training of autistic children and adolescents. *Journal of Autism and Developmental Disorders, 10*(3), 311-321.

Ogletree, B. T., & Oren, T. (1998). Structured yet functional: An alternative conceptualization of treatment for communication impairment in autism. *Focus on Autism and Other Developmental Disabilities, 13*(4), 228-233.

Piazza, C. C. (1996). Differential reinforcement of alternative behavior and demand fading in the treatment of escape-maintained destructive behavior. *Journal of Applied Behavior Analysis, 29*(4), 569-572.

Ramirez, J. (1998). Sensory integration and its effects on young children.

Richman, D. M., Wacker, D. P., Asmus, J. M., & Casey, S. D. (1998). Functional analysis and extinction of different behavior problems exhibited by the same individual. *Journal of Applied Behavior Analysis, 31*(3), 475-478.

Rogers, S. J. (1996). Brief report: Early intervention in autism. *Journal of Autism and Developmental Disorders, 26*(2), 243-246.

Rogers, S. J., & Dilalla, D. (1991). A comparative study on a developmentally based preschool curriculum on young children with autism and young children with other disorders of behavior and developmental. *Topics in Early Childhood Special Education, 11*, 29-48.

Rotholz, D. A., & Luce, S. C. (1983). Alternative reinforcement strategies for the reduction of self-stimulatory behavior in autistic youth. *Education and Treatment of Children, 6*(4), 363-377.

Sainato, D. M., Strain, P. S., Lefebvre, D., & Rapp, N. (1987). Facilitating transition times with handicapped preschool children: A comparison between peer-mediated and antecedent prompt procedures. *Journal of Applied Behavior Analysis, 20*(93), 285-291.

Schopler, E., Short, A., & Mesibov, G. (1989). Relation of behavioral treatment to normal functioning: Comment on Lovaas. *Journal of Consulting and Clinical Psychology, 57*(1), 162-164.

Sheinkopf, S. J., & Siegal, B. (1998). Home based treatment of young autistic children. *Journal of Autism and Developmental Disorders, 28*, 15-24.

Smith, M. D., & Coleman, D. (1985). Managing the aggressive and self-injurious behavior of adults disabled by autism. *Journal of the Association for Persons with Severe Handicaps (JASH), 10*(4), 228-232.

Smith, T., Eikeseth, S., Klevstrand, M., & Lovaas, O. I. (1997). Intensive behavioral treatment for preschoolers with severe mental retardation and pervasive developmental disorder. *American Journal on Mental Retardation, 102*(3), 238-249.

Stahmer, A. C., & Schreibman, L. (1992). Teaching children with autism appropriate play in unsupervised environments using a self-management treatment package. *Journal of Applied Behavior Analysis, 25*(2), 447-459.

Strain, P. S., & Cordisco, L. K. (1994). LEAP preschool. In S. L. Harris & J. S. Handleman (Eds.), *Preschool education programs for children with autism* (pp. 225-244). Austin, TX: PRO-ED.

Sugai, G., & White, W. J. (1986). Effects on using object self-stimulation as a reinforcer on the prevocational work rates of an autistic child. *Journal of Autism and Developmental Disorders, 16*(4), 459-471.

Thompson, R. H., Fisher, W. W., Piazza, C. C., & Kuhn, D. E. (1998). The evaluation and treatment of aggression maintained by attention and automatic reinforcement. *Journal of Applied Behavior Analysis, 31*(1), 103-116.

Volkmar, F. R. (1985). Compliance, "negativism," and the effects of treatment structure in autism: A naturalistic behavioral study. *Journal of Child Psychology and Psychiatry and Allied Disciplines, 23*(6), 865-877.

Weber, R. C., Thorpe, J. (1992). Teaching children with autism through task variation in physical education. *Exceptional Children, 59*(1), 77-86.

Wolery, M. (1988). Fading extra-stimulus prompts with autistic children using time delay. *Education and Treatment of Children, 11*(1), 29-44.

Wolf, M. M., Braukmann, C. J., & Ramp, K. A. (1987). Serious delinquent behavior as part of a significantly handicapping condition: Cures and supportive environments. *Journal of Applied Behavior Analysis, 20*(4), 347-359.

Wolf, M. M., Risley, T. R., & Mees, H. (1964). Application of operant procedures to the behavior problems of an autistic child. *Behavior Research and Therapy, 1,* 305-312.

Wong, S. E., Floyd, J., Innocent, A. J., & Woolsey, J. E. (1992). Applying a DRO schedule and compliance training to reduce aggressive and self-injurious behavior in an autistic man: A case report. *Journal of Behavior and Therapy in Experimental Psychiatry, 23*(2), 147.

Woods, T. S. (1981). *The development of stimulus control as a behaviour management technique.* Research Forum of the Annual International Conference of the Council for Exceptional Children, New York, April.

Woods, T. S. (1982). Reducing severe aggressive and self-injurious behavior: A nonintrusive, home based approach. *Behavioral Disorders, 7*(3), 180-188.

Zanolli, K. (1996). Teaching preschool age autistic children to make spontaneous initiations to peers using priming. *Journal of Autism and Developmental Disorders, 26*(4), 407-422.

Zanolli, K., & Dagget, J. (1998). The effects of reinforcement rate on the spontaneous social initiations of socially withdrawn preschoolers. *Journal of Applied Behavior Analysis, 31*(1), 117-125.

Zelazo, P. R. (1997). Infant-toddler information processing treatment of children with pervasive developmental disorder and autism: Part II. *Infants and Young Children, 10*(2), 1-13.

CONCLUSION

The foregoing chapters have shown that many children and families with special needs evidence a number of specific functional developmental deficits as well as areas of strength. Even within syndromes such as autism, each child tends to evidence his or her own unique profile. It was also shown that because each child and family evidences their own unique pattern, it is essential to employ a functional developmental approach that can tailor the assessment and intervention to a specific child and family, rather than fit the child into a standard assessment and treatment program. The chapters discussed how to observe, assess, and work with each area of functioning, both at home and at school, providing the infrastructure for a functional developmental approach (i.e., the Developmental, Individual Differences, Relationship-based [DIR] model).

Some functional developmental capacities, such as speech and language functioning and aspects of social and relationship skills, were seen to involve a great deal of research as well as clinical wisdom. Other capacities, such as visual-spatial thinking, were seen to be very important to work with, but were informed predominantly by clinical experience. The discussion showed that meeting the important goal of individualizing the approach to each child's and family's unique profile goes significantly beyond available research and requires a reliance on both research and clinical experience from each of the disciplines that work with children and families with special needs.

Importantly, both research and clinical experience were shown to point to the importance of working with all the functional developmental capacities, rather than only with surface behaviors or isolated cognitive skills. Such a comprehensive approach was observed to include work with such processing capacities as auditory processing and language, visual-spatial processing, motor planning and sequencing, and sensory modulation. It also included working with caregiver-child and family relationships on the capacities for shared attention; relating; engaging in basic problem-solving; reciprocal, affective, and gestural interactions; using ideas creatively, meaningfully, and logically; and reaching high levels of abstract, inferential, and empathetic thinking.

Systematizing the vast amount of clinical knowledge required to work with all the functional developmental capacities at the level of each child's and family's unique profile, as the foregoing chapters demonstrate, must, by necessity, be an ongoing, dynamic process. By its nature, such a process needs to involve all those who work with children and their families in sharing their observations and insights to build a growing body of clinical knowledge that can guide what to assess, how to intervene, and where to direct research. ∎